Ireland

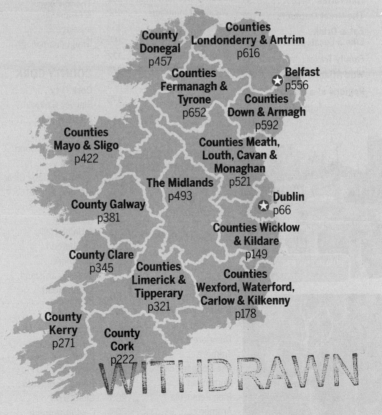

County Donegal
p457

Counties Londonderry & Antrim
p616

Counties Fermanagh & Tyrone
p652

★ Belfast
p556

Counties Down & Armagh
p592

Counties Mayo & Sligo
p422

Counties Meath, Louth, Cavan & Monaghan
p521

The Midlands
p493

★ Dublin
p66

County Galway
p381

Counties Wicklow & Kildare
p149

County Clare
p345

Counties Limerick & Tipperary
p321

Counties Wexford, Waterford, Carlow & Kilkenny
p178

County Kerry
p271

County Cork
p222

WITHDRAWN

Neil Wilson, Isabel Albiston,
Fionn Davenport, Belinda Dixon, Catherine Le Nevez

Contents

PLAN YOUR TRIP

DUBLIN CITY P66

KILLARNEY NATIONAL PARK P282

ON THE ROAD

Contents

SKELLIG MICHAEL P294, COUNTY KERRY

Contents

UNDERSTAND

SURVIVAL GUIDE

SPECIAL FEATURES

Welcome to Ireland

Ireland, a small island with a memorable punch, has breathtaking landscapes and friendly, welcoming people, that will leave visitors floored but looking for more.

Ireland of the Postcard

Everything you've heard is true: Ireland is a stunner. The locals need little prodding to proclaim theirs the most beautiful land in the world, and can support their claim with many examples. Everyone will argue over the must-sees, but you can't go wrong if you put the brooding loneliness of Connemara, the dramatic wildness of Donegal, the majestic mountains of Mourne, the world-famous scenery of counties Kerry and Cork, and the celebrated Causeway Coast in Northern Ireland on your to-visit list.

Tread Softly...

History is everywhere, from the breathtaking monuments of prehistoric Ireland at Brú na Bóinne, Slea Head in Kerry and Carrowmore in Sligo, to the fabulous ruins of Ireland's rich monastic past at Glendalough, Clonmacnoise and Cashel. More recent history is visible in the Titanic Experience in Cobh and the forbidding Kilmainham Gaol in Dublin. And there's history so young that it's still considered the present, best experienced on a black-taxi tour of West Belfast or an examination of Derry's colourful political murals.

A Cultural Well

It's become almost trite to declare that Ireland operates a cultural surplus. Its main strengths are literature and music, where Ireland has long punched above its weight, but it is well represented in most other fields, too. Wherever you go you will discover an abundance of cultural expression. You can attend a play by a literary great in Dublin, toe-tap your way through a traditional-music session in a west-of-Ireland pub, or get your EDM on at a club in Belfast. The Irish summer is awash with festivals celebrating everything from flowers in bloom to high literature.

Tá Fáilte Romhat

On the plane and along your travels you might hear it said: *tá Fáilte romhat* (taw fall-cha row-at) – you're very welcome. Or, more famously, *céad míle fáilte* (kade meela fall-cha) – a hundred thousand welcomes. Irish friendliness is an oversimplification of a character that is infinitely complex, but the Irish are nonetheless genuinely warm and welcoming, and there are few more enjoyable ways of gaining a greater understanding of the island's inhabitants than a chat with a local.

Why I Love Ireland

By Fionn Davenport, Writer

I have always cherished Ireland's unvarnished informality, whose primary measure is friendliness. It's the casual encounters that spark conversation; the unprompted offers of assistance to those who appear lost or in need of help; the warm welcome that most visitors are greeted with. Whether you're north or south, in Dublin or in the deepest countryside, Irish informality dictates that your comfort trumps other social conventions. Cross an Irish hearth and straight away you'll most likely be offered tea...or something stronger. Don't even think about refusing.

For more about our writers, see p736

Above: Galway City (p383)

Ireland

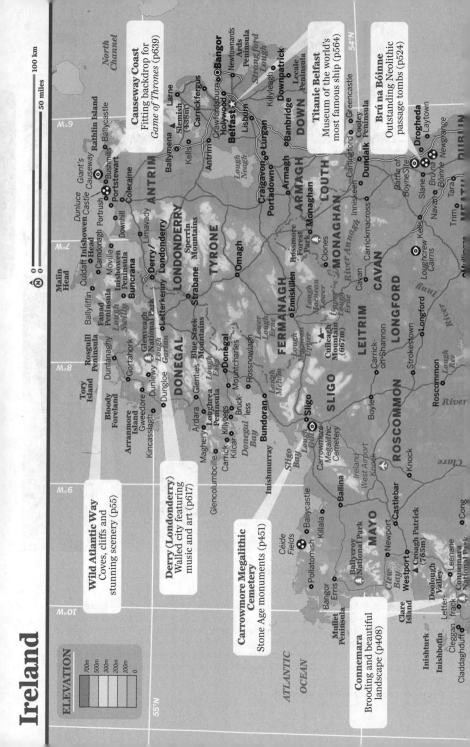

ELEVATION
- 700m
- 500m
- 300m
- 200m
- 100m
- 0

Wild Atlantic Way
Coves, cliffs and stunning scenery (p55)

Derry (Londonderry)
Walled city featuring music and art (p617)

Carrowmore Megalithic Cemetery
Stone Age monuments (p451)

Connemara
Brooding and beautiful landscape (p408)

Causeway Coast
Fitting backdrop for *Game of Thrones* (p639)

Titanic Belfast
Museum of the world's most famous ship (p564)

Brú na Bóinne
Outstanding Neolithic passage tombs (p524)

100 km
50 miles

ATLANTIC OCEAN

North Channel

54°N

55°N

M°01   M°8   M°9   M°7   M°9

ANTRIM
Rathlin Island, Ballycastle, Bushmills, Giant's Causeway, Dunluce Castle, Inishowen Head, Portrush, Portstewart, Coleraine, Ballymena, Kells, Slemish (438m), Antrim, Larne, Carrickfergus

DOWN
Bangor, Newtownards, Ards Peninsula, Strangford Lough, Killyleagh, Downpatrick, Lecale Peninsula, Crawfordsburn, Holywood, Belfast, Lisburn, Banbridge

ARMAGH
Craigavon, Lurgan, Portadown, Armagh

MONAGHAN
Rossmore Forest Park, Clones, Monaghan, Carrickmacross

LOUTH
Carlingford, Greencastle, Cooley Peninsula, Dundalk, Inniskeen, Battle of the Boyne Site, Drogheda, Laytown

CAVAN
Cuilcagh Mountain (667m), Cavan, Carrick-on-Shannon

LONDONDERRY
Culdaff, Carndonagh, Moville, Inishowen Peninsula, Buncrana, Derry/Londonderry, Limavady, Downhill, Sperrin Mountains, Strabane

TYRONE
Omagh

FERMANAGH
Enniskillen, Lough Macnean, Upper Lough Erne, Lower Lough Erne

LEITRIM
Carrick-on-Shannon

LONGFORD
Strokestown, Longford

DONEGAL
Malin Head, Ballyliffin, Fanad Peninsula, Lough Swilly, Rosguill Peninsula, Dunfanaghy, Gortahork, Letterkenny, Bloody Foreland, Gweedore, Glenveagh National Park, Lough Gartan, Dunlewy, Lough Beagh, Dungloe, Ardara, Glenties, Blue Stack Mountains, Lough Eske, Donegal, Mountcharles, Kincasslagh, Arranmore Island, Tory Island, Maghery, Loughrea Peninsula, Killybegs, Carrick, Kilcar, Bruckless, Rossnowlagh, Lough Melvin, Glencolumbcille

SLIGO
Inishmurray, Sligo Bay, Bundoran, Lough Gill, Sligo, Carrowmore Megalithic Cemetery, Boyle

ROSCOMMON
Roscommon, Knock, Ireland West Airport Knock, Castlebar

MAYO
Céide Fields, Pollatomish, Ballycastle, Killala, Ballina, Bangor Erris, Mullet Peninsula, Ballycroy National Park, Newport, Westport, Clew Bay, Croagh Patrick (765m), Clare Island, Achill Island, Doolough Valley, Leenane, Connemara National Park, Cong

CONNEMARA / GALWAY area
Inishturk, Inishbofin, Cleggan, Letterfrack, Claddaghduff

MEATH / DUBLIN area
Slane, Navan, Trim, Tara, Kells, Loughcrew Cairns, Mullingar, DUBLIN

Lough Neagh, Upper Lough Erne, Lower Lough Erne, River Shannon, River Erne, River Annagh, Lough Ree, River

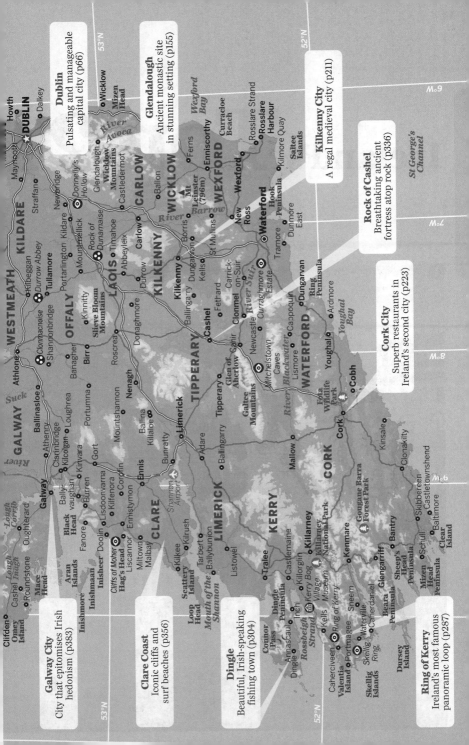

Dublin
Pulsating and manageable capital city (p66)

Glendalough
Ancient monastic site in stunning setting (p155)

Kilkenny City
A regal medieval city (p211)

Rock of Cashel
Breathtaking ancient fortress atop rock (p336)

Cork City
Superb restaurants in Ireland's second city (p223)

Galway City
City that epitomises Irish hedonism (p383)

Clare Coast
Iconic cliffs and surf beaches (p356)

Dingle
Beautiful, Irish-speaking fishing town (p304)

Ring of Kerry
Ireland's most famous panoramic loop (p287)

Ireland's Top 21

1

Dublin

1 Ireland's capital and largest city (p66) by some stretch is the main gateway into the country, and it has enough distractions to keep visitors engaged for at least a few days. From world-class museums and entertainment, to superb dining and top-grade hotels, Dublin has all the baubles of a major international metropolis. But the real clinchers are the Dubliners themselves, who are friendlier, more easygoing and more welcoming than the burghers of virtually any other European capital. And it's the home of Guinness.

Ha'penny Bridge (p95)

Dingle, County Kerry

2 Dingle (p304) is the quintessential Irish town in all its colourful beauty. Sharing its name with the picturesque, ruin-strewn peninsula jutting into the Atlantic from County Kerry, Dingle is a delight: fishing boats unload fish and shellfish that couldn't be any fresher if you caught it yourself, many pubs are untouched since their earlier incarnations as old-fashioned shops, artists sell their creations (including beautiful jewellery with Irish designs) at intriguing boutiques, and toe-tapping trad sessions take place around roaring pub fires.

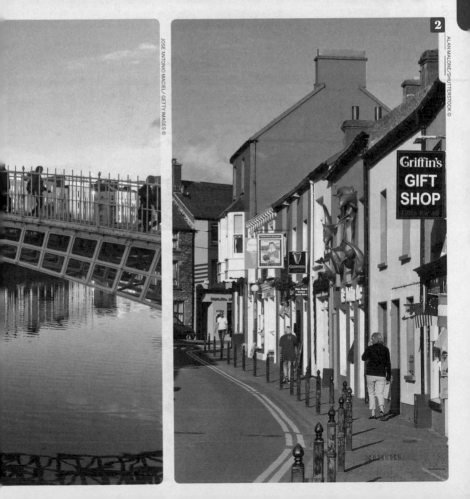

JOSE ANTONIO MACIEL / GETTY IMAGES ©

ALAN MALONE / SHUTTERSTOCK ©

Connemara, County Galway

3 A filigreed coast of tiny coves and beaches is the Connemara Peninsula's (p408) beautiful border with the wild waters of the Atlantic. Characterful roads lead you from one village to another, each with trad pubs and restaurants serving seafood chowder cooked from recipes that are family secrets. Inland the scenic drama is even greater. In fantastically desolate valleys, green hills, yellow wildflowers and wild streams reflecting the blue sky provide elemental beauty. Rambles take you far from other people, and back to a simpler time.

Causeway Coast

4 County Antrim's Causeway Coast is an especially dramatic backdrop for *Game of Thrones* filming locations. Put on your walking boots by the swaying Carrick-a-Rede rope bridge (pictured, p637), then follow the rugged coastline for 16.5 spectacular kilometres, passing Ballintoy Harbour (aka the Iron Islands' Lordsports Harbour) and the geological wonder of the Giant's Causeway (p636) with its outsized basalt columns, as well as cliffs and islands, sandy beaches and ruined castles, before finishing with a dram at the Old Bushmills Distillery.

VIOLLIAMELET/SHUTTERSTOCK ©

Wild Atlantic Way

5 Depending on what direction you travel, the craggy, crenellated Donegal coastline is either the dramatic finale of the Wild Atlantic Way (p55) or its breathtaking beginning. Ireland's northwestern corner is an untamed collection of soaring cliffs (the tallest in Europe), lonely, sheep-speckled headlands and, between them, secluded coves and long stretches of white, powdery sand. Among them, in the county's southwest, is Rossnowlagh (pictured; p463), one of Europe's premier surf beaches and a hotspot for big-wave surfers.

The Pub

6 Every town and hamlet has at least one: no matter where you go, you'll find that the social heart of the country beats loudest in the pubs, which are still the best places to discover what makes Ireland tick. In suitable surroundings – whether a traditional pub such as John Benny's (pictured; p309) in Dingle with flagstone floors and live music, or a more modern bar – take a moment or an evening to listen for that beating heart...and drink some decent beer in the process.

Ring of Kerry

7 Driving around the Ring of Kerry (p287) is an unforgettable experience in itself, but you don't need to limit yourself to the main route. Along this 179km loop around the Iveragh Peninsula, there are countless opportunities for detours. From near Killorglin it's a short hop up to the beautiful, little-known Cromane Peninsula. Between Portmagee and Waterville, you can explore the Skellig Ring, while the peninsula's interior offers mesmerising mountain views. And that's just for starters. Wherever your travels take you, remember to charge your camera batteries!

Valentia Island (p293)

Galway City

8 One word to describe Galway city (p383)? Craic! Ireland's liveliest city literally hums through the night at music-filled pubs where you can hear three old guys playing spoons and fiddles, or a hot young band. Join the locals as they bounce from place to place, never knowing what fun lies ahead but certain of the possibility. Add in local bounty such as the famous oysters and nearby adventure on the Connemara Peninsula and the Aran Islands, and the fun never ends.

Traditional Music

9 Western Europe's most vibrant folk music is Irish traditional music, which may have earned worldwide fame thanks to the likes of *Riverdance* but is best expressed in a 'trad session' – a loosely organised performance in an old-fashioned pub. The west of Ireland is particularly musical: from Donegal down to Kerry there are centres of musical excellence, none more so than Doolin (p370) in County Clare, the unofficial capital of Irish music, where you'll find pubs and 'music houses' – private dwellings known for their sessions and open to the public.

Glendalough, County Wicklow

10 St Kevin knew a thing or two about magical locations. When he chose a remote cave on a glacial lake nestled at the base of a forested valley as his monastic retreat (p155), he inadvertently founded a settlement that would later become one of Ireland's most dynamic universities and, in our time, one of the country's most beautiful ruined sites. The remains of the settlement (including an intact round tower, pictured), coupled with the stunning scenery, are unforgettable.

Walking & Hiking

11 Yes, you can visit the country easily enough by car, but Ireland is best explored on foot, whether you opt for a gentle afternoon stroll along a canal towpath or take on the challenge of any of the 43 waymarked long-distance routes. There are mountain hikes and coastal walks, such as the Causeway Coast Way (p637), and you can explore villages along the way or steer clear of civilisation by traipsing along lonely moorland and across barren bogs. All you'll need is a decent pair of boots and, inevitably, a rain jacket.

Titanic Belfast

12 The construction of the world's most famous ocean liner is celebrated in high-tech, multimedia glory at this wonderful museum (pictured; p564). Not only can you explore every detail of the *Titanic*'s construction, including a simulated 'fly-through' of the ship from keel to bridge, but you can place yourself in the middle of the industrial bustle that was Belfast's shipyards at the turn of the 20th century. The experience is heightened by the use of photography, audio and – perhaps most poignantly – the only footage of the actual *Titanic* still in existence.

11

POOGIE/SHUTTERSTOCK ©

12

MILOSZ MASLANKA/SHUTTERSTOCK ©

Clare Coast

13 Bathed in the golden glow of the late-afternoon sun, the iconic Cliffs of Moher (p365) are but one of the splendours of County Clare. From a boat bobbing below, the towering stone faces have a jaw-dropping dramatic beauty that's enlivened by scores of seabirds, including cute little puffins. Down south in Loop Head, pillars of rock towering above the sea have abandoned stone cottages, the existence of which is inexplicable. All along the coast are charming villages such as trad-session-filled Ennistymon and the surfer destination of Lahinch (pictured, p362).

A Gaelic Football or Hurling Match

14 It depends on whether you're in a football or hurling stronghold (some, such as County Cork, are both), but attending a match of the county's chosen sport is not just a unique Irish experience but also a key to unlocking local passions and understanding one of the cultural pillars of Ireland. Whether you attend a club football match in Galway, an intercounty hurling battle between old foes such as Kilkenny and Tipperary, or an All-Ireland final at Croke Park (p136), you cannot help but be swept up in the emotion of it all.

Kilkenny City

15 From its regal castle to its soaring medieval cathedral, Kilkenny (p211) exudes a permanence and culture that have made it an unmissable stop on journeys to the south and west. Its namesake county boasts scores of artisans and craftspeople and you can browse their wares at Kilkenny's classy shops and boutiques. Chefs eschew Dublin in order to be close to the source of Kilkenny's wonderful produce, and you can enjoy the local brewery's beers at scores of delightful pubs.

Brú na Bóinne, County Meath

16 Looking at once ancient and yet eerily futuristic, Newgrange's (pictured, p524) immense, round, white stone walls topped by a grass dome are one of the most extraordinary sights you'll ever see. Part of the vast Neolithic necropolis Brú na Bóinne (p524; the Boyne Palace), it contains Ireland's finest Stone Age passage tomb, predating Egypt's pyramids by some six centuries. Most extraordinary of all is the tomb's precise alignment with the sun at the time of the winter solstice.

PIERRE LECLERC/SHUTTERSTOCK ©

Rock of Cashel, County Tipperary

17 Soaring up from the green Tipperary pastures, this ancient fortress (p336) takes your breath away at first sight. The seat of kings and churchmen who ruled over the region for more than 1000 years, it rivalled Tara as a centre of power in Ireland for 400 years. Entered through the 15th-century Hall of the Vicars Choral, its impervious walls guard an awesome enclosure with a complete round tower, a 13th-century Gothic cathedral and the most magnificent 12th-century Romanesque chapel in Ireland.

Links Golf

18 If Scotland is the home of golf, then Ireland is where it goes on holiday. The best spots are along the sea, where the country's collection of seaside links are dotted in a steady string along virtually the entire Irish coastline, each carved into the undulating, marram-grass-covered landscapes. Some of the world's best-known courses, including 2019 Open host Royal Portrush (p632), share spectacular scenery with lesser-known gems, and each offers golfers the opportunity to test their skills against the raw materials provided by Mother Nature.

Cork City

19 The Republic's second city (p223) is second only in terms of size – in every other respect it will bear no competition. A tidy, compact city centre is home to an enticing collection of art galleries, museums and – most particularly – places to eat. From cheap cafes to top-end gourmet restaurants, Cork excels, which is hardly a surprise given the county's exceptional foodie reputation. At the heart of it is the simply wonderful English Market, a covered produce market that is an attraction unto itself.

Derry

20 History runs deep in Northern Ireland's second city (p617). The symbols of the country's sectarian past are evident, from the 17th-century city walls built to protect Protestant settlers, to the latter forcing the adoption of its Loyalist name, Londonderry. Explore its tormented past by walking the walls, visiting the Bogside and the famous murals that tell the tale of resistance and defiance, before losing yourself in Derry's superb live-music scene and terrific nightlife. You're almost certainly guaranteed a memorable night out.

Carrowmore Megalithic Cemetery, County Sligo

21 One of Europe's most significant megalithic monuments, the collection of stone circles, passage tombs and dolmens at Carrowmore (p451) is rich in superlatives: the oldest Stone Age monument in Ireland, and one of the largest cemeteries of its kind in Europe. Archaeologists continue to excavate new monuments and piece together clues as to the site's deeper meaning and connection to the world around it.

Need to Know (ROI)

For more information, see Survival Guide (p699)

Currency
Euro (€)

Language
English, Irish

Visas
Not required by most citizens of Europe, Australia, New Zealand, USA and Canada.

Money
Credit and debit cards are widely accepted.

Mobile Phones
All European and Australasian phones work in Ireland, as do North American phones not locked to a local network. Check with your provider. Prepaid SIM cards cost from €10.

Time
Western European Time (GMT/UTC November to March; plus one hour April to October).

When to Go

Belfast

Dublin
GO year-round, lots of indoor attractions

Galway
GO May–Sep

Kerry
GO May–Sep

Cork
GO May–Sep

High Season
(Jun–mid-Sep)
➡ Weather at its best.
➡ Accommodation rates at their highest (especially in August).
➡ Tourist peak in Dublin, Kerry and southern and western coasts.

Shoulder
(Easter–May, mid-Sep–Oct)
➡ Weather often good: sun and rain in May, often-warm 'Indian summers' in September.
➡ Summer crowds and accommodation rates drop off.

Low Season
(Nov–Easter)
➡ Reduced opening hours from October to Easter; some destinations close.
➡ Cold and wet weather throughout the country; fog can reduce visibility.
➡ Big city attractions operate as normal.

Useful Websites

Entertainment Ireland (www.entertainment.ie) Country-wide listings for every kind of entertainment.

Failte Ireland (www.discoverireland.ie) Official tourist-board website – practical info and a huge accommodation database.

Lonely Planet (www.lonelyplanet.com/ireland) Destination information, hotel bookings, traveller forum and more.

Important Numbers

Include area codes only when dialling from outside the area or from a mobile phone. Drop the initial 0 when dialling from abroad.

Republic of Ireland country code	353
International access code	00
Emergency (police, fire, ambulance)	999

Exchange Rates

The Republic of Ireland uses the euro.

Australia	A$1	€0.61
Canada	C$1	€0.67
Japan	Y100	€0.81
New Zealand	NZ$1	€0.59
UK	£1	€1.11
USA	US$1	€0.88

For current exchange rates see www.xe.com.

Daily Costs

**Budget:
Less than €80**

➡ Dorm bed: €14–25

➡ Cheap meal in cafe or pub: €10–18

➡ Intercity bus travel (200km trip): €14–25

➡ Pint of beer: €5–6.50 (more expensive in cities)

**Midrange:
€80–180**

➡ Double room in hotel or B&B: €100–180 (more expensive in Dublin)

➡ Main course in midrange restaurant: €17–30

➡ Car rental (per day): from €32

➡ Three-hour train journey: €60

**Top end:
More than €180**

➡ Four-star-hotel stay: from €200

➡ Three-course meal in good restaurant: around €70

➡ Top round of golf (midweek): from €100

Opening Hours

Banks 10am–4pm Monday to Friday (to 5pm Thursday)

Pubs 10.30am–11.30pm Monday to Thursday, 10.30am–12.30am Friday and Saturday, noon–11pm Sunday (30 minutes 'drinking up' time allowed); closed Christmas Day and Good Friday

Restaurants noon–10.30pm; many close one day of the week

Shops 9.30am–6pm Monday to Saturday (to 8pm Thursday in cities), noon–6pm Sunday

Arriving in Ireland

Dublin Airport Private coaches run every 10 to 15 minutes to the city centre (€6). Taxis take 30 to 45 minutes and cost €20 to €25.

Dublin Port Terminal Buses are timed to coincide with arrivals and departures; they cost €3.50 to the city centre.

Belfast International Airport Airport Express 300 bus runs hourly from Belfast International Airport (one way/return £8/11.50, 30 to 55 minutes). A taxi costs around £30.

George Best Belfast City Airport Airport Express 600 bus runs every 20 minutes from George Best Belfast City Airport (one way/return £2.60/4, 15 minutes). A taxi costs around £10.

Getting Around

Transport in Ireland is efficient and reasonably priced to and from major urban centres; smaller towns and villages along those routes are well served. Service to destinations not on major routes is less frequent and often impractical.

Car The most convenient way to explore Ireland's every nook and cranny. Cars can be hired in every major town and city. Drive on the left.

Bus The extensive network of public and private buses is the most cost-effective way to get around. There's service to and from most inhabited areas.

Bicycle Dublin operates a bike-share scheme with more than 100 stations spread throughout the city.

Train A limited (and expensive) network links Dublin to all major urban centres, including Belfast in Northern Ireland.

For much more on **getting around**, see p709

Need to Know (NI)

For more information, see Survival Guide (p699)

Currency
Pound sterling (£)

Language
English, Irish

Visas
Generally not needed for stays of up to six months. The UK is not a member of the Schengen Area.

Money
ATMs widely available. Credit cards accepted in most hotels and restaurants.

Mobile Phones
International roaming charges can be high, and you'll probably find it cheaper to get a UK number. This is easily done by buying a pay-as-you-go SIM card (from £5 including calling credit) and sticking it in your phone.

Time
Western European Time (UTC/GMT November to March; plus one hour April to October)

When to Go

High Season (May–Aug)

➡ June is the best time to spot puffins nesting at the Rathlin West Light Seabird Centre.

➡ Warm weather makes July the best month for hiking in the Mournes and Sperrins.

Shoulder (Mar–Apr, Sept–Oct)

➡ April can be a great time to visit Belfast, with spring flowers blooming throughout the city's parks and gardens.

➡ The Belfast International Arts Festival brings three weeks of theatre, music, dance and talks.

Low Season (Nov–Feb)

➡ Experience popular attractions such as Titanic Belfast and Carrick-a-Rede rope bridge without the crowds.

➡ Outside is chilly, but you can enjoy the warmth in snug pubs across the north.

Useful Websites

Lonely Planet (www.lonely planet.com/ireland/northern-ireland) Destination information, hotel bookings, traveller forum and more.

Culture Northern Ireland (www.culturenorthernireland. org) Entertainment news, reviews and listings.

Translink (www.translink.co.uk) Public transport information.

Northern Ireland Tourist Board (www.nitb.com) Official tourist site.

Important Numbers

All Northern Ireland landline numbers begin with 028, which you can omit when calling from another local landline. Drop the initial 'O' if you're calling from abroad.

UK country code	44
International access code	00
Emergency (police, fire, ambulance, mountain rescue, coast guard)	999

Exchange Rates

Australia	A$1	£0.55
Canada	C$1	£0.59
Eurozone	€1	£0.89
Japan	¥100	£0.73
New Zealand	NZ$1	£0.52
USA	US$1	£0.79

For current exchange rates, see www.xe.com.

Daily Costs
Budget: Less than £55

➡ Dorm beds: £18–25

➡ Cheap meals in cafes and pubs: £7–11

➡ Bus or train ticket: £3–12

Midrange: £55–120

➡ Double room in midrange hotel or B&B: £50–120

➡ Main course in midrange restaurant: £15–28

➡ Admission to museums: £7–17

Top end: More than £120

➡ Four-star-hotel room: from £130

➡ Three-course meal in a good restaurant: around £40

➡ Car rental per day: from £35

Opening Hours

Opening hours may vary throughout the year, especially in rural areas, where many places have shorter hours or close completely from October or November to March or April.

Banks 9.30am–4pm Monday to Friday; some 9.30am–1pm Saturday

Cafes 8.30am–5pm

Pubs & Bars noon–11pm Monday to Saturday (many to midnight or 1am Friday and Saturday), and noon–11pm Sunday

Restaurants noon–2.30pm and 6–9pm

Shops 9am–5.30pm Monday to Saturday and often 1–6pm Sunday

Arriving in Northern Ireland

Belfast International Airport Airport Express 300 bus runs to the Europa Bus Centre (one way/return £8/11, 30 to 55 minutes). A taxi costs about £30.

George Best Belfast City Airport Airport Express 600 bus runs to the Europa Bus Centre (one way/return £2.60/4, 15 minutes). A taxi fare to the city centre is about £10.

Victoria Ferry Terminal (Belfast) Bus 96 runs from Upper Queen St (£2, 20 minutes). A taxi costs about £10.

Larne ferry terminal Located 37km north of Belfast; trains connect the terminal at Larne Harbour with Belfast's Great Victoria St station (£7.70, one hour).

Getting Around

Car The easiest way to get around Northern Ireland is by car; roads are good and traffic is rarely a problem (although avoid routes in and around Belfast at rush hour).

Bus Buses serve urban areas and connect the province's main towns and cities, with less frequent services to most (but not all) rural villages.

Train Some towns are linked to Belfast by train.

For much more on **getting around**, see p709

First Time Ireland

For more information, see Survival Guide (p699)

Checklist*

➡ Make sure your passport is valid for at least six months past your arrival date

➡ Make all necessary bookings (accommodation, events and travel)

➡ Check the airline baggage restrictions

➡ Inform your debit-/credit-card company

➡ Arrange appropriate travel insurance

➡ Check if your mobile phone is compatible

What to Pack

➡ Good walking shoes, as there's plenty of walking to do

➡ Raincoat – you will undoubtedly need it

➡ UK/Ireland electrical adapter

➡ Finely honed sense of humour

➡ A hollow leg – all that beer has to go somewhere

➡ Irish-themed Spotify playlist

Top Tips for Your Trip

➡ Quality rather than quantity should be your goal: instead of a hair-raising race to see everything, pick a handful of destinations and give yourself time to linger. The most memorable experiences in Ireland are often the ones where you're doing very little at all.

➡ If you're driving get off the main roads when you can: some of Ireland's most stunning scenery is best enjoyed on secondary or tertiary roads that wind their narrow way through standout photo ops.

➡ Make the effort to greet the locals: the best experiences are to be had courtesy of the Irish themselves, whose helpfulness, friendliness and sense of fun has not been exaggerated.

What to Wear

You can wear pretty much whatever you want: smart casual is the most you'll need for fancy dinners, the theatre or the concert hall. Irish summers are warm but rarely hot, so you'll want something extra when the temperatures cool, especially in the evening. Ultimately the ever-changeable weather will determine your outfits, but a light waterproof jacket should never be beyond reach for the almost-inevitable rain.

Sleeping

From basic hostels to five-star hotels, you'll find every kind of accommodation in Ireland. Advance bookings are generally recommended and are an absolute necessity during the July–August holiday period.

Hotels From chain hotels with comfortable digs to Norman castles with rainfall showers and wi-fi – with prices to match.

B&Bs From a bedroom in a private home to a luxurious Georgian townhouse, the ubiquitous B&B is the bedrock of Irish accommodation.

Hostels Every major town and city has a selection of hostels, with clean dorms and wi-fi – some have laundry and kitchen facilities.

Money

ATMs are found pretty much everywhere. They're all linked to the main international money systems, allowing you to withdraw money with your own card, but be sure to check with your bank before you travel.

Credit and debit cards can be used almost everywhere except for some rural B&Bs that only accept cash. Make sure bars or restaurants will accept cards before you order. The most popular are Visa and MasterCard; American Express is only accepted by the major chains, and virtually no one will accept Diners or JCB. Chip-and-PIN is the norm for card transactions – only a few places will accept a signature.

The Republic of Ireland uses the euro (€). Northern Ireland uses the pound sterling (£), though the euro is also accepted in many places.

Bargaining

Ireland doesn't do bargaining.

Tipping

Hotels A tip of €1/£1 per bag is standard; tip cleaning staff at your discretion.

Pubs Not expected unless table service is provided, then €1/£1 for a round of drinks.

Restaurants For decent service 10%; up to 15% in more expensive places.

Taxis Tip 10% or round up fare to nearest euro/pound.

Toilet attendants Loose change; no more than 50c/50p.

Tea shop, Galway

Etiquette

Although largely informal in their everyday dealings, the Irish do observe some (unspoken) rules of etiquette.

Greetings Shake hands when meeting for the first time and when saying goodbye. The Irish expect a firm handshake with eye contact.

Conversation Generally friendly but often reserved, the Irish avoid conversations that might embarrass. They are very mistrustful of 'oversharers'. Not surprisingly politics and religion can be touchy topics in Northern Ireland: take your lead from locals and don't make any assumptions or assertions.

Round System The Irish generally take it in turns to buy a round of drinks for the whole group and everyone is expected to take part. The next round should be bought before the previous round is drunk.

Eating

Booking ahead is recommended in cities and larger towns; same-day reservations are usually fine except for top-end restaurants – book those two weeks in advance.

Restaurants From cheap eats to Michelin-starred feasts, covering every imaginable cuisine.

Cafes Open during the daytime (rarely at night), cafes are good for all-day breakfasts, sandwiches and basic lunches.

Pubs Pub grub ranges from toasted sandwiches to carefully crafted dishes as good as any you'll find in a restaurant.

Hotels All hotel restaurants accept nonguests. They're a popular option in rural Ireland.

What's New

Ireland has rediscovered the mojo that made it such a dynamic economic force in the 1990s. The tourist trade is booming and, in the Republic at least, the forces of liberalism continue to win battles against conservative traditionalism. Meanwhile, the spectre of Brexit casts a shadow over everything.

The Tourism Boom

The year 2018 was a bumper one for Irish tourism, with a record 11.2 million visitors to the island. To meet the growing demand, dozens of new hotels are being added to the country's stock – at the end of 2018, 21 hotels were under construction across the country (70% more than at the same time in 2017), with at least another 20 to be built by 2020.

More hotels won't necessarily mean lower prices, however, as the government has raised value added tax (VAT) on the hospitality industry back to 13.5% – up from the 9.5% lifeboat thrown in 2011 to help the sector weather the effects of the global financial crisis. Many hoteliers and restaurateurs have responded negatively, arguing that the rise puts pressure on operators' margins already stretched by rising wage and rent costs.

What is almost certain is that the VAT hike will be passed on to the consumer. Many cafes and restaurants have already raised their prices, while hotel and B&B owners will be forced to mitigate what is effectively a 50% increase in their VAT bill by bumping up their room rates even more than the standard rate of year-on-year inflation.

New Distilleries

The number of operational distilleries in Ireland has grown from just four in 2013 to 25 and counting as of mid-2019 (and there's another two dozen planned or already in development). Whiskey must be aged in the barrel for at least three years before it can be legally sold as Irish whiskey, so many distilleries have been turning out craft gin while they wait for the whiskey to mature – there are more than 30 Irish gin brands to choose from.

LOCAL KNOWLEDGE

WHAT'S HAPPENING IN IRELAND

Ireland's city skylines are once again dotted with cranes, just one of the more visible signs of the renewal that's continued apace over the last several years. New hotels are opening along with so many new cafes and restaurants that it's almost impossible to keep count, while the country's infrastructure is once again being improved after nearly a decade of stagnation.

But politics is the subject that casts a long shadow over many coffee-shop conversations, notably the looming spectre of Brexit (the UK's withdrawal from the European Union) and the fate of the 'Irish backstop', an insurance policy designed to ensure that the border between the Republic and Northern Ireland – the only land border between a post-Brexit UK and the EU – remains open as per the terms of the Good Friday Agreement, irrespective of the future relationship with the United Kingdom. Whatever the terms of the Withdrawal Agreement, the backstop will be part of it until a solution to the border question can be found.

Typical of this new wave is the state-of-the-art Clonakilty Distillery (p250) in West Cork. It opened in 2019, and produces gin infused with local rock samphire, as well as a triple-distilled single-pot still Irish whiskey made with grain grown on the owners' family farm nearby.

In Dublin, several new distilleries have opened up in the city's very own whiskey quarter, the Liberties. Teeling Distillery (p109) were the trailblazers, but have been followed by the Pearse Lyons Distillery (p109), the Dublin Liberties Distillery (p99) and Roe & Co (p109).

Sea-Inspired Food Tours

Ireland has cottoned on to the popularity of food tours, with a slew of new (and often unusual) offerings all around the island. The fad for wild food gets its feet wet on the Ring of Kerry, where new outfit Atlantic Irish Seaweed (p299) offers guided beach foraging for edible seaweed, followed by a tasting session of seaweed-based dishes and drinks. And a new factory tour (p436) on Achill Island, off the west coast, explains exactly how sea salt drawn from the waters around the island becomes the salt with which you might flavour your food. Plenty of samplings included.

Belfast's Asian Fusion Scene

There are a bunch of excellent new Asian/Asian-fusion restaurants in Belfast, notably Bia (p568), Jumon (p581) and Yügo (p580), an excellent new restaurant where Asian dishes are given an Irish twist.

14 Henrietta Street

Dublin's most complete Georgian street is home to this refurbished townhouse (p103). It is now a museum showcasing the history of the dwelling, from its construction in the 1740s as an elegant family home to its dereliction in the late 19th and early 20th centuries.

The Gobbins

Rockfalls and slips delayed its full opening, but this spectacular guided cliff walk (p648) on Islandmagee is finally complete, and you can now fully enjoy its collection of tubular bridges, rocky surfaces, tunnels, caves and narrow crevices.

LISTEN, WATCH AND FOLLOW

For inspiration and up-to-date news, visit www.lonely planet.com/ireland/travel-tips-and-articles.

Insta @lonelyplanet Inspiring images from our writers on the road.

Insta @chrishillphotographer Stunning landscapes from one of Ireland's leading photographers.

All the Food (www.allthefood.ie) Top Dublin food blog.

Life of Stuff (www.thelifeofstuff.com) Irish travel, culture and lifestyle blog.

Irish History Podcast (irishhistorypodcast.ie) A fascinating look at Ireland's past.

FAST FACTS

Food Trend Foraging and food tours

Mobile Phones 98 per 100 people

Language in the Republic, 1.7m people claim to be able to speak Irish Gaelic, but only 73,800 say they speak it every day.

Pop Republic of Ireland: 4,840,508; Northern Ireland: 1,810,863

REPUBLIC OF IRELAND   NORTHERN IRELAND   ENGLAND

≈ 35 people per sq km

Mayo Dark Sky Festival

A three-day festival (p435) focused on the celestial displays in Mayo's International Dark Sky Park. As well as stargazing there are talks, walks and workshops in Newport, Mulranny and Ballycroy.

Creative Hub, Wexford Town

In 2018 a brand new arts centre (p182) was established in an abandoned 20th-century mall; the shops are now full of artists, craftspeople and local musicians making (and selling) their work.

Accommodation

Find more accommodation reviews throughout the On the Road chapters (from p65)

Accommodation Types

Hotels From chain hotels with comfortable digs to Norman castles with rainfall showers and wi-fi – with prices to match.

B&Bs From a bedroom in a private home to a luxurious Georgian townhouse, the ubiquitous B&B is the bedrock of Irish accommodation.

Hostels Every major town and city has a selection of hostels, with clean dorms and wi-fi – some have laundry and kitchen facilities.

Camping Campsites range from rustic farm-based retreats in rural areas, to bustling, family-oriented places in seaside resorts.

Horse-Drawn Caravan Get back to nature by hiring a traditional horse-drawn caravan to explore the rural backroads of the country.

Canal Barge An unhurried way to see the countryside involves renting a barge on one of Ireland's canal systems.

Rental Accommodation Self-catering accommodation is often rented on a weekly basis and usually means an apartment, house or cottage where you look after yourself.

House Swap Several agencies facilitate international house swaps, and use of the family car is sometimes included.

PRICE RANGES

Accommodation prices can vary according to demand, or there may be different rates for online, phone or walk-in bookings. B&B rates are more consistent, but virtually every other accommodation will charge wildly different rates depending on the time of year, day, festival schedule and even your ability to do a little negotiating. The following price ranges are based on a double room with private bathroom in high season.

Republic of Ireland (excluding Dublin)
€ less than €80
€€ €80–€180
€€€ more than €180

Dublin
€ less than €150
€€ €150–€250
€€€ more than €250

Northern Ireland
£ less than £50
££ £50–£120
£££ more than £120

Best Places to Stay

Best on a Budget

Budget accommodation usually means hostels, so you'll find the widest choice in places that traditionally attract backpackers – cities such as Dublin, Belfast and Galway have a wide range of attractive and competitively priced spots. You'll also find a good choice in places which attract hikers, surfers and other outdoors enthusiasts – Donegal, Kerry and the west coast, for example.

Best budget accommodation:
➡ Isaacs Hostel (p120), Dublin
➡ Kinlay Hostel (p387), Galway
➡ Valley House (p437), Achill Island
➡ Sandrock Holiday Hostel (p490), Malin Head
➡ Vagabonds (p576), Belfast

Best for Families

The best family-oriented places tend to be holiday resorts, country hotels (though they can be expensive) and farmhouse B&BS within weekend getaway distance of cities like Dublin, Belfast, Galway and Cork – so consider looking at counties Wicklow, Kildare, Offaly, Cavan, Antrim, Down and Waterford, and regions such as West Cork, Connemara and the Ring of Kerry.

Best family accommodation:

➡ Sheila's Hostel (p227), Cork
➡ Slieve Russell Hotel (p550), Co Cavan
➡ Station House Hotel (p414), Clifden
➡ Aghadoe Heights Hotel (p277), Killarney
➡ Annaharvey Farm (p516), Tullamore
➡ Faithlegg (p198), Co Waterford

Best for Solo Travellers

Many guesthouses and hotels in Ireland charge much the same for a single traveller as for a couple sharing a double room; in fact, single rooms can be downright hard to find. If you want to meet other travellers, your best bet is backpacker hostels with buzzing common rooms, and convivial B&Bs where guests enjoy breakfast conversations around a communal kitchen table.

Best solo traveller accommodation:

➡ Black Sheep Hostel (p275), Killarney
➡ Olde Bakery (p248), Kinsale
➡ Top of the Rock Pod Pairc (p253), Skibbereen
➡ Fortwilliam Country House (p610), Hillsborough

Best Historic Hotels

Ireland has a rich legacy of country houses, castles and stately homes that have been converted into hotels. Places like these offer the chance to indulge in four-poster beds, Victorian baths, antique furniture and candlelit dining rooms, and to stroll through landscaped gardens that would once have been the preserve of the rich and powerful.

Best historic hotels:

➡ Glenlo Abbey Hotel (p390), Galway
➡ Cahernane House Hotel (p277), Killarney
➡ Belleek Castle (p443), Ballina
➡ Old Inn (p595), Crawfordsburn

DERICK HUDSON/SHUTTERSTOCK ©
Isaacs Hostel (p120), Dublin

Booking

Daft.ie (www.daft.ie) Online property portal includes holiday homes and short-term rentals.

Elegant Ireland (www.elegant.ie) Specialises in self-catering castles, period houses and unique properties.

Imagine Ireland (www.imagineireland.com) Holiday cottage rentals throughout the whole island, including Northern Ireland.

Irish Landmark Trust (www.irishlandmark.com) Not-for-profit conservation group that rents self-catering properties of historical and cultural significance, such as castles, tower houses, gate lodges, schoolhouses and lighthouses.

Lonely Planet (www.lonelyplanet.com/Ireland/hotels) Recommendations and bookings.

Dream Ireland (www.dreamireland.com) Lists self-catering holiday cottages and apartments.

If You Like...

Traditional Pubs

Everybody's got their favourite, so picking the best ones is a futile exercise. What can be done, however, is to select a handful that won't disappoint you, especially if you're looking for a traditional pub in the classic mould.

Blakes of the Hollow Ulster's best pint of Guinness in a Victorian classic. (p658)

John Benny's Stone slab floor, memorabilia on the walls and rocking trad sessions in this Dingle pub most nights. (p309)

McCarthy's A pub, restaurant and undertakers, all in one, in Fethard. (p344)

Tigh Neachtain In Galway, one of Ireland's best-known traditional pubs. (p393)

John Mulligan's The most famous of the capital's traditional pubs and a star of film and TV – where it usually plays itself. (p133)

Sean's Bar An ancient bar in Athlone with peat fires, sloping floors and lots of music. (p505)

Vaughan's Pub Superb bar in Kilfenora with an outstanding reputation for traditional music. (p375)

Great Views

Irish scenery is among the most spectacular in Europe, with breathtaking views and stunning landscapes throughout the whole country. There are the famous spots, of course, but they're not alone.

Binevenagh Lake Spectacular views over Lough Foyle, Donegal and the Sperrin Mountains from the clifftop at the height of Bishop's Rd. (p630)

Kilkee Cliffs Jaw-dropping views of soaring cliffs that aren't the Cliffs of Moher. (p359)

Powerscourt Estate The view of the Sugarloaf from the entrance road to this Palladian mansion is one of the best along the east coast. (p152)

Connor Pass Stand at the top of the 456m pass through the mountains of the Dingle Peninsula and inhale the views of the valley below. (p314)

Poisoned Glen The views down this Donegal valley are breathtaking; the final touch is the ruined church at the foot of the glen. (p476)

Priest's Leap A scenic mountain pass near the Beara Peninsula with sensational views of Bantry Bay and its eponymous town. (p263)

Sky Road Astonishing views over the sea from this dramatic coastal road just outside Clifden in Connemara. (p413)

Ancient Ruins

Thanks to the pre-Celts, Celts and early Christians, ancient and monastic sites are a feature of the Irish landscape. Thanks to the Vikings and Henry VIII, many of them are ruins, but no less impressive.

Glendalough Ruins of a once-powerful monastic city in tranquil surroundings. (p156)

Brú na Bóinne Europe's most impressive Neolithic burial site. (p524)

Clonmacnoise Ireland's finest monastic site. (p513)

Athassel Priory Sublime and haunting ecclesiastical ruin. (p337)

Carrowkeel Megalithic cemetery and majestic views. (p453)

Athenry A magnificent castle, Dominican priory, an original market cross and lengthy sections of town walls. (p420)

Devenish Island Ruins of an Augustinian monastery and near-perfect round tower on the biggest island in Lough Erne. (p660)

Dun Aengus Stunning Stone Age fort perched perilously on Inishmore's cliffs. (p398)

Literary Corners

Four Nobel laureates for literature are just the highlight of a rich literary tradition. Ireland is one of the English-speaking world's most notable heavyweights of the written word, a tradition that continues to thrive through contemporary writers and literary festivals.

Cape Clear Island International Storytelling Festival The storytelling tradition is kept alive by tales tall and long from all over the world. (p257)

Seamus Heaney Home Place A new museum and arts centre in the Nobel laureate's home town of Bellaghy, County Londonderry. (p649)

Cúirt International Festival of Literature Galway attracts writers from far and wide to its April literary showcase. (p386)

Dublin Literary Pub Crawl A fine selection of literary tours takes full advantage of the city's rich literary reputation. (p110)

Writers' Week The Irish literary festival, held in June in Listowel, the home town of John B Keane. (p319)

Town of Books Festival The Kilkenny town of Graiguenamanagh aspires to be Ireland's answer to Hay-on-Wye with this annual festival. (p221)

Yeats International Summer School Now in its sixth decade, this prestigious 10-day festival in Sligo town features lectures, workshops, drama, readings and walking tours. (p448)

Traditional Music

Western Europe's most vibrant folk music is kept alive by musicians who ply their craft (and are plied

Top: Powerscourt Estate (p152), County Wicklow

Bottom: Connor Pass (p314), County Kerry

with drink) in impromptu and organised sessions in pubs and music houses throughout the country. Even the strictly-for-tourists stuff will feature excellent performances.

An Droichead Excellent music sessions at a Belfast arts centre dedicated to Irish culture. (p586)

Matt Molloy's The Chieftain's fife player owns this Westport pub where the live *céilidh* (session of traditional music and dancing) kicks off at 9pm nightly. (p434)

Miltown Malbay Every pub in this County Clare town features outstanding Irish trad sessions. (p361)

Tig Cóilí Galway's best trad sessions are held in this pub whose name means 'house of music'. (p393)

Marine Bar Wonderful music three times a week at this 200-year-old pub on the Ring Peninsula. (p203)

Cobblestone The nightly sessions in this Smithfield pub are the best in the capital. (p132)

Tracing Your Roots

Roughly 80 million people worldwide can claim to be part of, or descended from, the Irish diaspora, with about 41 million of those in the USA alone. Most major towns have a heritage centre with a genealogical service.

Genealogical Office Based in the National Library in Dublin, this is the place to start the search for your Irish ancestors. (p98)

PRONI (Public Record Office of Northern Ireland) Belfast's purpose-built centre is the place to go to track down your Ulster family history. (p581)

Clare Heritage & Genealogy Centre Part of the Clare Heritage Centre Interpretative Museum in Corofin. (p376)

Cobh, The Queenstown Story Cobh's superb heritage museum houses a genealogy centre. (p240)

Dún na Sí Heritage Park A folk park 16km east of Athlone with an associated genealogical centre attached. (p504)

Ulster American Folk Park Ulster's rich links with the USA are explored in one of Northern Ireland's best museums. (p665)

Rothe House & Garden An excellent genealogical service is housed in this 16th-century merchant's house in Kilkenny city. (p213)

Family Days Out

There are plenty of family-friendly activities throughout the country, from heritage museums to zip lines across a forest canopy.

Castle Ward Estate *Game of Thrones* was filmed at this National Trust property, which also has an adventure playground and farm animals. (p603)

Lough Key Forest Park This 350-hectare adventure playland includes a 300m-long canopy walk and an outdoor adventure playground. (p501)

Tayto Park Lots of fun for all the family, including Europe's largest wooden inverted roller coaster, a zoo and a 5D cinema. (p533)

Great Western Greenway Flat and popular bike path from Westport to Achill with plenty of castles and sites to see along the way. (p434)

Fota Wildlife Park Huge outdoor zoo just outside Cork city with not a cage or fence in sight; the cheetah run is especially popular. (p236)

Tralee Bay Wetlands Centre When you're done learning about the habitats of this 3000-hectare reserve, you can hop aboard a boat for a 15-minute safari ride. (p316)

Golf

Ireland is one of the world's premier golf destinations. There are more than 400 courses spread throughout the island, but for a proper Irish golfing experience, tee it up on a links course by the sea.

Ballybunion Golf Club A perennial favourite with visiting celebrities and professionals – the course is as tough as the views are beautiful. (p320)

County Sligo Golf Course Stunning links on a peninsula in the shadow of Ben Bulben. (p450)

Lahinch Golf Club One of Ireland's most beloved links was laid out by Scottish soldiers in 1892. (p362)

Royal County Down Hallowed links designed by Old Tom Morris often rated as the best course in Ireland. (p604)

Royal Portrush A stunner that hosted the Open Championship in 1951 and 2019. (p632)

Waterville Golf Links A world-class links with views to match. (p298)

Month by Month

February

Bad weather makes February the perfect month for indoor activities. Some museums launch new exhibits, and it's a good time to visit the major towns and cities.

☆ Dublin International Film Festival

Most of Dublin's cinemas participate in the capital's film festival, a two-week showcase for new films by Irish and international directors. It features local flicks, arty international films and advance releases of mainstream movies.

☆ Six Nations Rugby

The Irish national rugby team (www.irishrugby.ie) plays its three home matches at the Aviva Stadium in Dublin's southern suburb of Ballsbridge. The season runs from February to April.

March

Spring is in the air, and the whole country is getting ready for arguably the world's most famous parade. Dublin's is the biggest, but every town in Ireland holds one.

☆ St Patrick's Day

Ireland erupts into one giant celebration on 17 March (www.stpatricks day.ie), but Dublin throws a five-day party around the parade (attended by over 750,000 people), with gigs and festivities that leave the city with a giant hangover.

April

The weather is getting better, the flowers are beginning to bloom and the festival season begins anew. Seasonal attractions start to open up around the middle of the month or at Easter.

☆ Circuit of Ireland International Rally

Northern Ireland's most prestigious rally-car race, known locally as the 'Circuit' (www.circuitofireland. net), sees more than 130 competitors throttle and turn through 550km of Northern Ireland and parts of the Republic over two days at Easter.

☆ Irish Grand National

Ireland loves horse racing, and the race that's loved the most is the Grand National, the showcase of the national hunt season. It takes place at Fairyhouse in County Meath on Easter Monday.

☆ World Irish Dancing Championships

There's far more to Irish dancing than *Riverdance*. Every April some 4500 competitors from all over the world gather to test their steps and skills against the very best. The location varies from year to year; see www.irishdancingorg.com.

May

The May Bank Holiday (on the first Monday) sees the first of the busy summer weekends as the Irish take to the roads to enjoy the budding good weather.

🎭 Cork International Choral Festival

One of Europe's premier choral festivals, with the winners going on to the Fleischmann International Trophy Competition, is held over five days between the end of April and the beginning of May.)

☆ North West 200

Ireland's most famous road race is also the country's biggest outdoor sporting event; up to 100,000 people line the triangular route to cheer on some of the biggest names in motorcycle racing. Held in mid-May. (p631)

🎭 Fleadh Nua

The third week of May sees the cream of the traditional-music crop come to Ennis, County Clare, for one of the country's most important festivals. (p347)

🎭 Cathedral Quarter Arts Festival

Belfast's Cathedral Quarter hosts a multidisciplinary arts festival, including drama, music, poetry and street theatre over 10 days at the beginning of the month. (p574)

🎭 Listowel Writers' Week

Well-known writers engaged in readings, seminars and storytelling are the attraction at the country's premier festival (www.writersweek.ie) for bibliophiles, which runs over five days in the County Kerry town of Listowel at the end of the month. There's also poetry, music and drama.

🎭 Father Ted Festival

Fans of the celebrated comedy dress up as their favourite characters and quote their favourite lines at this festival in Lisdoonvarna, culminating in tea and cake in the house where the TV show was shot. It takes place in early May. Gwan Gwan. (p376)

June

The bank holiday at the beginning of the month sees the country spoilt for choice for things to do. Weekend traffic gets busier as the weather gets better.

🎭 Cat Laughs Comedy Festival

Kilkenny gets very, very funny in early June (sometimes late May), with the country's premier comedy festival drawing comedians both known and unknown from around the globe. (p214)

🎭 Dublin LGBTQ Pride

Ireland's most important LGBTQ celebration sees 10 days of events, gigs, screenings and talks that culminate in a huge colourful parade through the capital. (p113)

🎭 Belsonic

Ormeau Park in Belfast hosts Northern Ireland's biggest music festival (www.belsonic.com), with a host of big international names keeping the 5000-or-so fans entertained over two weeks in mid-June.

☆ Irish Derby

Wallets are packed and fancy hats donned for the best flat-race festival in the country (www.curragh.ie), run during the first week of the month.

🎭 Bloomsday

Edwardian dress and breakfast of 'the inner organs of beast and fowl' are but two of the elements of this Dublin festival celebrating 16 June, the day on which James Joyce's *Ulysses* takes place; the real highlight is retracing Leopold Bloom's steps. (p113)

🏃 Mourne International Walking Festival

The last weekend of the month plays host to a walking festival in the Mourne Mountains of County Down, designated an area of outstanding natural beauty. (p607)

🎭 Cork Midsummer Festival

Cork city's largest celebration of the arts takes place over a week midmonth at various venues throughout the city. (p227)

July

There isn't a weekend in the month that a major festival doesn't take place, while visitors to Galway will find that the city is in full swing for the entire month.

🎺 Willie Clancy Summer School

Inaugurated to celebrate the memory of a famed local piper, this exceptional festival of traditional music sees the world's best players show up for gigs, pub sessions and workshops over nine days in Miltown Malbay, County Clare. (p361)

🎺 Galway International Arts Festival

Music, drama and a host of artistic endeavours are on the menu at the most important arts festival in the country, which sees Galway go merriment mad for the last two weeks of the month. (p386)

☆ Galway Film Fleadh

Irish and international releases make up the programme at one of the country's premier film festivals, held in early July. (p386)

☆ Longitude

A mini-Glastonbury in Dublin's Marlay Park, Longitude packs them in over three days in mid-July for a feast of EDM, nu-folk, rock and pop. In 2019 Grace Carter, Chasing Amy and Stormzy were the headliners. (p113)

🎺 Folkfest

Killarney gets all folksy in early July for this festival (http://folkfestkillarney.com) featuring music, beards and flannel from all over Ireland and abroad, including performers from Britain, the USA and elsewhere.

August

Schools are closed, the sun is shining (or not!) and Ireland is in holiday mood. Seaside towns and tourist centres are at their busiest as the country looks to make the most of its time off.

🎺 Féile An Phobail

The name translates simply as the 'people's festival' and it is just that: the largest community festival on the island takes place on the Falls Rd in West Belfast over 10 days. (p575)

🎺 Fleadh Cheoil na hÉireann

The mother of all Irish music festivals (www.fleadhcheoil.ie), held at the end of the month, attracts in excess of 400,000 music lovers and revellers to whichever town is playing host (in 2019 it was held in Drogheda, County Louth) – there's some great music amid the drinking.

☆ Galway Race Week

The biggest horse-racing festival west of the Shannon is not just about the horses; it's also a celebration of Irish culture, sporting gambles and elaborate hats. (p386)

🎺 Mary From Dungloe Festival

Ireland's second most important beauty pageant takes place in Dungloe, County Donegal, at the beginning of the month – though it's an excuse for a giant party, the young women really do want to be crowned the year's 'Mary'. (p473)

🎺 Puck Fair

Ireland's oldest festival is also its quirkiest: crown a goat king and celebrate for three days. Strange idea, but a brilliant festival that takes place in Killorglin, County Kerry, in mid-August. (p290)

☆ Rose of Tralee

The country's biggest beauty pageant divides those who see it as an embarrassing throwback to older days and those who see it as a throwback to older days. Wannabe Roses plucked from Irish communities throughout the world compete for the ultimate prize. (p317)

🎺 Kilkenny Arts Festival

One of Ireland's most important arts festivals brings musicians, artists, performers and writers to a variety of sites across Kilkenny city, including churches, castles, courtyards, townhouses and gardens. The 10-day event takes place in the middle of the month. (p214)

☆ All-Ireland Finals

The end of the summer sees the finals of the hurling and Gaelic football championships respectively, with 80,000-plus crowds thronging into Dublin's Croke Park for the biggest sporting days of the year.

September

Summer may be over, but September weather can be surprisingly good, so it's often the ideal time to enjoy the last vestiges of sun as the crowds dwindle.

Galway International Oyster & Seafood Festival

Over the last weekend of the month, Galway kicks off its oyster season with a festival celebrating the local catch. Music and beer have been the accompaniment since its inception in 1954. (p387)

Dublin Fringe Festival

Upwards of 100 different performances take the stage, the street, the bar and the car in the fringe festival that is unquestionably more innovative than the main theatre festival that follows it. (p113)

October

The weather starts to turn cold, so it's time to move the fun indoors again. The calendar is still packed with activities and distractions, especially over the last weekend of the month.

Dublin Theatre Festival

The most prestigious theatre festival in the country sees new work and new versions of old work staged in theatres and venues throughout the capital. (p113)

Wexford Opera Festival

Opera fans gather in Wexford's National Opera House, the country's only theatre built for opera, to enjoy Ireland's premier lyric festival, which tends to eschew the big hits in favour of lesser-known works. (p182)

Cork Jazz Festival

Ireland's best-known jazz festival sees Cork taken over by more than 1000 musicians and their multitude of fans during the last weekend of the month... even if some of the music sounds suspiciously like blues and rock. (p227)

Belfast International Arts Festival

Northern Ireland's top arts festival attracts performers from all over the world for the second half of the month; on offer is everything from visual arts to dance. (p575)

December

Christmas dominates the calendar as the country prepares for the feast with frenzied shopping and after-work drinks with friends and family arrived home from abroad. On Christmas Day nothing is open.

Christmas

This is a quiet affair in the countryside, though on 26 December (St Stephen's Day) the ancient custom of Wren Boys is re-enacted, most notably in Dingle, County Kerry, when groups of children dress up and go about singing hymns.

Christmas Dip

A traditional Christmas Day swim at the Forty Foot in the Dublin suburb of Sandycove sees a group of very brave swimmers go for a 20m swim to the rocks and back.

Itineraries

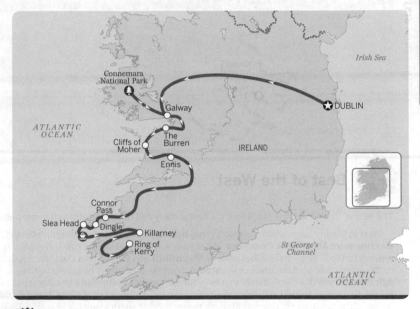

 **Iconic Ireland**

This 300km tourist trail takes you past some of Ireland's most famous attractions and through spectacular countryside.

Start with a whistle-stop tour of **Dublin**, including visits to Trinity College and the Book of Kells, then enjoy a sample of Guinness in its home town. The next day head west to **Galway**, from where you should take a drive through stunning, brooding **Connemara National Park** (which can be driven in a nice loop) before heading south through the moonlike landscape of **The Burren**. Take a detour to the **Cliffs of Moher**, then head to **Ennis**, a good spot to enjoy a bit of traditional Irish music. Keep going south through **Connor Pass** into County Kerry, stopping for a half-day in **Dingle**, then set out to visit its peninsula, taking in the views and prehistoric monuments of **Slea Head**. Via the ferry, continue on to **Killarney**, the perfect base from which to explore the famous **Ring of Kerry**, a much-trafficked 179km loop around the Iveragh Peninsula.

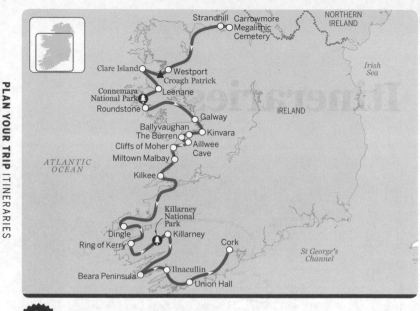

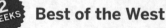

Best of the West

2 WEEKS

The west of Ireland is where you'll find the best scenery and the best traditional music pubs.

Start in County Sligo, where prehistory and panorama combine to wonderful effect at **Carrowmore Megalithic Cemetery**. Wind your way south along the coast, stopping at some of Ireland's best surf beaches such as **Strandhill** and Enniscrone. Continue south to the pub-packed heritage town of **Westport**. Southwest of here is magnificent **Croagh Patrick**, worth a climb if only to feast your eyes on island-studded Clew Bay from a height. Go west to Louisburgh, from where you can head offshore to craggy **Clare Island** (home of the pirate queen Grace O'Malley), before turning south along the beautiful Doolough Valley to **Leenane**, situated on Ireland's only fjord. This is the northern gateway to **Connemara National Park**, which you can explore via the beautiful coastal route, passing Kylemore Abbey, venturing onto Clifden's scenic Sky Road and then winding your way around the coast through pretty **Roundstone**. Alternatively you could savour the stunning wilderness of the inland route to **Galway**, where you should devote at least a day to exploring the city's colourful streets and wonderful pubs.

South of Galway the fishing villages of **Kinvara** and **Ballyvaughan** are at the edge of the strange, karst landscape of **The Burren**, home to all manner of flora and fauna, as well as big-ticket attractions such as the ancient **Aillwee Cave** and the **Cliffs of Moher**. Going south sample some of Ireland's traditional music by attending a session in one of the pubs in **Miltown Malbay**. Beach lovers should also stop in **Kilkee**, a favourite with surfers.

The easiest way to cross into County Kerry is via the ferry at Killimer. Take a day to explore the **Dingle Peninsula** with its rich menu of ancient sites and stunning views, before overnighting in **Dingle** – one of the prettiest towns along the entire west coast. Take another day to explore the world-famous **Ring of Kerry**, ending in **Killarney National Park**, right on the edge of **Killarney** itself. Take the scenic route across the middle of the **Beara Peninsula** and make your way to the Italianate **Ilnacullin** with its exotic flowers. Then follow the coast through Castletownshend and the fishing village of **Union Hall** to the city of **Cork**.

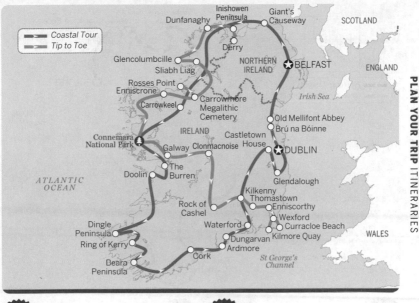

3 WEEKS Coastal Tour

This round-the-island tour takes in some of Ireland's scenic and heritage highlights.

Start in **Dublin**, then head north to the Neolithic necropolis at **Brú na Bóinne**. Continue on to the atmospheric **Old Mellifont Abbey** before crossing the border and heading to **Belfast**. Go along the Antrim coast to the **Giant's Causeway**. Continue around the coastline and head into Sligo to climb the Stone Age passage grave at **Carrowkeel** for views of Lough Arrow. Make your way to the southwest via **Connemara National Park**, one of Ireland's scenic highlights. Wonder at **The Burren** and check out traditional music in **Doolin** before delving into the music, scenery and heritage on the **Dingle Peninsula**. Explore the scenic wonderland of the **Ring of Kerry**. Discover more gorgeous landscapes on the **Beara Peninsula**, then visit Ireland's second city, **Cork**. Become acquainted with seaside **Ardmore**. Visit **Dungarvan** and its castle, and the Museum of Treasures in **Waterford**. Go through medieval **Kilkenny** and then check out handsome **Castletown House** in County Kildare. Cut east to see the monastic site at **Glendalough**. Finally, head back to Dublin.

2 WEEKS Tip to Toe

The full range of Ireland – from north to south – is on the menu in this itinerary.

Begin in Northern Ireland's second city, **Derry**, walking the city walls and exploring the Bogside district. Then cross into County Donegal and explore the **Inishowen Peninsula** before overnighting in **Dunfanaghy**. As you move down the coastline, visit the monastic ruins of **Glencolumbcille** and the sea cliffs at **Sliabh Liag**. Cross into County Sligo and visit the **Carrowmore Megalithic Cemetery**. The next day treat yourself to a round of golf at the County Sligo Golf Course at **Rosses Point**, or a seaweed bath in **Enniscrone**. You'll skirt the eastern edge of **Connemara National Park** as you travel south to **Galway**, from where you should strike out for **Clonmacnoise**. Move through the heart of the Midlands to another monastic gem, the **Rock of Cashel**. Medieval **Kilkenny** is only an hour away – visit its stunning castle before exploring nearby **Thomastown** and Jerpoint Abbey. Using **Wexford** as a base, explore **Curracloe Beach** and visit **Enniscorthy** and the excellent National 1798 Rebellion Centre. Or you could chill out and watch the fishermen draw in their lines in **Kilmore Quay**.

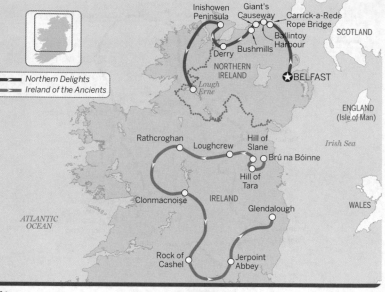

Northern Delights
Ireland of the Ancients

Northern Delights

1 WEEK

Explore the gorgeous landscapes and discover the fascinating history of this much-misunderstood province.

Start in **Belfast**, where you should visit Titanic Belfast and take a black-taxi tour, before heading north towards the Antrim Coast and the **Carrick-a-Rede Rope Bridge**. Head west towards the World Heritage–listed **Giant's Causeway**, a highlight of any trip to Northern Ireland; along the way, *Game of Thrones* fans can check out **Ballintoy Harbour**, which stood in for the Iron Islands' Lordsport Harbour in the TV series. The causeway coast finishes in the fascinating village of **Bushmills**, home to the famous distillery. **Derry** is worth a day – walk the city's walls and explore its more recent past in the Bogside district, and then cross the invisible border into the Republic by visiting the **Inishowen Peninsula** in County Donegal. Back in the North, finish your visit in **Lough Erne**, taking in White Island and the carved stones of Devenish Island.

Ireland of the Ancients

1 WEEK

The majesty and mystery of Ireland's ancient history are yours to discover on this route.

Begin at the stunning Neolithic tombs of Newgrange and Knowth in County Meath, in the heart of **Brú na Bóinne**. Nearby stand at the top of the celebrated **Hill of Tara**, a site of immense folkloric significance and seat of the high kings of Ireland until the 11th century. Across the plain is the **Hill of Slane**, where St Patrick lit a fire in 433 to proclaim Christianity throughout the land. To the west is the Neolithic monument of **Loughcrew**, a quieter alternative to Brú na Bóinne. Keep going west to County Roscommon. Just outside Tulsk village is **Rathcroghan**, the most important Celtic site in Europe. Head south to **Clonmacnoise**, the 6th-century monastic site in County Offaly, then continue through the heart of the country to the impressive **Rock of Cashel** in County Tipperary. Turn east and head through County Kilkenny, stopping at the Cistercian Jerpoint Abbey in the pretty village of **Thomastown**. From here travel northeast to Wicklow and magnificent **Glendalough**, where the substantial remains of a monastic settlement linger by two beautiful lakes.

Plan Your Trip
The Great Outdoors

There's no better way of experiencing this wildly beautiful country than by exploring its varied landscapes – and the rewards can be spectacular. From majestic craggy mountains to lush lakeside woods, from broad sandy beaches to blankets of wild bog stretching as far as the eye can see, Ireland's great outdoors will never disappoint.

Walking

Gentle hills, rocky ridges, wild moorlands, spectacular sea cliffs, remote islands, warm hospitality and the gloriously unpredictable weather – all are part of the wonderful experience of exploring Ireland on foot. There is something for everyone, from postprandial strolls to challenging 1000m peaks.

What to Bring

For short walks on waymarked trails all you will need is comfortable footwear, a rain jacket and some food and water.

Hikers venturing further into Ireland's hills and bogs should be properly equipped and cautious, as the weather can become vicious at any time of year.

➡ After rain, peaty soil can become boggy, so always wear stout shoes or boots and carry good waterproofs and extra food and drink.

➡ Always take a map and compass (and know how to use them). Don't depend on mobile phones (though carrying one with you is a good idea).

➡ Leave a note with your route and expected time of return with a trusted person (either at your accommodation, or in an email or text to a friend or family member), and let them know when you have returned safely.

Top Outdoor Tips

Best Time to Go

May, June and September are the best months for hiking and cycling – best chance of dry weather and less chance of midges.

Best Outdoor Experiences

Hike the Wicklow Way (Wicklow), climb Carrauntoohil (Kerry), cycle the Great Western Greenway (Mayo), mountain-bike at Davagh Forest (Tyrone), tee off at Royal Portrush (Antrim), sea kayak in Lough Hyne (Cork) and canoe the Lough Erne Canoe Trail (Fermanagh).

Essential Hill-Walking Gear

Hiking boots, good waterproofs, spare warm clothing, map, compass, mobile phone (but don't rely on it), first-aid kit, head torch, whistle (for emergencies), spare food and drink.

Safety

Check the weather forecast before setting out, let someone know your plans, set your pace and objective to suit the slowest member of your party, and don't be afraid to turn back if it's too difficult.

TOP FIVE IRISH HILL WALKS

What Ireland's mountains lack in height (its highest peak is a meagre 1040m) they more than make up for in stunning scenery and superb hill-walking opportunities.

Carrauntuohil (1040m; MacGillicuddy's Reeks, County Kerry) The ascent of Ireland's highest peak involves scrambling and challenging navigation; inexperienced hill walkers should hire a guide.

Slieve Donard (853m; Mourne Mountains, County Down) Northern Ireland's highest hill is a straightforward climb; its near neighbour Slieve Binnian is more interesting.

Errigal Mountain (752m; County Donegal) This pyramidal quartzite peak is one of Ireland's shapeliest hills.

Twelve Bens (729m; County Galway) Though small in stature, Connemara's craggy hills offer some of Ireland's toughest terrain. The Glencoaghan Horseshoe is often cited as the country's finest hill walk.

Mt Brandon (951m; County Kerry) The highest peak on the Dingle Peninsula has rugged trails that yield jaw-droppingly spectacular views.

Walking Guides & Maps

There are several good hiking guidebooks that cover Ireland, notably the Collins Press (www.collinspress.ie) series of walking guides.

The Ordnance Survey of Ireland (www.osi.ie) and the Ordnance Survey of Northern Ireland (www.nidirect.gov.uk/ordnance-survey-of-northern-ireland) cover the entire island with their 1:50,000 *Discovery/Discoverer* series (€8.99/£6.50 per sheet). There are also more detailed 1:25,000 *Adventure/Activity* maps (€12.99/£7.80) covering popular areas such as MacGillicuddy's Reeks and Killarney National Park, the Wicklow Mountains, the Mournes and the Causeway Coast.

Maps produced specifically for walkers include the following:

Harveys Superwalker (www.harveymaps.co.uk) Waterproof 1:30,000 hill-walking maps covering Connemara, the Mournes (1:25,000), the Wicklow Mountains and MacGillicuddy's Reeks.

EastWest Mapping (www.eastwestmapping.ie) Walkers' maps of the Wicklow Mountains, the Wicklow Way, the Comeragh Mountains and the Blackstairs Mountains and Barrow Valley.

Access to the Countryside

Unlike Scotland, England and Wales (and most other European countries), where there are public rights of way and/or a public right of access to most areas of uncultivated land, walkers and cyclists in Ireland have no rights of access to privately owned land, not even on wild moorland and mountains (unless it is part of a national park).

The absence of a legal framework has led to a rather fraught situation in recent years as the popularity of walking, mountaineering and mountain biking has increased, and numerous disputes have blown up across the country, forcing the closure or re-routing of some traditional walking routes.

Access has been negotiated with landowners for many national trails and way-marked walks (disputes over access is why many of these trails follow public roads for long distances). However, you will occasionally come across locked gates, barbed-wire fences or 'no walkers allowed' signs – these are legal and must be obeyed.

For more information on access rights and responsible walking see the following:

Keep Ireland Open (www.keepirelandopen.org) Voluntary body campaigning for rights of access to the countryside.

Leave No Trace (www.leavenotraceireland.org) Educational charity promoting responsible use of the outdoors.

Mountaineering Ireland (www.mountaineering.ie) Good information and advice on the Access Policy page.

Where to Walk

For a small country, Ireland is packed with choice – from seaside ambles to long-distance treks in mountain ranges.

Day Walks

You can take a leisurely day hike in just about any part of Ireland. Some suggestions:

Barrow Towpath (p208) Along the River Barrow in Counties Carlow and Kilkenny, pleasant walks can be had along the towpath from Borris to Graiguenamanagh and on to St Mullins.

Glendalough (p161) The wooded trails around this ancient monastic site in County Wicklow lure many a traveller from nearby Dublin for a few hours' rambling.

Lough Key Forest Park (p501) The woods around this lake in County Roscommon have a wonderful canopied trail.

Sky Road (p413) In County Galway, Clifden's Sky Road yields views of the Connemara coast; it's suitable for walking or cycling.

South Leinster Way The prettiest section of this waymarked way is a 13km hike between the charming villages of Graiguenamanagh and Inistioge in County Kilkenny.

Brandon Way Not to be confused with Mt Brandon in County Kerry, the smaller Brandon Hill (516m) in County Kilkenny has a path that wends up to the summit from woodlands and moorlands along the River Barrow.

Killarney National Park (p282) Superb short walks on the shores of Lough Leane in County Kerry, plus the slightly longer Muckross Lake Loop.

Killary Harbour (p418) Scenic walks along the shore of this long, fjord-like inlet of the sea in County Galway.

Glen of Aherlow (p335) Fine walking amid lush woodland and low hills in County Tipperary with grand views towards the high Galtee Mountains.

Fair Head (p644) Easy paths lead to the top of huge basalt sea cliffs in County Antrim, with a panorama that takes in Rathlin Island and the Scottish coast.

Coastal Trails

Ireland's coastline is naturally conducive to long and reflective walks, with or without shoes on. Here are five to get you started:

Arranmore Way (p474; County Donegal) This 14km trail makes a circuit of the wild sea-cliff scenery of this rocky island off the Donegal coast.

Causeway Coast Way (p637; County Antrim) A waymarked trail that follows Antrim's north coast. Particularly spectacular is the final 16.5km from Carrick-a-Rede to the Giant's Causeway.

Wexford Coastal Walk (County Wexford) Follow 221km of trails overlooking vast sandy beaches, bird-haunted backwaters and the bones of old shipwrecks.

Sheep's Head Lighthouse (p260; County Cork) A superb short walk leads from the road end to one of the country's most spectacularly sited lighthouses.

Tory Way (p480; County Donegal) A 12km looped trail around the rocky coast of Tory Island.

Waymarked Trails

The opening of the 1000km Ulster Way in the 1970s followed by the Wicklow Way in 1982 prompted the establishment of a network of 44 long-distance walking trails that total more than 5000km in length. Though many of these would take several days, or even weeks, to complete, you can easily walk shorter sections of each trail as you see fit.

Our top 10 of Ireland's long-distance trails:

Barrow Way (p208) A 114km wander through some of Ireland's loveliest riverside scenery between Lowtown in County Kildare and St Mullins in County Carlow.

Beara Way (p266) A moderately easy loop of 206km that follows historic routes and tracks on a stunning peninsula in West Cork.

Burren Way (p370) This 123km walk takes in County Clare's unique rocky landscape, the Cliffs of Moher and the musical town of Doolin.

Cavan Way (p551) Impressive topographic variety is packed into this short (26km) route, taking in bogs, Stone Age monuments and the source of the River Shannon.

Dingle Way (p310) A popular 179km route in County Kerry that loops around one of Ireland's most beautiful peninsulas.

East Munster Way (p343) Starting in County Tipperary and ending up in County Waterford, a 70km walk through forest and open moorland and along the towpath of the River Suir.

Kerry Way (p276) A 214km route that takes in Killarney National Park, the spectacular Macgillycuddy's Reeks and the Ring of Kerry coast.

Sheep's Head Way (p260) Sweeping seascapes and splendid isolation mark out this 93km off-the-beaten-track peninsular circuit.

Ulster Way (p660) A 1000km route, making a circuit around the six counties of Northern Ireland and Donegal. It can easily be broken down into smaller sections.

Wicklow Way (p157) Ireland's most popular walking trail is this 127km route, which starts in southern Dublin and ends in Clonegal in County Carlow.

MIDGES

Midges are tiny, 2mm-long, blood-sucking flies that appear in huge swarms in summer, and can completely ruin a holiday if you're not prepared to deal with them.

They proliferate from late May to mid-September, but especially mid-June to mid-August – which unfortunately coincides with the main tourist season – and are most common in the western and northern parts of Ireland, especially in boggy areas such as Connemara and Donegal.

Midges are at their worst during the twilight hours and on still, overcast days – strong winds and bright sunshine tend to discourage them. The only way to combat them is to cover up, particularly in the evening. Wear long-sleeved, light-coloured clothing (midges are attracted to dark colours) and, most importantly, use a reliable insect repellent.

Golf

With more than 400 courses dotted around the island, golf is one of Ireland's most popular pastimes and – for the most part – lacks the exclusivity that comes with the game in other parts of the world. There are plenty of parkland courses, but the more memorable golf experiences are to be had on seaside links courses – the Irish coastline is home to 30% of the world's links courses.

Most golf courses are privately owned, but all welcome non-member bookings and walk-ins – to avoid disappointment, book the better-known courses in advance. For the top courses, expect to pay €100 to €250 or more per round; lesser-known courses charge as little as €25, depending on when you play. Some courses will insist that you have a registered handicap from your home country. Most courses will also rent out clubs, but they're not usually very good.

A great option is to rent a customised set of clubs at Dublin or Cork airport through www.clubstohire.com, which you can drop back at the airport when you leave.

Our favourite courses:

Ballybunion Golf Club (p320), County Kerry

Royal Portrush Golf Club (p632), County Londonderry

County Sligo Golf Course (p450), County Sligo

Portmarnock Golf Club (p145), County Dublin

Waterville Golf Links (p298), County Kerry

Lahinch Golf Club (p362), County Clare

Killeen Castle (www.killeencastle.com; Dunsany; green fees from €55), County Meath

For more information, check out **Golf Ireland** (www.golf.discoverireland.ie), or the **Golfing Union of Ireland** (www.golfnet.ie), both of which offer booking services.

There are specials and discounted green fees available throughout the year – a good online resource is www.teetimes.ie, where you can book heavily discounted green fees at dozens of courses throughout the country.

Cycling

Ireland has a lot to offer the cycle tourist, not least in the huge network of minor roads that criss-cross even the wildest parts of the island. Take along a good map and a spirit of adventure (and decent waterproofs, of course) and you can clock up hundreds of kilometres of happy exploration.

Several operators offer guided and self-guided cycling tours in Ireland, including **Iron Donkey** (www.irondonkey.com) and **Ireland by Bike** (www.irelandbybike.com).

Where to Cycle

Great Western Greenway (p434) This 42km, mostly off-road and hugely popular cycleway stretches from Westport to Achill Island in County Mayo.

Killarney National Park (p282) The park offers an adventurous boat-and-bike trip via the lakes of Killarney and up through the impressive Gap of Dunloe.

Kingfisher Trail (p657) A waymarked, long-distance cycling trail stretching 370km along the back roads of Counties Fermanagh, Leitrim, Cavan and Monaghan.

Clifden Cycle Hub The 'capital' of Connemara in County Galway is the focus of four looped cycle routes, ranging from 16km to 40km in length, including the scenic Sky Road (p413).

Waterford Greenway (p201) A 46km, all-abilities trail that opened in in 2017 along the lines of a railway track between Waterford city and Dungarvan.

in the Dublin Mountains, offering varying degrees of gradient and difficulty. Access is at the bottom of Three Rock Mountain.

Mountain Biking

The lack of a legal right of access to private land has meant that off-road biking in Ireland lags behind the UK. That said, there are some excellent purpose-built trail centres, mostly in state forest parks on both sides of the border.

In many areas, local riders quietly work away at their own network of self-built trails; the local bike shop is a great source of information on these.

For more details, check out the following:

Biking.ie (www.biking.ie) Excellent resource, including trail details, rentals and tours in the Republic.

Mountain Bike NI (www.mountainbikeni.com) Full details of mountain-bike centres in Northern Ireland.

TrailBadger (www.trailbadger.com) Useful database of mountain-bike trails in Ireland.

Top MTB Trail Centres

Davagh Forest (p666) Forest trails for beginners, and rock slabs and drop-offs for experts, in the heart of County Tyrone.

Kilbroney Park (p607) With a thigh-crunching 27km red trail and a terrifying 19km black, Rostrevor in County Down is reckoned by some to offer the best mountain biking in Ireland.

Ballyhoura (p334) This mountain-bike centre in County Limerick has the biggest network of trails in the country, ranging from green to black, with the longest at more than 50km.

Ballinastoe (www.coillteoutdoors.ie/site/ballinastoe) This trail centre on the edge of the Wicklow Mountains south of Dublin has a superbly flowing, 14km blue trail. There are plenty more trails to explore in the nearby hills.

Bike Park Ireland (☑067-21961; www.bikeparkireland.ie; Fairymount Farm, Ballingarry; per day/half-day incl uplift €45/35, trails only €10; ☺9am-6pm Sat & Sun Apr-Oct; ⓐ) This purpose-built centre in County Tipperary has an uplift service to the top of the hill, and downhill trails for all levels of rider.

Ticknock MTB (www.dublinmountains.ie; Ticknock Forest, Sandyford) A 13km network of purpose-built single-track trails and forest roads

Water Sports

Surfing & Windsurfing

Surfing is all the rage on the coast, especially in the west. The most popular spots include the following:

County Donegal Bundoran, the unofficial capital of Irish surfing, hosts the Irish national championships in April. Along the coast there are at least half a dozen top-rated spots for beginners and advanced surfers. Windsurfing and kitesurfing are equally popular around Port-na-Blagh.

County Sligo Easkey and Strandhill are famous for their year-round surf, and have facilities for travellers who seek room and board (with the room being optional).

County Clare Nice breaks at Kilkee, Lahinch and Fanore.

County Waterford Tramore Beach is a coastal resort that's home to Ireland's largest surf school.

County Kerry Surfers flock to massive Inch Strand for its nicely sized, well-paced waves. Brandon Bay and Ballybunion are also top spots.

County Antrim The beaches around Portrush afford good surfing and bodysurfing. The swells are highest and the water warmest in September and October.

Canoeing & Sea Kayaking

Ireland's long, indented coastline provides some of the world's finest sea kayaking. There are sheltered inlets ideal for beginners, long and exciting coastal and island tours, and gnarly tidal passages that will challenge even the most expert paddler, all amid spectacular scenery and wildlife – encounters with seals, dolphins and even whales are relatively common. The **Irish Sea Kayaking Association** (www.iska.ie) lists providers of kayak tours and courses.

The country's inland lakes and waterways offer excellent Canadian canoeing. Northern Ireland has established a network of official **canoe trails** (www.canoeni.com), with infrastructure that includes access points, information boards, toilets and campsites. South of the border, waterways such as the Shannon,

Barrow and Grand Canal (see www. waterwaysireland.org) offer long-distance canoe-touring possibilities.

Scuba Diving

Ireland's west coast has some of the best diving in Europe. The best period for diving is roughly March to October, when visibility averages more than 12m, but can increase to 30m on good days.

Top dive locations include Kilkee (Mayo), Baltimore (Cork), Castlegregory (Kerry) and Arranmore Island and Rosguill (Donegal).

For more details about diving, contact **Comhairle Fó-Thuinn** (CFT; www. diving.ie), also known as the Irish Underwater Council; it publishes the dive magazine *SubSea* (available online).

Coasteering

If sometimes a simple clifftop walk doesn't cut the mustard, then coasteering might appeal. It's like mountaineering, but instead of going up a mountain, you go sideways along a coast – a steep and rocky coast – with waves breaking around your feet. And if the rock gets too steep, no problem – you jump in and start swimming. Coasteering centres provide wetsuits, helmets and buoyancy aids; you provide an old pair of training shoes and a sense of adventure.

Providers include the following:

Eclipse Ireland (www.eclipseireland.com) Operates mostly on the Beara Peninsula (Cork) and the Ring of Kerry.

Coasteering NI (www.coasteeringni.co.uk) Operates at Ballintoy in County Antrim near the Giant's Causeway.

Fishing

Fishing – whether in sea, lough or river – is one of Ireland's most popular pastimes. The country is justly famous for its salmon, sea-trout and brown-trout fishing, and for its superb sea angling.

The books *Rivers of Ireland* and *Loughs of Ireland* by Peter O'Reilly provide a comprehensive guide to fishing for trout and salmon in both Northern Ireland and the Republic of Ireland.

Top Irish angling experiences:

➡ Fly fishing for brown trout on the big limestone loughs of Corrib and Mask (County Galway); the annual mayfly hatch here attracts thousands of anglers from all over the world.

➡ Sea trout fishing in the Moy Estuary (County Mayo), one of the most productive sea trout fisheries in all of Britain and Ireland.

➡ Fishing for salmon on the Blackwater (Cork), Laune (Kerry) or Roe (Londonderry), three of Ireland's top salmon rivers.

➡ Shore fishing for sea bass in the southwest, or boat fishing for blue shark out of Kinsale – Ireland has some of Europe's finest sea angling.

Permits & Rod Licences

Neither a permit nor a licence is needed for sea angling.

Permits Fishing for brown trout in many of Ireland's most famous loughs, including Corrib, Mask and the Killarney lakes, is free. Most loughs and rivers, however, require a permit (ask at the local hotel or tackle shop). Day-ticket prices range from €3 to €20.

Rod licences In addition to a permit, a rod licence is required for all freshwater fishing in Northern Ireland (three/14 days £3.50/9). In the Republic a rod licence is needed only for salmon and sea-trout fishing (one day/three weeks €20/40). You can buy them from local tackle shops and some tourist offices.

For more information see www.fishing inireland.info.

Rock Climbing

Ireland's mountain ranges aren't high – Mt Carrantuohil in Kerry's Macgillycuddy's Reeks is the highest peak in the country at only 1040m – but they offer some excellent rock climbing, notably in the Mournes, the Reeks and around Glendalough in the Wicklow Mountains.

The cream of the country's climbing, however, is on its superb sea cliffs – from Malin Beg in Donegal and the cliffs on Achill Island, to the soaring basalt columns of Fair Head and perfect limestone crags of The Burren. *Rock Climbing in Ireland* (2014; €25/£20) by David Flanagan covers 400 of the country's best routes. For all other information, check out **Irish Climbing Online** (www.climbing.ie).

Plan Your Trip
Eat & Drink Like a Local

The 'local food' movement was pioneered in Ireland in the 1970s, notably at the world-famous Ballymaloe House. Since then the movement has gone from strength to strength, with dozens of farmers markets showcasing the best of local produce, and restaurants all over the country highlighting locally sourced ingredients.

Food Experiences
Meals of a Lifetime

Restaurant Patrick Guilbaud, Dublin (p125)

Mews, Baltimore, County Cork (p255)

Nash 19, Cork city (p231)

Campagne, Kilkenny city (p216)

Wilde's at the Lodge, Cong, County Mayo (p427)

Jacks' Coastguard Restaurant, Cromane Peninsula, County Kerry (p292)

Olde Post Inn, Butlersbridge, County Cavan (p549)

Restaurant 1826 Adare, Adare, County Limerick (p332)

MacNean House & Restaurant, Blacklion, County Cavan (p550)

Aniar, Galway city (p393)

Dare to Try

Ironically, while the Irish palate has become more adventurous it is the old-fashioned Irish menu that features some fairly challenging dishes. Dare to try the following:

Black pudding Made from cooked pork blood, suet and other fillings; a ubiquitous part of an Irish cooked breakfast.

The Year in Food
April–June

Freshly picked fruit and vegetables, such as asparagus and rhubarb, make an appearance.

West Waterford Festival of Food (p201) Three days of local produce and fine food in Dungarvan, including a seaside barbecue and a craft-beer garden.

Taste of Dublin (p113) The capital's best restaurants combine to serve up sample platters of their finest dishes amid music and other entertainment.

July–September

First of the season's new potatoes appear, along with jams and pies made with gooseberries, blackberries and loganberries.

Taste of West Cork Food Festival (p253) Skibbereen brings together its best producers to put on this week-long festival.

Galway International Oyster & Seafood Festival (p387) The last weekend in September sees plenty of oysters, washed down with lashings of Guinness.

October–December

October is apple-picking month, and the main potato crop is harvested.

Kinsale Gourmet Festival (p247) The unofficial gourmet capital of Ireland struts its culinary stuff over three days.

Top: Boxty

Bottom: Cashel Blue cheese

Boxty A Northern Irish starchy potato cake made with a half-and-half mix of cooked mashed potatoes and grated, strained raw potato.

Carrageen The typical Irish seaweed that can be found in dishes as diverse as salad and ice cream.

Corned beef tongue Usually accompanied by cabbage, this dish is still found on a traditional Irish menu.

Lough Neagh eel A speciality of Northern Ireland, typically eaten around Halloween; it's usually served in chunks with a white onion sauce.

Poitín It's rare to be offered a drop of the 'cratur', as illegally distilled whiskey (made from malted grain or potatoes) is called here. Still, there are pockets of the country – Donegal, Connemara and West Cork – with secret stills.

> **THE BEST IRISH CHEESES**
>
> **Ardrahan** Flavoursome farmhouse creation with a rich, nutty taste.
>
> **Corleggy** Subtle, pasteurised goat's cheese.
>
> **Gubbeen** The crumbly, oak-smoked variety is superb.
>
> **Durrus** A creamy, fruity cheese, loved by fine-food fans.
>
> **Cashel Blue** Creamy blue cheese from Tipperary.
>
> **Cooleeney** Award-winning Camembert-style cheese.

Local Specialities

To Eat

Potatoes Still a staple of most traditional meals and presented in a variety of forms. The mashed-potato dishes colcannon and champ (with cabbage and spring onion, respectively) are two of the tastiest recipes in the country.

Meat and seafood Beef, lamb and pork are common options. Seafood is widely available in restaurants and is often excellent, especially in the west. Oysters, trout and salmon are delicious, particularly if they're direct from the sea or river rather than a fish farm.

Soda bread The most famous Irish bread is made with bicarbonate of soda, to make up for soft Irish flour that traditionally didn't take well to yeast. Combined with buttermilk, it makes a superbly tasty bread, and is often on breakfast menus at B&Bs.

The fry Who can say no to a plate of fried bacon, sausages, black pudding, white pudding, eggs and tomatoes? For the famous Ulster fry, common throughout the North, simply add fadge (potato bread).

To Drink

Stout While Guinness has become synonymous with stout the world over, few outside Ireland realise that there are two other major brands competing for the favour of the Irish drinker: Murphy's and Beamish, both brewed in Cork city.

Tea The Irish drink more tea, per capita, than any other nation in the world and you'll be offered a cup as soon as you cross the threshold of any Irish home. Taken with milk (and sugar, if you want) rather than lemon, preferred blends are very strong and nothing like the namby-pamby versions that pass for Irish breakfast tea elsewhere.

Whiskey As recently as the 1990s there were only three working distilleries in Ireland – Jameson's, Bushmills and Cooley's. An explosion in artisan distilling has seen the number grow to more than 30, exhibiting a range and quality that will make the connoisseur's palate spin while winning over many new friends to what the Irish call *uisce beatha* (water of life).

Craft Distilleries

A handful of independently owned distilleries have opened in recent years, producing whiskies (and, in some cases, gin and rum) that have added a fine bit of diversity to the range of Irish spirits.

Blackwater Distillery A distillery in Cappoquin, County Waterford, that produces around 50 casks of whisky (without the 'e', in accordance with Munster tradition) a year.

Dingle Distillery (p305) Whiskey, a quintuple-distilled vodka and a London dry gin made on the edge of Dingle town.

Listoke Distillery & Gin School (p540) Gin distillery that gives you the chance to make your own.

West Cork Distillers (☏028-22815; www.westcorkdistillers.com; Marsh Rd; ⊘10am-2pm Sat) Blended, pot still and single malt whiskies, as well as liqueurs and vodka.

Slane Distillery (p529) The first batch of triple cask matured whiskey was made in 2017 at this new distillery.

IRELAND'S CRAFT BEERS

Although mainstream lagers are most pubs' best-selling pints, the craft-beer revolution has seen around 100 microbreweries come into operation all over the island, making artisan beers that are served in more than 600 of Ireland's pubs and bars. Here's a small selection to whet the taste buds:

Devil's Backbone (4.9% alcohol by volume) Rich amber ale from County Donegal brewer Kinnegar.

The Full Irish (6%) Single malt IPA by Eight Degrees Brewery outside Mitchelstown, County Cork.

O'Hara's Leann Folláin (6%) Dry stout with vaguely chocolate notes produced by Carlow Brewing Company in Moneybeg, County Carlow.

Metalman Pale Ale (4.3%) American-style pale ale by the much-respected Metalman Brewing Company in County Waterford – now available in cans.

Saturate (8.0%) A double IPA with a hefty kick, from County Wicklow–based Whiplash Beer, voted Irish beer of the year in 2018.

Twisted Hop (4.7%) Blond ale produced by Hilden, Ireland's oldest independent brewery, just outside Lisburn.

Teeling Distillery (p109) Dublin's first new distillery in 125 years was opened in 2015 by the same family that owns the Cooley Distillery in County Louth.

How to Eat & Drink

When to Eat

Irish eating habits have changed over the last couple of decades, and there are differences between urban and rural practices.

Breakfast Usually eaten before 9am, as most people rush off to work (though hotels and B&Bs will serve until 10am or 11am Monday to Friday, and till noon at weekends in urban areas). Weekend brunch is popular in bigger towns and cities.

Lunch Urban workers eat on the run between 12.30pm and 2pm (most restaurants don't begin to serve lunch until at least midday). At weekends, especially Sunday, the midday lunch is skipped in favour of a substantial mid-afternoon meal (called dinner), usually between 2pm and 4pm.

Tea Not the drink, but the evening meal – also confusingly called dinner. This is the main meal of the day for urbanites, usually eaten around 6.30pm. Rural communities eat at the same time but with a more traditional tea of bread, cold cuts and, yes, tea. Restaurants follow international habits, with most diners not eating until at least 7.30pm.

Supper A before-bed snack of tea and toast or sandwiches, still enjoyed by many Irish folk, though urbanites increasingly eschew it for health reasons. Not a practice in restaurants.

Where to Eat

Restaurants From cheap 'n' cheerful to Michelin-starred, Ireland has something for every palate and budget.

Cafes Ireland is awash with cafes of every description, many of which are perfect for a quick, tasty bite.

Hotels Even if you're not a guest, most hotel restaurants cater to outside diners. Top hotels usually feature good restaurants with prices to match.

Pubs Pub grub is ubiquitous, mostly of the toasted-sandwich variety. A large number, however, also have full menu service, with some being as good as any top restaurant.

Dining Etiquette

The Irish aren't big on restrictive etiquette, preferring friendly informality to any kind of stuffy to-dos. Still, the following are a few tips to dining with the Irish:

Children All restaurants welcome kids up to 7pm, but pubs and some smarter restaurants don't allow them in the evening. Family restaurants have children's menus; others have reduced portions of regular menu items.

Returning a dish If the food is not to your satisfaction, it's best to politely explain what's wrong with

Teeling Whiskeys on display at the distillery (p109)

it as soon as you can. Any respectable restaurant will offer to replace the dish immediately.

Paying the bill If you insist on paying the bill for everyone, be prepared for a first, second and even third refusal to countenance such an exorbitant act of generosity. But don't be fooled: the Irish will refuse something several times even if they're delighted with it. Insist gently but firmly and you'll get your way!

Finding the Best of Irish Food & Drink

www.bordbia.ie Irish Food Board website, with a comprehensive list of farmers markets (enter 'farmers markets' in the search box on the homepage).

www.goodfoodireland.ie Listings of top-quality Irish food and drink suppliers.

www.irishcheese.ie The Association of Irish Farmhouse Cheesemakers, with every small dairy covered.

www.slowfoodireland.com Organisation supporting small producers, with social events across Ireland.

Plan Your Trip
Family Travel

Ireland loves kids. Everywhere you go you'll find locals to be enthusiastic and inquisitive about your beloved progeny. This admiration, however, hasn't always translated into child services such as widespread and accessible baby-changing facilities, or high chairs in restaurants, especially in smaller towns and rural areas.

Keeping Costs Down

Accommodation

Hotels are often geared up for families and many will squeeze in a cot for no extra charge. Look out for B&Bs with family rooms, which often offer a double bed and two singles for not much more than the price of a double room.

Sightseeing

There are free or half-price tickets for little ones at most sights in Ireland; many of the more family-oriented attractions also offer family tickets (usually for two adults plus two children). For many big-ticket attractions (eg Titanic Belfast and Dublin Zoo) you can save substantial amounts of cash, as well as queuing time, by prepurchasing tickets online.

Eating

Children can get half portions at many restaurants. Ireland's farmers markets are a great way to sample the country's culinary delights. You'll find bread, cheese, charcuterie, smoked fish, fruit and vegetables – all ideal for picnics.

Transport

Children under five travel free on all public transport. Trains are ideal for families, as there's lots of room to move about and store all of your gear, including buggies and prams.

Children Will Love...

Animal Adventures

Ark Open Farm, Newtownards (p598) Get up close and personal with lambs, piglets and ducklings, all of which you can pet and feed.

Courtown Seal Rescue, County Wexford (☎053-942 4980; www.sealrescueireland.org; Courtown; tours by donation; ⊙10am-5pm) ✿ Meet orphaned, lost and injured seals before they're rehabilitated and returned to the wild.

Dolphinwatch, Loop Head (p358) Take a cruise and get up close to the Shannon Estuary's 200-odd bottlenose dolphins.

St Tola Irish Goat Cheese, The Burren (p366) Meet (and pet) the goats who produce the milk that turns into one of Ireland's best-known cheeses.

Outdoor Fun

Brave Maeve Story Trail, Bray (p164) A 1.5km walking trail along the seafront aimed at kids, who uncover the story of a young giant along the way.

Last Leprechauns of Ireland, Carlingford (p547) Enter a leprechaun cave in the company of a 'leprechaun whisperer' – is there a better invitation for adventurous young minds?

Killarney Riding Stables (p273) Learn to ride in one of Europe's most beautiful settings, along the lakes of Killarney National Park.

Slieve Gullion Forest Park, County Armagh
(p615) There's a fabulous and kid-friendly hike to the top of Slieve Gullion, from where the views are sublime.

Tasty Treats

Rowan Tree Cafe Bar (p349) Ennis. Child-friendly cafe, with a great range of dishes in kid-size portions, including local-goat-cheese fritters.

Hazel Mountain Chocolate (p395) Galway. A 45-minute session watching how chocolate is made is as close to Willy Wonka's chocolate factory as you'll get in Ireland.

Murphy's (p308) Dingle. Handmade ice cream with a range of classic and more unusual flavours, including Irish brown bread, sea salt, and elderflower.

Tankardstown House (p531) Slane. A rarity – a fine-dining restaurant that caters for children.

Rainy Day Escapes

Aillwee Cave, Ballyvaughan (p379) They've been keeping the rain out for more than two million years, and this extraordinary network of caves is a world unto itself.

Celtic & Prehistoric Museum, Slea Head (p311) The world's largest woolly mammoth skull and a 40,000-year-old bear skeleton are just some of the fabulous artefacts at this museum.

National Leprechaun Museum, Dublin (p105) More a romper room for kids with a sprinkling of folklore, but still a lot of fun.

Ulster Museum, Belfast (p566) A wealth of artefacts, from Egyptian mummies to swag salvaged from ships of the Spanish Armada.

Educational Experiences

King John's Castle, Limerick city (p324) The tour of a genuine medieval castle and its superb multimedia exhibit is highly educational.

Irish National Heritage Park, Wexford town (p182) A brilliant, educational day out learning the whole history of Ireland.

National Museum of Country Life, Castlebar (p444) Ireland's rural history told in fascinating, easy-to-digest manner.

Spike Island, Cobh (p237) Visit 'Ireland's Alcatraz', as this former prison island is dubbed.

Ulster Folk Museum, Belfast (p570) A fully reconstructed folk village shows how the Irish used to live.

Region by Region
Dublin & The East

For information on family travel in Dublin, see Dublin for Children (p112).

Beyond the city limits, County Wicklow makes for an easy day trip, and Powerscourt Estate (p152) is a great family-friendly attraction.

If your kids like horses, a visit to the Irish National Stud (p172) will be a thrill – the best time to visit is in the afternoon in springtime, as you can watch the foals getting walked back from the paddocks to the stables around 3pm.

The South

Counties Cork and Kerry are prime summer-holiday territory, with lots of sandy beaches to play on. As well as swimming you can get lessons in surfing, boardsailing and stand-up paddleboarding.

Outdoor activities are the name of the game in Killarney National Park (p282), with the prospect of boat trips and bicycle tours, as well as pony trekking, kayaking and rock climbing. Kells Bay Gardens (p293) are dotted with model dinosaurs and home to Ireland's longest rope bridge.

For older children, a boat trip to the spectacular Skellig Michael (p53) – a Star Wars movie location – would be unforgettable.

The West

The stunning coastal scenery of County Clare might not be a big draw for younger children, but exploring the stalagmites and stalactites beneath the ground is always popular – the limestone landscape of the Burren is riddled with spectacular subterranean chambers.

Be aware that boggy areas in the west – notably Connemara – can suffer badly from midges (tiny biting flies) in summer. Although they are not dangerous, they can be a nuisance; be prepared by wearing long-sleeved clothing and a hat and using insect repellent (Smidge brand is effective and pleasant to use).

Northern Ireland

Belfast is packed with fun activities for kids, from Belfast Zoo (p571) and Cave Hill (p570) adventure playground, to W5 (p566), an interactive hands-on science museum aimed specifically at the under-11s. The city was home to **CS Lewis**, and you can explore public art inspired by *The Lion, the Witch and the Wardrobe* in East Belfast. There's also the **Narnia Trail** near Rostrevor in County Down.

Good to Know

Look out for the 👪 icon for family-friendly suggestions throughout this guide.

Hotels Most big hotels can provide cots if given adequate notice; note that during busy periods their often-limited supply may quickly run out, so be sure to give plenty of notice. You'll have to check with smaller hotels and B&Bs, as many only have them on an ad hoc basis.

Eating Out There are no legal restrictions on kids in any restaurant or cafe, but in practice many places (especially in higher price brackets, but not exclusively so) would prefer if you left the kids at home, especially at busy times or in the evenings. Then, high chairs suddenly become unavailable: if you're booking ahead, be sure to specify if you need one.

Car seats Child seats are mandatory in rental cars for children aged nine months to four years. All main car-hire companies can provide them (around €50/£35 per week), but you'll need to book them in advance.

Changing diapers Most museums and attractions targeting families have decent baby-changing facilities. Elsewhere, modern shopping centres in cities all have baby-changing areas (in Ireland diapers are known as nappies).

Breastfeeding Although public breastfeeding is not a common sight (Ireland has one of the lowest rates of it in the world), you can do so with impunity pretty much everywhere without getting so much as a stare.

Useful Resources

Lonely Planet Kids (www.lonelyplanetkids.com) Loads of activities and family-travel blog content.

Failte Ireland (www.discoverireland.ie) Some good ideas for family-friendly things to see and do.

Northern Ireland Tourist Board (https://discovernorthernireland.com) Has a section dedicated to family travel.

Kids' Corner

Say What?

Hello.	Dia duit. *deea gwit*
Goodbye.	Slán leat. *slawn lyat*
Thank you (very much).	Go raibh (míle) *goh rev (meela)* maith agat. *mah agut*
My name is ...	...is ainm dom. *... is anim dom*

Did You Know? ℹ

- The submarine was invented by an Irishman (John Philip Holland).
- The longest place name in Ireland is Muckanaghederdauhaulia.

Have You Tried?

DALAIFOOD/SHUTTERSTOCK ©

Champ
Mashed potato mixed with chopped scallions

Plan Your Trip
Wild Atlantic Way

Ireland's western coastline is one of the world's most stunning shorelines – a 2500km necklace of jagged cliffs, crescent strands and latticed fields strung out from west Cork to northeastern Donegal. This official driving route is richly decorated with the panoramic pit stops you came to Ireland to experience.

Cork to Kerry

Ireland's southwest corner is packed with scenic highlights along its 463km coastline, skirting around the best known (and most explored) peninsulas in the country.

Highlights

Mizen Head (p257; Cork) The spectacular views from the rugged clifftop (cross the Mizen footbridge to get right to the edge) include the Fastnet Lighthouse, perched on a rock known as Ireland's Teardrop (this was the last sight of the country for emigrants leaving for America during the Famine).

Slea Head Drive (p311; Kerry) Only 47km long, this circular route around the tip of the peninsula is one of Ireland's best scenic drives. The main distraction from the stunning scenery is the heavy concentration of prehistoric sites dotted throughout the hills.

Worth Discovering

Dursey Island (p268; Cork) At the tip of the remote Beara Peninsula is a quiet island, blissfully free of shops, pubs and restaurants but worth visiting for its lighthouse, castle ruins and standing stones. Get here on a 10-minute cable-car ride, but remember that the handful of residents take precedence over tourists!

Need to Know

The Route

Split into five connected sections spread across nine counties: Cork, Kerry, Clare, Limerick, Galway, Mayo, Sligo, Leitrim and Donegal.

Clearly marked by nearly 4000 signposts featuring an aquamarine-coloured wave and punctuated by 157 'Discovery Points' where you can stop and learn about must-sees and lesser-known diversions in each area.

Direction

Car You can drive the route in either direction, but to stay closer to the sea – with the best views – drive south to north.

Bicycle The prevailing wind is southerly, so south to north is easier (even if the wind can't be relied to cooperate).

Information

For up-to-date information on everything to do with the Wild Atlantic Way, check out Failte Ireland's designated website at www.wildatlanticway.com.

Wild Atlantic Way

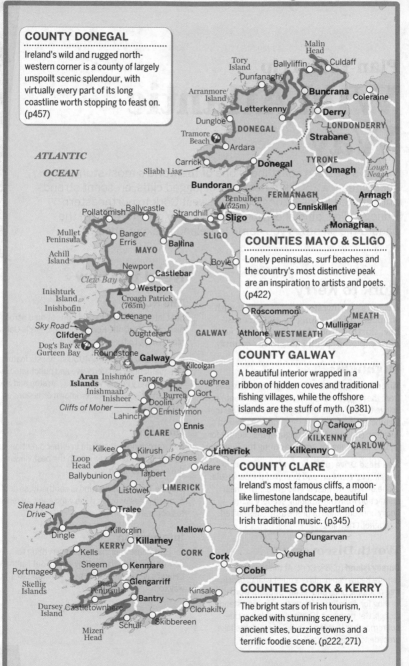

COUNTY DONEGAL

Ireland's wild and rugged north-western corner is a county of largely unspoilt scenic splendour, with virtually every part of its long coastline worth stopping to feast on. (p457)

COUNTIES MAYO & SLIGO

Lonely peninsulas, surf beaches and the country's most distinctive peak are an inspiration to artists and poets. (p422)

COUNTY GALWAY

A beautiful interior wrapped in a ribbon of hidden coves and traditional fishing villages, while the offshore islands are the stuff of myth. (p381)

COUNTY CLARE

Ireland's most famous cliffs, a moon-like limestone landscape, beautiful surf beaches and the heartland of Irish traditional music. (p345)

COUNTIES CORK & KERRY

The bright stars of Irish tourism, packed with stunning scenery, ancient sites, buzzing towns and a terrific foodie scene. (p222, 271)

SIGNATURE EXPERIENCES

The Wild Atlantic Way is interspersed with a series of 'signature experiences' designed to enhance your visit. They include the following:

Cork & Kerry A visit to Skellig Michael (p56), a rocky crag with the beehive huts of 8th-century monks, described by George Bernard Shaw as 'part of our dream world'.

Clare Take a guided tour (p370) of The Burren, as the local guides will give you a remarkable insight into 'Europe's largest rock garden', an area rich in flora and home to Neolithic monuments that predate the Egyptian pyramids.

Clare & Galway Explore Inisheer (p405), the smallest of the Aran Islands, by pony and trap. If it suits, catch the ferry (p397) to Doolin, in County Clare – if you time it right, you'll go by the Cliffs of Moher just as the sun is going down.

Sligo Take an oily soak in hand-harvested Atlantic seaweed and briny water, a traditional organic cure for stress and other ailments due to the high concentration of iodine in the seaweed. Voya Seaweed Baths (p450) in Strandhill are renowned.

Donegal Take the ferry out to the remote island of Tory (p479), where nearly everybody is a painter in the native art style developed in the 1950s. You'll most likely be met at the dock by the 'King' of the island, Patsy Dan...who happens to be a painter, too.

County Clare

Clare's coastline is justifiably renowned throughout Europe for its dramatic cliffs, shaped over aeons by the crashing waves of the relentless Atlantic.

Highlights

Loop Head (p358) This narrow shelf of headland, surrounded on both sides by the sea, has a long hiking trail between the tip and Kilkee. The views – of the Dingle Peninsula to the south and Galway and the Aran Islands to the north – are mesmerising.

Cliffs of Moher (p365) Ireland's most famous cliffs rise 203m from the sea and their majesty entirely justifies the busloads of visitors that come, gawp and leave in wonder. For the best views, head south for about 5km along the southerly trail to Hag's Head.

Worth Discovering

Lahinch (p362) The Blue Flag beach at Lahinch is a surfers' paradise thanks to its flooding tide. Nearby is one of the best golf courses in Ireland and, a little further afield, Ennistymon is a fine spot for traditional music.

County Galway

Wildness abounds in Galway, even beyond the crazy nights in its namesake city. Connemara is a stunning wilderness of bogs, mountains and glacial lakes, while the Aran Islands' dramatic desolation is at the heart of their beguiling beauty.

Highlights

Sky Road (p413) A 12km circular route from Clifden, Connemara's 'capital'. The scenery is staggering, especially northward towards remote Inishboffin and the islands of Clew Bay in Mayo. It's also a popular cycling route; you can hire bikes in Clifden.

Aran Islands (p396) Forty minutes by ferry (or 10 by plane) and you're in another century. Take your pick of three islands, each with their own distinctive features (Inishmor the most visited, Inisheer the smallest and Inishmaan the most isolated) but each giving the feeling of living at the edge of the world.

Worth Discovering

Dog's Bay & Gurteen Bay (p411) About 3km from Roundstone, the twin beaches of Dog's Bay and Gurteen Bay are among Ireland's most beautiful – two back-to-back crescents of brilliant white sand made entirely of tiny bits of seashells rather than the crushed limestone common on other beaches.

County Mayo to County Sligo

Less visited than their southern counterparts, Mayo and Sligo adorn the Wild Atlantic crown with some truly stunning and desolate landscapes, beautiful islands and a handful of superb beaches that are surfers' favourites.

Highlights

Achill Island (p436; Mayo) Ireland's largest offshore island is easily reached by a causeway from the mainland. Once there you'll have soaring cliffs and sandy beaches to explore as well as blanket bogs and even a mountain range.

Benbulben (p454; Sligo) On a clear day you won't miss the distinctive peak of Sligo's most famous mountain, which is like a table covered in a pleated tablecloth. Its beguiling look inspired WB Yeats.

Worth Discovering

Mullet Peninsula (p440; Mayo) Few spots in Ireland are as unspoilt and as unpopulated as this beautiful peninsula, which juts about 30km into the Atlantic. The eastern shores are lined with pristine beaches and the few people here speak Irish.

County Donegal

Wild, remote in parts and beautiful throughout, Donegal is the fitting end (or start) to the Wild Atlantic Way. Its jagged coastline of sheer cliffs, hidden coves and long stretches of golden sand are the stuff of myth and postcard – and an easy rival to any other county in the natural-beauty stakes.

Highlights

Sliabh Liag (p467) These spectacular, monochrome cliffs in southwestern Donegal get far less press than their southern equivalent, but they're taller, at 600m, and every bit as dramatic.

Malin Head (p489) Ireland's northernmost point is a rocky, weather-battered promontory topped by an early-19th-century Martello tower called Banba's Crown.

Worth Discovering

Tramore Beach (p199) An exhilarating 2km hike from the pretty village of Dunfanaghy takes you through some impressive dunes to a beautiful, usually empty strand; at the far end a path leads to Pollaguill Bay.

Regions at a Glance

The historic counties of Antrim, Armagh, Down, Fermanagh, Londonderry and Tyrone form Northern Ireland, which is part of the United Kingdom and (despite the lack of border controls) separate from the Republic of Ireland.

Dublin

Museums
Entertainment
History

Cultural Exhibits

The capital is the nation's primary repository of archaeological artefacts and artistic and cultural treasures. The National Museum's three Dublin branches are the place to start, while the city's multitude of galleries have art from the Renaissance to the current day.

Pubs & Nightlife

With 700-odd pubs, Dublin offers plenty of choice when deciding where to enjoy a pint of the city's most celebrated produce. Beyond Guinness and pub chatter there's theatre old and new, all manner of gigs and a host of sporting distractions.

A Story in Every Stone

Virtually every Dublin street is lined with monuments to its storied history, from the cobbled grounds of Trinity College to the bloodied walls of Kilmainham Gaol. A host of top-notch walking tours reveal each one, from the city's fine Georgian architecture to the less-than-salubrious characters that darkened its history.

p66

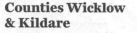

Counties Wicklow & Kildare

Scenery
Monastic Ruins
Activities

Mountain Views

There are splendid views pretty much everywhere in the Wicklow Mountains, especially at the top of the passes that cut through the range – on a clear day you can see five counties. In Kildare the fecund Bog of Allen offers another classic Irish landscape.

Ancient Monasteries

Not only are the ruins of Glendalough utterly absorbing, but their location alone, at the bottom of a glacial valley by two lakes, is absolutely enchanting and well worth the visit.

Walking Routes

Ireland's most popular walking trail, the Wicklow Way, cuts through the county north to south. Kildare is horse-breeding country, with walking paths that are a bit gentler but no less enjoyable.

p149

Counties Wexford, Waterford, Carlow & Kilkenny

Scenery
History
Food

Seaside Vistas

Emerald-green fields above ragged ebony cliffs that end in a cerulean sea: you will never tire of the vista. Should you need a break, perfect pockets of sand dot the coast, while Wexford's beaches stretch beyond the horizon. Inland, rural Ireland includes wild rivers and bucolic farms.

Viking Trails

You half expect to encounter a Viking as you wander the streets of Waterford and Wexford, where traces of the Middle Ages are all around you. Kilkenny's medieval past is impossible to miss, from its soaring cathedral to its great castle.

Local Produce

Head to Dungarvan, County Waterford, to enjoy Irish cooking at its best, and enjoy the region's wonderful produce in all towns, big and small.

p178

County Cork

Food
Scenery
History

Gourmet Treats

County Cork is the unofficial gourmet heartland of Ireland, from the fabulous eateries of Cork city to the wealth of local producers and foodie artisans of West Cork, where you can buy directly at the source and eat like a lord.

Peninsular Panoramas

The county's three western peninsulas – Mizen Head, Sheep's Head and Beara – have it all: mountain passes, lonely windswept hills, beautiful beaches and views that will stay with you long after you've returned home.

Story of Rebellion

'The Rebel County' wears its history, even the sorrowful kind, with pride. You can explore it all, from Famine memorials and sites of 17th-century battles, to the powerful tribute to its more recent fallen heroes.

p222

County Kerry

Scenery
Seafood
Traditional Music

An Irish Postcard

County Kerry is the very definition of scenic Ireland – the Connor Pass, the Dingle Peninsula and, particularly, the Ring of Kerry are the gold standard by which Irish landscapes are judged. Decide for yourself by picking up a postcard.

Fresh from the Sea

Kerry's intimate relationship with the sea means that the fresh catch of the day is exactly that – throughout the Dingle Peninsula you can eat fish fresh off the boat you've just watched dock.

Traditional Sounds

No Kerry town or village is complete without at least one pub featuring traditional music, played by musicians schooled in the respective styles of their region. It's the proper accompaniment to a visit to the county.

p271

Counties Limerick & Tipperary

Walking
History
Scenery

Heritage Trails

It's a long way to Tipperary, but keep going once you get there, tramping through the chequered Glen of Aherlow and along the more challenging Tipperary Heritage Trail, a 56km walk through beautiful valleys dotted with ancient ruins.

Castles & Monasteries

From the mighty monastic city of Cashel in County Tipperary to the impressive fortifications of King John's Castle in Limerick city, the varied fortunes of the region's history are easily discernible throughout the two counties.

Atmospheric Ruins

At its broadest point, the mighty Shannon makes for some beautiful vistas, while the rolling hills and farmland of County Tipperary, peppered with ancient ruins, offer the kind of views for which Ireland is renowned.

p321

County Clare

Scenery
Music
Pubs

Dramatic Cliffs

Rising from the stormy Atlantic in all their sheer dramatic glory, the Cliffs of Moher are an arresting sight not to be missed. Elsewhere on the Clare coast there are similar levels of drama and beauty, especially at Loop Head and the coastal roads leading to and from its spectacular views of the restless Atlantic.

Traditional Sessions

Clare plays Ireland's most traditional music, with few modern influences. At festivals, in pubs or even just around any corner, you can hear brilliant trad sessions by the county's surfeit of musicians.

Old-Fashioned Pubs

There is *no* town in Clare that doesn't have at least one wonderful old pub where the Guinness is ready, the peat is lit and the craic never ends.

p345

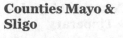

County Galway

Scenery
Food
Culture

Islands & Mountains

Hundreds of years of ceaseless toil have brought green accents to the otherwise barren rocks of the Aran Islands. The results are gorgeous, and a walk around these windswept and intriguing islands is one of Ireland's highlights. In spring, when the gorse blooms in brilliant yellow, the Connemara Peninsula's beauty astounds.

Fresh Oysters

Even as you read this, millions of succulent oysters are growing to the perfect size out in the tidal waters of Galway Bay. Local chefs excel at creating tasty treats with the water's bounty.

Gigs Everywhere

On any given night, Galway city's pubs and clubs hum with trad sessions, brilliant rock and tomorrow's next big band. It's a feast for the ears.

p381

Counties Mayo & Sligo

Islands
Megalithic Remains
Yeats Country

Coastal Scenery

There are reputed to be 365 islands in Mayo's Clew Bay, including one once owned by John Lennon. There's also Craggy Island, which isn't the island of *Father Ted* fame but rather the home of the notorious pirate queen, Grace O'Malley (or Granuaile).

Ancient Ruins

From the world's most extensive Stone Age monument at Céide Fields to the megalithic cemeteries at Carrowmore and Carrowkeel, the environs of Mayo's Ballycastle are a step back into prehistory.

Poetic Inspiration

County Sligo is Yeats country: he's buried in the church at Drumcliff, in the shadow of Benbulben. Throughout the county you'll find tributes to him in museums and heritage centres, and the landscapes reflected in his poetry.

p422

County Donegal

Wild Landscapes
Pristine Beaches
Surfing

Mountains & Cliffs

Untamed and almost impossibly wild, Donegal is the ultimate frontier country. From the wave- and wind-lashed cliffs and beaches to the mountainous interior, it's as brooding as it is beautiful.

Sweeping Coastlines

The county with the second-longest coastline has the country's best beaches, including surf-friendly Rossnowlagh, unspoilt Tramore and the red-tinged sands of Malinbeg. The multitude of coves hides an astonishing number of sandy hideaways.

Sea Activities

In Donegal you can learn to surf as well as take on some of the world's toughest breaks – with its great mix of beaches and abundance of surf centres, the county is arguably the best place in the country to ride the waves.

p457

The Midlands

Traditional Pubs
The Mighty River
Saints & Scholars

Authentic Atmosphere

Spread almost innocuously across the Midlands are some of the most atmospheric pubs in the country, including perhaps the most perfect pub in Ireland: Morrissey's of Abbeyleix in County Laois.

Shannon Cruises

What better way to explore the length and breadth of the country's belly than by cruiser along Ireland's longest river? See the sights and stop off along the way to eat in the riverbank restaurants that have sprouted for that purpose.

Saints & Scholars

The top monastic site in Ireland is Clonmacnoise, perched on the edge of the Shannon in County Offaly. Within its walled enclosure you'll find early churches, high crosses, round towers and graves in astonishingly good condition.

p493

Counties Meath, Louth, Cavan & Monaghan

History
Fishing
Scenery

Chieftains & Conflict

Irish history was lived and written across these counties, at the Hill of Tara, the Neolithic monuments of Brú na Bóinne and Loughcrew (all in Meath), the magnificent abbeys of Mellifont and Monasterboice, and in towns such as Drogheda (all in Louth).

Casting a Line

County Cavan's myriad lakes are famed for coarse fishing. County Monaghan isn't far behind, and if you fancy a little sea angling, towns such as Clogherhead and Carlingford in County Louth are the places to go.

Lakelands & Hills

These counties offer a variety of scenery, from the lakelands of Cavan and Monaghan to the fecund hills of County Meath. There are beautiful seaside views too, along the Louth coast as far up as scenic Carlingford.

p521

Belfast

History
Pubs
Music

Titanic Belfast

Belfast's shipbuilding heritage has been salvaged and transformed into Northern Ireland's most-visited museum – a fabulous multimedia experience centred on the construction of the world's most famous maritime disaster, which you can explore in virtual detail.

Victorian Gems

The Victorian classic pubs of the city centre are Belfast's most beloved treasure – the Crown might be the most famous, but equally beautiful are the John Hewitt and the Garrick, while older taverns such as White's and Kelly's have even more atmosphere.

Banging Tunes

From DJs spinning tunes in the Eglantine to sell-out gigs at the Odyssey, Belfast's music scene is top-notch. Best of the lot is probably the Belfast Empire, which features new bands and established acts nightly.

p556

Counties Down & Armagh

Activities
Wildlife
Food

Walking Festivals

With an impressive calendar of yearly events, including birdwatching meets, walking festivals and more strenuous activities such as rock climbing and canoeing, there's enough to do here to keep you busy every day of the year.

Birds & Seals

The bird-filled mudflats of Castle Espie in County Down are home to a wildfowl and wetlands centre that will entice even the most indifferent of ornithologists, while large colonies of grey seals are but the most obvious of visitors to Strangford Lough in County Armagh.

Gastro Goodness

You'll find first-rate dining in the restaurants and gastropubs of Hillsborough, Bangor and Warrenpoint. Many of the best places to eat are in the countryside, using seafood, beef, apples and other fine local ingredients.

p592

Counties Londonderry & Antrim

History
Scenery
Pop Culture

A Walled City

Derry, Ireland's only walled city, has a rich historical past, poignantly told along the walls that withstood a siege in 1688–89, in its storied museums and, most tellingly, in the political murals of the Bogside district, where history was played out on its very streets.

Giant's Footsteps

Virtually the entire length of the Antrim coast is scenic gold, but the real stars are the southern section around Carnlough Bay and the North's most outstanding tourist attraction, the surreal geological formations of the Giant's Causeway.

Game of Thrones

Game of Thrones fans will recognise Antrim's Dark Hedges as the Kingsroad, Mussenden Temple on the Causeway Coast as Dragonstone, Cushenden Caves as the spot where Melisandre gave birth to the shadow baby in season 2, and Ballintoy Harbour as the Iron Islands' Lordsports Harbour.

p616

Counties Fermanagh & Tyrone

Activities
Scenery
History

Walking & Fishing

Need something to do? How about fishing in the waters of County Fermanagh, or taking part in the Ulster American Folk Park's annual Appalachian and bluegrass festival? For something more spiritual, why not climb to the summit of Mullaghcarn, County Tyrone, along with other pilgrims?

From a Height

Whether you're boating on Lough Erne, staring out the windows at the top of the round tower on Devenish Island (both in County Fermanagh) or hiking across Tyrone's Sperrin Mountains, the scenery is beguiling, especially if you have any kind of decent weather.

Conflict & Connections

The towns of Omagh and Enniskillen speak volumes about the atrocities of violence, but Northern Ireland's history isn't just one of conflict – Tyrone's Ulster American Folk Park expertly tells the story of the province's strong links with the USA.

p652

On the Road

Dublin

POP 1,214,666 / AREA 114.99 SQ KM

Best Places to Eat

➡ Chapter One (p127)
➡ Clanbrassil House (p126)
➡ Greenhouse (p124)
➡ Pi Pizza (p122)

Best Places to Stay

➡ Merrion (p118)
➡ Grafton Guesthouse (p114)
➡ Cliff Townhouse (p114)
➡ Conrad Dublin (p118)
➡ Aloft Dublin City (p119)

Why Go?

Virtually synonymous with the same-named city at its heart, Dublin is by far the most populated county in Ireland, with roughly one quarter of the country's population living and working within its borders. Unsurprisingly, here you'll find the biggest concentration and range of hotels and restaurants, the largest choice of attractions and things to do, plus virtually all of the services that Ireland has available.

Beyond the city limits, County Dublin's collection of villages have for the most part retained their distinct character, despite being largely absorbed into the suburban conurbation: to the north, seaside towns such as Malahide and Howth are separated from the city proper by fields and, in Howth's case, a long beachy strand. In the south, Dalkey and Sandycove are pleasant seaside suburbs with a strong village feel.

When to Go

➡ March brings the marvellous mayhem of St Patrick's Festival, with 600,000 parade viewers.

➡ The Taste of Dublin and Forbidden Fruit festivals are in June, featuring the best of food and music.

➡ The last two weeks of September host the Dublin Fringe Festival, which is followed by the main theatre festival in October.

➡ Although impossible to predict, the best weather is often in September, to make up for a regularly disappointing August!

History

Dublin's been making noise since around 500 BC, when a bunch of intrepid Celts camped at a ford over the River Liffey, which is the provenance of the city's tough-to-pronounce Irish name, Baile Átha Cliath (Bawl-ya Aw-ha Kleeya; Town of the Hurdle Ford). The Celts went about their merry way for a thousand years or so, but it wasn't until the Vikings showed up that Dublin was urbanised in any significant way. By the 9th century raids from the north had become a fact of Irish life, and some of the fierce Danes chose to stay rather than simply rape, pillage and depart. They intermarried with the Irish and established a vigorous trading port at the point where the River Poddle joined the Liffey in a *dubh linn* (black pool). Today there's little trace of the Poddle, which has been channelled underground and flows under St Patrick's Cathedral to dribble into the Liffey by the Capel St (Grattan) Bridge.

The Normans arrived in the 12th century, and so began the slow process of subjugating Ireland to Anglo-Norman (then British) rule, during which Dublin generally played the role of Anglo-Norman, later British, bandleader. By the beginning of the 18th century, the squalid city packed with poor Catholics hardly reflected the imperial pretensions of its Anglophile burghers. The great and the good – aka the Protestant ascendancy – wanted big improvements, and they set about transforming what was in essence still a medieval town into a modern, Anglo-Irish metropolis. Roads were widened, landscaped squares laid out and new townhouses built, all in a proto-Palladian style that soon became known as Georgian after the kings then on the English throne. For a time, Dublin was the second-largest city in the British Empire and all was very, very good – unless you were part of the poor, mostly Catholic masses living in the city's ever-developing slums.

The Georgian boom came to a sudden and dramatic halt after the Act of Union (1801), when Ireland was formally united with Britain and its separate parliament closed down. Dublin went from being the belle of the imperial ball to the annoying cousin who just wouldn't take the hint, and slid quickly into economic turmoil and social unrest. During the Potato Famine (1845–51), the city's population was swollen by the arrival of tens of thousands of starving refugees from the west, who joined the ranks of an already downtrodden working class. As Dublin entered the 20th century, it was a dispirited place plagued by poverty, disease and more social problems than anyone cared to mention. It's hardly surprising that the majority of Dublin's citizenry were disgruntled and eager for change.

The first fusillade of transformation came during the Easter Rising of 1916, which caused considerable damage to the city centre. At first, Dubliners weren't too enamoured of the rebels, who caused more chaos and disruption than most locals were willing to put up with, but they soon changed their tune when the leaders were executed – Dubliners being natural defenders of the underdog.

As the whole country lurched radically towards full-scale war with Britain, Dublin was, surprisingly, not part of the main theatre of events. In fact, although there was an increased military presence, the odd shooting and the blowing up of some notable buildings – such as the Custom House in 1921 – in the capital it was business as usual for much of the War of Independence.

A year later, Ireland – minus its northern bit – was independent, but it then tumbled into the Civil War, which led to the burning of more notable buildings, including the Four Courts in 1922. Ironically, the war among the Irish was more brutal than the struggle for independence – O'Connell St became 'sniper row' and the violence left deep scars that took most of the 20th century to heal.

When the new state finally started doing business, Dublin was an exhausted capital. Despite slow and steady improvements, the city – like the rest of Ireland – continued to be plagued by rising unemployment, high emigration rates and a general stagnation that hung about like an impenetrable cloud. Dubliners made the most of the little they had, but times were tough.

The city has been in and out of recession for decades, but the dramatic dip that followed the sky-high good times of the Celtic Tiger was especially severe: Dublin is recovering more than the rest of the country, but recuperation has been slow.

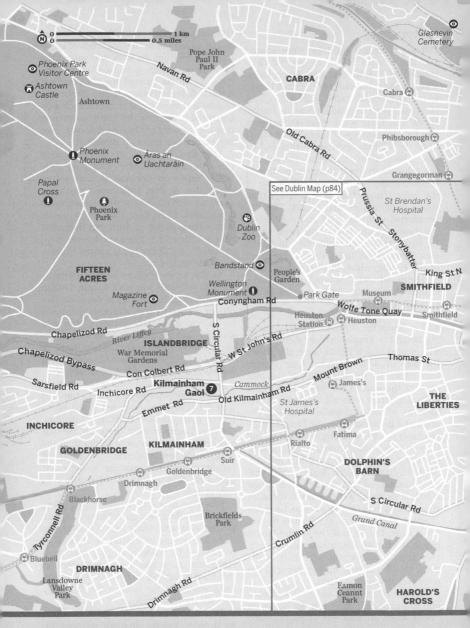

Dublin Highlights

1 **Trinity College** (p72) Staring in wonderment at the *Book of Kells*, the world's most famous illuminated gospel, in the Old Library of this university

2 **Chester Beatty Library** (p78) Basking in the glow of the magnificent collection.

3 **14 Henrietta Street** (p103) Exploring layers of Irish history in this restored Georgian townhouse.

4 **National Museum of Ireland – Archaeology** (p87) Uncovering the fascinating treasures of the most

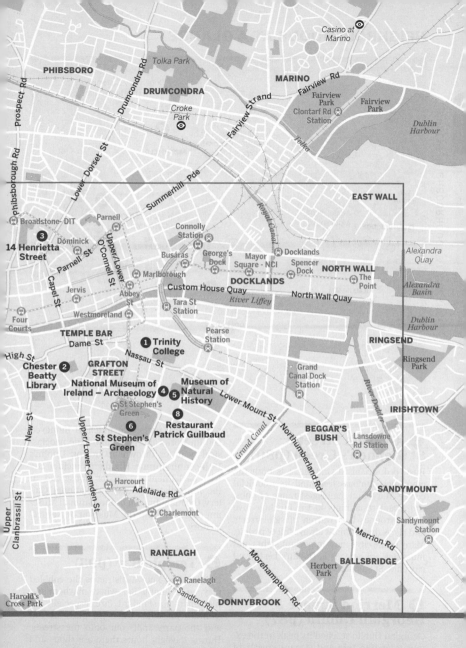

PHIBSBORO

Prospect Rd

Tolka Park

Drumcondra Rd

DRUMCONDRA

Casino at Marino

MARINO

Fairview Rd

Fairview Strand

Fairview Park

Clontarf Rd Station

Fairview Park

Croke Park

Tolka

Dublin Harbour

Phibsborough Rd

Lower Dorset St

Summerhill Pde

Royal Canal

EAST WALL

Broadstone- DIT

Dominick

Parnell

3

14 Henrietta Street

Parnell St

Upper/Lower O'Connell St

Connolly Station

Docklands

Alexandra Quay

Capel St

Jervis

Busáras

George's Dock

Mayor Square - NCI

Spencer Dock

NORTH WALL

Alexandra Basin

Marlborough

Abbey St

DOCKLANDS

The Point

Custom House Quay

Four Courts

Westmoreland

Tara St Station

River Liffey

North Wall Quay

Dublin Harbour

TEMPLE BAR

Dame St

1 Trinity College

Pearse Station

RINGSEND

High St

Nassau St

2 Chester Beatty Library

GRAFTON STREET

National Museum of Ireland – Archaeology

4 5 Museum of Natural History

Lower Mount St

Grand Canal Dock Station

Ringsend Park

New St

8 Restaurant Patrick Guilbaud

St Stephen's Green

Northumberland Rd

IRISHTOWN

Upper/Lower Camden St

6 St Stephen's Green

Grand Canal

BEGGAR'S BUSH

River Dodder

Lansdowne Rd Station

Harcourt

Adelaide Rd

SANDYMOUNT

Upper Clanbrassil St

Charlemont

Merrion Rd

Sandymount Station

RANELAGH

Morehampton Rd

Herbert Park

BALLSBRIDGE

Harold's Cross Park

Ranelagh

Sandford Rd

DONNYBROOK

---

important repository of Irish culture.

5 Museum of Natural History (p91) Visiting this antiquated museum.

6 St Stephen's Green (p82) Enjoying a sunny, summer afternoon on the grass.

7 Kilmainham Gaol (p79) Taking a trip through Ireland's

troubled history at this foreboding 18th-century prison.

8 Fine Dining (p121) Feasting on the superb cuisine offered by some of Dublin's very best restaurants.

NEIGHBOURHOODS AT A GLANCE

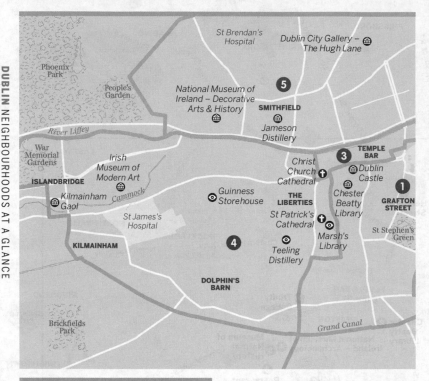

❶ Grafton Street & St Stephen's Green (p80)

Busy, pedestrianised Grafton St is both the city's most famous street and its unofficial centre. You'll find the biggest range of pubs, shops and restaurants in the bustling hive that surrounds it, a warren of side streets and alleys that is almost always full of people. Many of the city's most important sights and museums are here, as is Dublin's best-loved city park, St Stephen's Green.

❷ Merrion Square & Georgian Dublin (p87)

Georgian Dublin reached its peak in the exquisite architecture and elegant spaces of Merrion and Fitzwilliam Sqs. There are imposing public buildings, museums, and private offices and residences to be found as you wander through these areas. It is also round these parts that much of moneyed Dublin works and plays, amid the neoclassical beauties thrown up during Dublin's 18th-century prime. Highlights include the Irish parliament at Leinster House and, in the immediate vicinity, the National Gallery, the main branch of the National Museum of Ireland and the Museum of Natural History.

❸ Temple Bar (p93)

Dublin's best-known district is the cobbled playpen of Temple Bar, where mayhem and merriment is standard fare, especially on summer weekends when the pubs are full and the party spills out onto the streets. During daylight hours there are shops and galleries to discover, which at least lend some truth to the area's much-mocked title of 'cultural quarter'.

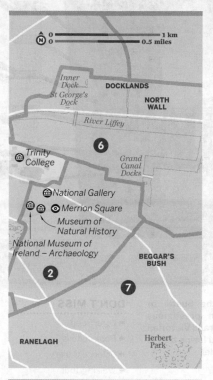

life and the multicultural melting pot that is contemporary Dublin. Beyond its widest, most elegant boulevard you'll find art museums and whiskey museums, bustling markets and some of the best ethnic eateries in town. Oh, and Europe's largest enclosed park – home to the president, the US ambassador and the zoo.

❻ Docklands (p105)

The gleaming modern blocks of the Docklands were first laid during the Celtic Tiger years of the late 1990s and came to a stuttering halt following the crash but have continued apace since then. Home to digital tech giants including Google, Facebook, Twitter and LinkedIn, the stretch from the Irish Financial Services Centre (IFSC) down to Grand Canal Dock on both sides of the Liffey has been dubbed the Silicon Docks. A couple of architectural beauties – notably a theatre designed by Daniel Libeskind – stand out among the modern buildings.

❼ Southside (p107)

The neighbourhoods that border the southern bank of the Grand Canal are less about sights and more about the experience of affluent Dublin – dining, drinking and sporting occasions, both watching and taking part. Here are the city's most desirable neighbourhoods and most precious postcodes: Dublin 4, which includes fancy schmancy Ballsbridge and Donnybrook, home to embassies and local potentates; and Dublin 6, covered by the elegant residential districts of Ranelagh, Rathgar and Rathmines, where the professional classes who still want a slice of city life reside.

❹ Kilmainham & the Liberties (p95)

Dublin's oldest and most traditional neighbourhoods, immediately west of the south city centre, have a handful of tourist big hitters, not least the Guinness Storehouse, Dublin's most-visited museum. Keeping watch over the ancient Liberties is St Patrick's Cathedral, the most important of Dublin's three (!) cathedrals, while further west is the country's premier modern-art museum and a Victorian prison that played a central role in Irish history.

❺ North of the Liffey (p100)

Grittier than its more genteel southside counterpart, the area immediately north of the River Liffey offers a fascinating mix of 18th-century grandeur, traditional city

TOP SIGHT
TRINITY COLLEGE

This calm and cordial retreat from the bustle of contemporary Dublin is Ireland's most prestigious university, a collection of elegant Georgian and Victorian buildings, cobbled squares and manicured lawns that is among the most delightful places to wander.

History

The college was established by Elizabeth I in 1592 on land confiscated from an Augustinian priory in an effort to stop the brain drain of young Protestant Dubliners, who were skipping across to continental Europe for an education and becoming 'infected with popery'. Trinity went on to become one of Europe's most outstanding universities, producing a host of notable graduates – how about Jonathan Swift, Oscar Wilde and Samuel Beckett at the same alumni dinner?

Front Square & Parliament Square

The elegant **Regent House entrance** on College Green is guarded by statues of the writer **Oliver Goldsmith**, 1728–74, and the orator **Edmund Burke**, 1729–97. The railings outside are a popular meeting spot.

Through the entrance, past the Students Union, are Front Sq and Parliament Sq, the latter dominated by the 30m-high **Campanile** (pictured), designed by Edward Lanyon and erected from 1852 to 1853 on what was believed to be the centre of the monastery that preceded the college. According to superstition, students who pass beneath it when the bells toll will fail their exams. To the north of the Campanile is a statue of **George Salmon**, the college provost from 1886 to 1904, who fought bitterly to keep women out of the college. He carried out his threat to permit them in 'over his dead body' by dropping dead when the worst happened. To the south of the Campanile is a statue of historian **WEH Lecky** (1838–1903).

DON'T MISS
➡ Long Room
➡ *Book of Kells*
➡ Science Gallery
➡ Walking Tour

PRACTICALITIES
➡ ☏ 01-896 1000
➡ www.tcd.ie
➡ College Green
➡ ⊙ 8am-10pm
➡ 🚌 all city centre, 🚊 Westmoreland or Trinity

Library Square & Old Library

On the far east of Library Sq, the red-brick **Rubrics Building** (Trinity College; ⊘closed to public; 🖳all Trinity College) dates from around 1690, making it the oldest building in the college. Extensively altered in an 1894 restoration, it underwent serious structural modification in the 1970s.

If you are following the less-studious-looking throng, you'll find yourself drawn south of Library Sq to the **Old Library** (www.tcd.ie; adult/student/family €11/11/28, fast-track €14/11/28; ⊘8.30am-5pm Mon-Sat, from 9.30am Sun May-Sep, 9.30am-5pm Mon-Sat, noon-4.30pm Sun Oct-Apr; 🖳all city centre, 🚏Westmoreland or Trinity), home to Trinity's prize possession and biggest crowd-puller, the astonishingly beautiful Book of Kells (p87).

Upstairs is the highlight of Thomas Burgh's building, the magnificent 65m **Long Room** with its barrel-vaulted ceiling. It's lined with shelves containing 200,000 of the library's oldest manuscripts, busts of scholars, a 14th-century harp and an original copy of the Proclamation of the Irish Republic.

Fellows' Square

West of the brutalist, brilliant **Berkeley Library** (Fellows' Sq; ⊘closed to public; 🖳all city centre, 🚏Trinity), designed by Paul Koralek in 1967 and now closed to the public, the **Arts & Social Science Building** (⊘closed to public; 🖳all city centre, 🚏Westmoreland) is home to the **Douglas Hyde Gallery** (www.douglashydegallery.com; ⊘11am-6pm Mon-Wed & Fri, to 7pm Thu, to 5.30pm Sat; 🖳all city centre) **FREE**, one of the country's leading contemporary galleries. It hosts regularly rotating shows presenting the works of top-class Irish and international artists across a range of media.

Science Gallery

Although it's part of the campus you'll have to walk along Pearse St to get into Trinity's newest attraction, the **Science Gallery** (www.sciencegallery.ie; Naughton Gallery, Pearse St; ⊘exhibitions usually 11am-7pm Tue-Fri, to 6pm Sat & Sun; 🖳all city centre) **FREE**. Since opening in 2008, it has proven immensely popular with everyone for its refreshingly lively and informative exploration of the relationship between science, art and the world we live in. Exhibits have touched on a range of fascinating topics including the science of desire and an exploration of the relationship between music and the human body. The ground-floor **cafe** (www.dublin.sciencegallery.com/cafe; sandwiches €8-9; ⊘8am-4pm Mon-Fri), bathed in floor-to-ceiling light, is a pretty good spot to take a load off.

A CATHOLIC BAN

Trinity was exclusively Protestant until 1793, but even when the university relented and began to admit Catholics, the Church forbade it; until 1970, any Catholic who enrolled here could consider themselves excommunicated.

For nearly two centuries students weren't allowed through the grounds without a sword – and duels with pistols were not uncommon in the 17th and 18th centuries.

Trinity College, Dublin

STEP INTO THE PAST

Ireland's most prestigious university, founded by Queen Elizabeth I in 1592, is an architectural masterpiece, mostly dating to the 18th and 19th centuries, and a cordial retreat from the bustle of modern life in the middle of the city. Step through its main entrance and you step back in time, the cobbled stones transporting you to another era, when the elite discussed philosophy and argued passionately in favour of empire.

Standing in Front Sq, the 30m-high **❶ Campanile** is directly in front of you with the **❷ Dining Hall** to your left. On the far side of the square is the Old Library building, the centrepiece of which is the magnificent **❸ Long Room**, which was the inspiration for the computer-generated imagery of the Jedi Archive in *Star Wars Episode II: Attack of the Clones*. Here you'll find the university's greatest treasure, the **❹ Book of Kells**. You'll probably have to queue to see this masterpiece, and then only for a brief visit, but it's very much worth it.

Just beyond the Old Library is the very modern **❺ Berkeley Library**, which nevertheless fits perfectly into the campus's overall aesthetic. Directly in front of it is the distinctive **❻ Sphere Within a Sphere**, the most elegant of the university's sculptures.

DON'T MISS

➡ Douglas Hyde Gallery, the campus's designated modern-art museum.

➡ A cricket match on the pitch, the most elegant of pastimes.

➡ A pint in the Pavilion Bar, preferably while watching the cricket.

➡ A visit to the Science Gallery, where science is made completely relevant.

Campanile
Trinity College's most iconic bit of masonry was designed in the mid-19th century by Sir Charles Lanyon; the attached sculptures were created by Thomas Kirk.

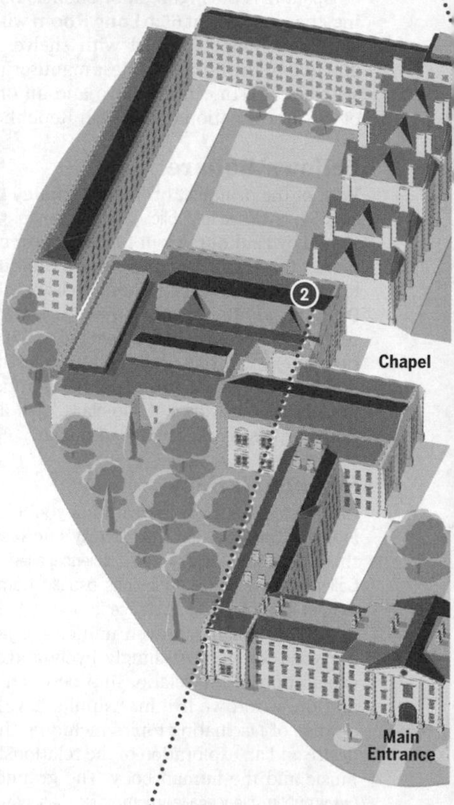

RPEDROSA/GETTY IMAGES ©

Chapel

Main Entrance

Dining Hall
Richard Cassels' original building was designed to mirror the Examination Hall directly opposite on Front Sq: the hall collapsed twice and was rebuilt from scratch in 1761.

Sphere Within a Sphere
Arnaldo Pomodoro's distinctive sculpture has an inner ball that represents the earth and an outer sphere that represents Christianity; there are versions of it in Rome, New York and Tehran.

Berkeley Library
Paul Koralek's brutalist library seems not to fit the general theme of the university, but the more you look at it the more you'll appreciate a building that is a modernist classic.

New Square

⑥

Old Library

⑤

Library Square

④

Fellows Square

③

①

Parliament Square

Long Room
At 65m long and topped by a barrel-vaulted ceiling, Thomas Burgh's masterpiece is lined with shelves groaning under the weight of 200,000 of the library's oldest books and manuscripts.

Book of Kells
Examine a page (or two) of the world's most famous illuminated book, which was produced by monks on the island of Iona around AD 800 before being brought to Kells, County Meath.

⊙ TOP SIGHT
GUINNESS STOREHOUSE

More than any beer produced anywhere in the world, Guinness has transcended its own brand and is not just the best-known symbol of the city but a substance with near spiritual qualities, according to its legions of devotees the world over. A visit to the factory museum where it's made is therefore something of a pilgrimage for many of its fans.

The mythology around Guinness is remarkably durable: it doesn't travel well; its distinctive flavour comes from Liffey water; it is good for you – not to mention the generally held belief that you will never understand the Irish until you develop a taste for the black stuff. All absolutely true, of course, so it should be no surprise that the Guinness Storehouse, in the heart of the St James's Gate Brewery, is the city's most-visited tourist attraction, an all-singing, all-dancing extravaganza that combines sophisticated exhibits, spectacular design and a thick, creamy head of marketing hype.

From Humble Beginnings...

In the 1770s, while other Dublin brewers fretted about the popularity of a new English beer known as porter – which was first created when a London brewer accidentally burnt his hops – Arthur Guinness started making his own version. By 1799 he decided to concentrate all his efforts on this single brew. He died four years later, aged 83, but the foundations for world domination were already in place.

At one time a Grand Canal tributary was cut into the brewery to enable special Guinness barges to carry consignments out onto the Irish canal system or to the Dublin port. When the brewery extensions reached the Liffey in 1872, the fleet of Guinness barges became a familiar sight. Pretty soon Guinness was being exported

DON'T MISS

➡ A drink of Guinness

➡ Gravity Bar view

➡ 1837 Bar & Brasserie

➡ Advertising exhibit

➡ Connoisseur Experience

PRACTICALITIES

➡ www.guinness-storehouse.com

➡ St James's Gate, S Market St

➡ adult/child from €18.50/16, Connoisseur Experience €55

➡ ⊙ 9.30am-7pm Sep-Jun, 9am-8pm Jul & Aug

➡ 🚌 13, 21A, 40, 51B, 78, 78A, 123 from Fleet St, 🚉 James's

as far afield as Africa and the West Indies. As the barges chugged their way along the Liffey towards the port, boys used to lean over the wall and shout 'bring us back a parrot'. Old school Dubliners still say the same thing to each other when they're going off on holiday.

The Essential Ingredients

One link with the past that hasn't been broken is the yeast used to make Guinness, essentially the same living organism that has been used since 1770. Another vital ingredient is a hop by the name of fuggles, which used to be grown exclusively around Dublin but is now imported from Britain, the US and Australia (everyone take a bow).

Guinness Storehouse Museum

The brewery is far more than just a place where beer is manufactured. It is an intrinsic part of Dublin's history and a key element of the city's identity. Accordingly, the quasi-mythical stature of Guinness is the central theme of the brewery's museum, the Guinness Storehouse, which is the only part of the brewery open to visitors.

It occupies the old Fermentation House, built in 1904. As it's a listed building, the designers could only adapt and add to the structure without taking anything away. The result is a stunning central atrium that rises seven storeys and takes the shape of a pint of Guinness. The head is represented by the glassed Gravity Bar (pictured), which provides panoramic views of Dublin to savour with your complimentary half-pint.

Before you race up to the top, however, you might want to check out the museum for which you've paid so handsomely. Actually, it's designed as more of an 'experience' than a museum. It has 1.6 hectares of floor space, featuring a dazzling array of audiovisual and interactive exhibits, which cover most aspects of the brewery's story and explain the brewing process in overwhelming detail.

On the ground floor, a copy of Arthur Guinness' original lease lies embedded beneath a pane of glass in the floor. Wandering up through the various exhibits, including 70-odd years of advertising, you can't help feeling that the now wholly foreign-owned company has hijacked the mythology Dubliners attached to the drink, and it has all become more about marketing and manipulation than mingling and magic.

THE GRAVITY BAR

The Gravity Bar (pictured), at the top of the building, offers a complimentary glass of Guinness. The views from the bar are superb, but the Guinness itself is as near-perfect as a beer can be. Die-hards can opt for the Connoisseur Experience, where a designated barkeeper goes through the histories of the four variants of Guinness – Draught, Original, Foreign Extra Stout and Black Lager – and provides delicious samples of each.

St Patrick's Tower, the large smock windmill on the extensive factory grounds, was originally built as part of the Roe Distillery, which once occupied 7 hectares on the north side of James's St and was Europe's largest producer of whiskey. Arthur Guinness didn't much care for whiskey, branding it the 'curse of the nation' (and his own brew the 'nurse of the nation'). The Roe distillery stopped producing whiskey in 1926 and was taken over by Guinness in 1949.

TOP SIGHT
CHESTER BEATTY LIBRARY

The world-famous Chester Beatty Library, housed in the Clock Tower at the back of Dublin Castle, is not just Ireland's best small museum, but one of the best you'll find anywhere in Europe.

This extraordinary collection, so lovingly and expertly gathered by New York mining magnate Alfred Chester Beatty, is breathtakingly beautiful and virtually guaranteed to impress.

Artistic Traditions

The collection is spread over two levels. On the 1st floor you'll find the Artistic Traditions Gallery, a compact but stunning collection of artworks from the Western, Islamic and East Asian worlds. Highlights include the finest collection of Chinese jade books in the world and illuminated European texts featuring exquisite calligraphy that stand up in comparison with the *Book of Kells*. Audiovisual displays explain the process of bookbinding, paper-making and printing.

Sacred Traditions

The 2nd floor is home to Sacred Traditions, a wonderful exploration of the world's major religions through decorative and religious art, enlightening text and a cool cultural-pastiche video at the entrance. The collection of Qur'ans dating from the 9th to the 19th centuries (the library has more than 270 of them) is considered by experts to be the best example of illuminated Islamic texts in the world. There are also outstanding examples of ancient papyri, including renowned Egyptian love poems from the 12th century, as well as the second-oldest biblical fragment ever found (after the Dead Sea Scrolls).

DON'T MISS

➡ Nara e-hon scrolls, The East Asian Collection, Sacred Traditions

➡ Ibn al-Bawwab Qur'an, The Qur'an Collection, Sacred Traditions

➡ New Testament papyri, The Western Collection, Sacred Traditions

PRACTICALITIES

➡ ☑ 01-407 0750

➡ www.cbl.ie

➡ Dublin Castle

➡ ⊙ 10am-5pm Mon-Fri, from 11am Sat & Sun Mar-Oct, 10am-5pm Tue-Fri, from 11am Sat & Sun Nov-Feb

➡ ▣ all city centre

TOP SIGHT
KILMAINHAM GAOL

If you have any desire to understand Irish history – especially the long-running resistance to British rule – then a visit to this former prison is an absolute must. It's played a role in virtually every act of Ireland's painful path to independence, and even today it still has the power to chill.

Early Days

It took four years to build, and the prison opened – or rather closed – its doors in 1796. The Irish were locked up for all sorts of misdemeanours, some more serious than others. A six-year-old boy spent a month here in 1839 because his father couldn't pay his train fare, and during the Famine it was crammed with the destitute imprisoned for stealing food and begging. But it is most famous for incarcerating 120 years of Irish nationalists.

Executions

The uprisings of 1798, 1803, 1848, 1867 and 1916 ended with the leaders' confinement here. Robert Emmet, Thomas Francis Meagher, Charles Stewart Parnell and the 1916 Easter Rising leaders were all visitors, but it was the executions in the stone breakers' yard in 1916 that most deeply etched the jail's name into the Irish consciousness. Of the 15 executions that took place between 3 May and 12 May after the revolt, 14 were conducted here. As a finale, prisoners from the Civil War were held here from 1922.

DON'T MISS
- ➜ Prison museum
- ➜ Stone breakers' yard
- ➜ Prison cells

PRACTICALITIES
- ➜ ☎ 01-453 5984
- ➜ www.kilmainhamgaolmuseum.ie
- ➜ Inchicore Rd
- ➜ adult/child €9/5
- ➜ ⏱ 9am-7pm Jun-Aug, 9.30am-5.30pm Oct-Mar, 9am-6pm Apr, May & Sep
- ➜ 🚌 69, 79 from Aston Quay, 13, 40 from O'Connell St

⊙ Sights

⊙ Grafton Street & St Stephen's Green

Trinity College   HISTORIC BUILDING
See p72.

Chester Beatty Library   MUSEUM
See p78.

Dublin Castle   HISTORIC BUILDING
(Map p88; ☑01-645 8813; www.dublincastle.ie; Dame St; guided tours adult/child €12/6, self-guided tours €8/4; ⊙9.45am-5.45pm, last admission 5.15pm; ▣all city centre) Despite its hotchpotch appearance, Dublin Castle was the stronghold of British power in Ireland for more than 700 years, beginning with the Anglo-Norman fortress commissioned by King John in 1204. Only the Record Tower (1258) survives from the original; most of what you see was built from the 18th century onwards – but its best bits are still impressive.

The castle was officially handed over to Michael Collins, representing the Irish Free State, in 1922, when the British viceroy is reported to have rebuked Collins on being seven minutes late. Collins replied, 'We've been waiting 700 years, you can have the seven minutes.'

As you walk into the grounds from the main Dame St entrance, there's a good example of the evolution of Irish architecture.

On your left is the Victorian Chapel Royal (occasionally part of the Dublin Castle tours), decorated with more than 90 heads of various Irish personages and saints carved out of Tullamore limestone. Beside this is the Norman Record Tower with its 5m-thick walls. It's currently closed to the public pending a long-awaited revamp. On your right is the Georgian Treasury Building, the oldest office block in Dublin, and behind you, yikes, is the uglier-than-sin Revenue Commissioners Building of 1960.

Heading away from that eyesore, you ascend to the Upper Yard. On your right is a figure of Justice with her back turned to the city, an appropriate symbol for British justice, reckoned Dubliners. Next to it is the 18th-century Bedford Tower, from which the Irish Crown Jewels were stolen in 1907 and never recovered. Opposite is the entrance for the tours.

The castle is now used by the Irish government for meetings and functions, and the best bits are only visible as part of a 70-minute guided tour (departing every 20 to 30 minutes, depending on numbers). Highlights include the State Apartments and St Patrick's Hall, where Irish presidents are inaugurated and foreign dignitaries toasted, as well as the room in which the wounded James Connolly was tied to a chair while convalescing after the 1916 Easter Rising, so that he could be executed by firing squad.

DUBLIN IN...

Two Days

If you've only got two days (whatever is taking you away better be worth it!), start with Trinity College (p72) and the *Book of Kells* before venturing into the Georgian heartland – amble through St Stephen's Green (p82) and Merrion Square (p87), and be sure to visit both the National Museum of Ireland – Archaeology (p87) and the National Gallery (p89). In the evening, try an authentic Dublin pub – Kehoe's (p128) off Grafton St will do nicely. The next day go west, stopping at the Chester Beatty Library (p78) on your way to the Guinness Storehouse (p76); if you still have the legs for it, the Irish Museum of Modern Art (p98) and Kilmainham Gaol (p79) will round off your day perfectly. Take in a traditional Irish music session at the Cobblestone (p132).

Four Days

Follow the two-day itinerary, but stretch it out with refuelling stops at some of the city's better pubs. Visit Glasnevin Cemetery (p108) and the Hugh Lane Gallery (p100). Become a whiskey expert at the Jameson Distillery (p103) and a literary (or beer) one with a Dublin Literary Pub Crawl (p110). Explore the northside's blossoming foodie scene – there's creative cafe food at Fegan's 1924 (p126) and superb pub grub at Legal Eagle (p127). Oh, and don't forget Temple Bar (p70), where there are distractions for every taste.

County Dublin

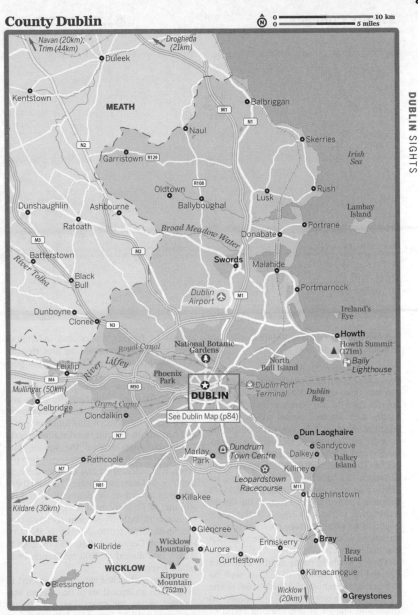

Another highlight is a visit to the medieval undercroft of the old castle, discovered by accident in 1986. It includes foundations built by the Vikings (whose long-lasting mortar was made of ox blood, eggshells and horsehair), the hand-polished exterior of the castle walls that prevented attackers from climbing them, the steps leading down to the moat and the trickle of the historic River Poddle, which once filled the moat on its way to join the Liffey.

There's a self-guided tour option, but that only includes the State Apartments. The castle has brochures in 17 languages, but the

Trinity College

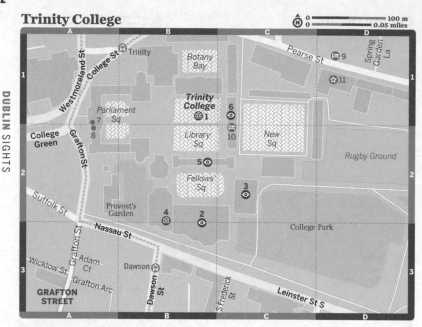

handiest guide is the free Dublin Castle app, available for all devices.

Little Museum of Dublin   MUSEUM
(Map p88; ☑ 01-661 1000; www.littlemuseum.ie; 15 St Stephen's Green N; adult/student €10/8; ⊙ 9.30am-5pm, to 8pm Thu, last admission 7pm; 🚌 all city centre, 🚊 St Stephen's Green) This award-winning museum tells the story of Dublin over the last century via memorabilia, photographs and artefacts donated by the general public. The impressive collection, spread over the rooms of a handsome Georgian house, includes a lectern used by JFK on his 1963 visit to Ireland and an original copy of the fateful letter given to the Irish envoys to the treaty negotiations of 1921, whose contradictory instructions were at the heart of the split that resulted in the Civil War.

There's a whole room on the 2nd floor devoted to the history of U2, as well as the personal archive of Alfred 'Alfie' Byrne (1882–1956), mayor of Dublin a record 10 times and known as the 'Shaking Hand of Dublin'. Visit is by guided tour, which goes on the hour every hour. The museum also runs the Green Mile walking tour (p110) of St Stephen's Green.

St Stephen's Green   PARK
(Map p92; ⊙ dawn-dusk; 🚌 all city centre, 🚊 St Stephen's Green) As you watch the assorted groups of friends, lovers and individuals splaying themselves across the nine elegantly landscaped hectares of Dublin's most popular green lung, St Stephen's Green, consider that those same hectares once formed a common for public whippings, burnings and hangings. These days, the harshest treatment you'll get is the warden chucking you out if you disturb the carefully tended flower beds.

The buildings around the square date mainly from the mid-18th century, when the green was landscaped and became the centrepiece of Georgian Dublin. The northern side was known as the Beaux Walk and it's still one of Dublin's most esteemed stretches, home to Dublin's original society hotel, the Shelbourne (p119). Nearby is the tiny **Huguenot Cemetery** (Map p92; ⊙ closed to public), established in 1693 by French Protestant refugees.

Railings and locked gates were erected in 1814, when an annual fee of one guinea was charged to use the green. This private use continued until 1877 when Sir Arthur Edward Guinness pushed an act through parliament opening the green to the public once again. He also financed the central park's gardens and ponds, which date from 1880.

The main entrance to the green today is beneath **Fusiliers' Arch**, at the top of Grafton St. Modelled to look like a smaller

Trinity College

◎ **Top Sights**

◎ **Sights**

⊕ **Activities, Courses & Tours**

⊜ **Sleeping**

⊕ **Entertainment**

version of the Arch of Titus in Rome, the arch commemorates the 212 soldiers of the Royal Dublin Fusiliers who were killed fighting for the British in the Boer War (1899–1902).

Spread across the green's lawns and walkways are some notable artworks; the most imposing of these is a **monument to Wolfe Tone**, the leader of the abortive 1798 Rising. Occupying the northeastern corner of the green, the vertical slabs serving as a backdrop to the statue have been dubbed 'Tonehenge'. At this entrance is a **memorial** to all those who died in the Potato Famine (1845–51).

On the eastern side of the green is a **children's playground** and to the south there's a fine old **bandstand**, erected to celebrate Queen Victoria's jubilee in 1887. Musical performances often take place here in summer. Near the bandstand is a **bust of James Joyce**.

Bank of Ireland   NOTABLE BUILDING
(Map p88; ☑ 01-671 1488; College Green; ⊘ 10am-4pm Mon-Wed & Fri, to 5pm Thu; ⊒ all city centre, ⊒ Westmoreland) A sweeping Palladian pile occupying one side of College Green, this magnificent building was the Irish Parliament House until 1801 and was the first purpose-built parliament building in the world. The original building – the central colonnaded section that distinguishes the present-day structure – was designed by Sir Edward Lovett Pearce in 1729 and completed by James Gandon in 1733.

When the parliament voted itself out of existence through the 1801 Act of Union, the building was sold under the condition that the interior would be altered to prevent it ever again being used as a debating chamber. It was a spiteful strike at Irish parliamentary aspirations, but while the central House of Commons was remodelled and offers little hint of its former role, the smaller **House of Lords** (admission free) survived and is much more interesting. It has Irish oak woodwork, a mahogany longcase parliament clock and a late-18th-century Dublin crystal chandelier. Its design was copied for the construction of the original House of Representatives in Washington, DC, now the National Statuary Hall. The House of Lords is open to visitors during banking hours.

**Bank of Ireland Cultural
& Heritage Centre**   MUSEUM
(Map p88; ☑ 01-670 6153; College Green; ⊘ 10am-4pm Mon-Sat, last entry 3.30pm; ⊒ all city centre, ⊒ Westmoreland) **FREE** Housed within the College Green complex of the Bank of Ireland is this 2018-opened cultural centre, which until 2021 is hosting Seamus Heaney: Listen Now Again, an exhibition dedicated to the poet and featuring manuscripts, letters, unpublished works, diaries, photographs and personal items, including the desk at which he wrote in the family home in Sandymount, a lamp that belonged to WB Yeats and a portrait by artist Louis le Brocquy. The exhibition is organised in tandem with the National Library.

City Hall   MUSEUM
(Map p88; www.dublincity.ie/dublincityhall; Dame St; adult/student/child €4/2/1.50; ⊘ 10am-5.15pm Mon-Sat; ⊒ all city centre) This beautiful Georgian structure was originally built by Thomas Cooley as the Royal Exchange between 1769 and 1779, and botched in the mid-19th century when it became the offices of the local government (hence its name). Thankfully, a renovation in 2000 has restored it to its gleaming Georgian best. The basement has an exhibit on the city's history.

The rotunda and its ambulatory form a breathtaking interior, bathed in natural light from enormous windows to the east. A vast marble statue of former mayor and Catholic emancipator Daniel O'Connell stands here as a reminder of the building's links with Irish nationalism (the funerals of both Charles Stewart Parnell and Michael Collins were held here). Dublin City Council still meets here on the first Monday of the month, gathering to discuss the city's business in the

Dublin

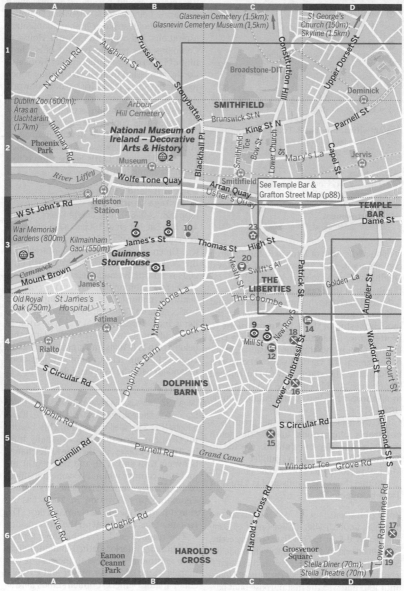

Council Chamber, which was the original building's coffee room.

There was a sordid precursor to City Hall on this spot in the shape of the Lucas Coffee House and the adjoining Eagle Tavern, in which the notorious Hellfire Club was founded by Richard Parsons, Earl of Rosse,

in 1735. Although the city abounded with gentlemen's clubs, this particular one gained a reputation for messing about in the arenas of sex and Satan, two topics that were guaranteed to fire the lurid imaginings of the city's gossip mongers.

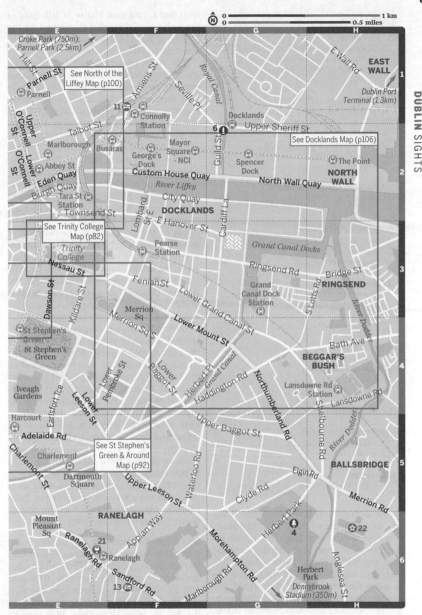

Located in the striking vaulted basement, **The Story of the Capital** is a multimedia exhibition that traces the history of the city from its earliest beginnings to its hoped-for future – with ne'er a mention of sex and Satan. More's the pity, as the info is quite overwhelming and the exhibits are a little text-heavy. Still, it's a pretty slick museum with informative audiovisual displays.

Museum of Literature Ireland MUSEUM
(MoLI; Map p92; ☎ 01-477 9810; www.moli.ie; 85-86 St Stephen's Green S; adult/child under 3/concession/family €8/free/6/17, guided tour €12; ⏰10am-

Dublin

6pm; 🚇 all city centre, 🚇 St Stephen's Green) Newly opened in September 2019, the Museum of Literature Ireland is a digital, interactive exploration of Ireland's deep literary heritage, from the Middle Ages to the present day. Highlights include Joyce's *Ulysses* notebooks as well as the very first print of the novel. The museum is in two stunning Georgian townhouses collectively known as Newman House, which in 1865 saw the establishment of the Catholic University of Ireland, the alma mater of Joyce, Pádraig Pearse and Eamon de Valera.

The college was founded as an alternative to the Protestant hegemony of Trinity College, which was then the only option available to those seeking third-level education

in Ireland. Newman House is still part of the college, which later decamped to the suburb of Belfield and changed its name to University College Dublin.

The house comprises two exquisitely restored townhouses. No 85, the granite-faced original, was designed by Richard Cassels in 1738 for parliamentarian Hugh Montgomery, who sold it to Richard Chapel Whaley, MP, in 1765. Whaley wanted a grander home, so he commissioned another house next door at No 86.

Aside from Cassels' wonderful design, the highlight of the building is the plasterwork, perhaps the finest in the city. For No 85, the artists were the Italian stuccodores Paolo and Filippo Lafranchini, whose work is best appreciated in the wonderfully detailed Apollo Room on the ground floor. The plasterwork in No 86 was done by Robert West, but it is not quite up to the high standard of next door. When the newly founded, Jesuit-run Catholic University of Ireland took possession of the house in 1865, alterations were made to some of the more graphic plasterwork, supplying the nude figures with 'modesty vests'.

During Whaley's residency, the house developed a certain notoriety, largely due to the activities of his son, Buck, a notorious gambler and hellraiser who once walked all the way to Jerusalem for a bet and somehow connived to have himself elected to parliament at the tender age of 17. During the university's tenure, however, the residents were a far more temperate lot. The Jesuit priest and wonderful poet Gerard Manley Hopkins lived here during his time as professor of classics, from 1884 until his death in 1889. Hopkins' bedroom is preserved as it would have been during his residence, as is the classroom where the young James Joyce studied while obtaining his Bachelor of Arts degree between 1899 and 1902.

City Assembly House   HISTORIC BUILDING
(Map p88; www.igs.ie; 58 S William St; ☉ 10am-6pm Mon-Sat; 🚇 all city centre) **FREE** This Georgian townhouse was built between 1766 and 1771 by the Society of Artists as the first purpose-built public exhibition room in the British Isles. During the 19th century it served as an unofficial city hall – Daniel O'Connell delivered one of his most famous speeches here in 1843 – but it is now the headquarters of the Irish Georgian Society, which is restoring it to its original purpose. It hosts occasional exhibitions.

⊙ Merrion Square & Georgian Dublin

Georgian Dublin's apotheosis occurred in the exquisite architecture and elegant spaces of Merrion and Fitzwilliam Sqs. Here you'll find the perfect mix of imposing public buildings, museums, and private offices and residences. It is round these parts that much of moneyed Dublin works and plays, amid the neoclassical beauties thrown up during Dublin's 18th-century prime. These include the home of the Irish parliament at Leinster House and, immediately surrounding it, the National Gallery, the main branch of the National Museum of Ireland and the Museum of Natural History.

★ Merrion Square   PARK

(Map p92; ⊙ dawn-dusk; 🚊 all city centre) Merrion Sq is the most prestigious and, arguably, the most elegant of Dublin's Georgian squares. Its well-kept lawns and tended flower beds are flanked on three sides by gorgeous Georgian houses with colourful doors, peacock fanlights, ornate door knockers and, occasionally, foot-scrapers, used to remove mud from shoes. Over the past two centuries they've been used by some notable residents.

The square, laid out in 1762, is bordered on its fourth side by the National Gallery (p89) and Leinster House (p92) – all of which, apparently, isn't enough for some. One former resident, WB Yeats (1865–1939), was less than impressed and described the architecture as 'grey 18th century'; there's just no pleasing some people.

Just inside the northwestern corner of the square is a colourful **statue of Oscar Wilde** (Map p92; ⊙ dawn-dusk).

★ National Museum of Ireland – Archaeology   MUSEUM

(Map p92; www.museum.ie; Kildare St; ⊙ 10am-5pm Tue-Sat, from 1pm Sun; 🚊 all city centre) FREE Established in 1877 as the primary repository of the nation's cultural and archaeological treasures, this is the country's most important museum. The original 1890 building is where you'll find stunning Celtic metalwork, Ireland's most famous crafted artefacts (the **Ardagh Chalice** and the **Tara Brooch**, from the 12th and 8th centuries respectively) and a collection of mummified bodies from the Iron Age, preserved to a disturbingly perfect degree by Ireland's peat bogs.

Also part of the Treasury is the exhibition **Ór-Ireland's Gold**, featuring stunning jewellery and decorative objects created by Celtic artisans in the Bronze and Iron Ages. Among them are the **Broighter Hoard**, which includes a 1st-century-BC large gold collar, unsurpassed anywhere in Europe, and an extraordinarily delicate gold boat. There's also the wonderful Loughnashade bronze war trumpet, which also dates from the 1st century BC.

The other showstopper is the collection of Iron Age 'bog bodies' in the

---

THE BOOK OF KELLS

The history of the *Book of Kells* is almost as fascinating as its illuminations. It is thought to have been created around AD 800 by the monks at St Colmcille's Monastery on Iona, a remote island off the coast of Scotland; repeated looting by marauding Vikings forced the monks to flee to Kells, County Meath, along with their masterpiece. It was stolen in 1007, then rediscovered three months later buried underground. The *Book of Kells* was brought to Trinity College for safekeeping in 1654, and is now housed in the Old Library (p73), with over half a million visitors queuing up to see it annually. The 680-page (340-folio) book was rebound in four calfskin volumes in 1953.

And here the problems begin. Of the 680 pages, only two are on display – one showing an illumination, the other showing text – hence the 'page of Kells' moniker. No getting around that one, though: you can hardly expect the right to thumb through a priceless treasure at random. No, the real problem is its immense popularity, which makes viewing it a rather unsatisfactory pleasure. Punters are herded through the specially constructed viewing room at near lightning pace, making for a quick-look-and-move-along kind of experience.

To really appreciate the book, you can get your own reproduction copy for a mere €22,000. Failing that, the Old Library bookshop stocks a plethora of souvenirs and other memorabilia, including Bernard Meehan's *The Book of Kells* (€17), which includes plenty of reproductions plus excellent accompanying text.

Temple Bar & Grafton Street

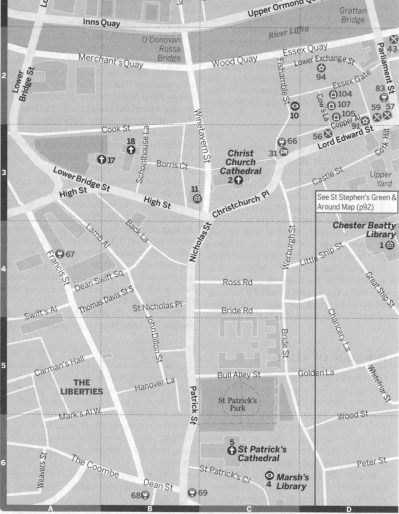

Kingship and Sacrifice exhibit – four figures in varying states of preservation dug out of the midland bogs. The bodies' various eerily preserved details – a tangle of hair, sinewy legs and fingers with fingernails intact – are memorable, but it's the accompanying detail that will make you pause: scholars now believe that all of these bodies were victims of the most horrendous ritualistic torture and sacrifice – the cost of being notable figures in the Celtic world.

Upstairs are **Medieval Ireland 1150–1550**, **Viking Ireland** – which features exhibits from the excavations at Wood Quay, the

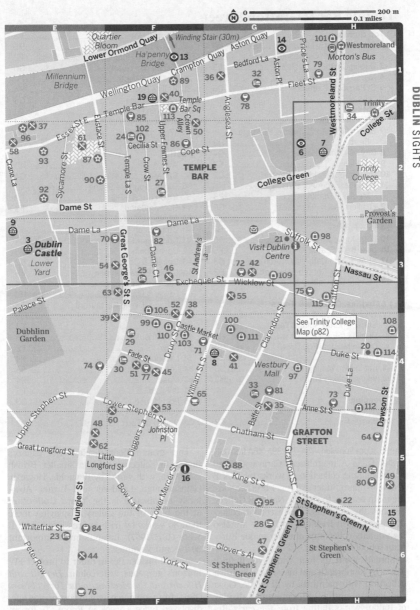

area between Christ Church Cathedral and the river – and **Ancient Egypt**, featuring items acquired from excavations conducted between 1890 and 1930.

The museum's sister museums are made up of the stuffed beasts of the Museum of Natural History (p91), the decorative arts

section at Collins Barracks (p101), and a country life museum (p444) in County Mayo, on Ireland's west coast.

★**National Gallery**   MUSEUM
(Map p92; www.nationalgallery.ie; Merrion Sq W; ⊙ 9.15am-5.30pm Tue-Wed, Fri & Sat, to 8.30pm Thu,

Temple Bar & Grafton Street

11am-5.30pm Sun-Mon; 🚌 4, 7, 8, 39A, 46A from city centre) **FREE** A magnificent Caravaggio and a breathtaking collection of works by Jack B Yeats – William Butler's younger brother – are the main reasons to visit the National Gallery, but not the only ones. Its excellent collection is strong in Irish art, and there are also high-quality collections of every major European school of painting.

Spread about its four wings you'll find: works by Rembrandt and his circle; a Spanish collection with paintings by El Greco, Goya and Picasso; and a well-represented display of Italian works dating from the early Renaissance to the 18th century. Fra Angelico, Titian and Tintoretto are among the artists represented, but the highlight is undoubtedly Caravaggio's *The Taking of Christ* (1602), which lay for over 60 years in a Jesuit house in Leeson St and was accidentally discovered by chief curator Sergio Benedetti.

The ground floor displays the gallery's fine Irish collection, plus a smaller British collection, with works by Reynolds, Hogarth, Gainsborough, Landseer and Turner. Absolutely unmissable is the **Yeats Collection** at the back of the gallery, displaying more than 30 works by Irish impressionist Jack B Yeats (1871–1957), Ireland's most important 20th-century painter.

A good insider tip: in order to protect FW Burton's gorgeous watercolour, *Hellelil and Hildebrand, the Meeting on the Turret Stairs* (1864) from too much light exposure, it is only displayed twice a week in Room 20, for an hour at a time on Thursdays at 5.30pm and Sundays at 2pm.

Entrance is via the light-filled modern **Millennium Wing** on Clare St or the refurbished entrance on Merrion Sq West. Here you'll also find a small collection of 20th-century Irish art, high-profile visiting collections (for which there are admission charges), an art reference library, a lecture theatre, a good bookshop and Fitzer's Café.

There are free tours at 6.30pm Thursday, 12.30pm Saturday and at 11.30am, 12.30pm and 1.30pm on Sunday. The gallery also has a free Masterpieces app featuring 80% of its collection.

★ Museum of Natural History   MUSEUM
(National Museum of Ireland – Natural History; Map p92; www.museum.ie; Upper Merrion St; ⊙10am-5pm Tue-Sat, from 1pm Sun; 🚌 7, 44 from city centre) FREE Affectionately known as the 'Dead Zoo', this dusty, weird and utterly compelling museum is a fine example of the scientific wonderment of the Victorian age. Its enormous collection of stuffed beasts and carefully annotated specimens has barely changed since Scottish explorer Dr David Livingstone opened it in 1857 – before disappearing into the African jungle for a meeting with Henry Stanley.

The Irish Room on the ground floor is filled with mammals, sea creatures, birds and some butterflies all found in Ireland at some point, including the skeletons of three 10,000-year-old Irish elk that greet you as you enter. The World Animals Collection, spread across three levels, has as its centrepiece the skeleton of a 20m-long fin whale found beached in County Sligo. Evolutionists will love the line-up of orang-utan, chimpanzee, gorilla and human skeletons on the 1st floor.

A newer addition is the Discovery Zone, where visitors can do some firsthand exploring of their own, handling taxidermy specimens and opening drawers. Other notables include a Tasmanian tiger (an extinct Australian marsupial, mislabelled as a Tasmanian wolf), a giant panda from China, and several African and Asian rhinoceros. The wonderful

St Stephen's Green & Around

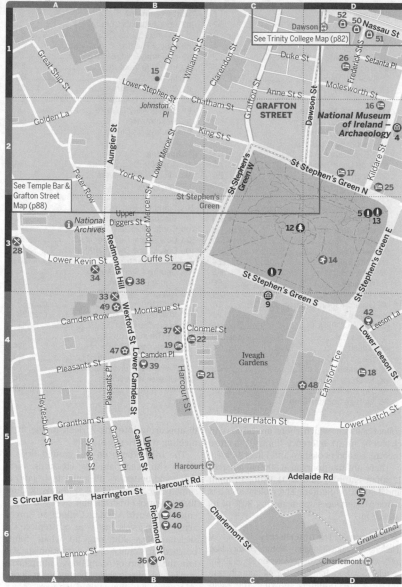

Blaschka Collection comprises finely detailed glass models of marine creatures whose zoological accuracy is incomparable.

Leinster House NOTABLE BUILDING
(Oireachtas Éireann; Map p92; ☎ 01-618 3271; www.oireachtas.ie; Kildare St; ☺ observation galleries 2.30-8.30pm Tue, from 10.30am Wed, 10.30am-5.30pm Thu Nov-May; ☒ all city centre) All the big decisions are made at the Oireachtas (Parliament). This Palladian mansion was built as a city residence for James Fitzgerald, the Duke of Leinster and Earl of Kildare, by Richard Cassels between 1745 and

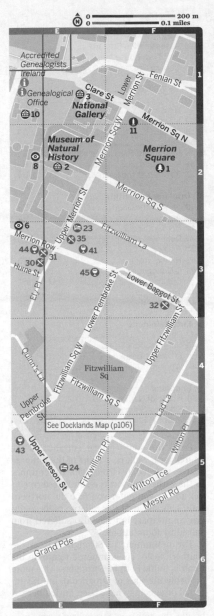

The Kildare St facade looks like a townhouse (which inspired Irish architect James Hoban's design for the US White House), whereas the Merrion Sq frontage resembles a country mansion. The obelisk in front of the building is dedicated to Arthur Griffith, Michael Collins and Kevin O'Higgins, the architects of independent Ireland.

The first government of the Irish Free State moved in from 1922, and both the Dáil (lower house) and Seanad (senate, or upper house) still meet here to discuss the affairs of the nation and gossip at the exclusive members bar. The 60-member Seanad meets for fairly low-key sessions in the north-wing saloon, while there are usually more sparks and tantrums when the 166-member Dáil bangs heads in a less-interesting room, formerly a lecture theatre, which was added to the original building in 1897. Parliament sits for 90 days a year.

⊙ Temple Bar

You can visit all of Temple Bar's attractions in less than half a day, but that's not really the point: this cobbled neighbourhood, for so long the city's most infamous party zone, is really more about ambience than attractions. If you visit during the day, the district's bohemian bent is on display. You can browse for vintage clothes, get your nipples pierced, nibble on Mongolian barbecue, buy organic food, pick up the latest musical releases and buy books on every conceivable subject. You can check out the latest art installations or join in a pulsating drum circle. By night – or at the weekend – it's a different story altogether, as the area's bars are packed to the rafters with revellers looking to tap into their inner Bacchus: it's loud, raucous and usually a lot of fun. Temple Bar is also Dublin's official 'cultural quarter', so you shouldn't ignore its more high-minded offerings like the progressive Project Arts Centre (p135), **Temple Bar Gallery & Studios** (Map p88; ✆ 01-671 0073; www.templebargallery.com; 5 Temple Bar; ⊙ 11am-6pm Tue-Sat; 🚌 all city centre) **FREE** and the Irish Film Institute (p136).

★ Christ Church Cathedral   CHURCH
(Map p88; www.christchurchcathedral.ie; Christ Church Pl; adult/student/child €7/5.50/2.50, with Dublinia €15/12.50/7.50; ⊙ 9.30am-5pm Mon-Sat, from 12.30pm Sun year-round, longer hours Mar-Oct; 🚌 50, 50A, 56A from Aston Quay, 54, 54A from Burgh Quay) Its hilltop location and eye-catching flying buttresses make this the most photogenic of Dublin's cathedrals. It

1748. Pre-arranged free **guided tours** (Map p92; ⊙ 10.30am, 11.30am, 2.30pm & 3.30pm Mon-Fri) **FREE** are available when parliament is in session (but not sitting); entry tickets to the observation galleries are available.

St Stephen's Green & Around

was founded in 1030 and rebuilt from 1172, mostly under the impetus of Richard de Clare, Earl of Pembroke (better known as Strongbow), the Anglo-Norman noble who invaded Ireland in 1170 and whose monument has pride of place inside.

Guided tours (Map p88; tour €11; ⊙ hourly 11am-noon & 2-4pm Mon-Fri, 2-4pm Sat) include the belfry, where a campanologist explains the art of bell-ringing and you can even have a go.

Once the original wooden church was replaced by the building you see today, the cathedral vied for supremacy with nearby St Patrick's Cathedral, but like its sister church it fell on hard times in the 18th and 19th centuries – the nave had been used as a market and the crypt housed taverns – and was virtually derelict by the time restoration took place. Today both Church of Ireland cathedrals are outsiders in a largely Catholic nation.

From the southeastern entrance to the churchyard, walk past ruins of the **chapter house**, which dates from 1230. The entrance to the cathedral is at the southwestern corner and as you enter you face the northern wall. This survived the collapse of its southern counterpart but has also suffered from subsiding foundations.

The monument to Strongbow is in the southern aisle. The armoured figure on the tomb is unlikely to be Strongbow (it's more probably the Earl of Drogheda), but his internal organs may have been buried here. A popular legend relates that the half figure beside the tomb is Strongbow's son, who was cut in two by his father when his bravery in battle was suspect.

The southern transept contains the superb baroque **tomb** of the 19th Earl of Kildare (died 1734). His grandson, Lord Edward

Fitzgerald, was a member of the United Irishmen and died in the abortive 1798 Rising.

An entrance just by the south transept descends to the unusually large arched **crypt**, which dates back to the original Viking church. Curiosities in the crypt include a glass display case housing a mummified cat chasing a mummified rat (known as Tom and Jerry), which were trapped inside an organ pipe in the 1860s! From the main entrance, a bridge, part of the 1871 to 1878 restoration, leads to Dublinia.

Dublinia: Experience Viking & Medieval Dublin
MUSEUM

(Map p88; ☑ 01-679 4611; www.dublinia.ie; Christ Church Pl; adult/student/child €10/9/6.50, with Christ Church Cathedral €15/12.50/7.50; ◑10am-5.30pm Mar-Sep, to 4.30pm Oct-Feb; ☐50, 50A, 56A from Aston Quay, 54, 54A from Burgh Quay) A must for the kids, the old Synod Hall, added to Christ Church Cathedral during its late-19th-century restoration, is home to the seemingly perennial Dublinia, a lively and kitschy attempt to bring Viking and medieval Dublin to life. Models, streetscapes and somewhat old-fashioned interactive displays do a fairly decent job of it, at least for kids.

The model of a medieval quayside and a cobbler's shop in **Medieval Dublin** are both excellent, as is the scale model of the medieval city. Up one floor is **Viking Dublin**, which has a large selection of objects recovered from Wood Quay, the world's largest Viking archaeological site. Interactive exhibits tell the story of Dublin's 9th- and 10th-century Scandinavian invaders, but the real treat is exploring life aboard the recreated longboat. You can also climb neighbouring **St Michael's Tower** and peek through its grubby windows for views over the city to the Dublin hills. There is also a cafe and the inevitable souvenir shop.

Icon Factory
ARTS CENTRE

(Map p88; ☑ 086 202 4533; www.iconfactorydublin.ie; 3 Aston Pl; ◑11am-6pm; ☐all city centre) FREE This artists' collective in the heart of Temple Bar hosts exhibitions on Ireland's cultural heritage. You'll find colourful, unique souvenirs celebrating the very best in Irish music and literature, and every sale goes towards the artists themselves. Take a stroll around their **Icon Walk** outside and get better acquainted with Irish playwrights, rock stars, sporting heroes and actors.

Ha'penny Bridge
BRIDGE

(Map p88; ☐all city centre) Dublin's most famous bridge is the Ha'penny Bridge, built in 1816. One of the world's oldest cast-iron bridges, it was built to replace the seven ferries that plied a busy route between the two banks of the river. Officially known as the Liffey Bridge, it gets its name from the ha'penny (half penny) toll that was charged until 1919 (for a time the toll was one-and-a-half pence, and so it was called the Penny Ha'penny Bridge).

Contemporary Music Centre
ARTS CENTRE

(Map p88; ☑ 01-490 1857; www.cmc.ie; 19 Fishamble St; ◑10am-5.30pm Mon-Fri; ☐all city centre) FREE Anyone with an interest in Irish contemporary music must visit the CMC's national archive where you can hear (and play around on an electronic organ) 10,000 samples from composers of this and the last century. There's also a good reference library where you can attend courses and meet composers.

◉ Kilmainham & the Liberties

Guinness Storehouse
BREWERY
See p76.

Kilmainham Gaol
MUSEUM
See p79.

WOMEN IN TRINITY COLLEGE

Despite being founded by a charter issued by a queen in 1592, Trinity College forbade women from attending until 1904 – and even dissuaded them from entering the college grounds at all. But a letter from King Edward VII in January 1904, authorising them to admit women to the degrees of Trinity College put an end to the board's resistance, even though the then-provost George Salmon was said to have declared that women would be admitted 'over his dead body'. He got his wish as he died a few days after the receipt of the king's letter, and only a few days before Isabel Marion Weir Johnston was officially enrolled as a student. She was forbidden from attending lectures and using the dining hall, and had to be off campus by 6pm. She was also prohibited from joining any of the major societies – so she started her own, the Elizabethan Society. Despite her pioneering efforts, most of the rules limiting women's activities were in place until the 1960s. Half a century later, women make up the majority of the student body.

MONICAMI/SHUTTERSTOCK ©

1. Poolbeg Lighthouse (p107)
Dating from 1768, this lighthouse gives you stunning views of Dublin Bay and the city.

2. Temple Bar (p93)
By day a bohemian, eclectic cobbled neighbourhood; by night loud, raucous, and a lot of fun.

3. Christ Church Cathedral (p93)
Founded in 1030, this impressive cathedral is Dublin's most photogenic.

4. Grand Canal Square
The magnificent Bord Gáis Energy Theatre here stages a broad variety of shows, from opera to comedy shows.

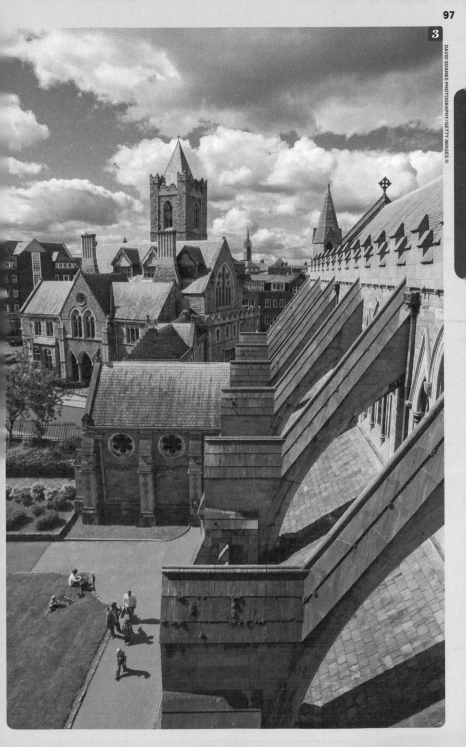

★ **St Patrick's Cathedral**   CATHEDRAL
(Map p88; ☑ 01-453 9472; www.stpatrickscathedral.
ie; St Patrick's Close; adult/student €8/7; ⊘ 9.30am-
5pm Mon-Fri, 9am-6pm Sat, 9-10.30am, 12.30-
2.30pm & 4.30-6pm Sun Mar-Oct, 9.30am-5pm Mon-
Fri, from 9am Sat, 9-10.30am & 12.30-2.30pm Sun
Nov-Feb; ▤ 50, 50A, 56A from Aston Quay, 54, 54A
from Burgh Quay) Ireland's largest church and
the final resting place of Jonathan Swift, St
Patrick's stands on the spot where St Patrick
himself reputedly baptised the local Celtic
chieftains in the 5th century. Fiction or not,
it's a sacred bit of turf upon which this cathedral was built between 1191 and 1270. The
adjacent park was once a slum but is now a
lovely garden to sit and catch some sunshine.

Like Christ Church Cathedral, the building has suffered a rather dramatic history
of storm and fire damage and has been altered several times (most questionably in
1864 when the flying buttresses were added,
thanks to the neo-Gothic craze that swept
the nation). Oliver Cromwell, during his
1649 visit to Ireland, converted St Patrick's
to a stable for his army's horses, an indigni-
ty to which he also subjected numerous other Irish churches. Jonathan Swift, author of
Gulliver's Travels, was the dean of the cathedral from 1713 to 1745, but after his tenure the cathedral was very neglected until

TRACING YOUR IRISH ANCESTORS

The **Genealogy Advisory Service**
(Map p92; ☑ 01-603 0200; ⊘ 9.30am-5pm
Mon-Fri, to 1pm Sat; ▤ all city centre) on
the 2nd floor of the **National Library
of Ireland** (Map p92; www.nli.ie; Kildare
St; ⊘ 9.30am-7.45pm Mon-Wed, to 4.45pm
Thu & Fri, 9.30am-12.45pm Sat) FREE will
advise you on how to trace your ancestry, which is a good way to begin your
research if you have no other experience. For information on commercial
agencies that will do the research for
you, contact the **Accredited Gene-
alogists Ireland** (AGI; Map p92; www.
accreditedgenealogists.ie; c/o the Genealogy Advisory Service, Kildare St; ▤ all city
centre). The files of the National Library
and the **National Archives** (Map p92;
☑ 01-407 2300; www.nationalarchives.ie;
Bishop St, Dublin 8; ⊘ 10am-5pm Mon-Fri;
▤ all city centre) are all potential sources of genealogical information.

its restoration in the 1860s. Also like Christ
Church, St Patrick's is a Church of Ireland
cathedral – which means that overwhelmingly Catholic Dublin has two Anglican
cathedrals!

Entering the cathedral from the southwestern porch you come almost immediately,
on your right, to the tombs of Swift and his
long-time companion Esther Johnson, aka
Stella. On the wall nearby are Swift's own
(self-praising) Latin epitaphs to the two of
them, and a bust of Swift.

The huge, dusty **Boyle Monument** to the
left was erected in 1632 by Richard Boyle,
Earl of Cork, and is decorated with numerous painted figures of members of his family. The figure in the centre on the bottom
level is the earl's five-year-old son Robert
Boyle (1627–91), who grew up to become a
noted scientist. His contributions to physics include Boyle's Law, which relates to the
pressure and volume of gases.

★ **Marsh's Library**   LIBRARY
(Map p88; www.marshlibrary.ie; St Patrick's Close;
adult/child €5/free; ⊘ 9.30am-5pm Mon & Wed-Fri,
from 10am Sat; ▤ 50, 50A, 56A from Aston Quay, 54,
54A from Burgh Quay) This magnificently preserved scholars' library, virtually unchanged
in three centuries, is one of Dublin's most
beautiful open secrets and an absolute highlight of any visit. Atop its ancient stairs are
beautiful dark-oak bookcases, each topped
with elaborately carved and gilded gables, and
crammed with 25,000 books, manuscripts
and maps dating back to the 15th century.

Founded in 1701 by Archbishop Narcissus
Marsh (1638–1713) and opened in 1707, the
library was designed by Sir William Robinson, the man also responsible for the Royal
Hospital Kilmainham. It's the oldest public
library in the country, and contains 25,000
books dating from the 16th to the early 18th
century, as well as maps, manuscripts (including one in Latin dating back to 1400)
and a collection of incunabula (books printed before 1500).

Irish Museum of Modern Art   MUSEUM
(IMMA; Map p84; Map p84; www.imma.ie; Military
Rd; ⊘ 11.30am-5.30pm Tue-Fri, from 10am Sat, from
noon Sun, tours 1.15pm Wed, 2.30pm Sat & Sun; ▤ 51,
51D, 51X, 69, 78, 79 from Aston Quay, ▤ Heuston)
FREE Ireland's most important collection of
modern and contemporary Irish and international art is housed in the elegant, airy
expanse of the Royal Hospital Kilmainham,
designed by Sir William Robinson and built

between 1684 and 1687 as a retirement home for soldiers. It fulfilled this role until 1928, after which it languished for nearly 50 years until a 1980s restoration saw it come back to life as this wonderful repository of art.

The building, which was inspired by Les Invalides in Paris, is a marvellous example of the Anglo-Dutch style that preceded the Georgian Age; at the time of its construction there were mutterings that it was altogether too fine a place for its residents.

Following Irish independence it was briefly considered as a potential home for the new Irish Parliament, but it ended up as a storage facility for the National Museum of Ireland. Restorations began on the occasion of its 300th birthday in 1984 and it opened in 1991. A major restoration between 2012 and 2013 gave it an extra bit of sparkle.

The blend of old and new comes together wonderfully, and you'll find such contemporary Irish artists as Louis le Brocquy, Sean Scully, Barry Flanagan, Kathy Prendergast and Dorothy Cross featured here, as well as a film installation by Neil Jordan. The permanent exhibition also features paintings from heavy-hitters Pablo Picasso and Joan Miró, and is topped up by regular temporary exhibitions. There's a good cafe and a bookshop on the grounds.

There are free guided tours of the museum's exhibits throughout the year.

Dublin Liberties Distillery DISTILLERY
(Map p84; https://thedld.com; 33 Mill St; adult/child €16/14; ⊗9.30am-6pm Mon-Thu, to 7pm Fri & Sat, 11am-7pm Sun Apr-Aug, 10am-5.30pm Mon-Sat, from 11am Sun Sep-Mar; ▣49, 54A from city centre) Housed in a 400-year-old building is Dublin's newest distillery venture, which opened in 2019 and cements the Liberties' newly established rep as a centre for whiskey production. There's a standard tour, where you learn about the distilling process and finish with a tasting of three whiskeys – the Dubliner, the Dublin Liberties and the Dead Rabbit – although these have all been distilled elsewhere as it'll be at least three years before any of the distillate can be called whiskey.

There's also an Experience tour (€32) where you get to taste six whiskeys, and plans are afoot for a Master Blender experience (€100).

War Memorial Gardens PARK
(www.heritageireland.ie; S Circular Rd, Islandbridge; ⊗8am-dusk Mon-Fri, from 10am Sat & Sun; ▣69, 79 from Aston Quay, 13, 40 from O'Connell St) FREE

THE TWO LUKES

In 2018 Dublin's legendary folk singer Luke Kelly (1940–1984) was immortalised in sculpture not once, but twice – on the same day. The first **figure** (Map p88; S King St; ▣all city centre, ▣St Stephen's Green) to be erected was a traditional bronze sculpture on South King St by John Coll, capturing Kelly mid-song while playing the banjo. The second **figure** (Map p84; ▣Mayor Square – NCI or Spencer Dock) is a 2m marble head with eyes closed and featuring 3000 strands of copper hair. It's on Sheriff St, where Kelly was born, and like all bold pieces of art has generated much comment, with some wits declaring that the artist did a great job capturing Kelly mid-orgasm.

Hardly anyone ever ventures this far west, but they're missing a lovely bit of landscaping in the shape of the War Memorial Gardens – by our reckoning as pleasant a patch of greenery as any you'll find in the heart of the Georgian centre. Designed by Sir Edwin Lutyens, the memorial commemorates the 49,400 Irish soldiers who died during WWI – their names are inscribed in the two huge granite bookrooms that stand at one end.

St Audoen's Church of Ireland CHURCH
(Map p88; ☑01-677 0088; www.heritageireland. ie; Cornmarket, High St; ⊗9.30am-4.45pm May-Oct; ▣50, 50A, 56A from Aston Quay, 54, 54A from Burgh Quay) Two churches, side by side, each bearing the same name, a tribute to St Audoen, the 7th-century bishop of Rouen (aka Ouen) and patron saint of the Normans. They built the older of the two, the Church of Ireland, between 1181 and 1212, and today it is the only medieval church in Dublin still in use. A free 30-minute guided tour departs every 30 minutes from 9.30am to 4.45pm. Attached to it is the newer, bigger, 19th-century **Catholic St Audoen's** (Map p88; Cornmarket, High St; ⊗Mass 1.15pm & 7pm Mon-Fri, 6pm Sat, 9.30am, 11am, 12.30pm & 6pm Sun; ▣50, 50A, 56A from Aston Quay, 54, 54A from Burgh Quay) FREE.

Through the Norman church's heavily moulded Romanesque Norman door, you can touch the 9th-century 'lucky stone' that was believed to bring good luck to business, and check out the 9th-century slab in the porch that suggests it was built on an even older church. As part of the tour you can

North of the Liffey

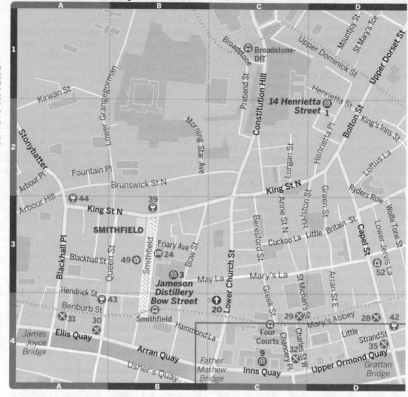

explore the ruins as well as the present church, which has funerary monuments that were beheaded by Cromwell's purists. Its tower and door date from the 12th century and the aisle from the 15th century, but the church today is mainly a product of a 19th-century restoration.

St Anne's Chapel, the visitor centre, houses a number of tombstones of leading members of Dublin society from the 16th to 18th centuries. At the top of the chapel is the tower, which holds the three oldest bells in Ireland, dating from 1423. Although the church's exhibits are hardly spectacular, the building itself is beautiful and a genuine slice of medieval Dublin.

The church is entered from the south off High St through **St Audoen's Arch**, which was built in 1240 and is the only surviving reminder of the city gates. The adjoining park is pretty but attracts many unsavoury characters, particularly at night.

◉ North of the Liffey

★**Hugh Lane Gallery, Dublin**   GALLERY
(Map p100; ☎ 01-222 5550; www.hughlane.ie; 22 N Parnell Sq; ⊗ 9.45am-6pm Tue-Thu, to 5pm Fri, 10am-5pm Sat, 11am-5pm Sun; 🚌 7, 11, 13, 16, 38, 40, 46A, 123 from city centre) **FREE** Whatever reputation Dublin has as a repository of world-class art has a lot to do with the simply stunning collection at this exquisite gallery, housed in the equally impressive Charlemont House, designed by William Chambers in 1763. Within its walls you'll find the best of contemporary Irish art, a handful of impressionist classics and Francis Bacon's relocated studio.

The gallery owes its origins to one Sir Hugh Lane (1875–1915). Born in County Cork, Lane worked in London art galleries before setting up his own gallery in Dublin in 1908. He had a connoisseur's eye and a good nose for the directions of the market, which enabled him to build up a superb collection, particularly strong in impressionists.

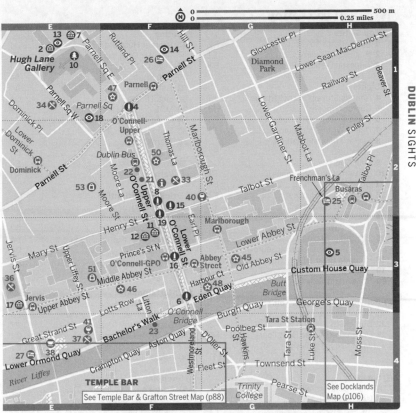

See Temple Bar & Grafton Street Map (p88)

See Docklands Map (p106)

Unfortunately for Ireland, neither his talents nor his collection were much appreciated. Irish rejection led him to rewrite his will and bequeath some of the finest works in his collection to the National Gallery in London. Later he relented and added a rider to his will leaving the collection to Dublin but he failed to have it witnessed, thus causing a long legal squabble over which gallery had rightful ownership.

The collection of eight paintings (known as the **Hugh Lane Bequest 1917**) was split in two in a 1959 settlement that sees half of them moving back and forth every six years. From 2015 the gallery has *Les Parapluies* by Auguste Renoir, *Portrait of Eva Gonzales* by Edouard Manet, *Jour d'Été* by Berthe Morisot and *View of Louveciennes* by Camille Pissarro.

Impressionist masterpieces notwithstanding, the gallery's most popular exhibit is the **Francis Bacon Studio**, which was painstakingly moved, in all its shambolic mess, from

7 Reece Mews, South Kensington, London, where the Dublin-born artist (1909–92) lived for 31 years. The display features some 80,000 items madly strewn about the place, including slashed canvases and the last painting he was working on.

The gallery is also home to a permanent collection of seven abstract paintings by Irish-born, New York–based Sean Scully, probably Ireland's most famous living painter.

At noon on Sundays, from September to June, the art gallery hosts concerts of contemporary classical music.

★ **National Museum of Ireland – Decorative Arts & History**   MUSEUM
(Map p84; www.museum.ie; Benburb St; ⏱10am-5pm Tue-Sat, from 2pm Sun; 🚌25, 66, 67, 90 from city centre, 🚉Museum) **FREE** Once the world's largest military barracks, this splendid early neoclassical grey-stone building on the Liffey's northern banks was completed in 1704 according to the design of Thomas

North of the Liffey

Burgh (he of Trinity College's Old Library). It is now home to the Decorative Arts & History collection of the National Museum of Ireland, with a range of superb permanent exhibits ranging from a history of the **1916 Easter Rising** to the work of iconic Irish designer **Eileen Gray** (1878–1976).

The building's central square held six entire regiments and is a truly awesome space, surrounded by arcaded colonnades and blocks linked by walking bridges. Following the handover to the new Irish government in 1922, the barracks were renamed to honour Michael Collins, a hero of the struggle for independence, who was killed that year in the Civil War; to this day most Dubliners refer to the museum as the **Collins Barracks**. Indeed, the army coat Collins wore on the day of his death (there's still mud on the sleeve) is part of the **Soldiers and Chiefs** exhibit, which

covers the history of Irish soldiery at home and abroad from 1550 to the 21st century.

The museum's exhibits include a treasure trove of artefacts ranging from silver, ceramics and glassware to weaponry, furniture and folk-life displays. The fascinating **Way We Wore** exhibit displays Irish clothing and jewellery from the past 250 years. An intriguing sociocultural study, it highlights the symbolism jewellery and clothing had in bestowing messages of mourning, love and identity. The old Riding School is home to **Proclaiming a Republic: The 1916 Rising**, which opened in 2016 as an enhanced and updated version of the long-standing exhibit dedicated to the rebellion. The display explores the complicated socio-historical background to the Rising and also includes visceral memorabilia such as firsthand accounts of the violence of the Black and Tans and post-Rising hunger strikes, and the handwritten death certificates of the Republican prisoners and their postcards from Holloway prison. Some of the best pieces are gathered in the **Curator's Choice** exhibition, which is a collection of 25 objects hand-picked by different curators and displayed alongside an account of why they were chosen.

★**14 Henrietta Street**   MUSEUM
(Map p100; ✆01-524 0383; www.14henriettastreet. ie; 14 Henrietta St; adult/child €9/6; ☺tours hourly 10am-4pm Wed-Sat, from noon Sun; ☒9, 13, 16, 40 from city centre) Explore one of Dublin's Georgian townhouses, carefully restored to gently peel back layers of complex social history over 250 years. Part museum, part community archive, it covers the magnificent elegance of upper-class life in the 1740s to the destitution of the early 20th century, when the house was occupied by 100 tenants living in near squalor. Access is by 75-minute guided tour only, which means visitors get the benefit of lots of interesting detail.

★**Jameson Distillery Bow Street** MUSEUM
(Map p100; www.jamesonwhiskey.com; Bow St; adult/student/child €19/18/11, masterclasses €60; ☺10am-5pm Mon-Sat, from 10.30am Sun; ☒25, 66, 67, 90 from city centre, ☒Smithfield) Smithfield's biggest draw is devoted to *uisce beatha* (ish-kuh ba-ha, 'the water of life'); that's Irish for whiskey. To its more serious devotees, that is precisely what whiskey is, although they may be put off by the slickness of this museum (occupying part of the old distillery that stopped production in 1971), which shepherds visitors through a compulsory tour of the recreated factory (the tasting at the end is a lot of fun) and into the ubiquitous gift shop.

If you're really serious about whiskey, you can deepen your knowledge with the Whiskey Makers or the Whiskey Shakers, two 90-minute masterclasses that deconstruct the creation of Jameson whiskeys and teach you how to make a range of whiskey-based cocktails. If you're just buying whiskey, go for the stuff you can't buy at home, such as the excellent Red Breast or the super-exclusive Midleton, a very limited reserve that is appropriately expensive.

General Post Office   HISTORIC BUILDING
(Map p100; ✆01-705 7000; www.anpost.ie; Lower O'Connell St; ☺8am-8pm Mon-Sat; ☒all city centre, ☒Abbey) It's not just the country's main post office, or an eye-catching neoclassical building: the General Post Office is at the heart of Ireland's struggle for independence. The GPO served as command HQ for the rebels during the 1916 Easter Rising and as a result has become the focal point for all kinds of protests, parades and remembrances, as well as home to an interactive **visitor centre** (Map p100; www.gpowitnesshistory.ie; adult/child €14/7; ☺10am-4.30pm Mon-Sat, from noon Sun).

The building – a neoclassical masterpiece designed by Francis Johnston in 1818 – was burnt out in the siege that resulted from the Rising, but that wasn't the end of it. There was bitter fighting in and around the GPO during the Civil War of 1922; you can still see the pockmarks of the struggle in the Doric columns. Since its reopening in 1929 it has lived through quieter times, although its role in Irish history is commemorated inside the visitor centre.

**James Joyce
Cultural Centre**   CULTURAL CENTRE
(Map p100; www.jamesjoyce.ie; 35 N Great George's St; adult/child €5/free; ☺10am-5pm Tue-Sat, from noon Sun Apr-Sep, closed Mon Oct-Mar; ☒3, 10, 11, 11A, 13, 16, 16A, 19, 19A, 22 from city centre) James Joyce is brought to virtual life in this beautifully restored Georgian house. As well as some wonderful interactive details, the exhibits include some of the furniture from Joyce's Paris apartment; a life-size recreation of a typical Edwardian bedroom (not Joyce's, but one similar to what he would have used); and the original door of 7 Eccles St, the home of Leopold and Molly Bloom in *Ulysses*, which was demolished in real life to make way for a private hospital.

Professor Denis Maginni, the exuberant, flamboyant dance instructor and 'confirmed bachelor' immortalised by James Joyce in *Ulysses*, taught the finer points of dance out of here, and if the house survived at all it's down to the efforts of Joycean scholar and gay rights activist Senator David Norris.

If the house lacks a lot of period detail, it's more than compensated for by the superb interactive displays, which include three short documentary films on various aspects of Joyce's life and work, and – the highlight of the whole place – computers that allow you to explore the content of *Ulysses* episode by episode and trace Joyce's life year by year. It's enough to demolish the myth that Joyce's works are an impenetrable mystery and render him as he should be to the contemporary reader: a writer of enormous talent who sought to challenge and entertain his audience with his wit and use of language.

While here, you can also admire the fine plastered ceilings, some of which are restored originals while others are meticulous reproductions of Dublin stuccodore Michael Stapleton's designs. The street has also been given a facelift and now boasts some of the finest Georgian doorways and fanlights in the city.

Walking **tours** (Map p100; ☑ 01-878 8547; adult/student €10/8; ⏰ 2pm Tue, Thu & Sat May-Sep, Sat only Oct-Apr) based on Joyce and his literary works run from the house.

St Michan's Church   CHURCH
(Map p100; ☑ 01-872 4154; Lower Church St; adult/child €6/4; ⏰ 10am-12.45pm & 2-4.45pm Mon-Fri, 10am-12.45pm Sat; 🚇 Smithfield) Macabre remains are the main attraction at this church, which was founded by the Danes in 1095 and named after one of their saints. Among the 'attractions' is an 800-year-old Norman crusader who was so tall that his feet were lopped off so he could fit in a coffin. Visits are by guided tour only.

St Michan's was the Northside's only church until 1686, a year after it was almost completely rebuilt (it was remodelled in 1825 and again after the Civil War), leaving only the 15th-century battlement tower as its oldest bit. The courtroom-like interior hasn't changed much since the 19th century: still in place is the organ from 1724, which Handel may have played for the first-ever performance of his *Messiah*. The organ case is distinguished by the fine oak carving of 17 entwined musical instruments on its front. A skull on the floor on one side of the altar is said to represent Oliver Cromwell. On the opposite side is the Stool of Repentance, where 'open and notoriously naughty livers' did public penance.

The tours of the underground vaults are the real draw, however. The bodies within are aged between 400 and 800 years, and have

---

ⓘ DUBLIN PASS
· ·
For heavy-duty sightseeing, the **Dublin Pass** (adult/child one-day €62/33, three-day €92/49) will save you a packet. It provides free entry to over 25 attractions (including the Guinness Storehouse), discounts at 20 others and guaranteed fast-track entry to some of the busiest sights. To avail of the free Aircoach transfer to and from the airport, download the app before you arrive. Otherwise, it's available from any Discover Ireland Dublin Tourism Centre.

---

been preserved by a combination of methane gas coming from rotting vegetation beneath the church, the magnesium limestone of the masonry (which absorbs moisture from the air) and the perfectly constant temperature. Although there are caskets strewn about the place, the main attractions are 'the big four' – mummified bodies labelled The Unknown (a female about whom nothing is known), The Thief (his hands and feet are missing; some say as punishment for his crimes), The Nun and The Crusader: if he is indeed 800 years old then he may have participated in the piratical free-for-all crusades of the 13th century that resulted in the sack of Constantinople but which weren't sanctioned by the church. Also in the crypt are the bodies of John and Henry Sheares, two brothers executed following the Rising of 1798 and – it is claimed – the remains of Robert Emmet, the fallen leader of the 1803 rebellion. Bram Stoker is said to have visited the crypt, which may have inspired him to write a story about a certain vampire who slept in a coffin...

Dublin Writers Museum   MUSEUM
(Map p100; www.writersmuseum.com; 18 N Parnell Sq; adult/child €7/6; ⏰ 9.45am-4.45pm Mon-Sat, 11am-4.30pm Sun; 🚌 3, 7, 10, 11, 13, 16, 19, 46A, 123 from city centre) Memorabilia aplenty and lots of literary ephemera line the walls and display cabinets of this elegant museum devoted to preserving the city's rich literary tradition up to 1970. The building, comprising two 18th-century houses, is worth exploring on its own; Dublin stuccodore Michael Stapleton decorated the upstairs gallery.

However, the curious decision to omit living writers limits its appeal – no account at all is given to contemporary writers, who would arguably be more popular with today's readers.

Although the busts and portraits in the gallery upstairs warrant more than a cursory peek, the real draws are the ground-floor displays, which include Samuel Beckett's phone (with a button for excluding incoming calls, of course), a letter from the 'tenement aristocrat' Brendan Behan to his brother, and a first edition of Bram Stoker's *Dracula*.

The **Gorham Library** next door is worth a visit, and there's also a calming Zen garden. The basement restaurant, Chapter One (p127), is one of the city's best.

While the museum focuses on the dearly departed, the **Irish Writers Centre** (Map p100; ☑ 01-872 1302; www.irishwriterscentre.ie; 19 N Parnell Sq; ⏰ 10am-9pm Mon-Thu, to 5pm Fri)

O'CONNELL STREET STATUARY

O'Connell St is lined with statues of Irish history's good and great. The big daddy of them all is the 'Liberator' himself, **Daniel O'Connell** (1775–1847; Map p100; Lower O'Connell St; 🚌 all city centre, 🚉 Abbey) whose massive bronze bulk soars above the street at the bridge end. The four winged figures at his feet represent O'Connell's supposed virtues: patriotism, courage, fidelity and eloquence. Dubs began to refer to the street as O'Connell St soon after the monument was erected– the 1880 statue was unveiled in 1882; its name was officially changed after independence.

Heading away from the river, past a monument to **William Smith O'Brien** (1803–64), leader of the Young Irelanders, is a statue that easily rivals O'Connell's for drama: just outside the GPO on Lower O'Connell St is the spread-armed figure of trade-union leader **Jim Larkin** (1876–1947; Map p100). His big moment came when he helped organise the general strike in 1913 – the pose catches him in full flow, urging workers to rise up for their rights. We're with you, comrade.

Next up and difficult to miss is the **Spire**, but just below it, on pedestrianised North Earl St, is the detached figure of **James Joyce** (Map p100), looking on the fast and shiny version of 21st-century O'Connell St with a bemused air. Dubs have lovingly dubbed him the 'prick with the stick' and we're sure Joyce would have loved the vulgar rhyme.

Further Upper O'Connell St is **Father Theobald Mathew** (1790–1856; Map p100; Upper O'Connell St) the 'apostle of temperance'. There can't have been a tougher gig in Ireland, but he led a spirited campaign against 'the demon drink' in the 1840s and converted hundreds of thousands to teetotalism.

The top of the street is completed by the imposing statue of **Charles Stewart Parnell** (1846–91;Map p100; Upper O'Connell St), the 'uncrowned king of Ireland', who was an advocate of Home Rule and became a political victim of Irish intolerance.

next door provides a meeting and working place for their living successors.

National Leprechaun Museum
MUSEUM

(Map p100; www.leprechaunmuseum.ie; Twilfit House, Jervis St; adult/child €16/10, Darkland Tour €18; ⏰ 10am-6.30pm, also 7-8.30pm Fri & Sat; 🚌 all city centre, 🚉 Jervis) Ostensibly designed as a child-friendly museum of Irish folklore, this is really a romper room for kids sprinkled with bits of fairy tale. Which is no bad thing, even if the picture of the leprechaun painted here is more Lucky Charms and Walt Disney than sinister creature of pre-Christian mythology.

There's the optical illusion tunnel (which makes you appear smaller to those at the other end), the room full of oversized furniture, the wishing wells and, inevitably, the pot of gold; all of which is strictly for the kids. But if Walt Disney himself went on a leprechaun hunt when visiting Ireland during the filming of *Darby O'Gill and the Little People* in 1948, what the hell do we know?

The summertime Darkland Tour, a nighttime storytelling session of dark and haunting tales of folklore, is a little more in keeping with the original purpose of most folklore tales – imparting moral lessons through a little bit of fear!

👁 Docklands

Custom House
LANDMARK

(Map p100; Custom House Quay; ⏰ 9am-5pm Mon-Fri; 🚌 all city centre) Georgian genius James Gandon (1743-1823) announced his arrival on the Dublin scene with this magnificent building constructed over 10 years between 1781 and 1791, just past Eden Quay at a wide section of the River Liffey. It's a colossal, neoclassical pile that stretches for 114m and is topped by a copper dome.

Best appreciated from the south side of the Liffey, its fine detail deserves closer inspection. Below the frieze are heads representing the gods of Ireland's 13 principal rivers; the sole female head, above the main door, represents the River Liffey. The cattle heads honour Dublin's beef trade, and the statues behind the building represent Africa, America, Asia and Europe. Set into the dome are four clocks and, above that, a 5m-high statue of Hope.

EPIC The Irish Emigration Museum
MUSEUM

(Map p106; 📞 01-906 0861; www.epicchq.com; CHQ Bldg, Custom House Quay; adult/child €15/7.50; ⏰ 10am-6.45pm, last entrance 5pm; 🚉 George's Dock) This is a high-tech, interactive exploration of emigration and its effect

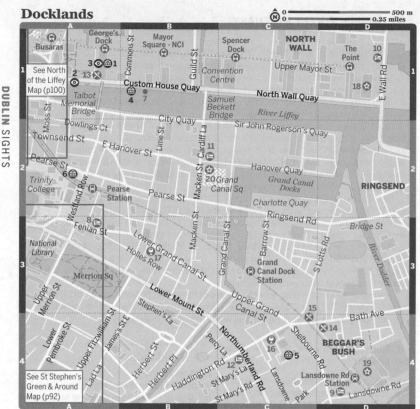

Docklands

Sights

1 EPIC The Irish Emigration Museum	A1
2 Famine Memorial	A1
3 Irish Family History Centre	A1
4 Jeanie Johnston	B1
5 National Print Museum	C4
6 Science Gallery	A2

Activities, Courses & Tours

7 City Kayaking Dublin	B1

Sleeping

8 Alex	A3
9 Ariel House	D4
10 Gibson Hotel	D1
11 Marker	B2

12 Schoolhouse Hotel	C4

Eating

13 Ely Bar & Grill	A1
14 Farmer Brown's	D4
15 Juniors Deli & Cafe	C4
Science Gallery Café	(see 6)

Drinking & Nightlife

16 Beggar's Bush	C4
17 Square Ball	B3

Entertainment

18 3 Arena	D1
19 Aviva Stadium	D4
20 Bord Gáis Energy Theatre	B2

on Ireland and the 70 million or so people spread throughout the world who claim Irish ancestry. Start your visit with a 'passport' and proceed through 20 interactive – and occasionally moving – galleries examining why they left, where they went and how they maintained their relationship with their ancestral home.

Famine Memorial MEMORIAL
(Map p106; Custom House Quay; ⌨all city centre) Just east of the Custom House (p105) is one of Dublin's most thought-provoking (and photographed) examples of public art: the set of life-size bronze figures (1997) by Rowan Gillespie known simply as *Famine*. Designed to commemorate the ravages of the Great Hunger (1845–51), their haunted, harrowed look testifies to a journey that was both hazardous and unwelcome.

The location of the sculptures is also telling, for it was from this very point in 1846 that one of the first 'coffin ships' (as they gruesomely came to be known) set sail for the USA. Steerage fare on the *Perseverance* was £3 and 210 passengers made that first journey, landing in New York on 18 May 1846, with all passengers and crew intact.

In June 2007 a second series of *Famine* sculptures by Rowan Gillespie was unveiled on the quayside in Toronto's Ireland Park by then Irish president Mary McAleese to commemorate the arrival of Famine refugees in the New World.

Jeanie Johnston MUSEUM
(Map p106; www.jeaniejohnston.ie; Custom House Quay; adult/student/child/family €10/9/6/28; ☉tours hourly 10am-4pm Apr-Oct, 11am-3pm Nov-Mar; ⌨all city centre, ⌨George's Dock) One of the city's most original tourist attractions is an exact working replica of a 19th-century 'coffin ship' – even if the original *Jeanie Johnston* suffered no deaths in 16 journeys between 1848 and 1855, carrying a total of 2500 passengers. A small on-board museum details the harrowing plight of a typical journey, which usually took around 47 days.

The ship also operates as a Sail Training vessel, with journeys taking place from May to September. If you are visiting during these times, check the website for details of when it will be in dock.

Irish Family History Centre CULTURAL CENTRE
(Map p106; ☏01-671 0338; www.irishfamily historycentre.com; CHQ Bldg, Custom House Quay; €12.50, incl EPIC The Irish Emigration Museum €24; 30/60min genealogist consultation €45/85; ☉10am-5pm Mon-Fri, from noon Sat; ⌨George's Dock) Discover your family history with interactive screens where you can track your surname and centuries of Irish emigration. The ticket price includes a 15-minute consultation with a genealogist, but additional 30-minute and hour-long sessions are also

POOLBEG LIGHTHOUSE

One of the city's most rewarding walks is a stroll along the Great South Wall to the **Poolbeg Lighthouse** (South Wall; ☉24hr; ⌨1, 47, 56A, 77A, 84N from city centre), that red tower visible in the middle of Dublin Bay. The lighthouse dates from 1768, but it was redesigned and rebuilt in 1820. To get there, take the bus to Ringsend from the city centre, and then make your way past the power station to the start of the wall (it's about 1km). It's not an especially long walk out to the lighthouse – about 800m or so – but it will give you a stunning view of the bay and the city behind you, a view best enjoyed just before sunset on a summer's evening.

DUBLIN SIGHTS

available. You can visit as part of the EPIC exhibition or buy a separate ticket.

⊙ Southside

National Print Museum MUSEUM
(Map p106; ☏01-660 3770; www.nationalprintmuseum.ie; Haddington Rd, Garrison Chapel, Beggar's Bush; ☉9am-5pm Mon-Fri, from 2pm Sat & Sun; ⌨4, 7 from city centre, ⌨Grand Canal Dock, Lansdowne Rd) **FREE** You don't have to be into printing to enjoy this quirky little museum, where personalised guided tours (11.30am daily and 2.30pm Monday to Friday) are offered in a delightfully casual and compelling way. A video looks at the history of printing in Ireland and then you wander through the various (still working) antique presses amid the smell of ink and metal.

The guides are excellent and can tailor the tours to suit your special interests – for example, anyone interested in history can get a detailed account of the difficulties encountered by the rebels of 1916 when they tried to have the proclamation printed. Upstairs there are lots of old newspaper pages recording important episodes in Irish history over the last century.

Herbert Park PARK
(Map p84; Ballsbridge; ☉dawn-dusk; ⌨5, 7, 7A, 8, 45, 46 from city centre, ⌨Sandymount, Lansdowne Rd) A gorgeous swathe of green lawns, ponds and flower beds near the Royal Dublin Society Showground (p137). Sandwiched between prosperous Ballsbridge and Donnybrook, the

park runs along the River Dodder. There are tennis courts and a kids' playground here too.

⊙ Beyond the City Centre

★ Phoenix Park   PARK

(www.phoenixpark.ie; ⊘24hr; ▣10 from O'Connell St, 25, 26 from Middle Abbey St) FREE Measuring 709 glorious hectares, Phoenix Park is one of the world's largest city parks; you'll find joggers, grannies pushing buggies, ladies walking poodles, gardens, lakes, a sporting oval and 300 fallow deer. There are also cricket and polo grounds, a motor-racing track and some fine 18th-century residences, including those of the Irish president and the US ambassador.

The deer were first introduced by Lord Ormond in 1662, when lands once owned by the Knights of Jerusalem were turned into a royal hunting ground. In 1745 the viceroy Lord Chesterfield threw it open to the public and it has remained that way ever since. (The name 'Phoenix' has nothing to do with the mythical bird; it is a corruption of the Irish *fionn uisce*, meaning 'clear water'.)

In 1882 the park played a crucial role in Irish history, when Lord Cavendish, the British chief secretary for Ireland, and his assistant were murdered outside what is now the Irish president's residence by an obscure nationalist group called the Invincibles. Lord Cavendish's home is now called Deerfield and is used as the official residence of the US ambassador.

Glasnevin Cemetery   CEMETERY

(Prospect Cemetery; www.glasnevintrust.ie; Finglas Rd; tours €13.50; ⊘10am-5pm, tours hourly 10.30am-4.30pm; ▣40, 40A, 40B from Parnell St) FREE The tombstones at Ireland's largest and most historically important burial site read like a 'who's who' of Irish history, as most of the leading names of the past 150 years are buried here, including Daniel O'Connell and Charles Stewart Parnell. It was established in 1832 by O'Connell as a burial ground for people of all faiths – a high-minded response to Protestant cemeteries' refusal to bury Catholics. The selection of themed tours are all highly recommended.

A modern replica of a round tower acts as a handy landmark for locating the tomb of O'Connell, who died in 1847 and was reinterred here in 1869 when the tower was completed. It opened to visitors in 2018 for the first time in nearly half a century; the reward for a climb to the top is a sweet view of the city. Charles Stewart Parnell's tomb is topped with a large granite rock, on which only his name is inscribed – a remarkably simple tribute to a figure of such historical importance. Other notable people buried here include Sir Roger Casement, executed for treason by the British in 1916; the Republican leader Michael Collins, who died in the Civil War; the docker and trade unionist Jim Larkin, a prime force in the 1913 general strike; and the poet Gerard Manley Hopkins.

The history of the cemetery is told in wonderful detail in the **Glasnevin Cemetery Museum** (museum €6.75, museum & tour €13.50; ⊘10am-5pm Oct-May, until 6pm Jun-Sep).

The best way to visit the cemetery is to take one of the daily **tours** that will (ahem) bring to life the rich and important stories of those buried in what is jokingly referred to by Dubs as 'Croak Park'.

Áras an Uachtaráin   HISTORIC BUILDING

(www.president.ie; Phoenix Park; ⊘guided tours hourly 10.30am-3.30pm Sat; ▣10 from O'Connell St, 25, 26 from Middle Abbey St) FREE The official residence of the Irish president, this white Palladian lodge was originally built in 1751 and has been enlarged a couple of times since, most recently in 1816. Tickets for the free one-hour tours can be collected from the **Phoenix Park Visitor Centre** (☎01-677 0095; www.phoenixpark.ie; ⊘10am-6pm Apr-Dec, 9.30am-5.30pm Wed-Sun Jan-Mar) FREE, the converted former stables of the papal nunciate (embassy), where you'll see a 10-minute introductory video before being shuttled to the Áras itself to inspect five state rooms and the president's study.

It was home to the British viceroys from 1782 to 1922, and then to the governors general until Ireland cut ties with the British Crown and created the office of president in 1937. Queen Victoria stayed here during her visit in 1849, when she appeared not to even notice the Famine. The candle burning in the window is an old Irish tradition, to guide the Irish diaspora home.

Dublin Zoo   ZOO

(www.dublinzoo.ie; Phoenix Park; adult/child/family €19.50/14/53; ⊘9.30am-6pm Mar-Sep, to dusk Oct-Feb; ⊞; ▣10 from O'Connell St, 25, 26 from Middle Abbey St) Established in 1831, the 28-hectare Dublin Zoo just north of the Hollow is one of the oldest in the world. It is well known for its lion-breeding program, which dates back to 1857, and includes among its offspring the lion that roars at the start of

DUBLIN DISTILLERIES

The Liberties might be dominated by the world-famous Guinness brewery, but Dublin's most traditional neighbourhood has rediscovered whiskey. In 2015 the **Teeling Distillery** (Map p84; www.teelingwhiskey.com; 13-17 Newmarket; tours €15-30; 10am-5.40pm; 27, 77A & 151 from city centre) **FREE** reopened after a hiatus of nearly 200 years (the original on nearby Marrowbone Lane operated between 1782 and 1822), followed in 2017 by the opening of the **Pearse Lyons Distillery** (Map p84; 01-825 2244; www.pearselyonsdistillery.com; 121-122 James's St; guided tours €20-30; 21A, 51B, 78, 78A, 123 from Fleet St), which began operations in the former St James's Church on James's St. Pearse Lyons and his wife Deirdre own a brewery and distillery in Kentucky (as well as the giant animal nutrition company Alltech), but this new project is close to Lyons' heart as his own grandfather is buried in the church's graveyard. In 2019 two more distilleries opened: the Dublin Liberties Distillery (p99) and **Roe & Co** (Map p84; www.roeandcowhiskey.com; 91 James's St; €19-25; 11am-7pm, last admission 5pm; 123 from city centre), whose owners Diageo also own Guinness.

The boilerplate tours are all similar: you learn about the distilling process and finish with a tasting; for extra you get a master distiller experience, which includes more detail and more whiskey. The problem with all the new arrivals is that it takes a minimum of three years before anything they make can be officially called whiskey, so until the casks have reached maturation the whiskey you're tasting is a blend of something distilled elsewhere, usually the Cooley Distillery in County Louth.

MGM films. You'll see these tough cats, from a distance, on the 'African Savannah', just one of several habitats that are home to over 400 animals. Tickets are cheaper online.

The zoo is home to 100 different species, and you can visit all of them across the eight different habitats, which range from an Asian jungle to a family farm, where kids get to meet the inhabitants up close and milk a (model) cow.

There are restaurants, cafes and even a train to get you around.

Croke Park Stadium & Museum MUSEUM
(www.crokepark.ie; Clonliffe Rd, New Stand, Croke Park; adult/child museum €7/6, museum & tour €14/9; 9.30am-6pm Mon-Sat, 10.30am-5pm Sun Jun-Aug, 9.30am-5pm Mon-Sat, 10.30am-5pm Sun Sep-May; 3, 11, 11A, 16, 16A, 123 from O'Connell St) This museum is all about the history and importance of Gaelic sports in Ireland and the role of the Gaelic Athletic Association (GAA) as the stout defender of a proud cultural identity. It helps if you're a sporting enthusiast.

The twice-daily tours (except match days) of the impressive Croke Park stadium are excellent, and well worth the extra cost. Admission to the tour includes a museum visit.

The stadium's other attraction is the **Skyline** (adult/child €20/12; half-hourly 10.30am-3.30pm Mon-Sat, from 11.30am Sun Jul & Aug, 11.30am & 2.30pm Mon-Fri, half-hourly 10.30am-2.30pm Sat, from 11.30am Sun Sep-Jun), a guided tour around Croke Park's roof.

National Botanic Gardens GARDENS
(www.botanicgardens.ie; Botanic Rd; 9am-5pm Mon-Fri, 10am-6pm Sat & Sun Mar-Oct, 9am-4.30pm Mon-Sat, 10am-4.30pm Sun Nov-Feb; 13, 13A, 19 from O'Connell St, 34, 34A from Middle Abbey St) **FREE** Founded in 1795, these 19.5-hectare botanic gardens are home to a series of curvilinear glasshouses, dating from 1843 to 1869 and created by Richard Turner, who was also responsible for the glasshouse at Belfast Botanic Gardens and the Palm House in London's Kew Gardens. Within these Victorian masterpieces you will find the latest in botanical technology, including a series of computer-controlled climates reproducing environments from different parts of the world.

Activities

★ Experience

Gaelic Games ADVENTURE SPORTS
(01-254 4292; www.experiencegaelicgames.com; St Mobhi Rd; per person €28-39; Mon-Sat Mar-Oct, Fri & Sat Nov- Feb; 4, 9 from O'Connell St) Ostensibly created as a uniquely Irish version of a corporate bonding exercise, this centre allows you to experience the trio of Gaelic games: hurling, Gaelic football and handball. The staff have an enormous passion for the sports and their pride and delight at showing them to visitors is infectious. Join one of the open sessions; groups of six or more can book private sessions.

National Aquatic Centre   SWIMMING
(☑ 01-646 4300; www.nationalaquaticcentre.ie; Snugborough Rd; adult/child & student €7.50/5.50, incl AquaZone €16/14; ☉ 6am-10pm Mon-Fri, 9am-8pm Sat & Sun; ☐ 38 & 38A from O'Connell St) The National Aquatic Centre is the largest indoor water park in the country. Besides its Olympic-sized competition pool, there's the AquaZone, with water roller coasters, wave and surf machines, a leisure pool and all types of flumes. It's a great day out for the family, but at weekends be prepared to join the line of shivering children queuing for slides.

City Kayaking Dublin   KAYAKING
(Map p106; ☑ 085 866 7787; www.citykayaking.com; Dublin City Moorings, Custom House Quay; adult/child €33/25; ☉ tours 9am-8pm May-Oct; ☐ all city centre, ☐ George's Dock) A great way to see the city is aboard a kayak on this 90-minute guided trip that takes you up the Liffey through the city centre. There's a 30-minute instruction and prep session beforehand; a change of clothes and a towel is advisable, as you will inevitably get a little wet. Book online.

🖝 Tours

★ Secret Street Tours   WALKING
(Map p84; www.secretstreettours.org; standard/ supporter/premium supporter €10/20/30) Former rough sleeper Derek McGuire leads this eye-opening and revealing two-hour tour of the Liberties beginning at St Patrick's Tower. The 1.3km route includes areas where McGuire slept rough for two years. Along the way, Derek shares homeless tips on staying safe and blending into crowds. Some of the proceeds go towards homeless charity the Simon Community.

★ Fab Food Trails   WALKING
(www.fabfoodtrails.ie; tours €60; ☉ 10am Sat) Highly recommended 2½- or three-hour tasting walks through the city centre's choicest independent producers. You'll visit up to eight bakeries, cheesemongers, markets and delis, learning about the food culture of each neighbourhood you explore. There is also a Food & Fashion walk. You meet in the city centre.

★ Green Mile   WALKING
(Map p88; ☑ 01-661 1000; www.littlemuseum.ie; Little Museum of Dublin, 15 St Stephen's Green N; adult/ student €15/13; ☉ 11am Sat & Sun; ☐ all city centre, ☐ St Stephen's Green) Excellent one-hour tour of St Stephen's Green led by local historian Donal Fallon. Along the way you'll hear tales of James Joyce, the park's history and the drafting of the Irish Constitution. Book ahead as tours fill up pretty quickly. The tour also includes admission to and a guided tour of the Little Museum of Dublin (p82).

★ Historical Walking Tour   WALKING
(Map p82; ☑ 01-878 0227; www.historicaltours.ie; Trinity College Gate; adult/student/child €14/12/ free; ☉ 11am & 3pm May-Sep, 11am Apr & Oct, 11am Fri-Sun Nov-Mar; ☐ all city centre) Trinity College history graduates lead this 'seminar on the street' that explores the Potato Famine, Easter Rising, Civil War and Partition. Sights include Trinity, City Hall, Dublin Castle and the Four Courts. In summer, themed tours on architecture, women in Irish history and the birth of the Irish state are also held. Tours depart from the College Green entrance.

1916 Rebellion Walking Tour   WALKING
(Map p88; ☑ 086 858 3847; www.1916rising.com; 23 Wicklow St; adult/child €15/9; ☉ 11.30am Mon-Sat, 1pm Sun Mar-Oct, 11.30am Fri & Sat, 1pm Sun Nov-Feb; ☐ all city centre) Superb two-hour tour starting in the International Bar, at 23 Wicklow St. Lots of information, humour and irreverence to boot. The guides – all Trinity graduates – are uniformly excellent and will not say no to the offer of a pint back in the International at tour's end. They also have a tour based around Michael Collins, hero of the War of Independence.

Dublin Musical Pub Crawl   WALKING
(Map p88; ☑ 01-475 8345; www.musicalpubcrawl. com; Anglesea St; adult/student €16/14; ☉ 7.30pm daily Apr-Oct, 7.30pm Thu-Sat Nov-Mar; ☐ all city centre) The story of Irish traditional music and its influence on contemporary styles is explained and demonstrated by two expert musicians in a number of Temple Bar pubs over 2½ hours. Meet upstairs in Oliver St John Gogarty's.

Dublin Literary Pub Crawl   WALKING
(Map p88; ☑ 01-670 5602; www.dublinpubcrawl.com; 9 Duke St; adult/student €14/12; ☉ 7.30pm daily Apr-Oct, 7.30pm Thu-Sun Nov-Mar; ☐ all city centre) A tour of pubs associated with famous Dublin writers is a sure-fire recipe for success, and this 2½-hour tour-performance by two actors is a riotous laugh. There's plenty of drink taken, which makes it all the more popular. It leaves from the Duke on Duke St; get there by 7pm to reserve a spot for the evening tour.

Pat Liddy Walking Tours   WALKING
(Map p88; ☑ 01-831 1109; www.walkingtours.ie; Visit Dublin Centre, 25 Suffolk St; tours €10-15; ☐ all city centre) A variety of guided walks on a host of

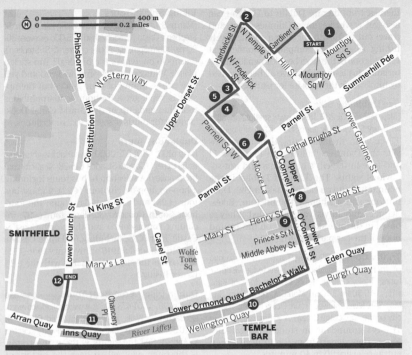

🏃 City Walk
A Walk on the Northside

START MOUNTJOY SQUARE
END ST MICHAN'S CHURCH
LENGTH 2.5KM; TWO HOURS

From **①** **Mountjoy Square**, take a left at the northwestern corner and walk down Gardiner Pl, turning right onto N Temple St. Up ahead is the fine but now deconsecrated Georgian **②** **St George's Church** (⊘ closed to public).

Take a left onto Hardwicke St and again onto N Frederick St. You'll spot the **③** **Abbey Presbyterian Church**, built in 1864.

The northern slice of Parnell Sq houses the **④** **Garden of Remembrance** (Map p100; www.heritageireland.ie; ⊘ 8.30am-6pm Apr-Sep, 9.30am-4pm Oct-Mar), opened in 1966 to commemorate the 50th anniversary of the 1916 Easter Rising. Facing the park is the excellent **⑤** **Hugh Lane Gallery, Dublin** (p100), home to some of the best modern art in Europe.

In the southern part of Parnell Sq is the **⑥** **Rotunda Hospital** (Map p100; ☑ 01-873 0700), a wonderful example of public architecture in the Georgian style and now a maternity hospital. The southeastern corner of the

square has the **⑦** **Gate Theatre** (p136), one of the city's most important theatres – and where Orson Welles began his acting career in 1931 as a 16-year-old.

Head down O'Connell St, passing by the 120m-high **⑧** **Spire** (p105). Erected in 2001, it has become an iconic symbol of the city. On the western side of O'Connell St, the stunning neoclassical **⑨** **General Post Office** (p103) towers over the street – this was the operational HQ for the 1916 Easter Rising: you can still see the bullet holes in the columns.

When you hit the river, turn right and walk along the boardwalk until you reach the city's most distinctive crossing point, the **⑩** **Ha'Penny Bridge** (p95), named for the charge levied on those who used it.

Continue along Ormond Quay to one of James Gandon's Georgian masterpieces, the **⑪** **Four Courts** (Map p88; ☑ 01-886 8000; ⊘ 9am-5pm Mon-Fri) FREE, home to the most important law courts in Ireland. Finally take a right onto Church St to admire **⑫** **St Michan's Church** (p104), a beautiful Georgian construction with grisly vaults populated by the remains of the long departed.

themes, from literary Dublin to U2. You can also get a whiskey or a Guinness tour and travel out to Howth for a tour of the lovely fishing village. The company's founder, Pat Liddy, is one of the city's best-known local historians – his tour guides have all been trained by him. Check the website for timings.

See Dublin by Bike   CYCLING
(Map p92; ☑ 01-280 1899; www.seedublinbybike. ie; Drury St Car Park; tours €30; 🖳 all city centre) Three-hour themed tours that start outside the Daintree Building on Pleasants Pl and take in the city's highlights and not-so-obvious sights. The Taste of Dublin is the main tour, but you can also take a U2's Dublin tour and a Literary Dublin tour. Bikes, helmets and hi-vis vests included. They're based in the bike storage area on the ground floor of the car park on Drury St.

Trinity College Walking Tour   WALKING
(Authenticity Tours; Map p82; www.tcd.ie/visitors/ tours; Trinity College; tours €6, incl Book of Kells €15; ⊙ 9.30am-3.40pm Mon-Sat, to 3.15pm Sun May-Sep, fewer midweek tours Oct & Feb-Apr; 🖳 all city centre, 🚌 College Green) A great way to see Trinity's grounds is on student-led walking tours. They depart from the College Green entrance every 20 to 40 minutes.

Viking Splash Tours   TOURS
(Map p88; ☑ 01-707 6000; www.vikingsplash.com; St Stephen's Green N; adult/child €25/13; ⊙ every 30-90min 10am-3pm; 🖳 all city centre, 🚌 St Stephen's Green) Go on, what's the big deal? You stick a plastic Viking's helmet on your head and yell 'yay' at the urging of your guide, but the upshot is you'll get a 1¼-hour semiamphibious tour that ends up in the Grand Canal Dock. 'Strictly for tourists' seems so…superfluous.

Dublin Bus Tours   BUS
(Map p100; ☑ 01-872 0000; www.dublinsightseeing. ie; 59 Upper O'Connell St; adult €15-28; 🖳 all city centre, 🚌 Abbey) A selection of bus tours including a hop-on, hop-off city tour (€22), a ghost-bus tour (€28) and two half-day tours: the four-hour South Coast & Gardens Tour (€27; including Powerscourt) and the North Coast & Castle Tour (€25; including Malahide Castle). In 2016 it added a 1916 anniversary tour (€15) that covers the sights associated with the 1916 Easter Rising.

Dublin Discovered Boat Tours   BOATING
(Map p100; ☑ 01-473 4082; www.dublindiscovered. ie; Bachelor's Walk; adult/student/child €15/13/9; ⊙ 10.30am-4.15pm Mar-Oct; 🖳 all city centre, 🚌 Abbey) 'See the sights without the traffic' is the pitch; you get to hear the history of

---

DUBLIN FOR CHILDREN

Kid-friendly? You bet. Dublin loves the little 'uns, and will enthusiastically 'ooh' and 'aah' at the cuteness of your progeny. But, alas, such admiration hasn't fully translated into child services such as widespread and accessible baby-changing facilities.

If your kids are between three and 14, spend an afternoon at **Ark Children's Cultural Centre** (Map p88; www.ark.ie; 11A Eustace St; 🖳 all city centre), which runs activities aimed at stimulating participants' interests in science, the environment and the arts – but be sure to book well in advance.

There are loads of ways to discover Dublin's Viking past, but Dublinia (p95), the city's Viking and medieval museum, has interactive exhibits that are specifically designed to appeal to younger visitors. And kids of all ages will love Viking Splash Tours (p112), where you board an amphibious vehicle, put on a plastic Viking hat and roar at passers-by as you do a tour of the city before landing in the water at the Grand Canal basin.

A perennial favourite is Dublin Zoo (p108), while the National Leprechaun Museum (p105) lets imaginations run wild among the optical illusions and oversized furniture.

While it's always good to have a specific activity in mind, don't forget Dublin's parks – from St Stephen's Green (p82) to Merrion Square (p87), from Herbert Park (p107) to Phoenix Park (p108), the city has plenty of green spaces where the kids can run wild.

Transport Children under five travel free on all public transport.

Pubs Unaccompanied minors are not allowed in pubs; accompanied children can remain until 9pm (until 10pm from May to September).

Resources Parents with young children should check out www.everymum.ie. An excellent site about family-friendly accommodation is www.babygoes2.com.

Dublin from a watery point of view aboard an (all-important) all-weather cruiser.

⚜ Festivals & Events

Temple Bar Trad Festival   MUSIC
(www.templebartrad.com; ⊘ Jan; 🚇 all city centre) Traditional music festival in the pubs of Temple Bar over the last weekend in January.

★ St Patrick's Festival   PARADE
(www.stpatricksfestival.ie; ⊘ mid-Mar) The mother of all festivals: 750,000-odd gather to 'honour' St Patrick over four days around 17 March on city streets and in venues.

Forbidden Fruit   MUSIC
(www.forbiddenfruit.ie;   1-/2-day ticket from €69.50/129; ⊘ Jun; 🚇 51, 51D, 51X, 69, 78, 79 from Aston Quay) A two-day alternative-music festival over the first weekend in June in the grounds of the Irish Museum of Modern Art. In 2019 Elbow, Laurent Garnier and Spiritualized performed here.

★ Dublin LGBTQ Pride   LGBT
(www.dublinpride.ie; ⊘ mid-Jun) One of the highlights of the festival calendar is this 10-day celebration of the LGBTIQ+ community, with events, gigs, screening and talks culminating in a massive rainbow-coloured parade through the city centre.

Bloomsday   LITERATURE
(www.jamesjoyce.ie; ⊘ 16 Jun) Every 16 June a bunch of oddballs wander around the city dressed in Edwardian gear, talking nonsense in dramatic tones. They're not mad – at least not clinically – they're only Bloomsdayers committed to commemorating James Joyce's epic novel *Ulysses* through readings, performances and recreated meals, including Leopold Bloom's famous breakfast of kidneys with a 'fine tang of faintly scented urine'. Yummy.

Taste of Dublin   FOOD & DRINK
(https://dublin.tastefestivals.com; Iveagh Gardens; €17.50-30.50, VIP tickets €47.50-71.50; ⊘ mid-Jun; 🚇 Harcourt) The capital's best restaurants combine to serve sample platters of their finest dishes amid music and other entertainment over three food-filled days. It's so popular that tickets are limited to four-hour increments, with different ticket prices reflecting the more popular times; VIP tickets include access to the champagne lounge, where you'll get a glass of bubbly and some chocolates.

EVENSONG IN THE CATHEDRALS

In a rare coming together, the choirs of St Patrick's Cathedral and Christ Church Cathedral both participated in the first-ever performance of Handel's *Messiah* in nearby Fishamble St in 1742, conducted by the great composer himself. Both houses of worship carry on their proud choral traditions, and visits to the cathedrals during evensong will provide enchanting and atmospheric memories. The choir performs evensong in St Patrick's at 5.30pm Monday to Friday and 3.15pm Sundays, while the Christ Church choir performs at 6pm on Wednesday and Thursday and 5pm Saturday (times may vary, so check ahead at www.christchurchcathedral.ie). If you're going to be in Dublin around Christmas, do not miss the carols at St Patrick's; call ahead for the hard-to-get tickets on ☎ 01-453 9472.

Longitude   MUSIC
(www.longitude.ie; Marlay Park; ⊘ Jul; 🚇 14, 14A, 16, 48A, 75 from city centre) A three-day alt-music festival in mid-July featuring old and new acts, art installations and food stalls.

★ Dublin Fringe Festival   THEATRE
(www.fringefest.com; ⊘ Sep) This two-week extravaganza features more than 100 events and over 700 performances, all designed to showcase the very best of upcoming theatrical talent. Originally set up to offer a stage to those shows considered too 'out there' for Dublin's main theatre festival, it's now every bit as popular and critically acclaimed.

★ Culture Night   CULTURAL
(www.culturenight.ie; ⊘ Sep) For one night in September museums, historic houses, private parks and other sites of cultural significance throw open their doors to the public. There are lectures, demonstrations, concerts, tours and other fun cultural events. All free, all absolutely wonderful. One of the best ways to experience the city.

Dublin Theatre Festival   THEATRE
(www.dublintheatrefestival.com; ⊘ Sep-Oct) For around three weeks between the end of September and early October most of the city's theatres participate in this festival, originally

founded in 1957 and today a glittering parade of quality productions and elaborate shows.

Dublin Book Festival LITERATURE
(www.dublinbookfestival.com; ⊗ mid-Nov) A three-day festival of literature with readings and talks, held in collaboration with the city's public libraries and the Unesco City of Literature office.

🛏 Sleeping

🛏 Grafton Street & St Stephen's Green

★Grafton Guesthouse BOUTIQUE HOTEL €
(Map p88; ☑ 01-648 0025; www.graftonguesthouse. com; 27 S Great George's St; s/d from €100/125; @🛜; 🚇all city centre, 🚇St Stephen's Green) Following a hefty refurbishment in 2018, Grafton Guesthouse is one of the standout budget hotels in the city. Exposed brick walls, subway-tiled bathrooms and period features give the rooms a distinct Brooklyn vibe, and it's bang in the middle of the action on George's St. Street-facing rooms are noisy, especially at weekends.

Kelly's Hotel BOUTIQUE HOTEL €
(Map p88; ☑ 01-648 0010; www.kellysdublin.com; 36 S Great George's St; r from €130; ❄@🛜; 🚇all city centre) A trendy boutique hotel in an original Victorian red-brick. The interiors are thoroughly modern: rooms are small and tastefully decorated with polished wooden floors and elegant minimalist furnishings. It's part of a complex that includes Grafton Guesthouse, two bars – **Hogan's** (Map p88; 35 S Great George's St; ⊗ 1.30pm-11.30am Mon-Wed, to 1am Thu, to 2.30am Fri & Sat, 2-11pm Sun) and the No Name Bar (p129) – and French restaurant L'Gueuleton (p124) next door. Front-facing rooms can be quite noisy.

Avalon House HOSTEL €
(Map p88; ☑ 01-475 0001; www.avalon-house.ie; 55 Aungier St; dm/s/d from €19/36/72; @🛜; 🚇15, 16, 16A, 16C, 19, 19A, 19C, 65, 65B, 83, 122) Pared-back dorms with high ceilings and old-fashioned sinks, metal-framed bunks and shared bathrooms give this an old-school look at odds with newer hostels, but it's popular – because of its location and nice common room. Book well in advance.

★Cliff Townhouse BOUTIQUE HOTEL €€
(Map p92; ☑ 01-638 3939; www.theclifftownhouse. com; 22 St Stephen's Green N; r from €220; @🛜;

🚇all city centre, 🚇St Stephen's Green) As pieds-à-terre go, this is a doozy: there are 10 exquisitely appointed bedrooms spread across a wonderful Georgian property whose best views overlook St Stephen's Green. Downstairs is Sean Smith's superb restaurant **Cliff Townhouse** (mains €20-34; ⊗ noon-2.30pm & 5pm-late Mon-Sat, noon-4pm & 6-9.30pm Sun).

Iveagh Garden Hotel HOTEL €€
(Map p92; ☑ 01-568 5500; www.iveaghgarden hotel.ie; r from €180; 🚇Harcourt) Instagrammers flock to this ever-so-stylish hotel on Harcourt St, with its art deco couches and geometric light fittings. Rooms vary from snug City Pods to lofty suites, some of which overlook the beautiful Iveagh Gardens.

Dean HOTEL €€
(Map p92; ☑ 01-607 8110; www.deanhoteldublin. ie; 33 Harcourt St; r/ste from €155/315; 🅿@🛜; 🚇10, 11, 13, 14, 15A, 🚇St Stephen's Green) Every room at this newish designer hotel comes with earplugs, vodka, wine and Berocca – so you know what to expect (light sleepers, beware). Take your pick from well-appointed and elegant Mod Pods (single bed on a couch), Punk Bunks (yup, bunk beds) or deluxe doubles (SupeRooms or Hi-Fis) and suites. The more expensive rooms come with Netflix and a turntable.

The hotel deliberately advertises as an upmarket party hotel that borrows its ethos (if not its look) from the Ace Hotel in New York and the Hoxton in London: sandwiched between two of the most popular nightclubs in town the rooms can get very noisy indeed, especially those on the 1st floor. The top floor is home to Sophie's (p123), a brasserie that turns into a popular bar after 11pm.

It has discounted parking arrangements with a car park that is a five-minute walk away.

Trinity Lodge GUESTHOUSE €€
(Map p92; ☑ 01-617 0900; www.trinitylodge.com; 12 S Frederick St; r from €180; 🛜; 🚇all city centre, 🚇St Stephen's Green) Martin Sheen's grin greets you upon entering this award-winning guesthouse, which he declared his favourite spot for an Irish stay. Marty's not the only one: this place is so popular it's added a second townhouse across the road, which has also been kitted out to the highest standards. Room 2 of the original house has a lovely bay window.

Discounted parking (€17.50) is available in an adjacent covered car park.

JAMES JOYCE & ULYSSES

Ulysses is the ultimate chronicle of the city in which, Joyce once said, he intended 'to give a picture of Dublin so complete that if the city one day suddenly disappeared from the earth it could be reconstructed out of my book'. It is set here on 16 June 1904 – the day of Joyce's first date with Nora Barnacle – and follows its characters as their journeys around town parallel the voyage of Homer's *Odyssey*.

The experimental literary style makes it difficult to read, but there's much for even the slightly bemused reader to relish. It ends with Molly Bloom's famous stream of consciousness discourse, a chapter of eight huge, unpunctuated paragraphs. Because of its sexual explicitness, the book was banned in the USA and the UK until 1933 and 1937 respectively.

As a testament to the book's enduring relevance and extraordinary innovation, it has inspired writers of every generation since. Joyce admirers from around the world descend on Dublin every year on 16 June to celebrate Bloomsday and retrace the steps of *Ulysses'* central character, Leopold Bloom. It is a slightly gimmicky and touristy phenomenon that is aimed at Joyce fanatics and tourists, but it's plenty of fun and a great way to lay the groundwork for actually reading the book.

Harrington Hall GUESTHOUSE €€
(Map p92; ☑ 01-475 3497; www.harringtonhall. com; 69-70 Harcourt St; r from €180; @ ⏰; ☐ Harcourt) Want to fluff up the pillows in the home of a former Lord Mayor of Dublin? The traditional Georgian style of Timothy Charles Harrington's home – he wore the gold chain from 1901 to 1903 – has thankfully been retained and this smart guesthouse stands out for its understated elegance. The 1st- and 2nd-floor rooms have their original fireplaces and ornamental ceilings.

Central Hotel HOTEL €€
(Map p88; ☑ 01-679 7302; www.centralhoteldublin. com; 1-5 Exchequer St; r from €150; @ ⏰; ☐ all city centre, ☐ St Stephen's Green) The rooms are a modern – if miniaturised – version of Edwardian luxury. Heavy velvet curtains and custom-made Irish furnishings (including beds with draped backboards) fit a bit too snugly into the space afforded them, but they do lend a touch of class. Note that street-facing rooms can get a little noisy. Location-wise, the name says it all.

Green HOTEL €€
(Map p92; ☑ 01-607 3600; www.thegreenhotel.ie; 1-5 Harcourt St; r from €180; ⓟ @ ⏰; ☐ all cross-city, ☐ St Stephen's Green) Fresh out of a big refurb (and rebrand), the former O'Callaghan hotel is now a much cooler spot simply known as the Green. With an ultra-slick new bar area, stylish rooms and a great location right on St Stephen's Green, it makes for a great base in the city.

Buswell's Hotel HOTEL €€
(Map p92; ☑ 01-614 6500; www.buswells.ie; 23-27 Molesworth St; s/d from €165/180; ⓟ ✳ @; ☐ all

cross-city, ☐ St Stephen's Green) This Dublin institution, open since 1882, has a long association with politicians, who wander across the road from Dáil Éireann (Irish Assembly) to wet their beaks at the hotel bar. The 69 bedrooms have all been given the once-over, but have kept their Georgian charm intact.

Dawson BOUTIQUE HOTEL €€
(Map p88; ☑ 01-612 7900; www.thedawson.ie; 35 Dawson St; r from €160; @ ⏰; ☐ all city centre, ☐ St Stephen's Green) A boutique hotel with a range of elegant rooms designed in a variety of styles, from classical French to more exotic Moroccan. Crisp white sheets throughout and luxe amenities in the bathrooms. There's also a fancy spa and the trendy **Sam's Bar** (www.samsbar.ie; 36 Dawson St; ⏱ 4pm-12.30am Mon-Wed, to 2.30am Fri & Sat, 4pm-12.30am Sun) below.

★ Westbury Hotel HOTEL €€€
(Map p88; ☑ 01-679 1122; www.doylecollection. com; Grafton St; r/ste from €430/580; ⓟ @ ⏰; ☐ all city centre, ☐ St Stephen's Green) Tucked away just off Grafton St is one of the most elegant hotels in town. The upstairs lobby is a great spot for afternoon tea or a drink, and the two restaurants on-site – Balfes and Wilde – are both exceptional.

Fitzwilliam Hotel HOTEL €€€
(Map p88; ☑ 01-478 7000; www.fitzwilliamhoteldublin.com; St Stephen's Green W; r from €350; ⓟ ✳ @ ⏰; ☐ all cross-city, ☐ Stephen's Green) You couldn't pick a more prestigious spot on the Dublin Monopoly board than this minimalist Terence Conrad–designed number overlooking the Green. Ask for a corner room

Where to Stay in Dublin

North of the Liffey

Within walking distance of sights and nightlife, but some locations not especially comfortable after dark.

Best For Backpackers

Transport 15 minutes by tram from city centre

Price Mostly budget

North of the Liffey

National Museum of Ireland – Decorative Arts & History

Jameson Distillery

Irish Museum of Modern Art

Kilmainham Gaol

Guinness Storehouse

Kilmainham & the Liberties

Limited choice of accommodation. Close to the Guinness Storehouse, but a longer trek to the city-centre attractions. Good restaurants.

Best For Guinness fans

Transport 20 minutes by bus to city centre

Price Mostly midrange

Kilmainham & the Liberties

Teeling Distillery

N 0 — 1 km
0 — 0.5 miles

Temple Bar
In the heart of the city's nightlife; close to everything, but can be noisy and crowded. Rooms are often small and less than pristine.

Best For The party crowd

Transport Short walk to city centre

Price Mostly budget

Docklands
Excellent contemporary hotels with good service, but an isolated neighbourhood that doesn't have a lot of life after dark.

Best For Business travellers

Transport Taxi recommended to city centre

Price Mostly midrange

Hugh Lane Gallery

Temple Bar

Christ Church Cathedral
Dublin Castle

Chester Beatty Library

St Patrick's Cathedral

Marsh's Library

Trinity College

Docklands

Grafton Street & Around

National Gallery

Merrion Square

Museum of Natural History

National Museum of Ireland – Archaeology

Southside
More bang for your buck, accommodation-wise; plenty of restaurants and decent nightlife but few sights.

Best For Boutique hotels, elegant B&Bs

Transport 15 minutes by tram or bus to city centre

Price Mostly midrange

Grafton Street & St Stephen's Green
Close to sights, nightlife and pretty much everything. Not always good value for money; rooms tend to be smaller.

Best For Convenience, shopping, weekend breaks

Transport Short walk to city centre

Price Mostly midrange

Merrion Square & Around

Southside

Merrion Square & Georgian Dublin
Lovely neighbourhood, elegant hotels and townhouse accommodation, but not a lot of choice. Also relatively quiet in the evenings.

Best For Romantic getaways

Transport One bus stop from city centre

Price Mostly top end

on the 5th floor (502 or 508), with balmy balcony and a view. The mezzanine-level Citron restaurant serves modern Irish cuisine. It's contemporary elegance at its very best.

Westin Dublin HOTEL €€€
(Map p88; ☑ 01-645 1000; www.thewestindublin.com; Westmoreland St; r from €350; P@☎; ☐ all city centre) Once a fancy bank branch, now a fancier hotel: rooms are decorated in elegant mahogany and soft colours that are reminiscent of the USA's finest. You will sleep on 10 layers of the Westin's own trademark Heavenly Bed, which is damn comfortable indeed. The old bank vault is now the basement bar.

Merrion Square & Georgian Dublin

★ **Number 31** GUESTHOUSE €€
(Map p92; ☑ 01-676 5011; www.number31.ie; 31 Leeson Close; r from €220; P☎; ☐ all city centre) The city's most distinctive property is the former home of modernist architect Sam Stephenson, who successfully fused 1960s style with 18th-century grace. Its 21 bedrooms are split between the retro coach house, with its modern rooms, and the more elegant Georgian house, where rooms are individually furnished with tasteful French antiques and big, comfortable beds.

Gourmet breakfasts with kippers, homemade breads and granola are served in the conservatory.

Alex HOTEL €€
(Map p106; ☑ 01-607 3700; www.thealexhotel.ie; 41-47 Fenian St; r from €229; @☎; ☐ Pearse) The first of the O'Callaghan Collection to get a rebrand in 2018, the Alex is a beautifully sleek hotel where gorgeous design meets decadent comfort. Think herringbone blankets on the bed, plump velvet cushions and retro rotary telephones. There's a cool co-working area in the lobby, along with excellent Cloud Picker coffee in the cafe.

Wilder Townhouse HOTEL €€
(Map p92; ☑ 01-969 6598; www.thewilder.ie; 22 Adelaide Rd; r from €180; P@☎; ☐ Harcourt) Set in a striking red-brick building, the Wilder has a delightfully quirky vibe, with cute little ornaments and tailor's mannequins in the rooms, which vary wildly in size. The bar is deliciously atmospheric, and you couldn't ask for a more peaceful location.

★ **Merrion** HOTEL €€€
(Map p92; ☑ 01-603 0600; www.merrionhotel.com; Upper Merrion St; r/ste from €410/900; P@☎☒; ☐ all city centre) This resplendent five-star hotel, in a terrace of beautifully restored Georgian townhouses, opened in 1988 but looks like it's been around a lot longer. Try to get a room in the old house (with the largest private art collection in the city), rather than the newer wing, to sample its truly elegant comforts.

Located opposite Government Buildings, its marble corridors are patronised by politicos, visiting dignitaries and the odd celeb. Even if you don't stay, book a table for the superb Art Afternoon Tea (€55 per person), with endless cups of tea served out of silver pots by a raging fire.

★ **Conrad Dublin** HOTEL €€€
(Map p92; ☑ 01-602 8900; www.conradhotels.com; Earlsfort Tce; r from €350; P@☎; ☐ all city centre) A €13 million refit has transformed this standard business hotel into an exceptional five-star property. The style is contemporary

---

ⓘ BOOKING SERVICES

Getting the hotel of your choice without a reservation can be tricky in high season (May to September), so always book your room in advance. You can book through Dublin Tourism's online booking service (www.visitdublin.com). Advance internet bookings are your best bet for deals.

All Dublin Hotels (www.irelandhotels.com/hotels) Decent spread of accommodation in the city centre and suburbs.

Daft.ie (www.daft.ie) If you're looking to rent in Dublin, this is the site to search.

Dublin Hotels (www.dublinhotels.com) Hotels in the city centre and beyond.

Dublin Tourism (www.visitdublin.com) Good selection of rated accommodation.

Hostel Dublin (www.hosteldublin.com) Good resource for hostel accommodation.

Lonely Planet (lonelyplanet.com/ireland/dublin/hotels) Recommendations and bookings.

During the summer months (and sometimes during term time), visitors can opt to stay in campus accommodation, which is both convenient and comfortable.

Trinity College (Map p82; ☑ 01-896 1177; www.tcd.ie/summeraccommodation; Accommodations Office, Trinity College; s/d from €85/140; ☺ May–mid-Sep; P @ ☎; ☐ all cross-city) The extensive range of student accommodation includes modern apartments with all mod cons and older (more atmospheric) rooms with shared bathrooms. They're on campus and just off it, on Pearse St.

Dublin City University (DCU; ☑ 01-700 5736; www.dcurooms.com; Larkfield Apartments, Campus Residences, Dublin City University; s/d from €80/110; P; ☐ 11, 11A, 11B, 13, 13A, 19, 19A from city centre) This accommodation is proof that students slum it in relative luxury. The modern rooms have plenty of amenities at hand, including a kitchen, a common room and a fully equipped health centre. The Glasnevin campus is only 15 minutes by bus or car from the city centre.

chic – marble bathrooms, wonderfully comfortable beds and a clutter-free aesthetic that doesn't skimp on mod cons (bedside docking stations for iPhones, USB sockets and HD flat-screen TVs) – and it works. The Coburg Brasserie (p125) is exceptional.

★ **Shelbourne**   HOTEL €€€
(Map p92; ☑ 01-676 6471; www.theshelbourne.ie; 27 St Stephen's Green N; r from €385; P @ ☎ ⛽; ☐ all city centre, ☐ St Stephen's Green) Dublin's most famous hotel was founded in 1824 and has been the preferred halting post of the powerful and wealthy ever since. Several owners and refurbs later it is now part of Marriott's Renaissance portfolio, and while it has a couple of rivals in the luxury stakes, it cannot be beaten for heritage.

Guests are staying in a slice of history: it was here that the Irish Constitution was drafted in 1921, and this is the hotel in Elizabeth Bowen's eponymous novel. Afternoon tea in the refurbished Lord Mayor's Lounge remains one of the best experiences in town.

🛏 Temple Bar

If you're here for a weekend of wild abandon and can't fathom anything more than a quick stumble into bed, then Temple Bar's choice of hotels and hostels will suit you perfectly. Generally speaking the rooms are small, the prices are large and you must be able to handle the late-night symphonies of die-hard revellers.

Barnacles   HOSTEL €
(Map p88; ☑ 01-671 6277; www.barnacles.ie; 19 Temple Lane S; dm/d from €15/120; P ☎; ☐ all city centre) If you're here for a good time, not a long time, then this bustling Temple Bar hostel is the ideal spot to meet fellow revel-

lers and tap up the helpful and knowledgeable staff for the best places to cause mischief. Rooms are quieter at the back.

Kinlay House   HOSTEL €
(Map p88; ☑ 01-679 6644; www.kinlaydublin.ie; 2-12 Lord Edward St; dm/tw from €25/60; ☎; ☐ all city centre) This former boarding house for boys has massive, mixed dormitories (for up to 24), and smaller rooms, including doubles. It's on the edge of Temple Bar, so it's occasionally raucous. Staff are friendly, and there are cooking facilities and a cafe. Breakfast is included.

Dublin Citi Hotel   HOTEL €€
(Map p88; ☑ 01-679 4455; www.dublincitihotel.com; 46-49 Dame St; r from €195; @ ☎; ☐ all city centre) An unusual turreted 19th-century building right next to the Central Bank is home to this midrange hotel. Rooms aren't huge, are simply furnished and have fresh white quilts. It's only a stagger (literally) from the heart of Temple Bar, hic.

★ **Morgan Hotel**   BOUTIQUE HOTEL €€€
(Map p88; ☑ 01-643 7000; www.themorgan.com; 10 Fleet St; r from €280; @ ☎; ☐ all city centre) Fresh out of a €15 million redesign in 2018, the Morgan is one of the sleekest hotels in town. The rooms are contemporary and calming, with a pale grey decor and slick marble bathrooms. The restaurant, 10 Fleet Street, is exceptional, as are the cocktails whizzed up with smoke and pizazz.

🛏 Kilmainham & the Liberties

★ **Aloft Dublin City**   HOTEL €€
(Map p84; ☑ 01-963 1800; www.alofthotels.com; 1 Mill St; r from €180; P ☎; ☐ 49, 54A from city centre) 'This must be the place' is emblazoned in

bright neon across the wall of the 7th-floor breakfast room, and you'd be hard pushed to disagree. Modern rooms adorned with cool local artwork; huge, floor-to-ceiling windows; and – back up on the 7th floor, where you'll also find the reception – a swish rooftop bar with fab views over the city.

Maldron Kevin Street
HOTEL €€

(Map p84; ☑ 01-906 8900; www.maldronhotelkevin street.com; Upper Kevin St; r from €200; 🛜; 🚌 49, 54A from city centre) Handy for all the sights you'll find within the Liberties – St Patrick's Cathedral, the Teeling Distillery and, of course, the Guinness Storehouse – the latest outpost from the Maldron group is modern and clean, if a little soulless. Still, it makes for a handy base, and you can often score great rates at the last minute.

🛏 North of the Liffey

There is a scattering of decent midrange options between O'Connell St and Smithfield, with a fair number of hostels in the mix. Gardiner St, to the east of O'Connell St, was the traditional B&B district of town, but with only a few exceptions it has been rendered largely obsolete by chain hotels throughout the city.

★ Generator Hostel
HOSTEL €

(Map p100; ☑ 01-901 0222; www.staygenerator.com; Smithfield Sq; dm/tw from €18/150; @🛜; 🚌 Smithfield) This European chain brings its own brand of funky, fun design to Dublin's hostel scene, with bright colours, comfortable dorms (including women-only) and a lively social scene. It even has a screening room for movies. Good location right on Smithfield Sq, next to the Jameson Distillery Bow Street (p103).

★ Isaacs Hostel
HOSTEL €

(Map p100; ☑ 01-855 6215; www.isaacs.ie; 2-5 Frenchman's Lane; dm/tw from €22/99; @🛜; 🚌 all city centre, 🚉 Connolly) The Northside's best hostel – actually the best in town – is it's the best in town – is in a 200-year-old wine vault just around the corner from the main bus station. With summer barbecues, live music in the lounge, internet access, colourful dorms and even a sauna, this terrific place generates consistently good reviews from backpackers and other travellers.

MEC Hostel
HOSTEL €

(Map p100; ☑ 01-873 0826; www.mechostel.com; 42 N Great George's St; dm/ste from €17/125; 🛜; 🚌 36, 36A from city centre) A Georgian classic on one of Dublin's most beautiful streets,

this popular hostel has a host of dorms and apartment-style suites, all with private bathroom. Facilities include a full kitchen, two lounges and a bureau de change. Breakfast is free and there's decent wi-fi throughout.

Address at Dublin 1
HOTEL €€

(Map p84; ☑ 01-704 0770; www.theaddressat dublin1.ie; Amiens St; r from €200; @🛜; 🚉 Connolly, 🚉 Connolly) Ostensibly part of the old North Star Hotel, the Address has surprisingly stylish and plush bedrooms, some of which overlook the passing trains gliding into Connolly Station – so give the commuters a little wave as they pass. The tiny rooftop lounge is an added bonus.

Morrison Hotel
HOTEL €€€

(Map p88; ☑ 01-887 2400; www.morrisonhotel.ie; Lower Ormond Quay; r €350; P@🛜; 🚉 all city centre, 🚉 Jervis) Space-age funky design is the template at this hip hotel, part of the Hilton Doubletree group. King-sized beds (with fancy mattresses), 40in LCD TVs, free wi-fi and deluxe toiletries are just some of the hotel's offerings. Probably the Northside's most luxurious address.

🛏 Docklands

Staying in the Docklands area means you'll be relying on public transport or taxis to get you in and out of the city centre.

Trinity City Hotel
HOTEL €€

(Map p82; ☑ 01-648 1000; www.trinitycityhotel.com; Pearse St; r from €220; @🛜; 🚉 Trinity) While the bedrooms have a slight corporate feel, the public spaces in Trinity City really shine, particularly the Brunswick Terrace and courtyard garden, where you can enjoy a drink alfresco (which is something of a rarity in Dublin).

Gibson Hotel
HOTEL €€

(Map p106; ☑ 01-618 5000; www.thegibsonhotel. ie; Point Village; r from €225; P@🛜; 🚌 151 from city centre, 🚉 The Point) Built for business travellers and out-of-towners taking in a gig at the 3 Arena (p134) next door, the Gibson is impressive: 250-odd ultramodern rooms decked out in deluxe beds, flat-screen TVs and internet work stations. You might catch last night's star act having breakfast the next morning in the snazzy restaurant area.

★ Marker
HOTEL €€€

(Map p106; ☑ 01-687 5100; www.themarkerhotel dublin.com; Grand Canal Sq; r/ste from €350/520; P@🛜🏊; 🚉 Grand Canal Dock) Behind the eye-catching chequerboard facade created by Manuel Aires Mateus are 187 swanky rooms and suites decked out in a wintry palette (washed-out citruses and cobalts) and starkly elegant furnishings, which give them an atmosphere of cool sophistication. The public areas are a little wilder and the rooftop bar is a summer favourite with the 'in' crowd.

🛏 Southside

Some of the city's most elegant B&Bs are scattered about these leafy suburbs, including a handful that can rival even the best hotels in town for comfort and service.

★ Ariel House   INN €
(Map p106; ✆ 01-668 5512; www.ariel-house.net; 52 Lansdowne Rd; r from €130; P ⚏; ☐ 4, 7, 8, 84 from city centre) Our favourite lodging in Ballsbridge is this wonderful Victorian-era property that is somewhere between a boutique hotel and a luxury B&B. Its 28 rooms are all individually decorated with period furniture, which lends the place an air of genuine luxury. A far better choice than most hotels.

★ Devlin   BOUTIQUE HOTEL €€
(Map p84; ✆ 01-406 6550; www.thedevlin.ie; 117-119 Ranelagh Rd; r from €150; P @ ⚏; ☐ 4, 15, 15A, 15B, 65, 83, 140 from city centre, 🚊 Beechwood) Following the lead of its hip sister hotel the Dean (p114), this Ranelagh outpost is an artsy spot in one of Dublin's fanciest boroughs. Though definitely on the small side, the rooms (or ModPods) are well designed, with navy-coloured walls, local artwork and a stash of Irish treats – there are Dyson hairdryers in the rooms and a cinema in the basement.

Schoolhouse Hotel   BOUTIQUE HOTEL €€
(Map p106; ✆ 01-667 5014; www.schoolhousehotel.com; 2-8 Northumberland Rd; r from €180; P ⚏; ☐ 5, 7, 7A, 8, 18, 27X, 44 from city centre) A Victorian schoolhouse dating from 1861, this beautiful building has been successfully converted into an exquisite boutique hotel that is (ahem) ahead of its class. Its 31 cosy bedrooms, named after famous Irish people, all have king-sized beds, big white quilts and loudly patterned headboards. The Canteen bar and patio bustles with local businessfolk in summer.

🍴 Eating

The choice of restaurants in Dublin has never been better. Every cuisine and every trend – from doughnuts on the run to kale with absolutely everything – is catered for, as the city seeks to satisfy the discerning taste buds of its diners.

🍴 Grafton Street & St Stephen's Green

While the options on Grafton St itself are minimal, the streets around it are packed with food joints to suit every taste and craving. Camden and Wexford Sts are a particular delight, with everything from funky cafes to swish restaurants attracting Dublin's foodie connoisseurs.

Loose Canon   CHEESE €
(Map p88; www.loosecanon.ie; 29 Drury St; toasties €7.50-8; ⊘ 10.30am-10pm Mon & Wed-Sat, to 5.30pm Tue, noon-10pm Sun; ☐ all city centre) Ostensibly a cheese shop with a few stools, at Loose Canon you can prop yourself up at the counter for a platter of cheese or Irish charcuterie, with a glass of vino chosen from the shelves of natural wines. The buttery toasties (toasted sandwiches) are generous, rich and filled with gooey Irish cheeses like smoked mozzarella or Corleggy goat's cheese.

Masa   MEXICAN €
(Map p88; ✆ 01-430 2841; www.masadublin.com; 2 Drury St; tacos €5-7; ⊘ noon-9.30pm Mon-Wed, to 10pm Thu, to 10.30pm Fri, 1-10.30pm Sat, 2-9pm Sun; ☐ all city centre) A quick and easy taco joint serving authentic soft corn tortillas filled with pulled pork, crispy fish and fried chicken. The *elotes* (corn on the cob slathered in cheese and chilli) are fantastic.

Cornucopia   VEGETARIAN €
(Map p88; www.cornucopia.ie; 19-20 Wicklow St; salads €6-10, mains €13-15; ⊘ 8.30am-9pm Mon, to 10pm Tue-Sat, noon-9pm Sun; 🍴; ☐ all city centre) Dublin's best-known vegetarian restaurant is a terrific eatery that serves wholesome salads, sandwiches, and a selection of hot main courses from a daily changing menu. There's live musical accompaniment Thursday and Friday evenings. The 2nd-floor dining-room windows overlooking the street below are a good spot for people-watching.

Pang   VIETNAMESE €
(Map p92; ✆ 01-563 8702; www.lovepang.ie; 6-11 Lower Kevin St; rolls €4, pho €9; ⊘ noon-8pm Mon-Sat; ☐ all city centre) Fresh and zingy Vietnamese rice paper rolls, *banh mi* (filled bread rolls) and *pho* (soup with noodles) are the name of the game here, all of which are as delicious as they are well priced. There are only six stools in the window, so you won't be lingering.

DUBLIN FOOD MARKETS

Dublin's choice of artisan street and covered markets continues to improve. If you're looking to self-cater, there are some excellent options for supplies, especially south of the river, including Fallon & Byrne, **Dollard & Co** (Map p88; ✆ 01-616 9606; www.dollardandco.ie; 2-5 Wellington Quay; pizza slice €4.50, mains €8-15; ⏰ 8am-9pm Mon-Thu, to 10pm Fri, 9am-10pm Sat, 10am-8pm Sun, pizzas until 4am; ▣ all city centre) and the **Temple Bar Food Market** (Map p88; www.facebook.com/TempleBarFoodMarket; Meeting House Sq; ⏰ 10am-5pm Sat; ▣ all city centre) – not to mention a fine selection of cheesemongers and bakeries. North of the river, the traditional **Moore Street Market** (Map p100; Moore St; ⏰ 8am-4pm Mon-Sat; ▣ all city centre) is the city's most famous, where the colour of the produce is matched by the language of the spruikers.

Eatyard (Map p92; www.the-eatyard.com; 9-10 S Richmond St; free admission; ⏰ noon-10pm Thu-Sat, to 8pm Sun Mar-Dec; ▣ 14, 15, 44, 65, 140, 142 from city centre, ▣ Harcourt) Spend an hour or two eating and drinking your way through a dozen or so of the city's best food vendors. There's always seasonal produce, and plenty of veggie/vegan options, as well as craft beer. The vendors rotate every few months and the market can close for a short time to accommodate this – confirm opening times online.

Dublin Food Co-op (Map p84; ✆ 01-454 4258; www.dublinfood.coop; The Old Chocolate Factory, Kilmainham Sq; ⏰ 8am-7pm Mon-Fri, 9am-6pm Sat & Sun; ▣ 49, 54A, 77X from city centre) From dog food to detergent, everything in this member-owned co-op is organic and/or ecofriendly. Thursday has a limited selection of local and imported fairtrade products, but Saturday is when it's all on display – Dubliners from all over drop in for their responsible weekly shop. There's an on-the-premises baker and even baby-changing facilities.

Daniel
CAFE €

(www.3fe.com; 19 Lower Clanbrassil St; toasties €4.80; ⏰ 7.30am-4pm Mon-Fri, from 9am Sat & Sun; ▣ 49, 54A, 77X from city centre) The latest cafe from Colin Harmon's 3fe, Dublin's best-known coffee roasters, is this sparsely decorated cafe. The menu reflects the decor: all that's on offer is toasties, pastries (from Bread Nation on Pearse St) and brownies. And coffee of course, with a selection of 3fe roasts.

Dublin Pizza Company
PIZZA €

(Map p88; ✆ 01-561 1714; www.dublinpizzacompany.ie; 32 Aungier St; pizzas €9-13; ⏰ noon-midnight Mon-Thu, to 3am Fri, 4pm-3am Sat, 4.30pm-midnight Sun; ▣ all city centre) A great place to grab a bite and go. Served from a wooden hatch, this is some of the best pizza in the city, helped by its woodfire oven and organic ingredients. If you'd rather sit down, you can take your pizza into the **Swan** (✆ 01-647 5272; www.theswanbar.com; 70 Aungier St; ⏰ 11am-11.30pm Mon-Thu, to 12.30am Fri & Sat, noon-11pm Sun pub just up the road, or get it delivered to **Fourth Corner** (Map p88; www.fourthcorner.ie; 50 Patrick St; ⏰ 4-11.30pm Mon-Thu, 1pm-12.30am Fri, 2pm-12.30am Sat & Sun; ▣ 49, 54A from city centre).

Wow Burger
BURGERS €

(Map p88; www.wowburger.ie; 8 Wicklow St; burgers €6-7; ⏰ noon-10pm Sun-Thu, to 11pm Fri & Sat; ▣ all city centre) The basement of **Mary's Bar** (www.marysbar.ie; ⏰ 11am-11.30pm Mon-Wed, to 12.30am Thu-Sat, noon-11pm Sun) is home to a reliable burger joint: hamburgers, cheeseburgers and a sinful bacon cheeseburger come in two sizes (double or single) and with a side of choice – the garlic-butter fries are terrific. Order at the bar, pick up at the counter and eat in the 1950s diner–styled room.

Fallon & Byrne
DELI €

(Map p88; www.fallonandbyrne.com; Exchequer St; mains €5-10; ⏰ 8am-9pm Mon-Fri, from 9am Sat, 11am-7pm Sun; ▣ all city centre) Dublin's answer to the American Dean & DeLuca chain is this upmarket food hall and wine cellar, which is where discerning Dubliners come to buy their favourite cheeses and imported delicacies, as well as to get a superb takeaway lunch from the deli counter. Upstairs is an elegant **brasserie** (Map p88; ✆ 01-472 1000; mains €19-34; ⏰ noon-3pm & 5.30-9pm Sun-Tue, to 10pm Wed & Thu, to 11pm Fri & Sat) that serves Irish-influenced Mediterranean cuisine.

★ Pi Pizza
PIZZA €€

(Map p88; www.pipizzas.ie; 73-83 S Great George's St; pizzas €9-16; ⏰ noon-10pm Sun-Wed, to 10.30pm Thu-Sat; ▣ all city centre) Reg White cut his pie-making teeth at flour + water in San Francisco before opening this fabulous restaurant in 2018, and it's already a contender for best pizzeria in town. The smallish menu has just eight pizzas, each an inspired interpretation of a Neapolitan classic. Highly recommended are the *funghi* (mushroom) or *broccolini,* 'white' pizzas made without the tomato layer.

Sisu Izakaya
JAPANESE €€

(Map p88; ☑ 01-475 7777; http://sisuizakaya.ie; 23-27 Lower Stephen St; mains €15-17.50; ⊘ noon-10pm Sun-Wed, to 11pm Thu-Sat; 🖳 all city centre) Japanese casual dining at its Dublin best is the order of the day at this wonderful new spot whose name translates as 'Sisu's Tavern'. Within its wood-panelled, low-lit interior you'll get a broad range of dishes, from rolls to ramen. The €10 lunch bento was, at the time of writing, the best in town.

Balfes
IRISH €€

(Map p88; ☑ 01-646 3353; www.balfes.ie; 2 Balfe St; mains €19-25; ⊘ 8am-10pm Mon-Thu, to 10.30pm Fri, 9am-10.30pm Sat, 9am-10pm Sun; 🖳 all city centre) This all-day brasserie has a chic New York vibe, with leather banquettes and a small heated terrace luring a perpetually stylish crowd. While the menu focuses on hearty bistro dishes like duck liver pâté and steaks cooked on the Josper grill, it caters well to the healthier diner – think protein pancakes and superfood salads.

Uno Mas
SPANISH €€

(Map p88; ☑ 01-475 8538; www.unomas.ie; 6 Aungier St; tapas €4-15, mains €20-34; ⊘ 5.30-9.30pm Mon, noon-2.30pm & 5.30-9.30pm Tue-Sat; 🖳 all city centre) Sister restaurant to Dublin favourite Etto (p124), Uno Mas quickly rose in the popularity stakes following its launch in late 2018. Expect to see dishes like octopus with kale, potato and violet garlic, alongside a tapas menu of *jamon croquetas* (ham croquettes) and *Padrón peppers.* Booking is essential, with more availability at lunch (two/three courses €24/28).

Port House
TAPAS €€

(Map p88; ☑ 01-677 0298; www.porthouse.ie; 64A South William St; tapas €5-9; ⊘ 11am-midnight; 🖳 all city centre) This dark cavern restaurant is full of flickering candlelight. The extensive, delicious Spanish tapas menu is best enjoyed with the impressive Iberian wines (which the friendly staff can help you navigate). It doesn't take bookings, so if you go at the weekend prepare to wait for a table.

Richmond
MODERN IRISH €€

(Map p92; ☑ 01-478 8783; www.richmondrestaurant. ie; 43 S Richmond St; mains €18-27; ⊘ 5.30-9.30pm Wed-Sat, to 9pm Sun, 11am-2.30pm Sat & Sun; 🖳 14,

15, 65, 83) At first glance the menu offers nothing particularly novel, just a nice selection of favourites from a burger to a roasted breast of duck. But it's the way it's prepared and presented that makes this place one of the best in town, and proof that expertise in the kitchen trumps everything else. Brunch is particularly recommended.

Sophie's @ the Dean
ITALIAN €€

(Map p92; ☑ 01-607 8100; www.sophies.ie; 33 Harcourt St; mains €14-34; ⊘ 7am-10.30pm Mon-Wed, to 11am Thu-Fri, 8am-1.30am Sat, 8am-10.30pm Sun; 🖳 10, 11, 13, 14, 15A, 🚈 Harcourt) There's perhaps no better setting in all of Dublin – a top-floor glasshouse restaurant with superb views of the city – in which to enjoy this quirky take on Italian cuisine. Delicious pizzas come with nontraditional toppings (smoked brisket with barbecue mustard?) and the 8oz fillet steak is done to perfection. A good spot for breakfast too.

Fade Street Social
MODERN IRISH €€

(Map p88; ☑ 01-604 0066; www.fadestreetsocial. com; 4-6 Fade St; mains €20-36, tapas €6-17; ⊘ 5-10.30pm Mon-Wed, 12.30-3pm & 5-10.30pm Thu, to 11pm Fri & Sat, to 10.30pm Sun; 🛜; 🖳 all city centre) 🍴 Two restaurants in one, courtesy of renowned chef Dylan McGrath. At the front, the buzzy tapas bar, which serves gourmet bites from a beautiful open kitchen; at the back, the more muted restaurant specialises in Irish cuts of meat – from veal to rabbit – served with homegrown organic vegetables. There's a bar upstairs too. Reservations recommended.

Opium
ASIAN €€

(Map p92; ☑ 01-475 8555; www.opium.ie; 26 Wexford St; mains €18-25; ⊘ noon-10pm Mon-Wed, to 2.30am Thu & Fri, 1pm-2.30am Sat, 1-10pm Sun; 🖳 14, 15, 65, 83) Modelled on Hakkasan in London, Opium is a late-night restaurant and bar that serves tasty pan-Asian cuisine with a soundtrack. When you're done dining you can retire to the cocktail bar or the late-night **club** (⊘ noon-11pm Mon-Thu, to 2.30am Fri & Sat, noon-11.30pm Sun). The Botanical Garden is a great outdoor space, too.

Brasserie Sixty6
FUSION €€

(Map p92; ☑ 01-400 5878; www.brasseriesixty6.com; 66-67 S Great George's St; mains €18-33; ⊘ noon-3pm & 4-10pm Mon-Fri, 10am-3pm & 4-10pm Sat & Sun; 🖳 all city centre) This New York–style brasserie's speciality is rotisserie chicken, done four different ways at any given time. For that special occasion, there's a whole roast pig (€390 to €490) – you need to order seven

VEGETARIAN FOOD

Vegetarians (and vegans) are finding it increasingly easier in Dublin, as the capital has veered away from the belief that food isn't food until your incisors have ripped fresh flesh from bone and towards an understanding that healthy eating leads to, well, longer lives.

There's a selection of general restaurants that cater to vegetarians beyond the token dish of mixed greens and pulses – places such as M&L (p126), **Yamamori** (Map p88; ☑ 01-475 5001; www.yamamori.ie; 71 S Great George's St; mains €19-24, lunch bentos €10; ☺ noon-10.30pm Sun-Thu, to 11.30pm Fri & Sat; ☑; ☐ all city centre) and **Chameleon** (Map p88; ☑ 01-671 0362; www.chameleonrestaurant.com; 1 Lower Fownes St; set menus €29-40, tapas €8-11; ☺ 4-11pm Wed-Sun; ☑; ☐ all city centre). The Wednesday night dinner at the **Fumbally** (Map p84; ☑ 01-529 8732; www.thefumbally.ie; Fumbally Lane; mains €7-12; ☺ 8am-5pm Tue-Fri, from 10am Sat, plus 7-9.30pm Wed; ☐ 49, 54A from city centre) always includes a tasty vegetarian option, while Assassination Custard (p126) strikes an even balance between meat and vegetarian dishes.

Solidly vegetarian places include **Blazing Salads** (Map p88; ☑ 01-671 9552; www.blazing salads.com; 42 Drury St; salads €5-10; ☺ 9am-6pm Mon-Sat; ☑; ☐ all city centre), with organic breads, Californian-style salads and pizza; Cornucopia (p121), Dublin's best-known vegetarian restaurant, serving wholesome salads, sandwiches and a selection of hot main courses; and **Govinda's** (Map p88; www.govindas.ie; 4 Aungier St; mains €10.45; ☺ noon-9pm Mon-Sat; ☑; ☐ all city centre), an authentic beans-and-pulses place run by the Hare Krishna.

days in advance and be in a group of 10. It also has a vegetarian menu and an early bird three-course menu for €31.50.

L'Gueuleton
FRENCH €€

(Map p88; ☑ 01-675 3708; www.lgueuleton.com; 1 Fade St; mains €20-31; ☺ 12.30-4pm & 5.30-10pm Mon-Wed, to 10.30pm Thu-Sat, noon-4pm & 5.30-9pm Sun; ☐ all city centre) Despite the tongue-twister name (it means 'gluttonous feast' in French), L'Gueuleton is a firm favourite with locals for its robust (meaty, filling) take on French rustic cuisine – it does a mean onion soup and the steak frites is a big crowd pleaser.

Avoca
CAFE €€

(Map p88; ☑ 01-677 4215; www.avoca.ie; 11-13 Suffolk St; mains €7-18; ☺ 9.30am-4.30pm Mon-Fri, to 5.30pm Sat, 10am-5pm Sun; ☐ all city centre) This top-floor cafe, part of the marvellous Avoca group, is very popular with discerning shoppers who enjoy a gourmet lunch: how about a Toonsbridge halloumi salad with kale, sweet potato, baba ganoush and dukkah, or falafel with bulgar pilaf, caramelised onion hummus, beetroot tzatziki and pitta? There's also a takeaway salad bar and hot-food counter in the basement.

★ Greenhouse
SCANDINAVIAN €€€

(Map p88; ☑ 01-676 7015; www.thegreenhous-erestaurant.ie; Dawson St; 2-/3-course lunch menu €45/55, 4-/6-course dinner menu €110/129; ☺ noon-2pm & 6-9.30pm Tue-Sat; ☐ all city centre, ☒ St Stephen's Green) Chef Mickael Viljanen might just be one of the most exciting chefs

working in Ireland today thanks to his Scandi-influenced tasting menus, which have made this arguably Dublin's best restaurant. The lunchtime set menu is one of the best bargains in town – a two-Michelin-starred meal for under €50. Reservations necessary.

Glovers Alley
IRISH €€€

(Map p88; ☑ 01-244 0733; www.gloversalley.ie; 128 St Stephen's Green; 3-course dinner €80, 2-course lunch €35; ☺ 6-9.30pm Tue-Sat & 12.30-2.15pm Thu-Sat; ☐ all city centre) Superstar chef Andy McFadden returned to Dublin to head up this fine-dining restaurant, where you'll find exceptional dishes served with style and panache. The menu changes regularly but you can expect dishes like Dublin Bay prawns with carrot, tarragon and lardo, and Sika deer with beetroot, endive and watercress. A fabulous addition to the Dublin dining scene.

✕ Merrion Square & Georgian Dublin

The area around Merrion Row is a culinary hotbed, whether it's casual lunches for the business trade or upmarket dining at restaurants that hold most of the city's Michelin stars. Sandwich bars and nondescript cafes make up the rest of the dining landscape.

★ Etto
ITALIAN €€

(Map p92; ☑ 01-678 8872; www.etto.ie; 18 Merrion Row; mains €18-24; ☺ noon-9.30pm Mon-Wed, to 10pm Thu-Fri, 12.30-10pm Sat; ☐ all city centre) Award-winning restaurant and wine bar that does contemporary versions of classic Italian cuisine. The ingredients are fresh, the presentation is exquisite and the service is just right. Portions are small, but the food is so rich you won't leave hungry. The only downside is the relatively quick turnover; lingering over the excellent wine would be nice. Book ahead.

★ Coburg Brasserie   FRENCH €€
(Map p92; ☑ 01-602 8900; www.thecoburgdublin. com; Conrad Dublin, Earlsfort Tce; mains €17-26; ☺ 6.30am-11pm; ⌨ all city centre) The French-inspired, seafood-leaning cuisine at this revamped hotel brasserie puts the emphasis on shellfish: the all-day menu offers oysters, mussels and a range of lobster dishes, from lobster rolls to lobster cocktail. The bouillabaisse is chock-full of sea flavours, and you can also get a crab and shrimp burger and an excellent yellowfin tuna Niçoise salad. Top-notch.

House   MEDITERRANEAN €€
(Map p92; ☑ 01-905 9090; www.housedublin.ie; 27 Lower Leeson St; small plates €9-12, mains €15-26; ☺ 8am-midnight Mon-Wed, to 3am Thu & Fri, 4pm-3am Sat; ⌨ 11, 46, 118, 145 from city centre) This gorgeous bar does a limited selection of main courses, but the real treats are the tapas-style sharing plates, which cover the full Mediterranean spread, from wild mushroom risotto and pulled pork to grilled halloumi and salt-and-pepper calamari.

Ely Wine Bar   IRISH €€
(Map p92; ☑ 01-676 8986; www.elywinebar.ie; 22 Ely Pl; mains €22-38; ☺ noon-11.30pm Mon-Fri, 5pm-12.30am Sat; ⌨ all city centre) 🍴 Scrummy organic burgers, nine-hour braised beef cheek and perfectly charred steaks are all on the menu in this basement restaurant. Meals are prepared with organic and free-range produce from the owner's family farm in County Clare, so you can rest assured of the quality. There's another branch (p128) in the Docklands.

★ Restaurant Patrick Guilbaud   FRENCH €€€
(Map p92; ☑ 01-676 4192; www.restaurantpatrick-guilbaud.ie; 21 Upper Merrion St; 2-/3-course set lunch €52/62, dinner menus €135-203; ☺ 12.30-2.30pm & 7-10.30pm Tue-Fri, 1-2.30pm & 7-10.30pm Sat; ⌨ 7, 46 from city centre) With two Michelin stars, this restaurant is understandably considered the best in the country by its devotees, who proclaim Guillaume Lebrun's French haute cuisine the most exalted expression of the culinary arts. If you like formal dining, this is as good as it gets: the lunch menu is an absolute steal, at least in this stratosphere. Innovative and beautifully presented.

The room itself is all contemporary elegance and the service expertly formal yet surprisingly friendly – the staff are meticulously trained and as skilled at answering queries and addressing individual requests as they are at making sure not one breadcrumb lingers too long on the immaculate tablecloths. Owner Patrick Guilbaud usually does the rounds of the tables himself in the evening to salute regular customers and charm first-timers into returning. Reservations are absolutely necessary.

L'Ecrivain   FRENCH €€€
(Map p92; ☑ 01-661 1919; www.lecrivain.com; 109A Lower Baggot St; 3-course lunch menus €47.50, 8-course tasting menus €115, mains €38-46; ☺ 12.30-3.30pm Fri, 6.30-10.30pm Mon-Sat; ⌨ 38, 39 from city centre) Head chef Derry Clarke is considered a gourmet god for the exquisite simplicity of his creations, which put the emphasis on flavour and the best local ingredients – all given the French once-over and turned into something that approaches divine dining. The Michelin people like it too and awarded it one of their stars.

✖ Temple Bar

Scattered among the panoply of overpriced and underwhelming eateries in Temple Bar are some excellent spots to get a bite that will suit a variety of tastes and pocket depths.

Sano Pizza   PIZZA €
(Map p88; ☑ 01-445 3344; www.sano.pizza; 2 Upper Exchange St; pizzas €6-12; ☺ noon-10pm Sun-Wed, to 11pm Thu-Sat, ⌨ all city centre) The authentic Neapolitan pizza served here is fantastic, with a chewy, charred crust and a sparse smattering of toppings — we love the *Sapori del Sud*, with spicy nduja pork, fennel sausage, broccoli and mozzarella. And it's a bargain to boot.

Klaw   SEAFOOD €
(Map p88; www.klaw.ie; 5a Crown Alley; mains €8-15; ☺ noon-10pm Mon-Wed & Sun, to 11pm Thu-Sat; ⌨ all city centre) There's nothing sophisticated about this crab-shack-style place except the food: Irish oysters served naked, dressed or torched; Lambay Island crab claws served with a yuzu aioli; or half a lobster. Whatever you go for it's all delicious; the 'shucknsuck' oyster happy hour is a terrific deal.

Bison Bar & BBQ   BARBECUE €
(Map p88; ☑ 01-533 7561; www.bisonbar.ie; 11 Wellington Quay; mains €14-22; ☺ noon-9pm; ⌨ all city centre) Beer, whiskey sours and finger-lickingly

good Texas-style barbecue – served with tasty sides such as slaw or mac 'n' cheese – is the fare at this boisterous restaurant. The cowboy theme is taken to the limit with the saddle chairs (yes, actual saddles); this is a place to eat, drink and be merry.

Queen of Tarts CAFE €
(Map p88; ✆01-670 7499; www.queenoftarts.ie; 4 Cork Hill; mains €5-13; ⊗8am-7pm Mon-Fri, from 9am Sat & Sun; ▣all city centre) This cute little cake shop does a fine line in tarts, meringues, crumbles, cookies and brownies, not to mention a decent breakfast: the smoked bacon and leek potato cakes with eggs and cherry tomatoes are excellent. There's another, bigger, branch around the corner on Cow's Lane.

★Banyi Japanese Dining JAPANESE €€
(Map p88; ✆01-675 0669; www.banyijapanese dining.com; 3-4 Bedford Row; lunch bento €11, small/large sushi platter €19/32; ⊗noon-10.30pm; ▣all city centre) This compact restaurant in the heart of Temple Bar has arguably the best Japanese cuisine in Dublin. The rolls are divine, and the sushi as good as any you'll eat at twice the price. If you don't fancy raw fish, the classic Japanese main courses are excellent, as are the lunchtime bento boxes. Dinner reservations are advised, particularly at weekends.

Roberta's INTERNATIONAL €€
(Map p88; ✆01-616 9612; www.robertas.ie; 1 Essex St E; mains €20-31; ⊗5-10pm Mon-Wed, to 10.30pm Thu & Fri, 11am-2.30pm & 5-10.30pm Sat, 11am-2.30pm & 5-10pm Sun; ▣all city centre) Inside this austere-looking protected building lies a beautiful red-brick restaurant with some of the most atmospheric views you can get in Dublin while dining, taking in both the River Liffey and the cobblestones of Temple Bar. The range of budget options makes it suitable for groups, and the cocktails are excellent.

✗ Kilmainham & the Liberties

★Assassination Custard CAFE €
(Map p92; ✆087 997 1513; www.facebook.com/assassinationcustard; 19 Kevin St; mains €7-9; ⊗noon-3pm Tue-Fri; ▣all city centre) It doesn't look like much, but this is one of the tastiest treats in town. The menu changes daily – think roasted cauliflower with toasted dukkah, or broccoli with spicy Italian nduja pork sausage and Toonsbridge ricotta. If you're feeling really adventurous, try the tripe sandwich. The name comes from a phrase coined by Samuel Beckett.

Clanbrassil Coffee Shop CAFE €
(Map p84; www.clanbrassilhouse.com; 6 Upper Clanbrassil St; mains €6-12; ⊗8am-3pm Mon-Fri, 9am-3.30pm Sat; ▣9, 16, 49, 54A from city centre) The daytime incarnation of Clanbrassil House next door, this cafe has a small but solid menu of sandwiches, bagels and pastries, made fresh each day.

★Clanbrassil House IRISH €€
(Map p84; ✆01-453 9786; www.clanbrassilhouse.com; 6 Upper Clanbrassil St; mains €19-28; ⊗5-10pm Tue-Fri, 11.30am-2.30pm & 5-10pm Sat; ▣9, 16, 49, 54A from city centre) With an emphasis on family-style sharing plates, this intimate restaurant consistently turns out exquisite dishes, cooked on a charcoal grill. Think rib-eye with bone marrow and anchovy, or ray wing with capers and brown shrimp butter. The hash brown chips are a thing of glory. Order the full feast menu (€50) for the chef's choice.

✗ North of the Liffey

★Fegan's 1924 CAFE €
(Map p100; ✆01-872 2788; www.fegans1924.com; 13 Chancery St; mains €6-9; ⊗7.30am-4pm Mon-Fri, from 11am Sat & Sun; ⊛; ▣25, 66, 67, 90 from city centre, ▣Four Courts) A slice of rural Ireland in the city centre: this wonderful cafe is all distressed furniture and rustic charm, but there's nothing old-fashioned about the food and coffee. Fluffy scrambled eggs, perfectly made French toast and excellent brews...this is a place designed for lingering. Weekends also feature 40-minute creative workshops for kids (€6 each). No cash; cards only.

Tram Cafe CAFE €
(Map p100; www.thetramcafe.ie; Wolfe Tone Sq; mains €5-6.50; ⊗8am-6pm Mon-Wed, to 9pm Thu & Fri, 10am-6pm Sat & Sun; ▣Jervis) The coffee and sandwiches are tasty, but it's the location that's special: a 1902 tram built by Brill in Philadelphia that lay in a field in County Cavan before being restored and transported to Dublin by its two owners. The 1920s musical soundtrack adds a touch of class.

M&L CHINESE €
(Map p100; ✆01-874 8038; www.mlchineserestaurant.com; 13/14 Cathedral St; mains €11-20; ⊗11.30am-10pm Mon-Sat, from noon Sun; ▣all city centre) Beyond the plain frontage and the cheap-looking decor is Dublin's best Chinese restaurant...by some distance. It's usually full of Chinese customers, who come for the authentic Szechuan-style cuisine – spicier than Cantonese and with none

of the concessions usually made to Western palates (no prawn crackers or curry chips).

Soup Dragon   FAST FOOD €
(Map p88; 01-872 3277; www.soupdragon.com; 168 Capel St; mains €5-8; 8am-5pm Mon-Fri; ; all city centre, Jervis) Queues are a regular feature outside this fabulous spot which specialises in soups on the go – it also does superb stews, sandwiches, bagels and salads. The all-day breakfast options are excellent – especially the mini breakfast quiche of sausage, egg and bacon. Bowls come in two sizes and prices include fresh bread and fruit.

★ Legal Eagle   IRISH €€
(Map p88; 01-555 2971; www.thelegaleagle.ie; 1/2 Chancery Pl; mains €22-30; 9.30am-4pm Mon & Tue, to 10pm Wed-Fri, noon-10pm Sat, noon-9pm Sun; Four Courts) With the aesthetic of an old Dublin pub, combined with a kitchen churning out top-notch comfort food, this is one of Dublin's best new restaurants. There's a wood oven for potato flatbreads topped with Toonsbridge mozzarella and oxtail, and the retro-influenced Sunday menu is a contender for the best roast in town.

Yarn   PIZZA €€
(Map p100; 01-828 0839; www.theyarnpizza.com; 37 Lower Liffey St; pizzas €9-15; 5-9pm Sun-Tue, to 10pm Wed-Sat; all city centre) With a 1st-floor terrace view of the Ha'Penny Bridge, this might be the city's coolest pizza joint. Add that it serves excellent drinks (pizza and Aperol, anyone?) and its credentials are rock solid. Oh, and the pizza – thin base, pomodoro San Marzano and delicious mozzarella – is delicious. It's the sister restaurant to the **Woollen Mills** (Map p100; 01-828 0835; www.thewoollenmills.com; 42 Lower Ormond Quay; sandwiches €10-11, mains €19-30; 9am-9pm Mon-Wed, to 10pm Thu & Fri, 9am-4pm & 5-10pm Sat, 11am-4pm & 5-9pm Sun; all city centre) – hence the name.

Fish Shop   FISH & CHIPS €€
(Map p100; 01-557 1473; www.fish-shop.ie; 76 Benburb St; fish & chips €15; noon-1pm Tue-Fri, 4-10pm Sat & Sun; 25, 25A, 66, 67 from city centre, Museum) A classic fish-and-chip shop with a gourmet, sit-down twist – not only is the fish the best you'll taste in battered form, but you'll wash it down with a fine wine from its carefully selected list. It's the original Fish Shop that moved from Queen St, where its fancier sister **restaurant** (Map p100; 01-430 8594; 6 Queen St; 4-course set menu €45; 6-10pm Wed-Sat; 25, 25A, 66, 67 from city centre, Smithfield) is now installed.

Winding Stair   IRISH €€
(Map p100; 01-873 7320; www.winding-stair.com; 40 Lower Ormond Quay; 2-course lunch €24, mains €25-32; noon-3.30pm & 5.30-10.30pm; all city centre) In a beautiful Georgian building that once housed the city's most beloved bookshop – the ground floor still is one (p139) – the Winding Stair's conversion to elegant restaurant has been faultless. The wonderful Irish menu (potted crab, haddock poached in milk, steamed mussels and gorgeous fat chips) coupled with an excellent wine list makes for a memorable meal.

★ Mr Fox   IRISH €€€
(Map p100; 01-874 7778; www.mrfox.ie; 38 W Parnell Sq; mains €20-30; noon-2pm & 5-9.30pm Tue-Sat; Parnell) In a gorgeous Georgian townhouse on Parnell Sq, the fantastic Mr Fox is cooking some of the finest food in the city. The plates celebrate Irish ingredients with a cheeky twist – think venison with black pudding, chestnut and blackberries, or pheasant with lentils and Toulouse sausage. A Michelin star can't be too far away.

★ Chapter One   IRISH €€€
(Map p100; 01-873 2266; www.chapterone restaurant.com; 18 N Parnell Sq; 2-course lunch €36.50, 4-course dinner €80; 12.30-2pm Fri, 5-10.30pm Tue-Sat; 3, 10, 11, 13, 16, 19, 22 from city centre) Flawless haute cuisine and a relaxed, welcoming atmosphere make this Michelin-starred restaurant in the basement of the Dublin Writers Museum our choice for the

best dinner experience in town. The food is French-inspired contemporary Irish; the menus change regularly; and the service is top-notch. The pre-theatre menu (€44) is great if you're going to the Gate (p136).

✕ Docklands

★ Juniors Deli & Cafe   ITALIAN €€
(Map p106; ☑ 01-664 3648; www.juniors.ie; 2 Bath Ave; mains €17-26; ☺ 8.30-10.30am, noon-2.30pm & 5.30-10pm Mon-Fri, 11am-3pm & 5.30-10pm Sat, 11am-3.30pm Sun; ☑ 3 from city centre, ☒ Grand Canal Dock) Cramped and easily mistaken for any old cafe, Juniors is hardly ordinary. Designed to imitate a New York deli, the food (Italian-influenced, all locally sourced produce) is delicious, the atmosphere always buzzing (it's often hard to get a table) and the ethos top-notch, which is down to the two brothers who run the place.

Ely Bar & Grill   FUSION €€
(Map p106; ☑ 01-672 0010; www.elywinebar.ie; CHQ Bldg, ISFC, George's Dock; mains €18-40; ☺ noon-10pm Mon-Fri, to 6pm Sun; ☒ George's Dock) 🍴 Homemade burgers, bangers and mash, and perfectly charred steaks are some of the meals served in this converted tobacco warehouse in the International Financial Services Centre (IFSC). Dishes are prepared with organic produce from the owner's family farm in County Clare, so you can be assured of the quality.

Workshop Gastropub   IRISH €€
(Kennedy's; ☑ 01-677 0626; www.theworkshop gastropub.com; 10 George's Quay; mains lunch €7-9, dinner €10-24; ☺ noon-3pm & 5-10pm Sun-Fri, noon-12.30am Sat; 🍴; ☑ all city centre, ☒ Tara St) Take a traditional pub and introduce a chef with a vision: hey presto, you've got a gastropub (surprisingly one of the few in the city) serving burgers, *moules frites* (mussels served with French fries) and sandwiches, as well as a good range of salads.

✕ Southside

★ Manifesto   ITALIAN €€
(Map p84; ☑ 01-496 8096; www.manifestorestaurant. ie; 208 Lower Rathmines Rd; pizzas €12-17, mains €19-25; ☺ 5-10pm; ☑ 14,15,140 from city centre) A table at this tiny Italian joint, which has a loyal legion of fans, is worth the wait. Pizzas are expertly charred with carefully curated toppings like tender-stem broccoli and Sicilian capers, and the wine list is inventive and vast, with a generous selection available by the glass.

★ Farmer Brown's   INTERNATIONAL €€
(Map p106; ☑ 01-660 2326; www.farmerbrowns.ie; 25A Bath Ave; brunch €7-12, dinner €15-28; ☺ 10am-4pm & 5-8.30pm; 📷; ☑ 7, 8 from city centre, ☒ Grand Canal Dock) The hicky-chic decor and mismatched furniture won't be to everyone's liking, but there's no disagreement about the food, which makes this spot our choice for best brunch in Dublin. From healthy smashed avocado to a stunning Cuban pork sandwich, it has all your lazy breakfast needs covered. Very much worth the effort. There's another branch in Rathmines.

Stella Diner   DINER €€
(☑ 01-496 7063; www.stelladiner.ie; 211 Lower Rathmines Rd; mains €8-20; ☺ 8am-10pm; ☑ 14, 15, 140 from city centre) Unsurprisingly, American comfort food is at the heart of this stylish spot, where diners tuck into hot dogs and burgers from red-leather booths. If you have a craving for American pancakes, these are some of the best in town – fluffy, light and accompanied by a generous jug of maple syrup. Unlimited filter coffee is a nice touch, too.

Farmer Brown's   INTERNATIONAL €€
(Map p84; ☑ 086 046 8837; www.farmerbrowns.ie; 170 Lower Rathmines Rd; mains €16-28; ☺ 10am-4pm & 5-10pm; ☑ 14, 15 from city centre) A second branch of the much-loved restaurant on Bath Ave, offering virtually the same delicious menu. Its juicy burgers are a contender for the best in the city.

🍸 Drinking & Nightlife

If there's one constant about life in Dublin, it's that Dubliners will always take a drink. Come hell or high water, the city's pubs will never be short of customers, and we suspect that exploring a variety of Dublin's legendary pubs and bars ranks pretty high on the list of reasons you're here.

Last orders are at 11.30pm from Monday to Thursday, 12.30am on Friday and Saturday and 11pm on Sunday, with 30 minutes' drinking-up time each night. However, many central pubs have secured late licences to serve until 1.30am or even 2.30am (usually pubs that double as dance clubs).

🍸 Grafton Street & St Stephen's Green

★ Kehoe's   PUB
(Map p88; 9 S Anne St; ☺ 11am-11.30pm Mon-Thu, to 12.30am Fri & Sat, 12.30-11pm Sun; ☑ all city centre) This classic bar is the very exemplar of a

traditional Dublin pub. The beautiful Victorian bar, wonderful snug and side room have been popular with Dubliners and visitors for generations, so much so that the publican's living quarters upstairs have since been converted into an extension – simply by taking out the furniture and adding a bar.

★ Grogan's Castle Lounge   PUB
(Map p88; www.facebook.com/groganscastlelounge; 15 S William St; ⊙10.30am-11.30pm Mon-Thu, to 12.30am Fri & Sat, 12.30-11pm Sun; 🖭 all city centre) Known simply as Grogan's (after the original owner), this is a city-centre institution. It has long been a favourite haunt of Dublin's writers and painters, as well as others from the alternative bohemian set, who enjoy a fine Guinness while they wait for that inevitable moment when they're discovered.

★ Long Hall   PUB
(Map p88; 51 S Great George's St; ⊙noon-11.30pm Mon-Thu, to 12.30am Fri & Sat, 12.30-11pm Sun; 🖭 all city centre) A Victorian classic that is one of the city's most beautiful and best-loved pubs. Check out the ornate carvings behind the bar and the elegant chandeliers. The bartenders are experts at their craft, an increasingly rare attribute in Dublin these days.

★ No Name Bar   BAR
(Map p88; www.nonamebardublin.com; 3 Fade St; ⊙1.30-11.30pm Mon-Wed, to 1am Thu, 12.30pm-2.30am Fri & Sat, noon-11pm Sun; 🖭 all city centre) A low-key entrance next to the trendy French restaurant L'Gueuleton (p124) leads upstairs to one of the nicest bar spaces in town, consisting of three huge rooms in a restored Victorian townhouse plus a sizeable heated patio area for smokers. There's no sign or a name – folks just refer to it as the No Name Bar.

Against the Grain   CRAFT BEER
(Map p92; www.galwaybaybrewery.com/against thegrain; 11 Wexford St; ⊙noon-midnight Mon-Thu, to 2am Fri & Sat, 12.30pm-midnight Sun; 🖭 all city centre) An excellent pub for the craft-beer fans, which is no surprise considering it's owned by the Galway Bay Brewery. There's a dizzying selection of ales and beers on tap, and the barkeeps are generous when it comes to offering tasters to help in your decision-making. Order some chicken wings for soakage if you plan on staying a while...

Network   COFFEE
(Map p88; www.networkcafe.ie; 39 Aungier St; ⊙7.30am-6pm Mon-Fri, from 9am Sat, 10am-5pm Sun; 🖭 all city centre) If you're a fan of latte art, you'll be swooning at the creations that come out of this cool little cafe on Aungier St. But, thankfully, it's not all Instagram-luring bluster – the coffee itself is exquisite.

Peruke & Periwig   COCKTAIL BAR
(Map p88; ✍01-672 7190; www.peruke.ie; 31 Dawson St; ⊙noon-midnight Sun-Thu, to 2.30am Fri & Sat; 🖭 all city centre) This teeny little Tardis of a bar has an eccentric apothecary vibe, with mixologists decked out in bow ties and a cocktail menu that reads like a novella. If the thought of trawling through pages of options seems exhausting, just tell the bar staff what you're into – their concoctions are always bang on the money.

Anseo   BAR
(Map p92; 18 Lower Camden St; ⊙4-11.30pm Mon-Thu, to 12.30am Fri & Sat, to 11pm Sun; 🖭14, 15, 65, 83) Unpretentious, unaffected and incredibly popular, this cosy alternative bar – which is pronounced 'an-*shuh*', the Irish for 'here' – is a favourite with those who live by the credo that to try too hard is far worse than not trying at all. The pub's soundtrack is an eclectic mix; you're as likely to hear Peggy Lee as Lee Perry.

Bestseller   WINE BAR
(Map p88; ✍01-671 5125; www.bestsellerdublin.com; 41 Dawson St; ⊙9am-6pm Mon-Wed, to 11pm Thu-Sat, 10am-4pm Sun; 🖭 all city centre, 🖭 St Stephen's Green) A daytime cafe and evening wine bar – this relaxing bohemian spot is surrounded by an eclectic mix of books and art. Housed in the previous headquarters of the National Bible Society, you'll still find its name above the door as well as a small selection of biblically inspired cocktails. There's reasonably priced hot food during the day or sharing platters at night.

Clement & Pekoe   CAFE
(Map p88; www.clementandpekoe.com; 50 S William St; ⊙8am-7pm Mon-Fri, 9am-6.30pm Sat, 11am-6pm Sun; 🖭 all city centre) Our favourite cafe in town is this contemporary version of an Edwardian tearoom. Walnut floors, art deco chandeliers and wall-to-wall displays of handsome tea jars are the perfect setting in which to enjoy the huge range of loose-leaf teas and carefully made coffees, along with a selection of cakes.

Bernard Shaw   BAR
(Map p92; www.thebernardshaw.com; 11-12 S Richmond St; ⊙noon-midnight Mon-Thu, to 12.30am Fri & Sat; 🖭14, 15, 65, 83) This deliberately ramshackle boozer is probably the coolest bar in town for its marvellous mix of music (courtesy of its

POURING THE PERFECT GUINNESS

Like the Japanese tea ceremony, pouring a pint of Guinness is part ritual, part theatre and part logic. It's a five-step process that every decent Dublin bartender will use to serve the perfect pint.

The Glass

A dry, clean 20oz (568mL) tulip pint glass is used because the shape allows the nitrogen bubbles to flow down the side, and the contour 'bump' about halfway down pushes the bubbles into the centre of the pint on their way up.

The Angle

The glass is held beneath the tap at a 45-degree angle – and the tap faucet shouldn't touch the sides of the glass.

The Pour

A smooth pour should fill the glass to about three-quarters full, after which it is put on the counter 'to settle'.

The Head

As the beer flows into the glass it passes through a restrictor plate at high speed that creates nitrogen bubbles. In the glass, the agitated bubbles flow down the sides of the glass and – thanks to the contour bump – back up through the middle, settling at the top in a nice, creamy head. This should take a couple of minutes to complete.

The Top-Off

Once the pint is 'settled', the bartender will top it off, creating a domed effect across the top of the glass with the head sitting comfortably just above the rim. Now it's the perfect pint.

Where to Find It?

Most Dublin pubs know how to serve a decent pint of Guinness. But for something really special, you'll need the expertise of an experienced bartender and the appropriate atmosphere in which to savour their creations. Everyone has their favourites: we recommend Kehoe's (p128), the Stag's Head (p130) and John Mulligan's (p133) on the southside; and Walshs (p132) on the northside.

owners, the Bodytonic production crew) and diverse menu of events, such as afternoon car-boot sales, storytelling nights and fun competitions like having a 'tag-off' between a bunch of graffiti artists. It also runs the excellent Eatyard (p122).

Stag's Head PUB

(Map p88; www.stagshead.ie; 1 Dame Ct; ⊙10am-11pm Sun-Thu, to 1am Fri & Sat; ᐇall city centre) The Stag's Head was built in 1770, remodelled in 1895 and thankfully not changed a bit since then. It's a superb pub: so picturesque that it often appears in films and also featured in a postage-stamp series on Irish bars. A bloody great pub, no doubt.

Sidecar COCKTAIL BAR

(Map p88; www.doylecollection.com; Balfe St; ⊙4pm-midnight Mon-Fri, from noon Sat & Sun; ᐇall city centre) This sleek and rather saucy cocktail bar is the place to take someone you want to impress – snifters of Prosecco are served while you browse the menu, or you can keep things simple with a martini, shaken (or stirred) right next to your table by a bow-tied waiter.

Merrion Square & Georgian Dublin

★Toner's PUB

(Map p92; ☎01-676 3090; www.tonerspub.ie; 139 Lower Baggot St; ⊙10.30am-11.30pm Mon-Thu, to 12.30am Fri & Sat, 11.30am-11.30pm Sun; ᐇ7, 46 from city centre) Toner's, with its stone floors and antique snugs, has changed little over the years and is the closest thing you'll get to a country pub in the heart of the city. Next door, Toner's Yard is a comfortable outside space. The shelves and drawers are reminders that it once doubled as a grocery shop.

The writer Oliver St John Gogarty once brought WB Yeats here, after the upper-class poet – who lived just around the corner – decided he wanted to visit a pub. After a silent sherry in the noisy bar, Yeats turned to his friend and said, 'I have seen the pub, now please take me home'. We always suspected he was a little too precious for normal people, and he would probably be horrified by the good-natured business crowd making the racket these days too. His loss.

★ **O'Donoghue's** PUB
(Map p92; www.odonoghues.ie; 15 Merrion Row; ☺10am-midnight Mon-Thu, to 1am Fri & Sat, 11am-midnight Sun; ☒all city centre) The pub where traditional music stalwarts The Dubliners made their name in the 1960s still hosts live music nightly, but the crowds would gather anyway – for the excellent pints and superb ambience, in the old bar or the covered coach yard next to it.

Hartigan's PUB
(Map p92; 100 Lower Leeson St; ☺2.30-11.30pm Mon-Thu, 1.30pm-12.30am Fri & Sat, 12.30pm-midnight Sun; ☒all city centre) This is about as spartan a bar as you'll find in the city, and the daytime home of some serious drinkers, who appreciate the quiet, no-frills surroundings. In the evening it's popular with students from the medical faculty of UCD.

Square Ball BAR
(Map p106; ☏01-662 4473; www.the-square-ball. com; 45 Hogan Pl; ☺noon-11.30pm Tue-Thu, to 12.30am Fri & Sat, noon-11pm Sun; ☒4, 7 from city centre) This bar is many things to many people: craft beer and cocktail bar at the front, sports lounge and barbecue pit at the back and an awesome vintage arcade upstairs. There are also plenty of board games, so bring your competitive spirit.

House BAR
(Map p92; ☏01-905 9090; www.housedublin.ie; 27 Lower Leeson St; ☺8am-midnight Mon, to 2am Tue & Wed, to 3am Thu & Fri, noon-3am Sat, noon-11pm Sun; ☒11, 46, 118, 145) Spread across two Georgian townhouses, this could be Dublin's most beautiful modern bar, with wood-floored rooms, comfortable couches and even log fires in winter to amp up the cosiness. In the middle there's a lovely glassed-in outdoor space that on a nice day bathes the rest of the bar with natural light. There's also an excellent menu.

Doheny & Nesbitt's PUB
(Map p92; ☏01-676 2945; www.dohenyandnesbitts.ie; 5 Lower Baggot St; ☺9am-12.30am Mon & Tue, to 1am Wed & Thu, to 2am Fri, 9.30am-2am Sat, 10.30am-midnight Sun; ☒all city centre) A standout, even in a city of wonderful pubs, Nesbitt's

is equipped with antique snugs and is a favourite place for the high-powered gossip of politicians and journalists; Leinster House is only a short stroll away.

Temple Bar

★ **Vintage Cocktail Club** BAR
(Map p88; ☏01-675 3547; www.vintagecocktailclub. com; Crown Alley; ☺5pm-1.30am Mon-Fri, from 12.30pm Sat & Sun; ☒all city centre) The atmosphere behind this inconspicuous, unlit doorway initialled with the letters 'VCC' is that of a Vegas rat pack hang-out or a '60s-style London members' club. It's so popular you'll probably need to book for one of the 2½-hour evening sittings, which is plenty of time to sample some of the excellent cocktails and finger food.

★ **Palace Bar** PUB
(Map p88; www.thepalacebardublin.com; 21 Fleet St; ☺10.30am-11.30pm Mon-Thu, to 12.30am Fri & Sat, 12.30-11.30pm Sun; ☒all city centre) With its mirrors and wooden niches, the Palace (established in 1823) is one of Dublin's great 19th-century pubs, still stubbornly resisting any modernising influences from the last half-century or so. Literary figures Patrick Kavanagh and Flann O'Brien were once regulars and it was for a long time the unofficial head office of the *Irish Times*.

Darkey Kelly's Bar & Restaurant IRISH PUB
(Map p88; ☏01-679 6500; www.darkeykellys.ie; 19 Fishamble St; ☺10.30am-11.30pm Mon-Thu, to 12.30am Fri & Sat, 12.30-11pm Sun; ☒all city centre) Once the home of Ireland's first female serial killer, Darkey's now boasts a killer whiskey selection instead. It has a range of craft beer, and is a compromise between the tourist bars of Temple Bar and local boozers. The pint prices are on the steep side, but there's a great buzz and traditional music is guaranteed.

This pub is built on the site of Darkey Kelly's 18th-century brothel. For years she was believed to have been burned at the stake in 1746 for the crime of witchcraft. In fact, papers discovered in 2010 showed she was executed after the bodies of five men were found in her vaults. Her motives are lost to history, but at her wake prostitutes from her brothel had a minor riot in Temple Bar, leading to 13 arrests.

Temple Bar BAR
(Map p88; ☏01-677 3807; www.thetemplebarpub. com; 48 Temple Bar; ☺10.30am-1.30am Mon-Wed, 10am-2.30am Thu-Sat, 11.30am-1am Sun; ☒all city centre) The most photographed pub facade in

Dublin, perhaps the world, the Temple Bar (aka Flannery's) is smack bang in the middle of the tourist precinct and is usually chock-a-block with visitors. It's good craic, though, and presses all the right buttons, with traditional musicians, a buzzy atmosphere and even a beer garden.

Kilmainham & the Liberties

★ Old Royal Oak   PUB
(11 Kilmainham Lane; ⊘ 5pm-midnight Mon-Thu, 3pm-1am Fri, 12.30pm-1am Sat, 12.30-11pm Sun; 🚌 68, 79 from city centre) Locals are fiercely protective of this gorgeous traditional pub, which opened in 1845 to serve the patrons and staff of the Royal Hospital (now the Irish Museum of Modern Art). The clientele has changed, but everything else remains the same, which makes this one of the nicest pubs in the city in which to enjoy a few pints.

Drop Dead Twice   BAR
(Map p88; www.dropdeadtwice.com; 18/19 Francis St; ⊘ 5-11.30pm Tue-Thu, to 12.30am Fri, noon-12.30am Sat, noon-11pm Sun; 🚌 51B, 51C, 78A, 123 from city centre) The taproom downstairs is a great little boozer, but upstairs things are a bit jazzier with the BYO cocktail lounge. Bring a bottle of your favourite spirit, pay for a sitting of two/three hours (€25/35) and the bartenders will whizz you up cocktails using their extensive ingredients. We've seen cocktails infused with peat smoke, homemade bitters and even bacon.

Fallon's   PUB
(Map p88; ☎ 01-454 2801; 129 The Coombe; ⊘ 10.30am-11.30pm Mon-Thu, to 12.30am Fri & Sat, 12.30-11pm Sun; 🚌 51B, 123, 206 from city centre) A fabulously old-fashioned bar that has been serving a great pint of Guinness since the end of the 17th century. Prizefighter Dan Donnelly, the only boxer ever to be knighted, was head bartender here in 1818. A local's local.

North of the Liffey

★ Cobblestone   PUB
(Map p100; www.cobblestonepub.ie; N King St; ⊘ 4.30-11.30pm Mon-Thu, 2pm-12.30am Fri & Sat, 1.30-11pm Sun; 🚌 Smithfield) It advertises itself as a 'drinking pub with a music problem', which is an apt description for this Smithfield stalwart – although the traditional music sessions that run throughout the week can hardly be described as problematic. Wednesday's Balaclava session (from 7.30pm) is for any

musician who is learning an instrument, with musician Síomha Mulligan on hand to teach.

Token   BAR
(Map p100; ☎ 01-532 2699; www.tokendublin.ie; 72-74 Queen St, Smithfield; ⊘ 4-11pm; 🚌 25, 26, 37, 39, 66, 67, 69, 70, 79A from city centre, 🚊 Smithfield, Red Line) This arcade-style bar is fitted out with retro video games and pinball machines. As well as a full bar, the restaurant serves generous portions of innovative, gourmet fast food. Book ahead for groups of more than four if you want to eat. Over 18s only.

Caffe Cagliostro   COFFEE
(Map p88; www.facebook.com/cagliostrodublin; Bloom's Lane; ⊘ 7am-6.30pm Mon-Thu, to 10pm Fri, from 8.30am Sat, 10am-6pm Sun; 🚊 Jervis) In the middle of the 'Italian Quarter' this tiny cafe serves brilliant Italian-style coffee at a reasonable price, alongside miniature doughnuts, cannoli and paninis. On Friday evenings the little patio turns into a *Spritzeria*, with drinkers tucking into Aperol spritzes and nibbles.

Confession Box   PUB
(Map p100; ☎ 01-874 7339; www.c11407968.wixsite. com/ryan; 88 Marlborough St; ⊘ 11am-11pm Mon-Fri, 10am-midnight Sat & Sun; 🚊 Abbey) This historic pub is popular with tourists and locals alike. Run by some of the friendliest bar staff you're likely to meet, it's also a good spot to brush up on your local history: the pub was a favourite spot of Michael Collins, one of the leaders in the fight for Irish independence.

Walshs   PUB
(Map p100; www.walshsstoneybatter.ie; 6 Stoneybatter; ⊘ 3-11pm Mon-Thu, to 12.30am Fri & Sat, 3-11pm Sun; 🚌 25, 25A, 66, 67 from city centre, 🚊 Museum) If the snug is free, a drink in Walshs is about as pure a traditional experience as you'll have in any pub in the city; if it isn't, you'll have to make do with the old-fashioned bar, where the friendly staff and brilliant clientele (a mix of locals and trendsetting imports) are a treat. A proper Dublin pub.

Grand Social   BAR
(Map p100; ☎ 01-874 0076; www.thegrandsocial.ie; 35 Lower Liffey St; ⊘ 4pm-12.30am Mon-Wed, to midnight Thu, noon-2.30am Fri & Sat, 3-11pm Sun; 🚌 all city centre, 🚊 Jervis) This multipurpose venue hosts club nights, comedy and gigs, and is a decent bar for a drink. It's spread across three floors, each of which has a different theme: the Parlour downstairs is a cosy, old-fashioned bar; the mid-level Ballroom is where the dancing is; and the upstairs Loft hosts events.

LGBTQ+ DUBLIN

Dublin is a pretty good place to be LGBTIQ+. Being gay or lesbian in the city is completely unremarkable, while in recent years members of the trans community have also found greater acceptance. However, LGBTIQ+ people can still be harrassed or worse, so if you do encounter any sort of trouble, call the Crime Victims Helpline (p141) or the Sexual Assault Investigation Unit (☑ 01-666 3430; www.garda.ie; ⊘24hr).

Resources include the following:

Gaire (www.gaire.com) Online message board and resource centre.

Gay Men's Health Project (☑ 01-660 2189; www.hse.ie/go/GMHS) Practical advice on men's health issues.

National LGBT Federation (☑ 01-675 5025; www.nxf.ie; 2 Upper Exchange St, Temple Bar; ▣ all city centre) Publishers of *Gay Community News*.

Outhouse (☑ 01-873 4932; www.outhouse.ie; 105 Capel St; ⊘10am-6pm Mon-Fri, noon-5pm Sat; ▣ all city centre) Top LGBTIQ+ resource centre, and a great stop-off point to see what's on, check noticeboards and meet people. It publishes the free *Ireland's Pink Pages*, a directory of gay-centric services, which is also accessible on the website.

Festivals & Events

International Dublin Gay Theatre Festival (www.gaytheatre.ie; ⊘May) The only event of its kind anywhere in the world, with more than 20 LGBTIQ-themed productions over two weeks in May.

Gaze International LGBT Film Festival (www.gaze.ie; ⊘Aug; ▣ all city centre) An international film and documentary festival held at the Irish Film Institute (p136).

Drinking & Nightlfe

Pantibar (Map p88; www.pantibar.com; 7-8 Capel St; ⊘4-11.30pm Mon-Thu, to 12.30am Fri & Sat, to 11pm Sun; ▣ all city centre) A raucous, fun gay bar owned by Rory O'Neill, aka Panti Bliss, star of 2015's acclaimed documentary *The Queen of Ireland,* about the struggle for equality that climaxes in the historic marriage referendum of May 2015. The bar has since become a place of LGBTQ pilgrimage – and no-holds-barred enjoyment. Its own brew, Panti's Pale Ale, is a gorgeous beer.

Street 66 (Map p88; www.street66.bar; 33 Parliament St; ⊘12.30pm-midnight Mon-Thu, to 2.30am Fri & Sat, noon-midnight Sun; ▣ all city centre) In late 2016 this place replaced the very popular LGBT Front Lounge and promised to be all things to all people: a dog-friendly coffee shop and bar dressed in upcycled chic that is LGBTQ-friendly. The front is the Dive Bar, the back the Disco Lounge. Better than most Temple Bar joints.

George (Map p88; www.thegeorge.ie; 89 S Great George's St; weekends after 10pm €5-10, other times free; ⊘2pm-2.30am Mon-Fri, from 12.30pm Sat, 12.30pm-1am Sun; ▣ all city centre) The purple mother of Dublin's gay bars is a long-standing institution, having lived through the years when it was the only place in town where the gay crowd could, well, be gay. Shirley's legendary Sunday-night bingo is as popular as ever, while Wednesday's Space N Veda is a terrific night of cabaret and drag.

Mother (Map p88; www.motherclub.ie; Copper Alley, Exchange St; €10; ⊘11pm-3.30am Sat; ▣ all city centre) The best club night in the city is ostensibly a gay night, but it does not discriminate: clubbers of every sexual orientation come for the sensational DJs – mostly local but occasionally brought in from abroad – who throw down a mixed bag of disco, modern synth-pop and other danceable styles.

🍺 Docklands

★ **John Mulligan's**　　　　PUB
(www.mulligans.ie; 8 Poolbeg St; ⊘noon-11.30pm Mon-Thu, 11am-12.30am Fri, 11.30am-12.30am Sat, 12.30-11pm Sun; ▣ all city centre) This brilliant old boozer is a cultural institution, established in 1782 and in this location since 1854. A drink (or more) here is like attending liquid services at a most sacred, secular shrine. John

F Kennedy paid his respects in 1945, when he joined the cast of regulars that seems barely to have changed since.

Southside

Taphouse
BAR

(Map p84; ☑ 01-491 3436; www.taphouse.ie; 60 Ranelagh Rd; ⊘ 12.30pm-11.30am Mon-Thu, to 12.30am Fri & Sat, to 11pm Sun; ⛴ Ranelagh) Locals refer to it by its original name of Russell's, but that doesn't mean that the regulars aren't delighted with the new owners' sprucing up of a village favourite. What they didn't change was the beloved balcony – the best spot to have a drink on a warm day.

Beggar's Bush
PUB

(Jack Ryan's; Map p106; www.beggarsbush.com; 115 Haddington Rd; ⊘ 10.30am-11pm Mon-Thu, to 12.30am Fri & Sat, 12.30-11pm Sun; ⛴ 4, 7, 8, 120 from city centre, ⛴ Grand Canal Dock) A staunch defender of the traditional pub aesthetic, Ryan's (as it's referred to by its older clientele) has adjusted to the modern age by adding an outside patio for good weather. Everything else has remained the same, which is precisely why it's so popular with flat-capped pensioners and employees from nearby Google.

☆ Entertainment

Believe it or not, there is life beyond the pub. There are comedy clubs and classical concerts, recitals and readings, marionettes and music – lots of music. The other great Dublin treat is the theatre, where you can enjoy a light-hearted musical alongside the more serious stuff by Beckett, Yeats and O'Casey – not to mention a host of new talents.

Theatre, comedy and classical concerts are usually booked directly through the venue. Otherwise you can buy through booking agencies such as **Ticketmaster** (Map p88; ☑ 0818 719 300; www.ticketmaster.ie; St Stephen's Green Shopping Centre; ⛴ all city centre, ⛴ St Stephen's Green), which sells tickets to every genre of big- and medium-sized show – but be aware that it levies a 12.5% service charge.

Live Music

★ Devitt's
LIVE MUSIC

(Map p92; ☑ 01-475 3414; www.devittspub.ie; 78 Lower Camden St; ⊘ from 9pm Mon & Tue, 9.30pm Wed & Thu, 7.45pm Fri & Sat, 6.30pm Sun; ⛴ 14, 15, 65, 83) Devitt's – aka the Cusack Stand – is one of the favourite places for the city's talented musicians to display their wares, with sessions

as good as any you'll hear in the city centre. Highly recommended.

★ Whelan's
LIVE MUSIC

(Map p92; ☑ 01-478 0766; www.whelanslive.com; 25 Wexford St; ⛴ 16, 122 from city centre) Perhaps the city's most beloved live-music venue is this midsized room attached to a traditional bar. This is the singer-songwriter's spiritual home: when they're done pouring out the contents of their hearts on stage, you can find them filling up in the bar along with their fans.

O'Donoghue's
TRADITIONAL MUSIC

(Map p92; ☑ 01-660 7194; www.odonoghues.ie; 15 Merrion Row; ⊘ from 7pm; ⛴ all city centre) There's traditional music nightly in the old bar of this famous boozer. Regular performers include local names such as Tom Foley, Joe McHugh, Joe Foley and Maria O'Connell.

Workman's Club
LIVE MUSIC

(Map p88; ☑ 01-670 6692; www.theworkmansclub. com; 10 Wellington Quay; free-€20; ⊘ 5pm-3am; ⛴ all city centre) A 300-capacity venue and bar in the former working-men's club of Dublin. The emphasis is on keeping away from the mainstream, which means everything from singer-songwriters to electronic cabaret. When the live music at the Workman's Club is over, DJs take to the stage, playing rockabilly, hip-hop, indie, house and more.

Bowery
LIVE MUSIC

(Map p84; www.facebook.com/thebowerydublin; 196 Lower Rathmines Rd; ⊘ 4-11.30pm Mon-Thu, to 12.30am Fri & Sat, to 11pm Sun; ⛴ 14, 65, 140 from city centre) With its burnished wood, intricate chandeliers and ship-shaped stage, this music venue is one of the best-looking bars in the city. It features live performances every night of the week, from ska to disco to reggae, and upstairs is an excellent people-watching spot.

Academy
LIVE MUSIC

(Map p100; ☑ 01-877 9999; www.theacademydublin. com; 57 Middle Abbey St; ⛴ all city centre, ⛴ Abbey) A terrific midsize venue, the Academy's stage has been graced by an impressive list of performers on the way up – and down – the ladder of success, from Ron Sexsmith to the Wedding Present.

3 Arena
LIVE MUSIC

(Map p106; ☑ 01-819 8888; www.3arena.ie; East Link Bridge, North Wall Quay; tickets €30-100; ⊘ 6.30-11pm; ⛴ The Point) The premier indoor venue in the city has a capacity of 23,000 and plays host to the brightest touring stars in the

LIVE MUSIC IN DUBLIN

Dubliners love their live music and are as enthusiastic about supporting local acts as they are about cheering touring international stars – even if the latter command the bigger crowds and ticket prices. You can sometimes buy tickets at the venue itself, but you're probably better off going through an agent. Prices for gigs range dramatically, from as low as €5 for a tiny local act to anywhere up to €90 for the really big international stars. The listings sections of both paper and online resources will have all the gigs.

Traditional & Folk Music

The best place to hear traditional music is in the pub, where the 'session' – improvised or scheduled – is still best attended by foreign visitors who appreciate the form far more than most Dubs and will relish any opportunity to drink and toe-tap to some extraordinary virtuoso performances.

Also worth checking out is the Temple Bar Trad Festival (p113), which takes place in the pubs of Temple Bar over the last weekend in January. For online info on sessions, check out www.dublinsessions.ie.

firmament. Drake, Boyzone and Steely Dan performed here in 2019.

Classical Music

National Concert Hall LIVE MUSIC
(Map p92; ☑ 01-417 0000; www.nch.ie; Earlsfort Tce; ☒ all city centre) Ireland's premier orchestral hall hosts a variety of concerts yearround, with an increasingly diverse roster of performances including author interviews and spoken-word events.

Bord Gáis Energy Theatre THEATRE
(Map p106; ☑ 01-677 7999; www.bordgaisenergy theatre.ie; Grand Canal Sq; ☒ Grand Canal Dock) Forget the uninviting sponsored name: Daniel Libeskind's masterful design is a three-tiered, 2100-capacity auditorium where you're as likely to be entertained by the Bolshoi or a touring state opera as you are to see *Dirty Dancing* or Barbra Streisand. It's a magnificent venue – designed for classical, paid for by the classics.

Theatre

Smock Alley Theatre THEATRE
(Map p88; ☑ 01-677 0014; www.smockalley.com; 6-7 Exchange St; ☒ all city centre) One of the city's most diverse theatres is hidden in this beautifully restored 17th-century building. It boasts a broad program of events (expect anything from opera to murder mystery nights, puppet shows and Shakespeare) and many events also come with a dinner option.

The theatre was built in 1622 and was the only Theatre Royal ever built outside London. It was reinvented as a warehouse and a Catholic church, and was lovingly restored in 2012 to become a creative hub once again.

Abbey Theatre THEATRE
(Map p100; ☑ 01-878 7222; www.abbeytheatre.ie; Lower Abbey St; ☒ all city centre, ☒ Abbey) Ireland's national theatre was founded by WB Yeats in 1904 and was a central player in the development of a consciously native cultural identity. Expect to see a mix of homegrown theatre from Irish playwrights, as well as touring performances from around the world.

Project Arts Centre THEATRE
(Map p88; ☑ 01-881 9613; www.projectartscentre.ie; 39 Essex St E; ☺ 45min before showtime; ☒ all city centre) The city's most interesting venue for challenging new work – drama, dance, live art or film. Three separate spaces allow for maximum versatility. You never know what to expect, which makes it all that more fun: we've seen some awful rubbish here, but we've also seen some of the best shows in town.

Vaults Live THEATRE
(Map p84; ☑ 01 541 1485; www.vaults.live; W John's Lane; adult/child from €25/17; ☺ 11am-5pm Wed-Sun; ☒ 13, 40, 123 from city centre) An immersive theatre performance in an old schoolhouse that takes you through six scenes from the darker side of Dublin history with incredibly detailed sets and impressive performances. The thrills and fun (go in a group if you can) will allow you to overlook the historical inaccuracies of the hour-long show.

Olympia Theatre THEATRE
(Map p88; ☑ 0818 719 330; www.olympia.ie; 72 Dame St; tickets €22.50-60; ☺ shows from 7pm; ☒ all city centre) This Victorian-era theatre specialises in light plays and, at Christmastime, pantomimes. It also hosts some terrific live gigs.

Gate Theatre
THEATRE

(Map p100; ☑ 01-874 4045; www.gatetheatre.
ie; 1 Cavendish Row; ☺ performances 7.30pm Tue-
Fri, 2.30pm & 7.30pm Sat; ☐ all city centre) The
city's most elegant theatre, housed in a late
18th-century building, features a repertory of
classic Irish, American and European plays.
Orson Welles and James Mason played here
early in their careers. Even today it is the only
theatre in town where you might see established international movie stars work on their
credibility with a theatre run.

Samuel Beckett Theatre
THEATRE

(Map p82; ☑ 01-896 2461; www.tcd.ie/beckett-
theatre; Regent House, Pearse St; ☐ all city centre)
The Trinity College Players' Theatre hosts
student productions throughout the academic year, as well as the most prestigious plays
from the Dublin Theatre Festival (p113).

Gaiety Theatre
THEATRE

(Map p88; ☑ 0818 719 388; www.gaietytheatre.
com; S King St; ☺ 7-10pm; ☐ all city centre) The
'Grand Old Lady of South King St' is more
than 150 years old and has for much of that
time thrived on a diet of fun-for-all-the-fam-
ily fare: West End hits, musicals, Christmas
pantos and classic Irish plays keep the more
serious-minded away, leaving more room for
those simply looking to be entertained.

Comedy

Chaplins Comedy Club
COMEDY

(www.chaplinscomedy.com; Chaplin's Bar, 2
Hawkins St; €10; ☺ 8-11pm Sat & select other days;
☐ all city centre) A regularly changing line-up
of up-and-coming and local talent look for
laughs at this all-seater club; failing that,
there's always pizza and craft beer to guarantee a decent night out. Shows start at
9pm.

Laughter Lounge
COMEDY

(Map p100; ☑ 01-878 3003; www.laughterlounge.
com; 4-8 Eden Quay; from €26; ☺ doors open 7pm;
☐ all city centre) Dublin's only specially designated comedy theatre is where you'll find
those comics too famous for the smaller pub
stages but not famous enough to sell out the
city's bigger venues. Think comedians on the
way up (or on the way down).

Ha'Penny Bridge Inn
COMEDY

(Map p88; ☑ 01-677 2515; www.hapennybridgeinn.
com; 42 Wellington Quay; €6; ☺ 10.30am-12.30am;
☐ all city centre) A traditional old bar that
features local comics on the rise upstairs at

the Unhinged Comedy Club on Sundays and
Wednesdays, and Irish music downstairs.

Cinema

★ Stella Theatre
CINEMA

(☑ 01-496 7014; www.stellatheatre.ie; 207-209
Lower Rathmines Rd; tickets from €19; ☺ 5pm-late
Mon-Fri, from 9am Sat & Sun; ☐ 14, 15, 140 from city
centre) A cinema night may not always be a
glamorous event, but at the Stella Theatre it
is. A narrow entrance opens up to sumptuous
art deco glory with comfortable leather seats
paired with tables and footstools. Leave extra time to order food that will be delivered
during the film or book ahead to go to the
cocktail club upstairs.

★ Light House Cinema
CINEMA

(Map p100; ☑ 01-872 8006; www.lighthousecinema.
ie; Smithfield Plaza; ☐ all city centre, ☐ Smithfield)
The most impressive cinema in town is this
snazzy four-screener in a stylish building just
off Smithfield Plaza. The menu offers a mix
of art-house and mainstream releases, docu-
mentaries and Irish films.

Irish Film Institute
CINEMA

(IFI; Map p88; ☑ 01-679 5744; www.ifi.ie; 6 Eustace
St; ☺ 11am-11pm; ☐ all city centre) The IFI has a
couple of screens and shows classics and new
art-house films. The complex also has a bar, a
cafe and a bookshop.

Savoy
CINEMA

(Map p88; ☑ 01-874 8822; www.imccinemas.ie; Upper O'Connell St; ☺ from 2pm; ☐ all city centre) The
Savoy is a five-screen, first-run cinema, and
has late-night shows at weekends. Savoy Cinema 1 is the largest in the city and its enormous
screen is the perfect way to view spectacular
blockbuster movies.

Sport

Croke Park
SPECTATOR SPORT

(☑ 01-819 2300; www.crokepark.ie; Clonliffe Rd;
☐ 3, 11, 11A, 16, 16A, 123 from O'Connell St) Hurling
and Gaelic football games are held from February to November at Europe's fourth-largest
stadium (capacity around 82,000), north of
the Royal Canal in Drumcondra; see www.
gaa.ie for schedules.

The stadium is also the administrative
HQ of the Gaelic Athletic Association (GAA),
the body that governs them. To get an idea of
just how important the GAA is here, a visit
to the museum (p109) is a must, though it
will help if you're a sporting enthusiast. The
twice-daily tours (except match days) of the
impressive stadium are excellent.

Aviva Stadium
STADIUM

(Map p106; ☎ 01-238 2300; www.avivastadium.ie; 11-12 Lansdowne Rd; ☒ Lansdowne Rd) Gleaming 50,000-capacity ground with an eye-catching curvilinear stand in the swanky neighbourhood of Donnybrook. Home to Irish rugby and football internationals.

Donnybrook Stadium
STADIUM

(www.leinsterrugby.ie; Donnybrook Rd; ☒10, 46A from city centre) This purpose-built 6000-capacity arena is shared by a bunch of rugby teams, including the Ireland Wolfhounds (the junior national side), the Ireland Women's Team, Leinster 'A' and local club sides Old Wesley and Bective Rangers. Tickets are easily available for virtually all games.

Parnell Park
SPECTATOR SPORT

(www.dublingaa.ie; Clantarkey Rd, Donnycarney; adult/child €15/5; ☒20A, 20B, 27, 27A, 42, 42B, 43, 103 from Lower Abbey St or Beresford Pl) The Dublin Gaelic team plays its league matches at Parnell Park.

Royal Dublin Society Showground
SPECTATOR SPORT

(RDS Showground; Map p92; ☎ 01-668 9878; www.rds.ie; Merrion Rd, Ballsbridge; ☒7 from Trinity College) This impressive, Victorian-era showground is used for various exhibitions throughout the year. The most important annual event here is the late-July **Dublin Horse Show**, which includes an international show-jumping contest. Leinster rugby also plays its home matches in the 35,000-capacity arena. Ask at the tourist office for other events.

The Royal Dublin Society Showground was founded in 1731 and has had its headquarters in a number of well-known Dublin buildings, including Leinster House from 1814 to 1925. The society was involved in the foundation of the National Museum, the National Library, the National Gallery and the National Botanic Gardens.

🛍 Shopping

If it's made in Ireland – or pretty much anywhere else – you can find it in Dublin. Grafton St is home to a range of largely British-owned high-street chain stores; you'll find the best local boutiques in the surrounding streets. On the northside, pedestrianised Henry St has international chain stores, as well as Dublin's best department store, Arnott's.

Traditional Irish products such as crystal and knitwear remain popular choices, and you can increasingly find innovative modern takes on the classics. But steer clear of the mass-produced junk whose joke value isn't worth the hassle of carting it home on the plane: trust us, there's no such thing as a genuine *shillelagh* (Irish fighting stick) for sale anywhere in town.

Non-EU residents are entitled to claim VAT (value-added tax) on goods (except books, children's clothing or educational items) purchased in stores operating the Cashback or Taxback return program. Fill in a voucher at your last point of exit from the EU to arrange refund of duty paid.

Most shops open from 9.30am to 6pm Monday to Saturday, with later hours – usually to 8pm – on Thursday. Many also open on Sunday, usually from noon to 6pm.

DUBLIN THEATRE TODAY

Despite Dublin's rich theatrical heritage, times are tough for the city's thespians. Once upon a time, everybody went to the theatre to see the latest offering by Synge, Yeats or O'Casey. Nowadays a night at the theatre is the preserve of the passionate few, which has resulted in the city's bigger theatres taking a conservative approach to their programming and many fringe companies having to make do with non-theatrical spaces to showcase their skills.

The theatre scene in Dublin is rarely without controversy – in 2019, more than 300 members of the theatre community signed a letter to the Minister for Culture, condemning the way in which the Abbey Theatre has been run since the appointment of new directors in 2016. Concerns were raised about the decrease in Irish-based actors employed by what is the national theatre, founded with the intent of supporting homegrown talent. As a result, it's likely future seasons will focus more on Irish productions, many of which more than hold their own on the world stage.

Theatre bookings can usually be made by quoting a credit-card number over the phone, then you can collect your tickets just before the performance. Expect to pay anything between €12 and €25 for most shows, with some costing as much as €30. Most plays begin between 8pm and 8.30pm. Check www.irishtheatreonline.com to see what's playing.

🄰 Grafton Street & St Stephen's Green

★ Irish Design Shop
ARTS & CRAFTS

(Map p88; ☑ 01-679 8871; www.irishdesignshop.com; 41 Drury St; ⊙ 10am-6pm Mon-Sat, 1-5pm Sun; ▣ all city centre) Beautiful, imaginatively crafted items – from jewellery to kitchenware – curated by owners Clare Grennan and Laura Caffrey. If you're looking for a stylish Irish-made memento or gift, you'll surely find it here.

★ Avoca Handweavers
ARTS & CRAFTS

(Map p88; ☑ 01-677 4215; www.avoca.ie; 11-13 Suffolk St; ⊙ 9.30am-6pm Mon-Wed & Sat, to 7pm Thu & Fri, 11am-6pm Sun; ▣ all city centre) Combining clothing, homewares, a basement food hall and an excellent top-floor cafe (p124), Avoca promotes a stylish but homey brand of modern Irish life – and is one of the best places to find an original present. Many of the garments are woven, knitted and naturally dyed at its Wicklow factory. There's a terrific kids' section.

★ Sheridan's Cheesemongers
FOOD

(Map p88; ☑ 01-679 3143; www.sheridanscheesemongers.com; 11 S Anne St; ⊙ 10am-6pm Mon-Fri, from 9.30am Sat; ▣ all city centre) If heaven were a cheese shop, this would be it. Wooden shelves are laden with farmhouse cheeses, sourced from around the country by Kevin and Seamus Sheridan, who have almost single-handedly revived cheese-making in Ireland.

★ Chupi
JEWELLERY

(Map p88; ☑ 01-551 0352; www.chupi.com; Powerscourt Townhouse, S William St; ⊙ 10am-6pm Mon-Wed, Fri & Sat, to 7pm Thu, noon-5pm Sun; ▣ all city centre) Exceptional modern jewellery inspired by the Irish landscape and worn by all the city's style fiends. The pretty shop also stocks Irish-designed clothing and accessories.

ⓘ ONLINE LISTINGS

Entertainment.ie (www.entertainment.ie) For all events.

MCD (www.mcd.ie) Biggest promoter in Ireland.

Nialler9 (www.nialler9.com) Excellent indie blog with listings.

Totally Dublin (www.totallydublin.ie) Comprehensive listings and reviews.

What's On In (www.whatsonin.ie) From markets to gigs and club nights.

Powerscourt Townhouse
SHOPPING CENTRE

(Map p88; ☑ 01-679 4144; www.powerscourtcentre.ie; 59 S William St; ⊙ 10am-6pm Mon-Wed & Fri, to 8pm Thu, 9am-6pm Sat, noon-6pm Sun; ▣ all city centre) This absolutely gorgeous and stylish centre is in a carefully refurbished Georgian townhouse, built between 1741 and 1744. These days it's best known for its cafes and restaurants but it also does a top-end, selective trade in high fashion, art, exquisite handicrafts and other chi-chi sundries.

Kilkenny Shop
ARTS & CRAFTS

(Map p92; ☑ 01-677 7066; www.kilkennyshop.com; 6 Nassau St; ⊙ 8.30am-7pm Mon-Wed, Fri & Sat, to 8pm Thu, 10am-6.30pm Sun; ▣ all city centre) A large, long-running repository for contemporary, innovative Irish crafts, including multi-coloured modern Irish knits, designer clothing and lovely silver jewellery. The glassware and pottery is beautiful and sourced from workshops around the country. A great source for traditional presents.

Design Centre
CLOTHING

(Map p88; ☑ 01-679 5718; www.designcentre.ie; Powerscourt Townhouse, S William St; ⊙ 10am-6pm Mon-Wed, Fri & Sat, to 8pm Thu; ▣ all city centre) Mostly dedicated to Irish designer womenswear, featuring well-made classic suits, evening wear and knitwear. Irish labels include Jill De Burca, Philip Treacy, Aoife Harrison and Erickson Beamon – a favourite with Michelle Obama.

Om Diva
VINTAGE

(Map p88; ☑ 01-679 1211; www.omdivaboutique.com; 27 Drury St; ⊙ 10am-6.30pm Mon-Wed, Fri & Sat, to 7.30pm Thu, noon-6pm Sun; ▣ all city centre) There are three floors of funky fashion in this cosy spot on Drury St – well-curated vintage in the basement, cutting-edge Irish design upstairs and contemporary style when you walk in. A one-stop shop for cool Dublin style.

Barry Doyle Design Jewellers
JEWELLERY

(Map p88; ☑ 01-671 2838; www.barrydoyledesign.com; 30 George's St Arcade; ⊙ 10am-6pm Mon-Sat; ▣ all city centre) Goldsmith Barry Doyle's upstairs shop is one of the best of its kind in Dublin. The handmade jewellery – using white gold, silver, and some truly gorgeous precious and semiprecious stones – is exceptional in its beauty and simplicity. Most of the pieces have Afro-Celtic influences.

Ulysses Rare Books
BOOKS

(Map p88; ☑ 01-671 8676; www.rarebooks.ie; 10 Duke St; ⊙ 9.30am-5.45pm Mon-Sat; ▣ all city centre) Our favourite bookshop in the city stocks

MARKETS

In recent years Dublin has gone gaga for markets, but the fluctuating rental crisis has seen many of them pushed from location to location, which means it can be hard to keep track of what's happening where. The best now happen in static businesses, such as at **Lucky's** (Map p84; 01-556 2397; www.luckys.ie; 78 Meath St; 11.30am-midnight Mon-Thu, to 1am Fri, 1pm-1am Sat, 1-11.30pm Sun; 13, 40, 123 from city centre) or the George (p133).

George's Street Arcade (Map p88; www.georgesstreetarcade.ie; btwn S Great George's & Drury Sts; 9am-6.30pm Mon-Wed, to 7pm Thu-Sat, noon-6pm Sun; all city centre) Dublin's best non-food market is sheltered within an elegant Victorian Gothic arcade. Apart from shops and stalls selling new and old clothes, secondhand books, hats, posters, jewellery and records, there's a fortune teller, some gourmet nibbles, and a fish and chipper that does a roaring trade.

Cow's Lane Designer Mart (Map p88; 10am-5pm Sat Jun-Sep; all city centre) A real market for hipsters, on the steps of Cow's Lane, this market brings together over 60 of the best clothing, accessory and craft stalls in town. Buy cutting-edge designer duds from the likes of Drunk Monk, punky T-shirts, retro handbags, costume jewellery by Kink Bijoux and even clubby babywear. It's open from June to September; the rest of the year it moves indoors to **St Michael's and St John's Banquet Hall** (Map p88; 10am-5pm Oct-May; all city centre), just around the corner.

Temple Bar Book Market (Map p88; Temple Bar Sq; 11am-5pm Sat & Sun; all city centre) Bad secondhand potboilers, sci-fi, picture books and other assorted titles invite you to rummage about on weekend afternoons. If you look hard enough, you're bound to find something worthwhile.

a rich and remarkable collection of Irish-interest books, with a particular emphasis on 20th-century literature and a large selection of first editions, including rare ones by the big guns: Joyce, Yeats, Beckett and Wilde.

Weir & Son's JEWELLERY
(Map p88; 01-677 9678; www.weirandsons.ie; 96-99 Grafton St; 9.30am-6pm Mon-Wed, Fri & Sat, to 8pm Thu; all city centre) The largest jeweller in Ireland, this huge shop on Grafton St first opened in 1869 and still has its original wooden cabinets and a workshop on the premises. There's new and antique Irish jewellery and a huge selection of watches, Irish crystal, porcelain, leather and travel goods.

Louis Copeland CLOTHING
(Map p88; 01-872 1600; www.louiscopeland.com; 18-19 Wicklow St; 9am-6pm Mon-Wed, Fri & Sat, to 8pm Thu, noon-5pm Sun; all city centre) Dublin's answer to the famed tailors of London's Savile Row, this shop makes fabulous suits to measure, and stocks plenty of ready-to-wear suits by international designers. There's another outlet on Capel St (Map p100; Jervis).

Temple Bar

★**Gutter Bookshop** BOOKS
(Map p88; 01-679 9206; www.gutterbookshop.com; Cow's Lane; 10am-6.30pm Mon-Wed, Fri &

Sat, to 7pm Thu, 11am-6pm Sun; all city centre) Taking its name from Oscar Wilde's famous line from *Lady Windermere's Fan* – 'We are all in the gutter, but some of us are looking at the stars' – this fabulous place is flying the flag for the downtrodden independent bookshop, stocking a mix of new novels, children's books, travel literature and other assorted titles.

★**Claddagh Records** MUSIC
(Map p88; 01-677 0262; www.claddaghrecords.com; 2 Cecilia St; 10am-6pm Mon-Sat, from noon Sun; all city centre) An excellent collection of good-quality traditional and folk music is the mainstay at this record shop. The profoundly knowledgable staff should be able to locate even the most elusive recording for you. There's also a decent selection of world music. There's another branch (01-888 3600) at 5 Westmoreland St; you can also shop online.

North of the Liffey

Winding Stair BOOKS
(Map p100; 01-872 6576; www.winding-stair.com; 40 Lower Ormond Quay; 10am-6pm Mon & Fri, to 7pm Tue-Thu & Sat, noon-6pm Sun; all city centre) This handsome old bookshop is in a ground-floor room when once upon a time it occupied the whole building, which is now given over to an excellent restaurant (p127) of the

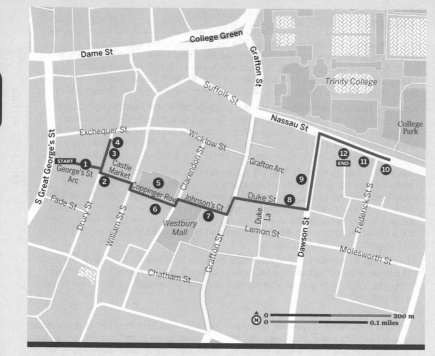

City Walk
A Retail Stroll

START GEORGE'S STREET ARCADE
END KNOBS & KNOCKERS
LENGTH 1.1KM; TWO HOURS

Start your retail adventure in the ❶ **George's Street Arcade** (p139), with its range of stalls selling all kinds of alternative wares.

Exit at the Drury St side and cross onto Castle Market, stopping to browse the high-end women's fashions in ❷ **Costume** (Map p88; ☑ 01-679 5200; www.costumedublin.ie; ⊙10am-6pm Mon-Wed, Fri & Sat, to 7pm Thu, 2-5pm Sun) or go north on Drury St to the homewares and handicrafts in ❸ **Industry** (Map p88; ☑ 01-613 9111; www.industryandco.com; ⊙8am-6pm Mon-Wed, to 7pm Thu, to 6.30pm Fri, 9am-6.30pm Sat, 10am-6pm Sun) or the excellent ❹ **Irish Design Shop** (p138).

From Castle Market, cross S William St and enter the ❺ **Powerscourt Townhouse Shopping Centre** (p138), an elegant retail space.

Exit the centre on S William St and walk south, taking the first left onto Coppinger Row. The eponymous ❻ **restaurant** (☑ 01-672 9884; www.coppingerrow.com; mains €21-29; ⊙noon-11pm) is a great spot for refuelling.

Continue east and cross Clarendon St. On Johnson's Ct, the southern side is lined with jewellery shops, including ❼ **Appleby** (☑ 01-679 9572; www.appleby.ie; ⊙9.45am-6pm Mon-Wed, Fri & Sat, to 6.30pm Thu).

Take a left on Grafton St and turn right onto Duke St: on your left is ❽ **Ulysses Rare Books** (p138), the city's most illustrious seller of rare books. The biggest bookshop in town is ❾ **Hodges Figgis** (☑ 01-677 4754; www.waterstones.com; ⊙9am-7pm Mon-Wed & Fri, to 8pm Thu, to 6pm Sat, noon-6pm Sun), around the corner on Dawson St.

From here walk down to Nassau St and take a right to ❿ **Kilkenny Shop** (p138), which has all kinds of locally produced handicrafts, knits, glassware and silverware.

If you still need to pick up some typically Irish gifts, retrace back along Nassau St, stopping at ⓫ **House of Names** (☑ 01-679 7287; www.houseofnames.ie; ⊙10am-6pm Mon-Wed, Fri & Sat, to 8pm Thu, 11am-6pm Sun), where you can get coasters with your family's coat of arms, and ⓬ **Knobs & Knockers** (☑ 01-671 0288; www.knobsandknockers.ie; ⊙9.30am-5.30pm Mon-Sat), for a replica Georgian door handle.

same name. Smaller selection, but still some excellent quality new- and old-book perusals.

Arnott's
DEPARTMENT STORE

(Map p100; ☑ 01-805 0400; www.arnotts.ie; 12 Henry St; ☺ 9.30am-7pm Mon-Wed, to 9pm Thu, to 8pm Fri, 9am-7pm Sat, 11am-7pm Sun; ☒ all city centre) Occupying a huge block with entrances on Henry, Liffey and Abbey Sts, this is our favourite of Dublin's department stores. It stocks virtually everything, from garden furniture to high fashion, and it's all relatively affordable.

ⓘ Information

DANGERS & ANNOYANCES

Dublin is a safe city by any standards, except maybe those set by the Swiss. Basically, act as you would at home.

➔ Don't leave anything visible in your car when you park.

➔ Skimming at ATMs is an ongoing problem; be sure to cover the keypad with your hand when you input your PIN.

➔ Take care around the western edge of Thomas St (onto James St), where drug addicts are often present.

➔ The northern end of Gardiner St and the areas northeast of there have crime-related problems.

EMERGENCY

Garda Station (☑ 01-676 3481; Harcourt Tce; ☺24hr; ☒ Harcourt) Largest police station in southside city centre.

Rape Crisis Centre (☑ 24hr 1800 778 888; www.drcc.ie; 70 Lower Leeson St; ☺8am-7pm Mon-Fri, 9am-4pm Sat; ☒ all city centre) In the unlikely event of a sexual assault, get in touch with the police and the Rape Crisis Centre.

Crime Victims Helpline (☑116006; 24hr) The gardaí's network of liaison services for victims of racial abuse or attacks as well as victims of homophobic attacks.

Domestic Violence & Sexual Assault Investigation Unit (p133) In the event of any kind of sexually related crime, call, or visit any garda station.

INTERNET ACCESS

Wi-fi and 3G/4G networks are making internet cafes largely redundant (except to gamers); the few that are left will charge around €6 per hour. Most accommodation has wi-fi service, either free or for a daily charge (up to €10 per day).

MEDICAL SERVICES

Should you experience an immediate health problem, contact the A&E (accident and emergency) department of the nearest public hospital; in an emergency, call an ambulance (☑ 999). There are no 24-hour pharmacies in Dublin; the latest any stay open is 10pm.

Caredoc (☑1850 334 999; www.caredoc.ie; ☺6pm-8am Mon-Fri, 24hr Sat & Sun) Doctors on call; available only outside of regular surgery hours.

City Pharmacy (☑01-670 4523; 14 Dame St; ☺9am-10pm; ☒ all city centre) Late-night pharmacy.

Dental Hospital (☑01-612 7200; 20 Lincoln Pl; ☺9am-5pm Mon-Fri; ☒7, 44) If you don't have an appointment, head in after noon.

Grafton Medical Centre (☑01-671 2122; www.graftonmedical.ie; 34 Grafton St; ☺8.30am-6pm Mon-Thu, to 5pm Fri; ☒ all city centre) One-stop shop with male and female doctors as well as physiotherapists. You'll usually need to give a day's advance notice, but same-day appointments are often available.

Health Service Executive (HSE; ☑01-679 0700, 1800 520 520; www.hse.ie; Dr Steevens' Hospital, Steevens' Lane; ☺9.30am-5.30pm Mon-Fri; ☒25A, 25B, 26, 66 from city centre) Central health authority with Choice of Doctor Scheme, which can advise you on a suitable GP from 9am to 5pm Monday to Friday. Also has information services for those with physical and mental disabilities.

Hickey's Pharmacy (☑01-679 0467; 21 Grafton St; ☺8am-8pm Mon-Wed & Fri, to 8.30pm Thu, 9am-8pm Sat, 10am-7pm Sun; ☒ all city centre) Well-stocked pharmacy on Grafton St.

Mater Misericordiae Hospital (☑01-830 1122; www.mater.ie; Eccles St; ☒120, 122 from city centre) Northside city centre, off Lower Dorset St.

St James's Hospital (☑01-410 3000; www.stjames.ie; James's St; ☒ James's) Dublin's main 24-hour accident and emergency department.

MONEY

The best exchange rates are at banks, although bureaux de change and other exchange facilities usually open for longer hours. There's a cluster of banks located around College Green opposite Trinity College and all have exchange facilities.

POST

The Irish postal service, An Post, is reliable, efficient and generally on time. Postboxes in Dublin are usually green and have two slots: one for 'Dublin only', the other for 'All Other Places'. There are a couple of post offices in the city centre, including **An Post** (Map p88; ☑ 01-705 8206; www.anpost.ie; St Andrew's St; ☺8.30am-5pm Mon-Fri; ☒ all city centre) and the General Post Office (p103).

TOURIST INFORMATION

A handful of official-looking tourism offices on Grafton and O'Connell Sts are actually privately run enterprises for paying members.

Visit Dublin Centre (Map p88; www.visitdublin.com; 25 Suffolk St; ☺9am-5.30pm Mon-Sat, 10.30am-3pm Sun; ☒ all city centre) The main

GUARANTEED IRISH ARTS & CRAFTS

Avoca Handweavers (p138) Our favourite department store in the city has myriad homemade gift ideas.

Irish Design Shop (p138) Wonderful handicrafts carefully sourced.

Barry Doyle Design Jewellers (p138) Exquisite handcrafted jewellery with unique contemporary designs.

Ulysses Rare Books (p138) For that priceless first edition or a beautiful, leather-bound copy of Joyce's *Dubliners*.

Louis Copeland (p139) Dublin's very own top tailor, with made-to-measure suits.

tourist information centre, with free maps, guides and itinerary planning, plus booking services for accommodation, attractions and events.

Dublin Discover Ireland Centre (Map p100; www.discoverireland.ie; 14 Upper O'Connell St; ⏱9am-5pm Mon-Sat; 🚆 all city centre) Failte Ireland's walk-in information centre for Dublin.

USEFUL WEBSITES

All the Food (www.allthefood.ie) Up-to-date restaurant reviews for Dublin.

Dublin Tourism (www.visitdublin.com) Official website of Dublin Tourism.

Dublintown (www.dublintown.ie) Comprehensive list of events and goings-on.

Failte Ireland (www.discoverireland.ie) Official tourist-board website.

Lonely Planet (www.lonelyplanet.com/ireland/dublin) Destination information, hotel bookings, traveller forum and more.

Old Dublin Town (www.olddublintown.com) Haphazard-looking website that's an excellent info resource for this city in flux.

ℹ Getting There & Away

AIR

Dublin Airport (☎01-814 1111; www.dublin airport.com) is 13km north of the city centre and has two terminals: most international flights (including most US flights) use Terminal 2; Ryanair and select others use Terminal 1. Both terminals have the usual selection of pubs, restaurants, shops, ATMs and car-hire desks.

BOAT

The **Dublin Port Terminal** (☎01-855 2222; Alexandra Rd; 🚌 53 from Talbot St) is 3km northeast of the city centre.

An express bus transfer to and from Dublin Port is operated by **Morton's Bus** (Map p88; www.mortonscoaches.ie; adult/child €3.50/2; ⏱7.15am, 12.30pm, 2pm & 7pm), leaving from Westmoreland St and timed to coincide with ferry departures. Otherwise, regular bus 53 serves the port from Talbot St. Inbound ferries are met by timed bus services that run to the city centre.

BUS

Dublin's central bus station, **Busáras** (Map p100; ☎01-836 6111; www.buseireann.ie; Store St; 🚆 Connolly) is just north of the River Liffey, behind the Custom House. It has different-sized luggage lockers costing from €6 to €10 per day.

It's possible to combine bus and ferry tickets from major UK centres to Dublin on the bus network. The journey between London and Dublin takes about 12 hours and costs from €32 return (but note it's €47 one way). For more London details, contact **Eurolines** (☎01-836 6111; https://eurolines.buseireann.ie).

From here, **Bus Éireann** (☎1850 836 6111; www.buseireann.ie) serves the whole national network, including buses to towns and cities in Northern Ireland.

CAR & MOTORCYCLE

Road access to and from Dublin is pretty straightforward. A network of motorways radiates outward from the M50 ring road that surrounds Dublin, serving the following towns and cities:

M1 North to Drogheda, Dundalk and Belfast.

M3 Northwest to Navan, Cavan and Donegal.

M4 West to Galway and Sligo.

M7 Southwest to Limerick; also (via M8) to Cork.

M9 Southeast to Kilkenny and Waterford.

M11 Southeast to Wexford.

TRAIN

All trains in the Republic are run by **Irish Rail** (Iarnród Éireann; ☎01-836 6222; www.irishrail. ie). Dublin has two main train stations: **Heuston Station** (☎01-836 6222; 🚆 Heuston), on the western side of town near the Liffey; and **Connolly Station** (☎01-703 2359; 🚆 Connolly, 🚆 Connolly Station), a short walk northeast of Busáras, behind the Custom House.

Connolly Station is a stop on the DART line into town; the Luas Red Line serves both Connolly and Heuston stations.

ℹ Getting Around

TO/FROM THE AIRPORT
Bus

It takes about 45 minutes to get into the city by bus.

Aircoach (☎01-844 7118; www.aircoach.ie; one way/return €7/10) Private coach service with three routes from the airport to more than

20 destinations throughout the city, including the main streets of the city centre. Coaches run every 10 to 15 minutes between 6am and midnight, then hourly from midnight until 6am.

Airlink Express Coach (☎01-873 4222; www. dublinbus.ie; one way/return €7/12) Bus 747 runs every 10 to 20 minutes from 5.45am to 12.30am between the airport, the central bus station (Busáras) and the Dublin Bus office on Upper O'Connell St. Bus 757 runs every 15 to 30 minutes from 5am to 12.25am between the airport and various stops in the city, including Grand Canal Dock, Merrion Sq and Camden St.

Dublin Bus (Map p100; ☎01-873 4222; www. dublinbus.ie; 59 Upper O'Connell St; ⊙9am-5.30pm Tue-Fri, to 2pm Sat, 8.30am-5.30pm Mon; ▣all city centre) A number of buses serve the airport from various points in Dublin, including buses 16 (Rathfarnham), 41 (Lower Abbey St) and 102 (Sutton/Howth); all cross the city centre on their way to the airport.

Taxi

There is a taxi rank directly outside the arrivals concourse of both terminals. It should take about 45 minutes to get into the city centre by taxi, and cost around €25, including an initial charge of €3.80 (€4.20 between 10pm and 8am and on Sundays and bank holidays). Make sure the meter is switched on.

BICYCLE

Relatively flat and compact, Dublin is ideal cycling territory. Getting from one end of the city centre to the other is a cinch, and a bike makes the nearby suburbs readily accessible. There is a (growing) network of cycle lanes, but encroachment by larger vehicles such as buses and trucks is a major problem in the city centre, so you'll have to keep your wits about you.

There are plenty of spots to lock your bike throughout the city, but be sure to do so thoroughly as bike theft can be a problem, and never leave your bike on the street overnight as even the toughest lock can be broken. Dublin City Cycling (www.cycledublin.ie) is an excellent online resource.

Bikes are only allowed on suburban trains (not the DART), either stowed in the guard's van or in a special compartment at the opposite end of the train from the engine.

Bike rental has become tougher due to the Dublinbikes scheme. The typical rental costs for a hybrid or touring bike are around €25 a day or €140 per week.

Cycleways (www.cycleways.com; 31 Lower Ormond Quay; ⊙8.30am-6pm Mon-Fri, from 10am Sat; ▣all city centre) An excellent bike shop that rents out hybrids and touring bikes during the summer months (May to September).

2Wheels (www.2wheels.ie; 57 S William St; ⊙10am-6pm Mon, Tue & Sat, to 8pm Wed, Thu

---

DUBLIN BY BIKE

One of the most popular ways to get around the city is with the blue bikes of Dublinbikes (www.dublinbikes.ie), a public bicycle-rental scheme with more than 100 stations spread across the city centre. Purchase a €5 three-day card (as well as a credit-card deposit of €150) online or at select stations where credit cards can be used. You'll be issued a ticket with an ID and PIN that you'll need to use to free a bike for use, which is then free of charge for the first 30 minutes and €0.50 for each half-hour thereafter.

& Fri, noon-6pm Sun; ▣all city centre) New bikes, all the gear you could possibly need and a decent repair service; but be sure to book an appointment as it is generally quite busy.

CAR & MOTORCYCLE

Traffic in Dublin is a nightmare and parking is an expensive headache. There are no free spots to park anywhere in the city centre during business hours (7am to 7pm Monday to Saturday), but there is plenty of paid parking, priced according to zone: €2.90 per hour in the yellow (central) zone down to €0.60 in the blue (suburban). Supervised and sheltered car parks cost around €4 per hour, with most offering a low-cost evening flat rate.

Clamping of illegally parked cars is thoroughly enforced, and there is an €80 charge for removal. Parking is free after 7pm Monday to Saturday, and all day Sunday, in most metered spots (unless indicated) and on single yellow lines.

Car theft and break-ins are an occasional nuisance, so never leave anything visible or of value in your car. When you're booking accommodation, check on parking facilities.

Car Rental

All the main agencies are represented in Dublin. Book in advance for the best rates, especially at weekends and during summer months, when demand is highest.

Motorbikes and mopeds are not available for rent. People aged under 21 are not allowed to hire a car; for the majority of rental companies you have to be at least 23 and have had a valid driving licence for a minimum of one year. Many rental agencies will not rent to people over 70 or 75.

The following rental agencies have several branches across the capital and at the airport:

Avis Rent-a-Car (☎01-605 7500; www.avis. ie; 35 Old Kilmainham Rd; ⊙8.30am-5.45pm Mon-Fri, to 2.30pm Sat & Sun; ▣23, 25, 25A, 26, 68, 69 from city centre)

Budget Rent-a-Car (☑ 01-837 9611; www.budget.ie; 151 Lower Drumcondra Rd; ☺9am-6pm; ☐ 41 from O'Connell St) Also at the **airport** (☑ 01-844 5150; ☺5am-12.30am).

Europcar (☑ 01-812 2800; www.europcar.ie; 1 Mark St; ☺8am-6pm Mon-Fri, 8.30am-3pm Sat & Sun; ☐ all city centre) Also at the **airport** (☑ 01-812 2880; ☺ 5am-1am).

Hertz Rent-a-Car (☑ 01-709 3060; www.hertz.com; 151 S Circular Rd; ☺ 8.30am-5.30pm Mon-Fri, 9am-4.30pm Sat, 9am-3.30pm Sun; ☐ 9, 16, 77, 79 from city centre) Also at the **airport** (☑ 01-844 5466; ☺5am-1am).

Thrifty (☑ 01-844 1944; www.thrifty.ie; 26 E Lombard St; ☺8am-6pm Mon-Fri, to 3pm Sat & Sun; ☐ all city centre) Also at the **airport** (☑ 01-840 0800; ☺ 5am-1am).

PUBLIC TRANSPORT
Bus

The office of Dublin Bus (p143) has free single-route timetables for all its services. Buses run from around 6am (some start at 5.30am) to about 11.30pm.

Fares are calculated according to stages (stops):

Stages	Cash Fare (€)	Leap Card (€)
1-3	2.15	1.55
4-13	3	2.25
over 13	3.30	2.50

A Leap Card (www.leapcard.ie), available from most newsagents, is not just cheaper but also more convenient, as you don't have to worry about tendering exact fares (required with cash, otherwise you will get a receipt for reimbursement, which is only possible at the Dublin Bus main office). Register the card online and top it up with whatever amount you need. When you board a bus, DART, Luas (light rail) or suburban train, just swipe your card and the fare is automatically deducted.

Nitelink

Nitelink late-night buses run from the College, Westmoreland and D'Olier Sts triangle. On Fridays and Saturdays, departures are at 12.30am, then every 20 minutes until 4.30am on the more popular routes, and until 3.30am on the less-frequented; there are no services from Sunday to Thursday. Fares are €6.60 (€4.50 with Leap Card). See www.dublinbus.ie for route details.

Luas (Light Rail)

The **Luas** (www.luas.ie) light-rail system has two lines: the Green Line (running every five to 15 minutes) runs from Broombridge in the north of the city down through O'Connell St and St Stephen's Green to Sandyford in south Dublin (via Ranelagh and Dundrum); the Red Line (every 20 minutes) runs from the Point Village to Tallaght via the north quays and Heuston Station.

There are ticket machines at every stop or you can use a tap-on, tap-off Leap Card, which is available from most newsagents. A typical short-hop fare (around four stops) is €2.80. Services run from 5.30am to 12.30am Monday to Friday, from 6.30am to 12.30am Saturday and from 7am to 11.30pm Sunday.

Taxi

All taxi fares begin with a flagfall of €3.80 (€4.20 from 10pm to 8am), followed by €1.14 per kilometre/€0.40 per minute thereafter (€1.50/0.53 from 10pm to 8am). In addition to these, there are a number of extra charges – €1 for each extra passenger and €2 for telephone bookings. There is no charge for luggage.

Taxis can be hailed on the street and found at taxi ranks around the city, including on the corner of Abbey and O'Connell Sts; College Green; in front of Trinity College; and St Stephen's Green at the end of Grafton St.

Numerous taxi companies, such as **National Radio Cabs** (☑ 01-677 2222; www.nrc.ie), dispatch taxis by radio. You can also try MyTaxi (www.mytaxi.com), a taxi app.

Train (DART)

The **Dublin Area Rapid Transport** (DART; ☑ 01-836 6222; www.irishrail.ie) provides quick train access to the coast as far north as Howth (about 30 minutes) and as far south as Greystones in County Wicklow. Pearse Station is convenient for central Dublin south of the Liffey, and Connolly Station for north of the Liffey. There are services every 10 to 20 minutes, sometimes more frequently, from around 6.30am to midnight Monday to Saturday. Services are less frequent on Sunday. A one-way DART ticket from Dublin to Dun Laoghaire or Howth costs €3.30 (€2.40 with a Leap Card).

There are also suburban rail services north as far as Dundalk, inland to Mullingar and south past Bray to Arklow.

AROUND DUBLIN

Without even the smallest hint of irony Dubliners will tell you that one of the city's best features is how easy it is to get out of – and they do, whenever they can. But they don't go especially far: for many the destination is one of the small seaside villages that surround the capital. To the north are the lovely villages of Howth and Malahide – slowly and reluctantly being sucked into the Dublin agglomeration – while to the south is Dalkey, which has long since given up the fight but still manages to retain that village vibe.

Malahide

POP 16,550

Malahide (Mullach Íde) was once a small village with its own harbour, a long way from the urban jungle of Dublin. The only thing protecting it from the northwards expansion of Dublin's suburbs is Malahide Demesne, 101 well-tended hectares of parkland dominated by a castle once owned by the powerful Talbot family.

The handsome village remains relatively intact, but the once-quiet marina has been massively developed and is now a bustling centre with a pleasant promenade and plenty of restaurants and shops.

◉ Sights & Activities

Malahide Castle   CASTLE
(⌂ 01-816 9538; www.malahidecastleandgardens. ie; adult/child €14/6.50; ◷ 9.30am-5.30pm; ▣ 42, 142 from city centre, ▣ Malahide) The oldest part of this hotchpotch castle, which was in the hands of the Talbot family from 1185 to 1976, is the three-storey 12th-century tower house. The facade is flanked by circular towers that were tacked on in 1765. The castle, now owned by Fingal County Council, is accessible via guided tour only (last tour 4.30pm; 3.30pm November to March). The impressive gardens are self-guided.

The castle is packed with furniture and paintings; highlights are a 16th-century oak room with decorative carvings, and the medieval Great Hall, which has family portraits, a minstrel's gallery and a painting of the Battle of the Boyne. Puck, the Talbot family ghost, is said to have last appeared in 1975.

★Portmarnock Golf Club   GOLF
(⌂ 01-846 2968; www.portmarnockgolfclub.ie; Golf Links Rd, Portmarnock; green fees weekday/weekend €225/250) Founded in 1894, this is one of the world's outstanding links courses and a former long-time host of the Irish Open. Visitor tee times are spread throughout the day, with 11.30am to 2.30pm reserved exclusively for members.

✕ Eating & Drinking

Malahide is one of north Dublin's great culinary hotspots, full of excellent restaurants serving virtually every kind of cuisine. The competition is fierce and expectations are so high that it's hard to eat badly here. All of the best places are in the town and the marina.

Greedy Goose   INTERNATIONAL €€
(⌂ 01-845 1299; www.greedygoose.ie; 15 Townyard Lane; menus €25-31; ◷ 5-11pm Mon-Fri, 1-11pm Sat & Sun; ▣ 42, 142 from city centre, ▣ Malahide) The menu at this pleasant restaurant overlooking the marina has dishes from all over the globe: take your pick from Thai crab cakes, chana masala, wild mushroom arancini and more. The food is best enjoyed as part of three separate menus: pick three dishes from one and eat portions like Spanish *raciones* – bigger than starters, smaller than mains.

Chez Sara   FRENCH €€
(⌂ 01-845 1882; www.chezsara.ie; 3 Old St; mains €19-24; ◷ 5pm-midnight Tue-Sun; ▣ 42, 142 from city centre, ▣ Malahide) Irish lamb, seafood linguine and beautifully cooked steak are just three of the highlights at this cosy French restaurant in the middle of the village.

Sale e Pepe   INTERNATIONAL €€
(⌂ 01-845 4600; www.saleepepe.ie; The Diamond, Main St; mains €17-29; ◷ 5-10.30pm Mon-Sat, 4-10.30pm Sun; ▣ 42, 142 from city centre, ▣ Malahide) Despite the name, there's only a handful of Italian dishes here on a menu that emphasises well-prepared steaks, homemade organic burgers and fish and chips.

Gibney's   PUB
(www.gibneys.com; 6 New St; ◷ 10.30am-11.30pm Mon-Thu, to 12.30am Fri & Sat, 11.30am-11pm Sun;

SANDYCOVE

Sandycove has a pretty little beach and a Martello tower, built by British forces as a look-out for signs of a Napoleonic invasion – it's now the James Joyce Tower & Museum.

There are really only two things to do here: visit the tower and, if you're brave enough, get into the water at the adjacent Forty Foot Pool. If you want to swim in the Forty Foot Pool in your birthday suit, do so before 9am; later swims are generally done wearing bathing suits.

From Dublin, Sandycove is easily reached by DART train. Alternatively, It's a 1km walk from Dalkey.

James Joyce Tower & Museum (☑ 01-280 9265; www.joycetower.ie; ⊙ 10am-6pm May-Sep, to 4pm Oct-Apr; ⊠ Sandycove & Glasthule) This tower is where the action begins in Joyce's epic novel *Ulysses*. The museum was opened in 1962 by Sylvia Beach, the Paris-based publisher who first dared to put *Ulysses* into print, and has photographs, letters, documents, various editions of Joyce's work and two death masks of Joyce on display. Tours are available by prior arrangement.

Forty Foot Pool (⊠ Sandycove & Glasthule) The Forty Foot Pool is an open-air, seawater bathing pool that took its name from the army regiment, the Fortieth Foot, that was stationed at Sandycove until the regiment was disbanded in 1904. At the close of the first chapter of *Ulysses*, Buck Mulligan heads off to the Forty Foot Pool for a morning swim. A morning wake-up here is still a local tradition, in summer and winter: the Christmas Day Dip is one of Dublin's most enduring traditions.

Pressure from female bathers eventually opened this public stretch of water – originally nudist and for men only – to both sexes, despite strong opposition from the 'forty foot gentlemen', who eventually agreed.

⊟ 42, 142 from city centre, ⊠ Malahide) Malahide's best-known and best-loved pub is a huge place, spread over a number of rooms and outdoor areas. At weekends it's always packed with locals.

ⓘ Getting There & Away

Malahide is 13km north of Dublin.

Bus Services 42 and 142 (€3.50) from Talbot St take around 45 minutes.

DART Stops in Malahide (€3.50).

Dalkey

POP 8083

Dublin's most important medieval port has long since settled into its role as an elegant dormitory village, but there are some revealing vestiges of its illustrious past, most notably the remains of three of the eight castles that once lorded over the area.

Dalkey is small enough that you can get around on foot. Most visitors will be arriving by DART, so start your exploration in the middle of town: the main sights are on Castle St, as are most of the cafes (or on the streets just off it). Coliemore Harbour is where you can get boat trips; overlooking the adjoining Bullock Harbour are the remains of Bullock Castle.

The waters around the island are popular with scuba divers; qualified divers can rent gear in Dun Laoghaire, further north, from **Ocean Divers** (www.oceandivers.ie; The Boat Yard, Dun Laoghaire Harbour, Dun Laoghaire; boat dives €45-69; ⊙ 9.30am-5pm Tue-Sat; ⊠ Dalkey).

⊙ Sights & Activities

Dalkey Castle & Heritage Centre MUSEUM (☑ 01-285 8366; www.dalkeycastle.com; Castle St; adult/child €10/8; ⊙ 10am-6pm Mon-Fri, from 11am Sat & Sun, closed Tue Sep-May; ⊠ Dalkey) Spread across Goat Castle and St Begnet's Church, this heritage centre has models, displays and exhibitions on Dalkey's history. There's a Living History tour in the format of a theatre performance, and a Writers' Gallery covering the town's rich literary heritage – from Samuel Beckett (who was born here) and Maeve Binchy (who was born near here) to Joseph O'Connor (who lives here). The centre also organises guided tours.

Dalkey Island ISLAND
Dalkey Island's main sight is **St Begnet's Holy Well** (⊠ Dalkey), but it's also a popular spot for fishing, with shoals of pollock, mackerel and coalfish feeding in its waters. It's also a lovely spot to spend a couple of hours with a picnic – but be sure to take everything off the island with you when you

leave. **Ken the Ferryman** (www.kentheferry man.com; Coliemore Harbour; adult/child €8/5; ⊘10am-6pm) provides transport to and from the island.

Dalkey Guided Tours TOURS
(www.dalkeycastle.com; Dalkey Castle & Heritage Centre; €10; ⊘11am & noon Wed & Fri Jun-Aug; ⓡDalkey) Historical and literary tours of Dalkey, including a Maeve Binchy–themed walk (the writer lived here) and a James Joyce–themed one. Tours are run out of the Dalkey Castle & Heritage Centre.

★**Dalkey Book Festival** LITERATURE
(www.dalkeybookfestival.org; ⊘mid-Jun) Salman Rushdie is an acknowledged fan, which must help this festival's organisers, Sian Smyth and David McWilliams, to always draw some big award-winning names – in 2019 Emma Dabiri, Stephen Fry and Jared Diamond were speakers.

✖ Eating & Drinking

Dalkey's culinary credentials are excellent, mostly because its affluent population wouldn't stand for anything else. There's a good choice of everything from healthy cafe bites to fine dining.

★**Select Stores** HEALTH FOOD €
(☑01-285 9611; www.facebook.com/selectstores dalkey; 1 Railway Rd; mains €6-12; ⊘8am-6pm Mon-Sat; ⓡDalkey) This long-established food emporium has been transformed into a one-stop shop for all things good for you: the award-winning kitchen rolls out veggie burgers, fresh juices, salads and, in the mornings, a range of healthy breakfasts. Bono is a fan, apparently.

Magpie Inn PUB FOOD €€
(☑01-202 3909; www.magpieinn.com; 115-116 Coliemore Rd; mains €15-24; ⊘12.30-11.30pm Mon-Thu, to 12.30am Fri & Sat, to 11pm Sun; ⓡDalkey) The main strength of the excellent menu here is, obviously, seafood, including a range of mouth-watering lunch options such as fresh Galway mussels *marinière* with toasted sourdough, and more substantial dinner mains like ale-battered fish with pea puree, tartar sauce and chips. Wash it all down with a choice of craft beer.

Finnegan's PUB
(www.finnegans.ie; 1 Sorrento Rd; ⊘noon-midnight; ⓡDalkey) There's a fabulous local atmosphere in this lovely traditional pub, which has been a staple here for over 40 years.

WORTH A TRIP

IRELAND'S EYE

A short distance offshore from Howth is **Ireland's Eye** (☑01-831 4200), a rocky seabird sanctuary with the ruins of a 6th-century monastery. There's a Martello tower at the northwestern end of the island, where boats from Howth land, while a spectacularly sheer rock face plummets into the sea at the eastern end. It's really only worth exploring if you're interested in birds, although the boat trip out here, with Doyle & Sons, affords some lovely views of Dublin Bay.

As well as the seabirds overhead, you can see young birds on the ground during the nesting season. Seals can also be spotted around the island. Further north of Ireland's Eye is Lambay Island, an important seabird sanctuary that cannot be visited.

ⓘ Getting There & Away

DART The best way to get to Dalkey is by train from Pearse or Connolly Stations – a one-way ticket costs €3.30 (€3 with a Leap Card).
Bus Service 7 takes a slow route from Mountjoy Sq through the Dublin city centre to Dalkey – the fare is €3.30.

Howth

POP 8706
Tidily positioned at the foot of a bulbous peninsula, the pretty port village of Howth (the name rhymes with 'both') is a major fishing centre, a yachting harbour and one of the most sought-after addresses in town.

Howth is divided between the upper headland – where the best properties are, discreetly spread atop the gorse-rich hill where there are some fine walks and spectacular views of Dublin Bay – and the busy port town, where all the restaurants are (as is an excellent weekend farmers market).

⊙ Sights & Activities

Howth Castle CASTLE
(⛴31, 31A from Beresford Pl, ⓡHowth) FREE Most of Howth backs onto the extensive grounds of Howth Castle, built in 1564 but much changed over the years, most recently in 1910 when Sir Edwin Lutyens gave it a modernist makeover. Today the castle is divided into four very posh and private residences (the grounds are open to the public). The **castle**

gardens (⊘24hr) FREE are worth visiting, as they're noted for their rhododendrons (which bloom in May and June), azaleas and a long, 10m-high beech hedge planted in 1710.

The original estate was acquired in 1177 by the Norman noble Sir Almeric Tristram, who changed his surname to St Lawrence after winning a battle at the behest (or so he believed) of his favourite saint. The family has owned the land ever since, though the unbroken chain of male succession came to an end in 1909.

On the grounds are the ruins of the 16th-century Corr Castle and an ancient dolmen (a tomb chamber or portal tomb made of vertical stones topped by a huge capstone) known as Aideen's Grave. Legend has it that Aideen died of a broken heart after her husband was killed at the Battle of Gavra near Tara in AD 184, but the the dolmen is at least 300 years older than that.

Also within the grounds are the ruins of St Mary's Abbey FREE, originally founded in 1042 by the Viking King Sitric, who also founded the original church on the site of Christ Church Cathedral. The abbey was amalgamated with the monastery on Ireland's Eye in 1235. Some parts of the ruins date from that time, but most are from the 15th and 16th centuries. The tomb of Christopher St Lawrence (Lord Howth), in the southeastern corner, dates from around 1470. See the caretaker or read the instructions on the gate for opening times.

★ Howth Summit Walk   WALKING
(🚈31, 31A from Beresford Pl, 🚉Howth) A 6km looped walk around the headlands begins at Howth DART station – follow the green arrow along the promenade and then turn right onto the cliff path. The walk takes you up to the summit before looping back down again. There are other, longer walks marked by blue, red and purple arrows (which partially overlap the green route).

✕ Eating

Howth Market   MARKET €
(☎01-839 4141; www.howthmarket.ie; 3 Harbour Rd, Howth Harbour; ⊘9am-6pm Sat, Sun & bank holidays; 🚈31, 31A from Beresford Pl, 🚉Howth) One of the best markets in greater Dublin, this is the place to come not only for fresh fish (obviously) but also for organic meat and veg, and homemade everything else, including jams, cakes and breads. A great option for Sunday lunch.

★ House   IRISH €€
(☎01-839 6388; www.thehouse-howth.ie; 4 Main St; mains €18-25; ⊘8.45am-9.30pm Mon-Thu, to 10.30pm Fri, 10am-10.30pm Sat, to 9.30pm Sun; 🚈31, 31A from Beresford Pl, 🚉Howth) A wonderful spot on the main street leading away from the harbour where you can feast on dishes such as squash and potato gnocchi or wild Wicklow venison with smoked black-pudding croquette, as well as a fine selection of fish. The brunch is one of the best you'll find on the north side of the city.

Octopussy's Seafood Tapas   SEAFOOD €€
(☎01-839 0822; www.octopussys.ie; 7-8 West Pier; tapas €8-17; ⊘noon-9pm; 🚈31, 31A from Beresford Pl, 🚉Howth) Best known for its tasty seafood tapas, Octopussy's is a firm local favourite. All of the seafood comes from the fish shop next door, which in turn buys it from the fishing boats that dock right in front. You can't get any fresher than that.

❶ Getting There & Away

DART The 20-minute train ride from Dublin city centre to Howth Village costs €3.25.

Bus Services 31 and 31A from Beresford Pl near Busáras run up to Howth Summit for €2.70.

Counties Wicklow & Kildare

POP 364,929 / AREA 3718 SQ KM

Best Places to Eat

➡ Strawberry Tree (p168)

➡ Hartes of Kildare (p174)

➡ Firehouse Bakery (p166)

➡ Mickey Finns Pub (p169)

➡ Dockyard No 8 (p165)

Best Places to Stay

➡ Heather House (p161)

➡ Hunter's Hotel (p167)

➡ Powerscourt Hotel & Spa (p154)

➡ Martinstown House (p174)

➡ Tinakilly Country House (p167)

Why Go?

Wicklow and Kildare may be neighbours and have a boundary with Dublin in common, but that's where the similarities end.

Immediately south of the capital is wild, scenic Wicklow. Its most dramatic natural feature is a gorse-and-bracken mountain spine that is the east coast's most stunning landscape, complete with deep glacial valleys, isolated mountain passes and, dotted throughout, some important historical treasures, including one of Ireland's most important early-Christian sites and a couple of 18th-century Palladian mansions.

To the west is flat, fertile Kildare, which also has a handful of elegant Palladian piles but is best known as horse country – of the thoroughbred kind. Some of the world's most lucrative stud farms are here, many with links to the horse-breeding centre of Kentucky in the USA. Kildare is also home to some of the best golf courses in Ireland and the country's largest outlet mall.

When to Go

➡ Your best chance of witnessing the birth of a thoroughbred foal at the Irish National Stud is between February and June.

➡ The Irish Derby takes place at the Curragh Racecourse in June; meets continue right up to October.

➡ The best weather for walking the Wicklow Way or exploring Wicklow's gardens is from June to September.

Counties Wicklow & Kildare Highlights

❶ Glendalough (p155) Stepping back in time at this evocative and scenic early-Christian monastic site.

❷ Powerscourt Estate (p152) Admiring the Italianate gardens, glorious views and Ireland's highest waterfall at this Enniskerry estate.

❸ Castletown House (p173) Taking the tour at Ireland's most impressive Palladian mansion, once owned by the country's richest man.

❹ Wicklow Way (p157) Hiking at least part of Ireland's most popular long-distance walking trail.

❺ Russborough House (p170) Examining the art and absorbing the aristocratic atmosphere of this magnificent mansion.

❻ Irish National Stud (p172) Learning about Ireland's long association with thoroughbred racehorses.

❼ Avoca Handweavers (p169) Shopping for crafts at the birthplace of one of the country's best-known brands.

❽ Bog of Allen (p176) Learning about conservation and biodiversity amid County Kildare's huge tracts of exploited peat bog.

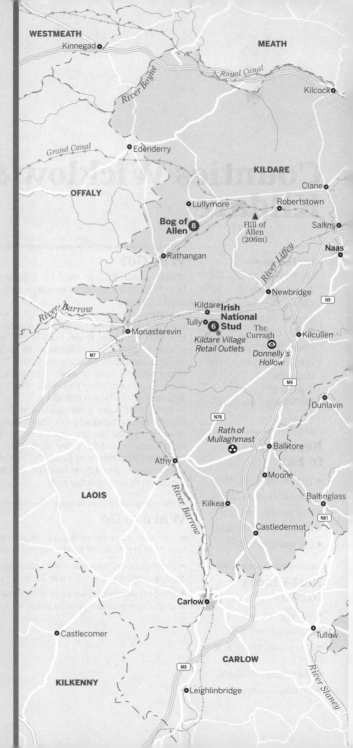

Swords

North Bull
Island

Howth

Howth
Peninsula

*Irish
Sea*

Maynooth

River Liffey

M4

Leixlip

**Castletown
House**

3

⭐ **DUBLIN**

Celbridge

*Dublin
Bay*

**Dun
Laoghaire**

Straffan

Sandycove

Dalkey

*Dalkey
Island*

Rathcoole

Killiney

Grand Canal

M7

Kill

Loughlinstown

Glencree

Kippure
Mountain
(752m)

Enniskerry

R117

Kilbride

N81

**Powerscourt
Estate**

2

Bray

*Bray
Head*

R759

River Liffey

Kilmacanogue

Blessington

Sally
Gap

*Powerscourt
Waterfall*

Great
Sugarloaf
Mountain
(503m)

M11

Greystones

**Russborough
House**

5

Ballymore
Eustace

*Poulaphouca
Reservoir*

Mt
Mullaghcleevaun
(848m)

Military Rd

River Glenmacnass

*Lough
Tay*

Kilpedder

Valleymount

Kilcoole

Hollywood

Wicklow
Mountains

*Lough
Dan*

Sraghmore

Mt Tonelagee
(816m)

Roundwood

*Vartry
Reservoir*

Table
Mountain
(700m)

Wicklow
Gap

Devil's
Glen

N11

Camaderry
Mountain
(700m)

Glendalough

1

Annamoe

Donard

Lugduff
(652m)

Turlough
Hill

Spink
Mountain
(550m)

Laragh

River Avonmore

Ashford

Rathnew

Ballinclea

Knockanarrigan

Glenmalure

Mullacor
(657m)

Drumgoff

WICKLOW

Glenealy

Wicklow

*Wicklow
Head*

Lugnaquilla
Mountain
(924m)

River Avonbeg

Vale of
Clara

Derrynamuck

Glen of
Imaal

Greenane

Rathdrum

Silver Strand

Rathdangan

Slieve Maan
(550m)

Aghavannagh

Carrickashane
Mtn (508m)

River Ow

Vale of
Avoca

**Avondale
House**

Ardmore
Point

*Meeting of
the Waters*

R754

Redcross

Brittas Bay

Aughrim

**Wicklow
Way**

4

Avoca

7

Mizen
Head

Maheramore

Tinahely

Woodenbridge

Clogga
Beach

*ATLANTIC
OCEAN*

River Bann

River Avoca

Arklow

Shillelagh

N11

Kilmichael
Point

Carnew

WEXFORD

M11

Ⓝ 0 ————————— 10 km
    0 ————————— 5 miles

COUNTY WICKLOW

Just south of Dublin, County Wicklow (Cill Mhantáin) is the capital's favourite playground, a wild expanse of coastline, woodland and daunting mountains through which runs the country's most popular walking trail. Stretching 127km from Dublin's southern suburbs to the rolling fields of County Carlow, the Wicklow Way leads walkers along disused military supply lines, old bog roads and forest trails. En route you can explore monastic ruins, lush gardens and some magnificent 18th-century mansions.

❶ Getting There & Away

BUS

St Kevins Bus (www.glendaloughbus.com) runs twice daily from Dublin and Bray to Roundwood and Glendalough. Dublin Bus runs regularly as far as Blessington.

CAR

The main routes are the N11/M11, which runs north–south through the county from Dublin to Wexford, and the N81, which runs down the western side of the Wicklow Mountains through Blessington into County Carlow.

TRAIN

The Dublin Area Rapid Transport (p144) suburban rail line runs southward from Dublin as far as Greystones, and there are regular train and bus connections from the capital to Wicklow town and Arklow.

Wicklow Mountains

As you leave Dublin and cross into Wicklow, the landscape changes dramatically. From Rathfarnham, still within the city limits, the Military Rd begins a 40km southward journey along the spine of the Wicklow Mountains, crossing vast sweeps of gorse-, bracken- and heather-clad moors, bogs and hills, dotted with small corrie lakes.

The highest peak in the range, Lugnaquilla (925m), is really more of a very large hill. The vast granite intrusion, an upwelling of molten rock that solidified some 400 million years ago, was shaped during the ice ages into the schist-capped mountains visible today. The wild topography is marvellously desolate and raw. Between the mountains are a number of deep glacial valleys – most notably Glenmacnass, Glenmalure and Glendalough – and corrie lakes such as Lough Bray Upper and Lower, and Lough Tay, gouged by ice at the head of the glaciers.

The Military Road

The R115, better known as the Military Road, was first built in the early 1800s by British forces to help suppress rebels in the wake of the 1798 Rising. The narrow road winds its way through the most remote parts of the mountains, offering some extraordinary views of the surrounding countryside. The best place to join it is at Glencree (from Enniskerry). It then runs south through the Sally Gap, Glenmacnass Valley and Laragh, then on to Glenmalure and Aghavannagh.

On the trip south you can divert east at the Sally Gap to look at Lough Tay and Lough Dan. Further south you pass the great waterfall at Glenmacnass before dropping down into Laragh, with the magnificent monastic ruins of Glendalough nearby. Continue south through the valley of Glenmalure and, if you're fit enough, climb to the top of Lugnaquilla.

Powerscourt Estate & Enniskerry

At the top of the '21 Bends', as the steep and winding R117 road from Bray is known, the handsome village of Enniskerry is home to upmarket shops and organic cafes. It's a far cry from the village's origins, when Richard Wingfield, earl of nearby Powerscourt, commissioned a row of terraced cottages for his labourers in 1760. These days you'd need to have laboured pretty successfully to get your hands on one of them.

There are **day tours** (Map p100; www.do dublin.ie; 59 Upper O'Connell St; adult/child €27/12; ⊙10.30am daily May-Sep, 10.30am Mon, Fri & Sat Apr, Oct & Nov, 10.30am Fri & Sat Mar) that take in both Glendalough and Powerscourt departing from Dublin.

◉ Sights & Activities

★ **Powerscourt Estate**   GARDENS
(☎01-204 6000; www.powerscourt.com; Bray Rd; house free, gardens adult/child Mar-Oct €10/5, Nov-Feb €7.50/3.50; ⊙9.30am-5.30pm Mar-Oct, to dusk Nov-Feb) Wicklow's most visited attraction is this magnificent 64-sq-km estate, whose main entrance is 500m south of Enniskerry. At the heart of it is an elegant Palladian mansion, but the real draws are the formal gardens and the stunning views that accompany them. Most of the house is not open to the public, but there's a fine cafe and

several gift and homewares shops, while the grounds are home to two golf courses and the best hotel (p154) in Wicklow.

The estate has existed more or less since 1300, when the LePoer (later anglicised to Power) family built themselves a castle here. The property changed Anglo-Norman hands a few times before coming into the possession of Richard Wingfield, newly appointed Marshall of Ireland, in 1603. His descendants were to live here for the next 350 years. In 1730 the Georgian wunderkind Richard Cassels (or Castle) was given the job of building a 68-room Palladian-style mansion around the core of the old castle. He finished the job in 1741, but an extra storey was added in 1787 and other alterations were made in the 19th century.

The Wingfields left in the 1950s, after which the house had a massive restoration. Then, on the eve of its opening to the public in 1974, a fire gutted the whole building. The estate was eventually bought by the Slazenger sporting-goods family, who have overseen a second restoration as well as the addition of all the amenities the estate now has to offer, including the two golf courses and the hotel, part of Marriott's Autograph collection.

The 20-hectare landscaped gardens are the star attraction, originally laid out in the 1740s but redesigned in the 19th century by gardener Daniel Robinson. Robinson was one of the foremost horticulturalists of his day, and his passion for growing things was matched only by his love of booze: the story goes that by a certain point in the day he was too drunk to stand and so insisted on being wheeled around the estate in a barrow.

Perhaps this influenced his largely informal style, which resulted in a magnificent blend of landscaped gardens, sweeping terraces, statuary, ornamental lakes, secret hollows, rambling walks and walled enclosures replete with more than 200 types of trees and shrubs, all designed to frame the stunning natural backdrop of the Great Sugarloaf mountain. Tickets come with a map laying out 40-minute and hour-long walks around the gardens. Don't miss the exquisite **Japanese Gardens** or the **Pepperpot Tower**, modelled on a 7.5cm-tall pepper pot owned by Lady Wingfield. The **animal cemetery** is the final resting place of the Wingfield pets and even one of the family's favourite milking cows. Some of the epitaphs are surprisingly personal.

The house itself is every bit as grand as the gardens, but with most areas closed to the public, there's not much to see beyond the bustle of the ground-floor cafe and gift shop.

A 6km drive to a separate part of the estate takes you to the 121m-high **Powerscourt Waterfall** (www.powerscourt.com/waterfall; adult/child €6/3.50; ⊙ 9.30am-7pm May-Aug, 10.30am-5.30pm Mar, Apr, Sep & Oct, 10.30am-4pm Nov-Feb) – walking from house to falls is not recommended as the route lies on narrow roads with no footpath. It's the highest waterfall in Ireland, and at its most impressive after heavy rain. A nature trail has been laid out around the base of the waterfall, taking you past giant redwoods, ancient oaks, beech, birch and rowan trees.

COUNTIES WICKLOW & KILDARE WICKLOW MOUNTAINS

WICKLOW MOUNTAINS NATIONAL PARK

Wicklow Mountains National Park covers just over 200 sq km of mountain, blanket bog and woodland. Within its boundaries are two nature reserves, owned and managed by the Heritage Service and legally protected by the Wildlife Act 1976. The larger reserve, west of the **Glendalough Visitor Centre** (☑ 0404-45352; www.heritageireland.ie; adult/child €5/3; ⊙ 9.30am-6pm mid-Mar–mid-Oct, to 5pm mid-Oct–mid-Mar), conserves the extensive heath and bog of the Glendalough Valley plus the Upper Lake and valley slopes on either side. The second, Glendalough Wood Nature Reserve, protects oak woods stretching from the Upper Lake as far as the Rathdrum road to the east.

Most of Ireland's native mammal species can be found within the confines of the park. Large herds of deer roam on the open hill areas, though these were introduced in the 20th century as the native red-deer population became extinct during the first half of the 18th century. The uplands are the preserve of foxes, badgers and hares. Red squirrels are usually found in the pine woodlands – look out for them around the Upper Lake.

The bird population of the park is plentiful. Birds of prey abound, the most common being peregrine falcons, merlins, kestrels, hawks and sparrowhawks. Hen harriers are a rarer sight, though they too live in the park. Moorland birds found in the area include meadow pipits and skylarks. Less common birds such as whinchats, ring ouzels and dippers can be spotted, as can red grouse, which are quickly disappearing in other parts of Ireland.

THE SALLY GAP

One of the two main east–west passes across the Wicklow Mountains, the Sally Gap is surrounded by some spectacular countryside. From the turn-off on the lower road (R755) a few kilometres north of Roundwood, the narrow R759 passes above the dark and dramatic **Lough Tay**, backed by steep scree slopes descending from Luggala (Fancy Mountain).

The almost fairy-tale estate of Luggala is owned by one **Garech de Brún**, member of the Guinness family and founder of Claddagh Records, a leading producer of Irish traditional and folk music. The small River Cloghoge links Lough Tay with Lough Dan just to the south. The R759 then continues to the Sally Gap crossroads, where it cuts across the Military Rd and heads northwest to Kilbride and the N81, following the young River Liffey, still only a stream here.

There are plenty of birds in the vicinity, including the chaffinch, cuckoo, chiffchaff, raven and willow warbler.

Great Sugarloaf   HILL

At 503m it's nowhere near Wicklow's highest summit, but the Great Sugarloaf is one of the most distinctive hills in Ireland, its conical peak visible for many kilometres around. The mountain towers over the small village of Kilmacanogue, on the N11 about 35km south of Dublin, and can be climbed from a car park on the L1031 minor road (off the R755 road, 7.5km south of Enniskerry). It's a steep but straightforward hike (one hour return).

Powerscourt Golf Club   GOLF

(☑ 01-204 6033; www.powerscourtgolfclub.com; Powerscourt Estate; green fees Apr-Oct €75, Nov-Mar €55; ⊘ 8am-dusk) You have a choice of two stunning par-72 courses here: the West Course, with streams and ravines, was designed by David McLay Kidd (who also designed Bandon Dunes in Oregon, USA) and is a shade tougher than the East Course, designed by Peter McEvoy, which is arguably the more scenic, with hedges, ancient oaks and beech trees.

🍴 Sleeping & Eating

Knockree Youth Hostel   HOSTEL €

(☑ 01-276 7981; www.anoige.ie/knockree-youth-hostel; off L1011, Lackandarragh; dm/d/f from

€21.50/55/102; ☎) In the wooded Glencree Valley, 5km southwest of Enniskerry, this An Óige hostel opened in 1938 in an 18th-century farmhouse and has since received a 21st-century extension. Dorms are single-sex or mixed; doubles and four-person family rooms have private bathrooms. A log fire warms the lounge, and there's a laundry and self-catering kitchen. Wi-fi is available in public areas.

Rates include a basic breakfast, and lunch and dinner packs can be arranged with several days' notice; otherwise bring supplies with you. The hostel is wheelchair accessible.

Coolakay House   B&B €€

(☑ 01-286 2423; www.coolakayhouse.ie; Waterfall Rd, Coolakay; s/d from €60/80; Ⓟ ☎) A great option for walkers along the Wicklow Way, this modern working farm is 4km south of Enniskerry off the R760. The light, airy bedrooms are well appointed and comfortable, the views are terrific and the breakfast sensational. March and April is lambing season and guests are encouraged to observe – and even name – a newborn lamb. Cash only.

★ Powerscourt Hotel & Spa   LUXURY HOTEL €€€

(☑ 01-274 8888; www.powerscourthotel.com; Powerscourt Estate; d/ste from €244/333; Ⓟ ☎ ☒) Wicklow's most luxurious hotel is this 200-room stunner on the grounds of the Powerscourt Estate (p152). Inside this Marriott-managed property, the decor is a thoroughly contemporary version of the estate's Georgian style. Rooms are massive; some have balconies. There's a gourmet restaurant (three-course evening menu €65), a lounge serving afternoon tea, a traditional bar and a holistic ESPA spa.

Poppies Country Cooking   CAFE €

(☑ 01-282 8869; www.facebook.com/poppiesireland; The Square; mains €6.50-12; ⊘ 8am-5pm Mon-Fri, to 6pm Sat & Sun) Hearty Irish breakfasts are served until noon at this poppy-red-painted cafe with a butter-yellow interior, while wholesome salads, filling sandwiches and daily specials such as shepherd's pie and veggie quiches make it a great option for lunch. You can also drop by for cakes, pastries and scones served with Kilmurry-made jam.

Johnnie Fox's   SEAFOOD €€

(☑ 01-295 5647; www.johnniefoxs.com; Glencullen; mains €15-26, seafood platters €28-130, 3-course Hooley menu €59.50; ⊘ kitchen 12.30-9.30pm, bar 11am-11.30pm Mon-Thu, to 12.30am Fri & Sat, noon-11pm Sun; ☎ ☑ ⛾) Just over the

County Dublin border, 5.5km northwest of Enniskerry, traditional 19th-century pub Johnnie Fox's fills with busloads of tourists for its knees-up Hooley Show of Irish music and dancing. But it's even more worthwhile entering its warren of rooms, nooks and crannies for standout seafood spanning Roaring Bay oysters, Dublin Bay prawns, Annagassan crab, Kilmore Quay lobster and more.

Vegetarian, kids and babies menus are available.

🛍 Shopping

Avoca Handweavers ARTS & CRAFTS
(📞 01-274 6900; www.avoca.com; Main St, Kilmacanogue; ⏱ 9am-6pm Mon-Fri, 9.30am-6pm Sat & Sun) Avoca has 13 branches across Ireland and a widespread reputation for creating stylish traditional rural handicrafts. Its operational HQ is set in a 19th-century arboretum 5km southeast of Enniskerry. The bustling shop is crammed with knitwear, textiles, ceramics, toys, homewares, foodstuffs and cookbooks; also here is an excellent cafe (dishes €6 to €15) utilising Avoca's own-grown produce.

❶ Getting There & Away

Car Enniskerry is 18km south of Dublin, just 3km west of the M11 along the R117.

Bus Dublin Bus (www.dublinbus.ie) services link Dublin (Dublin City University) with Enniskerry (€3.30, 1½ hours, hourly).

Roundwood

POP 948

The unassuming village of Roundwood makes a handy staging post for a meal and a rest for walkers on the Wicklow Way, which runs 2.5km past the town to the west.

🛏 Sleeping & Eating

Roundwood Caravan & Camping Park CAMPGROUND €
(📞 01-281 8163; www.dublinwicklowcamping.com; R755; campsite per adult/child €8/4, plus per tent/campervan €8; ⏱ mid-Apr–Sep; 🅿🛜) Located 500m north of the village and served by the twice-daily St Kevins Bus service between Dublin and Glendalough, Roundwood's campground has good shelter (though no views) and amenities including a kitchen, dining area and TV lounge.

Byrne & Woods IRISH €€
(📞 01-281 7078; www.byrneandwoods.com; Main St; mains €14-26; ⏱ 12.30-9pm Thu-Sat, to 8pm Wed & Sun) At this elegant restaurant housed in an old cottage in Roundwood, Wicklow rainbow trout, chargrilled Kildare rib-eye and roast Blessington duck are among the locally sourced dishes, and are accompanied by well-chosen wines. The service is excellent.

❶ Getting There & Away

St Kevins Bus (www.glendaloughbus.com) passes through Roundwood on its journey between Dublin (€13, one hour, two daily) and Glendalough (€5, 30 minutes).

Glendalough

If you've come to Wicklow, chances are that a visit to Glendalough (Gleann dá Loch, meaning 'Valley of the Two Lakes') is one of your main reasons. And rightly so, for this is one of the most beautiful corners of the whole country and the epitome of Ireland's rugged, romantic landscape.

The substantial remains of this important monastic settlement are certainly impressive, but an added draw is the splendid setting: two dark and mysterious lakes tucked into a long, glacial valley fringed by forest. It is, despite its immense popularity, a deeply tranquil and spiritual place, and you will have little difficulty in understanding why those solitude-seeking monks came here in the first place.

History

In AD 498 a young monk named Kevin arrived in the Glendalough Valley looking for somewhere to kick back, meditate and be at one with nature. He pitched up in what had been a Bronze Age tomb on the southern side of the Upper Lake and for the next seven years slept on stones, wore animal skins, maintained a near-starvation diet and – according to the legend – became bosom buddies with the birds and animals. Kevin's ecofriendly lifestyle soon attracted a bunch of disciples, all seemingly unaware of the irony that they were flocking to hang out with a hermit who wanted to live as far away from other people as possible. Over the next couple of centuries his one-man undertaking mushroomed into an established settlement and by the 9th century Glendalough rivalled Clonmacnoise as the island's premier monastic city. Thousands of students studied and lived in a thriving community that was spread over a considerable area.

Glendalough

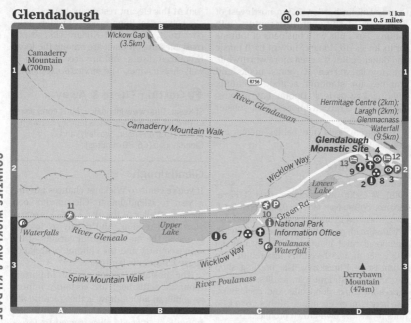

Glendalough

◎ Top Sights
1 Glendalough Monastic Site	D2

◎ Sights
Cathedral of St Peter & St Paul	(see 1)
2 Deer Stone	D2
3 Glendalough Visitor Centre	D2
4 Monastery Gatehouse	D2
Priest's House	(see 1)
5 Reefert Church	C3
Round Tower	(see 1)
6 St Kevin's Bed	C3
7 St Kevin's Cell	C3
St Kevin's Kitchen	(see 8)
8 St Kieran's Church	D2
9 St Mary's Church	D2
Teampall na Skellig	(see 6)

☉ Activities, Courses & Tours
10 Go Beyond Adventure	C2
11 Mine Workings Walk	A2

⊟ Sleeping
12 Glendalough Hotel	D2
13 Glendalough International Hostel	D2

Inevitably Glendalough's success made it a key target for Viking raiders, who sacked the monastery at least four times between 775 and 1071. The final blow came in 1398, when English forces from Dublin almost destroyed it. Efforts were made to rebuild and some life lingered on here as late as the 17th century when, under renewed repression, the monastery finally died.

◉ Sights

While the Upper Lake has the best scenery, the most fascinating buildings lie in the lower part of the valley east of the Lower Lake, huddled together around the heart of the ancient monastic site. A woodland trail and boardwalk link the two lakes; it takes about 20 to 30 minutes to walk from one to the other.

★ Glendalough Monastic Site
CHRISTIAN SITE
(www.glendalough.ie; ⊙24hr) FREE Nestled between two lakes, haunting Glendalough is one of the most significant monastic sites in Ireland and one of the loveliest spots in the country, centred on a 1000-year-old Round Tower, a ruined cathedral and a tiny church known as St Kevin's Kitchen. It was founded in the late 5th century by St Kevin, a bishop who established a monastery on the Upper

WALK: THE WICKLOW WAY – GLENDALOUGH TO AUGHRIM

The 127km Wicklow Way (www.wicklowway.com) is one of Ireland's most popular long-distance walks because of its remarkable scenery and its relatively fluid and accessible starting and finishing points – there are plenty of half- and full-day options along the way.

This section is 37km long and takes you through some of the more remote parts of the Wicklow Mountains and down into the southeastern foothills. There's relatively little road walking; the greater part of the day is through conifer plantations. The walk should take between 7½ and eight hours, with an ascent of 1035m.

From the **National Park Information Office** (☎ 0404-45425; www.wicklowmountains nationalpark.ie; Bolger's Cottage, Upper Lake car park; ☺ 10am-5.30pm May-Sep, to dusk Sat & Sun Oct-Apr) on the southern side of Glendalough's Upper Lake, climb the yellow-waymarked trail beside Lugduff Brook and **Poulanass Waterfall**. Veer left when you meet a forest track, then left again at a junction and cross two bridges. The Way leads northeast for about 600m then, from a tight right bend, heads almost directly southwards (via a series of clearly marked junctions), up through the conifer plantations, across Lugduff Brook again and beside a tributary, to open ground on the saddle between **Mullacor** (657m) and **Lugduff** (652m; 1¾ hours from Glendalough). From here on a good day, massive Lugnaquilla sprawls across the view to the southwest; in the opposite direction is Camaderry's long ridge above Glendalough, framed against the bulk of Tonelagee. Follow the raised boardwalk down, contour above a plantation and drop into it where a steep muddy and rocky path descends to a forest road; turn left.

If you're planning to stay at Glenmalure Hostel (p163), rather than go all the way down to the crossroads in Glenmalure, follow the Way from the left turn for about 1km southwards. At an oblique junction where the Way turns southeast, bear left in a westerly direction and descend steeply to the road in Glenmalure. The hostel is about 2km northwest.

To continue straight on along the Way from the left turn, follow forest roads south then southeast for 1.6km to a wide zigzag above open ground, then contour the steep slope, swing northeast and drop down to a minor road beside two bridges. Continue down to an intersection and Glenmalure; it's about 1¼ hours from the saddle.

The Way presses straight on (south) through the crossroads for 500m, across the River Avonbeg and past silent **Drumgoff Barracks**, built in 1803 but long since derelict, then right along a forest track. Keep left past a ruined cottage and start to gain height in two fairly long reaches; go through two left turns then it's down and across a stream. About 800m further on, turn right along a path to start the long ascent almost to the top of **Slieve Maan** (550m) via four track junctions, maintaining a southwesterly to south-southwesterly direction. Back on a forest track, the Way turns left (southeast) close to unforested ground to the west. With a few more convoluted turns, you're out of the trees and on a path between the plantation and the road (mapped as the Military Rd). The Way eventually meets the latter beside a small tributary of the River Aghavannagh (two hours from Glenmalure).

Walk down the road for about 250m, then turn off left along a forest track, shortly bearing left to gain height steadily on a wide path over **Carrickashane Mountain** (508m). Descend steeply to a wide forest road and continue down for about 1km. Bear right to reach a minor road and turn right. Leave the road 500m further on and drop down to another road – Iron Bridge is just to the right (an hour from Military Rd).

Walk 150m up to a road and turn left; follow this road down the valley of the River Ow for 7.5km to a junction – Aughrim is to the left, another 500m. Buses on the Dublin–Wexford route stop here.

Lake's southern shore and about whom there is much folklore.

During the Middle Ages, when Ireland was known as 'the island of saints and scholars', Glendalough became a monastic city catering to thousands of students and teachers. The site is entered through the only surviving monastic gateway in Ireland.

The Glendalough Visitor Centre (p153), opposite the Lower Lake car park, has historical displays and a good 20-minute audiovisual show. From the Upper Lake

Glendalough
A WALKING TOUR

A visit to Glendalough is a trip through ancient history and a refreshing hike in the hills. The ancient monastic settlement founded by St Kevin in the 5th century grew to be quite powerful by the 9th century, but it started falling into ruin from 1398 onwards. Still, you won't find more evocative clumps of stones anywhere.

Start at the ❶ **Main Gateway** to the monastic city, where you will find a cluster of important ruins, including the (nearly perfect) 10th-century ❷ **Round Tower**, the ❸ **cathedral** dedicated to Sts Peter and Paul, and ❹ **St Kevin's Kitchen**, which is really a church. Cross the stream past the famous ❺ **Deer Stone**, where Kevin was supposed to have milked a doe, and turn west along the path. It's a 1.5km walk to the ❻ **Upper Lake**. On the lake's southern shore is another cluster of sites, including the ❼ **Reefert Church**, a plain 11th-century Romanesque church where the powerful O'Toole family buried their kin, and ❽ **St Kevin's Cell**, the remains of a beehive hut where Kevin is said to have lived.

ST KEVIN

St Kevin came to the valley as a young monk in AD 498, in search of a peaceful retreat. He was reportedly led by an angel to a Bronze Age tomb now known as St Kevin's Bed. For seven years he slept on stones, wore animal skins, survived on nettles and herbs and – according to legend – developed an affinity with the birds and animals. One legend has it that, when Kevin needed milk for two orphaned babies, a doe stood waiting at the Deer Stone to be milked.

Kevin soon attracted a group of disciples and the monastic settlement grew, until by the 9th century Glendalough rivalled Clonmacnoise as Ireland's premier monastic city. According to legend, Kevin lived to the age of 120. He was canonised in 1903.

Round Tower
Glendalough's most famous landmark is the 33m-high Round Tower, which is exactly as it was when it was built a thousand years ago except for the roof; this was replaced in 1876 after a lightning strike.

Deer Stone
The spot where St Kevin is said to have truly become one with the animals is really just a large mortar called a *bullaun*, used for grinding food and medicine.

St Kevin's Kitchen
This small church is unusual in that it has a round tower sticking out of the roof – it looks like a chimney, hence the church's nickname.

St Kevin's Cell
This beehive hut is reputedly where St Kevin would go for prayer and meditation; not to be confused with St Kevin's Bed, a cave where he used to sleep.

Reefert Church
Its name derives from the Irish *righ fearta*, which means 'burial place of the kings'. Seven princes of the powerful O'Toole family are buried in this simple structure.

Upper Lake
The site of St Kevin's original settlement is on the banks of the Upper Lake, one of the two lakes that give Glendalough its name – the 'Valley of the Two Lakes'.

⑧

⑦

⑥

②

③

①

NORTH ↓

INFORMATION
At the eastern end of the Upper Lake is the National Park Information Office, which has leaflets and maps on the site, local walks etc. The grassy spot in front of the office is a popular picnic spot in summer.

Cathedral of St Peter & St Paul
The largest of Glendalough's seven churches, the cathedral was built gradually between the 10th and 13th centuries. The earliest part is the nave, where you can still see the *antae* (slightly projecting column at the end of the wall) used for supporting a wooden roof.

Main Gateway
The only surviving entrance to the ecclesiastical settlement is a double arch; notice that the inner arch rises higher than the outer one in order to compensate for the upward slope of the causeway.

(1.5km west of the visitor centre), several good hiking trails head into the hills.

Visitors swarm to Glendalough in summer, so it's best to arrive early and/or stay late, preferably on a weekday, as the site is free and open 24 hours. The lower car park gates are locked when the visitor centre closes.

LOWER LAKE

Monastery Gatehouse   GATE
The stone arch of the monastery gatehouse is the only surviving example of a monastic entranceway in the country. Just inside the entrance is a large slab with an incised cross.

Round Tower   TOWER
The 10th-century Round Tower is 33m tall and 16m in circumference at the base. The upper storeys and conical roof were reconstructed in 1876.

Cathedral of St Peter & St Paul   RUINS
The Cathedral of St Peter and St Paul, just southeast of the Round Tower, has a 10th-century nave; the chancel and sacristy date from the 12th century.

Priest's House   HISTORIC SITE
At the centre of the graveyard, to the southwest of the Cathedral of St Peter & St Paul, is the Priest's House. This odd building dates from 1170 but has been heavily reconstructed. It may have been the location of shrines to St Kevin. Later, during penal times, it became a burial site for local priests – hence the name.

St Kevin's Kitchen   CHURCH
Glendalough's trademark is St Kevin's Kitchen or Church, at the southern edge of the monastic site (p156). This compact structure, with a miniature round-tower-like belfry, protruding sacristy and steep stone roof, is a masterpiece. It was never a kitchen, instead getting its name because its belfry resembles a kitchen chimney. The oldest parts of the building date from the 11th century – the structure has been remodelled since; but it's still a classic early Irish church.

Deer Stone   MONUMENT
At the junction with Green Rd as you cross the river just south of the Glendalough monastic site (p156) is the Deer Stone, set in the middle of a group of rocks. Legend claims that when St Kevin needed milk for two orphaned babies, a doe stood here waiting to be milked. The stone is actually a *bullaun* (a stone used as a mortar for grinding medicines or food).

Many such stones are thought to be pre-historic, and they were widely regarded as having supernatural properties: women who bathed their faces with water from the hollow were supposed to keep their looks forever. The early churchmen brought the stones into their monasteries, perhaps hoping to inherit some of their powers.

St Mary's Church   CHURCH
The 10th-century St Mary's Church, to the southwest of the Round Tower, stands outside the walls of the Glendalough monastic site (p156) and belonged to local nuns. It has a lovely western doorway.

St Kieran's Church   RUINS
There are but scant remains of St Kieran's Church, the smallest at the site (p156). It's to the east of St Mary's Church.

UPPER LAKE

Reefert Church   CHURCH
The considerable remains of Reefert Church sit above the tiny River Poulanass, south of the Upper Lake car park. It's a small, plain, 11th-century Romanesque nave-and-chancel church with some reassembled arches and walls. Traditionally, Reefert (literally 'Royal Burial Place') was the burial site of the chiefs of the local O'Toole family. The surrounding graveyard contains a number of rough stone crosses and slabs, most made of shiny mica schist.

St Kevin's Cell   RUINS
Climb the steps at the back of the Reefert Churchyard and follow the path to the west and you'll find, at the top of a rise overlooking the Upper Lake, the scant remains of St Kevin's Cell, a small beehive hut.

Teampall na Skellig   RUINS
The original site of St Kevin's settlement, Teampall na Skellig is at the base of the cliffs towering over the southern side of the Upper Lake and accessible only by boat. There's no boat service to the site so you'll have to settle for looking at it from across the lake. The terraced shelf has the reconstructed ruins of a church and early graveyard. Rough wattle huts once stood on the raised ground nearby.

Scattered around are some early grave slabs and simple stone crosses.

St Kevin's Bed   MONUMENT
Just east of Teampall na Skellig, and 10m above the Upper Lake's waters, is the 2m-deep artificial cave called St Kevin's Bed,

said to be where Kevin lived. The earliest human habitation of the cave was long before St Kevin's era – there's evidence that people lived in the valley for thousands of years before any monks arrived.

🏃 Activities & Tours

The Glendalough Valley is all about walking. There are nine waymarked trails in the valley, the longest of which is about 10km, or about four hours' walking. Before you set off, drop by the National Park Information Office (p157) and pick up the relevant leaflet and trail map. It also has a number of excellent guides for sale – you won't go far wrong with Joss Lynam's *Easy Walks Near Dublin* or Helen Fairbairn's *Dublin & Wicklow: A Walking Guide*.

A word of warning: don't be fooled by the relative gentleness of the surrounding countryside or the fact that the Wicklow Mountains are really no taller than big hills. The weather can be merciless here, so be sure to take the usual precautions, have the right equipment and tell someone where you're going and when you should be back. For Mountain Rescue call 112 or 999.

The easiest and most popular walk is the gentle hike along the northern shore of the Upper Lake to the old lead and zinc **mine workings**, which date from 1800. The better route is along the lakeshore rather than on the road (which runs 30m in from the shore), a distance of about 2.5km one way from the Glendalough Visitor Centre. Continue up to the head of the valley if you wish.

Alternatively, you can walk up the **Spink** (from the Irish for 'pointed hill'; 380m), the steep ridge with vertical cliffs running along the southern flanks of the Upper Lake. You can go part of the way and turn back, or complete a circuit of the Upper Lake by following the top of the cliff, eventually coming down by the mine workings and going back along the northern shore. This circuit is about 6km long and takes around three hours.

The third option is a hike up **Camaderry Mountain** (700m), hidden behind the hills that flank the northern side of the valley. The path (not waymarked) begins opposite the entrance to the Upper Lake car park (near a 'Wicklow Mountains National Park' sign). Head straight up the steep hill to the north and you come out on open mountains with sweeping views in all directions. You can then continue west up the ridge to Camaderry summit. To the top of Camaderry and

back is about 7.5km and takes around four hours.

Wild Wicklow Tour   BUS
(☑ 01-280 1899; www.wildwicklow.ie; adult/child €33/28; ⊙ departs 8.50am) These award-winning day trips from Dublin to Glendalough via Avoca Handweavers (p155) and the Sally Gap (p154) never fail to generate rave reviews for atmosphere and all-round fun. There are a variety of pick-up points throughout Dublin; the first is at the Shelbourne hotel. Tours return to Dublin around 6pm.

Go Beyond Adventure   OUTDOORS
(☑ 087 935 3868; www.gobeyondadventure.ie; rock climbing per day from €80; ⊙ by reservation Mar-Oct) Go Beyond Adventure runs rock-climbing expeditions for all levels of experience; rates include equipment. Trips depart from the Upper Lake car park. Guided half-day to multiday hiking trips can also be arranged.

🛏 Sleeping & Eating

Glendalough International Hostel   HOSTEL €
(☑ 0404-45342; www.anoige.ie; The Lodge; dm/tw from €19.50/55; P 🕯) This modern hostel is conveniently situated near Glendalough's ancient monastic site, set within the scenic Glendalough Valley. All dorms have their own bathrooms and there's a decent cafeteria on the premises, as well as a self-catering kitchen and a drying room.

Glendalough Hermitage Centre   COTTAGE €
(☑ 087 935 6696; www.glendaloughhermitage.ie; Laragh; s/d €50/80) For spiritual R&R, five hermitages (really just plain one- and two-bed cottages) are rented out by St Kevin's Parish Church. Facilities are pretty basic but comfortable: there's a bathroom, electric blanket, small kitchen and an open fire supplemented by a storage heater. The cottages are 1.5km east of Glendalough in Laragh. Minimum stay is two nights. Cash only.

Visitors are welcome to join in morning and evening prayer, but the venture is not exclusively Catholic and all faiths and denominations are welcome.

★ Heather House   B&B €€
(☑ 0404-45157; www.heatherhouse.ie; Glendalough Rd, Laragh; d from €100; P 🕯) Understated country-style elegance radiates from the luxurious bedrooms at this superb-value B&B, around 2km east of Glendalough. There's a lovely garden at the back with a view along the wooded valley (two of the bedrooms are in self-contained garden chalets), and it's just

OFF THE BEATEN TRACK

GLENMACNASS WATERFALL

Desolate and utterly deserted, the Glenmacnass Valley – a stretch of wild bogland between the Sally Gap crossroads and Laragh that contains the **Glenmacnass Waterfall** (Military Rd; ⊘24hr) – is one of the most beautiful parts of the Wicklow Mountains, and the sense of isolation is quite dramatic. The highest mountain to the west is Mullaghcleevaun (848m), and River Glenmacnass flows south and tumbles over the edge of the mountain plateau in a great foaming cascade. It's 9.5km north of Glendalough. There's a car park near the top of the waterfall.

Be careful when walking on rocks near Glenmacnass Waterfall as a few people have slipped to their deaths here. There are fine walks up Mullaghcleevaun and in the hills to the east of the car park.

next door to the Wicklow Heather restaurant (where you check in).

Glendalough Hotel   HOTEL €€
(☑0404-45135; www.glendaloughhotel.com; Main St; s/d/f from €129/149/179; ℗🐾) There's no mistaking Glendalough's only hotel, conveniently located next door to the visitor centre. There is also no shortage of takers for its 44 chintzy bedrooms – it's a popular venue for weddings and tour groups. Some rooms have balconies; family rooms sleep four. Along with a bistro there's a more upmarket restaurant.

Cots and kids' menus are available.

Wicklow Heather   INTERNATIONAL €€
(☑0404-45157; www.wicklowheather.ie; Glendalough Rd, Laragh; mains €13-29; ⊘8am-9.30pm Mon-Thu, to 10pm Fri & Sat, to 9pm Sun) This long-established rustic family restaurant serves breakfast through to dinner amid the honeyed glow of polished wood. The globe-trotting menu ranges from Wicklow lamb, wild venison, Irish beef and fish (including excellent trout) to satay dishes, Cajun chicken, and tomato and basil arancini. Its Writers Room houses a display of Irish literary memorabilia; there's also a well-stocked whiskey bar.

ⓘ Information

The National Park Information Office (p157) provides info about Wicklow Mountains National Park, and is the place to pick up maps and leaflets about local hiking trails. It's located by the Upper Lake car park, 1.5km west of the Glendalough Visitor Centre (p153).

ⓘ Getting There & Away

St Kevins Bus (www.glendaloughbus.com) departs from the bus stop on St Stephen's Green North in Dublin at 11.30am and 6pm daily (one way/return €13/20, 1½ hours); from March to October the evening bus leaves at 7pm on Saturday and Sunday. It also stops at the Town Hall in Bray. Departures from Glendalough are at 7am and 4.30pm weekdays, and 9.45am and 5.40pm on weekends. Buy your ticket on the bus. On weekdays in July and August there's an additional service from Glendalough to Dublin departing at 9.45am.

Glenmalure

As you head deeper into the mountains southwest of Glendalough, near the southern end of the Military Rd, everything gets a bit wilder and more remote. Beneath the eastern slopes of Wicklow's highest peak, Lugnaquilla (925m), is Glenmalure, a dark and sombre valley flanked by scree slopes.

⊙ Sights & Activities

After coming over the mountains from Laragh to Glenmalure, turn northwest at the Drumgoff bridge. From there it's about 6km up the road beside the River Avonbeg to a car park where trails lead off in various directions.

You can walk up the hidden Fraughan Rock Glen west of the car park, and – for experienced hill walkers only – continue to the summit of **Lugnaquilla** (925m; allow six hours for the return trip).

The head of Glenmalure and parts of the neighbouring Glen of Imaal are off-limits. It's military land that's well marked with warning signs.

Greenan Maze   PARK
(☑086 884 5624; www.greenanmaze.com; Ballinanty; adult/child €8/7; ⊘10am-6pm daily Jun-Aug, Sat & Sun Apr, May & Sep) Finding your way out of this 2m-high Celtic hedge maze is harder than it looks. Watch others attempt it from the viewing tower; there's also a hedgeless, ground-level solstice maze for contemplation. Other attractions include three small museums (one on farming history, a bottle museum and a restored 16th-century farmhouse), a gentle nature trail taking in woodland, wetlands and ponds (and occasional

wild deer), and farm animals (lambs, piglets, draught horses and more). Also here are a craft shop and tearooms.

Cullen's Rock

MEMORIAL

(⊗24hr) FREE At the side of the Glenmalure road, 260m west of Drumgoff bridge, is Dwyer's or Cullen's Rock, commemorating both the Glenmalure battle and Michael Dwyer, a member of the United Irishmen who fought unsuccessfully against the English in the 1798 Rising and holed up here. Men were hanged from the rock during the Rising.

🛏 Sleeping & Eating

Glenmalure Hostel

HOSTEL €

(☑01-830 4555; www.anoige.ie; Baravore; dm from €20; ⊗daily Jun-Aug, Sat only Sep-May) No telephone (the listed number is An Óige head office), no electricity (lighting is by gas) and no running water, just a rustic two-storey former hunting lodge with 19 beds, a gas stove, water from the stream, and an open log fire. And a top literary connection – this place was the setting for JM Synge's play *The Shadow of a Gunman*.

You can take a car to the hostel if the river is low enough to drive across; if not, it's a 750m walk northwest from the parking area by the bridge. Otherwise, you can hike here from Laragh, following the Wicklow Way south over the hills to the Glenmalure Lodge Hotel, then continuing up the valley (14km in total).

Glenmalure Lodge

PUB FOOD €€

(☑0404-46188; www.glenmalurelodge.ie; mains €9-15.50; ⊗kitchen 7.30-10am & noon-9pm, bar 10am-11pm; 🐾) Hearty all-day pub food at Glenmalure Lodge includes steak and Guinness pie, lamb stew, leek and potato soup and a ploughman's lunch. Breakfast is available for guests and nonguests; hikers can also get packed lunches (€6.50) with sandwiches, fruit, chocolate and bottled water. Trad music often plays in the bar; upstairs are 14 simple but comfortable guest rooms (double/triple €60/90).

ⓘ Getting There & Away

The privately run Wicklow Way Bus (www. wicklowwaybus.com) picks up hikers from Rathdrum train station (serving Dublin) and drops off at Laragh, Glendalough Visitor Centre and Glenmalure Lodge among other places (€8, one hour, twice daily). It is not a scheduled service, and must be booked in advance.

Eastern Wicklow

The coastal towns and rolling valleys of eastern Wicklow play second fiddle to the mountains in terms of dramatic scenery, but have a subtle charm. Highlights include the seaside towns of Bray and Greystones, the historic jail in Wicklow town and the beautiful Vale of Avoca.

A string of beaches – Silver Strand, Brittas Bay and Maheramore – starts 16km south of Wicklow town. With high dunes, safe bathing and powdery sand, the beaches attract droves of Dubliners in good weather.

Bray

POP 32,600

Right on the County Dublin border and less than 25km from the centre of the capital, County Wicklow's biggest town stretches along a 1.6km sand and shingle beach fronted by a broad promenade.

Bray (Bré in Irish) evolved into a seaside resort after the arrival of the railway in 1854. Although tourism later declined when cheap flights made it easier for Dubliners to head to sunnier climes, grand buildings from its 19th-century heyday still line the waterfront and it remains a popular day-trip destination. Visitor numbers peak during late July, when Bray hosts the country's largest air show, the Bray Air Display.

MT USHER GARDENS

Wicklow's nickname, 'the Garden of Ireland', is justified by green idylls such as the 8-hectare **Mt Usher Gardens** (☑0404-49672; www.mountushergardens. ie; Ashford; adult/child €8/4; ⊗10am-5pm), just outside the unremarkable town of Ashford, about 10km south of Greystones on the N11. Trees, shrubs and herbaceous plants from around the world are laid out in Robinsonian style – ie according to the naturalist principles of famous Irish gardener William Robinson (1838–1935) – rather than in the formalist manner of preceding gardens.

There's also an Avoca cafe on the premises, as well as a 'shopping courtyard' where you can buy freshly baked goods, ice cream, plants, furniture, clothing, and art, including photography.

WORTH A TRIP

BALLYKNOCKEN HOUSE

Ballyknocken House & Cookery School (☏0404-44627; www.bally knocken.ie; Glenealy, Ashford; d/tr from €129/176; P☎) is a beautiful ivy-clad Victorian home, where each of the seven carefully appointed bedrooms has antique furnishings, and some with original, stencilled claw-foot tubs. Besides the home itself, the big draw is Catherine Fulvio's cooking classes (from €140), which run throughout the year; check the website for schedules. It's 10km west of Wicklow town off the R752.

⊙ Sights & Activities

★**Killruddery House & Gardens** HOUSE
(☏01-286 3405; www.killruddery.com; Southern Cross Rd; house & gardens adult/child €15.50/5.50, garden only €8.50/3; ⊙house 9.30am-6pm Sat-Thu May-Sep, Sat & Sun only Apr & Oct, gardens 9.30am-6pm daily May-Sep, Sat & Sun only Apr & Oct) A stunning mansion in the Elizabethan Revival style, Killruddery has been home to the Brabazon family (the earls of Meath) since 1618 and has one of the oldest gardens in Ireland, with a magnificent orangery built in 1852 and chock-full of statuary and plant life. Compulsory 45-minute guided tours lead you through the impressive house, designed by architects Richard Morrisson and his son William in 1820. It's 2km south of Bray just off the R768.

The house was reduced to its present-day still-huge proportions by the 14th earl in 1953; he was obviously looking for something a little more bijou.

An excellent farmers market sets up from 10am to 3pm on Saturdays year-round.

Brave Maeve Story Trail PUBLIC ART
(www.bray.ie; The Promenade; ⊙24hr; ☝) Along Bray's seafront promenade, this kids' walking trail links up five brightly coloured murals created by children's author and illustrator Chris Judge and 50 local children. Together, the murals tell the story of Maeve, a young giant who is searching for a home for her family, encountering monsters and mythical figures along the way. The trail is 1.5km long; download a free map from the website (there's also a free app).

Sea Life AQUARIUM
(☏01-286 6939; www.visitsealife.com; Strand Rd; adult/child €13.50/10.50; ⊙10am-6pm daily mid-Feb–late Nov, 11am-5pm Mon-Fri, 10am-6pm Sat & Sun late Nov–mid-Feb; ☝) Resident marine creatures at the only aquarium in Ireland's east coast include sharks, rays, eels, tropical and cold-water fish, piranhas, octopuses, turtles and sea horses. Feeding sessions take place throughout the day; kids can pet crabs, starfish and sea urchins in the rock-pool-style touch tank.

Online bookings can be up to 20% cheaper, and are recommended for weekends and school holidays.

Cliff Walk WALKING
(www.bray.ie) From the base of Bray Head, at the seafront's southern edge, a signposted path runs for 7km along the clifftop to Greystones. En route, look out for Black Harbour porpoises, dolphins and basking sharks. Birdlife includes sparrowhawks, kestrel falcons and hen harriers; on land, you might spot Ireland's only reptile, the viviparous lizard. You can return to Bray by train.

The track was built in the 1840s as a supply road during the construction of the railway.

Brennanstown Riding School HORSE RIDING
(☏01-286 3778; www.brennanstownrs.ie; Southern Cross Rd; 2hr trek adult/child from €70/50, 1hr lesson from €45/35; ⊙by reservation) Equipped with a large indoor training area as well as three outdoor areas, this riding school 2.5km southwest of Bray's town centre provides lessons and runs treks into the Wicklow Mountains for riders of all levels. All-day treks are available on request.

Everest Cycles CYCLING
(☏01-282 8660; www.everestcycles.ie; Unit 4, Industrial Yarns, Dublin Rd; bike hire per day/week €15/75; ⊙9.30am-6pm Mon-Sat) The hybrid road/mountain bikes for hire at this knowledgeable outfit are ideal for a day trip or a longer ride into the Wicklow Mountains. Rates include helmets; child seats are free. You can also rent bike racks to attach to your car (per day €20).

⚘ Festivals & Events

Bray Air Display AIR SHOW
(www.brayairdisplay.com; ⊙late Jul) Bray's famous air show – Ireland's largest – takes place over two days in late July. Overhead you'll see flyovers and aerobatic manoeuvres, while on the ground at the seafront park on Strand Rd there are artisan food, drink and craft stalls, a fun fair, music concerts, plus opportunities for helicopter flights.

🛏 Sleeping

Esplanade Hotel
HOTEL €€

(📞01-286 2056; www.esplanadehotel.ie; Strand Rd; s/d/tr/f from €94/99/109/119; 🛜) Topped by turrets, this red-brick Victorian hotel is a Bray landmark. The pick of the rooms are the 38 in the original seafront building (some with bay windows and period furnishings); another 56 occupy a modern extension. Food is served day and night in Oscar's Bar (mains €11.50 to €19.50) and evenings only at the Breakers Seaview Restaurant (mains €17 to €31.50).

Family rooms sleep up to four.

Strand Hotel
BOUTIQUE HOTEL €€

(📞01-548 2960; www.thestrandhotelbray.com; Strand Rd; d from €165; 🛜) Built in 1870 by Sir William and Lady Jane Wilde, this beautifully restored property was inherited by their son, poet and playwright Oscar, in 1876. Named for his works, its 10 unexpectedly contemporary rooms are reached by a sweeping timber staircase (there's no lift); some have sea views. Breakfast is served at the 1st-floor cafe, which opens to a panoramic terrace.

The ground-floor pub hosts regular live music.

🍴 Eating & Drinking

⭐ Dockyard No 8
CAFE €€

(📞01-276 1795; www.dockyardno8.ie; 8 Dock Tce; breakfast & lunch dishes €7-19, dinner mains €16-24; ⏱9am-4.30pm Sun-Wed, 9am-4.30pm & 5.30-9.30pm Thu-Sat; 🛜) By day this harbourside cafe opposite the shipyard is a fantastic spot for breakfast (ham hock eggs Benedict; Belgian waffles with smoked bacon) and lunch (chowder with chorizo; seafood baskets with calamari, tiger prawns and daily-caught fish), especially when the retractable roof opens up. At dinner, refined mains might include Parma-ham-wrapped cod on white-bean cassoulet.

Platform Pizza
PIZZA €€

(📞01-538 4000; www.platformpizzabar.com; Strand Rd; pizzas €12.50-15.75; ⏱noon-10pm Sun-Thu, to 11pm Fri & Sat; 🛜🍴🪑) Wood-fired pizzas at this hip restaurant have won it a host of awards, including 'Ireland's Best Pizza'. Toppings include stracciatella cheese with roast tomato and artichokes, and smoked pancetta with wild mushrooms and mascarpone. There are craft cocktails and local craft beers, and kids' menus include pizzas and design-your-own-dessert options, and come with a cute activity sheet. Takeaway is available.

While the pizzas take top billing, lunch and dinner dishes include flatbreads, pastas, gourmet salads and more substantial dishes (eg roast chicken or pan-fried sea bass).

⭐ Harbour Bar
PUB

(www.theharbourbar.ie; 1-4 Dock Tce; ⏱1-11.30pm Mon-Thu, to 12.30am Fri, noon-12.30am Sat, noon-11pm Sun; 🛜) Four former fisherman's terraces make up this maze of rooms with vintage maritime bric-a-brac (and a resident cat). Craft-beer options by local brewers include County Wickow's Wicklow Wolf (made in Bray), Larkin's Brewing (from nearby Kilcoole), and County Kildare's Whiplash (from Cellbridge). The beer garden gets rammed on sunny days; live music plays from Wednesday to Sunday.

It's been a pub since 1872; James Joyce, Katharine Hepburn, Peter O'Toole, Laurence Olivier, Roddy Doyle and U2's Bono are among its past patrons.

ℹ Information

Tourist Office (📞01-286 7128; www.bray.ie; Civic Offices, Main St; ⏱10am-1pm & 2-4.30pm Tue-Fri) Provides information on Bray and the surrounding area.

ℹ Getting There & Away

BUS

Bus Éireann (www.buseireann.ie) serves Dublin (€3.60, 30 minutes, hourly).

Dublin Bus (www.dublinbus.ie) serves Dublin Heuston (€3.30, one hour, every 10 minutes Monday to Friday, every 15 minutes Saturday, four services on Sunday).

St Kevins Bus (www.glendaloughbus.com) has two daily services to/from Dublin (€3, 40 minutes), continuing to Roundwood (€5, 25 minutes) and Glendalough (€9, 40 minutes).

Aircoach (www.aircoach.ie) has a direct service to Dublin Airport (€12, 1¼ hours, hourly).

TRAIN

DART (www.irishrail.ie) suburban trains run from Dublin (€3.60, 50 minutes, up to eight per hour) and continue to Greystones (€2.25, 10 minutes).

Greystones

The upmarket coastal town of Greystones, 33km south of Dublin, was originally a fishing village and Victorian seaside resort, and the seafront around the little harbour is idyllic. In summer the bay is dotted with dinghies and windsurfers, and there are two sandy beaches – the South Beach is a Blue Flag one – as well as a scenic cliff walk to Bray.

The town itself rewards a little exploration, with vintage shops, boutiques, cafes and some excellent restaurants.

Druid's Glen Resort
GOLF

(☑ 01-287 0812; www.druidsglenresort.com; Newtownmountkennedy; green fees from €60) The four-time host of the Irish Open is known locally as the 'Augusta of Europe'. It's a beautiful, forested championship golf course with some spectacular holes. It's 8km south of Greystones.

A second course, Druid's Heath, is considered a tougher test.

On-site accommodation (double/family/suite from €185/200/360) rambles over 140 contemporary, countrified rooms; also here is a luxury spa.

★ Firehouse Bakery
BAKERY, CAFE €

(☑ 01-287 6822; www.thefirehouse.ie; Old Delgany Inn, R762, Delgany; breads & pastries €2.50-5.50, dishes €7.50-13.50; ☺ 8.30am-5pm Mon-Fri, 9.30am-5pm Sat & Sun; ☜ ☑) ✎ Pastries are piled high on the counters at this bakery/cafe 3km southwest of Greystones. Breakfast (eg sautéed wild Wicklow Mountains mushrooms and poached eggs on sourdough baked in a wood-fired oven) is served to noon; lunch dishes include spectacular pizzas (such as blue cheese and pear or smoked aubergine, tomato and mint sour cream). Coffee comes from on-site roastery Roasted Brown.

The attached deli sells produce from local artisans, farmers and foragers, plus freshly caught seafood. Upstairs is gourmet restaurant Pigeon House.

Happy Pear
CAFE €

(www.thehappypear.ie; Church Rd; dishes €2.80-7.50; ☺ 9am-5pm Mon-Fri, to 6pm Sat & Sun; ☜ ☑) Half of Greystones seem to meet each other for a chat at this hugely popular cafe, deli and organic grocery. Enjoy your porridge with fruit and seeds, washed down with a soy latte, in the upstairs dining area, in the cosy outdoor courtyard, or at a pavement table where you can watch the world go by.

Pigeon House
IRISH €€

(☑ 01-287 7103; www.pigeonhouse.ie; Old Delgany Inn, R762, Delgany; mains lunch €8-16, dinner €14-30; ☺ noon-4pm Tue & Wed, noon-4pm & 5.30-9.30pm Thu & Fri, 10am-4pm & 5.30-9.30pm Sat & Sun; ☜ ☑) ✎ Rustic-contemporary Pigeon House, 3km southwest of Greystones, has a stunning interior of reclaimed timbers, richly coloured walls and a glassed-in kitchen showcasing the

culinary action. Book ahead for fine dining of an evening (offerings include duck-liver parfait with pear-and-raisin chutney; and pan-fried sea bream with samphire gnocchi). Gastropub-style lunch choices span ploughman's lunches with Wicklow blue cheese and caramelised onions to seafood skillets.

Hungry Monk
IRISH €€

(☑ 01-201 0710; www.thehungrymonk.ie; Church Rd; mains €14-23; ☺ 5-11pm Tue-Sat, 12.30-8.30pm Sun) An excellent wine bar, bistro and restaurant on Greystones' main street, the Hungry Monk serves crowd-pleasing classics prepared from premium Irish produce. Expect dishes such as a Wicklow lamb burger with rosemary, slow roast belly of Carlow pork and Dublin Bay prawn scampi, along with blackboard specials that include a 'pie of the day'.

🛈 Getting There & Away

Bus Éireann (www.buseireann.ie) operates buses from Dublin (Georges Quay) to Greystones (€11, 1½ hours, hourly). Aircoach (www.aircoach.ie) has a direct service to Dublin Airport (€12, 1½ hours, hourly).

DART (www.irishrail.ie) commuter trains link Greystones with Dublin Connolly station (€6.20, one hour, up to three per hour) via Bray (€2.25, 10 minutes).

Wicklow Town

POP 10,584

Busy Wicklow town has a working harbour and a commanding position on the crescent curve of a wide bay, which stretches north for about 12km and includes a long pebble beach that makes for a fine walk. It's a service hub rather than a tourist town and, unless you have your own transport, it doesn't make an especially good base for exploring inland.

Wicklow's Historic Gaol
HISTORIC BUILDING

(☑ 0404-61599; www.wicklowshistoricgaol.com; Kilmantin Hill; adult/child incl tour €9.50/6.50, night tour €15; ☺ 10.30am-4.30pm Feb-Nov, 11am-3.30pm Dec & Jan) Wicklow's infamous jail was notorious throughout Ireland for the brutality of its keepers and the harsh conditions suffered by its inmates. The smells, vicious beatings, shocking food and disease-ridden air have long since gone, but adults and children alike can experience a sanitised version of what the prison was like – and stimulate the secret sadist buried deep within – on a highly entertaining tour of the prison, now one of Wicklow's most popular tourist attractions.

The prison was opened in 1702 to house inmates sentenced under the repressive Penal Laws and continued in this role until 1877, when it was reduced to the status of a remand prison (a bridewell), before closing in 1924. The building fell into ruin before finally being restored in the 1990s in recognition of its historic significance.

Actors play the roles of various jailers and prisoners, adding to the sense of drama already heightened by the various exhibits, which include the gruesome dungeon and a life-size treadmill that prisoners would have to turn for hours on end as punishment.

The prison also has a **genealogical library**, where you can scour digital databases for details of Irish ancestry. Tours are every 10 minutes except between 1pm and 2pm. Regular adult-only night tours come complete with ghouls, snacks and a glass of wine.

🛏 Sleeping

Town lodgings are not that great, so if you are planning on staying in the area, you're better off staying in one of the beautiful country homes within a few kilometres of town.

★ Tinakilly Country
House & Restaurant HERITAGE HOTEL €€
(☑ 0404-69274; www.tinakilly.ie; Rathnew; d/ste from €139/169; P⌨) This magnificent Victorian Italianate house 4km northwest of Wicklow town is one of the most elegant country homes in the county. You have a choice between a period room in the west wing (original antiques, and four-poster and half-tester canopy beds) or a sumptuous suite with a view in the east wing. Massage and beauty treatments are available.

The restaurant (mains €14 to €28) utilises local produce, much of it from its own gardens, in dishes such as goat's cheese mousse with hazelnut praline and beetroot dust, venison Wellington, or brown bread berry pudding.

★ Hunter's Hotel HOTEL €€
(☑ 0404-40106; www.hunters.ie; Newrath Bridge, Rathnew; d/tr from €160/190; P⌨) Just outside Rathnew, 5km northwest of Wicklow town on the R761, this exquisite former coaching inn (one of Ireland's oldest) has 16 romantic rooms furnished with antiques. There are flowering gardens, and an attached fine-dining restaurant serves breakfast, lunch, afternoon tea and dinner (two/three courses for €29.50/36.50).

Wicklow Head Lighthouse COTTAGE €€€
(☑ 01-670 4733; www.irishlandmark.com; Dunbar Head; cottage €312; P) Dating from 1781, this six-storey-high stone lighthouse has octagonal rooms with 1m-thick walls and arched windows providing views of the Wicklow Mountains and the Irish Sea, which surrounds it on three sides. Below the top-floor kitchen (reached by 109 stairs; no lift) are two bedrooms, a lounge room and bathroom. Note there's no TV or wi-fi. The minimum stay is two nights.

ⓘ Getting There & Away

Bus Éireann (www.buseireann.ie) runs from Dublin (Georges Quay) to Wicklow town (€11, 1½ hours, hourly).

Rathdrum
POP 1586

The quiet village of Rathdrum, sitting above the River Avonmore at the foot of the Vale of Clara, is famed as the birthplace of nationalist hero Charles Stewart Parnell, whose story is told at nearby Avondale House and in the memorial park at the south end of the main street. Otherwise there's little of interest for visitors, but there are a couple of worthwhile sights and some good walks in the surrounding area.

◉ Sights & Activities

Kilmacurragh Botanic Gardens GARDENS
(☑ 0404-48844; www.botanicgardens.ie; Kilbride; ⊘ 9am-5pm daily Mar-Sep, 9am-4.30pm Mon-Fri, 10am-4.30pm Sat & Sun Oct-Feb) FREE Surrounding the ruins of an 18th-century mansion are these ornamental gardens, originally laid out in 1712 and replanted in the 19th century to reflect the wilder, antiformal style of William Robinson (1838–1935); particularly notable are the South American conifers, the colourful rhododendrons and the avenue of yews. The gardens are 7km east of Rathdrum.

Avondale House HOUSE
(☑ 0404-46111; www.heritageisland.com; Avondale Forest Park) This fine Palladian mansion was the birthplace and Irish headquarters of Charles Stewart Parnell (1846–91), the 'uncrowned king of Ireland' and one of the key figures in the Irish independence movement. Avondale House was designed by James Wyatt in 1779. Its highlights include a stunning vermilion-hued library and the American Room, dedicated to Parnell's eponymous

grandfather, admiral of the USS *Constitution* during the War of 1812. The house is closed for renovations until 2020 but the gardens remain open dawn to dusk year-round.

Wicklow Adventures   OUTDOORS
(☑ 086 727 2872; www.wicklowadventures.ie; Hidden Valley Holiday Park; 1hr guided kayak tour €30, bike hire per day €15; ⊙ by reservation) Guided kayak tours run by Wicklow Adventures take you downstream along the River Avonmore from Laragh to Rathdrum; prices include transport and use of wetsuits and life vests. The company also hires mountain bikes (complete with hi-vis jackets, helmets, bike locks and maps), and offers self-guided tours downhill from Sally Gap (€40 including transport), passing Glenmacnass Waterfall and Glendalough.

Railway Walk   WALKING
(www.coillte.ie) You can hike to Avondale House (p167) from Rathdrum village via this 2km-long trail. The start is hard to find, at the back of a small industrial estate on the far side of the tracks from Rathdrum train station, but thereafter it's a pleasant woodland walk along the banks of the River Avonmore, passing beneath two impressive railway viaducts.

🛏 Sleeping & Eating

Hidden Valley Holiday Park   CAMPGROUND €
(☑ 086 727 2872; www.irelandholidaypark.com; Lower Main St, Glasnaget North; camping per tent/adult/child €16/6/5, glamping/log cabin from €60/80; ℗ 🛜) The River Avonmore flows through this peaceful camping ground, with riverside pitches and safe, shallow swimming. Simple glamping cabins sleeping up to six come with fridges and outdoor picnic tables; log cabins sleeping up to five have bathrooms and kitchenettes. Kids' activities include crazy golf, kayaking and pedalos. Wi-fi is in public areas only. Located 1km north of the village.

Outdoor cinema nights, with beanbags and popcorn, take place in summer.

Brook Lodge & Wells Spa   SPA HOTEL €€€
(☑ 0402-36444; www.brooklodge.com; Macreddin; d/ste from €178/258; ℗ 🛜 ⌷) ✎ This luxurious country-house hotel has 86 beautifully appointed rooms ranging from standard bedrooms with sleigh beds and deep baths to loft-style mezzanine suites. There are two swimming pools, a sumptuous spa (treatments from €40), a Serail mud chamber, Finnish baths and outdoor hot tubs, plus a par-72 golf course designed by Paul McGinley. It's 12km southwest of Rathdrum.

★ Strawberry Tree   IRISH €€€
(☑ 0402-36444; www.brooklodge.com; Brook Lodge, Macreddin; dinner menu €65; ⊙ 7-9pm daily Jul & Aug, Tue-Sun Mar-Jun, Sep & Oct, Sat & Sun Nov-Feb) ✎ There's organic, and then there's certified organic – and this elegant country-style restaurant at Brook Lodge was Ireland's first to be classified as such. Everything is grown on nearby organic farms or foraged from the nearby fields, woods, river and sea. The menu lists the provenance of ingredients used in dishes such as Glenmalure venison with game consommé, or beech-smoked wood pigeon with chestnut terrine.

Bates Restaurant   BISTRO €€
(☑ 0404-29988; www.batesrestaurant.com; 3 Market Sq; mains €18-27; ⊙ 6-8.30pm Wed-Fri, 5.30-9.30pm Sat, 12.30-8pm Sun; ⌷) Housed in a coaching inn that first opened its doors in 1785, this terrific restaurant is hidden down a side alley beside a pub. It puts a premium on exquisitely prepared meat and fish dishes, including a 17oz chateaubriand steak for two (€50). Bookings are recommended for weekend evenings.

A two-course kids' menu costs €10.

ⓘ Information

The small **tourist office** (☑ 0404-46262; www.visitwicklow.ie; Market Sq; ⊙ 9.30am-5pm Mon-Fri) has leaflets and information on the town and surrounding area, including the Wicklow Way.

ⓘ Getting There & Away

Trains serve Rathdrum from Dublin Connolly (€9.50, 1½ hours, five daily) on the main Dublin–Rosslare Harbour line.

Bus Éireann (www.buseireann.ie) links Dublin (Georges Quay) with Rathdrum (€13, two hours, two per day) via Bray (€12, one hour) and Wicklow town (€6, 20 minutes) and on to Avoca (€3.30, 10 minutes).

Vale of Avoca

One of the most scenic spots in County Wicklow is the Vale of Avoca, a darkly wooded valley that begins where the Rivers Avonbeg and Avonmore come together to form the River Avoca. The aptly named Meeting of the Waters was made famous by Thomas Moore's 1808 poem of the same name.

The tiny village of Avoca (Abhóca in Irish) is best known as the birthplace of the superstar of all Irish cottage industries, Avoca Handweavers.

Wicklow Brewery
BREWERY

(📱0404-41661; www.wicklowbrewery.ie; Main St, Redcross; tour €15; ⊗brewery beer hall 2-11pm Sat & Sun, tours by reservation) 🍴 Engaging hour-long tours at this craft brewery guide you through the brewing process, from milling local grains to mashing, whirlpooling, fermenting, maturing and, finally, kegging. Beers are preservative-free and use the brewery's own well water. St Kevins Red Ale and the spicy Gingerknut IPA are standouts. Tours include five tastings (often featuring experimental brews). On weekends you can stop by the brewery's beer hall for a pint; live-music concerts regularly take place amid the kettles and tanks.

Its brews are also available on tap and by the bottle at the attached Mickey Finns Pub.

★Avoca Handweavers
ARTS & CRAFTS

(📱0402-35105; www.avoca.com; Main St; ⊗shop 9.30am-5pm, cafe 9.30am-4pm Mon-Fri, to 5pm Sat & Sun, mill 9.30am-4.30pm) Ireland's oldest working mill is the birthplace of Avoca Handweavers, a company that is now famous across Ireland and the world. The mill has been turning out woollen and other fabrics since 1723, and many of Avoca's clothing and homewares (blankets, cushion covers and more) are produced here and sold in the neighbouring shop.

You're free to wander around the weaving sheds and to chat with the weavers. The cafe serves warming soups, salads, sandwiches and pastries. Arrive early or late to avoid coach tour groups.

🛏 Sleeping & Eating

Woodenbridge Hotel
INN €€

(📱0402-35146; www.woodenbridgehotel.com; R752, Woodenbridge; s/d from €96/103; 🅿🛜) First licensed as a coaching inn in 1608, the Woodenbridge has hosted Sir Walter Scott, Eamon de Valera, Michael Collins and countless other travellers on the old Dublin–Wexford road. The original inn has 29 spacious rooms; another 40 rooms are in the adjacent contemporary riverside Lodge. Many rooms in both buildings open to balconies with views of the vale.

Food is served at the Goldmines Bar, which has live music on weekends, and at the Redmond restaurant (three-course menu €34; open nightly April to September, weekends only October to March), where dishes might include black pudding and wild boar roulade or nettle-stuffed roast partridge.

★Mickey Finns Pub
PUB FOOD €€

(📱0404-41661; www.wicklowbrewery.ie; Main St, Redcross; mains €13-25; ⊗kitchen 12.30-9.30pm, bar to midnight; 🛜🍴) Many dishes at this cosy, low-ceilinged pub incorporate beers brewed at the adjacent Wicklow Brewery and come with pairing suggestions, such as Wicklow Black Stout beef pie paired with a Black 16, or the artisan 8oz burger with maple-smoked bacon and Helles Lager chutney accompanied by a Hopknut Pale Ale. There's trad music on Wednesdays year-round.

Free Hooley Nights on Saturdays from July to August feature Irish dancing, music and storytelling.

The kids' menu has half-portions of adult dishes.

❶ Information

Tourist Office (📱0402-35022; www.visit wicklow.ie; Old Courthouse, Main St; ⊗9am-4pm Mon-Fri) Pick up information about local walks here in Avoca village.

❶ Getting There & Away

Bus Éireann (www.buseireann.ie) links Dublin (Georges Quay) with the Meeting of the Waters (€14, 1¾ hours, two per day) and Avoca village (€14, two hours).

Western Wicklow

West of the Wicklow Mountains the landscape is more rural than rugged, especially towards the borders of Kildare and Carlow. The wild terrain of the county's east gives way to rich pastures; east of Blessington the countryside is dotted with private stud farms where some of the world's most expensive horses are trained in secrecy.

The main attraction in this part of Wicklow is the magnificent Palladian pile at Russborough House, just outside Blessington. If it's wild scenery you're after, you'll find it around Kilbride and the upper reaches of the River Liffey, as well as further south in the Glen of Imaal.

Blessington

POP 5520

Lined with pubs, shops and 18th-century townhouses, Blessington makes a convenient base for exploring western Wicklow. The main attractions nearby are Russborough House and Poulaphouca Reservoir. Also known as Blessington Lake, the 20.2-sq-km

IRELAND'S ANCIENT EAST

Ancient Ireland

Ireland's 5000-year-old history has left an abundance of prehistoric sites scattered across the country. The richly decorated passage tombs of Newgrange and Howth at Brú na Bóinne (p524) are the most famous, but there are thousands more to be discovered, from impressive burial cairns to simple dolmens and standing stones:

Browne's Hill Dolmen (Hacketstown Rd/R726; ⊙ dawn-dusk) `FREE`

Loughcrew Megalithic Centre (p537)

Uisneach (p504)

Corlea Trackway (p502)

Cavan Burren Park (p550)

Vikings

Viking raiders arrived in southeast Ireland in the 9th century, burning villages, carrying off prisoners and robbing monasteries of their gold. But eventually they settled in the country, establishing harbour towns such as Waterford and Wexford and setting up a rich trading economy. Their influence can be seen in many parts of Ireland:

Irish National Heritage Park (p182)

Lough Gur Heritage Centre (p333)

Reginald's Tower (p194)

Waterford Medieval Museum (p193)

Dunmore Cave (☑ 056-776 7726; www.heritageireland.ie; Ballyfoyle; adult/child €5/3; ⊙ 9.30am-6pm Jun-Aug, to 5pm Mar-May, Sep & Oct, to 5pm Wed-Sun Nov-Feb)

Castles & Conquests

Beginning in the 12th century, Norman invaders from England and Wales sought to occupy Ireland and subdue the native people, building a network of impressive castles to help control their territories:

Rock of Dunamase (p520)

---

reservoir is Ireland's biggest artificial lake, created in 1940 by damming the River Liffey to generate hydroelectric power and provide water for the growing city of Dublin. It's a major venue for fishing and boating.

◉ Sights & Activities

Russborough House HISTORIC BUILDING
(☑ 045-865 239; www.russborough.ie; off N81, Russelstown; guided tour adult/child €12/6, parklands €5/free; ⊙ 10am-5pm Mar-Dec, parklands to 6pm Mar-Dec) Magnificent Russborough House is one of Ireland's finest stately homes, a Palladian palace built for Joseph Leeson (1705–83), later the first Earl of Milltown and, later still, Lord Russborough. Since 1952 the house has been owned by the Beit family, who founded the De Beers diamond-mining company and stocked the mansion with a remarkable art collection, including masterpieces by Velázquez, Vermeer, Goya, Rubens and others. Admission includes a 45-minute guided tour of the house. It's 5km southwest of Blessington.

Russborough was built between 1741 and 1751 to the design of Richard Cassels, who was at the height of his fame as an architect. Poor old Richard didn't live to see it finished, but the job was well executed by Francis Bindon. The house remained in the Leeson family until 1931, but it was only after the Beits bought the pile that the drama began.

In 1974 the IRA stole 16 of the paintings, all of which were later recovered. In 1984 Loyalist paramilitaries followed suit, hiring Dublin criminal Martin Cahill to mastermind the heist. Although most of that haul was also recovered, some pieces were damaged beyond repair. In 1988 Beit donated the most valuable works to the National Gallery, but that didn't stop two more break-ins, in 2001 and 2002: one of the stolen paintings was a Gainsborough that had already been taken – and recovered – twice

Trim Castle (p534)

Cahir Castle (p340)

Athlone Castle (p503)

Birr Castle (p509)

Sacred Ireland

Famously known as the 'land of saints and scholars', Ireland was a cradle of early Christianity. From the arrival of St Patrick in the 5th century to the Dissolution of the Monasteries in the 16th, there is a fantastic legacy of high crosses, churches, abbeys and monasteries, many in a state of picturesque ruin:

Clonmacnoise (p513)

St Declan's Monastery (p203)

Monasterboice (p542)

Fore Valley (p508)

Hill of Tara (p532)

Big Houses & Hard Times

Aristocrats of the 18th and 19th centuries competed with each other to show off how wealthy they were, commissioning fashionable architects to design ever-larger and more extravagant mansions. When the aristocracy fell on hard times in the 20th century, many properties were bequeathed to the state and opened to the public:

Castletown House (p173)

Curraghmore Estate (☑086 821 1917; www.curraghmorehouse.ie; Portlaw; house tours €12, shell house tours €10, gardens €6, combination ticket €18; ☉10.30am-4.30pm Wed-Sun Easter-Sep)

Huntington Castle (p210)

Russborough House (p170)

Belvedere House & Gardens (p506)

---

before. Thankfully all of the paintings were recovered after both attempts, but where a succession of thieves couldn't succeed, the cost of upkeep did: in 2015 the owners announced they were going to auction off 10 of the paintings, a decision that caused much consternation as the family had always maintained that the collection was to be held in trust for the Irish people.

On the tour of the house, which is decorated in typical Georgian style, you'll see all the (remaining) important paintings, which, given the history, is a monumental exercise in staying positive.

Its 80-hectare parklands encompass an 18th-century walled garden, a hedge maze, themed walking trails (including a wildlife trail where you can spot badgers, foxes, hares and swans), and a birds of prey centre (adult/child €8/6) with 40 species, including owls and golden eagles.

Blessington Lake Boat Hire　FISHING
(☑087 355 2403; www.blessingtonlakeboathire. com; Bog Rd, Ballyknockan; boat hire per day €75; ☉by reservation) Rents out boats with outboard motors for fishing or cruising on Blessington Lake, which is home to brown and rainbow trout as well as being one of Ireland's prime pike fisheries. This outfit also sells fishing permits (€5 per day) and rents out fishing tackle (€15). It's 12km southeast of Blessington.

🛏 Sleeping & Eating

**Rathsallagh House
& Country Club**　HOTEL €€€
(☑045-403 112; www.rathsallagh.com; Dunlavin; s/d from €150/200; 🅿�) This fabulous country manor was converted from Queen Anne stables after the main house was burned down during the 1798 Rising. Luxury reigns here, with 29 splendidly appointed rooms, exquisite country-house dining (five-course dinner

OFF THE BEATEN TRACK

BALTINGLASS ABBEY

Founded by Cistercian monks in 1148 and inhabited for nearly four centuries, the 56m-long, now-ruined **Baltinglass Abbey** (www.visitwicklow.ie; Church Lane, Baltinglass; ☺24hr) incorporates both Cistercian and Irish Romanesque architecture, with animal and human motifs inscribed on the stones. In the nave, its six surviving Gothic arches are supported by alternate square and round pillars; also still intact is the abbey's tower.

It's 12km southeast of Ballitore on the River Slaney's eastern bank; there are superb views from the western bank, where you'll find picnic tables.

menu €40) and a par-72 golf course designed by Peter McEvoy and Christy O'Connor Jr. It's 23km southwest of Blessington, off the R756.

Ballymore Inn   GASTROPUB €€
(☑045-864 585; www.ballymoreinn.com; Main St, Ballymore Eustace; mains €13-32; ☺12.30-9.30pm; ☎☑☑☺) ✆ Utilising produce from local farms and its own polytunnels and gardens, plus seafood delivered daily from Duncannon, this unexpected find 7.5km southwest of Blessington has extensive vegetarian, vegan and kids' menus, as well as meat and fish dishes. Expect creations such as sweet potato and chive-stuffed peppers, grilled steaks with homemade mustard, and on-the-bone black sole with fennel-and-ginger sauce.

Mosaic floor tiles, a cast-iron open fire and leather banquettes grace the dining room; there's a cavernous back bar and outdoor picnic tables in sunny weather.

🛍 Shopping

Ring Fort Gallery   JEWELLERY
(www.facebook.com/RingFortIrishjewellery; Unit 2, Blessington Craft Centre, Main St; ☺10am-6pm Tue-Sat) Watch jeweller Kieran Cunningham handcrafts bracelets, brooches, earrings, necklaces, rings, tiaras, torcs (solid necklaces) and pins here at his gallery/shop. Honed since 1977, his traditional Celtic techniques include chiselled scroll effects and hammered finishes. You can buy pre-made pieces or get them custom made.

Charles Camping   SPORTS & OUTDOORS
(☑045-865 351; www.charlescamping.ie; Main St; ☺9.30am-6pm Mon-Sat, 2-6pm Sun) Everything you need for a camping trip – tents, maps, cooking equipment, portable heaters, waterproofs and other clothing – is stocked at this Blessington camping shop. It's also a great source of information for walking in Wicklow, and sells fishing permits.

ℹ Information

Tourist Office (☑045-865 850; www.visitwicklow.ie; Unit 5, Blessington Craft Centre, Main St; ☺9.30am-5pm Mon, Tue & Thu, noon-5pm Wed, 10am-3pm Fri) Tucked away behind the Credit Union building, just west of Main St.

ℹ Getting There & Away

Dublin Bus (www.dublinbus.ie) runs from Poolbeg St in Dublin to Blessington (€3.30, 1½ hours, every two hours).

COUNTY KILDARE

Some of Ireland's best grazing farmland has made County Kildare (Cill Dara) prime agricultural real estate, especially for the horse-racing set: the county is dotted with stud farms where champion racehorses are reared and trained. In recent decades it has had to contend with Dublin's ever-expanding commuter belt, which has swallowed up many of its towns and villages.

The county isn't especially stocked with must-see attractions, but there are enough diversions to justify a day trip from the capital or a stop on your way out west.

Kildare Town

POP 8634

Built around a compact, triangular square beneath an impressive cathedral, Kildare town is closely associated with Ireland's second-most important saint, Brigid. Although there aren't a lot of attractions within the town itself, it's a popular shopping destination, home to designer outlet centre Kildare Village, and is a centre for equestrian enthusiasts, with the Irish National Stud and the Curragh Racecourse both nearby.

⊙ Sights

**Irish National
Stud & Gardens**   STABLES, GARDENS
(☑045-521 617; www.irishnationalstud.ie; Tully Rd; adult/child €12.50/7; ☺9am-6pm early Feb-Oct, last entry 5pm) The Irish National Stud, 1.5km south of town, is the big attraction in Kildare – visitors have included Queen Elizabeth II.

CASTLETOWN HOUSE

Magnificent **Castletown House** (☑ 01-628 8252; www.castletown.ie; Celbridge; house adult/child €8/3.50, with guided tour €10/5, grounds free; ⊙ house 10am-6pm daily Mar-Oct, to 5.30pm Wed-Sun Nov–mid-Dec, grounds dawn-dusk year-round) is Ireland's single-most imposing Georgian estate, and a testament to the vast wealth enjoyed by the Anglo-Irish gentry during the 18th century. Hour-long guided tours beginning at noon and 3pm provide an insight into how the 1% lived in the 18th century; otherwise you can wander at will. Don't miss a stroll down to the river for grand views back to the house. Castletown is signposted from junction 6 on the M4.

The house was built between the years 1722 and 1732 for William Conolly (1662–1729), speaker of the Irish House of Commons and, at the time, Ireland's richest man. Born into relatively humble circumstances in Ballyshannon, County Donegal, Conolly made his fortune through land transactions in the uncertain aftermath of the Battle of the Boyne (1690).

The job of building a palace fit for a prince was entrusted to Sir Edward Lovett Pearce (1699–1733) – hence the colonnades and terminating pavilions. His design was an extension of a preexisting 16th-century Italian palazzo-style building, created by Italian architect Alessandro Galilei (1691–1737) in 1718, but Conolly wanted something even grander, hence Pearce's appearance on the job in 1724. A highlight of the opulent interior is the Long Gallery, replete with family portraits and exquisite stucco work by the Francini brothers.

Conolly didn't live to see the completion of his wonder-palace. His widow, Katherine, continued to live at the unfinished house after his death in 1729, and instigated many improvements. Her main architectural contribution was the curious 42.6m obelisk, known locally as the Conolly Folly. Her other offering was the Heath Robinson–esque (or Rube Goldberg–esque, if you prefer) Wonderful Barn, six teetering storeys wrapped by an exterior spiral staircase, on private property just outside Leixlip, which is closed to the public.

Castletown House remained in the family's hands until 1965, when it was purchased by Desmond Guinness, who restored the house to its original splendour. His investment was continued from 1979 by the Castletown Foundation. In 1994 Castletown House was transferred to state care and today it is managed by the Heritage Service.

Owned and managed by the Irish government, the immaculately kept centre breeds high-quality stallions to mate with mares from all over the world. You can wander the paddocks and go eye-to-eye with famous stallions, or take a 45-minute guided tour (four daily; included in admission). Around 3pm in the spring, you'll see the foals being walked back to their stables.

The stud was founded by Colonel Hall Walker (of Johnnie Walker whiskey fame) in 1900. He was remarkably successful with his horses, but his eccentric breeding technique relied heavily on astrology: the fate of a foal was decided by its horoscope and the roofs of the stallion boxes opened on auspicious occasions to reveal the stars above and hopefully influence the horses' fortunes.

Guided tours take place every hour on the hour, with access to the intensive-care unit for newborn foals. If you visit between February and June, you might even see a foal being born. Alternatively, the foaling unit shows a 10-minute video with all the action. Given that most of those foals are now geldings, they probably have dim memories of their time in the Teasing Shed, the place where stallions are stimulated before 'covering' a mare. The fee for having a mare inseminated by the stud's top stallion can be as much as €120,000.

Other attractions on-site include lakeside walks, a 'fairy trail' for kids and the **Irish Horse Museum**, a celebration of championship horses and the history of horse racing. You can also visit Colonel Hall Walker's **Japanese Gardens** (part of the complex), considered to be the best of their kind in Europe. Created between 1906 and 1910, they trace the journey from birth to death through 20 landmarks, including the Tunnel of Ignorance, the Hill of Ambition and the Chair of Old Age.

St Brigid's Cathedral CATHEDRAL

(☑ 045-521 229; www.kildareheritage.com; Market Sq; cathedral/round tower €2/7; ⊙ 10am-1pm Mon-Sat, 2-5pm Mon-Sun May-Sep) The solid presence of 13th-century St Brigid's Cathedral looms over Kildare's Market Sq. Look out for a fine stained-glass window that depicts Ireland's three principal saints: Patrick, Brigid and Colmcille. The church also contains the restored tomb of Walter Wellesley, Bishop of Kildare, which disappeared soon after his death in 1539 and was found in 1971. One of its carved figures has been variously interpreted as an acrobat or a sheila-na-gig (a carved female figure with exaggerated genitalia).

The 10th-century **round tower** in the grounds is Ireland's second highest at 32.9m, and one of only two in Ireland that you can climb (the other is in Kilkenny), provided the guardian is around. Its original conical roof has been replaced with an unusual Norman battlement. Near the tower is a **wishing stone** – put your arm through the hole and touch your shoulder and your wish will be granted. On the north side of the cathedral are the heavily restored foundations of an ancient **fire temple**.

🛏 Sleeping & Eating

★ Martinstown House HOTEL €€€

(☑ 045-441269; www.martinstownhouse.com; Ballysax; r from €175; ⓟ 🐾) This beautiful 18th-century country manor is built in the frilly Strawberry Hill Gothic style and set in a 69-hectare estate and farm surrounded by attractive woodland. Its seven rooms are filled with antiques; children aren't permitted. You can arrange for memorable dinners 24 hours in advance (€50); ingredients come from the kitchen garden. It's 10km southeast of Kildare town.

Agapé CAFE €

(☑ 045-533711; Station Rd; dishes €4-10.50; ⓒ 8am-6pm Mon-Sat) That's *ah-gap-ay* (as in Greek for unconditional love), not *ah-gayp* (as in

open-mouthed in astonishment), though the quality of the freshly prepared food in this little cafe will leave you pleasantly surprised. There's a full coffee bar and a menu of salads, soups, sandwiches and hot specials such as veggie lasagne.

★ Hartes of Kildare GASTROPUB €€

(☑ 045-533 557; www.hartesofkildare.ie; Market Sq; mains lunch €9.50-16, dinner €18-28.50; ⓒ noon-3.45pm & 5-9pm Tue-Thu, noon-3.45pm & 5-9.45pm Fri & Sat, noon-8.30pm Sun; 🛜 🍴) Kildare hotspot Hartes has exposed brick walls, gleaming timber furniture and brilliant gastropub fare. Lunch dishes including corned beef and Knockanore cheddar toasties are the precursors for gourmet evening mains such as chestnut- and sausage-stuffed butter-roasted chicken or six-hour-braised lamb shoulder with Ardsallagh goat's cheese parcels. Three-hour cookery classes (covering 'traditional Irish breads' or 'Wicklow mountain roasts') start from €65.

Kids dine free between 5pm and 6.30pm Tuesday to Friday; at other times, they get half-portions of adult meals for €9.

🛍 Shopping

Kildare Village SHOPPING CENTRE

(www.kildarevillage.com; Nurney Rd; ⓒ 10am-7pm Mon-Wed, 10am-8pm Thu, Fri & Sun, 9am-8pm Sat) Shoppers come from all over the country to buy discounted designer brands at this village-like outlet mall, the biggest of its kind in Ireland – more than 100 high-street brands are represented. The brick and timber architecture is inspired by the county's stud farms, with horse boxes converted into gourmet food trucks; there are also cafes and restaurants.

ⓘ Information

The **Tourist Office & Heritage Centre** (☑ 045-530 672; www.kildareheritage.com; Market Sq; ⓒ 9.30am-1pm & 2-5pm Mon-Sat Feb-Oct) has a free exhibition outlining Kildare's history. There's also local art for sale.

ⓘ Getting There & Away

Bus Éireann (www.buseireann.ie) service 126 runs between Kildare and Dublin (Connolly Luas stop; €13, 1½ hours, hourly); one service per day stops at the Irish National Stud.

Kildare is a major rail hub, with direct trains to destinations including Dublin Heuston (€12.90, 30 minutes, up to four per hour), Kilkenny (€10.50, one hour, six daily) and Waterford (€13,

---

GRAND CANAL TOWPATH

The Grand Canal towpath is ideal for leisurely walkers and there are numerous access points, with none better than Robertstown if you fancy a canalside ramble. The village is the hub of the Kildare Way and the Barrow towpath trails, the latter stretching all the way to St Mullins, 95km to the south in County Carlow. From County Carlow it's possible to connect with the South Leinster Way at Graiguenamanagh, or the southern end of the Wicklow Way at Clonegal, north of Mt Leinster.

A variety of leaflets detailing the paths can be picked up at most regional tourist offices. **Waterways Ireland** (www.waterwaysireland.org) is also a good source.

1¾ hours, six daily), and indirect services to Cork, Galway and Limerick cities, among others.

The Curragh

Stretching from Kildare town to Newbridge, the Curragh is one of the country's largest tracts of unfenced grassland and the centre of the Irish horse-racing industry. The name derives from the Irish for 'place of the running horse', and they've been doing just that on this rolling sward since the 1700s, although there are tales of chariot races as far back as the 13th century. If you get up early or pass by in the late evening, you'll see thoroughbreds exercising on the wide-open spaces surrounding the world-famous Curragh Racecourse.

The service town of Newbridge (Droichead Nua), at the east end of the Curragh, is best known for its shopping centres and silverware.

You'll find several swish bars and restaurants at the Curragh Racecourse, and plenty of cafes, restaurants and takeway options in Kildare town and Newbridge.

Curragh Racecourse HORSE RACING
(☑ 045-441 205; www.curragh.ie; R413, Newbridge; tickets €20; ⊙ mid-Apr–Oct) Hosting its first recorded race in 1727 and officially inaugurated in 1868, the Curragh is the oldest and most prestigious racecourse in the country, and one of the finest flat-racing courses in the world. Even if you're not the horsey type, it's worth experiencing the passion and atmosphere of a day at the races here. It's 3km southwest of central Newbridge.

Museum of Style Icons MUSEUM
(☑ 045-431 301; www.newbridgesilverwarevisitor centre.com; Newbridge Silverware, Athgarvan Rd, Newbridge; ⊙ 9am-5.30pm Mon-Sat, 10am-5.30pm Sun) FREE Housed inside the Newbridge Silverware showroom, beneath a sparkle of glitter balls, is this unexpected display of star-studded memorabilia. There are exhibits showcasing dresses, suits and stage costumes that were once worn by Audrey Hepburn, The Beatles, Victoria Beckham, Elizabeth Taylor and Princess Diana, among others.

Newbridge Silverware FACTORY
(☑ 045-431 301; www.newbridgesilverwarevisitor centre.com; Athgarvan Rd, Newbridge; showroom free, guided tour adult/child €12/free; ⊙ 9am-5.30pm Mon-Sat, 10am-5.30pm Sun) Founded in 1934, Newbridge Silverware produces and sells vast quantities of silver jewellery, silver-plated

ARTHUR'S LAST RESTING PLACE

The 10m-tall stump of an 8th-century round tower marks the ancient Christian site of **Oughterard Round Tower & Cemetery** (Oughterard; ⊙ dawn-dusk) FREE, 7km southeast of Straffan. Its name in Irish means 'high place', and there are sweeping views of the green Kildare countryside from here. The cemetery is best known for its most famous resident – a vault amid the ruins of the 14th-century church is the last resting place of Arthur Guinness (1724–1803), the brewer who created the world-famous black beer.

cutlery, homewares and engravable gift items. Guided factory tours lasting 30 minutes take place at 10.30am, 11.30am and 2pm daily; they're best on weekdays when you'll see the machines in action.

⊙ Getting There & Away

The M7 from Dublin cuts through the middle of the Curragh (take exit 12 for the racecourse and Newbridge).

Bus Éireann (www.buseireann.ie) runs between Dublin's Busáras bus station and Newbridge (€11, 1¼ hours, up to four per hour), continuing to Kildare town (€4.30, 25 minutes). Dublin Coach (www.dublincoach.ie) runs special buses from Dublin Airport and Dublin to the Curragh on race days; you must reserve 72 hours in advance online.

Trains link Newbridge with Dublin Heuston (€10.50, 35 minutes, up to four per hour) and Kildare town (€5.50, five minutes, up to four per hour).

Maynooth

POP 14,585

Bustling Maynooth (Maigh Nuad) is dominated by the local campus of the National University of Ireland (NUIM), whose students make up two-thirds of its population and add a touch of liveliness to this otherwise demure country town lined with stone-fronted houses and shops.

The main sights – the castle, college and museum – are clustered together at the western end of Main St, a 1km walk north from the train station.

WORTH A TRIP

BOG OF ALLEN

Run by the nonprofit Irish Peatland Conservation Council, the **Bog of Allen Nature Centre** (☑ 045-860 133; www.ipcc.ie; R414, Lullymore; adult/child €5/free; ☺ 9am-5pm Mon-Fri year-round, occasional weekends May-Sep) ✎ celebrates the amazing biodiversity of Ireland's bogs, and traces the history of peat extraction and the threat it poses to wildlife and the environment. The garden at the back has the largest carnivorous plant collection in Ireland, including sundews, butterworts and pitcher plants, and ponds filled with frogs and newts. A nearby boardwalk extends into Lodge Bog, one of the last surviving untouched fragments of the Bog of Allen.

Developed on an area of cutaway bog, where peat has been extracted for commercial purposes, the award-winning, family-oriented **Lullymore Heritage & Discovery Park** (☑ 045-870 238; www.lullymoreheritagepark.com; off R414, Lullymore; adult/child park €9/7.50, railway €5/2.50; ☺ 10am-6pm daily Apr-Sep, Sat & Sun only Feb-Mar; 🚼) offers a huge range of activities. A woodland trail leads past various points of interest including a recreation of an Iron Age hut and an enchanting fairy village. Boardwalks lead out over the half-drowned bog to wildlife hides. There's also a pet farm, crazy golf, an adventure playground and a heritage railway providing 15-minute rides.

Set aside at least half a day to make the most of a visit.

◉ Sights & Activities

St Patrick's College   UNIVERSITY
(☑ 01-708 6404; www.visitmaynooth.com; Main St; guided tours adult/child €8/4; ☺ tours 11am-5.30pm Jun-Aug) Part of NUI Maynooth, and turning out Catholic priests since 1795, St Patrick's College & Seminary is Ireland's second-oldest university (after Trinity College, Dublin). The college buildings are impressive – Gothic architect Augustus Pugin had a hand in designing them – and the grounds contain a number of lofty Georgian and neo-Gothic buildings, gardens and squares. It's worth taking the guided tour to see the **College Chapel**, the world's largest choir chapel, with stalls for more than 450 choristers.

The college was founded so that aspiring priests didn't have to skip off to seminary school in France – and so get infected with strains of republicanism and revolution. In 1898 it was made a Pontifical College (which meant that its curriculum was determined and controlled by the Holy See) and in 1910 it became part of the then recently established National University of Ireland. The college's student body remained exclusively clerical until 1966 when lay students were finally admitted, but even today, despite being part of the bigger university, it remains largely autonomous and its 80-odd male seminarians are distinct from the university's 8500 other students.

**National Science
& Ecclesiology Museum**   MUSEUM
(☑ 087 915 2003; www.maynoothcollege.ie; St Patrick's College; entry by donation; ☺ 2-4pm Wed & 2-6pm Sun Jun-Aug) Father Nicholas Callan (1799–1864), Professor of Natural Philosophy at St Patrick's College in the mid-19th century, was a pioneer of research into electromagnetism and the inventor of the induction coil. This small museum preserves his original experimental apparatus, along with a large collection of historic scientific instruments and three centuries worth of ecclesiastical objects associated with the college.

Maynooth Castle   CASTLE
(☑ 01-628 6744; www.heritageireland.ie; Parson St; ☺ 10am-6pm mid-May–Sep, to 4pm Oct–mid-May) **FREE** At the west end of the town centre you can see the ruined gatehouse, keep and great hall of this 13th-century castle, once home to the Fitzgerald family. The castle was dismantled in Cromwellian times, when the Fitzgeralds moved to Kilkea Castle. Entry is by a 45-minute guided tour only; there's a small exhibition on the castle's history in the keep.

Carton House   GOLF
(☑ 01-651 7727; www.cartonhouse.com; green fees from €60) Two outstanding courses make Carton House one of eastern Ireland's premier golfing destinations. The O'Meara Course has broad fairways and strategically placed greens; the Montgomerie Course is more challenging, with bunkers positioned to swallow all but the most accurate shots. Carton House is 2.5km east of Maynooth via the R148 along the Royal Canal.

🛌 Sleeping & Eating

NUI Maynooth   ACCOMMODATION SERVICES €
(📞01-708 6400; www.maynoothcampus.com; Accommodation Office, St Patrick's College; s/d from €37/62; 🅿🛜) The National University of Ireland campus can accommodate 1000 guests in seven room types, ranging from a traditional college room to doubles in an apartment in the purpose-built university village. Most are in the mid-1970s North Campus, but better rooms are in the South Campus, strewn around the courts and gardens of atmospheric St Patrick's College. Availability is best in the summer months.

Carton House   HISTORIC HOTEL €€€
(📞01-505 2000; www.cartonhouse.com; d/ste from €250/340; 🅿🛜🏊) Dating from 1739, the former country manor of the Fitzgerald earls of Kildare (their city pile was Leinster House, now the Irish Parliament) is now an exquisite hotel. Rooms are split between the grander suites of the original Richard Cassels–designed mansion and the business-style accommodation in the modern extension. From Maynooth, follow the R148 2.5km east towards Leixlip along the Royal Canal.

Carton House's spa has a large indoor swimming pool and treatments that use organic Pevonia botanicals.

Also here are two renowned golf courses.

Bistro 53   BISTRO €€
(📞01-628 9001; Main St; mains €12.50-26.50; ⊙kitchen noon-3pm & 5-9.30pm, bar to 11.45pm; 🛜) Exposed timber beams, buffed Chesterfield sofas and lilac banquettes create a stylish setting for bistro dishes (cognac-sautéed lambs liver, wild venison stew, roast suckling pig and grilled black sole) and wines from across Europe. Live acoustic sets are played on weekends.

❶ Getting There & Away

Dublin Bus (www.dublinbus.ie) runs a service to Maynooth (€3.30, 50 minutes, every two hours) departing from Merrion Sq in Dublin.

Maynooth has regular trains to Dublin (€4.90, 40 minutes, up to four per hour) and Sligo town (€18, 2¾ hours, every two hours).

Ballitore to Castledermot

The R448 road between Kilcullen and Carlow runs just east of the M9, linking the small villages of Ballitore, Moone and Castledermot and a handful of off-the-beaten-track sights.

Quaker Museum   MUSEUM
(📞059-862 3344; www.kildare.ie; Mary Leadbeater House, Main St; entry by donation; ⊙10am-1pm & 2-5pm Wed, Fri & Sat, 12.30-4pm & 4.45-8pm Thu) Set in a tiny, restored Meeting House of the Society of Friends (which also houses the local library), this small museum documents the lives of Ballitore's Quaker community, including the former owner, Mary Leadbeater, who was known for her aversion to war.

On the southern edge of the village there's a Quaker cemetery.

Moone High Cross   CHRISTIAN SITE
(www.kildareheritage.com; Moone; ⊙dawn-dusk) **FREE** Housed within the ruins of a 13th-century abbey, the unusually tall and slender Moone High Cross – Ireland's second-highest, at 5.3m – is a masterpiece dating from the 8th or 9th century. It displays carved biblical scenes with the confidence and exuberance of a comic strip, among them Daniel in the lions' den and the flight into Egypt. The cross is situated on a minor road 1km west of Moone village, accessed via an inconspicuous wooden door in a stone wall.

Moone High Cross Inn   PUB
(📞059-862 4112; www.moonehighcrossinn.com; Bolton Hill, Moone; ⊙10am-11pm Sun-Thu, to midnight Fri & Sat) This charming 19th-century inn, 2km south of Moone, is famed for its craic and live music, which have attracted celebrity visitors including Bono, Sandra Bullock and Clint Eastwood (not all at the same time!). It serves good pub grub (there's always a pot of leek and potato soup on the stove), and has five simple B&B bedrooms (from €85).

Castledermot Monastery   RUINS
(St James' Church, Church Lane, Castledermot; ⊙dawn-dusk) **FREE** Castledermot village was once home to a vast ecclesiastical settlement, but all that remains of St Diarmuid's 9th-century monastery is a 20m round tower topped with a medieval battlement. Nearby are two well-preserved, 10th-century granite high crosses, a 12th-century Romanesque doorway and a medieval Scandinavian 'hogsback' gravestone, the only one in Ireland. Reach the ruins by passing through the rusty gate on all-too-busy Main St (N9), then walking along the tree-lined avenue to St James' church.

At the southern end of town, the ruins of an early-14th-century **Franciscan friary** can be seen alongside the road.

Counties Wexford, Waterford, Carlow & Kilkenny

POP 422,062 / AREA 7192 SQ KM

Best Places to Eat

➜ Tannery (p202)

➜ The House Restaurant (p204)

➜ Sha-Roe Bistro (p210)

➜ Campagne (p216)

➜ The Hollow (p189)

➜ La Côte (p183)

Best Places to Stay

➜ Cliff House Hotel (p204)

➜ Lawcus Farm (p217)

➜ Hanora's Cottage (p206)

➜ Faithlegg (p198)

➜ Mulvarra House (p210)

➜ Rosquil House (p215)

Why Go?

Counties Wexford, Waterford, Carlow and Kilkenny are (along with the southern chunk of Tipperary) referred to collectively as the 'sunny southeast'. This being Ireland the term is, of course, relative. But it *is* the country's warmest, driest region. A tiara of golden-sand beaches adorns the counties of Wexford and Waterford, and there are plenty more eye-catching gems, including picturesque thatched cottages, elegant seaside towns and dramatic windswept peninsulas. If you're looking for real sparkle, check out the world-acclaimed Waterford crystal. Deeper inland, the verdant valley of the River Barrow separates the riverside villages and arts and crafts studios of County Kilkenny from the country houses and flower-filled gardens of County Carlow. Kilkenny city is the urban star with its imposing castle, cathedral, medieval lanes and cracking pubs and restaurants. And thanks to that 'sunny southeast' climate, these four counties offer some of Ireland's best outdoor pursuits.

When to Go

➜ The summer and early autumn months of June to September are the best times for enjoying the region's superb beaches, seafront cafes and alfresco-restaurant terraces.

➜ From spring (April) to autumn (October), the weather is at its most comfortable for hiking and walking, although be sure to pack waterproof gear and warm clothing.

➜ When the weather starts getting chilly in October and November, the region's arts scene heats up with indoor festivities. It's especially great for music lovers, with Wexford's world-acclaimed opera festival and Kilkenny's trad music Celtic Festival.

COUNTY WEXFORD

County Wexford's navigable rivers and fertile farmland have long lured invaders and privateers. The Vikings founded Ireland's first major town on the wide, easy-flowing River Slaney, which cuts through the middle of the county. Today the Viking city of Wexford is a centre for opera and art, complementing a beach-fringed coastline and a rural hinterland dotted with cute villages and thatched cottages.

Wexford Town & Around

POP 20,188

Wexford's rich and bloody history includes being founded by the Vikings and nearly obliterated by Oliver Cromwell. Its claustrophobic maze of medieval streets is lined with a mixture of old-time pubs, modern steel-and-glass facades and repurposed buildings, such as Creative Hub, a disused shopping mall now converted into an arts centre.

Arty Wexford has plenty of craft shops and galleries – and innovative restaurants – but the biggest cultural attraction is the world-famous Wexford Opera Festival, a 12-day autumn extravaganza that presents rarely performed works to packed audiences in the town's shiny National Opera House.

History

The Vikings named it Waesfjord (meaning 'harbour of mudflats') and its handy location near the mouth of the River Slaney encouraged landings as early as AD 850. The town was captured by the Normans in 1169; traces of their fort can still be seen in the grounds of the Irish National Heritage Park (p182).

Cromwell included Wexford in his destructive Irish tour of 1649–50. Around 1500 of the town's then 2000 inhabitants were killed, including all the Franciscan friars. During the 1798 Rising, rebels made a determined, bloody stand here before being defeated.

⊙ Sights

Selskar Abbey   RUINS

(Westgate) After Henry II murdered his former ally Thomas Becket, he did penance at Selskar Abbey, founded in 1190. Basilia, the sister of Richard Fitz Gilbert de Clare (better known as Strongbow), is thought to have married one of Henry II's lieutenants in the abbey. Its present ruinous state is a result of Cromwell's visit in 1649. Admission is only by guided tour, run by

Wexford Walking Tours (p182) – gather at the Westgate off Spawell Rd.

St Iberius' Church   CHURCH

(North Main St; ⊙ 10am-5pm May-Sep, to 3pm Oct-Apr) St Iberius' Church was built in 1660. The Renaissance-style frontage is worth a look, but the real treat is the Georgian interior with its finely crafted altar rails and 18th-century monuments in the gallery. Oscar Wilde's forebears were rectors here. The church is also famed for its superb acoustics, and is an occasional venue for concerts.

★ Johnstown Castle Gardens   GARDENS

(www.irishagrimuseum.ie; Johnstown Castle Estate, Johnstown; adult/child €3/1, incl Irish Agricultural Museum €8/4; ⊙ 9am-6.30pm Jul & Aug, to 5.30pm Mar-Jun, Sep & Oct, to 4.30pm Nov-Feb) Parading peacocks guard the splendid 19th-century Johnstown Castle, the former home of the once-mighty Fitzgerald and Esmonde families (the estate was gifted to the nation in 1945). Situated 7km southwest of Wexford town, the empty castle (not open to public) is surrounded by 20 hectares of beautiful wooded gardens complete with an ornamental lake, a sunken Italian garden, statues and waterfalls.

Irish Agricultural Museum   MUSEUM

(⌨ 053-918 4671; www.irishagrimuseum.ie; Johnstown Castle Estate, Johnstown; adult/child incl castle gardens €8/4; ⊙ 9am-6pm Mon-Fri, 11am-6pm Sat & Sun Jul & Aug, 9am-5pm Mon-Fri, 11am-5pm Sat & Sun Mar-Jun, Sep & Oct, 9am-4pm Mon-Fri, 11am-4pm Sat & Sun Nov-Feb) The outbuildings of Johnstown Castle, whose gardens (p179) are a must-see, house a fascinating collection of early Ferguson tractors, farm machinery, Irish country furniture and recreated farmhouse kitchens. The exhibition on the Great Famine is one of the best explanations of this national tragedy anywhere in Ireland. It's 7km southwest of Wexford town.

Wexford Wildfowl Reserve   NATURE RESERVE

(⌨ 076 100 2660; www.wexfordwildfowlreserve.ie; off R741, North Slob; ⊙ 9am-5pm) The North Slob (from the Irish *slab*, meaning 'mud' or 'mire') is a large area of reclaimed land to the north of Wexford harbour, drained by ditches and protected by Dutch-style dykes. It's prime birdwatching territory – home to 35% of the world's population of Greenland white-fronted geese each winter, some 10,000 in total. There's an observation tower, assorted hides and a visitor centre with detailed exhibits. It's 7km northeast of Wexford town.

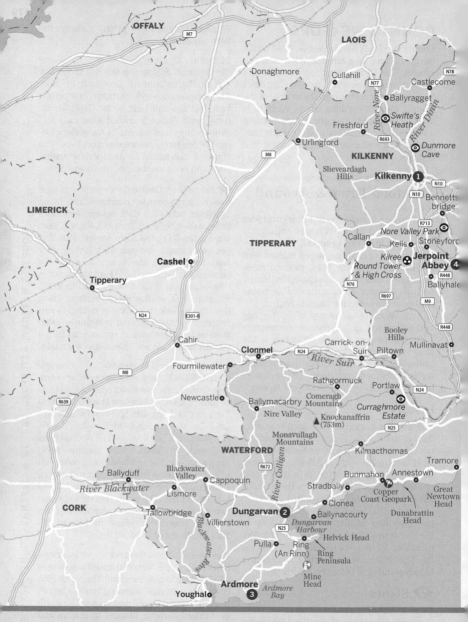

Counties Wexford, Waterford, Carlow & Kilkenny

Highlights

1 **Kilkenny** (p211) Soaking up the culture of one of Ireland's most vibrant cities.

2 **Dungarvan** (p200) Savouring the gourmet delights of West Waterford in this lively town.

3 **Ardmore** (p203) Appreciating County Waterford's coastal beauty around historic Ardmore.

4 **Jerpoint Abbey** (p219) Exploring this 12th-century abbey's evocative ruins in Kilkenny's countryside.

5 **Curracloe Beach** (p183) Walking to the end of this beach

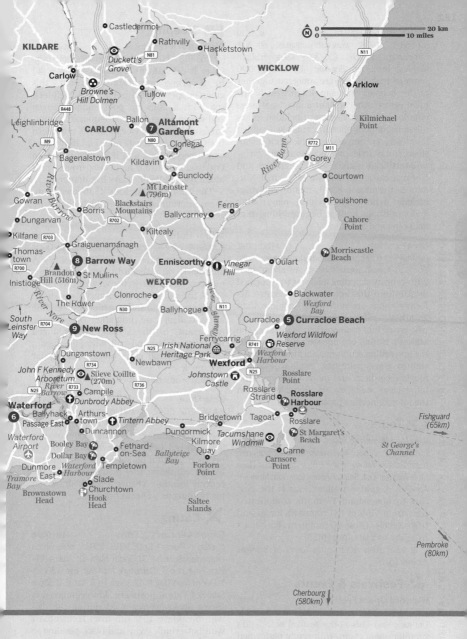

KILDARE

● Castledermot
● Rathvilly
● Hacketstown

WICKLOW

N81

● Duckett's Grove

Carlow

Browne's Hill Dolmen

● Tullow

N11

● Arklow

R448

Kilmichael Point

Leighlinbridge

CARLOW

● Ballon

⑦ Altamont Gardens

M9

● Bagenalstown

N80

● Clonegal

R772 M11

● Kildavin

● Bunclody

● Gorey

River Bann

● Courtown

Gowran

Borris

▲ Mt Leinster (796m)

Blackstairs Mountains

R702

● Ferns

● Poulshone

Cahore Point

Dungarvan

● Ballycarney

Kilfane R703

● Kiltealy

Morriscastle Beach

Thomastown

R700

Graiguenamanagh

⑧ Barrow Way

Enniscorthy

❶ Vinegar Hill

● Oulart

Brandon Hill (516m) ▲ St Mullins

WEXFORD

● Blackwater

Inistioge

River Nore

Clonroche

Wexford Bay

The Rower

N30

Ballyhogue

N11

Curracloe

⑤ **Curracloe Beach**

South Leinster Way R704

⑨ **New Ross**

River Slaney

Ferrycarrig

Wexford Wildfowl ✚ Reserve

R741

Dunganstown

Newbawn

N25

Irish National Heritage Park

Wexford

Wexford Harbour

John F Kennedy Arboretum R734

▲ Slieve Coillte (270m)

N25

R733 ● Campile

R736

Johnstown Castle

Rosslare Point

Rosslare Strand

Waterford

⑥ ● Ballyhack

Passage East

Arthurstown

❶ Tintern Abbey

● Bridgetown

● Tagoat

Rosslare Harbour

Rosslare

Fishguard (65km)

❶ Dunbrody Abbey

Duncannon

Duncormick

Tacumshane Windmill

St Margaret's Beach

Waterford Airport

Booley Bay

Fethard-on-Sea

Kilmore Quay

● Carne

St George's Channel

Dollar Bay

Ballyteige Bay

Forlorn Point

Carnsore Point

Dunmore East

Waterford Harbour

Templetown

Tramore Bay

● Slade

Churchtown

Brownstown Head

Hook Head

Saltee Islands

Pembroke (80km)

Cherbourg (580km)

0 ─── 20 km
0 ─── 10 miles

near Wexford: a seemingly endless vision of white powder.

⑥ **Waterford City** (p193) Reliving the days of the Vikings and Normans in Waterford's excellent museums.

⑦ **Altamont Gardens** (p208) Tiptoeing through the flowers in County Carlow's most beautiful gardens.

⑧ **Barrow Way** (p208) Cycling along the towpath between Graiguenamanagh and St Mullins.

⑨ **Dunbrody Famine Ship** (p191) Learning about Ireland's history aboard this replica immigrant ship.

Irish National Heritage Park
MUSEUM

(☑053-912 0733; www.irishheritage.ie; off N11, Ferrycarrig; adult/child €10/5; ⊗9.30am-6.30pm May-Aug, to 5.30pm Sep-Apr; ⓐ) Over 9000 years of Irish history are squeezed together at this open-air museum 5.5km west of the town centre. After a short audiovisual presentation, take a guided tour (included in admission, but book ahead) or audio self-guided tour (€2), encompassing a Neolithic farmstead, stone circle, ring fort, monastery, *crannóg* (artificial island), Viking shipyard and Norman castle (on the site of original Norman fort remains). Family-friendly activities include archery, an adventure playground, and workshops such as blacksmithing, flint knapping and foraging.

Creative Hub
ARTS CENTRE

(☑053-919 6369; www.wexfordartscentre.ie; Mallin St; ⊗10.30am-5.30pm Mon-Sat) An abandoned 20th-century shopping mall was transformed in 2018 into this innovative arts centre. Its former shops are now home to more than 25 artists, craftspeople and local musicians who create and promote their work here. The Maker's House is a one-stop shop showcasing and selling sculptures, furniture, mirrors, stained glass, paintings, fashion, jewellery, music recordings and more. Concerts, exhibitions and one-off events often take place in the interconnecting passageways.

👉 Tours

Wexford Walking Tours
WALKING

(☑053-912 2288; www.wexfordwalkingtours.net; town/Selskar Abbey tour €7/5; ⊗town tour 11am Mon-Wed Apr-Oct, Selskar Abbey tour 3pm Mon-Sat Apr-Oct) A guided walking tour is the best way to understand Wexford's complicated past, from Vikings to Cromwell's forces and Irish Rebels. These 90-minute walks depart from the tourist office (p185).

It also runs 40-minute tours of Selskar Abbey (p179).

🎉 Festivals & Events

Wexford Opera Festival
MUSIC

(☑053-912 2144; www.wexfordopera.com; ⊗late Oct-early Nov) This 12-day festival is Ireland's premier opera event, with rarely performed operas and shows playing to packed audiences at the National Opera House (p185). Fringe street theatre, poetry readings and exhibitions give the town a festive atmosphere, and many local bars run amateur singing competitions. Book tickets in advance.

🛏 Sleeping

Clayton Whites Hotel
SPA HOTEL €€

(☑053-912 2311; www.claytonwhiteshotel.com; Abbey St; d/f/ste from €134/154/204; ⓟ✳️🐕🛜❄️) In a prime town-centre location, this green-copper-fronted hotel has a high-tech spa with a 20m lap pool, sauna, Jacuzzi and steam room, and contemporary rooms, some with estuary views. There's a modern Irish restaurant, a cafe and the Library Bar, which serves food and hosts live music on Friday and Saturday nights year-round, plus Mondays and Wednesdays in summer.

The Young Viking Kids' Club keeps children entertained; cots and high chairs are available.

Talbot Hotel
HOTEL €€

(☑053-912 2566; www.talbotwexford.ie; The Quay; s/d/tr/ste from €119/129/139/209; ⓟ🐕🛜❄️) A landmark on Wexford's waterfront, this modern hotel has water views from many of its 107 rooms. Facilities include a steam room, sauna, gym and 15m indoor pool. Dine at its Gallery cafe, upmarket Oyster Lane restaurant, or the stylish, high-ceilinged Ballast Bank bar and grill, with pub classics such as fish and chips along with regular live music.

Family amenities include a kids' club.

Blue Door
B&B €€

(☑053-912 1047; www.bluedoor.ie; 18 Lower George St; s/d/f from €50/70/100; 🛜) Behind the eponymous cobalt-blue door of this 200-year-old Georgian townhouse, homely bedrooms with a period feel are brightened by tall windows; they're quiet despite the central location. Owner Derrick draws on his training as a chef at breakfast.

🍴 Eating

Simon Lambert & Sons
PUB FOOD €

(Simon's Place; ☑053-918 0041; www.simon lambertandsons.ie; 37 South Main St; mains €8-10; ⊗kitchen 9.30am-4pm Mon-Sat, bar 9.30am-11.30pm Mon-Thu, to 12.30am Fri & Sat, 6-11.30pm Sun; 🛜) This atmospheric, low-ceilinged pub serves above-average food during the day, with breakfasts that run from French toast with buttermilk syrup and black pudding to full Irish fry-ups, complete with excellent coffee. The lunch menu features dishes such as Yellowbelly beer–marinated pork *blaa* (local, floury bread roll) or crumbed goat's cheese and pear salad, alongside a grand selection of craft beers.

Stable Diet Cafe
CAFE **€**

(☎ 053-914 9012; www.stabledietcafe.com; 100 South Main St; mains €8-12; ⊙ 8.30am-5pm Mon-Sat) This bright and busy cafe is a Wexford institution, famous for its home-baked breads, scones and cakes. Breakfast choices include potato cakes with smoked salmon, homemade spicy baked beans or savoury filled croissants, while the lunch menu consists of freshly made soups (eg broccoli and blue cheese), salads and sandwiches.

★ Greenacres
BISTRO, DELI **€€**

(☎ 053-912 2975; www.greenacres.ie; 7 Selskar St; mains lunch €11.50-19.50, dinner €17.50-26.50; ⊙ 9am-10pm Mon-Sat; �) Eating, shopping, culture...this place has it covered! Irish cheeses and local produce are beautifully displayed in the food hall, the wine selection is the best south of Dublin, and the gourmet bistro produces innovative dishes from premium ingredients such as wild pigeon, rock oysters and smoked rabbit. The upper floors house an excellent art gallery.

Crust
PIZZA **€€**

(☎ 053-912 3685; www.crustpizza.ie; 93 South Main St; pizzas €11.50-15.50; ⊙ 5-10pm Mon-Fri, 12.30-10pm Sat & Sun; ϐ⏵) Neapolitan-style pizzas baked in Wexford's first wood-fired oven are topped with artisan Irish cheeses (Toonsbridge mozzarella, Coolea cheddar and Cashel Blue), meats (Richie Doyle sausages, Gubbeen chorizo and salami), Wicklow mountain herbs and wild Wexford mushrooms. Overlooking the open kitchen, the exposed-stone seating area with industrial lighting is great for enjoying a Wexford-brewed Yellowbelly beer. Takeaway is also available.

Owner/chef Richard Whitty initially trained at Ireland's renowned Ballymaloe Cookery School then later in Italy at Naples' Associazione Verace Pizza Napoletana (True Neapolitan Pizza Association).

Cistín Eile
IRISH **€€**

(☎ 053-912 1616; 80 South Main St; lunch mains €9-14, 3-course dinner €37.50; ⊙ noon-3pm Mon & Tue, noon-3pm & 6-9pm Wed-Sat; ϐ) ⌀ Bring a hearty appetite when you visit this always-busy restaurant – as the motto on the wall says, *Is maith an t-anlann an t-ocras* (hunger makes a great sauce). Expect the daily menu of locally sourced artisan produce to include slow-cooked beef, bacon and cabbage, mashed potatoes, foraged salad leaves, intense flavours and generous helpings.

WORTH A TRIP

CURRACLOE BEACH

Soft white sand, gentle surf and lack of development are the big draws of the 11km-long, Blue Flag–rated **Curracloe Beach**. Families flock here on sunny days, but with its vast size you can easily find a spare hectare of the beach to call your own. The strand doubled for Omaha Beach in the famous D-Day opening scenes of the movie *Saving Private Ryan* (1998). It's 11km northeast of Wexford, signposted at various points along the R741, R742 and R743.

There are good walking trails through the pine forests and sand dunes of Raven Nature Reserve at the south end, and it's possible to cycle to the beach from Wexford town, via waymarked cycle route 2 – ask for a map at the Wexford Tourist Office.

★ La Côte
SEAFOOD **€€€**

(☎ 053-912 2122; www.lacote.ie; Custom House Quay; mains €22.50-34, 3-course dinner menu €33; ⊙ 5.30-9.30pm Tue-Sat) 'The Coast' has raked in awards – notably Irish Seafood Restaurant of the Year – for its innovative takes on the finest of local seafood, such as turbot with oyster mousse, John Dory with squid ink bulgur (cracked wheat), or lemon sole with a Wexford mussel reduction. Big picture windows, timber floors and pale-blue-painted walls give it a breezy beach-house vibe.

Gluten-free dishes are available, and there's always at least one inventive vegetarian dish on the menu, such as toasted oat and pearl barley risotto with ramsons, roast garlic and crème fraiche.

🍷 Drinking & Nightlife

Sky & the Ground
PUB

(www.facebook.com/TheSkyAndTheGround; 112 South Main St; ⊙ 2-11.30pm Mon-Thu, to 12.30am Fri & Sat, to 11pm Sun) The Sky & the Ground is a perennial Wexford favourite. Its decor is classic, with a roaring fire and walls covered in old enamel signs, while its upstairs outdoor deck makes a great summer hang-out. There are often live-music sessions.

Centenary Stores
PUB

(☎ 053-912 4424; www.thestores.ie; Charlotte St; ⊙ 10am-11pm Sun-Thu, to midnight Fri & Sat) One of Wexford's livelier spots, this former warehouse is a mix of old and new. A

Wexford Town

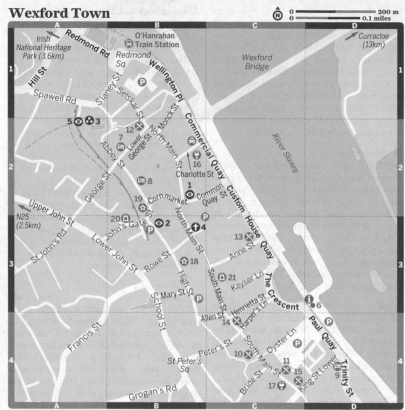

Ⓝ 0 ┣━━━━━━━━┫ 200 m
    0 ┣━━━━━━━━┫ 0.1 miles

Wexford Town

◉ Sights
1 Bull Ring...................................B2
2 Creative Hub............................B3
3 Selskar Abbey..........................A2
4 St Iberius' Church....................B3
5 Westgate.................................A2

✪ Activities, Courses & Tours
6 Wexford Walking Tours...........D3

⬛ Sleeping
7 Blue Door.................................B2
8 Clayton Whites Hotel..............B2
9 Talbot Hotel............................D4

✕ Eating
10 Cistín Eile...............................C4
11 Crust......................................C4

12 Greenacres..............................B2
13 La Côte...................................C3
14 Simon Lambert & Sons...........C4
15 Stable Diet Cafe.....................C4

⬛ Drinking & Nightlife
16 Centenary Stores....................B2
17 Sky & the Ground....................C4

✪ Entertainment
18 National Opera House..............B3
19 Wexford Arts Centre...............B2

⬛ Shopping
20 Blue Egg Gallery.....................B3
Bull Ring Market...................(see 1)
21 Wexford Book Centre..............C3

downstairs dark-wood pub with basic food and a long-standing local clientele contrasts with a pulsating designer nightclub, the Backroom (open 9pm to 2am Thursday to Sunday), that attracts a spirited, youthful crowd. Sunday lunchtime trad-music sessions take place in summer.

⭐ Entertainment

★ **National Opera House**   OPERA
(☑ box office 053-912 2144; www.nationalopera house.ie; High St; ☎) Opened in 2008, Wexford's gleaming opera house packs more architectural punch inside than out, but sports state-of-the-art acoustics and superb views from the top-floor bar. In addition to hosting the Wexford Opera Festival (p182) in autumn, it stages year-round theatre productions and concerts.

Wexford Arts Centre   ARTS CENTRE
(☑ 053-912 3764; www.wexfordartscentre.ie; Cornmarket; ☎) Housed in the 18th-century market hall, this centre hosts exhibitions, theatre (including occasional productions in Irish), dance and music, and has a good cafe.

🛍 Shopping

Wexford Book Centre   BOOKS
(☑ 053-912 3543; www.thebookcentre.ie; 5 South Main St; ☺9am-6pm Mon-Sat, 1-5pm Sun) Pick up local guides and maps at this bookshop, which also has an excellent selection of Irish fiction and nonfiction.

Blue Egg Gallery   ARTS & CRAFTS
(☑ 053-914 5862; www.blueegggallery.ie; 22 John's Gate St; ☺11am-5.30pm Tue-Sat) One of several commercial galleries and craft shops in town, the Blue Egg concentrates on contemporary Irish crafts in a range of materials, including ceramics, metal and glass.

Bull Ring Market   MARKET
(www.facebook.com/TheBullringMarketWexford; ☺9am-5pm Fri & Sat) The lively twice-weekly market at the Bull Ring has crafts, vintage clothes, antiques, jewellery, homewares, toys and accessories, along with food and drink stalls.

ℹ Information

Wexford Tourist Office (☑ 053-912 3111; www.visitwexford.ie; Quay Front; ☺9am-5pm Mon-Sat; ☎) Has maps and leaflets showing local walks and cycling routes.

ℹ Getting There & Around

BUS
Buses depart from **O'Hanrahan Station** (☑ 053-912 2522; www.irishrail.ie; Redmond Sq).
Bus Éireann (www.buseireann.ie) destinations include:
Dublin (€20, two hours, hourly)
Enniscorthy (€7.70, 20 minutes, hourly)

Rosslare Harbour (€6, 25 minutes, six daily Monday to Saturday, five Sunday)
Waterford (€12.50, one hour, seven daily)
Wexford Bus (www.wexfordbus.com) operates to/from Dublin Airport (€21, 2¾ hours, hourly) via Enniscorthy (€8, 25 minutes) and Dublin city centre (€18, two hours).

TAXI
Wexford Cabs (☑ 053-912 3123; 3 Charlotte St) Provides a 24-hour taxi service, including trips to Rosslare Harbour and Dublin Airport.

TRAIN
Trains from O'Hanrahan Station (p185) service Dublin Connolly Station (€16, 2½ hours, five daily) and Rosslare Harbour (€4.50, five daily, 20 minutes).

Rosslare Harbour

POP 1123
Busy Rosslare Harbour has connections to Wales and France from the Europort ferry terminal, home also to the Rosslare Europort train station. The road leading uphill from the harbour is the N25. There are some lovely sandy beaches in the area, in particular Rosslare Strand, which make it worth spending some time here before catching your train or ferry.

Rosslare Strand   BEACH
(Rosslare Strand) This glorious white-sand and pebbled beach stretches for 6.5km and has a Blue Flag rating. Protected by offshore sandbars, its shallow waters make it ideal for

GUINNESS BOOK OF RECORDS

During a wildfowling trip to the Slobs near Wexford in 1951, the chairman of Guinness Brewery, Sir Hugh Beaver, shot at but missed a golden plover. This provoked a spirited debate over whether it, or the red grouse, was Europe's fastest game bird. Sir Hugh realised that similar debates regularly cropped up all over the world, and that publishing definitive answers could prove profitable.

He was right about that – the first *Guinness Book of Records* was an immediate bestseller when it was published in 1955, and today it is itself a record-holder, as the world's biggest-selling copyrighted book – but wrong about Europe's fastest game bird (it's actually the spur-wing goose).

families; lifeguards patrol here from June to August. Its southern tip is 1.5km north of Rosslare Harbour.

Sleeping & Eating

St Martin's Rd (signposted Rosslare Harbour Village, on the right approaching from Wexford) is lined with B&Bs that cater to ferry passengers with early/late starts. Behind Rosslare Strand, 8km northwest, Strand Rd has hotels.

Coast Rosslare Strand
HOTEL €€

(053-913 2010; www.coastrosslarestrand.com; Strand Rd, Rosslare Strand; d/f from €129/160; P🐾) Just 200m west of the beach, and 8.5km northwest of the ferry port, this triple-storey hotel received a makeover in 2018 following the success of its sister property, Coast Kilmore Quay (p187). Painted a distinctive gull-grey inside and out, it has simple but spacious rooms, and a popular bar and restaurant (mains €13.50 to €24.50) hosting regular live music.

★ Karoo Farmshop & Cafe
CAFE, DELI €€

(053-915 8585; www.karoo.ie; Killinick; cakes & pastries €2-4.50, mains €9-17; 9am-4pm Mon, to 5pm Tue-Sat, 10am-4pm Sun; 🐾) Behind shelves filled with local breads, cheeses, cured meats, eggs, seafood, fruit, veggies and preserves, Karoo's cafe is a fabulous spot for all-day breakfasts, gourmet salads (black pudding, chorizo and sun-dried tomatoes), toasties (Wexford brie and cranberry chutney), burgers (falafel, lamb with blue cheese) and mains such as sea bass with lemon-and-dill cream sauce. It's 9km west of Rosslare Harbour.

Coffee made from Dublin-roasted beans is brewed to perfection; spectacular cakes include dark chocolate and pistachio.

Getting There & Away

BOAT

Rosslare ferries link Ireland to Wales and France (note that the frequency of sailings may be reduced in winter).

Cherbourg (France) Stena Line (www.stena line.ie) sails to/from France three times a week (foot passenger from €90, car and driver from €175, 18 hours).

Fishguard (Wales) Stena Line runs to/from Wales twice daily (foot passenger from €51, car and driver from €165, 3¼ hours).

Pembroke (Wales) Irish Ferries (www.irish ferries.com) offers two crossings daily (foot passenger €39, car and driver from €161, 3½ hours).

BUS

Bus Éireann (www.buseireann.ie) has services to numerous Irish towns and cities, including Dublin (€22, three hours, one daily Monday to Friday), and Cork (€26, 3¾ hours, six daily) via Wexford (€6, 25 minutes) and Waterford (€19, 1½ hours).

TRAIN

Irish Rail (www.irishrail.ie) runs four trains daily on the Rosslare Europort–Dublin Connolly Station route (€17, three hours) via Wexford (€4.50, 20 minutes).

South of Rosslare Harbour

A maze of minor roads meanders among the flatlands and tidal lagoons that spread from Rosslare Harbour to Kilmore Quay. Traditional Wexford thatched cottages – with mud walls, half-hipped roofs and small, square porches – brighten the roadsides, and a sandy beach is never far away.

Our Lady's Island
RUINS

(www.ourladysisland.ie; 24hr) Lady's Island Lake encloses Our Lady's Island, the site of an early Augustinian priory, which still has an annual pilgrimage in August/September. Pilgrims make nine circuits of the island, many of them barefoot (in olden times they used to crawl). Outside of pilgrimage season, the 2km pilgrim path is a lovely walk, passing the priory graveyard, which blooms with wild garlic in spring. Rare roseate terns breed in the lake's brackish waters, separated from the sea by a barrier beach.

Tacumshane Windmill
WINDMILL

(www.meylersmillhouse.com/the-windmill; Tacumshane) FREE Tacumshane Windmill is a rare survivor of the mills that once dotted this landscape, and is the only complete windmill in the Republic of Ireland. Built in 1846 using timber washed up on local beaches, it sports a cute thatched cap. It's on a minor road, 4km west of Our Lady's Island; ask for the key at the neighbouring **Meyler's Millhouse Bar & Restaurant** (053-913 1700; mains €14-27; kitchen 5-9pm Fri & Sat, 12.30-8pm Sun, bar 4-11pm Mon-Fri, 2pm-midnight Sat, 12.30-10pm Sun; 🐾).

O'Leary's Farm B&B
B&B €€

(053-913 3134; www.olearysfarm.com; Killilane, Kilrane; s/d/tr from €45/76/114; P🐾) This working 40-hectare organic farm offers four homely guest rooms, three with sea views. The delightful sitting room has a fireplace, a piano and plenty of books. Breakfast includes vegan, vegetarian and gluten-free options, with the farm's produce and homemade bread. It's 5km south of the Europort, 300m west of sandy Carne Beach. Cash only.

Lobster Pot
SEAFOOD €€€

(☑ 051-913 1110; www.lobsterpotwexford.com; Ballyfane, Carne; mains bar €7-15, restaurant €24-30; ☺ restaurant 6-9pm Tue-Sun, bar food noon-7.30pm Tue-Sun, closed Jan) Locals and visitors alike pack the Lobster Pot's warren of rooms and beer garden in summer (at which time it doesn't take bookings). Lobster is a highlight of its super-fresh seafood, and the chowder – brimming with cockles, mussels, prawns, salmon, crab and cod – is among the finest on the planet. It's 1.5km south of Our Lady's Island.

ⓘ Getting There & Away

You'll need your own wheels – motorised or otherwise – to access this maze of back roads. Distances are ideal for exploring by bicycle.

Kilmore Quay

POP 372

Kilmore Quay is part commercial fishing port, and part picturesque village lined with thatched cottages, where the cry of gulls and smell of the ocean provide the appropriate atmosphere for sampling the local seafood. The harbour is the jumping-off point for Ireland's largest bird sanctuary, the Saltee Islands.

⊙ Sights & Activities

Sea anglers can fish for sea bass, plaice and flounder from the shore, or charter one of half a dozen boats from the harbour (details at www.visitkilmorequay.com) for wreck and reef fishing.

Ballyteigue Burrow Nature Reserve
NATURE RESERVE

(www.npws.ie; ☺ 24hr) FREE The beach and sand dunes of Ballyteigue Burrow Nature Reserve stretch for 9km northwest from Kilmore Quay, covering 227 hectares in all. It's the summer home of chattering terns and serenading skylarks. The salt marsh and mudflats behind the dunes are an important habitat for overwintering birds such as golden plovers, black-tailed godwits and pale-bellied brent geese. The reserve also supports protected plant species including wild asparagus and perennial glasswort, and the lichen *Fulgensia fulgens*, found nowhere else in Ireland.

Ballycross Apple Farm
FARM

(☑ 053-913 5160; www.ballycross.com; adult/child €4/3; ☺ noon-6pm Sat & Sun Apr-Oct, to 5pm Sat & Sun Nov & Dec; ⓯) This working farm gets top marks from kids for its pedal-powered tractors and go-karts, animal-feeding sessions and signposted walking trails that run via woodland, riverbanks and orchards. The farm shop sells apples, apple juice, chutneys and jams, and the cafe serves delicious homemade waffles and pancakes. It's 8km north of Kilmore Quay, on a minor road 2km southwest of Bridgetown.

Saltee Islands
ISLAND

(www.salteeislands.info) Once the haunt of privateers, smugglers and 'dyvers pyrates', the Saltee Islands now have a peaceful existence as one of Europe's most important bird sanctuaries. More than 220 species have been recorded here, most of them passing migrants; the main breeding populations include chough, gannet, guillemot, razorbill, kittiwake, puffin and Manx shearwater. Boats make the 4km trip from Kilmore Quay harbour, but landing is weather-dependent. Book through **Declan Bates** (☑ 087 252 9736, 053-912 9684; Kilmore Quay Harbour; day trips €30).

The 90-hectare Great Saltee and the 40-hectare Little Saltee (closed to visits) were inhabited as long ago as 3500 to 2000 BC. From the 13th century until the Dissolution of the Monasteries, they were the property of Tintern Abbey (p188), after which various owners were granted the land. The islands are now privately owned.

The best time to visit is the spring and early-summer nesting season. The birds leave once the chicks can fly; by early August it's eerily quiet. There are no toilets or other facilities on the islands (landing often means getting your feet wet), and no shelter, so bring rain gear.

⚔ Festivals & Events

Seafood Festival
FOOD & DRINK

(www.kilmorequayseafoodfestival.com; ☺ early Jul) A four-day festival of music, exhibitions, guided nature walks, kayak races and, of course, local seafood.

▨ Sleeping & Eating

Coast Kilmore Quay
HOTEL €€

(☑ 053-914 8641; www.coastkilmorequay.com; R739; d/f from €125/159; ⓟ ⓢ) An old roadside motel 500m north of the beach and village centre has been upcycled with storm-grey,

DON'T MISS

TINTERN ABBEY

Tintern Abbey (☑051-562 650; www.heritageireland.ie; Saltmills; adult/child €5/3, with Colclough Walled Garden €9/5; ⊗10am-5.30pm Jun-Aug, 9.30am-5pm Apr, May, Sep & Oct) is named after its Welsh counterpart, from where its first monks hailed. The atmospheric remains of the abbey enjoy a lovely setting amid 40 hectares of woodland. Unusually for an abbey, it has a long history as a private residence. Following the Dissolution of the Monasteries in the early 16th century, Tintern was granted to Staffordshire nobleman Anthony Colclough, and his descendants continued to live here until 1959. The abbey is 11km north of Fethard-on-Sea, signposted off the R733.

William Marshal, Earl of Pembroke, founded the Cistercian abbey in the early 13th century after he nearly perished at sea and swore to establish a church if he made it ashore. The cloister walls, nave, crossing tower, chancel and south transept still stand tall, along with the conversions made by generations of Colcloughs to create a country residence out of a ruined abbey.

Walking trails wind into the surrounding woods, past lakes and streams and more crumbling ruins, including a small single cell church, to the beautiful, 200-year-old Colclough Walled Garden (☑083 306 4159; www.colcloughwalledgarden.com; Tintern Abbey, Saltmills; adult/child €5/3, with Tintern Abbey €9/5; ⊗10am-6pm Apr-Sep, to 4pm Oct-Mar), which has been replanted and restored to its former glory.

driftwood-brown and bright-white colour schemes while retaining the convenience of parking right outside your room. Its contemporary bar and quieter restaurant share an all-day menu (mains €12.50 to €24.50). Live music is played regularly. Kids' facilities include a playground; family rooms sleep four.

There's a second, larger sister property, Coast Rosslare Strand (p186), near Rosslare Harbour.

Mary Barry's SEAFOOD €€
(☑053-913 5982; www.marybarrys.ie; R739; mains €15-25; ⊗kitchen noon-8.30pm Mon-Thu, to 9.30pm Fri & Sat, to 9pm Sun, bar to 11pm Mon-Thu, to midnight Fri-Sun; 🅿️♿) Cosy pub Mary Barry's, with low ceilings, timber panelling, burgundy paintwork, ships wheels and crackling fireplaces, is 4.5km northeast of Kilmore Quay. Dishes incorporate locally caught seafood (scallops with black pudding crumb; tiger prawn and smoked haddock gratin), with a live tank of lobsters and oysters in season. Its adjacent bar hosts regular trad sessions.

❶ Getting There & Away

Wexford Bus (www.wexfordbus.com) runs to/from Wexford town four times daily Monday to Saturday (€8, 35 minutes).

Hook Peninsula

The road that leads around the long, tapering finger of the Hook Peninsula is signposted as the Ring of Hook coastal drive. Around every other bend is a quiet beach, a crumbling fortress, a stately abbey or a seafood restaurant, and the world's oldest working lighthouse stands tall at the peninsula's tip.

Strongbow passed here on his way to capture Waterford in 1170, reputedly instructing his men to land 'by Hook or by Crooke' (the latter referring to the nearby settlement of Crooke) – the origin of the popular phrase.

Hook Head Adventures OUTDOORS
(☑087 661 2299; www.hookheadadventures.ie; Main St, Fethard-on-Sea; tours €30-100; ⊗by reservation) Among the activities offered by Hook Head Adventures are sunset and sea-cave kayaking trips, coasteering, SUP (stand-up paddleboarding) trips and treks in the Comeragh Mountains.

❶ Information

Tourist Office (Hook Tourism; ☑051-262 900; www.hookpeninsula.com; Main St, Fethard-on-Sea; ⊗9.30am-5.30pm daily Jun-Aug, Mon-Fri only Sep-May) Has information on the Hook Peninsula and can make activity and accommodation bookings.

Duncannon & Around

POP 305

The small holiday town of Duncannon slopes down to a sandy beach that's transformed into a surrealist canvas during August's Duncannon Sand Sculpting Festival.

About 5.5 km northwest of Duncannon is pretty Ballyhack, where the car ferry makes the short crossing to Passage East in County Waterford. The village is dominated by the 15th-century Ballyhack Castle, a Knights Hospitallers tower house containing a small exhibition on the Crusades.

Sights & Activities

Duncannon Fort
FORT

(☑051-389 530; www.duncannonfort.ie; tour adult/child €6/1.50; ⊙11.30am-4.30pm Jun-Aug) Star-shaped Duncannon Fort, just west of Duncannon village, was built in 1588 to stave off a feared attack by the Spanish Armada, and was later used by the Irish army as a WWI training base (most buildings here date from this period). There are four guided tours a day, each lasting around 45 minutes.

Dunbrody Abbey
HISTORIC BUILDING

(☑086 275 9149; www.dunbrodyabbey.com; Campile; abbey ruin adult/child €4/1, maze & museum €7/4; ⊙11am-6pm Jul & Aug, to 5.30pm May, Jun & Sep) Beside the R733, 9km north of Duncannon, ruined Dunbrody Abbey is a remarkably intact Cistercian abbey founded by Strongbow in 1170 and completed in 1220. Across the road from the ruins is a museum with a huge doll's house, minigolf and an entertaining yew-hedge maze made up of over 1500 trees. There are also tearooms and a craft shop.

Hooked Kitesurfing
KITESURFING

(☑087 675 5567; www.hookedkitesurfing.ie; Duncannon Beach; half-day/2-day kitesurfing lesson €100/340, SUP lesson €40, kayak/SUP hire per hr €15; ⊙by reservation Apr-Sep) Duncannon's wide bay and Atlantic winds make it a great place to learn to kitesurf. Gentler SUP lessons are also available, and you can also hire a kayak or SUP.

Festivals & Events

Duncannon Sand Sculpting Festival
CULTURAL

(www.hookpeninsula.com; Duncannon Beach; ⊙mid-Aug) At this festival, held over two days in mid-August, giant sand sculptures are accompanied by fishing, crabbing and oyster-eating competitions, a local food market, sporting events such as beach volleyball, a kids' treasure hunt, and live music.

Sleeping & Eating

★Glendine Country House
GUESTHOUSE €€

(☑051-389 500; www.glendinehouse.com; Arthurstown; s/d from €65/98; P🖥) Staying at this 1830-built country house 5km north of

Duncannon is like visiting friends with impeccable taste. Bay windows overlook grounds with fallow deer, Highland cattle and Jacob sheep, and paintings by local artists line the walls. Named for local castles, the rooms typically have hardwood floors, chandeliers and antiques; try for room 9 and its canopied king-sized bed.

Cots and high chairs are available if you have little ones.

★The Hollow
SEAFOOD €€

(☑051-389 230; www.facebook.com/TheHollowBar; Ramsgrange; restaurant mains €13-26, takeaway dishes €6-10; ⊙noon-3pm & 5-10pm) This one-time rural pub, 5.5km from Duncannon, is now an exquisite restaurant with blue-and-grey velveteen chairs and marine-green walls. Depending on the day's catch, you might find scallops seared in chilli-and-lime butter, gin-flambéed prawns, or on-the-bone black sole with wild nettle tartar. Alternatively, order fish and chips, scampi or calamari at its takeaway kiosk and dine in its garden.

Getting There & Away

Bus Éireann (www.buseireann.ie) runs four times daily Monday to Saturday to Waterford city (€10, one hour) via New Ross (€8.50, 30 minutes).

The **Passage East Ferry** (☑051-382 480; www.passageferry.ie; one way pedestrian/bicycle €2, car €8; ⊙7am-9pm Mon-Sat, 9.30am-10pm Sun Jun-Aug, 7am-8pm Mon-Sat, 9.30am-8pm Sun Sep-May) shuttles between Ballyhack, 5.5km northwest of Duncannon, and Passage East, County Waterford.

Hook Head

The 10km journey southwest from the village of Fethard-on-Sea to Hook Head takes in a hypnotic stretch of horizon, with few houses between the flat, open fields of the tapering peninsula. Views extend across Waterford Harbour and, on a clear day, to the Comeragh and Galtee Mountains.

There are tiny, charming hamlets, such as Slade (where most of the activity is in the swirl of seagulls above the ruined castle and harbour). Beaches include the wonderfully secluded Dollar Bay and Booley Bay, just beyond Templetown en route to Duncannon.

Sights

★Hook Lighthouse
LIGHTHOUSE

(☑051-397 055; www.hookheritage.ie; R734, Hook Head; €9; ⊙9.30am-7pm Jul & Aug, to 6pm Jan-Jun, to 5.30pm Sep-Dec) On its southern tip, Hook

WORTH A TRIP

WEXFORD & THE KENNEDYS

In 1848 Patrick Kennedy escaped a famine-stricken County Wexford aboard an emigrant ship similar to the Dunbrody Famine Ship (p191) in New Ross. Hoping to find better prospects in America, he succeeded beyond his wildest dreams: his descendants included rum-runners, senators and a US president.

The family's Irish roots are remembered at two sites near New Ross, signposted from the Famine ship on a 24km driving route known as the Emigrant Trail: the Kennedy Homestea, where John F Kennedy's great-grandfather Patrick Kennedy was born, and the woodland park John F Kennedy Arboretum, dedicated to the memory of the late US president.

John F Kennedy Arboretum (☎ 051-388 171; www.heritageireland.ie; Ballysop; adult/child €5/3; ⏱ 10am-8pm May-Aug, to 6.30pm Apr & Sep, to 5pm Oct-Mar) This beautiful woodland park, dedicated to the memory of JFK, the late US president, has 4500 species of trees and shrubs spread across 252 hectares of woods and gardens, where walking trails meander among groves of eucalyptus, redwood, oak, magnolia and many other iconic species. The park has a small visitors centre, a tearoom (open May to September) and a picnic area. A miniature train tootles around in the summer months. It's 12km south of New Ross, signposted off the R733.

Kennedy Homestead (☎ 051-388 264; www.kennedyhomestead.ie; Dunganstown; adult/child €7.50/6; ⏱ 9.30am-5.30pm) The birthplace of Patrick Kennedy is a farm that still looks much as it must have done when he departed for America in 1848. When JFK visited in 1963 and hugged the current owner's grandmother, it was his first public display of affection, according to his sister, Jean. A museum examines the Kennedy dynasty's history on both sides of the Atlantic. It's on a minor road 7km south of New Ross, signposted from the R733.

Head is capped by the world's oldest working lighthouse, with a modern light flashing atop a 13th-century tower. Access is by half-hour guided tour, which includes a climb up the 115 steps for great views. The visitors centre has a cafe, while the grassy grounds and surrounding shore are ideal for picnics and walks.

It's said that monks first lit a beacon on the head in the 5th century, and that the first Viking invaders were so happy to have a guiding light that they left them alone. In the early 13th century William Marshal erected a more permanent structure, which is still standing today beneath the lighthouse's neat, black-and-white-striped exterior.

Loftus Hall   HISTORIC BUILDING
(☎ 051-397 728; www.loftushall.ie; R734; adult/child daytime tour €12/3, adult-only evening tour €66, gardens only adult/child €4/free; ⏱ noon-5pm daily late Jun-Aug, noon-4pm Sat & Sun Sep-late Jun, evening tours by reservation) Situated 3.5km northeast of Hook Head, this crumbling manor house gazes across Waterford Harbour to Dunmore East. Dating from the 1600s and rebuilt in the 1870s, Loftus Hall is reputed to be one of Ireland's most haunted houses. Its 45-minute historical daytime tours (ages five and above) depart up to six times a day, while monthly 'paranormal lockdown' evening tours

(over-18s only) run from 8.30pm to 2.30am. Its 2-hectare walled gardens shelter box hedges, bulbs and a fairy trail.

Check the website for special events such as Halloween.

🏃 Activities

There are brilliant, blustery **walks** on both sides of Hook Head. Poke around the tide pools while watching for surprise showers from blowholes on the western side of the peninsula. The rocks here are carboniferous limestone, rich in **fossils**. Search carefully and you may find 350-million-year-old brachiopod shells, lacy bryozoans and tiny disclike pieces of crinoids, ancient relatives of the sea urchin. The slabs beneath the seaward side of Hook Lighthouse (p189) are a good place to look.

At low tide there's a good walk between Grange and Carnivan beaches, past caves, rock pools and **Baginbun Head**, which, surmounted by a 19th-century Martello tower, is where the Normans first landed in 1169 to begin their conquest of Ireland. It's a good vantage point for **birdwatching**: more than 200 species have been recorded passing through. You might even spot dolphins or whales in the estuary.

New Ross & Around

POP 8040

The big attraction at New Ross (Rhos Mhic Triúin) is the opportunity to board a 19th-century Famine ship. But New Ross' historical links stretch back much further – to the 12th century, when it developed as a Norman port on the River Barrow. A group of rebels tried to seize the town during the 1798 Rising. They were repelled by the defending garrison, leaving 3000 dead and much of the place in tatters.

Today it's not a pretty town, but the eastern bank retains some intriguingly steep and narrow streets, and the remains of a medieval abbey. Ask at the tourist office for a map of the town's **history trail** (allow 1½ hours).

◉ Sights & Activities

★ Dunbrody Famine Ship   MUSEUM
(☑ 051-425 239; www.dunbrody.com; The Quay; adult/child €11/6; ⊙ 9am-6pm) Called 'coffin ships' due to their fatality rate, the leaky, smelly boats that hauled a generation of Irish emigrants to America are reimagined on board this replica ship on the New Ross waterfront. The emigrants' sorrowful yet often inspiring stories are brought to life by costumed actors during 45-minute tours. A 10-minute introductory film provides historical background about the mid-19th-century Ireland they were leaving.

Galley River Cruising Restaurant   CRUISE
(☑ 051-421 723; www.rivercruises.ie; North Quay; cruises for lunch/afternoon tea/dinner €25/12/40; ⊙ Apr-Oct) This floating restaurant offers scenic cruises along the 'Three Sisters' rivers – the Suir, Nore and Barrow – heading upstream to Inistioge or St Mullins or downstream towards Waterford, depending on the tide. Two-hour, four-course lunch cruises depart at 12.30pm, 1½-hour afternoon-tea cruises set off at 3pm, and three-hour, four-course dinner cruises leave at 6pm.

🛌 Sleeping & Eating

Brandon House Hotel   SPA HOTEL €€
(☑ 051-421 703; www.brandonhousehotel.ie; N25 Ring Rd; d/f from €86/126; P🐾) This Victorian red-brick manor certainly lives up to its reputation as family-friendly, with kids happily bounding around the place. Winning elements include river views, open log fires, a library bar and spacious modern rooms, and a spa with a sauna, eucalyptus steam room,

Jacuzzis and plunge pools. It's signposted off the N25 Ring Rd on New Ross' southern edge. Family rooms sleep four.

MacMurrough Farm Cottages   COTTAGE €€
(☑ 051-421 383; www.macmurrough.com; MacMurrough; 2-person cottage from €60; ⊙ mid-Mar-Oct; P🐾) A strutting rooster serves as an alarm clock at Brian and Jenny's remote hilltop farm. The two well-priced self-catering cottages are located in the former stables and have full kitchens, wood stoves, washing machines, cots and high chairs; one even has a piano. The farm is 3.5km northeast of New Ross' centre.

Cafe Nutshell   CAFE €
(☑ 051-422 777; www.facebook.com/cafenutshell; 8 South St; mains €8-17; ⊙ 9am-6pm Mon-Sat) Scones, breads and buns are all baked on Nutshell's premises, and lunch specials such as broccoli pasta bake, spinach-and-ham quiches or lamb-and-Guinness pie come with an array of fresh salads. There's a great range of smoothies, juices and organic wines. The adjacent health-food shop and deli are handy for picnic provisions.

ℹ Information

New Ross Tourist Office (☑ 051-425 239; www.discoverireland.ie; The Quay; ⊙ 9am-6pm Apr-Sep, to 5pm Oct-Mar) Located in the same building as the Dunbrody Famine Ship ticket office.

ℹ Getting There & Away

Bus Éireann (www.buseireann.ie) services depart from The Quay. Buses travel to/from Waterford city (€9.50, 30 minutes, 12 daily Monday to Saturday, six Sunday) via New Ross to Wexford town (€10.50, 35 minutes). A service also links New Ross with Dublin (€18.50, 2¾ hours, three daily).

Enniscorthy

POP 11,381

County Wexford's second-largest town, Enniscorthy (Inis Coirthaidh) has a warren of steep streets descending from Augustus Pugin's cathedral to a Norman castle and the River Slaney. The town is inextricably linked to some of the fiercest fighting of the 1798 Rising, when rebels captured the town and set up camp at Vinegar Hill.

◉ Sights

National 1798 Rebellion Centre   MUSEUM
(☑ 053-923 7596; www.1798centre.ie; Parnell Rd; adult/child €7/3; ⊙ 9am-5pm daily Jun-Sep, closed

Sat & Sun Oct-May) This exhibition does a fine job of explaining the background to one of Ireland's pivotal historical events. It covers the French and American revolutions, which helped spark Wexford's abortive uprising against British rule in Ireland, before chronicling the Battle of Vinegar Hill. One of the most bloodthirsty battles of the 1798 Rising and a turning point in the struggle, it took place just outside Enniscorthy. A visit here provides context for a walk up Vinegar Hill itself.

Joint tickets for the centre and Enniscorthy Castle are available (adult/child €10/5) from April to September.

Enniscorthy Castle   CASTLE

(☑ 053-923 4699; www.enniscorthycastle.ie; Castle Hill; adult/child €6/3; ⊙ 9.30am-5pm Mon-Fri, noon-5pm Sat & Sun Apr-Sep, 10am-4pm Mon-Fri, noon-5pm Sat & Sun Oct-Mar) This stout, four-towered keep was originally built by the Normans; like much else in these parts, it was surrendered to Cromwell in 1649. During the 1798 Rising, rebels used this castle as a prison, and from 1901 to 1953 it was the family home of local businessman and landowner Henry J Roche. It now houses a museum about the history of both town and castle, and has a rooftop deck with spectacular views.

From April to September, joint tickets for the castle and the National 1798 Rebellion Centre (p191) are available (adult/child €10/5).

Vinegar Hill   HISTORIC SITE

(www.vinegarhill.ie; ⊙ dawn-dusk) `FREE` Scene of one of the most important battles of Ireland's 1798 rebellion against British rule, this hill just outside Enniscorthy is topped with a memorial to the Rising, and dotted with explanatory signs about the battlefield. A battle re-enactment takes place on the first weekend in August each year. Access is from a car park on the east side of the hill, reached via Drumgoold Rd; it's 2km east of Enniscorthy Castle, about a 30-minute walk.

🎇 Festivals & Events

Strawberry Festival   FOOD & DRINK

(www.enniscorthytourism.com/events; ⊙ late May/early Jun) Celebrating the favourite crop of Ireland's sunny southeast, this eclectic event has been going strong since 1967. Held over three days, it includes an agricultural show, a farmers market, cookery demonstrations, children's events, live music and the crowning of the Strawberry Queen. Pubs extend

their hours, bands are booked, and strawberries and cream are on sale everywhere.

🛏 Sleeping & Eating

Riverside Park   HOTEL €€

(☑ 053-923 7800; www.riversideparkhotel.com; The Promenade; d/tr from €89/99; P 🐕 🕿) Enjoy strolls along the grassy banks of the river from this superbly positioned hotel, where a dramatic lobby in a circular tower sets the scene. Comfortable rooms are decorated in neutral creams and browns, and most have balconies and river views. This is a popular hotel for weddings, so Saturdays may be booked up and/or noisy!

Woodbrook House   GUESTHOUSE €€

(☑ 053-925 5114; www.woodbrookhouse.ie; Killann; s/d from €105/170; ⊙ Easter-Jun & Aug-Sep; P 🕿) 🍴 Rebuilt after sustaining damage in the 1798 Rising, this glorious Georgian country house has a superb setting beneath the Blackstairs Mountains. The lobby features a gravity-defying spiral staircase that still amazes, just as it did over 200 years ago. Green practices are used throughout and you can make arrangements for dinner (€50; organic, of course). It's 14km northwest of Enniscorthy.

★ The Wilds   CAFE €

(☑ 053-923 7799; www.thewilds.ie; 23 Weafer St; dishes €6-13; ⊙ 9am-5pm Tue-Fri, 10am-5pm Sat, 11am-4pm Sun; 🕿) 🍴 Using only organic, free-range and local produce from small-scale farms, the Wilds serves brilliant dishes such as pork-and fennel sausage rolls with spicy homemade relish, baked potatoes with hazelnut pesto, and daily soups including artichoke and parsnip. The setting is a pearl-grey-painted dining room with bare boards and vintage furniture, while the attached design shop sells art, crafts, cosmetics, clothing and homewares.

Kids are well catered for, with smaller dishes and their own hot chocolate.

Farmers Market   MARKET €

(www.wexfordfarmersmarkets.com; Abbey Sq Car Park; ⊙ 9am-2pm Sat) Enniscorthy's farmers market sells local and organic goods and prepared foods. Look for Carrigbyrne cheese.

Galo Chargrill Restaurant   PORTUGUESE €€

(☑ 053-923 8077; 19 Main St; mains €17-26.50; ⊙ 5-11pm Wed, noon-3pm & 5-11pm Thu-Sat, noon-9pm Sun) In warm weather, the front of this small restaurant opens up like the lid on a can of sardines, and even on dull days the spicy chargrills – such as peri-peri chicken or pork skewers – provide a burst of southern European sunshine.

ℹ Information

Tourist Office (☑ 053-923 4699; www.ennis corthytourism.com; Castle Hill; ⊙ 9.30am-5pm Mon-Fri, noon-5pm Sat & Sun Apr-Sep, 10am-4pm Mon-Fri, noon-5pm Sat & Sun Oct-Mar) Inside Enniscorthy Castle.

ℹ Getting There & Away

BUS

Bus Éireann (www.buseireann.ie) runs to Dublin (€18, two hours, hourly) and Wexford town (€7.70, 20 minutes, hourly).

Wexford Bus (www.wexfordbus.com) runs from Enniscorthy to Wexford town (€8, 25 minutes, hourly) and Carlow (€5, 50 minutes, six daily).

TRAIN

The train station is on the eastern bank of the river. Services run to Dublin Connolly (€14.50, 2¼ hours, four daily) and Wexford (€6.90, 20 minutes, five daily).

COUNTY WATERFORD

Diverse County Waterford harbours seaside settlements along its sandy coastline, from pretty fishing villages to surf meccas. You'll also find historic churches, cathedrals and castles, a warren of walking trails in the beautiful Nire Valley, concealed among the Comeragh and Monavullagh Mountains, and lively Waterford city, with its maze of medieval lanes and well-preserved Georgian architecture.

Waterford City

POP 53,504

Waterford (Port Láirge) is Ireland's oldest city – it celebrated its 1100th anniversary in 2014 – with a history that dates back to Viking times. Taking its name from the Old Norse *vedrarfjord* ('winter haven' or 'windy harbour' are just two of several possible translations) it remains a busy port city on a tidal reach of the River Suir, and is famous as the home of Waterford crystal.

Although the city has been extensively redeveloped, notably along the waterfront, it retains vestiges of its Viking and Norman past in the narrow streets and town walls of the so-called Viking Triangle, where three museums tell the story of Ireland's Middle Ages better than in any other city in the country.

The Waterford Greenway (p201) links the city to Dungarvan via a 46km all-abilities walking and cycling trail.

History

Waterford was established as a Viking port around 914. Its original city walls were extended by King John in 1210, making it Ireland's most powerful city. In the 15th century it resisted the forces of two pretenders to the English Crown, Lambert Simnel and Perkin Warbeck, and in 1649 defied Cromwell. In 1650 his forces returned and Waterford surrendered. Although the city escaped the customary slaughter, Catholics were either exiled to the west or shipped as slaves to the Caribbean, and the population dramatically declined.

⊙ Sights & Activities

The wedge of ancient streets northwest of The Mall – the **Viking Triangle** (www.waterford vikingtriangle.com) – is home to three excellent museums: the Medieval Museum, the Bishop's Palace (p194) and Reginald's Tower (p194), collectively called **Waterford Treasures**. Together they cover 1000 years of local history. If you only have time to visit one attraction here, make it the Medieval Museum.

A wide 18th-century street, **The Mall** is built on reclaimed land that was once a tidal inlet. Its stateliest buildings are John Roberts' 1788 **City Hall** and the beautifully refurbished **Theatre Royal** (☑ 051-874 402; www.theatreroyal .ie; ⊙ box office 10am-4pm Mon-Fri, noon-4pm Sat & performance days 6-8pm), arguably Ireland's most intact 18th-century theatre. In the middle of the waterfront stands the 1860s **clock tower** (The Quay), a famous local landmark.

Crumbling fragments of the old city wall include **Beach Tower**, at the top of Jenkin's Lane, and **Half Moon Tower**, just off Patrick St.

★ **Medieval Museum**   MUSEUM
(www.waterfordtreasures.com; Cathedral Sq; adult/ child €7/free, with Bishop's Palace €10/free; ⊙ 9.15am-6pm Mon-Fri, 9.30am-6pm Sat, 11am-5pm Sun Jun-Aug, 9.15am-5pm Mon-Fri, 10am-5pm Sat, 11am-5pm Sun Sep-May) Housed in a stunning modern structure that incorporates several medieval buildings and part of the city wall in its basement (all on display), this museum documents Waterford's medieval history in glowing detail. The highlights of the collection are the extraordinary 15th-century **cloth-of-gold church vestments**,

Waterford

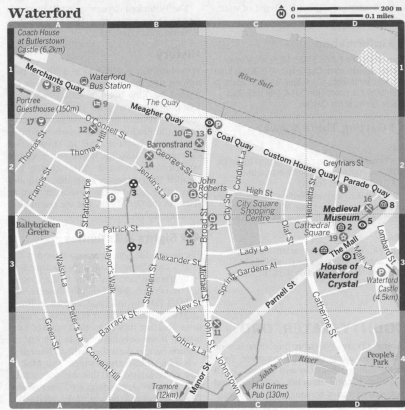

made from silk woven in Florence and embroidered in Bruges around 1460. Hidden beneath Christ Church Cathedral and forgotten for 123 years, they are a rare survivor and one of the great treasures of medieval Europe.

Other outstanding exhibits include the **Great Parchment Book of Waterford**, an original document that records in fascinating detail what medieval life was like, including cases of petty crime and the impact of the plague, and a **ceremonial sword** and two maces gifted to the city by England's Edward IV in 1462.

Bishop's Palace   MUSEUM
(☎ 0761 102 501; www.waterfordtreasures.com; The Mall; adult/child €7/free, with Medieval Museum €10/free; ⊙ 9.15am-6pm Mon-Fri, 9.30am-6pm Sat, 11am-5pm Sun Jun-Aug, 9.15am-5pm Mon-Fri, 10am-5pm Sat, 11am-5pm Sun Sep-May) The Bishop's Palace, a Georgian mansion dating from 1741, covers Waterford's history from 1700 to 1970 and displays a wide-ranging selection of city

treasures, from period furniture, oil paintings and Georgian silverware to old photos recording the 1960s heyday of Irish showbands. Most interesting is the original dining room set with period tableware, including the world's oldest surviving piece of Waterford crystal, a decanter dating from 1789.

Reginald's Tower   MUSEUM
(☎ 0761 102 501; www.waterfordtreasures.com; The Quay; adult/child €5/3; ⊙ 9.30am-5.30pm late Mar-late Dec, to 5pm early Jan-late Mar) Ireland's oldest complete building and the first to use mortar, 13th-century Reginald's Tower, the city's key fortification, is an outstanding example of medieval architecture. Its 3m- to 4m-thick walls were built on the site of a Viking wooden tower. Over the years the building served as an arsenal, a prison and a mint; it now houses a museum recording the city's Viking and early medieval history. The sparse exhibits include the tiny but exquisite **Waterford Kite Brooch**, made around 1100.

Waterford

⊙ Top Sights
1 House of Waterford Crystal.................D3
2 Medieval Museum................................D3

⊙ Sights
3 Beach Tower...B2
4 Bishop's Palace...................................D3
5 City Hall...D3
6 Clock Tower...C2
7 Half Moon Tower.................................B3
8 Reginald's Tower.................................D2

⊙ Sleeping
9 Dooley's Hotel......................................A1
10 Granville Hotel....................................B2

⊗ Eating
11 Bodega!...C4

12 Candied Hazelnut...............................A2
13 Carter's Chocolate Cafe.....................B2
14 La Bohème...B2
15 Momo..B3
16 Munster Bar..D2

⊙ Drinking & Nightlife
17 Henry Downes Bar...............................A2
18 Metalman..A1

⊙ Entertainment
19 Theatre Royal......................................D3

⊙ Shopping
20 Waterford Book Centre.......................B2
21 Waterford City Food & Craft
   Market...C3

★ **House of Waterford Crystal** FACTORY
(☑ 051-317 000; www.waterfordvisitorcentre.com;
The Mall; adult/child €13/6.50; ⊙ 9am-4.15pm
Mon-Sat, 9.30am-4.15pm Sun Apr-Oct, shorter
hours Nov-Mar) This large modern complex
combines a retail shop and cafe with a factory offering a 90-minute tour that shows
how world-famous Waterford crystal is produced. The highlight is the blowing room
where you can watch skilled artisans trans-
form blobs of red-hot molten glass into delicate crystalware. The tour ends, inevitably,
in the shop, where twinkling displays range
from a €30 bottle coaster to a €30,000 crystal version of Cinderella's carriage.

The first Waterford glass factory was established at the western end of the riverside
quays in 1783. Centuries later, after the boom
of the 1980s and 1990s, the company fell on
hard times and in 2009 was purchased by
an American investment firm; in 2015 it was
acquired by Finland's Fiskars Corporation.
Today pieces are produced in Ireland and
further afield in Europe to strict Waterford
standards.

⭐ Tours

★ **Jack Burtchaell's**
Guided Walking Tour WALKING
(☑ 051-873 711; www.jackswalkingtours.com; adult/
child €7/free; ⊙ 11.45am & 1.45pm mid-Mar–mid-
Oct) Jack's 'gift of the gab' brings Waterford's
nooks and crannies to life, effortlessly squeezing 1000 years of history into one hour. Tours
leave from near the tourist office (p197) – confirm the exact location there – and pick up
walkers from various hotels en route.

★☆ Festivals & Events

Waterford Harvest
Food Festival FOOD & DRINK
(www.waterfordharvestfestival.ie; ⊙ mid-Sep) Held
over three days in mid-September, this festival features food markets, taste workshops,
celebrity-chef clinics and open-air picnics,
as well as a *blaa*-eating competition, where
contestants devour the area's signature soft,
fluffy bread rolls.

🛏 Sleeping

Portree Guesthouse B&B €
(☑ 051-874 574; www.portreeguesthouse.ie; 10
Mary St; s/d/tr/q from €53/72/82/113; ⓟ⑨)
This large, 24-room Georgian B&B is on a
quiet street, but close to the city centre. It is
well run by a couple of Londoners, and the
rooms are spick and span. There's a garden
and library, a cosy sitting room with plenty of tourist information and brochures,
plus 24-hour coffee and tea. Popular with
groups.

★ **Granville Hotel** HOTEL €€
(☑ 051-305 555; www.granvillehotel.ie; Meagher Quay; d from €140; ⓟ⑨) The floodlit
18th-century building overlooking the waterfront is the Granville, one of Ireland's
oldest hotels. Brocaded bedrooms (some
with river views) maintain a sense of Georgian elegance, as do the public areas with
their showstopping stained glass, historical
prints and antiques. Star turns at breakfast
are the organic porridge with Baileys and
the perfect eggs Benedict.

Dooley's Hotel
HOTEL €€

(☑ 051-873 531; www.dooleys-hotel.ie; Merchants Quay; d from €142; @ 🖙) Locally owned and run like clockwork, Dooley's is a Waterford institution that has hosted family holidays, weddings and social gatherings since 1947. It sports smartly refurbished bedrooms, and the breakfast is a belt notch up from most hotel buffets, and includes organic porridge, fresh fruit compote and cooked options. The on-site Thai Therapy Centre offers various treatments.

Coach House at Butlerstown Castle
B&B €€

(☑ 086 223 8102; www.butlerstowncastle.com; Butlerstown; d from €99; ⊘ Apr-Oct; P 🖙) Dating from the 19th century, this stone-built B&B is as appealing inside as it is out, with deep, studded-leather armchairs to sink into, toasty open fires to warm up by, canopied beds to drift off in and pancakes to wake up to. It's 7.5km southwest of Waterford on the L4047, signposted off the R680.

★ Waterford Castle
CASTLE €€€

(☑ 051-878 203; www.waterfordcastleresort.com; The Island, Ballinakill; d/lodge from €278/300; P 🖙) Getting away from it all is an understatement at this turreted mid-19th-century castle set on its own private island (a free car ferry at Ballinakill on the eastern edge of town provides round-the-clock access). All 19 castle rooms have hand-painted tiles and claw-foot baths, and some have four-poster beds. There are also 45 contemporary self-catering lodges on the island.

Both guests and nonguests can dine on organic fare in the sublime oak-panelled Munster Restaurant (three-course dinner €68), or play a round of golf on the hotel's own par-72 course (green fees €35 to €45).

✗ Eating

Candied Hazelnut
VEGAN €

(☑ 051-876 583; www.thecandiedhazelnut.com; 11 O'Connell St; mains €6-9; ⊘ 5.30-9pm Wed-Sat, noon-4pm Sun; 🖙 🍴) Colourful art decorates the exterior and interior walls of this little bistro, whose cooking is 100% plant based. Start off with pistachio pâté or wild garlic and broccoli soup, before moving on to mains like hazelnut gnocchi with shallot and white-wine sauce or 'shepherdless pie', and finishing with desserts such as flourless blueberry and dark-chocolate cake.

Live acoustic sets are often played.

Carter's Chocolate Cafe
CAFE €

(☑ 051-841 802; www.facebook.com/thechoccafe; 8 Barronstrand St; dishes €2.50-6.50; ⊘ 8am-6.30pm Mon-Sat, 11am-5.30pm Sun) In addition to Ireland's famous Lily O'Brien's chocolates (and wonderfully warming hot chocolate), this shop/cafe has sweet treats such as berry crumble, macaroons and rich, dark carrot cake. Savoury snacks include gourmet sandwiches.

★ Momo
BISTRO €€

(☑ 051-581 509; www.momorestaurant.ie; 47 Patrick St; mains lunch €8.50-15, dinner €17-25; ⊘ noon-9pm Tue-Thu, to 10pm Fri & Sat, 1-8pm Sun; 🖙 🍴) This buzzing bistro is so popular that you might struggle to find a table, so book ahead to dine on creative dishes that incorporate local produce such as Waterford goat's cheese and beetroot risotto, port-wine-marinated beef ribs with roast apple, or smoked-cod pie topped with kale mash. Kids' dishes (€7) might include spiced lamb koftas or lemon- and herb-marinated chicken.

Munster Bar
PUB FOOD €€

(☑ 051-874 656; www.themunsterbar.com; Bailey's New St; mains €8.50-20; ⊘ kitchen noon-9pm Mon-Sat, to 7pm Sun, bar to 11.30pm Sun-Thu, to 12.30am Fri & Sat) Set in a building dating from 1822, this pub and restaurant has a snug, complete with roaring fire, and a spacious bar in the former coach house. Enjoy traditional pub food such as Irish stew with bread and butter, steak-and-Guinness pie, and sausages with colcannon (mashed potato dish). It's the perfect casual end to a long day's touring.

Bodega!
IRISH €€

(☑ 051-844 177; www.bodegawaterford.com; 54 John St; mains lunch €11-19, dinner €16.50-29; ⊘ 5-10pm Mon-Wed, noon-3pm & 5-10pm Thu-Sat) 🖉 Although the colourful Mediterranean-style decor lends it a Spanish air, the latest Bodega! incarnation is contemporary Irish with an emphasis on local produce. Alongside dishes such as crispy pork belly with apple and black pudding slaw are lighter options such as goat's cheese tartlets and warm crab sandwiches on sourdough. Keeping it local is a long list of Irish craft brews.

★ La Bohème
FRENCH €€€

(☑ 051-875 645; www.labohemerestaurant.ie; 2 George's St; mains €22-32.50; ⊘ 5.30-11pm Tue-Thu & Sat, noon-3pm & 5.30-11pm Fri) In the kitchen basement of a Georgian townhouse, La Bohème's intimate dining rooms have barrel-vault roofs and arches. The kitchen combines French flair with fresh Irish produce, resulting in dishes like Waterford crab brûlée, Cappoquin guinea fowl with artichoke and tarragon mousseline, and Irish Breakfast tea-poached pears with Wexford strawberry sorbet. There's an extensive wine cellar.

The three-course early bird menu is a bargain at €31.

🍷 Drinking & Nightlife

★ Phil Grimes Pub   PUB
(📞 051-875 759; 60 Johnstown; ⏱ 4-11.30pm Sun-Thu, to 12.30am Fri & Sat) Located on the southern edge of the city centre, this is a genuine local boozer with a friendly atmosphere and a loyal clientele who throng here to enjoy a range of Irish and international craft beers, a fantastic line-up of live-music gigs, and regular quiz and movie nights.

Metalman   CRAFT BEER
(www.metalmanbrewing.com; 15 Merchants Quay; ⏱ 5-11.30pm Mon-Thu, to 12.30am Fri, 2pm-12.30am Sat, 2-11pm Sun; 📶) Behind a black-and-cream facade on the quayfront is the taproom of Waterford city's Metalman Brewing Co. Beers include Ironmonger (amber IPA), Moonbeam (stout) and Blaager (lager brewed with crumbs from Waterford city's sweet, doughy *blaa* bread), as well as guest beers from around the Emerald Isle. Look out for sci-fi film screenings (with free popcorn), trivia quizzes and board-game nights.

Henry Downes Bar   PUB
(📞 051-874118; 10 Thomas St; ⏱ 5-11.30pm Mon-Thu, to midnight Fri-Sun, also noon-2.30pm Sat & Sun; 📶) For a change from stout, drop into Downes, which has been blending and bottling its own No 9 Irish whiskey since 1797. Have a dram in one of a series of character-filled rooms, or buy a bottle to take away. This place is a real one-off – they even have a squash court out the back, as well as a full-sized billiard table.

🛍 Shopping

As well as its famous crystal, available from House of Waterford Crystal (p195), Waterford has a wealth of local craftspeople creating textiles, paintings, jewellery, pottery, papier mâché, candles, and furniture built from recycled materials. Great George's St, Blackfriars, Broad St and Patrick St are good starting points.

Waterford Book Centre   BOOKS
(📞 051-873 823; www.thebookcentre.ie; 25 John Roberts Sq; ⏱ 9am-6pm Mon-Sat, 1-5pm Sun)

Waterford Book Centre has three floors of books – including an excellent selection of Irish classics – and a cafe.

Waterford City
Food & Craft Market   MARKET
(John Roberts Sq; ⏱ 10am-4pm Sat) Crafts on sale at this excellent market include pottery, jewellery and hand-turned wood. There are many ready-to-eat dishes; look out for the breads, cakes, biscuits and more by Mary Doherty of Granny Maddock's Pantry.

ℹ Information

Tourist Office (📞 051-875 823; www.discoverireland.ie; 120 Parade Quay; ⏱ 9am-5pm Mon-Sat) The best source of info in Counties Waterford and Wexford.

ℹ Getting There & Away

AIR
Waterford Airport (www.flywaterford.com), 9km south of the city centre, has no passenger services, but there are hopes for their revival – check the website for updates.

BOAT
If you're driving or cycling between Wexford and Waterford along the coast, the Passage East Ferry (p189) from Ballyhack to Passage East across the River Suir saves a long detour via New Ross. The crossing takes five minutes, with several departures per hour.

BUS
There are frequent Bus Éireann (www.buseireann.ie) services to:
Dublin (€17, 2½ hours, 14 daily)
Dublin Airport (€21, three hours, 11 daily)
Tramore (€2.80, 45 minutes, twice hourly)
Wexford (€12.50, one hour, six daily)

The Dublin Coach (www.dublincoach.ie) M9 Express service runs every two hours, linking Waterford to:
Cork (€10, two hours)
Dublin (€10, 2½ hours)
Dungarvan (€5, 50 minutes)
Kilkenny (€5, 45 minutes)

Suirway (www.suirway.com) services to Dunmore East (€4, 30 minutes, every 90 minutes) depart from the bus stop on Merchants Quay, outside the main **Waterford Bus Station** (📞 051-879 000; Merchants Quay).

TRAIN
Waterford's Plunkett train station is across the river from the city centre. Direct trains:
Carlow (€10.50, 1¼ hours, seven daily)

SOUTHEAST COUNTY WATERFORD

This hidden corner of the county makes an easy day trip from Waterford city, its winding back roads best explored by bike.

Situated 12km east of Waterford is the estuary village of **Passage East**, from where car ferries shuttle back and forth to Ballyhack in County Wexford. It's a pretty little fishing village with cottages set around a square near the harbour.

A little-travelled 12km-long minor road wiggles south between Passage East and Dunmore East. At times single-vehicle width and steep, it offers occasional glimpses across undulating fields to the estuary, and passes **Woodstown Beach**, a perfect sandy strand ideal for family picnics, sandcastle building and seashell collecting.

Majestic 18th-century mansion **Faithlegg** ([☎] 051-382 000; www.faithlegg.com; Faithlegg; d/ste from €149/189; [P][🎧][🏊]) has 14 rooms in the original building, and another 66 in its newer wing. Flapjacks on arrival, sensational breakfasts including individual triple-tiered silver trays of warm-from-the-oven pastries, house-made yoghurts and smoothie shots, a gourmet restaurant, bar (serving Faithlegg's own Ice House Lager), golf course, swimming pool, gym and spa are just some of its standout features.

There's a kids' club, a playground and babysitting services on request.

Dublin Heuston (€18, 2¼ hours, eight daily)
Kilkenny (€7.50, 35 minutes, seven daily)
Tipperary (€5.30, 1½ hours, two daily)

Dunmore East

POP 1808

Strung out above a coastline of red sandstone cliffs scalloped with concealed coves full of squawking kittiwakes, Dunmore East (Dún Mór) is a long-time weekend and summer retreat for locals from Waterford, 17km to the northwest.

There are two parts, separated by the town park – the **Upper Village** is poised above the fishing harbour to the south, while the **Lower Village** clusters in a hollow behind Lawlors Strand to the north.

In the 19th century, the town was a port of call for the steam packets that carried mail between England and the south of Ireland. Legacies include picturesque thatched cottages along the main street and an unusual Doric **lighthouse** (1825) overlooking the commercial fishing harbour.

◉ Sights & Activities

The town slumbers through the winter months but comes alive in summer when bathers congregate at a series of half a dozen tiny cove beaches beneath the cliffs. Among them, **Lawlors Strand** (the largest) and neighbouring **Councillor's Strand** at the north end of town are close to pubs and cafes, while the smaller **Mens Cove** and **Ladies Cove** – at either end of the town's central park – speak of earlier, more prudish

times (no segregation today, though). They offer safe swimming, and good snorkelling along the rocks between the coves.

Going west, the 16.5km **scenic drive** to the seaside frivolities of Tramore is packed with enough natural thrills (rolling green hills, soaring coastal vistas, herds of cattle crossing the road...) to more than match the resort's carnival appeal.

Dunmore East Adventure Centre OUTDOORS ([☎] 051-383 783; www.dunmoreadventure.com; Stoney Cove; equipment hire per hr €25, activity sessions per 2hr from €40) Located in the first cove north of the fishing harbour, this place hires out equipment for kayaking and SUP. It also runs sailing, kayaking, canoeing and windsurfing courses for children and adults, plus land-based activities such as archery and rock climbing on an outdoor wall. In summer, an inflatable water park with slides is set up in the bay.

✵ Festivals & Events

Bluegrass Festival MUSIC
([☎] 051-878 832; www.discoverdunmore.com/events; ⊙late Aug) In high summer the air thrums for four days with banjos as local pubs provide the stage for one of Ireland's liveliest music festivals.

🛏 Sleeping & Eating

Avon Lodge B&B B&B €€
([☎] 051-385 775; www.avonlodge.ie; 6 The Garage; s/d from €50/80; [P][🎧]) This suburban-style family home has clean, comfortable, spacious rooms with pine furniture, brightened by punchy

colour schemes with coordinated fabrics. It's just off the Waterford road, a 400m uphill walk west of Lawlors Strand.

Haven Hotel
HOTEL €€

(☑ 051-383 150; www.thehavenhotel.com; Dock Rd; d/f from €130/150; ⊘ Mar-Oct; 🅿 �🛜) Built in the 1860s as a summer house for the Malcolmson family, whose coat of arms can still be seen on the fireplaces, the Haven remains an elegant retreat, with 18 rooms, six of which are in the adjacent garden house. The bridal suite has a four-poster bed, and there's a casual in-house restaurant, bar, and outdoor picnic tables overlooking the glittering sea.

Bay Cafe
CAFE €

(☑ 087 674 3572; Dock Rd; dishes €4-12.50; ⊘ 9am-5pm) With views over the harbour and out to sea, this arty cafe serves interesting twists on casual cafe fare. Open-faced seafood sandwiches are the house speciality; it also serves a great seafood chowder, hot specials such as Irish stew, and breakfast until noon. Seagulls swoop on the picnic tables out front, so watch out if you're dining alfresco.

Lemon Tree Cafe
IRISH €€

(☑ 051-383 164; www.lemontreecatering.ie; Coxtown Rd; mains lunch €8-12.50, dinner €12-24.50; ⊘ 9am-5pm Tue-Thu, to 9pm Fri & Sat, to 4pm Sun; 🛜🐕) On the southwestern edge of town, this hybrid cafe/bistro is a great place for breakfast (until noon), lunch (mainly soups, salads and sandwiches) and organic coffee. The evening menu has an emphasis on seafood, such as pan-fried sea bass, sizzling garlic prawns and local steamed crab. Its deli counter's takeaway dishes range from lentil nutloaf to seafood pie.

❶ Getting There & Away

Suirway (www.suirway.com) buses connect Dunmore East with Waterford city (€4, 30 minutes, every 90 minutes Monday to Saturday year-round, plus five on Sunday July and August).

Tramore

POP 10,381

In summer the seafront that stretches below the steep town of Tramore (Trá Mhór in Irish, meaning 'big beach') is a whirl of fairground rides, amusement arcades, candy floss stalls and all the other tack of an old-style seaside resort. In winter, it's considerably quieter.

◉ Sights

Tramore Bay is hemmed in by **Great Newtown Head** to the west and **Brownstown Head** to the east. Their 20m-high concrete pillars (three on Great Newtown and two on Brownstown) were erected by Lloyds of London in 1816 after a shipping tragedy: 363 lives were lost when the *Seahorse* mistook Tramore Bay for Waterford Harbour and was wrecked.

Tramore Strand
BEACH

Tramore's broad, 5km-long strand is backed by 30m-high sand dunes at the eastern end. The Blue Flag–rated beach is patrolled by lifeguards from June to August. It's one of Ireland's premier surfing spots, suitable for all levels of experience, thanks to slow-forming waves.

🏃 Activities

The town has year-round surf schools that also arrange eco-walks around the Back Strand, one of Europe's largest intertidal lagoons, and various other activities.

Several places along the prom offer surfing lessons and equipment hire, including wetsuits and (much-needed) boots, gloves and hoods during winter.

On the west side of the bay is a delightful, sheltered swimming spot at Guillamene Cove. Access is from Newtown Glen Rd (signposted Newtown & Guillamene Swimming Club); there's a car park, toilets and picnic tables.

Oceanics Surf School
SURFING

(☑ 051-390 944; www.oceanics.ie; Red Cottage, Riverstown Rd; lesson adult/child €35/25) Besides providing lessons and courses, Oceanics organises surf parties and summer camps for teens and younger children.

It also runs a 2½-hour walking tour of town (€10) and a three-hour coasteering tour (€50).

Freedom Surf School
SURFING

(☑ 051-386 773; www.freedomsurfschool.com; The Gap; 2hr group/private lessons €35/85) As well as surfing courses, this school runs 90-minute SUP tours for €35, and hires surfboards, wetsuits and bodyboards (per day €25/15/10).

Tramore Golf Club
GOLF

(☑ 051-386 170; www.tramoregolfclub.com; Newtown Hill; green fees from €40) Established in 1894, Tramore Golf Club is one of Ireland's oldest courses, with a par-72 18-hole championship course and a newer nine-hole course. It has hosted several championships, including the Irish Close Championship on four occasions, most recently in 2015.

🛏 Sleeping & Eating

★**Beach Haven House**   HOSTEL, B&B €
(☑ 051-390 208; www.beachhavenhouse.com; Tivoli Tce; hostel dm/tw/q from €25/65/100, B&B s/d/q from €75/100/150, apt from €110; ☺ B&B & apt year-round, hostel Mar-Nov; ℗🖥) American Avery and his Irish wife Niamh have all budgets covered with their B&B, hostel and apartments (two-night minimum stay). The B&B and apartments are tastefully decorated with light wood and earth colours, while the hostel is basic but has excellent facilities, including a comfortable sitting room. Avery fires up the barbecue during the summer months.

Seagull Bakery   BAKERY €
(www.seagullbakery.ie; 4 Broad St; breads & pastries €1.80-4.50; ☺ 8am-4pm Wed-Sat) Artisan baker Sarah Richards' brilliant-white-painted shop is piled high with white, wholemeal, three-seed, seaweed and rye sourdough loaves, soda bread, focaccia and filled pizza pockets, plus sweet pastries such as iced cinnamon scrolls, salted caramel slices, and apple, plum and hazelnut oaties. The coffee is excellent; Sarah also brews fermented kombucha tea. There's a handful of window-side bench seats but no tables.

Vee Bistro   INTERNATIONAL €€
(☑ 051-386 144; www.facebook.com/theveebistro; 1 Lower Main St; mains €12-15; ☺ 9am-4.30pm Mon-Wed, to 9.30pm Thu-Sat, to 6.30pm Sun; 🖥) This busy restaurant with tribal art and abstract canvases on the walls has a good breakfast menu that includes stacks of pancakes with bacon and maple syrup. Casual bistro-style dishes served at lunch and dinner span the globe, from fish and chips to prawn and chorizo hotpot, wild mushroom bruschetta and burgers (including a vegan option).

ⓘ Getting There & Away

Bus Éireann (www.buseireann.ie) services run between Tramore and Waterford city (€2.80, 45 minutes, twice hourly).

The Copper Coast

On a sunny day, the azure waters, impossibly green hills and grey-green, rust-red and yellow-ochre sea cliffs create a vibrant palette of colour along the beautiful Copper Coast, as the R675 winds its way from one stunning vista to another between Tramore and Dungarvan.

There are lots of little coves and beaches to discover – Stradbally Cove is a hidden treasure – and, just before you reach Dungarvan, there is the beautiful, pristine stretch of sand that is Clonea Strand, near Ballynacourty.

Copper Coast Geopark   NATURE RESERVE
(www.coppercoastgeopark.com) Inscribed on Unesco's World Heritage list in 2004, this 20km stretch of rugged coastline, centred on the village of Bunmahon, takes its name from the copper-mining industry that flourished here in the 19th century. The most visible legacy of the area's mining history is the Cornish-style winding-engine house at Tankardstown, 1km east of Bunmahon, and you'll find a Geological Garden on the eastern edge of Bunmahon.

Up the hill from here is the Copper Coast Geopark Centre (☑ 051-292 828; Knockmahon Church, Bunmahon; ☺ 11am-5pm Sat & Sun) FREE, housing an exhibition about the history and geology of copper mining. You can pick up information on the self-guided Copper Coast Trail, as well as trail cards describing walks in the area.

The area's 460-million-year-old mudstones, sandstones and lavas were contorted by an ancient continental collision, and invaded by hot, metal-rich fluids, which cooled to form quartz veins rich in copper minerals.

Dungarvan

POP 9227

Brightly painted buildings ring Dungarvan's picturesque harbour, where the River Colligan meets the sea. This famously foodie town is home to some outstanding restaurants, a renowned cookery school and the annual West Waterford Festival of Food.

St Garvan founded a monastery here in the 7th century, but most of the centre dates from the early 19th century when the Duke of Devonshire rebuilt the streets around Grattan Sq. Overlooking the bay are a dramatic ruined castle and an Augustinian abbey.

Clonea Strand is a sandy beach, popular with families, located 6km to the east.

⊙ Sights

Dungarvan Castle CASTLE
(☑058-48144; www.heritageireland.ie; Castle St; ⊙10am-6pm late May-late Sep) FREE Ongoing renovation is helping to restore this stone fortress to its former Norman glory. The oldest part of the castle, once inhabited by King John's constable Thomas Fitz Anthony, is the unusual 12th-century shell keep, built to defend the mouth of the river. The 18th-century British army barracks house a visitor centre with various exhibits. Admission is by (free) guided tour only.

Waterford County Museum MUSEUM
(☑058-45960; www.waterfordmuseum.ie; 2 St Augustine St; ⊙10am-5pm Mon-Fri) FREE This small, well-presented museum covers maritime heritage (with relics from shipwrecks), Famine history, local personalities and various other titbits, all displayed in an 18th-century grain store.

Old Market House Arts Centre GALLERY
(☑058-48944; www.facebook.com/oldmarket house; Lower Main/Parnell St; ⊙11am-1.30pm & 2.30-5pm Tue-Fri, 1-5pm Sat, hours can vary) FREE Housed in a whitewashed, black-trimmed stone building dating from the 17th century, these light, airy galleries showcase contemporary art by local artists.

🏃 Activities & Courses

★Waterford Greenway CYCLING
(www.visitwaterfordgreenway.com) The all-abilities, 46km Waterford Greenway cycle trail follows an old railway line between Waterford city (at the car park near WIT Arena, just off the N25 at the ring road) and Dungarvan (at the car park near Shandon roundabout). Heading east–west provides the easiest descent. The route takes in three spectacular viaducts and a tunnel, and has great sea views at Knock, 8km east of Dungarvan.

A good short trip is to cycle east from Dungarvan along the coast to Clonea, through the Ballyvoyle tunnel to O'Mahony's pub (30 to 40 minutes' riding), and back again.

It's possible to hire bicycles in Dungarvan and drop them off in Waterford, or vice versa. Outlets offering one-way bicycle rental include **Waterford Greenway Bike Hire** (☑085 111 3850; www.waterfordgreenway.com; 1 Davitt's Quay; road/electric/kid's bike per day €24/40/10; ⊙9am-6pm).

TRIANGLE OF GOLF

There are three championship golf courses within five minutes' drive of Dungarvan: **West Waterford Golf & Country Club** (www.westwater-fordgolf.com), **Dungarvan Golf Club** (www.dungarvangolfclub.com) and the **Gold Coast Golf Club** (www.gold coastgolfclub.com). All three are part of the Dungarvan Golf Triangle initiative, whereby keen golfers can play three courses for the price of two (€69). Each of the courses can provide more information, including directions and maps.

★Tannery Cookery School COOKING
(☑058-45420; www.tannery.ie; 6 Church St; courses from €75) Looking like a futuristic kitchen showroom (you can see it through the huge windows on the side street), this school is run by best-selling author and chef Paul Flynn. Courses range from the three-hour 'A Simple Dinner Party' (€75) to the popular three-day 'Masterclass' (€590), while others cover bread making, seafood, Italian cuisine and cooking on an Aga.

✯ Festivals & Events

West Waterford Festival of Food FOOD & DRINK
(www.westwaterfordfestivaloffood.com; ⊙late Apr) West Waterford's abundant fresh produce is celebrated at this hugely popular three-day festival. It features cooking workshops and demonstrations, talks by local producers, farmers markets, guided walks and a craft-brew beer garden.

Dungarvan TradFest MUSIC
(www.comeraghs.com; ⊙early Jun) This lively four-day festival of traditional music and dance runs over the June bank holiday weekend and is held in local pubs and hotels, and on a public stage in Grattan Sq. It's famous for its annual bucket singing competition (look it up!).

🛏 Sleeping

Tannery Townhouse GUESTHOUSE €€
(☑058-45420; www.tannery.ie; 2 Church St; d from €120; P🐾🛜) Under the same management as the Tannery restaurant, this boutique guesthouse spans two buildings just across the street. Its 14 rooms are modern and stylish, and have fridges stacked with juices, fruit and

muffins so you can enjoy a continental breakfast in your own time.

Treetops B&B
B&B €€

(☑089 231 1012; www.treetopsbnb.com; Kilgobnet; d from €105; P🐾) Up in the hills 6km northwest of Dungarvan, with sweeping views above the treeline to the town and bay beyond, this 2018-opened B&B is run by husband-and-wife team Vivian and Bryony (and their adorable poodle, Pip). The three ultra-comfortable rooms have king-size beds, Egyptian cotton sheets and state-of-the-art bathrooms. Guests can use the barbecue on the terraced gardens' upper level.

Wrens, kinglets and finches frequent the gardens, as does the occasional deer.

Park Hotel
HOTEL €€

(☑058-42899; www.parkhoteldungarvan.com; Shandon Rd; d/f/townhouse from €100/120/299; P🐾🅿) Along the western bank of the River Colligan on Dungarvan's northern edge, this smart, modern hotel has 86 bright, spacious rooms, and 15 self-catering townhouses sleeping up to five, with full kitchens, gas fireplaces and courtyards. Guests can use the attached leisure centre, with a 20m pool, sauna and steam room. Family-friendly amenities include cots, high chairs and a kids' club.

It's a major venue for the Dungarvan TradFest (p201), so book well ahead if you plan on attending the festival.

🍴 Eating & Drinking

Pubs line the waterfront. Look for locally produced craft beers from the **Dungarvan Brewing Company** (☑058-24000; www.dungarvanbrewingcompany.com; Westgate Business Park; tour €15; ☺tours 3pm & 5pm Wed & Fri mid-Apr–mid-Sep), including the crisp and hoppy Helvick gold blonde ale.

Dungarvan Farmers Market
MARKET €

(www.facebook.com/DungarvanMarket; Grattan Sq; ☺9.30am-2pm Thu) Dungarvan's farmers market is a minor festival of artisan breads, cheeses (including Knockalara Farmhouse cheese, made near Lismore), bacon, farm vegetables and hot food such as burgers from food truck Bear Grillz.

Meades
CAFE €

(☑087 411 6714; www.meadescafe.com; 22 Grattan Sq; mains €5-10; ☺8am-6pm Mon-Sat; 🛜🍴) Enjoying an ace position on the town's main square, this cafe has a cheerful vibe with a kids' corner, sofas to lounge on, papers to

read and a menu spanning savoury tartlets to homemade soups, salads and cottage pie. The breakfast special is a *blaa* with crispy bacon, black pudding and country relish.

Merry's Gastro Pub
GASTROPUB €€

(☑058-24488; www.merrysgastropub.ie; Lower Main/Parnell St; mains €11-25; ☺kitchen noon-9.30pm, bar noon-midnight; 🛜🍴) Lots of polished, dark wood and gleaming brass and copper reflected in antique mirrors create a romantic, old-fashioned atmosphere in this traditional pub gone gastro – the menu runs from barbecued ribs and fish and chips, to pork belly with cumin and fennel braised in local Dungarvan Brewing Company ales, which are served here.

Mini versions of pub classics for kids cost €4.50 to €6.50.

★Tannery
MODERN IRISH €€€

(☑058-45420; www.tannery.ie; 10 Quay St; 2-/3-course menu lunch €26/33, dinner €45.50/58.50; ☺5.30-9.30pm Tue-Thu, 12.30-2.30pm & 5.30-9.30pm Fri & Sat, 12.30-3pm Sun, plus 5.30-9.30pm Sun Jul & Aug) At this old tannery building, lauded chef Paul Flynn creates seasonally changing dishes that focus on just a few flavours, such as charred trout with lemon-and-fennel arancini (rice balls) or crab crème brûlée. There's intimate seating downstairs and in the buzzing, loftlike room upstairs. Service is excellent. From Tuesday to Sunday, buffet breakfasts (€19.50) are available for nonguests and guests of the Tannery Townhouse (p201).

Moorings
PUB

(☑058-41461; www.themoorings.ie; Davitt's Quay; ☺11am-midnight; 🛜) Beautiful original wood panelling and a snug create a cosy atmosphere in the creaky period interior at this waterfront bar. Outside there's a great beer garden beneath the walls of Dungarvan Castle where you can enjoy local beers on tap and DJs on weekends. It also has solid traditional food (including superb seafood chowder) and B&B accommodation (single/double/family room €60/90/120).

ⓘ Information

Tourist Office (☑058-41741; www.dungarvantourism.com; Main/Parnell St; ☺9.30am-5pm Mon-Fri, 10am-5pm Sat) A helpful resource with stacks of informative brochures; the inconspicuous entrance is next to the SuperValu supermarket.

ⓘ Getting There & Away

Bus Éireann (www.buseireann.ie) picks up and drops off on Davitt's Quay on the way to and from Waterford city (€5, 50 minutes, hourly), Cork city (€7, 1½ hours, hourly), and Youghal (€12, 35 minutes, hourly), which has connections to Ardmore.

Cyclists (and walkers) can take the Waterford Greenway trail (p201) to Waterford city; outlets offering one-way bicycle rental include Waterford Greenway Bike Hire (p201).

Ring Peninsula

Just 15 minutes' drive south of Dungarvan, the Ring Peninsula (An Rinn, meaning 'the headland') is one of Ireland's best-known Gaeltacht (Irish-speaking areas). En route, views across Dungarvan Bay to the Monavullagh Mountains and the cliffs of the Copper Coast drift away to the northeast. You could easily spend a day exploring quiet country lanes here, with the promise of a hidden beach or fine old pub around the next corner, or hiking out to enjoy the panorama from Helvick Head.

Dún Ard   B&B €€

(☑ 058-46782; www.dunard.ie; Na Céithre Gaotha, Ring; d from €105; 🅿🌐) This B&B is perched high above Dungarvan Bay on the western edge of Ring village and set in an upmarket development, with a plain exterior that's deceiving. Rates for its four rooms reflect the quality, spaciousness and finish you find in a top-end hotel. Breakfast choices include porridge with Baileys, and the guest lounge opens to a wraparound terrace with sea views.

An Seanachaí   PUB FOOD €€

(☑ 058-70957; www.anseanachai.ie; off N25, Pulla; mains €12.50-27; ⊘kitchen 9am-7pm Mon & Tue, to 9pm Wed-Fri & Sun, to 10pm Sat, bar to 10pm Sun-Thu, to midnight Fri & Sat; 🌐) The rough-hewn walls of the 'Old Storyteller' could certainly tell a few stories of their own. Parts of this thatched-roof pub date back to its earliest incarnation as an 18th-century farm. It's an atmospheric spot for a pint, a meal (wood-fired pizzas are a speciality), regular live music, or fortnightly storytelling sessions (9pm on Saturday). It's 8km southwest of Dungarvan.

On the grounds it has 12 three-bedroom townhouses; rates start from €125 per night.

★ Marine Bar   PUB

(☑ 058-46520; www.marinebar.ie; off N25, Pulla; ⊘4pm-midnight Mon-Thu, 2pm-1am Fri & Sat, 2-11.30pm Sun) Sure, there's good traditional food at this two-centuries-old pub 8km

southwest of Dungarvan, but the real reason to stop by is the craic. Year-round, traditional sessions rock the place from 9.30pm on Monday, Friday and Saturday, while locals contest the traditional Irish card game '45' on Wednesday evenings (anyone can join in).

Criostal na Rinne   ARTS & CRAFTS

(☑ 058-46174; www.criostal.ie; Baile na nGall, Ring; ⊘9.30am-5.30pm Mon-Fri year-round, plus 10am-5pm Sat & noon-5pm Sun Mar-Sep) Former Waterford Crystal craftsman Eamonn Terry returned home to the Ring Peninsula to set up his own workshop, where you can buy deep-prismatic-cut, full-lead crystal vases, bowls, clocks, jewellery and even chandeliers. The studio is signposted off the main road in An Rinn village, near the Spar grocery store.

Ardmore

POP 434

The appealing seaside village of Ardmore may look unassuming these days, but it was once one of the most important Christian settlements in Ireland. St Declan is thought to have introduced Christianity to southeast Ireland in the 5th century, well before St Patrick arrived, establishing his monastery on the hill above the harbour. The cathedral that was built here in the 12th century is among Ireland's most remarkable examples of Romanesque architecture.

Today's visitors come mainly to enjoy the beaches (both the town strand and secluded Ballyquin Beach), as well as water sports and bracing coastal walks.

◉ Sights & Activities

★ St Declan's Monastery   RUINS

(Tower Hill; ⊘24hr) FREE The ruins of Ireland's oldest Christian settlement occupy a striking setting on a hill above Ardmore, strewn with gravestones both ancient and new. The most prominent landmark is the 30m-high round tower, one of the best examples in Ireland. But the most remarkable is the roofless shell of Ardmore Cathedral, in particular the Romanesque arcading on the west gable, decorated with worn but still wonderful 12th-century stone carvings of biblical scenes – very unusual in Ireland.

Inside the cathedral are two Ogham stones featuring the earliest form of writing in Ireland, one with the longest such inscription in the country, and a number of medieval grave slabs. The oldest building on the site is the 8th-century **Oratory of St Declan**, which was restored in 1716; the saint is said to be buried beneath a hollow in its southeast corner.

Ardmore Cliff Walk WALKING

A 5km loop walk leads from St Declan's Monastery – follow 'cliff walk' signs – to the 19th-century lookout tower on Ardmore Head, from where a clifftop path leads back into town along the coast. The footpath passes the wreck of the crane barge *Samson*, blown ashore in 1987, wedged at the foot of the cliffs, and **St Declan's Church & Well**.

🛏 Sleeping & Eating

Newtown Farm Guesthouse B&B €€

(📋 024-94143; www.newtownfarm.com; Grange; d from €90; 🅿🛜) This peaceful B&B with magnolia-shaded rooms (two with balconies) is located on a dairy farm with views over gardens, fields and the distant sea. Its breakfast menu includes homemade scones, local cheeses and smoked salmon. It's just off the N25, 8km north of Ardmore.

★ Cliff House Hotel LUXURY HOTEL €€€

(📋 024-87800; www.cliffhousehotel.ie; Cliff Rd; d/ste from €350/490; 🅿🛜🏊) All the bedrooms at this cutting-edge hotel, built into the hillside, overlook Ardmore Bay. Some suites even have two-person floor-to-ceiling glass showers so you don't miss a second of those sea views. More sea views extend from the indoor swimming pool, the outdoor Jacuzzi and spa, the bar and summer terrace serving lunch, dinner and snacks, and Michelin-starred The House Restaurant.

Ardmore Gallery & Tearoom CAFE €

(📋 024-94863; www.ardmoregalleryandtearoom. ie; Main St; dishes €3.50-11.50; 🕘9.30am-6.30pm daily Apr-Sep, 1-5pm Sat & Sun only Oct-Mar) A winning combination, the gallery displays local art while the teashop sells delicious cakes, plus soup and savoury treats during the summer months. Jewellery, hand-painted silk scarves and knitwear are also for sale. Ask about occasional art workshops.

★ The House Restaurant GASTRONOMY €€€

(📋 024-87800; www.cliffhousehotel.ie; Cliff House Hotel; 3-course menu €88, with wine €130, 7-course tasting menu €110, with wine €172; 🕘6.30-9.30pm Tue-Sat May-Sep, 6.30-9.30pm Wed-Sat Oct-Apr; 🛜) Exquisitely presented set-menu dishes (no à la carte) have earned chef Martijn Kajuiter a Michelin star. Offerings include organic Irish smoked salmon with buttermilk and dill oil,

West Cork scallops with sea spinach and Irish caviar, Kilmore Quay turbot with Lismore chanterelles and bee pollen, and pecan caramel rum mousse in a milk chocolate sphere.

Its panoramic dining room at Ardmore's Cliff House Hotel has stupendous sea views.

White Horses SEAFOOD €€€

(📋 024-94040; Main St; mains lunch €9-17, dinner €25-35; 🕘12.30-3.30pm & 6-10pm Tue-Sun May-Sep, Fri-Sun only Oct-Apr, closed Jan–mid-Feb) Energetically run by three sisters, this bistro set in a former grocery shop concentrates on fresh local seafood. Push the boat out and try the Dublin Bay prawns, served on plates handmade in Ardmore. Enjoy a drink on the bench at the front, or a meal at a sunny lawn table out the back.

🔒 Shopping

Ardmore Pottery & Gallery CERAMICS

(📋 024-94152; www.ardmorepottery.com; Cliff Rd; 🕘10am-6pm Mon-Sat, 2-6pm Sun Apr-Oct, hours can vary) Fronted by a cottage garden, this cosy little house above the harbour sells beautiful pottery, much of it in lovely shades of blue and cream. Other locally produced goods include warm hand-knitted socks.

ⓘ Getting There & Away

Bus Éireann (www.buseireann.ie) runs one to three times daily to Youghal (€5, 20 minutes) and Cork city (€15, 1¾ hours); there are no connections east to Dungarvan except via Youghal.

Cappoquin & Around

POP 699

Slinking up a steep hillside, the small market town of Cappoquin sits at the foot of the rounded, heathery Knockmealdown Mountains. To the west lies the picturesque valley of the River Blackwater, one of Ireland's most famous and prolific salmon fisheries.

Cappoquin House & Gardens HISTORIC BUILDING

(www.cappoquinhouseandgardens.com; garden €5; 🕘garden 10am-4pm Mon-Sat) This magnificent 1779 Georgian mansion with formal gardens overlooking the River Blackwater is the private residence of the Keane family, who have lived here for around 200 years. The best time to visit is May and June, when the gardens are ablaze with colourful rhododendron, azalea and oleander blossoms. The house is closed to the public. The entrance to the estate is just north of Cappoquin, at a set of huge black iron gates.

Dromana Gate   HISTORIC BUILDING
(Dromana Estate) The Dromana Drive from Cappoquin to Villierstown, 9km to the south, follows the Blackwater valley through the Dromana Estate. At a bridge over the River Finisk stands this remarkable Hindu-Gothic gate, inspired by the Brighton Pavilion in England. A temporary version was erected here in 1826 to welcome home the estate's owner, Henry Villiers-Stuart, and his wife after their honeymoon (part of which was spent in Brighton). He liked it so much he had a permanent version built in 1830.

River Blackwater   FISHING
(day ticket €20) The Blackwater is one of Ireland's finest salmon rivers, and the 6km stretch around Cappoquin offers good value and easy access. You can get advice, permits, licences and fishing tackle from **Titelines Tackle & Gift Shop** (☑058-54152; 19 Main St; ⊙9am-1pm & 2-5.30pm Mon-Fri, 9am-1pm Sat).

ⓘ Getting There & Away

Bus Éireann (www.buseireann.ie) runs from Waterford city to Cappoquin (€17, 1½ hours, once on Sunday only) en route to Lismore (€3.30, 10 minutes).

Lismore
POP 1374

The quiet, elegant town of Lismore on the River Blackwater was once the location of a great monastic university founded in the 7th century and frequented by statespeople and luminaries from all over Europe. Prince John of England built the first castle here in 1182, and in the 17th century the estate belonged for a while to the family of Robert Boyle, the father of modern chemistry, before passing through marriage to the dukes of Devonshire.

Present-day Lismore Castle – a vast, battlemented mansion, spreading along a steep slope above the river – dates mostly from the 19th century, and is still the family home of the 12th Duke of Devonshire. Adele Astaire, sister of dance legend Fred, married the son of the 9th Duke and lived here from 1932 to 1944. The castle is not open to the public, but the gardens are one of the county's most popular attractions.

★ Lismore Castle Gardens   GARDENS
(☑058-54061; www.lismorecastlegardens.com; Castle St; adult/child €8/6.50; ⊙10.30am-5.30pm mid-Mar–mid-Oct, last entry 4.30pm) Although Lismore Castle itself is not open to the public, the 3 hectares of ornate and manicured gardens are well worth a visit. Thought to be the oldest landscaped gardens in Ireland, they are divided into the walled Jacobean upper garden and the less formal lower garden, the latter dotted with **modern sculpture**, including two chunks of the Berlin Wall. Highlights include a splendid **yew walk**, where Edmund Spenser is said to have written *The Faerie Queen*.

There's a contemporary **art gallery** beside the upper garden. The gardens are used as an opera venue during the annual **Blackwater Valley Opera Festival** (www.blackwatervalleyoperafestival.com; ⊙late May-early Jun).

Ballyrafter Country House Hotel   HOTEL €€
(☑058-54002; www.ballyrafterhouse.com; Ballyrafter; s/d/tr from €90/110/140; ▣ 🕈) Built for the Duke of Devonshire in the early 19th century, this country-house hotel 1km across the river from Lismore has grand views of the town's castle. Rooms are traditionally furnished and there's an in-house restaurant (open daily March to November, Saturday evenings only from December to February). The owners can arrange salmon fishing on nearby River Blackwater (including licences, equipment and guides).

Lismore Farmers Market   MARKET €
(www.facebook.com/LismoreMarket; Castle Ave; ⊙11am-4pm Sun Apr-Sep) 🍴 The upmarket surrounds on the approach to Lismore Castle attract a fab collection of vendors to this market, with stalls selling artisan food and local arts and crafts. You can enjoy freshly prepared sandwiches, barbecued sausages and other goodies in the park or at tables set up on the gravel path.

Summerhouse Cafe   CAFE €
(Main St; dishes €2-7; ⊙10am-5pm Tue-Sat; 🕈) Sweet treats at this red-and-yellow-painted cafe span buttery scones with homemade mulberry jam to apple and rhubarb crumble, hazelnut-and-cranberry cookies, and an enticing array of cakes such as carrot and cardamom. Savoury options include quiches and soups such as wild mushroom, as well as sandwiches and salads.

Booley House
TRADITIONAL MUSIC

(☑ 058-60456; www.thebooleyhouse.com; St Michael's Hall, Ballyduff; adult/child €15/10; ☺ 8.15pm Wed late Jul-Aug) During summer, this weekly 90-minute show of traditional Irish music and dance takes place in St Michael's Hall in the village of Ballyduff, 10km west of Lismore. Details of upcoming shows are available from the **Lismore Heritage Centre** (☑ 0761-102 157; www.discoverlismore.com; Main St; adult/child €5/3.50; ☺ 9am-5.30pm Mon-Fri, 10am-5pm Sat, noon-5pm Sun Mar-Nov, weekdays only Dec-Feb) in Lismore's town centre.

ⓘ Information

Tourist Office (☑ 058-54975; www.discover lismore.com; Main St; ☺ 9am-5.30pm Mon-Fri, 10am-5pm Sat, noon-5pm Sun Mar-Oct, weekdays only Nov-Feb) Inside the Lismore Heritage Centre.

ⓘ Getting There & Away

Bus Éireann (www.buseireann.ie) runs from Lismore to Cappoquin (€3.30, 10 minutes), Dungarvan (€7.70, 50 minutes) and Waterford city (€16, 1¾ hours) once on Sunday only.

Northern County Waterford

Some of the most scenic parts of County Waterford are in the north around Ballymacarbry. The **Nire Valley Drive** (signposted from Ballymacarbry) leads 9.5km deep into the Comeragh and Monavullagh Mountains; the last few kilometres of narrow, twisting road end at a car park where there are several waymarked walks into the hills (see www.visitwaterford.com).

The **Sgilloge Lakes walk** is an easy two-hour return trip to a pair of tiny glacial lakes in one of the dramatic corries, or *coums* (glacial hollows), that give the Comeragh hills their name. The views west to the Galtee Mountains are dramatic, especially towards sunset.

Clonanav Fly-Fishing Centre
FISHING

(☑ 052-613 6765; www.flyfishingireland.com; Clonanav, Ballymacarbry; guided fishing per day €350-400; ☺ 9am-5pm Tue-Fri, 10am-4pm Sat) From March to September, the Rivers Nire, Tar and Suir offer superb trout fishing. Permits (€30 to €70 per day, depending where you fish and what you're fishing for) can be arranged through this centre, which also has a fly-fishing school (per day €160), and leads guided trips.

Nire Valley Walking Festival
CULTURAL

(www.nirevalley.com; ☺ Oct) Held on the second weekend in October, this two-day festival features guided walks for all and traditional music in pubs.

🛏 Sleeping

★ Hanora's Cottage
GUESTHOUSE €€

(☑ 052-613 6134; www.hanorascottage.com; Nire Valley Dr, Ballymacarbry; d/ste from €130/160; 🅿 🛜) This gorgeous 19th-century cottage sits between the bubbling River Nire and a picturesque church. The luxurious rooms have beautiful country furnishings and Jacuzzis, and there's an outdoor deck overlooking the river. Everything in the gourmet restaurant (three-course dinner €39; 6.30pm to 8.30pm Monday to Saturday) is made on the premises. Hanora's is signposted 6km east of Ballymacarbry. No children.

Glasha Farmhouse B&B
B&B €€

(☑ 052-613 6108; www.glashafarmhouse.com; Ballymacarbry; s/d/f from €60/120/160; 🅿 🛜) Olive O'Gorman takes meticulous pride in maintaining the Regency-style bedrooms at her luxury farmhouse overlooking the Comeragh and Knockmealdown Mountains. Some wonderful walks fan out around the farm (including one that takes in the local pub!); afterwards, reward yourself with dinner served by candlelight (€35 to €40) in the conservatory. The farm is 4.5km northwest of Ballymacarbry.

COUNTY CARLOW

The focus of Ireland's second-smallest county is the River Barrow, Ireland's second-longest river, which flows south from Carlow town through several picturesque villages to the monastic hamlet of St Mullins, its towpath followed by the lovely Barrow Way walking trail. The Blackstairs Mountains dominate the southeast, their rounded ridges forming the backdrop to many a view, and their underlying granite cropping up everywhere as building stone – most notably as the capstone for Europe's largest prehistoric dolmen, the Browne's Hill dolmen.

The county's landed gentry have left a legacy of grand estates and country houses, many of which are now home to some of Ireland's most interesting gardens.

Carlow Town

POP 24,272

The narrow streets of Carlow's compact town centre stretch along the main drag of Tullow St, from the ruins of the castle on the banks of the River Barrow to the cathedral.

◉ Sights

Carlow County Museum MUSEUM
(☑ 059-913 1554; www.carlowmuseum.ie; cnr College & Tullow Sts; ⊙ 10am-5pm Mon-Sat, 2-4.30pm Sun Jun-Aug, 10am-4.30pm Mon-Sat Sep-May) **FREE** Housed in an atmospheric former convent with original stained-glass windows, this thoroughly engaging museum focuses on the lives of local people through the ages. There are some real one-offs, such as the trapdoor from the county gallows, dating from the early 1800s, and a 6m-high exquisitely carved pulpit from Carlow Cathedral, which the bishop apparently decided to replace with a more modern version (to the chagrin of many locals).

⌂ Sleeping & Eating

Clink Boutique Hotel BOUTIQUE HOTEL €€
(☑ 059-918 2418; www.theclinkboutiquehotel.com; 39 Dublin St; d/tr/f from €110/160/190; ☞) Centrally located near Carlow's courthouse, the Clink opened in 2017 with stylish, well-lit rooms that vary in size (some are minuscule, others spacious) and a cool in-house restaurant and cocktail bar, Cell 38½, specialising in steaks and burgers.

Barrowville Townhouse B&B €€
(☑ 059-914 3324; www.barrowville.com; Kilkenny Rd; s/d from €85/98; ☞) This 18th-century townhouse has been meticulously converted into a classy B&B with seven elegant rooms with private bathrooms. Enjoy local free-range eggs with smoked salmon or cured bacon for breakfast in the airy conservatory overlooking the semiformal gardens.

Mimosa TAPAS €
(☑ 059-917 0888; www.mimosawinebar.com; College St; tapas €6-9; ⊙ 5-11pm Wed, Thu & Sun, to midnight Fri & Sat; ☞) International tapas dishes – mini lamb empanadas, black pudding crostini, panko-crumbed squid with wasabi mayo, roast carrot hummus and caramelised goat's cheese – are accompanied by wines (by the bottle or glass) from around the globe and feisty house cocktails such as El Jefe (tequila, Grand Marnier, pineapple juice and Tabasco). The heated outdoor dining terrace overlooks the garden.

Carlow Farmers Market MARKET €
(www.facebook.com/CarlowFarmersMarket; Potato Market; ⊙ 9am-2pm Sat) Fittingly, Carlow's market is held at the old Potato Market. Look out for Carlow Farmhouse cheese, breads, organic fruits, vegetables and meats, homemade pesto at the olive stall, plus handcrafted chocolates and locally produced cider.

★**Lennons** CAFE, BISTRO €€
(☑ 059-917 9245; www.lennons.ie; Visual Centre for Contemporary Art, Old Dublin Rd; mains lunch €8-13.50, dinner €19-28.50; ⊙ 10.30am-5pm Mon-Wed, 10.30am-5pm & 5.45-9.30pm Thu-Sat, noon-4pm Sun; ☞) Carlow's best dining is amid the arty surrounds of the **Visual Centre for Contemporary Art** (☑ 059-917 2400; www.visualcarlow.ie; Old Dublin Rd; ⊙ 11am-5.30pm Tue-Sat, 2-5pm Sun) **FREE**. It's a sleek and stylish space with a patio bordering the grassy grounds of St Patrick's College. Lunch features creative sandwiches, salads and hot specials, while dinner is more refined, with a seasonal menu that showcases local artisan produce. Book a table at weekends.

ⓘ Information

Carlow Tourist Office (☑ 059-913 0411; www.carlowtourism.com; College St; ⊙ 10am-5pm Mon-Sat) A useful source of county-wide information.

ⓘ Getting There & Around

BUS

Bus Éireann (www.buseireann.ie) runs to Dublin (€15, 1½ hours, 13 per day), Kilkenny (€10, 50 minutes, two daily Monday to Saturday, one Sunday) and Waterford (€15, 1½ hours, 13 per day).

TAXI

Carlow Cabs (☑ 059-914 0000; www.carlowcabs.com)

TRAIN

The train station is on Station Rd, northeast of the town centre. Trains run to Dublin Heuston (€10.50, one hour, 10 daily), Waterford (€10.50, 1¼ hours, seven daily) and Kilkenny (€6.40, 35 minutes, seven daily).

Around Carlow Town

Although the entire county could be considered a day trip from Carlow town, the following places are quite close.

THE BARROW WAY

The River Barrow, Ireland's second-longest river (after the Shannon), flows for 192km from the Slieve Bloom hills of Laois to meet the tide at St Mullins, and flow on into the sea at Waterford harbour. It was made navigable in the 18th century, and linked to Dublin's Grand Canal via the Barrow Line canal.

Its towpath is followed by the **Barrow Way** (www.irishtrails.ie). This national way-marked trail leads for 114km from Lowtown (near Robertstown) in County Kildare to St Mullins, with more than half of its length in County Carlow. It passes through a bucolic landscape of riverside villages, Victorian lock-keepers cottages, old stone bridges and boat-crowded quays, offering the chance of spotting wildlife such as otter, heron, little egret and kingfisher.

It would take four days to hike the whole way, but shorter sections make for a great half-day hike or bike route, notably the lovely 7.5km stretch between St Mullins and Tinnahinch (across the river from Graiguenamanagh in County Kilkenny; allow 1½ hours walking or 30 minutes cycling, each way).

★ **Altamont Gardens**   GARDENS
(☑ 059-915 9444; www.heritageireland.ie; The Pottle, Altamont; ⊙ 9am-6.30pm Apr-Sep, to 5pm Mar & Oct, to 4.30pm Feb & Nov, to 4pm Dec & Jan) FREE One of Ireland's most magnificent landscaped gardens, Altamont covers 16 hectares on the banks of the River Slaney. Carefully selected plantings are arranged in naturalistic settings where peacocks, swans, squirrels and wild hare abound, surrounding an ornamental water-lily lake. The gardens are off the N80, 5km east of Ballon (there's no public transport to the estate).

Walkways meander among flower beds, shrubberies, mature trees (some more than 250 years old), rhododendrons and azaleas, before finally leading down a flight of 100 granite steps to a gorgeous bluebell-filled wood beside the river – a great spot for a picnic.

It was first laid out in the 18th century; the present gardens are largely the work of plant collector Fielding Lecky Watson, who bought the estate in 1924, and his daughter Corona North, who bequeathed them to the nation after her death in 1999.

Duckett's Grove   GARDENS
(☑ 085 113 6075; www.facebook.com/TheTeaRooms AtDuckettsGrove; ⊙ dawn-dusk) FREE Dominated by the jackdaw-haunted ruins of a Gothic fantasy of a country house, the former seat of the Duckett family (the house burned down in 1933) was taken over by Carlow County Council in 2005. The walled gardens have been restored as a public park, which is filled with the scents of lavender and fruit blossom in early summer, while the outbuildings house craft workshops and a seasonal tearoom. The gardens are 11km northeast of Carlow, signposted off the R726 and L1009.

Borris & Around

POP 1011

This Georgian village has a charming main street running uphill from the Black River, lined on one side with pastel-painted Georgian cottages and on the other by the grounds of Borris House, the ancestral home of the High Kings of Leinster.

◉ Sights & Activities

Borris House   HISTORIC BUILDING
(☑ 059-977 1884; www.borrishouse.ie; Main St; house tour & grounds adult/child €10/free, grounds only €5/free; ⊙ house by appointment, grounds noon-4pm Wed-Sun May-Sep) This impressive Tudor Gothic mansion, the ancestral home of the McMorrough Kavanaghs, High Kings of Leinster, was modelled in 1810–20 around the earlier shells of an 18th-century house and a 15th-century castle. The highlight of the interior is the ornate stucco plasterwork by Michael Stapleton, whose work can also be seen in Trinity College and Powerscourt House in Dublin. Visits to the house are by guided tour only, which must be booked in advance.

Kilgraney House Herb Gardens   GARDENS
(☑ 059-977 5283; www.kilgraneyhouse.com; Borris Rd, Kilgraney; €5; ⊙ by appointment 2-6pm Sat & Sun May-Aug) These delightful gardens are home to a heady cocktail of medicinal and kitchen herbs growing in orderly profusion; the recreated medieval monastic herb garden is a favourite. Admission includes herbal tea tastings; the herbs are also used in the kitchens

of the inn and restaurant here. It's 7km northwest of Borris, signposted off the R705.

Go with the Flow
KAYAKING, CANOEING

(☑ 087 252 9700; www.gowiththeflow.ie; R729; guided tour from €35, kayak/canoe hire per day from €40; ☺ by reservation Apr-Oct) Go with the Flow runs various guided kayaking and canoeing trips (starting from 2½ hours) along the local waterways. En route you'll see herons, otters, egrets, kingfishers and swans. It also hires out kayaks and canoes and can set you up for self-guided trips (including multiday trips with either wild camping or B&B stays). Transportation to/from Borris is possible.

Barrels and dry bags are provided.

📇 Sleeping & Eating

Kilgraney Country House
B&B €€€

(☑ 059-977 5283; www.kilgraneyhouse.com; Borris Rd, Kilgraney; d/cottage/ste from €170/190/200; ☺ Mar-Oct; ℗🔊) The River Barrow flows gently through the valley below this lovely Georgian manor. The owners have created a fabulous interior, decorated using items collected from their travels to places such as the Philippines. There's a spa, herb gardens, and a restaurant serving a six-course menu (€50; Friday and Saturday evenings only). It's off the R705 halfway between Borris and Bagenalstown.

Cottages sleep up to six people, and come with full kitchens. Suites, also with kitchens, sleep three.

Lorum Old Rectory
B&B €€€

(☑ 059-977 5282; www.lorum.com; Borris Rd, Kilgraney; s/d from €130/180; ☺ Feb-Nov; ℗🔊) Halfway between Borris and Bagenalstown off the R705, this historic manor house, dating from 1863, sits on a prominent knoll to the east of the road. The gardens provide peaceful views from each of the four rooms, some of which have four-poster beds. Book ahead for largely organic four-course dinners (€50 per person), served at an antique mahogany table.

⭐Step House Hotel
IRISH €€

(☑ 059-977 3209; www.stephousehotel.ie; 66 Main St; brasserie mains €11-24, restaurant mains €20-29; ☺ brasserie & restaurant noon-9pm Wed-Sat, 4-9pm Sun; 🔊) The Step House Hotel's handsome 1808 Brasserie & Bar, all polished mahogany, red-leather benches and green-glass lampshades, is an elegant yet relaxed place to enjoy sophisticated pub classics such as traditional seafood chowder and a house burger with honey-cured bacon and smoked paprika aioli. Its more upmarket Cellar Restaurant serves refined dishes such as cured mackerel with cucumber chutney and black-sesame-seed wafer.

M O'Shea
PUB

(☑ 059-977 3106; Main St; ☺ noon-11pm) Surprises abound in this tidy warren of rooms, which combines a grocery shop, hardware store and an old-fashioned pub where spare electrical parts, wellies and bits of machinery hang from the ceiling. There are occasional live-music sessions, and decent food is also served.

❶ Getting There & Away

Borris is on the east–west R702 road, which links the M9 with the N11 in County Wexford. Kilbride Coaches (www.kilbridecoaches.com) run twice daily Monday to Saturday from Kilkenny to Borris (€6, 40 minutes) and on to Graiguenamanagh (€4, 15 minutes).

St Mullins

POP 180

The tranquil settlement of St Mullins, just a few houses and a pub scattered around a hummocky village green, gives no indication of its illustrious past. Founded by St Moling (St Mullin) in the 7th century, near the holy waters of St Moling's Well (signposted from the village car park), this was once an important monastic site.

In the 12th and 13th centuries it became a major Anglo-Norman settlement (those hummocks on the green are the remains of a motte-and-bailey castle), but for some reason the village never grew into a town. Today it's a beautiful and peaceful place, a centre for angling, canoeing, and walks and bike rides along the river.

The village hosts St James Pattern Day, an annual pilgrimage and Mass held on the Sunday preceding (or falling on) 25 July.

⭐St Mullins Monastery
RUINS

(☺ dawn-dusk) FREE This important monastic site, founded in the 7th century by St Moling, was the burial place of the Kings of Leinster. Its remains include four church buildings dating from the 10th to the 15th centuries, a round tower stump and a 9th-century high cross. Nearby is the grave of General Thomas Cloney, a hero of the 1798 Rising, and a monument raised by 'St Mullins exiles in New York', marking the tomb of Art, King of Leinster (1357-1416).

★ **Mulvarra House**   B&B €€

(☑051-424 936; www.mulvarra.com; d/tr/f from €75/95/115; P🖤) 🖉 Most of the bedrooms in this modern, comfortable B&B on a hillside above the village have balconies with glorious views over the River Barrow, which offers lovely evening walks along its banks. You can also indulge in body treatments such as hot stone massages, and yoga, meditation and traditional arts and crafts workshops. Mostly organic breakfasts use produce grown on-site.

Old Grainstore   COTTAGE €€

(☑051-424 440; www.oldgrainstorecottages.ie; The Quay; cottages per 3 nights/week from €300/500; P🖤) Martin and Emer O'Brien eschewed corporate life to convert this former grain warehouse on the River Barrow into four self-catering cottages sleeping two to five people. Stylish yet cosy interiors have book-filled shelves and wood-burning stoves (gas and electricity are charged according to meter readings). Minimum stay is three nights.

Fishing and walking information is available at the neighbouring Mullicháin Café (☑051-424 440; www.oldgrainstorecottages.ie; The Quay; dishes €2.50-14; ⊙11am-5pm Tue-Sun Mar-Oct).

Clonegal

POP 193

The picturesque village of Clonegal has a tiny green beside an 18th-century stone bridge over the River Derry, whose crystal-clear, limestone-filtered waters are thick with waving ribbons of green ranunculus and plump brown trout.

It is the southern terminus of Ireland's inaugural long-distance walking trail, the Wicklow Way, and is home to Huntington Castle, the atmospheric setting for Stanley Kubrick's 1975 movie *Barry Lyndon*.

Huntington Castle   CASTLE

(☑053-937 7160; www.huntingtoncastle.com; house tours & gardens adult/child €10/5, gardens only €6/2.50; ⊙house tours hourly 2-5pm May-Sep, gardens 10am-5pm May-Sep) The core of Huntington Castle is a spooky, dusty old tower house built in 1625 by Sir Laurence Esmonde, now surrounded by Georgian terraces and flamboyantly castellated Victorian extensions. Related to the Esmondes by marriage, the Durdin-Robertson family still live here today and offer 40-minute guided tours of the house's Jacobean hall, Victorian

kitchens and living quarters, complete with entertaining ghost stories.

The oddest part of the tour is the Temple of Isis in the basement, the idiosyncratic headquarters of the Fellowship of Isis, an order dedicated to the worship of the 'divine feminine', founded by family member Olivia Robertson in 1976.

The gardens combine the formal with rural fantasy and include a fabulous 500-year-old Yew Walk, an avenue of lime trees planted in 1680 and a 17th-century fishpond. Facilities include an adventure playground, a tearoom and a gift shop.

★ **Sha-Roe Bistro**   IRISH €€

(☑053-937 5636; www.sha-roe.ie; Main St; mains €19-26; ⊙7-8.30pm Thu-Sat, 12.30-2.30pm Sun Feb-Dec) Tucked inside an 18th-century building, award-winning chef Henry Stone's restaurant has a huge open fireplace and a pretty courtyard at the back, providing a rustic setting for contemporary cuisine based on produce from the surrounding orchards and farms. Offerings include Carlow Farmhouse cheese souffle, wild garlic risotto, and Blessington lamb shoulder with local herbs. Book at least two weeks ahead.

❶ Getting There & Away

Drivers will find Clonegal signposted along a series of winding local roads 4.5km east of Kildavin on the N80. Hikers can take Bus Éireann service 132 from Dublin to Kildavin (€18, 1¾ hours, two daily Sunday to Friday, one Saturday) and walk the 4.5km (one hour) to Clonegal.

COUNTY KILKENNY

County Kilkenny's centrepiece is its namesake city. An enduring gift from the Normans, it seduces visitors with medieval alleys winding between an imposing castle and a historic cathedral, craft studios, traditional pubs and riverside walks.

The county too is a delight, a place of rolling hills where you'll soon run out of adjectives for shades of green. Tiny roads navigate the valleys alongside trout-filled rivers, moss-covered stone walls and relics of centuries of Irish religious history. Shamrock-cute Inistioge village may be star of many a movie but it is the real deal, as are country towns such as Graiguenamanagh, Bennettsbridge and Thomastown. It's no surprise that so many artists and craftspeople have set up shop here.

Much of the county is easily visited on a day trip from Kilkenny city, best explored with your own wheels.

Kilkenny City

POP 26,512

Kilkenny is the Ireland of many visitors' imaginations. Built from dark-grey limestone flecked with fossil seashells, Kilkenny (from the Irish 'Cill Chainnigh', meaning the Church of St Canice) is also known as 'the marble city'. Its picturesque 'Medieval Mile' of narrow lanes and historic buildings strung between castle and cathedral along the bank of the River Nore is one of the southeast's biggest tourist draws. It's worth braving the crowds to soak up the atmosphere of one of Ireland's creative crucibles – Kilkenny is a centre for arts and crafts, and home to a host of fine restaurants, cafes, pubs and shops.

History

In the Middle Ages Kilkenny was intermittently the unofficial capital of Ireland, with its own Anglo-Norman parliament. In 1366 the parliament passed the Statutes of Kilkenny, aimed at preventing the adoption of Irish culture and language by the Anglo-Norman aristocracy – they were prohibited from marrying the native Irish, taking part in Irish sports, speaking or dressing like the Irish or playing any Irish music. Although the laws remained on the books for more than 200 years, they were never enforced with any great effect and did little to halt the absorption of the Anglo-Normans into Irish culture.

During the 1640s Kilkenny sided with the Catholic royalists in the English Civil War. The 1641 Confederation of Kilkenny, an uneasy alliance of native Irish and Anglo-Normans, aimed to bring about the return of land and power to Catholics. After Charles I's execution, Cromwell besieged Kilkenny for five days, destroying much of the southern wall of the castle before the ruling Ormonde family surrendered. The defeat signalled a permanent end to Kilkenny's political influence over Irish affairs.

Today tourism is Kilkenny's main economic focus, but the city is also the regional centre for more traditional pursuits such as agriculture – you'll see farmers on tractors stoically dodging tour buses.

◉ Sights & Activities

★ Kilkenny Castle
CASTLE

(☑056-770 4100; www.kilkennycastle.ie; The Parade; adult/child €8/4; ⊘9am-5.30pm Jun-Aug, 9.30am-5.30pm Apr, May & Sep, 9.30am-5pm Mar, 9.30am-4.30pm Oct-Feb) Rising above the River Nore, Kilkenny Castle is one of Ireland's most visited heritage sites. Stronghold of the powerful Butler family, it has a history dating back to the 12th century, though much of its present look dates from Victorian times.

During the winter months (November to January) visits are by 40-minute guided tours only, with guided and self-guided tours from February to October. Highlights include the Long Gallery with its painted roof and carved marble fireplace.

The first structure on this strategic site was a wooden tower built in 1172 by Richard Fitz Gilbert de Clare, the Anglo-Norman conqueror of Ireland better known as Strongbow. In 1192 Strongbow's son-in-law, William Marshal, erected a stone castle with four towers, three of which survive. The castle was bought by the powerful Butler family (later earls and dukes of Ormonde) in 1391, and their descendants continued to live here until 1935. Maintaining the castle became such a financial strain that most of the furnishings were sold at auction. The property was handed over to the city in 1967 for the princely sum of £50.

For most visitors, the focal point of a visit is the Long Gallery, which showcases portraits of Butler family members, the oldest dating from the 17th century. It is an impressive hall, with a 19th-century timber roof vividly painted with Celtic, medieval and Pre-Raphaelite motifs by John Hungerford Pollen (1820–1902), who also created the magnificent Carrara marble fireplace, delicately carved with scenes from Butler family history.

The basement Butler Gallery (☑056-776 1106; www.butlergallery.com; ⊘10am-5.30pm May-Nov, 10am-1pm & 2-4.30pm Dec-Feb, 10am-1pm & 2-5pm Mar & Apr) **FREE**, featuring contemporary artwork in temporary exhibitions, is expected to relocate to its new Barrack Lane premises in 2020. Also in the basement is a popular summertime tearoom housed in the castle kitchen. You can access the Butler Gallery and cafe without paying the castle admission.

The Kilkenny Castle Park (www.kilkenny castle.ie; Castle Rd; ⊘8.30am-8.30pm May-Aug, to 7pm Apr & Sep, shorter hours Oct-Mar), 21 hectares of public parkland extending to the southeast of the castle, frames a fine view of

Kilkenny

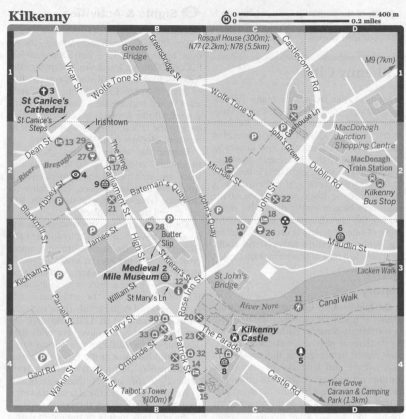

Mt Leinster, while a Celtic-cross-shaped rose garden lies northwest of the castle. A gate on the north side of the park leads steeply down to the riverside, where you can walk back into town at St John's Bridge.

★ **Medieval Mile Museum** MUSEUM
(☑ 056-781 7022; www.medievalmilemuseum.ie; 2 St Mary's Lane; adult/child self-guided tour €6.80/3, 45min guided tour €12/5; ⊗10am-6pm Apr-Oct, 11am-4.30pm Nov-Mar) Dating from the early 13th century, St Mary's Church has been converted into a fascinating modern museum that charts the history of Kilkenny in medieval times. Highlights include the Rothe Chapel, lined with ornate 16th- and 17th-century tombs carved from local limestone, remnants of the 17th-century timber roof above the crossing, and a selection of 13th- and 14th-century grave slabs. A huge interactive map of Kilkenny allows you to explore maps and documents relating to the medieval city.

★ **St Canice's Cathedral** CATHEDRAL
(☑ 056-776 4971; www.stcanicescathedral.ie; Coach Rd; cathedral/round tower/combined adult €4.50/4/7, child €3.50/4/6.50; ⊗9am-6pm Mon-Sat, 1-6pm Sun Jun-Aug, shorter hours Sep-May) Ireland's second-largest medieval cathedral (after St Patrick's in Dublin) has a long and fascinating history. The first monastery was built here in the 6th century by St Canice, Kilkenny's patron saint. The present structure dates from the 13th to 16th centuries, with extensive 19th-century reconstruction, its interior housing ancient grave slabs and the tombs of Kilkenny Castle's Butler dynasty. Outside stands a 30m-high round tower, one of only two in Ireland that you can climb.

Records show that a wooden church on the site was burned down in 1087. The existing structure was raised between 1202 and 1285, but then endured a series of catastrophes and resurrections. The first disaster, the collapse of the church tower in 1332, was associated with Dame Alice Kyteler's

Kilkenny

⊙ Top Sights
1	Kilkenny Castle	C4
2	Medieval Mile Museum	B3
3	St Canice's Cathedral	A1

◎ Sights
4	Black Freren Gate	A2
	Butler Gallery	(see 1)
5	Kilkenny Castle Park	C4
6	Maudlin Castle	D3
7	Maudlin Tower	C3
8	National Design & Craft Gallery	C4
9	Rothe House & Garden	A2

⊕ Activities, Courses & Tours
10	Kilkenny Cycling Tours	C3
11	Nore Linear Park	C3
12	Pat Tynan Walking Tours	B3

⊜ Sleeping
13	Bregagh House	A2
14	Butler Court	B4
15	Butler House	B4
16	Celtic House	C2

17	Kilkenny Tourist Hostel	B2
18	Langton House Hotel	C3

⊗ Eating
19	Campagne	C1
20	Farmers Market	B4
21	Foodworks	B2
22	Hungry Moose	C2
23	Rinuccini	B4
24	The Cutting Vedge	B4
25	Zuni	B4

⊙ Drinking & Nightlife
26	Bridie's General Store	C3
27	John Cleere's	A2
28	Kyteler's Inn	B3
29	O'Hara's Brewery Corner	A2

⊚ Shopping
30	Kilkenny Book Centre	B4
31	Kilkenny Design Centre	C4
32	Rudolf Heltzel Goldsmith	B4
33	Truffle Fairy	B4

conviction for witchcraft. Her maid Petronella was also convicted, and her nephew, William Outlawe, was implicated. The unfortunate maid was burned at the stake, but Dame Alice escaped to London and William saved himself by offering to reroof part of St Canice's Cathedral with lead tiles. His new roof proved too heavy, however, and brought the church tower down with it.

In 1650 Cromwell's forces defaced and damaged the church, using it to stable their horses. Repairs began in 1661; the beautiful roof in the nave was completed in 1863.

Inside, highly polished ancient **grave slabs** are set on the walls and the floor. On the northern wall, a slab inscribed in Norman French commemorates Jose de Keteller, who died in 1280; despite the difference in spelling he was probably the father of Alice Kyteler. The **stone chair of St Kieran** embedded in the wall dates from the 13th century. The fine 1596 monument to Honorina Grace at the western end of the southern aisle is made of beautiful local black limestone. In the southern transept is the handsome black **tomb of Piers Butler**, who died in 1539, and his wife, Margaret Fitzgerald. Tombs and monuments (listed on a board in the southern aisle) to other notable Butlers crowd this corner of the church. Also worth a look is a model of Kilkenny as it was in 1642.

Apart from missing its crown, the 9th-century **round tower** is in excellent condition. Inside is a tight squeeze and you'll need both hands to climb the 100 steps up steep ladders (under 12s not admitted).

Walking to the cathedral from Parliament St leads you over Irishtown Bridge and up **St Canice's Steps**, which date from 1614; the wall at the top contains fragments of medieval carvings. The leaning tombstones scattered about the grounds prompt you to look, at the very least, for a black cat.

Rothe House & Garden   MUSEUM
(☑ 056-772 2893; www.rothehouse.com; 16 Parliament St; house & garden adult/child €7.50/4.50, garden only €4/2; ⊙ 10.30am-5pm Mon-Sat, noon-5pm Sun) Dating from 1594, this is Ireland's finest example of a Tudor merchant's house, complete with a restored medieval garden. Built around a series of courtyards, it now houses a museum with a rather sparse display of local artefacts, including a rusted Viking sword and a grinning stone head sculpted by a Celtic artist. The highlight is the delightful walled garden, divided into fruit, vegetable and herb sections and a traditional orchard, as it would have been in the 17th century. There's also a genealogy centre here.

In the 1640s the wealthy Rothe family played a part in the Confederation of Kilkenny, and Peter Rothe, son of the original builder, had all his property confiscated. His sister was able to reclaim it, but just before the Battle of the Boyne (1690) the family

KILKENNY CITY WALLS

Parts of Kilkenny's medieval city walls, mostly dating from the 14th and 15th centuries, can still be seen in several places, notably at **Talbot's Tower** (cnr Ormonde Rd & New St), **Maudlin Tower** (Maudlin St) and the **Black Freren Gate** (Abbey St) – the only surviving city gate. **Maudlin Castle** (Maudlin St), dating from around 1500, is a more substantial tower house and once protected the eastern approach to the city.

supported James II and so lost the house permanently. In 1850 a Confederation banner was discovered in the house; it's now in the National Museum in Dublin.

National Design & Craft Gallery   GALLERY
(☑056-779 6147; www.ndcg.ie; Castle Yard; ⊙10am-5.30pm Tue-Sat, from 11am Sun) FREE Contemporary Irish crafts are showcased at the imaginative National Design & Craft Gallery, set in former stables across the road from Kilkenny Castle, next to the shops of the Kilkenny Design Centre (p216). Ceramics dominate, but exhibits often feature furniture, jewellery and weaving from the members of the Crafts Council of Ireland. Family days are held the second Saturday of every month, with a tour of the gallery and free hands-on workshops for children. Check the website for additional workshops and events.

Nore Linear Park   WALKING
This network of footpaths allows walkers to hike southeast along the banks of the River Nore as far as the ring road (2.5km) and return on the opposite side. Ask the tourist office (p217) for a map or see www.trail kilkenny.ie.

The **Canal Walk**, on the southwest bank, leads under the castle and on past mill races, weirs and the ruins of 19th-century woollen mills, some of which continued working until the 1960s. The **Lacken Walk**, on the northeast side, begins on Maudlin St.

☞ Tours

Kilkenny Cycling Tours   CYCLING
(☑086 895 4961; www.kilkennycyclingtours.com; 16 John St; adult/child tours from €25/12.50, bike hire €20/10; ⊙10am-6pm) Explore the city and surrounds on a bike during a two-hour guided tour that can include a lunch option.

Prebooking is essential, at least 48 hours in advance. Bikes are also available to hire.

Pat Tynan Walking Tours   WALKING
(☑087 265 1745; www.kilkennywalkingtours.ie; adult/child €10/8; ⊙11am & 2pm Mon-Sat, 11.15am & 12.30pm Sun Apr-Oct, by appointment Nov-Mar) Entertaining, informative 70-minute walking tours through Kilkenny's narrow lanes, steps and pedestrian passageways. Meet at the tourist office (p217).

✵ Festivals & Events

Cat Laughs Comedy Festival   COMEDY
(www.thecatlaughs.com; ⊙May-Jun) World-famous comedians, including Irish stars such as Dara Ó Briain and Aisling Bea, perform in Kilkenny's hotels and pubs over a long weekend in late May/early June.

Kilkenny Rhythm & Roots   MUSIC
(www.kilkennyroots.ie; ⊙Apr-May) More than 30 pubs and other venues participate in hosting this major music festival over three days in late April/early May. Its emphasis is on country and 'old time' American roots music.

Kilkenny Arts Festival   ART
(www.kilkennyarts.ie; ⊙Aug) In early to mid-August the city comes alive for 10 action-packed days of theatre, cinema, music, literature, visual arts, children's events and street spectacles.

🛏 Sleeping

Kilkenny city has a wide range of accommodation, from camping grounds and backpacker hostels to luxury hotels. Book well ahead at weekends, in summer and during festivals.

**Tree Grove Caravan
& Camping Park**   CAMPGROUND €
(Kilkenny Camping; ☑086 830 8845; www.kilkenny camping.com; New Ross Rd; sites campervan €17-30, hiker €8-9, camping pod from €70; ⊙Mar–mid-Nov; P🅿🛜) Set in a small park, this well-organised camping ground 2.5km southeast of Kilkenny is a pleasant 20-minute walk along the river from the city centre. Simple beehive-shaped timber camping pods sleep two.

Bregagh House   B&B €
(☑056-772 2315; www.bregaghhouse.com; 18 Dean St; s/d/tr from €49/70/105; P🛜) Conveniently located near St Canice's Cathedral, this modern B&B is a good bet, with comfortable soundproof guest rooms and filling hot (or continental) breakfasts. There's ample on-site parking, and a conservatory overlooking

a pretty back garden with a magnificent copper beech tree.

Kilkenny Tourist Hostel HOSTEL €€
(📞056-776 3541; www.kilkennyhostel.ie; 35 Parliament St; dm/tw/q from €18/48/88; @ 🛜) Inside an ivy-covered 1770s Georgian townhouse, this fairly standard 60-bed IHH hostel has a sitting room warmed by a turf fire, and a timber- and leadlight-panelled dining room adjoining the self-catering kitchen. Excellent location, but a place for relaxing rather than partying.

⭐ Rosquil House GUESTHOUSE €€
(📞056-772 1419; www.rosquilhouse.com; Castlecomer Rd; d/tr/f from €95/120/130, 2-person apt from €80; P🛜) Rooms at this immaculately maintained guesthouse are decorated with dark-wood furniture and pretty paisley fabrics, while the guest lounge is similarly tasteful, with sink-into sofas, brass-framed mirrors and leafy plants. The breakfast is above average, with homemade granola and fluffy omelettes. There's also a well-equipped and comfortable self-catering apartment (minimum three-night stay).

Butler Court INN €€
(📞056-776 1178; www.butlercourt.com; 14 Patrick St; d €85-140; P🛜) Not to be confused with the grand Butler House a few doors uphill, this place was originally the mail-coach yard for Kilkenny Castle. Wrapping around a flower-filled courtyard, contemporary rooms have Canadian-cherry parquet floors, and eye-catching photography or Celtic art on the walls. A continental breakfast, including fresh fruit and filtered coffee, is stocked in your in-room fridge.

Langton House Hotel HOTEL €€
(📞056-776 5133; www.langtons.ie; 67 John St; d/ste from €120/140; P✳️🛜) In the same family since the 1930s, but constantly evolving, this Kilkenny icon has 34 corporate-style rooms with dark wood and sombre-toned furnishings. The beige-tiled bathrooms have superb high-power pressure showers. There's a fine restaurant and a popular pub stocking 90 different Irish whiskeys.

Celtic House B&B €€
(📞056-776 2249; www.celtic-house-bandb.com; 18 Michael St; d from €85; 🛜) Artist and author Angela Byrne extends one of Ireland's warmest welcomes at this homely and comfortable B&B. Some of the brightly decorated bedrooms come with sky-lit bathrooms, others

have views of Kilkenny's castle, and Angela's landscapes adorn many of the walls. Book ahead.

⭐ Butler House HOTEL €€€
(📞056-772 2828; www.butler.ie; 16 Patrick St; d/ste from €200/275; P🛜) You can't stay in Kilkenny Castle, but this 1786-built mansion is the next best thing. Once the home of the earls of Ormonde, the hotel today combines modern design with aristocratic trappings including sweeping staircases, marble fireplaces, an art collection and magnificent gardens. The generous rooms are individually decorated, and, to remind you that you're staying amid history, the floors creak.

🍴 Eating

Kilkenny city offers a huge choice for all budgets. It's best to book a table on weekends at the top-end restaurants.

The Cutting Vedge VEGETARIAN, VEGAN €
(📞087 243 6754; www.facebook.com/helencostelloes; 4 Ormonde St; dishes €5-11; ⏰9am-5pm Mon-Fri, 10am-5pm Sat; 🍽️) ✔️ At the cutting edge of the worldwide trend for vegetarian and vegan cuisine, this brilliant cafe, opened in 2018, kicks off at breakfast with dishes such as tofu burritos, followed at lunch by white bean goulash; cauliflower and leek crumble; potato and basil Wellington; almond-crusted courgette and daily soups such as parsnip and watercress. Sandwiches are served on organic oatmeal bread.

Everything is made from scratch, with a zero-waste policy.

Farmers Market MARKET €
(Mayors Walk, The Parade; ⏰10am-3pm Thu) Kilkenny's weekly farmers market is a showcase for local produce.

⭐ Zuni IRISH €€
(📞056-772 3999; www.zuni.ie; 26 Patrick St; mains breakfast & lunch €8-15, dinner €19.50-28.50; ⏰8-11.15am, 12.30-2.30pm & 6-9.30pm; 🛜) ✔️ Among Kilkenny's most stylish and busiest restaurants, Zuni is sophisticated yet informal, with a kitchen that elevates humble comfort food such as black pudding scotch eggs, confit duck terrine, spinach-wrapped cod and parsnip parcels and savoury beetroot cheesecake.

⭐ Foodworks BISTRO, CAFE €€
(📞056-777 7696; www.foodworks.ie; 7 Parliament St; mains €17.50-26.50, 3-course dinner menus €26-29; ⏰noon-9pm Wed & Thu, to 9.30pm Fri & Sat, to

5pm Sun; 🐷🍴) 🖉 The owners of this cool and casual bistro keep their own pigs and grow their own salad leaves, so it would be churlish not to try their pork loin stuffed with black pudding, or pressed pig's trotter – and you'll be glad you did. Delicious food, excellent coffee and friendly service make this a justifiably popular venue; it's best to book a table.

Its excellent kids' menu (mains €7 to €9.50) includes grilled cod and chips, stone-baked pizzas, and local sausages with gravy and mash.

Hungry Moose   BURGERS €€
(☑ 056-775 1469; www.facebook.com/thehungry moosekilkenny; 60 John St; burgers €15-20; ⊙ noon-9.30pm Sun-Thu, to 10pm Fri & Sat; 🐷🍴) Winner of Ireland's Best Burger 2018 for its house-speciality Hungry Moose (smoked bacon, dill pickles, aged Canadian Moose cheddar and beer-battered onion rings), this Kilkenny hotspot has another seven beef varieties as well as fish, veggie and vegan burgers, all served with chunky, skinny or curly fries. Reclaimed timbers kit out the stripped-back dining space (no takeaways).

Sides include corn on the cob with chilli-infused butter, kimchi slaw and fried jalapeño poppers; craft beers come from around the country and as far afield as Hawaii.

Kids burgers can be made to order.

Rinuccini   ITALIAN €€
(☑ 056-776 1575; www.rinuccini.com; 1 The Parade; mains €17-29, 2-/3-course lunch menu €24/29; ⊙ noon-2.30pm & 5-10pm Mon-Sat, noon-9pm Sun) Follow a short flight of steps down to the candlelit basement of this long-standing local treasure for classical Italian cuisine, including house specials *gamberoni Rinuccini* (fresh Kilmore Quay langoustines with a cream, brandy and Dijon mustard sauce) and *porchetta Rinuccini* (garlic- and herb-rolled pork belly with Marsala wine sauce).

★**Campagne**   GASTRONOMY €€€
(☑ 056-777 2858; www.campagne.ie; 5 Gashouse Lane; 3-course lunch & early bird menu €38, 3-course dinner menu €60; ⊙ 6-10pm Wed & Thu, 12.30-2.30pm & 6-10pm Fri & Sat, 12.30-2.30pm Sun, closed late Jun-early Jul & mid-Jan–early Feb) 🖉 Chef Garrett Byrne was awarded a Michelin star for this bold, stylish restaurant in his native Kilkenny. He's passionate about supporting local and artisan producers, and adds a French accent to memorable culinary creations such as black-pudding-stuffed pigs

trotters or rhubarb-crumble souffle. The early bird menu (to 9pm Wednesday to Friday, to 6pm Saturday) is a serious bargain.

🍷 Drinking & Nightlife

★**Kyteler's Inn**   PUB
(☑ 056-772 1064; www.kytelersinn.com; 27 St Kieran's St; ⊙ 11am-11.30pm Mon-Thu, to 2am Fri & Sat, 12.15pm-midnight Sun) Dame Alice Kyteler's old house was built back in 1224 and has seen its share of history: she was charged with witchcraft in 1323. Today the rambling bar incorporates the original building, vaulted ceiling and arches. There's a beer garden and a large upstairs room for live music (nightly from March to October), ranging from trad to blues.

O'Hara's Brewery Corner   PUB
(☑ 056-780 5081; www.carlowbrewing.com/our-pub; 29 Parliament St; ⊙ 1-11.30pm Mon-Thu, to 12.30am Fri & Sat, to 11pm Sun) Kilkenny's best venue for craft brews is a long, narrow beer hall of a place owned by Carlow Brewing Company, with a wide selection of ciders and ales, including Carlow's own IPA.

Bridie's General Store   PUB
(☑ 056-776 5133; www.facebook.com/bridiesbar; 72 John St; ⊙ 11am-10pm Sun-Wed, 6pm-2am Thu-Sat) Top design talent was employed by the Langton's empire to create this reproduction trad grocery-pub. The front is a beguiling retail potpourri of souvenirs, jokes, toys, preserves and deli items. Step through the swinging doors to the pub with polished timber and beautiful tiles. Out back is a classy, partly covered beer garden.

John Cleere's   PUB
(☑ 056-776 2573; www.cleeres.com; 28 Parliament St; ⊙ noon-12.30am) One of Kilkenny's finest venues for live music, theatre and comedy, this long bar has blues, jazz and rock, as well as trad-music sessions on Mondays and Wednesdays. Food such as Irish stew is served throughout the day.

🔒 Shopping

★**Kilkenny Design Centre**   ARTS & CRAFTS
(☑ 056-772 2118; www.kilkennydesign.com; Castle Yard; ⊙ 9am-6pm) Top-end Irish crafts and artworks from artisans county-wide are sold at this design centre. Look for John Hanly wool blankets, Cushendale woollen goods, Foxford scarves and Bunbury cutting boards.

Rudolf Heltzel Goldsmith JEWELLERY
(☎056-772 1497; www.rudolfheltzel.com; 10
Patrick St; ⊘9.30am-1pm & 2-5.30pm Mon-Sat)
Originally from Germany, Rudolf Heltzel
has been creating fine-art jewellery in Kilkenny since 1968, and now works with his
son Christopher creating intricate and unusual pendants and rings, hand-fashioned
from gold, platinum, silver and a range of
precious and semiprecious stones (including agate, chalcedony, onyx, labradorite and
moonstone).

Kilkenny Book Centre BOOKS
(☎056-776 2117; www.thebookcentre.ie; 10 High
St; ⊘9am-6pm Mon-Sat, 1-5pm Sun) Kilkenny's
largest bookshop stocks plenty of Irish-
interest fiction and nonfiction, periodicals
and a good range of maps. There's a cafe
upstairs.

ⓘ Information

Kilkenny Tourist Office (☎056-775 1500;
www.visitkilkenny.ie; Rose Inn St; ⊘9am-5pm
Mon-Sat, 10am-4pm Sun) Stocks guides and
walking maps.

ⓘ Getting There & Around

BICYCLE
Kilkenny Cycling Tours (p214) hires out bikes.

BUS
Bus Éireann (www.buseireann.ie) and Dublin
Coach (www.dublincoach.ie) services run to the
bus stop (Dublin Rd) at the train station and the
stop on Ormonde Rd (nearer the town centre).
Bernard Kavanagh Coaches (www.bernard
kavanaghcoaches.ie) going to Dublin Airport
stop at Ormonde Rd only.
Carlow (€10, 35 minutes, two daily Monday to
Saturday, one Sunday) Bus Éireann.
Cork (€15, 2½ hours, every two hours) Dublin
Coach M9 Express.
Dublin (€10, 1½ hours, every two hours) Dublin
Coach M9 Express.
Dublin Airport (€20, 2½ hours, every two
hours) Bernard Kavanagh Coaches.
Waterford (€5, 40 minutes, every two hours)
Dublin Coach M9 Express.

TRAIN
Kilkenny's **MacDonagh Train Station** (Dublin
Rd) is a 10-minute walk (800m) northeast of the
town centre. Trains run to Dublin Heuston (€13,
1½ hours, seven daily) and Waterford (€7.50, 35
minutes, seven daily).

Kells & Around

Kells (not to be confused with Kells in County Meath) is a mere hamlet with a fine stone
bridge on a tributary of the Nore. However,
in Kells Priory, the village has one of Ireland's
most evocative and romantic monastic sites.

Kells is 15km south of Kilkenny city on
the R697; there's no public transport here.

⊙ Sights

★Kells Priory RUINS
(⊘dawn-dusk) FREE This fortified Augustinian
monastery is the best sort of ruin, where you
can amble around whenever you like, with
no tour guides, set hours or fees. Most days
you stand a chance of exploring the site alone
(apart from some nosy sheep); at dusk with
a clear sky the old priory is simply beautiful.
The ruins are 500m east of Kells on the Stoneyford road; from the car park, head to the
right of the walls to find the main entrance.

The earliest remains of the monastic site
date from the late 12th century, while the bulk
of the present ruins are from the 15th century.
In a sea of rich farmland, a carefully restored
protective wall connects seven dwelling towers. Within the walls are the remains of an
Augustinian abbey and the foundations of
several chapels and houses. It's unusually well
fortified and the heavy curtain walls hint at a
troubled history. Indeed, within a single century from 1250, the abbey was twice fought
over and burned down by squabbling warlords. Its permanent decline began when it
was suppressed in 1540 as part of King Henry
VIII's campaign to dissolve all Catholic monasteries in England, Wales and Ireland.

Kilree Round Tower
& High Cross HISTORIC SITE
(⊘dawn-dusk) FREE Signposted across the
road from the Kells Priory car park, 2.5km
south of Kells, are a 29m-high round tower,
an ancient church and a Celtic high cross,
said to mark the grave of a 9th-century
Irish high king, Niall Caille. He apparently
drowned in the Kings River at Callan during
the 840s while attempting to save a servant,
and his body washed up near Kells. His final resting place lies outside the church
grounds, as he wasn't a Christian.

⌂ Sleeping & Eating

★Lawcus Farm GUESTHOUSE €€
(☎056-772 8949; www.lawcusfarmguesthouse.com;
Stoneyford; s/d/f from €80/100/160; P⊙) ⌀

Bought as a thatched ruin, this 18th-century farmhouse 3km east of Kells has been rebuilt to create an enchanting place to stay. Rooms typically have stone walls, rustic antiques and quirky curiosities, while breakfast features the farm's own eggs, sausages and ham. The property is bordered by the Kings River; fishing is available for guests, as are free bikes.

Hidden in a small copse away from the main house, this two-person timber tree house has a small kitchenette and veranda but no TV or wi-fi; the minimum stay is two nights (€250 for the first two nights, €100 for subsequent nights).

Fenelly's

CAFE €

(www.facebook.com/fenellysbridgest; 11 Upper Bridge St, Callan; dishes €4-9.50; ⊗7.30am-3pm Mon, Tue, Thu & Fri, 10am-4pm Sat; 🛜🅿) In a former pub and undertakers, Fenelly's is revitalising the quaint little village of Callan with local art exhibitions, film screenings, storytelling, theatre, workshops and Saturday morning trad-music sessions. The biggest draws, though, are its sensational Cork-roasted coffee and cooking at both breakfast (eg Turkish eggs with feta and chorizo) and lunch (such as vegetarian Massaman curry with basmati rice).

It's 9km west of Kells.

Knockdrinna Farm Shop & Cafe

CAFE, DELI €

(☑083 800 7474; www.knockdrinna.com; Main St, Stoneyford; dishes €5-9.50; ⊗10am-5pm Tue-Sat, 10.30am-3.30pm Sun; 🅿) 🍴 This gourmet cafe and deli 3.5km east of Kells is a tiny tour de force of locally produced cheeses (including its own), cured meats, smoked fish, salads and much more. Assemble a picnic, or get a table indoors or in the sunny courtyard for an all-day breakfast or lunch of sandwiches, wraps, toasties and specials such as beef and Guinness pie.

It also runs four-hour cheese-making courses (€90 including lunch) and sells cheese-making kits.

🔒 Shopping

Bridge Pottery

CERAMICS

(☑056-772 9156; www.thebridgepottery.com; off N76, Burnchurch; ⊗10am-6pm Mon-Sat) Hidden away on a country lane 6.5km northwest of Kells, this rural pottery is the base for Mark Campden, who turns out colourful majolica pieces with meticulous hand-painted decoration, while his partner Caroline Dolan creates elegant vases, bowls, mugs and jugs in tin-glazed earthenware.

Bennettsbridge & Around

POP 685

Just 9km south of Kilkenny city on the R700, charming little Bennettsbridge takes its name from the elegant 18th-century stone bridge that spans the River Nore. The village is home to a couple of craft studios and shops.

St Mary's Church

RUINS

(www.heritageireland.ie; Main St, Gowran; ⊗tower & church 10am-5.30pm mid-May–Aug) Built in the 13th century on the site of a former monastery, St Mary's is ruined today but the well-preserved remains include its tower, which can be climbed, and rebuilt chancel, with a 1.5m-high Ogham stone, and several stone effigies including one that's believed to be the oldest in Ireland to have a date inscribed on it (1253). It's 9.5km northeast of Bennettsbridge on the R448 in Gowran's village centre.

Nore Valley Park

FARM

(☑056-772 7229; www.norevalleypark.com; Annamult; adult/child €8/7.50; ⊗9am-6pm Mon-Sat Mar-Oct; 🅷) At this 73-hectare farm, children can pet goats, cuddle rabbits, feed lambs, turkeys and ducks, navigate a maze (in the former barn), play crazy golf and jump on a straw bounce. There's a tearoom and picnic area; on-site camping (per tent/adult/child €10/5/4) includes farm entry. It's 4km south of Bennettsbridge, along Annamult Rd on the west side of the river.

Nicholas Mosse Irish Country Shop

CERAMICS

(☑056-772 7505; www.nicholasmosse.com; Annamult Rd; ⊗10am-6pm Mon-Sat, 1.30-5pm Sun) Across the river from the village in an old mill, this pottery shop specialises in handmade spongeware – ceramics decorated with sponged patterns – exported worldwide to retail outlets such as Tiffany's. Short audiovisual displays explain the manufacturing process.

The cafe here is renowned for its scones, and is the best choice locally for lunch.

Moth to a Flame

ARTS & CRAFTS

(☑056-772 7826; www.mothtoaflame.ie; Kilkenny Rd; ⊗9am-6pm Mon-Sat) Established in 1999, this workshop creates beautifully coloured and textured candles of all sizes, from bedside-table to church-altar scale.

ⓘ Getting There & Away

Kilbride Coaches (www.kilbridecoaches.com) runs buses from Kilkenny city to Bennettsbridge (€4, 15 minutes, twice daily Monday to Saturday), continuing to Thomastown (€4, 15 minutes), Inistioge (€4.50, 30 minutes) and New Ross (€5.50, one hour).

Bus Éireann (www.buseireann.ie) also runs a service from Kilkenny city (€4.30, 20 minutes, two daily Monday to Saturday, one Sunday), continuing to Carlow town (€11, 55 minutes).

Thomastown & Around

POP 2445

Named after 14th-century Welsh mercenary Thomas de Cantwell, who became a local lord, Thomastown retains some fragments of its medieval town walls. Down by the bridge (built in 1792) over the River Nore you can find **Mullin's Castle**, the most prominent survivor of no fewer than 14 towers that once stood along the town perimeter. There's good **trout fishing** here; get a permit at Simon Treacy Hardware, just along from the bridge.

Like the rest of Kilkenny, the area has a vibrant craft scene – look out for Clay Creations (p220).

⊙ Sights

★ **Jerpoint Abbey**   RUINS
(☏056-772 4623; www.heritageireland.ie; R448; adult/child €5/3; ⊙9am-5.30pm Mar-Sep, to 5pm Oct, 9.30am-4pm Nov) One of Ireland's finest Cistercian ruins, Jerpoint Abbey was established in the 12th century, with the tower and cloister dating from the late 14th or early 15th century. It is famous for its untypically large number of medieval stone carvings – look for the series of unusual and often amusing figures, both human and animal, carved on the pillars around the cloister. The abbey enjoys a lovely rural setting 2.5km southwest of Thomastown.

Faint traces of a 15th- or 16th-century painting remain on the northern wall of the church. This chancel area also contains a tomb thought to belong to hard-headed Felix O'Dulany, Jerpoint's first abbot and bishop of Ossory, who died in 1202.

Jerpoint Park   HISTORIC SITE
(☏086 606 1449; www.jerpointpark.com; Belmore House, Jerpoint; €10; ⊙10am-5pm May-Sep, hours can vary) Jerpoint Park is a working farm on the site of a 12th-century medieval town, where 35-minute guided tours (10.30am and 2.30pm) use cutting-edge archaeological techniques to reveal in detail the settlement that once stood here. This includes the ruined Church of St Nicholas where, according to local legend, St Nicholas (or Santa Claus) is buried. There are also sheepdog demonstrations, and, from mid-March to September, angling on the River Nore (rod hire available). It's 3km southwest of Thomastown.

Jerpoint Glass Studio   WORKSHOP
(www.jerpointglass.com; Glenmore, Stoneyford; ⊙10am-5.30pm Mon-Sat, noon-5pm Sun Apr-Sep, 10am-5pm Mon-Sat Oct-Mar) FREE The nationally renowned Jerpoint Glass Studio is housed in an old stone-walled farm building, where you can watch workers craft molten glass into exquisite artistic and practical items (demos on weekdays only, 10am to 4pm Monday to Thursday, to 1pm Friday). It's 6km west of Thomastown on the L4206 towards Stoneyford.

Goatsbridge Trout Farm   FARM
(☏086 818 8340; www.goatsbridgetrout.ie; L4206, Jerpoint; tour per person €15; ⊙tour by appointment 9am-5.30pm Mon-Fri) Goatsbridge trout is sold across Ireland and beyond, and here you can visit the source. Guided one-hour tours of the fish farm show you the ponds and smokery. You can also stock up on hot- and cold-smoked trout, caviar, pâté and fresh fish at its farm shop, and buy picnic hampers.

Mount Juliet   GOLF
(☏056-777 3071; www.mountjuliet.ie; Mount Juliet Estate, Jerpoint; green fees €55-100) Designed by Jack Nicklaus, par-72 Mount Juliet is a three-time host of the Irish Open and home to the Paul McGinley Golf Academy, established by the winning Irish Ryder Cup captain. Set over 245 wooded hectares, 6km southwest of Thomastown, the estate also has an equestrian centre, gym, spa, two restaurants, wine masterclasses and palatial rooms (doubles/suites from €250/550).

✕ Eating

★ **Blackberry Cafe**   CAFE €
(www.theblackberrycafe.ie; Market St; dishes €5.50-9; ⊙9.30am-5.30pm Mon-Sat year-round, plus 10am-5pm Sun Jun-Aug; ⊕) ✎ Warming soups come with pumpkin-seed-speckled soda bread at this bright cafe, whose menu highlights also include breakfast baps with dry-cured bacon and sausage, superb thick-cut sandwiches, gourmet sausage rolls and quiches (with goat's cheese and pine nuts or

sun-dried tomato and ham). Much is organic; tarts and cakes are baked daily. Between noon and 2pm, it gets packed to bursting.

For €4.75, kids get a half sandwich, a chocolate florentine and locally made apple juice.

🛍 Shopping

Truffle Fairy CHOCOLATE
(www.trufflefairy.ie; Chapel Lane; ⊙10am-5pm Mon-Sat, 11.30am-5pm Sun) 🍴 Ethically sourced single-origin cacao and local, organic ingredients are used to make truffles (varieties include strawberry and whiskey, cinnamon mulled wine, gold leaf and blackberry, and lavender and rose) and caramels (orange and cardamom, and Irish sea salt), along with brownies, muffins, flourless chocolate cake and magnificently thick, rich, hot chocolate. There are a couple of tables inside and out.

It has a second shop in Kilkenny city (www.trufflefairy.ie; Ormonde St; ⊙10am-5pm Tue-Sat) 🍴.

Clay Creations CERAMICS
(📞087 257 0735; www.bridlyonsceramics.com; Low St; ⊙10am-5.30pm Wed, Thu & Sat, 10am-1pm & 3.30-5.30pm Fri, by appointment Tue) Clay Creations displays the quixotic ceramics and sculptures of award-winning local artist Brid Lyons.

❶ Getting There & Away

Kilbride Coaches (www.kilbridecoaches.com) runs buses from Kilkenny to Thomastown (€4.50, 30 minutes, twice daily Monday to Saturday), continuing to Inistioge (€3.50, 15 minutes) and New Ross (€5.50, 45 minutes).

From Thomastown station, 1km west of town on Station Rd, seven trains daily travel to Dublin (€16, 1¾ hours), Kilkenny city (€6.90, 10 minutes) and Waterford city (€6.90, 20 minutes).

Inistioge

POP 260

Tiny Inistioge (*in*-ish-teeg) is a delight, with its tranquil village square, riverside park and 18th-century, 10-arch stone bridge spanning the River Nore (fishing permits available from O'Donnell's pub on the square). The Nore Valley Walk heads north along the riverbank to Thomastown, or try the Nature Walk signposted south from the square.

The R700 from Thomastown makes for a lovely scenic drive along the Nore valley, and features views of the ruined 13th-century Grennan Castle.

Kilbride Coaches (www.kilbridecoaches.com) runs buses from Kilkenny to Inistioge (€5, 45 minutes, twice daily Monday to Saturday), continuing to New Ross (€4.50, 30 minutes).

Woodstock Gardens GARDENS
(📞056-779 4373; www.woodstock.ie; €4; ⊙9am-7pm Apr-Sep, 10am-4pm Oct-Mar) Thickly wooded Woodstock Gardens is a beauty of a park with huge landscaped terraces, a walled garden, an arboretum (including two 40m-tall redwoods), walking trails and a cafe (open 11am to 5pm from April to September). From Inistioge's Woodstock Arms, follow Main St 500m up the hill towards Woodstock Estate and enter the large gates (despite appearances, it's a public road), then continue along the road for another 1.5km until you reach the car park. Cash only.

Woodstock Arms PUB €€
(📞056-775 8440; www.woodstockarms.ie; The Square; s/d/tr from €50/85/100; 📶) This picturesque pub has tables on the square and seven basic bedrooms that are squeaky clean; the triples are particularly spacious. Breakfast is served in a pretty little room out the back with wooden tables and traditional local china.

Graiguenamanagh

POP 1545

Graiguenamanagh (greg-nuh-*mah*-na; known locally as just Graig) is the kind of place where you could easily find yourself staying longer than planned. Spanning the Barrow, an ancient six-arch stone bridge is illuminated at night and connects the village with the smaller township of Tinnahinch on the County Carlow side of the river (look for the darker stones at the Carlow end of the bridge – a legacy of being rebuilt after getting blown up during the 1798 Rising).

There are good walks near town, notably the riverside Barrow Way (p208).

◉ Sights & Activities

Duiske Abbey CHURCH
(📞059-972 4238; Main St; ⊙9am-6pm May-Sep, to 5pm Oct-Apr) FREE Founded in 1204, this was once Ireland's largest Cistercian abbey, and is still very much a working parish church. In the grounds stand two Celtic high crosses (from the 7th and 9th centuries), brought here in the last century for protection. Around the corner, the Abbey Centre (open 9am to 1pm weekdays only) houses a small

exhibition of Christian art, plus pictures of the abbey in its unrestored state.

Graiguenamanagh Bike Hire CYCLING
(☑086 408 4008; www.watersideguesthouse.com; The Quay; per day mountain/electric bike €20/25; ☉by reservation 9am-6pm) The classic summer outing in Graig is to walk or cycle along the grassy River Barrow towpath to the pretty village of St Mullins. The Waterside Guesthouse on the quayside rents mountain and electric bikes, and can provide advice on local walks.

🎪 Festivals & Events

Town of Books Festival LITERATURE
(www.graiguenamanaghtownofbooks.com; ☉late Aug) Graiguenamanagh's narrow streets spill over with booksellers, authors and bibliophiles during this three-day festival in August.

🛏 Sleeping & Eating

Waterside GUESTHOUSE €€
(☑059-972 4246; www.watersideguesthouse.com; The Quay; s/d from €65/98; 🕸) Overlooking the boats tied up along the River Barrow, this inviting guesthouse occupies a converted 19th-century grain store. Its 10 renovated bedrooms have exposed timber beams, and the cafe/restaurant (mains €17 to €24.50; open March to October only) is well regarded for its interesting modern Irish menu and its regular 'After Dinner Live' music acts featuring anything from jazz to bluegrass.

🍷 Drinking & Nightlife

Mick Doyle's PUB
(☑059-972 4203; www.mickdoyles.ie; Main St; ☉11.30am-11pm Mon-Sat, 12.30-10.30pm Sun)

One of Graig's hidden treasures is this unchanged-for-generations shop-pub on Main St. Doyle's is the sort of place where you can buy a bag of potatoes, get some fly-fishing lures and pick up some gardening implements, before settling down for a pint and some craic. Live music plays on the weekends.

🛍 Shopping

Cushendale Woollen Mill ARTS & CRAFTS
(☑059-972 4118; www.cushendale.ie; Mill Rd; ☉9am-12.30pm & 1.30-5.30pm Mon-Fri, 10am-1pm Sat) Cushendale produces knitting yarns, blankets, tweed and winter woollies, which are on sale at the neighbouring shop; ask for an informal, behind-the-scenes peek at the mill's century-old machinery in action. It's up the hill west of Duiske Abbey.

Duiske Glass ARTS & CRAFTS
(www.duiskeglasskilkenny.ie; High St; ☉10am-5pm Mon-Sat) This small studio creates contemporary and traditional crystal, with many designs hand-cut using the old intaglio method of engraving. The gift shop also stocks Irish glassware, ceramics, leather goods and accessories.

ⓘ Getting There & Away

Kilbride Coaches (www.kilbridecoaches.com) runs two buses daily, Monday to Saturday, from Kilkenny bus station (€6, 55 minutes) to Graig, via Borris in County Carlow (€4, 15 minutes).

County Cork

POP 417,210 / AREA 7508 SQ KM

Best Places to Eat

➡ Black Pig Wine Bar (p248)

➡ Nash 19 (p231)

➡ Manning's Emporium (p262)

➡ Square Table (p236)

➡ Mews (p255)

➡ Ocean Wild (p267)

Best Places to Stay

➡ Montenotte Hotel (p229)

➡ Ballymaloe House (p242)

➡ Top of the Rock Pod Pairc (p253)

➡ Blairscove House (p261)

➡ Old Presbytery (p248)

➡ Gallán Mór (p261)

Why Go?

Everything good about Ireland can be found in County Cork. Surrounding the country's second city – a thriving metropolis made glorious by location and its almost Rabelaisian devotion to the finer things of life – is a lush landscape dotted with villages that offer days of languor and idyll. The city's understated confidence is grounded in its plethora of food markets and ever-evolving cast of creative eateries, and in its selection of pubs, entertainment and cultural pursuits.

Further afield, you'll pass inlets along eroded coastlines and a multitude of perfectly charming old fishing towns and villages. The scenery is every bit as enchanting as the best bits of Ireland, particularly along the Mizen Head, Sheep's Head and Beara Peninsulas, where you can hike wild hills and touch Ireland's ancient past.

When to Go

➡ Springtime is heralded in Baltimore with a fiddle fair, followed by a seafood and jazz festival.

➡ Peak season for whale-spotting around the Cork coastline, and the best weather for sea-kayak trips.

➡ Autumn sees food festivals galore, notably in Skibbereen and Kinsale.

CORK CITY

POP 208,670

Ireland's second city is first in every important respect – at least according to the locals, who cheerfully refer to it as the 'real capital of Ireland'. It's a liberal, youthful and cosmopolitan place that was badly hit by economic recession but is now busily reinventing itself with spruced-up streets, revitalised stretches of waterfront, and – seemingly – an artisan coffee bar on every corner. There's a bit of a hipster scene, but the best of the city is still happily traditional – snug pubs with live-music sessions, restaurants dishing up top-quality local produce, and a genuinely proud welcome from the locals.

The compact city centre is set on an island in the River Lee, surrounded by waterways and packed with grand Georgian avenues, cramped 17th-century alleys, modern masterpieces such as the opera house, and narrow streets crammed with pubs, shops, cafes and restaurants, fed by arguably the best foodie scene in the country.

History

Cork has a long and bruising history, inextricably linked with Ireland's struggle for nationhood.

The story begins in the 7th century, when St Fin Barre (also spelt Finbarr and Finbarre) founded a monastery in the midst of a *corcach* (marshy place). By the 12th century the settlement had become the chief city of the Kingdom of South Munster, having survived raids and sporadic settlement by Norsemen. Irish rule was short-lived and by 1185 Cork was in the possession of the English. Thereafter it changed hands regularly during the relentless struggle between Irish and Crown forces. It survived a Cromwellian assault only to fall to that merciless champion of Protestantism, William of Orange.

During the 18th century Cork prospered, with butter, beef, beer and whiskey exported around the world from its port. A mere century later famine devastated both county and city, and robbed Cork of tens of thousands (and Ireland of millions) of its inhabitants by death or emigration.

The 'Rebel City's' deep-seated Irishness ensured that it played a key role in Ireland's struggle for independence. Mayor Thomas MacCurtain was killed by the Black and Tans (British auxiliary troops, so-named because their uniforms were a mixture of army khaki and police black) in 1920. His successor, Terence MacSwiney, died in London's Brixton prison after a hunger strike. The British were at their most brutally repressive in Cork – much of the centre, including St Patrick's St, the City Hall and the Public Library, was burned down. Cork was also a regional focus of Ireland's Civil War in 1922–23.

Today it's a young city, thanks in part to its university: 40% of the population is under 25, and at just 11%, it has the lowest percentage of over 65s in Europe.

◎ Sights

The best sight in Cork is the city itself – soak it up as you wander the streets. A new conference and events centre, complete with 6000-seat concert venue, tourist centre, restaurants, shops, galleries and apartments, was scheduled to open in 2019, but the project has been delayed by financial problems. It will eventually be the focus of the new **Brewery Quarter** (the former Beamish & Crawford brewery site, fronted by the landmark mock-Tudor 'counting house'), a block west of the English Market.

Shandon, perched on a hillside overlooking the city centre to the north, is a great spot for the views alone, but you'll also find galleries, antique shops and cafes along its old lanes and squares. Those tiny old row houses, where generations of workers raised huge families in very basic conditions, are now sought-after urban pieds-à-terre. Pick up a copy of the *Cork Walks – Shandon* leaflet from the tourist office (p235) for a self-guided tour of the district.

★ **Cork City Gaol**   MUSEUM
(☑021-430 5022; www.corkcitygaol.com; Convent Ave; adult/child €10/6; ⊙9.30am-5pm Apr-Sep, 10am-4pm Oct-Mar) This imposing former prison is well worth a visit, if only to get a sense of how awful life was for prisoners a century ago. An audio tour (€2 extra) guides you around the restored cells, which feature models of suffering prisoners and sadistic-looking guards. Take a bus to University College Cork (UCC), and from there walk north along Mardyke Walk, cross the river and follow the signs uphill (10 minutes).

The tour is very moving, bringing home the harshness of the 19th-century penal system. The most common crime was that of poverty; many of the inmates were sentenced to hard labour for stealing loaves of bread. Atmospheric evening tours take place every weekday at 5.45pm (€12, booking required).

County Cork Highlights

1 **Cork city** (p223) Revelling in Cork's brilliant selection of restaurants, pubs, music and theatre.

2 **Sheep's Head Peninsula** (p260) Hiking out to the tip of this windswept and wonderfully remote finger of land.

3 **Ballymaloe Cookery School** (p242) Catching a culinary demonstration or taking a cookery class.

4 **Kinsale** (p245) Meandering through medieval streets and along the coast to mammoth Charles Fort.

5 **Ilnacullin** (p264) Spotting seals and sea eagles

as you sail from Glengarriff to this magical island.

6 **Fastnet Rock** (p256) Braving the Atlantic waves on a thrilling boat trip around this famous landmark.

7 **Healy Pass** (p266) Driving the switchback road across the Beara Peninsula's most spectacular pass.

8 **Lough Hyne** (p254) Joining a guided sea-kayak

tour by moonlight on this lovely marine lake.

9 **Bantry House & Garden** (p262) Stepping back into a world of fading aristocratic splendour.

The prison closed in 1923, reopening in 1927 as a radio station that operated until the 1950s. The on-site Governor's House has been converted into a **Radio Museum** (www.corkcitygaol.com/radio-museum; incl Cork City Gaol adult/child €10/6; 🖥️) where, alongside collections of beautiful old radios, you can hear the story of radio pioneer Guglielmo Marconi's conquest of the airwaves.

Crawford Art Gallery
GALLERY

(☑ 021-480 5042; www.crawfordartgallery.ie; Emmet Pl; ⊗ 10am-5pm Mon-Wed, Fri & Sat, to 8pm Thu, 11am-4pm Sun) FREE Cork's public gallery houses a small but excellent permanent collection covering the 17th century through to the modern day, though the works on display change from year to year. Highlights include paintings by Sir John Lavery, Jack B Yeats and Nathaniel Hone, and Irish women artists Mainie Jellett and Evie Hone.

The Sculpture Galleries contain snow-white plaster casts of Roman and Greek statues, created under the direction of Antonio Canova in the early 19th century, and gifted to King George IV by Pope Pius VII in 1818. London's Royal Academy lacked the space to store or exhibit them, so they were given to Cork 'to enable the artists of the sister kingdom to establish an adequate school of study'.

Cork Public Museum
MUSEUM

(☑ 021-427 0679; www.corkcity.ie/en/things-to-do/attractions/cork-public-museum; Fitzgerald Park, Mardyke Walk; ⊗ 10am-4pm Tue-Fri, 11am-4pm Sat, 2-4pm Sun) FREE Located in a Georgian mansion with a modern extension, this museum recounts Cork's history. The diverse collection of local artefacts tells the story from the Stone Age right up to local football legend Roy Keane, with a particularly interesting exhibit on medieval Cork and the growth of the city. There's a good cafe around the back.

University College Cork
UNIVERSITY

(UCC; ☑ 021-490 1876; http://visitorscentre.ucc.ie; College Rd; ⊗ 9am-5pm Mon-Fri, noon-5pm Sat) FREE Established in 1845 as one of three 'queen's colleges' (the others are in Galway and Belfast) set up to provide nondenominational alternatives to the Anglican Protestant Trinity College in Dublin, UCC's campus spreads around an attractive collection of Victorian Gothic buildings, gardens and historical attractions, including a 19th-century astronomical observatory. Self-guided audio tours are available from the visitor centre.

Stone Corridor
MUSEUM

(☑ 021-490 1876; www.ucc.ie; UCC Visitors Centre, Main Quad, College Rd; ⊗ 9am-5pm Mon-Sat) FREE This covered walkway on the north side of University College Cork's Victorian Gothic main quad houses Ireland's biggest collection of Ogham stones, carved with runic inscriptions dating from the 4th to the 6th century AD.

Lewis Glucksman Gallery
GALLERY

(☑ 021-490 1844; www.glucksman.org; University College Cork, Western Rd; suggested donation €5; ⊗ 10am-5pm Tue-Sat, 2-5pm Sun; 🚻) This award-winning building is a startling construction of limestone, steel and timber, built in 2004 by Dublin architects O'Donnell and Tuomey. Three floors of galleries display the best in both national and international contemporary art and installation. The on-site **Bobo cafe** (☑ 021-490 1848; www.glucksman.org/visit/cafe; mains €6-13; ⊗ 10am-5pm Tue-Sat, noon-5pm Sun) is excellent.

Elizabeth Fort
FORT

(☑ 021-497 5947; www.elizabethfort.ie; Barrack St; ⊗ 10am-5pm Mon-Sat & noon-5pm Sun, closed Mon Oct-May) FREE Originally built in the 1620s, and serving as a *garda* (police) station from 1929 to 2013, this small star-shaped artillery fort once formed an important part of the city's defences. Newly opened to the public, it offers an insight into Cork's military history, and there are good views across the city from the ramparts. Guided tours (per person €3) at 1pm provide additional context.

St Fin Barre's Cathedral
CATHEDRAL

(☑ 021-496 3387; www.corkcathedral.webs.com; Bishop St; adult/child €6/3; ⊗ 9.30am-5.30pm Mon-Sat year-round, 1-2.30pm & 4.30-5pm Sun Apr-Oct) Spiky spires, gurning gargoyles and elaborate sculpture adorn the exterior of Cork's Protestant cathedral, an attention-grabbing mixture of French Gothic and medieval whimsy. The grandeur continues inside, with marble floor mosaics, a colourful chancel ceiling and a huge pulpit and bishop's throne. Quirky items include a cannonball blasted into an earlier medieval spire during the Siege of Cork (1690). The cathedral sits about 500m southwest of the centre, on the spot where Cork's 7th-century patron saint, Fin Barre, founded a monastery.

Most of the cathedral's ostentation is the result of an architectural competition held in 1863 and won by William Burges. Once victory was assured Burges promptly redrew his plans – with an extra choir bay and taller towers – and his £15,000 budget went out the window. Luckily, the bishop appreciated such perfectionism and spent the rest of his life fundraising for the project. Local legend says that the golden angel on the eastern side will blow its horn when the Apocalypse is due to start...

Cork Butter Museum   MUSEUM
(☑ 021-430 0600; www.corkbutter.museum; O'Connell Sq; adult/child €4/1.50; ☺10am-5pm Mar-Oct) Cork has a long tradition of butter manufacturing – in the 1860s it was the world's largest butter market, exporting butter throughout the British Empire – and the trade's history is told through the displays and dioramas of the Cork Butter Museum. The square in front of the museum is dominated by the neoclassical front of the Old Butter Market, and the striking, circular Firkin Crane (p234) building, where butter casks were once weighed (it now houses a dance centre).

Tours

Cork Walks   WALKING
(☑ 021-492 4792; Daunt Sq) FREE There are four waymarked, self-guided tours covering the City Island, South Parish, University and Shandon districts, all beginning at an information board in Daunt Square. You can pick up a leaflet and map at the tourist office (p235).

Cork Culinary Tour   FOOD
(☑ 087 706 8391; www.bonner-travel.com/itinerary/cork-culinary-tour; per person €65) A four-hour tour of Cork's food markets and eating places, including tasting sessions with food and drink sellers and ending with lunch in one of the city's many restaurants.

Atlantic Sea Kayaking   KAYAKING
(☑ 028-21058; www.atlanticseakayaking.com; Lapp's Quay; per person €50; ☺Mar-Sep) Offers guided 'urban kayaking' trips around Cork's waterways from 6.30pm to 9pm (book in advance, minimum two people). It also offers a full-day expedition in two-seater kayaks to Cobh and Spike Island (p237; per person €100).

Cork City Tour   BUS
(☑ 021-430 9090; www.corkcitytour.com; adult/child €15/5; ☺Mar-Nov) A hop-on, hop-off open-top bus linking the city's main points of interest. Longer tours (€25 per adult) head to the Jameson Experience (p241) in Midleton.

Festivals & Events

Cork World Book Fest   LITERATURE
(www.corkworldbookfest.com; ☺late Apr) This huge literary festival combines talks and readings by Irish and international writers with book stalls, music, street entertainment, workshops, film screenings and more.

Cork Midsummer Festival   PERFORMING ARTS
(www.corkmidsummer.com; ☺Jun) A week-long arts festival celebrating music, theatre, dance, literature and visual arts.

Cork Oyster & Seafood Festival   FOOD & DRINK
(www.corkoysterfestival.com; ☺Sep) Seafood is king at this three-day event which includes cooking demos, tastings, a Gourmet Trail, an oyster-shucking contest and live music at venues across town.

Cork Folk Festival   MUSIC
(www.corkfolkfestival.com; ☺Sep-Oct) A long weekend of foot-stomping fiddle, hushed ballads and big-name headline acts such as Martin Simpson, Dick Gaughan and Kate Rusby.

Cork Jazz Festival   MUSIC
(www.guinnessjazzfestival.com; ☺late Oct) Cork's biggest festival has an all-star line-up of jazz, rock and pop in venues across town.

Cork Film Festival   FILM
(www.corkfilmfest.org; ☺Nov) Eclectic, week-long program of international films.

Sleeping

The city has a good range of accommodation, but rooms can be hard to find during major festivals.

City Centre & Around

Whether you stay on the main island, or to the north in Shandon or around MacCurtain St, staying here means you're right in the heart of the action.

Sheila's Hostel   HOSTEL €
(☑ 021-450 5562; www.sheilashostel.ie; 4 Belgrave Pl, off Wellington Rd; dm/tw/f from €16/50/80; @🖥) Sheila's heaves with young travellers, and no wonder given its excellent central location, but it's also a great choice for family travel. Facilities include a sauna, lockers, laundry service, a movie room and a barbecue. Cheaper twin rooms share bathrooms. Breakfast is €3 extra.

Cork City

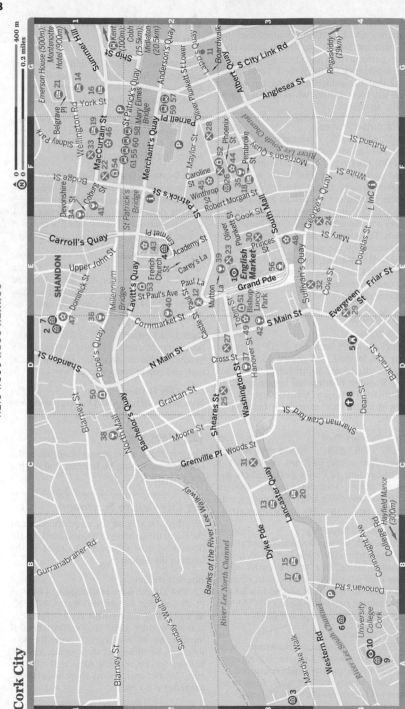

400 m
0.2 miles

Emerson House (500m);
Monerotte
Hotel (900m)

Kent
(100m);
Cobh
(15.5km);
Midleton
(20.5km)

Boardwalk

Ringaskiddy (19km)

S City Link Rd

Anglesea St

Albert Quay

Summer Hill

Ship St

Kent

York St

Belgrave
Pl

Wellington Rd

MacCurtain St

St Patrick's Quay

Merchant's Quay

Parnell Pl

Anderson's Quay

Oliver Plunkett St Lower

Lapp's Quay

Sidney Park

Devonshire St

Bridge St

St Patrick's
Bridge

Emmet Pl

Maylor St

Caroline
St

Winthrop
St

Robert Morgan St

Phoenix
St

Pembroke
St

Morrison's Quay

River Lee South Channel

Rutland St

White St

George's Quay

L.InC

Carroll's Quay

Upper John St

SHANDON

Dominick St

Millennium
Bridge

Lavitt's Quay

French
Church St

St Paul's Ave

Academy St

Carey's La

Paul La

Paul St

Mutton
La

Cook St

English
Market

Oliver
Plunkett
St

Princes
St

South Mall

Grand Pde

Sullivan's Quay

Cove St

Mary St

Douglas St

George's Quay

Evergreen St

Friar St

Shandon St

Pope's Quay

North Mall

Blarney St

Bachelor's Quay

Cornmarket St

Castle St

Tobin St

Bishop
Lucey
Park

S Main St

N Main St

Grattan St

Moore St

Sheares St

Washington St

Cross St

Hanover St

Sharman Crawford St

Dean St

Barrack St

Gurranabraher Rd

Sunday's Well Rd

Blarney St

Grenville Pl

Woods St

Lancaster Quay

Dyke Pde

Western Rd

Banks of the River Lee Walkway

River Lee North Channel

Donovan's Rd

College Rd

Connaught Ave

Hayfield Manor
(300m)

University
College
Cork

Mardyke Walk

River Lee South Channel

2 7
47
36
50
38
17 15

34
41
33 22 54
19
46
21 14 16

11
28
57 59
58 60 55 61
52
44
26 35 45
18

23 39
30
56
51 49 42
53
40 12
27 25 37
13
20
31

48
32
29
24

5
8

3
6
10 9

Cork City

Brú Bar & Hostel HOSTEL €
(☏021-455 9667; www.bruhostel.com; 57 Mac-Curtain St; dm/tw from €25/70; @🖥) This buzzing hostel has a fantastic bar, popular with backpackers and locals alike for its live music. The dorms (each with a bathroom) have four to six beds and are basic but clean – ask for one on the upper floors to avoid bar noise. Breakfast is included.

★ Auburn House B&B €€
(☏021-450 8555; www.auburnguesthouse.com; 3 Garfield Tce, Wellington Rd; s/d €58/90; P🖥) There's a warm family welcome at this neat B&B, which has smallish but well-kept rooms brightened by window boxes. Try to bag one of the back rooms, which are quieter and have sweeping views over the city. Breakfast

includes vegetarian choices, and the location near the fun of MacCurtain St is a plus.

Isaac's Hotel HOTEL €€
(☏021-450 0011; www.isaacscork.com; 48 Mac-Curtain St; s/d/apt from €105/153/222; @🖥) The central location is the real selling point at this hotel housed in what was once a Victorian furniture warehouse (ask for a room away from the busy street). As well as plain, functional bedrooms, there are self-contained apartments, which come with kitchen and washing machine. There's no air-con, so some rooms can get uncomfortably hot on sunny summer days.

★ Montenotte Hotel BOUTIQUE HOTEL €€€
(☏021-453 0050; www.themontenottehotel.com; Middle Glanmire Rd; d/f from €189/229; P🖥⌘)

WORTH A TRIP

BLACKROCK CASTLE

Blackrock Castle ([✓] 021-435 7924; www.bco.ie; Blackrock; adult/child €7/5; ⊙10am-5pm; [P] [♿]) is a restored 16th-century castle that now, rather incongruously, hosts a small hands-on science centre, an inflatable planetarium and a pleasant courtyard cafe. Kids love it and the view from the tower is worth the jaunt. It's on the south bank of the River Lee, 5.5km east of the city centre; take bus 202 from Parnell Pl to Blackrock Pier, from where it's a five-minute walk.

Built as a private residence for a wealthy merchant in the 1820s, the Montenotte has been reimagined as a boutique hotel that skilfully blends its 19th-century legacy with bold designer colour schemes. The hilltop location commands superb views, especially from the roof-terrace bar and restaurant, and guests can enjoy the hotel's sunken Victorian garden, private cinema and luxurious spa.

Imperial Hotel   HOTEL €€€
([✓] 021-427 4040; www.imperialhotelcork.com; South Mall; r from €180; [P] [@] [🛜]) Having celebrated its bicentenary in 2013 – Thackeray, Dickens and Sir Walter Scott have all stayed here – the Imperial knows how to age gracefully. Public spaces resonate with period detail – marble floors, elaborate floral bouquets and more – while the 125 bedrooms feature writing desks, understated decor and modern touches including a luxurious spa and a digital music library.

Irish Free State commander-in-chief Michael Collins spent his last night alive here; you can ask to check into his room.

🛏 Western Road & Around

Western Rd runs southwest from the city centre to the large UCC campus; it has the city's biggest choice of B&Bs. You can take a bus from the central bus station or walk (10 to 30 minutes).

★ Garnish House   B&B €€
([✓] 021-427 5111; www.garnish.ie; 18 Western Rd; d/f from €126/165; [P] [🛜]) Attention is lavished on guests at this award-winning B&B where the legendary breakfast menu (30 choices) ranges from grilled kippers to French toast. Typical of the touches here is freshly cooked porridge, served with creamed honey and

your choice of whiskey or Baileys; enjoy it out on the garden terrace. The 14 rooms are very comfortable; reception is open 24 hours.

Blarney Stone Guesthouse   B&B €€
([✓] 021-427 0083; www.blarneystoneguesthouse.com; Western Rd; s/d from €119/129; [P] [🛜]) The white facade of this tall Victorian townhouse conceals a dazzling interior crammed with polished period furniture, glittering Waterford crystal chandeliers and curlicued gilt mirrors. The Victorian theme does not extend to the facilities, though – creature comforts include power showers, fast wi-fi, satellite TV and hearty breakfasts.

Anam Cara   B&B €€
([✓] 085 864 5216; www.guesthousescork.com; 31 Palace View, Western Rd; r from €105; [P] [🛜]) Although it's just a 10-minute walk west of the city centre, this cute little Georgian-style cottage has a homely, country-house feel. There's a busy road out the front, but the rooms at the back are quiet. Delicious breakfasts are served in the next-door tearoom.

★ River Lee Hotel   HOTEL €€€
([✓] 021-425 2700; www.doylecollection.com; Western Rd; r from €269; [P] [🛜] [🏊]) This modern riverside hotel brings a touch of luxury to the city centre. It has gorgeous public areas with huge sofas, a designer fireplace, a stunning five-storey glass-walled atrium and superb service. There are well-equipped bedrooms (nice and quiet at the back) and possibly the best breakfast buffet in Ireland.

Hayfield Manor   HOTEL €€€
([✓] 021-484 5900; www.hayfieldmanor.ie; Perrott Ave, College Rd; r from €315; [P] [🛜] [🏊]) Roll out the red carpet and pour yourself a sherry for *you have arrived*. Just 1.5km southwest of the city centre but with all the ambience of a country house, Hayfield combines the luxury and facilities of a big hotel with the informality and welcome of a small one. The beautiful bedrooms offer a choice of traditional decor or contemporary styling.

🍴 Eating

Cork's food scene is reason enough to visit the city. Dozens of restaurants and cafes make the most of County Cork's rightly famous local produce, ranging from beef and pork to seafood and dairy, while the renowned English Market (p232) – a cornucopia of fine food – is a national treasure. Well-established places like Nash 19 showcase the best of Irish produce, while newcomer Ichigo Ichie (p232) has added top-end Japanese cuisine to an already heady mix.

Tara's Tea Room
TEAHOUSE €

(☑021-455 3742; www.facebook.com/tarastearoom; 45 MacCurtain St; mains €9-15; ☺9am-6pm Mon-Sat, 10am-5pm Sun; ☏) You'll search long and hard to find a cuter cafe in Ireland than this place. The vintage decor manages to be kitsch yet charming and food is served on vintage china plates. Good for a meal or just a freshly made cake and cup of tea (using real leaves of course). Service is prompt and smiling.

Crawford Gallery Cafe
CAFE €

(☑021-427 4415; www.crawfordgallerycafe.com; Crawford Art Gallery, Emmet Pl; lunch mains €10-15; ☺8.30am-4pm Mon-Sat, 11am-4pm Sun; ☏) An attractive neoclassical room at the back of the city art gallery houses this top-notch cafe. It is managed by the good people from Ballymaloe (p242), which means you can expect a deliciously fresh, locally sourced menu that includes the likes of eggs Benedict for breakfast, or crab, chilli and coriander tagliatelle for lunch.

Filter
CAFE €

(☑021-455 0050; filtercork@gmail.com; 19 George's Quay; mains €4-7; ☺8am-6pm Mon-Fri, 9am-5pm Sat, 10am-3pm Sun; ☏) ✔ The quintessential Cork espresso bar, Filter is a carefully curated shrine to coffee nerdery, from the rough-and-ready retro decor to the highly knowledgable baristas serving up expertly brewed shots made with single-origin, locally roasted beans. The sandwich menu is a class act too, offering a choice of fillings that includes pastrami, chorizo and ham hock on artisan breads.

Cork Coffee Roasters
CAFE €

(☑021-731 9158; www.facebook.com/CorkCoffee; 2 Bridge St; mains €3-6; ☺7.30am-6.30pm Mon-Fri, 8am-6.30pm Sat, 9am-5pm Sun; ☏) In this foodiest of foodie towns it's not surprising to find a cafe run by artisan coffee roasters. The brew on offer in this cute and often crowded corner is some of the best in Cork, guaranteed to jump start your morning along with a buttery pastry, scone or tart.

Quay Co-op
VEGETARIAN €

(☑021-431 7026; www.quaycoop.com; 24 Sullivan's Quay; mains €8-11; ☺11am-9pm Mon-Sat, noon-9pm Sun; ☏🖶) ✔ Flying the flag for alternative Cork, this cafeteria offers a range of self-service vegetarian dishes, all organic, including big breakfasts and rib-sticking soups and casseroles. It also caters

for gluten-, dairy- and wheat-free needs, and is amazingly child-friendly.

★Paradiso
VEGETARIAN €€

(☑021-427 7939; www.paradiso.restaurant; 16 Lancaster Quay; 2-/3-course menus €39/47; ☺5.30-10pm Mon-Sat; ☏) ✔ A contender for best restaurant in town of any genre, Paradiso serves contemporary vegetarian dishes, including vegan fare: how about corn pancakes filled with leek, parsnip and Dunmanus cheese with fennel-caper salsa and smoked tomato? Reservations are essential.

Rates for dinner, bed and breakfast, staying in the funky upstairs rooms, start from €180/220 per single/double.

★Nash 19
INTERNATIONAL €€

(☑021-427 0880; www.nash19.com; Princes St; mains €12-22; ☺7.30am-4pm Mon-Fri, from 8.30am Sat) ✔ A superb bistro and deli where locally sourced food is honoured at breakfast and lunch, either sit-in or take away. Fresh scones draw crowds early; daily lunch specials (soups, salads, desserts etc), free-range chicken pie and platters of smoked fish from Frank Hederman (p241) keep them coming for lunch – the Producers Plate (€22), a sampler of local produce, is sensational.

★Market Lane
IRISH €€

(☑021-427 4710; www.marketlane.ie; 5 Oliver Plunkett St; mains €14-25; ☺noon-9.30pm Mon-Wed, to 10pm Thu, to 10.30pm Fri & Sat, 1-9.30pm Sun; ☏🖶) ✔ It's always hopping at this bright corner bistro. The menu is broad and hearty, changing to reflect what's fresh at the English Market: perhaps roast hake with wild garlic velouté, or beetroot, walnut and feta cakes? No reservations for fewer than six diners; sip a drink at the bar till a table is free. Lots of wines by the glass.

Miyazaki
JAPANESE €€

(☑021-431 2716; www.facebook.com/miyazakicork; 1A Evergreen St; mains €12-15; ☺1-3.30pm & 5-9pm Tue-Sun) Here's something you don't see every day – a takeaway food joint run by a Michelin-starred chef! You can sample Takashi Miyazaki's superb dishes – the menu includes sushi rolls, donburi (rice bowls with your choice of topping), Japanese curries, udon noodles, dashi etc – without forking out for the full theatrical experience at his main restaurant (p232) across the river.

Liberty Grill
DINER €€

(☑021-427 1049; www.libertygrill.ie; 32 Washington St; mains lunch €10-16, dinner €12-29; ☺8am-9pm

THE ENGLISH MARKET

The **English Market** (www.englishmarket.ie; main entrance Princes St; ⊗ 8am-6pm Mon-Sat) – so called because it was set up in 1788 by the Protestant or 'English' corporation that then controlled the city (there was once an Irish Market nearby) – is a true gem, with its ornate vaulted ceilings, columns and polished marble fountain. Scores of vendors set up colourful and photogenic displays of the region's very best local produce, including meat, fish, fruit, cheeses and takeaway food.

On a sunny day, take your lunch to nearby Bishop Lucey Park, a popular alfresco eating spot.

The **Farmgate Cafe** (☎ 021-427 8134; www.farmgatecork.ie; mains €8-14; ⊗ 8.30am-5pm Mon-Sat) 🍽 is an unmissable experience at the heart of the English Market, perched on a balcony overlooking the food stalls below, the source of all that fresh local produce on your plate – everything from crab and oysters to the lamb in your Irish stew. Go up the stairs and turn left for table service, or right for counter service.

Mon-Thu, to 10pm Fri & Sat; 🕏) A gleaming white outpost on an otherwise drab street of brick facades, the Liberty Grill is popular for its locally sourced menu of crowd pleasers, such as traditional breakfasts, burgers, sandwiches, salads and slightly more ambitious dinner fare. Think of it as a diner for foodies.

Jacques Restaurant　　　MODERN IRISH €€
(☎ 021-427 7387; www.jacquesrestaurant.ie; 23 Oliver Plunkett St; mains lunch €8-15, dinner €23-29; ⊗ 10am-4pm Mon, to 10pm Tue-Sat) 🍽 The Barry sisters draw on a terrific network of local suppliers built up over three decades to help them provide the freshest Cork food cooked simply, without frills. The menu changes daily: roast venison with turnip and parmesan gratin, perhaps, or West Cork scallops with almond and raisin salsa. Two-course dinners (€28) served Tuesday to Thursday, and pre-6.30pm Friday and Saturday.

Ichigo Ichie　　　JAPANESE €€€
(☎ 021-427 9997; www.ichigoichie.ie; 5 Fenns Quay, Sheares St; per person €120-135; ⊗ 6-10.30pm Tue-Sat) More theatre than restaurant, this bold venture by chef Takashi Miyazaki immerses diners in the art and craft of Japanese *kappou* cuisine – an elaborate multicourse meal prepared and plated by the chef as you watch; expect a dozen courses spread over three hours or so. The restaurant was awarded a Michelin star in 2019. Miyazaki also has a takeaway restaurant (p231).

🍷 Drinking & Nightlife

In Cork pubs, locally brewed Murphy's and Beamish stouts, not Guinness, are the preferred pints.

Given the city's big student population, the small selection of nightclubs does a thriving trade. Entry ranges from free to €15; most are open until 2am on Fridays and Saturdays.

Local microbreweries include the long-established Franciscan Well, whose refreshing Friar Weisse beer is popular in summer, and relative newcomer Rising Sons, whose Mi Daza stout is a new take on an old recipe.

★ Sin É　　　PUB
(☎ 021-450 2266; www.facebook.com/sinecork; 8 Coburg St; ⊗ 12.30-11.30pm Mon-Thu, to 12.30am Fri & Sat, to 11pm Sun) You could easily spend an entire day at this place, which is everything a craic-filled pub should be – long on atmosphere and short on pretension (Sin É means 'that's it!'). There's music every night from 6.30pm May to September, and regular sessions Tuesday, Friday and Sunday the rest of the year, most of them traditional but with the odd surprise.

★ Franciscan Well Brewery　　　PUB
(☎ 021-439 3434; www.franciscanwellbrewery.com; 14 North Mall; ⊗ 1-11.30pm Mon-Thu, to 12.30am Fri & Sat, to 11pm Sun; 🕏) The copper vats gleaming behind the bar give the game away: the Franciscan Well brews its own beer (and has done since 1998). The best place to enjoy it is in the enormous beer garden at the back. The pub holds regular beer festivals together with other small independent Irish breweries.

★ Mutton Lane Inn　　　PUB
(☎ 021-427 3471; www.facebook.com/mutton.lane; Mutton Lane; ⊗ 10.30am-11.30pm Mon-Thu, to 12.30am Fri & Sat, 12.30-11pm Sun) Tucked down the tiniest of alleys off St Patrick's St, this inviting pub, lit by candles and fairy lights, is

one of Cork's most intimate drinking holes. It's minuscule, so try to get in early to bag the snug, or perch on the beer kegs outside.

The Oval
PUB

(☑ 021-427 8952; www.corkheritagepubs.com/pubs/the-oval; 25 South Main St; ⊙ 3-11.30pm Sun-Thu, to 12.30am Fri & Sat) Come early to grab the seats by the crackling open fire, but even if you're not lucky this time round, it's still a great place to park for a few hours with the perfect pint of stout, enjoying the buzzing atmosphere or an in-depth chat with drinking companions. It's been serving locals for more than 250 years; long may it continue.

Arthur Mayne's Pharmacy
WINE BAR

(☑ 021-427 9449; www.corkheritagepubs.com/pubs/arthur-maynes; 7 Pembroke St; ⊙ 10am-2am Sun-Thu, to 3am Fri & Sat) This unusual wine bar's former life as a pharmacy has been lovingly preserved – the window displays are full of vintage cosmetics and memorabilia. The staff are knowledgeable and always happy to recommend a wine pairing from the extensive menu. Combine all that with the delicious sharing plates and soft candlelight and you have an excellent date spot.

Abbot's Ale House
PUB

(☑ 021-450 7116; www.facebook.com/abbotsalehouse; 17 Devonshire St; ⊙ 4-11.30pm Mon-Thu, to 12.30am Fri & Sat, to 11pm Sun) A low-key, two-floor drinking den, whose small size contrasts with its huge beer list. There are always several beers on tap and another 300 in bottles. Good for preclubbing.

Rising Sons
MICROBREWERY

(☑ 021-241 4764; www.risingsonsbrewery.com; Cornmarket St; ⊙ noon-late; 🐕) This huge, warehouse-like, red-brick building houses an award-winning microbrewery. The industrial decor of exposed brick, riveted iron and gleaming copper brewing vessels recalls American West Coast brewpubs. It turns out 50 kegs a week, some of them full of its lip-smacking trademark stout, Mi Daza, and has a food menu that ranges from pizza to weekend brunch.

Bierhaus
PUB

(☑ 021-455 1648; www.thebierhauscork.com; Pope's Quay; ⊙ 3-11.30pm Mon-Thu, 3pm-12.30am Fri & Sat, 3-11pm Sun; 🐕) A convivial bar with one of the best selections of beer in town. More than 220 varieties, both local and international, are on offer, mostly bottled but with no fewer than 16 guest brews on tap.

☆ Entertainment

Cork's cultural life is generally of a high calibre. To see what's happening, check out the *WhazOn?* listings website (www.whazon.com).

Cork's musical credentials are impeccable. Besides theatres and pubs that feature live music, there are also places that are dedicated music venues, and bars known particularly for their live gigs. For full listings, refer to *WhazOn?*, PLUGD Records (p234), and the event guide at www.peoplesrepublicofcork.com.

★ Cork Opera House
OPERA

(☑ 021-427 0022; www.corkoperahouse.ie; Emmet Pl; tickets €30-50; ⊙ box office 10am-5.30pm Mon-Sat, pre-show to 7pm Mon-Sat & 6-7pm Sun) Given a modern makeover in the 1990s, this leading venue has been entertaining the city for more than 150 years with everything from opera and ballet to stand-up comedy, pop concerts and puppet shows. Around the back, the Half Moon Theatre presents contemporary theatre, dance, art and occasional club nights.

LGBTQ+ CORK

Cork has an out and proud gay scene that rivals Dublin's. Most nightlife venues are concentrated in the west end of the city centre, and most are mixed-crowd, all-welcome places.

Chambers Bar (☑ 086 703 7018; www.facebook.com/ChambersCork; Washington St; ⊙ 6pm-2am Wed & Thu, 4.30pm-2.30am Fri & Sat, 6-11.30pm Sun) Cork's biggest and liveliest gay bar, with DJs playing till 2am, themed entertainment nights and outrageous cocktails.

Cork Pride (www.corkpride.com; ⊙ Jul-Aug) Week-long festival with events throughout the city.

Emerson House (☑ 086 834 0891; www.emersonhousecork.com; 2 Clarence Tce, Summer Hill North; s/d from €70/90; 🅿 🐕) Gay and lesbian B&B in an elegant Georgian house. Host Cyril is a mine of information.

Gay Cork (www.gaycork.com) What's-on listings and directory.

L.InC (☑ 021-480 8600; www.linc.ie; 11A White St; ⊙ 11am-3pm Tue & Wed, to 8pm Thu) Resource centre for lesbians and bisexual women.

TRACING YOUR ANCESTORS

Genealogy services in County Cork:

Cobh Heritage Centre (p240) Housed in the Queenstown Story museum.

Mallow Heritage Centre (☑022-50302; www.mallowheritagecentre.com; 27/28 Bank Pl, Mallow; ☺10.30am-1pm Mon-Fri, 2-4pm Mon-Thu) Covers north and east Cork.

Skibbereen Heritage (p253) Located in the town's heritage centre.

★**Triskel Arts Centre** ARTS CENTRE
(☑021-472 2022; www.triskelart.com; Tobin St; tickets €8-30; ☺box office 10am-5pm Mon-Sat, 1-9pm Sun; ☎) A fantastic cultural centre housed partly in a renovated church building. Expect a varied program of live music, visual art, photography and theatre at this intimate venue. There's also a cinema (from 6.30pm) and a great cafe.

Crane Lane Theatre LIVE MUSIC
(☑021-427 8487; www.cranelanetheatre.ie; Phoenix St; tickets free-€5; ☺2pm-2am Mon-Fri, noon-2am Sat & Sun) Part pub, part vintage ballroom, this atmospheric venue is decked out in 1920s to 1940s decor, with a courtyard beer garden as a central oasis. It stages a wide range of live music gigs and DJ nights, most with free admission.

Everyman Theatre THEATRE
(☑021-450 1673; www.everymancork.com; 15 Mac-Curtain St; tickets €15-40; ☺box office noon-5pm Mon-Sat, preshow to 7.30pm Mon-Sat, 4-7.30pm Sun) Acclaimed musical and dramatic productions are the main bill here, but there's also the occasional comedy act or live band (it's a great venue for gigs that require a little bit of respectful silence).

Fred Zeppelins LIVE MUSIC
(☑086 260 7876; 8 Parliament St; ☺4-11.30pm Mon-Thu, to 12.30am Fri & Sat, to 11pm Sun; ☎) There's a hard edge to this dark den of a bar, popular with goths, rockers and anyone who feels uncomfortable leaving the house without a packet of Rizlas. It's been on the go since 1997, and is known for its live gigs (lots of tribute bands) and DJs at weekends, plus occasional open-mike nights.

Cyprus Avenue LIVE MUSIC
(☑021-427 6165; www.cyprusavenue.ie; Caroline St; tickets €8-23; ☺7.30pm-late) This midsized venue is one of the best spots in town to see all kinds of gigs, from heartfelt singer-songwriters to top local bands on their way to the big time (and some once-famous bands on their way down).

Firkin Crane DANCE
(☑021-450 7487; www.firkincrane.ie; O'Connell Sq, Shandon; tickets free-€20) One of Ireland's premier centres for modern dance.

🅐 Shopping

St Patrick's St is the retail spine of Cork, housing all the major department stores and malls. But pedestrianised Oliver Plunkett St is the retail heart; it and the surrounding narrow lanes are lined with small, interesting shops.

Vibes & Scribes BOOKS
(☑021-427 9535; www.vibesandscribes.ie/books; 21 Lavitt's Quay; ☺10am-6.30pm Mon-Sat, 12.30-6pm Sun) Stocks a vast selection of new, secondhand and remaindered books, including lots of Irish interest titles.

Village Hall VINTAGE
(www.facebook.com/thevillagehallcork; 4 St Patrick's Quay; ☺10am-6pm) This Aladdin's cave is stuffed to the brim with unusual vintage clothing, vinyl records, eclectic furniture and assorted oddities. Despite being full of knick-knacks to browse through, it maintains a stylish interior and you could find yourself spending a couple of hours here. There's also delicious coffee and cake to sustain you during your shopping.

PLUGD Records MUSIC
(☑021-472 6300; www.plugdrecords.com; Triskel Arts Centre, Tobin St; ☺noon-7pm Mon-Sat; ☎) Stocks all kinds of music on vinyl and CD and is the place to keep up with Cork's ever-changing music scene.

20 20 Gallery ART
(☑021-439 1458; www.2020artgallery.com; Griffith House, North Mall; ☺noon-5pm Tue-Sat) Commercial fine-art gallery selling paintings, ceramics and photographic prints by a broad range of Irish artists.

Pro Musica MUSIC
(☑021-427 1659; www.promusica.ie; 20 Oliver Plunkett St; ☺9am-6pm Mon-Sat) A focal point and meeting place for Cork's musicians, with a full range of instruments from electric guitars to

clarinets, recording equipment, sheet music and a noticeboard.

ℹ Information

Cork City Tourist Office (☎1850 230 330; www.purecork.ie; 125 St Patrick's St; ⊙9am-5pm Mon-Sat; ☎) Information desk, and free city maps and self-guided walk leaflets.

General Post Office (☎021-485 1042; Oliver Plunkett St; ⊙9am-5.30pm Mon-Sat)

Mercy University Hospital (☎021-427 1971; www.muh.ie; Grenville Pl) Has a 24-hour emergency department.

People's Republic of Cork (www.peoples republicofcork.com) Picking up on the popular nickname for the liberal-leaning city, this indie website provides excellent info.

Free wi-fi is available throughout the city centre's main streets and public spaces, including the bus and train stations.

Webworkhouse.com (☎021-427 3090; www.webworkhouse.com; 8A Winthrop St; per hr €1.50-3; ⊙24hr) Internet cafe; also offers low-cost international phone cards.

ℹ Getting There & Away

AIR

Cork Airport (☎021-431 3131; www.corkairport.com) is 8km south of the city on the N27. Facilities include ATMs and car-hire desks for all the main companies. Airlines servicing the airport include Aer Lingus, Ryanair and Jet2.com. There are flights to Edinburgh, Cardiff, London (Heathrow, Gatwick, Luton and Stansted), Paris and several other cities in Britain and across Europe.

Bus Éireann (☎1850 836 611; www.bus eireann.ie) service 226A shuttles between the train station, bus station and Cork Airport every half-hour between 6am and 10pm (€2.80/5.60 one-way/return, 30 minutes). A taxi to/from town costs €22 to €26.

BOAT

Brittany Ferries (☎021-427 7801; www.brittanyferries.ie; 42 Grand Pde) sails to Roscoff (France) weekly from the end of March to October. The crossing takes 14 hours; fares vary widely. The ferry terminal is at Ringaskiddy, 15 minutes by car southeast of the city centre along the N28. Taxis cost €30 to €38. Bus Éireann runs a service from Cork (South Mall) to link up with departures (€8, 40 minutes); confirm times on its website.

BUS

Bus Éireann operates from the **bus station** (cnr Merchant's Quay & Parnell Pl), while **Aircoach** (☎01-844 7118; www.aircoach.ie), **Dublin Coach** (☎01-465 9972; www.dublincoach.ie), **GoBus** (☎091-564 600; www.gobus.ie; ☎) and **Citylink** (☎091-564 164; www.citylink.ie; ☎) services depart from St Patrick's Quay, across the river.

TRAIN

Kent Train Station (☎021-450 6766) is north of the River Lee on Lower Glanmire Rd, a 10- to 15-minute walk from the city centre. Bus 205 runs into the city centre (€2.20, five minutes, every 15 minutes).

The train line goes through Mallow, where you can change for the Tralee line, and Limerick Junction, for the line to Ennis (and Galway), then on to Dublin.

Dublin €59, 2¼ hours, eight daily

Galway €57, four to six hours, seven daily, two or three changes

Killarney €25, 1½ to two hours, nine daily

Waterford €33, three to five hours, five daily, one or two changes

ℹ Getting Around

BICYCLE

Cycle Scene (☎021-430 1183; www.cyclescene.ie; 396 Blarney St; per day/week from

BUS TIMETABLE

DESTINATION	BUS COMPANY	FARE (€)	DURATION (HR)	FREQUENCY
Dublin	Bus Éireann	16.50	3¾	6 daily
Dublin	Aircoach	17	3	hourly
Dublin	GoBus	18	3	6-9 daily
Dublin Airport	Aircoach	20	3½	hourly
Dublin Airport	GoBus	28	3¼	6-9 daily
Galway	Citylink	20	3	5 daily
Kilkenny	Dublin Coach	15	2½	8 daily
Killarney	Bus Éireann	19	1½	hourly
Limerick	Citylink	16	1½	5 daily
Waterford	Dublin Coach	10	2	9 daily

€15/85) rents bikes and accessories, including electric bikes (€35 a day).

BUS

Most places are within easy walking distance of the centre. Single bus tickets costs €2.20 each; a day pass is €5.40. Buy all tickets on the bus.

CAR

Street parking requires scratch-card parking discs (€2 per hour, in force 8.30am to 6.30pm Monday to Saturday), available from many city centre shops. Be warned – traffic wardens are ferociously efficient. There are several signposted car parks around the central area, with charges around €2 per hour and €12 overnight.

You can avoid city centre parking problems by using Black Ash Park & Ride on the South City Link Rd, on the way to the airport. Parking costs €5 a day, with buses into the city centre at least every 15 minutes (10-minute journey time).

TAXI

Cork Taxi Co-op (☑ 021-427 22 22; www.corktaxi.ie)

Yellow Cabs Cork (☑ 021-427 22 55; www.yellowcabscork.com)

AROUND CORK CITY

Blarney Castle

If you need proof of the power of a good yarn, then join the queue to get into the 15th-century **Blarney Castle** (☑ 021-438 5252; www.blarneycastle.ie; Blarney; adult/child €18/8; ⊙ 9am-7pm Mon-Sat, to 6pm Sun Jun-Aug, shorter hours Sep-May; **P**), one of Ireland's most popular tourist attractions. Everyone's here, of course, to plant their lips on the **Blarney Stone**, which supposedly gives one the gift of gab – a cliché that has entered every lexicon and tour route. Blarney is 8km northwest of Cork and buses run hourly from Cork bus station (€5.60 return, 20 minutes).

The Blarney Stone is perched at the top of a steep climb up claustrophobic spiral staircases. On the battlements, you bend backwards over a long, long drop (with safety grill and attendant to prevent tragedy) to kiss the stone; as your shirt rides up, coachloads of onlookers stare up your nose. Once you're upright again, don't forget to admire the stunning views before descending. Try not to think of the local lore about all the fluids that drench the stone other than saliva. Better yet, just don't kiss it.

The custom of kissing the stone is a relatively modern one, but Blarney's association with smooth talking goes back a long time. Queen Elizabeth I is said to have invented the term 'to talk blarney' out of exasperation with Lord Blarney's ability to talk endlessly without ever actually agreeing to her demands.

The famous stone aside, **Blarney Castle** itself is an impressive 16th-century tower set in gorgeous grounds. Escape the crowds on a walk around the **Fern Garden** and **Arboretum**, investigate toxic plants in the Harry Potterish **Poison Garden** or explore the landscaped nooks and crannies of the **Rock Close**.

★ **Square Table**   IRISH €€€
(☑ 021-438 2825; www.thesquaretable.ie; 5 The Square, Blarney; mains €20-30; ⊙ 6-9pm Wed & Thu, to 10pm Fri & Sat, 12.30-4pm Sun) The sisters who run this cosy little restaurant are passionate about Irish produce, as shown in a menu that puts local seafood, pork and beef, Gubbeen chorizo, Ballyhoura mushrooms and platters of Irish-made salami, black pudding and Irish cheeses front and centre. Best to book in advance.

Fota Island

Fota Island lies in Cork Harbour, connected by short bridges to the mainland and Great Island, 10km east of Cork on the road to Cobh. Formerly the private estate of the Smith-Barry family, it is now home to gardens, golf courses and Ireland's only wildlife park.

The train from Cork to Fota (€3.10, 13 minutes, hourly) continues to Cobh.

Fota House Arboretum & Gardens   HOUSE
(☑ 021-481 5543; www.fotahouse.com; Carrigtwohill, Fota Island; house tours adult/child €9/3.50, house & gardens €13.50/6; ⊙ 10am-5pm daily Mar-Sep, Sat & Sun Feb & Oct-Dec; **P**) Guided tours of Regency-style Fota House focus on the original kitchen and ornate plasterwork ceilings, but the real highlight here is the 150-year-old arboretum and gardens (self-guided tour of garden only costs €3). There's a Victorian fernery set amid blocks of fluted limestone, a magnolia walk, a walled garden and a host of beautiful trees, including huge Japanese cedars overlooking the lily pond.

Fota Wildlife Park   ZOO
(☑ 021-481 2678; www.fotawildlife.ie; Carrigtwohill, Fota Island; adult/child €16.70/11.20, parking €3;

SPIKE ISLAND

A low-lying green island in Cork Harbour, **Spike Island** (☑021-237 3455; www.spikeisland cork.com; adult/child incl ferry €20/10; ⊙ferry departures 10am-3pm Jun-Aug, noon & 2pm May & Sep, Sat & Sun only Feb-Apr & Oct) was once an important part of the port's defences, topped by an 18th-century artillery fort. In the second half of the 19th century, during the Irish War of Independence, and from 1984 to 2004 it served as a prison, gaining the nickname 'Ireland's Alcatraz'. Today you can enjoy a guided walking tour of the former prison buildings, then go off and explore on your own; the ferry departs from Kennedy Pier, Cobh.

The guided tour takes in the modern prison, the old punishment block, the shell store (once used as a children's prison) and No 2 bastion with its massive 6in gun. Other highlights include the **Gun Park**, with a good display of mostly 20th-century artillery; the **Mitchell Hall**, with an exhibit on the *Aud*, a WWI German gun-running ship that was sunk in the entrance to Cork Harbour; and the **Glacis Walk**, a 1.5km trail that leads around the walls of the fortress, with great views of Cobh town and the harbour entrance. You'll need around four hours to make the most of a visit. There's a cafe and toilets on the island.

⊙10am-6pm; P🖶) Kangaroos bound, cheetahs run, and monkeys and gibbons leap and scream on wooded islands at this huge outdoor zoo, where the animals roam without a cage or fence in sight. A tour train (on wheels, not tracks) runs a circuit round the park every 15 minutes in high season (one-way/return €1/2), but the 2km circular walk offers a more close-up experience. Last admission is 1½ hours before closing.

Fota Island Resort GOLF
(☑021-488 3700; www.fotaisland.ie; Fota Island; green fees €45-110) Three championship golf courses sprawl within the 315-hectare Fota Island Resort – Deerpark, Belvelly and Barryscourt – anchored by one of Ireland's best known golfing hotels. The resort has hosted the Irish Open three times, most recently in 2014, and welcomes visitors; it's best to book your round in advance. The beautiful old stone clubhouse, set in a converted farmhouse overlooking the lake, is an atmospheric place for a postgolf drink.

Cobh
POP 12,800
Cobh (pronounced 'cove') is a charming waterfront town on a glittering estuary, dotted with brightly coloured houses and overlooked by a splendid cathedral. It's popular with Corkonians looking for a spot of R&R, and with cruise liners – each year around 90 visit the port, the second-largest natural harbour in the world (after Sydney Harbour in Australia).

It's a far cry from the harrowing Famine years when more than 70,000 people left Ireland through the port in order to escape the ravages of starvation (from 1848 to 1950, no fewer than 2.5 million emigrants passed through). Cobh was also the final port of call for the *Titanic;* a poignant museum commemorates the fatal voyage's point of departure.

Cobh is on the south side of Great Island. Visible from the waterfront are Haulbowline Island, once a naval base, and the greener Spike Island, formerly a prison and now a tourist attraction.

History

For many years Cobh was the port of Cork, and it has always had a strong connection with Atlantic crossings. In 1838 the *Sirius,* the first steamship to cross the Atlantic, sailed from Cobh. The *Titanic* made its last stop here before its disastrous voyage in 1912, and, when the *Lusitania* was torpedoed off the coast of Kinsale in 1915, it was here that many of the survivors were brought and the dead buried. Cobh was also the last glimpse of Ireland for tens of thousands who emigrated during the Famine.

In 1849 Cobh was renamed Queenstown after Queen Victoria paid a visit. The name lasted until Irish independence in 1921 when, unsurprisingly, the local council reverted to the Irish original.

The world's first yacht club, the Royal Cork Yacht Club, was founded here in 1720, but currently operates from Crosshaven on the other side of Cork Harbour. The beautiful Italianate Old Yacht Club now houses an arts centre.

1. Lot's Wife (p254), Baltimore
This white beacon marks the entrance to Baltimore's busy little harbour.

2. Eyeries (p269), West Cork
A cluster of brightly coloured houses overlooking Coulagh Bay, Eyeries is often used as a film set.

3. Bridge at Mizen Head (p259)
Connecting the Signal Station to the mainland, this 45m-high bridge gives access to astounding cliff scenery.

4. Castletownbere (p266)
A busy fishing port, Castletownbere is home to Dunboy Castle.

◉ Sights & Activities

Cobh, The Queenstown Story   MUSEUM
(☑ 021-481 3591; www.cobhheritage.com; Lower Rd; adult/child €10/6; ⊙ 9.30am-6pm mid-Apr–mid-Oct, 9.30am-5pm Mon-Sat, 11am-5pm Sun mid-Oct–mid-Apr) The howl of the storm almost knocks you off-balance, there's a bit of fake vomit on the deck, and the people in the pictures all look pretty miserable – that's just one room at Cobh Heritage Centre. Housed in the old train station (next to the current station), this interactive museum is way above average, chronicling Irish emigrations across the Atlantic in the wake of the Great Famine.

Other exhibits include some shocking stuff on the fate of convicts, shipped to Australia in transport ships 'so airless that candles could not burn'. Scenes of sea travel in the 1950s, however, might actually make you nostalgic for a more gracious way of travelling the world. There's also a genealogy centre and a cafe. The last admission is one hour before closing.

Titanic Experience Cobh   MUSEUM
(☑ 021-481 4412; www.titanicexperiencecobh.ie; 20 Casement Sq; adult/child €10/7; ⊙ 9am-6pm Apr-Sep, 10am-5.30pm Oct-Mar; ♠) The original White Star Line offices, where 123 passengers embarked on (and one lucky soul absconded from) the RMS *Titanic*, now house this powerful insight into the ill-fated liner's final voyage in 1912. Admission is by tour, which is partly guided and partly interactive, with holograms, audiovisual presentations and exhibits; allow at least an hour. The technical wizardry is impressive but what's most memorable is standing on the spot from where passengers were ferried to the waiting ship offshore, never to return.

Michael Martin's Walking Tours   WALKING
(☑ 021-481 5211; www.titanic.ie; tours from €13) Michael Martin's 1¼-hour guided Titanic Trail walk leaves from the Commodore Hotel (4 Westbourne Pl) at 11am and 2pm, with a free sampling of stout at the end. Martin also runs a ghoulish Ghost Walk (8pm start).

St Colman's Cathedral   CATHEDRAL
(☑ 021-481 3222; www.cobhcathedralparish.ie; Cathedral Pl; admission by donation; ⊙ 8am-6pm May-Oct, to 5pm Nov-Apr) Dramatically perched on a hillside terrace above Cobh, this massive French Gothic Cathedral is out of all proportion to the town. Its most exceptional feature is the 47-bell carillon, the largest in Ireland, with a range of four octaves. The biggest bell weighs a stonking 3440kg – about as much as a full-grown elephant! You can hear carillon recitals at 4.30pm on Sundays between May and September.

The cathedral, designed by EW Pugin, was begun in 1868 but not completed until 1915. Much of the funding was raised by nostalgic Irish communities in Australia and the USA.

Cobh Museum   MUSEUM
(☑ 021-481 4240; www.cobhmuseum.com; High Rd; adult/child €4/2; ⊙ 11am-1pm & 2-5pm Mon-Sat, 2.30-5pm Sun Apr-Oct) Model ships, paintings, photographs and curious artefacts tracing Cobh's history fill this small but engaging museum. It's housed in the 19th-century Scottish Presbyterian church overlooking the train station.

🛏 Sleeping & Eating

Gilbert's   GUESTHOUSE €€
(☑ 021-481 1300; www.gilbertsincobh.com; 11 Pearse Sq; s/d/penthouse €89/100/180; ♠) The four rooms at this boutique guesthouse in Cobh's town centre are fresh and contemporary with handmade furniture, pure-wool blankets and rain showers. Rates don't include breakfast, but the penthouse suite has a kitchenette. Gilbert's Bistro, one of Cobh's better restaurants, is just downstairs.

Knockeven House   B&B €€
(☑ 021-481 1778; www.knockevenhouse.com; Rushbrooke; d/f from €120/160; ℗) Knockeven is a splendid Victorian house with huge bedrooms done out with period furniture, overlooking a magnificent garden full of magnolias and camellias. Breakfasts are great too – homemade breads and fresh fruit – and are served in the sumptuous dining room. The decor takes you back to 1st-class passage on a vintage liner. It's 1.5km west of Cobh's centre.

★ Seasalt   CAFE €
(☑ 021-481 3383; www.facebook.com/Seasalt Cobh; 17 Casement Sq; mains €7-10; ⊙ 9am-5pm Mon-Sat, 10am-5pm Sun) This stylish cafe, run by a Ballymaloe-trained chef, brings fresh local produce to brunch dishes such as Gubbeen chorizo hash, or eggs Royale with Belvelly smoked salmon, and lunch specials like croque madame with West Cork ham and Dubliner cheese. Salads are fresh and inventive, and tart of the day could be spinach and feta, or roast tomato, pesto and mozzarella.

BELVELLY SMOKEHOUSE

No trip to Cork is complete without a visit to an artisan food producer, and the effervescent Frank Hederman is more than happy to show you around **Belvelly Smokehouse** (☑ 021-481 1089; www.frankhederman.com; Belvelly; free for individuals, charge for groups; ☺ by reservation 10am-5pm Mon-Fri) 🖉, the oldest traditional smokehouse in Ireland – indeed, the only surviving one. The smokehouse is 19km east of Cork on the R624 towards Cobh; call ahead to arrange a visit.

Alternatively, stop by Frank's stall at the **Cobh** (☑ 086 199 7643; www.facebook.com/cobhfarmers; The Promenade; ☺ 10am-2pm Fri) 🖉 or Midleton (p243) farmers markets; you can also buy his produce at Cork's English Market (p232).

Seafood and cheese are smoked here – even butter – but the speciality is fish, particularly salmon. In a traditional process that takes 24 hours from start to finish, the fish is filleted and cured before being hung to smoke over beech woodchips. The result is subtle and delectable.

Titanic Bar & Grill   IRISH €€
(☑ 021-481 4585; www.titanicbarandgrill.ie; 20 Casement Sq; mains €11-28; ☺ noon-3pm Mon & Tue, noon-3pm & 6-8.30pm Wed-Sat, noon-5pm Sun; 🖭) Around the back of the Titanic Experience, with a huge deck overlooking the harbour, this is a stunning spot for something to eat. The menu lives up to the stylish glossy timber surrounds with posh versions of pub-grub classics such as fish and chips, bangers and mash, and steak with pepper sauce.

🍸 Drinking & Nightlife

Roaring Donkey   PUB
(☑ 021-481 1739; www.facebook.com/RoaringDonkeyCobh; Orilia Tce; ☺ 5-11.30pm Mon-Thu, to 12.30am Fri, 3pm-12.30am Sat, 3-11pm Sun) It's a steep walk from the seafront but the pay-off is plenty of craic – and often live music – at the wonderfully named Roaring Donkey (allegedly so called because former patrons' donkeys made their presence known outside). It's 500m north of Cobh Pier.

ℹ️ Information

Tourist Office (☑ 021-481 3301; www.visitcobh.com; Market House, Casement Sq; ☺ 9am-5pm Mon-Fri) Housed in the building with an archway through it, opposite the Titanic Experience.

ℹ️ Getting There & Away

Car By road, Cobh is 23km southeast of Cork, off the main N25 Cork–Rosslare road; Great Island is linked to the mainland via a causeway.
Ferry From Carrigaloe, 3.5km northwest of Cobh, the Passage West Ferry (p249) provides a handy shortcut to Passage West, 14km southeast of Cork city. The cross-river journey takes just five minutes. It's particularly useful if you're heading to or from the southern side of Cork city, or Kinsale, and want to skip the city traffic.
Train Hourly trains connect Cobh with Cork (€6, 25 minutes) via Fota.
Bus CobhConnect (www.cobhconnect.ie) buses run hourly from St Patrick's Quay in Cork to Park Rd in Cobh (uphill from St Colman's Cathedral; €4, 30 minutes).

Midleton & Around
POP 12,495

Aficionados of a particularly fine Irish whiskey will recognise the name Midleton, and the main reason to linger in this bustling market town is to visit the old Jameson whiskey distillery, along with a meal at one of the town's famously good restaurants. The surrounding region is full of pretty villages, craggy coastlines and heavenly rural hotels such as Ballymaloe House (p242).

👁 Sights

Jameson Experience   MUSEUM
(☑ 021-461 3594; www.jamesonwhiskey.com; Old Distillery Walk; tours adult/child €22/11; ☺ shop 10am-6pm; 🅿) Coachloads pour in to tour this restored 200-year-old distillery building. Exhibits and 75-minute tours (run between 10am and 4pm) explain the process of taking barley and creating whiskey (Jameson is today made in a modern factory in Cork). There's a well-stocked gift shop, and the **Malt House Restaurant** (open noon to 3pm) has live music on Sundays.

🛌 Sleeping

There are some good places to stay in town, but most visitors overnight in Cork city or

THE GOURMET HEARTLAND OF BALLYMALOE

Drawing up at wisteria-clad **Ballymaloe House** (📞 021-465 2531; www.ballymaloe.ie; Shanagarry; r from €280; 🅿 📶 ♨ 🐕) you know you've arrived somewhere special. The Allen family has been running this superb hotel and restaurant in the old family home for decades. Rooms are individually decorated with period furnishings and breakfast goodies include bread from their own bakery, eggs from the farm and honey from their own hives. The house is 12km southeast of Midleton, off the R629.

Myrtle Allen (1924–2018) was a legend in her own lifetime, acclaimed internationally for her near single-handed creation of fine Irish cooking. The menu at Ballymaloe House's celebrated restaurant (three-course lunch €45, five-course dinner €80, open 1pm to 2pm and 7pm to 9.30pm) changes daily to reflect the availability of produce from its own farms and other local sources. The hotel also runs wine and gardening weekends.

Nonresidents can get a taste of local produce at the **Ballymaloe Cafe** (📞 021-465 2032; www.ballymaloeshop.ie/ballymaloe-cafe; mains €8-14; ⏰ 10am-5pm) 🍴 , next door to the hotel. The always busy Cafe serves freshly prepared seasonal and organic produce from its own farms and gardens (and from elsewhere in County Cork), including tasty quiche, salads, open sandwiches and daily blackboard specials. The neighbouring shop (open 9am to 6pm) sells foodstuffs, kitchenware, crafts and gifts.

TV personality Darina Allen, daughter-in-law of the late Myrtle Allen, runs the famous **Ballymaloe Cookery School** (📞 021-464 6785; www.ballymaloecookeryschool.com; Shanagarry). Darina's own daughter-in-law, Rachel Allen, is also a high-profile TV chef and author, and regularly teaches at the school. Demonstrations cost €75; lessons, from half-day sessions (€95 to €145) to 12-week certificate courses (€12,595), are often booked out well in advance. It's 3km east of Ballymaloe House. For overnight students, there are pretty cottages amid the 40 hectares of grounds.

head for one of the lovely country-house hotels in the nearby countryside.

An Stór Midleton Townhouse
B&B €

(📞 021-463 3106; www.anstortownhouse.com; Drury's Lane; s/d/f from €50/70/116; 🅿 📶) Housed in a former wool store, this place straddles the boundary between upmarket hostel and budget guesthouse, offering competitively priced accommodation in bright, recently redecorated rooms. Family rooms have a double bed and either two or four bunk beds. Breakfast is provided, and there's a self-catering kitchen too. The location is bang in the town centre.

Oatencake Lodge B&B
B&B €€

(📞 021-463 1232; www.oatencakelodge.com; Cork Rd; s/d €50/90; 🅿 📶) This suburban villa offers superb-value accommodation in crisp, clean, Ikea-furnished bedrooms. The owners are warm and welcoming, and ready with advice on the local area. It's a 10-minute walk into Midleton town centre, and there's a bus stop at the door for travel into Cork city.

✕ Eating

Midleton was one of the hotbeds of Cork's 'eat local' food scene that emerged in the last decades of the 20th century, pioneered by the late Myrtle Allen of nearby Ballymaloe House and championed by the original Farmgate Restaurant – parent of the more famous Farmgate Cafe in Cork city's English Market – and by one of Ireland's oldest farmers markets.

BiteSize
BAKERY €

(📞 021-463 6456; www.bitesize.ie; 35 Main St; snacks €2-5; ⏰ 8am-6pm Mon-Sat, 9am-6pm Sun; 📶 ♿) This artisan bakery in the middle of the high street is the ideal place to start the day with a Danish pastry served Scandi-style (ie with a luxurious dollop of whipped cream) and a perfectly poured cappuccino. For lunch you'll find soups, sandwiches and savoury tarts, plus cakes galore to take away.

★ Farmgate Restaurant
IRISH €€

(📞 021-463 2771; www.farmgate.ie; Broderick St; mains lunch €13-20, dinner €20-30; ⏰ 9am-5pm Tue-Sat, 5.30-9.30pm Thu-Sat) 🍴 The original, sister establishment to Cork city's Farmgate Cafe (p232), the Midleton restaurant offers the same superb blend of traditional and modern Irish cuisine. Squeeze through the deli (open 9am to 6pm Tuesday to Saturday) selling amazing baked goods and local produce to the subtly lit, art-clad, 'farmhouse shed' cafe-restaurant, where you'll eat as well as you would anywhere in Ireland.

Greenroom
CAFE €€

(☑021-463 9682; www.sagerestaurant.ie/green room; 8 Main St; mains €9-16; ☺9am-9pm Tue-Thu, to 10pm Fri & Sat, 11am-7pm Sun; 🛜☑🖢) ⌀ Tucked behind the Sage restaurant, this cafe is one of the town's social hubs, with a popular breakfast menu (excellent poached eggs on sourdough toast) and a convivial outdoor courtyard bar where you can enjoy a drink or two before tucking into gourmet burgers, chicken wings or fish and chips.

Sage
IRISH €€€

(☑021-463 9682; www.sagerestaurant.ie; 8 Main St; mains €21-29; ☺5.30-9pm Tue-Thu, to 9.30pm Fri, noon-3pm & 5.30-9.30pm Sat, noon-3.30pm & 4.30-8.30pm Sun) ⌀ Stylish modern decor set off with polished wood and copper make an elegant setting for relaxed fine dining at this deservedly popular restaurant. Simple-sounding dishes such as homemade black pudding with egg yolk and mushroom, or beer-brined chicken breast with barley and smoked cheese, turn out to be colourful miniature works of art. Reservations strongly recommended.

🛍 Shopping

Midleton Farmers Market
MARKET

(Main St; ☺9am-1pm Sat) ⌀ Midleton's farmers market is one of Cork's oldest and best, with bushels of local produce on offer and producers who are happy to chat. It's behind the big roundabout at the north end of Main St.

ℹ Information

The **tourist office** (☑021-461 3702; www.ring ofcork.ie; Distillery Walk; ☺10am-5pm Mon-Fri Apr-Oct, to 4pm Nov-Mar) is by the entrance gate to the Jameson Experience.

ℹ Getting There & Away

Midleton is 20km east of Cork. The train station is 1.5km (20 minutes' walk) north of the Jameson Experience (p241). There are frequent trains from Cork (€6, 25 minutes, at least hourly).

There are also frequent buses from Cork bus station (€7.70, 30 minutes, every 15 to 45 minutes). You'll need a car to explore the surrounding area.

Youghal
POP 7965

The ancient seaport of Youghal (Eochaill; pronounced 'yawl'), at the mouth of the Blackwater River, has a rich history that may not be instantly apparent, especially if you coast past on the N25. In fact, even if you stop, it may just seem like a humdrum Irish market town. But take a little time and you'll sniff out some of its once-walled past and enjoy views of the wide Blackwater estuary.

The town was a hotbed of rebellion against the English in the 16th century, when Youghal was granted to Sir Walter Raleigh during the Elizabethan Plantation of Munster; he was mayor of Youghal in 1588-89 and he spent brief spells living here in his house, Myrtle Grove. Later, Oliver Cromwell wintered here in 1649 as he sought to drum up support for his war in England and quell insurgency among the pesky Irish.

◉ Sights & Activities

Youghal Heritage Centre, in the same building as the tourist office (p244), has an interesting exhibition on the town's history. Pick up a **Youghal Walking Trail** leaflet, which will guide you around the various historical sites.

Youghal has two Blue Flag **beaches**, ideal for building sandcastles modelled after the Clock Gate. Claycastle (2km) and Front Strand (1km) are both within walking distance of town, off the N25.

Clock Gate Tower
HISTORIC BUILDING

(☑024-20769; www.youghalclockgate.ie; 89 N Main St; tours adult/child €9.50/5; ☺11am-4pm daily Jun-Sep, Thu-Sat Mar-May & Oct) The curious Clock Gate straddles the middle of Youghal's main street. Built in 1777, it served as a town gate, clock tower and jail; several prisoners taken in the 1798 Rising were hanged from its windows. One-hour guided tours (tickets from the nearby tourist office) lead you through four floors of exhibits to a rooftop viewpoint while telling the tale of Youghal's colourful past.

Blackwater Cruises
BOATING

(☑087 988 9076; www.blackwatercruises.com; The Quays; adult/child €20/10; ☺Apr-Nov) Runs 90-minute cruises upstream from Youghal along the lovely Blackwater River, past ruined castles and abbeys as far as grand Ballynatray House.

🛏 Sleeping & Eating

★Roseville
B&B €€

(☑087 294 7178; www.rosevilleyoughal.com; New Catherine St; d from €118; 🛜) Despite being right in the middle of town, this B&B feels like a secret hideaway with its two luxurious guest suites beautifully furnished in modern

YOUGHAL TOWN WALK

Youghal's history is best understood through its landmarks. Heading along Main St from the south, the curious Clock Gate Tower (p243) was built in 1777, and served as a town gate, clock tower and jail; several prisoners taken in the 1798 Rising were hanged from its windows.

The beautifully proportioned Red House, on North Main St, was designed in 1706 by the Dutch architect Leuventhen, and features some Dutch Renaissance details. Across the road is the 15th-century tower house Tynte's Castle (North Main St; ⊘ closed to the public), which originally had a defensive riverfront position.

A few doors further along, at the side street leading to the church, are six almshouses built by Englishman Richard Boyle, who bought Walter Raleigh's Irish estates and became the first Earl of Cork in 1616 in recognition of his work in creating 'a very excellent colony'.

Built in 1220, St Mary's Collegiate Church incorporates elements of an earlier Danish church dating back to the 11th century. The Earl of Desmond and his troops, rebelling against English rule, demolished the chancel roof in the 16th century.

Hidden behind high walls to the north of the church, 15th- to 18th-century Myrtle Grove (not open to the public) is the former home of Raleigh, and a rare Irish example of a late medieval Tudor-style house.

The churchyard is bounded to the west by a fine stretch of the old town wall – follow the parapet until you can descend stairs to the outer side, then enter the next gate along to descend back to Main St through the 17th-century College Gardens, now restored and in use as a public park.

style with country farmhouse touches, and opening onto a private walled garden. Sumptuous breakfasts include eggs all ways, and fruit and vegetable smoothies.

Aherne's Townhouse   INN €€
(☑ 024-92424; www.ahernes.net; 163 North Main St; d/f from €145/200; @ 🕏) The 12 rooms here are extremely well appointed; larger ones have small balconies, where you can breathe in the sea air. Rates include a fabulous breakfast (fresh-squeezed OJ, free-range eggs, locally caught fish) that will keep you going all day. The establishment includes an upmarket seafood restaurant and a stylish, cosy bar.

Sage Cafe   CAFE €
(☑ 024-85844; www.facebook.com/sagecafe youghal; 86 North Main St; mains €7-14; ⊘ 9.30am-5.30pm Mon-Sat; 🖉) 🕏 Everything at this luscious little cafe is homemade: cod and chips, lentil-and-nut loaf, quiche, cakes and more. Vegetarians in particular will be in heaven.

**Aherne's Seafood
Bar & Restaurant**   SEAFOOD €€
(☑ 024-92424; www.ahernes.net; 163 North Main St; bar meals €14-25, restaurant mains €29-34; ⊘ bar meals noon-9.30pm, restaurant 6.30-9.30pm; 🕏🖩) Three generations of the same family have run the award-winning Aherne's. Seafood is the star, but there are also plenty of meat and poultry

dishes. Besides the upmarket restaurant there's a cosy bar, all mahogany and polished brass, where you can enjoy fresh local seafood with wine by the glass. Kids' menu available.

ⓘ Information

Tourist Office (☑ 024-20170; www.youghal.ie; Market Sq; ⊘ 9am-5pm daily May-Sep, to 4pm Mon-Fri Oct-Apr) Housed in an attractive old market house on the waterfront, down from the clock tower, the Youghal Visitor Centre has tourist info, a small heritage centre and free town maps.

ⓘ Getting There & Away

Bus Éireann (p235) runs services to Cork (€13, 50 minutes, hourly) and Waterford (€19, 1½ hours, hourly).

KINSALE TO CAPE CLEAR

The West Cork coast begins the slow build-up of beauty that culminates in counties further west and north, but what you find here is already lovely. Picturesque villages, ancient stone circles and some fine sandy beaches mark the meandering coastal route from Kinsale to Clonakilty and on to Skibbereen and Baltimore. Rather than follow the main N71 all the way, take the R600 and explore the maze of minor roads along the coast – perfect for aimless wandering.

Kinsale

POP 5280

The picturesque yachting harbour of Kinsale (Cionn tSáile) is one of many colourful gems strung along the coastline of County Cork. Narrow, winding streets lined with galleries and gift shops, lively bars and superb restaurants, and a handsome natural harbour filled with yachts and guarded by a huge 17th-century fortress, make it an engrossing place to spend a day or two.

History

Granted a royal charter by the English King Edward II in 1334, Kinsale became a major port trading in wine and salt throughout the 15th century, and was also a provisioning port for the English navy.

In September 1601 English ships besieged a Spanish fleet anchored at Kinsale. Irish forces, which had appealed to the Spanish king to help them against the English, marched the length of the country to liberate the ships, but were defeated in the **Battle of Kinsale** on Christmas Eve. For the Catholic Irish, the immediate consequence was that they were banned from Kinsale; it would be another 100 years before they were allowed back in. Historians now cite 1601 as the beginning of the end of Gaelic Ireland.

After 1601 the town developed as a naval harbour, ship-building port and garrison town. In the early 18th century Alexander Selkirk departed from Kinsale Harbour on a voyage that left him stranded on a desert island, providing Daniel Defoe with the inspiration for *Robinson Crusoe*.

The town is also associated with the sinking of the *Lusitania* on 7 May 1915 off the Old Head of Kinsale – some of the bodies were brought ashore and buried here (many more are in Cobh), and the inquest into the disaster took place in Kinsale Courthouse. A memorial stands near the Old Head Signal Tower, which houses a Lusitania Museum.

◉ Sights

★ **Charles Fort** FORT
(☑ 021-477 2263; www.heritageireland.ie; Summercove; adult/child €5/3; ⊘ 10am-6pm mid-Mar–Oct, to 5pm Nov–mid-Mar; ℗) One of Europe's best-preserved star-shaped artillery forts, this vast 17th-century fortification would be

worth a visit for its spectacular views alone. But there's much more here: the 18th- and 19th-century ruins inside the walls make for some fascinating wandering. It's 3km southeast of Kinsale along the minor road through Scilly; if you have time, hike there along the lovely coastal Scilly Walk (p247).

Built in the 1670s to guard Kinsale Harbour, the fort was in use until 1921, when much of it was destroyed as the British withdrew. Displays explain the typically tough lives led by the soldiers who served here and the comparatively comfortable lives of the officers.

Old Head Signal Tower & Lusitania Museum MUSEUM
(☑ 021-419 1285; www.oldheadofkinsale.com; Signal Tower, Old Head of Kinsale; adult/concession €5/3.50; ⊘ 10am-6pm daily Easter-Oct, Sat & Sun only Mar-Easter; ℗) This 200-year-old signal tower houses a museum dedicated to the RMS *Lusitania*, which was torpedoed by a German U-boat in 1915 with the loss of 1200 lives. You can walk to the nearby clifftops for impressive views south towards the Old Head, the nearest point of land to the disaster; a privately owned golf club (p247) prevents you from reaching the lighthouse at the tip of the headland. The tower is 13km south of town via the R604.

Desmond Castle CASTLE
(☑ 021-477 4855; www.heritageireland.ie; Cork St; adult/child €5/3; ⊘ 10am-6pm Apr-Sep) Kinsale's roots in the wine trade are on display at this early-16th-century fortified house that was occupied by the Spanish in 1601. Since then it has served as a customs house, a prison for French and American captives, and a workhouse during the Famine. There are lively exhibits detailing its history, and a small wine museum that tells the story of the Irish wine-trading families, including names such as Hennessy (of brandy fame), who fled to France because of British rule.

Courthouse & Regional Museum MUSEUM
(☑ 021-477 7930; Market Sq; suggested donation €3; ⊘ 10am-2pm Tue-Sat Apr-Oct) Based in the 17th-century courthouse that was used for the inquest into the sinking of the *Lusitania*, this eclectic museum contains local curiosities as diverse as Michael Collins' hurley (hurling stick), and shoes belonging to the 8ft-tall Kinsale Giant, Patrick Cotter O'Brien (1760–1806).

St Multose Church CHURCH
(Church of Ireland Church; ☑ rectory 021-477 2220; www.kinsale.cork.anglican.org; Church St) This is

Kinsale

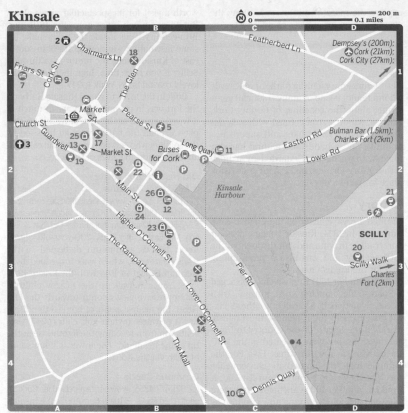

Kinsale

◉ Sights
1 Courthouse & Regional
   Museum...................................A1
2 Desmond Castle...............................A1
3 St Multose Church............................A2

✤ Activities, Courses & Tours
4 Kinsale Harbour Cruises..................C4
5 Mylie Murphy's...............................B2
6 Scilly Walk......................................D2

🛏 Sleeping
7 Cloisters B&B..................................A1
8 Giles Norman Townhouse................B3
9 Old Presbytery...............................A1
10 Olde Bakery....................................C4
11 Perryville House..............................C2
12 Pier House......................................B2

✖ Eating
13 Bastion...A2
14 Black Pig Wine Bar.........................B4
15 Finn's Table...................................B2
16 Fishy Fishy Cafe.............................B3
17 Leona's@Nine Market Street...........A2
18 OHK Cafe.......................................B1

🍸 Drinking & Nightlife
19 Folk House.....................................A2
20 Harbour Bar...................................D3
21 Spaniard Bar..................................D2

🛍 Shopping
22 Farmers Market..............................B2
23 Giles Norman Gallery......................B3
24 Granny's Bottom Drawer.................B2
25 Kinsale Crystal...............................A2
26 Koko Kinsale..................................B2

one of the country's oldest Church of Ireland
churches, built around 1190 by the Normans
on the site of a 6th-century church. Not

much of the interior is original, but the exterior is beautifully preserved. Inside, a flat
stone carved with a round-handed figure was

traditionally rubbed by fishermen's wives to bring their husbands home safe from the sea. Several victims of the *Lusitania* sinking are buried in the graveyard.

🏃 Activities

Scilly Walk   WALKING
You haven't 'done' Kinsale till you've done Scilly Walk, a lovely coastal trail that leads out to Charles Fort (p245). Follow Lower Rd to the Spaniard Bar (p249), descend to the waterfront and follow the harbourside path until it climbs to join High Rd. Descend to the Bulman Bar (p249) for a pint before climbing up to the fort.

Return along High Rd – this is Kinsale's 'Golden Mile', lined with millionaires' holiday homes and superb views over the harbour (round trip 6km).

Old Head Golf Links   GOLF
(☑021-477 8444; www.oldhead.com; Old Head of Kinsale; green fees €200-350) This exclusive golf resort is magnificently situated on a clifftop promontory 15km south of Kinsale via the R600 and R604. The remains of De Courcy castle frame the entrance, and the fifth tee is perched beside the iconic black-and-white striped Old Head lighthouse; beside the sixth green you'll see its predecessor, a ruined 17th-century lighthouse.

Mylie Murphy's   FISHING
(☑021-477 2703; 14 Pearse St; ⏰9.30am-6pm Mon-Sat) You can rent fishing rods here for €10 per day and bikes for €15 a day.

👉 Tours

Kinsale Food Tours   FOOD & DRINK
(☑085 107 6113; www.kinsalefoodtours.com; €60) These 2½-hour guided tours of Kinsale combine a bit of local history and folklore with tasting stops at a range of eateries, and chats with local food producers and restaurateurs. Must be booked at least 48 hours in advance.

Dermot Ryan's Heritage Town Walks   WALKING
(☑021-477 2729; www.kinsaleheritage.com; adult/child €5/free; ⏰10.30am) One-hour walking tours with entertaining storyteller Dermot Ryan depart from the tourist office (p250); tours starting at 3pm can be arranged by appointment.

Kinsale Harbour Cruises   BOATING
(☑086 250 5456; www.kinsaleharbourcruises.com; Pier Rd; adult/child €13/5; ⏰Mar-Oct) Runs boat trips to Charles Fort, James Cove and up the River Bandon. Departure times vary through the year and are weather dependent – check the website or with the tourist office (p250) for details. Boats leave from the slip beside the marina.

✨ Festivals & Events

Kinsale Regatta   SAILING
(www.facebook.com/KinsaleRegatta; ⏰Aug) The August Bank Holiday weekend sees Ireland's oldest regatta take place (it was first held in 1796). Three days of events include yacht races, children's dinghy racing, a long-distance swim and a range of land-based entertainment.

Kinsale Gourmet Festival   FOOD & DRINK
(www.kinsalerestaurants.com; ⏰Oct) Three days of tastings, cookery demonstrations and competitions kick off with the Cork Heat of the All-Ireland seafood chowder cook-off (the final takes place in Kinsale in April).

Kinsale Fringe Jazz Festival   MUSIC
(www.kinsale.ie/events; ⏰Oct) An offshoot of the Cork Jazz Festival (p227), with chilled-out entertainment at around 20 venues in town over the October bank-holiday weekend.

🛏 Sleeping

Dempsey's   HOSTEL €
(☑021-477 2124; www.dempseyhostel.com; Eastern Rd; dm €15-25, f €60-100; 🛜) This basic hostel is nothing special, but it's the town's cheapest option, with separate male and female dorms, family rooms, a kitchen, and picnic tables in the front garden. It's the bright-blue house by the petrol station on the R600 road from Cork, 750m northeast of the centre.

★ Pier House   B&B €€
(☑021-477 4169; www.pierhousekinsale.com; Pier Rd; d €100-140; 🅿🛜) Set back from the road in a sheltered garden, this is a lovely place to rest your head. Pristine rooms, decorated with shell-and-driftwood sculptures, have black-granite bathrooms with power showers and underfloor heating; four open to balconies with garden and harbour views.

Giles Norman Townhouse   GUESTHOUSE €€
(☑021-477 4373; www.gilesnorman.com/townhouse; 45 Main St; ⏰r from €150; 🛜) Upstairs from the Giles Norman Gallery (p249) (where you check in) are these plush, luxurious guest rooms in shades of grey and white that set off perfectly the photographic prints created by the eponymous owner; the rooftop Studio

suite (€230) is the pick of the lot. Perks include espresso machines, elegant bathrooms with organic toiletries, and discounted gallery purchases. Breakfast not provided.

Cloisters B&B
B&B €€

(☑ 021-470 0680; www.cloisterskinsale.com; Friars St; s/d from €60/110; ☜) Little touches make the difference at this blue-shuttered B&B near Desmond Castle. Chocolates await your arrival, rooms are squeaky-clean, and the orthopaedic mattresses are so comfy that only the creative breakfasts will tempt you out of bed.

Olde Bakery
B&B €€

(☑ 021-477 3012; www.theoldebakerykinsale.com; 56 Lower O'Connell St; r from €100; ☜) A short walk southeast of the centre is this very friendly place that was once the British garrison bakery. Rooms are a reasonable size and terrific breakfasts around the kitchen table get everyone chatting.

★ Old Presbytery
B&B €€€

(☑ 021-477 2027; www.oldpres.com; 43 Cork St; r from €175; ☺ closed Jan–mid-Feb; P ☜) ✐ The 18th-century Old Presbytery has glided gracefully into the 21st century with a painstaking refurbishment that has maintained its character while incorporating solar heating. Choose the deluxe double only if you have no plans to see anything of Kinsale: with its sunroom and balcony, you'll never want to leave. The organic breakfasts, cooked by landlord and former chef Phillip, are the stuff of legend.

Perryville House
BOUTIQUE HOTEL €€€

(☑ 021-477 2731; www.perryvillehouse.com; Long Quay; r from €250; ☺ closed Nov-Feb; P ☜) It's top-to-bottom grandeur at family-run Perryville, whether you're pulling up outside its imposing wrought iron–balconied facade or taking afternoon tea in the drawing room. All the rooms exude comfort; move up the rate card and the beds go from queen to king, and balconies and sea views appear.

✕ Eating

Kinsale has been labelled the gourmet centre of southwest Ireland, and for such a small place it certainly packs more than its fair share of international-standard restaurants. Most are situated near the harbour and within easy walking distance of the town centre, and you can eat well on any budget.

OHK Cafe
CAFE €

(O'Herlihy's; ☑ 087 950 2411; www.oherlihys kinsale.com; The Glen; mains €6-12; ☺ 9am-3.30pm

Tue-Sat, 10am-4pm Sun; ☑ ☺) The black sheep of Kinsale's cafe family, OHK occupies an artfully distressed dining room and serves a Mediterranean-inspired menu that includes off-the-beaten-track breakfast options such as Portuguese sardines, or Serrano ham and Manchego cheese on sourdough toast. Lunchtime salad plates are both hearty and healthy, with sides of hummus and pomegranate seed garnishes.

★ Black Pig Wine Bar
IRISH €€

(☑ 021-477 4101; www.facebook.com/theblackpig winebar; 66 Lower O'Connell St; mains €10-19; ☺ 5.30-11pm Wed, Thu & Sun, to 11.30pm Fri & Sat) ✐ This candlelit hideaway is set in an 18th-century coach house with a charming cobbled courtyard out the back, and offers a mouth-watering menu of gourmet nibbles, charcuterie platters and cheese boards sourced from artisan local suppliers. The award-winning wine list offers no fewer than 200 wines by the bottle and 100 by the glass, including many organic varieties. Reservations recommended.

Leona's@Nine Market Street
BISTRO €€

(☑ 021-470 9221; www.ninemarketstreet.ie; 9 Market St; mains €11-28; ☺ 10am-4pm Mon-Thu, to 9pm Fri & Sat, 11am-4pm Sun; ☑) Black-and-white floor tiles, warm golden wood and old photographs set the relaxed mood at this appealing little cafe-cum-bistro. Freshly prepared breakfasts and lunch dishes such as Thai fish cakes, falafel salads and soups are complemented by daily specials such as a Wagyu beef burger. There are three comfy, good-value guest bedrooms upstairs (double from €70).

★ Finn's Table
MODERN IRISH €€€

(☑ 021-470 9636; www.finnstable.com; 6 Main St; mains €30-40; ☺ 6-10pm Mon, Tue & Thu-Sat) ✐ Owning a gourmet restaurant in Kinsale means plenty of competition, but John and Julie Finn's venture is more than up to the challenge. Elegant but unstuffy, Finn's Table offers a warm welcome, and its menu of seasonal, locally sourced produce rarely fails to please. Seafood (including lobster when in season) is from West Cork, while meat is from the Finn family's butchers.

★ Bastion
MODERN IRISH €€€

(☑ 021-470 9696; www.bastionkinsale.com; cnr Main & Market Sts; mains €18-35; ☺ 5-10pm Wed-Sun; ☑) ✐ Holder of a Michelin Bib Gourmand since 2016, this place offers diners a relaxed and informal entry into the world of haute cuisine. Waitstaff will guide you through the concise à la carte menu of local oysters, beef, fish and venison, but it's best to go for the seven-course tasting menu (€78) or the five-course early-bird menu (pre-6pm; €58).

★ **Fishy Fishy Cafe**   SEAFOOD €€€
(☑ 021-470 0415; www.fishyfishy.ie; Crowley's Quay; mains €20-28; ☺ noon-9pm Mar-Oct, shorter hours rest of year) ✎ One of the most famous seafood restaurants in the country, Fishy Fishy has a wonderful setting with stark white walls splashed with bright artwork and striking steel fish sculptures, and a terrific decked terrace at the front. All the fish is caught locally, and dishes include lobster thermidor, gourmet fish pie, and a surf'n'turf tapas menu.

Drinking & Nightlife

★ **Folk House**   BAR
(☑ 021-477 2382; www.facebook.com/folkhouse kinsale; Guardwell; ☺ 4.30pm-midnight Mon-Fri, 12.30pm-12.30am Sat & Sun) A rustic huddle of cosy nooks makes the Folk House an inviting spot to settle down by the fire with your choice of craft beers from around the world, or to stand at the bar and soak up the craic. From Thursday to Sunday there's a swirl of live music, which could be anything from indie or ska to folk or traditional Irish.

Spaniard Bar   PUB
(☑ 021-477 2436; www.thespaniard.ie; River Rd, Scilly; ☺ 10.30am-11.30pm Mon-Thu, to 12.30am Fri & Sat, 12.30-11.30pm Sun) The food is good, but the real appeal of this old pub (it feels like it dates back to the Armada) lies in the quiet corners where you can smell the peat fire and catch fragments of hushed conversations, and, on sunny days, the outdoor tables with views across the harbour.

Bulman Bar   PUB
(☑ 021-477 2131; www.thebulman.ie; Summercove; ☺ 12.30-11.30pm Mon-Thu, to 12.30am Fri & Sat, to 11pm Sun; ☎) ✎ Escape from central Kinsale to this harbourside gastropub in the picturesque hamlet of Summercove, where salty informality is a style in its own right. Sip chilled white wine at outdoor tables or sup beers and seafood chowder in the wood-panelled interior. It's 2km southeast of Kinsale town centre, on the way to Charles Fort. No food on Mondays.

Harbour Bar   PUB
(Scilly Walk, Scilly; ☺ 6-11.30pm, hours may vary) It might look permanently closed from the outside, but inside it's like being in someone's

front room (actually, it *is* someone's front room! Tim, the landlord's). Battered old sofas, a fire stoked in the hearth, characters in every corner and garden benches with harbour views are all part of the charm. Serves bottled drinks only.

Shopping

Farmers Market   MARKET
(☑ 085 722 0259; www.facebook.com/kinsale farmersmarket; Short Quay; ☺ 10am-2pm Wed) ✎ Sets up on the wee square across from the tourist office; this is the place to buy artisan foods straight from the producer.

Giles Norman Gallery   ART
(☑ 021-477 4373; www.gilesnorman.com; 45 Main St; ☺ 10am-6pm) Evocative black-and-white landscape photographs of Ireland from a master of the genre. Prints start at €20 unframed and €30 framed.

Granny's Bottom Drawer   HOMEWARES
(☑ 021-477 4839; www.grannysbottomdrawer.com; 53 Main St; ☺ 9am-9pm Mon-Fri, to 7pm Sat & Sun May-Sep, 10am-6pm daily Oct-Mar) Top-quality Irish linen, woollens, leather goods, damask, furniture and vintage-style homewares.

Kinsale Crystal   GLASS
(☑ 021-477 4493; www.kinsalecrystal.ie; Market St; ☺ 9am-5.30pm Mon-Fri, 10am-6pm Sat, noon-6pm Sun) Exquisite work by an ex-Waterford craftsperson who stands by the traditional 'deep-cutting, high-angle' style. A million tiny sparkles greet you as you enter.

Koko Kinsale   CHOCOLATE
(☑ 087 611 0209; www.kokokinsale.com; Pier Rd; ☺ 9am-5pm Mon-Sat, noon-5pm Sun) Handmade chocolates and crystallised orange and ginger are among the enticing wares at this artisan chocolatier.

> ⓘ **PASSAGE WEST FERRY**
> ●●●●●●●●●●●●●●●●●●●●●●●●●●●●●●●●●●●●●●
> From Carrigaloe, 3.5km northwest of Cobh, the **Passage West Ferry** (☑ 021-481 1485; www.crossriverferries.ie; pedestrian/cyclist/car one way €1.50/1.50/6; ☺ 6.30am-9.30pm) provides a handy shortcut to Passage West, 14km southeast of Cork city. The cross-river journey takes just five minutes. It's particularly useful if you're heading to or from the southern side of Cork city, or Kinsale, and want to skip the city traffic.

COUNTY CORK KINSALE

ℹ Information

Tourist Office (☏ 021-477 2234; www.kinsale.
ie; cnr Pier Rd & Emmet Pl; ⊙ 9.15am-5pm
Tue-Sat year-round, 9.15am-5pm Mon Apr-Oct,
10am-5pm Sun Jul & Aug) Has a good map
detailing walks in and around Kinsale.

ℹ Getting There & Around

Bus Éireann (☏ 021-450 8188; www.buseireann.
ie) service 226 connects Kinsale with Cork bus
station (€9.50, one hour, hourly) via Cork Airport, and continues to Cork train station. The bus
stop is on Pier Rd, near the tourist office.

Kinsale Cabs (☏ 021-477 2642; www.kinsale
cabs.com; Market Sq) A taxi from Cork Airport
to Kinsale can cost from €35 to €45. Also
arranges golfing tours of West Cork.

You can rent bikes from Mylie Murphy's (p247)
for €15 a day.

Clonakilty

POP 4590

Cheerful, brightly painted Clonakilty is a
bustling market town which serves as a
hub for the scores of beguiling little coastal
villages that surround it. You'll find smart
B&Bs, good restaurants and cosy pubs
alive with music. Little waterways coursing
through town add to the charm.

Clonakilty is famous for two things: it's the
birthplace of Irish Free State commander-
in-chief Michael Collins, embodied in a large
statue on the corner of Emmet Sq; and it's
the home of the most famous black pudding
in the country.

Roads converge on Astna Sq, dominated by a 1798 Rising monument. Also in
the square is the Kilty Stone, a piece of the
original castle that gave Clonakilty (Cloich
na Coillte in Irish, meaning 'castle of the
woods') its name.

IRELAND'S BEST BLACK PUDDING

Clonakilty's most treasured export
is its black pudding, a sausage made
from pig's blood, oatmeal and onion
that features on most local restaurant
menus. The best place to buy it is from
butcher **Edward Twomey** (☏ 023-883
4835; www.clonakiltyblackpudding.ie; 16
Pearse St; ⊙ 9am-6pm Mon-Sat), who sells
different varieties based on an original
recipe from the 1880s.

◉ Sights

Clonakilty Distillery   DISTILLERY
(☏ 023-884 0635; www.clonakiltydistillery.ie; The
Waterfront; tours from €15; ⊙ noon-5.30pm Sun-Tue,
11am-6.30pm Wed-Sat; P👶) The state-of-the-
art Clonakilty Distillery opened its doors to
the public in 2019, producing triple-distilled
single pot still Irish whiskey made with grain
grown on the owners' family farm nearby.
There are three tours daily; book in advance
via the website.

**West Cork Model
Railway Village**   AMUSEMENT PARK
(☏ 023-883 3224; www.modelvillage.ie; Inchydoney Rd; adult/child incl road train tour €12/7.50;
⊙ 10am-6pm Jul-Aug, 11am-5pm Sep-Jun; P👶)
You can't help but smile at the West Cork
Model Railway Village. It features a vast
outdoor recreation of the West Cork Railway as it was during the 1940s, with superb
miniature models of the main towns in West
Cork. There's also a road train that provides
a 20-minute guided circuit of Clonakilty.

Inchydoney Beach   BEACH
(P) Inchydoney, signposted 5km south of
Clonakilty, has two gorgeous golden strands
either side of a rocky peninsula set on a
scenic inlet. You can rent surfboards on the
beach (€15 for two hours).

🛏 Sleeping

Bay View House   B&B €€
(☏ 023-883 3539; www.bayviewclonakilty.com; Old
Timoleague Rd; s/d from €55/90; P🛜) This spacious modern villa offers immaculate B&B
accommodation, a genial welcome and great
breakfasts. Rooms 5 and 6 and the cosy
landing lounge offer fantastic views over
fields that slope down to Clonakilty Bay. It
is 300m east of the town centre, just off the
main N71 roundabout into town.

Emmet Hotel   HOTEL €€
(☏ 023-883 3394; www.emmethotel.com; Emmet
Sq; d/f from €129/149; 🛜) This lovely Georgian
hotel on the elegant main square successfully mixes period charm and old-world service
with the perks of a modern hotel. The 20
rooms are large and plush; the on-site restaurant, bistro and bar all serve up tasty Irish
food made from organic and local ingredients.

O'Donovan's Hotel   INN €€
(☏ 023-883 3250; www.odonovanshotel.com;
Pearse St; s/d from €70/120; 🛜🍽) Behind a
vintage exterior beats the heart of a classic

old-fashioned hotel. Rooms are straightforward, but service is friendly and you can't beat the central location. A WWII plaque out the front will intrigue Americans in particular (it commemorates the crew of a crashed USAF Flying Fortress who stayed here in 1943).

★ **Inchydoney Island**
Lodge & Spa RESORT €€€
(☑ 023-883 3143; www.inchydoneyisland.com; Inchydoney; r from €210; @🅿️🛜🏊) A superb seawater spa is at the heart of this sprawling resort 5km south of Clonakilty, where the service is outstanding, the food at the French-inspired restaurant is delicious, and luxurious rooms overlook the ocean from private balconies and terraces.

🍴 Eating & Drinking

Lettercollum Kitchen Project DELI €
(☑ 023-883 6938; www.lettercollum.ie; 22 Connolly St; mains €4-10; ⊙ 10am-6pm Tue-Fri, to 5pm Sat) 🍃 This busy artisan bakery and deli turns out fresh breads, savoury tarts, pastries and pies daily, and also serves salads and hot dishes such as Thai curry and vegetable lasagne. Pick your pastries then order prepared dishes at the counter; there's barely space for six people to sit down, so plan on guzzling your goodies elsewhere.

Hart's Coffee Shop CAFE €
(☑ 023-883 5583; www.hartscafeclonakilty.com; 8 Ashe St; mains €7-11; ⊙ 10am-5.30pm Mon-Sat; 🛜) This welcoming cafe is a popular meeting place, serving hearty breakfasts, excellent coffee and a tempting selection of hot lunch dishes that include curried squash and sweet potato soup, club sandwiches, beef and chorizo stew and homemade fish cakes.

★ **Scannells** MODERN IRISH €€
(☑ 023-883 4116; www.scannellsbar.com; Connolly St; mains €12-16; ⊙ food served noon-4pm Mon-Sat; 🛜) The sheltered, flower-filled garden at this gastropub is absolutely hopping, rain or shine, thanks to an ambitious menu that ranges from superb West Cork steak sandwich with hand-cut chips (or salad), to trad seafood chowder and organic salads with halloumi, chia seeds and toasted almonds.

★ **De Barra's Folk Club** PUB
(☑ 023-883 3381; www.debarra.ie; 55 Pearse St; tickets free-€25; ⊙ 10am-11.45pm Mon-Thu, to 12.30am Fri & Sat, noon-11.30pm Sun) A convivial, jostling atmosphere – with walls splattered

MICHAEL COLLINS

Born on a farm just outside Clonakilty, Michael Collins is one of County Cork's most famous sons. He played a central role in the War of Independence with Britain, and in 1922 became commander-in-chief of the army of the newly founded Irish Free State.

The useful map and leaflet *In Search of Michael Collins*, available at the Clonakilty tourist office (p251), outlines places in the district associated with him; you can dig deeper into his life at the **Michael Collins Centre** (☑ 023-884 6107; www.michaelcollinscentre.com; Castleview; adult/child €5/3; ⊙ 10.30am-5pm Mon-Fri, 11am-2pm Sat mid-Jun–mid-Sep; 🅿️).

A visit to the Michael Collins Centre (p251) is an excellent way to make sense of his life and the times in which he lived. A tour reveals photos, letters and a reconstruction of the 1920s country lane where Collins was killed, complete with armoured vehicle. The centre runs tours of the crucial locations in Collins' life (book in advance). It's signposted off the R600 between Timoleague and Clonakilty.

with photos and press cuttings, dramatic masks and musical instruments – provides the setting for the cream of local folk music and one of Ireland's top trad venues. Nightly sessions usually begin around 9pm.

🛍 Shopping

Etain Hickey ARTS & CRAFTS
(☑ 023-882 1479; www.facebook.com/EtainHickey Collections; 40 Ashe St; ⊙ 10.30am-6pm Tue-Sat, hours may vary) A treasure trove of Irish-made and designed art and crafts, including Fair Trade gifts, unusual jewellery, and ceramics made by Ms Hickey herself.

Farmers Market MARKET
(☑ 087 135 6848; www.facebook.com/clonmarket; Pearse St; ⊙ 9am-3pm Fri) 🍃 Clonakilty's compact farmers market combines local produce with hot-food stalls. It sets up in a car park, down an alley beside O'Donovan's Hotel.

ℹ Information

The **tourist office** (☑ 023-883 3226; www. clonakilty.ie; Ashe St; ⊙ 9am-1.30pm & 2-5pm Mon-Thu & Sat) is towards the east end of the main street, in the centre of town.

DROMBEG STONE CIRCLE

On an exposed hillside, with fields falling away towards the coast and cattle lowing in the distance, the **Drombeg Stone Circle** (⊙24hr; P) FREE is superbly atmospheric. Its 17 stones, oriented towards the winter solstice sunset, once guarded the cremated bones of an adolescent. The 9m-diameter circle probably dates from the 5th century AD, and is a sophisticated Iron Age update of an earlier Bronze Age monument. To get here, take the signposted turn off the R597, approximately 4km west of Rosscarbery.

Just beyond the stones are the remains of a hut and an Iron Age cooking pit, known as a *fulachta fiadh*. Experiments have shown that its heated rocks would boil water and keep it hot for nearly three hours – long enough to cook meat.

ℹ Getting There & Around

There are buses to Cork (€14, 1¼ hours, seven daily) and Skibbereen (€11, 40 minutes, six daily). The bus stop is on Pearse St in the town centre.

MTM Cycles (☑ 023-883 3584; 33 Ashe St; ⊙8.30am-6pm Mon-Sat) hires out bikes for €10/50 per day/week. A nice ride is to Duneen Beach, about 13km south of town.

Glandore & Union Hall

POP 270

The picturesque waterside villages of Glandore (Cuan Dor) and Union Hall burst into life in summer when fleets of yachts race in the sheltered inlet of Glandore Harbour; in winter they are just quiet backwaters.

Union Hall, southwest of Glandore across a long, narrow causeway, was named after the 1801 Act of Union that abolished the separate Irish parliament. The 1994 film *War of the Buttons*, about two battling gangs of youngsters, was filmed here. There's an ATM, a post office and a general store.

Union Hall is famous as a fishing harbour, and as the home of **Union Hall Smoked Fish** (☑ 028-33125; www.unionhallsmokedfish.com; Main St, Union Hall; ⊙8.30am-5pm Mon-Fri), which produces excellent smoked salmon. There are two neighbouring pub-restaurants nearby in Glandore, both of which serve fresh local seafood with a fantastic view over the harbour.

🏃 Activities

Cork Whale Watch　　　WILDLIFE WATCHING
(☑086 327 3226; www.corkwhalewatch.com; Reen Pier; adult/child €50/40) Runs four-hour whale-watching cruises out of Reen Pier, 4km south of Union Hall: one trip daily year-round (weather dependent), two trips daily June to August. Cash only. Parking on right 200m before pier.

Atlantic Sea Kayaking　　　KAYAKING
(☑028-21058; www.atlanticseakayaking.com; Reen Pier; half-day from €50) Runs half- and full-day marine safaris by sea kayak from Reen Pier, 4km south of Union Hall. No previous experience needed. Also offers magical moonlight kayak tours on Castletownshend Bay and Lough Hyne (p254).

🛏 Sleeping & Eating

Bay View House　　　B&B €€
(☑028-33115; www.facebook.com/BayviewBedand breakfast; Main St, Glandore; s/d €50/80) Perched above the sea, Bay View House has seriously spectacular views across the bay. Try to snag Room 1 for the best panorama of all. Bright colours, tidy pine furniture and gleaming bathrooms add to the appeal, and Glandore's twin pub-restaurants are just a stumble away.

Shearwater B&B　　　B&B €€
(☑028-33178; www.shearwaterbandb.com; Keelbeg, Union Hall; r from €85; ⊙Apr-Oct; P 🕸) A warm welcome awaits at this bright and attractive B&B, just a short stroll east from the centre of Union Hall. Hearty breakfasts are served in a spacious sunroom, and on a terrace with killer views across the harbour; all of the five bedrooms share that gorgeous view.

★ Glandore Inn　　　PUB FOOD €€
(☑028-34494; www.glandoreinn.ie; Main St, Glandore; mains €12-25; ⊙noon-12.30am, food served till 9pm; 🕸) 🌿 Picture-postcard views over the harbour, especially from the outdoor tables, and a superlative menu make this one of West Cork's best pubs for eating out. Fresh seafood is sourced from Union Hall harbour (clearly visible across the water). The interior's rustic nautical charm has a contemporary edge, and there are Irish craft beers on tap.

Hayes Bar　　　PUB FOOD €€
(☑028-33214; www.facebook.com/hayesbarand kitchen; Main St, Glandore; mains €9-20; ⊙10am-11.30pm Mon-Sat, 11am-11pm Sun, food served noon-9pm, closed Nov; 🕸🌿) 🌿 This perfect

seaside pub has log fires in winter, and in summer tables spill out across the street to make the most of the harbour views. There's excellent pub grub on the menu. Standards such as seafood chowder, fish pie and boeuf bourguignon are complemented by more adventurous dishes like crab cannelloni and Mexican-inspired hake Veracruz.

ⓘ Getting There & Away

Six daily buses between Skibbereen (€4, 15 minutes) and Clonakilty (€7.60, 25 minutes) stop in nearby Leap (3km north), from where most B&B owners will pick you up if you arrange it in advance.

Skibbereen

POP 2780

Today Skibbereen (Sciobairín) is a pleasant, workaday market town, with an attractive, upmarket centre on the banks of the River Ilen.

During the Famine, however, Skibb was hit perhaps harder than any other town in Ireland, with huge numbers of the local population emigrating or dying of starvation or disease. 'The accounts are not exaggerated – they cannot be exaggerated – nothing more frightful can be conceived.' So wrote Lord Dufferin and GF Boyle, who journeyed from Oxford to Skibbereen in February 1847 to see if reports of the Famine were true. Their eyewitness account makes horrific reading; Dufferin was so appalled by what he saw that he contributed £1000 (about €100,000 in today's money) to the relief effort.

The main landmark in town is a statue in the central square, dedicated to heroes of Irish rebellions against the British.

⊙ Sights

Sky Garden GARDENS
(www.lissardestate.ie/skygarden; Liss Ard Estate; €5; ⊙noon-5pm specific days May-Aug; ℗) The Victorian country estate of Liss Ard is home to the remarkable Sky Garden, a piece of landscape art created by American artist James Turrell in 1992. You enter through a tunnel and emerge at the bottom of a grass-lined, oval crater, so that all you can see is sky. There's a plinth where two people can lie toe-to-toe and contemplate the heavens. Open days vary each year – check Liss Ard's Facebook page. The estate is 2km southeast of Skibbereen on the R596.

Skibbereen Heritage Centre MUSEUM
(☑028-40900; www.skibbheritage.com; Upper Bridge St; adult/child €6/3; ⊙10am-6pm Mon-Sat May-Sep, Tue-Sat mid-Mar–Apr & Oct, closed Nov–mid-Mar; ℗) Constructed on the site of the town's old gasworks, the Skibbereen Heritage Centre houses a haunting exhibition about the Famine, with actors reading heartbreaking contemporary accounts; a visit here puts Irish history into harrowing perspective. There's also a smaller exhibition about nearby Lough Hyne (p254), the first marine nature reserve in Ireland, plus a genealogical centre.

Festivals & Events

Taste of West Cork Food Festival FOOD & DRINK
(www.atasteofwestcork.com; ⊙Sep) If you're in town in mid-September, don't miss this foodie extravaganza, which includes a lively farmers market, cookery demonstrations, competitions, food-tastings, talks, exhibitions and children's events.

Sleeping & Eating

Top of the Rock Pod Pairc CAMPGROUND
(☑086 173 5134; www.topoftherock.ie; Drimoleague; tent site for car & 2 adults €20, pod from €59; ⊙year-round; 🕸) 🖋 This gorgeous campsite, 14km north of Skibbereen, is a haven of peace, its hilltop location offering grand views of the Mullaghmeesha hills. As well as tent sites and a couple of campervan pitches, there are seven comfortable camping pods and a cute two-person caravan. Goats, lambs, ducks and chickens wander freely, and the friendly owners light a communal campfire most nights.

Bridge House B&B €€
(☑028-21273; www.bridgehouseskibbereen.com; 46 Bridge St; s/d from €55/85; 🕸) Mona Best has turned her entire house into a work of art, filling the rooms with fabulous Victorian tableaux and period memorabilia. The whole place bursts at the seams with cherished clutter, crazed carvings, dressed-up dummies and fragrant fresh flowers; personalised service extends to champagne breakfasts for guests celebrating a birthday – not bad for a B&B!

West Cork Hotel HOTEL €€
(☑028-21277; www.westcorkhotel.com; Ilen St; r from €159; ℗🕸🐾) This stolid veteran has 30 comfortable, refurbished rooms in an attractive location next to the River Ilen. An old railway bridge across the river serves as an

LOUGH HYNE

This beautiful lough is one of Ireland's natural wonders, and became the country's first marine nature reserve in 1981. Its glacier-gouged depths were originally filled with fresh water until rising sea levels breached one end around 4000 years ago. It is now linked to the sea by a narrow tidal channel known as the Rapids, where the tide pours in and out twice a day in a rush of white water.

There are lovely walks along the loughside road and in the neighbouring **Knock-omagh Wood Nature Reserve**. A waymarked nature trail leads up a steep hill through the forest; you're rewarded with stunning views at the top.

Atlantic Sea Kayaking (p252) offers guided sea-kayak tours of the lough, including superbly atmospheric 2½-hour 'starlight paddles' after dark.

The lough is 6km northeast of Baltimore and 8km southwest of Skibbereen, signposted off the R595 between the two towns, and an easy bike ride from either.

outdoor terrace, and rooms at the back have pastoral views.

Antiquity Bookshop Cafe
VEGAN €

(☑ 085 756 9746; www.facebook.com/AntiquityCafe; 44 Bridge St; mains €6-12, dinner €18; ☺ 10am-4pm Tue-Sat, plus 6-10pm Fri; 🐾🍴) West Cork's first all-vegan eatery puts a lot of thought into its food, so you can expect more than just salad. Things like aromatic butterbean stew, or open sandwiches with stewed mushrooms and pesto. And the icing on the vegan cake? It's also a bookshop, with a huge selection of rare and secondhand books.

Kalbo's
INTERNATIONAL €

(☑ 028-21515; www.kalboscafe.com; 26 North St; mains €6-12; ☺ 9am-5pm Mon-Sat; 🐾🍴) 🍽 This place uses locally sourced produce and a deft hand in the kitchen to produce breakfast dishes such as vanilla pancakes with fresh berries, and lunch specials that include goat's cheese salad with caramelised pears, Castletownbere crab salad and more.

Glebe Gardens
BISTRO €€

(☑ 028-51948; www.glebegardens.com/skibbereen; 68 Bridge St; mains lunch €7-15, dinner €19-23; ☺ 10am-5pm Mon-Sat, 6-9pm Thu-Sat; 🅿🍴) 🍽 Whether lounging over breakfast in the sofas at the back, or enjoying a candlelit dinner, you can be sure that the food served here uses locally sourced produce where possible – many of the ingredients for inventive vegetarian dishes like spiced cauliflower with tahini yoghurt, pomegranate and dukkah come from the restaurant's own gardens (p255) near Baltimore.

Farmers Market
MARKET

(www.skibbereenmarket.com; The Fairfield, Bridge St; ☺ 9.30am-2pm Sat) 🍽 One of Ireland's biggest and liveliest farmers markets, a showcase for the best of West Cork food and drink; there's often live music laid on as well.

🛈 Getting There & Away

Bus Éireann (www.buseireann.ie) runs buses to Cork seven times daily Monday to Saturday, and five times on Sunday (€19, two hours). It also goes to Schull three times daily Monday to Saturday and once on Sunday (€7.60, 30 minutes).

Local Link Cork (www.locallinkcork.ie) operates a subsidised minibus service west to Bantry (€4, one hour, once daily Monday to Friday).

Baltimore

POP 323

Crusty old sea dog Baltimore is a classic maritime village with a long history, its busy little harbour full of fishing boats and pleasure yachts. The focus of life here is the central terrace overlooking the harbour, the ideal spot to sup a pint or slurp an ice cream while watching the boats go by. All around spreads a multitude of holiday cottages, catering to the summer swell of sailing folk, sea anglers, divers, and visitors to nearby Sherkin and Cape Clear Islands.

A white-painted landmark beacon (aka **Lot's Wife**) stands on the headland 2km southwest of town, marking the entrance to Baltimore Harbour and making a good objective for a pleasant walk, especially at sunset.

Baltimore's sheltered natural harbour has long been a favourite of mariners, and was best known in the 17th century as the haunt of pirates. The most famous date in its history is 20 June 1631, when the village was sacked by a fleet of Barbary pirates who carried off more than 100 prisoners to a life of slavery. The remaining villagers fled to

Skibbereen, and Baltimore lay abandoned for many decades afterwards.

Sights & Activities

Baltimore Castle
MUSEUM

(Dun na Sead; ✍028-20735; www.baltimorecastle. ie; adult/child €5/free; ⏰11am-6pm Mar-Oct) Baltimore harbour is dominated by the stone tower of 13th-century castle of Dun na Sead (Fort of the Jewels). Inside, the great hall houses seasonal art displays and exhibits on the town's and the castle's history, but the main attraction is the view from the battlements.

Baltimore Sea Safari
BOATING

(✍028-20753; www.baltimoreseasafari.ie; Ferry Pier) Trips in a fast rigid-hulled inflatable boat (RIB) along the West Cork coast to see sea cliffs and wildlife, including whales and dolphins; take a 20-minute harbour cruise (€10 per person) or a two-hour wildlife safari (€30). Cash or cheque only.

Aquaventures Dive Centre
DIVING

(✍028-20511; www.aquaventures.ie; Stone House B&B, Lifeboat Rd) This outfit leads half-day guided snorkelling tours (€45/35 per adult/child, including equipment) suitable for family groups (minimum age six years), exploring marine wildlife on the local coastline or at nearby Lough Hyne. It also offers 3½-hour sunset whale-watching boat trips out to Fastnet Rock (per person €40).

Festivals & Events

Baltimore Pirate Weekend
CULTURAL

(www.baltimore.ie/events; ⏰Jun) A long weekend of family-oriented fun, with boat trips, outdoor activities, treasure hunts, music and dancing, all in memory of a notorious event in Baltimore's history, when the port was attacked by Barbary pirates in 1631.

Seafood & Wooden Boat Festival
FOOD & DRINK

(www.baltimore.ie/events; ⏰May) A showcase for local restaurants and seafood producers. Jazz bands perform in the square and traditional wooden sailboats race around the harbour.

Fiddle Fair
MUSIC

(www.fiddlefair.com; ⏰2nd weekend of May) Sessions from international and local musicians.

Sleeping & Eating

Rolf's Country House
GUESTHOUSE €€

(✍028-20289; www.rolfscountryhouse.com; Baltimore Hill; s/d €110/160, cottages per week from €760; ⏰Apr-Oct; P🛜) Upmarket Rolf's, in a much-restored and extended old farmhouse in restful gardens on the upper fringes of town, does the lot: there are 10 smartly decorated private rooms, a clutch of two-bedroom self-catering cottages, helpful staff and a charming restaurant. The place is signposted from the R595 as you approach the village centre.

Casey's of Baltimore
HOTEL €€

(✍028-20197; www.caseysofbaltimore.com; Skibbereen Rd; r from €150; P@🛜) Ten of the 14 spiffy guest rooms here have estuary views, and all have huge beds. The hotel is right at the entrance to town (should you be arriving by chopper, there's a helipad). Food also comes with fantastic views, especially from the terrace. Seafood includes mussels fresh from the hotel's own shellfish farm in Roaringwater Bay.

Waterfront
HOTEL €€

(✍028-20600; www.waterfronthotel.ie; The Quay; s/d from €100/160; @🛜) Smack in the middle of town, this hotel has 13 bright and airy rooms; ask for one with a view of the sea. Its restaurant, the **Lookout** (Chez Youen; mains €20-40; ⏰6.30-9.30pm Wed-Mon Aug, Wed-Sat Jun, Jul & Sep, Fri & Sat May), also has equally splendid sea views and fresh seafood.

Glebe Gardens & Café
MODERN IRISH €€

(✍028-20579; www.glebegardens.com; Skibbereen Rd; mains €10-16; ⏰10am-5pm Wed-Sun Easter-Oct, Sat & Sun only Nov-Easter; P🛜) 🍴 The beautiful gardens here are an attraction in themselves (admission is €5). If you're dining, lavender and other herbs add fragrant aromas that waft over the tables inside and out. Food, sourced from the gardens and a list of local purveyors, is simple and fresh – eggs Florentine at breakfast, inspired sandwiches or a cheese and charcuterie platter at lunch.

★Mews
IRISH €€€

(✍028-20572; www.mewsrestaurant.ie; tasting menu €95; ⏰6.30-10.30pm Wed-Sat May-Sep) 🍴 Hidden away in an alley across from Baltimore Castle, this place looks like a top designer has reimagined an old fisherman's cottage. Similar creativity and attention to detail is lavished on the food – a carefully crafted palette of seasonal produce, local seafood, Irish cheeses and foraged herbs and seaweed – so much so that it was awarded a Michelin star in 2019. Book ahead.

WORTH A TRIP

FASTNET ROCK

Named 'Ireland's Teardrop' because it was the last sight of the 'ould country' for emigrants sailing to America, the Fastnet Rock is the most southerly point of Ireland.

This isolated fang of rock, topped by a spectacular lighthouse, stands 6.5km southwest of Cape Clear Island, and in good weather is visible from many places on the coastline from Baltimore to Mizen Head. Its image – usually with huge waves crashing around it – graces a thousand postcards, coffee-table books and framed art photographs.

The Fastnet lighthouse, widely considered the most perfectly engineered lighthouse in the world, was built in 1904 from ingeniously interlocked blocks of Cornish granite – there are exhibits about its construction at Mizen Head Visitor Centre (p259) and Cape Clear Heritage Centre.

From May to August, **Fastnet Tour** (☑ 028-39159; www.fastnettour.com; adult/family €40/90; ☺ May-Aug) operates boat trips to the rock (no landing), departing from Schull and Baltimore and travelling via Cape Clear Island. Tours are weather-dependent and last from 11am to 5pm.

Bushe's Bar   PUB
(☑ 028-20125; www.bushesbar.com; The Quay; sandwiches €3-11; ☺ noon-11pm) Seafaring paraphernalia drips from the ceiling at this genuinely character-filled old bar. The benches and tables outside on the main square are the best spots in town for a sundowner. Famous crab sandwiches are served when fresh crab has been landed at the quay.

❶ Information

There's an information board at the harbour, or check out www.baltimore.ie.

❶ Getting There & Away

Four buses daily Monday to Friday, and two on Saturday, link Skibbereen and Baltimore (€4.90, 20 minutes).

From June to August you can take a passenger ferry (p257) to Schull via Cape Clear Island (one-way fare €18); you can take a bike with you (€2 extra) and return by road, or stay overnight and return via Cape Clear the following day.

Cape Clear Island

POP 147

With its lonely inlets, pebble beaches, and gorse- and heather-clad cliffs, Cape Clear Island (Oileán Chléire) is an escapist's heaven – albeit one that is only 5km long and just over 1.5km wide at its broadest point. But that's just as well, as you'll want time to appreciate this small, rugged Gaeltacht (Irish-speaking) area, the southernmost inhabited island in the country.

Facilities are few (no banks or ATMs), but there's one small grocery store, two pubs and a restaurant, all within a few minutes

walk of the ferry, which docks in the bay on the north side of the island.

◉ Sights & Activities

Information boards near the harbour highlight a couple of marked walking trails, while unmarked roads wander all over the island. The remains of a 12th-century church and holy well are near the pier. On the coast to the west the ruins of 14th-century Dunamore Castle, the stronghold of the O'Driscoll clan, can be seen perched on a rock.

Cape Clear is one of the top birdwatching spots in Ireland, particularly known for seabirds including Manx shearwater, guillemot, gannet, fulmar and kittiwake. Tens of thousands of migrating birds can pass hourly, especially in the early morning and at dusk. The best time of year for twitching here is October. The bird observatory is in the white house by the harbour (turn right at the end of the pier and it's 100m along).

Mara Farm   FARM
(☑ 086 408 7665, 028-39121; www.marafarm.ie; ☺ 1-5pm Jun-Sep, hours vary) **FREE** Take a tour of Mara Farm to see Kerry cattle, Kerry bog ponies and rare-breed pigs, and enjoy home-baked goodies at the farm shop and cafe. It's 1km southeast of the ferry harbour, on the road towards the signal tower.

Cape Clear Heritage Centre   MUSEUM
(☑ 028-39100; www.capeclearmuseum.ie; adult/child €2/1; ☺ 11am-1pm & 2-6pm Jul & Aug, shorter hours Jun & Sep) This small museum has exhibits on the island's history and culture, and fine views north across the water to Mizen Head. It's 1km east of the ferry harbour (signposted).

Chléire Goats FARMING
(☑087 797 3056; www.capeclearisland.ie/Goat Farm) FREE Once you're this isolated, you might as well learn something, and Ed and his assistant Vanessa at Chléire Goats, west of the heritage centre, can teach you everything you need to know about goat husbandry. They make goat's-milk ice cream and goat's cheese, and run half-day (€35) to five-day (€155) courses on goat keeping.

You can drop in between 10.30am and noon daily to watch the goats being milked, and to buy some ice cream; it's 1km east of the ferry harbour, just before the heritage centre.

🎭 Festivals & Events

Cape Clear Island International Storytelling Festival PERFORMING ARTS
(☑028-39157; www.capeclearstorytelling.com; ⊙early Sep) Draws hundreds of people for traditional storytelling, workshops and walks.

🛏 Sleeping & Eating

Accommodation on the island is limited to a hostel, a campground, and a handful of B&Bs and self-catering options. As such, all accommodation must be booked in advance.

Eating places on the island are limited to two pubs and a restaurant. Check opening hours in advance if you intend to rely on these for food.

Cape Clear Bird Observatory HOSTEL €
(☑028-39181; www.birdwatchireland.ie; North Harbour; per person €25) The bird observatory offers basic self-catering accommodation for just seven people (one single, one twin and one quad), just a few minutes' walk from the ferry. There's a kitchen, shared bathroom and an extensive natural history library.

Cape Clear Hostel HOSTEL €
(☑028-41968; http://capeclearhostel.ie; South Harbour; per person €20-28; ⊙Easter-Sep) This large cream-coloured building with lovely sea views, a 10- to 15-minute walk from the ferry, was once the coastguard station. It now houses a hostel with four- to 10-bed dorms, a spacious self-catering kitchen, a laundry and an amazing collection of model ships in bottles. No wi-fi or internet.

Chléire Haven CAMPGROUND €
(☑028-39982; www.yurt-holidays-ireland.com; South Harbour; tent sites per adult/child €10/5, yurt per night from €135; ⊙Apr-Sep) 🌿 This appealing campground overlooking the South Harbour offers the chance to stay in a Mongolian yurt (sleeping up to six people), complete with log-burning stove; a bell tent (per adult/child €20/10); or your own tent (limited number of pitches available). All accommodation must be booked in advance, even if you're bringing your own tent.

Ard Na Gaoithe B&B €€
(Cape Clear Island B&B; ☑028-39160; www.cape clearbandb.ie; The Glen; s/d from €60/90; 🖥) Set on an organic farm overlooking the South Harbour, a 20-minute walk from the ferry (up a steep hill), this cottage-style B&B has restful rooms in a simple, sturdy house. There are cats in the garden, and free tea and scones on arrival.

ℹ Information

Tourist Information Point (☑028-39100; www.capeclearisland.ie/TouristInformation; North Harbour; ⊙11am-1pm & 2-6pm Jul-Aug, shorter hours Jun & Sep) Beyond the pier, next to Sean Rua's restaurant; includes a craft shop.

ℹ Getting There & Away

A **passenger ferry** (☑028-39159; www.cape clearferries.com; adult/child return €18/8) makes the 45-minute crossing from Baltimore to Cape Clear Island three or four times a day in summer, and twice a day in winter.

From June to August, the same outfit runs a high-speed ferry from Schull to Cape Clear (adult/child €18/8 return, 25 minutes) with two sailings daily Tuesday to Sunday in July and August, and on Tuesday, Thursday and Sunday only in June.

MIZEN HEAD PENINSULA

From Skibbereen the N71 rolls west through Ballydehob, the gateway to the cliff-bound Mizen Head Peninsula. From here the R592 leads southwest to the pretty yachting harbour of Schull and onward through ever-smaller settlements to the hamlet of Goleen.

Even here the Mizen (rhymes with 'prison') isn't done. Increasingly narrow roads head further west to spectacular Mizen Head itself, and to the hidden delights of Barleycove Beach and Crookhaven. Without a decent map you may well reach the same crossroads several times.

Heading back from Goleen, you can bear north to join the scenic coast road that follows the edge of Dunmanus Bay for most of the way to Durrus. The R591 heads north through Durrus for Bantry, while the L4704 turns west to Ahakista and the Sheep's Head Peninsula.

Schull

POP 700

The yachting and creative crowds (often the same folk) have turned the small fishing village of Schull (pronounced 'skull') into a buzzing little hotspot, crammed with craft shops and art galleries.

⊙ Sights & Activities

Walks in the area include a 13km return trip up **Mt Gabriel** (407m). It was once mined for copper, and there are Bronze Age remains and 19th-century mine shafts and chimneys.

For a gentler stroll try the short 2km foreshore path from the pier out to **Roaringwater Bay** for a view of the nearby islands.

Planetarium   PLANETARIUM
(☑028-28315; www.schullplanetarium.com; Schull Community College, Colla Rd; adult/child €6/4; ☉Jul-Sep; ℗) Founded by a German visitor who fell in love with Schull, the Republic's only planetarium is tucked around the back of Schull Community College at the south end of the village. During summer the 45-minute star show is on three or four times a week at 8pm (5pm on Fridays only in September); call or check the website to confirm times.

Schull Sea Safari   WILDLIFE WATCHING
(☑086 269 2101; www.schullseasafari.ie; per person €60) These small-boat tours last 3½ hours and visit the local seal colony before going on to tour the West Cork coast as far as Sherkin and Cape Clear Islands, always looking out for marine wildlife. Departs from Schull Pier. Sea-kayaking tours also available.

✦✦ Festivals & Events

Schull Regatta   SAILING
(www.shsc.ie; ☉early Aug) Five days of yacht racing, jokingly named Calves Week in reference to England's more famous Cowes Week, culminate in a weekend regatta that includes an outdoor market, children's sports, crab-fishing competitions and a fireworks display. Usually held after the August bank holiday.

⌇ Sleeping & Eating

There are a couple of good eateries in the village, but try to time your visit to coincide with Sunday's country market to get a real feel for the local food scene.

Summerfield Camping   CAMPGROUND €
(☑086 725 2031; www.campinginschullsummerfield.com; Colla Rd; per person €9; ☉Apr-Sep; ☎) It's basically the garden of a villa at the west end of the village, but the facilities are fine and the pitches are pleasantly sheltered. Can get a bit crowded in July and August.

Grove House   B&B €€
(☑087 249 4722; www.grovehouseschull.com; Colla Rd; s/d from €70/80; ℗☎) This beautifully restored Georgian mansion – Jack B Yeats once stayed here – is decorated in an easy-going period style with antiques, and handmade rugs scattered on polished pine floors. It also has a terrific **restaurant** (mains €9 to €23, open for lunch and dinner Monday to Saturday) where Swedish influences combine with Irish staples.

Hackett's Bar   PUB FOOD €
(☑028-28625; Main St; mains €8-13; ☉food served noon-3pm daily, 6-9pm Fri & Sat; ☎🍴) The town's social hub, Hackett's rises above the norm with a creative pub menu of organic dishes prepared from scratch, including crab and soda bread sandwiches and huge bacon and cheese toasties on sourdough bread. Black-and-white photos and tin signs adorn the crooked walls and there's a mishmash of old kitchen tables and benches on the worn stone floor.

Newman's West   CAFE €
(☑028-27776; www.facebook.com/newmans.west; Main St; mains €9-16; ☉9am-11pm; ☎) This yachtie cafe-cum-wine bar (with many good choices by the glass) and art gallery serves soups, salads and enormous chunky sandwiches filled with local cheese and salami.

GUBBEEN FARM FOODS

Farmed by the same family for six generations, Gubbeen Farm near Schull was one of the pioneers of Irish artisan cheese production, starting out in 1979. The dairy was joined by a smokehouse in 1989, and later by a market garden, while pedigree pigs and poultry were added to the livestock mix.

Gubbeen now turns out ham, salami, chorizo, free-range eggs and organic vegetables, as well as some of Ireland's finest cheeses – Extra Mature Smoked Gubbeen is highly recommended.

The farm is not open to the public, but you can visit the Gubbeen stall at farmers markets in Schull (p259), Skibbereen (p254) and Bantry (p263).

Daily specials might include Bantry Bay mussels and chowder. The adjoining original pub, TJ Newman's, is a charmer.

🔒 Shopping

Country Market   MARKET
(www.facebook.com/schullcountrymarket; Pier Road Car Park; ⊙10am-2pm Sun Easter-Sep) Schull's popular market showcases the work of the village's artists and craftspeople, and draws producers and purveyors from around the region.

Enibas   JEWELLERY
(📞028-28868; www.enibas.com; Main St; ⊙10am-6pm Mon-Sat) A pioneer of West Cork arts and crafts, designer Sabine Lenz (yes, the shop is her name spelt backwards) has been creating unique and inspiring gold and silver jewellery in her Schull studio (behind the shop) for more than 25 years.

ℹ️ Getting There & Away

BOAT
In summer only, a passenger **ferry** (📞028-39159; www.capeclearferries.com; adult/child return €18/8; ⊙Jun-Aug) links Schull and Cape Clear Island, with two sailings daily Tuesday to Sunday in July and August, and on Tuesday, Thursday and Sunday only in June.

BUS
There are two buses daily from Cork to Schull (€21, 2½ hours), via Clonakilty and Skibbereen.

There's also a Local Link Cork (www.locallink cork.ie) minibus (Tuesdays and Fridays only) that links Bantry to Durrus, Goleen and Schull (must be booked in advance).

Mizen Head

On a clear day the undulating coastal route from Schull to Goleen enjoys great views out to Cape Clear Island and the Fastnet lighthouse. The landscape becomes wilder around the hamlet of Toormore where a road branches north towards Durrus. Keeping straight on leads to Goleen, where narrowing roads run out to the remote harbour hamlet of Crookhaven and the impressive cliffs of Mizen Head itself.

Mizen Head Signal Station   HISTORIC SITE
(📞028-35115; www.mizenhead.ie; Mizen Head; adult/child €7.50/4.50; ⊙10am-6pm Jun-Aug, 10.30am-5pm mid-Mar–May, Sep & Oct, 11am-4pm Sat & Sun Nov–mid-Mar; 🅿️🚻) Completed in 1909 to help warn ships off the rocks, Mizen Head signal station is perched high above

crashing waves and contorted sea cliffs on a small island connected to the mainland by a spectacular 45m-high bridge. From the visitors centre (you have to pay the admission fee to get to the island), it's a 10-minute walk via 99 steps to reach the station, which houses exhibits on the station's history and on marine wildlife – keep a weather eye open for whales and dolphins.

Various ramps and steps lead to different viewpoints and photo opportunities; if you're pushed for time, the best cliff scenery is from Dunlough Bay View (across the bridge and up the steps to the right). Back at the visitors centre there are displays about local ecology and history, and on the building of the Fastnet lighthouse. There's also a modest cafe.

Barleycove Beach   BEACH
(🅿️) Vast sand dunes hemmed in by two long bluffs dissolve into the surf, forming West Cork's finest beach. Rarely crowded, it's a great place for youngsters, with gorgeous stretches of golden sand and a safe bathing area where a stream flows down to the sea. Access is via a long boardwalk and floating pontoon bridge (open from May to September) from the car park on the road to Crookhaven.

Goleen

Goleen is the largest settlement in these parts – though that's not saying much – with an impressive neo-Gothic church, four pubs, four shops and a petrol station.

There are maybe half-a-dozen B&Bs around the village, most of them open in summer only.

Heron's Cove   B&B €€
(📞028-35225; www.heronscove.com; Harbour Rd; s/d from €60/90; 🅿️🛜) 🍴 A delightful location on the shores of the tidal inlet of Goleen Harbour makes this fine restaurant and B&B a top choice. Rooms are brightly decorated and several have balconies overlooking the inlet. The small **restaurant** (three-course dinner €33, open 7pm to 9.30pm June to September, by reservation October to May) has an excellent menu of organic and local food.

Fortview House   B&B €€
(📞028-35324; www.fortviewhouse.ie; Gurtyowen, Toormore; s/d €50/100; ⊙Apr-Oct; 🅿️🛜) On a working farm, this lovely house has three antique-filled, flower-themed bedrooms. Hostess Violet's breakfast is gourmet standard (hot potato cakes with crème fraîche and smoked salmon), with eggs from the

garden's cheerfully clucking hens. The house is 9km northeast of Goleen, along the R591 towards Durrus.

ⓘ Information

Mizen Information & e-Centre (☑ 028-35000; www.facebook.com/mizenecentre; Main St; ⊙ 10.30am-5pm; 🛜) Provides tourist information, coffee, free wi-fi and internet access.

ⓘ Getting There & Away

Bus Éireann (www.buseireann.ie) has two buses a day from Skibbereen (€13, 1¼ hours) via Schull. Goleen is the end of the line for bus service on the peninsula.

Local Link Cork (www.locallinkcork.ie) also runs a minibus service from Bantry to Goleen (€4, one hour) via Schull once daily on Tuesday and Friday, and from Skibbereen on Wednesdays (€4, 45 minutes).

Crookhaven

The westerly outpost of Crookhaven feels so remote that you imagine it's more easily reached by boat than by road. And so it is for some people – in summer there's a big yachting presence. Outside summer it's very quiet.

In its heyday Crookhaven's natural harbour was an important anchorage and communications hub with a population of 700 (today it's around 30). Mail from America was collected here, and a telegraph line to Cork was installed in 1863, delivering news of transatlantic shipping.

It's worth the trip to enjoy a meal in the rustic bar of the **Crookhaven Inn** (☑ 028-35309; www.thecrookhaveninn.com; mains €12-25; ⊙ food served 12.30-8.30pm Sun-Thu, to 9pm Fri & Sat Apr-Sep, Fri-Sun only Oct-Dec & Mar; 🅿🛗), a popular local watering hole.

SHEEP'S HEAD PENINSULA

The drive from Mizen Head along the north side of the Mizen Head Peninsula leads to the crossroads village of Durrus – little more than a cluster of houses – at the head of Dunmanus Bay, where you can continue straight on to Bantry, or turn west to explore the Sheep's Head Peninsula, the least visited of West Cork's three peninsulas.

The Sheep's Head Peninsula has a rugged charm all its own – and yes, there are plenty of sheep. The road west from Durrus passes through Ahakista (Atha an Chiste), which has a couple of pubs including the charming, tin-roofed Ahakista Bar.

Beyond Ahakista the landscape gets progressively more barren and rocky as the road becomes narrower and more twisty. A link road with terrific views, called the **Goat's Path Road**, runs between Kilcrohane and Gortnakilly (on the south and north coasts respectively) over the western flank of **Mt Seefin** (345m), which offers an exhilarating 1km stride to the summit.

For tourist information see www.living thesheepsheadway.com.

⊙ Sights & Activities

Heading west beyond Kilcrohane, the road clambers up over high moors to end at a remote parking area with a tiny tearoom called **Bernie's Cupán Tae** (www.livingthesheepshead way.com/cupan-tae; Tooreen; mains €3-6; ⊙ 10am-4pm Fri-Sun Apr-Sep, hours vary), famous for its scones and salmon sandwiches. From here, a superb **waymarked walk** leads for 2km to the Sheep's Head lighthouse at the very tip of the peninsula, amid jaw-dropping sea-cliff scenery (allow 1½ to two hours round trip). Many more walks are listed on the Sheep's Head Way website (www.thesheepsheadway.ie).

Kilravock Garden   GARDENS
(☑ 027-61983; www.kilravock.garden; Ahakista Rd; adult/child €6/3; ⊙ by appointment May-Sep) Travel a world of plants at Kilravock Garden, which has been transformed over two decades from a field of scrag and stone to a feast of exotic plants by one green-fingered couple. Look out for the tiny blue sign on the Ahakista road, 2km west of Durrus.

Sheep's Head Cycle Route   CYCLING
(www.thesheepsheadway.ie) The 120km Sheep's Head Cycle Route runs anticlockwise from Ballylickey, round the coastline of the peninsula, back onto the mainland and down to Ballydehob. There are opportunities to take shortcuts or alternative routes (eg over the Goat's Path Rd, or along the coast from Ahakista to Durrus). The *Sheep's Head Cycle Route* brochure is available from local tourist offices and bookshops.

Sheep's Head Way   WALKING
(www.thesheepsheadway.ie) The Sheep's Head Way is a 93km-long walking route around the peninsula, on a mix of minor roads and footpaths; use Ordnance Survey map sheets 85 and 88. It can be extended to 150km by

linking from Bantry to Drimoleague. There are no campsites on the Sheep's Head Peninsula, but camping along the route is allowed with permission from the landowner.

Durrus Farmhouse   FOOD
(☑ 027-61100; www.durruscheese.com; Coomkeen; ⊙ by appointment 9am-1pm Mon-Fri) 🍴 West Cork has earned an international reputation for its marvellous cheese, thanks to the likes of Durrus Farmhouse, whose produce is sold all over Ireland and the wider world. You can visit the farm and watch the cheese-making process through a viewing window (must be booked in advance). The farm is 4km north of Durrus, along a minor road off the Ahakista road.

🛏 Sleeping & Eating

★ **Gallán Mór**   B&B €€
(☑ 027-62732; www.gallanmor.com; Kealties; s/d from €90/130, 2-night minimum stay; ℗ 🛜) Pampering is the name of the game at this gorgeous boutique B&B where the stylishness and comfort of the bedrooms is matched only by the beauty of the views. Breakfast on locally sourced bacon and eggs, home-baked bread, and honey from your hosts' own bees, and relax in an outdoor wood-fired hot tub. It's just over halfway from Durrus to Ahakista.

Fuschia Cottage   B&B €€
(☑ 027-61411; www.fuschiabandb.com; Gerahies; s/d from €65/88; ℗ 🛜) This 19th-century farmhouse has been lovingly restored and extended to create a warm and welcoming B&B, with homely bedrooms, a wood-burning stove in the lounge, and a conservatory and outdoor terrace overlooking beautifully landscaped gardens. It's on the north side of the peninsula, 11km southwest of Bantry.

★ **Blairscove House**   B&B €€€
(☑ 027-61127; www.blairscove.ie; R591; B&B d/f from €190/230; ⊙ daily Easter-Oct, Fri & Sat only Oct-Easter; ℗ 🛜) Set in 2 hectares of land overlooking the bay, this magnificent Georgian country house looks like it belongs in a style magazine. Superbly appointed suites are ranged around an exquisite courtyard, and can be taken on a B&B or self-catering basis. The Loft apartment (which sleep two) has lovely sea views. Blairscove is 2km southwest of Durrus on the R591.

The **restaurant** (three-course dinner €65, open 6pm to 9pm Tuesday to Saturday, mid-March to October), in a chandeliered hall, gives local produce an international treatment.

Heron Gallery, Cafe & Gardens   CAFE €
(☑ 027-67278; www.facebook.com/herongallerycafe; Glen Lough Rd, Ahakista; snacks €3-5, mains €8-11; ⊙ 10.30am-5.30pm Easter–mid-Sep; ℗ 🛜 🍴 👶) Filled with colourful works of art and cute gifts, the Heron Gallery is a charming place to pause. The wholesome, mostly vegetarian menu includes lunch dishes such as falafel, caramelised red onion and goat's cheese tart, and soups such as Thai-spiced parsnip, while cakes and scones are available all day. Wildflowers bloom in the gardens.

Ahakista Bar   PUB
(Tin Pub; ☑ 086 845 0175; www.facebook.com/TheTinPub; Ahakista; ⊙ 1.30-11pm May-Oct, hours may vary; ♿) This charming, tin-roofed stone cottage, known locally as the Tin Pub, has flowering gardens at the back that tumble down to the waterfront, with picnic tables where you can sip a cold one while soaking up the gorgeous view.

❶ Getting There & Away

Local Link Cork (www.locallinkcork.ie) minibuses run a circular route from Bantry via the Goat's Path Rd to Kilcrohane and Durrus (one-way/return €4/6), twice daily on Tuesday and Thursday only (once in each direction).

BANTRY

POP 2722

Framed by the Sheep's Head hills and the craggy Caha Mountains, magnificent, sprawling Bantry Bay is one of the country's most attractive seascapes. Sheltered by islands at the head of the bay, Bantry town is neat and respectable, with narrow streets of old-fashioned, one-off shops and a picturesque waterfront.

Pride of place goes to Bantry House (p262), the former home of one Richard White, who earned his place in history when, in 1798, he warned authorities of the imminent landing of Irish patriot Wolfe Tone and his French fleet, in support of the United Irishmen's rebellion. In the end storms prevented the fleet from landing and the course of Irish history was definitively altered – all Wolfe Tone got for his troubles was a square and a statue bearing his name.

⊙ Sights

★ **Bantry House & Garden** HISTORIC BUILDING
(☑027-50047; www.bantryhouse.com; Bantry Bay;
house & garden adult/child €11/3, garden only €6/
free; ⊙10am-5pm daily Jun-Aug, Tue-Sun mid-Apr–
May, Sep & Oct; P) With its melancholic air of
faded gentility, 18th-century Bantry House
makes for an intriguing visit. From the Gobe-
lin tapestries in the drawing room to the columned splendour of the library, it conjures
up a lost world of aristocratic excess. But
the gardens are its greatest glory, with lawns
sweeping down towards the sea, and the
magnificent Italian garden, with its staircase
of 100 steps, at the back, offering spectacular
views. The entrance is 1km southwest of the
town centre on the N71.

The house has belonged to the White
family since 1729 and every room brims
with treasures brought back from each generation's travels. The entrance hall is paved
with mosaics from Pompeii, French and
Flemish tapestries adorn the walls, and Japanese chests sit next to Russian shrines. Upstairs, worn bedrooms look out wanly over
an astounding view of the bay. Experienced
pianists are invited to tinkle the ivories of
the ancient grand piano in the library.

If it looks like the sort of place you can
imagine staying in, you're in luck – the owners offer B&B accommodation in one of the
wings.

⚜ Festivals & Events

Bantry Walking Festival WALKING
(www.facebook.com/bantrywalkingfestival; ⊙Jun)
Three days of guided walks in Bantry and
the surrounding West Cork countryside;
many of the walks are suitable for all the
family to take part in.

West Cork Literary Festival LITERATURE
(www.westcorkmusic.ie/literaryfestival; ⊙Jul) A
week's worth of readings, workshops, talks
by famous authors and children's events.

West Cork Chamber Music Festival MUSIC
(www.westcorkmusic.ie/chambermusicfestival;
⊙Jun-Jul) A major festival of concerts, talks
and musical masterclasses held over a week
at Bantry House and several other venues in
the town centre.

🛌 Sleeping

Eagle Point Camping CAMPGROUND €
(☑027-50630; www.eaglepointcamping.com; Glengarriff Rd, Ballylickey; campsites per person from

€12; ⊙mid-Apr–late Sep; P�🛜) A superb campground with an enviable location on a pine-
fringed promontory 6km north of Bantry.
Most of the 125 sites have sea views, and
there's direct access to the pebbly beaches
nearby for swimming and water sports. Wi-fi
at reception only.

Mill Apartments APARTMENT €€
(☑027-50278; bbthemill@eircom.net; Glengarriff Rd;
apt from €220; P🛜) These modern, four- to
six-bed holiday apartments, on the immediate outskirts of town, ooze individuality. The
rooms are beautifully decorated in understated country house style, the kitchens are well
equipped and the living areas are enlivened
by a collection of Indonesian puppets and artworks by the irrepressible owner, Tosca.

Bantry House HISTORIC HOTEL €€€
(☑027-50047; www.bantryhouse.com; Bantry Bay; d
from €189; ⊙Apr-Oct; P🛜) The six guest rooms
in this aristocratic mansion are decorated
with antiques and contemporary furnishings
– when you're not playing croquet, lawn tennis or billiards you can lounge in the library,
once the doors of the historic house have
closed to the public (guests have free access
to the house). Rooms 22 and 25 have views of
both the garden and the bay.

Sea View House Hotel HOTEL €€€
(☑027-50073; www.seaviewhousehotel.com; Ballylickey; s/d/f from €120/150/215; P🛜) You'll
find everything you'd expect from an old
country house hotel here: aristocratic ambience, tastefully decorated public rooms,
expansive service and 25 cosy, smart bedrooms. The hotel is on the N71 in Ballylickey,
5km north of Bantry.

✕ Eating

★ **Manning's Emporium** CAFE €
(☑027-50456; www.manningsemporium.ie; N71,
Ballylickey; mains €8-13; ⊙10am-5pm Sun-Thu, to
9pm Fri & Sat; P🛜) 🌿 This gourmet deli and
cafe is an Aladdin's cave of West Cork's finest
food. Grab a menu, choose a table, and order
at the counter – tasting plates are the best
way to sample the local artisan produce and
farmhouse cheeses on offer. Foodie events
take place regularly. It's on the N71 in Ballylickey (on the right approaching from Bantry).

Wood-fired pizza is available Friday to
Sunday.

★ **Organico** CAFE €
(☑027-55905; www.organico.ie; 2 Glengarriff Rd;
mains €7-11; ⊙9am-6pm Mon-Sat; 🛜🌿) 🌿 This

PRIEST'S LEAP

If you're a faint-hearted driver, don't even think about heading up the vertiginous, single-track road to Priest's Leap, 17km northwest of Bantry. In fact, if your GPS points you this way (as a shortcut between Bantry and Kenmare), think again. If you're feeling intrepid, however, this wild ride rewards with monumental views across the mountains to Bantry Bay.

The road is a classic challenge for cyclists, climbing almost 400m in 4.5km, and is exceptionally steep in parts; any fit rider will make it to the top, but unless your thighs are Tour de France material you'll be off and pushing the bike at three or four places. And make sure your brakes are in good order for the descent.

From Bantry, take the N71 north for 8km and turn right after the bridge at the head of the bay (brown signpost saying 'Priest's Leap'). Turn left at the first bridge, and left again at the second bridge (look for the white sign saying 'Priest's Leap'), then take the first right. A long straight gets increasingly steep, before relenting a bit, but with big drops on the left.

The summit of the pass is marked by a wind-buffeted crucifix. The story goes that in 1601 Father James Archer was rallying Cork and Kerry's clans to resist the English. Enemy troops spotted him on the old road to Kerry and gave chase until he and his horse leapt from the top of the pass and landed in Bantry.

bright and lively wholefood shop and cafe serves tinglingly fresh salads, sandwiches and soups, and lunch specials such as falafel platters with hummus and tahini. Great coffee and cakes too.

O'Connors Seafood Restaurant   SEAFOOD €€
(☑ 027-55664; www.oconnorseafood.com; Wolfe Tone Sq; mains lunch €10-20, dinner €18-26; ⊗ noon-3pm & 5.30-9pm, closed Tue & Wed Oct-Mar; ♠) ✦ West Cork scallops with black pudding and roasted parsnip purée; Union Hall hake pan-roasted and topped with lemon butter drizzle; Bantry Bay mussels done four ways: these are among the innovative dishes here that make the most of the area's renowned seafood. The early-bird menu (5.30pm to 6.30pm) offers two/three courses for €20/25.

Fish Kitchen   SEAFOOD €€
(☑ 027-56651; http://thefishkitchen.ie; New St; mains lunch €10-14, dinner €16-28; ⊗ noon-3pm & 5.30-9pm Tue-Sat) This outstanding little restaurant above a fishmonger's shop does seafood to perfection, from the live-tank local oysters (served with lemon and Tabasco sauce) to Bantry Bay mussels in white wine. If you don't fancy seafood, it does a juicy steak too. Friendly, unfussy and absolutely delicious.

🍷 Drinking & Nightlife

Ma Murphy's   PUB
(☑ 027-50242; www.mamurphys.com; 7 New St; ⊗ noon-12.30am Mon-Sat, to midnight Sun) You can still buy cornflakes and sugar at this time-warp grocery-pub, open since 1840.

The regulars are always up for a chat, and there are occasional live music sessions.

Crowley's   PUB
(☑ 027-50029; Wolfe Tone Sq; ⊗ noon-11pm Sun-Thu, to 12.30am Fri & Sat) Crowley's is one of the best bars in town for live music and features traditional bands on Wednesday nights.

Snug   PUB
(☑ 027-50057; www.thesnug.ie; Wolfe Tone Sq; ⊗ 11am-11pm Mon-Sat, 12.30-11pm Sun; ♠) A cosy local favourite on the waterfront known for its excellent pub grub (mains €15 to €28), which includes grilled steaks, seafood platters and a grand Sunday roast.

🛍 Shopping

Bantry Market   MARKET
(Wolfe Tone Sq; ⊗ 9.30am-1pm Fri) ✦ Wolfe Tone Sq takes on a heady mix of aromas for the weekly farmers market. Fresh fruit, organic veg, bread, cheese, charcuterie and other local produce fill most stalls, but there's also clothing, bric-a-brac and farming tools. The market morphs into an even bigger and busier affair on the first Friday of the month.

ℹ Information

Tourist Office (☑ 027-50229; www.visitbantry.ie; Wolfe Tone Sq; ⊗ 10am-6pm Mon-Sat Apr-Oct) Staffed by volunteers, so hours may vary.

ℹ Getting There & Away

Bus Éireann (www.buseireann.ie) runs four to six buses daily between Bantry and Cork (€22, two hours), and four daily to Glengarriff (€5.30, 20 minutes). The summer-only bus 282 allows you to continue from Glengarriff to Kenmare (one daily each direction, Monday to Saturday).

Local Link Cork (☑ 027-52727; www.locallink cork.ie; 5 Main St) is a minibus service that runs a useful series of circular routes from Bantry to Glengarriff, Dunmanway, Durrus, Goleen, Schull, Skibbereen and outlying villages. There's a set price of €4/6 one-way/return. Service is not frequent; check the website for timetables.

BEARA PENINSULA

After Kerry and Dingle, the Beara Peninsula is the third major 'ring' (circular driving route) in Ireland's southwest. Its intricate coast and sharp-featured mountains are a geologist's paradise of exposed and contorted rock strata, making for dramatic scenery at almost every turn.

You can easily drive the 137km Ring of Beara in one day, but you would miss the spectacular **Healy Pass Road** (R574), which cuts across the peninsula from Adrigole in Cork to Lauragh in County Kerry. In fact, if pressed for time, skip the rest and do the pass.

The south side, along Bantry Bay, is a string of working fishing villages. The north side, in contrast, has only a few small hamlets dotted along craggy roads with grand views north to the mountains of Kerry. At the tip is a cable car linking the peninsula to tiny **Dursey Island**.

The northeastern part of the peninsula lies in County Kerry, but most is within County Cork.

Glengarriff

POP 138

Tucked away in the thickly wooded, northernmost corner of Bantry Bay, Glengarriff (Gleann Garbh; www.glengarriff.ie) is a 19th-century resort village strung along the N71 Cork to Killarney road. It's the starting point for boat trips to the pretty island of Ilnacullin, and for driving tours around the Ring of Beara.

In the second half of the 19th century, Glengarriff became a popular retreat for prosperous Victorians, who sailed from England to Cork, took the train to Bantry (the line closed in 1961), then crossed over to the village in a paddle steamer. In 1850 the road to Kenmare was blasted through the mountains and a

link with Killarney was established, further increasing Glengarriff's popularity.

⊙ Sights

★**Ilnacullin**   GARDENS
(Garinish Island; ☑027-63040; www.garinishisland.ie; adult/child €5/3, plus ferry fare; ☺9.30am-5.30pm Jul & Aug, shorter hours Apr-Jun, Sep & Oct, closed Nov-Mar) This horticultural miracle of an island was created in the early 20th century when the island's owner commissioned architect Harold Peto to design a garden on the then-barren outcrop. Topsoil was shipped in, landscaped gardens laid out, and subtropical species planted; camellias, magnolias and rhododendrons now provide a seasonal blaze of colour. **Harbour Queen** (☑087 234 5861, 027-63116; www.harbourqueenferry.com; adult/child return €12/6; ☺Apr-Nov) and **Blue Pool** (☑027-63333; www.bluepoolferry.com; adult/child return €10/5; ☺Apr-Nov) run 10-minute ferry trips to the island past colonies of basking seals and a nesting site for white-tailed eagles.

The centrepiece of the island is a magical **Italianate garden**; nearby a cypress avenue leads to a faux-Grecian temple with a stunning view of Sugarloaf Mountain. There are more views from the island's highest point, a 19th-century **Martello tower**, one of hundreds built around the coast to watch out for a possible Napoleonic invasion.

Glengarriff Woods
Nature Reserve   NATURE RESERVE
(☑027-63636; www.glengarriffnaturereserve.ie; ☺24hr; ℗) FREE The valley of the Glengarriff River, to the northwest of Glengarriff village, was once the private estate of the Earl of Bantry. As such its ancient oak woodland has survived, the thick tree cover maintaining humid conditions that allow ferns and mosses to flourish. The reserve is rich in wildlife – look out for red squirrels and siskins in the woods, and otters and kingfishers along the river. Waymarked walking trails radiate from the main car park 1km north of the village.

There are five trails of varying lengths, from 500m to 3km, covering woodland, mountain, river and meadow. The purple-waymarked **Glengarriff Wood Loop** combines the best of all five in one route (8km, allow three hours).

Ewe Experience   GARDENS
(☑027-63840; www.theewe.com; N71, Tooreen; adult/child €7.50/6; ☺10am-6pm Jun-Aug; ℗) 🖉 More than 20 years in the making, this interactive sculpture garden is imaginative,

thought-provoking and humorous, with nature and art working together to provide an unforgettable walk in the woods. From the sheep in the vintage car to the pig blissing out in a bubble bath, a kilometre of trails takes you past dozens of intriguing sculptures, installations, puzzles and games, which weave together art, nature, science, music and poetry. The gardens are 4.5km northwest of Glengarriff on the N71.

🏃 Activities

The rough and rocky **Caha Mountains** rising to the north and west make for challenging hill walking, despite their small size, but there are plenty of gentler strolls in and around town, too. Mature woodlands of oak and Scots pine in the **Blue Pool Park** offer some easy waymarked trails along the shore between village and pier where seals, perched on submerged rocks, appear to float on the water.

A maze of minor roads extends northwest from Glengarriff Woods Nature Reserve, serving holiday cottages and remote farms, and ideal for exploring by bike. **Pooleen**, where picnic tables stand beside a natural bathing pool in the Glengarriff River, makes a good objective. Only the fit and hardy will venture to road's end at **Barley Lake**, a wild hill lough visited mainly by trout anglers (don't even think about driving it in anything less than a 4WD).

🛏 Sleeping & Eating

Blue Pool Hostel   HOSTEL €
(☑ 087 911 2050; www.bluepoolhostel.ie; Main St; dm/tw €20/48; 🛜) Opened in 2017, this bright and attractive hostel is right in the centre of the village, and has a six- and a 10-bed dorm, four twins and a three-bed, female-only room. There's an open fire in the common room and an outdoor terrace off the kitchen at the back. Breakfast (with fresh, not instant, coffee!) is included.

Coomarkane Visitor Centre   CAMPGROUND €
(☑ 027-63826; www.coomarkanevisitorcentre.com; Coomarkane; campsites/cabins per person €10/30; P) 🚭 This lovely rural retreat is hidden away in the Caha Mountains beyond Glengarriff Woods Nature Reserve, 6km west of the village. There's only room for six tents, plus two log cabins (which sleep three and five), each with its own firepit. Ideal for hikers and cyclists. It's signposted along a minor road which leads off the R572, 500m south of Glengarriff.

Bay View Boutique B&B   B&B €€
(☑ 027-63030; www.bayviewbedandbreakfast. ie; Reenmeen; r from €99; P 🛜) This spacious modern villa on the eastern edge of Glengarriff has been converted into a chic and elegant B&B, with bedrooms that look fresh from a Sunday colour supplement photo shoot. There's a lovely terrace and garden out back with sweeping views across the bay; try to snag one of the deluxe rooms (from €120), whose balconies share that view.

Eccles Hotel   HISTORIC HOTEL €€
(☑ 027-63003; www.eccleshotel.com; Glengarriff Harbour; s/d from €80/120; ⊗ closed Nov-Mar; P 🛜) Just east of the centre, this grande dame of West Cork hotels has a long and distinguished history (since 1745), counting the British War Office, WM Thackeray, George Bernard Shaw and WB Yeats as former guests. The public areas retain some 19th-century grandeur, though some bedrooms are on the small side. Ask for a bayside room on the 2nd floor for the best views.

Casey's Hotel   HOTEL €€
(☑ 027-63010; www.caseyshotelglengarriff.ie; Main St; r from €130; P @ 🛜) Old-fashioned Casey's has been welcoming guests since 1884 (Eamon de Valera stayed here). The 19 rooms have been modernised a bit but are still small. It's got stacks of atmosphere, and the vast terrace is a treat. The bar serves classics such as beef and Guinness pie; the restaurant ups the ante with posh seafood and steak dishes.

Harbour Bar   GASTROPUB €€
(☑ 027-63093; www.eccleshotel.com; Eccles Hotel, Glengarriff Harbour; mains €14-18; ⊗ food served noon-9pm; P 🛜 ♿) The vintage bar at the Eccles Hotel adds a sophisticated twist to the idea of pub grub – alongside classics such as fish and chips and beefburgers, you'll find the likes of salt cod croquettes with burnt orange and garlic mayo, and seafood *fritto misto* with shaved fennel and dill mayo.

MacCarthy's Bar   PUB FOOD €€
(☑ 027-63000; www.glengarriffpark.com; 14 Main St; mains €12-27; ⊗ food served noon-3pm & 6-9pm; 🛜 ♿) MacCarthy's is a traditional, Victorian-style wood-panelled bar with a menu of hearty pub grub; the house speciality is a steaming pan of succulent Bantry Bay mussels in a white wine and herb sauce.

ℹ Getting There & Away

Bus Éireann (www.buseireann.ie) runs the following services:

COUNTY CORK GLENGARRIFF

THE BEARA WAY

This 206km waymarked walk (see www.irishtrails.ie) forms a loop around the Beara Peninsula and takes around nine days. The peninsula is relatively unused to mass tourism and makes a pleasant contrast to the Ring of Kerry to the north.

The Beara Way mostly follows old roads and tracks and rarely rises above 340m. There's no official start or finish point, and the route can be walked in either direction. It could easily be reduced to seven days by skipping Bere and Dursey Islands and, if you start at Castletownbere, you could reach Kenmare in five days or less.

There's an online guide to the walk (and the peninsula itself) at Beara Tourism (www.bearatourism.com).

Bantry €5, 25 minutes, up to five daily
Castletownbere €10, 50 minutes, one or two daily
Cork €22, 2½ hours, up to five daily
Kenmare Bus 282, €12.40, 45 minutes, one daily Monday to Saturday, July and August
See also Local Link Cork (www.locallinkcork.ie).

Glengarriff to Castletownbere

The folded bedding of the peninsula's underlying sandstone bedrock becomes evident as you drive west from Glengarriff towards Castletownbere. On the highest hills, Sugarloaf Mountain and Hungry Hill, rock walls known as 'benches' snake backwards and forwards across the slopes. They can make walking on these mountains quite challenging, and dangerous in fog. Take a map (Ordnance Survey sheets 84 and 85 cover the area) and compass if venturing into the hills, and seek local advice.

Adrigole is no more than a scattered strip of houses and a harbour where Wild Atlantic Wildlife (☑ 083 115 6672; www.wildatlanticwildlife.ie; The Boat House, Adrigole; ☉ Jun-Aug) rents out kayaks (€12 per hour) and Canadian canoes (€20 per hour).

From Adrigole, a narrow, switchback road climbs 11km north across the other-worldly Healy Pass to Lauragh. The road passes through wild mountain scenery offering spectacular views of crags and lakes, especially on the steep descent on the north side.

Castletownbere & Around

POP 860

Busy Castletownbere (Baile Chais Bhéara) is a fishing port first and a tourist town second. And that gives it great appeal for those looking for the 'real' Ireland, although that's not to say it doesn't have some worthwhile sights, notably Dunboy Castle and the world-famous pub MacCarthy's Bar.

On Main St and the Square, you'll find ATMs as well as cafes, pubs and grocery stores.

There's a developing food scene on the Beara, and Castletownbere is at the centre of it. There's a farmers market (The Square; ☉ 10am-2pm 1st Thu of month year-round, every Thu May-Sep), a couple of artisan delis and coffee shops, and a growing number of excellent restaurants.

⊙ Sights

Dunboy Castle RUINS
FREE The ruins of this 15th-century castle, a former stronghold of the O'Sullivan Beare clan, sit on a promontory overlooking the southern entrance to the sheltered harbour of Bere Haven, a fantastic spot for a summer picnic. The castle was destroyed by English forces during the Siege of Dunboy in 1602. Dunboy is at the end of a narrow road (the L8935), which leaves the main road 2.5km southwest of Castletownbere (parking space for two or three cars).

On the way to the castle, you pass the fenced-off shell of Puxley Mansion, a grand Victorian manor house that was once home to a copper-mining magnate and provided the inspiration for Clonmere in Daphne du Maurier's 1943 novel Hungry Hill. The manor was burnt out by the IRA in 1921; there have been attempts to restore it as a hotel, but it has lain abandoned since 2008.

Bere Island ISLAND
(www.bereisland.net) Only 12km by 7km, Bere Island has around 200 permanent residents and attracts scores more to summer holiday homes. There are ruined Martello towers, craggy coves good for swimming, and a 19km loop of the Beara Way to hike. Bere Island Ferry (☑ 027-75009; www.bereislandferries.com; passenger/car return €8/25; ☉ every 90min Mon-Sat Jun-Sep, less often Sun & Oct-May) leaves from town but drops you in a remote part of the island. Murphy's Ferry Service (☑ 027-75014; www.murphysferry.com;

pedestrian/car return from €8/25; ⊙ 6-8 crossings daily), departing from Pontoon pier, 5km east of Castletownbere, docks to the island's main village, **Rerrin**, which has a shop, a pub, a cafe and accommodation.

🛏 Sleeping

Dzogchen Beara   COTTAGES €
(☑ 027-73032; www.dzogchenbeara.org; Garranes; dm/f €20/50, cottages per 2 nights from €260; P) Solitude and sea views set the mood at the remote Dzogchen Beara meditation centre, where a Buddhist temple is under construction (scheduled for completion in 2020). Accommodation (open to all) is available in self-catering cottages with wood-burning stoves overlooking the Atlantic, or in a homely farmhouse hostel; there's a good cafe here too. It's 9km southwest of Castletownbere.

The retreat runs seminars and workshops, and guests can attend meditation sessions.

Berehaven Lodge   COTTAGE €€
(☑ 027-71464; www.berehavenlodge.com; Millcove; per 2 nights €375, per week from €750; P 🔊) This complex of cosy self-catering cottages occupies an enviable setting overlooking the sea 6km east of Castletownbere. Each 'lodge' has three bedrooms, a Jacuzzi, an outdoor deck and an open-plan living area with a log fire. Also on-site are an attractive bar and restaurant, with regular summer barbecues on the terrace.

Old Medical Hall   B&B €€
(☑ 086 1732 606; www.theoldmedicalhall.com; s/d from €55/100; 🔊) Housed in a former pharmacy store, this renovated and centrally located B&B offers five homely and comfortable rooms with luxury bathrooms. There's a cosy tearoom on the ground floor, and the owner can arrange bike hire for guests.

Beara Coast Hotel   HOTEL €€
(☑ 027-71446; www.bearacoast.com; Cametringane Point; r from €135; P 🔊) It may look plain and pedestrian from the outside, but this beautifully modernised hotel has certainly had fun with the colour palette inside. Spacious bedrooms are bright and cheerful, and many have balconies with a view across the harbour. The location is quiet, but only a short walk from the town centre's pubs and restaurants.

It's a popular wedding venue, so weekdays are best for availability.

Sea Breeze   B&B €€
(☑ 027-70508; www.seabreez.com; Derrymihin; s/d €65/100; P 🔊) This grand villa of a place perches above the main Glengarriff road 1km east of town, looking out across the harbour to Bere Island. The residents' lounge, garden terrace and half of the bedrooms make the most of that sea view, while the other bedrooms enjoy a vista of the Caha Mountains. Breakfast options include bagels with cream cheese and smoked salmon.

🍴 Eating & Drinking

Fuchsia Cafe   CAFE €
(☑ 083 885 2552; www.facebook.com/fuchsia cafe; The Square; mains €5-12; ⊙ 9am-5pm Tue-Fri, to 4pm Sat, 10am-2pm Sun; 🔊) Vibrant colours (it's painted fuchsia-pink) and vibrant flavours characterise this cheerful cafe on the bustling village square. The menu runs from breakfast fry-ups (including veggie versions, served till noon) to lip-smacking lunch dishes such as homemade burgers and pulled pork focaccia sandwiches. The coffee is damn fine too.

★ Ocean Wild   SEAFOOD €€
(☑ 027-71544; www.oceanwild.ie; West End; mains €19-30; ⊙ 6-10pm Thu-Mon Jun-Sep & Dec; P) 🍴 Opened in 2017 by local sisters Mairead and Eileen (one the chef, the other front of house), Ocean Wild has quickly established a reputation as the Beara's top seafood restaurant. Expect dishes such as pan-roasted hake with lemon, olives and capers, or monkfish in Thai red curry sauce, as well as perfectly grilled steak and slow-cooked lamb shank.

Berehaven Lodge   INTERNATIONAL €€
(☑ 027-71306; www.berehavenlodge.com; Millcove; mains €15-33; ⊙ 10am-9pm Apr-Oct, shorter hours Nov-Mar; P 🍴) The restaurant at this complex of self-catering cottages, 6km east of Castletownbere, is open to all. The dining room has an outdoor terrace overlooking the sea where the South African chef does wonderful things with a barbecue on Fridays in summer. Otherwise, the menu serves up favourite dishes from Ireland and around the world (fish and chips, steaks, French onion soup, crab claws etc).

★ MacCarthy's Bar   PUB
(☑ 027-70014; www.maccarthysbar.com; Main St; ⊙ 9.30am-11.30pm Mon-Thu, to 12.30am Fri & Sat, 12.30-11pm Sun) If you're carrying an original

COUNTY CORK CASTLETOWNBERE & AROUND

GOUGANE BARRA FOREST PARK

Gougane Barra is a truly magical spot, with craggy mountains and pine forests sweeping down to a mountain lake, the source of the River Lee. St Fin Barre, the founder of Cork, established a monastery here in the 6th century. He had a hermitage on the island in **Gougane Barra Lake** (Lough an Ghugain), which is now approached by a short causeway. The small chapel on the island has fine stained-glass representations of obscure Celtic saints.

Beyond the lake, a loop road runs through the forest park (€5 entry per vehicle, coins only), but you're better off slowing down and walking the well-marked network of paths and **nature trails** through the woods. The park is signposted on the R584, which runs between the N71 at Ballylickey and Macroom on the N22.

You're really out in the sticks here, and the only place to air your hiking boots is the **Gougane Barra Hotel** (☑ 026-47069; www.gouganebarrahotel.com; s/d from €79/122; ⊗ Apr-Oct; P 🕾). There's a restaurant in the hotel, a **cafe** (☑ 026-47031; mains €4-7; ⊗10am-6pm Apr-Oct; P) and a pub next door.

copy of the late Pete McCarthy's bestseller, *McCarthy's Bar*, you'll be excited to see the front-cover photo in real life (the spelling was changed to match Pete's name for the cover pic). There's good food and drink, frequent live music and a grand wee snug inside the door, and the craic is mighty.

ℹ Information

Tourist Office (☑ 027-70054; www.beara tourism.com; Main St; ⊗ 9am-5.30pm Mon-Sat Jun-Sep, Fri & Sat only Oct-May) In the grounds of St Peter's Church.

ℹ Getting There & Away

Local bus service providers include **O'Donoghue's** (☑ 027-70007) and **Harrington's of Ardgroom** (☑ 027-74003; www.harringtonsbus. com). See also Bus Éireann (www.buseireann. ie) and Local Link Cork (www.locallinkcork.ie) timetables.

Bantry O'Donoghue's (€14, one hour, twice daily on Monday, once on Tuesday, Friday and Saturday); Bus Éireann (€14.20, 70 minutes, once on Monday, Wednesday and Friday).

Cork Harrington's of Ardgroom (€25, 2¼ hours, daily except Thursday) – booking a seat is recommended; O'Donoghue's (Thursday); Bus Éireann (€25, 3¼ hours, once or twice daily).

Glengarriff O'Donoghue's (€10.50, one hour, twice daily on Monday, and once on Tuesday, Friday and Saturday); Bus Éireann (€10.90, 50 minutes, once or twice daily).

Kenmare Bus Éireann's 282 Ring of Beara service (€14.20, 1½ hours, twice daily Monday to Saturday, July and August only).

Dursey Island

POP 4

Tiny Dursey Island, at the end of the peninsula, is reached by Ireland's only cable car, a rickety 1960s contraption that sways precariously 30m above Dursey Sound. In a perfect photo op, livestock take precedence over humans in the queue.

The island, just 6.6km long by 1.5km wide, is a wildlife **sanctuary**, and dolphins and whales can sometimes be seen in the surrounding waters. The **Beara Way** loops round the island for 14km (allow four hours for the complete loop), and the **signal tower** is an obvious destination for a shorter walk (8km round trip).

There's nowhere to eat on the island – bring your own food and drink. The nearest places for a meal are Allihies and Castletownbere, or you can get fish and chips from the **Dursey Deli** (Murphy's Mobile Catering; ☑ 086 366 2865; mains €4-11; ⊗12.30-7pm Sat & Sun May-early Sep, hours may vary) food truck, which can usually be found at the cable car parking area on summer weekends.

ℹ Getting There & Away

The Dursey **cable car** (☑ 028-21766; www. durseyisland.ie; adult/child return €10/5; ⊗9.30am-1pm & 1.30-5pm Mon-Thu, to 9.30pm Fri-Sun Jun-Aug, less frequently Sun & Sep-May) shuttles back and forth every 15 minutes or so during operating hours; passenger numbers (maximum six per trip) may be limited during busy periods – check website for details. It runs continuously in summer, and at set times only the rest of the year.

On Tuesday only, Local Link Cork (www.local linkcork.ie) minibuses run a circular route from Castletownbere to Allihies and the Dursey cable car (€4, 30 minutes or one hour), once in each direction.

Northside of the Beara

The entire north side is the scenic highlight of the Beara Peninsula. A series of minor roads – often steep and twisting single-lane tracks with few passing places – snake around the ins and outs of the rugged coastline. Boulder-strewn fields tumble dramatically towards the ocean and it all feels blissfully remote – your only company along some stretches are flocks of sheep.

Allihies

The isolated village of Allihies (Na hAilichí), whose colourfully painted houses grace many a postcard and guidebook cover, has dramatic vistas, plenty of walks and a fascinating history of copper mining.

Copper-ore deposits were first identified on the Beara in 1810. While mining quickly brought wealth to the Puxley family, who owned the land, it brought low wages and dangerous, unhealthy working conditions for the labour force, which at one time numbered 1300. Experienced Cornish miners were brought into the area, and the dramatic ruins of engine houses are reminiscent of Cornwall's coastal tin mines. As late as the 1930s, more than 30,000 tonnes of pure copper were exported annually, but by 1962 the last mine was closed.

The beautiful white strand of **Ballydonegan beach**, just southwest of the village, is largely made of crushed quartz washed out from the old mine workings.

Allihies Copper Mine Museum MUSEUM
(☑ 027-73218; www.acmm.ie; Main Rd; adult/child €6/2; ☺10am-5pm Easter-Oct) Allihies' history as a copper mining area is chronicled in this engaging museum, the result of years of work by the community; there's also tourist information and a cafe. Pick up a copy of the museum leaflet and follow the **Copper Mine Trail**, a waymarked hike among the remains of the old workings.

Allihies Seaview Guesthouse GUESTHOUSE €€
(☑ 027-73004; www.allihiesseaview.com; Main Rd; s/d €60/110; ℗) Clean, tidy and basic, the 10 spacious rooms in this two-storey yellow building have an abundance of pine; some have views north over the sea. The tempting spread at breakfast will help fuel your rambles.

O'Neill's PUB FOOD €€
(☑ 027-73008; www.oneillsbeara.ie; Main Rd; mains €12-25; ☺food served noon-8.30pm; ☎) The most appealing pub in town, with a distinctive bright-red facade and some polished wooden benches and picnic tables out the front. Pub grub standards intermingle with fresh local seafood; the haddock and chips could feed two people.

Allihies to Lauragh

Heading north and east from Allihies, the wild coastal road (R575), lined with fuchsias and rhododendrons, twists and turns for about 12km to **Eyeries**. This cluster of brightly coloured houses overlooking Coulagh Bay is often used as a film set. The village is also home to **Milleens Cheese** (☑ 086 210 5267; www.milleenscheese.com; ☺by appointment), from pioneering producer Veronica Steele. She welcomes visitors to her farm; phone ahead.

From Eyeries, forsake the R571 for even smaller coastal roads to the north and east, with sublime views of the Ring of Kerry hills to the north, rejoining the R571 at the crossroads of Ardgroom (Ard Dhór). From here, a minor road leads inland to dramatic **Glenbeg Lough**; ask at the village pub in Ardgroom for information on trout fishing here.

The village of **Lauragh** (Laith Reach) – barely more than a junction at the northern end of the Healy Pass road – and the whole northeastern corner of the peninsula lie in County Kerry.

Gleninchaquin Park FARM
(☑ 087 634 9282; www.gleninchaquin.com; Tuosist; adult/family €6/15; ☺10am-5pm; ℗♿☺) This working sheep farm offers a whole range of things to do, from waymarked history and geology walks to trout fishing and feeding the lambs (in spring), all in an extraordinarily beautiful setting, high in a valley overlooked by a bridal-veil waterfall. It's signposted off the R571 halfway between Lauragh and Kenmare. Cash only.

Derreen Gardens GARDENS
(☑ 064-668 3588; www.derreengarden.com; R573, Lauragh; adult/child €7/2; ☺10am-6pm; ℗) Derreen Gardens were planted by the fifth Lord Lansdowne around the turn of the 20th century. Mossy paths weave through an

abundance of interesting plants, including spectacular New Zealand tree ferns, colourful rhododendrons and red cedars, and you may see seals on the shore. There's a cafe (open 11am to 5pm Easter to October).

Pedals & Boots Cafe
CAFE €

(☑ 064-668 3101; www.pedalsandboots.ie; R571, Lauragh; mains €5; ⊙ 10am-5pm Mon-Sat mid-Apr–Jun & Sep, daily Jul-Aug; P 🐾) This cosy cafe, complete with wood-fired stove, serves up home-baked cakes and scones, soups and sandwiches. You can hire bikes here too (€16/12 per day/half day), and get information on local walking and cycling routes.

★ Josie's Lakeview House
MODERN IRISH €€

(☑ 064-668 3155; www.josiesrestaurant.ie; Clogherane; mains lunch €10-16, dinner €15-26; ⊙ 10.30am-7.30pm; P 🐾 ♿) Captivating views over Glanmore Lake accompany scrumptious, home-cooked food at Josie's, set on a hill above the water. Choose from salads and sandwiches for lunch, cakes at tea, or a heartier rack of lamb or local seafood specials at night; ask about B&B in the garden chalet (double room €90) to prolong the experience. Josie's is 4km south of Lauragh; follow the signs.

❶ Getting There & Away

In July and August only, **Bus Éireann's** (☑ 021-450 8188; www.buseireann.ie) 282 Ring of Beara service has two buses a day between Kenmare and Lauragh (€7.90, 40 minutes), Ardgroom (€12.40, 55 minutes) and Eyeries (€14.20, 1¼ hours).

See also Local Link Cork (www.locallinkcork.ie).

County Kerry

POP 147,554 / AREA 4807 SQ KM

Best Places to Eat

➡ Out of the Blue (p308)

➡ Smuggler's Inn (p298)

➡ Heather (p285)

➡ Boathouse Bistro (p302)

➡ Jacks' Coastguard Restaurant (p292)

➡ Reel Dingle Fish Co (p308)

Best Places to Stay

➡ Cahernane House Hotel (p277)

➡ Mannix Point Camping & Caravan Park (p292)

➡ Park Hotel (p302)

➡ Pax House (p307)

➡ Black Sheep Hostel (p275)

➡ Meadowlands Hotel (p317)

Why Go?

County Kerry contains some of Ireland's most iconic scenery: surf-pounded sea cliffs and soft golden strands, emerald-green farmland criss-crossed by tumbledown stone walls, mist-shrouded bogs and cloud-torn mountain peaks.

With one of the country's finest national parks as its backyard, the lively tourism hub of Killarney spills over with colourful shops, restaurants and pubs loud with spirited trad music. The town is the jumping-off point for Kerry's two famed loop drives: the larger Ring of Kerry skirts the mountainous, island-fringed Iveragh Peninsula. The more compact Dingle Peninsula is like a condensed version of its southern neighbour, with ancient prehistoric ring forts and beehive huts, Christian sites, sandy beaches and glimpses of a hard, unforgiving land.

Kerry's exquisite beauty makes it one of Ireland's most popular tourist destinations. But if you need to escape from the crowds, there's always a mountain pass, an isolated cove or an untrodden trail to discover.

When to Go

➡ Lots of festivals take place throughout the county during the warmer months, particularly from June to August (when you'll need to book accommodation well ahead).

➡ Some of the highlights on Kerry's annual calendar include Listowel's Writers' Week in May/June and Dingle town's races and regatta in August. Killorglin's famous Puck Festival, which dates to the 17th century, also takes place in August.

➡ Many sights and businesses, including some accommodation, close in the low season. But even in the depths of winter, you'll find storytellers and musicians taking part in impromptu sessions in pubs throughout the county.

County Kerry Highlights

❶ Gap of Dunloe (p285) Exploring the Killarney Lakes and starkly beautiful Gap of Dunloe by boat and bike.

❷ Carrauntoohil (p286) Hiking to the 1040m summit of Ireland's highest peak.

❸ Kells Bay House & Gardens (p293) Swaying on Ireland's longest rope bridge.

❹ Lough Leane (p283) Fishing on Killarney's beautiful Lough Leane.

❺ Slea Head (p311) Hiring a bike and cycling around scenic Slea Head.

❻ Waterville Golf Links (p298) Teeing off at these spectacularly sited links.

❼ Saint's Road (p312) Discovering early Christian monuments along this path.

❽ Skellig Michael (p294) Taking a boat trip to the remote monastic ruins.

❾ Tralee Bay Wetlands Centre (p316) Cruising through fresh and saltwater habitats on a boat.

KILLARNEY

POP 14,504

A town that's been in the business of welcoming visitors for more than 250 years, Killarney is a well-oiled tourism machine fuelled by the sublime scenery of its namesake national park set amid sublime scenery that spans lakes, waterfalls and woodland beneath a skyline of 1000m-plus peaks. Competition keeps standards high and visitors on all budgets can expect to find good restaurants, great pubs and comfortable accommodation.

Mobbed in summer, Killarney is perhaps at its best in late spring and early autumn when the crowds are manageable, but the weather is still good enough to enjoy its outdoor activities.

History

The Killarney area has been inhabited since at least the early Bronze Age, when copper ore was mined on Ross Island. In the 7th century St Finian founded a monastery on Inisfallen in Lough Leane, and the region became a focus for Christianity. The lands around the lough were occupied by the Gaelic clans of McCarthy Mór and the O'Donoghues of Ross, who built Ross Castle, before coming into the possession of the Herberts of Muckross and the Earls of Kenmare.

It wasn't until the mid-18th century that Sir Thomas Browne, the 4th Viscount Kenmare (1726–95), began to develop the region as an Irish version of England's Lake District. It was later bolstered by the arrival of famous visitors including Sir Walter Scott (1825) and Queen Victoria and Prince Albert (1861), as well as the railway (1853). By 1895 Killarney was on the Thomas Cook package-tour itinerary.

⊙ Sights & Activities

Killarney's biggest attraction, in every sense, is nearby Killarney National Park (p282). The town itself can easily be explored on foot in an hour or two.

★**Killarney House
& Gardens**   HISTORIC BUILDING
(www.facebook.com/killarneynationalpark; Muckross Rd; ⊘8.30am-7.30pm May-Sep, 9am-5.30pm Oct-Apr) FREE Dating from the early 18th century, Killarney House was once part of a much larger residence that was later demolished; it was restored in 2016 and now houses the Killarney National Park visitor centre. There are free guided tours of the house every half-hour, and seasonal guided walks in the vast gardens, which sweep majestically towards a gorgeous view of the Kerry mountains.

The house was originally the stable block of a much larger French-chateau-style mansion built for the landowning Browne family in the 1720s; the chateau was demolished in the 1870s when the family moved to then newly built Knockreer House nearby. When that was destroyed by fire in 1913, the stables were remodelled as a family residence, but abandoned in the 1950s. Despite its proximity to the centre of Killarney, the house lay empty and unused for half a century.

Knockreer House & Gardens   GARDENS
FREE The original Knockreer House, built for the Earl of Kenmare in the 1870s, burned down in 1913; the present house was built on the same site in 1958 and is now home to a national-park education centre. It isn't open to the public, but its terraced gardens have magnificent views across the lakes to the mountains.

From the park entrance opposite St Mary's Cathedral, follow the path forking right, past the cute thatched cottage of **Deenagh Lodge**, built in 1834.

St Mary's Cathedral   CATHEDRAL
(www.killarneyparish.com; Cathedral Pl; ⊘8am-6.30pm) Built between 1842 and 1855, St Mary's Cathedral is a superb example of neo-Gothic revival architecture. Designed by Augustus Pugin, the cruciform building was inspired by Ardfert Cathedral, near Tralee. Check the website for Mass times.

Killarney Golf & Fishing Club   GOLF
(☑064-663 1034; www.killarneygolfclub.com; Mahony's Point; green fees €60-125) This historic club, which has hosted the Irish Open on several occasions, has three championship golf courses with lakeside settings and mountain views. It's 3.4km west of Killarney on the N72.

O'Neill's   FISHING
(☑064-663 1970; www.facebook.com/oneillsofkillarney; 6 Plunkett St; ⊘9.30am-10pm Mon-Fri, to 9pm Sat, 10.30am-8pm Sun) Information, tackle, permits, licences and rental equipment (rod hire per day €10) can be obtained at O'Neill's, which looks like a gift shop but is a long-established fishing centre.

Killarney Riding Stables   HORSE RIDING
(☑064-663 1686; www.killarney-riding-stables.com; Ballydowney; horse riding per 1/2/3hr €45/75/95;

Killarney

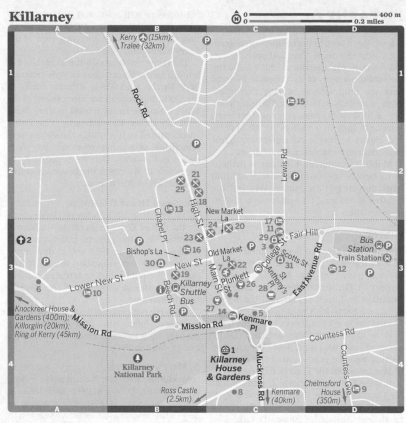

8am-6pm) Scenic trails take in Killarney National Park and lakes on treks offered by the well-run Killarney Riding Stables complex. It's 1.5km west of the centre on the N72.

👉 Tours

Jaunting Car Tours   TOURS
(☑ 064-663 3358; www.killarneyjauntingcars. ie; Kenmare Pl; per jaunting car €40-80) Killarney's traditional horse-drawn jaunting cars provide tours from the town to Ross Castle and Muckross Estate, complete with amusing commentary from the driver (known as a 'jarvey'). The cost varies depending on distance; cars can fit up to four people. The pickup point, nicknamed 'the Ha Ha' or 'the Block', is on Kenmare Pl.

Gap of Dunloe Tours   TOURS
(☑ 064-663 0200; www.gapofdunloetours.com; 7 High St; ⊙ Mar-Oct) Gap of Dunloe Tours can arrange a walking tour (€17.50), highly recommended bike-and-boat circuit (€20), or

bus-and-boat tour (€35) taking in the Gap. Buses depart from O'Connor's pub (p280).

Killarney Guided Walks   WALKING
(☑ 087 639 4362; www.killarneyguidedwalks.com; adult/child €12/6) Guided two-hour walks through the national-park woodlands leave at 11am daily from opposite St Mary's Cathedral (p273) at the western end of New St; advance bookings are required from November to April. Tours meander through Knockreer gardens, then to spots where Charles de Gaulle holidayed, David Lean filmed *Ryan's Daughter* and Brother Cudda slept for 200 years. Tours are available at other times on request.

Corcoran's   BUS
(☑ 064-663 6666; www.corcorantours.com; 8 College St; ⊙ Mar-Oct) If you're pushed for time, this well-organised outfit offers half-day coach tours that take in Killarney, Ross Castle, Muckross House and Torc Waterfall

Killarney

(€21), or the Gap of Dunloe (€28). It also offers day-long tours of the Ring of Kerry (€20) and Dingle and Slea Head (€25).

Deros Tours BUS
(☑064-663 1251; www.derostours.com; 22 Main St; ⊙Mar-Oct) Runs enjoyable bus trips to the Gap of Dunloe (€32), Ring of Kerry (€27) and Dingle and Slea Head (€27).

✵ Festivals & Events

Killarney Mountain Festival OUTDOORS
(www.killarneymountainfestival.com; ⊙Mar) Three days of cultural and historical walks and talks, film screenings, guest speakers, photography and art exhibits, and family fun, focused on the theme of outdoor activities and adventure sports.

The Gathering MUSIC
(www.inec.ie/festival/the-gathering; ⊙late Feb/early Mar) On the go for more than 20 years, this is a rousing five days of traditional Irish music, ranging from intimate fireside sessions to large-scale foot-stomping concerts.

Rally of the Lakes SPORTS
(www.rallyofthelakes.com; ⊙early May) A major date on Ireland's motor-sports calendar, this on-road rally sees drivers take death-defying twists and turns around the lakes and mountains over the May bank-holiday weekend. During the rally campsites and accommodation will be packed, and local roads (including the Healy Pass in County Cork and the N71 Killarney–Kenmare route) may be temporarily closed.

🛏 Sleeping

You'll find dozens of B&Bs just outside the centre on Rock, Lewis and Muckross Rds. The town also has some excellent hostels and high-end hotels, as well as scores of generic hotels aimed at tour groups and wedding parties, plus several campsites. Many places offer bike hire (around €15 per day) and discounted tours. Book ahead everywhere in summer.

★**Black Sheep Hostel** HOSTEL €
(☑064-663 8746; www.blacksheephostel.ie; 68 New St; dm/apt from €23/110; ☎) ⚑ This hostel was designed by travellers, and it shows – custom-made bunks with built-in lockers, reading lights, charging points and privacy curtains; a fully equipped kitchen with free breakfast, an organic garden with free-range chickens (eggs for breakfast!), and a comfortable lounge with sofas, fireplace, communal guitar and library. Three-night minimum from May to October.

★**Fleming's White Bridge Caravan & Camping Park** CAMPGROUND €
(☑064-663 1590; www.killarneycamping.com; White Bridge, Ballycasheen Rd; unit plus 2 adults

€28, hiker/cyclist €12; ⊙mid-Mar–Oct; 🛜🐾) A lovely, sheltered family-run campsite 2.5km southeast of the town centre off the N22, Fleming's has a games room, bike hire, campers' kitchen, laundry and free trout fishing on the river that runs alongside it. Reception can arrange bus, bike and boat tours.

Neptune's Killarney Town Hostel HOSTEL €
(📞 064-663 5255; www.neptuneshostel.com; Bishop's Lane, New St; dm €18-22, s/d €35/54; @ 🛜) Basic but adequate, this hostel has a great central location without being too noisy (it's set well back from the street). Its best aspect is the staff's unfailing helpfulness – they provide local advice and will sort out bus and boat tours for you. There's a laundry service; rates include breakfast.

Shire HOSTEL €
(📞 064-667 1605; www.theshirekillarney.com; Lewis Rd; dm/d from €18/98; 🛜) This place falls somewhere between hostel and B&B. There are three comfortable (if a little oddly shaped) private rooms with bathrooms and a couple of dorms. Check in at the adjacent *Lord of the Rings*–themed cafe-bar, a handy spot for a pint of Guinness and the venue for breakfast (not included in price).

★ Crystal Springs B&B €€
(📞 064-663 3272; www.crystalspringsbandb.com; Ballycasheen Cross, Woodlawn Rd; s/d from €98/120; 🅿🛜) The timber deck of this wonderfully relaxing B&B overhangs the River Flesk, where trout anglers can fish for free. Rooms are

THE KERRY WAY

The 214km Kerry Way (www.kerryway. com) is the Republic's longest way-marked footpath. Starting and ending in Killarney, it winds through the spectacular Macgillycuddy's Reeks, Ireland's highest mountain range, before continuing around the Kerry coast through Cahersiveen, Waterville, Caherdaniel, Sneem and Kenmare.

It takes around 10 days to complete the whole route; with less time it's worth hiking the first three days as far as Glenbeigh, from where a bus or a lift could return you to Killarney. Accommodation along the trail is listed on the website. Ordnance Survey 1:50,000 maps 78, 83 and 84 cover the walk.

richly furnished with patterned wallpapers and walnut timber; private bathrooms (most with spa bath) are huge. The glass-enclosed breakfast room also overlooks the rushing river. It's about a 15-minute stroll into town.

Cots, highchairs and babysitting can be arranged.

Algret House B&B €€
(📞 064-663 2337; www.algret.com; Countess Grove; s/d/f from €60/110/150; 🅿🛜) Knotted pine and polished wood dominate the decor of this light, bright and spacious modern villa, on a quiet side street just a five-minute walk south of the town centre. Friendly hosts make staying here a real pleasure.

Kingfisher Lodge B&B €€
(📞 064-663 7131; www.kingfisherlodgekillarney. eu; Lewis Rd; d/tr from €100/118; ⊙mid-Feb–Nov; 🅿🛜) Lovely gardens are a highlight at this immaculate B&B, whose guest rooms are done up in rich, warm colours. Showers are good and powerful, and breakfasts hearty. Owner Donal Carroll is a certified walking guide with a wealth of knowledge on hiking in the area.

Killarney Plaza Hotel HOTEL €€
(📞 064-662 1111; www.killarneyplaza.com; Kenmare Pl; s/d/ste from €140/175/275; 🅿@🛜🐾) Although it dates only from 2002, this large 198-room hotel channels the style of the art deco era. Classically furnished guest rooms and public areas are in keeping with its luxury reputation; besides the marble lobby and lavishly tiled indoor pool, there's a sauna, steam room and spa.

Killarney Haven APARTMENT €€
(📞 064-663 3570; www.killarney-selfcatering.com; Monsignor O'Flaherty Rd; 2-person apt from €165; 🅿🛜) The decor may be slightly dated, but these well-equipped self-catering apartments are clean and comfortable (some have balconies) and have a great location in the town centre, complete with secure parking.

Chelmsford House B&B €€
(📞 087 918 4161; www.chelmsfordhouse.com; 1 Muckross View; r from €85; 🅿🛜) Set on a rise to the south of town (a 10-minute stroll away), this B&B enjoys a superb view of the Kerry mountains (and even a glimpse of Lough Leane). All three rooms have private bathrooms; one has a balcony. There's a minimum two-night stay. Kids under 10 aren't permitted.

MUCKROSS LAKE LOOP TRAIL

You could easily spend most of a day ambling around this waymarked 9.5km loop trail (anticlockwise only for cyclists), which takes in some of the most photogenic parts of Killarney National Park. Starting from Muckross House, you head west through lovely lakeshore woods (with lots of side trails to explore) to reach postcard-pretty Brickeen Bridge, which spans the channel linking Lough Leane and the Middle Lake.

Continue to the sylvan glades that surround the Meeting of the Waters, where channels from all three of Killarney's lakes merge. Don't miss the 10-minute side trail (no bikes) to Old Weir Bridge, where you can watch tour boats powering through the narrow, rocky channel beneath its twin arches (here, a swiftly flowing current links the Upper and Middle Lakes).

On the return leg along the south shore of Middle Lake, the trail passes through woods before reaching the N71 Killarney–Kenmare road. Here, walkers have the option of climbing uphill on the other side of the road to visit **Torc Waterfall** before returning to Muckross House. Cyclists have to follow the main road east for 1km before regaining the off-road trail. Between the road and Muckross House you can detour along the **Old Boathouse Nature Trail**, which leads around a scenic peninsula.

Maps and details are available from Killarney tourist office (p281) and Muckross House ticket office (p282).

★ **Cahernane House Hotel**   HERITAGE HOTEL €€€
(☏ 064-663 1895; www.cahernane.com; Muckross Rd, Muckross; d/ste from €230/310, 4-course dinner menu €60; [P][🐕]) A tree-lined driveway leads to this magnificent manor 2km south of town, dating from 1877. A dozen of its 38 antique-furnished rooms (some with claw-foot bath or Jacuzzi) are in the original house; garden-wing rooms have balcony or patio. Fishing is possible in the River Flesk, which flows through the grounds. Its restaurant (nonguests by reservation) is sublime.

The manor's wine cellar has an atmospheric bar stocked with Irish whiskey, gin, craft beer and cider.

Fairview   GUESTHOUSE €€€
(☏ 064-663 4164; www.fairviewkillarney.com; College St; s/d/f from €199/229/239; [P][@][🐕]) Reflected in polished wooden floors, the individually decorated rooms (some with classical printed wallpaper, some with contemporary sofas and glass) at this boutique guesthouse offer more bang for your buck than bigger, less personal places. A veritable feast is laid on at breakfast.

Great Southern   HERITAGE HOTEL €€€
(☏ 064-663 8000; www.greatsouthernkillarney.com; East Avenue Rd; s/d/ste from €215/225/295; [P][@][🐕][🏊]) Hidden behind high ivy-clad walls in the town centre, the grand Georgian-style Great Southern first opened its doors in 1854 as the Railway Hotel; its marble-columned lobby and the pick of its rooms, in the 1852 wing, have retained their period opulence. The health club has a spa, vast swimming pool, gym and two tennis courts.

Aghadoe Heights Hotel   SPA HOTEL €€€
(☏ 064-663 1766; www.aghadoeheights.com; Aghadoe; d/f/ste from €222/334/419; [P][@][🐕][🏊]) A glassed-in swimming pool overlooking the lakes is the centrepiece of this contemporary hotel. Guests and nonguests can also soak up the views from the bar and **Lake Room Restaurant** (mains €28-32; ⊙6.30-9.30pm; [🍴]) and luxuriate at the spa's 10 treatment rooms and four-chamber thermal suite. Heavenly beds have memory-foam mattresses. Some rooms have balconies; interconnecting rooms are available for families.

There are board games for rainy days and a tennis court.

✕ Eating

Killarney has good cafes and restaurants in all price ranges. As elsewhere in Kerry, fresh seafood stars on many menus. In summer, evening bookings are recommended at high-end and/or popular places.

Curious Cat Café   CAFE €
(☏ 087 663 5540; www.facebook.com/curiouscatcafe; 4 New Market Lane; mains €9-15; ⊙9am-9pm Fri & Sat, to 4pm Sun & Mon) Tucked away on New Market Lane, with cable-drum tables out the front, this quirky little cafe serves a varied menu that ranges from breakfast smoothies with banana-chocolate bread, to sweet and savoury pancakes, to homemade

HRISTO ANESTEV/SHUTTERSTOCK ©

1. Inch Strand (p303)
A 5km-long beach that attracts surfers, land-yachters, anglers and film directors.

2. Kerry Bog Village Museum (p290)
A recreation of a 19th-century bog village, here you'll see thatched homes and meet native animals.

3. Carrauntoohil (p286)
Ireland's highest peak is a part of Macgillycuddy's Reeks mountain range.

4. Killorglin (p290)
Home of the lively Puck Fair in August, for the rest of the year Killorglin is a quiet town on the River Laune.

soups and lunch dishes such as chicken wings with blue-cheese dip and steak sandwiches. Good coffee too.

Look out for its feisty sangria in the warmer months.

Khao
ASIAN €

(☑064-667 1040; www.facebook.com/khao killarney; 66 High St; mains €11-12; ☺noon-10.30pm; ☑) Fiery spices waft from this cosy spot, which sizzles up authentic stir-fries and wok-fried noodles along with rich curries, rice dishes and noodle soups. All of its produce is organic, and vegetarian choices abound. The two-course lunch menu (€10), served between noon and 5pm weekdays, is a fantastic deal. Takeaway is available.

Petit Délice
CAFE €

(www.facebook.com/petitdelicekerry; 41-42 High St; dishes €3-6; ☺8am-4pm; ☎) Be prepared to wait if you want to get one of the upcycled wooden-box seats at this rustic, always-busy and authentically French cafe-patisserie. Indulge yourself with a breakfast of café au lait, baguette with butter and jam, and a selection of croissants and *pains chocolats*.

Jam
CAFE €

(☑064-663 7716; www.jam.ie; Old Market Lane; mains €4-11; ☺8am-5pm Mon-Sat; ☎☝) Duck down the alley to this local hideout for deli sandwiches, coffee and cake, and a changing menu of hot lunch dishes such as shepherd's pie. It's all made with locally sourced produce. There are a few tables set up out the front in summer.

★Murphy Brownes
INTERNATIONAL €€

(☑064-667 1446; www.facebook.com/murphy brownesrestaurant; 8 High St; mains €14-25; ☺5-9.30pm Mar-early Jan) Elegant and candlelit, but pleasantly informal, this place is ideal for a relaxing dinner. Service is smiling and attentive without being overbearing, and the crowd-pleasing menu is a mix of Irish and international favourites, with local mussels, Kerry lamb shank and fish and chips sitting alongside beef lasagne, chicken curry and Caesar salad.

Treyvaud's
IRISH €€

(☑064-663 3062; www.treyvaudsrestaurant.com; 62 High St; mains €10-30; ☺5-10pm Mon, from noon Tue-Thu & Sun, to 10.30pm Fri & Sat) Mustard-fronted Treyvaud's has a strong reputation for subtle dishes that merge trad Irish with European influences. The seafood chowder – a velvet stew of mussels, prawns and Irish salmon – makes a filling lunch; dinner mains incorporating local ingredients include roast cod with horseradish mash and tomato-and-caper salsa, and a hearty beef and Guinness stew.

Brícín
IRISH €€

(☑064-663 4902; www.bricin.ie; 26 High St; mains €19-28; ☺6-9pm Tue-Sat early Mar-Dec) Decorated with fittings from a convent, an orphanage and a school, this Celtic-themed restaurant doubles as the de facto town museum, with Jonathan Fisher's 18th-century views of the national park taking pride of place. Try the house speciality, boxty (traditional potato pancake). Early-bird two-/three-course dinner (€25/27) available before 6.45pm.

Gaby's Seafood Restaurant
SEAFOOD €€€

(☑064-663 2519; www.gabys.ie; 27 High St; mains €30-50; ☺6-10pm Mon-Sat) Gaby's is a refined dining experience serving superb seafood in a traditional manner. Peruse the menu by the fire before drifting past the wine racks to the low-lit dining room to savour exquisite dishes such as lobster in cognac and cream. The wine list is long and the advice unerring.

🍸 Drinking & Nightlife

Killarney is awash with pubs, most of which put on live music several times a week and nightly in summer.

★Celtic Whiskey Bar & Larder
BAR

(☑064-663 5700; www.celticwhiskeybar.com; 93 New St; ☺10.30am-11.30pm Mon-Thu, to 12.30am Fri & Sat, to 11pm Sun; ☎) Of the thousand-plus whiskeys stocked at this stunning contemporary bar, over 500 are Irish, including 1945 Willie Napier from County Offaly and 12-year-old Writers' Tears from County Carlow. One-hour tasting sessions and masterclasses (from €15) provide an introduction to the world of Irish whiskey. A dozen Irish craft beers are on tap; sensational **food** (mains €9-27; ☺food served noon-9.45pm) is available too.

★O'Connor's
PUB

(www.oconnorstraditionalpub.ie; 7 High St; ☺noon-11.30pm Sun-Thu, to 12.30am Fri & Sat; ☎) Live music plays every night at this tiny traditional pub with leaded-glass doors, one of Killarney's most popular haunts. There are more tables upstairs, and in warmer weather the crowds spill out onto the adjacent lane.

Lir Café
CAFE

(☑064-663 3859; www.lircafe.com; Kenmare Pl;
⊙8am-9pm Mon-Sat, to 7pm Sun; 🖥) Contemporary Lir Café brews some of Killarney's best coffee. Food is limited to toasties, cakes, biscuits and the real treat, handmade chocolates, including Baileys truffles.

Courtney's
PUB

(www.courtneysbar.com; 24 Plunkett St; ⊙2-11.30pm Sun-Thu, to 12.30am Fri & Sat Jun-Sep, from 5pm Mon-Thu Oct-May) Inconspicuous on the outside, this cavernous 19th-century pub bursts at the seams with regular Irish music sessions (nightly in summer). Rock, blues, reggae and indie bands perform year-round on Fridays, with DJs taking over on Saturdays. This is where locals come to see their old mates perform and to kick off a night on the town.

Killarney Grand
BAR

(www.killarneygrand.com; Main St; ⊙7.30pm-2.30am Mon-Sat, to 1.30am Sun) The various bars and clubs at this Killarney institution host traditional live music from 9pm to 11pm, rock bands from 11.30pm to 1.30am and a disco from 11pm. Admission is free before 11pm and €5 to €10 afterwards.

🛍 Shopping

Variety Sounds
MUSICAL INSTRUMENTS

(☑064-663 5755; 7 College St; ⊙9am-6pm Mon-Sat, from noon Sun) A good range of traditional instruments are stocked at this eclectic music shop along with sheet music and hard-to-find recordings.

Killarney Outdoor Store
SPORTS & OUTDOORS

(☑064-662 6927; New St; ⊙10am-6pm Mon-Sat, from noon Sun) Crams a vast amount of outdoor clothing, camping and climbing gear into a small space.

Dungeon Bookshop
BOOKS

(99 College St; ⊙8am-8pm Mon-Sat, from 9am Sun) This secondhand bookshop is hidden above a newsagent (take the stairs at the back of the shop).

Brícín
ARTS & CRAFTS

(www.bricin.ie; 26 High St; ⊙10am-9pm Mon-Sat) Interesting local craftwork, including jewellery and pottery, are stocked alongside touristy wares (shamrock aprons and mugs) at Brícín, which also houses a traditional Irish restaurant.

ℹ Information

The closest accident and emergency unit is at **University Hospital Kerry** (☑066-718 4000; www.hse.ie; Cloon More) in Tralee, 32km northwest of Killarney.

SouthDoc (☑1850 335 999; www.southdoc. ie; Upper Park Rd; ⊙6pm-8am Mon-Fri, 1pm Sat-8am Mon) provides a family doctor service outside normal hours, for urgent medical needs. The clinic is 500m east of Killarney's centre, just east of the roundabout on the N22.

Killarney's **tourist office** (☑064-663 1633; www.killarney.ie; Beech Rd; ⊙9am-5pm Mon-Sat; 🖥) can handle most queries and is especially good with transport intricacies.

ℹ Getting There & Away

AIR
The nearest airport to Killarney is **Kerry Airport** (KIR; ☑066-976 4644; www.kerryairport.ie), at Farranfore, 17km north of Killarney on the N22. There are daily flights to Dublin and London's Luton and Stansted airports, and less frequent services to Berlin and Frankfurt in Germany.

The small airport has a restaurant, bar, bureau de change and ATM. Virtually all the major car-hire firms have desks at the airport.

BUS
Bus Éireann operates from the **bus station** on Park Rd. For Dublin you need to change at Cork – the train is much faster.

Cork €18.05, two hours, hourly

Limerick €14.25, 1¼ hours, four or five daily

Tralee €10.45, 40 minutes, hourly

Waterford €24.70, 4¾ hours, five daily

TRAIN
Killarney's **train station** (☑064-663 1067; Fair Hill) is behind the bus station, just east of the centre.

There are one or two direct services per day to Cork and Dublin; otherwise you'll have to change at Mallow.

Cork €25, 1½ hours

Dublin €62, 3¼ hours

Tralee €11.35, 40 minutes, every two hours

ℹ Getting Around

TO/FROM THE AIRPORT
Bus Éireann (www.buseireann.ie) has hourly services between Killarney and Kerry Airport (€5.50, 20 minutes).

Tralee–Killarney trains (www.irishrail.ie) stop at Farranfore station (€8.80, 20 minutes, every two hours), 1.3km southwest of the airport (a 10-minute walk at minimum).

A taxi to Killarney costs about €20.

BICYCLE

Bicycles are ideal for exploring the scattered sights of the Killarney region, many of which are accessible only by bike or on foot.

Many of Killarney's hostels and hotels offer bike rental. Alternatively, try **O'Sullivan's Bike Hire** (☑ 064-663 1282; www.killarneyrentabike.com; Beech Rd; per day/week from €15/85).

BUS

The **Killarney Shuttle Bus** (☑ 087 138 4384; www.killarneyshuttlebus.com; single €2-5, day pass €10; ⊗ Mar-Oct) runs daily from the tourist office (p281) to all the main tourist spots, including Gap of Dunloe, Ross Castle, Muckross House, Torc Waterfall and Ladies' View. Buy tickets from the driver. A day pass giving unlimited travel on the shuttle bus offers the best value.

CAR & MOTORCYCLE

Killarney's town centre can be thick with traffic at times.

Budget (☑ 064-663 4341; www.budget.ie; International Hotel, Kenmare Pl; ⊗ 9am-6pm Mon-Fri, to 3pm Sat) is the only car-hire outfit with an office in town. Otherwise contact the companies at Kerry Airport. **Enterprise** (☑ 064-663 1393; www.enterprise.ie; Gleneagles Hotel, Muckross Rd; ⊗ 9am-5pm Mon-Fri, to 11.45am Sat) has an office on Muckross Rd, 2km south of the centre.

TAXI

The taxi rank is on College St. Taxi companies include **Killarney Taxi & Tours** (☑ 085 280 3333; www.killarneytaxi.com).

AROUND KILLARNEY

Aghadoe

On a hilltop 5km west of town, Aghadoe's sweeping views of the Killarney lakes, mountains and Inisfallen Island have made jaws drop for centuries. At the eastern end of the hilltop meadow are the ruins of a Romanesque church and 13th-century Parkavonear Castle. Parkavonear's keep, still standing, is one of the few cylindrical keeps built by the Normans in Ireland.

There's no public transport, but several tour buses stop here.

Killarney National Park

Sprawling over 10,236 hectares, the sublime **Killarney National Park** (www.killarneynationalpark.ie) FREE is an idyllic place to explore.

Ross Castle and Muckross House draw big crowds, but it's possible to escape amid Ireland's largest area of ancient oak woods, with panoramic views of its highest mountains and the country's only wild herd of native red deer.

The core of the national park is the Muckross Estate, donated to the state by Arthur Bourn Vincent in 1932; the park was designated a Unesco Biosphere Reserve in 1982. The **Killarney Lakes** – Lough Leane (the Lower Lake, or 'Lake of Learning'), Muckross (or Middle) Lake and the Upper Lake – make up about a quarter of the park, and are surrounded by natural oak and yew woodland, and overlooked by the high crags and moors of **Purple Mountain** (832m) to the west and **Knockrower** (552m) to the south.

⊙ Sights

★**Ross Castle**   CASTLE

(☑ 064-663 5851; www.heritageireland.ie; Ross Rd; adult/child €5/3; ⊗ 9.30am-5.45pm early Mar-Oct; P) Lakeside Ross Castle dates to the 15th century, when it was a residence of the O'Donoghue family. The entertaining 45-minute guided tour combines an easily digested history lesson with real insight into life in medieval Ireland. The castle is a lovely 2.6km walk or bike ride southwest of the St Mary's Cathedral pedestrian park entrance; you may well spot deer along the way.

★**Muckross House**   HISTORIC BUILDING

(☑ 064-667 0144; www.muckross-house.ie; Muckross Estate; adult/child €9.25/6.25, incl Muckross Traditional Farms €15.50/10.50; ⊗ 9am-7pm Jul & Aug, to 6pm Apr-Jun, Sep & Oct, to 5pm Nov-Mar; P) This impressive Victorian mansion is crammed with fascinating objects (70% of the contents are original). Portraits by John Singer Sargent adorn the walls alongside trophy stag heads and giant stuffed trout, while antique Killarney furniture, with its distinctive inlaid scenes of local beauty spots, graces the grand apartments along with tapestries, Persian rugs, silverware and china specially commissioned for Queen Victoria's visit in 1861. It's 5km south of Killarney, signposted from the N71.

The house, built as a hunting and fishing lodge for the Herbert family in 1843, is set in beautiful gardens that slope down to the Middle Lake. At the gate, jaunting cars wait to run you through deer parks and woodland to Torc Waterfall and Muckross Abbey (about €20 each return; haggle for a discount).

FISHING AROUND KILLARNEY

Trout Fishing for brown trout in the lakes of Killarney National Park is free (no permit needed). The season runs from 15 February to 12 October. Fishing from the bank is allowed, but the best sport is to be had from a boat, which you can hire at **Ross Castle** (p283) or at **Sweeney's** (📞 064-664 4207; www.theinvicta.com; Invicta B&B, Tomies, Beaufort), at the west end of Lough Leane, for €40 a day (including outboard motor, up to three people).

Salmon The River Laune, which flows from Lough Leane to the sea, is one of Ireland's best salmon rivers. The season runs from 17 January to 30 September, with the best fishing from late July onward. Both a permit (one day €20) and a state rod licence (one day/three weeks €20/40) are required. You can also fish for salmon in the Killarney lakes (no permit needed, but state rod licence is still required).

O'Neill's (p273) angling centre in Killarney provides information, rents rods and tackle, and sells permits and licences.

A block situated behind the main house contains a craft shop and studios where you can see potters, weavers and bookbinders at work; the nearby visitor centre has a cafe.

⭐**Muckross Abbey** RUINS
(Muckross Estate; ⊘ 24hr) **FREE** Signposted 1.5km northeast of Muckross House, this well-preserved ruin (actually a friary, though everyone calls it an abbey) was founded in 1448 and burned by Cromwell's troops in 1652. There's a square-towered church and a small, atmospheric cloister with a giant yew tree in the centre (legend has it that the tree is as old as the abbey). In the chancel is the tomb of the McCarthy Mòr chieftains, and an elaborate 19th-century memorial to local philanthropist Lucy Gallwey.

Muckross Traditional Farms MUSEUM
(📞 064-663 0804; www.muckross-house.ie; Muckross Estate; adult/child €9.25/6.25, incl Muckross House €15.50/10.50; ⊘ 10am-6pm Jun-Aug, from 1pm Apr, May & Sep, from 1pm Sat & Sun Mar & Oct) These recreations of 1930s farms evoke authentic sights, sounds and smells – cow dung, hay, wet earth and peat smoke, and a cacophony of chickens, ducks, pigs and donkeys. Costumed guides bring the traditional farm buildings to life, and the petting area allows kids to get close to piglets, lambs, ducklings and chicks. Allow at least two hours to do justice to the self-guided tour. A free shuttle loops around the farms, which are just east of Muckross House (p282).

Inisfallen ISLAND
The first monastery on Inisfallen (the largest of the islands in Lough Leane) was founded by St Finian the Leper in the 7th century.

The extensive ruins of a 12th-century **Augustinian priory** and an oratory with a carved Romanesque doorway stand on the site of St Finian's original. You can hire a motorboat with boater (around €10) from Ross Castle for the 10-minute trip to the island.

Inisfallen's fame dates from the early 13th century when the Annals of Inisfallen were written here. Now in the Bodleian Library at Oxford, they remain a vital source of information on early Munster history.

🏃 Activities

The park offers superb opportunities for walking, cycling and fishing.

Killarney's tourist office (p281) stocks walking guides and maps. Killarney Guided Walks (p274) leads guided explorations.

Killarney Lake Tours CRUISE
(MV Pride of the Lakes; 📞 064-663 2638; www.killarneylaketours.ie; Ross Castle Pier; adult/child €10/5; ⊘ Apr-Oct) One-hour tours of Lough Leane in a comfortable, enclosed cruise boat depart four times daily (11am, 12.30pm, 2.30pm and 4pm) from the pier beside Ross Castle, taking in the island of Inisfallen (no landing) and O'Sullivan's Cascade (a waterfall on the west shore).

For €30 per person, including the cruise, a jaunting car will pick you up from your accommodation and take you through Killarney National Park to the castle.

Ross Castle Traditional Boats BOATING
(📞 085 174 2997; Ross Castle Pier; ⊘ 9.30am-5pm Apr-Oct, by reservation Nov-Mar) The open boats at Ross Castle offer engaging trips with boaters who define the word 'character'. Rates are around €10 per person for a trip to Inisfallen

Around Killarney

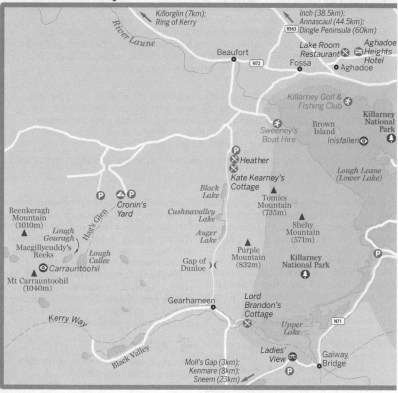

or the Middle Lake and back; it's €20 for a tour of all three lakes.

Outdoors Ireland   ADVENTURE
(☑ 086 860 4563; www.outdoorsireland.com) Guided kayak tours of the Killarney lakes lasting three/seven hours (€60/100 per person; no previous experience needed) generally depart from Ross Castle Pier. The company also runs three-hour sunset kayak trips (€60) and two-day beginner rock-climbing courses (€200).

ⓘ Getting There & Away

There are two pedestrian/bike entrances in Killarney town: opposite St Mary's Cathedral (p273), with 24-hour access; and the so-called Golden Gates at the roundabout on Muckross Rd (open 8am to 7pm June to August, to 6pm April, May and October, to 5pm November to March).

Vehicle access is via Ross Rd on the southern edge of Killarney town centre, leading to Ross

Castle car park; and the Muckross Estate entrance on the N71 5km south of Killarney, leading to the Muckross House car park; parking is free.

ⓘ Getting Around

Walking, cycling and boat trips are the best ways to explore the park.

From the cathedral entrance it's 2.5km (a 30-minute walk) to Ross Castle; to reach Muckross Estate on foot or by bike you have to follow the cycle path beside the N71 south for 3km where it veers off towards the lake (it's 5km all up to Muckross House).

Jaunting cars depart from Kenmare Pl in Killarney town centre, and from the Jaunting Car Entrance to Muckross Estate, at a car park 3km south of town on the N71. Expect to pay around €15 to €20 per person for a tour from Killarney to Ross Castle and back. There are no set prices; haggle for longer tours.

park here, where you can rent jaunting cars (cash only).

★**Heather**   CAFE €€
(☑ 064-664 4144; www.moriartys.ie/heather; mains €9-18; ⊙ 10.30am-5pm; P 🛜 ☑) 🍴 In a glorious setting, this light-filled cafe adjoins a farm that provides produce from its fields and polytunnels, while seafood and meat are locally and sustainably sourced. Fantastic food includes sweet treats such as Skelligs white chocolate and roasted-hazelnut cake to gourmet sandwiches and filling dishes like Kerry lamb burger or chickpea, spinach and potato curry.

The attached gift shop sells quality Irish crafts.

Kate Kearney's Cottage   PUB FOOD €€
(☑ 064-664 4146; mains €10-24; ⊙ kitchen noon-9pm, bar to 11.30pm Mon-Thu, to 12.30am Fri & Sat, to 11pm Sun; P 🖶) This 19th-century pub at the northern end of the Gap of Dunloe serves decent pub classics including sausage and mash, Irish stew, steaks and burgers, and has a kids' menu. Kitchen hours can be reduced at short notice, so call ahead if you're counting on dining here. The bar hosts live Irish music every night in summer.

Lord Brandon's Cottage   CAFE €
(Gearhameen; dishes €3-8; ⊙ 8am-3pm Apr-Oct) At the Gap's southern end, the road twists steeply down to the remote Black Valley and Lord Brandon's Cottage, a 19th-century hunting lodge surrounded by lush, green water meadows with a simple open-air cafe and a dock for boats to Ross Castle, near Killarney. By car, it's reached via a steep minor road from the R568 near Moll's Gap.

❶ Getting There & Away

The traditional way to explore the Gap is via a tour from Killarney – by bus to Kate Kearney's Cottage, then either on foot or by jaunting car through the Gap to Lord Brandon's Cottage on the Upper Lake, and finally by boat to Ross Castle and then bus back to town (€30 per person, plus €20 for jaunting car). Most hostels, hotels and pubs in Killarney can set up these tours, or try Gap of Dunloe Tours (p274).

Despite a road sign at Kate Kearney's Cottage implying that cars are forbidden, it is perfectly legal to drive through the Gap of Dunloe – it's a public road. However, driving the Gap is not recommended, at least from Easter to September. The road is very narrow, steep and twisting, and is usually crowded with walkers, cyclists, ponies and

Gap of Dunloe

The Gap of Dunloe is a wild and scenic mountain pass – studded with crags and bejewelled with lakes and waterfalls – that lies to the west of Killarney National Park, squeezed between Purple Mountain and the high summits of Macgillycuddy's Reeks.

Although it's outside the national park boundary, it's been a vital part of the Killarney tourist trail since the late 18th century when, inspired by the Romantic poets, wealthy tourists came in search of 'sublime' and 'savage' landscapes.

During this period, the legend of Kate Kearney first arose: Kate, a fabled local beauty based on a popular song, supposedly lived in a cottage in the pass and dispensed *poteen* (illegally distilled whiskey) to weary travellers. The 19th-century pub at the northern end of the Gap is still known as Kate Kearney's Cottage; there's a busy car

BY BOAT AND BIKE THROUGH THE GAP

A boat trip through the lakes followed by a bike ride through the Gap of Dunloe is the classic Killarney region experience. Your hostel, hotel or campsite can arrange it for you (boat €20 per person, plus bike hire €12 to €15 per day).

Boats depart near Ross Castle (p282) at 11am, with bikes propped in the bow. The 1½-hour cruise alone justifies the price; ask your boater about the highest/lowest water level ever seen in the lakes, and sit back to enjoy the story.

You cruise past Inisfallen (p283) with its ruined monastery then turn south to sail under pretty Brickeen Bridge and reach the Meeting of the Waters. The boat then surges up a rocky channel beneath the Old Weir Bridge – after prolonged dry weather, when lake levels are low, passengers may have to get out and walk a short distance while the boat gets hauled up this shallow, fast-flowing section.

The Long Range is next, a winding channel that is half-lake, half-river, uncoiling beneath the crags of Eagle's Nest mountain (golden eagles once nested here) before entering the long, narrow Upper Lake.

After disembarking at Lord Brandon's Cottage (p285) around 12.30pm (where there's a cafe and toilets), you begin the bike section with a 4.5km climb to the head of the Gap. It's a steady uphill, but not too steep, and there's no shame in getting off and pushing for a bit. At the summit you're rewarded with stunning views in both directions, and a 6.5km downhill run to Kate Kearney's Cottage (p285), where there's a cafe, pub and toilets.

From here, you follow signs for Killarney along minor roads to the N71, then a cycle path that first hugs the side of the main road before veering off through the golf course and the northern part of Killarney National Park to end near the town centre opposite St Mary's Cathedral.

The total distance cycled is 23km; allowing time for stops and an hour for lunch, you should be back in Killarney by 3.30pm. Hikers can also do this route – allow three hours to walk the 11km from Lord Brandon's to Kate Kearney's, and take the Killarney Shuttle Bus (p282) from the latter back into town (departs at 4.30pm, confirm times in advance).

jaunting cars; the drivers of the latter will give you short shrift. Early morning, or after 5pm is best.

Macgillycuddy's Reeks

Macgillycuddy's Reeks is Ireland's highest mountain range, encompassing 11 of the country's 14 summits that exceed 900m in altitude. The name dates from the 18th century – the MacGillycuddy clan were local landowners, and 'reeks' is dialect meaning 'stacks' (a reference to the layered nature of the rocks here).

The usual approach to the hills is from Cronin's Yard (☑ 064-662 4044; www.cronins-yard.com; Mealis, Beaufort; camping/pods per person €10/15; P), where there's a car park (€2), tearoom (packed lunches available on request), showers and toilets, a free basic campsite and a couple of nifty camping pods. It's at the road's end (OS reference 836873), reached from the N72 via Beaufort, west of Killarney; follow signs for the Gap of Dunloe at first, but keep straight on where the Gap is signposted left. After 4km you'll reach Kissane Foodstone and petrol station; 50m further on, over

the bridge, Cronin's is signposted on the left (a further 3km from Kissane). The Killarney Shuttle Bus (p282) runs here twice daily.

There's an alternative trailhead at Lisleibane – continue past the Cronin's Yard turn-off for 1.5km and turn left (signposted Carrauntoohil Lisleibane) on a narrow winding road which ends after 2.5km at a large parking area (free).

You can get a taste of the Reeks at close quarters by following the waymarked loop trail from Cronin's Yard into Hag's Glen, the beautiful approach valley that leads to loughs Callee and Gouragh below the towering east face of Carrauntoohil (round-trip 8km).

There are several routes up Carrauntoohil (1040m), Ireland's highest peak, but none of them are easy. Even the most straightforward requires good hill-walking and navigation skills, while others are serious scrambling or rock-climbing routes. The traditional route to the summit is via the Devil's Ladder, a gruelling trudge up a badly eroded and unpleasantly loose gully path at the far end of Hag's Glen. The easiest descent is via the **Zig-Zags** to the east of the Devil's Ladder.

An alternative route ascends via **Brother O'Shea's Gully** (some rock scrambling and good route-finding ability required), a steep and challenging route through spectacular scenery on the mountain's north side. Experienced hillwalkers can follow the directions in Adrian Hendorff's guidebook, *The Dingle, Iveragh & Beara Peninsulas: A Walking Guide*. If you're the slightest bit unsure, hire a guide – **Kerry Climbing** (☑ 087 932 3527; www.kerryclimbing.ie; per person €65-85) and **Hidden Ireland Adventures** (☑ 087 221 4002; www.hiddenirelandadventures.com; per person €75; ☺ Wed & Sat) both offer guided ascents of Carrauntoohil year-round, weather permitting (booking is essential).

Climbing Carrauntoohil should never be attempted without a map and compass (and the skills to use them), proper hillwalking boots, waterproofs and spare food and water. Use Harvey's 1:30,000 *MacGillycuddy's Reeks Superwalker* map, or the 1:25,000 Ordnance Survey Adventure Series map (*MacGillycuddy's Reeks & Killarney National Park*).

Moll's Gap

Built in the 1820s to replace an older track to the east (the Old Kenmare Rd, now followed by the Kerry Way hiking trail), the vista-crazy N71 Killarney to Kenmare road (32km) winds between rock and lake, with plenty of lay-bys to stop and admire the views (and recover from the switchback bends). Watch out for the buses squeezing along the road.

About 17km south of Killarney is the panoramic viewpoint **Ladies' View** (N71).

A further 5km south is the summit of the pass at Moll's Gap, which is worth a stop for great views and refreshments at **Avoca Cafe** (☑ 064-663 4720; www.avocahandweavers.com; N71, Moll's Gap; mains €5-9; ☺ 9.30am-5pm Mon-Fri, from 10am Sat & Sun Mar-Nov; � 🖶).

Strawberry Field   CAFE €
(PancakeCottage; ☑ 064-6682977; www.strawberry field-ireland.com; Sneem Rd, Moll's Gap; mains €5-9; ☺ 11am-6pm Apr-early Sep, closed Tue late Jun-early Sep; 🅿 🖶) This 200-year-old stone-built cottage, brightly painted in sunshine yellow and strawberry pink, serves up a tantalising menu of homemade soups, scones, and sweet and savoury pancakes, all freshly prepared to order; old favourites such as

lemon and sugar sit alongside more adventurous flavourings like Gorgonzola, spinach, chopped nuts and maple syrup. Good coffee and hot chocolate too.

RING OF KERRY

This 179km circuit of the Iveragh (pronounced *eev*-raa) Peninsula winds past pristine beaches, medieval ruins, mountains and loughs, with ever-changing views of the island-dotted Atlantic, particularly between Waterville and Caherdaniel in the peninsula's spectacular southwest.

The smaller but equally scenic Skellig Ring, which spins off the loop, is less travelled as the roads are too narrow for tour buses.

Centred on the Ring, the 700-sq-km Kerry International Dark-Sky Reserve (www.kerry darksky.com) was designated in 2014. Low light pollution offers fantastic stargazing when skies are clear.

If you want to get further off the beaten track, explore the interior of the peninsula – on foot along the eastern section of the Kerry Way from Killarney to Glenbeigh, or by car or bike on the minor roads that cut through the hills, notably the Ballaghisheen Pass between Killorglin and Waterville, or the Ballaghbeama Gap from Glenbeigh to Gearha Bridge on the R568.

❶ Getting Around

Although you can cover the Ring in one day by car or three days by bicycle, the more time you take, the more you'll enjoy it.

The road is narrow and twisty in places, notably between Killarney and Moll's Gap. Tour buses travel the Ring in an anticlockwise direction. Getting stuck behind one is tedious, so consider driving clockwise; just watch out on blind corners.

From late June to late August, Bus Éireann (www.buseireann.ie) runs a once-daily Ring of Kerry loop service (280). Buses leave Killarney at 11.30am (Tralee at 10.50am), arriving back at Killarney at 4.45pm (Tralee 5.35pm). En route, stops include Killorglin (€8, 30 minutes), Cahersiveen (€16, 1½ hours), Waterville (€18, 1¾ hours) and Caherdaniel (€21, 2¼ hours).

Year-round, Bus Éireann service 279A runs daily between Killarney and Waterville (€18, 1¾ hours), via Killorglin (€8, 30 minutes) and Cahersiveen (€16, 1½ hours).

LocalLink Kerry (☑ 066-714 7002; www. locallinkkerry.ie) minibuses run between Killorglin and Waterville (€8, 1½ hours) via Cahersiveen (€6, one hour), three to four times daily (once

1. King Puck statue (p290), Killorglin **2.** Kenmare (p300)
3. Valentia Island (p293) **4.** Derrynane National Historic Park
(p299), Caherdaniel

YOUNGOGOO/SHUTTERSTOCK ©

JUDITH LIENERT/SHUTTERSTOCK ©

Ring of Kerry

Windswept beaches, Atlantic waves crashing against rugged cliffs and islands, medieval ruins, soaring mountains and glinting loughs are some of the stunning distractions along the twisting 179km Ring of Kerry circle drive around the Iveragh Peninsula.

Killorglin

Even if you're racing around the ring, don't miss its first town (heading anticlockwise). The riverside village of Killorglin is home to a salmon smokehouse, some standout restaurants and, in August, the historic Puck Fair Festival.

Kenmare

A fitting last (or first) stop on the ring, Kenmare is a microcosm of Kerry's greatest charms. A beautiful location on the bay (from where boat trips depart), colourful shops and gracious architecture are cornerstones of this classic Irish town.

Skellig Ring

A ring within the ring, this 18km loop off the main route offers an escape from the crowds. The wild, scenic drive links Portmagee and Waterville via a Gaeltacht (Irish-speaking) area centred on Ballinskelligs (Baile an Sceilg).

Valentia Island

Islands are a scenic highlight on the ring. Some are accessible by boat, but picturesque Valentia Island is even easier to reach, via a short bridge. There's also a summer car-ferry service departing just south of Cahersiveen.

Caherdaniel

The ring's scenery is at its most rugged around Caherdaniel. Highlights here include the Derrynane National Historic Park with its stately house and palm-filled gardens, horse riding, a Blue Flag beach and water sports galore.

Ring of Kerry

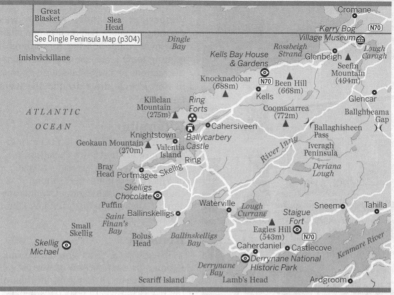

on Sunday), with one or two continuing to Caherdaniel (€10, two hours).

Killorglin

POP 2199

Travelling anticlockwise from Killarney, the first town on the Ring is Killorglin (Cill Orglain, meaning Orgla's Church). For most of the year, it's quieter than the waters of the River Laune that lap against its 1885-built eight-arched bridge, where salmon leap and little egrets paddle in the shallows.

In August, however, there's an explosion of time-honoured ceremonies at the famous pagan festival, the Puck Fair (a statue of **King Puck** – a goat – stands on the north side of the river). Author Blake Morrison documents his mother's childhood here in *Things My Mother Never Told Me.*

Kerry Bog Village Museum MUSEUM
(www.kerrybogvillage.ie; Ballincleave, Glenbeigh; adult/child €6.50/4.50; ⊙9am-6pm; P) This museum recreates a 19th-century bog village, typical of the small communities that carved out a precarious living in the harsh environment of Ireland's ubiquitous peat bogs. You'll see the thatched homes of the turfcutter, blacksmith, thatcher and labourer, as well as a dairy, and meet Kerry bog ponies (a native breed) and Irish wolfhounds. It's on the N70, 8.3km southwest of Killorglin near Glenbeigh; buy a ticket at the neighbouring Red Fox Inn if no one's at the gate.

Puck Fair CULTURAL
(Aonach an Phuic; www.puckfair.ie; ⊙mid-Aug) First recorded in 1603, with hazy origins, this lively three-day festival centres on the custom of installing a billy goat (a poc, or puck), the symbol of mountainous Kerry, on a pedestal in the town, its horns festooned with ribbons. Other entertainment ranges from a horse fair to street theatre, concerts and fireworks; the pubs stay open until 3am.

🛏 Sleeping & Eating

There's a handful of good restaurants and a bakery on and around Lower Bridge St, as well as an outstanding seafood restaurant, Jacks' Coastguard Restaurant (p292), in nearby Cromane.

KRD Fisheries (☑066-976 1106; www.krd fisheries.com; Tralee Rd; ⊙9am-1pm & 2-5pm Mon-Fri, to 1pm Sat, to 11am Sun) 🐟 sells smoked salmon direct from its factory premises. Self-caterers will also find decent-size supermarkets.

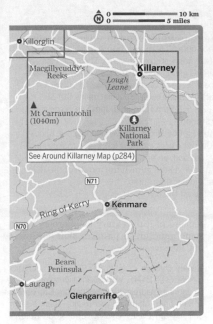

See Around Killarney Map (p284)

Coffey's River's Edge
B&B €€

(☑066-976 1750; www.coffeysriversedge.com; Lower Bridge St; s/d from €70/100; ⓟ🖅) You can sit out on the balcony overlooking the River Laune at this contemporary B&B with 10 spotless spring-toned rooms and hardwood floors. Cots are available. It's in a central location next to the bridge.

Jack's Bakery
BAKERY €

(Lower Bridge St; dishes €2.50-8; ⊙8am-6.45pm Mon-Fri, to 6pm Sat, 9am-2pm Sun) 🖉 Jack Healy bakes amazing artisan breads, and also serves killer coffee and beautiful sandwiches (using homemade pâtés) at this popular spot. There's no indoor seating, but a couple of tables are set up on the pavement in good weather.

Bianconi
GASTROPUB €€

(☑066-976 1146; www.bianconi.ie; Lower Bridge St; mains €10-28; ⊙kitchen 11.30am-10pm Mon-Sat, 6-9pm Sun; 🖅) This Victorian-style pub has a classy ambience and an equally refined menu. Its spectacular salads, such as Cashel Blue cheese, apple, toasted almonds and pancetta, are a meal in themselves. Upstairs, stylishly refurbished guest rooms (singles/doubles from €95/125) have olive and truffle tones and luxurious bathrooms (try for a roll-top tub).

Giovannelli
ITALIAN €€€

(☑087 123 1353; www.giovannellirestaurant.com; Lower Bridge St; mains €19-34; ⊙6.30-9pm Mon-Sat) Northern Italian native Daniele Giovannelli makes all his pasta by hand at this simple but intimate little restaurant. Highlights of the blackboard menu might include seafood linguine with mussels in the shell and beef ravioli in sage butter. Wonderful wines are available by the bottle and glass.

ⓘ Information

The **tourist office** (☑066-976 1451; www.reeksdistrict.com; Library Pl; ⊙9am-1pm & 1.30-5pm Mon-Fri) sells maps, walking guides, fishing permits and souvenirs.

Cahersiveen

POP 1041

The main town of the Iveragh Peninsula, Cahersiveen (pronounced caar-suh-*veen;* from *cathair saidhbhín,* Little Sarah's Ring Fort) began life as a fishing harbour and market town but fell on hard times at the end of the 20th century.

But the last few years have seen a determined effort to reinvent the town as a tourism centre. The main street and waterfront areas have been spruced up, the former barracks has been beautifully restored as a heritage centre, there are some excellent places to stay and eat, and the surrounding countryside is a delight to explore.

The town is indelibly linked with the fight for Irish independence – it was the birthplace of Daniel O'Connell, 'the Great Liberator', and was where the first shots of the 1867 Fenian Rising were fired.

⊙ Sights & Activities

Waymarked local walks include the Bentee Loop (9km), which starts in Cahersiveen and leads to the 376m summit of Bentee, the conical hill just south of town, with superb views of Valentia Island and the hills of the Iveragh Peninsula.

Casey Cycles (p292) offers bike rental and cycling-route advice.

Ring Forts
RUINS

(Ballycarbery) FREE Some 3km northwest of Cahersiveen, two extraordinary stone ring forts situated 600m apart are reached from a shared parking area. Cahergal, the larger and more impressive, dates from the 10th

CROMANE PENINSULA

Unless you know it's here, you wouldn't chance upon **Cromane**, home to Ireland's largest natural mussel beds (up to 8000 tonnes are harvested each year). The village sits at the base of a narrow shingle spit, with open fields giving way to spectacular water vistas and multihued sunsets. Some of the area's best seafood is served at **Jacks' Coastguard Restaurant** (☑ 066-976 9102; www.jackscromane.com; Cromane; mains €19-36, 5-course tasting menu €65, 3-course Sun lunch €29; ☺ 6-9pm Thu-Sun, 1-3pm Sun, hours can vary; P) , in a 19th-century coastguard station.

Southwest of Cromane is **Dooks Golf Club** (☑ 066-976 8205; www.dooks.com; Knockaunroe, Glenbeigh; green fees €100-140; ☺ Apr-Oct), one of the oldest links golf courses in Ireland, opened in 1889. A little further along the road, an unsignposted lane (look for the green postbox) leads to **Dooks Beach**, a little-visited gem at the mouth of the River Caragh, with gorgeous views of the Kerry and Dingle mountains.

Cromane is 9km west of Killorglin, signposted off the N70.

century and has stairways on the inside walls, a *clochán* (circular stone building, shaped like an old-fashioned beehive), and the remains of a roundhouse. The smaller, 9th-century **Leacanabuile** contains the outlines of four houses. Both have a commanding position overlooking Ballycarbery Castle (p292) and Valentia Harbour, with superb views of the Kerry mountains.

Old Barracks Heritage Centre MUSEUM
(☑ 066-401 0430; www.theoldbarrackscahersiveen. com; Bridge St; adult/child €4/2; ☺ 10am-5pm Mon-Sat, 11am-4pm Sun Mar-Nov; P) Established in response to the Fenian Rising of 1867, the Royal Irish Constabulary barracks at Cahersiveen were built in an eccentric Bavarian-Schloss style, complete with pointy turret and stepped gables. Burnt down in 1922 by anti-Treaty forces, the imposing building has been restored and now houses fascinating exhibitions on the Fenian Rising and the life and works of local hero Daniel O'Connell.

The **town park**, which stretches along the riverbank behind the heritage centre, contains the outline of the ancient ring fort that gave the town its name.

O'Connell's Birthplace RUINS
At the bridge across the Carhan River on the eastern edge of town, a neat little memorial park remembers Daniel O'Connell (1775–1847), 'the Great Liberator', a political leader who campaigned for Catholic emancipation and Irish independence. He was born in the ruined cottage that stands on the far bank of the river.

Ballycarbery Castle CASTLE
(Ballycarbery) FREE The atmospheric – and decidedly dangerous-looking – ivy-strangled remains of 16th-century Ballycarbery Castle stand amid green pastures 3km northwest of Cahersiveen.

Casey Cycles CYCLING
(☑ 066-947 2474; www.bikehirekerry.com; New St; touring/road/electric bikes per day €16/35/40; ☺ 9am-6pm Mon-Sat year-round, 10am-1.30pm Sun Jul-Aug) Casey Cycles rents good-quality touring bikes, road bikes and e-bikes, and provides information on local cycling routes. Good objectives include the ring forts at Cahergall, or Valentia Island, easily reached via the ferry (p293) just west of town.

★★ Festivals & Events

Cahersiveen Festival of Music & the Arts MUSIC
(www.celticmusicfestival.com; ☺ early Aug) Celtic bands, busking competitions and Irish set-dancing star at this family-friendly festival held over the August bank holiday weekend.

🛏 Sleeping & Eating

★ **Mannix Point Camping & Caravan Park** CAMPGROUND €
(☑ 066-947 2806; www.campinginkerry.com; Mannix Point, Cahersiveen; hikers €8.50, vehicle plus 2 adults from €26; ☺ late-Apr–mid-Sep; 🐾) Mortimer Moriarty's award-winning waterfront campsite is one of Ireland's finest, with 42 pitches, an inviting kitchen, a campers' sitting room with peat fire (no TV, but regular music sessions and instruments if you haven't brought your own), laundry facilities, squeaky-clean showers (€1), a barbecue area and even a birdwatching platform. Sunsets here are stunning.

San Antoine B&B €
(☎066-947 2521; www.sanantoine.com; Garrane-bane; s/d/tr/f from €50/90/110/125; P☎) At the western edge of town, this spotless and spacious B&B sports a large terrace and breakfast room, both with views towards sea and hills. The owners can help arrange boat trips to Skellig Michael, and advise on local walks and bike rides.

Sive Hostel HOSTEL €
(☎087 275 4561; https://sive-hostel.business.site; 15 East End; dm €23, s/d/tr from €40/60/80; ☎) Simple and sweet, this homely hostel has good-value private rooms, some in a cute stone cottage at the back, a rooftop balcony with great views and a lovely courtyard area. There's bike storage and a drying room.

★**Quinlan & Cooke** SEAFOOD €€
(☎066-947 2244; www.qc.ie; 3 Main St; mains €18-27; ☺food served 6-9pm, bar 3-10pm Thu-Mon Easter-Sep, shorter hours Oct-Easter; ☎🍴) 🍴
This is a modern take on a trad pub, so you can drop in for pints and craic in the after-noon, and stay for dinner. Some of the finest food on the Ring pours forth, particularly locally sourced seafood from the owner's fishing fleet, including fish and chips, and crab and prawn bisque. Hours can vary, so call to confirm.

Upstairs there are 10 boutique guest **bed-rooms** (d/ste from €140/230; P☎).

Camo's CAFE €€
(☎066-948 1122; www.camos.ie; 24 Church St; mains lunch €7-12, dinner €15-25; ☺10am-6pm Mon-Wed, 10am-5pm & 6.30-9pm Thu & Fri, 11am-5pm & 6.30-9pm Sat; ☎🍴) During the day, this friendly neighbourhood spot serves dishes such as oak-smoked salmon sandwiches on home-baked brown bread, and a delicious black pudding and blue-cheese salad. At night, seafood (sizzling prawns and chorizo, pan-fried hake) is the highlight of a menu that also includes forays into fusion cuisine.

ⓘ Getting There & Away

Bus Éireann (www.buseireann.ie) has daily ser-vice to Killarney (€16, 1½ hours) and Waterville (€5, 25 minutes), plus a daily Ring of Kerry loop service (p287) from late June to late August.

Valentia Island Car Ferry (☎087 241 8973; one-way/return car €8/12, cyclist €2/3, pedes-trian €1.50/2; ☺7.45am-10pm Mon-Sat, from 9am Sun Jul & Aug, 7.45am-9.30pm Mon-Sat, from 9am Sun Apr-Jun, Sep & Oct) links Caher-siveen with Valentia Island from April to October.

DON'T MISS

KELLS BAY HOUSE & GARDENS

Opened in 1837 as a hunting lodge, the magnificent estate of **Kells Bay House & Gardens** (☎066-947 7974; www.kellsgardens.ie; off N70, Kells Bay; adult/child €8/6; ☺9am-9pm Jun-Aug, to 7pm Feb-May, Sep & Oct, to 4.30pm Nov & Dec; P) sprawls over 17 hectares incorporat-ing a waterfall, beach and six different gardens, ranging from palms to a pri-meval fern forest with dinosaurs carved from fallen trees. Ireland's longest rope bridge, the 33.5m Skywalk, sways pre-cariously 11m above the River Delligeen-agh, which swirls through the property.

Walled kitchen gardens and farm animals provide ingredients for its Thai restaurant (mains €10 to €16). It's also possible to stay here (double/suite from €92/145).

Valentia Island
POP 665

Laced with narrow roads, Valentia is a beau-tiful and undervisited corner of Kerry with a rich and fascinating history. Its Latin-sounding name is actually an anglicised version of the Irish *Béal Inse,* meaning 'the mouth of the island' (a reference to the shel-tered harbour entrance), though the Irish name of the island itself, Oileán Dairbhre, means 'island of oak trees'.

Valentia is renowned for its high-quality slate, which was first quarried here in 1816 – Valentia slate was used to roof London's Houses of Parliament and Westminster Cathedral, and Paris' Palais Garnier opera house. The quarry, abandoned in 1911, re-opened in 1999 and produces slate objects including billiard-table bases.

The island measures just 11km long by 3km wide; Knightstown, at the eastern end of the island, is its only village.

◉ Sights

Glanleam House & Gardens GARDENS
(☎066-947 6176; gardens €5; ☺10am-7pm mid-Mar–Oct) Built as a linen mill in the 1770s, this estate was transformed from 1808 when its owner established its 16-hectare gardens with exotic plants from around the world including bamboo and the tallest tree ferns in Europe.

SKELLIG ISLANDS

The twin wave-battered pinnacles of the Skellig Islands (Oileáin na Scealaga) are the site of Ireland's most remote and spectacular ancient monastery. The 12km sea crossing can be rough, and the climb up to the monastery is steep and tiring. Due to the sheer (and often slippery) terrain and sudden wind gusts, it's not suitable for young children or people with limited mobility. Bring something to eat and drink, and wear sturdy shoes with good grip and weatherproof clothing.

The jagged, 217m-high rock of **Skellig Michael** (Michael's Rock; like St Michael's Mount in Cornwall and Mont St Michel in Normandy; www.heritageireland.ie; ⊘mid-May–Sep) FREE is the larger of the two Skellig Islands and a Unesco World Heritage site. Early Christian monks established a community and survived here from the 6th until the 12th or 13th century. The monastic buildings perch on a saddle in the rock, some 150m above sea level, reached by 618 steep steps cut into the rock face.

The astounding 6th-century oratories and beehive cells vary in size; the largest cell has a floor space of 4.5m by 3.6m. You can see the monks' south-facing vegetable garden and their cistern for collecting rainwater. The most impressive structural achievements are the settlement's foundations – platforms built on the steep slope using nothing more than earth and drystone walls.

Influenced by the Coptic Church (founded by St Anthony in the deserts of Egypt and Libya), the monks' determined quest for ultimate solitude led them to this remote, windblown edge of Europe. Not much is known about the life of the monastery, but there are records of Viking raids in AD 812 and 823. Monks were kidnapped or killed, but the community recovered and carried on. In the 11th century a rectangular oratory was added to the site, but although it was expanded in the 12th century, the monks abandoned the rock around this time.

After the introduction of the Gregorian calendar in 1582, Skellig Michael became a popular spot for weddings. Marriages were forbidden during Lent, but since Skellig used the old Julian calendar, a trip to the islands allowed those unable to wait for Easter to tie the knot. In the 1820s two lighthouses were built on the island, together with the road that runs around the base.

Skellig Michael famously featured as Luke Skywalker's Jedi temple in *Star Wars: The Force Awakens* (2015) and *Star Wars: The Last Jedi* (2017), attracting a whole new audience to the island's dramatic beauty (p297).

Now partly restored, part still atmospherically overgrown, trails meander along its beach, river and through the forest. Accommodation is available in the manor house (p296).

Tetrapod Trackway
HISTORIC SITE

(Dohilla; P) FREE This string of small depressions in an exposed sandstone bedding surface next to the sea may not be as spectacular as dinosaur footprints, but these fossil tracks – left behind by a metre-long amphibious creature around 360 million years ago – are among the world's oldest physical evidence of a vertebrate creature moving on land. Even if geology isn't your thing, the setting is beautiful, with views to the Blasket Islands and the Dingle Peninsula. It's 4.3km northwest of Knightstown.

Valentia Island Heritage Centre
MUSEUM

(☎066-947 6411; School Rd, Knightstown; adult/child €4/free; ⊘10.30am-5.30pm May-Sep) Inside the old school on the road towards Geokaun Mountain, this intriguing local museum has a treasure trove of artefacts that tell the tale of the island's history more eloquently than any textbook – from school chemistry sets and slate-quarrying tools to fossils and old photographs, with pride of place going to the Morse key used to test the world's first transatlantic telegraph cable.

Skellig Experience
MUSEUM

(☎066-947 6306; www.skelligexperience.com; adult/child €5/3, incl cruise €35/20; ⊘10am-7pm Jul & Aug, to 6pm May, Jun & Sep, to 4.30pm Fri-Wed Mar, Apr, Oct & Nov; P) Immediately across the bridge from Portmagee, this distinctive building with a turf-covered roof contains exhibitions on the life of the Skellig Michael monks, the history of the island's lighthouses and its wildlife. From April to September, it also runs two-hour **cruises** around the islands (no landing), and is a good place to get advice on visiting the Skelligs.

There are no toilets on the island.

Small Skellig is long, low and craggy: from a distance it looks as if it's shrouded in a swirling snowstorm. Close up you realise you're looking at a colony of over 23,000 pairs of breeding gannets, the second-largest breeding colony in the world. Most boats circle the island so you can see the gannets and you may see basking seals as well. Small Skellig is a bird sanctuary; no landing is permitted.

Getting to Skellig Michael

Boat trips to the Skelligs usually run from mid-May to September (dates are announced each year by Heritage Ireland), weather permitting (there are no sailings on two days out of seven, on average). You can depart from Portmagee, Ballinskelligs or Caherdaniel. There is a limit on the number of daily visitors, with boats licensed to carry no more than 12 passengers each, so it's wise to book ahead; it costs around €100 per person. Check to make sure operators have a current licence; the OPW (Office of Public Works; www.opw.ie) can provide advice.

Morning departure times depend on tide and weather, and last around five hours in total with two hours on the rock, which is the bare minimum to visit the monastery, look at the birds and have a picnic. The crossing takes about 1½ hours from Portmagee, 35 minutes to one hour from Ballinskelligs and 1¾ hours from Caherdaniel.

If you just want to see the islands up close and avoid actually having to clamber out of the boat, consider a 'no landing' cruise with operators such as Skellig Experience (p120) on Valentia Island.

The Skellig Experience heritage centre (p120), local pubs and B&Bs will point you in the direction of boat operators, including the following.

Force Awakens (p124) Star Wars–themed tours; based in Ballinskelligs.

Sea Quest (☑ 087 236 2344; www.skelligsrock.com; per person €100; ☺ mid-May–Sep) Based in Portmagee; also runs a nonlanding wildlife-watching eco-cruise.

Skellig Tours (☑ 087 689 8431; www.skelligtours.com; Bunavalla Pier, Bealtra; Skellig tour €100; ☺10am mid-May–Sep) Based at Bunavalla Pier, near Caherdaniel.

In March, April, October and November the centre opens six days a week, but the exact days change each year – check ahead.

Geokaun Mountain VIEWPOINT
(www.geokaun.com; car/cyclist/hiker €5/2/2; ☺6am-11pm) The local landowner has transformed the island's highest point, Geokaun (266m), into a network of easy walking trails and viewpoints, with a breathtaking outlook over the Fogher Cliffs. It's possible to drive all the way to the top, so visitors with limited mobility don't miss out on the views. At quieter times the site is unstaffed, and entry is via an automatic barrier (payment with coins only).

Telegraph Field MONUMENT
Valentia Island was chosen as the eastern terminus of the first transatlantic telegraph cable, from Heart's Content, Newfoundland. A monument at Telegraph Field, at the western end of the island, commemorates the establishment of the first permanent communications link between Europe and North America in 1866. The telegraph station here continued in operation until 1966, when satellite technology provided a faster alternative.

Prior to the cable, it took two weeks to transmit information, as communications were sent by boat.

Sleeping & Eating

Valentia Island

Caravan & Camping CAMPGROUND €
(☑ 087 967 3673; www.valentiaislandcamping.com; Farranreach, Knightstown; vehicle plus 2 adults €24, hiker or cyclist €8; ☺ Apr-Sep; ☏☺) Set on the southwestern edge of Knightstown, this campsite has good facilities, including a campers' kitchen and games room, and owners who are unstintingly helpful and welcoming.

★ **Atlantic Villa**   B&B €€
(☑ 087 212 6798; www.atlanticvilla.ie; Knightstown; s/d from €50/80; ᴾ 🅢) Built in 1873 for the superintendent of the transatlantic telegraph cable between Valentia and Newfoundland, this historic house has a blazing open fire and six lovingly restored rooms rich in period atmosphere – some with sea views – and modern comforts that include superb gourmet breakfasts and a sauna. Packed lunches can be arranged, as well as saunas and seaweed baths.

Produce for breakfast comes from its own gardens, with eggs supplied by its chickens. One- and two-bedroom self-catering cottages (€375/450 per week) are located on the property.

Glanleam House   B&B €€
(☑ 066-947 6176; mail@glanleam.com; Glanleam; d from €120; ᴾ 🅢) An overgrown road leads to this Georgian manor house, built in 1770 for the owner of a linen mill. It has four antique-furnished guest rooms and an impressive country-house-style library with ornamental fireplace. There are also four self-catering cottages sleeping up to six (from €160, two-night minimum stay); the Boathouse, right on the seafront, is particularly attractive.

Royal Valentia   HOTEL €€
(☑ 066-947 6144; www.royalvalentia.ie; Knightstown; s/d/f from €79/99/169; ᴾ 🅢) Established in the 1830s, this Victorian hotel has been given a modern makeover with 30 bright, uncluttered rooms (some with four-poster beds and many with harbour views). Family rooms sleep four. Its lively bar, serving pub food (mains €14 to €25), is the heart and soul of the local community.

Pod Coffee Shop   CAFE €
(☑ 066-947 6995; www.podcrepesandgifts.word press.com; 2 Market St, Knightstown; crêpes €5-12; ☉ noon-6pm Mon & Tue, from 10.30am Wed-Sun mid-Jun–Sep; 🅢) Sweet crêpes such as lemon and sugar or apple and cinnamon are served alongside savoury galettes made from buckwheat flour (Cashel Blue cheese, walnuts and honey; Portmagee crab, cheese and spinach). The attached gift shop stocks local art, crafts, soaps and deli items; on sunny days tables are set up on the terrace.

Valentia Island Farmhouse Dairy   ICE CREAM €
(☑ 066-947 6864; http://valentiaicecream.ie; Kilbeg East; ice cream per 1/2/3 scoops €3/5.50/7.50; ☉ 11am-7pm Jul & Aug, to 6pm Jun; ᴾ 🅱) 🍦 Dairy cattle on this working farm provide the milk for all-natural handmade ice cream in flavours such as cinnamon, caramel, mint choc-chip and strawberry, using berries also grown on the farm. Milk-free sorbets span rhubarb to cucumber. Its terrace overlooks the fields and sea beyond; there's a children's indoor/outdoor play area.

Horse-and-trap tours of the island are available for €9 per person (up to seven adults), minimum charge €30.

ⓘ Information

The island's **tourist office** (☑ 066-947 6985; www.valentiaisland.ie; 3 Watch House Cottage, Knightstown; ☉ 10am-4.30pm May-Sep, 9am-5pm Mon-Fri Oct-Apr) is in Knightstown.

ⓘ Getting There & Away

Valentia is not served by public transport.

A bridge links the island with Portmagee on the mainland.

From April to October, the Valentia Island Car Ferry (p293) shuttles back and forth between Knightstown and Reenard Point, 5km southwest of Cahersiveen. The crossing takes five minutes, with departures every 10 minutes.

Portmagee

POP 123

Portmagee's much-photographed single street is a rainbow of colourful houses. On summer mornings, the small harbour comes to life with boats embarking on the choppy crossing to the Skellig Islands (p291).

From the village, a bridge leads to Valentia Island (p293).

★ **Portmagee Heights**   B&B €€
(☑ 066-947 7251; www.portmageeheights.com; New Rd; s/d from €80/90; ᴾ 🅢) A location at the top of a hill just west of the village means that three of the five bedrooms at this luxurious B&B enjoy fantastic views across the harbour to Valentia Island. Tasteful modern decor with striking colour combinations add to the designer feel of the place, and the welcome is as warm as the freshly baked bread.

Moorings   GUESTHOUSE €€
(☑ 066-947 7108; www.moorings.ie; s/d/tr from €90/120/165; 🅢) The Moorings is a friendly local bar and restaurant. It has 16 guest rooms, split between superior sea-view choices and simpler options, decorated in soothing neutral tones enlivened by red cushions and coverlets. Cots and pullout sofas are available for kids.

STAR WARS SIGHTS

Star Wars aficionados will want to make a pilgrimage to the dizzyingly steep, starkly beautiful monastic island of Skellig Michael (p291), which made its dramatic big-screen debut in 2015's *Star Wars: The Force Awakens*, and reprised its role as Luke Skywalker's Jedi temple in 2017's *Star Wars: The Last Jedi*. Superfans can even travel to the island with a boat-tour company called **Force Awakens** (☑087 238 5610; www.theskelligs forceawakens.com; Ballinskelligs Pier; per person €100).

Other *Star Wars* filming locations in Kerry include Sybil Head (Ceann Sibeal) on the Dingle Peninsula, 4.5km northwest of Ballyferriter. Elsewhere in Ireland, shooting took place in the area around Loop Head Lighthouse (p358), 26km southwest of Kilkee, County Clare; Brow Head, 3km southwest of Crookhaven, County Cork; and Hell's Hole, a plunging, fissured chasm on the Inishowen Peninsula, 6km northwest of Malin Head, County Donegal.

Moorings Restaurant   SEAFOOD €€€
(☑066-947 7108; www.moorings.ie; mains €24-35; ⊘6-10pm Wed-Sun Apr-Oct; ⛨) This nautical-themed restaurant specialises in locally landed seafood, used in dishes such as hake with lemon-butter sauce, and a fresh seafood platter (€35) with lobster, Cromane mussels, garlic prawns, Portmagee crab claws and grilled fish. There's a good kids' menu.

Bridge Bar   BAR
(☑066-947 7108; www.moorings.ie; mains €13-18; ⊘8am-11.30pm Mon-Sat, to 11pm Sun, kitchen to 9pm; ⛨) The focus of Portmagee's village life is the raspberry-coloured Bridge Bar, a local gathering point that hosts traditional Irish music and dancing sessions every Friday and Sunday year-round, plus Tuesdays in July and August. Excellent fish and chips are among the standouts of its bar menu; breakfast is served till noon.

Skellig Ring

Branching off the Ring of Kerry, this little-travelled 18km route links Portmagee, Valentia Island and Waterville via a Gaeltacht (Irish-speaking) area centred on Ballinskelligs (Baile an Sceilg).

The area is wild and beautiful, with the ragged outline of Skellig Michael never far from view. This dramatic island housed a remote monastery between the 6th and 12th centuries and is now an important site for puffins, gannets and guillemots. Its starring role as a location in *Star Wars: The Force Awakens* and *Star Wars: The Last Jedi* means it hogs the limelight, but elsewhere on the Skellig Ring you'll find historic resorts, colourful houses, walking trails and a history that takes in ancient vertebrates and the transatlantic telegraph.

Kerry's Most
Spectacular Cliffs   NATURAL FEATURE
(Foilnagearagh; per person €4; ⊘9am-5pm) Its hyperbolic name – and recreated dry-stone *clochán* with fake birds perched on top – aside, the view is indeed spectacular from this privately owned walk along 305m-high cliffs, which look out over Skellig Michael and surrounding islands. The 800m-long path is fenced and has coin-operated binoculars. Admission includes parking; a cafe opens from Easter to September.

Skelligs Chocolate   FACTORY
(☑066-947 9119; www.skelligschocolate.com; St Finian's Bay; ⊘10am-5pm Mon-Fri year-round, from 11am Sat & Sun Apr-Sep; ᴾ⛨) FREE At these gleaming open-plan premises, you can get an overview of chocolate production and taste the wares too. Samples are free, and chocolates are sold in boxes, bags, and in dishes – along with heavenly hot chocolate – at the rather industrial on-site cafe (open Easter to September).

Skelligs Watersports   WATER SPORTS
(☑086 389 4849; www.skelligsurf.com; Ballinskelligs Beach; ⊘10am-6pm mid-May–Sep) At Ballinskelligs Beach, Skelligs Watersports hires out surfboards, stand up paddleboards (SUPs), kayaks and windsurfers (per day from €20), and gives surfing and windsurfing lessons (€35 per two hours including wetsuits).

Ballinskelligs Priory   RUINS
The sea and salty air are eating away at the atmospheric ruins of this medieval priory, a monastic settlement that was probably built by the Skellig Michael monks after they fled their isolated outpost in the 12th century. The ruins are 400m south of the car park for Ballinskelligs Beach.

Waterville

POP 538

Waterville is an old-fashioned seaside resort strung along the N72 at the head of Ballinskelligs Bay, and is known for its golf and fishing. The renowned Waterville Golf Links (p298) welcomes visitors, but the Hogs Head Golf Course at the other end of town, designed by Robert Trent Jones II and opened in 2018, is members only.

Silent-movie star Charlie Chaplin famously holidayed in Waterville in the 1960s with his extended family, returning every year for more than a decade to the Butler Arms Hotel. A bronze statue of Chaplin beams out from the seafront, and the Charlie Chaplin Comedy Film Festival is held here in late August.

Nearby Lough Currane has long been famed for the quality of its sea-trout fishing, particularly from May to July. However, the annual run of sea trout has declined since 2016, following the establishment of several salmon farms offshore (sea lice from the farms infect the wild fish).

No permit is required, but you'll need a state rod licence (www.fishinginireland. info) and a rental boat, which is €55 a day, or €140 a day for a *ghillie* (fishing or hunting guide) such as Vincent Appleby at **Salmon & Sea Trout Fishing** (☑ 087 207 4882; www. salmonandseatrout.com; fishing per day €140; ☺ by appointment).

★ **Waterville Golf Links** GOLF
(☑ 066-947 4102; www.watervillegolflinks.ie; green fees €75-230) Tiger Woods, Mark O'Meara and Payne Stewart are just some of the golfing greats who have teed off at the par 72 Waterville Golf Links. One of Ireland's most magnificently sited courses, with sweeping bay and mountain views, it was designed by Eddie Hackett together with Jack Mulcahy and Claude Harmon.

Sea Synergy WATER SPORTS
(☑ 087 785 0929; www.seasynergy.org; Seaview Tce; exhibition €3.50, activities per person from €25; ☺ 11am-6pm May-Sep, shorter hours Oct-Apr; ⚐) This outfit raises awareness of the marine environment and the challenges faced by wildlife through its in-house exhibition, 'sea safari' beach walks, and a range of activities that include guided kayaking and stand-up paddleboarding trips along the coast and on nearby Lough Currane.

Charlie Chaplin Comedy Film Festival FILM
(www.chaplinfilmfestival.com; ☺ late Aug) Over four days in late August, the Charlie Chaplin Comedy Film Festival features screenings, workshops, street entertainment, a lookalike contest and a parade.

🛏 Sleeping & Eating

Butler Arms Hotel HISTORIC HOTEL €€
(☑ 066-947-4156; www.butlerarms.com; New Line Rd; s/d from €145/160; P🐾) The castellated towers of the Butler Arms have dominated the north end of the village since 1884, and the hotel has provided accommodation for many famous guests through the years – Walt Disney in the 1940s, Charlie Chaplin in the 1960s, Mark Hamill and Daisy Ridley of *Star Wars* fame in 2014 and 2015. Expect luxurious rooms and top-notch service.

Brookhaven House B&B €€
(☑ 066-947 4431; www.brookhavenhouse.com; New Line Rd; d/f from €109/140; P🐾) The pick of Waterville's B&Bs is the contemporary Brookhaven House, run by a friendly family. Spick-and-span rooms with views towards either Waterville Golf Links or Ballinskelligs Bay have comfy beds; there's a sunny breakfast room with a view of distant hills.

★ **Smuggler's Inn** IRISH €€
(☑ 066-947 4330; www.smugglersinn.ie; Cliff Rd; 3-course lunch & early-bird menu €30, mains €20-27; ☺ noon-2.45pm & 6-9.30pm; 🐾) At this diamond find near Waterville Golf Links owner and chef Henry Hunt's gourmet creations incorporate fresh seafood and locally farmed poultry and meat, followed by artistic desserts (including homemade ice cream), served in a conservatory dining room. Half-board meals are available at the inn's upstairs rooms (doubles from €100); cooked-to-order breakfasts include a catch of the day.

If you're staying overnight, try for room 15, with a glassed-in balcony overlooking Ballinskelligs Bay.

Caherdaniel

POP 76

The road between Waterville and Caherdaniel climbs high over the ridge of Beenarourke, providing grandstand views of some of the finest scenery on the Ring of Kerry. The panorama extends from the scattered islands of Scarriff and Deenish to Dursey and the hills of the Beara Peninsula.

Caherdaniel, a tiny hamlet hidden among the trees at the head of Derrynane Bay, is the ancestral home of Daniel O'Connell, 'the Liberator', whose family made money smuggling from their base by the dunes. The area has a Blue Flag beach, good hikes and activities including horse riding and water sports. Lines of wind-gnarled trees add to the wild air.

⊙ Sights & Activities

★ Derrynane National Historic Park   HISTORIC SITE
(☑066-947 5113; www.derrynanehouse.ie; Derrynane; adult/child €5/3; ⊙10.30am-6pm mid-Mar–Sep, 10am-5pm Oct, to 4pm Sat & Sun Nov–early-Dec; P) Derrynane House was the home of Maurice 'Hunting Cap' O'Connell, a notorious local smuggler who grew rich on trade with France and Spain. He was the uncle of Daniel O'Connell, the 19th-century campaigner for Catholic emancipation, who grew up here in his uncle's care and inherited the property in 1825, when it became his private retreat. The house is furnished with O'Connell memorabilia, including the impressive triumphal chariot in which he lapped Dublin after his release from prison in 1844.

Other items on display include O'Connell's ornately sculpted oak chair from his time as Lord Mayor of Dublin (look for the gold collars and ruby eyes of the carved Irish wolfhounds), the duelling pistols with which he killed a man in 1815, and the iron bed in which he died during a pilgrimage to Rome in 1847.

The **gardens**, warmed by the Gulf Stream, nurture subtropical species including 4m-high tree ferns, gunnera ('giant rhubarb') and other South American plants. A network of walking trails leads through the woods towards the beach; kids can pick up a copy of the **Derrynane Fairy Trail** (www.irishfairytrails.com) at the cafe and track down two dozen 'fairy houses' hidden among the trees.

Staigue Fort   HISTORIC SITE
(€1 donation; ⊙dawn-dusk) This Iron Age structure, built around AD 300 to 400, is one of the biggest and best-preserved ring forts in Ireland, with near-intact walls some 4m thick and up to 5.5m in height. The site is reached via 4km of very narrow road, signposted off the main N70 6km east of Caherdaniel. The local farmer asks for a €1 donation to cover maintenance costs on the access path.

Derrynane Beach   BEACH
Derrynane's Blue Flag beach is one of the most beautiful in Kerry, with scalloped coves of golden sand set between grassy dunes and whaleback outcrops of wave-smoothed rock. From the car park at Derrynane House, you can walk 1km along the beach to explore **Abbey Island** and its picturesque cemetery – look inside the ruined chapel to find the tomb of Daniel O'Connell's wife, Mary.

Atlantic Irish Seaweed   FOOD & DRINK
(☑086 106 2110; www.atlanticirishseaweed.com; per person €60) A three-hour 'seaweed discovery workshop' involves a guided walk along the Derrynane foreshore at low tide, foraging for edible seaweed (instruction on identification and sustainable harvesting is provided), followed by a lunch (tasting session) of seaweed-based dishes and drinks. Workshops are tide- and weather-dependent, and booking is essential.

Derrynane Sea Sports   WATER SPORTS
(☑087 908 1208; www.derrynaneseasports.com; Derrynane Beach) Derrynane Sea Sports offers sailing, windsurfing and water-skiing lessons for all levels (from €40 per person). Equipment hire spans stand-up paddleboards, surfboards, windsurfers (€10 to €20 per hour), canoes, small sailboats (€25 to €40) and snorkelling gear. Snorkelling tours (€40 per person) last two hours. In July and August ask about fun half-day pirate camps for children (€95).

Eagle Rock Equestrian Centre   HORSE RIDING
(☑066-947 5145; www.eaglerockcentre.com; Ballycarnahan; horse riding per hr €40) Guided horseback treks take you along Derrynane Beach and through the woods of Derrynane National Historic Park.

🛏 Sleeping & Eating

Wave Crest   CAMPGROUND €
(☑066-947 5188; www.wavecrestcamping.com; hiker €10, vehicle & 2 adults €29; P @ 🛜) Just 1.6km southeast of Caherdaniel, this year-round campground has a superb setting right on the rocky waterfront with front-row sunset views. From June to August, there's an on-site cafe and an attached shop selling fishing supplies, beach equipment, basic food supplies and wine. Book ahead during high season.

Travellers' Rest Hostel   HOSTEL €
(☑066-947 5175; www.hostelcaherdaniel.com; dm/d from €18.50/43; ⊙Mar–early-Nov) All low

ceilings, gingham curtains and dried flowers in the grate, Travellers' Rest has the quaint feel of a country cottage, with an open fire and a self-catering kitchen (breakfast isn't included; bring supplies as there are no supermarkets nearby). Shower early: there are just two shared bathrooms. Call at the petrol station opposite if there's nobody about.

Olde Forge
B&B €€

(☑ 066-947 5140; www.theoldeforge.com; s/d/f from €60/80/120; P🖥) Fantastic views of Kenmare Bay and the Beara Peninsula unfold from this ivy-covered B&B, both from the garden terrace out front and from most of the spacious and comfortable bedrooms. Family rooms sleep two adults and one or two children. It's 1.2km southeast of Caherdaniel on the N70.

Blind Piper
PUB FOOD €€

(☑ 066-947 5126; www.blindpiperpub.ie; mains €13-24; ⊙ kitchen noon-7pm Mon-Thu, to 8pm Fri-Sun, bar to midnight daily; ⊕) This local institution is a great family pub with a lovely beer garden set beside the tiny Coomnahorna River, serving quality pub fare like deep-fried monkfish and rib-eye steak. On Thursday evenings from 9.30pm and most weekends from June to August, locals and visitors crowd inside, and music sessions strike up.

Sneem
POP 288

From Castlecove to Kenmare the main N70 Ring of Kerry road swings inland, and coastal panoramas are replaced with distant views of MacGillycuddy's Reeks.

The main village here is Sneem (An tSnaidhm). Its Irish name translates as 'the knot', which is thought to refer to the River Sneem that twists, knot-like, into nearby Kenmare Bay. The river splits the village in two, with separate village squares on either side and a picturesque waterfall tumbling below the old stone bridge.

There are no real sights, but it's a popular place for Ring of Kerry tour buses to pause so passengers can stretch their legs before the road dives into the woods for the 27km stretch to Kenmare.

Sneem has a couple of cafes and pubs. From June to September, a weekly **farmers market** (Bridge St; ⊙ 11am-4pm Tue Jun-Sep) 🍃 sets up in the centre.

The **tourist office** (☑ 064-667 5807; South Sq; ⊙ 11.30am-5.30pm May-Sep) is in the Joli Coeur craft shop.

★ **Parknasilla Resort & Spa**
HOTEL €€€

(☑ 064-667 5600; www.parknasillaresort.com; Parknasilla; d/f/ste from €169/195/325; P@🖥🏊) On the tree-fringed shores of the Kenmare River with views to the Beara Peninsula, this hotel has been wowing guests (including George Bernard Shaw) since 1895. From the modern, luxuriously appointed bedrooms to the top-grade spa, private 12-hole golf course, elegant restaurant and supervised kids' play area, everything here is done just right. It's 3km southeast of Sneem.

If you can't tear yourself away, it also rents two-bedroom villas by the week (from €1400).

Village Kitchen
IRISH €

(☑ 064-664 5281; www.facebook.com/village kitchensneem; 3 Bridge St; mains €7-14; ⊙ 10am-9pm Jun-Aug, to 6pm Mon-Sat Sep-May; 🖥🍴) Near the bridge, this family-run restaurant has been dishing up breakfast, lunch and dinner to locals and visitors alike for decades. The menu runs from seafood chowder and fish specials to steak sandwiches and Irish stew.

Kenmare
POP 2376

Kenmare (pronounced 'ken-*mair*') is the thinking person's Killarney. Ideally positioned for exploring the Ring of Kerry (and the Beara Peninsula), but without the coach-tour crowds of its more famous neighbour, Kenmare (Neidín, meaning 'little nest' in Irish) is a pretty spot with a neat triangle of streets lined with craft shops, galleries, cafes and good-quality restaurants.

One of the few planned towns in Ireland, Kenmare was laid out on an X-shaped street plan in the late 18th century by the Marquis of Lansdowne as the showpiece of his Kerry estates. It earned its living as a market town and fishing port, and from ironworks, lead mining and quarrying. The Market House and the Lansdowne Arms Hotel still survive from this period – pick up a copy of the *Kenmare Heritage Trail* from the tourist office (p303) to discover more.

◎ Sights & Activities

Walking opportunities abound. The tourist office (p303) has details of walks around Kenmare Bay and into the hills, on sections of the Kerry Way and Beara Way. Kenmare

Bookshop (p303) is a great resource with plenty of walking guides, maps and advice.

Cycling is also popular; **Finnegan's Cycle Centre** (☑064-664 1083; www.finnegans cycles.com; 37 Henry St; hybrid/electric bike per day €15/30; ⊙10am-6pm Mon-Sat) rents out wheels.

Kenmare Heritage Centre   MUSEUM
(☑064-664 1233; The Square; ⊙10am-5.30pm Mon-Sat Apr-Oct, by appointment Nov-Mar) **FREE** Kenmare's old courthouse is home to an exhibition telling the history of the town from its origins as Neidín, through its establishment as a market town by the Marquis of Lansdowne to the founding of the Poor Clare Convent in 1861, which still stands behind Holy Cross Church. Local women were taught needlepoint lacemaking at the convent and their lacework garnered international fame; the upstairs **Kenmare Lace and Design Centre**, which keeps the same hours, has displays.

They include designs for 'the most important piece of lace ever made in Ireland' (in a 19th-century critic's opinion).

Holy Cross Church   CHURCH
(Old Killarney Rd; ⊙8am-8pm Easter–mid-Oct, shorter hours mid-Oct–Easter) Begun in 1862 and consecrated in 1864, this church has a splendid wooden roof with 14 angel carvings. Intricate **mosaics** adorn the aisle arches and the edges of the stained-glass window over the altar. The architect was Charles Hansom, collaborator and brother-in-law of Augustus Pugin (the architect behind London's Houses of Parliament).

Installing the rooster atop the spire allowed Hansom to 'crow' over the landlord who had refused him permission to build in his first choice of location in the Square.

Dromquinna Stables   HORSE RIDING
(☑064-664 1043; www.dromquinna-stables.com; Sneem Rd; treks per hr €30; ⊙mid-Mar–mid-Oct) One-hour, 90-minute and two-hour treks follow trails up into the hills and along Kenmare Bay's beaches with views over the Beara and Iveragh Peninsulas from this stable, which has been in the same family for generations. The stables are 4.5km west of Kenmare on the N70.

It also offers lessons (30/60 minutes €15/25) and a Saturday pony club for kids (2½ hours €20), where they can discover horse grooming, tacking and riding.

Star Outdoors   WATER SPORTS
(☑064-664 1222; www.staroutdoors.ie; Dauros) Along with one-hour wildlife cruises (€18/10 per adult/child) on Kenmare River, Star Outdoors offers activities including kayak rental (per hour €22/38 single/ double) and wakeboarding and waterskiing (per 15 minutes €60). Its base is 6.5km southwest of Kenmare on the R571.

Seafari   BOATING
(☑064-664 2059; www.seafariireland.com; Kenmare Pier; adult/child €25/12.50; ⊙Apr-Oct; ⚫) Warm up with complimentary tea, coffee and rum – and the captain's sea shanties – on an entertaining two-hour cruise to see Ireland's biggest seal colony and other wildlife, including white-tailed eagles. Binoculars (and lollipops!) are provided. Cash only.

✦ Festivals & Events

Kenmare Fair   CULTURAL
(⊙mid-Aug) Dating back more than two centuries, the Kenmare Fair takes place on 15 August every year, when folk from all over Ireland descend on the town to trade in sheep, cattle and ponies, as well as crafts, bric-a-brac and artisan foods.

🛏 Sleeping

Kenmare Fáilte Hostel   HOSTEL €
(☑087 711 6092; www.kenmarehostel.com; Shelbourne St; dm/s/d from €21/48/56; ⊙May-Oct; ⚫) Perfectly located in a Georgian townhouse, this hostel is fitted out with quality furnishings and equipment – there's even an Aga cooker in the kitchen – a pleasant change from the utilitarianism of most budget accommodation. Wi-fi is available in common areas only, however, and there's a 1.30am curfew.

★ Dromquinna Manor   TENTED CAMP €€
(☑064-664 2888; www.dromquinnamanor.com; Sneem Rd; d/f €160/190; ⊙May-Aug; ⚫) This country estate on the shores of Kenmare River, 4.5km west of Kenmare, has 14 sturdy safari-style tents, luxuriously outfitted with plush double beds and antique furniture (but shared showers and toilets), on a gorgeous landscaped site sloping down to the sea. A picnic-hamper breakfast is delivered each morning. There are also converted Victorian potting sheds (from €190) to rent.

★ Brook Lane Hotel   BOUTIQUE HOTEL €€
(☑064-664 2077; www.brooklanehotel.com; Sneem Rd; s/d/f from €125/165/200; ⚫⚫) Chic rooms warmed by underfloor heating are individually decorated with bespoke furniture and luxurious fabrics at this contemporary olive-green

property on the northwestern edge of town. Public areas mix vintage and designer pieces. Run by the same owners as Kenmare's superb restaurant No 35 (p302), its adjoining stone-and-brick gastropub, Casey's, is first-rate. It's a 750m stroll from the centre.

Hawthorn House
B&B €€

(☑ 064-6641035; www.hawthornhousekenmare.com; Shelbourne St; s/d/f from €60/120/150; ᴘ 🛜) This stylish house has eight spacious pine-furnished rooms, all named after local towns and decked out with fresh flowers. It's set back from busy Shelbourne St behind a low wall.

Park Hotel
HERITAGE HOTEL €€€

(☑ 064-664 1200; www.parkkenmare.com; Shelbourne St; d/ste from €440/740; ᴘ 🛜 ➰) Overlooking Kenmare Bay, this 1897 Victorian mansion has every conceivable luxury: an indoor swimming pool, heavenly spa, tennis and croquet courts and even its own cinema. Antiques and original art fill its 46 rooms and suites, which have goose-down duvets and pillows. Those in the deluxe category face the water, while superior rooms and suites have balconies and patios.

Local produce is on the menu at its restaurant, which serves lunch, high tea and dinner (five-course menu €80). Adjoining rooms and cots are available for families, who are welcomed with open arms.

Sheen Falls Lodge
HISTORIC HOTEL €€€

(☑ 064-664 1600; www.sheenfallslodge.ie; Knockduragh; d/ste from €370/650; ⊙ Feb-Dec; ᴘ @ 🛜 ➰) The Marquis of Landsdowne's former summer residence still feels like an aristocrats' playground, with a fine-dining modern Irish restaurant, cocktail bar, spa, and 66 rooms and sumptuous suites with Italian-marble bathrooms. It's all in a glorious setting beside a waterfall on the River Sheen with views across Kenmare Bay to Carrantuohil. Amenities are many – salmon fishing or clay-pigeon shooting, anyone?

Its cellar has over 10,000 different wines from 18 different countries.

✕ Eating & Drinking

Dining options are especially good here, both at daytime cafes and gastropubs and elegant evening restaurants.

The weekly **farmers market** (www.facebook.com/kenmaremarket; The Square; ⊙ 10am-4pm Wed) 🥐 sets up in the town square, with stalls of vegetables, cheese, honey, gourmet ice cream, bread, smoked salmon and other artisan produce.

Jam
CAFE €

(☑ 064-664 1591; www.jam.ie; 6 Henry St; mains €7-12; ⊙ 8am-5pm Mon-Sat) Cheerful and bustling Jam makes a great breakfast venue, with a menu that includes granola with fruit, pancakes with bacon and maple syrup, and scrambled eggs on toast, along with an excellent flat white. There are good cakes and pastries, and a range of hot lunch dishes such as Irish stew, shepherd's pie and lasagne.

★ Boathouse Bistro
BISTRO €€

(☑ 064-664 2889; www.dromquinnamanor.com; Dromquinna Manor, Sneem Rd; mains €15-28; ⊙ 12.30-9pm daily mid-Mar–Sep, Fri-Sun only Oct–mid-Mar; ᴘ) 🥐 At the water's edge, this blue-and-white 1870s boathouse 4.5km west of Kenmare has been stunningly converted to a beach-house-style bistro specialising in local seafood delivered daily to its own wharf. Expertly cooked dishes (Kenmare Bay crab claws in chilli and garlic butter, beer-battered fish and chips) are accompanied by a great selection of by-the-glass wines and craft gins.

The bistro is part of a country estate that includes luxury camping accommodation (p301).

★ Tom Crean Fish & Wine
IRISH €€

(☑ 064-664 1589; www.tomcrean.ie; Main St; mains €17-31; ⊙ 5-9.30pm Thu-Mon Sep-Jun, daily Jul & Aug; 🛜) 🥐 Named for Kerry's pioneering Antarctic explorer, and run by his granddaughter, this venerable restaurant uses only the best of local organic produce, cheeses and fresh seafood. Sneem lobster is available in season, the oysters *au naturel* capture the scent of the sea, and the seafood gratin served in a scallop shell is divine.

Upstairs, the 19th-century townhouse has boutique rooms with king-size beds (doubles from €75).

No 35
IRISH €€

(☑ 064-664 1559; www.no35kenmare.com; 35 Main St; mains €21-26, 3-course set menu €34; ⊙ 5.30-9.30pm Mon, Tue & Fri, from 12.30pm Sat & Sun) 🥐 Hand-cut limestone walls, exposed timber beams, stained-glass windows and an open fire set the stage for some of Kenmare's most creative cuisine. All-Irish produce features in dishes like slow-cooked rare saddleback pork (from the owners' own farm) with caraway-spiced swede, and market fish with capers and hazelnuts. Great Irish craft beers and ciders are served alongside a well-chosen wine list.

Mews

IRISH €€€

(☎ 064-664 2829; www.themewskenmare.com; 3-4 Henry Ct; mains €20-33; ☺ 6-9pm Tue-Sun) Two of Kerry's top restaurateurs helm this stylish, palm-filled spot hidden in a laneway off Henry St. Vermouth-cream chowder with citrus oil, Kerry beef fillet with a parsnip rösti and clove-poached pear with home-made peanut-brittle ice cream are among the menu highlights. There's a three-course early-bird menu (€34, before 7pm).

Puccini's Coffee & Books

CAFE

(29 Henry St; ☺ 8.30am-4pm Mon-Fri, from 9.15am Sat, closed 12.30-1pm daily; ☎) Puccini's is a tiny coffee bar and bookshop with just a handful of stools at the window counters, but it's the social hub of Kenmare on weekday mornings as folk drop in for an expertly prepared espresso before work.

🛍 Shopping

Kenmare has many quality craft shops and art galleries – the *Kenmare Art Spots* leaflet, available from the tourist office (and the galleries themselves), lists half a dozen you can visit.

Soundz of Muzic

MUSICAL INSTRUMENTS

(www.soundzofmuzic.ie; 9 Henry St; ☺ 11am-5.30pm Mon-Sat, to 4pm Sun) Traditional instruments (accordions, harmonicas, banjos, tin whistles and more) are stocked alongside modern ones (including electric fiddles) at this decades-old shop. It also sells sheet music, CDs and vinyl, and DVDs of live performances.

Kenmare Bookshop

BOOKS

(www.facebook.com/kenmarebookshop; Shelbourne St; ☺ 10am-5.30pm) Irish history and literature, bestsellers and kids' books are stocked at this independent shop, as well as a good selection of maps and local walking guides.

ℹ Information

Kenmare's seasonal **tourist office** (☎ 1850 230 330; The Square; ☺ 9.30am-12.30pm & 1.30-5.30pm Mon-Wed, Fri & Sat Mar-Oct) has stacks of information about the town, its surrounds and the Ring of Kerry. Pick up free maps detailing a heritage trail around town and longer walks.

ℹ Getting There & Away

Bus Éireann (www.buseireann.ie) runs between Kenmare and Killarney (€12.40, 45 minutes, one to three daily), and runs a daily Ring of Kerry loop service (p287) from late June to late August.

The summer-only bus service 282 runs from Glengarriff to Kenmare (€16, 45 minutes, one daily late June to late August).

Finnegan's Coach & Cab (☎ 064-664 1491; www.kenmarecoachandcab.com) runs a variety of Ring of Kerry tours and taxi services.

DINGLE PENINSULA

One of the highlights of the Wild Atlantic Way, the Dingle Peninsula (Corca Dhuibhne) culminates in the Irish mainland's westernmost point. In the shadow of sacred Mt Brandon, a maze of fuchsia-fringed *boreens* (country lanes) weaves together an ancient landscape of prehistoric ring forts and beehive huts, early Christian chapels, crosses and holy wells, picturesque hamlets and abandoned villages.

But it's where the land meets the ocean – whether in a welter of surf-pounded rocks, or where the waves lap secluded, sandy coves – that Dingle's beauty truly reveals itself.

Centred on charming Dingle town, the peninsula has long been a beacon for those of an alternative bent, attracting artists, craftspeople, musicians and idiosyncratic characters who can be found in workshops, museums, festivals and unforgettable trad sessions throughout Dingle's tiny settlements.

ᗕ Tours

Killarney-based tour operators including Corcoran's (p274), Deros Tours (p275) and **Wild Kerry Day Tours** (☎ 064-663 1052; www.wildkerry-daytours.ie; Ross Rd) offer day trips to the Dingle Peninsula. Walking and cycling tours are possible with **Go Visit Ireland** (☎ 066-976 2094; www.govisitireland.com).

Inch Strand & Annascaul

Inch Strand is a 5km-long sand spit and dune system extending into Dingle Bay. This stupendous beach has attracted film directors as well as surfers, land-yachters and anglers – it has appeared in the movies *Ryan's Daughter* (1970), *Excalibur* (1981) and *Far and Away* (1992), among others.

The dunes are a great spot for windswept walks, birdwatching and bathing. The west-facing Blue Flag beach (lifeguarded in summer) is also a hot surfing spot; waves average 1m to 3m. You can learn to ride them with **Offshore Surf School** (☎ 087 294 6519;

Dingle Peninsula

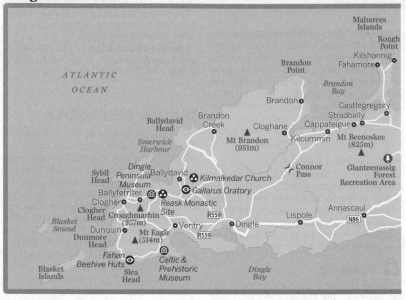

www.offshoresurfschool.ie; lessons adult/child per 2hr from €25/20, board & wetsuit hire per 2hr €15; ⊙9am-6pm Apr–mid-Oct).

Cars are allowed on the beach, but don't end up providing others with nonstop laughs by getting stuck.

Inch Beach House
GUESTHOUSE €
(☑066-915 8118; www.inchbeach.com; d/tr/f from €90/150/180, cottage per week €1280; P🅿🛜) Breezy Inch Beach House is all skylights, sea views, light colours and modern fittings. Rooms come with king-size beds; higher-priced rooms directly face the beach and have bathtubs and showers. It also has nine three-bedroom self-catering cottages available on a weekly basis.

Sammy's
CAFE €
(☑066-915 8118; www.facebook.com/sammy sinchbeach; Inch Beach; mains €7-15; ⊙10am-6pm Mon-Thu, to 9pm Fri-Sun, shorter hours Oct-Easter; 🛜🛗) Sammy's, at the entrance to the beach, is the nerve centre of the area. The beach-facing bar-restaurant serves a vast range of dishes from sandwiches to burgers, fish and chips, and steak. Fish fingers are among the favourites on the kids' menu. There's a shop selling ice creams and souvenirs, and trad sessions during summer.

South Pole Inn
PUB
(☑066-915 7388; www.facebook.com/southpole inn; Main St; ⊙noon-11.30pm Mon-Thu, to midnight Fri & Sat, to 11pm Sun; 🛗) Antarctic explorer Tom Crean ran this sky-blue inn in his retirement. Now it's a regular Crean museum and gift shop, as well as a cracking pub serving Killarney-brewed Expedition Ale and average pub grub (mains €10 to €18; food served to 9pm). It's in the residential village of Annascaul, 16km east of Dingle town.

Dingle Town

POP 1440

Framed by its fishing port, the Dingle Peninsula's charming little 'capital' manages to be quaint without even trying. Some pubs double as shops, so you can enjoy Guinness and a singalong among hats and hardware, horseshoes and wellies. It has long drawn runaways from across the world, making it a cosmopolitan and creative place. In summer its hilly streets can be clogged with visitors; in other seasons its authentic charms are yours for the savouring.

Although Dingle is one of Ireland's largest Gaeltacht towns, the locals have voted to retain the name Dingle rather than go by the officially sanctioned – and signposted – Gaelige name of An Daingean.

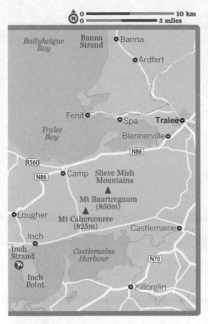

◉ Sights

Dingle is one of those towns whose very fabric is its main attraction. Wander up and down the streets and back alleys, stroll along the pier, and pop into shops, pubs, and art and craft galleries and see what you find.

Dingle Oceanworld   AQUARIUM
(☑ 066-915 2111; www.dingle-oceanworld.ie; The Wood; adult/child/family €15.50/10.75/47; ⊙10am-7pm Jul & Aug, to 6pm Sep-Jun) Dingle's aquarium is a lot of fun, and includes a walk-through tunnel and a touch pool. Psychedelic fish glide through tanks that recreate such environments as Lake Malawi, the River Congo and the piranha-filled Amazon. Reef sharks and stingrays cruise the shark tank; water pumped from the harbour fills the Ocean Tunnel tank where you can spot native Irish species such as dogfish, mullet, plaice, conger eels and the spectacularly ugly wreckfish.

Dingle Distillery   DISTILLERY
(☑ 066-402 9011; www.dingledistillery.ie; Ventry Rd; tour €15; ⊙ tours noon-4pm Mar-Sep, from 2pm Oct-Feb) An offshoot of Dublin's Porterhouse microbrewery, this small-scale craft distillery went into operation in 2012, and began bottling its distinctive single malt whiskey in 2016. It also produces award-winning artisan gin and vodka.

An Díseart   CULTURAL CENTRE
(☑ 066-915 2476; www.diseart.ie; Green St; ⊙9am-5pm Mon-Sat) FREE Set in a neo-Gothic former convent, this Celtic cultural centre has impressive stained-glass windows by Dublin artist Harry Clarke (1889–1931) depicting 12 scenes from the life of Christ (audio guide available).

🏃 Activities

Dingle Traditional Rowing   BOATING
(Naomhòg Experience; ☑ 087 699 2925; www.dingle rowing.com; Dingle Marina; lessons €25) *Naomhòg* is the Kerry name for a *currach*, a traditional Irish boat made from a wooden frame covered with tarred canvas (originally animal hides). They were used by the Blasket islanders for fishing, and are now maintained and raced by local enthusiasts. You can book a one-hour session in Dingle Harbour (minimum two people) to learn how to row one.

It also runs harbour tours and sunset cruises (€25 per person per hour, minimum two people).

Dingle Boat Tours   CRUISE
(☑ 066-915 1344, 087 672 6100; www.dingleboat tours.com; Dingle Marina; ferry adult/child return €50/25, ecotour €60/30; ⊙Apr-Sep) Dingle Marine & Leisure operates a 50-minute passenger ferry from Dingle Marina to Great Blasket Island (p313), and a 4½-hour ecotour with a one-hour stop on the island. En route look out for seals, dolphins, gannets, puffins, whales and, if you're lucky, basking sharks.

Other options include fishing trips (adult/child from €35/25 for two hours including tackle), one-hour trips to see Fungie the dolphin (€15/8) and a 3½-hour cruise around the Skellig Rocks (per person €100, no landing).

Dingle Dolphin Tours   CRUISE
(☑ 066-915 2626; www.dingledolphin.com; The Pier; adult/child €16/8) Boats run by the Dingle Boatmen's Association cooperative leave the pier daily for one-hour trips to see Dingle's most famous resident, Fungie the dolphin. It's free if Fungie doesn't show, but he usually does. The ticket office is next to the tourist office.

Wild SUP Tours   WATER SPORTS
(☑ 083 476 6428; www.wildsuptours.com; Strand St; half-/full-day tour €49/115; ⊙Apr-Oct) This outfit offers stand-up paddleboard adventures around the Dingle coastline. All equipment is provided and the full-day tours include a picnic lunch.

COUNTY KERRY DINGLE TOWN

Dingle Town

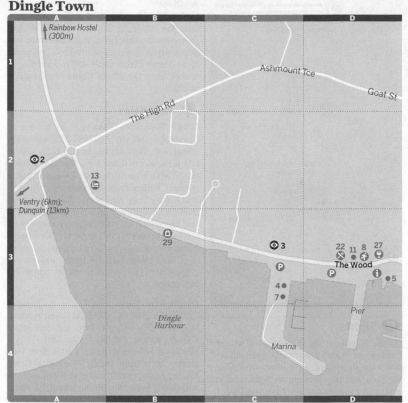

Mountain Man Outdoor Shop CYCLING
(☑ 087 297 6569; www.themountainmanshop.com;
Strand St; bike rental per hr/day €4/15) Mountain
Man rents bikes and runs guided cycling tours
(from €30) around the Dingle Peninsula, with
themes ranging from archaeology to food.

Dingle Surf SURFING
(☑ 066-915 0833; www.dinglesurf.com; Green St;
lessons adult/child €30/25; ☺ shop noon-5pm
Thu-Sat) Dingle Surf offers half-day surfing
and stand-up paddleboarding lessons for
beginners at Brandon Bay (on the north side
of the peninsula, transport included), and
sells gear including Dingle Surf–branded
T-shirts, hoodies and beanies.

Irish Adventures ADVENTURE SPORTS
(☑ 087 419 0318; www.irishadventures.net) This
outfit offers guided adventure trips including
rock climbing on the local sea cliffs (half-/
full-day €60/110 per person), and kayaking
in Dingle Harbour with Fungie the dolphin
(half-day per person €55). It also runs sunset

kayaking trips (three hours, €55), and kayaking on the Killarney lakes (three hours, €55).
Most trips depart from the pier.

★ Festivals & Events

Dingle Regatta SPORTS
(www.facebook.com/dingleregatta2016; ☺ mid-
Aug) Crews of four race traditional Irish
naomhóg around the harbour. It's Kerry's
largest event of its kind and inspired the
trad song of the same name.

Dingle Races SPORTS
(www.dingleraces.ie; N86, Ballintaggart; ☺ mid-Aug)
Held over the second weekend in August,
Dingle's horse-racing meet brings crowds
from far and wide. The racetrack is at Ballintaggart, 2km southeast of the centre.

Dingle Food & Wine Festival FOOD & DRINK
(www.dinglefood.com; ☺ early Oct) Held over
four days, this fabulous foodie fest features a
'taste trail' with sampling at over 70 locations

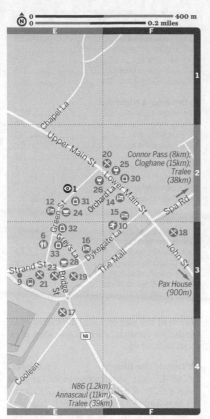

around town, plus a market, cooking demonstrations, workshops and a foraging walk. There are also beer, cider, whiskey and wine tastings, a bake-off competition and street entertainment, as well as children's events.

🛏 Sleeping

This tourist town has hostels, hotels and loads of midrange B&Bs. A number of pubs also offer accommodation.

Rainbow Hostel   HOSTEL €
(📞066-915 1044; www.rainbowhosteldingle.com; Milltown; dm/d/tr from €17/44/66, camping per person €10; 🅿@🛜🎿) This brightly refurbished bungalow, set in large gardens 1.5km northwest of town on the road towards Brandon Creek, offers basic but comfortable accommodation in doubles, twins, triples and dorms (12-bed mixed and six-bed female-only), and is the nearest place to town where you can pitch a tent (a 20- to 30-minute walk).

Hideout Hostel   HOSTEL €
(📞066-915 0559; Dykegate Lane; dm/d from €22/60; 🅿@🛜) Converted from a former guesthouse, this central hostel has inherited private bathrooms in all rooms. Top-notch facilities include two lounges, bike storage and a well-equipped kitchen. Rates include light breakfast (tea, coffee, toast and cereal). Switched-on owner Mícheál is a fount of local info.

Grapevine Hostel   HOSTEL €
(📞066-915 1434; www.grapevinedingle.com; Dykegate Lane; dm/d from €20/60; 🛜) Near the centre of town, this dinky hostel has eight-, three- and two-bed rooms with wooden bunks and private bathrooms (with minimalist sliding doors). The TV-free, fire-lit lounge is a good spot for visiting musicians to get a singalong going. Book well ahead.

★Castlewood House   BOUTIQUE HOTEL €€
(📞066-915 2788; www.castlewooddingle.com; The Wood; s/d/f €130/150/198; 🅿🛜) Book well ahead to secure a berth at Dingle's top hotel, a haven of country-house quiet and sophistication, yet less than 10 minutes' stroll from the town centre. Decor is stylish but understated; the luxury bedrooms have sea views and marble bathrooms with spa baths, while art and antiques adorn the public areas. Breakfast is a thing of beauty.

An Capall Dubh   B&B €€
(📞066-915 1105; www.ancapalldubh.com; Green St; d/tw/f €130/130/180; 🅿🛜) Entered via a 19th-century coaching gateway leading into a cobbled courtyard where breakfast is served in fine weather, this airy B&B has five simple rooms furnished with light timbers and checked fabrics.

★Pax House   B&B €€€
(📞066-915 1518; www.pax-house.com; Upper John St; d €130-230; ⊗Mar-Dec; 🅿🛜) From its highly individual decor (including contemporary paintings) to the outstanding views over the estuary from the glass-framed terrace and balconies opening from some rooms, Pax House is a treat. Breakfast incorporates produce grown in its own garden; families can be accommodated with fold-out beds. It's 1km southeast of the town centre.

Dingle Benner's Hotel   HOTEL €€€
(📞066-915 1638; www.dinglebenners.com; Main St; s/d/f from €129/199/259; 🅿🛜) A Dingle institution, melding old-world elegance, local charm and modern comforts in the quiet

Dingle Town

bedrooms, lounge, library and (very popular) Mrs Benner's Bar. Family rooms sleep four. Rooms in the 300-year-old wing have the most character; those in the new parts are quieter and more spacious.

✖ Eating

In a county famed for its seafood, Dingle still stands out. There are some superb restaurants and cafes, as well as excellent pub fare.

Dingle's weekly **farmers market** (www. facebook.com/dinglefarmersmarket; cnr Bridge St & Dykegate Lane; ⊙9am-3pm Fri) 🍽 takes place year-round.

★ Reel Dingle Fish Co   FISH & CHIPS €
(📞066-915 1713; Bridge St; mains €5-15; ⊙1-10pm) 🍽 Locals queue along the street to get hold of the freshly cooked local haddock (or cod, or monkfish, or hake, or mackerel...) and chips at this tiny outlet. Reckoned to be one of the best chippies in Kerry, if not in Ireland.

Murphy's   ICE CREAM €
(www.murphysicecream.ie; Strand St; 1/2/3 scoops €4.50/6.50/8.50; ⊙11.30am-10pm May-Oct, to 8pm Nov-Apr; 🖥) Made here in Dingle, Murphy's sublime ice cream comes in a daily changing range of flavours that include brown bread, sea salt, Dingle gin and whiskey-laced Irish coffee, along with sorbets made with rainwater. In addition to a second Dingle

branch at the pier opposite the tourist office (p310), its runaway success has seen it expand Ireland-wide.

★ Out of the Blue   SEAFOOD €€€
(📞066-915 0811; www.outoftheblue.ie; The Wood; mains €19-39; ⊙5-9.30pm Mon-Sat, 12.30-3pm & 5-9.30pm Sun) 🍽 Occupying a bright blue-and-yellow waterfront fishing shack, this rustic spot is one of Dingle's top restaurants, with an intense devotion to fresh local seafood (and only seafood). If staff don't like the catch, they don't open, and they resolutely don't serve chips. Highlights might include Dingle Bay prawn bisque with lobster or chargrilled whole sea bass flambéed in cognac.

Chart House   IRISH €€€
(📞066-915 2255; www.thecharthousedingle.com; The Mall; mains €22-32; ⊙6-10pm Jun-Sep, hours vary Oct-Dec & mid-Feb–May) Window boxes frame this free-standing stone cottage, while inside dark-red walls, polished floorboards and flickering candles create an intimate atmosphere. Creative cooking uses Irish produce: Cromane mussels and Dingle Bay prawns, Annascaul black pudding and Brandon Bay crab, fillet of Kerry beef and Cashel Blue cheese. Book up to several weeks ahead at busy times.

The Irish cheeseboard comes with a glass of vintage port.

Doyle's SEAFOOD €€€
(☑ 066-915 2674; www.doylesrestaurantdingle.ie; 4 John St; mains €25-33; ⊙ 5-9.30pm Mon-Sat, to 7.30pm Sun) Cherry-red-painted Doyle's serves some of the best seafood in the area (which in these parts is really saying something). Starters such as Dingle Bay crab claws or oysters *au naturel* team up with mains like fennel-scented Spanish fish stew, seafood linguine and roast monkfish cassoulet.

Global Village Restaurant INTERNATIONAL €€€
(☑ 066-915 2325; www.globalvillagedingle.com; Upper Main St; mains €24-30, 6-course tasting menu €65, with wine €100; ⊙ 5.30-9.30pm Mar-Oct) With the sophisticated feel of a continental bistro, this restaurant offers a fusion of global recipes gathered by the well-travelled owner-chef, but uses local produce, such as West Kerry lamb and Blasket Sound lobster. The wine list is excellent, as are the Irish and international craft beers, and there's even a vegan tasting menu (€60).

🍸 Drinking & Entertainment

Dingle has scores of pubs, many with live music.

★ Dick Mack's PUB
(www.dickmackspub.com; Green St; ⊙ 11am-11.30pm Mon-Thu, to 12.30am Fri & Sat, noon-11pm Sun) Stars in the pavement bear the names of Dick Mack's celebrity customers. Ancient wood and snugs dominate the interior, while the courtyard out back hosts a warren of tables, chairs and characters, plus artisan food trucks in summer. In 2017 the adjacent 19th-century brewhouse was restored and now creates the pub's very own craft beers.

Bean in Dingle COFFEE
(www.beanindingle.com; Green St; ⊙ 8am-5pm Mon-Sat, 10am-3pm Sun; 🗢) Coffee specialist Bean in Dingle roasts its own Brazilian, Ethiopian and Guatemalan blend of beans. There's a communal table and a handful of seats; arrive early before it sells out of its sweet and savoury pastries – flaky sausage rolls, sugar-dusted cinnamon scrolls and a daily vegan special such as raw chocolate and caramel slice.

John Benny's PUB
(☑ 066-915 1215; www.johnbennyspub.com; Strand St; ⊙ noon-11pm, kitchen to 9.30pm) A toasty cast-iron wood stove, stone slab floor, memorabilia on the walls, great staff and no intrusive TV make this one of Dingle's most enjoyable traditional pubs. Glenbeigh oysters and Cromane mussels are highlights of its excellent pub menu (mains €13 to €20). Local musos pour in most nights for rockin' trad sessions.

Curran's PUB
(Main St; ⊙ 10am-11pm) One of Dingle's most traditional shop-pubs, stocking everything from wellies to bags of potatoes, Curran's has nooks and crannies including original stained-glass snugs. Its Guinness is some of the best for miles around. Spontaneous trad sessions regularly take place.

My Boy Blue COFFEE
(www.facebook.com/myboybluedingle; Holyground; ⊙ 8.30am-5pm Mon, Tue & Thu-Sat, 10am-4pm Sun; 🗢) This bright and artsy corner spot is the place to head for some of Dingle's best coffee, supplied by the 3FE roastery in Dublin. Good choice of cakes and snacks too.

Foxy John's PUB
(Main St; ⊙ 10am-11pm; 🗢) Foxy John's is a classic example of Dingle's shop-pubs, stocking hardware and outdoor clothing alongside stout and whiskey. It even rents bikes (€15 per day).

FUNGIE THE DOLPHIN

In 1983 a bottlenose dolphin swam into Dingle Bay and local tourism hasn't been quite the same since. Showing an unusual affinity for human company, he swam around with the local fishing fleet. Eventually somebody got the idea of charging tourists to go out on boats to see the friendly dolphin (nicknamed Fungie). Today up to 12 boats at a time and more than 1000 tourists a day ply the waters with Dingle's mascot, now a cornerstone of the local economy; there's even a bronze statue of him outside the tourist office (p310).

In the wild, bottlenose dolphins live for an average of 25 years, though they have been known to live to over 40 in captivity. As Fungie has been around for more than 35 years (yes, it's still the same dolphin, recognisable by his distinctive markings), speculation is rife about how long it will be before he finally glides into the deep for the last time. And what will Dingle do without its dolphin?

THE DINGLE WAY

The 179km Dingle Way (www.dingleway. com) loops around the peninsula, beginning and ending in Tralee; it normally takes eight days to hike. Much of it is on low-lying minor roads and farm tracks, but the most impressive section climbs to 660m, above huge sea cliffs, as it crosses Masatiompan, the northern spur of Mt Brandon.

Ordnance Survey 1:50,000 sheets 70 and 71 cover the route.

Blue Zone JAZZ
(www.facebook.com/bluezonedingle; Green St; ⊙5.30-10.30pm Thu-Tue) Upstairs from Dingle Record Shop (p310), this great late-night hangout is part jazz venue, part pizza restaurant and part wine bar, with moody blue and red surrounds.

🛍 Shopping

Quaint shops sell quality goods made by local artisans, from jewellery to pottery, textiles, candles and art.

Little Cheese Shop FOOD
(www.facebook.com/thelittlecheeseshop; Grey's Lane; ⊙11am-6pm Mon-Fri, to 5pm Sat) Swiss-trained cheesemaker Maja Binder's tiny shop overflows with aromatic cheeses from all over Ireland, including her own range of Dingle Peninsula Cheeses.

Brian de Staic JEWELLERY
(www.briandestaic.com; The Wood; ⊙9.30am-5.30pm Mon-Sat) This renowned local designer's exquisite modern Celtic work includes symbols such as the Hill of Tara, crosses and standing stones, as well as jewellery inscribed with Ogham script. All of de Staic's jewellery is individually handcrafted.

Dingle Candle ARTS & CRAFTS
(www.dinglecandle.com; Main St; ⊙10am-5.30pm Mon-Sat May-Sep, shorter hours Oct-Apr) Hand-poured, long-burning candles made in Dingle come in 12 different scents inspired by the peninsula, including fuchsia, honeysuckle, smoky turf fire, Atlantic salt and sage, and peated whiskey. Browse too for body scrubs, shower mousses, bath salts and perfumes, which are also handmade here.

Dingle Record Shop MUSIC
(www.dinglerecordshop.com; Green St; ⊙11am-5pm Mon-Sat) Tucked off Green St, this jammed music hub has all the good stuff you can't download yet. Live bands play every couple of weeks; podcasts recorded in-store are available online. Hours can be erratic.

Lisbeth Mulcahy HOMEWARES
(www.lisbethmulcahy.com; Green St; ⊙9.30am-7pm Mon-Sat, noon-4pm Sun Jun-Sep, 10am-5pm Mon-Sat Oct-May) Beautiful wall hangings, rugs and scarves are created on a 150-year-old loom by this long-established designer. Also sold here are ceramics by her husband, who has a workshop at Louis Mulcahy Pottery (p313), 17km west of Dingle on Slea Head.

An Gailearaí Beag ARTS & CRAFTS
(www.angailearaibeag.com; Main St; ⊙11am-5pm) Often staffed by the artists themselves, this little gallery is a showcase for the work of the West Kerry Craft Guild, selling ceramics, paintings, wood carvings, photography, batik, jewellery, stained glass and more.

ℹ️ Information

Busy but helpful, Dingle's **tourist office** (☑1850 230 330; www.dingle-peninsula.ie; The Pier; ⊙9am-5pm Mon-Sat) has maps, guides and plenty of information on the entire peninsula.

ℹ️ Getting There & Away

Buses **stop** (The Tracks) outside the car park behind the supermarket. Four to six Bus Éireann (www.buseireann.ie) buses a day serve Tralee (€14, one hour) year-round.

Getting to Killarney by bus by means a change in Tralee (€15.20, two hours, three daily).

Dingle Shuttle Bus (☑087 250 4767; www.dingleshuttlebus.com) runs a minibus service between Kerry airport and destinations on the Dingle Peninsula (book in advance) and offers private Dingle Peninsula and Ring of Kerry tours.

ℹ️ Getting Around

Dingle is easily covered on foot. Bike-hire places include Foxy John's (p309), **Paddy's Bike Shop** (☑066-915 2311; www.paddysbikeshop.com; Dykegate Lane; bike rental per day/week from €15/75; ⊙9am-7pm May-Sep, to 6pm Mar, Apr & Oct) and the Mountain Man Outdoors Shop (p306).

Parking is free throughout town, with metered parking at the harbour.

Dingle Cabs (☑087 660 2323; www.dinglecabs.com) operates a local taxi service, and can arrange Kerry, Cork and Shannon airport transfers as well as private guided tours of Dingle Peninsula.

Slea Head Drive

A host of superbly preserved structures from Dingle's ancient past including beehive huts, ring forts, inscribed stones and early Christian sites are a highlight of Slea Head, set against staggeringly beautiful coastal scenery. The landscape is especially dramatic in shifting mist, although it's obliterated when thick sea fog rolls in.

Dunmore Head is the westernmost point of the Irish mainland; just to its south is the picturesque cove of Coumeenoole Beach. There are other good beaches at Ventry, Clogher and Wine Strand near Ballyferriter.

The signposted Slea Head Drive is a 47km loop that passes through the villages of Ventry, Dunquin, Ballyferriter and Ballydavid to the west of Dingle town, and takes in all the main sights. Including time for sightseeing, it's at least a half-day drive or one or two days by bike.

Dingle Slea Head Tours (☑087 218 9430; www.dinglesleaheadtours.com; per person from €30) runs guided three-hour minibus tours of Slea Head Drive. There's a minimum of four people; drivers pick you up from your accommodation in Dingle town.

◉ Sights

Celtic & Prehistoric Museum   MUSEUM
(☑087 770 3280; Kilvicadownig, Ventry; €5; ⊙10am-5.30pm mid-Mar-Oct; ℗) This museum squeezes in an astonishing collection of Celtic and prehistoric artefacts, including the world's largest woolly mammoth skull and tusks, as well as a 40,000-year-old cave bear skeleton, Viking horse-bone ice skates, stone battle-axes, flint daggers and jewellery. It started as the private collection of owner Harry Moore, a US expat musician (ask him to strike up a Celtic tune). It's 4km southwest of Ventry.

Fahan Beehive Huts   HISTORIC SITE
(Fahan; adult/child €3/free; ⊙8am-7pm Easter-Sep, shorter hours Oct-Easter) Fahan, on the roadside 7.5km southwest of Ventry, once had some 48 drystone *clochán* dating from AD 500, although the exact dates are unknown. Today five structures remain, including two that are fully intact. The huts are on the slope of Mt Eagle (516m), which still has an estimated 400-plus huts in various states of preservation.

Blasket Centre   CULTURAL CENTRE
(Ionad an Bhlascaoid Mhóir; ☑066-915 6444; www.blasket.ie; adult/child €5/3; ⊙10am-6pm Easter-Oct; ℗) This wonderful interpretative centre celebrates the rich cultural life of the now-abandoned Blasket Islands. It is housed in a striking modern building with a long, white hall ending in a picture window looking directly at the islands. Great Blasket's rich community of storytellers and musicians is profiled along with its literary visitors like playwright JM Synge, author of *The Playboy of the Western World*. The more prosaic practicalities of island life are covered by exhibits on boatbuilding and fishing.

The centre has a good cafe with a view of the islands, and a useful bookshop.

Dingle Peninsula Museum   MUSEUM
(Músaem Chorca Dhuibhne; ☑066-915 6333; www.westkerrymuseum.com; Ballyferriter; admission by donation; ⊙10am-5pm Easter & Jun-mid-Sep, by appointment rest of year; ℗) Set in a 19th-century schoolhouse, this local museum has displays on the history, geology, archaeology and ecology of the peninsula. It's in the centre of the tiny village of Ballyferriter (Baile an Fheirtearaigh), which was named after Piaras Ferriter, a poet and soldier who emerged as a local leader in the 1641 rebellion and was the last Kerry commander to submit to Cromwell's army.

Reask Monastic Site   RUINS
(An Riaisc; ⊙24hr) FREE The remains of this 5th- or 6th-century monastic settlement are one of the peninsula's more evocative archaeological sites, with low stone walls among close-cropped turf and drifts of white daisies revealing the outlines of beehive huts, storehouses and an early Christian oratory. At least 10 stone crosses have been found, including the beautiful **Reask Stone** decorated with Celtic motifs. The site is signposted 'Mainistir Riaisc' just off the R559, 2km east of Ballyferriter.

★**Gallarus Oratory**   HISTORIC SITE
(www.heritageireland.ie; Gallarus; ℗) FREE Gallarus Oratory is one of Ireland's most beautiful ancient buildings, its smoothly constructed dry-stone walls in the shape of an upturned boat. It has withstood the elements in this lonely spot beneath the brown hills for some 1200 years. There's a narrow doorway on the western side and a single, round-headed window on the east. Gallarus is clearly signposted off the R559, 8km northwest of Dingle town, and is 400m east of the (paid) Gallarus Visitor Centre car park.

Alternatively, free parking for half-a-dozen cars is available on the roadside at the public path leading to the oratory from the south.

Gallarus Visitor Centre VISITOR CENTRE
(www.gallarusoratory.ie; Gallarus; €3; ⊘9am-6pm Easter-Oct) This privately owned visitor centre and car park is next to Gallarus Oratory. The only reason for paying the fee is to use the car park (the audiovisual presentation is missable).

★ Kilmalkedar Church RUINS
(Kilmalkedar; ⊘24hr) FREE The Dingle Peninsula's most important Christian site, Kilmalkedar has a beautiful setting with sweeping views over Smerwick Harbour. Built in the 12th century on the site of a 7th-century monastery founded by St Maolcethair, the roofless church is a superb example of Irish Romanesque architecture, its round-arched west door decorated with chevron patterns and a carved human head. In the graveyard you'll find an Ogham stone and a carved stone sundial. It's 2km northeast of Gallarus.

🏃 Activities

Walking, cycling and horse riding are all possible here, as is swimming in warmer weather. Dingle-based Irish Adventures (p306) runs rock-climbing trips.

Mt Brandon WALKING
At 952m, Mt Brandon (Cnoc Bréanainn) is Ireland's ninth-highest summit. It stands in splendid isolation to the north of Dingle, a complex ridge bounded by spectacular cliffs and glacial lakes to the northeast, and falling steeply into the sea to the northwest. The shortest and easiest is via the old pilgrim path from Ballybrack.

The car park is signposted off the R549, 11km north of Dingle town. There are many other routes to the top listed in local walking guides.

From the car park the path leads arrow-straight towards the top, passing numbered wooden crucifixes marking the 14 Stations of the Cross, before deviating to the right for a single zigzag before the summit, which is marked by a huge cairn and a 15th cross. In clear weather the views are stupendous. Descend by the same route (total 8.5km, allow three hours).

Saint's Road WALKING
(www.discoverireland.ie/activities-adventure/cosan-na-naomh-the-saint-s-road/70393) A waymarked 18km walking trail, the Saint's Road (Cosàn na Naomh; www.irishtrails.ie) follows the route of an ancient pilgrim path from the beach at Ventry to Ballybrack (An Baile Breac) at the foot of Mt Brandon via Gallarus Oratory (p311), Kilmalkedar Church and several other early Christian sites.

From Ballybrack experienced hillwalkers can continue via the stations of the cross to the summit of Mt Brandon.

Long's Riding Stables HORSE RIDING
(☑087 225 0286; www.longsriding.com; Ventry; 1/2hr ride from €45/80) Horse treks head along Ventry beach or into the hills above the bay.

🛏 Sleeping & Eating

Dingle Camping & Caravan Site CAMPGROUND €
(Campaíl Teach An Aragail; ☑086 819 1942; www.dingleactivities.com/camping; Gallarus; hiker €11, vehicle plus 2 adults €24; ⊘Apr-Sep; 🅿🛜) A 450m walk west of Gallarus Oratory (p311), this sheltered, 42-pitch campground is just a 1km stroll east of beautiful Wine Strand beach. The owner is a great source of information on local activities, especially walking.

Old Pier B&B B&B €€
(☑066-915 5242; www.oldpier.com; Feothanach, Ballydavid; r from €90; 🅿🛜🐾) With a clifftop setting looking out across Smerwick Harbour to the triple peaks of the Three Sisters, the Old Pier enjoys the perfect sunset location. Bedrooms are decorated with bright summery colours and local artwork, and breakfast is served in a dining room that makes the most of that superlative view. Evening meals available by prior arrangement.

Ceann Trá Heights B&B €€
(☑066-915 9866; maryceanntra@gmail.com; Ventry; d/tr from €85/110; ⊘Easter-Oct; 🅿🛜) An ideal base for exploring the area, this comfortable, modern five-room guesthouse has a great location overlooking Ventry Bay (rooms 1 and 2 have stunning sea views). An open fire warms the cosy sitting room in chilly weather.

Louis Mulcahy Cafe CAFE €
(Caifé na Caolóige; www.louismulcahy.com; Clogher, Ballyferriter; mains €7-11; ⊘10.30am-4.30pm; 🅿) 🌿 The bright, contemporary cafe at Louis Mulcahy Pottery serves fresh homemade fare using Dingle Peninsula produce and herbs from its own gardens. Open sandwiches topped with organic smoked salmon, plus soups, panini and cakes are all served on its own pottery, along with warming coffee and hot chocolate.

Tigh TP SEAFOOD €€
(TP's Pub; 087 246 0507; www.dingleactivities.
com; mains €11-25; kitchen noon-9pm Easter-
Oct, 5-8pm Fri & Sun, 1-8.30pm Sat Nov-Easter) At
the north end of Wine Strand, this beachfront pub serves fantastic local seafood,
from Dingle Bay prawn-topped chowder to
lobster, crab and Brandon Bay hake, and
hosts regular wine and whiskey tastings.
Trad music plays on weekends in summer
and spontaneously throughout the year. Basic but comfortable accommodation (dorm/
double from €20/85) is available on-site.

★**Tig Bhric &**
West Kerry Brewery MICROBREWERY
(Beoir Chorca Dhuibhne; 087 682 2834; www.
westkerrybrewery.ie; An Riasc, Ballyferriter; noon-
11pm Wed-Sun;) Small-batch brews such
Carraig Dubh porter and Riasc red ale use
hand-drawn well water and botanicals such
as elderflower, rosehip and blackcurrants
from the brewpub's lush gardens, which are
strewn with sculptures by owner-brewer
Adrienne Heslin. The 19th-century pub hosts
live music and has four guest rooms (double
from €65) with private bathrooms, rustic
timber furniture and wrought-iron beds.

🛍 Shopping

Louis Mulcahy Pottery CERAMICS
(066-915 6229; www.louismulcahy.com; Clogher, Ballyferriter; 9am-5.30pm Mon-Fri, from
10am Sat & Sun year-round, longer hours Easter-Oct) One of Ireland's most acclaimed potters, Louis Mulcahy produces a wide range
of contemporary and traditional designs.
To learn how to create them yourself, book
a Potter Experience where you make your
own pot (fired/unfired €19.90/9.90, weekdays Easter to September). Behind-the-
scenes tours (€7.50 per person, minimum
four people) are also available. Upstairs, the
gourmet cafe is excellent.

🛈 Getting There & Away

Your own wheels are best for exploring. Most
traffic travels in a clockwise direction including
tour buses, so allow plenty of time if you're
driving in summer. Several places in Dingle town
rent out bikes.

Bus Éireann (www.buseireann.ie) has two
services from Dingle town to Dunquin (€6.90,
30 minutes) on Monday and Thursday, and two
services from Dingle town to Ballydavid (€5.20,
20 minutes) on Tuesday and Friday.

Blasket Islands

The Blasket Islands (Na Blascaodaí), 5km
offshore, are the most westerly part of Ireland. At 6km by 1.2km, Great Blasket (An
Blascaod Mór) is the largest and most visited.
Day trippers come to explore the abandoned
settlements, watch the seabirds, picnic on
Trá Bán (a gorgeous white-sand beach near
the pier) and hike the island's many trails.

Dingle Boat Tours (p305) and Blasket
Islands Eco Marine Tours (086 335 3805;
www.marinetours.ie; Ventry Pier, Ventry; full-/half-
day tour €70/55; Apr-Oct) run seasonal boat
trips. Confirm ahead as adverse weather can
cause cancellations.

All of the Blaskets were lived on at one
time or another; there is evidence of Great
Blasket being inhabited during the Iron Age
and early Christian times. The last islanders
left for the mainland in 1953 after they and
the government agreed that it was no longer
viable to live in such harsh and isolated conditions, although today a few people make
their home out here for part of the year.

Note there are no camping facilities on
the islands; just a handful of self-catering
cottages.

Blasket Island Experience COTTAGE €€
(086 057 2626; www.greatblasketisland.net;
Great Blasket Island; s/d/f from €80/100/150) If
you're looking for luxury, look elsewhere.
These three restored cottages on Great
Blasket island have no electricity, no hot
running water and certainly no TV. Instead
you have a cold-water supply, gas cookers,
wood-burning stoves and candles...and the
chance to enjoy a break from the modern
world with an island almost to yourself.

Access is by boat from Dunquin Harbour
(adult/child €35/15) and takes approximately 20 minutes. Departures depend on tide
and weather, so guests must be flexible.

Cloghane & Around
POP 297

Cloghane (An Clochán) is a delightful little
slice of Dingle. The village's few buildings
shelter in the lee of Mt Brandon, looking out
to Brandon Bay and across the water to the
Stradbally Mountains beyond.

The 5km drive out to Brandon Point from
Cloghane follows ever-narrower single-track
roads, culminating in cliffs with fantastic views south and east. Sheep wander

CONNOR PASS

Topping out at 456m, the R560 across the Connor (or Conor) Pass from Dingle town to Cloghane and Stradbally is Ireland's highest public road. On a foggy day you'll see nothing but the tarmac just in front of you, but in fine weather it offers phenomenal views of Dingle Harbour to the south and Mt Brandon to the north. The road is in good shape, despite being narrow in places and steep and twisting on the north side (large signs portend doom for buses and trucks; caravans are forbidden).

The summit car park yields views down to glacial lakes in the rock-strewn valley below, where you can see the remains of walls and huts where people once lived impossibly hard lives. From the smaller, lower car park on the north side, beside a waterfall, you can make a 10-minute climb to hidden Pedlar's Lake and the kind of vistas that inspire mountain climbers.

The pass is a classic challenge for cyclists; it's best to start in Dingle town, from where the road climbs 400m over a distance of 7km. The climb from the north is more brutal, and has the added problem of being single track at the final, steepest section, so you'll be holding up the traffic.

the constantly eroding hillsides, oblivious to their precarious positions.

Féile Lúghnasa   CULTURAL
(www.cloghanebrandon.com/feile-lughnasa-festival; ⊙ late Jul) On the last weekend in July, Cloghane celebrates the ancient Celtic harvest festival Lúghnasa with theatre performances and traditional events such as sheep shearing, a blessing of the boats at Brandon Pier and a pilgrimage to Mt Brandon's summit.

Mount Brandon Hostel   HOSTEL €
(☑ 085 136 3454; www.mountbrandonhostel.com; dm/s/d €23/35/57, apt for 2 nights €220; ⊙ Mar-Jan; P @ ☎) A patio overlooks the bay from this small, simple hostel with scrubbed wooden floors and furniture. Most rooms have private bathrooms. An apartment with kitchen sleeps up to four people (minimum two-night stay).

O'Connor's Guesthouse   B&B €€
(☑ 066-713 8113; www.cloghane.com; d/tr/f from €70/120/145, camping per person €7; P @ ☎) Book ahead to bag a simple room or a table in this welcoming village pub, which serves food made using local produce (from 8.30am to 8.30pm), ranging from salmon to steak (mains €8 to €16). Landlord Michael has loads of local info and can also explain why there's an aeroplane engine out the front.

Murphy's Bar   PUB
(☑ 086 343 0267; www.murphysbarbrandon.com; Brandon Pier; ⊙ 2-11.30pm Mon-Thu, to 1am Fri, from noon Sat, 12.30-11.30pm Sun) Set on the pier at Brandon, 4km north of Cloghane, this classic pub has been in the same family for five generations, offering live music,

a peat fire and a smooth pint of Murphy's stout. In summer, sit outside with a crab sandwich and a cold one, and soak up the view across Brandon Bay.

ⓘ Getting There & Away

Bus Éireann (www.buseireann.ie) runs to/from Tralee (€13, one hour) twice daily on Fridays only. No buses link Cloghane with Dingle town.

Castlegregory & Around

At the base of Rough Point Peninsula, Castlegregory (Caislean an Ghriare), which once rivalled Tralee as a busy local centre, is today a quiet village with lovely views of the hills to the south.

However, things change when you drive up the sand-blown road along the broad spit of land between Tralee Bay and Brandon Bay. Up here, it's a water-sports playground. A prime windsurfing location, the peninsula also offers adrenaline-inducing windsurfing and kitesurfing, while divers can swim among shoals of pollack amid the kelp forests and anemone-encrusted rocks of the Maharees Islands.

Accommodation on the little peninsula is limited – mostly camping, caravans and self-catering – but Dingle town (29km southwest) and Tralee (32km east) are both close by.

There are only a couple of places to eat, and just the one grocery store in Castlegregory, so stock up in Dingle or Tralee.

Jamie Knox Watersports   WATER SPORTS
(☑ 066-713 9411; www.jamieknox.com; Sandy Bay; equipment rental per hr €5-15; ⊙ lessons Apr-Oct,

shop year-round) Jamie Knox offers surf, wind-surf, stand-up paddleboarding, canoe and pedalo hire and instruction, and also rents wetsuits. Surf lessons on Brandon Bay start at €30 for a 'taster'. Kids won't want to miss bouncing on the inflatable water trampoline (€5 per hour) moored in the bay. There's also a surf-equipment shop nearby (usually open 10am to 5pm).

Waterworld   DIVING
(☑066-713 9292; www.waterworld.ie; Harbour House, Scraggane Pier; ⊙9am-6pm year-round) The Maharees Islands (north of Castlegregory), Brandon Point and the Blasket Islands offer some of the best scuba-diving in Ireland. For qualified divers, Waterworld, based at **Harbour House** (s/d from €60/100; P🖥🌐), runs daily boat trips to the best sites (€35 per dive) and half-day Try-a-Dive packages (€80 per person) for complete beginners.

★**Gregory's Garden**   IRISH €€
(☑087 213 0866; Main St, Castlegregory; mains €16-26; ⊙5.30-9pm Wed-Sun May-Sep) 🍴 This cute cottage restaurant in the middle of Castlegregory village takes the claims of 'locally sourced produce' very seriously indeed, pairing the likes of Dingle-whiskey-cured salmon, Kerry lamb and Brandon Bay crab with vegetables, herbs and salad leaves plucked from the chef's very own kitchen garden. Early-bird menu offers three courses for €20 (pre-6.30pm). Booking essential.

Spillane's   PUB FOOD €€
(☑066-713 9125; www.spillanesbar.com; Fahamore; mains €10-25; ⊙food served 1-9pm daily Jun-Aug, from 5pm Mon-Sat & 2-8pm Sun Mar-May, Sep & Oct; P🚻) 🍴 Outside tables look across Brandon Bay to the mountains at this laid-back pub idyllically located out near the tip of the peninsula. Seafood is a speciality (the breaded scampi is a revelation), but it also does excellent pizzas and house-made burgers with hand-cut chips.

❶ Getting There & Away

Bus Éireann (www.buseireann.ie) runs from Tralee to Castlegregory (€9.50, 35 minutes) twice daily on Fridays only.

NORTHERN KERRY

Consisting mainly of farmland, Northern Kerry's landscapes can't compare to the spectacular Killarney region, the Ring of

GLANTEENASSIG FOREST

Southeast of Castlegregory, the 450 hectares of forest, mountain, lake and bog that make up the **Glanteenassig Forest Recreation Area** (www.coillte.ie/site/glanteenassig; ⊙8am-10pm May-Aug, to 6pm Sep-Apr) FREE are a magical, off-the-tourist-trail treasure. There are two lakes; you can drive on an unsurfaced road up to the higher one, which is encircled by a plank boardwalk (too narrow for wheelchairs or prams). It's 4.5km south of Aughacasla on the northern coast road (R560).

Make sure you're out before closing time (check signs at the car park); there's a call-out fee to have the gates unlocked.

Kerry or the Dingle Peninsula. But there are some interesting places that merit a stop: Kerry's county town, Tralee, has a great museum; Ballybunion is home to a world-class golf club and sweeping beaches; and the town of Listowel has strong literary connections.

❶ Getting There & Away

Tralee is the main transport hub, with bus and train services.
Shannon Ferry Limited (☑068-905 3124; www.shannonferries.com; cars €20, motorcyclists, cyclists & pedestrians €5; ⊙7.30am-8.30pm Mon-Sat, from 9.30am Sun Apr-Sep, longer hours Jun-Aug, shorter hours Oct-Mar; 🌐) runs a ferry between Tarbert in County Kerry and Killimer in County Clare, departing hourly on the half-hour from Tarbert and on the hour from Killimer. Journey time is 20 minutes. The ferry dock is clearly signposted 2.2km northwest of Tarbert. Taking the ferry saves a 134km detour via Limerick by road.

Tralee & Around

POP 23,691
Although it's the county town, Tralee is down-to-earth and more engaged with the business of everyday life than the tourist trade, but a great museum and a family-friendly wetlands centre make it well worth a stop.

Founded by the Normans in 1216, Tralee has a long history of rebellion. In the 16th century the last ruling earl of the Desmonds was captured and executed here. His head was sent to Elizabeth I, who spiked it on

TRACING YOUR ANCESTORS

County Kerry currently has no genealogy centre, but you can search census returns, old newspapers and other archives at **Tralee Library** (☑ 066-712 1200; www.kerrylibrary.ie; Moyderwell; ☺ 10am-5pm Mon, Wed, Fri & Sat, to 8pm Tue & Thu; ☎) and **Killarney Library** (☑ 064-663 2655; www.kerrylibrary.ie; Rock Rd; ☺ 10am-5pm Mon, Wed, Fri & Sat, to 8pm Tue & Thu; ☎).

There are also some church records available free of charge on the Irish Genealogy (www.irishgenealogy.ie) website.

London Bridge. The Desmond castle once stood at the junction of Denny St and the Mall, but any trace of medieval Tralee that survived the Desmond Wars was razed during the Cromwellian period.

Elegant Denny St and Day Pl are the oldest parts of town, with 18th-century Georgian buildings, while the Square, just south of the Mall, is a contemporary open space.

⊙ Sights

★ **Banna Strand**   BEACH
(Banna) A favourite weekend getaway for Tralee residents, Banna is one of the biggest and best Blue Flag beaches in Ireland, a 6km stretch of fine golden sand backed by 10m-high dunes, with fantastic views southwest to Mt Brandon and the Dingle hills. The beach is 13km northwest of Tralee, signposted off the R551 Ballyheigue road.

A monument 500m south of the main car park marks the spot where the Irish revolutionary leader **Roger Casement** was landed from a German U-boat, shortly before the Easter Rising of 1916.

★ **Tralee Bay**
Wetlands Centre   NATURE RESERVE
(☑ 066-712 6700; www.traleebaywetlands.org; Ballyard Rd; adult/child €5/2, guided tour €10/5; ☺ 10am-7pm Jul & Aug, to 5pm Sep, Oct & Mar-Jun, 11am-4pm Nov-Feb; ℗ ⓖ) ✎ A 15-minute nature-safari boat ride is the highlight of a visit to Tralee's wetlands centre. You can also get a good overview of the reserve's 3000 hectares, encompassing saltwater and freshwater habitats, from the 20m-high viewing tower (accessible by lift), and spot wildlife from bird hides. A light-filled cafe overlooks the main lake, which has pedal boats (€15

per 30 minutes) and rowing boats (€10 per 30 minutes) for hire.

★ **Kerry County Museum**   MUSEUM
(☑ 066-712 7777; www.kerrymuseum.ie; 18 Denny St; adult/child €5/free; ☺ 9.30am-5.30pm Jun-Aug, to 5pm Tue-Sat Sep-May) An absolute treat, Kerry's county museum has excellent interpretive displays on Irish historical events and trends, with an emphasis on County Kerry. The Medieval Experience recreates life (smells and all) in Tralee in 1450, while the Tom Crean Room celebrates the local early-20th-century explorer who accompanied both Scott and Shackleton on epic Antarctic expeditions. It's housed in the neoclassical Ashe Memorial Hall.

Blennerville Windmill
& Visitor Centre   WINDMILL
(☑ 066-712 1064; www.blennerville-windmill.ie; Blennerville; adult/child €7/3; ☺ 9am-6pm Jun-Aug, 9.30am-5.30pm Apr, May, Sep & Oct; ℗) Blennerville, 3.4km southwest of Tralee's centre on the N86 to Dingle, used to be the city's chief port, though the harbour has long since silted up. A 19th-century grain windmill here has been restored and is the largest working mill in Ireland and Britain. Its modern visitor centre houses exhibitions on flourmilling, as well as on the thousands of emigrants who boarded 'coffin ships' from what was then Kerry's largest embarkation point.

Ardfert Cathedral   CATHEDRAL
(☑ 066-713 4711; www.heritageireland.ie; adult/child €5/3; ☺ 10am-6pm late Mar-Sep) The impressive remains of 13th-century Ardfert Cathedral are notable for the beautiful and delicate stone carvings on its Romanesque door and window arches. Set into one of the interior walls is an effigy, said to be of St Brendan the Navigator, who was educated in Ardfert and founded a monastery here. Other elaborate medieval grave slabs can be seen in the visitor centre. Ardfert is 9km northwest of Tralee on the Ballyheigue road.

Crag Cave   CAVE
(☑ 066-714 1244; www.cragcave.com; Castleisland; adult/child €15/6; ☺ 10am-6pm daily mid-Mar–Oct, Wed-Sun Nov & Dec, Fri-Sun Jan–mid-Mar; ℗ ⓖ) This cave was discovered in 1983, when problems with water pollution led to a search for the source of the local river. In 1989, 300m of the 4km-long cave were opened to the public; admission is by 30-minute guided tour involving 72 steps. The remarkable rock formations include a stalagmite shaped (to some) like a statue of

Tralee

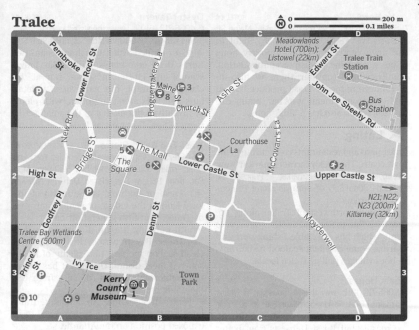

the Madonna. There are play areas for kids, a restaurant and a gift shop. The cave is signposted 18km east of Tralee.

✦ Festivals & Events

Rose of Tralee CULTURAL
(www.roseoftralee.ie; ☉ Aug) The hugely popular Rose of Tralee is a beauty pageant open to Irish women (and women of Irish descent) from around the world (the eponymous 'roses'). More than just a beauty contest, it's a five-day-long festival bookended by a gala ball and a 'midnight madness' parade led by the newly crowned Rose of Tralee, followed by a fireworks display.

Kerry Film Festival FILM
(www.kerryfilmfestival.com; ☉ Oct) The five-day Kerry Film Festival includes a short film competition and screenings at venues around town.

🛏 Sleeping

★ Meadowlands Hotel HOTEL €€
(☎ 066-718 0444; www.meadowlandshotel.com; Oakpark Rd; s/d/f from €95/125/178; P🐾) Strolling distance from town but far enough away to be quiet, Meadowlands is an unexpectedly romantic four-star hotel with stunning vintage-meets-designer public areas. Rooms have autumnal hues and

Tralee

◎ Top Sights
1 Kerry County Museum B3

✪ Activities, Courses & Tours
2 O'Halloran Cycles D2

🛏 Sleeping
3 Ashe Hotel B1

🍴 Eating
4 Chez Christophe B2
5 Quinlan's Fish B2
6 Roast House B2

🍷 Drinking & Nightlife
7 Baily's Corner B2
8 Roundy's B1

✪ Entertainment
9 Siamsa Tíre A3

🛍 Shopping
10 Farmers Market A3

service is spot-on. Its beamed-ceilinged bar (mains €13 to €29), serving top-notch seafood (the owners have their own fishing fleet), is at least as popular with locals as it is with visitors.

Ask about discounted rates.

Ashe Hotel HOTEL €€
(☑ 066-710 6300; www.theashehotel.ie; Maine St; s/d/f/ste from €80/105/145/200; ☎) Right in the town centre, this contemporary hotel offers good-value, stylish accommodation. Family rooms sleep four; there are also interconnecting rooms. Local produce is used in the gastropub menu at its bar (mains €10 to €20), which also has a kids' menu.

✕ Eating

Cafes, pubs and restaurants concentrate in the town centre. The weekly **farmers market** (www.facebook.com/traleefarmersmarket; Prince's St; ⊙ 10am-2.30pm Sat) 🍴 sprawls along Prince's St on Saturdays.

Heading northwest of Tralee along the coast, it's 7km to Spa and another 6km on to Fenit, which has a sizeable fishing port and marina. Some excellent seafood restaurants in both villages pull in Tralee locals.

Roast House CAFE €
(☑ 066-718 1011; www.theroasthouse.ie; 3 Denny St; mains €8-13; ⊙ 9am-5pm Mon-Sat; ☎🪑) The name comes from its own custom-built coffee roaster, but Roast House is even better known for its food, which spans breakfasts of homemade buttermilk pancakes with bacon and maple syrup to lunch dishes like barbecue pulled-pork sandwiches, sloppy joes, and curry-spiced mushroom and quinoa burger.

★ Quinlan's Fish SEAFOOD €€
(☑ 066-712 3998; www.kerryfish.com; The Mall; mains €10-19; ⊙ noon-9pm Sun-Thu, to 10pm Fri & Sat) 🍴 Quinlan's is Kerry's leading chain of fish shops, with its own fleet so you know everything here is fresh. The fish and chips are great; alternatives include Dingle Bay squid and chips with sweet-chilli sauce. Lighter pan-fried options are available. The Delftblue, scrubbed-timber and exposed-brick premises have a handful of wine-barrel tables, or head to Tralee's Town Park.

Chez Christophe FRENCH €€
(☑ 087 414 0974; laursodriscoll@gmail.com; 6 Courthouse Lane; mains €9-21; ⊙ 12.30-3pm & 5-10pm Wed-Fri, noon-10pm Sat; ☎) French native Christophe uses Kerry produce to create delicious dishes such as prawn and crabclaw cassoulet, and smoked fillet of beef with goat's-cheese mash, as well as a small choice of pizzas. The dining room has classic French bistro light fittings and a bookcase-lined wall. There's a two-/three-course early-bird menu for €16/19, before 7pm.

Oyster Tavern SEAFOOD €€
(☑ 066-713 6102; www.theoystertavern.ie; Spa; mains €16-30; ⊙ 5-10pm Mon-Sat, noon-9pm Sun; 🅿☎🪑) Grilled Atlantic salmon, pan-fried Kerry Head crab claws, Dingle Bay prawn scampi and lobster in season star at this classy restaurant, but carnivores, vegetarians and kids aren't forgotten, with plenty of inventive options. It's in the small settlement of Spa, 7km west of Tralee.

West End Bar & Bistro SEAFOOD €€
(☑ 066-713 6246; www.westendfenit.ie; West End, Fenit; mains €10-25; ⊙ kitchen 5.30-9pm Mon-Sat, from 1.30pm Sun, closed Mon-Thu Nov-Apr; 🪑) 'Fresh or nothing' is the motto of this local icon in the village of Fenit, 13km west of Tralee. The fifth-generation bar serves a mouth-watering line-up of seafood, including Tralee Bay prawn cocktail and Kerry Head scallop mornay, plus plenty of locally sourced meat dishes. Upstairs it has simple but comfortable rooms (doubles from €80 including breakfast).

Fenit's Irish name, An Fhianait, translates as 'the Wild Place', in reference to its exposed position on the Atlantic.

🍷 Drinking & Entertainment

★ Roundy's BAR
(5 Broguemakers Lane; ⊙ 6pm-midnight Thu-Sun) Ingeniously converted from a terrace house (with a tree still growing right through the courtyard-garden-turned-interior), this hip little bar has cool tunes, regular DJs spinning old school funk and live bands.

Baily's Corner PUB
(30 Lower Castle St; ⊙ 9am-11.30pm Mon-Thu, to 12.30am Fri & Sat, 4-11pm Sun; ☎) Filled with rugby paraphernalia, Baily's Corner has an ornate stained-glass-topped timber bar and a superb selection of whiskeys and gins. It's deservedly popular for its regular trad sessions, with local musicians performing original material.

Siamsa Tíre THEATRE
(☑ 066-712 3055; www.siamsatire.com; Town Park; tickets €15-35; ⊙ booking office 10am-6pm Mon-Sat & preperformance) Siamsa Tíre, the National Folk Theatre of Ireland, recreates dynamic aspects of Gaelic culture through song, dance, drama and mime. There are several shows a week year-round.

ℹ Information

University Hospital Kerry (p281) has an accident and emergency department.

Tourist office (☏ 066-712 1288; traleetio@ failteireland.ie; Denny St; ☺9am-5pm Mon-Sat) In the same building as the Kerry County Museum (p316).

ⓘ Getting There & Away

Bus Éireann (www.buseireann.ie) operates from the **bus station** (John Joe Sheehy Rd) next to the train station, 1km east of the town centre. Destinations include the following.

Cork €20, 2¼ hours, hourly

Killarney €10.45, 40 minutes, hourly

Limerick €14.25, two hours, hourly

Listowel €9.50, 30 minutes, hourly

Irish Rail (www.irishrail.ie) services include trains every two hours via Mallow to Cork (€32.50, 2½ hours) and Killarney (€11.35, 40 minutes), and one direct train to Dublin (€62, 3¾ hours) with additional services that require a change in Mallow.

ⓘ Getting Around

There's a taxi rank on the Mall, or try **Windmill Cabs** (☏ 087 236 1687; www.windmillcabs.ie).

O'Halloran Cycles (☏ 066-712 2820; 83 Boherbee; bike rental per day from €15; ☺9am-6pm Mon-Sat) hires out bikes.

Listowel

POP 4820

Listowel has more literary credentials than your average provincial town, with connections to such accomplished scribes as John B Keane, Maurice Walsh, George Fitzmaurice, Brendan Kennelly and Bryan MacMahon. They're featured at the Kerry Writers' Museum, and on a literary mural on Church St, opposite the police station. Keane is remembered with a statue on the opposite side of the square, in which he seems to be hailing a cab.

The town's tidy Georgian streets are arranged around an attractive main square with a Norman castle overlooking the River Feale.

◉ Sights

Kerry Writers' Museum   MUSEUM
(Seanchaí; ☏ 068-22212; www.kerrywriters museum.com; The Square; adult/child €8/3; ☺9.30am-5.30pm Mon-Fri, 10.30am-4pm Sat Jun-Sep, 10am-4pm Mon-Fri Oct-May) The Writers' Exhibition in this Georgian building celebrates Listowel's heritage of literary observers of Irish life. Rooms are devoted to local greats such as John B Keane and Bryan MacMahon, with simple, haunting tableaux narrating their lives, and recordings of them

reading their work, a reflection of Ireland's tradition of storytelling. There's a cafe and a performance space where events are regularly staged in summer.

Listowel Castle   CASTLE
(☏ 086 385 7201; www.heritageireland.ie; The Square; ☺9.30am-6pm mid-May–mid-Sep) **FREE** Standing between the town square and the river, this 12th-century castle was once the stronghold of the Fitzmaurices, the Anglo-Norman lords of Kerry. It was the last castle in Ireland to succumb to the Elizabethan attacks during the Desmond revolt. What remains of the castle has been thoroughly restored. Admission is by guided tour only.

Lartigue Monorailway   MUSEUM
(☏ 068-24393; www.lartiguemonorail.com; John B Keane Rd; adult/child €6/3; ☺1-4.30pm Easter weekend & May-Sep) Designed by Frenchman Charles Lartigue, this unique survivor of Victorian railway engineering once ran between Listowel and Ballybunion along the coast. The renovated section of line is short (less than a kilometre) but fascinating, with manual turntables at either end for swinging the train around.

🎊 Festivals & Events

Writers' Week   LITERATURE
(www.writersweek.ie; ☺late May/early Jun) Bibliophiles flock to Listowel for five days of readings, poetry, music, drama, seminars, storytelling and other events held at various locations around town. The festival attracts an impressive list of writers, which have included Booker Prize–winning Colm Tóibín, along with John Montague, Jung Chang, Roddy Doyle, Rebecca Miller and Terry Jones.

🛏 Sleeping & Eating

Listowel Arms Hotel   HOTEL €€
(☏ 068-21500; www.listowelarms.com; The Square; d/f/ste from €140/155/220; 🅿🛜) Overlooking the river, Listowel's principal hotel is a family-run affair in a Georgian building that balances grandeur with country charm, with 42 antique-furnished rooms. Nonguests are welcome at its Writers Bar, which often has music in summer, and Georgian Restaurant (three-course dinner €35, open 6pm to 9pm), which specialises in the fresh fish of the day.

★Lizzy's Little Kitchen   CAFE €
(☏ 087 149 7220; www.facebook.com/lizzyslittle kitchen; 12 William St; mains €7-10; ☺9am-4pm Tue-Sat; 🚸) 🌱 This busy wee place is a top spot

for lunch, whether squeezed around one of the old wooden tables or perched at the window counter. The menu is gourmet-style cafe food made from fresh local produce, including hot lunch specials such as deep-fried goujons of hake with salad, and vegan chickpea, spinach and sweet-potato curry.

🛍 Shopping

Woulfe's Bookshop   BOOKS
(☑ 068-21021; 7 Church St; ⊙ 10am-6pm Mon-Sat) As befits a writers' town, Listowel is blessed with an excellent independent bookshop in the shape of Woulfe's, stacked with a huge selection of titles.

ℹ Information

Listowel's **tourist office** (☑ 068-22212; www.listowel.ie; ⊙ 9.30am-5.30pm Mon-Sat Jun-Aug, 10am-4pm Mon-Fri Sep-Nov & Mar-May) is housed in the Kerry Writers' Museum (p319).

ℹ Getting There & Away

Bus Éireann (www.buseireann.ie) services run every two hours from Listowel to Tralee (€9.50, 40 minutes) and Limerick (€15, 1½ hours).

Ballybunion

POP 1413

The beach town of Ballybunion is best known for its eponymous golf club; a statue of a club-swinging Bill Clinton in the middle of town commemorates his visit to the course in 1998. Two pretty beaches, Ballybunion North (also known as Ladies Beach) and Ballybunion South (Men's Beach), have Blue Flag ratings; a signposted **Cliff Walk** links the two.

Overlooking the southern beach are the restored remains of **Ballybunion Castle** (aka Fitzmaurice Castle), the 16th-century seat of the Fitzmaurices, with views to the Dingle Peninsula and Loop Head, County Clare, on a clear day.

Ballybunion Golf Club   GOLF
(☑ 068-27146; www.ballybuniongolfclub.ie; Sandhill Rd; green fees €80-230; ⊙ Apr-early Oct) Ballybunion Golf Club is reputed as one of the finest links courses in the world. Weekends (and bank holidays) are reserved for members, but visitors can book tee times to play the par 71, 1893-established Old Course on weekday mornings, or the par 72 Cashen Course on weekday mornings and afternoons.

Teach de Broc   GUESTHOUSE €€
(www.ballybuniongolf.com; Links Rd; d from €155; ⊙ Apr-Oct; P🎁) Framed by flowers, this low-rise boutique inn next to the golf club has 14 spacious rooms that are thoughtfully appointed (hypo-allergenic pillows, free bottled water, USB chargers) and stylishly decorated in cream, gold and oyster-grey tones. Its on-site **Strollers Bar & Bistro** (☑ 068-27581; mains bar €8-15, restaurant €17-29; ⊙ bar meals 4-9pm Sun, restaurant 6-9pm Mon-Sat Apr-Oct) is Ballybunion's best place to eat.

ℹ Getting There & Away

Ballybunion is 15km northeast of Listowel on the R553.

Bus Éireann (☑ 01-836 6111; www.buseireann.ie) links Ballybunion with Listowel (€5.50, 20 minutes, three daily Monday to Friday, two on Saturday).

Counties Limerick & Tipperary

POP 354,450 / AREA 6995 SQ KM

Best Places to Eat

➡ Restaurant 1826 Adare (p332)

➡ Mustard Seed at Echo Lodge (p332)

➡ Hook & Ladder (p328)

➡ Mikey Ryan's (p337)

➡ Country Choice (p344)

Best Places to Stay

➡ Aherlow House Hotel (p335)

➡ No 1 Pery Square (p327)

➡ Raheen House Hotel (p342)

➡ Dunraven Arms (p332)

➡ Apple Caravan & Camping Park (p341)

Why Go?

From marching ditties to rhyming verse, the names Tipperary and Limerick are part of the Western lexicon, but both counties are relatively unexplored by visitors.

County Limerick is closely tied to its namesake city, which has a history as dramatic as Ireland's. In a nation of hard knocks, it has had more than its fair share. The city's streets have tangible links to the past and a gritty, honest vibrancy, while treasures abound in its lush, green countryside.

In contrast, Tipperary town is minor. But amid the county's rolling hills, rich farmland and deep valleys bordered by soaring mountains, it's a peaceful place that's perfect for following a river to its source or climbing a stile to reach a lonely ruin.

In both counties, ancient Celtic sites, medieval abbeys and other relics endure in solitude, awaiting discovery. And even Limerick and Tipperary's best-known sights retain a rough, inspiring dignity.

When to Go

➡ As the third-largest city in Ireland, with a sizeable student population, Limerick city bustles year-round, but is at its liveliest during the warmer months, from around April to October.

➡ April to October is also the best time to explore the rural villages, towns and countryside of both counties, when opening hours for attractions are longest (some attractions close during the rest of the year) and the weather is at its best.

➡ Most of the counties' festivities take place from April to October too, including wonderful walking festivals in the Glen of Aherlow.

Counties Limerick & Tipperary Highlights

1 **Rock of Cashel** (p336) Exploring the extensive remains of medieval churches at this impressive ancient religious stronghold

2 **Glen of Aherlow** (p335) Journeying through tranquil bucolic landscapes and hiking to high mountain lakes.

3 **Hunt Museum** (p324) Discovering Bronze and Iron Age, medieval and modern art treasures.

4 **Cahir Castle** (p340) Walking the walls and climbing the keep of Cahir's storybook, riverside castle.

Map Labels

Portumna

River Shannon

Little Brosna River

Birr

Kinnitty

Terryglass

N52

OFFALY

N62

Clonenagh
Mountrath

Portlaoise

M7

Borrisokane

N65

Cloughjordan

N65

Roscrea

R445

Borris-in-
Ossory

R445

LAOIS

Dromineer

Portroe

Nenagh

Arra
Mountains

R498

Moneygall

Toomyvara

N62

Abbeyleix

Durrow

M7

M8

River Nore

Kilkenny

Silvermine
Mountains

R503

TIPPERARY

River Suir

Templemore

Urlingford

Thurles

N75

N62

Holy Cross
Abbey

R660

M8

Famine
Warhouse

Ballingarry

KILKENNY

Dundrum

R601

R691

Dualla

Killenaule

Callan

Tipperary
Racecourse

Limerick
Junction

**Rock of
Cashel** ❶ **Cashel**

R692

N76

Golden

N74

Athassel
Priory

M9

Tipperary

R664

N74

R663

Bansha

Rockwell
College

New Inn

Fethard

Slievenamuck
Hills

Newtown

❷ **Glen of
Aherlow**

Knockgraffon
Motte

Galbally

Ballylanders

Galtee
Mountains

Cahir ❹

N24

Clonmel

N76

Carrick-
on-Suir

N24

River Suir

M8

River Tar

Ardfinnan

Comeragh
Mountains

WATERFORD

**Mitchelstown
Cave** ❼

Burncourt

Ballyporeen

Clogheen

Newcastle

River Tar

N8

Knockmealdown
Mountains

Kilmacthomas

N25

Scale

20 km
10 miles

---

❺ **Adare** (p331) Deliberating over mouth-watering menus in this heritage town's thatched-cottage restaurants.

❻ **Foynes Flying Boat Museum** (p330) Taking in Shannon Estuary vistas and discovering the glamorous history of 1940s transatlantic flying boats.

❼ **Mitchelstown Cave** (p341) Delving into a dazzling underworld of limestone passages and stalactite-laden caverns.

COUNTY LIMERICK

Limerick's low-lying farmland is framed on its southern and eastern boundaries by swelling uplands and mountains. Limerick city is boisterously urban in contrast and has enough historic and cultural attractions for a day's diversion. About 15km south of the city are the haunting archaeological sites around Lough Gur, while about the same distance southwest of the city is the cute thatched village of Adare.

Limerick City

POP 58,319

'There once was a city called Limerick...' Umm, no, can't think of anything that rhymes with Limerick. And no one is quite sure why those humorous five-line verses are named after this Irish city, though the term dates from the late 19th century.

Limerick straddles the tidal reaches of Ireland's longest river, the Shannon, where it swings west to join the Shannon Estuary. Following the city's tough past, as narrated in Frank McCourt's *Angela's Ashes,* its medieval and Georgian architecture received a glitzy makeover during the Celtic Tiger era, but the economic downturn hit hard.

The city is recovering rapidly, however. Limerick was chosen as the first-ever Irish City of Culture in 2014, and the subsequent investment saw a rejuvenated waterfront complete with stylish boardwalk. There's a renovated castle, an art gallery and a developing foodie scene to complement its traditional pubs, plus locals who can't wait to welcome you.

History

Viking adventurers established a settlement on an island in the River Shannon in the 9th century. They fought with the native Irish for control of the site until Brian Ború's forces drove them out in 968 and established Limerick as the royal seat of the O'Brien kings. Brian Ború finally destroyed Viking power and presence in Ireland at the Battle of Clontarf in 1014. By the late 12th century, invading Normans had supplanted the Irish as the town's rulers. Throughout the Middle Ages the two groups remained divided.

From 1690 to 1691 Limerick acquired heroic status in the saga of Ireland's struggle against occupation by the English. After their defeat in the Battle of the Boyne in 1690, Jacobite forces withdrew west behind the famously strong walls of Limerick town until the Treaty of Limerick guaranteed religious freedom for Catholics. The English later reneged and enforced fierce anti-Catholic legislation, an act of betrayal that came to symbolise the injustice of British rule, while Limerick gained the nickname 'Treaty City'.

During the 18th century the old walls of Limerick were demolished and a well-planned and prosperous Georgian town developed. Such prosperity had waned by the early 20th century, however, as traditional industries fell on hard times. Several high-profile nationalists hailed from here, including Eamon de Valera.

⊙ Sights

Limerick's main places of interest cluster to the north on King's Island (the oldest part of Limerick and once part of Englishtown), to the south around the Crescent and Pery Sq (the city's noteworthy Georgian area), and all along the riverbanks.

If you have time, the best approach (on foot) from the city centre to King John's Castle is to cross Sarsfield Bridge and follow the riverside walk north to Thomond Bridge – there are great views across the river to the city and castle.

★ **King John's Castle**   CASTLE
(☑ 061-711 222; www.kingjohnscastle.com; Nicholas St; adult/child €13/9.50; ⊙ 9.30am-6pm Apr-Sep, to 5pm Oct-Mar) An obdurate and brooding Norman mass looming over the River Shannon, Limerick's showpiece castle, with its vast curtain walls and towers, was built on the orders of King John of England between 1200 and 1212. The massive twin gate towers still stand to their full height. A multimedia experience that provides an excellent potted history of Ireland in general, and Limerick in particular, is followed by exposed archaeology in the undercroft and a tour of the courtyard and fortifications.

Upstairs from the cafe, don't miss the exhibitions on the castle's archaeology and the development of Georgian Limerick, or the view from the top of the gate towers, though the best views of the castle itself are from the riverside walk on the far side of the Shannon. Book online for discounts.

★ **Hunt Museum**   MUSEUM
(www.huntmuseum.com; Custom House, Rutland St; adult/child €7.50/free, free on Sun; ⊙ 10am-5pm Mon-Sat, from 2pm Sun; ⊛) Although named for its benefactors, this museum,

opened in 1997, is also a treasure hunt. Visitors are encouraged to open drawers and poke around the finest collection of Bronze Age, Iron Age, medieval and modern art treasures outside Dublin. Highlights include a Syracusan coin claimed to have been one of the 30 pieces of silver paid to Judas for his betrayal of Christ, a Renoir study, a Gauguin painting, a Giacometti drawing and works by Picasso and Jack B Yeats.

There's also a tiny but exquisite bronze horse once attributed to Leonardo da Vinci (but now considered a much later copy), Cycladic sculptures, an alabaster vase from ancient Egypt dated to the 3rd century BC and a smattering of pieces from the Far East. The 2000-plus items are from the private collection of the late John and Gertrude Hunt, antique dealers and consultants, who championed historical preservation throughout the region. Free one-hour guided tours from the dedicated and colourful volunteers are available. The museum has a good cafe.

Limerick City Gallery of Art   GALLERY

(www.gallery.limerick.ie; Carnegie Bldg, Pery Sq; ⊘10am-5.30pm Mon-Wed, Fri & Sat, to 8pm Thu, noon-5.30pm Sun) **FREE** Limerick's art gallery adjoins the peaceful People's Park (p325) in the heart of Georgian Limerick. Among its permanent collection of paintings from the last 300 years are works by Sean Keating and Jack B Yeats. Temporary exhibitions of conceptual and thought-provoking contemporary art fill the other well-lit galleries. The gallery is the home of EVA International (www.eva. ie; ⊘Sep-Nov), Ireland's contemporary art biennial held across the city in even-numbered years. Check the website for dates.

There's a good cafe (open 9.30am to 5pm) looking across the park.

Frank McCourt Museum   MUSEUM

(www.frankmccourtmuseum.com; Leamy House, Hartstonge St; adult/child €5/2.50; ⊘11am-4.30pm Mon-Fri year-round, 2-4pm Sat & Sun Apr-Aug) This museum dedicated to Frank McCourt (p328), author of *Angela's Ashes*, can be found in his former school building in Limerick's Georgian quarter. The museum contains a recreation of a 1930s classroom and of the McCourt household, plus an assortment of memorabilia.

People's Park   PARK

(www.limerick.ie; Pery Sq; ⊘8am-dusk Sep-Apr, to 9pm May-Aug) This lovely wooded park in Pery Sq at the heart of Georgian Limerick is an excellent place for collapsing onto

the grass with a chunky novel when the sun pops out. Check out the restored 19th-century red-and-white drinking fountain. The statue on the column in the middle of the park is of Thomas Spring Rice, a former MP for Limerick.

St Mary's Cathedral   CATHEDRAL

(⌨061-310 293; www.saintmaryscathedral.ie; Bridge St; adult/child €5/free; ⊘9am-5pm Mon-Thu, to 4pm Fri & Sat, from 1.30pm Sun) Limerick's ancient cathedral was founded in 1168 by Donal Mór O'Brien, king of Munster. Parts of the 12th-century Romanesque western doorway, nave and aisles survive, and there are splendid 15th-century black-oak misericords (for supporting 'clerical posteriors') in the Jebb Chapel, unique examples of their kind in Ireland and each fabulously carved with creatures and mythical animals. Check the website for upcoming musical events.

Thomond Park Stadium   STADIUM

(⌨061-421 109; www.thomondpark.ie; Cratloe Rd; adult/child combined tour & museum €10/8; ⊘9am-5pm Mon-Fri, also Sat & Sun for prebooked groups of 6 or more) From 1995 until 2007, the Munster province rugby team was undefeated in this legendary stadium; it was also the venue for their famous victories over New Zealand's All Blacks in 1978 and 2016. Tours of the hallowed ground include the dressing rooms, dugouts and pitch, and its memorabilia-filled museum. It's an easy 1km walk northwest of the centre along High St.

The museum is open on match days from 2½ hours before kickoff (museum-only admission adult/child €5/3).

🏃 Activities

⭐**Limerick City Kayaking Tours**   KAYAKING

(⌨086 330 8236; www.limerickadventures.com; Rutland St; short/long tour €25/35; ⊘Sat & Sun) Departing from behind the Hunt Museum, these 1½- or 2½-hour kayak tours take you along the River Shannon and beneath the walls of King John's Castle, offering an entirely new perspective on the city. Book in advance; no previous experience needed. Tour times depend on the tide and weather.

Limerick Walking Tours   WALKING

(⌨061-312 833; www.huntmuseum.com/limerick-walking-tours; per person €10) Highly popular and entertaining guided walks around town with knowledgeable Declan, who moonlights at the Hunt Museum. Tours start and finish outside Brown Thomas on Patrick St,

Limerick

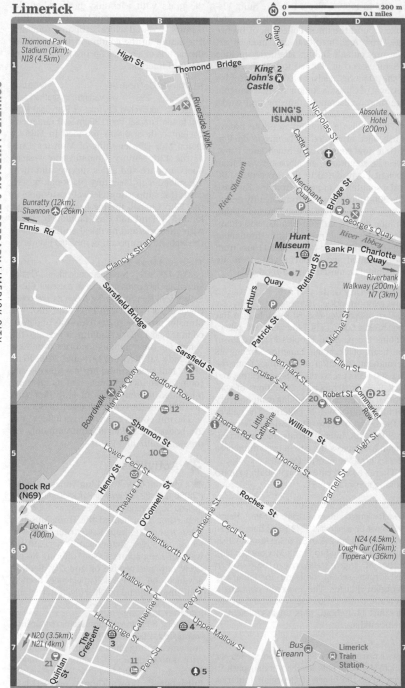

0   200 m
0   0.1 miles

Thomond Park
Stadium (1km);
N18 (4.5km)

High St

Thomond Bridge

Church St

King John's Castle 2

KING'S ISLAND

Nicholas St

Absolute Hotel
(200m)

Castle Ln

14

River Shannon

6

Merchants Quay

Bridge St

19 13

George's Quay

River Abbey

Riverside Walk

Bunratty (12km);
Shannon (26km)

Ennis Rd

Clancy's Strand

Hunt Museum
1
7

Bank Pl

Rutland St

22

Charlotte Quay

Riverbank
Walkway (200m);
N7 (3km)

Arthurs Quay

Sarsfield Bridge

Patrick St

Michael St

Ellen St

Sarsfield St

15

Denmark St

Cruise's St

9

Boardwalk

17

Harvey's Quay

Bedford Row

12

8

Thomas Rd

Little Catherine St

William St

20

Robert St

Cormarket Row

23

18

Shannon St

16

10

High St

Lower Cecil St

Henry St

Theatre Ln

O'Connell St

Thomas St

Parnell St

**Dock Rd
(N69)**

Dolan's
(400m)

Roches St

Glentworth St

Catherine St

Cecil St

N24 (4.5km);
Lough Gur (16km);
Tipperary (36km)

Mallow St

Catherine St

Pery St

Upper Mallow St

Hartstonge St

The Crescent

3

4

Bus
Éireann

Limerick Train Station

N20 (3.5km);
N21 (4km)

21

Quinlan St

11

Pery Sq

5

Limerick

near the intersection with Sarsfield St. Book by phone or email.

Angela's Ashes Walking Tour WALKING
(☏083 300 0111; www.limerick.ie; per person €10) Noel Curtin runs entertaining and informative walking tours of the city covering locations featured in *Angela's Ashes,* departing from the Frank McCourt Museum (p325) at 2.30pm. Book a tour at the tourist office (p330).

Riverbank Walkway WALKING
Opened in 2016, this 3km all-abilities walkway links the city centre to the University of Limerick campus, following a picturesque route along a former canal and later the south bank of the River Shannon. It begins from Lock Quay, just east of Abbey Bridge.

🛏 Sleeping

The city has a decent range of quality, midrange accommodation – aim to stay near the city centre for convenience and the nightlife.

Alexandra Tce on O'Connell Ave (which runs south from O'Connell St) has several midrange B&Bs. Ennis Rd, leading northwest towards Shannon, also has a selection, although most are at least 1km from the centre.

⭐ **No 1 Pery Square** HOTEL €€
(☏061-402 402; www.oneperysquare.com; 1 Pery Sq; club/period r from €145/195; P🐾) Treat yourself to a night in Georgian Limerick at this elegant hotel right on the corner of Pery Sq. Choose between very well-presented club rooms (each named after an Irish poet) in the modern extension and one of the four

period rooms in the classic Georgian townhouse, each a feast of huge sash windows, high ceilings and capacious bathrooms.

George Boutique Hotel HOTEL €€
(☏061-460 400; www.georgelimerick.com; Shannon St; s/d/tr/f from €129/139/164/179; P🐾) 'Boutique' might be overstating things a bit, but the rooms at this brisk, buzzing and centrally located hotel – with a decor of blond wood, caramels and browns, and the occasional splash of designer colour – are stylish and comfortable. It's frequently booked solid, so reserve well in advance.

Savoy HOTEL €€
(☏061-448 700; www.savoylimerick.com; Henry St; r from €175; P@🐾) This five-star hotel is beginning to show its age and feels more like four-star, but it's smart enough, with comfy king-size beds and a turn-down service, a spa that specialises in Thai massages, a small swimming pool and a couple of topnotch in-house restaurants.

Absolute Hotel HOTEL €€
(☏061-463 600; www.absolutehotel.com; Sir Harry's Mall; d from €120; P@🐾) Exposed brick walls, polished limestone bathrooms and contemporary art give this gleaming hotel overlooking the River Abbey a smart, modern edge. There's a light-filled atrium in the lobby and a cocooning in-house spa, plus a bar and grill. Check in early: secure parking is free but limited.

Boutique HOTEL €€
(☏061-315 320; www.theboutique.ie; Denmark St; s/d from €75/85; @🐾) Rotating works of art

FRANK MCCOURT

Since the 1990s, no name has been so closely intertwined with Limerick as Frank McCourt (1930–2009). His poignant autobiographical novel *Angela's Ashes* was a surprise publishing sensation in 1996, bringing him fame and honours (including the Pulitzer Prize).

Although he was born in New York City, McCourt's immigrant family returned to Limerick four years later, unable to survive in America. His childhood was filled with the kinds of deprivations that were all too common at the time: his father was a drunk who later vanished, three of his six siblings died in childhood, and at age 13 he dropped out of school to earn money to help his family survive.

At age 19, McCourt returned to New York and later worked for three decades as a high-school teacher. Among the subjects he taught was writing. From the 1970s he dabbled in writing and theatre with his brother Malachy. He started *Angela's Ashes* only after retiring from teaching in 1987. Its early success was thanks to a bevy of enthusiastic critics, but in Limerick the reaction was mixed, with many decrying the negative portrait it painted of the city.

Today McCourt's legacy in Limerick is celebrated. Limerick city's tourist office (p330) has information about city sights related to the book, you can join Angela's Ashes walking tours (p327), visit the Frank McCourt Museum (p325) and drink in South's (p329), one of the watering holes mentioned in the book.

by Limerick-based Claire De Lacy, a fish tank in the lobby and a glassed-in breakfast room on the 1st-floor balcony set this groovy hotel apart from the pack. Its central location in the heart of the city's nightlife district means it can get noisy on weekends – be aware that it caters to stag and hen parties!

X Eating

Limerick has many excellent eateries focusing on fresh Irish produce, an excellent weekly food market (p329), and a small street-food scene with a Wednesday **street-food market** (Harvey's Quay Boardwalk; mains €4-7; ⊘11am-4pm Wed May-Sep) on the boardwalk in summer.

★ Hook & Ladder   CAFE €€

(☑061-413 778; www.hookandladder.ie; 7 Sarsfield St; mains €11-15; ⊘8am-5pm Mon-Wed, to 6pm Thu-Sat, 9am-5pm Sun) A haven of understated style and a champion of local produce, this cafe set in a converted bank building epitomises Limerick's foodie scene. Exquisite sandwiches include Doonbeg crab with lemon mayo on honey and pumpkin-seed bread, while hot lunch dishes range from sausage and mash to falafel and hummus wrap. There are associated cookery schools in Limerick and Waterford.

★ Azur   IRISH, EUROPEAN €€

(☑061-314 994; www.azurrestaurant.ie; 8 George's Quay; mains €13-27; ⊘5-9pm Tue-Thu, to 9.30pm Fri & Sat, 11am-8pm Sun; 🕏🕭) Georgian architecture meets modern design at this elegant

venue – one of Limerick's best dining experiences. Service is professional but relaxed, the wine list is exemplary, and the menu lends a continental twist to the finest Irish produce, such as roast cod with wild garlic gnocchi and pea velouté, or chicken fillet with chorizo and chickpea cassoulet. Also does Sunday brunch.

La Cucina Centro   ITALIAN €€

(☑061-517 400; www.lacucina.ie; Henry St; mains €10-15; ⊘10am-9pm Mon-Wed, to 10pm Thu & Fri, from noon Sat, to 8pm Sun; 🕏) If you have a hankering for Italian comfort food, this modern diner is the place to head – hearty helpings of authentic pizza and pasta dishes sit alongside quality burgers, chicken salads and fish and chips.

Curragower Bar   GASTROPUB €€

(☑061-321 788; www.curragower.com; Clancy's Strand; mains €10-25; ⊘food served noon-8pm Mon-Tue, to 9pm Wed-Sun; 🕏) Ask a local for a lunch recommendation and they'll likely send you over the river to this appealing pub, which sports a superb outdoor terrace with views across the river to King John's Castle, and a menu that leans heavily towards Irish seafood, from rich and creamy chowder to baked sole with potted prawn, parsley root and pomegranate.

🍸 Drinking & Nightlife

Pubs such as Flannery's are famous for their range of Irish whiskeys, but craft beers are making an impact. Ales from Limerick's own Treaty City Brewery (www.treatycity brewing.com) can be found at several bars, including Flannery's and Nancy Blake's.

★ Nancy Blake's
PUB

(☑061-416 443; www.facebook.com/nancyblakes bar; 19 Upper Denmark St; ⊙11am-midnight Mon & Tue, to 2am Wed-Sun) There's sawdust on the floor and peat on the fire in the cosy front bar of this wonderful old pub, but be sure to head out the back to enjoy a vast covered drinking zone that often features live music or televised sports.

Flannery's Bar
PUB

(☑061-436 677; www.flannerysbar.ie; 17 Upper Denmark St; ⊙10am-11pm Sun-Wed, to 2am Thu-Sat) Housed in a former soap factory, this large and lively pub is a magnet for connoisseurs of Irish whiskey – there are more than 100 varieties on offer, and you can book a tasting session for €20 per person. Don't miss the roof terrace, a real suntrap on a summer afternoon.

Locke Bar
PUB

(☑061-413 733; www.lockebar.com; 3 George's Quay; ⊙9am-11.30pm Mon-Thu, to 12.30am Fri & Sat, 10am-11pm Sun; 🐧🍴) With its attractive riverside setting, a maze of stone-walled and wood-panelled rooms, outdoor tables overlooking the water, and a menu that runs from breakfast to dinner, the Locke is rightly one of Limerick's most popular pubs. Hosts the Big Limerick Seisiún (session) nightly, with traditional Irish music and dancing from 5pm to 7pm and 9pm to 11pm.

South's
PUB

(WJ South; ☑061-314 669; www.facebook.com/southspublimerick; 4 Quinlan St; ⊙8.30am-11.30pm Mon-Thu, to 12.30am Fri, from 9.30am Sat, 12.30-11pm Sun) Frank McCourt's father knocked 'em back in South's (Frank himself had his first pint here) and the *Angela's Ashes* connection is worked for all it's worth – even the toilets are named Frank and Angela. Check out the fabulous (though reproduction) neoclassical interior.

☆ Entertainment

Lime Tree Theatre
THEATRE

(☑061-953 400; www.limetreetheatre.ie; Mary Immaculate College, Courtbrack Ave; ⊙box office 2-5.30pm Mon-Fri) This 510-seat state-of-the-art theatre is set on a college campus on the southern edge of the city. It stages drama, music and comedy performances by local and international artists, and in 2017 premiered a musical version of *Angela's Ashes* (now touring Ireland and the UK).

University Concert Hall
CONCERT VENUE

(UCH; ☑061-331 549; www.uch.ie; University of Limerick; ⊙box office 10am-5pm Mon-Fri, longer hours on performance dates) Permanent home of the Irish Chamber Orchestra, with regular concerts from visiting acts, plus opera, drama, comedy and dance. The campus is 4.5km east of the city.

Dolan's
LIVE MUSIC

(☑061-314 483; www.dolanspub.com; 3 Dock Rd; tickets €10-55; ⊙noon-2am Mon-Fri, from 10am Sat & Sun) Limerick's best spot for live music promises authentic trad sessions and an unbeatable gig list – including occasional big-name artists such as Paul Young and Lloyd Cole – as well as cutting-edge stand-up comedians in two adjoining venues.

🛍 Shopping

Milk Market
MARKET

(www.milkmarketlimerick.ie; Cornmarket Row; ⊙10am-3pm Fri, from 8am Sat, from 11am Sun) 🍴 Pick from organic produce and artisan foods including local fruits and vegetables, preserves, baked goods and farmhouse cheeses, browse the flower and craft stalls, or grab a bite at one of the hot-food tables at this busy market held in Limerick's old market buildings. There's usually traditional live music as well.

TRACING YOUR ANCESTORS

Genealogical centres in Counties Limerick and Tipperary can help trace your ancestors; contact the centres in advance to arrange a consultation.

Limerick Genealogy (☑061-496 542; www.limerickgenealogy.com; Dooradoyle Rd, Lissanalta House, Dooradoyle) Professional genealogical research service.

Tipperary Family History Research (☑062-80555; www.tfhr.org; Mitchell St, Excel Heritage Centre, Tipperary town) Family research in Tipperary.

Tipperary South Genealogy Centre (☑062-61122; www.tipperarysouth.rootsireland.ie; Brú Ború Heritage Centre, Cashel) Comprehensive family-history research service.

WORTH A TRIP

LIMERICK CITY TO TARBERT VIA THE SCENIC N69

The narrow, peaceful N69 road follows the Shannon Estuary along the Wild Atlantic Way west from Limerick for 58km to Tarbert in northern County Kerry. There are some fantastic views of the broadening estuary and seemingly endless rolling green hills laced with stone walls.

At the small village of Clarina, west of Mungret on the N69, hang a right to head north for around 1.5km to a crossroads, then turn left and you'll see the haunting ruin of Carrigogunnell Castle (⊙dawn-dusk) FREE high up on a ridge. You'll soon see a road to your right that heads past the castle, beyond the hedgerow and the fields. The 15th-century castle was blown up with gunpowder in 1691 and the fabulous wreck famously adorns the back cover of the U2 album *The Unforgettable Fire*.

Further along off the N69 is the village of Askeaton, with evocative ruins including the mid-1300s Desmond Castle (⊙weekends by appointment May-Oct), perched dramatically on an island in the River Deel next to the Hellfire Gentlemen's club, once home to an 18th-century brothel and drinking club. Restoration of the ruins started in 2007 and is ongoing, with no public access to the site. On the edge of town is the atmospheric 1389-built Franciscan friary (⊙dawn-dusk) FREE, with a beautifully preserved cloister. The Askeaton Tourist Office (☑086 085 0174; askeatontouristoffice@gmail.com; The Square; ⊙limited hours, call to check) has details of the town's historic sites that you can freely wander (depending on restoration works) and can arrange eye-opening free guided tours lasting about one hour, led by the very knowledgeable Anthony Sheehy.

At Foynes is the fascinating Foynes Flying Boat Museum (☑069-65416; www. flyingboatmuseum.com; adult/child €12/6; ⊙9.30am-6pm Jun-Aug, to 5pm mid-Mar-Jun & Sep–mid-Nov; ℗). From 1939 to 1945 this was the landing place for the flying boats that linked North America with the British Isles. Big Pan Am clippers – there's a replica here – would set down in the estuary and refuel.

Celtic Bookshop   BOOKS
(☑061-401 155; http://celticbookshop-limerick.ie; 2 Rutland St; ⊙noon-5pm Mon-Sat) Crammed with specialist titles on local and Irish topics.

❶ Information

Limerick Tourist Office (☑061-317 522; www. limerick.ie; 20 O'Connell St; ⊙9am-5pm Mon-Sat, hours vary) Helpful staff provide advice and information on Limerick and the rest of Ireland.

Main Post Office (Lower Cecil St; ⊙9am-5.30pm Mon & Wed-Sat, from 9.30am Tue)

University Hospital Limerick (☑061-301 111; www.hse.ie; Dooradoyle) Has a 24-hour accident and emergency department; south of the city centre.

❶ Getting There & Away

AIR

Shannon Airport (p708) in County Clare handles domestic and international flights.

The airport is 26km northwest of Limerick, about 30 minutes by car. Regular Bus Éireann (€8.50, 50 minutes, twice hourly) buses connect Limerick's bus and train station with Shannon Airport. A taxi from the city centre to the airport costs around €35 to €45.

BUS

Bus Éireann (☑061-313 333; www.buseireann. ie) services operate from the bus and train stations near the city centre. Destinations include Galway, Killarney, Rosslare, Ennis, Shannon, Derry and most other centres. **Citylink** (☑091-564 164; www.citylink.ie) buses stop on Henry St between Cecil and Glentworth Sts; **JJ Kavanagh & Sons** (☑0818 333 222; www. jjkavanagh.ie) buses stop at Arthurs Quay.

Regular services run from Limerick to the following:

Cork Bus Éireann (€16, 1¾ hours, hourly); Citylink (€16, 1½ hours, five daily).

Dublin JJ Kavanagh & Sons (€15, 3¼ hours, four daily).

Dublin Airport JJ Kavanagh & Sons (€20, 3½ hours, four daily); Eireagle (www.eireagle.com) has 10 luxury wi-fi-equipped coaches daily (€25, 2½ hours), leaving from Arthurs Quay.

Galway Citylink (€16, 1½ hours, five daily).

Tralee Bus Éireann (€15, two hours, every two hours).

TRAIN

Irish Rail (www.irishrail.ie) has regular services from Limerick Railway Station, including to Dublin Heuston (€48, 2½ hours, hourly), Ennis (€11.35, 40 minutes, nine daily) and Galway

(€23, two hours, four daily). Other routes, including Cork, Tralee, Tipperary, Cahir and Waterford, involve changing at Limerick Junction, 20km southeast of Limerick.

ℹ Getting Around

Limerick city is compact enough to get around on foot or by bike. To walk across town from St Mary's Cathedral to the train station takes about 15 minutes.

Taxis can be found at Arthurs Quay, at the bus and train stations, and in Thomas St, or try **Castletroy Cabs** (☑ 061-332 266; www.castletroycabs.com).

Limerick's Coca-Cola Zero **bike-share scheme** (www.bikeshare.ie/limerick.html), with 23 stations around town is, for visitors, €3 (€150 deposit) for three days. The first 30 minutes of each hire is free.

Adare & Around

POP 1129

Overtouted as 'Ireland's prettiest village', Adare's fame centres on its string of thatched cottages built by 19th-century English landlord, the Earl of Dunraven, for workers constructing Adare Manor. Today the pretty cottages house craft shops and fine restaurants, while prestigious golf courses nearby cater to golf enthusiasts. The Irish name for Adare is Áth Dara – the Ford of the Oak.

The village is 16km southwest of Limerick. Tourists arrive here by the busload, clogging the roads (the busy N21 is the village's main street). As it's thronged with visitors at weekends, book accommodation and restaurants in advance.

◉ Sights & Activities

Before the Tudor Dissolution of the monasteries (1536–39), Adare had three flourishing religious houses, the ruins of which can still be seen, but the main attraction here is the row of thatched cottages lining the main street.

Adare Castle   CASTLE
(Desmond Castle; ☑ tour bookings 061-396 666; www.heritageireland.ie; tours adult/child €10/8; � tours hourly 11am-5pm Jul-Sep) Dating from around 1200, this picturesque Norman ruin changed hands several times before being entirely wrecked by Cromwell's troops in 1657, by which time its strategic importance had slipped away. Highlights include the **great hall** with its early-13th-century windows, and the huge kitchen and bakery.

Tours must be booked through the Adare Heritage Centre. When tours aren't on, you can view the castle from the busy main road, or more peacefully from the riverside footpath or the Augustinian Priory grounds.

Franciscan Friary   RUINS
(Adare Golf Club; � 9am-5pm) The ruins of this friary, founded by the Earl of Kildare in 1464, stand serenely in the middle of Adare Golf Club beside the River Maigue. Public access is assured, but let them know at the clubhouse that you intend to visit. A track leads away from the clubhouse car park for about 400m – watch out for flying golf balls. There's a handsome tower and a fine sedilia (row of seats for priests) in the southern wall of the chancel.

Adare Heritage Centre   MUSEUM
(☑ 061-396 666; www.adareheritagecentre.ie; Main St; � 9am-6pm) FREE In the middle of Adare, exhibits here explain the history and medieval context of the village's buildings in entertaining fashion. Quality Irish crafts are on sale and there's also a busy cafe.

Augustinian Priory   ABBEY
(� 9am-5pm Mon-Sat) North of Adare village, on the N21 and close to the bridge over the River Maigue, is the Church of Ireland parish church, once the Augustinian priory, founded in 1316 and also known as the Black Abbey. The interior of the church is agreeable enough, but the real joy is the atmospheric little cloister.

A pleasant, signposted riverside path, with wayside seats, starts from just north of the priory gates. Look for a narrow access gap and head off alongside the river. After about 250m, turn left along the road to return to the centre of Adare.

Adare Golf Club   GOLF
(☑ 061-605 200; www.adaremanor.com/golf; green fees €300-375) This prestigious golf club enjoys a spectacular setting within the vast and serene grounds of Adare Manor.

🛌 Sleeping

Adare Village Inn   INN €
(☑ 087 251 7102; www.adarevillageinn.com; Upper Main St; s/d weekday €45/60, weekend €50/70; P🐾) This cordial place has five excellent-value rooms which are cosy and comfortable and come with power showers. Run by Seán Collins, the inn is a few doors down from his namesake bar (p333), where you check

WORTH A TRIP

BALLINGARRY

Attractive village Ballingarry is home to one of County Limerick's hidden dining gems, **Mustard Seed at Echo Lodge** (☑ 069-68508; www.mustardseed.ie; Ballingarry; 4-course dinner €64; ⊘ 7-9.15pm mid-Feb–mid-Jan; P 🕏). Produce is picked fresh from this 19th-century former convent's orchards and kitchen gardens, and incorporated into seasonal dishes like wood pigeon with apple and parsnip puree and smoked pearl barley, or venison cooked with coffee and Szechuan pepper. Ballingarry is on the R519, 13km southwest of Adare.

To avoid having to move too far afterwards, book one of the lodge's elegant, country-style rooms, some with four-poster bed (double from €180).

in, round the corner from Main St towards Rathkeale Rd.

★ Dunraven Arms
INN €€

(☑ 061-605 900; www.dunravenhotel.com; Main St; r from €165; 🕏🛋) This jewel of an inn, built in 1792, exudes old-fashioned charm, with cottage-style gardens, hanging baskets, open fires and a comfortable lobby. Smart bedrooms are decorated with antiques, high-thread-count linens and – for the choosy – four-poster beds. Service is warm and helpful, and there's a great restaurant and bar.

Berkeley Lodge
B&B €€

(☑ 061-396 857; www.adare.org; Station Rd; s/d/f €70/90/135; P🕏) This detached house around 400m north of the village centre has six homely and antique-styled rooms – each in a different colour – with great breakfasts. It's just a three-minute walk to the heritage centre, pubs and restaurants.

Adare Manor
HOTEL €€€

(☑ 061-605 200; www.adaremanor.com; Main St; r from €700; P@🕏🛋) Built in the mid-19th century for the Earl of Dunraven, this magnificent manor house now houses a luxury hotel. After extensive renovations in 2017 it sports a new bedroom wing and a huge ballroom to complement an already elegant property dripping in antique furniture and class. The manor's superb Oakroom Restaurant and lavish high tea are also open to nonguests.

✕ Eating

Good Room Cafe
CAFE €

(☑ 061-396 218; www.thegoodroomadare.ie; Main St; mains €9-11; ⊘ 8.30am-5.30pm Mon-Sat, from 10am Sun; 🖟) This homely but busy place prepares inventive breakfasts, soups, salads, hot sandwiches, bruschetta, baked goods, homemade jams, kids' menus and huge cups of coffee in a thatched-cottage location. It's always busy, so arrive early before its famous scones sell out.

★ Restaurant 1826 Adare
MODERN IRISH €€

(☑ 061-396 004; www.1826adare.ie; Main St; mains €20-27; ⊘ 6-9.30pm Wed-Sat, 3-8pm Sun; 🖟) 🍽 One of Ireland's most highly regarded chefs, Wade Murphy continues to wow diners at this art-lined 1826-built thatched cottage. His passion for local seasonal produce is an essential ingredient in dishes such as pan-seared halibut with Connemara clams and pickled samphire. A three-course early-bird menu (€36) is served daily until 7pm.

Wild Geese
IRISH €€

(☑ 061-396 451; www.thewild-geese.com; Main St; mains lunch €7-16, dinner €22-32; ⊘ 11am-3pm & 6-9.30pm Tue-Sat, 12.30-3pm Sun; 🍽) The ever-changing menu at this inviting cottage restaurant celebrates the best of southwest Ireland's bounty, from lunch of crab cakes followed by cod fillet with creamed leeks, to dinner dishes of succulent scallops and sumptuous racks of lamb. The service is genial, preparations are imaginative and the bread basket is divine.

Maigue Restaurant
IRISH €€

(☑ 061-605 900; www.dunravenhotel.com; Main St; mains restaurant €16-28, bar €14-17; ⊘ 7-9.30pm daily, 12.30-2.30pm Sun) The restaurant in the charming Dunraven Arms hotel has an ambitious menu (roast chicken with caramelised fennel and celeriac puree, hake with lemon and chervil velouté), but the food in its sedate, wood-panelled Hunter's Bar (beef burger, fish and chips) offers a worthy and more affordable alternative. Hours can vary; reservations are advised.

Blue Door
IRISH €€

(☑ 061-396 481; www.bluedooradare.com; Main St; mains lunch €10-22, dinner €21-27; ⊘ noon-5pm & 5.30-10pm; 🖟) Hearty salads, open sandwiches and lasagne appear on the lunch menu at this upmarket thatched cottage restaurant, while dinner ups the ante with dishes such as confit of duck with black pudding and Guinness sauce, and pan-seared scallops with saffron cream.

Oakroom Restaurant
IRISH €€€

(☎ 061-605 200; www.adaremanor.com/dining; Adare Manor; afternoon tea €55, 3-course dinner €90; ⊙ afternoon tea 1.30-3.30pm, dinner 6-9.30pm) Dine like a lord at the atmospheric restaurant of Adare Manor, where dinner service is lit only by candles. The superb Irish menu is backed by a fabulous setting with views overlooking the grounds and the River Maigue. Alternatively, try the afternoon tea served on tiered plates in the stately drawing room. Dress code: smart casual.

🍸 Drinking & Nightlife

Seán Collins
PUB

(www.seancollinsbaradare.com; Upper Main St; ⊙ 10am-11.30pm Mon-Thu & Sun, 10.30am-1.30am Fri & Sat) A friendly, family-run pub with good craic, good food (served 12.30pm to 9.30pm), and live music on Monday and Friday at 8.30pm.

Bill Chawke's Lounge Bar
PUB

(☎ 061-396 160; www.billchawke.com; Main St; ⊙ 9am-11.30pm Mon-Thu, to 12.30am Fri & Sat, to 11pm Sun) Decked out in GAA (hurling and Gaelic football) memorabilia, this place has a good beer garden and hosts regular trad-music sessions and singalongs.

ⓘ Information

The Adare Village website (www.adarevillage.com) is a handy source of information.

Tourist Office (☎ 061-396 255; www.adare heritagecentre.ie/tourist-point; Adare Heritage Centre, Main St; ⊙ 9am-6pm)

ⓘ Getting There & Away

Hourly Bus Éireann (p330) services link Limerick with Adare (€5, 25 minutes). Many continue on to Tralee (€9, two hours, every two hours). Others serve Killarney (€9, two hours, every two hours).

Lough Gur

The area surrounding this picturesque, horseshoe-shaped lake is rich in Neolithic, Bronze Age and medieval archaeological sites. Short walks along the lake's edge lead to burial mounds, standing stones, ancient enclosures and other points of interest (admission free) and the whole area is ideal for walking and picnics.

Lough Gur Heritage Centre
MUSEUM

(☎ 087 285 2022; www.loughgur.com; adult/child €5/3; ⊙ 10am-8pm Mon-Fri, from noon Sat & Sun

Feb-Oct, to 4pm Nov-Jan; 🅿) This thatched replica of a Neolithic hut contains a helpful information desk and good exhibits on prehistoric monuments and settlements in the surrounding area, plus a small museum displaying Neolithic artefacts and a replica of the bronze Lough Gur shield dating from around 1000 BC (the original is in the National Museum in Dublin). It's a good idea to come here first to get some context before exploring the surrounding sites.

Grange Stone Circle
ARCHAEOLOGICAL SITE

(⊙ dawn-dusk) FREE This stone circle, known as the Lios, is a superb 4000-year-old circular enclosure made up of 113 embanked upright stones, the largest prehistoric circle of its kind in Ireland. It's a 3km walk or drive southwest of the heritage centre; there's roadside parking and access to the site is free (there's a donation box).

ⓘ Getting There & Away

There is no public transport to Lough Gur, which is 21km south of Limerick. Driving from Limerick, take the R512 road south towards Kilmallock 16km to find the Grange stone circle.

Around 1km further south along the R512, at Holycross garage and post office, a left turn takes you another 2km to the main car park beside Lough Gur itself, from where it's a short walk to the Lough Gur Heritage Centre.

Kilmallock & Around

POP 1668

Kilmallock was Ireland's third-largest town during the Middle Ages (after Dublin and Kilkenny), and is today the country's best-preserved medieval town. It developed around a 13th-century abbey and from the 14th to the 17th centuries was the seat of the Earls of Desmond. The village lies beside the River Lubach, 26km south of Limerick and a world away from the city's urban racket.

Coming into Kilmallock from Limerick, the first thing you'll see (to your left) is a medieval stone mansion – one of 30 or so that housed the town's prosperous merchants and landowners. Further on, the main street bends around the four-storey King's Castle, a 15th-century tower house with a ground-floor archway through which the pavement now runs.

Kilmallock Museum
MUSEUM

(☎ 063-91300; Sheares St; ⊙ 10am-1pm & 2-4pm Mon-Thu, to 5pm Fri & Sat, noon-5pm Sun) FREE

A lane leads down from the main street (opposite the King's Castle) to this tiny museum, which houses a random collection of historical artefacts and a model of the town in 1597. The museum is the base for the history trail around town, and provides tourist information.

Kilmallock Abbey   HISTORIC SITE

FREE A footbridge leads across the river from Kilmallock Museum to the atmospheric ruins of this 13th-century Dominican friary. Much of the arcaded cloister remains standing, as does the church tower, and in the choir stands the arched wall-tomb of the White Knight, Edmund John Fitzgibbon (1552–1608).

★ Kilmallock Medieval Tours   HISTORY

(☑ 087 395 2895; www.facebook.com/kilmallock medievaltours; adult/child €10/free; ⊙ 9am-5pm Sat & Sun) Historian Trevor McCarthy, dressed in full medieval garb, provides entertaining guided walking tours of Kilmallock's medieval buildings. Tours must be booked in advance.

Ballyhoura Trail Centre   MOUNTAIN BIKING

(www.coillte.ie/site/ballyhoura; parking €5, coins only) **FREE** The most extensive, purpose-built mountain-bike centre in the Republic, Ballyhoura has cross-country trails ranging from 6km to a thigh-burning 51km in length. There are showers, toilets, bike hire and a cafe at the car park.

COUNTY TIPPERARY

Landlocked Tipperary boasts the sort of fertile soil that farmers dream of – the Golden Vale, between Tipperary town and Cashel, with the best dairy farming in the country. The central area of the county is low-lying, but rolling hills spill over from adjoining counties and an upper-crust gloss still clings to equestrian traditions here, with fox hunts in full legal cry during the winter season.

Walking and cycling opportunities abound, especially in the Glen of Aherlow, south of Tipperary town. But the real crowd-pleasers are the iconic Rock of Cashel (p336) and Cahir Castle (p340). In between, you'll find bucolic charm along pretty much any country road you choose.

Tipperary Town

POP 4979

Tipperary (Tiobrad Árann) has a famous name, largely due to the WWI marching song. And indeed, you may find it a long way to Tipperary as the N24 and a web of regional roads converge on the centre (there's no bypass) and traffic often moves at the same speed as the armies at the Somme.

'Tipp town' itself is a bit sad and run-down, and has no real sights; there's no need to detour here, though you may pass through on your way to the Glen of Aherlow.

Brazil's   IRISH €€

(☑ 062-80503; www.brazilsrestaurant.com; Brazils Lane, Main St; mains €7-21; ⊙ 9am-5.30pm Mon-Sat, noon-5pm Sun; 🖥🚹) Whether you squeeze into the ground-floor cafe for breakfast or coffee and cake, or head upstairs to the more formal restaurant for lunch (good steak sandwiches, superb fish and chips) or dinner (baked hake fillet with a herb crust, maple-glazed chicken breast, Thai green curry), Brazil's is the best – and most popular – eatery in town.

Tipperary Racecourse   HORSE RACING

(☑ 062-51357; www.tipperaryraces.ie; Limerick Rd; adult/child €10/free; ⊙ Apr-Oct) Tipperary Racecourse is one of Ireland's leading tracks. It's 3km northwest of Tipperary town and has regular meetings during the year; see the local press for details. The course is within walking distance of Limerick Junction station. On race days there are minibus pickups from Tipperary town; phone for details.

Danny Ryan Music   MUSIC

(☑ 062-51128; www.dannyryanmusic.ie; 20 Bank Pl; ⊙ 10am-1pm & 2-6pm Mon, Tue & Thu-Sat, to 1pm Wed) This colourfully painted shop has a superb selection of traditional musical instruments.

ⓘ Getting There & Away

Most buses stop on Abbey St beside the river. Bus Éireann (www.buseireann.ie) runs up to eight buses daily on the Limerick (€11, 35 minutes) to Waterford route via Cahir and Clonmel.

To reach the train station, head south along Bridge St. Tipperary is on the Waterford–Limerick Junction line. There are two daily services to Cahir (€8.20, 25 minutes), Clonmel, Waterford (€19.70, 1½ hours) and Rosslare Harbour. Connect for Cork, Kerry and Dublin at **Limerick Junction** (☑ 062-51406), barely 3km from Tipperary station along the Limerick road.

Glen of Aherlow & Galtee Mountains

The broad, fertile valley of the Glen of Aherlow, slung between the wooded Slievenamuck Hills and the shapely Galtee Mountains, is the most scenic part of County Tipperary and one of Ireland's hidden delights.

A beautiful and leisurely 25km scenic drive through the Glen is signposted from Tipperary town. At the eastern end of the Glen, between Tipperary and Cahir, the village of Bansha (An Bháinseach) marks the start of a 20km trip west to Galbally, an easy bike ride or scenic drive along the R663 that takes in the best of the glen's landscapes.

The R663 from Bansha and the R664 south from Tipperary converge at Newtown at the Coach Road Inn, a fine old pub that's popular with walkers. Hidden around the back of the pub, the enthusiastically staffed Glen of Aherlow tourist office (062-56331; www.aherlow.com; Coach Rd, Newtown; 9am-5pm Mon-Fri, 10am-4pm Sat May-Sep) is an excellent source of information on the area, including hiking trails.

Activities

Renowned for its walking, the terrain around the glen ranges from the lush banks of the River Aherlow to spruce forests in the Slievenamuck Hills and the windswept, rocky grasslands of the high Galtees. For spectacular views, head 1.6km north of Newtown on the R664 to a lookout adjacent to the statue of Christ the King (a local landmark). Waymarked woodland trails fan out from here.

Lake Muskry
WALKING
(www.aherlow.com/walking; Rossadrehid) Lake Muskry is a small but scenic lough in a glacier-carved hollow high in the Galtees at around 490m, and is the destination for one of Aherlow's most popular hikes. From the tiny hamlet of Rossadrehid, on the southern edge of the glen, a narrow road leads uphill to a parking area with an information board. The walk begins here.

It follows a rough but easily followed path with green waymarks (11km round-trip; allow three to four hours).

Sleeping & Eating

Ballinacourty House Camping Park & B&B CAMPGROUND, B&B €
(087 327 8573; www.camping.ie; Ballinacourty; campsites/s/d €10/60/80; Apr-Sep; P) Set

against the spectacular backdrop of the Galtee Hills, this attractive site is 10km west from Bansha. It has excellent facilities, as well as a fine garden, a much-loved restaurant serving classic Irish fare, a wine bar and a tennis court. An old stone house has been renovated and offers B&B accommodation.

Homeleigh Farmhouse B&B €
(062-56228; www.homeleighfarmhouse.com; Newtown; s/d €60/90; P) Just west of Newtown and the Coach Road Inn on the R663, this working farm rents out simple rooms with views onto fields and garden. Furnishings are traditional and you can arrange for dinner (€30 per person).

Aherlow House Hotel HOTEL €€
(062-56153; www.aherlowhouse.ie; Newtown; d/lodge from €75/149; P) Up a pine-forested lane from the R663, a 1928 hunting lodge has been turned into an atmospheric woodland retreat. There are 29 rooms with king size beds and 15 contemporary countrified self-catering lodges (minimum two-night stay). There's a flowing bar, a fine restaurant and glorious mountain views from the terrace.

Treetop Restaurant & Bar IRISH €€
(062-56153; www.aherlowhouse.ie; Aherlow House Hotel, Newtown; mains €15-25, 3-course dinner €39; 6.30-9pm Fri & Sat, 12.30-5pm Sun;) The formal restaurant at Aherlow House Hotel serves fine Irish and European cuisine in a congenial and intimate dining environment (reservations recommended). Bar meals are available from 12.30pm to 9.30pm daily, and there's a summer terrace with superb views of the Galtee Mountains.

Getting There & Away

The Local Link Tipperary (076 106 6140; www.locallinktipperary.ie) bus from Cahir to Tipperary town and Cashel stops in Bansha (€3, 15 minutes, two daily Monday to Friday). From here it's a long walk or bike ride into the hills – 12km to Ballinacourty camping ground (p335). A car will enable you to explore far and wide between walks.

Cashel
POP 4422
It's little wonder that Cashel (Caiseal Mumhan) is such a fabulous draw (the Queen included it on her historic visit in 2011). The iconic religious buildings that crown the blustery summit of the Rock of Cashel (p336) seem to emerge from the craggy landscape itself and the neighbouring market town of

Cashel rewards rambles around its charming streets.

◉ Sights

Download a free audio-guide tour of the town from the tourist office website (www.cashel.ie).

★ Rock of Cashel   HISTORIC SITE
(☑ 062-61437; www.heritageireland.ie; adult/child €8/4, incl Cormac's Chapel €11/7; ⊙9am-7pm early Jun–mid-Sep, to 5.30pm mid-Mar–early Jun & mid-Sep–mid-Oct, to 4.30pm mid-Oct–mid-Mar; ℗) The Rock of Cashel is one of Ireland's most spectacular historic sites: a prominent green hill, banded with limestone outcrops, rising from a grassy plain and bristling with ancient fortifications. Sturdy walls circle an enclosure containing a round tower, a 13th-century Gothic cathedral and the finest 12th-century Romanesque chapel in Ireland, home to some of the land's oldest frescoes.

It's a five-minute stroll from the town centre up to the Rock, from where fantastic views range over the Tipperary countryside.

The word 'cashel' is an Anglicised version of the Irish word *caiseal,* meaning 'fortress' (related to the English 'castle', from the Latin *castellum*). In the 4th century the Rock of Cashel was chosen as a base by the Eóghanachta clan from Wales, who went on to conquer much of Munster and become kings of the region. For some 400 years it rivalled Tara as a centre of power in Ireland. The clan was associated with St Patrick, hence the Rock's alternative name of St Patrick's Rock. In the 10th century the Eóghanachta lost possession of the rock to the O'Brien (Dál gCais) tribe under Brian Ború's leadership. In 1101 King Muircheartach O'Brien presented the Rock to the Church to curry favour with the powerful bishops and to end secular rivalry over possession of the Rock with the Eóghanachta, by now known as the MacCarthys.

Numerous buildings must have occupied the cold and exposed Rock over the years, but it is the ecclesiastical relics that have survived even the depredations of the Cromwellian army in 1647. The vast medieval cathedral was used for worship until the mid-1700s. Among the graves are a 19th-century high cross and mausoleum for local landowners, the Scully family; the top of the Scully Cross was razed by lightning in 1976.

But the undoubted highlight of the Rock is the early-12th-century Cormac's Chapel, an exquisite gem of Romanesque architecture with beautifully carved doorways and

the precious remains of colourful wall paintings. Access is by 45-minute guided tour only (€3 extra, book at entrance).

Brú Ború   MUSEUM
(☑ 062-61122; www.bruboru.ie; The Kiln; adult/child €5/3; ⊙9am-5pm Mon-Fri, longer hours Jul–mid-Aug) This privately run cultural centre is next to the car park below the Rock of Cashel, and offers absorbing insights into Irish traditional music, dance and song. The centre's main attraction, the Sounds of History exhibition, relates the story of Ireland and its music through imaginative audio displays; various other musical events take place in summer.

Hore Abbey   RUINS
(⊙dawn-dusk) FREE The formidable ruin of 13th-century Hore Abbey (also known as Hoare Abbey or St Mary's) stands in flat farmland 1km west of the Rock of Cashel. Originally Benedictine and settled by monks from Glastonbury in England at the end of the 12th century, it later became a Cistercian house. Now an enjoyably gloomy, jackdaw-haunted ruin, the abbey was gifted to the order by a 13th-century archbishop who expelled the Benedictine monks after dreaming that they planned to murder him.

Cashel Folk Village   MUSEUM
(☑ 087 915 1316; www.cashelfolkvillage.ie; St Dominic St; adult/child €7/4; ⊙10.15am-7.30pm Mon-Sat, 11am-5.30pm Sun mid-Mar–mid-Oct, by appointment mid-Oct–mid-Mar) An engaging exhibition of old buildings, shopfronts and memorabilia from around the town. It's all a bit amateurish and slipshod, but in a charming, heart-warming way.

Cashel Heritage Centre   MUSEUM
(☑ 062-61333; www.cashel.ie; Main St; ⊙9.30am-5.30pm Mon-Sat mid-Mar–mid-Oct, Mon-Fri only rest of year) FREE Located in the town hall alongside the tourist office, the displays here include a scale model of Cashel in the 1640s with an audio commentary.

🛏 Sleeping

Cashel Holiday Hostel   HOSTEL €
(☑ 062-62330; www.anoige.ie; 6 John St; dm/s/d from €15/30/50; 🖥) In a vividly coloured three-storey Georgian terrace just off Main St, this central budget option has dorms in one end and private rooms in the other. Amenities include a kitchen, a laundry, a library, bike storage and a comfy and homely lounge.

★ **Cashel Lodge & Camping Park**   B&B, CAMPGROUND €€

(☑ 062-61003; www.cashel-lodge.com; Dundrum Rd; campsites per person €10, s/d from €45/85; P🖤) This converted 200-year-old coach house northwest of Cashel on the R505 (follow the signs for Dundrum) is a friendly and superb-value place with exposed stone-and-timber-beam interiors and terrific views of the Rock and Hore Abbey. As well as the B&B, there's a small campground.

Baileys Hotel   BOUTIQUE HOTEL €€

(☑ 062-61937; www.baileyshotelcashel.com; Main St; s/d from €90/130; P🖤) Clean, contemporary lines and dark wood contrasting with light walls give this restored, centrally located Georgian townhouse an elegant ambience. Rooms are smart, but neutrally styled. Rates include breakfast and lock-up parking, and there's a great in-house **restaurant and bar** (mains €10-20; ⊙ food served noon-9.30pm).

Copperfield House   B&B €€

(☑ 062-61075; www.copperfieldhouse.ie; Boherclogh St; s/d €60/120; P🖤) This spacious suburban villa is just a five-minute walk from the town centre, and has four individually decorated guest rooms (one with garden balcony), a TV lounge and a lovely bright breakfast room with a view of the garden. Delicious breakfasts include homebaked bread. Cash only.

✖ **Eating**

Apart from the Rock, Cashel is best-known in Ireland and beyond for award-winning Cashel Blue farmhouse cheese, Ireland's first-ever blue cheese, still handmade locally.

★ **Mikey Ryan's**   GASTROPUB €€

(☑ 062-62007; www.mikeyryans.ie; 76 Main St; mains lunch €9-16, dinner €17-30; ⊙ food served noon-3pm & 6-9.30pm; 🖤🖤) This long-established bar has been given a glitzy gastropub makeover, with a bright, sun-drenched dining room at the back, and a gorgeous garden complete with barbecue and horse-box bar. The delicious farmhouse-style food is sourced from local farmers and artisan producers, and Cashel Blue cheese makes several appearances on the menu – in pesto, on pizza and topping a burger.

Cafe Hans   CAFE €€

(☑ 062-63660; Dominic St; mains €15-26; ⊙ noon-5.30pm Tue-Sat; 🖤) Competition for the 32 seats is fierce at this gourmet cafe run by the same family as Chez Hans along the street.

There are fantastic salads, open sandwiches (including succulent prawns with tangy Marie Rose sauce) and filling fish, shellfish, lamb and vegetarian dishes, accompanied by a discerning wine selection and mouthwatering desserts. No credit cards. Enter via Moor Lane.

Arrive before or after the lunchtime rush or plan on waiting for a table.

Chez Hans   IRISH €€€

(☑ 062-61177; www.chezhans.net; Dominic St; mains €28-39, 2-/3-course Sun lunch €28/35; ⊙ 6-10pm Wed-Sat, 12.30-3.30pm Sun) Since 1968 this former church has been a place of worship for foodies from Ireland and beyond. Still as fresh and inventive as ever, the restaurant has a regularly changing menu and gives its blessing to all manner of Irish produce, including steamed Galway mussels, beetroot risotto with deep-fried goat's cheese and steamed halibut with fennel puree. No credit cards.

ⓘ **Information**

Tourist Office (☑ 062-61333; www.cashel.ie; Town Hall, Main St; ⊙ 9.30am-5.30pm Mon-Sat mid-Mar–mid-Oct, Mon-Fri only mid-Oct–mid-Mar) Helpful office with reams of info on the area.

ⓘ **Getting There & Away**

Bus Éireann (www.buseireann.ie) runs eight buses daily between Cashel and Cork (€16, 1¾ hours) via Cahir (€6, 20 minutes, six daily). The bus stop for Cork is at the northeast end of Main St. The Dublin stop (€16, 2½ hours, six daily) is opposite.

Not-for-profit service Local Link Tipperary (p335) runs buses twice daily Monday to Friday, linking Cashel with Cahir (€3, 20 minutes) and Tipperary town (€3, 35 minutes).

Parking in town is cheaper and less crowded than the car park below the Rock.

Around Cashel

Athassel Priory   RUINS

(Golden; ⊙ dawn-dusk) FREE Reached over a stile and across grassy (sometimes muddy) fields, the atmospheric ruins of Athassel Priory sit in the shallow and verdant River Suir Valley, 7km southwest of Cashel. The original buildings date from 1205, and Athassel was once one of the richest and most important monasteries in Ireland. What survives is substantial: the gatehouse and portcullis gateway, the cloister (ruined but recognisable) and large stretches of walled enclosure, as well as some medieval tomb effigies.

Rock of Cashel

A TOUR OF THE COMPLEX

For more than 1000 years the Rock of Cashel was a symbol of power and the seat of kings and clergymen who ruled over the region. Exploring this monumental complex offers a fascinating insight into Ireland's past.

Enter via the 15th-century **① Hall of the Vicars Choral**, built to house the male choristers who sang in the cathedral. Exhibits in its undercroft include rare silverware, stone reliefs and the original St Patrick's Cross. In the courtyard you'll see the replica of **② St Patrick's Cross**. A small porch leads into the 13th-century Gothic **③ cathedral**. To the west of the nave are the remains of the **④ Archbishop's Residence**. From the cathedral's north transept on the northeastern corner is the Rock's earliest building, an 11th- or 12th-century **⑤ Round Tower**. Nestled in the southeast corner of the cathedral is the compelling **⑥ Cormac's Chapel**, Ireland's earliest surviving Romanesque church. It dates from 1127 and the medieval integrity of its trans-European architecture survives. Inside the main door on the left is the sarcophagus said to house King Cormac, dating from between 1125 and 1150. Before leaving, take time for a close-up look at the Rock's **⑦ enclosing walls and corner tower**.

Hall of the Vicars Choral

Head upstairs from the ticket office to see the choristers' restored kitchen and dining hall, complete with period furniture, tapestries and paintings beneath a fine carved-oak roof and gallery.

Ticket Office

Entrance

Undercroft

Dormitory of Vicars Choral

TOP TIPS

→ Good photographic vantage points for framing the mighty Rock are on the road into Cashel from the Dublin Rd roundabout or from the little roads just west of the centre.

→ The best photo opportunities, however, are from inside the atmospheric ruins of Hore Abbey, 1km to the west.

Enclosing Walls & Corner Tower

Constructed from lime mortar around the 15th century, and originally incorporating five gates, stone walls enclose the entire site. It's thought the surviving corner tower was used as a watchtower.

St Patrick's Cross

In the castle courtyard, this cross replicates the eroded Hall of the Vicars Choral original – an impressive 12th-century crutched cross depicting a crucifixion scene on one face and animals on the other.

GEORGE MUNDAY/GETTY IMAGES ©

Archbishop's Residence

The west side of the cathedral is taken up by the Archbishop's Residence, a 15th-century, four-storey castle, which had its great hall built over the nave, reducing its length. It was last inhabited in the mid-1700s.

Cathedral

A huge square tower with a turret on the southwestern corner soars above the cathedral. Scattered throughout are monuments, a 16th-century altar tomb, coats of arms panels, and stone heads on capitals and corbels.

ANTON IVANOV/SHUTTERSTOCK ©

Turret

④

③

⑤

⑥

Choir

Scully Cross

Cormac's Chapel

Look closely at the exquisite doorway arches, the grand chancel arch and ribbed barrel vault, and carved vignettes, including a trefoil-tailed grotesque and a Norman-helmeted centaur firing an arrow at a rampaging lion.

ROBERT ZAHLER/SHUTTERSTOCK ©

Round Tower

Standing 28m tall, the doorway to this ancient edifice is 3.5m above the ground – perhaps for structural rather than defensive reasons. Its exact age is unknown but may be as early as 1101.

ATTILA JANDI/SHUTTERSTOCK ©

FAMINE WARHOUSE

A relic of one of Ireland's darkest chapters, the **Famine Warhouse** (📞 087 908 9972; www.heritageireland.ie; Ballingarry; ⏱ 2.30-5.30pm Wed-Sun Apr-Sep, 2-4pm Sat & Sun Oct-Mar) FREE today sits seemingly benignly amid typical farmland a few kilometres northeast of Ballingarry. During the 1848 rebellion, rebels led by William Smith O'Brien besieged police who had barricaded themselves inside and taken children hostage. Police reinforcements arrived, the rebels fled and the rebellion died out. Besides exhibits about the incident, there are also displays detailing the Famine and the mass exodus of Irish emigrants to America.

The warhouse is 30km northeast of Cashel on the R691 about midway to Kilkenny. Be careful navigating as County Tipperary has two Ballingarrys; the wrong one is over by Roscrea. Opening hours are variable; call ahead before committing to a visit.

To get here, take the N74 to the village of Golden, then head 2km south along the narrow L4304 road signed 'Athassel Abbey'. Roadside parking is limited and quite tight.

Holy Cross Abbey CHURCH
(📞 086 166 5869; www.holycrossabbey.ie; Holycross; tours €5; ⏱ tours 2.30pm Wed & Sun Mar-Sep) The pretty village of Holycross, with its thatched cottages, eight-arch stone bridge across the River Suir, and village green dotted with ducks, is 15km north of Cashel. Its magnificently restored Cistercian abbey, founded in 1168, proudly displays two relics of the True Cross, and Ireland's only intact medieval chapter-house doorway. Look for the ornately carved sedilia near the altar and pause to appreciate the early form of 'stadium seating'. Phone ahead to book a tour.

Cahir

POP 3593

At the eastern tip of the Galtee Mountains, 15km south of Cashel, Cahir (An Cathair; pronounced 'care') is a compact and attractive town that encircles a sublime castle. Walking paths follow the verdant banks of the River Suir, one of Ireland's finest trout-fishing streams.

⊙ Sights & Activities

For trout fishing along the River Suir, check out www.cahiranddistrictanglersassociation.com for more information.

★ **Cahir Castle** HISTORIC SITE
(📞 052-744 1011; www.heritageireland.ie; Castle St; adult/child €5/3; ⏱ 9am-6.30pm mid-Jun-Aug, 9.30am-5.30pm Mar-mid-Jun & Sep-mid-Oct, to 4.30pm mid-Oct-Feb) Cahir's castle enjoys a river-island site with massive walls, towers and keep, mullioned windows, original fireplaces and a dungeon. Founded by Conor O'Brien in 1142, and passed to the Butler family in 1375, it's one of Ireland's largest castles. In 1599 the Earl of Essex shattered its walls with cannon fire, an event illustrated by a large model. The impressive **Banqueting Hall** has a huge set of antlers pinned to its white walls, and you can climb the **Keep**.

The castle, originally built to protect a salmon fishery and important river crossing, eventually surrendered to Cromwell in 1650 without a struggle; its future usefulness may have discouraged the usual Cromwellian 'deconstruction' – it is largely intact and still formidable. It was restored in the 1840s and again in the 1960s when it came under state ownership.

A 15-minute audiovisual presentation puts Cahir in context with other Irish castles. The buildings within the castle walls are sparsely furnished, although there are good displays, including an exhibition on 'Women in Medieval Ireland'. There are frequent guided tours.

Swiss Cottage HISTORIC BUILDING
(📞 052-744 1144; www.heritageireland.ie; Cahir Park; adult/child €5/3; ⏱ 10am-6pm mid-Mar-Oct) A 30-minute walk along a riverside path from Cahir Castle car park leads to this thatched cottage, surrounded by roses, lavender and honeysuckle. A lavish example of Regency Picturesque, the cottage was built in 1810 as a retreat for Richard Butler, 12th Baron Caher, and his wife, and was designed by London architect John Nash, creator of the Royal Pavilion at Brighton. The 30-minute (compulsory) guided tours are thoroughly enjoyable.

The *cottage-orné* style emerged during the late 18th and early 19th centuries in England in response to the prevailing taste for the picturesque. Thatched roofs, natural wood and carved weatherboarding were characteristics and most examples were built as ornamental features on estates. The cottage was restored in the 1980s under the direction of Irish designer Sybil Connolly.

🛏 Sleeping & Eating

Don't miss the **farmers market** (www.face book.com/cahirfarmersmarket; Castle car park; ☺9am-1pm Sat) 🖉 on Saturday mornings, where you can browse some of the county's finest produce.

★Apple Caravan & Camping Park   CAMPGROUND €

(☑052-744 1459; www.theapplefarm.com; Moorstown; campsites per adult/child from €7.50/5; ☺May-Sep; 🅿🛜) 🖉 Set amid orchards on the N24 between Cahir (6km) and Clonmel (9km), this peaceful and picturesque campground has a tennis court, a camp kitchen in a converted apple store and spring water from its own well. New arrivals are welcomed with a bottle of the farm's own fresh apple juice.

Even if you're not pitching up here, it's worth dropping by its farm shop (open 8am to 5pm Monday to Saturday, from 10am Sunday), which sells apples, jams and juices as well as fruity ice creams.

Cahir House Hotel   HOTEL €€

(☑052-744 3000; www.cahirhousehotel.ie; The Square; s/d from €75/115; 🅿@🛜) Set in an imposing Georgian building on a prominent corner of the square, this landmark hotel has elegant rooms, a long menu of bar food, a spa, and helpful and efficient staff. The guestbook records visits by Mae West, Douglas Fairbanks, Walt Disney and Jackie Kennedy among other famous names.

Tinsley House   B&B €€

(☑052-744 1947; www.tinsleyhouse.com; The Square; d/f from €80/100; ☺Apr-Sep; 🛜) This light, bright and charming B&B on the Square offers four period-furnished rooms and a sweet roof garden. The owner, Liam Roche, is an expert on local history and can recommend walks and other activities.

Lazy Bean Cafe   CAFE €

(☑052-744 2038; www.thelazybeancafe.com; The Square; mains €7-10; ☺9am-6pm; 🛜🍽) The most popular place in town for a bite to eat, this bustling old-fashioned cafe serves all-day breakfasts, choose-your-own sandwiches, wraps, bagels and panini, and rounds it off with top-notch coffee, hot chocolate and cake.

Galileo   ITALIAN €€

(☑052-744 5689; www.galileocafe.com; Church St; mains €12-25; ☺noon-10pm Mon-Sat, 1-9pm Sun) Serving excellent pizza and pasta to Cahir locals for more than a decade, Galileo is a smart and stylish Italian restaurant, with modern decor and efficient, friendly service. The restaurant has no licence, so BYO.

❶ Information

Tourist Office (☑052-744 1453; www.tipperary. com; Castle car park; ☺9.30am-1pm & 1.45-5.30pm Tue-Sat Apr-Oct) Has information about the town and region.

❶ Getting There & Away

Cahir is a hub for several Bus Éireann (www.bus eireann.ie) routes, including Dublin–Cork, Limerick–Waterford, Galway–Waterford, Kilkenny–Cork and Cork–Athlone.

There are six buses per day to Cashel (€6, 20 minutes).

Buses stop in the car park beside the castle.

From Monday to Saturday, the train from Waterford to Limerick Junction stops in Clonmel and Cahir (€16.50, one hour, twice daily).

Mitchelstown Cave

Hollowed out of a narrow band of limestone along the southern side of the Galtee Mountains, the **Mitchelstown Cave** (☑052-746 7246; www.mitchelstowncave.com; Burncourt; adult/ child/family €9/3.50/20; ☺10am-4.45pm mid-May-Aug, to 4.30pm Sep & Oct, to 4pm Feb–mid-May & Nov, shorter hours Dec-Jan) is superior to Kilkenny's Dunmore Cave and yet less developed for tourists. There are nearly 3km of passages with spectacular chambers full of textbook formations with names such as the Pipe

---

TIPPERARY HERITAGE WAY

Extending 56km from the Vee Gap viewpoint near Clogheen in the south to Cashel in the north, the waymarked Tipperary Heritage Way (www.irishtrails. ie) passes some beautiful river valleys and ruins. The 30km north from Cahir to Cashel is the best segment, featuring the verdant lands around the River Suir and traversing close to highlights such as Athassel Priory (p337). The best stretches around Golden are off road. Expect to see a fair amount of wildlife as the paths and very minor roads follow the waters and penetrate woodlands. Ordnance Survey Discovery series maps 66 and 74 cover the route.

Organ, Tower of Babel, House of Commons and Eagle's Wing. The cave is 16km southwest of Cahir, signposted from the N8 to Mitchelstown. Tours take about 30 minutes.

Year-round, the cave temperature remains a constant 12°C, making it feel warm in winter and chilly in summer.

Clonmel & Around

POP 17,140

Spread along the banks of the broad River Suir, Clonmel (Cluain Meala; 'Meadows of Honey') is Tipperary's largest and busiest town.

Laurence Sterne (1713–68), author of *A Sentimental Journey Through France and Italy* and *The Life and Opinions of Tristram Shandy, Gentleman*, was born here. However, Clonmel's commercial cheerleader was Italian-born Charles Bianconi (1786–1875). At age 16, Bianconi's father sent him to Ireland in an attempt to break his liaison with a woman. Bianconi later channelled all his frustrated passion into setting up a coach service between Clonmel and Cahir; his company quickly grew to become a nationwide passenger and mail carrier. For putting Clonmel on the map, Bianconi was twice elected mayor.

The East Munster Way (p343) walking route passes through Clonmel.

Directly south of Clonmel, over the border in County Waterford, are the Comeragh Mountains. There's a scenic driving route south to Ballymacarbry and the Nire Valley on the R671 road.

◉ Sights

Turning south down Bridge St, crossing the river and following the road around brings you to **Lady Blessington's Bath**, a picturesque stretch of the river that's perfect for picnicking.

Main Guard HISTORIC BUILDING
(☏ 052-612 7484; www.heritageireland.ie; Sarsfield St; ☺ 9am-5pm Tue-Sun Apr-Sep, hours vary) FREE The beautifully restored Main Guard is a Butler courthouse dating from 1675 and based on a design by Christopher Wren, with an elegant columned loggia facing the street. Inside, exhibits include a model of Clonmel as a walled 17th-century town.

County Courthouse HISTORIC BUILDING
(Nelson St) The refurbished County Courthouse, south of Parnell St, was designed by

Richard Morrison in 1802. It was here that the Young Irelanders of 1848, including Thomas Francis Meagher, were tried and sentenced to transportation to Australia.

South Tipperary County Museum MUSEUM
(www.tipperarycoco.ie/museum; Mick Delahunty Sq; ☺ 10am-4.45pm Tue-Sat) FREE Informative displays on the history of County Tipperary from Neolithic times to the present are covered at this well-put-together museum, which also hosts changing exhibitions.

🛏 Sleeping & Eating

★ **Raheen House Hotel** HOTEL €€
(☏ 052-612 2140; www.raheenhouse.ie; Raheen Rd; r from €125; P ☞) Grand but homely, this gorgeous old country-house hotel offers high ceilings, massive rooms, some fine four-poster beds, wooden floors, a bar, a conservatory and two huge gardens with maples, magnolias and a vast cypress. There's also a walled garden, roaring fires in winter and a self-catering lodge (from €200).

Hotel Minella HOTEL €€
(☏ 052-612 2388; www.hotelminella.com; Coleville Rd; s/d from €130/150; P ☞ ☒) This family-run luxury hotel sits amid extensive grounds on the south bank of the River Suir, 2km east of the town centre. Its 90 rooms are divided between an 1863 mansion and a modern wing; the latter has almost every kind of convenience, including two suites with outdoor hot tubs on private terraces overlooking the river.

Niamh's CAFE, DELI €
(www.niamhs.com; 1 Mitchell St; mains €9-14; ☺ 8.30am-5pm Mon-Fri, to 4.30pm Sat; ☞ 🖶) This long, slender, smart and bustling deli and cafe does a brisk trade, serving a wide range of appealing lunch options, comfort food (gourmet burgers, pan-fried pork and lasagne, plus creative sandwiches) and breakfasts. Free coffee refills, with a smile.

Mani IRISH €€
(☏ 052-617 0007; www.mani.ie; 20 Parnell St; mains €14-30; ☺ 5-9.30pm Tue-Thu, 12.30-2.30pm & 5-10pm Fri & Sat, 12.30-8pm Sun; ☞) This relaxed yet stylish restaurant places seasonal Irish produce front and centre in dishes such as pan-fried hake (landed at Kilmore Quay in County Wexford) with garlic mash and star anise beurre blanc, and chargrilled Tipperary beef sirloin with sweet-onion confit and brandy and green-peppercorn sauce.

EAST MUNSTER WAY

This 70km walk (www.irishtrails.ie) travels through forest and open moorland, along small country roads and a lovely river towpath. It's clearly laid out with black markers bearing yellow arrows and could be managed in three days, starting at Carrick-on-Suir and finishing at Clogheen, both in County Tipperary.

The first day takes you to Clonmel following the old towpath on the Suir for significant portions of the route. At Kilsheelan Bridge you leave the river to Harney's Crossroads, then wander through Gurteen Wood and the Comeragh foothills to Sir Thomas Bridge where you rejoin the river.

On the second day, the Way first leads south into the hills and then descends to Newcastle and the river once more. The third day sees a lot of very atmospheric walking along the quiet River Tar to Clogheen.

Ordnance Survey Discovery series maps 74 and 75 cover the route.

Befani's Restaurant & Townhouse   MEDITERRANEAN €€

(☑ 052-617 7893; www.befani.com; 6 Sarsfield St; tapas €7-8, mains €16-29; ☺ 9-11am, 12.30-2.30pm & 5.30-9.30pm; ☜) Befani's brings a touch of the Mediterranean to Clonmel. Breakfasts include veggie omelettes and mushrooms on toast, at lunchtime there's a mouth-watering tapas menu, while dinner dishes include seafood *fritto misto,* braised beef with Toulouse sausage, and pan-fried salmon with sun-dried tomato and pesto mash. Guest rooms upstairs offer B&B accommodation (single/double €45/75).

🍸 Drinking & Nightlife

Phil Carroll   PUB

(☑ 052-612 5215; www.facebook.com/philcarrolls bar; Parnell St; ☺ 5pm-1am) This diminutive place is Clonmel's most atmospheric old boozer, with a vintage exterior of black gloss and gold, and a charming interior that's crammed with character.

Sean Tierney   PUB

(☑ 052-612 4467; www.seantierneys.com; 13 O'Connell St; ☺ noon-11pm) Wander this narrow old pub's warren of rooms and floors until you find a spot that's just right. The ground-level bar is always alive with craic.

❶ Information

Tourist Office (☑ 052-612 2960; Main Guard, Sarsfield St; ☺ 9.30am-1pm & 2-4.30pm Mon-Fri) Very helpful staff; adjoins Main Guard.

❶ Getting There & Away

BUS

Buses stop at the train station. Bus Éireann (www.buseireann.ie) has buses to destinations including Cahir (€6.50, 15 minutes, hourly), Cork

(€24, two hours, three daily; change at Cahir) and Waterford (€10.50, one hour, six daily).

TRAIN

The **train station** (☑ 052-612 1982) is on Prior Park Rd past Oakville Shopping Centre, 1km north of the town centre. From Monday to Saturday, the train from Waterford to Limerick Junction stops in Clonmel (€13.05, 50 minutes, twice daily).

Fethard

POP 1545

An appealingly quaint little village with impressive medieval ruins scattered about its compact, linear centre, Fethard (pronounced 'feathered') is located 14km north of Clonmel on the River Clashawley. One of Ireland's most complete medieval town walls is the village's principal feature.

◉ Sights

Holy Trinity Church   CHURCH

(Main St) This church and churchyard occupy a captivating time warp. The main part of the building dates from the 13th century, though its ancient walls have been blighted with mortar for weatherproofing. A ruined chapel and sacristy adjoin the south end of the church, while old gravestones descend in ranks to a refurbished stretch of medieval town wall complete with a guard tower and a parapet, from where you can look down on the gentle River Clashawley between its horse-trod banks.

The interior of the church has an aisled nave and a chancel of typical medieval style, but is sparsely furnished. Within the church ceiling is the oldest scientifically dated timber roof in Ireland. If the church is closed, ask for keys at the neighbouring Horse Country Experience museum (p344).

Horse Country Experience
MUSEUM

(☑ 052-613 0439; www.fhcexperience.ie; Tholsel, Main St; adult/child €7.50/3.50; ☺10am-4pm Tue-Sat) Housed in Fethard's 17th-century Tholsel (town hall), this museum traces the role of the horse in Irish history and culture, from military steeds and plough horses to horse racing and stud farms. Exhibits also explore the history of Fethard and the surrounding region. Twice weekly in summer there are guided tours of nearby Coolmore Stud (adult/child €10/8, book in advance).

Sheila-na-gig
HISTORIC SITE

On the way down to Watergate Bridge from Main St is a fine sheila-na-gig (a sexually explicit medieval depiction of a woman) embedded in the old town wall to your left. You can stroll along the river bank here, provided the resident geese are feeling friendly.

✕ Eating & Drinking

★ Dooks Fine Foods
CAFE, DELI €

(☑ 052-613 0828; www.facebook.com/dooksfine foods; Kerry St; mains €5-14; ☺ 7.30am-5pm Tue-Fri, from 9am Sat, to 3pm Sun) A slice of culinary sophistication poised at the west end of sleepy little Fethard, Dooks is a cornucopia of all that is good to eat – breakfast sausages flavoured with rosemary, fennel and orange, lunchtime focaccia topped with garlic- and buttermilk-marinated chicken, salads scattered with nasturtium petals...or just drop in for sublime coffee and blissful cake.

McCarthy's
PUB FOOD €

(☑ 052-613 1149; www.mccarthyshotel.net; Main St; mains €8-13; ☺ food served noon-3pm daily, 6-9pm Wed-Sun) A classic multifunctional Irish country pub, McCarthy's proclaims itself as bar, restaurant and undertaker ('we'll wine you, dine you and bury you'). Closely spaced wooden booths and tables are wedged among a thicket of bric-a-brac dating to 1840, under a wood-panelled ceiling. The menu of hearty pub grub runs from lasagne and burgers to chicken curry and fish and chips.

Nenagh & Around

POP 8968

In the far north of Tipperary County, beyond the Silvermine Mountains, pretty Nenagh is a historic market town and the site of a dominant castle (☑ 067-33850; www.heritage ireland.ie; O'Rahilly St; ☺10am-1pm & 2-4.30pm Tue-Sat Apr-Oct) FREE. Its role as the administrative centre of north Tipperary has left a legacy of impressive courthouse and prison buildings (the latter no longer in use).

Nenagh is also a gateway to the eastern shore of Lough Derg, a popular swimming, fishing and boating area – Lough Derg Water Sports (☑ 086 411 4822; www.loughderg watersports.com; Kilgarvan Quay, Brockagh; per person €35-45; ☺ Apr-Sep), 21km to the north of town, operates guided kayak tours. An interesting, scenic lakeside drive from Nenagh is the 24km R494, which winds around to Killaloe and Ballina.

There's tourist information at Nenagh Heritage Centre.

Nenagh Heritage Centre
MUSEUM

(☑ 067-33850; www.tipperarycoco.ie/heritage/nenagh-heritage-centre; Kickham St; ☺10am-4pm Tue-Fri) FREE The 1840 Governor's House is an unusual octagonal stone building that was once at the centre of a 19th-century prison complex. Today it holds the Nenagh Heritage Centre, which houses a local history museum, tourist information and genealogy services.

★ Country Choice
CAFE, DELI €

(☑ 067-32596; www.countrychoice.ie; 25 Kenyon St; mains €5-12; ☺ shop 9am-5pm Tue-Sat, cafe to 4pm) Country Choice is a place of pilgrimage for lovers of really great Irish artisan foods. Sample the superb lunch menu in the cafe or just have a coffee, but ready yourself to browse the extensive deli area with homemade preserves, farmhouse cheeses and myriad other treats. Baskets of fruit sit out front of the shop, luring you in.

Steeples
CAFE €

(☑ 067-64592; www.steeples.ie; 1 O'Rahilly St; mains €5-10; ☺9am-5pm Mon-Sat, 10am-3pm Sun) Part bookshop, part cafe, this place combines appealing junk-shop decor – ancient stove, old piano, glass-fronted display cases, mismatched furniture – with an all-day breakfast menu that includes a few Tex-Mex touches, including excellent huevos rancheros and corn cakes.

ⓘ Getting There & Away

Frequent Bus Éireann (www.buseireann.ie) services run to Limerick city (€8.30, 50 minutes, nine daily).

Nenagh's train station has four services daily to Limerick city (€13.05, one hour); connect in Ballybrophy for Dublin, Cork and Tralee.

County Clare

POP 118,817 / AREA 3440 SQ KM

Best Places to Eat

➡ Gallagher's of Bunratty (p353)

➡ Wooden Spoon (p355)

➡ Barrtrá Seafood Restaurant (p363)

➡ Cheese Press (p364)

➡ Long Dock (p359)

➡ Cafe Linnalla (p380)

Best Places to Stay

➡ Gregan's Castle Hotel (p380)

➡ Old Ground Hotel (p348)

➡ Wild Atlantic Lodge (p379)

➡ Loop Head Lighthouse Keeper's Cottage (p359)

➡ Coast Lodge (p361)

➡ Rowan Tree Hostel (p347)

Why Go?

County Clare combines spectacular windswept landscapes and vibrant Irish culture. The ocean relentlessly pounds Clare's coast year-round, eroding rock into fantastic formations, and fashioning sheer rock crags including those at the iconic Cliffs of Moher and at ends-of-the-earth Loop Head. Right along the coast, the waves are a magnet for surfers, and surf schools set up on many of Clare's beaches in summer.

Stretching down to the shore – and out as far as the Aran Islands, linked to Doolin in summer by ferries – is the moonscape-like bare limestone expanse of the Burren, which blazes with wildflowers in spring.

If the land is hard, Clare's soul certainly isn't: traditional Irish culture and music flourish here. And it's not just a show for tourists, either. In larger towns and even the tiniest of villages you'll find pubs with trad-music sessions year-round.

When to Go

➡ While the unsettled seas of winter have a drama that will fill your days with a raw intensity, the county shines during the more temperate months when long walks along the soaring cliffs of the coast and among the desolate rocks of the Burren don't require full foul-weather gear.

➡ County Clare's pubs hum year-round to the beats of trad sessions, so even in winter you'll find the craic – often warmed in the countryside by a peat fire.

➡ Musical highlights on Clare's festival calendar include Doolin's Russell Memorial Weekend in February; Ennis' Fleadh Nua in May; and one of Ireland's best traditional music festivals, Miltown Malbay's Willie Clancy Summer School, in July.

County Clare Highlights

1 **Music Pubs** (p372) Joining locals at spirited trad sessions in age-old inns.

2 **Cliffs of Moher** (p365) Boarding a late-afternoon boat to see Clare's iconic cliffs.

3 **Loop Head** (p358) Driving the peninsula's narrow roads to the headland.

4 **Poulnabrone Dolmen** (p377) Encountering the pick of the Burren's many photogenic prehistoric sites.

5 **Vandeleur Walled Garden** (p356) Wandering through these grand old gardens.

6 **Hazel Mountain Chocolate** (p380) Sampling artisan chocolate on a tour of this cottage-housed factory.

7 **Aillwee Cave** (p379) Delving 600m under the mountain at this cavernous series of tunnels.

8 **Burren Perfumery & Floral Centre** (p377) Savouring the scents of Clare's wild spaces at this fragrant cottage-factory.

9 **Loop Head Summer Hedge School** (p358) Unleashing your inner artist during these creative, outdoor classes.

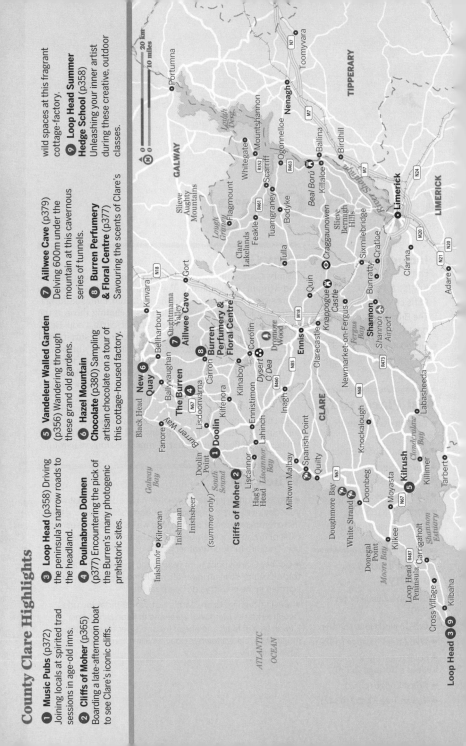

ENNIS

POP 25,276

Clare's charming commercial hub, Ennis (Inis), lies on the banks of the fast-moving River Fergus, which flows east, then south into the Shannon Estuary.

The town's medieval origins are recalled by its irregular, narrow streets, but the most important surviving historical site is Ennis Friary, founded in the 13th century by the O'Briens, kings of Thomond, who also built a castle here in the 13th century. Much of the wooden town went skywards in a 1249 fire, and Ennis was then razed by one of the O'Briens in 1306.

Today formal sights are few, but the town centre, with its narrow, pedestrian-friendly streets, is enjoyable to wander. Handily situated 23km north of Shannon Airport, it makes an ideal base for exploring the county: you can reach any part of Clare in under two hours from here.

◉ Sights & Activities

★ Ennis Friary   CHURCH

(☑ 065-682 9100; www.heritageireland.ie; Abbey St; adult/child €5/3; ⊙ 10am-6pm Easter-Sep, to 5pm Oct) North of the Square, Ennis Friary was founded by Donnchadh Cairbreach O'Brien, a king of Thomond, between 1240 and 1249. A mix of structures dating between the 13th and 19th centuries, the friary has a graceful five-section window dating from the late 13th century, a McMahon tomb (1460) with alabaster panels depicting scenes from the Passion, and a particularly fine *Ecce Homo* panel portraying a stripped and bound Christ.

Objects associated with the Passion to look for include the rooster rising from a cooking pot, three dice, nails and various tools. The panel was possibly painted in earlier centuries. On the other side of the nave is a devotional relief carving of St Francis of Assisi (displaying stigmata), patron of the Franciscans who arrived in Ennis in the early 13th century. Further fascinating carvings associated with Jesus Christ and his crucifixion are displayed in glass cabinets in the nave.

Clare Museum   MUSEUM

(☑ 065-682 3382; www.clarelibrary.ie; Arthur's Row; ⊙ 9.30am-1pm & 2-5.30pm Mon-Sat Jun-Sep, Tue-Sat Oct-May) FREE At this diverting little museum, the 'Riches of Clare' exhibition tells the story of Clare from 8000 years ago to the present day using authentic artefacts grouped into five themes: earth (geology, seasons and agriculture), power (such as hill forts and tower houses), faith (Christianity's influence), water (the county's relationship with the River Shannon and the Atlantic) and energy (particularly Clare's musical and sporting prowess).

Daniel O'Connell Monument   MONUMENT

(The Square) Set on a soaring column, a statue of Daniel O'Connell (aka the 'Great Liberator') presides over the Square.

O'Connell's election to the British parliament by a huge majority in 1828 forced Britain to lift its ban on Catholic MPs and led to the Act of Catholic Emancipation a year later.

Ennis Cathedral   CATHEDRAL

(☑ 065-682 4043; www.ennisparish.com; O'Connell St; ⊙ 7.30am-8pm Mon-Fri, 9am-7pm Sat & Sun) FREE Consecrated in 1843, this impressive structure had its tower and spire added in 1874, and was elevated to the status of a cathedral in 1990. A highlight is its 1930-built organ.

Tierney's Cycles   CYCLING

(☑ 065-682 9433; www.clarebikehire.com; 17 Abbey St; bike rental per day/week from €24/85; ⊙ 9.30am-6pm) Tierney's rents well-maintained road and racing bikes. Hire includes a lock and a repair kit.

Ennis Walking Tours   WALKING

(☑ 087 648 3714; www.enniswalkingtours.com; adult/child €10/5; ⊙ 11am Mon, Tue & Thu-Sat May-Oct) Tales of famine, murder, riots and rebellion bring to life the story of Ennis' history on these excellent 75-minute walking tours, departing from the tourist office (p351) on Arthur's Row.

★★ Festivals & Events

Fleadh Nua   CULTURAL

(www.fleadhnua.com; ⊙ May) Singing, dancing and workshops are part of this lively eight-day traditional-music festival.

Ennis Trad Festival   MUSIC

(www.ennistradfest.com; ⊙ early–mid-Nov) Traditional music in venues across town keeps the tunes flowing during November's five-day festival.

🛏 Sleeping

★ Rowan Tree Hostel   HOSTEL €

(☑ 065-686 8687; www.rowantreehostel.ie; Harmony Row; dm €25-29, d €79-89, f €125; 🔊) Balconies overlooking the swift-flowing River Fergus; bright, airy dorms; and doubles

Ennis

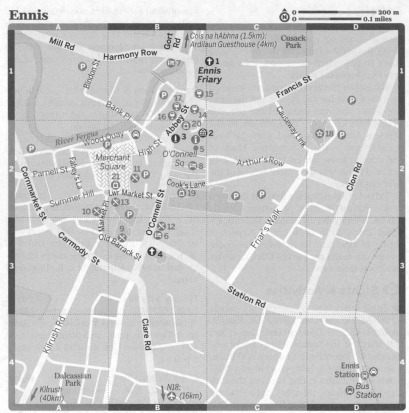

with Egyptian linen add to the appeal at this town-centre hostel. It's set in a grand 1740-built former gentlemen's club, and fantastic facilities include a kitchen, a laundry and the excellent Cafe Bar in the former ballroom.

Ardilaun Guesthouse
B&B €

(☑ 065-682 2311; purcells.ennis@eircom.net; Ballycoree; s/d €44/68; ᴘ🛜) Drop a line into the River Fergus or just watch the sunset from the rear deck of this B&B around 3km north of the centre, off the R458. Pluses include an onsite fitness room and sauna, and friendly owners who can help arrange transport into town.

Temple Gate Hotel
HOTEL €€

(☑ 065-682 3300; www.templegatehotel.com; The Square; s/d/f from €131/131/191; ᴘ🛜) The soaring cathedral-ceilinged lobby at this epicentral 70-room hotel was once part of the 19th-century Sisters of Mercy convent. Upper-floor rooms (reached by a lift) have

views over Ennis' rooftops, but try to avoid ground-floor rooms facing the car park at the rear. There's an on-site restaurant and a great bar, the Preachers Pub, which also serves quality bar food.

★ Old Ground Hotel
HOTEL €€€

(☑ 065-682 8127; www.oldgroundhotelennis.com; O'Connell St; s €130, d €180-200, ste €230-275; 🛜) Entered through a lobby of polished floorboards, cornice-work, antiques and open fires, this prestigious landmark dates back to the 1800s. The 83 rooms vary greatly in size and decor, which ranges from historic to cutting-edge. Kids under 16 staying in their parents' room are charged €25 per night. The ground-floor Poet's Corner Bar (p350) is one of Ennis' best pubs.

✕ Eating

Most of Ennis' pubs serve food, some of good quality; there are also some excellent delis and cafes.

Ennis

The Ennis farmers market (www.ennisfarmers market.com; Roslevan Shopping Centre, Tulla Rd; ⊙8am 2pm Fri) is some 3km northeast of town and features prime produce, the vast majority of which comes from County Clare or within 30 miles of the market.

Food Heaven CAFE €
(☑065-682 2722; www.food-heaven.ie; 21 Market St; dishes €6-12; ⊙8.30am-6pm Mon-Sat; ⊛) The aptly named Food Heaven rustles up creative, fresh fare right from the American-style breakfast pancakes, via lunchtime open crayfish sandwiches through to afternoon teas. Be ready to queue at lunch for its renowned handmade sausage rolls.

Souper CAFE €
(☑065-682 3901; 10 Merchant Sq; soups from €4.50; ⊙9am-5pm Mon-Sat; ⊘) The choice of soups changes daily at this cosy cafe, which dishes up warming bowls of creamy garden pea, French onion with croutons, vegan leek and potato, and chicken and tarragon. Paninis, wraps and sandwiches fill any gaps.

Ennis Gourmet Store DELI €
(☑065-684 3314; www.ennisgourmet.com; 1 Old Barrack St; dishes €8-16; ⊙10am-8pm Mon-Wed, to 10pm Thu-Sat, noon-6pm Sun) Gourmet produce – from Burren smoked salmon and whiskey marmalade to fine French wines – fills the shelves of this delightful deli. Simple but delicious dishes change daily but might include cauliflower soup, roast beetroot salad or warm mackerel on brioche.

Town Hall IRISH €€
(☑065-682 8127; www.flynnhotels.com; O'Connell St; mains lunch €9-17, dinner €19-28; ⊙10am-9.45pm Mon-Sat, to 9.30pm Sun; ⊛) At this smart bistro attached to the neighbouring Old Ground Hotel local ingredients take centre stage: Clare lamb, Fergus Bay crab, Sixmilebridge free-range pork and Shannon Estuary monkfish. Scones, jam and coffee are served for afternoon tea, while candlelit tables create an intimate ambience at night.

Rowan Tree Cafe Bar FUSION €€
(☑065-686 8669; www.rowantreecafebar.ie; Harmony Row; mains €8-14; ⊙10.30am-11pm; ⊛⊘⊕) A one-time ballroom, the dining room here has high ceilings, fairy lights and 18th-century wooden floors, while tables outside have river views. Global-themed dishes are packed with local, seasonal ingredients; treats include St Tola's goat-cheese fritters, west-coast crab linguini, and lamb and feta burgers. A cracking Sunday brunch draws the crowds.

The extensive children's menu features healthy options, with free mini-bowls of mash and soup for the under-twos.

▼ Drinking & Entertainment

As the capital of a renowned music county, Ennis pulses with pubs featuring trad music a couple of times a week year-round and often nightly during summer. Custy's Music Shop (p350) is a great place to find out about live gigs; the tourist office also collates weekly listings.

TRADITIONAL MUSIC IN COUNTY CLARE

Clare is one of Ireland's best counties for traditional music. Musicians here stick resolutely to the jigs and reels of old, often with little vocal accompaniment, without more modern influences such as rock or polkas that are often heard elsewhere. You'll find pubs with trad sessions at least one night a week in almost every town and village, including the following:

Doolin A famous trio of pubs have nightly trad-music sessions. However, tourist crowds can be intense, evaporating any sense of intimacy. An atmospheric alternative is a trad session at the private home of musician Christy Barry, aka Doolin Music House (p373).

Ennis You can bounce from one music-filled pub (p349) to another most nights, especially in summer, in Clare's largest town.

Ennistimon The charming village of Ennistimon (p363) has ancient pubs attracting top local talent.

Kilfenora This small Burren village has a big musical heritage on show at local pub Vaughan's (p375), with set dancing in its adjacent barn.

Miltown Malbay This tiny village hosts the annual Willie Clancy Summer School (p361), one of Ireland's best music festivals. Talented locals perform in pubs throughout the year.

Nora Culligans   PUB
(☑065-682 4954; www.noraculligans.com; Abbey St; ⏱4-11.30pm Mon-Thu, to 2am Fri, noon-2am Sat, noon-midnight Sun; ⏥) Magnificently restored, cavernous Nora Culligans retains original features including the front bar's ornate two-storey-high whiskey cabinets and timber panelling in the back bar. It's an atmospheric venue for live music across a diverse array of genres, from jazz and blues to acoustic singer-songwriters and reggae as well as trad.

Brogan's   PUB
(☑065-684 4365; www.brogansbarandrestaurant. com; 24 O'Connell St; ⏱noon-midnight) On the corner of Quinns Row, Brogan's rambles from one room to the next, with musicians playing traditional instruments such as tin whistles, fiddles, accordions and more most nights.

Food (mains €7 to €14; served noon to 9pm) ranges from artisan sausage sandwiches to west Clare mussels poached in white wine.

Poet's Corner Bar   PUB
(☑065-682 8127; www.flynnhotels.com; Old Ground Hotel, O'Connell St; ⏱11am-11.30pm Mon-Thu, to 12.30am Fri & Sat, noon-11pm Sun; ⏥) It's partly the regular trad sessions (Wednesday to Sunday, May to September; Friday and Saturday, October to April), partly the timber panels and snugs, and partly the chatty, welcoming vibe that help make the pub in the Old Ground Hotel (p348) a favourite with locals and visitors.

Retro pub food (mains €10 to €25; food served to 9pm) ranges from poached salmon on brown treacle bread to prime Irish steaks.

Cois na hAbhna   TRADITIONAL MUSIC
(☑065-682 4276; www.coisnahabhna.ie; Gort Rd; ⏱opening hours vary) Traditional Irish music, dancing, singing and Irish language are showcased at this important regional resource centre for Comhaltas Ceoltóirí Éireann (CCÉ; Society of the Musicians of Ireland), 1.5km north of town. Check online for renowned Summer Seisiún shows (Wednesday and Friday, late June to August), which combine formal and informal traditional entertainment, plus a wide range of classes year-round.

Books, DVDs and CDs are also on sale.

Glór   PERFORMING ARTS
(☑065-684 3103; www.glor.ie; Causeway Link; ⏱box office 10am-5pm Mon-Sat) In a striking modern building, Clare's cultural centre hosts theatre, dance, traditional music, film, photography, art and more.

🛍 Shopping

⭐ **Scéal Eile Books**   BOOKS
(☑065-684 8648; www.scealeilebooks.ie; 16 Lower Market St; ⏱11am-6pm Mon-Sat) A delight to explore, this emerald-green-painted bookshop overflows with new and secondhand literature, including rare titles across all genres from poetry to sci-fi and travel. A stove at the rear, ensconced between two armchairs, creates a wonderfully cosy atmosphere. Book readings and cultural events regularly take place. It also buys secondhand books.

Custy's Music Shop   MUSICAL INSTRUMENTS
(☑065-682 1727; www.custysmusic.com; Cook's Lane; ⏱9am-6pm Mon-Sat) A must-stop shop for Irish music, with instruments, musical

paraphernalia and a wealth of info about the local scene.

Ennis Bookshop
BOOKS

(☑ 065-708 1300; www.ennisbookshop.ie; 13 Abbey St; ⊙ 10am-6pm Mon-Sat) Independent Ennis Bookshop has a strong kids' section, fiction and nonfiction, and a vast range of stationery.

❶ Information

Ennis' **tourist office** (☑ 1850 230 330; www. visitennis.com; Arthur's Row; ⊙ 9.30am-5.30pm Tue-Fri, 9am-5pm Sat) is housed in the same building as the Clare Museum.

❶ Getting There & Away

BUS

Bus Éireann (www.buseireann.ie) services operate from the **bus station** (Station Rd) beside the train station. Connect in Galway or Limerick for Dublin.

Destinations include the following:

Cork Bus 51; €19, three hours, hourly

Doolin Bus 350; €9.50, 50 minutes, five daily, via Corofin, Ennistimon, Lahinch, Liscannor and Cliffs of Moher

Galway Bus 51; €9.50, 1½ hours, hourly, via Gort

Limerick Bus 51; €7, one hour, hourly, via Bunratty

Shannon Airport Bus 51; €8.50, 30 minutes, hourly

TRAIN

Irish Rail (www.irishrail.ie) trains serve Limerick (€6, 40 minutes, nine daily), where you can connect to trains to places further afield, including Dublin.

The line to Galway (€7.50, 1¼ hours, four to five daily) takes in some superb Burren scenery.

❶ Getting Around

There's a big car park southeast of the tourist office on Friar's Walk and one alongside the river just off Abbey St.

Taxi stands are at the **train station** (Quin Rd) and Wood Quay, or call **Burren Taxis** (☑ 065-682 3456).

Tierney's Cycles (p347) rents well-maintained road and racing bikes.

AROUND ENNIS

Dysert O'Dea

The centrepiece of Dysert O'Dea (☑ 065-683 7401; www.dysertcastle.com; adult/child €7/3; ⊙ 10am-6pm May-Sept), a fascinating historic site

where St Tola founded a monastery in the 8th century, is the four-storey, 15th-century O'Dea Castle. Today it houses the Clare Archaeology Centre, which has a rooftop castle walk and a museum displaying local artefacts. A 5km history trail around the castle passes some two-dozen ancient monuments, from ring forts and high crosses to a prehistoric cooking site. Dysert O'Dea is just off the R476, 5km south of Corofin.

The site's church dates from the 12th century, as does the high cross, the White Cross of St Tola, depicting Daniel in the lion's den on one side and a crucified Christ above a bishop carved in relief on the other. Look for carvings of animal and human heads in a semicircle on the southern doorway of the Romanesque church. There are also the 5m-high remains of a round tower. In 1318 the O'Briens, who were kings of Thomond, and the Norman de Clares of Bunratty fought a pitched battle nearby, which the O'Briens won, thus postponing the Anglo-Norman conquest of Clare for some two centuries.

Dromore Wood

Extending along a lovely river, Dromore Wood (☑ 085 808 5199; www.heritageireland.ie; Ruan; ⊙ woods 8am-7.30pm Jun-Aug, to 6pm Sep-May, visitor centre 10am-5pm Wed-Sun May-Aug) encompasses some 400 hectares of picturesque Irish woodland as well as the ruins of the lakeside 17th-century O'Brien Castle and two ring forts. Dromore Wood is 9.3km east of Corofin; you'll need your own transport.

Craggaunowen

Ireland's award-winning prehistoric park, Craggaunowen (www.shannonheritage.com; off R469; adult/child/family €10/8/28; ⊙ 10am-5pm Easter-early Sep), features rarities such as *crannóg* dwellings (artificial islands), recreated Celtic farms, and a 5th-century ring fort, as well as authentic artefacts, including a 2000-year-old oak road. You'll also encounter Craggaunowen Castle (a small, well-preserved medieval fortified house), a souterrain (underground passage) and animals such as wild boars and rare Soay sheep. Craggaunowen is some 10km southeast of Quin.

In a specially built display hall, the Brendan Boat is a leather-hulled vessel built by Tim Severin and sailed across the Atlantic in the 1970s to recreate St Brendan's reputed journey to America in the 6th century.

Quin

POP 951

The tiny village of Quin (Chuinche) was the site of the Great Clare Find of 1854 – the most important discovery of prehistoric gold in Ireland. Only a few of the several hundred torcs, gorgets and other pieces made it to the National Museum in Dublin; most were sold and melted down.

Quin Friary   RUINS
(Quin Abbey; www.monastic.ie/visitor-info; off R469; ⊙10am-4pm Tue-Sat, 9am-3pm Sun) FREE Impressively intact, this Franciscan friary was founded in 1433 using part of the walls of an older Clare castle built in 1280. Despite many periods of persecution, Franciscan monks lived here until the 19th century. The splendidly named Fireballs MacNamara, a notorious duellist and member of the region's ruling family, is buried here. An elegant bell tower rises above the main body of the friary and its charming cloister. Beside the friary is the 13th-century Gothic Church of St Finghin.

Knappogue Castle   LIVE PERFORMANCE
(☑061-711 222; www.shannonheritage.com; R469; banquet adult/child €63/35; ⊙by reservation 6.30-8.30pm Apr-Oct) The only way to visit this stately 15th-century castle 3.5km southeast of Quin is to attend a touristy but fun medieval banquet. Following a cup of mead (honey wine) and harp music, you'll sit down to a four-course meal accompanied by live entertainment. Knappogue's walls are intact, and it has a fine collection of period furniture and fireplaces, and restored formal gardens.

The castle was built in 1467 by the MacNamaras, who held sway over a large part of Clare from the 5th to mid-15th centuries and littered the region with 42 castles. It was confiscated by Cromwellian forces in 1659 and bestowed upon a parliamentarian, Arthur Smith, which is one of the reasons it was spared destruction. The MacNamara family regained the castle after the Restoration in 1660 and it was finally restored by a Texan architect after he purchased it in 1966. Shannon Development now administers the site.

EASTERN & SOUTHEASTERN CLARE

Away from the Atlantic coast and the rugged Burren, Clare rolls through low-lying green countryside with gentle hills.

The county's eastern boundary is the River Shannon and the long, inland waterway of Lough Derg, which stretches 48km from Portumna in County Galway to just south of Killaloe. Lakeside villages here seem a world away from the rugged, evocative west of Clare, but it's a picturesque landscape of water, woods and panoramic views.

Southeastern Clare, where the Shannon swells into its broad estuary, is largely farmland.

Shannon Airport

Shannon Airport, halfway between Ennis and Limerick City, was once a vital fuelling stop for piston-engine planes lacking the range to make it between the North American and European mainlands.

Shannon Airport   AIRPORT
(SNN; ☑061-712 000; www.shannonairport.ie; ⊛) Ireland's third-busiest airport has ATMs, currency exchange, car-rental desks, taxis and a tourist office (⊙7am-11pm) near the arrivals area. Numerous flights serve North America (with US pre-clearance facilities), the UK and Europe.

From Shannon Airport, direct Bus Éireann (www.buseireann.ie) services include bus 51, which runs hourly to the following destinations:

Cork €14, 2½ hours

Ennis €8.50, 30 minutes

Galway €10, two hours

Limerick €8.50, 50 minutes

Bunratty

POP 349

Bunratty (Bun Raite) is home to a splendid castle that abuts a theme park recreating an Irish village of yore. It's a double act that draws in countless visitors, particularly given its proximity to Shannon Airport, 13km to the west.

Bunratty Castle & Folk Park   CASTLE
(☑061-711 222; www.bunrattycastle.ie; adult/child/family €16/12/45; ⊙9am-5.30pm) Dating from the 15th century, square, hulking Bunratty Castle is only the latest of several edifices to occupy its location beside the River Ratty. Vikings founded a settlement here in the 10th century, and later occupants included the Norman Thomas de Clare in the 1250s. It's accessed via the folk park, a reconstructed

traditional Irish village with smoke coiling from thatched-cottage chimneys, a forge and working blacksmith, weavers, post office, grocery-pub, small cafe and more. Tickets are 10% cheaper online.

The present castle was built in 1425 by the energetic MacNamara family, falling shortly thereafter to the O'Briens, in whose possession it remained until the 17th century. Fully restored in 1954 and loaded with 14th- to 17th-century furniture, paintings, wall tapestries and antlers, the castle is home to a **dungeon**, a **main hall** and the magnificent and colossal **Great Hall**.

A few of the 30 buildings in the folk park were brought here from elsewhere, but most are recreations. In peak season, employees in period garb explain the more family-friendly and rose-tinted aspects of the late 19th century. Faux but fun.

Medieval banquets (p353) in the castle and traditional Irish evenings (p353) in the folk park's corn barn are other crowd pleasers.

📥 Sleeping & Eating

Cahergal Farmhouse
B&B €€

(📞 061-368 358; www.cahergal.com; Newmarket-on-Fergus; s/d/f from €75/100/150; 🅿🛜) At Cahergal you can wake up to the gentle clucking of chickens on a working farm. With bucolic views, floral drapes and Irish landscape prints, rooms are charmingly old-fashioned. Breakfasts are hearty and facilities include a tennis court. It's 14km northwest of Bunratty.

The owners can arrange horse riding, farm tours for guests and take kids to meet the animals.

Briar Lodge
B&B €€

(📞 061-363 388; www.briarlodgebunratty.com; Hill Rd; s/d/f from €55/75/103; 🕒mid-Mar–mid-Oct; 🅿🛜) On a very quiet and secluded cul-de-sac some 2.4km northwest of Bunratty, this traditionally styled house with a conifer-filled front garden has five pretty rooms, some with wallpaper feature walls, and welcoming, cordial owners.

Durty Nelly's
PUB FOOD €€

(📞 061-364 861; www.durtynellys.ie; Bunratty House Mews; snacks from €6, mains €14-29; 🕒kitchen noon-10pm, bar to 11.30pm) Having opened way back in 1620, mustard-yellow Durty Nelly's once served the guards at neighbouring Bunratty Castle. A warren of snugs, timber beams and peat fires, it also has an astonishing collection of badges donated by firefighters, police and service personnel from

all over the world. Impressive food includes duck breast with black cherry sauce.

Superb castle and river views extend from the upstairs terrace.

★ Gallagher's of Bunratty
SEAFOOD €€€

(📞 061-363 363; www.gallaghersofbunratty.com; Old Bunratty Rd; mains €15-40; 🕒5.30-9.30pm daily, plus 12.30-3pm Sun) Stone walls, exposed beams, timber panelling and a wood stove make this thatched cottage as enchanting inside as it is out. But the real reason to book is for some of Ireland's most magnificent seafood, such as saffron-infused John Dory with samphire, whole Dover sole, or garlicky hot buttered crab claws. The set meals (two/three courses €32/37) are excellent value.

The adjacent JP Clarke's Country Pub serves lunch and dinner daily, and has an extensive gin, whiskey and craft-beer selection.

☆ Entertainment

Irish Evening at Bunratty
LIVE PERFORMANCE

(📞 061-711 222; www.shannonheritage.com/IrishEvening; adult/child €43/35; 🕒7-9.30pm Apr-Oct) High-spirited Irish nights lift the roof of a corn barn in the folk park adjacent to Bunratty Castle. Waitstaff serve Irish classics (stews, poached salmon, apple pie) amid traditional storytelling, music and dancing, while wine gets you in the mood for the singalong.

Bunratty Castle Medieval Banquet
LIVE PERFORMANCE

(📞 061-711 222; www.bunrattycastle.ie; adult/child from €63/35; 🕒5.30pm & 8.45pm) Candlelit medieval banquets at Bunratty Castle are replete with harp-playing maidens, court jesters and meaty medieval fare (vegetarian options available) washed down with goblets of mead. The banquets are extremely popular with groups, so book well ahead.

You can often find savings online; the earlier sitting is cheaper.

❶ Getting There & Away

Bus Éireann (www.buseireann.ie) services include bus 343, which runs hourly to Ennis (€8, one hour) and Limerick (€4, 25 minutes).

Killaloe & Ballina

POP 4116

Facing each other across the River Shannon, Killaloe and Ballina are really one destination, even if they have different personalities (and counties). A fine 13-arch, one-lane bridge (1770) spans the river, linking the pair.

WORTH A TRIP

WILDE IRISH CHOCOLATES

At the heady open-plan factory of Wilde Irish Chocolates ((☑ 061-922 080; www.wildeirishchocolates.com; Tuamgraney; ⊙ by arrangement) you can watch chocolates being made and packed, and taste developmental and best-selling products (over 80 to date, including chocolate, spreads, fudges such as malted honeycomb and chocolate, and hot chocolate preparations). The factory is in the village of Tuamgraney, 16km northwest of Killaloe; call ahead to arrange a visit.

Look out for its chocolates at Killaloe's farmers market (Between the Waters; ⊙ 11am-3pm Sun), and at shops in Doolin (p373) and Limerick city.

Killaloe (Cill Da Lúa) is picturesque Clare at its finest, lying on the western banks of lower Loch Deirgeirt, the southern extension of Lough Derg, where the lough narrows at one of the crossings of the River Shannon.

Not as quaint as Killaloe, Ballina (Béal an Átha) is in County Tipperary and has some of the better pubs and restaurants. It lies at the end of a scenic drive from Nenagh along Lough Derg on the R494.

◉ Sights & Activities

Killaloe Cathedral   CHURCH
(St Flannan's Cathedral; ☑ 061-374 779; www.cathedral.killaloe.anglican.org; Royal Pde, Killaloe; tower €2; ⊙ 9am-6pm Easter-Sep, to 5pm Oct-Easter) Built by the O'Brien family on top of a 6th-century church, Killaloe Cathedral dates from the early 13th century. Astonishing carvings decorate the Romanesque southern doorway (on your right as you enter). Nearby is the c AD 1000 Thorgrim's Stone, a shaft of a stone cross unusually inscribed with both the old Scandinavian runic and Irish Ogham scripts. Other highlights include a 13th-century font.

Brian Ború Heritage Centre   MUSEUM
(☑ 061-360 788; www.discoverkillaloe.ie; Lock House, Bridge St, Killaloe; ⊙ 10am-5pm May–mid-Sep) FREE Inside the former lock keeper's cottage on the little islet Between the Waters, the Brian Ború Heritage Centre celebrates the local boy made good as the king who, according to the political spinmeisters of his time, both unified Ireland and freed it from the Vikings. Displays also illustrate the nautical heritage of the surrounding lakes and rivers.

The centre is also home to the town's tourist office (p355).

Beal Ború   HISTORIC SITE
(Brian Ború's Fort; R463, Killaloe) The remains of this early-medieval ring fort are believed by some to have been Kincora, the fabled palace of the famous Irish king Brian Ború. His forces defeated the Vikings at the Battle of Clontarf in 1014, although Ború himself was slain in the fight. Traces of Bronze Age settlement have also been discovered here. It's just over 2km north of Killaloe's town centre.

TJ's Angling Centre   FISHING
(☑ 061-376 009; www.tjsangling.com; Main St, Ballina; fishing equipment rental per day from €15; ⊙ 8am-5.30pm Mon-Sat, to 6pm Sun) TJ's rents out fishing equipment (€50 deposit required) and is a great source of advice. You can hook trout and pike right here in town, but the best fishing is from the lake; guided half-/full-day fishing trips including gear cost €120/180 for two people.

Spirit of Killaloe   CRUISE
(☑ 086 814 0559; www.killaloerivercruises.com; Lakeside Dr, Ballina; adult/child €15/8; ⊙ daily, weather permitting) Scenic hour-long cruises aboard this 50-seat boat head out on Lough Derg's peaceful waters, passing sights including Beal Ború. Advance reservations are essential.

⌱ Sleeping

B&Bs abound in the area, especially on the roads along Lough Derg. Book ahead in summer. Many places close from November to March.

Kingfisher Lodge   B&B €
(☑ 061-376 911; www.kingfisherlodge-ireland.com; Lower Ryninch, Ballina; s/d/f €50/70/105; ℗ 🛜) A bit of a rarity: a smart B&B with its own boathouse and deck beside Lough Derg. Comfy bedrooms look out onto almost a hectare of gardens, while Room 3 (with twin beds) has a full-length balcony. Smoked kippers are a highlight of the breakfast menu.

★ Kincora House   B&B €€
(☑ 061-376 149; www.kincorahouse.com; Church St, Killaloe; s/d from €50/90; ℗ 🛜) Set on a hill in the heart of Killaloe, this neat-as-a-pin townhouse was once a pub/general store. Many original features have been retained, while historic black-and-white photos of Clare decorate the walls. The heritage-style

rooms feature smart power showers, big squishy sofas and bright rugs on tile floors.

Lakeside Hotel
HOTEL €€

(☑ 061-376 122; www.lakesidehotel.ie; Lakeside Dr, Ballina; s €70, d €70-100, f from €110; [P][🛜][🏊]) With sweeping views across the water to the arched bridge and Killaloe Cathedral, this gentrified hotel is surrounded by flowering gardens. The 43 rooms vary greatly in size, shape and decor; prices work in direct ratio to the view. All let you use the fun figure-of-eight 40m-long water slide and large indoor swimming pool as well as the on-site gym.

Eating & Drinking

There are cafes, pubs and restaurants in both Killaloe and Ballina. Killaloe also has a large supermarket, and there's a 20-stall farmers market (Between the Waters; ⊘ 11am-3pm Sun) on Sundays.

★ Wooden Spoon
CAFE €

(☑ 061-622 415; Bridge St, Killaloe; dishes €4-9; ⊘ 9am-5pm; 🍴) Strewn with old cookbooks, the Wooden Spoon is so popular queues regularly stretch out the door. Savoury dishes include towering jacket potatoes stuffed with Mediterranean vegetables and goat cheese. Sweet treats take in mini-pavlovas, chocolate-and-raspberry brownies, and inspired cake combos like hazelnut-and-carrot or apple-beetroot.

Gluten-free and vegan options are plentiful; it also brews excellent Cork-roasted Badger & Dodo coffee.

Tuscany Bistro
ITALIAN €€

(☑ 061-376 888; www.tuscany.ie; Main St, Ballina; mains €14-34, pizzas €12-16; ⊘ 4-9pm Wed-Fri, 12.30-10pm Sat, 12.30-9pm Sun; 🛜🍴) The flavours of west Italy come to west Ireland in this small, stylish bistro, where the chairs are striped and timber floors gleam. The list of pastas, pizzas and expertly cooked mains is extensive; highlights include seafood risotto and the acclaimed fish stew.

A strong kids' menu (two courses €10) and high chairs make it a great choice for families.

Liam O'Riains
PUB

(☑ 087 665 8262; Main St, Ballina; ⊘ 4pm-midnight Mon-Fri, 1pm-midnight Sat & Sun; 🛜) The lively trad sessions at this much-loved, stone-fronted pub ensure it's a linchpin of the local community. The music flows from Thursday to Sunday between late April and early September, and spontaneously throughout the rest of the year.

Goosers
PUB

(☑ 061-376 791; www.goosers.ie; Main St, Ballina; ⊘ noon-10pm Mon-Sat, 12.30-9.30pm Sun) Stone floors and peat fires sit under the thatched roof of this cheerful pub on Ballina's main street. Roadside picnic tables out front are the setting for an alfresco pint with views across the river to Killaloe.

❶ Information

The **tourist office** (☑ 061-360 788; www.discover killaloe.ie; Brian Ború Heritage Centre, Bridge St, Killaloe; ⊘ 10am-5pm May–mid-Sep) shares space with the Brian Ború Heritage Centre.

❶ Getting There & Away

Both towns have parking beside the river.

Bus Éireann (www.buseireann.ie) links Killaloe and Ballina with Limerick (€6.50, 50 minutes, one to four daily, Monday to Saturday).

Mountshannon

POP 200

On the southwestern shores of Lough Derg, Mountshannon (Baile Uí Bheoláin) was founded in 1742 by an enlightened landlord to house a largely Protestant community of flax workers. The harbour hosts fishing boats and visiting yachts and cruisers in summer, and is the main launch pad for trips to Holy Island (p355), one of Clare's finest early Christian settlements.

Some fantastic fishing abounds around Mountshannon, mainly for brown trout, pike, perch and bream. Ask at your lodging about boat hire and equipment or contact TJ's Angling Centre in Ballina.

Holy Island
ISLAND

Lying 2km offshore from Mountshannon, Holy Island (Inis Cealtra) is the site of a monastic settlement thought to have been founded by St Cáimín in the 7th century. Operators who will take you over to the island include local historian Gerard Madden (☑ 086 874 9710; www.holyisland.ie; Royal Pde, Killaloe; adult/child €12/7; ⊘ by reservation Apr-Sep), who runs two-hour tours from Mountshannon's pier.

The island has a round tower over 27m tall, along with the ruins of several churches, a hermit's cell and some early Christian gravestones dating from the 8th to 12th centuries.

One of the chapels possesses an elegant Romanesque arch and, inside, an old Irish inscription that translates as 'Pray for Tornog, who made this cross'.

The Vikings treated this monastery roughly in the 9th century, but it flourished under the protection of Brian Ború and others. During the 17th century as many as 15,000 people would make Easter pilgrimages here.

🛏 Sleeping

Hawthorn Lodge
B&B €

(☎ 061-927 120; www.mountshannon-clare.com; R352; s/d from €52/75; P🕸) The welcome at this tidy, family-friendly country cottage has a genuine warmth.The three clean rooms with private bathrooms have comfy beds warmed by electric blankets. Kids under five stay free; high chairs and cots are also available.

It's just under 1km northeast of Mountshannon.

Sunrise B&B
B&B €€

(☎ 061-927 343; www.sunrisebandb.com; s/d/f from €55/75/120; 🕸) The setting alone might draw you here: sitting amid rural hills just north of Mountshannon, you can see Lough Derg and the Arra Mountains from the terrace and sunny breakfast room. Bedrooms are stylish, while owner Vera is full of useful local tips.

ℹ Getting There & Away

Mountshannon has limited public transport; Bus Éireann (www.buseireann.ie) runs one bus a week to Limerick (bus 346; €13, 1½ hours).

SOUTHWESTERN & WESTERN CLARE

Your best days in the county's west may be spent on the smallest roads you can find.

South of the plunging Cliffs of Moher to the beach resort of Kilkee, the land flattens, with vistas that sweep across pastures and dunes to the horizon. Some of Ireland's finest surf rolls in to shore near the low-key beach towns of Lahinch, Miltown Malbay and Doonbeg.

Kilkee is the main town of the Loop Head Peninsula. Beautiful and dramatic in equal measure, its soaring cliffs stretching to the lighthouse-crowned tip are major milestones on an already breathtaking shore.

Inland, don't miss the charming heritage town of Ennistimon and its surging cascades.

ℹ Getting There & Away

BOAT
Shannon Ferry Limited (☎ 065-905 3124; www.shannonferries.com; cars €20, motorcyclists,

cyclists & pedestrians €5; ⊘7am-9pm Mon-Sat, 9am-9pm Sun Jun-Aug, 7am-8pm Mon-Sat, 9am-8pm Sun Apr, May & Sep, 7am-7pm Mon-Sat, 9am-7pm Sun Oct-Mar) runs a ferry between Killimer in County Clare and Tarbert (p315) in County Kerry, departing hourly on the hour from Killimer and on the half-hour from Tarbert. Journey time is 20 minutes. It's a great shortcut, saving you 134km by road via Limerick.

BUS
Bus Éireann (www.buseireann.ie) services include Galway city to Ennis (bus 51; €9.50, 1½ hours, hourly) via Gort, and Ennis to Doolin (bus 350; €9.50, 50 minutes, five daily), via Corofin, Ennistimon, Lahinch, Liscannor and Cliffs of Moher.

Kilrush
POP 2719

Overlooking the Shannon Estuary and the hills of Kerry to the south, the lively town of Kilrush (Cill Rois) has a strikingly wide main street that reflects its origins as a port and market town in the 19th century.

From the west coast's biggest marina at Kilrush Creek, ferries run 3km offshore to Scattery Island, home to magnificent early Christian ruins. Cruises also depart from the marina to view bottlenose dolphins living in the estuary, which is an important calving region for the mammals.

◉ Sights & Activities

A 1.5km signposted walking trail, the **Dolphin Trail**, leads west from Kilrush's central square and is dotted with information panels, sculptures and murals.

★ Vandeleur Walled Garden
GARDENS

(☎ 065-905 1760; www.vandeleurwalledgarden.ie; Killimer Rd; ⊘10am-5pm Tue-Sat) FREE Within a 170-hectare forest 800m south of the centre, this stunning 'lost' garden was the private domain of the Vandeleur family – merchants and landowners who engaged in harsh evictions and forced emigration of local people in the 19th century. Today woodland trails wind around the surrounding forest, which has a colourful array of plants, including magnolias, acacias, acers, monkey puzzle trees, bamboo, banana trees, hydrangeas and a beech maze.

The Woodland Bistro rustles up tasty snacks, often using ingredients grown on the site.

Shannon Dolphin Centre
MUSEUM

(www.shannondolphins.ie; Merchants Quay; ⊘10am-6pmMay–mid-Sep) FREE The 170-plus bottlenose

SCATTERY ISLAND

The uninhabited, windswept and treeless Scattery Island (☑ 087 995 8427; www.heritage ireland.ie; ⊙ visitor centre 10am-6pm late May-late Sep), in the estuary 3km southwest of Kilrush, was the site of a Christian settlement founded by St Senan in the 6th century. Its 36m-high round tower, the best preserved in Ireland, has its entrance at ground level instead of the usual position high above the foundation. The evocative ruins of six medieval churches include the 9th-century **Cathedral of St Mary** (Teampall Naomh Mhuire) – part of **St Senan's Monastery**.

Also here are a **lighthouse** and an **artillery battery**, built during the Napoleonic wars, at the southern end of the island. A free exhibition on the history and wildlife of the Heritage Service–administered island is housed in the Scattery Island Visitor Centre. The centre also provides free 45-minute tours to St Senan's Monastery.

Scattery Island Ferries (☑ 085 250 5512; www.scatteryislandtours.com; adult/child return €20/10; ⊙ late May-Aug) runs boats from Kilrush to the island; the journey takes 15 to 20 minutes. There's no strict timetable as the trips are subject to tidal and weather conditions, but there are usually two sailings a day between June and September. Time spent on the island is usually between two and five hours. Buy tickets at the small kiosk at **Kilrush Marina** (☑ 065-905 2072; www.kilrushmarina.ie; Kilrush Creek) and bring a decent pair of walking shoes.

dolphins swimming out in the Shannon are monitored by this dedicated research facility. In addition to learning about its latest work, you can listen to acoustic recordings and watch a 20-minute film about the playful cetaceans, a population unique to the area.

West Clare Railway
RAIL
(☑ 087 791 9289; www.westclarerailway.ie; N67; steam ticket adult/child €15/8, diesel €10/5; ⊙ 1-4pm May-Sep, days vary) A 2km vestige of the historic West Clare Railway line survives near Moyasta, 5km northwest of Kilrush. A beautiful steam-powered train was privately restored by Jackie Whelan, who now runs occasional Steam and Diesel Days, when the train shuttles back and forth over the open land. Call ahead for the schedule.

Dolphin Discovery
CRUISE
(☑ 065-905 1327; www.discoverdolphins.ie; Kilrush Marina; adult/child €26/14; ⊙ late May–mid-Oct) These two-hour boat rides on the Shannon offer plenty of dolphin-spotting opportunities. Trips depart depending on weather and demand.

🛏 Sleeping & Eating

Kilrush has a hostel, pub accommodation and several B&Bs. There are also good options in Kilkee, 14km northwest.

Cafes are scattered throughout town; pubs also serve food. Self-caterers will find supermarkets as well as a weekly farmers' market on the main square.

Katie O'Connor's Holiday Hostel
HOSTEL €
(☑ 065-905 1133; www.katieshostel.com; 50 Frances St; dm/d/tr from €22/40/50; ⊙ mid-Mar–Oct; 🐾) Dating from the 18th century, this tall townhouse once belonged to the powerful Vandeleur family. Today it's a well-equipped IHH-affiliated hostel with clean dorms and private rooms with bathrooms.

Other bonuses include a barbecue and picnic tables, plus bike storage. Bike hire costs €15 per day.

Potter's Hand
CAFE €
(☑ 065-905 2968; 3 Vandeleur St; dishes €3-8; ⊙ 9am-5pm Tue-Sat, to 4.30pm Mon; 🚲🍴) The Potter's Hand is the kind of calm, cool cafe you wish was on your own doorstep. Shelves stacked with books sit beside counters showcasing crumbly fruit scones and homemade treats: coffee and walnut, and plum and polenta cakes, and nutty protein balls.

Buttermarket Cafe
CAFE €
(☑ 065-905 1822; Burton St; mains €5-12; ⊙ 10am-4pm Mon-Thu, to 5pm Fri & Sat, 11am-4pm Sun; 🐾) A courtyard that's a sun trap in fine weather might draw you here. That or hot specials including stews and shepherd's pie, or drinks spanning salted caramel lattes, cinnamon hot chocolates, and mint-mocha frappuccinos.

Crotty's
PUB
(☑ 065-905 2470; www.crottyspubkilrush.com; Market Sq; ⊙ 9am-11.30pm Sun-Fri, to 12.30am Sat; 🐾) Crotty's brims with character, thanks to an old-fashioned high bar, intricately tiled

DON'T MISS

CLARE'S OTHER CLIFFS

On the way to and from the southern tip of Loop Head, take in the jaw-dropping sea vistas and drama of the sensational cliffs along the coast roads.

Heading west, from Carrigaholt drive south down central Church St for around 2km till you reach a junction with brown Loop Head Drive signs pointing right. This scenic route is the Coast Rd (L2002). It bounces beside a rocky shore, past reed beds and alongside green fields, offering splendid panoramas of the sea. It runs through the village of Rhinevilla, eventually rejoining the R487 at Kilbaha before surging onto the lighthouse at Loop Head.

Heading east from Loop Head Lighthouse, drive back along the R487 for a few minutes until signs point left along another Coast Rd (L2000). From here you make your way to Kilkee. You'll rejoin the R487 but can head north again along small roads north from just after either Oughterard or Cross for stunning views of soaring coastal cliffs.

floors and a series of snugs decked out with retro furnishings. Trad sessions take place at 9.30pm on Tuesday and Wednesday; less traditional bands play most weekends.

Crotty's serves basic pub fare (mains €10 to €22), and has five heritage-style guest rooms upstairs (doubles from €85).

❶ Getting There & Around

Bus Éireann has four buses Monday to Saturday and two on Sunday to Ennis (bus 336; €13, one hour) and Kilkee (€4.70, 15 minutes).

Hardware shop and garden centre Gleeson's (☑ 065-905 1127; www.irishlandmark.com; 2-4 Henry St; bike rental per day/week from €15/70; ⊘ 9am-5pm Mon-Sat) rents out bikes.

Loop Head Peninsula

A sliver of land between the Shannon Estuary and the pounding Atlantic, windblown Loop Head Peninsula has an ends-of-the-earth feel. As you approach along the R487, sea begins to appear on both flanks as land tapers to a narrow shelf. On a clear day, the lighthouse-capped headland at Loop Head (Ceann Léime), Clare's southernmost point, has staggering views to counties Kerry and Galway. The often-deserted wilds of the head are perfect for exploration, but be extra careful near the cliff edge.

On the northern side of the cliff near the point, a dramatic crevice has been cleaved into the coastal cliffs where you'll first hear and then see a teeming bird-breeding area. Guillemots, choughs and razorbills are among the squawkers nesting in the rocky niches.

A long hiking trail runs along the cliffs to the peninsula's main town, Kilkee. A handful of other tiny settlements dot the peninsula. The website www.loophead.ie is an excellent source of local information.

◉ Sights & Activities

Loop Head Lighthouse   LIGHTHOUSE
(www.loophead.ie; Loop Head; adult/child €5/2; ⊘ 10am-6pm mid-Mar–early Nov) On a 90m-high cliff, this 23m-tall working lighthouse, complete with a Fresnel lens, rises up above Loop Head. Guided tours (included in admission) take you up the tower and onto the balcony – in fine weather you can see as far as the Blasket Islands and Connemara. There's been a lighthouse here since 1670; the present structure dates from 1854. It was converted to electricity in 1871 and automated in 1991.

It's possible to stay at the neighbouring former lighthouse keeper's cottage.

**★Loop Head
Summer Hedge School**   ARTS & CRAFTS
(☑ 086 819 7726; www.carmeltmadigan.com; Cross Village; per 1/2/3/4 days €75/100/270/310; ⊘ early Jul–mid-Aug) Occasional seashore safaris (adult/family €20/60) feature among the acclaimed courses led by local artist, writer and naturalist Carmel Madigan. They'll see you immersed in the landscape and developing new skills and knowledge encompassing everything from stone art and paintings to habitats, seaweed and sealife.

Loop Head Walking Tours   WALKING
(☑ 086 826 0987; www.loopheadwalkingtours.ie; from €25; ⊘ by request) Friendly local expert Martin runs guided walks around the peninsula's cliffs and lanes, ranging from a couple of hours to a half-day hike to Loop Head Lighthouse itself. Email ahead to see if there's room on a tour.

Dolphinwatch   CRUISE
(☑ 065-905 8156; www.dolphinwatch.ie; The Square, Carrigaholt; tours adult/child €35/20; ⊘ Apr-Oct) Some 200 resident bottlenose dolphins frolic in the Shannon Estuary; they're

best encountered on Dolphinwatch's two-hour cruises, on which you might also see minke and fin whales in autumn. Sailings depend on tides and weather conditions. Boats depart from Carrigaholt's Castle Pier; it's best to park by Dolphinwatch's booking office a few hundred metres away, as accessing the pier itself by car is tricky.

Dolphinwatch also runs Loop Head sunset cruises and geology tours.

Sleeping & Eating

Pure Camping CAMPGROUND €
(☑ 065-905 7953; www.purecamping.ie; Querrin; pitches per 2 adults €24, bell tents €60-85, cabins €90-105; ⊗ May-Sep) It's luxury all the way at this boutique campsite tucked in among the Loop Head fields. To spacious pitches, furnished canvas bell tents and four-person wooded cabins, add yoga classes, a pizza oven and a sauna. And all just a 15-minute walk from the sea.

★ **Loop Head Lighthouse Keeper's Cottage** COTTAGE €€
(☑ 01-670 4733; www.irishlandmark.com; Loop Head; 2 nights €460-548) Staying at the former Loop Head Lighthouse keeper's home gives you a real feel for what life was once like out here. Managed by the Irish Landmark Trust, the 19th-century cottage sleeps five, and has no TV or wi-fi – all the better then for enjoying the radio, books, board games and warming wood stove. There's also central heating and a fully kitted-out kitchen. The minimum stay is two nights.

★ **Long Dock** SEAFOOD €€
(☑ 065-905 8106; www.thelongdock.com; West St, Carrigaholt; mains €12-25; ⊗ 11am-9pm, closed Mon-Wed Nov-Feb) With stone walls and floors, and a roaring fire, this treasure of a pub has a seriously good kitchen. Seafood is the order of the day – you'll see the folks who work out in the estuary drinking at the bar. Specialities include Loop Head monkfish, Carrigaholt crab, Shannon Estuary sea bass and house-cured salmon, along with sensational chowder.

Shopping

Kilbaha Gallery & Crafts ARTS & CRAFTS
(☑ 065-905 8843; www.kilbahagallery.com; R487, Kilbaha; ⊗ 10am-6pm daily Mar-Sep, Sat & Sun Oct-Dec; 🐾) Paintings, sculptures, photography, crafts, books and postcards at this delightful shop are all made by local artists. Up the back, its little light-filled cafe (dishes from €3) serves fantastic coffee, cakes, scones with homemade jam and freshly churned cream, herbal teas and warming hot chocolate.

ⓘ Getting There & Around

Regular buses serve Kilkee, but there is no public transport elsewhere on the peninsula.

If you want to explore the peninsula by bike, hire cycles from Gleeson's (☑ 065-905 1127; 2-4 Henry St; bike rental per day/week from €15/70; ⊗ 9am-5pm Mon-Sat) in Kilrush.

Kilkee
POP 972
The Loop Head Peninsula's main town, Kilkee (Cill Chaoi), sits on a sweeping semicircular bay with high cliffs on the northern end and weathered rocks to the south.

St George's Head, to the north, has good cliff walks and scenery. South of the bay, reached by the coastal path from Kilkee's West End area, **Duggerna Rocks** form an unusual natural amphitheatre, with natural swimming pools known as the **Pollock Holes**. Further south is a huge sea cave.

Kilkee first became popular in Victorian times when rich families built seaside retreats here. Its wide golden beach gets thronged in warmer months. The waters are highly tidal, with wide-open sandy expanses replaced by pounding waves in just a few hours.

Nevsail Watersports ADVENTURE SPORTS
(☑ 086 330 8236; www.nevsailwatersports.ie; Seafront; adult/child per 2hr from €35/30) A pop-up unit beside the lifeguard's hut on Kilkee seafront is the base for a wealth of kayak and stand-up paddleboard (SUP) sessions, plus coasteering and snorkelling combo tours.

Sleeping

Kilkee has plenty of guesthouses and B&Bs, though during the high season rates can soar and you may have a problem finding a vacancy if you haven't booked ahead. Closures are common in winter.

Stella Maris Hotel HOTEL €€
(☑ 065-905 6455; www.stellamarishotel.com; O'Connell St; s/d/tr/f from €95/110/170/190; 🐾) Follow the red tartan carpet to 20 contemporary rooms in an old cherry-coloured building in Kilkee's heart. Local producers, including the butcher run by the same family, supply its excellent restaurant (mains €8 to €26), which is warmed by an open fire.

A few rooms have sea views; request one when you book.

Strand Guest House
INN €€

(☑065-905 6177; www.thestrandkilkee.com; Strand; s/d/tr from €80/98/135; ☺Feb-Oct; ☏) The Strand is aptly named: it's directly across from the beach with superb views of the sand. The six bedrooms are simply decorated, but cheerful and well maintained. Views also extend from its inviting bistro-bar.

Surprising fact: Che Guevara stayed here in 1961.

✖ Eating & Drinking

Kilkee is well known for its seafood, served at some excellent cafes, pubs and restaurants throughout town. A small farmers market (☑086 823 5598; O'Connell St; ☺10am-2pm Sun May-Sep) sets up in the public car park on O'Curry St each Sunday.

★ Diamond Rocks Cafe
CAFE €

(☑086 372 1063; www.diamondrockscafe.com; West End; dishes €6-14; ☺10am-5pm) Before heading off on a cliff walk, fuel up at this contemporary cafe opening to a huge terrace at the water's edge. Food is well above the norm for places found in stunning spots, and encompasses daily changing specials such as asparagus and goat's cheese quiche, and Guinness beef stew.

It's set at the far western end of the coast road that hugs Kilkee's shore.

★ Murphy Blacks
IRISH €€

(BiaBaile; ☑085 875 4886; www.murphyblacks.ie; The Square; mains €17-25; ☺6-9pm Tue-Sat) The county's produce stars on Murphy Blacks' menu: Clare lamb cooked in cider and cream; Loop Head crab hotpot; St Tola goat's cheese tart. It's regularly booked out, so reserve. Tables outside are a summer-night treat.

Pantry
CAFE €€

(☑065-905 6576; www.pantrykilkee.ie; O'Curry St; mains €9-18; ☺8.30am-6pm Easter-Sep; ☑) A former home-economics teacher gets top marks for this cafe-bakery, where breakfast features organic porridge with cinnamon stewed apricots, lunch brings tiger prawn sandwiches on treacle bread, and afternoons usher in belt-busting carrot cake.

Ask about a program of cooking classes in winter; they cover gluten-free food, baking and family meals.

Strand Bistro & Cafe
BISTRO €€

(☑065-905 6177; www.thestrandkilkee.com; Strand; mains €8-26; ☺9am-5pm Mon, 11am-10pm Wed-Sun Easter-Sep, 6-10pm Fri, noon-4pm & 6-10pm Sat, noon-4pm Sun Oct-Easter) Feel the sea spray on your face at the outside tables of this friendly beach cafe, bar and bistro. Dishes range from seafood chowder, fish and chips, and gourmet burgers, to linguine with red pesto and prawns. It also has a decent wine list and some fine old whiskeys. Upstairs are six well-maintained guest rooms.

Naughton's Bar
PUB

(☑086 649 3307; www.naughtonsbar.com; 45 O'Curry St; ☺noon-midnight Sun-Thu, 10am-2am Fri & Sat Easter-Sep, 5pm-midnight Fri-Sun Oct-Easter) Dating from 1856, today Naughton's combines a traditional pub, a contemporary cocktail bar and a buzzing pavement terrace, making it a focal point for Kilkee nightlife.

Cracking pub fare (mains €16 to €25) includes plenty of seafood such as Guinness-battered monkfish or garlic-laced west Clare crab claws – book ahead for dinner.

ⓘ Getting There & Away

Bus Éireann (www.buseireann.ie) has two to five buses daily to Ennis (bus 336; €17, one hour) via Kilrush (€6, 15 minutes).

Kilkee to Ennistimon

North of Kilkee the land flattens, with vistas that sweep across pastures and dunes. The N67 runs inland for some 32km until it reaches Quilty. Take the occasional lane to the west and search out unfrequented places such as White Strand, north of Doonbeg. **Ballard Bay** is 8km west of Doonbeg, where an old telegraph tower looks over some fine cliffs, while the remains of a promontory fort can be found at **Donegal Point**. There's good fishing all along the coast, and safe beaches at Seafield, Lough Donnell and Quilty. Off the coast of Quilty, look for **Mutton Island**, a barren expanse that once served as a prison, sporting an ancient tower and fantastic views.

Doonbeg
POP 262

Doonbeg (An Dún Beag) is a tiny seaside village 11km northeast of Kilkee. A Spanish Armada ship, the *San Esteban,* was wrecked on 20 September 1588 near the mouth of the River Doonbeg. The survivors were later executed at Spanish Point, near Miltown Malbay. It was one of many Spanish ships in the area to meet such a fate. Doonbeg offers some decent surfing for those who want to flee the Lahinch crowds, but there are no rental shops or surf schools based here.

White Strand
BEACH

(Killard Rd) Secluded White Strand (Trá Ban) offers relatively safe swimming sheltered from the Atlantic swells. With a Blue Flag rating, the 250m beach is patrolled by lifeguards in summer. It's 4km northwest of the village. Clare Kayak Hire (⏰085 148 5856; www.clare kayakhire.com; White Strand; kayak rental per hr from €15, tours from €35; ⏱10am-5pm Sat & Sun May, 9am-6pm Jun-Aug) sets up here from May to August.

Doonbeg Castle
RUINS

The ruined 16th-century tower next to the stone bridge over the River Doonbeg is all that remains of Doonbeg Castle – its entire garrison was hanged in 1595 by the O'Briens, who had lost the castle 10 years earlier.

Doughmore Bay
BEACH

A long, sweeping 2km stretch of golden sand, Doughmore Bay is 4km north of the village. There's often good surf here; rent equipment in Lahinch.

Its southern end, behind the dunes, is dominated by Trump International Golf Links.

Morrissey's
INN €€

(⏰065-905 5304; www.morrisseysdoonbeg.com; Main St; s/d from €70/110; ⏱late Mar-Oct; 🎧) Stylish Morrissey's is a coastal haven, a riverside pub with six elegant rooms featuring king-size beds and large soaking tubs. Its restaurant (6pm to 9pm Wednesday to Sunday; 12.30pm to 2pm Sunday) is renowned for gastropub fare (mains €16 to €24), especially seafood from homemade scampi to succulent Doonbeg crab claws. It has a scenic terrace.

Miltown Malbay

POP 829

Miltown Malbay has a thriving music scene and hosts the annual Willie Clancy Summer School, one of Ireland's great traditional music events. The town was a favoured resort for well-to-do Victorians, though it isn't actually on the sea: the beach is 2km southwest at Spanish Point.

An Ghiolla Finn Gift Shop (⏰065-708 5107; Main St; ⏱10.30am-5pm Mon-Sat mid-Mar–Oct) doubles as the tourist office. It also opens on some summer Sundays.

Spanish Point
BEACH

With dazzling views of the setting sun, this lovely beach also offers excellent walks north of the point amid the low cliffs, vast ledges of stone, rock pools, coves and isolated beaches.

CLARE'S BEST MUSIC FESTIVAL

....

Miltown Malbay's tribute to native son Willie Clancy, one of Ireland's greatest pipers, is one of the best traditional-music festivals in the country. During the nine-day Willie Clancy Summer School (⏰065-708 4148; www.scoilsamhraidh willieclancy.com; ⏱Jul), which usually begins in the first or second week of July, impromptu sessions occur day and night and the town pubs are packed. Workshops and classes underpin the event.

★ Coast Lodge
INN €€

(⏰065-708 5687; www.coastlodge.ie; R482, Spanish Point; d/f/apt from €126/136/140; 🅿🎧) Opposite the beach at Spanish Point, this beautifully appointed inn has luxurious rooms overlooking the ocean or adjacent golf course. Although the cottage-style apartments don't have standout views, they come with spacious lounges, full kitchens, laundries and patios with picnic tables.

Craft beers are served at the piano bar; the attached restaurant (mains €14 to €17) serves upmarket, seafood-focused bistro fare.

Old Bake House
BISTRO €€

(⏰065-708 4350; www.theoldbakehouse.ie; Main St; mains lunch €5-14, dinner €17-27; ⏱noon-9pm Sun-Thu, to 10pm Fri & Sat, reduced winter hours) Blackboard menus line the walls at the Old Bake House, which serves light dishes like soup and open sandwiches at lunch and dinner mains including salmon with creamed leek, and Moroccan spiced chicken. Live music plays on Fridays and Saturdays from 7pm.

Hillery's
PUB

(⏰065-708 4188; Main St; ⏱3pm-1am) Opened in 1891, Miltown Malbay's oldest pub has stained-glass windows and framed photos on the walls. Live trad sessions take place every weekend year-round and most nights in summer. Its Facebook page features updates on upcoming gigs.

Friel's Bar
PUB

(Lynch's; ⏰065-708 5883; Mullagh Rd; ⏱6pm-midnight Mon-Thu, to 1am Fri & Sat, 2pm-midnight Sun) This old-style charmer has walls crammed with photos and books, and regular trad sessions most nights in summer and on Friday, Saturday and Sunday evenings in winter.

Although called Friel's, the sign for Lynch's, picked out in black text on a white background, is much bigger.

SURF'S UP!

Like swells after a storm, Clare's surfing scene keeps getting bigger and better. On weekends in Lahinch the exposed beach break, with both left-hand and right-hand waves, attracts hundreds of surfers.

Conditions are excellent for much of the year, with the bay's cliffs funnelling regular and reliable sets. Beginners will find the northern end gentler. Watch out for rocks and rips.

There are plenty of surf shops where you can rent gear and get lessons from around €35 per two-hour session. Board and (much-needed) wetsuit rental starts at €20 for two hours.

As the waters fill in Lahinch, surfers are seeking out less crowded spots along the coast such as Doonbeg and Fanore.

ℹ️ Getting There & Away

Bus Éireann (www.buseireann.ie) bus 333 runs once a day, Monday to Saturday, north and south along the coast, taking in Spanish Point beach (€3, five minutes), and heading inland to Ennis (€15, 1¼ hours).

Lahinch

POP 638

On protected Liscannor Bay, Lahinch (Leacht Uí Chonchubhair; often spelt 'Lehinch' on road signs) has long owed its living to beach-seeking summer tourists and visitors to venerable Lahinch Golf Club, which dates from the 19th century and remains one of the country's finest.

More recently this old holiday town has become one of the epicentres of Ireland's burgeoning surfing scene. Surf schools and stores cluster near the seafront.

🏃 Activities

⭐ **Lahinch Golf Club**   GOLF

(065-708 1003; www.lahinchgolf.com; green fees May-Sep Old Course €230, Castle Course €40, cheaper rates Oct-Apr) First marked out through the dunes in 1892 by British Army officers of the Black Watch Regiment, Lahinch's renowned par-72 Old Course was designed by Old Tom Morris in 1894, and reworked by Alister MacKenzie in the 1920s, then by Martin Hawtree in 1999. The flatter par-70 Castle Course overlooks ruined Dough Castle.

Goats have roamed the fairways since the early 20th century, when their ancestors belonged to a local caddie. They act as a barometer of sorts: when they're out in the dunes, conditions are favourable, but if you see them around the clubhouse, adverse weather is likely on its way.

⭐ **Wild Kitchen**   WALKING

(087 687 7890; www.wildkitchen.ie; €30; ⊙ hours vary) For forager Oonagh a walk on the shore or hills is like a stroll down a supermarket isle. On these two-hour walks you'll learn about incredible edibles such as seaweeds dilisk and truffle of the sea, and wild treats such as watercress, pignuts and samphire. Places are limited; book well in advance.

Dive Academy Scuba School   DIVING

(085 725 7260; www.diveacademy.info; Promenade; pool/ocean dives incl gear from €35/45; ⊙ by reservation) Learn to scuba dive in this PADI-accredited dive school's 170,000L aquarium tank (€85) or join open water and shore dives, classes and courses, including the day-long Try Ocean Diving (€130).

You can warm up in the academy's hot showers, sauna and steam room afterwards.

Green Room   SURFING

(086 142 2988; www.thegreenroom.ie; Marine Pde; per 2hr €35; ⊙ 9am-5.30pm) Shop for surf gear, clothing and accessories, rent boards (€15/20 per two hours/day) and wetsuits (€10/15), or learn to ride the waves with Green Room's surf school (two hours €35).

Bodyboard (€10/15) and stand-up paddleboard (€15/20) hire is also available.

Clare Surf Safari   SURFING

(087 634 5469; www.claresurfsafari.com; ⊙ by reservation) Mobile operator Clare Surf Safari picks you up in its van from your accommodation and takes you to the Clare beaches with the best conditions of the day. Lessons, including transport, cost €40/70 per two hours/full day. Book ahead as the van only carries five people.

Lahinch Surf School   SURFING

(087 960 9667; www.lahinchsurfschool.com; Promenade; per 2hr €35; ⊙ by reservation mid-Jan–Nov) Champion surfer John McCarthy offers lessons ranging in duration from two hours up to various multiday packages.

Ben's Surf Clinic SURFING
(☑086 844 8622; www.benssurfclinic.com; Promenade; ⊙9am-9pm Apr-Sep, 10am-4pm Oct-Mar) Ben's runs lessons (per two hours €35) and rents out boards and wetsuits (two hours €20). You can also rent stand-up paddleboards and kayaks (each €25 for two hours including wetsuits).

It also organises rock-climbing trips in the Burren (€35 for two hours), with access to hundreds of crags.

🍴 Sleeping & Eating

Atlantic Hotel HOTEL €€
(☑065-708 1049; www.atlantichotel.ie; Main St; d from €100; ⓢ) In the bedrooms at the grand old Atlantic you're likely to find mini-chandeliers and leather-topped desks that'd be right at home in a well-established bank. It's more peaceful than many places as it doesn't accept hen and stag parties, but there can occasionally be a little bar noise.

O'Looneys IRISH €€
(☑065-708 1414; www.olooneys.ie; Promenade; mains €10-20; ⊙kitchen 11am-9pm mid-Mar–Oct) The best views of Lahinch's pounding breaks and spectacular sunsets are from the terrace at this contemporary dual-level bar, cafe and club. Decent pub classics range from chowder to fish and chips, burgers and steaks.

★**Barrtrá**
Seafood Restaurant SEAFOOD €€€
(☑065-708 1280; www.barrtra.com; off N67; mains €27; ⊙5.30-9pm Wed-Sat, noon-7pm Sun May-Sep, 5.30-9pm Fri & Sat, noon-7pm Sun Oct-Apr; ☑) 🌱 The kitchen gardens surrounding this whitewashed country cottage provide ingredients for exquisite dishes such as fennel-stuffed plaice with shellfish bisque. Views over the pastures to the sea unfold from the beautiful glass conservatory dining room. Its five-course surprise menu (€50; vegetarian €45) is a fantastic feast. Barrtrá is also open for lunch (12.30pm to 4.30pm) daily in July and August.

It's some 5km south of Lahinch.

🛍 Shopping

Lahinch Surf Shop SPORTS & OUTDOORS
(☑065-708 1543; www.lahinchsurfshop.com; Promenade; ⊙11am-5pm Tue-Sun) In a dramatic surfside location, Lahinch Surf Shop sells boards, clothing and accessories.

Lahinch Bookshop BOOKS
(☑065-708 1300; Main St; ⊙9.30am-6pm Wed-Sat, 10.30am-6pm Sun) Lahinch Bookshop stocks hiking maps for the nearby Burren, as well as fiction and nonfiction for when the swell's not running.

❶ Getting There & Away

Bus Éireann (www.buseireann.ie) bus 350 runs four times daily to the following destinations:
Doolin €5, 25 minutes
Ennis €10, 35 minutes
Ennistimon €2.40, five minutes
Galway €19, 2½ hours

Bus 333 runs once a day, Monday to Saturday, south along the coast to Doonbeg (€9.50, 55 minutes).

Ennistimon

POP 1045

One of Clare's most charming market towns, Ennistimon (Inis Díomáin; sometimes spelt Ennistymon) has a postcard-perfect main street lined with brightly coloured shopfronts and traditional pubs that host fantastic trad sessions throughout the year. From the roaring Cascades (p363), the stepped falls on the River Inagh, there are picturesque walks downstream.

★**Cascades** WATERFALL
Best seen by walking through the arch by Byrne's Inn, Ennistimon's cascades are quite a sight after heavy rain when they surge, beer-brown foaming, and you risk getting drenched on windy days in the flying drizzle. Beyond the cascades, a pretty riverside walk takes you beyond the Falls Hotel.

Courthouse Studios & Gallery ARTS CENTRE
(☑065-707 1630; www.thecourthousegallery.com; Parliament St; ⊙noon-5pm Tue-Sat May-Sep, to 4pm Nov-May) FREE Rotating exhibitions from local and international artists are displayed over two floors of these studios, which are located in a renovated 19th-century courthouse.

🍴 Sleeping & Eating

The town features some superb eateries, with restaurants and cafes congregating along Main St. The farmers market (Market Sq; ⊙10am-2pm Sat) sets up weekly on Market Sq.

★**Byrne's Inn** INN €€
(☑065-707 1080; www.byrnes-ennistymon.ie; Main St; d from €105; ⓟⓢ) Facing Main St out front and the rushing waters of the town's Cascades out back, this historic guesthouse has one of Ennistimon's most colourful

ⓘ THE ATM HUNT

It's easy to get caught cashless in western Clare. Many small towns are ATM-free zones, so stock up with money when you can. You'll find ATMs in Ennistimon, Kilkee, Kilrush and Lahinch.

facades, in vibrant shades of violet, orange, aqua and sky-blue. Up the steep stairs are six large, stylish, contemporary rooms – some with Cascades views.

Downstairs, its restaurant (mains lunch €5-16, dinner €8-24; ⊙ 10am-9pm, closed Mon Oct-Mar) is the town's best.

Falls Hotel   HOTEL €€
(☑ 065-707 1004; www.fallshotel.ie; off N67; s/d/f/tr €100/150/190/225; P ⑤ ≋) Built on the ruins of an O'Brien castle on the western edge of town, the vast, Georgian Falls Hotel was once the family home of Caitlín MacNamara, who married Dylan Thomas. Today it houses a large indoor pool, a spa and 142 modern rooms overlooking the rushing River Inagh and 20 hectares of wooded grounds.

Self-catering apartments sleeping two people start at €235; cots and high chairs are available.

★Cheese Press   DELI €
(☑ 085 760 7037; Main St; ⊙ 8am-6pm Mon-Sat) Everything you need for a riverside picnic or a packed lunch for a Burren hike is on offer at this enticing deli. Organic Irish cheeses include St Tola Irish goat cheese (p366), Abbey Brie, Ballyhooly Blue, Burren Gold, Smoked Gubbeen and Bay Lough Cheddar. It also has smoked salmon and hams, relishes and house-baked bread, and the best coffee in town.

Oh La La   CRÊPES €
(☑ 065-707 2500; Parliament St; galettes €6-13, crêpes €3.50-8; ⊙ 10am-5pm Mon-Sat, 11am-5pm Sun; ☑⌖) At this brightly coloured little crêperie, savoury buckwheat galettes include Clonakilty black pudding with apple compote and crème fraiche, and Burren smoked salmon with capers and leeks. Sweet crêpes span chestnut cream with honey-roasted cashews to white chocolate with rhubarb jam.

🍷 Drinking & Nightlife

Ennistimon's wonderful old pubs are a highlight of a visit. Trad sessions take place most nights in summer and regularly throughout the rest of the year.

★Eugene's   PUB
(☑ 065-707 1777; Main St; ⊙ 10.30am-11.30pm Mon-Thu, to 12.30am Fri & Sat, 12.30-11pm Sun) Hand-painted timber panels, including portraits of James Joyce and the cast of cult TV show *Father Ted* (who drank here during filming), frame the extraordinary facade of this treasure of a pub. Intimate and cosy, the interior has a great whiskey collection, vintage trad-festival posters and some fab stained glass. Trad music plays at least several times a week year-round.

Cooley's House   PUB
(☑ 065-707 1712; Main St; ⊙ 10.30am-11.30pm Mon-Thu, to 12.30am Fri & Sat, noon-11pm Sun) Trad musicians perform most nights in summer and several nights a week in winter at this sociable and low-ceilinged old pub.

🛍 Shopping

★Irish Hand Weaves   ARTS & CRAFTS
(☑ 087 648 5937; www.irishhandweaves.ie; Main St; ⊙ 10am-5pm Tue-Fri, 11am-5pm Sat, to 4pm Sun) You'll likely find weaver Jean Moran behind her loom in this studio-workshop, surrounded by her creations. Browse local craftspeople's work, or learn the skills yourself in her spinning and weaving taster sessions (from €30).

ⓘ Getting There & Away

Bus Éireann (www.buseireann.ie) bus 350 runs four times daily to the following destinations:
Doolin €5, 30 minutes
Ennis €8.50, 30 minutes
Galway €19, 2½ hours
Lahinch €2.40, five minutes

Liscannor & Around

POP 113

The small seaside village of Liscannor (Lios Ceannúir) looks out over Liscannor Bay southeast towards Lahinch. There are no sights as such, but it's a pretty spot to stop and has a couple of excellent pubs.

Liscannor has given its name to a type of local slate-like rippled stone used for floors, walls and even roofs.

Atlantic View   B&B €
(☑ 065-708 1214; www.accommodation-cliffs-of-moher.com; s/d/f €45/60/90; P ⑤) There's a

country-cottage feel to the rooms at this prim-rose-yellow B&B set in farmland 5km north of Liscannor. Floral prints grace sea-view bedrooms, stately furniture fills the lounge and home-baked bread appears at breakfast time.

Cliffs of Moher Hotel HOTEL €€
(☑ 065-708 1924; www.cliffsofmoherhotel.com; Main St; d €150-190, f from €170; P 🛜) Although 6km southeast of the cliffs' visitor centre (p366), this spiffing hotel is handily sited at the southern end of the Cliffs of Moher Coastal Walk. Its 23 rooms have memory-foam mattresses, Nespresso machines and original Irish art on the walls. Some have balconies with cracking views over Liscannor Bay.

Trad sessions play regularly (nightly in summer) at its bar, which serves quality local gastropub fare (mains €15 to €25).

Vaughan's Anchor Inn SEAFOOD €€
(☑ 065-708 1548; www.vaughans.ie; Main St; mains €16-30; ⊙ kitchen noon-9pm daily, bar 11am-midnight Mon-Sat, to 11pm Sun Easter-Oct, winter hours vary) Superb seafood is the centrepiece at this elegant pub-restaurant, but it also serves flavoursome roasted venison and beef. When it rains, you can settle by the peat fire; when it shines (sometimes 15 minutes later), you can take in the air at a picnic table.

Vaughan's also has compact but smart rooms (doubles from €105).

Joseph McHugh's Bar PUB
(☑ 065-708 1106; www.josephmchughspub.ie; Main St; ⊙ 11am-11.30pm Mon-Thu, to 12.30am Fri & Sat, to 11pm Sun) Lots of courtyard tables, County Clare–brewed craft beers from Western Herd Brewing Company, excellent pizzas (from €13) served to 9pm and regular trad sessions give this beautiful old timber-lined pub considerable appeal.

Cliffs of Moher

In good visibility, the Cliffs of Moher (Aillte an Mothair, or Ailltreacha Mothair) are staggeringly beautiful. The entirely vertical cliffs rise to a height of 214m, their edge abruptly falling away into a ceaselessly churning Atlantic.

In a progression of vast heads, the dark sandstone and siltstone strata march in a rigid formation. Views stretch to the Aran Islands and the hills of Connemara. Sunsets here see the sky turn a kaleidoscope of amber, amethyst, rose pink and deep garnet red.

ⓘ DODGING THE CROWDS AT THE CLIFFS OF MOHER

As with many dramatic natural sights, lots of people (naturally) want to visit. Luckily it really is possible to dodge the coach-party crowds.

Board a Boat Yes, you're still surrounded by people, but seeing the 214m cliffs from the bottom makes the crowds feel small. Book trips from nearby Doolin.

Hike from Doolin It takes 2½ hours minimum to walk from Doolin along difficult, exposed trails. But if you're fit and have the right kit, you'll love it.

Moher Walk Another challenging hike for the well-equipped; a 5km trail from the visitor centre south to spectacular Hag's Head.

Walk 20 Minutes Many visitors gather at the main viewing platform; walking south takes you to a puffin-viewing spot and, beyond, fewer crowds.

One of Ireland's blockbuster sights, it includes a high-tech visitor centre, a 19th-century lookout tower and a wealth of walking trails. Visiting by boat can bring the best views.

The cliffs' fame guarantees a steady stream of visitors, which can surge in summer – up to 10,000 people on busy August bank–holiday weekends. But the tireless Atlantic winds, and expansive walking options, help thin out the crowds. A vast, grass-covered visitor centre (p366) with innovative exhibits, is embedded into the side of a hill. The main walkways and viewing areas along the cliffs have a 1.5m-high wall to prevent visitors getting too close to the crumbling, often slippery edge.

You're rewarded with epic views if you walk even a short way north or south along the cliffs. Note the hiking trails are strenuous, encompassing narrow, exposed cliff paths with steep ascents and descents. Proper boots and kit are a must.

To the north, you can follow the Doolin Trail, via the 1835-built stone observation post O'Brien's Tower, to the village of Doolin (8km; 2½ hours).

Heading south, past the end of the 'Moher Wall', a 5km trail runs along the cliffs to Hag's Head – few venture this far, yet the views are uninhibited. Forming the southern end of the Cliffs of Moher, Hag's Head

WORTH A TRIP

ST TOLA GOAT CHEESE

Creamy St Tola Irish goat's cheese (☑ 065-683 6633; www.st-tola.ie; off L1094; adult/child €10/5; ⊘ tours by reservation) is served at some of Ireland's finest restaurants, with award-winning lines including ash log, Greek-style feta and Gouda-style hard cheese. Call ahead to see if you can join a tour on which you'll pet the goats, watch them being fed, see a cheese-making demonstration and taste the products. The farm is 11km southeast of Ennistimon (16km northwest of Ennis), signposted off the N85.

is a dramatic place from which to view the cliffs. There's a huge sea arch at the tip of Hag's Head and another arch visible to the north. The old signal tower on the head was erected in case Napoleon tried to attack the western coast of Ireland. From Hag's Head, you can continue on to Liscannor for a total walk of just under 12km (about 3½ hours).

The entire 20km-long Liscannor to Doolin walking path via the cliffs is signposted as the Cliffs of Moher Coastal Walk; it's likely to take four to five hours. Seasonal shuttle buses link stops along this route.

Look out for migrating minke and humpback whales in autumn. With binoculars you can spot the more than 30 species of birds – including adorable puffins, which appear between late March and mid-July.

For awe-inspiring views of the cliffs and wildlife, consider a cruise. Boat operators in Doolin (p373), including Doolin 2 Aran Ferries and the Doolin Ferry Co, offer popular tours of the cliffs.

The cliffs are enabled with free wi-fi. It's possible to exit (but not enter) the car park once it closes for the day.

Cliffs of Moher Visitor Centre VISITOR CENTRE (☑ 065-708 6141; www.cliffsofmoher.ie; R478; adult/child incl parking €8/free; ⊘ 8am-9pm May-Aug, to 7pm Mar, Apr, Sep & Oct, 9am-5pm Nov-Feb) Covered in turf and cut into the hillside, the cliffs' state-of-the-art visitor centre has engaging exhibitions covering the fauna, flora, geology and climate of the cliffs, and an interactive genealogy board with information on local family names. Free information booklets on the cliffs are available, or download the app online. Booking an off-peak visit (8am to 11am and 4pm to close) online, 24 hours in advance, brings the adult entrance fee down to €4.

The soulless ground-floor cafe, Puffin's Nest (sandwiches from €4.50; ⊘ 8am-8.45pm May-Aug, to 6.45pm Mar, Apr, Sep & Oct, 9am-4.45pm Nov-Feb), seems designed to urge you up to the pricier cafe above, aptly named Cliffs View (cake €5, mains €11-14; ⊘ 8am-8.45pm May-Aug, to 6.45pm Mar, Apr, Sep & Oct, 9am-4.45pm Nov-Feb), which has a Murphy's ice-cream stand.

ⓘ Getting There & Away

Bus 350 (www.buseireann.ie) runs to the cliffs. There are up to five services a day from June to mid-September and at least two daily from mid-September to May.

Doolin €3.30, 15 minutes
Ennis €13, 50 minutes
Lahinch €4, 10 minutes
Galway €17, 2¼ hours

Numerous private tour operators run tours to the cliffs from as far afield as Galway, Dublin and Cork.

The seasonal Cliffs of Moher Coastal Walk Shuttle Bus (☑ 065-707 5599; www.cliffsofmohercoastalwalk.ie; one-way €8; ⊘ 6 services daily, Mar-Oct; 🛱) connects the Cliffs of Moher with Doolin and Liscannor.

THE BURREN

Stretching across northern Clare, the rocky, windswept Burren region is a unique striated lunar-like landscape of barren grey limestone that was shaped beneath ancient seas, then forced high and dry by a great geological cataclysm. It covers 250 sq km of exposed limestone, and 560 sq km in total.

Wildflowers in spring give the Burren brilliant, if ephemeral, colour amid its stark beauty. Villages throughout the region include the music hub of Doolin on the west coast, Kilfenora inland and charming Ballyvaughan in the north, on the shores of Galway Bay.

South of Ballyvaughan, a series of severe bends twists up Corkscrew Hill (180m), which was built as part of a Great Famine relief scheme in the 1840s. Nearby photogenic prehistoric sites include Gleninsheen Wedge Tomb (p377), Poulnabrone Dolmen (p377) and Caherconnell Fort (p377).

Throughout the region, there are fantastic opportunities for walking and rock climbing.

History

Despite its apparent harshness, the Burren supported quite large numbers of people in ancient times, and has more than 2500 historic sites. Chief among them is the

The Burren

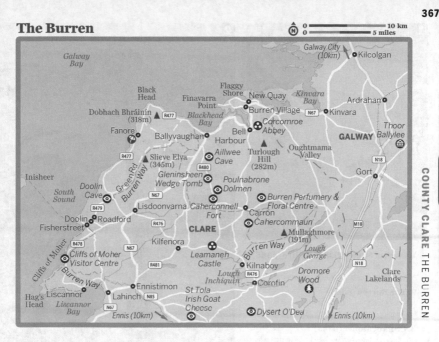

5000-year-old Poulnabrone Dolmen (p377), part of a Neolithic/Bronze Age tomb, and one of Ireland's iconic ancient monuments.

Around 70 prehistoric tombs are in evidence today. Many are wedge-shaped graves, stone boxes tapering both in height and width, and about the size of a large double bed. The dead were placed inside, and the whole structure covered in earth and stones. Gleninsheen Wedge Tomb (p377), 7km south of Ballyvaughan, is a prime example. Ring forts are strewn throughout the Burren. There are almost 500, including Iron Age stone forts such as Cahercommaun (p377) near Carron.

Geology

The Burren (*boireann* is the Irish term for 'rocky country') is one of Europe's largest areas of karst landscape (ie formed limestone that has been dissolved and eroded by rainwater). The limestone rock was orignally laid down in shallow tropical seas near the equator more than 300 million years ago, and carried to its present location by continental drift.

Uplift associated with the opening of the Atlantic Ocean 50 million years ago raised the limestone beds above sea level, and repeated glaciation in the past million years or so scraped away the overlying sandstone and shale to expose the bare limestone.

Since then rainwater has eroded and dissolved the limestone to create classic karst landscape features such as caves, underground rivers, seasonal lakes (turloughs) and limestone pavements – large expanses of naked rock with a criss-cross network of dissolution cracks known as 'clints and grykes'.

Flora & Fauna

Soil may be scarce on the Burren, but the small amount that gathers in the cracks and faults is well drained and nutrient-rich. This, together with the mild Atlantic climate, supports an extraordinary mix of Mediterranean and Arctic-alpine plants. Of Ireland's native wildflowers, 75% are found here, including 23 species of beautiful orchids, the creamy-white burnet rose, the little starry flowers of mossy saxifrage and the magenta-coloured bloody cranesbill. Lime-detesting plants such as heathers can be found living alongside those that thrive on lime. One of the biggest threats to this diversity is the proliferation of hazel scrub and blackthorn, which needs to be controlled.

The Burren is a stronghold of Ireland's most elusive mammal, the rather shy weasel-like pine marten. Badgers, foxes and even stoats are common throughout the region. Otters and seals inhabit the shores around Bell Harbour, New Quay and Finavarra

GARETH MCCORMACK/ALAMY STOCK PHOTO ©

1. Cliffs of Moher Visitor Centre (p366)
Cut into the hillside, the centre provides information on geology, fauna, flora and even local genealogy.

2. The Burren (p366)
The rocky, windswept Burren region is a unique landscape, perfect to explore on foot.

3. Cliffs of Moher (p365)
On a clear day the staggeringly beautiful vertical cliffs can afford views to the Aran Islands.

4. Poulnabrone Dolmen (p377)
Also known as the Portal Tomb, the 5000-year-old burial site was excavated in 1986.

Point. The Burren Code is an initiative to educate people as to how they can protect the environment of the Burren when they visit.

🏃 Activities

The Burren is a walker's paradise. The stark, beautiful landscape, plentiful trails and ancient sites are best explored on foot. 'Green roads' are the old highways of the Burren, crossing hills and valleys to some of the remotest corners of the region. Many of these unpaved ways were built during the Famine as part of relief work, while some may date back thousands of years. Now used mostly by hikers and the occasional farmer, some are signposted.

Beginning in Lahinch and ending in Corofin, the **Burren Way** is a 123km waymarked network of walking routes along a mix of roads, lanes and paths. There are also seven waymarked trails through the national park, taking from 30 minutes to three hours to hike.

Guided nature, history, archaeology and wilderness walks are great ways to appreciate this unique region. Typically the cost of the walks averages €10 to €35 and there are many options, including private trips. Operators include Burren Guided Walks & Hikes, Heart of Burren Walks and Burren Wild Tours.

The **Burren National Park** (www.burren nationalpark.ie) also runs free guided walks; its website lists dates and has a downloadable hiking map.

Burren Wild Tours   WALKING
(☑087 877 9565; www.burrenwalks.com; €35; ⊙by appointment) John Connolly offers a broad range of walks, from gentle to more strenuous. Themes include heritage, botany and folklore.

Heart of Burren Walks   WALKING
(☑087 292 5487; www.heartofburrenwalks.com; €30; ⊙by reservation Tue-Sat) Local Burren author Tony Kirby leads walks and archaeology hikes lasting 2½ hours. Cash only.

Burren Guided Walks & Hikes   WALKING
(☑065-707 6100, 087 244 6807; www.burrenguided walks.com; from €20; ⊙by reservation) Longtime guide Mary Howard leads groups on a variety of rambles, off-the-beaten-track hikes and rugged routes.

ℹ Information

BOOKS & MAPS

There is a wealth of literature about the Burren. In Ennis' bookshops and local visitor centres, look out for publications such as Charles Nelson's *Wild Plants of the Burren and the Aran Islands*. The *Burren Journey* books by George Cunningham are excellent for local lore. *The Burren and the Aran Islands: A Walking Guide* by Tony Kirby is an excellent, up-to-date resource.

The Burren Series of Ramblers' Guides and Maps published by Tír Eolas (www.tireolas.com) features three illustrated, fold-out maps: *Bally-vaughan* (€4), *Kilfenora* (€3) and *O'Brien Country* (€3; which covers Doolin, Lisdoonvarna and the Cliffs of Moher). The booklet *The Burren Way* has good walking routes. Ordnance Survey Ireland Discovery series maps 51 and 57 cover most of the area.

VISITOR INFORMATION

The Burren Centre (p375) in Kilfenora is an excellent resource, as are the Burren **Tourist Office** (☑065-682 7693; www.burrennational park.ie; Clare Heritage Centre, Church St; ⊙9.30am-5pm Apr-Sep) and the Clare Heritage & Genealogy Centre (p376) in Corofin.

Online, informative sites include the following:
Burren Ecotourism (www.burren.ie)
Burren Geopark (www.burrengeopark.ie)
Burren National Park (www.burrennational park.ie)
Burrenbeo Trust (www.burrenbeo.com)

ℹ Getting There & Away

On its Limerick–Galway route 350, which runs via Ennis, Bus Éireann (www.buseireann.ie) stops at key Burren destinations, including Ballyvaughan, Corofin, Doolin, Fanore and Lisdoonvarna.

Kilfenora has limited services to Ennis and some coastal Clare destinations, while New Quay has limited services to Galway city. For Carron, you'll need your own transport.

ℹ Getting Around

With your own car, you can cover a fair amount of the Burren in a day and explore some of the many unnamed back roads.

Cycling is an excellent way of getting off the main roads; ask about rentals at your accommodation or try e-whizz (p375) for bike hire.

Doolin

POP 280

Doolin is hugely popular as a centre of Irish traditional music, with year-round trad sessions at its famous trio of music pubs. Located 6km northeast of the Cliffs of Moher in a landscape riddled with caves and laced with walking paths, it's also a jumping-off point for cliff cruises and ferries out to the Aran Islands.

Without a centre, this scattered settlement consists of three smaller linked villages. Charming Fisherstreet has some picturesque traditional cottages; there are dramatic surf vistas at the harbour 1.5km west along the coast. Doolin itself is about 1km east on the little River Aille. Roadford is another 1km east. None of the villages has more than a handful of buildings.

While the music pubs give Doolin a lively vibe, the heavy concentration of visitors means standards don't always hold up to those in some of Clare's less-frequented villages (p350).

◉ Sights & Activities

Doolin Pier is the departure point for memorable, one-hour cruises to the 214m Cliffs of Moher, 6km to the southwest. They're recommended not only for views of towering cliffs that loom ever-closer, but also great wildlife-spotting opportunities. Doolin 2 Aran Ferries (☑ 065-707 5949; www.doolin2aranferries.com; Doolin Pier; €15; ☺ mid-Mar–Oct) and the Doolin Ferry Co (☑ 065-707 5555; www.doolinferry.com; Doolin Pier; €15; ☺ mid-Mar–Oct) are two firms running popular trips.

★ Doolin Cave   CAVE
(☑ 065-707 5761; www.doolincave.ie; R479; adult/child €15/8; ☺ 10am-6pm Mar-Oct, 11am-4pm Sat & Sun Nov-early Jan) The Great Stalactite, the longest in Europe at 7.3m, is the big draw of Doolin Cave. Tour times vary seasonally, but are usually on the hour. Glacial clay from deep within the cave is used by on-site potter Caireann Browne, who sells her works here. The property also has a 1km-long farmland trail featuring rare animal breeds, and a cafe. The caves are around 4km north of town.

Tickets are 20% cheaper if bought online in advance.

Doonagore Castle   CASTLE
(off R478) Looking every inch a fairy-tale stronghold, round, turreted Doonagore Castle dates from the 16th century. The ruin was restored by architect Percy Leclerc in the 1970s for an American client whose family still owns it. The interior is closed to the public, but aim to pass by at sunset for photos set against a multihued sky. It's some 2km south of Doolin.

Doolin Cliff Walk   WALKING
(☑ 065-707 4170; www.doolincliffwalk.com; €10; ☺ 10am May-early Nov) This tremendous three-hour cliff walk sets off each morning from outside Gus O'Connor's pub in Fisherstreet past Doonagore Castle, ending at the Cliffs

of Moher Visitor Centre (p366), from where you can get a bus back to Doolin. Due to the precipitous terrain, it's not recommended for kids or those with limited mobility or vertigo.

★彡 Festivals & Events

Russell Memorial Weekend   MUSIC
(☑ 065-707 4168; www.michorussellweekend.ie; ☺ Feb) Held on the last weekend in February, this festival celebrates the work of legendary Doolin musician Micho Russell and his brothers, and features workshops, dancing classes and trad-music sessions throughout town.

⨶ Sleeping

Doolin has scores of good-value hostels and B&Bs. If you're planning on catching trad-music sessions, choose your location carefully, as you may find yourself staying a very long way from the pubs you most want to visit, and roads in the area are narrow and unlit.

★ Doolin Inn & Hostel   HOSTEL €
(☑ 087 282 0587; www.doolinhostel.ie; Fisherstreet; dm/d/tr/q from €30/75/90/125; Ⓟ@🖙) In a great Fisherstreet location, this friendly, family-run property is split between two neighbouring buildings. On the hill, the main building houses the inn, with immaculate, neutrally toned B&B accommodation, reception and a great cafe stocking craft beers. The hostel, with five- to 12-bed dorms, is directly across the street.

No hen or stag parties ensure a low-key, sociable atmosphere.

Aille River Hostel   HOSTEL €
(☑ 065-707 4260; www.ailleriverhosteldoolin.ie; Doolin; dm €21-23, d €52-58, campsites per adult €10; ☺ Mar-Dec; Ⓟ🖙) In a picturesque spot by the river, this converted, cosy, 17th-century farmhouse is a great choice, with peat fires and free laundry. There are 24 beds and a camping area; if you don't have your own tent, ask about tepee rental.

Rainbow Hostel   HOSTEL €
(☑ 065-707 4415; rainbowhostel@eircom.net; Roadford; dm/d/tr from €20/50/66; Ⓟ🖙) With a lovely stove in its lounge, wooden ceilings and colourful rooms, this cottagey IHH-affiliated hostel has 24 beds in an old farmhouse by the road. It also rents out bikes (€10 per day).

Nagles Camping
& Caravan Park   CAMPGROUND €
(☑ 065-707 4458; www.doolincamping.com; Fisherstreet; campsites per 2 adults €20; ☺ mid-Mar–mid-Oct; Ⓟ🖙) Let the nearby pounding surf

lull you to sleep at this grassy expanse 100m from the pier. The spaces for caravans, campervans and tents are open to the elements, so pin those pegs down hard. Timber glamping pods (from €70) have a small double bed, single bed, kitchenette and porch.

★ O'Connors Guesthouse & Riverside Camping
INN €€

(☑ 065-707 4498; www.oconnorsdoolin.com; Doolin; s €55-70, d €70-100, campsites per 2 adults €16-20; ☺ late Feb-Nov; ᴘ ᐧ) On a bend in the River Aille, this working farm has an L-shaped barn-style guesthouse with 10 spick-and-span rooms, two of which are equipped for visitors with limited mobility. Next door, tent pitches, and caravan and campervan sites, some right by the river, are available at its campground, along with glamping yurts, tepees and cool retro caravans (€80 to €100).

Twin Peaks
B&B €€

(☑ 086-812 7049; www.twinpeaksdoolin.com; Fisherstreet; s/d €65/90; ᴘ ᐧ) The rural views and soothing feel at this simple but smart B&B belie the fact that it's just a few minutes' walk from Fisherstreet's huddle of shops and pubs. Warmly welcoming hosts who're happy to advise on the best places to eat and drink are another plus.

Cullinan's Guesthouse
INN €€

(☑ 065-707 4183; www.cullinansdoolin.com; Doolin; d €120-140; ☺ Mar-Nov; ᴘ ᐧ) Owned by well-known fiddle-playing James Cullinan, this mustard-coloured inn on the River Aille has eight spotless, comfortable, pine-furnished rooms. A couple of rooms are slightly smaller than the others, but have river views.

It has a lovely back terrace for enjoying the views and a well-regarded restaurant.

Sea View House
B&B €€

(☑ 087 267 9617; www.seaview-doolin.ie; Fisherstreet; d €120-200; ☺ mid-Mar–Oct; ᴘ ᐧ) Sweeping views extend from higher-priced rooms at this aptly named house on high ground above Fisherstreet village, and from the timber deck. Rooms have dark wood furniture, floral curtains and colourful prints; the common lounge has a telescope for surveying the panorama.

Hotel Doolin
HOTEL €€

(☑ 065-707 4111; www.hoteldoolin.ie; Doolin; d/f/tr €145/188/205; ᴘ ᐧ) ✿ The supremely comfortable, streamlined rooms at this contemporary hotel have elegant dark-wood furniture and Voya Irish seaweed toiletries. On the ground floor, the stylish lounge opens to a patio and lawns. Look out for deals online.

It has a classy evening restaurant (mains €16 to €28), a pizzeria (pizzas €13), a residents-only bar, and an in-house pub, Fitz's, which also serves food.

✕ Eating

Irish classics such as bacon and cabbage and seafood chowder are served at Doolin's pubs throughout the day until about 9.30pm. Doolin also has a handful of restaurants and cafes, some open only in summer.

There are no supermarkets (or ATMs), so stock up on supplies before you arrive.

Doolin Cafe
CAFE €

(☑ 065-707 4795; www.doolincafe.ie; Roadford; mains €3.50-11; ☺ 9am-6pm Wed-Mon mid-Mar–late Oct; ᐧ ᐧ) Locals love to gather at the picnic tables outside the Doolin Cafe. Bumper breakfasts are served until 1pm and include vegan, vegetarian and seafood options. Soups and salads star at lunch, while pastries and cakes tempt you throughout the day.

Cullinan's
MODERN IRISH €€€

(☑ 065-707 4183; www.cullinansdoolin.com; Doolin; mains €22-29; ☺ 6-9pm Mon, Tue & Thu-Sat Easter–mid-Oct) The brief menu at this superb restaurant is accompanied by a long wine list. Dishes change depending on what's fresh, but expect plates such as baked monkfish with almond pesto, marinated Burren lamb, and brandy-poached strawberry and mascarpone crème brûlée. Book.

⚑ Drinking & Entertainment

Doolin's famed music pubs – Gus O'Connor's in Fisherstreet and McGann's and McDermott's in Roadford – have sessions throughout the year, as does Fitz's. To experience trad music in intimate surrounds, reserve ahead to visit the Doolin Music House.

★ Gus O'Connor's
PUB

(☑ 065-707 4168; www.gusoconnorsdoolin.com; Fisherstreet; ☺ 9am-midnight Mon-Thu, to 2am Fri-Sun) Right on the river where it runs into the sea, this sprawling place dating from 1832 has a rollicking atmosphere when the music is in full swing. On some summer nights you won't squeeze inside. Music plays from 9.30pm nightly from late February to November and at weekends year-round.

The breakfasts and classic pub food served at both lunch (mains €8 to €17) and dinner (€13 to €27) are well above average.

McGann's
PUB

(☎065-707 4133; www.mcgannspubdoolin.com; Roadford; ⊘10am-11.30pm Mon-Wed, to 12.30am Thu-Sat, to 11pm Sun; 🕸) McGann's has all the classic touches of a full-on Irish music pub, with action often spilling onto the street. Inside you'll find locals playing darts in its warren of small rooms, some with peat fires. Trad sessions take place most nights year-round.

Upstairs are a batch of simple bedrooms with private bathrooms (doubles from €65).

McDermott's
PUB

(MacDiarmada's; ☎065-707 4328; www.mcdermotts pub.com; Roadford; ⊘10am-11am Sun-Wed, to 12.30am Thu-Sat) This traditional pub is a rowdy favourite. Picnic tables face the street, inside renowned music sessions kick off at 9pm nightly from Easter to October, and several nights a week the rest of the year.

Bar food (mains €12 to €23) is served daily from 1pm to 9pm.

Fitz's
PUB

(☎065-707 4111; www.hoteldoolin.ie; Doolin; ⊘noon-11.30pm Mon-Thu, to 12.30am Fri & Sat, to 11pm Sun) At Hotel Doolin (p372), relative newcomer Fitz's has trad sessions twice nightly from April to October and at least three times a week from November to March. Sample its superb whiskey selection, fine craft beers and ciders, or own-brewed Dooliner beer.

Bar food (mains €9 to €24) is first rate. Ingenious cocktails include MV Plassy on the Rocks, named after the Aran Islands shipwreck (p406), a Burren martini and a Father Jack Espresso (in honour of the cantankerous priest from *Father Ted*).

★Doolin Music House
TRADITIONAL MUSIC

(☎086 824 1085; www.doolinmusichouse.com; R478, Caherkinalla; €20; ⊘by reservation 7-8.30pm Mon, Wed & Fri) For a change from Doolin's crowded music pubs, book ahead to visit local musician Christy Barry's cosy home, which is filled with artworks by his artist partner Sheila. By the open fire, Christy plays traditional tunes, tells stories relating to Irish musical history and welcomes questions. The price includes a glass of wine and snacks. It's 4km east of Doolin.

🛍 Shopping

Clare Jam Shop
FOOD

(☎065-707 4778; www.clare-jam-shop.business. site; off R478; ⊘9am-6pm) 🥄 Jams (such as wild blueberry; strawberry and champagne; and blackberry and apple), marmalades

(including Irish whiskey), jellies (such as rose petal), chutneys (tomato and rhubarb) and mustards (including Guinness mustard) are homemade using traditional open-pan boiling methods at this sweet little hilltop cottage 3.5km southwest of Fisherstreet (3km north of the Cliffs of Moher). Many ingredients are handpicked in the Burren.

Doolin Chocolate Shop
CHOCOLATE

(☎061-922 080; www.wildeirishchocolates.com; Fisherstreet; ⊘11am-7pm May-Oct, shorter hours Nov-Apr) Lavender and rose, seaweed and lime, and hazelnut and raisin are among the chocolate flavours made by Clare company Wilde Irish Chocolates, which has its factory (Tuamgraney; ⊘by arrangement) in Tuamgraney near Lough Derg in the county's east. This shop also sells white and dark chocolate spreads, and fudge such as porter or Irish cream liqueur.

❶ Information

The town's **tourist information point** (☎065-707 5649; Doolin; ⊘8am-8pm Easter-Sep) is alongside the central Hotel Doolin. The website www.doolin.ie has comprehensive tourist information.

❶ Getting There & Away

BOAT

From mid-March to October, **Doolin Pier** (off R439) is one of two ferry departure points to the Aran Islands (the other is **Rossaveal Ferry Terminal** (Rossaveal), 37km west of Galway city, where services are year-round). Sailings can be affected if high seas or tides make the dock inaccessible.

Doolin 2 Aran Ferries (☎065-707 5949; www. doolin2aranferries.com; Doolin Pier; ⊘mid-Mar–Oct) and **Doolin Ferry Co** (O'Brien Line; ☎065-707 5555; www.doolinferry.com; Doolin Pier; ⊘mid-Mar–Oct) each have sailings to Inisheer (one way/return €10/20, 30 minutes, three to four daily), Inishmore (€15/25, 1¼ hours, two to three daily) and Inishmaan (€15/25, from 45 minutes, two to three daily). Interisland ferry tickets cost €10 to €15 per crossing.

There are various combination tickets and online discounts.

BUS

Bus Éireann (www.buseireann.ie) bus 350 runs to the following destinations:
Ballyvaughan €8, one hour, five daily
Cliffs of Moher €3.30, 15 minutes, two to five daily
Ennis €9.50, 50 minutes, five daily
Galway €19, two hours, five daily

ⓘ Getting Around

Accommodation providers sometimes offer bike rental; otherwise hire bicycles from Doolin Rent a Bike (☑ 086 109 1850; www.doolinrentabike.ie; Fisherstreet; rental per day from €14; ⊙ 8am-7pm Jul & Aug, shorter hr Sep-Jun).

The seasonal Cliffs of Moher Coastal Walk Shuttle Bus (p366) connects Doolin and its villages with the Cliffs of Moher and Liscannor.

Lisdoonvarna

POP 829

For centuries people have been visiting Lisdoonvarna (Lios Dún Bhearna), often just called 'Lisdoon', for its mineral springs. The village is more down at heel today than in its Victorian heyday, but it makes a good base for exploring the area.

◉ Sights & Activities

Burren Smokehouse   FOOD
(☑ 065-707 4432; www.burrensmokehouse.ie; Kincora Rd; ⊙ 9am-6pm May-Aug, 10am-4pm Sep-Apr) FREE Learn about the ancient Irish art of oak-smoking salmon during a seven-minute video presentation at this local smokehouse. Then tuck into the free tastings of salmon, other smoked fish and cheese, before trying to resist buying everything in the deli shop.

Spa Well   SPRING
At the town's southern end is a spa well, with a sulphur spring, a Victorian pumphouse and a wooded setting. The iron, sulphur, magnesium and iodine in the water are believed to be good for rheumatic and glandular complaints.

Walking trails head off east beside the river to two other well sites. They emerge, near the Roadside Tavern and the Burren Smokehouse.

⌂ Sleeping & Eating

Lisdoonvarna has a hostel and a couple of inns. Book ahead if you're heading here for the Father Ted Festival (p376), on the May bank holiday weekend, or September's Matchmaking Festival (p375).

Sleepzone Burren Hostel   HOSTEL €
(☑ 065-707 4036; www.sleepzone.ie; Kincora Rd; dm/d/f €19/70/90; P ⃰) The rooms in this modern, friendly hostel set in a former hotel range from six-bed dorms to family rooms that sleep up to five people. Facilities include a self-catering kitchen, a book-filled guest lounge and a large lawn.

A shuttle-bus service links it with Sleepzone's sister property in Galway city (p387).

★ Sheedy's Hotel & Restaurant   INN €€
(☑ 065-707 4026; www.sheedys.com; Main St; d from €150; ⊙ mid-Mar–Sep; P ⃰) Stately 18th-century country house Sheedy's has 11 beautifully furnished rooms with checked fabrics and sage-coloured walls. The long front porch has comfy chairs for looking out over the gardens. Nonguests are welcome at its restaurant (mains €18 to €29), which serves dinner Monday to Saturday, 6.30pm to 8.30pm by reservation, and its bar.

Whiskey-soaked porridge with Baileys is on the menu at breakfast.

Wild Honey Inn   INN €€
(☑ 065-707 4300; www.wildhoneyinn.com; Kincora Rd; d €140-185; ⊙ early Mar-Nov; P ⃰) In an 1840s roadside mansion, Wild Honey has 14 stylish rooms, some opening onto private terraces over the gardens. Its acclaimed restaurant (three courses from €44) serves seasonal dishes teaming French flair with Irish ingredients (dinner from 6pm Wednesday to Saturday, plus Tuesday May to September).

★ Roadside Tavern   PUB
(☑ 065-707 4084; www.roadsidetavern.ie; Kincora Rd; ⊙ noon-11.30pm Mon-Thu, to 12.30am Fri & Sat, to 11pm Sun Mar-Oct, shorter hours Nov-Feb) The Roadside offers pure Clare craic. Third-generation owner Peter Curtin proudly presides over trad sessions, which play nightly in summer and on Friday and Saturday evenings in winter. Peter also kickstarted the in-house Burren Brewery, which makes superb gold lagers, red ales and stout that's best sampled along with the tavern's award-winning food.

Fish from the nearby Burren Smokehouse is incorporated in dishes, which are served between March and October (mains from €13; noon to 4pm and 6pm to 9pm Monday to Friday, noon to 9pm Saturday and Sunday).

ⓘ Getting There & Away

Bus Éireann (www.buseireann.ie) bus 350 runs at least four times daily to the following destinations:
Ballyvaughan €6, 45 minutes
Doolin €2.40, 15 minutes
Ennis €13, 1¼ hours
Galway €16, two hours

Kilfenora

POP 175

Kilfenora (Cill Fhionnúrach) lies on the southern fringe of the Burren, 8.5km southeast of Lisdoonvarna. It's a small place, with low polychromatic buildings surrounding the compact centre.

The town has a strong musical tradition: the **Kilfenora Céilí Band**, Ireland's oldest *céilidh* band, featuring fiddles, banjos, squeezeboxes and more, has been playing here for over a century.

◉ Sights

Burren Centre   MUSEUM
(☑065-708 8030; www.theburrencentre.ie; Main St; adult/child €6/4; ⊙9.30am-5.30pm Jun-Aug, 10am-5pm Mar-May, Sep & Oct) At the Burren Centre, a 12-minute film gives you an overview of the Burren's flora, fauna and geology, while interactive exhibits detail its formation and evolution right up to the present day. Exhibits also cover the Kilfenora Céilí Band. You'll also find a tearoom and a large shop stocking Irish-made crafts.

Kilfenora Cathedral   RUINS
(off Main St; ⊙9.30am-5.30pm Jun-Aug, 10am-5pm Mar-May, Sep & Oct) FREE Built in 1189, Kilfenora's cathedral was once an important place of pilgrimage. St Fachan (or Fachtna) founded the monastery here in the 6th century, and it later became the seat of Kilfenora diocese, the smallest in the country. Loop around the more recent Protestant church and enter the oldest part of the ruins, under a glass roof to protect them from the elements. The chancel contains two primitive carved figures on top of two tombs and three ancient stone crosses.

The high crosses have explanatory captions on stainless-steel plaques alongside. They include the impressive 800-year-old **Doorty Cross** measuring 4.2m high; it lay broken in two until the 1950s, when it was re-erected.

Leamaneh Castle   RUINS
(junction R476 & R480) This magnificent, allegedly haunted ruin stands on a rise 6.2km east of Kilfenora. Built in 1480 as a tower house and converted to a mansion in 1650, it's the erstwhile home of Máire Rúa (Red Mary) who – according to local anecdote – got through 25 husbands, dispatching at least one to a grisly death on horseback off the Cliffs of Moher, before being incarcerated in a hollow tree by her enemies.

West Cross   MONUMENT
In a field accessed via a stile, 130m west of Kilfenora's cathedral (p375) ruins, is the 4.6m-high West Cross, which depicts Christ's crucifixion.

LISDOONVARNA MATCHMAKING FESTIVAL

Lisdoonvarna was once a centre for *basadóiri* (matchmakers) who, for a fee, would fix up a person with a spouse. Most of the (mainly male) hopefuls would hit town in September, feet shuffling, cap in hand, after the hay was in. Today, the **Lisdoonvarna Matchmaking Festival** (☑065-707 4005; www.matchmakerireland.com; ⊙weekends Sep) is billed as Europe's largest singles' festival, with music, dancing and partying on September weekends.

☕ Drinking & Nightlife

★**Vaughan's Pub**   PUB
(☑065-708 8004; www.vaughanspub.ie; Main St; ⊙10.30am-11.30pm, hours can vary) With a big reputation in Irish music circles, Vaughan's has music in the bar every night during the summer and several times a week the rest of the year. The adjacent barn hosts terrific set-dancing sessions on Sunday between 9.30pm and 11.30pm.

Pub food (mains from €10) is served until 9pm.

Linnane's Pub   PUB
(☑065-708 8157; Main St; ⊙10.30am-11.30pm, hours can vary) A much-loved local hosting regular live music, including evening trad sessions most Wednesdays with the Kilfenora Céilí Band.

❶ Getting There & Around

Bus Éireann (www.buseireann.ie) bus 333 runs once a day between Monday and Saturday to Ennis (€8.50, 40 minutes) and coastal destinations, including Doonbeg (€13, 1¼ hours).

e-whizz (☑065-708 8846; www.e-whizz.com; The Burren Hub, The Sq) Hires out both standard and electric bikes (€20 to €35 per day) and offers a series of guided and self-guided tours (€40 to €70). Also delivers further afield.

Corofin & Around
POP 776

Corofin (Cora Finne), also spelt Corrofin, is a traditional village on the southern fringes of the Burren. The surrounding area features a number of turloughs (small lakes) and several O'Brien castles, including two on the shores of nearby **Lough Inchiquin**.

THE IMMORTAL FATHER TED

Father Ted, the enduring 1990s TV comedy, is set around the high jinks of three Irish priests living on the fictional Craggy Island.

Aside from the opening shot of the Plassy (p406) shipwreck on the Aran Island of Inisheer, most of the locations used in the show are around Kilfenora, including Vaughan's Pub (p375), and Ennistimon, where Eugene's (p364) pub was used both as a location and the cast's watering hole. The lonely Father Ted (p376) house is in Kilnaboy; book in advance to stop in for tea.

Inspired by the great success of Inishmore's Tedfest (p399), the good people of Lisdoonvarna have organised their own **Father Ted Festival** (www.tedtours.com; ☺ early May), with costume parties, contests, tours and more. Year-round, **Ted Tours** (☑ 065-708 8846; www.tedtours.com; Burren Centre; adult/child €29/24; ☺ 1.30pm Sat Mar-Oct, plus Thu Jul & Aug) visits local filming locations, departing from Kilfenora.

Father Ted's House   FILM LOCATION
(☑ 087 404 8475; www.fathertedshouse.com; Glanquin House, Cloon, Kilnaboy; per person €10; ☺ by reservation) Fans of TV comedy *Father Ted* will jump at the chance to visit the building that provided the exterior shots of the series' parochial house. Advance bookings are essential; phone bookings are requested only between 6pm and 8pm Monday to Friday. Payment is by cash only, and includes tea, cake and biscuits, and organic jams from the gardens. It's 9.5km north of Corofin. The house can also be visited on a tour with Ted Tours.

Clare Heritage Centre
Interpretative Museum   MUSEUM
(www.clareroots.com; Church St; adult/child €4/2; ☺ 9am-5pm Mon-Fri Easter-Oct) Many of the displays inside early-1700s St Catherine's Church cover the horrors of the Great Famine, which led to mass emigration. More than 200,000 people lived in Clare before the Famine; today the county's population remains nearly half that.

Across the street, the Clare Heritage & Genealogy Centre (☑ 065-683 7955; ☺ 9am-5pm Mon-Fri), which administers the museum, can help you trace your ancestors.

Corofin Hostel & Camping Park   HOSTEL €
(☑ 065-683 7683; www.corofincamping.com; Main St; campsites per 2 adults €25, s/d/q €30/50/80; ☺ May-Aug; P ☎) Campsites out the back have nice open spaces, and inside there are 30 beds at this friendly hostel right in the village centre. It has a cosy open fire in the sitting room, a laundry and a self-catering kitchen. Camping includes free hot showers.

Lakefield Lodge   B&B €
(☑ 065-683 7675; www.lakefieldlodgebandb.com; R476; s/d from €50/75; ☺ Apr-Oct; P ☎) Gardens surround this bungalow with four comfy rooms on the southern edge of the village. Conveniently situated for Burren hikes, it also provides a wealth of info for anglers.

Guests can rent a boat (with/without a motor €45/35 per day, including fishing equipment).

Fergus View   B&B €€
(☑ 065-683 7606; www.fergusview.com; R476, Kilnaboy; s/d from €55/84; ☺ Easter-Oct; ☎) The River Fergus flows right past this 19th-century residence, which has six rooms and breakfasts that use organic produce, including local cheese, homemade yoghurt and herbs from the garden. It's 3.5km north of Corofin.

ⓘ Getting There & Away

Bus Éireann (www.buseireann.ie) bus 350 runs four times a day to Ennis (€9, 25 minutes) and Galway (€22, 2¾ hours).

Central Burren

Several roads dotted with sights cross the heart of the Burren. The scenery along the R480 as it passes through the region is harsh but inspiring, highlighting the barren Burren at its best. Remarkable prehistoric stone structures litter the area.

South from Ballyvaughan, the R480 branches off the N67 at the sign for Aillwee Caves, passing Gleninsheen Wedge Tomb and the outstanding Poulnabrone Dolmen before reaching the magnificent Leamaneagh Castle ruins, where it joins the R476, which runs southeast to Corofin. At any point along here, try a small road – especially those to the east – to plunge into otherworldly solitude.

Originally a Famine relief road built in the 1800s, the N67 to Lisdoonvarna rewards visitors with sweeping views of the stark Burren landscape.

★**Poulnabrone Dolmen** HISTORIC SITE
(R480) FREE Also known as the Portal Tomb, Poulnabrone Dolmen is one of Ireland's most photographed ancient monuments. Built more than 5000 years ago, the other-worldly dolmen (a large slab perched on stone uprights) stands amid a swath of rocky pavements; the capstone weighs 5 tonnes. The site is 9km south Ballyvaughan and visible from the R480; there's a large free parking area and excellent displays.

Poulnabrone was excavated in 1986, and the remains of at least 22 people were found, as well as pieces of pottery and jewellery. Radiocarbon dating suggests that they were buried between 3800 and 3200 BC. When the dead were originally entombed here, the whole structure was partially covered in a mound of earth, which has since worn away. A highly informative Office of Public Works staff member is often on duty.

★**Gleninsheen Wedge Tomb** HISTORIC SITE
(R480) FREE One of Ireland's most famous prehistoric grave sites, Gleninsheen lies beside the R480 7km south of Ballyvaughan. It's thought to date from 4000 to 5000 years ago. A magnificent gold gorget (a crescent of beaten gold that hung round the neck) found here and dating from the late Bronze Age is now on display at the National Museum in Dublin.

Note: the access gate to the tomb is sometimes locked, and signage is poor.

Caherconnell Fort HISTORIC SITE
(065-708 9999; www.caherconnell.com; R480; adult/child €6/4, sheepdog demonstration €5/3, combination ticket €9.60/5.60; 10am-6pm Jul & Aug, to 5.30pm May, Jun & Sep, 10.30am-5pm mid-Mar–Apr & Oct) For a close-up look at a well-preserved, drystone *caher* (walled fort) of the late Iron Age–early Christian period, stop at this privately run heritage attraction 10km south of Ballyvaughan. Exhibits detail how the evolution of these defensive settlements may have reflected territorialism and competition for land among a growing, settling population. The visitor centre also has information on many other monuments in the area. Fun sheepdog demonstrations take place throughout the day.

It also runs two-, four- and six-week residential archaeological field schools for a range of skill levels. Prices start at €2400 for two weeks.

Carron & Around

In the heart of the Burren, the tiny village of Carron (Irish: An Carn; often spelt Carran) is a wonderfully remote spot. Vistas of the rocky moonscape stretch in all directions from its elevated position. Wildflowers that bloom in this bare, ethereal landscape are made into perfumes at the area's Burren Perfumery & Floral Centre.

★**Burren Perfumery & Floral Centre** VISITOR CENTRE
(065-708 9102; www.burrenperfumery.com; 9am-7pm Jul & Aug, 10am-6pm May, Jun & Sep, to 5pm Oct-Apr, cafe to 5pm Apr-Sep) The Burren's wildflowers are the inspiration for the subtle scents at this wonderful perfumery and floral centre, which creates scented items such as perfumes, candles and soaps that are beautifully packaged in handmade paper. A 10-minute audiovisual presentation details the area's diverse flora, including many fragrant orchids that grow between the rocks. You're free to wander its flower and herb gardens, which provide ingredients for dishes and herbal teas served at its tearoom.

Cahercommaun HISTORIC SITE
Perched on the edge of an inland cliff about 3km south of Carron is the triple ring fort of Cahercommaun, built around AD 800 and inhabited by people who hunted deer and grew small amounts of grain. The remains of a souterrain (underground passage) lead from the fort to the outer cliff face. From Carron, head south on the L1014 and turn towards Kilnaboy. After 1.7km, a 600m-long walking trail on the left leads up to the fort.

★**Clare's Rock Hostel** HOSTEL €
(065-708 9129; www.claresrock.com; L1014; dm/d/tr/q €20/54/66/70; May-Sep;) The 30 beds in this IHH hostel built from rough-hewn grey Burren stone sit in spacious, squeaky-clean rooms with commanding views over the waters of Carron Polje. Excellent facilities include a self-catering kitchen, a drying room and a laundry, and giant chess and chequerboards outside.

All of its power comes from solar panels and its own wind turbine.

Cassidy's PUB FOOD €€
(065-708 9109; www.cassidyspub.com; L1014; mains €9-23; kitchen noon-9pm Mon-Sat, 11am-8pm Sun, winter hours vary;) Cassidy's raises its own livestock for famed dishes such

towering Dolmen beef and goat burgers. Idyllic views extend from the terrace of the historic building, while trad music and dancing takes place on Fridays year-round and spontaneously on summer nights.

The pub stays open until 11.30pm Monday to Thursday, 12.30am Friday and Saturday, and 11pm Sunday.

Fanore

POP 111

Fanore (Fan Óir, meaning 'The Golden Slope') is less a village and more a stretch of coastline with a shop, a pub and a few houses scattered along the scenic R477, which hugs the barren coast as it curves past the Aran Islands into Galway Bay. Scenery aside, the beach and the chance to swim and surf might draw you here.

◉ Sights & Activities

The nearby shelves of limestone are popular with rock climbers; contact Ben's Surf Clinic (p363), surprisingly, in Lahinch for trips.

Surfers flock here throughout the year. The rocky coastline offers excellent fishing.

Fanore Beach   BEACH
With an extensive backdrop of grass-covered dunes, this Blue Flag–rated beach off the R477 is patrolled by lifeguards in summer and is a surfing hotspot. Its golden sands have exposed limestone outcrops – part of the Burren – at low tide. Signs identify hiking trails along the coast and up into the dramatic hills. You'll find showers and toilets open in summer in a small block by the car park.

Aloha Surf School   SURFING
(☑ 087 213 3996; www.surfschool.ie; Fanore Beach; 2hr lessons from €35, equipment rental per 2hr from €20; ☺ Apr-Sep, by appointment Oct-Mar) Aloha offers classes for all ages and abilities. You can rent surfboards, wetsuits and boots, as well as stand-up paddleboards and kayaks.

Siopa Fan Óir   FISHING
(☑ 065-707 6131; www.fanoreshop.com; R477; fishing equipment rental per half day from €18; ☺ 9am-6pm Mon-Sat, to noon Sun, hours can vary) This well-stocked shop rents out rods and has fishing tackle, walking maps, boogie boards and cheap sand buckets. Its helpful owner, Mick, is often out fishing himself, so call in advance.

🛏 Sleeping & Eating

Rocky View Farmhouse   B&B €
(☑ 065-707 6103; www.rockyviewfarmhouse.com; off R477; s/d €50/75; P🐾) 🐾 At the heart of the coastal Burren, this charming farmhouse has a guest lounge, four bright, airy, TV-free rooms and views out to the Aran Islands. Organic food grown on the property is used at breakfast, served in a sunny conservatory. Cash only.

Orchid House   B&B €€
(☑ 065-707 6975; www.orchidhouse.net; R477; s/d from €50/80; P🐾) 🐾 All four spotless, contemporary rooms come with sea views at this traditional-style stone cottage set on a working farm 1km south of Fanore. The owners are keen conservationists: solar power provides hot water, and home-grown fruit and vegetables appear at breakfast in scones, fruit salads and jams.

O'Donohue's   PUB
(☑ 065-707 6119; R477; ☺10am-11pm Mon-Thu, noon-midnight Fri & Sat, to 11pm Sun Apr-Oct, 8-11pm Fri-Sun Nov-Mar, hours can vary) You can't miss O'Donohue's – it's the bright blue building with a painted fish drinking a pint of Guinness on the side that's visible for miles around. It's the heart and soul of the community, so expect a great whiskey selection, summertime pub grub (mains from €13) and lively trad-music sessions, especially at weekends from April to October.

ℹ Getting There & Away

Bus Éireann (www.buseireann.ie) bus 350 runs four times a day north to Galway (€17, 1½ hours), and south to Doolin (€7, 30 minutes) and Ennis (€16, 1½ hours).

Northern Burren

Low farmland stretches south from County Galway to the bluff limestone hills of the Burren, which begin west of Kinvara and Doorus in County Galway.

From Oranmore in County Galway to Ballyvaughan, the coastline wriggles along small inlets and peninsulas; some, such as New Quay, are worth a detour. Here narrow roads traverse low rocky hills dotted with old stone ruins that have yielded to nature.

Inland near Bell Harbour is the largely intact Corcomroe Abbey, while the three ancient churches of Oughtmama lie up a quiet side valley. Galway Bay forms the

THE RUINS OF CORCOMROE ABBEY

Moody and evocative, marvellously ruined **Corcomroe Abbey** (Corcomroe Rd, Bellharbour; ⊘dawn-dusk) sits in a quiet green hollow, 2km inland from Bellharbour, surrounded by the stark grey Burren hills. The former Cistercian abbey began its long decline in the 15th century, but the surviving vaulting in the presbytery and transepts is impressively intact and some striking Romanesque carvings remain.

The abbey was founded in 1195 by Donal Mór O'Brien. His grandson, Conor na Siudaine O'Brien (died 1268), king of Thomond, is said to occupy the tomb in the northern wall, and there's a crude carving of him below the effigy of a bishop holding a crosier, the pastoral staff that was carried by a bishop or abbot. Often-touching modern graves crowd the ruins.

backdrop to some outstanding scenery: bare stone hills shining in the sun, with small hamlets and rich patches of green wherever there's soil.

Buses to and from Galway pass through the area on the N67. Just over the border in Galway, Kinvara makes a good base for this region.

Ballyvaughan & Around

POP 191

An ideal base for exploring the northern Burren, Ballyvaughan (Baile Uí Bheacháin) has a picturesque location between the rocky hills and Galway Bay's translucent waters.

Just west of the village centre, Ballyvaughan's quay was built in 1829 at a time when boats traded with the Aran Islands and Galway, exporting grain and bacon and bringing in peat – a scarce commodity in this barren landscape. From the quay, a signposted track leads to a seashore bird shelter offering fine views of the tidal shallows.

To the village's south, at the foothills of the Burren, you can visit the two-million-year-old Aillwee Cave.

★**Aillwee Cave**   CAVE
(☑065-707 7036; www.aillweecave.ie; off R480; cave adult/child €11/5, raptor exhibit €9/7, combined ticket €17/10; ⊘10am-6.30pm Jul & Aug, to 5.30pm Mar-Jun, Sep & Oct, to 5pm Nov-Feb) Aillwee's extraordinary caves were carved out by water some two million years ago. The main cave penetrates 600m into the mountain, widening into larger caverns, one with its own waterfall. Near the entrance are the remains of a brown bear, extinct in Ireland for over 10,000 years. Aillwee Cave has a cafe and a shop selling local Burren Gold cheese.

A large raptor exhibit includes captive hawks and owls.

🛏 Sleeping & Eating

Ballyvaughan is one of the loveliest places to stay in the Burren. Several B&Bs and inns are close to the village centre.

Pubs in Ballyvaughan serve quality fare. It also has a cafe and a small supermarket. Local produce is sold at the farmers market (St John's Hall car park; ⊘10am-2pm Sat May-Oct).

★**Wild Atlantic Lodge**   INN €€
(☑065-707 7003; www.thewildatlanticlodge.com; Main St; d/tr/f from €100/140/180; ℙ🛜) The Wild Atlantic Lodge overflows with comfort and charm, from the soft woollen blankets in the warm-hued rooms to the huge Burren photographs covering the walls. Breakfast is served in its airy Wildflower Restaurant and Bar, which delivers a mellow soundtrack and outstanding food (mains €13 to €24); beef and lamb from its own farm are scented with Burren-foraged herbs.

You'll find it in the centre of Ballyvaughan village.

Cappabhaile House   B&B €€
(☑083 858 0018; www.cappabhaile.com; N67; d €110, f €130-155) At Cappabhaile House you sink into serenity. Set in 5 hectares of gorgeous Burren countryside 3km south of Ballyvaughan, it's surrounded by the sounds of birdsong and cows. Styling is country-life chic: quality furnishings in warm colours sit beside stripped floorboards and polished wood.

Breakfast treats include omelettes cooked to order and platters of Irish cheese.

Ballyvaughan Lodge   B&B €€
(☑065-707 7292; www.ballyvaughanlodge.com; N67; s/d €70/110; ℙ🛜) Little touches make a big difference at Ballyvaughan Lodge: fragrant lilies, freshly ground coffee and breakfasts that include poached eggs and locally smoked salmon, and mushrooms on toast with blue cheese. Add polished floorboards, bright rugs and very comfy beds and you have a winner.

★ **Gregan's Castle Hotel** HOTEL €€€
(☑ 065-707 7005; www.gregans.ie; N67; d €240-325, ste €377-447; ℗ 🖥) This hidden Clare gem is housed in a grand 18th-century manor, 5km south of Ballyvaughan at the aptly named, twisting Corkscrew Hill. The 21 rooms and suites combine antiques with contemporary countrified furnishings (and purposely no TVs); some open to private garden areas.

Nonguests are welcome by reservation at its glass-paned gourmet restaurant (four courses €75), which serves exquisite dishes like hand-dived barbecue scallops and wild garlic-laced Kilshanny lamb.

★ **Monks at the Pier** SEAFOOD €€
(☑ 065-707 7059; www.monksballyvaughan.com; The Pier; mains €15-50; ⊙ noon-10pm Jun-Aug, to 9pm Sep-May) Although vegetarians and carnivores eat well here, seafood is the star at this whitewashed restaurant warmed by log-burning stoves. Think black Head Bay clams steamed in white wine; Burren smoked salmon and Liscannor crab salad; red ale-battered fish with triple-fried chips; natural and grilled oysters (per half dozen €12 to €16); and spectacular lobster (€50) and seafood platters (€32).

ⓘ Information

Inside a large gift shop behind the supermarket, Ballyvaughan's **visitor centre** (☑ 065-707 7464; www.ballyvaughantourism.com; N67; ⊙ 10am-1.30pm & 2-6pm, reduced hours Oct-Apr) has a good selection of local guides and maps.

ⓘ Getting There & Away

Bus Éireann (www.buseireann.ie) bus 350 runs four times a day to Galway (€14, one hour), Doolin (€8.50, one hour) and Ennis (€16, two hours).

New Quay & Around

Stretching along the Finavarra Peninsula, New Quay (Ceibh Nua) is a narrow, fertile strip of land between Galway Bay and the stark, rocky Burren.

The **Flaggy Shore**, west of New Quay, is a particularly scenic stretch of coastline where limestone terraces step down to the sea. The road hugs the shoreline then curves south past **Lough Muirí**, where you're likely to see wading birds and swans. Otters also inhabit the area.

★ **Hazel Mountain Chocolate** FACTORY
(☑ 065-707 8847; www.hazelmountainchocolate.com; Oughtmama, off L1014; tour adult/child €15/10; ⊙ shop 10am-5pm, tour days vary) 🍫 Book ahead to watch chocolate being made in small batches using rare Trinitario cacao beans and raw sugar on a 45-minute tour of this heavenly smelling cottage-housed chocolate factory in a picturesque hillside location. If you don't catch a tour, peer through the factory's glass viewing windows from the chocolate-filled shop. Its on-site organic cafe (dishes €8 to €14; Wednesday to Sunday) uses chocolate in creations like parsnip, cacao butter and white-pepper soup, and grilled halloumi and chocolate-and-plum-chutney toasties.

Its Galway city shop (p395) has a cacao brew bar.

★ **Cafe Linnalla** ICE CREAM €
(☑ 065-707 8167; www.linnallaicecream.ie; Finavarra Point; scoops from €3; ⊙ 11am-7pm daily Apr-Oct, noon-5pm Sat & Sun Nov-Mar) Own-grown and foraged ingredients infuse the innovative artisan ice cream crafted at this remote dairy farm overlooking Galway Bay. Treats include scoops, cakes and sundaes featuring blackcurrants, rhubarb, gorse, hazelnuts and sloes.

Time your drive out here to avoid early mornings or late afternoons, or prepare to find yourself stuck on the narrow road amid the cows that provide the ice cream's milk.

Linnane's Lobster Bar SEAFOOD €€
(☑ 065-707 8120; www.linnanesbar.com; mains €14-24, whole lobster €38; ⊙ 12.30-8pm daily mid-Mar–Sep, Fri-Sun Oct–mid-Mar) Net-fresh seafood is sourced from the docks adjoining this unpretentious local bar with views over the water. The seafood chowder is an awesome starter, or opt for oysters, platters of house-smoked fish and succulent lobster in season.

Russell Gallery ART
(☑ 065-707 8185; www.russellgallery.net; New Quay; ⊙ 11am-6pm Mon-Sat, noon-6pm Sun Apr-Sep) Top-notch art and glass works by Irish artists are for sale at this airy gallery alongside photographs and books on the region. It doubles as a cafe and wine bar; there are seats out on the grass in fine weather.

Look out for the striking pieces of raku ceramics, influenced by the moods of the Burren and the surrounding sea.

ⓘ Getting There & Away

The area is spread out, so having your own wheels makes things easier.

Bus Éireann (www.buseireann.ie) bus 350 runs once a day to Galway (€14, 50 minutes) and Doolin (€16, one hour).

County Galway

POP 258,058 / AREA 6148 SQ KM

Best Places to Eat

➡ Loam (p393)

➡ Moran's Oyster Cottage (p419)

➡ Pullman Restaurant (p393)

➡ Aniar (p393)

➡ O'Dowd's (p412)

Best Places to Stay

➡ Glenlo Abbey Hotel (p390)

➡ Inis Meáin (p405)

➡ House Hotel (p387)

➡ Clifden Eco Camping (p413)

➡ Kinlay Hostel (p387)

➡ Blue Quay Rooms (p414)

Why Go?

County Galway's exuberant namesake city is a swirl of colourful shop lined streets filled with buskers and performance artists, enticing old pubs that hum with trad music sessions throughout the year, and an increasingly sophisticated food scene that celebrates local produce.

Some of Ireland's most picturesque scenery fans out from Galway's city limits, particularly along the breathtaking Connemara Peninsula. Tiny roads wander along a coastline studded with islands, dazzling white sandy beaches and intriguing villages; the interior shelters heath-strewn boglands, glassy lakes, looming mountains and isolated valleys. In the county's east, towns with medieval remains give way to rolling farmland.

Offshore, the wild and beautiful eroded swaths of the Aran Islands possess a desolate and windswept yet entrancing aura, and offer a glimpse into Irish life of centuries past.

When to Go

➡ With its excellent restaurants, roaring pubs, cultural pursuits and student life, Galway city is a year-round destination, with a packed calendar of festivals.

➡ Elsewhere, in rural parts of the county, the months of April to October offer the best weather and fewest closures.

➡ Visitor numbers are highest and bookings hardest to come by in high summer (July and August).

➡ The shoulder seasons of May, June and September see fewer crowds.

➡ Moody in the depths of winter (when many establishments close), the Aran Islands may be unreachable during storms at any time of year.

➡ In scenic Connemara, many country inns close during the winter months, particularly December and January.

County Galway Highlights

1 Galway city (p393)
Catching high-spirited trad sessions in atmospheric pubs.

2 Dun Aengus (p397)
Pondering the ruins of this prehistoric fort on Inishmore.

3 Inisheer (p402) Visiting ancient holy sites and springs, plus a famous shipwreck, on the Arans' smallest island.

4 Dunguaire Castle (p417)
Climbing to the roof of this 16th-century castle to gaze out over Galway Bay.

5 Inishbofin (p413)
Escaping to the sparsely inhabited island of Inishbofin, off the Connemara coast.

6 Kylemore Abbey (p414)
Exploring the historic walled gardens at this 19th-century neo-Gothic abbey.

7 Roundstone (p408)
Delighting in sandy toes on

Galway's gorgeous beaches, such as Gurteen.

8 Sky Road (p410)
Catching the sun dipping into the Atlantic from this scenic loop outside Clifden.

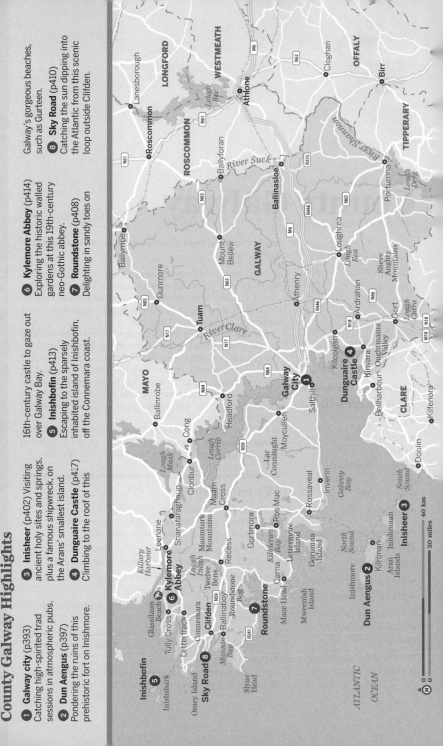

GALWAY CITY

POP 79,934

Arty, bohemian Galway (Gaillimh) is one of Ireland's most engaging cities. Brightly painted pubs heave with live music, while restaurants and cafes offer front-row seats for observing buskers and street theatre. Remnants of the medieval town walls lie between shops selling handcrafted Claddagh rings, books and musical instruments, bridges arch over the salmon-stuffed River Corrib, and a long promenade leads to the seaside suburb of Salthill, on Galway Bay, the source of the area's famous oysters.

While it's steeped in history, the city buzzes with a contemporary vibe, thanks in part to students, who make up around a fifth of the population. Its energy and creativity have seen it designated a European Capital of Culture for 2020.

History

Galway's Irish name, Gaillimh, originates from the Irish word *gaill,* meaning 'outsiders' or 'foreigners', and the term resonates throughout the city's history.

From humble beginnings as the tiny fishing village Claddagh at the mouth of the River Corrib, it grew into an important town when the Anglo-Normans, under Richard de Burgo (also spelt de Burgh or Burke), captured territory from the local O'Flahertys in 1232. Its fortified walls were built from around 1270.

In 1396 Richard II granted a charter transferring power from the de Burgos to 14 merchant families or 'tribes' – hence Galway's enduring nickname: City of the Tribes. (Each of the city's roundabouts is named for one of the tribes.)

Galway maintained its independent status under the ruling merchant families, who were mostly loyal to the English Crown. Its coastal location encouraged a huge trade in wine, spices, fish and salt with Portugal and Spain. Its support of the Crown, however, led to its downfall; the city was besieged by Cromwell in 1651 and fell the following year. Trade with Spain declined and Galway stagnated for centuries.

The early 1900s saw Galway's revival as tourists returned to the city and student numbers grew. In 1934 the cobbled streets and thatched cabins of Claddagh were tarred and flattened to make way for modern, hygienic buildings, and construction has boomed since.

◉ Sights

★ Galway City Museum   MUSEUM
(☑091-532 460; www.galwaycitymuseum.ie; Spanish Pde; ⊙10am-5pm Tue-Sat, plus noon-5pm Sun Easter-Sep) FREE Exhibits at this modern, three-floor museum engagingly convey the city's archaeological, political, cultural and social history. Look out for an iconic Galway hooker fishing boat, a collection of *currachs* (boats made of a framework of laths covered with tarred canvas) and sections covering Galway's role in the revolutionary events that shaped the Republic of Ireland.

Also check out regular gallery tours, talks and workshops, and rotating displays of works by local artists. The ground-floor cafe, with its Spanish Arch views, is a perfect rest stop.

★ Spanish Arch   HISTORIC SITE
The Spanish Arch is thought to be an extension of Galway's medieval city walls, designed to protect ships moored at the nearby quay while they unloaded goods from Spain. It was partially destroyed by the tsunami that followed the 1755 Lisbon earthquake. Today it reverberates with buskers and drummers, and the lawns and riverside form a gathering place for locals and visitors on sunny days, as kayakers negotiate the tidal rapids of the River Corrib.

A 1651 drawing of Galway clearly shows its extensive fortifications, but depredation by Cromwell and William of Orange, and subsequent centuries of neglect, saw the walls almost completely disappear. One surviving portion has been cleverly incorporated into the modern shopping mall **Eyre Square Centre** (☑091-568 302; www.eyresquarecentre.com; cnr Merchants Rd & Eyre Sq; ⊙8.30am-7pm Mon-Wed & Sat, to 9pm Thu & Fri, 10.15am-7pm Sun).

Galway Market   MARKET
(www.galwaymarket.com; Church Lane; ⊙8am-6pm Sat, noon-6pm Sun) Galway's bohemian spirit comes alive at its street market, which has set up in this spot for centuries. Saturdays are the standout for food, when farmers sell fresh produce alongside stalls selling arts, crafts and ready-to-eat dishes. Additional markets take place from noon to 6pm on bank holidays, Fridays in July and August and every day during the Galway International Arts Festival (p386). Buskers add to the festive atmosphere.

Connemara

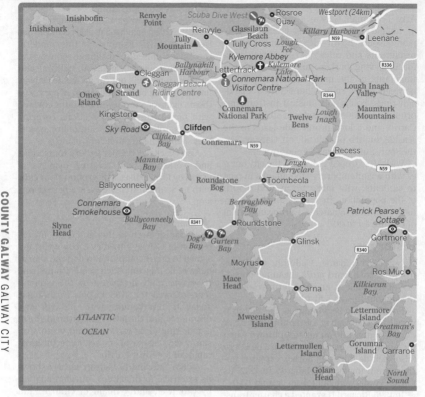

Fishery Watchtower MUSEUM
(www.galwaycivictrust.ie; off Wolfe Tone Bridge; ⊙10am-4pm Tue-Fri, 11am-3pm Mon & Sat) **FREE**
Constructed in the 1850s, this butter-coloured Victorian tower was used to monitor fish stock levels (and poachers). Now restored, the unique trilevel building contains a tiny museum that gives an overview of Galway's salmon-fishing industry through displays including photos, along with fantastic views over the waterways.

Galway Cathedral CHURCH
(Catholic Cathedral of Our Lady Assumed into Heaven & St Nicholas; ☑091-563 577; www.galwaycathedral.ie; Gaol Rd; by donation; ⊙8.30am-6.30pm) Rising over the River Corrib, imposing Galway Cathedral is one of the city's finest buildings. Highlights include a beautifully decorated dome, attractive Romanesque arches, intricate mosaics and rough-hewn stonework emblazoned with copious stained glass. Regular musical events showcase the

superb acoustics; look out for concerts, organ recitals, Gregorian chanting and Sunday morning Mass (11am), when the choir sings.

Concert dates and ticket information are posted online. From the Spanish Arch, a riverside path runs upriver and across the Salmon Weir Bridge to the cathedral.

Hall of the Red Earl ARCHAEOLOGICAL SITE
(www.galwaycivictrust.ie; Druid Lane; ⊙9am-4.45pm Mon-Fri, 11am-3pm Sat) **FREE** In the 13th century, when the de Burgo family ruled Galway, Richard – the Red Earl – erected a large hall as a seat of power, where locals would arrive to curry favour. After the 14 tribes took over, the hall fell into ruin. It was lost until the 1990s, when expansion of the city's Custom House uncovered its foundations, along with more than 11,000 artefacts including clay pipes and gold cufflinks. The Custom House was built on stilts overhead, leaving the old foundations open.

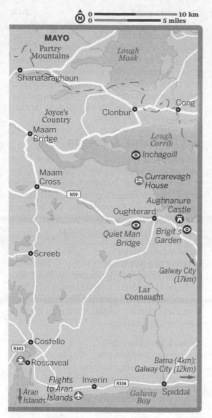

MAYO

Partry Mountains
Lough Mask
Shanafaraghaun
Joyce's Country
Cong
Clonbur
Maam Bridge
Lough Corrib
Inchagoill
Maam Cross
N59
Currarevagh House
Aughnanure Castle
Oughterard
Quiet Man Bridge
Brigit's Garden
Screeb
Galway City (17km)
Lar Connaught
Costello
R343
Rossaveal
Barna (4km); Galway City (12km)
Flights to Aran Islands
Inverin
R336
Aran Islands
Galway Bay
Spiddal

Interpretive panels detail the history of the city, the de Burgo family, and the replica artefacts on display. Volunteers are often on hand to give a verbal explanation of the ruins and their significance, and an insight into Galway life some 900 years ago.

Eyre Square   PARK

Galway's central public square is busy in all but the harshest weather. A welcoming open green space with sculptures and pathways, its lawns are formally named Kennedy Park in commemoration of JFK's June 1963 visit to Galway, though locals always call it Eyre Sq. Guarding the upper side of the square is the **Browne Doorway**, an imposing, if forlorn, fragment from the home of one of the city's merchant rulers. Dating from 1627, it was relocated here from Abbeygate St in 1905.

The street running along the southwestern side of the square is pedestrianised and lined with seating, while the eastern side is taken up almost entirely by the Victorian-era, grey limestone **Hotel Meyrick** (☑ 091-564 041; www.hotelmeyrick.ie; d €178-213, ste €229-278; P ☎).

Lynch's Castle   HISTORIC BUILDING

(Shop St; ⊘10am-4pm Mon-Wed & Fri, to 5pm Thu) **FREE** Now an AIB Bank, this excellent example of a town castle was built around 1500 (the exact date is unknown). The facade's stonework includes ghoulish gargoyles and the coats of arms of Henry VII, the Lynches (the most powerful of the 14 ruling Galway tribes) and the Fitzgeralds of Kildare. On the ground floor, interpretive panels cover its history and architecture; the magnificent fireplace is a highlight.

Atlantaquaria   AQUARIUM

(☑ 091-585 100; www.nationalaquarium.ie; Promenade, Salthill; adult/child €12/7.50; ⊘10am-5pm Mon-Fri, to 6pm Sat & Sun, closed Mon & Tue Nov–mid-Feb) More than 150 freshwater and sea-dwelling creatures from local waters swim in Ireland's largest native-species aquarium, including seahorses, sharks and rays. There's also a floor-to-ceiling ocean tank, fin whale skeleton and model submarine. Talks, tours and feeding sessions take place daily; check times online. Tickets are valid all day, so you can come and go as you please.

Salthill Promenade   WATERFRONT

A favourite pastime for Galwegians and visitors alike is walking along the Salthill Prom, the 2km-long seaside promenade running from the edge of the city along Salthill. Local tradition dictates 'kicking the wall' across from the diving boards (a 30- to 45-minute stroll from town) before turning around.

☞ Tours

If you're short on time, bus tours departing from Galway are a good way to see Connemara, the Burren and the Cliffs of Moher, while boat tours take you to the heart of Lough Corrib. Tours can be booked directly or at the Galway tourist office (p396).

Lally Tours   BUS

(☑ 091-562 905; www.lallytours.com; 4 Forster St; tours adult/child €30/20) Entertaining, informative day-long bus tours of Connemara, plus County Clare's Burren and the Cliffs of Moher, depart from Galway Coach Station (p396).

Galway Food Tours   FOOD & DRINK

(☑ 086 733 2885; www.galwayfoodtours.com; 21 Shop St; €50; ⊘daily Wed-Sun) Galway's vibrant foodie scene shines through on these

THE SALMON WEIR

Upstream from Salmon Weir Bridge, which crosses the River Corrib just east of Galway Cathedral, the river cascades down the Salmon Weir, one of its final descents before reaching Galway Bay. The weir controls the water levels above it, and when the salmon are running you can often see shoals of them waiting in the waters before rushing upriver to spawn. The salmon and sea-trout seasons usually span February to September, but most fish pass through during May and June.

It's a popular spot for anglers, even with May and June's restriction of one fish per day, as a fish can exceed 7kg. Contact Inland Fisheries Ireland (www.fisheriesireland.ie) for permits and licences.

two-hour gourmet walking tours. Tastings include sushi, local cheeses, artisan breads and Galway Bay oysters. Booking is required. Tours leave from outside Griffin's Bakery.

Other tours include a six-hour pub trawl of Galway and Connemara, plus food-themed cycling and whiskey tours. All tours are also available in French.

Walking Tours of
Medieval Galway WALKING
(☑091-564 946; www.galwaycivictrust.ie; ⊗2pm Tue & Thu May-Sep) FREE In the warmer months, the Dúchas na Gaillimhe (Galway Civic Trust) runs free 90-minute guided walking tours of Galway's medieval centre. Tours depart from the Hall of the Red Earl (p384). Donations are welcomed.

City Sightseeing Galway BUS
(☑091-562 905; https://csgalway.palisis.com; Eyre Sq; 48hr tickets adult/child €12/7; ⊗10.30am-3pm Mar-Oct) Hop-on, hop-off open-top bus tours of the city and its environs set out from Eyre Sq. Buses run every 90 minutes and make 14 stops including Salthill. Two children travel free with every adult.

Galway Tour Company BUS
(☑091-566 566; www.galwaytourcompany.com; adult/child from €30/20) A variety of tours of County Clare's Burren, the Aran Islands and Connemara depart from the Galway Coach Station (p396).

Corrib Princess CRUISE
(☑091-563 846; www.corribprincess.ie; Waterside, Woodquay; adult/child €17/8; ⊗May-Sep) Ninety-minute cruises aboard an open-top 157-seat boat pass castles and other historic landmarks along the River Corrib en route to the Republic's largest lake, Lough Corrib. In season, there are two or three departures per day.

Boats leave from Woodquay, just beyond the Salmon Weir Bridge.

🎭 Festivals & Events

Galway Food Festival FOOD & DRINK
(www.galwayfoodfestival.com; ⊗Easter) The area's sublime food and drink are celebrated for five days over the Easter weekend during the Galway Food Festival. Food and foraging tours, talks, cookery demonstrations and a market are among the highlights.

Cúirt International
Festival of Literature LITERATURE
(www.cuirt.ie; ⊗Apr) Top-name authors converge on Galway over eight days in late April for one of Ireland's premier literary festivals, featuring poetry slams, theatrical performances and readings.

Galway Film Fleadh FILM
(www.galwayfilmfleadh.com; ⊗early Jul) Early July sees the six-day Galway Film Fleadh set screens alight with new, edgy works.

Galway International Arts Festival ART
(www.giaf.ie; ⊗mid-late Jul) Catch performances and exhibits by top drama groups, musicians and bands, comedians, artists and much more during this two-week fiesta of theatre, comedy, music and art.

Galway Race Week SPORTS
(www.galwayraces.com; ⊗late Jul-early Aug) Galway Race Week draws tens of thousands of punters for a week of partying. Races in Ballybrit, some 7km northeast of the city centre, are the centrepiece of Galway's most boisterous festival. Thursday's Ladies Day is a highlight, with best dressed and best hat competitions. Shuttle buses (return €9) link Galway city with the racecourse.

Galway Pride Festival LGBT
(www.galwaypride.com; ⊗mid-Aug) Started in 1989, Galway's Pride Festival (Ireland's first) runs for six days in mid-August and includes a flamboyant parade of floats through the city's streets. Dance, music, workshops, talks and family events also feature.

Galway International Oyster & Seafood Festival FOOD & DRINK
(www.galwayoysterfest.com; South Park; ⊙late Sep) Going strong since 1954, the world's oldest oyster festival draws thousands of visitors. Events include the World Oyster Opening Championships, live music, a masquerade carnival and family activities.

Galway Christmas Market CHRISTMAS MARKET
(www.galwaytourism.ie; Eyre Sq; ⊙mid-Nov–mid-Dec) Stalls selling traditional Christmas fare and gifts glow with candles and fairy lights during this enchanting Christmas market.

🛏 Sleeping

Galway's festivals mean accommodation fills far in advance, particularly on weekends: book ahead. B&Bs line the major approach roads (College Rd, a 15-minute walk from the centre, has an especially high concentration). To take full advantage of Galway's tightly packed attractions, though, try for a room in the centre itself. Most B&Bs on College Rd have on-site parking but few central accommodation providers do, although many offer good deals at car parks.

★Kinlay Hostel HOSTEL €
(📞091-565 244; www.kinlaygalway.ie; Merchants Rd; dm/d/q €33/98/84; @🛜) The central location, cosy lounge, mellow vibe, pool table and smart kitchen and eating area make this large, brightly lit hostel a winner. Dorms vary in size but all the beds have individual curtains, lights and power and USB sockets. Tuesday night brings a pub crawl.

Snoozles Forster Street HOSTEL €
(📞091-530 064; www.snoozleshostelgalway.ie; Forster St; dm €25-30, d €120; @🛜) Dorms (with four, six or 10 beds) and private rooms all have bathrooms at this sociable 130-bed hostel near the train and bus stations. Continental breakfast is free and facilities include a kitchen, barbecue terrace, pool table and lounge with piano, fiddles and guitars.

Sleepzone HOSTEL €
(📞091-566 999; www.sleepzone.ie; Bóthar na mBan; dm €17-30, d/tr/q from €60/69/119; @🛜) In a bright red and yellow building, this big, busy backpacker base has over 200 beds in equally colourful dorms (most with their own bathrooms) and private rooms. Tea, coffee and toast are included. There's a large self-catering kitchen along with a coin-operated laundry and several lounges. Buses link it with its sister hostel in Connemara (p419).

Galway City Hostel HOSTEL €
(📞091-535 878; www.galwaycityhostel.com; Frenchville Lane, Eyre Sq; dm €33; @🛜) The awards keep rolling in for this cheery, orange-trimmed spot directly across from the train station, thanks to beds with electrical sockets and USB ports, privacy curtains in the bigger rooms, free continental breakfast, free printing, bike hire and a same-day laundry service. They'll also arrange tours, while live trad music plays in the downstairs bar.

In August, beds in all dorms, from four- to 16-bed, are the same price; beds in the bigger dorms fall to €19 in low season.

★Heron's Rest B&B €€
(📞091-539 574; www.theheronsrest.com; 16A Longwalk; d €179-199; 🛜) The thoughtful hosts of this B&B in a lovely row of houses on the banks of the Corrib provide binoculars and deck chairs so you can sit outside and enjoy the views – views also extend from all three snug but cute double-glazed rooms. Breakfasts incorporate organic local produce; other touches include complimentary decanters of port.

Gourmet picnic baskets can be arranged on request.

★House Hotel BOUTIQUE HOTEL €€
(📞091-538 900; www.thehousehotel.ie; Spanish Pde; d €205-285; 🛜) Inside a former warehouse in the liveliest part of the city, Galway's hippest hotel has a stunning lobby with retro-styled furnishings and modern art, accented with bold shades like fuchsia pink. The 40 soundproofed rooms are small but plush, with vivid colour schemes and quality fabrics. Bathrooms come with toiletries by Irish designer Orla Kiely.

The on-site restaurant and cocktail bar are always buzzing, especially on Friday and Saturday nights when there's live music.

Adare Guesthouse GUESTHOUSE €€
(📞091-582 638; www.adareguesthouse.ie; 9 Father Griffin Pl; s/d/f €75/130/150; P🛜) 🍃

GALWAY'S WEST END

For many Galwegians, the West End is the real Galway. Sitting just west of the River Corrib, the cluster of cafes, bistros, pubs and independent shops has an even more bohemian vibe than the rest of the city (which is saying something). Begin explorations by strolling over Wolfe Tone Bridge, cutting right up Raven Tce, into Upper Dominick St and on from there.

Galway City

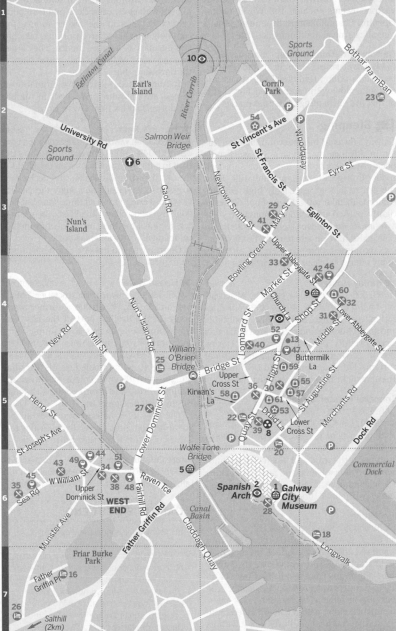

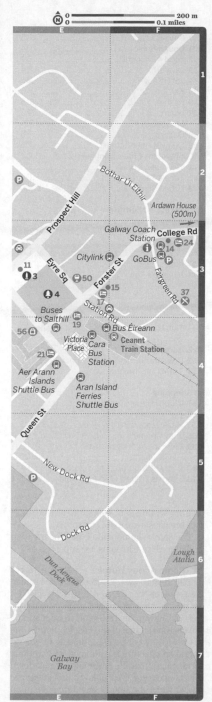

Overlooking a football pitch and children's playground, this beautifully kept guesthouse has generously sized rooms and service that runs like clockwork. Sift through 16, often organic, menu choices at breakfast including French toast with caramelised plums, smoked salmon and scrambled eggs, and buttermilk pancakes with honeyed pears.

Prices fall dramatically, by as much as €60 per double, from October to March.

Ardawn House
B&B €€

(☑ 091-568 833; www.ardawnhouse.com; College Rd; s/d/tr/f €55/95/140/190; P🖥) Green shrubs frame the front door of this red-brick house towards the end of the B&B-lined College Rd strip. Inside, antique-style furniture sits in elegant, sparingly decorated bedrooms, while at breakfast the homemade preserves are served amid gleaming silverware and china plates.

Cots are provided free of charge.

Residence Hotel
BOUTIQUE HOTEL €€

(☑ 091-569 600; www.theresidencehotel.ie; 14 Quay St; d/tr from €139/169; 🖥) The Residence is surrounded by Quay St's music-filled pubs. Its 20 rooms are small but strikingly decorated, with street-art-style murals above the beds. Amenities include streaming TV service, pod espresso machines and luxury smellies.

Light sleepers should ask for a quieter upper-floor room (reached by a lift).

Stop
B&B €€

(☑ 091-586 736; www.thestopbandb.com; 38 Father Griffin Rd; s/d/tr/f from €60/110/150/200; 🖥) Done up with contemporary artworks, stripped floorboards and bold colours, this design-conscious B&B delivers snug rooms where aesthetically pleasing space-saving tricks include hangers instead of wardrobes and streamlined work desks. Gourmet breakfast includes freshly squeezed orange juice and there's a handy supermarket right across the street.

St Judes
B&B €€

(☑ 091-521 619; www.st-judes.com; 110 Lower Salthill Rd; s/d €98/130; P🖥) In this elegant, double-fronted 1920s stone manor house, three individually furnished rooms feature antique-style chairs, polished floorboards and gleaming bathrooms. It's set in a peaceful residential area to the west of the city centre.

St Martins
B&B €€

(☑ 091-568 286; 2 Nun's Island Rd; s/d €55/85; 🖥) The nearest thing to staying with your own Irish relatives is checking into this welcoming

Galway City

B&B. Run by warm-hearted Mary, the impeccably kept older-style house has a gorgeous flower-filled garden overlooking the rushing River Corrib, and four cosy rooms complete with hot-water bottles.

Mary's hearty breakfasts will set you up for the day.

Huntsman Inn   INN €€
(☑ 091-562 849; www.huntsmaninn.com; 164 College Rd; r €130-140; 🅿🐕) On Lough Atalia, 1.5km northeast of central Galway, the Huntsman suits those who'd rather not stay in the city's busy heart. Its 12 rooms are streamlined and contemporary, with generous bathrooms. There's a well-regarded restaurant

and bar serving craft beers; the terrific gourmet breakfasts are extra (€8 to €11).

The smoky homemade baked beans with grilled local mushrooms are superb.

★ Glenlo Abbey Hotel   HISTORIC HOTEL €€€
(☑ 091-519 600; www.glenloabbeyhotel.ie; Kentfield Bushy Park, off N59; d €357-448, ste €538-984; 🐕) Set on the shores of Lough Corrib, 4km northwest of Galway, this 1740-built stone manor is the ancestral home of the Ffrench family, one of Galway's 14 tribes. Exceptionally preserved period architecture is combined with antique furnishings, marble bathrooms, duck-down duvets and king-sized pillows. Breakfasts are lavish, while the hotel's fine-dining Pullman

Restaurant (p393) occupies original *Orient Express* train carriages.

The vast grounds include a never-completed abbey with a walled garden, started by the family in 1790, as well as a nine-hole golf course (green fees €45) – the fourth hole sits on an island in the lough that's reached by a bridge. Booking a week in advance, online, brings 10% off the standard price.

G Hotel
DESIGN HOTEL €€€

(☏091-865 200; www.theghotel.ie; Wellpark, Old Dublin Rd; d €355-435, ste €515-1550; P✳🖥) Contrasting with its business-complex location near Lough Atalia, the stunning G Hotel has avant-garde interiors designed by Galwegian milliner-to-the-stars Philip Treacy, including a grand salon with 300 suspended silver balls, a Schiaparelli-pink cocktail lounge, and an award-winning restaurant with huge, seashell-shaped, purple banquettes. Shell-motif cushions feature in the sand-toned rooms; you can watch TV from the bathtub of most suites. The on-site spa looks out on a bamboo-planted forest.

Kids get a personalised cookie with milk on arrival. Valet parking is free.

✖ Eating

Seafood is Galway's speciality, and Galway Bay oysters star on many menus. The smorgasbord of eating options ranges from its wonderful market (p383) to adventurous new eateries redefining Irish cuisine, and a burgeoning restaurant scene in the West End (p387).

★ Sheridans Cheesemongers
DELI €

(☏091-564 829; www.sheridanscheesemongers. com; 14 Churchyard St; platters €9-18; ⊘shop 10am-6pm Mon-Fri, 9am-6pm Sat, wine bar 1pm-midnight Wed-Fri, noon-midnight Sat, 5pm-midnight Tue & Sun) Heavenly aromas waft from this fabulous cheesemongers filled with superb local and international cheeses. But the real secret is up a narrow flight of stairs at its wonderfully convivial wine bar. Sample from an Italian-influenced wine list while nibbling on platters of cheeses and charcuterie.

Urban Grind
CAFE €

(☏091-375 000; www.urbangrind.ie; 8 West William St; dishes €3.50-8.50; ⊘8am-6pm Mon-Fri, 9am-6pm Sat) Creative hub Urban Grind whips up fantastic breakfasts (cinnamon porridge; organic ciabatta with grilled chorizo and poached egg) and lunches (black- and white-bean tortilla with avocado and lime mayo;

glazed beef brisket with horseradish relish), and brews some of Galway's best coffees and loose-leaf teas. Craft beers and boutique wines are served until 11pm Thursday to Saturday in summer.

Breakfast is served until 11.30am on weekdays and all day on Saturday.

Dough Bros
PIZZA €

(☏091-395 238; www.thedoughbros.ie; Middle St; pizza €9-12; ⊘noon-9.30pm Sun-Wed, to 10pm Thu-Sat; 🖥) Beginning life as a food truck, this wood-fired pizza maker has found a permanent home. The bright-green-fronted space overflows with regulars, including plenty of students, who come for its perfect crusts, fresh, flavour-loaded toppings, craft beers and casual vibe. It doesn't take bookings, but you can order pizzas to take away.

Java's
BISTRO €

(☏091-533 330; 17 Upper Abbeygate St; mains €7.50-8.50; ⊘11am-midnight Sun-Wed, to 1am Thu-Sat; 🖉) We may be in western Ireland, but this is as northern France as they come. In this authentic Breton crêperie, savoury and sweet French pancakes have fillings ranging from goat's cheese with lardons, to pear with salted caramel. The cracking Irish breakfast crêpe comes with black pudding.

TGO Falafel Bar
VEGETARIAN €

(☏091-865 924; 11 Mary St; mains €7-9; ⊘noon-9pm; 🖉) 🌿 Galway's hipsters, vegetarians and vegans love the street-food creations rustled up by this ethics-conscious relative newcomer, thanks to fresh, flavourful vegan burgers, 'not dogs', beetroot arancini and carrot gravlax. Eat upstairs or take away.

Tuco's Taqueria
TACOS €

(☏091-563 925; www.tuco.ie; 6 Upper Abbeygate St; dishes €7-8; ⊘noon-9pm; 🖉) At this student favourite, you first choose from tacos, burritos or enchiladas, then select your fillings (meat, vegetarian or vegan), extras (guacamole, sour cream etc) and finally your salsa: Smokie Chipotle (hot), Roja (hotter) or Tuco's Terror (hottest; have a drink handy!).

Food 4 Thought
VEGETARIAN €

(☏091-565 854; 5 Lower Abbeygate St; mains €6-12; ⊘7.30am-5.30pm Mon-Fri, 8am-6pm Sat, 12.30-4.30pm Sun; 🖥🖉) Besides providing organic, vegetarian and vegan sandwiches, savoury scones and wholesome dishes such as cashew-nut roast, this place is great for finding out about energy workshops and

LEARN TO COOK MICHELIN-STYLE

Run by JP McMahon, owner/chef of Michelin-starred Aniar restaurant, the themes of the inspiring day-long courses at Aniar Boutique Cookery School (☑091-535 947; www.aniarrestaurant.ie; 53 Lower Dominick St; day courses €225) include tapas, dinner parties, fish, bread and wild food. Prepare to make your own butter and cheese, cure meat and fish, and pickle your own veg. Lunch and a glass of wine are included; bring a container to take your creations away.

Other options include a six-session Understanding Food course (€500), and day-long courses on contemporary Irish cooking, gastropub classics, and the perfect Christmas dinner.

yoga classes around town. The free filter coffee refills are plentiful.

Tables are set up on the pavement terrace in the warmer months.

★ **Cava Bodega** TAPAS €€
(☑091-539 884; www.cavarestaurant.ie; 1 Middle St; tapas €7-14; ⊙5-10pm Mon-Thu, 4-11pm Fri, noon-11.30pm Sat, noon-9.30pm Sun; ⏛) More than 50 regional Spanish tapas dishes are given a gourmet twist by star chef JP McMahon, whose other ventures include Michelin-starred Aniar. Showstoppers include turf-smoked salmon, duck fritter with seaweed jam and a harissa-infused Connemara mountain lamb, along with over 100 Spanish wines.

On Friday and Saturday, the bodega's bar stays open late.

★ **John Keogh's** GASTROPUB €€
(Lock Keeper; ☑091-449 431; www.johnkeoghs.ie; 22 Upper Dominick St; mains €11-24; ⊙kitchen 5-9pm Mon-Fri, 1-9pm Sat & Sun) Dark-wood panelling, snugs, stained glass, antique mirrors, book-lined shelves and blazing open fires set the scene for standout gastropub fare. John Keogh's doesn't take reservations, so arrive early to dine on mussels with home-baked soda bread and garlic aioli, or Irish oysters with a Guinness shot.

End with a Roscommon-brewed Sheep Stealer ale or rare whiskey at the bar.

★ **Oscar's** SEAFOOD €€
(☑091-582 180; www.oscarsseafoodbistro.com; Upper Dominick St; mains €16-30; ⊙5.30-9.30pm

Mon-Sat) The menu changes daily at this outstanding seafood restaurant but it might include monkfish poached in saffron and white wine and served with cockles, seaweed-steamed Galway Bay lobster with garlic-lemon butter, or lemon sole with samphire. The intensely flavoured fish soup is a delight.

Head chef Micheal O'Meara also authors a range of seafood gastronomy books.

★ **Ard Bia at Nimmo's** IRISH €€
(☑091-561 114; www.ardbia.com; Spanish Arch, Longwalk; cafe dishes €7-12, dinner mains €20-28; ⊙cafe 10am-3.30pm Mon-Fri, to 3pm Sat & Sun, restaurant 6-9pm; ⏛) Casually hip Ard Bia ('High Food' in Irish) is decorated with works by local artists and upcycled vintage furniture. Organic, local, seasonal produce (some foraged) features firmly – you might sample Cork monkfish, Burren smoked haddock or Galway goat's yoghurt. Opt for the upstairs restaurant or a street-level cafe serving flavour-packed breakfasts, brunches and lunches.

Kai MODERN IRISH €€
(☑091-526 003; www.kaicaferestaurant.com; 20 Sea Rd; mains lunch €12, dinner €19-28; ⊙cafe 9.30am-3pm Mon-Fri, 10.30am-3pm Sat, restaurant 6.30-10.30pm Tue-Sat; ⏛) Set in an olive-green building with exposed stone, bare timbers, fresh flowers and a glass-roofed atrium, this rustic West End spot is a fantastic place for daytime coffee, gourmet sandwiches and salads, and craft beer. Or come for adventurous evening meals such as monkfish with madras broth, perhaps followed by saffron sorbet. Reserve for dinner.

McDonagh's FISH & CHIPS €€
(☑091-565 001; www.mcdonaghs.net; 22 Quay St; cafe & takeaway mains €7-16, restaurant mains €15-30; ⊙cafe & takeaway noon-11pm Mon-Sat, 2-9pm Sun, restaurant 5-10pm Mon-Sat) A trip to Galway isn't complete without a meal here. Galway's best fish-and-chip shop fries up shoals of battered cod, plaice, haddock, whiting and salmon, accompanied by homemade tartar sauce. It's divided into two parts, with a takeaway counter and sociable cafe where diners sit elbow-to-elbow at long communal wooden tables, and a more upmarket restaurant.

Kasbah BISTRO €€
(☑085 734 0164; www.kasbahwinebar.ie; 2 Quay S; mains €5-28; ⊙food served 5-11.30pm Wed-Thu, 5pm-12.30am Fri, noon-4pm Sat) Set beside Galway's famous Tigh Neachtain pub (and also providing its bar food), the Kasbah flies the flag for fresh, locally sourced ingredients. So

you might be munching on creamy Atlantic chowder at lunch, or on Roscommon Black Angus rib-eye steak for dinner. They're winners either way.

Outside food-serving hours the wine bar is open until 12.30am on Saturday, and 11.30pm on Sunday.

Quay Street Kitchen IRISH €€
(⌨ 091-865 680; The Halls, Quay St; mains €12-22; ⊙noon-10pm; ⓐ⌨) Vegetarian and vegan dishes such as beer-battered organic tofu are a highlight of this small, busy restaurant on bustling Quay St. It also caters well for seafood fans (cider-steamed Connemara mussels, potted crab on crusty bread) and carnivores (Irish lamb shanks, beef and Guinness stew).

★Loam GASTRONOMY €€€
(⌨ 091-569 727; www.loamgalway.com; Fairgreen Rd; 2/3/7/9 courses €45/55/119/159; ⊙6-10pm Tue-Sat) ⌨ Enda McEvoy is one of the most groundbreaking chefs in Ireland today (with a Michelin star to prove it), producing inspired flavour combinations from home-grown, locally sourced or foraged ingredients: dried hay, fresh moss, edible flowers, wild oats, forest gooseberries, Salthill sea vegetables and hand-cut peat (which McEvoy uses in his extraordinary peat-smoked ice cream).

The on-site wine bar opens at 5pm and closes at 10pm Tuesday to Saturday.

★Pullman Restaurant FRENCH €€€
(⌨ 091-519 600; www.glenloabbeyhotel.ie; Glenlo Abbey Hotel, Kentfield Bushy Park, off N59; 2/3 courses €61/69; ⊙6.30-10pm daily Mar-Oct, 6.30-9.30pm Fri & Sat Nov–early-Feb; ⌨) One of the two original 1927 *Orient Express* train carriages at Glenlo Abbey Hotel (p390) was used in the filming of Agatha Christie's *Murder on the Orient Express* and was also part of Winston Churchill's 1965 funeral cortège. Sepia lamps, inlaid wood panelling, plush upholstery, white tablecloths and piped 1940s and 1950s music create an impossibly romantic setting for fine dining.

Expect dishes such as broth with bladderwrack, miso and mussels, and duck with fermented gooseberry and trout caviar. Vegetarians will delight in the entire menu devoted to their needs.

★Aniar IRISH €€€
(⌨ 091-535 947; www.aniarrestaurant.ie; 53 Lower Dominick St; 6/8/10 courses €72/89/99, with wine pairings €107-169; ⊙6-9.30pm Tue-Thu, 5.30-9.30pm Fri & Sat) ⌨ Terroir specialist Aniar is passionate about the flavours and food producers of Galway and west Ireland. Owner and chef JP McMahon's multicourse tasting menus have earned him a Michelin star, yet the casual spring-green dining space remains refreshingly down to earth. The wine list favours small producers. Reserve at least a couple of weeks in advance.

To discover the secrets behind classic and contemporary Irish cuisine, book a course at the on-site Aniar Boutique Cookery School

ⓘ Drinking & Nightlife

Galway's pub selection is second to none. The city is awash with traditional pubs offering live music, along with stylish wine and cocktail bars. Expect throngs of revellers, especially on weekends and throughout the summer.

Look out for craft beers by local success story Galway Hooker (www.galwayhooker. ie), named for the iconic local fishing boats, on tap around town.

The city's West End (p387) has a lively bar scene, popular with locals.

★Tigh Neachtain PUB
(www.tighneachtain.com; 17 Upper Cross St; ⊙11.30am-midnight Mon-Thu, to 1am Fri, 10.30am-1am Sat, 12.30-11.30pm Sun) Painted a bright cornflower blue, this 19th-century corner pub – known simply as Neáchtain's (*nock-tans*) or Naughtons – has a wraparound terrace for watching Galway's passing parade, and a timber-lined interior with a roaring open fire, snugs and atmosphere to spare. Along with perfectly pulled pints of Guinness and 130-plus whiskeys, it has its own range of beers brewed by Galway Hooker.

A short menu of quality bar food (mains €7 to €15) comes courtesy of Kasbah next door. Lunch might be an intensely flavoured fish chowder; evenings bring oysters and platters of meat and cheese.

★Tig Cóilí PUB
(⌨ 091-561 294; www.tigcoiligalway.com; Mainguard St; ⊙10.30am-11.30pm Mon-Thu, to 12.30am Fri & Sat, 12.30-11pm Sun) Two live *céilidh* (traditional music and dancing session) a day (at 6pm and 9.30pm) draw the crowds to this authentic fire-engine-red pub just off High St. Decorated with photos of those who have played here, it's where musicians go to get drunk or drunks go to become musicians...or something like that. A gem.

★Garavan's PUB
(⌨ 091-562 537; www.garavans.ie; 46 William St; ⊙11am-11.30pm Mon-Thu, to 12.30am Fri & Sat,

CLADDAGH RINGS

The fishing village of Claddagh has long been subsumed into Galway's city centre, but its namesake rings survive as a timeless reminder.

Popular with people of Irish descent everywhere, the rings depict a heart (symbolising love) between two outstretched hands (friendship), topped by a crown (loyalty). Jewellery shops selling Claddagh rings include Ireland's oldest, Thomas Dillon's Claddagh Gold (p396).

12.30-11pm Sun) Irish whiskeys are the speciality of this genteel old boozer. Incredible 'tasting platters' generally cost €11 to €14 – choices include an Irish Writers' platter, featuring the favourite tipples of Samuel Beckett, James Joyce and WB Yeats. Or splash out on the Grand Masters' platter (€95), with an 18-year-old blended Kilbeggan, 26-year-old Teeling single malt gold reserve and 1964 Dungourney pure pot still.

Look out for its whiskey-tasting events.

★ Crane Bar   PUB

(☑091-587 419; www.thecranebar.com; 2 Sea Rd; ☺10.30am-1am Mon-Thu, to 1am Fri, 12.30pm-1am Sat, to 11.30pm Sun) West of the Corrib, this atmospheric, always crammed two-storey pub is the best spot in Galway to catch an informal *céilidh*, with music nightly on both levels.

O'Connor's   PUB

(☑091-523 468; www.oconnorsbar.com; Upper Salthill Rd, Salthill; ☺7.30pm-late) Antiques fill every nook, cranny, wall and ceiling space of this 1942-established pub: clocks, crockery, farming implements, gas lights, sewing machines, fishing equipment, a stag's head and an almost life-size statue of John Wayne from *The Quiet Man*. Trad music and singalongs take place nightly.

Chalked blackboards feature quips including that the closest the pub gets to serving food is 'whiskey soup with ice croutons'.

Buddha Bar   COCKTAIL BAR

(☑091-563 749; www.buddhabar.ie; 14 Mary St; ☺5-11.30pm Mon, Wed & Thu, to 12.30am Fri & Sat, to 11pm Sun) Neighbouring the **Asian Tea House** (☑091-563 749; www.asianteahouse.ie; 15 Mary St; mains €11-24; ☺5-10.30pm; ☑), this lantern-lit bar decorated with Buddha statues mixes inventive cocktails such as the Shanghai Kiss (passion-fruit liqueur, sake, mango-infused vodka and orange juice) and Lotus Espresso (vanilla-infused vodka, coffee, Kahlúa and cinnamon), and serves five different Asian beers.

Nova   GAY & LESBIAN

(☑091-725 693; www.novabargalway.com; 1 West William St; ☺4-11.30pm Mon-Thu, 3pm-2am Fri, noon-2am Sat, 12.30-11.30pm Sun; ☎) Rainbow flags and motifs adorn Galway's premier LGBTQ bar, where Wednesday is student night, DJs spin dance music on Friday, Saturday brings drag acts, and cocktails are suggestively named.

O'Connell's   PUB

(☑091-563 634; www.oconnellsbargalway.com; 8 Eyre Sq; ☺10.30am-11.30pm Mon-Thu, to 12.30am Fri & Sat, 12.30-11pm Sun) Right on Eyre Sq, this traditional, garrulous pub has a great, huge heated beer garden, which is home to two outdoor bars and regular music events. Original floor tiles, stained-glass windows and a pressed-tin ceiling are among its preserved features; historical photos line the walls.

From Thursday to Saturday the Dough Bros (p391) serve pizza in the garden.

King's Head   PUB

(☑091-566 630; www.thekingshead.ie; 15 High St; ☺11am-11.30pm Sun-Thu, to 2am Fri & Sat) Sprawling over three floors, this vast, ancient pub dating from the 13th century has medieval details including cut-stone windows, fireplaces and the walls of Bank's Castle. There are live events nightly.

The building has a fascinating past. It was seized from the Mayor of Galway, Thomas Lynch Fitz-Ambrose, in 1654 by Colonel Peter Stubbers, who led Cromwell's army to Ireland and is suspected to have beheaded King Charles I in 1649 (hence the pub's name).

Monroe's Tavern   PUB

(☑091-583 397; www.monroes.ie; 14 Upper Dominick St; ☺10am-11.30pm Mon-Sat, noon-11.30pm Sun) Often photographed for its classic two-storey black-and-white facade, Monroe's has been at the heart of local nightlife for more than 50 years. Expect a buzzing vibe, live music nightly and an eclectic range of gigs.

Bierhaus   BAR

(☑091-376 944; www.bierhausgalway.com; 2 Henry St; ☺4pm-midnight Sun-Thu, to 1am Fri & Sat) At any one time 20 stouts, ales, Pilsners, wheat beers and ciders from around Europe rotate on the taps of this beer specialist, in addition to over 60 bottled varieties. There are also beer-based and traditional cocktails.

Soak them up with snacks such as smoked mackerel po' boys.

Róisín Dubh
PUB

(☑091-586 540; www.roisindubh.net; 9 Upper Dominick St; ⊙5pm-2am Sun-Thu, to 2.30am Fri & Sat) Emerging acts play here before they hit the big time. It's *the* place to hear bands but it's also renowned for regular stand-up comedy, along with a silent disco on Tuesday (and Wednesday when university's in session). Thursday brings the renowned, eclectic music mix of Strange Brew, open-mike nights take place on Sunday and the covered rooftop terrace is always crammed.

☆ Entertainment

Most pubs in Galway have live music at least a couple of nights a week, whether in an informal trad session or a headline act. Róisín Dubh is the best place for new bands; Tig Cóilí (p393) excels at trad sessions.

★ Druid Performing Arts Company
THEATRE

(☑091-568 660; www.druid.ie; Druid Lane) Internationally renowned, the Druid Performing Arts Company was established in 1975 and is famed for staging experimental works by young Irish playwrights, as well as new adaptations of classics. When it's not touring, its Galway home is the Mick Lally Theatre, situated in an old tea warehouse.

Town Hall Theatre
THEATRE

(☑091-569 777; www.tht.ie; Courthouse Sq) With a 400-seat main auditorium and 52-seat studio space, the Town Hall Theatre features Broadway and West End shows, orchestras, dance and occasional films.

It was built in 1820 as a courthouse and later used as a town hall and a cinema, before being revived in 1996 as Galway's municipal theatre.

Trad on the Prom
LIVE PERFORMANCE

(☑091-582 860; www.tradontheprom.com; Leisureland Theatre, Lower Salthill Rd, Salthill; adult from €32; ⊙mid-May–mid-Oct) A festival of Irish dancing and music, this long-running summer extravaganza is led by Máirín Fahy, a local diva of the fiddle. The glossy production is performed several nights per week in a venue near the Salthill Promenade.

🔒 Shopping

Speciality shops dot Galway's narrow streets, stocking cutting-edge fashion, Irish woollens, outdoor clothing and equipment, local jewellery, books, art and, of course, music.

★ Charlie Byrne's Bookshop
BOOKS

(☑091-561 766; www.charliebyrne.com; Cornstore, Middle St; ⊙9am-6pm Mon-Wed & Sat, to 8pm Thu & Fri, noon-6pm Sun) A civic treasure, the rambling rooms at Charlie Byrne's are crammed with over 100,000 new, secondhand, thirdhand, discounted and out-of-print books, including a trove of Irish interest (and Irish language) fiction and nonfiction. Look out for events including book launches and storytelling sessions.

Hazel Mountain Chocolate
CHOCOLATE

(www.hazelmountainchocolate.com; Middle St; ⊙11am-6.30pm) Truffles using Burren-produced Hazel Mountain chocolate (p380) are made on-site daily at this airy, contemporary shop behind a duck-egg-blue facade. It doubles as a cacao brew-bar serving its signature hot chocolate with toasted marshmallows and sweet treats such as chocolate-rhubarb brownies and chocolate-coffee cake with cardamom glaze.

Judy Greene's
ARTS & CRAFTS

(☑091-561 753; www.judygreenepottery.com; Kirwan's Lane; ⊙9.30am-6pm Mon-Sat) Handthrown pottery by Galway artist Judy Greene incorporates designs inspired by Ireland's flora and landscapes. Also displayed in her boutique are jewellery items made from Connemara green marble, plus clothing and artworks by Irish artists and designers.

The store is easily missed, tucked away at the end of Kirwan's Lane.

P Powell & Sons
MUSICAL INSTRUMENTS

(☑091-562-295; www.powellsmusic.ie; 53 William St; ⊙9am-5.30pm Mon-Thu & Sat, to 6pm Fri, 1.30-5.30pm Sun) You can pick up everything from bodhráns (hand-held goatskin drums) and harmonicas to tin whistles and sheet music at this wonderfully traditional crimson-coloured shop, with black trim and letters picked out in gold.

Kiernan Moloney Musical Instruments
MUSICAL INSTRUMENTS

(☑091-566 488; www.moloneymusic.com; 17 High St; ⊙10am-6pm Tue-Thu, to 7pm Fri, to 5.30pm Sat) Stringed instruments including fiddles and harps are the speciality of this dealer in fine instruments, which handles sales, rentals and repairs. It also stocks a small range of wind instruments. The shop sometimes opens on Sunday and Monday.

It's on the 1st floor; duck into the alley, then take the stairs immediately on the right.

Thomas Dillon's Claddagh Gold JEWELLERY
(☑ 091-566 365; www.claddaghring.ie; 1 Quay St; ⏰10am-5pm Mon-Sat, noon-4pm Sun) Established in 1750, this is Ireland's oldest jewellery shop, with vintage examples of Claddagh rings (p394), featuring two hands holding a heart topped by a crown, wax blanks and traditional tools in its small back-room 'museum'. Admission is free.

ⓘ Information

Galway's large, efficient **tourist office** (☑1850 230 330; www.discoverireland.ie; Forster St; ⏰9am-5pm Mon-Sat) can help arrange tours and has plentiful information on the city and region.

ⓘ Getting There & Away

BUS

Bus Éireann (www.buseireann.ie) operates daily services to all major cities in the Republic and the North from **Cara Bus Station** (☑ 091-562 000; Station Rd), near the train station. Hourly services include the following:

Cork Bus 51, €20, 4½ hours

Dublin Bus 20/X20, €16, 3½ hours

Dublin Airport Bus 20/X20, €19, four hours

Shannon Airport Bus 51, €10, 1¾ hours

Citylink (www.citylink.ie; 17 Forster St; ⏰office 9am-6pm Mon-Sat, 10am-6pm Sun; 📶) services depart from **Galway Coach Station** (New Coach Station; Fairgreen Rd), northeast of Eyre Sq. Destinations include the following:

Clifden (Connemara) €14, 1½ hours, six daily

Cork €18, three hours, five to eight daily

Dublin €13, 2½ hours, hourly

Dublin Airport €18, three hours, hourly

Limerick €14, 1¼ hours, five daily

GoBus (☑091-564600; www.gobus.ie; 📶) also has frequent services from Galway Coach Station to Dublin (€13, 2½ hours) and Dublin Airport (€18, 2½ hours).

Shuttle buses serve **Connemara Regional Airport** (Aerfort Réigiúnach Chonamara; NNR; ☑ 091-593 034; Inverin), for Aer Arann (p397) flights to the Aran Islands, and the ferry dock at Rossaveal for Aran Island ferries (p397).

TRAIN

From the **train station** (www.irishrail.ie; Station Rd), just off Eyre Sq, there are six to nine direct trains daily to/from Dublin's Heuston Station (€18, 2½ hours), and three to five daily to Ennis (€8, 1¼ hours). Connections with other train routes can be made – some involve changing at Athlone (€11, one hour, four to 10 daily).

ⓘ Getting Around

BICYCLE

Galway's Coca-Cola Zero bike-share scheme (www.bikeshare.ie/galway.html) has 22 stations around town and 195 bikes. For visitors, €3 (with €150 deposit) gets you a three-day pass. Otherwise, the first 30 minutes of each hire is free; up to two hours costs €1.50.

On Yer Bike (☑ 091-563 393; www.onyourbike-cycles.com; 42 Prospect Hill; per day from €25; ⏰9.30am-6.30pm Mon-Fri, 11am-4pm Sat) Offers bike hire, sales and repairs.

West Ireland Cycling (☑ 087 205 6904; www.westirelandcycling.com; Unit 1, Bridgewater Court, Fairhill Rd; bike rental per day/week €20/125; ⏰9.30am-6pm Apr-Sep, closed Sun Oct-Mar) Rents mountain, electric, racing and touring bikes as well as accessories like child trailers, children's seats and panniers. It also organises seven-day, self-guided bike tours throughout the region (€825 including accommodation).

BUS

You can walk to almost everything in Galway, including out to Salthill, but you'll also find frequent buses departing from Eyre Sq. For Salthill, take Bus Éireann bus 401 (€2, 15 minutes).

CAR & MOTORCYCLE

Parking on Galway's streets is metered. There are several multistorey and pay-and-display car parks around town – look out for 24-hour parking deals. Traffic jams can be lengthy during peak hours.

TAXI

Taxi ranks are located on Eyre Sq, on Bridge St and next to the bus and train **stations** (Station Rd). Alternatively, order one from **City Taxis** (☑091-525 252; www.citytaxisgalway.com; ⏰24hr).

ARAN ISLANDS

Easily visible from the coast of Counties Galway and Clare, the rocky, wind-buffeted Aran Islands have a desolate beauty that draws countless day trippers. Visitors who stay longer experience the sensation that they're far further removed from the Irish mainland than the 40-minute ferry ride or 10-minute flight would suggest.

An extension of the limestone escarpment that forms The Burren in Clare, the islands have shallow topsoil scattered with wildflowers, grass where livestock grazes and jagged cliffs pounded by surf. Ancient forts here are some of the oldest archaeological remains in Ireland.

Inishmore (Irish: Inis Mór) is the largest island and home to the only town, Kilronan. Inishmaan (Inis Meáin) preserves its age-old traditions and evokes a sense of timelessness. Inisheer (Inis Oírr), the smallest island, has a strong trad culture.

History

Little is known about the people who built the massive Iron Age stone structures on Inishmore and Inishmaan. Commonly referred to as 'forts', they are believed to have served as pagan religious centres. Folklore holds that they were built by the Firbolgs, a people who invaded Ireland from Europe in prehistoric times. It's thought that people came to the islands to farm, a major challenge given the rocky terrain. Early islanders augmented their soil by hauling seaweed and sand up from the shore and fished the surrounding waters on long *currachs*, which remain a symbol of the Aran Islands.

Early Christianity

Christianity reached the islands remarkably early, and some of the oldest monastic settlements were founded by St Enda (Éanna) in the 5th century. Enda appears to have been an Irish chief who converted to Christianity and spent some time studying in Rome before seeking out a suitably remote spot for his monastery.

From the 14th century, control of the islands was disputed by two Gaelic families, the O'Briens and the O'Flahertys. The English took over during the reign of Elizabeth I, and in Cromwell's times a garrison was stationed here.

Modern Isolation

In the 1600s conflicts brought destruction and disruption to Galway city. As its importance as a port waned, so did the fortunes of the Aran Islands, which relied on the city for trade. Their isolation meant that islanders maintained a traditional lifestyle well into the 20th century. Up to the 1930s, people wore traditional Aran dress: bright red skirts and black shawls for women, and baggy woollen trousers and waistcoats with *crios* (colourful belts) for men. The classic heavy cream-coloured Aran sweater, featuring complex patterns, originated here, and is still hand-knitted on the islands.

Air services began in 1970, changing island life forever, and today fast ferries make a quick (if sometimes rough) crossing.

ℹ️ ISLAND-HOPPING IN THE ARANS

Between mid-March and the end of October, interisland ferries mean you can visit all three islands in a day, starting at one and returning from another. Linking the route and connecting with your preferred mainland port can be complex – discuss plans with ferry firms or the Inishmore tourist office (p403).

Farming has all but died out on the islands and tourism is now the primary source of income. While Irish remains the official tongue, most locals speak English with visitors and converse with each other in Irish.

ℹ️ Getting There & Away

AIR

All three islands have landing strips. The mainland departure point is Connemara Regional Airport (p396), 30km west of Galway city, linked by a prebooked **shuttle bus** (☑ 091-593 034; www.aerarannislands.ie; Merchants Rd).

Aer Arann Islands (☑ 091-593 034; www.aerarannislands.ie; one-way/return €25/49) Offers flights aboard tiny fixed-wing prop planes to each of the islands up to six times a day. The flights take about 10 minutes and can be done as a day trip. The airline also offers scenic flights (per person from €75) in July and August and by arrangement year-round, flying over the Cliffs of Moher, Galway Bay and the Aran Islands.

BOAT

Year-round, **Aran Island Ferries** (☑ 091-568 903; www.aranislandferries.com; one-way/return €15/25) has sailings to Inishmore (40 minutes, two to three daily), Inishmaan (45 minutes, two daily) and Inisheer (55 minutes, two daily). Crossings are subject to cancellation in high seas. Boats leave from Rossaveal Ferry Terminal (p373), 38km west of Galway city, linked by **shuttle bus** (☑ 091-568 903; www.aranisland-ferries.com; Queen St). Contact the company in advance to arrange bike transport.

From mid-March to October, Doolin 2 Aran Ferries (p373) and Doolin Ferry Co (p373) run ferries to the Arans from Doolin, County Clare; they also run interisland ferries.

Inishmore

POP 762

Most visitors who venture out to the Aran Islands don't make it beyond the largest, and closest to Galway, Inishmore (Inis Mór) and

Inishmore

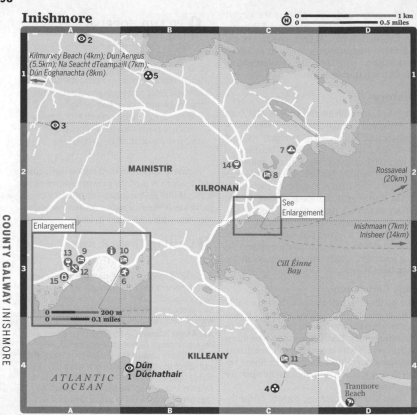

its most spectacular prehistoric stone fort, Dun Aengus, perched on the island's towering cliffs. Inishmore is 14km long and 4km at its widest stretch. Boats arrive and depart from Inishmore's main settlement, **Kilronan** (Cill Rónáin), on the southeastern side of the island. The arid landscape to its west is dominated by stone walls, boulders, scattered buildings and the odd patch of deep-green grass and potato plants.

Today, tourism turns the wheels of the island's economy: from May to September tour vans greet each ferry and flight, offering a ride around the sights.

⊙ Sights

★ Dun Aengus   HISTORIC SITE

(Dún Aonghasa; ☑ 099-61008; www.heritageireland. ie; adult/child €5/3; ⊙ 9.30am-6pm Apr-Oct, to 4pm Nov-Mar) Standing guard over Inishmore, Dun Aengus, 7km west of Kilronan, has three massive drystone walls that run right up to sheer

drops to the ocean below. Originally built around 1100 BC, it was refortified around 700 AD and is protected by remarkable *chevaux de frise,* fearsome and densely packed defensive limestone spikes. Displays at its small **visitor centre** provide context and a 900m walkway wanders uphill to the fort itself.

Powerful swells pound the 87m-high cliff face. A complete lack of railings or other modern additions that would spoil this incredible site means that you can not only go right up to the cliff's edge, but also potentially fall to your doom below – take care.

★ Dún Dúchathair   HISTORIC SITE

(Black Fort) FREE Many locals pick this ruined ancient fort, dating from the Iron Age or early medieval period, as their favourite Inishmore historic sight. It's dramatically perched on a clifftop promontory 2km southwest of Kilronan with terraced walls up to 6m high surrounding the remains of a *clochán* (early Christian beehive-shaped hut). Its name,

Inishmore

meaning the Black Fort, comes from the dark limestone prevalent on this part of the island.

Dún Eochla
HISTORIC SITE

FREE Atop the island's highest point, at 100m, historic fort Dún Eochla has a double ring of circular walls, and is thought to date from the early medieval era. It's signposted 2.8km west of Kilronan.

Teampall Chiaráin
RUINS

(Church of St Kieran) The highlight of this small church is on the eastern side – a beautifully carved boundary cross with a circular hole at the top. It was possibly used as a sundial; drawing an item of clothing through the hole is said to bring fertility and good luck. It's thought the church was founded in the 12th century by St Kieran (aka St Ciarán), who studied under St Enda and later established his own monastery at Clonmacnoise.

Teampall Chiaráin is set 1.5km northwest of Kilronan.

Na Seacht dTeampaill
HISTORIC SITE

FREE The scattered early Christian ruins known as the Na Seacht dTeampaill (Seven Churches) actually comprise just two ruined churches. The biggest is the 13m by 5m Teampall Bhreacáin (St Brecan's Church), which dates from the 8th to 13th century. You'll also find monastic houses and fragments of several 8th-century high crosses.

Dún Eoghanachta
HISTORIC SITE

FREE Probably built around 900 AD, Dún Eoghanachta has one towering circular wall that's 5m high, nearly 5m thick and 30m in diameter.

Teampall Bheanáin
RUINS

(Church of St Benen) Tiny Teampall Bheanáin dates from the 11th century. Measuring just

3m by 3m, it's thought to have been a hermitage. Unusually for a religious structure, it's oriented on a north–south axis rather than east–west. The views over Cill Éinne Bay are outstanding.

It's just over 2km southeast of Kilronan.

Wormhole
NATURAL POOL

(Poll na bPeist) Access to this extraordinary rectangular natural tidal pool is via a 750m clifftop walk southeast from Dun Aengus, or via a 1km signposted walking path from the hamlet of Gort na gCapall. Dubbed 'Serpent's Lair', the pool is a regular on the Red Bull Cliff Diving World Series circuit, when daredevil divers plunge from nearly triple the height of an Olympic tower-dive platform. Take care as the area can be dangerous in wild weather and high seas.

🎊 Festivals & Events

Tedfest
CULTURAL

(www.tedfest.org; ⊙ late Feb) Book a bed early if you're heading to this four-day carnival of nonsense celebrating the cult TV show *Father Ted* – it's a huge hit.

Pátrún
CULTURAL

(⊙ Jun) On the last weekend of June a centuries-old, three-day festival celebrates St Enda, the island's patron saint. Prepare for Galway hooker and *currach* races, a triathlon, sandcastle competitions, loads of Irish music and dancing on the pier.

🛏 Sleeping

After the last day trippers have left in summer, the island assumes a wonderful serenity. Advance bookings are advised, particularly in high season. Many B&Bs and inns close during winter.

COUNTY GALWAY INISHMORE

400

1

LISANDRO LUIS TRARBACH/SHUTTERSTOCK ©

1. The *Plassy* Wreck (p406) 2. Kilronan (p398), Inishmore
3. Inishmaan (p404) 4. Inisheer (p405)

3

2

LISANDRO LUIS TRARBACH/SHUTTERSTOCK ©

Aran Islands Scenery

Blasted by the wind and washed over by waves, the eroded, striated slivers of rock known as the Aran Islands hold a fascination for travellers. Their exposed landscapes are home to descendants of unimaginably hardy folk who forged their own culture of survival.

Aran Islands

Left to nature, the Arans would be bare rocks in the Atlantic. But generations of islanders have gathered and spread seaweed and sand by hand over the centuries, creating fertile fields.

Inishmore

On a summer weekend a thousand day trippers come to Inishmore to see one of Ireland's most impressive ancient wonders. Dun Aengus (p398) has been guarding a bluff over the Atlantic for more than 3000 years.

4

Inishmaan

Escape the crowds on Inishmaan, the least visited of the Arans. You'll see few others on walks across the dramatic countryside, where every path seems to pass the mysterious remains of past lives and end on a beach trod only by you.

Inisheer

An old castle, ancient churches and a magical spring are just a few of the highlights of Inisheer, the smallest of the Arans. Centuries of history are preserved in rock.

The Plassy Wreck

Star of the opening sequence of the comedy TV classic *Father Ted,* the *Plassy* (p406) was driven ashore on Inisheer by storms in 1963. Its rusting hulk attracts walkers and is the perfect embodiment of the timeless force of the elements.

ARAN GOAT CHEESE

You've encountered the produce on countless west Ireland menus; now meet the goats that make **Aran Goat Cheese** (☑ 087 222 6776; www.arangoat-cheese.com; Oughill; tours €15-30) possible. Call ahead to join a tour of this tiny dairy where some 160 Nubian and Saanen goats produce 1000L of milk a week so you can sample delights like soft goat's cheese, a feta-like product and Gouda.

Kilronan Hostel
HOSTEL €

(☑ 099-61255; www.kilronanhostel.com; Kilronan; dm from €24; ☺ late Feb–late Oct; @ 🖥) You'll see Kilronan Hostel perched above Tí Joe Mac's pub (p403) even before your ferry docks 200m east at the pier. It's a friendly place with lots of pluses: squeaky-clean dorms, a harbour-view terrace complete with barbecue, a kitchen and free continental breakfast. Owner Dave will even lend you a double kayak for free.

Ard Mhuiris
B&B €

(☑ 099-61208; Kilronan; s/d €75/90; 🖥) Peacefully situated a five-minute stroll from the centre of town, Martin and Cait's very tidy B&B is last in a line of cottages before fields and then the sea, with great ocean views. Martin can also take you on island tours by request. Cash only.

⭐ Aran Islands
Camping & Glamping
CAMPGROUND €€

(☑ 086 189 5823; www.irelandglamping.ie; Frenchman's Beach; campsites per person €10, glamping hut €150-160) 🖉 At this smart, modern campground with direct access to a sweeping white-sand beach, you can stay in a beehive-shaped glamping hut inspired by an early Christian stone *clochán*. Sleeping up to four people, the nine timber huts have bathrooms, kitchenettes, double beds and pull-out sofas, along with sea views from the front decks. The site's green credentials include solar power.

Facilities for those pitching tents include a communal camp kitchen, showers and a common room. It's 750m north of Kilronan.

⭐ Kilmurvey House
B&B €€

(☑ 099-61218; www.aranislands.ie/kilmurvey-house; Kilmurvey; s/d from €60/95; ☺ Apr–mid-Oct; 🖥) There's a dash of grandeur about Kilmurvey House, where 12 spacious rooms sit in an imposing, 18th-century stone mansion.

Breakfasts are convivial affairs, with homemade granola, porridge with whiskey and own-baked scones. It's a 500m stroll east to swim at pretty **Kilmurvey Beach**.

Children under 16 aren't permitted.

Pier House Guest House
INN €€

(☑ 099-61417; www.pierhousearan.com; Kilronan; d from €95; 🖥) You won't have time to lose your sea legs on the 50m walk from the ferry to this two-storey inn set on a small rise. The 12 rooms are decorated in rich shades of red, and come with tea- and coffee-making facilities. The sun terrace at the front is the perfect spot to watch harbour life go by. No under 16s.

Tigh Fitz
INN €€

(☑ 099-61213; www.tighfitz.com; s/d €95/120; 🖥) With their striped or floral fabrics, the rooms are simple, but the views are anything but – windows here frame stone-wall-laced-fields, azure seas and a rocky shore. It's some 2km southeast of Kilronan (ferry pickups can be arranged), but within a 30-minute stroll of sandy Tramore beach.

🍴 Eating & Drinking

Seafood is widespread along with vegetables grown in organic garden plots. Most cafes and restaurants are in Kilronan, as are the pubs, which serve some excellent food. Self-caterers can pick up supplies at the town's small **Spar supermarket** (☑ 099-61203; www.spar.ie; Kilronan; ☺ 9am-6pm Mon-Sat, to 5pm Sun; 🖥).

⭐ Bayview Restaurant
INTERNATIONAL €€

(☑ 086 792 9925; www.bayviewrestaurantinishmore.com; mains lunch €8-15, dinner €19-35; ☺ noon-9pm; 🖥 ♿) At Bayview there's local art on the walls, and a deal of artistry on the plates. Beautifully presented dishes might feature Aran goat's cheese with baked mushroom tapenade, whole lobster, chargrilled steaks or the day's catch with bursts of coriander or lime.

Kids are well catered for. Winter hours can vary.

Teach Nan Phaidi
CAFE €€

(☑ 099-20975; Kilmurvey; mains €5-12; ☺ 11am-5pm) At tiny, thatched Nan Phaidi, picnic tables and a riot of flowers sit in front of whitewashed walls, and happy diners tuck into award-winning treats. These might range from zesty, home-baked orange cake to fresh mackerel salad, or a flavourful beef and Guinness stew.

★**Tí Joe Watty's Bar** PUB
(☑086 049 4509; www.joewattys.ie; Kilronan;
☺noon-midnight Sun-Thu, 11.30am-12.30am Fri &
Sat Apr-Oct, 4pm-midnight Mon-Fri, noon-midnight
Sat & Sun Nov-Mar) Warmed by peat fires, the
island's oldest and most popular pub has trad
sessions every night in summer from 9pm
or 10pm, and weekends the rest of the year.
Wednesday's darts night is a local fixture.
There's a large beer garden and an extensive
list of Irish gins, craft beers and whiskeys.

Its seafood-focused menu (mains €14 to
€25) is excellent; book for dinner in summer.

The Bar PUB
(☑099-61130; www.inismorbar.com; Kilronan;
☺noon-11pm Sun-Thu, 11.30am-midnight Fri & Sat)
The buzzing Bar provided last pints for those
emigrating from Galway to the USA, hence
its former name, the American Bar (and its
photos of Elvis, Bob Dylan et al). Live music
plays nightly from May to mid-October, and
weekends year-round.

Quality food (mains €8 to €24), spanning
burgers and mussels steamed in wine, is
served from 10.30am to 9.30pm.

Tí Joe Mac's PUB
(Kilronan; ☺11am-11pm Mon-Thu, 11am-12.30am Fri
& Sat, noon-10pm Sun; ☎) Informal music sessions, open fires and a broad terrace with harbour views make Tí Joe Mac's a local favourite.

🛍 Shopping

Kilmurvey Craft Village ARTS & CRAFTS
(Kilmurvey; ☺hours vary) You'll see local knitters handcrafting traditional Aran sweaters
at this charming collection of traditional
thatched cottages. Woollens, Irish linen,
carved stonework and jewellery incorporating Celtic designs are among the local arts
and crafts for sale. It tends to be open daily

in the summer; check with the tourist office
if you're making a special trip.

Man of Aran Gift Shop GIFTS & SOUVENIRS
(☑085 710 5254; Kilronan; film per adult/child
€5/3; ☺9am-8pm Easter-Sep, winter hours vary;
☎) At Kilronan's main crossroads, this eclectic shop stocks souvenirs from T-shirts
to stained glass and Celtic-design jewellery,
and screens the iconic film *Man of Aran* five
times daily in its tiny 24-seat theatre. It also
has wi-fi (free with purchase) and a fine little coffee bar serving Italian brews.

ℹ Information

The Spar supermarket has the Aran Islands' only
ATM, but it's not unknown for it to run out of
cash, especially in summer.

The welcoming **tourist office** (☑099-61263;
www.aranislands.ie; ☺10am-5pm, to 6pm Jul &
Aug) is on the waterfront 50m northwest of the
ferry pier in Kilronan.

ℹ Getting Around

➤ From May to September, minibuses offer 2½-
hour tours of the island (€15) to ad hoc groups.
The drive – with commentary – between
Kilronan and Dun Aengus (p398) takes about
45 minutes each way. You can also negotiate
for private and customised tours.

➤ To see the island at a gentler pace, pony
traps with a driver are available from Easter to
September for trips between Kilronan and Dun
Aengus; the return journey costs between €50
and €100 for up to four people.

➤ Many places to stay have bicycles for use
or rent; alternatively, **Aran Bike Hire** (☑099-
61132; www.aranislandsbikehire.com; Inishmore Pier; mountain & road bike rental per day
€10, electric bikes from €30, deposit €20-30;
☺10am-5pm) rents out road, mountain and
electric bikes. They'll deliver your bicycles

FATHER TED'S DIVINE INSPIRATION

Devotees of the late 1990s cult British TV series Father Ted might recognise Inisheer
from the opening sequence showing the Plassy (p406) shipwreck on 'Craggy Island' –
the show's fictional island setting off Ireland's west coast. However, apart from this single
shot, the sitcom was mostly filmed in London studios, with additional location shots in
Counties Clare, Wicklow and Dublin. Alas, the parochial house (p376) and Vaughan's Pub
(p375) are nowhere to be found here (instead you'll find them in County Clare).

This hasn't stopped the Aran Islands from embracing the show as their own. Although
there has been some grumbling from its smaller neighbours, Inishmore has seized upon
Ted-mania for itself and each year hosts the wildly popular festival Tedfest (p399), when
accommodation on the island fills up fast.

Meanwhile, County Clare now has a competing Father Ted Festival (p376) in Lisdoonvarna. As Ted might say: 'Oh feck!'

(or, if you prefer to cycle, deliver your bags) to accommodation anywhere on the island.

Inishmaan

POP 183

The least-visited of the islands, with the smallest population, Inishmaan (Inis Meáin) is a rocky respite, roughly 5km long by 3km wide. Early Christian monks seeking solitude were drawn to Inishmaan, as was the author JM Synge, who spent five summers here over a century ago. The island they knew largely survives today: stoic cows and placid sheep, impressive old forts and warm-hearted locals, who speak Irish to each other exclusively.

Inishmaan's scenery is breathtaking, with a jagged coastline of startling cliffs, empty beaches and fields criss-crossed by a lattice-work of stone walls. Most buildings spread out along the road that runs east-west across the centre. You can easily walk to any place on the island, enjoying the stark scenery and sweeping views on the way. Inishmaan's down-to-earth islanders are largely unconcerned with the prospect of attracting the tourist dollar, so facilities are scarce.

⊙ Sights

Dún Chonchúir   HISTORIC SITE

(Conor's Fort) FREE Glorious views of Inishmaan's limestone valleys and maze of stone walls extend from this ruined elliptical stone fort, which sits on the island's highest point. Built sometime between the 1st and 7th centuries AD, its walls reach over 6m in height.

Dún Fearbhaigh   HISTORIC SITE

FREE The well-preserved ruins of this stone fort are 200m west of the Cill Cheannannach church ruins; the fort similarly dates from around the 8th century.

Synge's Chair   VIEWPOINT

At the desolate western end of the island, Synge's Chair is a viewpoint at the edge of a sheer limestone cliff with the surf from Gregory's Sound booming below. The cliff ledge is often sheltered from the wind; do as Synge did and find a stone perch to take it all in. The formation is two minutes' walk from the end of the lane. On the walk out to Synge's Chair, a sign points the way to a *clochán*, hidden behind a house and shed.

Teach Synge   HISTORIC BUILDING

(☑ 099-73036; €3; ⊙ by appointment Apr–mid-Sep) Now a small museum, this 300-year-old

thatched cottage, on the road just before you head up to Dún Chonchúir, is where the writer JM Synge (1871–1909) spent his summers between 1898 and 1902.

Church of the Holy Mary of the Immaculate Conception   CHURCH

(Séipéal Naomh Mhuire gan Smal; ⊙ 10am-7pm Apr–mid-Sep, to 5pm mid-Sep–Mar) Built in 1939, this small church has beautiful stained-glass windows designed by the studio of Harry Clarke and an altar by James Pearse (the father of Pádraig Pearse, aka Patrick Pearse, who led the Easter Rising in 1916).

🛏 Sleeping & Eating

Some B&Bs serve evening meals, usually using organic local produce. Food is also on offer at the acclaimed Inis Meáin inn and the pub, while the **shop** (⊙ 10am-6pm Mon-Fri, to 2pm Sat) sells grocery staples.

Cois Cuain   B&B €€

(☑ 087 972 8796; www.coiscuain.com; s/d/f €40/80/90; ⊙ Apr-Sep) You'll get spotless rooms, a fine breakfast and a wealth of tips on exploring Inishmaan at this traditional, whitewashed stone Aran house. It's within easy striking distance of the beach, the pub and eateries, and they'll even run you a seaweed bath on request.

Tig Congaile   B&B €€

(☑ 099-73085; www.bbinismean.com; s/d from €50/80; ☎) 🍴 The spacious rooms here have gleaming bathrooms and broad island views. An air of relaxation pervades, helped by the yoga classes and holistic massages on offer. The restaurant (mains €16 to €30) delights in delivering freshly ground Guatemalan coffee and dishes packed with own-grown and foraged produce – potatoes scattered with seaweed, fresh fish on wild garlic. Dining times vary; book ahead.

Eco initiatives include solar power, and captured rainwater and seaweed fertiliser for the garden.

An Dún   B&B €€

(☑ 087 680 6251; www.inismeainaccommodation. ie; d from €103; ⊙ Mar-Oct; ☎) At modern An Dún the five comfortable cheery rooms come with wide sea views. Local cuisine such as pillowy potatoes (fertilised with seaweed), luscious smoked salmon and fresh local fish are served at its restaurant (three-course dinner menu €37); nonguests are welcome but need to book.

Kids under 12 aren't accepted. An Dún is at the foot of the Dún Chonchúir historic site.

★ **Inis Meáin** INN €€€
(☑ 086 826 6026; www.inismeain.com; d 2/3/5 nights from €1000/1350/2300; ☺ Mar-Sep; ⏝) 🍃 Everything about Inis Meáin gives a boutique twist to Aran's wild heart. Five suites sit among curving, stacked stone walls, wraparound windows, crisp styling and cinematic views. The acclaimed restaurant (dinner at 8pm Wednesday, Friday and Saturday) is bold enough to deliver pared-down combinations of own-grown veg, freshly harvested shellfish and home-reared meat. Booking is required; four courses cost €75.

If you'd like a suite, book early – they sell out pretty much instantly when launched each October. Prices fall by as much as €750 per booking outside July and August.

Teach Ósta PUB
(☑ 099-73003; ☺ noon-late) A local linchpin, the island's only pub has outdoor tables with great views. Live music plays most nights in July and August, with spontaneous weekend sessions throughout the rest of the year. Pub food (mains €12 to €16) generally stops around 7pm and isn't always available in the winter months, though the bar often keeps going until the wee hours.

🛍 Shopping

★ **Cniotáil Inis Meáin** CLOTHING
(Inis Meáin Knitting Co; ☑ 099-73009; www.inis meain.ie; ☺ 10am-4pm Mon-Fri) One of the island's main employers was founded more than 40 years ago and today exports fine woollen garments – including iconic Aran sweaters – to some of the world's most exclusive shops. You can buy the same items at this factory shop (tax free for visitors from outside the EU). Call to confirm hours before visiting.

ℹ Getting Around

➜ Enjoy a fact-filled one- to two-hour minibus or pony-trap tour of the island (€10 to €15 per person). Look out for them at the **airstrip** (IIA) and pier.

➜ Check to see whether Inishmore-based Aran Bike Hire will have bike rentals at the pier.

Inisheer

POP 281

Inisheer (Inis Oírr), the smallest of the Aran Islands at roughly 3km wide by 3km long, has a palpable sense of enchantment, enhanced by the island's wildflower–strewn landscapes, deep-rooted mythology and enduring traditional culture.

The wheels of change turn very slowly here. Electricity wasn't fully reliable until 1997. Given that there's at best 15cm of topsoil to eke out a living farming, the slow conversion of the economy to tourism has been welcome. Day trippers from Doolin (as many as 1000 on a balmy summer weekend), 8km across the water, enliven the hiking paths all summer long. Facilities are still limited, however, so visitors need to come prepared.

ARTISTIC ARAN

The Aran Islands have sustained a strong creative streak, partly as a means of entertainment during long periods of isolation. Artists and writers from the mainland have similarly long been drawn to the elemental nature of island life.

Dramatist JM Synge (1871–1909) spent a lot of time on the islands. His play *Riders to the Sea* (1905) is set on Inishmaan, while his renowned *The Playboy of the Western World* (1907) also draws upon his island experiences. Synge's highly readable book *The Aran Islands* (1907) is the classic account of life here and remains in print.

American Robert Flaherty came to the islands in the early 1930s to film *Man of Aran*, a dramatic account of daily life. He was something of a fanatic about the project and got most of the locals involved in its production. The film remains a classic that's deeply evocative of island life.

The noted 1996 play *The Cripple of Inishmaan*, by Martin McDonagh, involves tragic characters and a strong desire to leave the island in 1934.

Map-maker Tim Robinson has written a wonderful two-volume account of his explorations on Aran, called *Stones of Aran: Pilgrimage* and *Stones of Aran: Labyrinth*.

Local writer Liam O'Flaherty (1896–1984), from Inishmore, wrote several harrowing novels, including *Famine* (1937) and *Insurrection* (1950).

◉ Sights & Activities

Wandering the lanes with their ivy-covered stone walls is the best way to experience the island. There are two, circular waymarked National Looped Trails, one of 8km, one of 13km.

Well of Enda   HISTORIC SITE

(Tobar Éanna) Some locals still carry out a pilgrimage known as the Turas to the Well of Enda (also known as Éinne or Endeus), a bubbling spring in a remote rocky expanse in the southwest. The ceremony involves, over the course of three consecutive Sundays, picking up seven stones from the ground nearby and walking around the small well seven times, putting one stone down each time, while saying the rosary until an elusive eel appears from the well's watery depths.

If, during this ritual, you're lucky enough to see the eel, it's said your tongue will be bestowed with healing powers, enabling you to literally lick wounds better.

O'Brien's Castle   HISTORIC BUILDING

(Caisleán Uí Bhriain) FREE Built in the 14th century on the island's highest point, this tower house was constructed within the remains of a ring fort called Dún Formna, dating from as early as the 1st century AD. The 100m climb rewards with a sweeping panorama across clover-covered fields to the beach and harbour. The views are especially dramatic at sunset. You're free to walk around the ruins.

Plassy   SHIPWRECK

A steam trawler launched in 1940, the *Plassy* was thrown up on to the rocks on 8 March 1960 and driven on to the island a couple of weeks later after another storm. Its cargo of whiskey was never recovered but miraculously, all on board were saved. The Tigh Ned (p407) pub has a collection of photographs and documents detailing the rescue. An aerial shot of the wreck was used in the opening sequence of the cult TV series *Father Ted*.

Áras Éanna   ARTS CENTRE

(☑ 099-75150; www.discoverinisoirr.com; ⊙ hours vary, Jun-Sep) Inisheer's large community arts centre sits out on an exposed stretch of the northern side of the island and hosts visiting artist events, cultural programs and performances.

Teampall Chaoimháin   HISTORIC BUILDING

Named for Inisheer's patron saint, who is buried close by, the roofless 10th-century Church of St Kevin and its small cemetery perch on a tiny bluff near the Strand. On the eve of St Kevin's 14 June feast day, a Mass is

---

WALKING INISHEER'S COAST

As well as the island's two official, circular trails, you can also circumnavigate Inisheer's 12km shoreline in about five hours, gaining a far deeper understanding of the island than from hurried visits to the main sights.

From the Inisheer ferry **pier**, walk west along the narrow road parallel to the shore and go straight on to the small fishing pier at the northwest corner of the island. Continue along the road with the shingle shore on one side and a dense patchwork of fields, enclosed by the ubiquitous stone walls, on the other. Look for tide pools and grey seals resting in the sun.

About 1km from the acute junction, turn left at the painted sign; about 100m along the paved lane is the Well of Enda (p406).

Continue southwest as the path becomes a rough track. After about 600m, head roughly south across the limestone pavement and strips of grass to the shore. Follow the gently sloping rock platform around the southwestern headland (Ceann na Faochnaí) and walk east to the **lighthouse** near Fardurris Point (two hours from the ferry pier).

Stay with the coast, turning northeast. You'll see the wreck of the Plassy in the distance. When necessary, use stiles to cross walls and fences around fields. Note that the grass you see grows on about 5cm of topsoil created by islanders who cleared rocks by hand and then stacked up seaweed over decades.

Head north, following the track, which then becomes a sealed road at the northern end of Lough More. Continue following the road along the northern shore of the island, past the **airstrip** (INQ).

At the airstrip you can diverge for Teampall Chaoimháin and O'Brien's Castle. Otherwise rest on the lovely sands of the curving **beach** and check out the nearby **Cnoc Rathnaí**, a Bronze Age burial mound (1500 BC) that is remarkably intact considering it was submerged by sand until the 19th century, when it was rediscovered.

held here in the open air at 9pm. The sick sleep here for a night hoping to be healed.

Cill Ghobnait
CHURCH

(⊙9am-5pm) This tiny 9th-century church is named after St Gobnait (locally spelt Ghobnait), who fled here from Clare to escape a family feud. Gobnait is the patron saint of bees and beekeepers, and is believed to have cured the sick using honey.

✷ Festivals & Events

Craiceann
MUSIC

(www.craiceann.com; ⊙late Jun) Inisheer reverberates to the thunder of traditional rhythms at the end of June with bodhrán classes, workshops and concerts. Craiceann takes its name from the Irish word for 'skin', referring to the goatskin used to make these circular drums. The festival features top talent, and nightly drumming sessions take place in the pubs.

▦ Sleeping & Eating

Inisheer has B&Bs, pub accommodation and a hostel; book well in advance in summer and especially during Craiceann week in June.

Seafood is the island's speciality. Pubs tend to serve food, but confirm opening hours, particularly outside the Doolin ferry season (mid-March to October). Some places only accept cash and Inisheer has no ATM, so plan ahead.

Brú Radharc Na Mara Hostel
HOSTEL €

(☑099-75024; www.bruhostelaran.com; dm/d €25/70; ⊙Apr-Sep; @🛜) The name translates as Seaview Hostel, and this sweet sleep spot 100m west of the pier doesn't disappoint. It offers a large kitchen, a warming fireplace, book swap, bike hire (€10 per day) and those eponymous ocean views. A continental breakfast is thrown in.

Dorms have four or six beds; private rooms have their own bathrooms.

Radharc an Chaisleán
B&B €

(☑099-75983; Castle Village; s/d/f from €55/75/85) With views looking on to Inisheer's 14th-century O'Brien's Castle, family-friendly Radharc an Chaisleán comes complete with an array of children's toys. It's open all year, but you'll need to book ahead in the winter.

★ South Aran House & Restaurant
B&B €€

(☑099-75073; www.southaran.com; s/d €65/84; ⊙Apr-Oct; 🛜) ✔ There's an idyllic feel to this rustic B&B; lavender grows outside windows framing broad Atlantic views, and the

GUIDED WALKS IN CONNEMARA
••••••••••••••••••••••••••••••••••••••

Maps of the many walking trails in Connemara are sold at bookshops and tourist offices. However, to really appreciate the region's unique geology, natural beauty and ancient history, you may want to go with a guide. **Connemara Adventure Tours** (☑095-42276; www.connemaraadventuretours.com; tours from €655; ⊙Apr-Oct) runs five- and seven-day walking and cycling tours themed around history and food. Meals and accommodation are included.

four bedrooms have underfloor heating and wrought-iron beds. Breakfasts feature apple fritters with potato cakes and the evening restaurant (mains €17 to €25) showcases local seafood and organic produce; booking required.

Guests must be over 18. Regular events include cookery and foraging courses (from €30 per person).

Tigh Ruairí
PUB €€

(Rory's; ☑099-75002; d €55-94; 🛜) Rory Conneely's atmospheric digs have 20 rooms with private bathrooms and dark-wood furniture; many have views across the water. The cosy pub downstairs serves pub fare (mains €10 to €14) and hosts live music sessions in summer.

★ Teach an Tae
CAFE €

(☑099-75092; www.cafearan.ie; dishes €5-12; ⊙11am-5pm May-early Nov) ✔ Wild island raspberries and blackberries, home-grown salads, eggs from the cafe's chickens and apples from its heritage orchard are used in dishes here. Treats include net-fresh local mackerel, a herby Aran goat's cheese tart and an Irish porter cake that's laced with Guinness. Cash only.

Tigh Ned
PUB FOOD €

(☑099-75004; www.tighned.com; dishes €7-15; ⊙kitchen noon-4pm Apr-Oct, bar 10am-11.30pm Apr-Oct) That the daily seafood special is caught by the owner speaks volumes. Snug, welcoming Tigh Ned's has been here since 1897 dishing up inexpensive sandwiches, cottage pie and, of course, fish and chips. They're best enjoyed in Ned's harbour-view beer garden or inside listening to lively trad tunes (weekends, June to August).

Shopping

Cleas ARTS & CRAFTS

(☑ 099-75979; www.cleas-teoranta.com; ⊙ 9am-5.30pm Mon-Fri) A one-stop shop of Inisheer's traditional crafts, at Cleas you'll find willow baskets, model Aran *currachs*, brightly coloured belts and hand-harvested seaweed products.

Cleas also offers occasional basket-weaving workshops (call for details) and weekly, 1½-hour guided walks (€5), which set off from the shop at noon on Tuesdays, March to September.

❶ Information

In July and August a small **kiosk** (www.discover inisoirr.com; ⊙ 10am-6pm Jul & Aug) at the ferry pier provides tourist information.

❶ Getting Around

➡ **Rothaí Inis Oírr** (☑ 099-75049; www.rothai-inisoirr.com; bike rental per day from €10; ⊙ 9am-7pm) rents out road bikes, mountain bikes and 21-speed bikes, and has a good free map. Many accommodation places also rent out bikes to nonguests.

➡ In summer, you can take a tour of the island on a pony trap (€10 to €15 per hour per person); drivers meet arriving ferries.

CONNEMARA

The name Connemara (Conamara) translates as 'Inlets of the Sea' and the roads along the peninsula's filigreed shoreline bear this out as they wind around the coves of this breathtaking stretch of Ireland's jagged west coast.

From Galway city, a slow, shore-side route passes hidden beaches and seaside hamlets. At the start of the Gaeltacht region, west of Spiddal, the scenery becomes increasingly dramatic, with parched fields rolling to fissured bays.

Connemara's starkly beautiful interior, traversed by the N59, is a kaleidoscope of rusty bogs, lonely valleys and shimmering black lakes. At its heart are the Maumturk Mountains and the pewter-tinged quartzite peaks of the Twelve Bens mountain range, with a network of scenic hiking and biking trails. Everywhere the land is laced by stone walls.

❶ Information

➡ Galway city's tourist office (p396) has lots of information on the area.

➡ Online, Connemara Tourism (www.connemara.ie) and Go Connemara (www.goconnemara.com) have region-wide info and links.

❶ Getting There & Around

Organised bus tours from Galway city with companies such as Lally Tours (p385) offer a good, if condensed, overview of the region.

BUS

➡ Bus Éireann (www.buseireann.ie) serves most of Connemara. Services can be sporadic – a handful operate May to September only, or July and August only.

➡ Citylink (www.citylink.ie) has several buses a day linking Galway city with Clifden via Oughterard and going on to Cleggan and Letterfrack.

➡ For stop-offs between towns, you might be able to arrange a drop-off with the driver.

CAR & MOTORCYCLE

Your own wheels are the best way to get off this scenic region's beaten track. Watch out for the narrow roads' stone walls and meandering Connemara sheep – characterised by their thick creamy fleece and coal-black face and legs.

The main road from Galway is the N59, which heads northwest via Oughterard to Clifden then swings northeast up to Letterfrack and Connemara National Park and on to Killary Harbour before crossing into County Mayo.

An alternative route between Galway and Clifden is via the R336 and R340; you can either join the N59 near Recess, or continue along the coast via the R342 then R341 to Roundstone, Ballyconneely and Derrygimla and on to Clifden. Side roads lead to tiny inlets, little coves and remote beaches. In the south, the low, bleak islands of Lettermore, Gorumna and Lettermullen are linked by bridges.

Oughterard & Around

POP 1318

The charmingly down-to-earth village of Oughterard (Uachtar Árd) sits on the shore of the Republic's biggest lake, Lough Corrib. Some 64km long and covering around 175 sq km, the lake virtually cuts off western Galway from the rest of the country and encompasses more than 360 islands.

Immediately west of Oughterard, the countryside opens up to sweeping panoramas of lakes, mountains and bogs.

◉ Sights & Activities

★ Aughnanure Castle
CASTLE

(☑ 091-552 214; www.heritageireland.ie; off N59; adult/child €5/3; ⊙9.30am-6pm Mar-Oct) The 'Fighting O'Flahertys' were based at this superbly preserved 16th-century fortress 4km east of Oughterard. The clan controlled the region for hundreds of years after they fought off the Normans. Today their six-storey **tower house** stands on a rocky outcrop overlooking Lough Corrib and has been extensively restored.

Surrounding the castle are the remains of an unusual double *bawn* (area surrounded by walls outside the main castle); there's also the remains of the banqueting hall and a small, now isolated **watchtower** with a conical roof. The River Drimneen once enclosed the castle on three sides, while today the waterway washes through a number of natural caverns and caves beneath the castle.

Inchagoill
ISLAND

The largest island on Lough Corrib, Inchagoill lies about 5km offshore from the lake's edge, some 8km north of Oughterard. The island is a lonely place dotted with ancient remains. In the summer **Corrib Cruises** (☑ 087 994 6380; www.corribcruises.com; Oughterard Pier; adult/child €28/14; ⊙noon Wed-Mon Jul & Aug) runs day cruises. Alternatively, rent your own boat from Molloy's Boats (p410).

Inchagoill's most fascinating sight is a 6th-century obelisk called **Lia Luguaedon Mac Menueh** (Stone of Luguaedon, Son of Menueh), which identifies a burial site. It stands about 75cm tall, near the Saints' Church. It's claimed that the Latin writing on the stone is the second-oldest Christian inscription in Europe, after those in the catacombs in Rome.

The prettiest church is the Romanesque **Teampall na Naoimh** (Saints' Church), probably built in the 9th or 10th century, with carvings around its arched doorway. **Teampall Phádraig** (St Patrick's Church) is a small oratory of a very early design, with some later additions.

Glengowla Mines
MINE

(☑ 091-552 021; www.glengowlamines.ie; off N59, Glengowla East; adult/child €11/4.50; ⊙10am-6pm mid-Mar–Oct) These 19th-century mines 3km west of Oughterard yielded silver, lead and glistening quartz. As well as marvelling at some of the treasures unearthed, visitors learn about the tough existence of workers here until the mine closed in 1865. You can also try

---

THE QUIET MAN BRIDGE

One of the most photogenic locations from the iconic 1952 John Wayne and Maureen O'Hara film, the eponymous Quiet Man Bridge is some 7km west of Oughterard off the N59. Looking much as it did in the film, the picture-perfect little arched span (whose original name was Leam Bridge) would be a lovely spot even without screen immortality. Purists will note, however, that the scene based here included close-ups from a set in Hollywood.

---

gold-panning and feed horses and donkeys at the adjacent working farm. Sheepdog herding and peat-cutting demonstrations can be arranged with prior notice for an additional €5.

Brigit's Garden
GARDENS

(☑ 091-550 905; www.brigitsgarden.ie; off N59, Pollagh, Rosscahill; adult/child €8/5; ⊙10am-5.30pm Mar-Oct, to 5pm Nov-Feb) 🌱 Covering 4.5 hectares of woodland and meadowland, and with traditional architecture including a reed-thatched *crannóg* roundhouse, tranquil Brigit's Garden is dedicated to Celtic myth and heritage. Four gardens represent seasonal Celtic festivals: **Samhain** (winter), **Imbolc** (spring), **Bealtaine** (summer) and **Lughnasa** (autumn). There's also a huge **sundial** (Ireland's largest) and a sustainability zone with solar panels, a wood pellet boiler and a polytunnel. Salads and herbs from the gardens are used at the on-site cafe. It's 9km southeast of Oughterard.

Knockillaree Riding Centre
HORSE RIDING

(☑ 087 960 4517; www.connemarahorseriding.com; Rusheeney Rd; treks per 1/2hr €35/65, lessons adult/child €25/20; ⊙by appointment) Treks lasting one to five hours head out along mountain trails or through woodland along the shores of Lough Corrib. Lessons are available for riders of all levels, with ponies for kids.

The centre can also organise riding in an approved yard for people with disabilities.

🛏 Sleeping & Eating

Currarevagh House
HOTEL €€

(☑ 091-552 312; www.currarevagh.com; Glann Rd; s €95-140, d €150-190; ⊙mid-Mar–Oct; P🐾) Set in 73 hectares on the shores of Lough Corrib, 19th-century Currarevagh House is a magnificent 12-bedroom mansion. Fresh flowers fill the halls, rooms have high ceilings, and the

FISHING ON LOUGH CORRIB

Lough Corrib is world-famous for its salmon and wild brown trout, and Oughterard is one of Ireland's principal angling centres. The highlight of the fishing calendar is the mayfly season, when zillions of the small bugs hatch over a few days (usually in May) and drive the fish – and anglers – into a frenzy. Salmon begin running around June.

Hotels and lodges around Lough Corrib can usually arrange fishing equipment, as can boat-rental companies such as **Molloy's Boats** (☑ 091-866 954; Baurisheen; motor/row-boat per day €70/40, motorboat with guide €150; ☺ by appointment). **Tuck's Angling Shop** (☑ 091-552 335; Main St; ☺ 9am-6pm Mon-Sat) offers tackle, bait and advice.

grounds are wonderful for rambling. Breakfast and afternoon tea are included in the price. It's around 6km north of Oughterard.

Four-course evening meals (€50) feature local ingredients such as trout.

Connemara Lake Hotel   HOTEL €€
(☑ 091-866 016; www.theconnemaralakehotel.com; Main St; s/d/f from €75/80/150; ☎) Anglers love this bright, white hotel in the centre of Oughterard. Not only can it organise boat and equipment hire, it will also arrange for your catch to be cooked by the chef, or shipped to the **Connemara Smokehouse** (☑ 095-23739; www.smokehouse.ie; Bunowen Pier, Ballyconneely; tours free; ☺ 9am-1pm & 2-5pm Mon-Fri) to be smoked and sent on to your home.

The bike storage and drying room for wet clothes come in handy too.

Ross Lake House Hotel   GUESTHOUSE €€€
(☑ 091-550 109; http://rosslakehotel.com; Rosscahill; s/d/ste from €128/181/194; ☺ Easter-Oct; P ☎) Undulating lawns and bird-filled woodlands surround this beautiful ivy-clad Georgian house, which blazes red in autumn when the leaves change colour. Its 13 large rooms have antique furniture (some with four-poster beds). There's even a tennis court.

Kids under 12 stay for half-price.

Greenway Cafe   IRISH €€
(☑ 091-866 645; Main St; mains lunch from €8, dinner €14-22; ☺ 9am-9pm Tue-Sat, noon-4pm Sun, reduced hours winter) Most of the ingredients at this award-wining eatery are sourced from the Connemara region – Killary Harbour mussels (served with mint), Lough Corrib trout (with roast rhubarb) and Twelve Bens lamb (with wild mushrooms).

Powers Thatched Pub   PUB FOOD €€
(☑ 091-557 597; Main St; mains €14-20; ☺ kitchen noon-8.30pm, bar 9am-midnight) The only thatched building on the main road, this comfy pub has open fires, welcoming service and an impressive menu of seafood (freshly caught trout, mussels and smoked haddock chowder) and meat (lamb burger with preserved lemon). The homemade treacle bread is divine. Traditional music plays on Wednesday, Saturday and Sunday.

ⓘ Getting There & Away

➡ Bus Éireann (www.buseireann.ie) bus 419 runs one to eight times daily to/from Galway city (€9, 35 minutes) and Clifden (€15.50, two hours). Three times a week it also runs to Roundstone (€14, 50 minutes).

➡ Citylink (www.citylink.ie) has six services daily to/from Galway (€9, 35 minutes) and Clifden (€12, 55 minutes).

Lough Inagh Valley & Around

Lough Inagh Valley's stark landscape is beguiling, with the moody skies reflected in the waters of Loughs Derryclare and Inagh. The R344 enters the valley from the south, just west of the hamlet of Recess. On the western side is the brooding **Twelve Bens** mountain range.

At the north end of the valley, the R344 meets the N59, which loops around Connemara to Leenane and Killary Harbour. A track near the northern end leads west off the road up a blind valley, which is well worth exploring. It's fantastic walking country but trails can get busy in summer, so set out early.

⌂ Sleeping & Eating

Lough Inagh Lodge can provide evening meals for guests. Otherwise there are no restaurants or shops; your nearest options are in Clifden, 20km to the west, or Roundstone, 19km to the southwest.

Ben Lettery Hostel HOSTEL €
(☑086 849 3712; www.anoige.ie; N59, Ballynahinch; dm/d/q €20/50/96; ☺Jun-Aug; P🐾) A peat fire adds to the warm welcome at this seasonally opening, 40-bed YHA hostel. With a tidy, homely kitchen and drying room, it's an excellent base for exploring the valley.

Check-in is between 5pm and 9pm. It's 12km east of Clifden; Citylink buses stop here on request.

Lough Inagh Lodge LODGE €€
(☑095-34706; www.loughinaghlodgehotel.ie; off R344; s/d from €140/170; P🐾) Set in huge grounds against a hill, this atmospheric lodge has rich colour schemes, an oak-panelled dining room and open log fires. Several of its 13 grand rooms face the lake. You can also dine (mains €17 to €33) in style.

It's midway up the Lough Inagh Valley, 9km north of Recess.

Ballynahinch Castle Hotel LUXURY HOTEL €€€
(☑095-31006; www.ballynahinch-castle.com; off R341; s/d/ste from €320/340/490; P🐾) With fishing on private lakes and the River Owenmore running through the vast, mountain-ringed property, ivy-draped Ballynahinch Castle is ideally set up for anglers. Its 48 luxurious rooms include riverside suites with four-poster beds. The gatehouse Owenmore Restaurant (three-course menu €70) offers fine dining; bar meals are available at the manor's Fisherman's Pub (mains €20 to €36).

Fly-fishing lessons and guides cost €160 per half day; equipment hire per half/full day is from €50/70.

Roundstone

POP 214

Clustered around a boat-filled harbour, picture-perfect Roundstone (Cloch na Rón) is the kind of Irish village you hoped to find. Colourful terrace houses and inviting pubs overlook the shimmering recess of Bertraghboy Bay, which is home to dramatic tidal flows, lobster trawlers and traditional *currach*.

The scalloped coastline here harbours some spectacular beaches. The Errisbeg Peninsula, 3km southwest of Roundstone, has two. **Gurteen Bay** (sometimes spelt Gorteen Bay) has a sweep of golden sand. After a further 800m, there's a turn for **Dog's Bay**, a dazzling white strand formed from tiny crushed seashells. Together the pair

---

WORTH A TRIP

PÁDRAIG PEARSE'S COTTAGE

Pádraig Pearse (Patrick Pearse; 1879–1916) wrote some of his short stories and plays on the shore of a remote lake in a small thatched **cottage** (Ionad Cultúrtha an Phiarsaigh; www.heritageireland.ie; R340, Ros Muc; adult/child €5/3; ☺9.30am-6pm Easter-Sep, to 4pm Oct-Easter), which he built in 1909. Pearse led the Easter Rising with James Connolly in 1916; after the revolt he was executed by the British. In 2016 a state-of-the-art, A-frame **visitor centre** detailing Pearse's life and writing opened a short walk away. Allow an hour here all up.

Note that the cottage's location is sometimes spelt Rosmuc on signs.

---

form the two sides of the dog-bone-shaped sand spit and tombolo.

◉ Sights & Activities

Roundstone Musical Instruments WORKSHOP
(☑095-35808; www.bodhran.com; Monastery Rd; ☺9.15am-7pm Jul-Sep, 10.30am-6pm Mon-Sat Oct-Jun) At the village's southern edge, you can watch Malachy Kearns, Ireland's only full-time maker of traditional bodhráns, hand-crafting goat-skin drums in his workshop. Other traditional Irish instruments are also for sale here, along with sheet music and recordings.

Roundstone Outdoors KAYAKING
(☑087 943 3440; www.bogbeanconnemara.com; Main St; ☺by appointment) One of the best ways to explore Roundstone's beautiful coastline is to get out on the water. Roundstone Outdoors offers kayak lessons (per hour €30), introductory stand-up paddleboarding (SUP) sessions (per two hours €35) and 2½-hour kayak tours (from €40). It also rents out kayaks and stand-up paddleboards (two hours €35).

Mt Errisbeg WALKING
Looming above Roundstone is Mt Errisbeg (Iorras Beag; 300m), the only significant hill along this section of coastline. The scenic walk to the top takes about two hours; just follow small Fuchsia Lane past O'Dowd's (p412) pub in the centre of the village. From the summit, a panorama radiates across the bay to the distant humps of the Twelve Bens.

ROUNDSTONE BOG

Away from the coast, an alternative route between Roundstone and Clifden winds through the protected Roundstone Bog. The bumpy unnamed road passes through magnificently eerie, water-logged desolation that's often shrouded in low cloud; locals who believe the bog is haunted won't drive this road at night. In summer you might still see peat being harvested by hand. The road runs west from a junction on the R341 about 4km north of Roundstone. It rejoins the R341 at Ballinaboy.

🛏 Sleeping

Gurteen Beach Caravan & Camping Park   CAMPGROUND €

(📞095-35882; www.facebook.com/gurteenbay1975; off R341; campsites per 2 adults €20; ⊗Easter-Oct; 🅿🖥) In this idyllic spot just 50m from Gurteen Beach you'll find 80 pitches for caravans and tents, a camp kitchen, a laundry, a shop (May to September) selling groceries and ice cream, and a games room with TV. Showers cost €1. It's 3km southwest of Roundstone.

Wits End B&B   B&B €

(📞095-35813; www.roundstoneaccommodation.com; Main St; s/d from €50/75; 🖥) With a name like this you'd expect cheerful hosts, and so it proves at this bright-pink, flower-pot-framed B&B. Rooms may be simple but most overlook the water, and in the sea-view breakfast room unflappable Eileen serves up a full fry-up or smoked salmon and scrambled eggs.

Island View B&B   B&B €€

(📞095-35701; www.islandview.ie; Main St; s €55-60, d €80-100; 🖥) For spick-and-span, bay-view rooms with fresh flowers, a cosy guest lounge, homemade scones and a complimentary afternoon tea, head to this delightful B&B in the centre of Roundstone.

Roundstone House   INN €€

(📞095-35864; www.roundstonehousehotel.com; Main St; s/d from €85/140; ⊗Apr-Oct) There are views across the bay from the front rooms of this elongated, family-run inn. All 12 rooms have tea- and coffee-making facilities and subtle furnishings. Service couldn't be friendlier.

You can enjoy pints and top-notch local seafood at its attached pub, Vaughan's (12.30pm to 9pm, mains €10 to €28), out on the terrace.

🍴 Eating & Drinking

Bog Bean Cafe   CAFE €

(📞087 943 3440; www.bogbeanconnemara.com; Main St; dishes €5-12; ⊗9am-5.30pm Thu-Tue Easter-Sep, 9.30am-4.30pm Thu-Sun Oct-Easter; 🖥) Cork-roasted Badger & Dodo coffee, full Irish breakfasts and sweet treats such as rhubarb-and-raspberry slice make this cheerful cafe worth a stop. Or refuel on Connemara smoked-salmon sandwiches or local crab salad dressed with lime.

Upstairs are six charming, colourful B&B rooms with private bathrooms (doubles €75 to €85, family rooms from €100).

★O'Dowd's   SEAFOOD €€

(📞095-35809; www.odowdsseafoodbar.com; Main St; mains €14-29; ⊗restaurant 5-9.30pm, bar menu noon-9.30pm; 🖥) 🦞 Roundstone lobster, Aran Islands hake, plaice and sea bass, local crab and mackerel smoked in-house are sourced off the old stone dock directly opposite this wonderfully authentic old pub and restaurant, while produce comes from its garden. There's a strong list of Irish craft beers and ciders.

Its neighbouring summertime cafe (dishes €5.50-11.50; ⊗9am-6pm Mar-Oct; 🖥) serves breakfast and lunch.

Shamrock Bar   PUB

(📞095-35797; www.facebook.com/theshamrockroundstone; Main St; ⊗11am-11.30pm Mon-Thu, to 12.30am Fri & Sat, to 10.30pm Sun; 🖥) Roundstone's best bet for live music is this red-trimmed, timber-lined pub on the main street, where musicians play at weekends throughout the year and most nights in July and August.

As well as trad, it also has jazz on many summer Sunday afternoons.

ℹ Getting There & Away

Bus Éireann (www.buseireann.ie) bus 419 stops at Roundstone three times a week en route between Galway city (€16, 1½ hours) and Clifden (€8, 35 minutes).

Clifden & Around

POP 1597

A definitive stop on any tour of Connemara, the region's 'capital', Clifden (An Clochán, meaning 'stepping stones'), is an appealing Victorian-era town presiding over the head of the narrow bay where the River Owenglin tumbles into the sea.

◉ Sights & Activities

This is pony country and rides along the beaches are popular. Cycling is also a great way to explore the scenic landscapes.

★ Sky Road   SCENIC DRIVE

Signposted from the N59 heading north out of Clifden, this aptly named 15km driving and cycling route traces a dizzying loop out to the township of Kingston and back, taking in rugged, stunningly beautiful coastal scenery en route. Set out clockwise from the southern side for the best views, which peak at sunset.

En route there are several viewpoints where you can park.

Station House Museum   MUSEUM

(☑095-21494; Station House Courtyard, off Low Rd; adult/child €3/2; ⊘10am-5pm Mon-Sat, noon-6pm Sun Easter–Oct) Located in a former train shed, this small, absorbing museum has displays on the local ponies and pivotal aspects of Clifden's history, including the Galway to Clifden Connemara Railway (in service from 1895 to 1935) and Guglielmo Marconi's transatlantic wireless station at Derrigimlagh.

Derrigimlagh Discovery Point   HISTORIC SITE

(Marconi Rd, off R341) FREE A wealth of interactive exhibits dot this 5km scenic loop walk around windswept bogland: crystal radio sets let you listen to recordings from the 1907 station established here by Guglielmo Marconi – the messages it transmitted were the earliest transatlantic wireless communications. Artistic panels also mark the area's other claim to fame: in 1919 British aviators John Alcock and Arthur Brown completed the world's first transatlantic flight when they crash-landed into the bog.

Both aviators survived and were awarded the honour of Knight Commander of the British Empire (KBE) a week later by King George V. The trailhead is 6km south of Clifden.

The wireless station operated until 1922, when it was attacked by Republican forces and compensation from the Free State government for its repair didn't eventuate.

Connemara Heritage & History Centre   MUSEUM

(☑095-21808; www.connemaraheritage.com; N59, Lettershea; adult/child €8.50/4.25; ⊘10am-6pm Apr-Oct) Farmer Dan O'Hara lived here in the 1840s until his eviction from the farm and subsequent emigration to New York, where he ended up selling matches on the street. Its present owners have restored the property, turning it into a window onto lost traditional ways, including cutting peat by hand. It's 7km east of Clifden, with last admission an hour before closing.

There's a craft shop and tearoom on-site.

★ Errislannan Manor   HORSE RIDING

(☑095-21134; www.errislannanmanor.com; per hr from €35; ⊘by appointment Mon-Fri Mar-Oct) Guides provide lessons and lead treks along the beach and up into the hills on the iconic local ponies. All abilities are catered for and children's lessons are a speciality (per half hour €25).

It's 7.5km from Clifden: take the Ballyconneely Rd (the R341) south for 4km, turn northwest on to the Errislannan Peninsula and look out for the signs.

All Things Connemara   CYCLING

(Clifden Bike Shop; ☑095-22630; www.bikeelectric.ie; Market St; ⊘9am-6pm) Road and electric bikes (per half/full day €25/44) for exploring the region are in excellent condition at All Things Connemara, which also sells a diverse range of products solely from the region (clothes, stationery, fishing lures, Connemara marble jewellery, organic seaweed, music and more).

Blue Water Fishing   FISHING

(☑095-21073; www.seafishingireland.net; Clifden Harbour; fishing per day €60, tackle €20; ⊘by appointment) Shore fishing, reef fishing and shark and tuna fishing in season are offered by experienced skipper John Brittain aboard the 13m single-hull *Cygnus Cyfish*. Trips are also possible from Cleggan.

✷ Festivals & Events

Connemara Pony Show   SPORTS

(☑095-21863; www.cpbs.ie; ⊘mid-Aug) The area's famous ponies are exhibited at Clifden's showgrounds during the annual Connemara Pony Show. Other events during the show include Irish dancing.

🛌 Sleeping

★ Clifden Eco Camping   CAMPGROUND €

(☑095-44036; www.clifdenecocamping.ie; Claddaghduff Rd; campsites/campervan sites per 2 adults €21/24; ⊘Easter-Oct; P🗪) 🚭 You're just paces from a gorgeous white-sand beach at Ireland's first climate-neutral campground. The well-maintained facilities tucked into the dunes include a kitchen, campfires and a natural spring. You can book sea-kayaking trips and hire bikes, too. It's 10km northwest of Clifden.

OMEY ISLAND

Following the rugged coastline north-west of Clifden brings you to the tiny village of Claddaghduff (An Cladach Dubh), which is signposted off the road to Cleggan. If you turn west here down by the Catholic church, you will come out on Omey Strand, where horse races take place in summer.

At low tide you can drive or walk across the sand to Omey Island, a low islet of rock, grass and sand. Swimming is possible at its white sandy beaches, and walking is popular. Now uninhabited, there's a handful of abandoned houses. Omey's last resident, professional stuntman Pascal Whelan (whose film credits include *Butch Cassidy and the Sundance Kid* and *Crocodile Dundee*), died in 2017; he is buried in the island's cemetery. Tide times are displayed on the noticeboard in the car park; the route is marked by blue road signs bearing white arrows. Don't be tempted to cross between half tide and high tide, or if there's water on the route. And be sure to time it so you can get back. From Clifden it's a 26km round trip.

★ **Blue Quay Rooms**   B&B €€

(☑ 087 621 7616; www.bluequayrooms.com; Beach Rd; d €70-100; Ⓟ🖸) Painted a vivid shade of blue, this boutique property is even more stunning inside. Adorned with a brass ship's wheel, the nautical-themed lounge has black-and-white chequerboard floor tiles, designer fabrics and fresh flowers. Rooms also blend vintage and contemporary furnishings; all but one have harbour views.

No kids under 12.

Dolphin Beach   B&B €€

(☑ 095-21204; www.dolphinbeachhouse.com; Lower Sky Rd; r from €110; Ⓟ🖸) 🍽 The Atlantic views are superb from this stylish B&B tucked away off the Lower Sky Rd 5km west of Clifden, especially from the front terrace and atrium dining room. High-ceilinged rooms have chic, countrified furnishings. Organic vegetables from its own gardens are used at breakfast.

Children under 12 aren't permitted.

Quay House   HOTEL €€

(☑ 095-21369; www.thequayhouse.com; Beach Rd; s €90-120, d €140-160; ⊙Apr-Oct; Ⓟ🖸) Set right beside the water in an 1820s property built for the harbour master, rambling Quay House has 15 elegant antique-filled rooms with proper bathtubs. Some have working fireplaces; all but three have harbour views. Despite the rich heritage there's a relaxed, cosy feel. It's a 650m stroll into town.

One ground-floor room is equipped for visitors with limited mobility.

Station House Hotel   HOTEL €€

(☑ 095-21699; www.clifdenstationhouse.com; off Galway Rd/N59; s/d/ste €80/130/164, f €139-142; Ⓟ🖸🏊) In the former train station complex, this 1998-constructed hotel was built in the style of an old steam-train utility shed. Large rooms have warm red fabrics; children under 12 stay free. The kids' club and indoor swimming pool are a hit with families.

There's also a spa, gym and sauna, and a bar in the historic red-brick station waiting room.

Abbeyglen Castle Hotel   CASTLE €€€

(☑ 095-21201; www.abbeyglen.ie; Sky Rd; d €284; Ⓟ🖸) Complete with crenellations and turrets, this 1832-built castle, amid landscaped grounds on the scenic Sky Road (p413), is straight out of a fairy tale. Spacious rooms and suites, complimentary afternoon tea with scones, a tennis court and a billiards room are among its amenities. On Tuesdays its restaurant (mains €22 to €40) hosts an Irish night with trad music followed by storytelling.

A three-course dinner menu costs €53. Nonguests are welcome but need to book ahead.

🍴 Eating & Drinking

Connemara Hamper   DELI €

(☑ 095-21054; www.connemarahamper.com; Market St; dishes €4-9; ⊙9.30am-6pm Mon-Sat, plus noon-6pm Sun Jul & Aug) Irish farmhouse cheeses, Connemara smoked salmon, pâtés, dips, jams and chutneys, plus cakes, biscuits and hearty pies, make this terrific deli your one-stop picnic shop. It sells organic wines too.

Steam Cafe   CAFE €

(☑ 095-30600; Station House Courtyard; mains €5-12; ⊙9.30am-5.30pm Tue-Sat Apr-Oct; 🖸) Tables scattered in the tucked-away courtyard draw you into a cheery cafe, full of natural light. Along with Clifden's best coffee, it serves scones with homemade jam, soups such as curried carrot, fantastic open crab sandwiches and creative cakes like Guinness and blueberry.

★ Mitchell's SEAFOOD €€
(⌨095-21867; www.mitchellsrestaurantclifden.com; Market St; mains lunch €8-16, dinner €18-28; ⊙noon-9pm Mar-Oct) Seafood from the surrounding waters takes centre stage at this elegant spot, from velvety chowder and open crab sandwiches at lunchtime to intricate dinner mains. The highlight is a standout seafood platter (€26), piled high with Ros A Mhil prawns, Killary mussels, Oranmore oysters, Connemara smoked salmon and Cleggan crab. Strong wine list. Book ahead.

The three-course set menu (€29), available Sunday to Friday, is a great deal.

Off the Square IRISH €€
(⌨095-22281; www.offthesquare.ie; Main St; mains €10-23; ⊙9.15am-10pm;) Surf meets turf on the menu of this busy town-centre bistro. Full Irish breakfasts and casual lunches (smoked salmon on soda bread; Irish stew) give way to more complex meals at night featuring fish from Clifden's pier, Cleggan lobsters, Aughrismore oysters and crab, and Connemara black-faced lamb. A decent kids' menu makes it a good family option.

Lowry's Bar PUB
(⌨095-21347; www.lowrysbar.ie; Market St; ⊙10.30am-11.30pm Mon-Thu, to 12.30am Fri & Sat, noon-11.30pm Sun) Back-lit bottles behind the bar create a beautiful setting for a time-worn, third-generation-run local pub. A place to enjoy céilidh sessions at least a couple of nights a week (nightly from Easter to October) and a 100-strong whiskey collection.

🛍 Shopping

Clifden has a burgeoning arts and crafts scene. Several boutiques in the town centre stock work by local artists, including All Things Connemara (p413) and Connemara Blue, which also runs glassmaking workshops.

Clifden Bookshop BOOKS
(⌨095-22020; www.clifdenbookshop.com; Main St; ⊙9.30am-6pm Mon-Fri, 10am-6pm Sat, noon-4pm Sun) Local history, memoirs, Irish literature and plant and wildlife guides are among the titles at this well-stocked bookshop, along with maps and children's books.

Connemara Blue GLASS
(⌨095-30782; www.connemarablue.com; Market St; ⊙10am-5pm) You can't miss this chic atelier/gallery: bubblegum-pink walls and bright blue trim lead to the glinting array of glass coasters, plates, bowls, vases and sculptures in traditional and contemporary designs that are made on-site. Learn how to create pieces yourself on its glassmaking courses (per one/three hours €30/75).

ℹ Information

Helpful staff at Clifden's seasonal **tourist office** (⌨01-605 7700; www.visitclifden.com; Galway Rd/N59; ⊙10am-5pm Easter–mid-Oct) can suggest activities including walking routes.

ℹ Getting There & Around

➜ Citylink (www.citylink.ie) bus 923 connects with Galway city (€16, 90 minutes, six daily).
➜ Bus Éireann (www.buseireann.ie) bus 419 also runs to Galway (€16, two hours, one to four services daily). Three times a week it stops at Roundstone (€8, 35 minutes) en route.

All Things Connemara (p413) and **Mannion's Bikes** (⌨095-21160; www.clifdenbikes.com; Bridge St; ⊙9am-6pm Mon-Sat, 10am-1pm & 5-6pm Sun) rent bikes.

Cleggan
POP 208

With a charming, boat-lined dock, the tiny fishing port of Cleggan (An Cloiggean), 11km northwest of Clifden, is the gateway to the island of Inishbofin. West of Cleggan, narrow looping roads follow the spectacular shoreline.

Citylink (www.citylink.ie) bus 923 connects Cleggan with Clifden (€5.50, 30 minutes, three to four daily) and Galway (€17, 2¼ hours, three daily).

Island Discovery (⌨095-45819; www.inishbofinislanddiscovery.com; adult/child return €20/10) ferries run from Cleggan to Inishbofin.

Cleggan Beach Riding Centre HORSE RIDING
(⌨083 388 8135; www.clegganridingcentre.com; ⊙by appointment) Three-hour treks across the sand to Omey Island (€70), 90-minute beach or moorland rides (€45) and lessons (from €35 per hour) are offered by this friendly riding centre in Cleggan's east.

Oliver's SEAFOOD €€
(⌨095-44640; www.oliversoncleggganpier.ie; Cleggan Pier; mains lunch €10-14, dinner €18-35; ⊙kitchen 12.30-3pm & 6-9pm; 🐕) At much-loved Oliver's bar, specials depend on the catch, so your seafood feast might be locally landed lobster, pan-seared scallops or sea bass with ginger and lime. Or plump for the garlicky crab claws. Traditional music kicks off on Wednesdays and Thursdays from 7pm.

Upstairs are five simple B&B rooms (double/family from €70/100), full of sea breezes and, when the sun obliges, Connemara light.

Inishbofin

POP 170

Situated 9km from the mainland, the tranquil island of Inishbofin measures just under 6km long by 4km wide, and its highest point is a mere 86m above sea level. You can walk or cycle its narrow, deserted lanes, green pastures and sandy beaches, with farm animals and seals for company.

Its history is more tumultuous: St Colman exiled himself to Inishbofin in AD 665, after he fell out with the Church over its adoption of a new calendar. He set up a monastery northeast of the harbour, where the more recent ruins of a small 14th-century church still stand. Grace O'Malley, the famous pirate queen, used Inishbofin as a base in the 16th century, and Cromwell's forces captured the island in 1652, using it to jail priests and clerics.

◉ Sights & Activities

Inishbofin offers excellent walking, cycling and horse riding. The island has three looped routes; you can download maps for the routes from the island's Community Centre website.

The ruined 14th-century chapel on the site of St Colman's monastery is a highlight of the 8km **Cloonamore Loop**. Spectacular views over Counties Galway, Mayo and Clare feature on the 5km **Middlequarter Loop**. The 8km **Westquarter Loop** takes in the Atlantic coast, with views of the island's blowholes, sea arch and seal colony.

All three loops start and finish at the pier.

Inishbofin Heritage Museum MUSEUM
(⊙noon-1.30pm & 2.30-5pm Easter-Sep) FREE Inishbofin's small but evocative museum gives a comprehensive overview of the island's history. Displays include fishing, farming and tradespeople's tools as well as items from traditional Irish homes (crockery, clothing, furniture and more) and more than 200 photos of islanders over the years. Hours can vary.

Parish Church of St Colman CHURCH
(⊙8am-5pm) The interior of this small, charming church 300m east of the pier is illuminated by the soft light of its stained glass.

Inishbofin Equestrian Centre HORSE RIDING
(☑087 950 1545; www.inishbofinequestriancentre. com; ⊙9am-6pm) Offers horse-riding lessons

(from €35 per hour) catering for all ages and abilities and treks (€30 per hour) around the island. Evening rides are possible by request.

Kings Bicycle Hire CYCLING
(☑095-45833; Inishbofin Pier; bike rental per day €15; ⊙10am-5pm Jun-Aug & by appointment) The island's mostly flat terrain is well suited for cycling – albeit not very far given its tiny size.

✻ Festivals & Events

Inishbofin Arts Festival CULTURAL
(www.inishbofin.com; ⊙mid-May) Accordion workshops, archaeological walks, art exhibitions and concerts feature during this festival held over the May bank holiday weekend.

⊨ Sleeping & Eating

Self-caterers should stock up on the mainland, although Inishbofin's post office has a small grocery shop. There are around nine restaurants and bars, most located at the island's hotels. Many places only accept cash and the island has no ATM – come prepared.

Inishbofin Island Hostel HOSTEL €
(☑095-45855; www.inishbofin-hostel.ie; campsites per person €12, dm/d €18/50, f €50-100; ⊙Easter-Sep) A clutch of new glamping pods (per night €50) add a bit of pizzazz at this snug 38-bed hostel, with its six-bed dorms and private rooms with shared bathroom facilities. Good amenities include a conservatory with panoramic views, self-catering kitchen, barbecue, laundry and lounge with solid-fuel stove.

It's 1km east of the pier.

Inishbofin House Hotel HOTEL €€
(☑095-45888; www.inishbofinhouse.ie; d €110-140, f from €180; ⊙Apr-Sep; ☎) The emphasis in this swish modern hotel is on relaxation: a comfy bed in a serene guest room, in the library, in the large lounge overlooking a cove. Standard rooms look out on to farmland; sea-view rooms (some with balconies) cost more. Seafood is the mainstay of the hotel's restaurant (mains €18 to €30).

Inishbofin House Hotel is 400m east of the pier.

Lapwing House B&B €€
(☑095-45996; www.inishbofin.com/bandb/lap wing.html; d from €80; ☎) Named after the local bird species that breeds on the island, this lovely family-run B&B in a whitewashed building 500m north from the pier has just two rooms (one double and one twin), each with a private bathroom. Views extend over the sheep-flecked hillside to the harbour.

Homemade breakfast pancakes come with maple syrup.

❶ Information

The island's website (www.inishbofin.com) and **Community Centre** (☑095-45895; www.inishbofin.com; ☺9am-11pm Mon-Thu, to 5pm Fri, noon-4pm Sat & Sun; 🛜) are good resources for local information.

❶ Getting There & Away

Ferries from Cleggan to Inishbofin take 30 to 45 minutes and are run by Island Discovery (p415). In low season there are two ferries a day, increasing to three from June to August. Dolphins often swim alongside the boats, and basking sharks can often be spotted in April. Confirm ahead, as ferries may be cancelled when seas are rough.

Letterfrack & Around

POP 192

Founded by Quakers in the mid-19th century, Letterfrack (Leitir Fraic) is a crossroads with a few pubs and B&Bs. But the forested setting and nearby coast are a magnet for outdoors adventure seekers. A 4km walk to the peak of **Tully Mountain** (356m) takes 40 minutes and offers uplifting ocean views.

⊙ Sights & Activities

★**Kylemore Abbey**   HISTORIC BUILDING
(☑095-52001; www.kylemoreabbey.com; off N59; adult/child €13/free; ☺9am-7pm Jul & Aug, 9.30am-5.30pm Sep & Oct, 9am-6pm Apr-Jun, 10am-4.30pm Nov-Mar) Photogenically perched on the shores of Pollacapall Lough, 4km east of Letterfrack, Kylemore is a crenellated 19th-century neo-Gothic fantasy. It was built for a wealthy English businessman, Mitchell Henry, who spent his honeymoon in Connemara. Ground-floor rooms are open to visitors, and you can wander down to the lake and the **Gothic church**. Admission includes entry to the extravagant **Victorian walled gardens**, around a 20-minute walk away (linked by a free shuttle bus from April to October).

Run by Benedictine nuns, the abbey served as the Kylemore Abbey School from 1923 to 2010, teaching Catholic girls. There's a cafe and a teahouse on the grounds, which also offer hikes and woodland walks.

★**Connemara National Park**   NATIONAL PARK
(☑076-100 2528; www.connemaranationalpark.ie; off N59; ☺24hr) **FREE** Immediately southeast

of Letterfrack, Connemara National Park spans 2000 dramatic hectares of bog, mountains, heath and woodlands.

The park encloses a number of the **Twelve Bens**, including Bencullagh, Benbrack and Benbaun. The heart of the park is **Gleann Mór** (Big Glen), through which the River Polladirk flows. There's fine walking up the glen and over the surrounding mountains along with short self-guided walks.

Guided nature walks (p417) led by park rangers depart from the visitor centre (p418).

DK Connemara Oysters   FACTORY
(☑087 918 6997; www.dkconnemaraoysters.com; Ballinakill Bay; adult/child €15/5; ☺11am & 4pm Fri-Sun Easter-Sep) On these hour-long tours you'll get a real sense of the skill and sheer hard work that goes into producing Connemara's famous oysters. Then try your hand at shucking, grading and, of course, tasting them, fresh from the sea. Book ahead.

Connemara Guided Walks   WALKING
(☑076-100 2528; www.connemaranationalpark.ie) **FREE** National park rangers lead free guided walks from the Connemara National Park visitor centre (p418). Themes vary and include flora, fauna, history, geology and children's activities. Check the park's online events pages for details.

🍴 Sleeping & Eating

Letterfrack has pubs and a small supermarket, but there are many more dining options in Clifden.

Letterfrack Lodge   HOSTEL €
(Connemara National Park Hostel; ☑095-41222; off N59; dm/d/tr/q €25/90/110/160; ℗🛜) Close to the Letterfrack crossroads, this stone-fronted hostel has spacious dorms as well as private rooms with their own bathrooms. There's a big self-catering kitchen-dining room, and friendly staff are a great source of info on walks throughout the region.

Laundry facilities, bike hire and storage are available.

Rosleague Manor   HOTEL €€€
(☑095-41101; www.rosleague.com; N59; s/d €145/210, f & ste €249; ☺Easter–mid-Nov; ℗🛜) Rose-pink Rosleague Manor is gloriously sited – overlooking Ballynakill Harbour and the Twelve Bens mountain range. Richly coloured rooms, furnished with antiques and original artworks, make it feel like a romantic hideaway, as do walking trails through private woods, a Victorian conservatory and

CONNEMARA'S NORTH COAST

The north coast of Connemara is awash with gorgeous beaches, raw mountain vistas and stark views out to the moody sea.

Bypass the N59 for a series of small roads that follows the twists and turns along the coast for about 15km. Start at Letterfrack, where a narrow track (the L5102) leads northwest. Follow various small roads, sticking as close to the water as you can, and keeping an eye out for sheep. The land here seems to be in the midst of a dissolution into the sea.

At **Renvyle** you can pause for the night. **Renvyle Beach Caravan & Camping** (☑ 095-43462; www.renvylebeachcaravanpark.com; campsites per 2 people €22; ⊙ Easter-Sep; P 🔊) has campsites on a grassy expanse with direct access to a sandy beach. **Renvyle House** (☑ 095-46100; www.renvyle.com; s/d/tr/f from €102/204/255/323; P 🔊 🐾) is a luxurious 68-room converted country house–hotel set on 80 hectares.

Continue east, past a few fine country pubs at the tiny junction of **Tully Cross**. Stick to the coast and stop often – especially on sunny days – to marvel at the dazzling colours: rich cobalt sea, cerulean sky, emerald-green grass, brown hills, slate-grey rocks and white-sand beaches. The beach horse-racing sequences for *The Quiet Man* were shot at **Lettergesh**.

Look for a turn to **Rosroe Quay**, where a magnificent crescent of sand awaits at **Glassilaun Beach**. If you're drawn to the beauty of the water, **Scuba Dive West** (☑ 095-43922; www.scubadivewest.com; Glassilaun Beach, Renvyle; shore/boat dives incl gear from €45/70, snorkelling per 2hr €35) runs highly recommended courses and dives around the surrounding coastlines and islands.

Continue southeast along the final 5km stretch of road leading back to the N59. It runs along **Lough Fee**. In spring when the gorse explodes in yellow bloom, the views here are breathtaking.

an excellent restaurant (two/three courses €35/49). It's 2km west of Letterfrack.

Fruit, vegetables and herbs come from its own kitchen gardens.

ℹ Information

The **Connemara National Park Visitor Centre** (☑ 076-100 2528; www.connemaranationalpark.ie; off N59, Letterfrack; ⊙ 9am-5.30pm Mar-Oct) is in a beautiful setting 300m south of the Letterfrack crossroads, and offers an introduction to the park's flora, fauna and geology.

ℹ Getting There & Away

Citylink (www.citylink.ie) bus 923 serves Letterfrack from Galway (€15, two hours, three daily), via Clifden (€5.50, 20 minutes).

Leenane & Killary Harbour

Dotted with mussel rafts, long, narrow Killary Harbour is often referred to as Ireland's only fjord. Slicing 16km inland and more than 45m deep in the centre, it certainly looks like a fjord, although some scientific studies suggest it may not actually have been glaciated. The small village of Leenane (also spelt Leenaun) sits on its

shore, while **Mt Mweelrea** (814m) towers to its north.

The Leenane village website, www. leenanevillage.com, is a good source of information.

◉ Sights & Activities

Aasleagh Falls   WATERFALL
(Eas Liath) The tumbling waters of these low, wide waterfalls are framed by a series of rapids and pools, where you're likely to see salmon fishers trying their luck. From the parking bays, look out for the footpaths leading beside the Erriff River to the falls.

Sheep & Wool Centre   MUSEUM
(☑ 095-42323; www.sheepandwoolcentre.com; Leenane; adult/child €5/3; ⊙ 9.30am-6pm mid-Mar-Oct) On Leenane's main street, just north of the bridge, sits a compelling little museum dedicated to sheep and wool. It has spinning and weaving demonstrations, and covers the history of dyeing. The on-site shop sells locally made handicrafts as well as topographical walking maps.

Joyce Country Sheepdogs   FARM
(☑ 094-954 8853; www.joycecountrysheepdogs.ie; Shanafaraghaun; adult/child €10/5; ⊙ 11am, 1pm & 3.30pm Mon-Sat Mar-Sep) Book in advance to see the amazing herding feats performed by

the sheepdogs on this working farm. From Leenane, it's 14km east: take the R336 and turn on to the L1301.

Connemara Seaweed Baths
BATHHOUSE

(☑095-42408; www.connemaraseaweedbaths. com; Leenane Hotel, N59; per hr €25; ⊙10am-6pm Easter-Sep) Rejuvenating seaweed baths at this complex in the Leenane Hotel use salt-water and seaweed cut by hand daily. Six of its eight free-standing baths have views out over the harbour.

Treatments start with sweating in the steam room to open your pores before sub-merging yourself in the bath, then finish with a bracing ice-cold shower to lock in the minerals.

Killary Adventure Centre
ADVENTURE SPORTS

(☑095-43411; www.killaryadventure.com; off N59; half-day activities per adult/child from €49/32; ⊙10am-5pm) ✎ Sea kayaking, gorge walk-ing, SUP, water-skiing, rock climbing, high ropes, archery, orienteering, day hikes and clay-pigeon shooting are among the activities offered by this adventure centre 6km west of Leenane. Decent dorms (€23 to €28) and double rooms (€70 to €78) come with under-floor heating.

Power is supplied by wind turbines; it also has a biomass boiler.

Killary Fjord Boat Tours
BOATING

(☑091-566 736; www.killaryfjord.com; N59; adult/child €24/13; ⊙late Mar-Oct) From Nancy's Point, 3km west of Leenane, Killary Fjord Boat Tours offers 1½-hour cruises of Killary Harbour. Dolphins leap around the boat, which passes by a mussel farm and stops at a salmon farm. There are up to four cruises daily in season.

Kids under 11 travel free. Tickets are €1.50 cheaper if you prebook online.

🛏 Sleeping & Eating

Sleepzone Connemara
HOSTEL €

(☑095-42929; www.sleepzone.ie; off N59; campsites per 2 people €24, dm/s/d/q from €19/39/49/59; ⊙Mar-Oct; P🐕) Direct access down to the water, clean dorms and pri-vate rooms, and a bar and barbecue terrace make this 100-bed hostel a winner. There's a self-catering kitchen, but bring supplies as there are no shops nearby. It's 6km west of Leenane; shuttle buses run to its sister hostel in Galway (p387).

Guests get discounts at the nearby Killary Adventure Centre.

GALWAY OYSTERS

Some of County Galway's finest sea-food, including lobster (€45) in season, is served in **Moran's Oyster Cottage** (☑091-796 113; www.moransoystercottage. com; The Weir, Kilcolgan; mains €14-29, half-dozen oysters €13-16; ⊙noon-9.30pm Sun-Thu, to 10pm Fri & Sat; 🐕), an atmos-pheric thatched pub and restaurant, set in a quiet cove. A terrace overlooks Dunbulcaun Bay, where the oysters are reared before they arrive on your plate. It's signposted 2km west of the N18 There's a good, pared-down kids' menu.

The long-established **Clarenbridge Oyster Festival** (www.clarenbridge. com; ⊙Sep) takes place in Clarenbridge, 17km southeast of Galway city, over four days in September.

Leenane Hotel
HOTEL €€

(☑095-42249; www.leenanehotel.com; N59; s €65, d €115-145; ⊙Easter-Sep; P🐕) Despite dating from the 19th century, there's a smart mod-ern feel to the 66 rooms of this stately hotel on the western fringes of Leenane. An open peat fire warms the bar, while the restaurant (mains €7 to €25) serves regional specialities including seafood and lamb. Balcony rooms with harbour views cost €10 extra.

The hotel is also home to the Connemara Seaweed Baths.

Blackberry Cafe
BISTRO €€

(☑095-42240; www.blackberryrestaurant.ie; Leenane; mains lunch €8-25, dinner €16-25; ⊙noon-4.30pm & 6-9pm Wed-Mon Apr-Sep; 🐕) Conne-mara smoked salmon, creamy chowder and oysters (€12.50 for six) are on offer during the day at this smart wood-floored cafe with wa-ter views in the centre of Leenane. Dinners are more elaborate affairs (prime sirloin; su-preme of chicken). Cash only; it also opens on Tuesdays from June to August.

Gaynor's
PUB

(☑095-42261; Leenane; ⊙10.30am-11.30pm Mon-Thu, to 12.30am Fri & Sat, 12.30-11pm Sun) A crackling peat fire, dark-wood panelling and spontaneous trad sessions make this cosy pub an essential stop. Pavement picnic ta-bles overlook the harbour; hearty pub fare (dishes €6 to €18) includes Irish lamb stew. It also doubles as the town's petrol station.

The pub played a starring role in the 1990 Irish film *The Field*.

ⓘ Getting There & Away

➤ Bus Eireann (www.buseireann.ie) bus 419 stops at Leenane once a week, en route between Galway (€14, 1¼ hours) and Clifden (€13, 55 minutes).

EASTERN GALWAY

Lough Corrib separates eastern Galway from the dramatic landscape of the county's western coast, and the regions are markedly different. To Galway city's south, pretty Kinvara on Galway Bay is a stepping stone to County Clare. Inland there are some interesting sights around the working town of Gort, while farming country unfolds east of Galway city.

Kinvara

POP 734

The small stone harbour of Kinvara (sometimes spelt Kinvarra) sits at the southeastern corner of Galway Bay, which accounts for its Irish name, Cinn Mhara: 'Head of the Sea'. Filled with vividly painted buildings, the charming village makes an excellent pit stop between Galway city and County Clare.

★ **Dunguaire Castle**   HISTORIC BUILDING
(www.shannonheritage.com; off N67; adult/child €7/4; ⊙10am-5pm Apr–mid-Sep) Erected around 1520 by the O'Hynes clan, Dunguaire Castle sits on the fringes of Kinvara on the former site of the 6th-century royal palace of Guaire Aidhne, the king of Connaught. Lady Christabel Ampthill restored the castle after buying it for the equivalent of €500 and lived here from the 1950s to the 1970s. Climb to the roof for glorious views of Galway Bay and Kinvara.

Lady Ampthill's bedroom was in the crafts studio, with her living room at the very top, beneath a new pitched roof.

A touristy medieval banquet (adult/child €57/35) takes place at 5.30pm and 8.45pm daily, and must be prebooked online.

Fleadh na gCuach   MUSIC
(Cuckoo Festival; ⊙early May) Held over the early May bank holiday weekend, this traditional music festival features over 100 musicians performing at upward of 50 organised sessions. Spin-off events include a parade and lessons in traditional Irish dancing.

Cruinniú na mBáid   SPORTS
(Gathering of the Boats; www.galwaytourism.ie; ⊙mid-Aug) As many as 100 Galway hooker

sailing boats race each year in the Cruinniú na mBáid 'Gathering of the Boats'.

🛏 Sleeping & Eating

Kinvara Guesthouse   B&B €€
(✆091-638 562; http://kinvaraguesthouse.ie; The Square; s/d/tr/f from €65/105/125/140; ☎) Smart modern styling, ceramics, bold colours and fresh flowers brighten this welcoming 22-room guesthouse right on the central square. Dinner, bed and breakfast deals are available with the **Pier Head** (✆091-638 188; The Quay; mains lunch €13-20, dinner €17-30; ⊙noon-9.30pm) bar and restaurant.

Ishka   CAFE €
(✆091-637 934; www.ishkakinvara.com; The Quay; dishes €5-12; ⊙9am-5pm) From tasty soups and pastas to Burren smoked salmon and seafood chowder, the flavours of west Ireland infuse the dishes at this welcoming harbourside cafe. Breakfast, including a warm salad of chorizo, sun-dried tomatoes and organic poached eggs, is served all day.

★ **Green's Bar**   PUB
(✆091-637 110; Main St; ⊙5-11.30pm Sun-Thu, to 12.30am Fri & Sat) With more than a hundred different whiskeys on shelves behind its bar, which looks ready to collapse, this 1865 pub is quite a sight. Painted peppermint-green on the outside, with darker lime-green trim, it's home to spontaneous sessions of traditional music several times a week.

There's a discounted whiskey of the week along with various whiskey-tasting platters.

ⓘ Getting There & Away

Bus Éireann (www.buseireann.ie) links Kinvara with Galway city (€9.50, 30 minutes, four daily) and towns in County Clare including Doolin (€13, 1½ hours, five daily).

Athenry

POP 4445

Athenry (Áth an Rí; pronounced 'Athenrye') constitutes one of Ireland's most intact collections of medieval architecture – two-thirds of the lengthy town walls survive. However, the impressive heritage is overshadowed by the modern, industrial town.

Athenry takes its name from a nearby ford (áth in Irish) that crosses the River Clare east of the settlement and which was the meeting point for three kingdoms, hence its Irish name, which translates as Ford of the Kings. The town's name is synonymous with the stirring song 'The Fields of Athenry', composed by Pete St John in the 1970s, which recounts incarceration resulting from the Famine.

Heritage-rich Athenry features a magnificent **castle** (☑091-844 797; www.heritageireland.ie; adult/child €5/3; ⊙9.30am-6pm Easter-Sep), the medieval parish **Church of St Mary's**, a **Dominican Priory** (☑091-844 661; Bridge St; ⊙by appointment), an original **market cross** and the **North Gate**, which you can drive through. The Arts & Heritage Centre has free downloadable walking-tour maps.

Arts & Heritage Centre   MUSEUM
(☑091-844 661; www.athenryheritagecentre.com; St Mary's, the Square; adult/child €5/4.50, Medieval Experience €8/6.50; ⊙10.30am-5pm May-Sep, hours vary Oct-Apr) Athenry's rich history is delivered with colourful flourishes here – the gruesome details of medieval life include a ghoulish array of torture implements. The Medieval Experience lets you dress up in period costume and practise archery. Call ahead as the heritage centre may be shut for school visits.

You can download a free walking-tour map of the town from the website.

ⓘ Getting There & Away

Car Athenry is beside the Galway–Dublin M6 motorway.

Bus Buslink (www.buslink.ie) serves Galway (€7, 40 minutes, up to eight daily). There's an additional Nightlink service on Friday and Saturday nights.

Train Frequent rail services (www.irishrail.ie) run daily to Galway (€8, 20 minutes) and Dublin (€33, 2¼ hours).

Gort & Around

POP 2994

Central to the workaday town of Gort is the Square, with its personable Christ the King statue and shop-filled streets radiating out. Most sights, however, are just outside town, including those connected with the great poet WB Yeats and his patron, Lady Augusta Gregory.

★**Thoor Ballylee**   HISTORIC BUILDING
(☑091-631 436; www.yeatsthoorballylee.org; Peterswell; adult/child €7/3.50; ⊙10am-6pm May-Aug) In an idyllic setting by a stream, this 16th-century Norman tower was the summer home of WB Yeats from 1921 to 1929 and was the inspiration for one of his

best-known works, *The Tower*. It adjoins a whitewashed cottage with forest-green trim, which contains an exhibition on Yeats' life and work. From Gort, it's 7.2km northeast off the N66.

Kilmacduagh   HISTORIC SITE
(off R460) FREE The extensive ruins at the monastic site of Kilmacduagh, 6km southwest of Gort, include a well-preserved 34m-high round tower, the remains of a small 14th-century cathedral (Teampall Mór MacDuagh), an oratory dedicated to St John the Baptist and other little chapels. The original monastery is thought to have been founded by St Colman MacDuagh at the beginning of the 7th century.

Kiltartan Gregory Museum   MUSEUM
(☑091-632 346; www.kiltartangregorymuseum.org; Kiltartan Cross; adult/child €3/1; ⊙11am-5pm Jun-Aug, plus 1-5pm Sun May & Sep) A charming stone schoolhouse built in 1892 now contains this museum, which traces the life of WB Yeats' literary patron, Lady Augusta Gregory, through photographs, manuscripts and objects from her former home at **Coole Park** (Coole-Garryland Nature Reserve; ☑091-631 804; www.coolepark.ie; Coole Haven; ⊙8am-7.30pm May-Oct, to 6pm Nov-Apr) FREE. The schoolhouse was designed by Lady Gregory's brother, Frank Persse. It's 4km north of Gort.

ⓘ Getting There & Away

Bus Bus Éireann (www.buseireann.ie) has hourly services to Galway city (€6, 50 minutes) and Ennis (€11, 35 minutes).

Train Services (www.irishrail.ie) link Gort with Galway (€13, 50 minutes) and Ennis (€8.20, 20 minutes) five times daily.

Counties Mayo & Sligo

POP 196,042 / AREA 7424 SQ KM

Best Places to Eat

➡ Wilde's at the Lodge (p427)

➡ Pantry & Corkscrew (p433)

➡ Hargadons (p449)

➡ Stoked (p451)

➡ Eithna's by the Sea (p456)

Best Places to Stay

➡ Belleek Castle (p443)

➡ Stella Maris (p441)

➡ Go Explore Hostel (p430)

➡ Glass House (p448)

➡ Delphi Lodge (p428)

Why Go?

Despite their natural wonders and languid charm, Counties Mayo and Sligo remain a well-kept secret, offering all of Ireland's wild, romantic beauty but without the crowds. Mayo is the more rugged of the two, with scraggy peaks, sheer cliffs, heather-covered moors and beautiful offshore islands where life is dictated by the elements. Sligo is more pastoral and its lush fields, fish-filled lakes and flat-topped mountains inspired William Butler Yeats to compose some of Ireland's most ardent verse.

Both counties boast grand stretches of golden sands and legendary breaks that lure the surfing cognoscenti from around the globe. Visit and you'll find all this plus an improbable bounty of prehistoric sites, elegant Georgian towns, abandoned manor houses, charming fishing villages and good old-fashioned warm-hearted country hospitality.

When to Go

➡ The weather-beaten shores of Mayo and Sligo can be whipped by brutal winds and rain in winter, when only the hardiest tourists and surfers make it here.

➡ If you're interested in catching a swell, spring and autumn are your best shot, with September and October favoured by those in the know.

➡ In summer the region bursts into life with oodles of festivals. In July and August you'll get the pick of the crop with Yeats festivals in Sligo and a variety of small traditional-music festivals elsewhere. Plus the weather is often balmy.

COUNTY MAYO

Mayo has wild beauty and haunting landscapes, but you'll find few tourists here, which means there are plenty of untapped opportunities for exploration by car, foot, bicycle or horseback. Life here has never been easy and the Potato Famine (1845–51) ravaged the county and prompted mass emigration. Consequently many people with Irish ancestry around the world can trace their roots to this once-blighted land.

Cong

POP 145

Sitting on a sliver-thin isthmus between Lough Corrib and Lough Mask, Cong conjures up romantic notions of the traditional Irish village. Time seems to have been in reverse ever since the evergreen classic *The Quiet Man* was filmed here in 1951. In fact, much effort has been made to recreate Cong as it looked for the film. Across from the tourist office there's even a statue of Sean Thornton (John Wayne) and Mary Kate Danaher (Maureen O'Hara).

The wooded trails between the lovely old abbey and stately Ashford Castle offer a respite from crowds; continue further and you find the Cong area is honeycombed with limestone caves, each associated with a colourful legend.

Look out for the gaunt roofless church with tower as you travel down through Ballinarobe on the way to Cong. From Cong, a gorgeous and straightforward car journey travels in a scenic loop around Lough Mask.

⊙ Sights

Ashford Castle Estate HISTORIC SITE
(☑ 094-954 6003; www.ashfordcastle.com; grounds adult/child €10/5; ⊙ grounds 9am-dusk) Just beyond Cong Abbey, the village abruptly ends and the woodlands surrounding Ashford Castle begin. First built in 1228 as the seat of the de Burgo family, owners over the years included the Guinness family (of stout fame). Arthur Guinness turned the castle into a regal hunting and fishing lodge, which it remains today. Although the only way to look inside its restored interior is to stay (p426) or dine here, the surrounding estate is open to the public.

The 140 hectares of parkland, covered with forests, streams and a golf course, are great to explore. Walking through the Kinlough Woods gets you away from the golfers and out to the shores of **Lough Corrib**. You can also stroll along the riverbanks to the monk's fishing house near Cong Abbey. Occasionally there is no entry to the estate due to private functions.

Cong Abbey HISTORIC SITE
(Mainistir Chonga; ☑ 094-954 6542; Abbey St; ⊙ dawn-dusk) FREE The evocatively weathered shell of Cong's 12th-century Augustinian abbey is scored by a cross-hatch of lines from centuries of exposure to the elements. Nevertheless, several finely sculpted features have survived, including a carved doorway, windows, lovely medieval arches and the ruined cloisters.

Founded in 1135 by Turlough Mór O'Connor, high king of Ireland and king of Connaught, the abbey occupies the site of an earlier 7th-century church that was destroyed in a fire; the 12th-century abbey was later attacked by the Norman knight William de Burgh and rebuilt in the early 13th century (it is these ruins you see today). The community once gathered in the chapter house to confess their sins publicly.

From the abbey, moss-encrusted trees guard a path to the river and the diminutive and roofless 16th-century **monk's fishing house** FREE, built midway over the river (near the bridge). Cross the bridge and all manner of rambling opportunities await in the forest.

Pigeonhole Cave CAVE
This cave, in a pine forest about 1.5km west of Cong, can be reached via a signposted walking loop from the abbey. Steep stone steps lead down into the cave, where subterranean water flows in winter. Watch for the white trout of Cong – a mythical woman who turned into a fish to be with her drowned lover.

Quiet Man Museum MUSEUM
(☑ 094-954 6089; www.quietmanmuseum.com; Circular Rd; adult/child €5/4, location tour €15; ⊙ 10am-4pm Apr-Oct) Modelled on Sean Thornton's White O' Morn' Cottage from *The Quiet Man* film, the museum offers a location tour – good for film fanatics and those with a postmodern fascination for the way reality bends to fiction.

🏃 Activities

Corrib Cruises CRUISE
(☑ 087 283 0799; www.corribcruises.com; Lisloughery Pier; adult/child from €20/10) Cruises on Lough Corrib run from both Lisloughery Pier and Ashford Castle Pier, 15 minutes away by boat. A 75-minute history cruise

ATLANTIC OCEAN

Benwee Head
Portacloy
Downpatrick Head
Dun Briste ❶
Lacka Bay
Erris Head
Broad Haven Bay
Rossport
Belderrig
Ballycastle
Lackan Strand ❹
Doonamo Point
Belmullet
Pollatomish
R314
Céide Fields ✪
Killala
Carrowmore Lough
River Owenmore
Blacksod Bay
Bangor Erris
N59
Dahybaun Lough
Crossmolina
Mullet Peninsula
Inishkea
Aghleam
Blacksod
N59
Ballcroy National Park ⬇
Nephin Beg (628m) ▲
Castlehill
Lough Conn
Lahardane
Achill Head
Dugort
Ballycroy
Mt Nephin (806m) ▲
Pontoon
Keem
Keel
Achill Island ❸
Achill Sound
Nephin Beg Range
MAYO
Dooega
Curraun Peninsula
Mulranny
Lough Feeagh
Carrigahowley Castle
Turlough
❼ 🏰
Newport
Great Western Greenway
Clew Bay
Castlebar
Mt Knockmore (462m) ▲
Clare Island
Louisburgh
Westport
N5
Roonagh Quay
Murrisk
Knappagh
Ballintubber
Inishturk
Killadoon
Cregganbaun
❷ **Croagh Patrick**
N59
Srah
Partry
Doolough Valley ❻
Bengorm (702m) ▲
Delphi
Tourmakeady
Lough Mask
Ballinrobe
Inishbofin
Rosroe Quay
Killary Harbour
Leenane
Partry Mountains
Curramore
Inishshark
Shanafaraghaun
Neale
Cleggan
Letterfrack
Clonbur
Cong
GALWAY
Lough Corrib
Clifden
Lough Inagh

0 — 20 km
0 — 10 miles

Counties Mayo & Sligo Highlights

❶ **Dun Briste** (p440)
Staring out over raging waves to this vast sea stack cleaved from the coast by a huge storm.

❷ **Croagh Patrick** (p430)
Following in St Patrick's footsteps up the conical peak.

❸ **Achill Island** (p436)
Discovering Blue Flag beaches,

a haunted deserted village and a sea-salt factory.

❹ **Lackan Strand** (p442)
Exploring the glory of this beautiful beach.

THE FIRST BOYCOTT

It was near the unassuming little village of Neale, near Cong, that the term 'boycott' came into use. In 1880 the Irish Land League, in an effort to press for fair rents and improve the lot of workers, withdrew field hands from the estate of Lord Erne, who owned much of the land in the area. When Lord Erne's land agent, Captain Charles Cunningham Boycott, evicted the striking labourers, the surrounding community began a campaign to ostracise him. Not only did farmers refuse to work his land, people in the town also refused to talk to him, provide services or sit next to him in church. The incident attracted the attention of the London papers, and soon Boycott's name was synonymous with such organised, nonviolent protests. Within a few months, Boycott fled Ireland.

departs each morning year-round; there are two-hour island cruises in the afternoons between June and September. They visit Inchagoill, the island at the centre of Lough Corrib with 5th-century monastic ruins.

There are also boats to/from Oughterard in County Galway.

Ashford Outdoors   KAYAKING
(☑ 094-954 6507; www.ashfordoutdoors.com; Ashford Equestrian Centre, Ashford Castle Estate; tours from adult/child €75/55, bike rental per day from adult/child €40/30) Pedal the shores and then paddle the waters of Ashford Castle Estate and Lough Corrib on these tours by bike, kayak, stand-up paddleboard (SUP), horse and pony.

Lakeshore Angling Centre   FISHING
(☑ 094-954 1389; www.lakeshoreholidays.com) Provides fishing services for all types of river and lake anglers, from novice to professional; also offers a range of other activities, from trekking to horse riding, mountain biking and water sports. It's about 10km north of Cong.

🛏 Sleeping

Lakeland House   HOSTEL €
(Cong Hostel; ☑ 094-954 6089; www.quietman-cong.com; Quay Rd, Lisloughrey; campsites per 2 adults €25, dm/d/f €20/55/75; ℗ 🛜) In this well-run hostel a mini-cinema screens Cong's iconic *The Quiet Man* film *every* night. The four-bed dorms and doubles are simple but bright and comfortable. You can borrow fishing rods, and there's even a freezer for your catch.

Breakfast is included, except for campers.

Nymphsfield House   B&B €
(☑ 094-954 6320; www.nymphsfieldhouse.com; R345, Gortaroe; s €50, d €70-80; 🛜) Just northeast of Cong (a pretty 10-minute or 1km walk), in the vicinity of several good B&Bs, this family-run B&B offers a warm welcome and a breakfast menu featuring cooked-to-order

omelettes, smoked salmon and waffles. You'll also find a place to store your fishing gear.

Michaeleen's Manor   B&B €
(☑ 094-954 6089; www.michaeleensmanor.com; Quay Rd, Lisloughrey; s/d/f €55/75/115; ℗ 🛜) One for fans of *The Quiet Man* film: each of 12 comfy rooms here is named after a character in the movie and is decorated with memorabilia and quotations. The lush garden even has a large fountain replica of Galway's Quiet Man Bridge. It's about 2km east of Cong.

Ryan's Hotel   HOTEL €€
(☑ 094-954 6243; www.ryanshotelcong.ie; Main St; s from €85, d €110-120; 🛜) From the earth-tone checked carpets to the sketches of fishing flies on the walls, Ryan's is every inch a Lough Corrib hotel. Add a genuinely warm welcome, cosy bars, a village-centre location and a quality breakfast menu and you have a winner.

★ Lodge at Ashford Castle   HOTEL €€€
(☑ 094-954 5400; www.thelodgeac.com; Quay Rd; d €289-323, ste €395-540; 🛜) Built in the 1820s by the owners of nearby, prestigious Ashford Castle, the lodge has rich, contemporary colours, plush furnishings, handmade toiletries and dreamy lake views. The suites are magnificent: some boast private terraces and mini-balconies, while others have rain showers and range over two floors.

The lodge's renowned eatery, Wilde's at the Lodge, delivers fine dining at its best.

Ashford Castle   HOTEL €€€
(☑ 094-954 6003; www.ashfordcastle.com; d €675-950, ste €1725-5000; 🛜) High-end luxury, exquisite interiors and superb personalised service define Ashford Castle, once home to the Guinness family. Old-world elegance is everywhere, from the vaulted wine cellars and refined billiard room to the state-of-the-art spa. The 140-hectare estate is home to horse riding, fishing, falconry and golf, and eating options range from fine dining to afternoon tea.

Eating & Drinking

Fennel Seed Restaurant
IRISH €€

(☑094-954 6004; www.ryanshotelcong.ie; Main St, Ryan's Hotel; bar food €13-22, mains €16-29; ⊙6-9pm Mon-Sat, 1-7pm Sun) Denis Lenihan's culinary skills enjoy widespread acclaim, so make sure you don't miss the signature 'smoky bake' pie, stuffed with trout, salmon, mackerel, haddock and knockout flavour. Bar food is served in the adjoining Crowe's Nest Pub until 7pm.

★ Wilde's at the Lodge
IRISH €€€

(☑094-954 5400; www.thelodgeac.com; Quay Rd, Lisloughrey Lodge; 5 courses €65; ⊙6.30-9pm Thu-Sun plus 1-3.30pm Sun; 🐾) Chef Jonathan Keane and his team forage the mussels, wild herbs and flowers that adorn the dishes at this exquisite restaurant within the vast grounds of Ashford Castle. Produce and meat come from organic local suppliers for a much-lauded, seasonally changing menu, bringing the chance to sample many dishes served on small plates.

The restaurant takes its name from Sir William Wilde (father of Oscar), who loved the Lough.

Pat Cohan's
PUB

(☑094-954 5620; www.patcohanbar.ie; Abbey St; ⊙10am-11pm) In a case of life imitating art, this one-time grocery store was disguised in the film The Quiet Man as the fictional Pat Cohan's. But as The Quiet Man craziness only grows, it has now become that pub.

Information

The **tourist office** (☑016-057 700; www.discoverireland.ie; Abbey St; ⊙9am-5pm Tue-Sat Mar-Sep, winter hours vary) is in the old courthouse building opposite Cong Abbey.

Getting There & Away

Bus Éireann (www.buseireann.ie; Main St) bus 422 runs three times a day to Castlebar (€9, 40 minutes), Ballinrobe (€3, 15 minutes) and Headford (€6, 25 minutes). For services to Westport, change at Castlebar and for Galway, change at Headford.

Doolough Valley

The R335 from Leenane in County Galway to Westport is one of Ireland's most beautiful scenic routes. Largely untouched by housing, cut turf or even stone walls, the desolate Doolough Valley is a sublime journey, the steep sides of the surrounding mountains simply sliding into the steely grey waters of Doo Lough as sheep graze placidly on the hills – they occasionally park themselves in the middle of the road, too.

This is also one of Ireland's most poignant spots – the site of the Doolough Tragedy – a Famine catastrophe that occurred in 1849.

Choose a dry and clear day to tackle the road as curtains of rain can greatly diminish the views. If you have time, wander down the side roads to the north and west of the valley to reach glorious, often-deserted beaches.

Delphi

This swath of mountainous moorland along the spectacular R335 is miles from any significant population, allowing you to set about the serious business of relaxing and, if you fancy it, taking endless photographs.

The southern end of the Doolough Valley was named by its most famous resident, the second Marquis of Sligo, who was convinced that it resembled the land around Delphi, Greece. If you can spot the resemblance, you've a better imagination than most. However,

COUNTIES MAYO & SLIGO DOOLOUGH VALLEY

THE DOOLOUGH TRAGEDY

Marked today by a grim memorial cross in the Doolough Valley that serves as its epitaph, the Doolough Tragedy still casts a black shadow across the sublime landscape, even on the sunniest of days.

On 30 March 1849, in the midst of the Potato Famine, hundreds of starving men, women and children set off from Louisburgh for Delphi Lodge, where they had heard they would be reassessed for famine relief. The reassessment took place the next day, but there was no food for them upon their arrival, so the long walk back to Louisburgh commenced. The weather was freezing and bitter and the people so malnourished and weak that the 16-mile return journey on foot took its toll and many people died. Corpses were left by the side of the road, some – it was said – with their mouths stuffed with grass in a desperate last bid for sustenance.

Every year, a Famine Walk to Louisburgh from Delphi commemorates the disaster.

the beauty of creeks babbling over boggy countryside against a backdrop of stark sun- and cloud-dappled hillsides is undeniable.

Delphi Resort
LODGE €€

(☎ 095-42208; www.delphiadventureresort.com; off R335; dm €15-17, d €129, ste €199-229; P @ 🛜) There's a bed for most budgets at the modern, multipurpose Delphi Resort, from standard guest rooms, loft rooms and larger suites (some with enormous timber decks) to luxury six-bed dorms with bathrooms where each bunk has its own USB charger and reading light. A cavernous pub-restaurant serves great bar food (mains €12 to €29).

Spa treatments use hand-harvested seaweed and the property's own mountain spring water. There's a good **cafe** (mains from €7; ⊗ 9.30am-5.30pm; 🛜) here as well.

Delphi Lodge
HISTORIC HOTEL €€€

(☎ 095-42222; www.delphilodge.ie; off R335; s from €150, d €265-295, f €295, ste €295; P @) Dwarfed by the mountainous backdrop, this wonderful 1830s Georgian mansion beside Fin Lough was built by the Marquis of Sligo. The 13-room country hotel features beautiful interiors, colossal 405-hectare grounds, delicious food (six-course dinner €65) and a serious lack of pretension. It's popular with fishers (half-day with fishing tutor €180) and those seeking relaxation and escape.

Louisburgh
POP 434

The northern gateway to the Doolough Valley is the appealing village of Louisburgh, founded under curious circumstances in 1795. Based on a simple four-street system known as the Cross, the town was designed and built as a living memorial to a relative of the first Marquis of Sligo, Lord Altamont (John Browne) – his kinsman was killed at the 1758 Battle of Louisburgh in Nova Scotia.

In addition to the lovely beach at Carrowmore, there are also some excellent surf beaches nearby, like Carrownisky.

West and south of Louisburgh you'll find a web of narrow unmarked roads that wander through the scruffy countryside. The rewards come when you hit the water.

◉ Sights & Activities

Granuaile Heritage Centre
& Famine Exhibition
MUSEUM

(☎ 098-66341; www.granuaile.org; Church St; adult/ child €5/2.50; ⊗ 10am-5pm Mon-Fri) Acquire an illuminating glimpse into the life and times of Grace O'Malley (Gráinne Ní Mháille or Granuaile; 1530–1603), the infamous pirate queen of Connaught, as well as details of the horrors of the local Famine.

Old Head
BEACH

(off R335) Head east from Louisburgh for a couple of kilometres and look out for the turning north to the pleasant and secluded beach at Old Head.

Carrowmore
BEACH

The sheltered, broad beach at Carrowmore, just west of Louisburgh village, offers good views of Croagh Patrick and has a lifeguard on duty in summer.

Surf Mayo
SURFING

(☎ 087 778 6821; www.surfmayo.com; Carrownisky Beach, Louisburgh; lessons adult/child from €30/25, surfboard & wetsuit rental per day €20; ⊗ varies) Offers surfing lessons and camps at Carrownisky Beach, and rents out gear, including SUPs (stand-up paddleboards).

🛏 Sleeping & Eating

Ponderosa
B&B €

(☎ 098-66440; www.ponderosamayo.com; Tooreen Rd; s/d from €45/60; ⊗ Apr-Oct; 🛜) Just 400m east of the Louisburgh town centre, this three-room purple-and-white B&B is set in a modern bungalow, with a long front lawn.

West View
HOTEL €€

(☎ 098-23817; bookings@thewestviewhotel.ie; Chapel St; d €120; P 🛜) You'll find lashings of contemporary style in this small inn right in the centre of town, along with bright, comfy rooms and staff who are keen to please. The bar has trad-music sessions some nights.

Good Grazing
DINER €

(☎ 098-23578; Chapel St; meals €7; ⊗ 5-10pm Sat-Thu, 9.30am-11pm Fri) A surfboard propped up in a corner and a pool table in the middle help lend this diner a laid-back air. Irish ingredients pack a menu that's strong on burgers, hot dogs and fries. The Facebook page features regular menu updates.

Louisburgh 74
CAFE €

(☎ 087 152 8682; www.facebook.com/pg/louisberg74; Chapel St; mains €6; ⊗ 9.30am-6pm; 🖍) The unmistakable vibe of a proper neighbourhood cafe pervades this eatery, where folks chat surrounded by pine tables and bookcases. There's a firm focus on home cooked cakes and scones, and the coffee is first rate.

THE PIRATE QUEEN

The life of Grace O'Malley (Gráinne ní Mháille or Granuaile, c 1530–1603) reads like fantasy adventure fiction. Twice widowed and twice imprisoned for acts of piracy, she was a fearsome presence in the troubled landscape of 16th-century Ireland.

Her unorthodox life was the stuff of legend and mythology; hundreds of stories testify to her unequalled courage, skill and dogged determination to protect her clan against virtually anyone else – from rival chieftains to the English army.

Born into a powerful seafaring family that controlled most of the Mayo coastline and traded internationally, the independent Grace soon decided she should join the family business. Legend has it that while still a child she asked her father if she could join a trip to Spain, but was refused on the grounds that seafaring was not for girls. She promptly shaved off her hair, dressed in boys clothing, returned to the ship and announced that she was ready to sail. Her family nicknamed her Gráinne Mhaol (pronounced grawn-ya wail; bald Grace), a name that stuck for the rest of her life.

A Life of Notoriety

At 15 Grace was married off to Donal O'Flaherty, a querulous local chieftain, but using her smarts she soon eclipsed her husband in politics and trade. The O'Flahertys were banned from trading in Galway, one of the largest ports in the British Isles. Grace got around this by waylaying cargo vessels en route to port and demanding payment for safe passage. If they refused, she had them looted.

After her husband's death, Grace settled on Clare Island but continued marauding around the Irish and Scottish coasts. Closer to home, the only part of Clew Bay not under her control was Rockfleet, so in 1566 Grace married Richard an-Iarrain (aka Iron Dick of the Burke) to gain control of his castle (p435). Despite some marital ups and downs (she tried to 'dismiss' him once she controlled his tower), they remained together until his death 17 years later.

By the 1570s Grace's blatant piracy had come to English attention and many attempts were made to capture her. Eventually she was brought to London in 1593, whereupon Queen Elizabeth I granted her a pardon and offered her a title: which she declined, saying she was already Queen of Connaught.

Grace O'Malley died in 1603 and is thought to be buried in the abbey (p429) on Clare Island.

🛍 Shopping

Books@One BOOKS
(📞 098-66885; www.facebook.com/booksatone; Main St; ⊙ 10am-5pm Mon-Sat, noon-4pm Sun) This excellent community nonprofit bookshop is a tremendous place for a browse, and serves as a kind of cafe and social hub too.

ℹ Getting There & Away

Bus Éireann (www.buseireann.ie) bus 450 links Louisburgh with Westport one to three times a day, Monday to Saturday (€8, 30 minutes).

Clare Island

POP 159

Clew Bay is dotted with some 365 islands, of which the largest is mountainous Clare Island, 5km offshore but half a world away. Dominated by rocky Mt Knockmore (462m), its varied terrain is terrific for walking and

climbing, and swimming can be enjoyed at safe, sandy beaches. The island is also one of the dwindling number of places where you can find choughs.

Clare Island has the windswept ruins of the Cistercian Clare Island Abbey (c 1460) and **Granuaile's Castle**, both associated with the pirate queen Grace O'Malley. The island is also a great place to retreat from the world and reflect upon the beauty of Ireland. Among the many stirring hikes, there's a self-guided **archaeological walk** or you can climb **Knockmore**, a 462m hill. Spectacular views enthral visitors.

★ **Clare Island Abbey** ABBEY
(St Brigid's Abbey) The chancel roof of 13th-century Clare Island Abbey is dotted with faded fragments of murals, dating from around 1500. Look out too for the tomb reputed to be that of Grace O'Malley, where a stone inscribed with her family motto formidably

declares: 'Invincible on land and sea'. The abbey is in the south of the island; it's often locked – get the key from O'Malley's Post Office (how fitting), some 30m away.

Displays help you decipher the mural fragments. Once your eyes adjust to the light, you'll make out sections of hunting and fishing scenes, as well as wrestlers, a harpist and a pelican.

🛌 Sleeping

★ **Go Explore Hostel** HOSTEL €
(☑ 098-26307, 087 410 8706; www.goexplorehostel.ie; dm weekday/weekend €25/30; ⊘ Jun-Aug, plus Wed-Sun May & Sep; 🕏) This terrific hostel is a delight, with voluminous windows and a terrace overlooking the water, while vintage features include a large 1840s fireplace. The pub draws drinkers from around the island, with the call of decent beer, good food (mains €8 to €20) and frequent live-music sessions. All manner of adventure activities and classes keep guests occupied.

The hostel also opens for the Easter holidays; in the wind-lashed winter months, it's group bookings only.

Macalla Farm B&B €
(☑ 087 250 4845; www.macallafarm.ie; s/d €50/70, retreats per 2/7 days from €480/780) A haven of calm, Macalla Farm is an organic oasis in the northeast of the island. It offers lessons and retreats focusing on yoga, mindfulness, natural food and connecting with horses. Guests enjoy organic vegetarian meals, and the fact that there is no wi-fi. Camping is also possible at a €20 discount.

Granuaile House B&B €€
(☑ 098-26250; www.granuailehouse.net; s/d from €60/80; 🕏) This fine guesthouse right bedside Clare Harbour has been accommodating people since 1909. These days it offers smart, bright rooms, a warm, relaxed welcome and captivating views directly overlooking the sandy bay.

★ **Clare Island Lighthouse** B&B €€€
(☑ 087 668 9758; www.clareislandlighthouse.com; ste €250-300; 🕏) With its ends-of-the-earth feel, views onto jagged cliffs and regular blasts of salt spray, there's a dash of magic about this boutique retreat on the island's north coast. Facilities in the sleek suites vary: one has a sauna, others open fires or underfloor heating. The Tower Suite has a spiral staircase leading to a circular bedroom in the old lantern room.

ℹ Information

There's an unstaffed **tourist information point** (www.clareisland.info; ⊘ dawn-dusk) at the harbour, with free island maps and info on activities.

ℹ Getting There & Around

Clare Island Ferries (☑ 086 851 5003, 098-23737; www.clareislandferry.com; adult/child return €17/12) and **O'Malley Ferries** (☑ 098-25045, 086 887 0814; www.omalleyferries.com; adult/child return €17/12) run boats from Roonagh Quay, 8km west of Louisburgh to Clare Harbour. There are around eight sailings daily in July and August, and two to four sailings daily the rest of the year.

You can often pick up a taxi at the harbour and rent bikes (about €15 per day); your accommodation may also be able to arrange transport.

Inishturk Island

POP 51

Ruggedly beautiful Inishturk lies 14km off Mayo's western coast. It's sparsely populated and little visited, despite the two sandy beaches on its eastern side, impressive cliffs, wonderful flora and fauna, and a rugged, hilly landscape that's ideal for walking. In fact, ambling along the island's maze of country roads is a perfect way to adapt to the deeply relaxed pace of life here.

If you want to stay, there are several guesthouses on the island, including the recommended **Teach Abhainn** (☑ 098-45510; teachabhainn@hotmail.com; s/d €45/80; ⊘ Apr-Oct; 🕏), around 1.5km west of the harbour.

Food can be found at the **Community Club** (☑ 087 131 7426; ⊘ noon-12.30am) south of the pier.

ℹ Getting There & Away

O'Malley Ferries (☑ 098-25045; www.omalleyferries.com) runs one to three ferries daily from Roonagh Quay, near Louisburgh (adult/child return €9/6). The crossing takes 50 minutes.

Croagh Patrick

St Patrick couldn't have picked a better spot for a pilgrimage than this conical mountain (also known as 'the Reek'). On a clear day, the tough two-hour climb rewards with stunning views over Clew Bay and its sandy islets.

It was on Croagh Patrick that Ireland's patron saint fasted for 40 days and nights, and where he reputedly banished venomous snakes. Climbing the 764m holy mountain is an act of penance for thousands of believers on the last Sunday of July (Reek Sunday). The truly contrite take the ancient 35km pilgrim's route, Tóchar Phádraig (Patrick's Causeway), from Ballintubber Abbey and ascend the mountain barefoot. The 7km trail taken by the less repentant begins at the village of Murrisk.

National Famine Memorial   MONUMENT
Opposite the car park on the far side of the road is the National Famine Memorial, a spine-chilling sculpture of a three-masted ghost ship wreathed in swirling skeletons, commemorating the lives lost on so-called 'coffin ships' used to help people escape the Famine.

Croagh Patrick Hike   WALKING
(Teach na Miasa, Murrisk) The main 7km trail up Croagh Patrick ascends the mountain from the signed car park in the west end of Murrisk. The steep trail is rocky in parts and it gets crowded on sunny weekends. At the summit you'll find a 1905 whitewashed church and a 9th-century oratory fountain. Views are sublime. The average return trip takes three to four hours. Murrisk is 8km west of Westport.

You can hire walking sticks for €3 at the cafe beside the car park.

Croagh Patrick Stables   HORSE RIDING
(☑ 086 121 7590; www.croaghpatrickstables.com; rides per 2hr from €30; ☺ 9am-6pm Mon-Sat) From its base right at the foot of the Holy Mountain, Croagh Patrick Stables offers treks along beaches and fields as well as lessons for all abilities.

Westport

POP 6198

Bright and vibrant even in the depths of winter, Westport is a photogenic Georgian town with tree-lined streets, riverside walkways and a great vibe. With an excellent choice of accommodation, fine restaurants and pubs renowned for their music, it's a hugely popular place yet has never sold its soul to tourism.

Westport is Mayo's nightlife hub, and its central location makes it a convenient and enjoyable base for exploring the county.

◉ Sights

Westport Quay, the town's harbour, is on Clew Bay, 2km west of the centre. It's a picturesque spot with shops and cafes. In town, the **Octagon** is a major landmark, punctuated by a Doric column.

Westport House   HISTORIC BUILDING
(☑ 098-27766; www.westporthouse.ie; Quay Rd; adult/child house only €14/7, house & pirate adventure park €25/20; ☺ 10am-6pm Jun-Aug, to 4pm Mar-May & Sep-Nov, hours vary Dec-Feb; ⊞) Built in 1730 on the ruins of Grace O'Malley's 16th-century castle, this charming Georgian mansion 2km west of the centre retains much of its original contents and has some stunning period-style rooms. Set in glorious gardens, the overall effect is marred somewhat by its commercial focus, but children love the **Pirate Adventure Park**, complete with a swinging pirate ship, 'pirate's playground', roller-coaster-style flume ride through a water channel, and Gracy's Bouncy Castle.

Tickets are 5% cheaper if bought in advance online.

Clew Bay Heritage Centre   MUSEUM
(☑ 098-26852; www.westportheritage.com; Westport Quay; adult/child €3/free; ☺ 10am-5pm Mon-Fri Jun & Sep, 10am-5pm Mon-Fri, 3-5pm Sun Jul & Aug, 10.30am-2pm Mon-Fri Oct-May) Set in a 19th-century stone building 2km west of town, this museum traces the history, customs and traditions of Westport and Clew Bay.

⚡ Activities & Tours

The area around Westport is superb for cycling, with gentle coastal routes or more challenging mountain trails to test your legs, all within a short distance of town. The Great Western Greenway (p434), a 42km cycling route between Westport and Achill, begins 500m from the centre of town off the N59.

The tourist office (p435) has an excellent brochure detailing local walks for all skill levels.

★ Clew Bay Bike Hire   CYCLING
(☑ 098-37675; www.clewbaybikehire.ie; Distillery Rd; adult/child per day €20/15; ☺ 9am-6pm) Offers advice on routes and trails in the area and has shops in Westport and along the Great Western Greenway in Newport, Mulranny and Achill. Its shuttle service means you can start the trail at any point and be picked up on completion (per adult/child €15/free).

During summer, it also offers half-day sea-kayaking tours (per person €60, minimum four people, private tour €130 per person).

★ Guided Walks of Historic Westport   WALKING
(☑ 098-26852; www.westportheritage.com; Bridge St; per person €5; ☺ 11am Wed Jul-Sep) Local

Westport

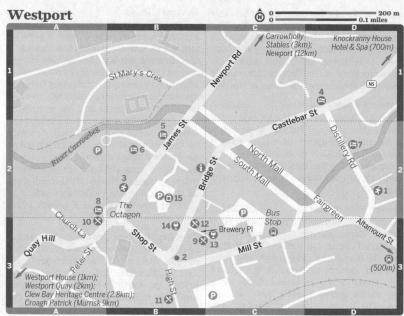

historians lead 90-minute walks around Westport. They start at Westport's historic clock tower in the centre of town.

Westport Walking Tours
WALKING

(☑ 087 410 1363; www.westportwalkingtours.ie; from €5; ⊙ times vary) Tours of the town include two-hour walking tours, and a meander around the pick of the local pubs, sampling craft beers. Check times and departure points online.

Croagh Patrick Walking Holidays
WALKING

(☑ 098-26090; www.walkingguideireland.com; 7-day walks from €800; ⊙ Apr-Aug) Highly customisable walks in the countryside surrounding Westport that usually last seven days. You can include St Patrick's holy site and/ or a beach. Fees include accommodation, breakfast and lunch.

Clewbay Cruises
BOATING

(☑ 098-39192; www.clewbaycruises.com; Westport Quay; adult/child €20/10; ⊙ May-Oct) Enjoy views of Clew Bay on 90-minute cruises.

Carrowholly Stables
HORSE RIDING

(☑ 098-27057; www.carrowholly-stables.com; near Carrowholly; per hr adult/child €30/25) All skill levels are catered for at this recommended outfit, which offers horse and pony treks on the beach and beside Clew Bay. The stables

are 3km northwest of the town centre, near the village of Carrowholly.

🛏 Sleeping

Westport is Mayo's main city, and while there's an abundance of B&Bs and hotels, rooms are in short supply during summer and special events.

Old Mill Holiday Hostel
HOSTEL €

(☑ 098-27045; www.oldmillhostel.com; off James St; dm/d/f from €18/50/75; 🛜) There's an appealing feel to the rooms in this converted stone mill. Dorms range from four to 12 bed, while the family rooms sleep up to four. The communal areas are inviting and there's a handy kitchen and laundry. It's central too.

★ St Anthony's Riverside B&B
B&B €€

(☑ 098-28887; www.st-anthonys.com; Distillery Rd; s from €90, d €100-115; 🅿 🛜) It may be in the middle of Westport, but a tall hedge and thick, twisted vines give this genteel, 19th-century B&B a tucked-away feel. Rooms have clean lines and restful, light colours, some also have Jacuzzis. There's a large garden to relax in and breakfast is excellent.

Clew Bay Hotel
HOTEL €€

(☑ 098-28088; www.clewbayhotel.com; James St; s/d from €85/130; 🛜) Some of the small but stylish rooms at this central, family-run,

Westport

three-star hotel come with river views. Bathrooms and furnishings are first-rate, while the modern pub is popular for contemporary takes on classic fare. Parking costs €3 a day.

Guests get a free pass to the leisure centre across the car park, with its swimming pool, sauna and gym.

Wyatt Hotel HOTEL €€
(☎098-25027; www.wyatthotel.com; The Octagon; s from €69, d €110-218; P✿⃝) The Wyatt is a local landmark. Plumb in the centre of Westport, painted a sunflower yellow and stretching around one side of the central Octagon, it has been accommodating travellers in style for centuries. Standard rooms are comfortable; restyled and fresh superior rooms have large beds, walk-in showers and lavish amenities.

Prices can fall by as much as €40 per double on weekdays in low season.

Castlecourt Hotel HOTEL €€
(☎098-55088; www.castlecourthotel.ie; Castlebar St; s €128, d €128-163, ste/f €180/150; @✿⃝) The spacious but still cosy rooms at this grand hotel in the town centre blend contemporary style with classic elegance. It has a gym, a 20m indoor pool and a very snazzy spa.

Knockranny House Hotel & Spa BOUTIQUE HOTEL €€€
(☎098-28600; www.knockrannyhousehotel.ie; off N5; r €100-160, ste €170-300; ✳@✿⃝) Open fires take the chill out of the air at this modern hotel, where more than 100 rooms and suites each feature plush classic furnishings and styles. Amenities include an indoor pool and spa facilities. Westport's centre is 1.5km west, a 15-minute walk.

The restaurant, La Fougère, is renowned for innovative cuisine and an extensive wine list. Afternoon tea (per person €19, 2.30pm

to 5.30pm daily) in the Brehon Bar is another favourite.

✕ Eating

Westport is packed with superb restaurants and cafes: just wander along Bridge St and the little laneways off it to make some tasty discoveries. Book for dinner in summer and on weekends.

Creel CAFE €
(☎098-26174; The Quay; mains €5-12; ⊙10am-4pm Wed-Thu, 9.30am-5pm Fri-Sun) With its lively chatter, superb cakes and all-day brunches, Creel conjures up inventive treatments with traditional Mayo ingredients. Lunch might be a warming chicken noodle soup or a vivid, seed-scattered salad; puddings span rhubarb crumble to lemon meringue pie.

★Pantry & Corkscrew IRISH €€
(☎098-26977; www.thepantryandcorkscrew.com; The Octagon; mains €17-24; ⊙5-10pm daily May-Sep, Wed-Sun Oct-Apr; ♪) The heart of Mayo's slow-food movement is found at this narrow storefront with a turquoise exterior and interior walls crammed with pictures. The kitchen works culinary magic with seasonal, local and organic produce to rustle up stout-braised beef, maple-glazed pork and arancini with jalapeño and Aran Islands feta. Book ahead.

The early-evening menu (5pm to 6.30pm; two/three courses €22/25) is superb value.

★An Port Mór IRISH €€
(☎098-26730; www.anportmor.com; 1 Brewery Pl; mains €14-22, 5 courses €39; ⊙5-9pm Sun-Thu, to 9.30pm Fri & Sat; ♪) Proprietor-chef Frankie Mallon's little restaurant packs a big punch. It's an intimate place with a series of long narrow rooms and a menu featuring gutsy flavours, excellent meats and much-lauded seafood (try the excellent Clew Bay scallops). Just about everything is procured from the region.

GREAT WESTERN GREENWAY

Following the route of the old Westport–Achill Railway (which ran from 1895 to 1937), the Great Western Greenway (www.greenway.ie) is a terrific reason to travel through this part of Mayo. The 42km trail penetrates gorgeous countryside and waterfront scenery, consisting of three main sections, none of which requires more than moderate effort.

Westport to Newport This 11km section through pretty, lush countryside starts off the N59, 500m northeast of Westport's centre, and ends at the N59, 2km before Newport. This is the easiest section.

Newport to Mulranny This 18km section is the most popular and passes close to many sights along Clew Bay. It's off the N59 just north of Newport and ends in Mulranny.

Mulranny to Achill This 13km section starts right in Mulranny and ends about 1km short of Achill Island (many tourist maps show the trail going all the way), after which you ride along roads. It has some sweeping water views.

You can easily rent bicycles all along the Greenway. Two Westport-based operators, Clew Bay Bike Hire (p431) and **Westport Bikes 4 Hire** (☑ 086 088 0882; www.westportbikes4 hire.com; James St; adult/child per day €20/15; ⊙ 9am-6pm), offer uber-convenient pickup and drop-off services that let you cycle all or part of the Greenway one way, and be driven the other way.

The two-course early-bird menu (€24), served nightly between 5pm and 6pm, is superb value.

Helm SEAFOOD €€
(☑ 098-26398; www.thehelm.ie; The Quay; mains €12-22; ⊙ 8am-9.30pm) Fittingly for a pub set beside a boat-backed quay, Helm showcases the freshest Irish seafood, with chefs working with fish caught between Rossaveal in County Galway and Ballina in County Mayo. Regulars on the menu include salmon stuffed with spinach and prawns, and perfectly cooked black sole on the bone.

Sage EUROPEAN €€
(☑ 098-56700; www.sagewestport.ie; 10 High St; mains €18-26; ⊙ 5.30-9.30pm Thu-Tue; 🐾) A wave of aromas hits you as you walk through the door of this stylish restaurant, run by Shteryo Yurukov and Eva Ivanova. Foraged, wild and local ingredients are the mainstays, as are innovative flavour combinations – crab claws with wild garlic, a bitter coastline salad and free-range chicken with wild mushroom sauce.

There's an early-evening menu (two/three courses €22/26) and the vast majority of dishes are coeliac friendly.

Sol Rio MEDITERRANEAN €€
(☑ 098-28944; www.solrio.ie; Bridge St; mains lunch €10, dinner €14-22; ⊙ cafe 9am-6pm, restaurant noon-3pm & 6-10pm; 🐾) The extensive menu here ranges from pizza and pasta to organic meat and fish. Carefully chosen ingredients are combined cleverly, whether

you pause at the simple cafe downstairs or the more stylish restaurant upstairs. The deli is famous for its egg-custard pastries.

🍷 Drinking & Nightlife

Westport is thronged with pubs, many of them with regular live music.

★**Matt Molloy's** PUB
(☑ 098-27663; www.mattmolloy.com; Bridge St; ⊙ 12.30-11.30pm Mon-Thu, to 12.30am Fri & Sat, to 11pm Sun; 🐾) Matt Malloy, the fife player from the Chieftains, runs this old-school pub where Mayo's musical heritage comes vividly to life. Head to the back room most nights and you'll probably catch live *céilidh* (traditional music and dancing). Or perhaps a veteran musician will simply slide into a chair and croon a few classics. Great microbrews on tap add to the allure.

Gallery WINE BAR
(☑ 083 109 1138; www.thegallerywestport.com; 9 Brewery Pl; ⊙ 4-11.30pm Tue-Thu, 4pm-midnight Fri, 2pm-midnight Sat) With its ranks of vinyl, twin turntables, shelves stacked with books and comfy chairs, the Gallery is the hang-out of choice for Westport's cool crowd. Add live music, board games, tapas and an array of wines and you may stay longer than planned.

🛍 Shopping

Wandering Westport's centre, you'll discover little boutiques and a surprising number of bookshops.

Market
MARKET

(James St, car park; ☺8.30am-1pm Thu) Fresh produce from the region.

Custom House Studios
ART

(☑098-28735; www.customhousestudios.ie; Westport Quay; ☺10am-5pm Mon-Fri, 1-4.30pm Sat & Sun) Local artists display their creations at this inviting gallery, which also has special exhibitions.

ℹ Information

Mayo's main **tourist office** (☑098-25711; www.westporttourism.com; Bridge St; ☺9am-5.45pm Mon-Fri year-round, plus 10am-4pm Sat Easter-Oct) has a lot of walking and cycling info.

ℹ Getting There & Away

BUS

Bus Éireann (www.buseireann.ie) services include Galway (bus 456; €11, 1½ hours, five daily); for Sligo, take a bus to Knock (bus 440; €9, one hour, two daily) or Charlestown (bus 440; €9, one hour, two to four daily) and change. Buses depart from Mill St.

TRAIN

There are four to five daily trains to Dublin (€21, 3¼ hours).

Newport

POP 626

Newport is a picturesque 18th-century village on the Newport River. The trains on the Westport–Achill Railway stopped in 1937, but a striking seven-arch viaduct built in 1892 remains a popular spot with walkers and cyclists.

Newport – or at least a ruined house by Drumgoney Lough (Leg O' Mutton Lake) just outside town – is actress (and former Princess of Monaco) Grace Kelly's ancestral home, drawing dedicated fans from far and wide.

The Bangor Trail ends here, while the wonderful Great Western Greenway heads west to Achill, 31km away along the former rail line.

◉ Sights & Activities

Newport is an attractive riverine place in its own right, though most sights of note lie beyond town.

Burrishoole Abbey
HISTORIC SITE

(off N59; ☺dawn-dusk) From a distance, the eerie shell of this wind-battered 1470-built Dominican abbey near the water is quite a sight. Leaving Newport in a northwest direction along the N59 towards Achill Island, a sign points the way to this stunning abbey, and from there it's a further 1km to the car park.

Carrigahowley Castle
CASTLE

(Rockfleet Castle; off N59) Carrigahowley Castle (also called Rockfleet Castle), an intact 15th-century tower off the N59, is associated with Grace O'Malley. She married her second husband, Richard an-Iarrain, to gain control of this castle, and famously fought off an English attack here. Moodily set on a boggy tidal area, the castle was her principal stronghold, and in her later years she settled here permanently. The castle is currently closed for safety reasons.

The other structures of the castle have vanished. Legend says that Grace fed the rope from her ship through the hole in the south wall, tying it to her bed.

Clew Bay Bike Hire
CYCLING

(☑098-37675; www.clewbaybikehire.ie; Georges St; adult/child per day €20/15; ☺9am-6pm) This excellent bike-hire operator has four locations scattered along the 42km Great Western Greenway (p434), which runs between Westport and Achill Island. Its shuttle buses (per adult/child €15/free) save you cycling back.

🛌 Sleeping & Eating

★ Newport House
HISTORIC HOTEL €€€

(☑098-41222; www.newporthouse.ie; off Main St; s €135-155, d €220-280; ☺Apr–mid-Oct; 🖥) Cloaked in ivy that turns crimson in autumn, the gorgeous Georgian mansion that is Newport House is one of Ireland's most romantic country retreats. Traditional furnishings meet burnished wood and gilt mirrors to elegant but comfortable effect. Bedrooms are in the main house or beside the courtyard; one was once a holiday home of an Irish Prime Minister.

MAYO DARK SKY FESTIVAL

Stargazers, environmentalists and romantics head to Mayo's International Dark Sky Park for the **Mayo Dark Sky Festival** (www.mayodarkskyfestival.ie; ☺early Nov), a three-day celebration of inky blackness and celestial displays. Expect a wealth of talks, walks, workshops and stargazing in and around Newport, Mulranny and Ballycroy.

★ **Kelly's Kitchen** CAFE €
(☎ 098-41647; 17 Main St; mains €8-20; ⊘ 9am-5pm Mon-Sat) The fare of Sean Kelly's much-loved artisan butcher shop (next door) can be sampled here for breakfast and lunch, or stop for a coffee, a sandwich or some delicious seafood chowder. The huge – and stunning – photograph of Grace Kelly on the wall near the door celebrates the film star's ancestral connection to Newport.

Blue Bicycle Tea Rooms CAFE €
(☎ 098-41145; www.bluebicycletearooms.com; Main St; mains from €7; ⊘ 10.30am-6pm May-Oct) Grab a snack or pause for a true respite in this cafe, packed with old-world charm. It features sandwiches, salads, soups, baked treats and more, all sourced locally.

❶ Information

Newport Tourist Office (☎ 098-41895; tourism@newportmayo.ie; Main St; ⊘ 10.30am-5pm Mon-Sat Jun-Sep, closed Sat Oct-May)

❶ Getting There & Away

Bus Éireann (www.buseireann.ie) bus 440 stops at Newport once daily, en route between Westport (€4, 20 minutes) and Achill Island (€10, 40 minutes).

Achill Island

POP 2440

With five Blue Flag beaches, Ireland's largest offshore island, Achill (An Caol), is linked to the mainland by a short bridge. Despite the accessibility, there's plenty of remote-island feel: soaring cliffs, rocky headlands, sheltered sandy beaches, broad expanses of blanket bog and rolling mountains. It also has its share of history, having been a frequent refuge during Ireland's various rebellions.

Achill is at its most dramatic during winter, when high winds and lashing seas make the island seem downright inhospitable. The year-round population, though, remains as welcoming as ever. In summer, heather, rhododendrons and wildflowers bloom, splashing the island with colour.

The village of Keel is the island's main centre of activity – which is a relative term; shops and services also cluster at the end of the bridge onto the island, at Achill Sound.

◉ Sights

Instead of following the main road (R319) from Mulranny to Achill Island, take the signposted Ocean Rd, which curves clockwise around the Curraun Peninsula. The narrow road passes an odd fortified tower and as it hugs the isolated southern edge the views across Clew Bay and out to sea are simply stunning.

After you cross the bridge onto Achill, cut left again on leaving Achill Sound, to pick up the Atlantic Drive, signed Wild Atlantic Way. It follows the island's remote southern shore, passing through the little fishing hamlet of **Dooega**, with its sheltered beach.

★ **Keem Bay Beach** BEACH
(Ⓟ) Tucked away at the far west of the island, Keem Bay is Achill's most remote Blue Flag beach. The crescent of golden sands sits at the foot of steep cliffs, hemmed in by rock on three sides. Spiralling down to this perfect cove feels like finding the pot of gold at the end of an Irish rainbow. Beautiful.

It's a stunning drive here from Keel, 8km to the east, taking in expansive views across the water as the road climbs beside steep cliffs.

★ **Trawmore Beach** BEACH
(Keel) Running 3km southeast from Keel, beautiful, Blue Flag, golden-sand Trawmore is among Achill's most photographed beaches. Be aware that there are dangerous rips from its centre to the eastern end (under the Minaun Cliffs). If you're swimming, heed the signs and stick to the western half.

The strand is also good for bracing walks with a backdrop of pounding surf.

★ **Slievemore Deserted Village** HISTORIC SITE
(⊘ dawn-dusk) FREE The bleak remains of more than 80 houses in this deserted village at the foot of Mt Slievemore are slowly being reduced to rock piles, a poignant reminder of the island's past hardships and a vanished way of life. Research into why the village was abandoned is ongoing; some historians think that the Potato Famine helped prompt villagers to emigrate or move closer to the sea and its alternative food sources. The adjacent graveyard compounds the desolation.

★ **Achill Sea Salt** VISITOR CENTRE
(☎ 098-47856; www.achillislandseasalt.ie; Bunacurry; adult/child €7/free; ⊘ tours noon Thu & Fri) At the O'Malley's factory, tours reveal just how the family magics Achill's mineral-rich waters into flavoursome flakes of crunchy salt. After seeing demos on the

crystallisation of brine and sampling regular and smoked versions on cherry tomatoes, it will be hard to resist a quick purchase in the on-site shop. Booking essential.

Grace O'Malley's Castle
CASTLE

(Kildownet Tower; Kildownet; ⏰ dawn–dusk) FREE
The 40ft-high, 15th-century tower house rising beside the shore at Kildownet is associated with Grace O'Malley. Entering through a steel turnstile is an eerie experience – it reveals a tall hollow shell with slits for windows and a square hole in the roof.

Don Allum Monument
MONUMENT

(Dooagh) FREE In the village of Dooagh's main car park sits a slender, inscribed stone noting the epic achievement of Don Allum, the first person to row across the Atlantic Ocean in both directions. He landed here in September 1987 after 77 days at sea. He made the entire journey in a 6m-long, open plywood boat, dubbed the *QE3*, which had no satellite navigation or communication systems. Opposite the monument, **Lourdie's bar** (The Pub; ☎ 098-43109; Dooagh; ⏰ 12.30pm-12.30am Mon-Sat, to 11.30pm Sun) has associated memorabilia.

Mulranny
VILLAGE

Rising from a narrow isthmus, the hillside village of Mulranny overlooks a wide Blue Flag beach on the road from Newport to Achill Sound and on the cusp of the Curraun Peninsula. It's a prime vantage point for counting the 365 or so seemingly saucer-sized islands that grace Clew Bay.

🏃 Activities

Achill Island is a wonderful place for walking and the views are terrific. Ramblers can climb **Mt Slievemore** (671m) or take on the longer climb of **Mt Croaghaun** (664m), Achill Head and a walk atop what locals claim are Europe's highest sea cliffs. There's also a good 4.3km loop starting at the beach in Dooagh in the south. Achill Tourism (p439) produces 14 excellent downloadable guides to walks around the island.

Achill has many additional scalloped bays tame enough for swimming, including the Blue Flag beaches at Keem Bay, **Dooega**, **Silver Strand** (Dugort) and **Golden Strand** (Dugort) – find the last two at Dugort in the north. Except in the height of the holiday season, these beaches are often deserted.

Pure Magic Achill Island (p438) runs lessons in kite-surfing (per three hours €130)

and stand-up paddleboarding (per hour €40). It also does SUP rental (per hour €15).

Achill Bikes
CYCLING

(☎ 087 243 7686; www.achillbikes.com; Dooagh; adult/child rental per day from €20/14) Rents out a variety of bikes, including electric ones, per day for €50. Also offers advice on routes. Weekly rates are also available.

Calvey's Equestrian Centre
HORSE RIDING

(☎ 087 988 1093; www.calveysofachill.com; Slievemore; adult/child per 1½hr from €50/60) Calvey's arranges a wide variety of lessons, including taster sessions for novices, a four-day summer camp (€140) and, for experienced riders, a two-hour gallop (adult/child €60/70) on the sand.

⭐ Festivals & Events

Achill Island hosts several festivals during the year, including ones devoted to traditional Irish music, cycling, painting, boating and more. See www.achilltourism.com for the latest.

Scoil Acla Festival
CULTURAL

(☎ 085 881 9548; www.scoilacla.ie; ⏰ late Jul-early Aug) Traditional Irish music resonates for a week during this festival, which also has Irish dancing, culture and music workshops.

🛌 Sleeping

Achill's B&Bs are scattered along the main road from the bridge all the way to Keel, and you'll also find places to stay dotted along the shores.

⭐ Valley House
HOSTEL €

(☎ 085 216 7688; www.valley-house.com; The Valley; campsites per 2 people €21, dm/d €20/50; @🐾) Amid unruly gardens, this remote 32-bed hostel in a creaking old mansion has atmosphere to spare. JM Synge based his play *The Playboy of the Western World* on misadventures here and the subsequent film *Love and Rage* (1999) was also partially shot here.

Bonuses include scones for breakfast and a pub with patio tables. Breakfast for campers is another €5.

Keel Sandybanks Caravan & Camping Park
CAMPGROUND €

(☎ 098-43211; www.achillcamping.com; Keel; campsites per 2 adults €17-22, caravan per 2 nights from €195; ⏰ mid-Apr–Sep; 🐾) There are views of Keel beach from this campground, just a

Achill Island

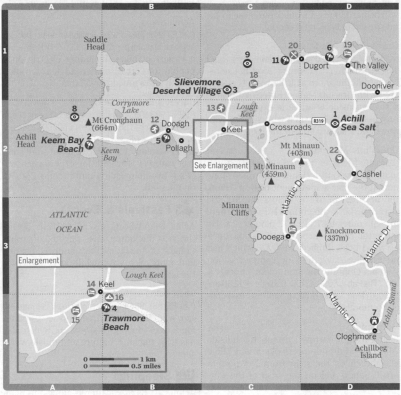

Achill Island

short stroll from town. If you're not keen on canvas, you can try a four-person caravan, which comes with bathrooms and TVs.

★ **Pure Magic Achill Island** GUESTHOUSE €€
(☏085 243 9782; www.puremagic.ie; Slievemore Rd; s/d/f from €60/80/120; ☏) There's a fun

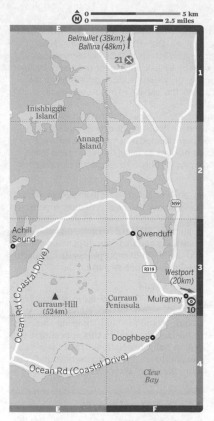

vibe at this lively 10-room spot near Dugort thanks to a buzzing bar and cafe with excellent pizza. Bedroom themes range from Moroccan and Brazilian to French, and you can arrange lessons in kite-surfing (per three hours €130) and stand-up paddleboarding (per hour €40) and rent out stand-up paddleboards (per hour €15).

Achill Cliff House
Hotel & Restaurant   GUESTHOUSE €€
(☑ 098-43400; www.achillcliff.com; Keel; d €120-150; ⑳) Sweeping views out to sea – even from the breakfast room – make this family-run guesthouse a great retreat. Furnishings are smart but comfy and the restaurant (mains €19 to €25) delivers superb fresh local seafood and creative takes on Irish classics.

Bervie   B&B €€
(☑ 098-43114; www.bervie-guesthouse-achill.com; Keel; s €80, d €110-150, f €165-225; ⑳) Former coastguard station Bervie occupies a spot

plumb on the shore. It's a friendly place with 14 bright and cosy rooms, many with ocean views, and direct access to the beach from its well-tended garden. A playroom with a pool table chips in for wet days. Lauded evening meals are available on request.

✕ Eating & Drinking

Cottage   CAFE €
(☑ 098-43966; Dugort; mains €6-17; ☺ 10am-6pm Jun-Sep; ☑) The perfect pause to soak up the charms of the little seaside village of Dugort, the Cottage offers fab coffees and baked goods plus a tasty variety of sandwiches, seafood, and vegetarian and vegan specials. Relax outside at a picnic table with views.

★ Chalet   SEAFOOD €€
(☑ 087 230 7893; www.keembayfishproducts.ie; Keel; mains €17-30; ☺ 6-10pm summer, shorter hours rest of year) The proprietors of Keem Bay Fish Products have been serving up their acclaimed smoked local salmon and other delicacies at this restaurant for decades. The menu changes with what's fresh, but expect a meal of the very best seafood.

Mickey's Bar   SEAFOOD €€
(☑ 098-45116; www.lavellesseasidehouse.com; Dooega; mains €9-15; ☺ food served 6-8pm May-Sep) Friendly village pub Mickey's draws the locals for gossip, the occasional sing-a-long and simple but excellent seafood: smoked salmon, mussels and crab claws.

It sits next door to the **Lavelles Seaside House** (s/d from €55/80; ☎) B&B.

Lynott's   PUB
(☑ 086 084 3137; R319, Cashel; ☺ hours vary) This tiny, traditional thatched roadside pub with flagstone floors and ancient benches is the real deal. There's no TV or radio or even a hint of a ham-and-cheese toastie, just plenty of craic; music sessions are held here on Fridays at 10pm.

It's set back from the road and easy to miss: look for the sign with a finger pointing left off the R319 as you exit the village of Cashel, heading west.

ⓘ Information

There's an ATM in the village of Achill Sound.

There are post offices in Keel and Achill Sound.

Achill Tourism (☑ 098-20400; www.achilltourism.com; Davitt Quarter, Achill Sound; ☺ 9am-5.30pm Mon-Fri, to 4pm Sat) Offers good walking and cycling information and a wealth of tips on island life.

DUN BRISTE

An astonishing sea stack that's lashed by foaming sea, **Dun Briste** (Downpatrick Head; www.dunbriste.com) is Mayo's top natural sight. Legend attests that St Patrick drove all the vipers from Ireland onto the stack on Downpatrick Head, leaving the mainland snake-free. Try to choose a clear day for a visit to amplify the visuals. You can drive most of the way up to the sea edge, but then you'll need to walk the last 400m or so. Dun Briste is 6km northeast of Ballycastle.

The sea stack was shorn from the mainland in 1393 by a severe storm that left poor unfortunates stranded upon it (later rescued). Indeed, the remains of buildings survive on the stack to this day. A viewing area has been constructed by a huge **blowhole** set back slightly from the cliff edge. It has numerous plaques detailing the history and folk-lore of the area. During storms, seawater is dramatically blasted through the blowhole.

❶ Getting There & Around

Bus Éireann (www.buseireann.ie) bus 440 runs daily Monday to Saturday to Achill from West-port (€14), with stops that include Dooagh, Keel, Dugort, Cashel, Achill Sound, Mulranny and Newport. On Sunday, services onto the island only go as far as Achill Sound.

Exploring Achill Island by car brings much greater flexibility.

Bangor Erris

POP 306

The little village of Bangor Erris is the start or end point of the 40km Bangor Trail, which connects Bangor and Newport via Ballycroy National Park and the Nephin Beg Mountains. It's an extraordinary hike that takes walkers through some of the bleakest, most remote and deeply inspiring landscapes in Ireland. It is very difficult and includes long stretches of tough, but magnificent, bog-walking.

Hillcrest House   B&B €

(☑ 097-83494; www.hillcresthousemayo.com; Main St; s €40, d €60-70; ☞) Comfortable rooms and a drying room make this a very good choice for walkers or those on fishing holidays or just touring the gorgeous north Mayo countryside. The friendly owner, Evelyn, is full of handy tips, kids get 25% off and there's a lovely garden out back.

Ballycroy National Park

This huge and scenic park – comprising some of Europe's greatest areas of blanket bog – is home to magnificent natural diversity, including peregrine falcons, corncrakes and whooper swans. A short nature trail with interpretation panels leads from the **visitor centre** (☑ 098-49888; www.ballycroynationalpark.

ie; off N59, Ballycroy; ☺ 10am-5.30pm Mar-Oct) **FREE** across the bog, revealing superb and frequently sublime views to the surrounding mountains. Staff can recommend more ambitious hikes and there are displays on whaling and the ubiquitous purple heather. Ballycroy is 45km north of Newport on the N59.

Ginger & Wild   CAFE €

(☑ 087 666 6633; off N59, Ballycroy; snacks from €4; ☺ 10am-5pm Mar-Oct; ☞) Views of Achill Island, mountains and shore do their best to upstage the food in this appealingly airy cafe in Ballycroy National Park Visitor Centre. But the quiches, soups, scones and cakes more than hold their own.

Mullet Peninsula

Dangling some 30km into the Atlantic, this thinly populated Gaeltacht (Irish-speaking) peninsula feels more cut off than many islands, and has a similar sense of loneliness. However, you'll find pristine beaches along its sheltered eastern shore, plenty of religious sites plus lots of sheep – often fully blocking the road. The main settlement is the busy town of Belmullet (Béal an Mhuirthead).

The road south (R313) from Belmullet loops round the tip of the peninsula, becoming the L5230/5231 before rejoining itself at Aghleam. Along the way it passes the Blue Flag beach at **Elly Bay** and stunning **Mullaghroe Beach**. There are several sights associated with St Deirbhile in the south of the peninsula, including **St Deirbhile's Church** (St Dervla's Church) and **Deirbhile's Twist**.

You'll find all the main services in Belmullet, including bank, ATM, post office and **tourist office** (☑ 097-20494; www.visiterris.ie; Chapel St; ☺ 9am-4pm Mon-Sat Jun-Aug, 9am-4pm Mon-Fri Sep-May).

🛏 Sleeping & Eating

★ Leim Siar
B&B €€

(📞 097-85004; www.leimsiar.com; Blacksod; s/d from €50/80; 📶) 🚲 Leim Siar means Jump West in Irish – a fitting name for a B&B just a short walk from the Blacksod lighthouse. A remote, end-of-the-earth feel combines with all the modern comforts: bright rooms, underfloor heating, fantastic breakfasts and cracking views. Bike rental costs €10 per day.

★ Talbot's
HOTEL €€

(📞 097-20484; www.thetalbothotel.ie; Barrack St, Belmullet; s/d/ste from €95/150/210; 📶) The kind of uber-designer flourishes that could go horribly wrong are pulled off with elan at Talbot's – some rooms sport pink and gold baroque beds, black flock wallpaper and swirly gilt mirrors; others are as luxurious but more restrained. Some have Jacuzzis too.

Talbot's Seafood Lodge
PUB €€

(📞 097-20484; www.thetalbothotel.ie; Barrack St, Belmullet; mains €10-18; ⊙9am-9pm) Fishing-themed decor festoons this welcoming restaurant-bar where local seafood is firmly to the fore, with lobster, crab claws and an excellent fish pie all on offer. Or opt for a cheaper pizza.

ℹ Getting There & Away

Bus Éireann (www.buseireann.ie) bus 446 runs once a day from Ballina to Belmullet (€15, one hour), continuing on to Blacksod (€19, 1¼ hours).

Ballycastle & Around

POP 219

The main draw of the beautifully sited village of Ballycastle, consisting of a sole sloping street, is its megalithic tombs – one of the greatest concentrations in Europe – and some gorgeous coastal scenery, including one of Ireland's top photogenic experiences: the raw, isolated sea stack of Dun Briste at Downpatrick Head.

★ Céide Fields
ARCHAEOLOGICAL SITE

(📞 096-43325; www.heritageireland.ie; off R314; adult/child €5/3; ⊙visitor centre 10am-6pm Jun-Sep, to 5pm Easter-May & Oct, last tour 1hr before closing) An exposed hillside 8km northwest of Ballycastle is home to one of the world's most extensive Stone Age monuments. So far stone-walled fields, houses and megalithic tombs – about half a million tonnes of stone – have been found, the legacy of a farming community nearly 6000 years old. The **visitor centre**, in a glass pyramid overlooking

WORTH A TRIP

DOWNPATRICK HEAD DETOUR

For a spectacular short looping detour off the main road (R314) to Killala, take the coast road north out of Ballycastle, passing **Downpatrick Head**, where you can view one of Mayo's most amazing sights, the sea stack of Dun Briste (p440). Here is some of Mayo's most dramatic shoreline, with no end to the excitement. Look for the narrow lane to the head that takes you right up to the surf. Continue east and south, with **Lackan Bay** on your left until you rejoin the R314.

If driving west from Killala, look for the turn to Kilcummin 4.5km northwest of town and do the route in reverse.

the site, gives a fascinating glimpse into these times. Be sure to take a **guided tour** of the site to fully appreciate the findings.

It was only during the 1930s that a local, Patrick Caulfield, was digging in the bog when he noticed a lot of piled-up stones buried beneath it. A full realisation of what lay under the sod didn't happen for another four decades, when his son Seamus began exploration of the area. Excavations are ongoing.

★ Stella Maris
HOTEL €€€

(📞 096-43322; www.stellamarisireland.com; Killerduff; r €155-195; ⊙Easter-Oct; 📶) With a turret at each end and a long glass-fronted veranda in between, Stella Maris is a charismatic sight. Dating from 1853, it was originally a British Coast Guard station, and later a convent. Today, upmarket rooms combine antiques, stylish modern furnishings and killer views of a lonely stretch of coast. Stella Maris is 2.5km northwest of Ballycastle

Mary's Cottage Kitchen
CAFE €

(📞 096-43361; Main St; snacks from €4; ⊙10am-5pm Wed-Sun) Mary makes everyone feel welcome at this charming place with good coffee, fresh-baked goods, lunch items, chocolate treats and a back garden, where campers have been known to overnight.

Killala & Around

POP 562

The town of Killala itself is pretty enough, but it's really renowned for its glorious namesake bay nearby.

It's claimed that the ever-busy St Patrick founded Killala, and the Church of Ireland church sits on the site of the first Christian church in Ireland. The most noticeable sight, though, is the town's 25m-high round tower, which soars over Killala's heart.

★ **Lackan Strand**   BEACH
Lackan Bay's beach is a stunning and vast expanse of golden sand – it's particularly beautiful as the sun goes down, making it one of Ireland's most gorgeous bays. There's good surf here and plenty of places to get lost. Follow the R314 about 4.5km northwest from Killala, then turn at the signpost for Kilcummin.

★ **St Mary's Well**   RELIGIOUS SITE
(Tobar Mhuire; off R314; ⊙24hr) St Mary's is one of Ireland's most transfixing holy wells. An apparition of the Virgin Mary has drawn pilgrims here for centuries, and today a tumbledown 18th-century chapel covers the spot. A large thorn tree, garlanded with rosary beads and crucifixes, sprouts from the roof; inside, waters spill from an old stone vault, overseen by a statue of the Virgin.

St Mary's Well is a signed 1km walk from the approach road to Rosserk Abbey, off the R314.

The site, near the confluence of the Rosserk and Moy rivers, is particularly beautiful when the wildflowers are out.

Round Tower   TOWER
Right at the centre of things and at the heart of Killala, the town's gorgeous 12th-century limestone round tower is perfectly preserved, although it was struck by lightning in the 19th century and repaired.

Rosserk Abbey   HISTORIC BUILDING
(off R314; ⊙dawn-dusk) Dipping its toes into the River Rosserk, this sublime Franciscan abbey dates from the mid-15th century. An eye-catching double piscina (perforated stone basin) is in the chancel: look for the exquisite carvings of a 2ft-high round tower (very rare to see one carved in this way) and two angels on either side of a Gothic arch.

The abbey is 4km south of Killala off the R314. Look for the signposts and then follow narrow farming lanes for another 5km.

Lackan Trail   WALKING
(www.mayowalks.ie; Lackan Church, car park) Follow beautiful Lackan Bay and discover ancient ring forts and megalithic tombs on this moderate and looping 8km walk that begins in the car park of the parish church at Lackan Strand.

An optional 3km extension includes sweeping views of the region. Both trails are marked by fingerpost signs.

❶ Getting There & Away
From Monday to Friday Bus Éireann (www.buseireann.ie) bus 445 runs three times a day between Killala and Ballina (€5, 20 minutes).

Ballina
POP 10.171
Mayo's third-largest town, Ballina, is synonymous with salmon. If you find yourself here during fishing season, you'll be joined by droves of green-garbed waders, poles in hand, heading for the River Moy – which pumps right through the heart of town.

In addition to its excellent museum, Ballina is very much worth a visit to explore, spend the night at, or dine in the astonishing Belleek Castle.

◉ Sights

Belleek Castle   CASTLE
(☑096-22400; www.belleekcastle.com; Castle Rd; adult/child €10/7.50; ⊙tours 11am, 2pm & 4pm) Take a fascinating tour of this restored castle, built between 1825 and 1831 on the site of a medieval abbey. The castle was bought in the 1960s by fossil collector Marshall Doran, who gave it an eclectic and eccentric interior, some of it nautical (including the Spanish Armada bar). The tour also visits the Banquet Hall and Marshall Doran's collection of fossils, weaponry and armour. En route you will also encounter the last wolf shot in Connaught.

To fully get in the castle mood, check in for the night, as the grand place also serves as a hotel; there's also a fine restaurant.

Jackie Clarke Collection   MUSEUM
(☑096-73508; www.clarkecollection.ie; Pearse St; ⊙10am-5pm Tue-Sat) FREE Starting when he was 12, the late Jackie Clarke was a businessman who amassed an extraordinary collection of 100,000 items covering 400 years of Irish history. With a lovely walled garden and housed in an 1881 bank building, this well-curated museum brims with eclectic surprises.

Foxford Woollen Mill   HISTORIC BUILDING
(☑094-925 6104; www.foxfordwoollenmills.com; tours €5; ⊙tours 10am-6pm Mon-Sat, noon-6pm Sun Apr-Nov) Founded in 1892, the Foxford mill was set up to ease post-Famine suffering and provide much-needed work. It remained open until 1987, during which time its woven goods

achieved great acclaim. Now operated by locals, it employs a fraction of the hundreds who previously worked here. Besides sweaters and scarves (under €35) made in the mill, the shop sells a huge amount of imported goods. Foxford is midway between Ballina and Castlebar at the junction of the N26 and N58.

🏃 Activities

Salmon fishing is the main draw in Ballina, so most activities centre on angling on the River Moy. A list of fisheries and permit contacts is available at the tourist office. The season is February to September, but the best salmon fishing is June to August.

Ridge Pool Tackle Shop FISHING
(☑ 086 875 3648; Emmet St; ⊙ 9am-5pm Mon-Sat) Information, supplies and licences are available at Ridge Pool Tackle Shop. Fly-casting lessons can also be arranged.

🎉 Festivals & Events

Ballina Salmon Festival CULTURAL
(www.ballinasalmonfestival.ie; ⊙ Jul) A summer fixture for more than 50 years, the popular five-day festivities include parades, dances, an arts show and fishing competitions.

🛏 Sleeping & Eating

Belleek Park CAMPGROUND €
(☑ 096-71533; www.belleekpark.com; off R314; campsites per adult €11; P 🐾) Landscaped parkland, spacious pitches and a wealth of facilities, including tennis courts, football areas and a games room, make this campground some 3km north of Ballina popular with families. The three-person log cabins (per week €350 to €600) come complete with bathroom, kitchen and bed linen.

★ Belleek Castle HOTEL €€€
(☑ 096-22400; www.belleekcastle.com; Castle Rd; r €200-250; 🐾) Your chance to kip in a castle – imposing Belleek is eclectically decorated in ornate period style, with plush rooms successfully pairing four-poster beds with flat-screen TVs. This dollop of luxury is permeated with a gorgeous sense of seclusion and is set in vast grounds by the River Moy. Breakfast included.

It's also a fine place for dinner in the Library Restaurant, while fascinating tours are run throughout the day for visitors.

Mount Falcon
Country House Hotel LUXURY HOTEL €€€
(☑ 096-74472; www.mountfalcon.com; Foxford Rd; r from €180; 🐾🏊) Hidden away on 40 hectares between Lough Conn and the River Moy lies this stunning place to stay. Rooms in the gorgeous 1870s mansion ooze old-world grandeur, while those in the modern extension have a more contemporary edge. Anglers will be hooked by the exclusive fishery, while the tranquil tempo is endlessly relaxing. Find it 5km south of Ballina. Special offers reduce prices to around €150 per night.

Ice House Hotel BOUTIQUE HOTEL €€€
(☑ 096-23500; www.icehousehotel.ie; The Quay; r €125-307; 🐾) Up-close views of the serene River Moy estuary are the main draw at this 32-room hotel that combines an elegant restored namesake heritage building with a pared-down, modern wing and a spa, right by the water. It's 2km northeast of the centre and close to good waterfront pubs.

★ Clarke's Seafood Delicatessen DELI €
(☑ 096-21022; www.clarkes.ie; O'Rahilly St; treats from €5; ⊙ 9am-6pm Mon-Sat) Couldn't catch a salmon? The wizards at award-winning Clarke's will sell you their house oak-smoked salmon in myriad forms, plus all manner of other picnic-friendly fishy creations. If you have caught your own fish, they'll smoke it for you too.

★ Library Restaurant IRISH €€€
(☑ 096-22400; www.belleekcastle.com; Belleek Castle; mains €28-34, 8 courses €73; ⊙ 2.30-9pm) Set in the splendid manor house of Belleek Castle, the Library serves up elegant, acclaimed modern Irish cuisine that showcases local meat, fish and game. It also delivers a sumptuous afternoon tea (per person €34) and a great-value three-course early-evening menu (€34), between 5.30pm and 6.30pm.

ℹ Information

The **tourist office** (☑ 096-72800; www.northmayo.ie; 44 Lower Pearse St; ⊙ 10am-5pm Mon-Sat, closed Sat Oct-Apr) is in the centre of town, opposite the Jackie Clarke Collection museum.

ℹ Getting There & Away

BUS

The **bus station** (www.buseireann.ie; Kevin Barry St) has Bus Éireann (www.buseireann.ie) services including to Ballycastle (€9.50, 30 minutes, two buses daily Monday to Friday) and Sligo (€16, 1½ hours, three to six daily).

If you're heading to Westport there's a change at Castlebar.

TRAIN

The train station is on Station Rd at the west end of Hill St. Ballina is on a branch of the main Westport–Dublin line, so you'll have to change at Manulla Junction. There are four connections a day to Dublin Heuston (€22, 3½ hours).

Lahardane

POP 178

In the shadow of Mt Nephin (806m), this charming little village is most famed for the 14 local people (the Addergoole Fourteen) aboard the RMS *Titanic* when it went down in 1912. Eleven of the 14 perished; their deaths are commemorated in one of the stained-glass windows of St Patrick's Church and in the Titanic Memorial Park.

Lahardane locals helped General Humbert in the 1798 Uprising against the English, and Father Andrew Conroy helped lead French and Irish forces along the Windy Gap to Castlebar. After the revolt was put down, Father Conroy was executed for his troubles and a marvellous high cross stands in commemoration of his bravery, near the Titanic Memorial Park, along the R315, with Mt Nephin in the background.

St Patrick's Church   CHURCH

(cnr The Windy Gap & R315; ⊙ 8am-5pm) Bursting at the seams with worshippers on Sundays, this small church has a magnificent stained-glass window depicting a girl being lowered in a lifeboat down the side of the doomed *Titanic*. It commemorates the 11 local lives lost in the disaster. For maximum effect, wait for the sun to come streaming through.

Every year on 15 April, at 2.20am, relatives of the victims chime the bell in the churchyard to commemorate the vessel's loss.

Titanic Memorial Park   MEMORIAL

(R315) With the bow of the RMS *Titanic* cast in bronze and statues of several of the 14 local passengers who were on the ship when it went down, this memorial garden is a place of quiet and poignant repose. The park was created in 2012 to commemorate the 100th anniversary of the sinking of the *Titanic*.

Nephin Whiskey Emporium   DRINKS

(⌂ 087 695 5002; www.nephinwhiskey.com/village-store; R315; ⊙ hours vary) 🕭 This start-up distillery is creating peated single malt Nephin whiskey employing local barley and locally cut turf; it's triple distilled in traditional copper pot stills and matured in unique, handmade casks. The shop also sells all manner of Nephin-branded hoodies, jackets and T-shirts, plus handmade sticks for walkers.

Castlebar & Around

POP 12,068

Mayo's county town, Castlebar, is a traffic-thronged hub of shops and services, but there are useful facilities and some good hotels, and its proximity to some big sights makes it a handy short-term base. Most places of interest lie outside the town centre.

◎ Sights

⭐**National Museum of Country Life**   MUSEUM

(⌂ 094-903 1755; www.museum.ie; off N5, Turlough Park; ⊙ 10am-5pm Tue-Sat, 1-5pm Sun & Mon) FREE The extensive and engrossing displays of this riverside museum delve into Ireland's fascinating rural traditions and skills. It's set in a modern, photogenic facility that overlooks a lake in the lush grounds of 19th-century **Turlough Manor**. A branch of the National Museum of Ireland, the museum explores everything from the role of the potato to boat building, herbal cures and traditional clothes. It has a good cafe and a shop; it's 8km northeast of Castlebar. The lovely Turlough Round Tower is visible from the grounds.

⭐**Ballintubber Abbey**   CATHEDRAL

(⌂ 094-903 0934; www.ballintubberabbey.ie; Ballintubber; donation requested; ⊙ 9am-midnight, tours 9.30am-5pm Mon-Fri, by arrangement Sat & Sun) FREE Imposing Ballintubber Abbey is the only church in Ireland founded by an Irish king that remains in use. It's reputed to have been established in 1216 next to the site of an earlier church founded by St Patrick after he came down from Croagh Patrick. Its history is tumultuous: the abbey was burned by Normans, seized by James I and suppressed by Henry VIII. It's signposted off the N84, 13km south of Castlebar.

The **nave roof** was burned down by Cromwell's soldiers in 1653 and not fully restored until 1966, but the **apse** was the site of services for hundreds of years, in all manner of weather; indeed, the abbey has provided Mass continuously to the present day for 800 years, the only church in Ireland to have done so.

The ruined **cloister** is also a sublime sight, while Grace O'Malley's son, Tiobóid na Long (the 1st Viscount of Mayo), is buried in the vault. Guided tours and a 25-minute video help tell the abbey's story. **Tóchar Phádraig** (Patrick's Causeway), the ancient

35km pilgrim's route to Croagh Patrick, begins at the end of the churchyard.

Moore Hall   HISTORIC BUILDING
(✆ 098-25293; www.moorehall.net; Lough Carra; ⏰ dawn-dusk) **FREE** With towering walls engulfed in ivy and empty windows, Moore Hall is an astonishing and atmospheric ruin. Set beside Lough Carra, it was built in the 1790s and burned down in 1923 during the Civil War, its priceless library of old books and splendid panelling going up in flames. The surrounding woodland is a joy to explore. You can also wander around the totally overgrown walled garden, which may, along with the house, be eventually restored.

Turlough Round Tower   HISTORIC BUILDING
(off N5) Stretching up 23m and featuring a single lofty window, the magnificent Turlough Round Tower, a short distance northeast of the National Museum of Country Life, is a robust 11th-century structure crowning a hilltop beside a ruined 18th-century church.

✖ Eating

★Rua Deli & Cafe   IRISH €
(✆ 094-928 6072; www.caferua.com; Spencer St; mains €9-12; ⏰ 8.30am-6pm Mon-Sat; 🖥) Artisan, organic, local food packs the shelves and tables of this gourmet deli-cafe. Picnic goodies include Carrowholly cheese, Ballina smoked salmon and luscious salads. Upstairs, amid artfully mismatched furniture, Mayo produce is teamed with global flavours such as harrisa, pesto and toasted seeds.

A second cafe – the original, indeed – is on New Antrim St.

❶ Getting There & Away

BUS
Buses stop on Stephen Garvey Way. Bus Éireann (www.buseireann.ie) services include those to Westport (€5.70, 15 minutes, nine to 12 daily) and Ballina (€12, 45 minutes, nine daily).

TRAIN
Castlebar is on the line between Dublin (€22, three hours) and Westport (€7, 20 minutes). There are four to five trains each way daily. The station is 1km southeast of town on the N84 towards Ballinrobe.

Knock

POP 972
Knock was little more than a downtrodden rural village until 1879, when reports of a divine apparition made it one of the world's most sacred Catholic shrines. It's now a pilgrimage site and dominates the little village. Otherwise, it's large and blandly modern – the appeal here is spiritual rather than physical.

The **tourist office** (✆ 094-938 8100; www.knock-shrine.ie; ⏰ 9am-5pm) across from the shrine is patiently helpful.

Knock Marian Shrine   HISTORIC SITE
(✆ 094-938 8100; www.knockshrine.ie; ⏰ chapel 8am-9pm) A place of pilgrimage for decades, the Knock shrine includes five churches and a museum set amid landscaped grounds. The complex has evolved thanks to reports of religious apparitions, including those of the Virgin Mary, in the 19th century. Today a modern **chapel** encloses a depiction of the apparition carved from snow-white marble. A segment of **stone** from the original church mounted on the outside wall has been rubbed smooth by the hands and lips of the faithful.

The story that led to Knock's development goes thus: on the evening of 21 August 1879, in drenching rain, two young Knock women were startled by a vision of the Virgin Mary, Joseph, St John the Evangelist and a sacrificial lamb upon an altar, freeze-framed in dazzling white light against the southern gable of the parish church. The women were soon joined by 13 more villagers, all gazing at the heavenly apparition for around two hours as the daylight faded. A Church investigation confirmed it as a bona fide miracle, and a sudden rush of other Vatican-approved miracles followed as the sick and disabled claimed amazing recoveries upon visiting the spot.

Besides the sacred chapel, there's the vast 1970s **Basilica of Our Lady, Queen of Ireland**, which can accommodate more than 10,000 people. Pilgrims can fill their drinking bottles from the 18 Holy Water Fonts outside the chapel.

Knock Museum   MUSEUM
(✆ 094-937 5034; www.knock-shrine.ie/museum; adult/child €4/3; ⏰ 10am-5pm) This small museum follows the story of the first witnesses to the vision of Mary in the parish church in 1879, through to the miraculous cures attributed to this event and the repeated Church investigations as to its legitimacy. Audio guides are available in seven languages.

❶ Getting There & Away

AIR
Ireland West Airport Knock (NOC; ✆ 094-936 8100; www.irelandwestairport.com; off N17),

20km northeast of the village, has services to eight UK airports, plus seasonal flights to European destinations. The airport website lists bus services to Westport and Galway.

BUS

Bus Éireann (www.buseireann.ie) bus 440 runs to Westport (€9, one hour, two daily); its bus 64 links Knock and Ireland West Airport Knock with Galway city (€14, 1½ hours, 10 daily).

COUNTY SLIGO

County Sligo packs as much poetry, myth and folklore into its countryside's lush splendour as any shamrock lover and archaeologist could hope for. It was Sligo that most inspired the Nobel laureate, poet and dramatist William Butler Yeats (1865–1939). Ever fascinated by Irish mysticism, he was intrigued by places such as prehistoric Carrowmore Megalithic Cemetery, Knocknarea Cairn, iconic and hulking Benbulben and cute little Innisfree Island.

And it's no complacent backwater: there's a vibrant and creative food culture, and the coast's surf is internationally renowned.

Sligo Town

POP 19,199

Pedestrian streets lined with inviting shopfronts, stone bridges spanning the River Garavogue, and *céilidh* sessions spilling from pubs contrast with contemporary art and glass towers rising from prominent corners of compact Sligo. It makes a fantastic, low-key and easily manageable base for exploring Yeats country, and the countryside out of town is gorgeous.

⊙ Sights

★ **Model**   GALLERY
(☑071-914 1405; www.themodel.ie; The Mall; admission varies; ⊙10am-5pm Tue-Sat 10.30am-3.30pm Sun) The Model houses an impressive collection of contemporary Irish art including works by Jack B Yeats (WB's brother and one of Ireland's most important modern artists) and Louis le Brocquy.

There are also galleries for temporary exhibitions and installations. The centre has a lively program of experimental theatre, music and film, and an excellent cafe.

Sligo Abbey   HISTORIC BUILDING
(☑071-914 6406; www.heritageireland.ie; Abbey St; adult/child €5/3; ⊙10am-6pm Apr-Oct) This

handsome Dominican friary was built around 1252 but burned down in the 15th century, to be later rebuilt. Friends in high places saved the abbey from the worst ravages of the Elizabethan era, and rescued the sole sculpted altar to survive the Reformation. The doorways reach only a few feet high at the abbey's rear; the ground around it was swollen by the mass graves from years of famine and war.

Yeats Memorial Building   MUSEUM
(☑071-914 2693; www.yeatssociety.com; Hyde Bridge; €3; ⊙10am-5pm Mon-Fri) In a pretty setting in a former 1895 bank, the **WB Yeats Exhibition** has details of his life, draft manuscripts and special summer programs. Admission includes a tour of the collection.

The small cafe has tables overlooking the River Garavogue.

Sligo County Museum   MUSEUM
(☑071-911 1679; www.sligoarts.ie; Stephen St; ⊙9.30am-12.30pm Tue-Sat, plus 2-4.50pm Tue-Sat May-Sep) FREE The major draw of Sligo's small county museum is the Yeats room, which features photographs, letters and newspaper cuttings connected with WB Yeats. Also on display are paintings by his brother, Jack B Yeats, George Russell and Sean Keating.

WB Yeats Statue   STATUE
(off Hyde Bridge) Erected in 1989, this abstract statue of Yeats – with broken glasses – in front of the 1863 Ulster Bank (a building he admired) is the source of much local mirth.

🏃 Activities

★ **Sea Trails**   WALKING
(☑087 240 5071; www.seatrails.ie; walks from €20) Led by the resourceful and knowledgeable Auriel, this highly recommended company runs interesting walks concentrating on Yeats, ancient features and natural beauty in and near the coast, including Armada sights and the stunning local geology. She also runs heritage horseback tours (adult/child €60/40), which are suitable for beginners.

Auriel has a BA degree in Archaeology and Geography and a master's degree in Maritime Archaeology, plus many years working in the field of heritage.

Chain Driven Cycles   CYCLING
(☑071-912 9008; www.chaindrivencycles.com; 23 High St; per day/week from €15/45; ⊙10am-6pm Tue-Fri, to 5pm Sat, noon-6pm Mon) Offers hybrid-, electric- and road-bike hire. Rates include helmet.

Sligo Town

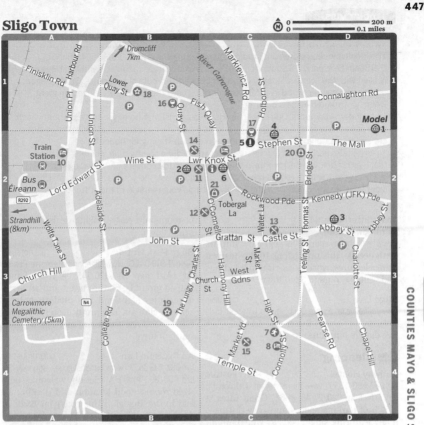

Sligo Town

⊚ Top Sights
1 Model D1

⊚ Sights
2 Michael Quirke's Studio B2
3 Sligo Abbey D2
4 Sligo County Museum C2
5 WB Yeats Statue C2
6 Yeats Memorial Building C2

⊕ Activities, Courses & Tours
7 Chain Driven Cycles C4

⊟ Sleeping
8 An Crúiscin Lan C4
9 Glass House C2
10 Railway Hostel A2

⊗ Eating
11 Fabio's B2
12 Hargadons C2
13 Kate's Kitchen C3
14 Lyons Cafe B2
15 Montmartre C4

⊙ Drinking & Nightlife
16 Harp Tavern B1
17 Thomas Connolly C2

⊕ Entertainment
18 Blue Raincoat Theatre Company B1
19 Hawk's Well Theatre B3

⊚ Shopping
20 Bookmart D2
21 Liber C2

✷ Festivals & Events

Tread Softly CULTURAL
(www.treadsoftly.ie; ⊗late Jul) Poetry, music, drama and art characterise this 10-day celebration of the life and work of WB Yeats. It's held in conjunction with the Yeats International Summer School.

MICHAEL QUIRKE – THE WOODCARVER OF WINE STREET

The inconspicuous storefront studio of **Michael Quirke** (☑071-914 2624; Wine St; ⊙9.30am-12.30pm & 3-5.30pm Mon-Sat) **FREE**, woodcarver, raconteur and local legend, is filled with the scents of locally felled timbers and off-cuts of sycamore. Quirke began cutting and carving wood in 1968. Today he still uses the same saw he used on meat when he worked here as a butcher.

A modern-day Yeats, Quirke's art is inspired by Irish mythology, a subject about which he is passionate and knowledgeable, and as he carves he readily chats with the customers and the curious who enter his shop and end up staying for hours.

As he talks and carves, Quirke frequently pulls out a county map, pointing to places (such as his beloved Carrowmore) that spring from the conversation, leading you on your own magical, mystical tour of the county. Should he ask you your favourite animal, consider your answer carefully, as he's likely to carve you a version of the critter on the spot.

Yeats International
Summer School   LITERATURE
(www.yeatssociety.com; ⊙ Jul-Aug) Now into its sixth decade, this prestigious 10-day festival brings lectures, workshops, drama, readings and walking tours to Sligo town.

Sligo Live   CULTURAL
(www.sligolive.ie; ⊙ late Oct) Sligo's biggest cultural event is this live-music festival over five days in autumn.

🛏 Sleeping

Railway Hostel   HOSTEL €
(☑087 690 5539; www.therailway.ie; 1 Union Pl; dm/s/tw from €20/27/46; P🕏) Great rates, a clutch of parking spaces and cosy dorms – many featuring single beds as well as bunk beds – sit inside this cheery hostel, where the train-themed decor meshes with the name. A basic breakfast of tea, coffee and cereal is included in the price.

★Glass House   HOTEL €€
(☑071-919 4300; www.theglasshouse.ie; Swan Point; s €103, d €112-129, ste €138-155; 🕏) You can't miss this cool and contemporary four-star hotel in the centre of town, its sharp glass facade jutting skyward. Inside, the food areas have good river views, there are two bars and the 116 well-equipped rooms come in a choice of zesty colours.

Clayton Hotel   HOTEL €€
(☑071-911 9000; www.claytonhotelsligo.com; Clarion Rd; d/f from €115/125; 🏊) Looking vaguely reminiscent of a Harry Potter film set, the huge, historic, grey-stone Clayton bristles with Hogwarts-esque turrets, gables and mini-spires. The rooms are massive, as are the grounds; you'll also find a swimming pool, spa and loads of facilities for kids. A wealth of room-only, early-booking deals can bring prices down.

Sligo Park Hotel   HOTEL €€
(☑071-919 0400; www.sligoparkhotel.com; Pearse Rd; s/d/f from €110/120/145; P🕏🏊) Landscaped grounds, mature trees, and an array of facilities help lend this modern hotel a country-club air. The pretty, tastefully decorated rooms are bright and modern. It's 3km south of town.

An Crúiscín Lan   GUESTHOUSE €€
(☑087 233 1573; www.bandbsligo.ie; Connolly St; s/d €50/85; P🕏) A friendly welcome, fair-sized rooms, good location and parking all add to the appeal at this convivial B&B, as do the porridge and Irish fry-ups for breakfast. Some rooms share bathrooms.

🍴 Eating

★Fabio's   ICE CREAM €
(☑087 177 2732; Wine St; treats from €2.50; ⊙11am-6pm Mon-Thu, to 6.30pm Fri & Sat, noon-6pm Sun) Local hero Fabio makes arguably Ireland's best Italian gelato and sorbets from mostly local and natural ingredients. The frequently changing flavour offer is remarkable: from white chocolate and pistachio crunch to raspberry lime sorbet. In summer he's often open till 7pm.

★Lyons Cafe   IRISH €
(☑071-914 2969; www.lyonscafe.com; Quay St; mains €8-16; ⊙9am-6pm Mon-Sat) The cafe in Sligo's flagship department store, Lyons, first opened in 1926, but the food served in the airy, 1st-floor eatery is bang up to date. Acclaimed chef and cookbook author Gary Stafford offers a fresh and seasonal menu that's inventive yet casual.

The gourmet sandwiches feature superb artisan bread baked by the in-store bakery on the ground floor.

Kate's Kitchen   CAFE €
(☑ 071-914 3022; www.kateskitchen.ie; 3 Castle St; mains from €7; ☺ 8.30am-5.30pm Mon-Sat) Only the best local foodstuffs are served at this welcoming, contemporary cafe-store. All the ingredients for a prime picnic are there along with prepared foods. The tiny cafe is a cheery spot for punchy coffee and homemade lunch.

★ Hargadons   PUB FOOD €€
(☑ 071-915 3709; www.hargadons.com; 4/5 O'Connell St; mains €10-25; ☺ food noon-3.30pm & 4-9pm Mon-Sat) You'll have a hard time leaving this superb 1868 inn with its winning blend of old-world fittings and gastropub style. The uneven floors, peat fire, antique signage, snug corners and bowed shelves laden down with ancient bottles lend it a wonderful charm. The great-value food is renowned, transforming local ingredients such as oysters with continental flair.

The menu changes with the seasons, many of the wines come from the pub's vineyard in France and the stock of microbrews is strong. The three-course lunch (€10) is a bargain. Trad music chips in some nights too.

Montmartre   FRENCH €€
(☑ 071-916 9901; www.montmartrerestaurant.ie; 1 Market Yard; mains €17-26; ☺ 5-11pm Tue-Sat) Tucked away on a back road by the market sits an excellent French restaurant serving unpretentious but top-quality food. The menu spotlights local meats, but seafood lovers are well catered for too. Book ahead.

The 'smart eater' menu, available all evening Tuesday to Thursday, and 6pm to 7pm on Friday and Saturday, is excellent value (two/three courses €22/27).

🍺 Drinking & Entertainment

Harp Tavern   PUB
(☑ 071-914 2473; Quay St; ☺ noon-11.30pm Sun-Thu, to 1am Fri & Sat) This all-around good pub has a glowing stove, a genuinely welcoming vibe, good bar food and live music on Friday, Saturday and Sunday nights. See the Facebook page for updates on upcoming gigs.

Thomas Connolly   PUB
(☑ 071-919 4920; www.thomasconnollysligo.com; Markievicz Rd & Holborn St; ☺ 11am-11.30pm Sun-Thu, to 12.30pm Fri & Sat) Join the locals amid the faded photos, mottled mirrors, craft beer

and live music ranging from trad to jazz at this magnificent historic pub.

Blue Raincoat Theatre Company   THEATRE
(☑ 071-917 0431; www.blueraincoat.com; Lower Quay St) A former abattoir is home to innovative theatre company Blue Raincoat, whose program includes original productions plus Yeats in the summer.

Hawk's Well Theatre   THEATRE
(☑ 071-916 1518; www.hawkswell.com; Temple St) This well-regarded 340-seat theatre presents concerts, dance and drama for children and adults.

🛍 Shopping

★ Liber   BOOKS
(☑ 071-914 2219; www.liber.ie; 35 O'Connell St; ☺ 9am-6pm Mon-Sat) The section on local literary legend WB Yeats at this fabulous bookshop is extensive; staff are also happy to advise on books about County Sligo's history and other local authors. There's an eclectic range of music CDs and vinyl too.

Bookmart   BOOKS
(www.bookmart.ie; 6 Bridge St; ☺ 10am-6pm Mon-Sat) A treasure trove of titles, from duffed-up Asimov to Dylan Thomas, and Sylvia Plath to Primo Levi, share space on stuffed shelves in Bookmart, overseen by friendly, helpful staff.

Look out for poetry readings too (8pm on the first Thursday of the month), and other cultural events.

ℹ Information

The **tourist office** (☑ 071-916 1201; www.sligotourism.ie; cnr O'Connell & Wine Sts; ☺ 9am-5pm Mon-Fri, 9.30am-5pm Sat, closed Sat Nov-Apr) has information on the whole northwest region, plus good walking info and loads of maps and literature. In August the office also opens on Sunday (10am to 2pm).

ℹ Getting There & Away

BUS
Bus Éireann (☑ 1850 836 611; www.buseireann.ie; Lord Edward St) leaves from the bus station situated below the train station. Destinations include Ballina (€16, 1½ hours, three to four daily) and Donegal town (€16, 1¼ hours, six daily).

TRAIN
Trains leave Sligo MacDiarmada station in Lord Edward St for Dublin's Connolly station (€21, three hours, six to eight daily) via Boyle, Carrick-on-Shannon and Mullingar.

Around Sligo Town

Rosses Point

POP 883

Grassy dunes roll down to the golden strand at the appealing seaside town of Rosses Point. Benbulben (525m), Sligo's most recognisable mountain, looms in the distance. Offshore, the unusual – and jaunty – Metal Man lighthouse-statue points the way into harbour, while Coney and Oyster Islands add to the picturesque scene.

Rosses Point has two sweeping Blue Flag beaches and one of Ireland's most challenging and renowned golf links. The First and Second Beaches are on the west-facing side of the headland; the Second Beach is the longer of the two.

County Sligo Golf Course GOLF
(☑ 071-917 7134; www.countysligogolfclub.ie; Rosses Point; 18 holes €175-195; ☺ mid-Mar–Oct) Established in 1894, the County Sligo Golf Course has a breathtaking position on the peninsula tip and is one of Ireland's most challenging links courses, attracting golfers from all over the world. Interwoven with the dune systems, it's possibly Ireland's most picturesque course.

Yeats Country Hotel HOTEL €€
(☑ 071-911 7100; www.yeatscountryhotel.com; Rosses Point; d/f €139/148; ☒) A commanding presence on Rosses Point overlooking the beach and County Sligo Golf Course makes this huge three-star hotel a big hit with familes and golfers. Many of the large, modern rooms have fine sea views. There's a popular restaurant; food is also served at its two bars.

Prices fall by as much as €60 a double in low season.

Little Cottage Cafe CAFE €
(☑ 071-911 7766; off R291; mains from €4.50; ☺ 9.30am-5pm) At this charming little light-filled bungalow join other satisfied customers enjoying hand-roasted coffee, excellent breakfasts and imaginative lunches that might include spicy sweet potato and coconut soup, or falafel drizzled with lime yoghurt.

Strandhill

POP 1753

The great Atlantic rollers that sweep Strandhill's shore make this long, red-gold beach a magnet for surfers. The town is also located not far from Knocknarea Cairn, one of the most important archaeological sites in the county, which also makes for a terrific hike.

🏃 Activities

Although it's not ideal for swimming, there are excellent long walks along the beach both north and south. The views of the surf are spectacular and you can wander up into the dunes. Surfing is naturally the principal draw for a large contingent of visitors.

Voya Seaweed Baths SPA
(☑ 071-916 8686; www.voyaseaweedbaths.com; Shore Rd; bath from €28; ☺ 10am-8pm) Don't just smell seaweed on the beach – immerse yourself in it at this beachfront location. Fifty-minute sessions include access to your own steam and shower room, plus a toasty seaweed bath. Couples and friends can share a room (€55).

From September to June, the baths close an hour earlier (at 7pm) from Monday to Thursday.

Perfect Day Surf & SUP School SURFING
(☑ 087 202 9399; www.perfectdaysurfing.ie; Shore Rd; lessons adult/child from €35/25; ☺ Apr-Oct) Look out for the big yellow van on Strandhill's shoreline to book stand-up paddleboarding (SUP) and surfing lessons (including women-only and kids' sessions) with small class sizes.

Strandhill Surf School SURFING
(☑ 071-916 8483; www.strandhillsurfschool.com; Shore Rd; lessons adult/child from €35/25; ☺ Apr-Oct) Offers gear hire, lessons and summer surf camps for children; check out the conditions via its live webcam.

🛏 Sleeping

Surf & Stay Lodge & Hostel LODGE €
(☑ 085 851 0889; www.surfnstay.ie; Shore Rd; hostel dm €25, d €50, lodge s €55, d €50-85; ☎) Surfers thaw out by the open fire in the common room of the 34-bed hostel portion of this two-building complex. Rooms in the adjoining lodge are B&B-style and, while small, are comfortable; some share bathrooms. The beach is close and there's an on-site surf school.

Surfing lessons cost from €25 to €40; stand-up paddleboard sessions start at €40.

Ocean Wave Lodge B&B €
(☑ 071-916 8115; www.oceanwavelodge.com; Top Rd; dm/s/d/f €20/35/60/70; P ☎) This large modern house uphill from the beach has minimalist but comfortable rooms. Breakfast is included and there's a self-catering kitchen and a large lounge area too.

CARROWMORE & KNOCKNAREA

One of the largest Stone Age cemeteries in Europe, **Carrowmore Megalithic Cemetery** (☑ 071-916 1534; www.heritageireland.ie; adult/child €5/3; ⊙ 10am-6pm Apr-Oct, final admission 5pm; ℗) is finally receiving the renown it deserves and is Sligo's must-see attraction. Some 30 monuments, including passage tombs, stone circles and dolmens, adorn the rolling hills of this haunting site, which is thought to predate Newgrange in County Meath by 700 years. To get here, follow the R292 southwest from Sligo for 4km and follow the signs.

Ongoing excavations continue to uncover more areas of interest both within the public site and on adjoining private land.

Discoveries about the meaning of Carrowmore are both continuing and dramatic, particularly in terms of how the many features of the site relate to the surrounding hills and mountain. Among the numbered sites, 51 has been found to get direct sunlight at dawn each 31 October, or Halloween. Many people claim to feel strong powers here and you'll likely see a few spiritual pilgrims on the site.

The site is some 2.5km wide. In it dolmens appear delicately balanced, and many monuments have been altered over the centuries. Look out for the prominent Circle Seven, which has been partly reconstructed and so gives a strong impression of how it would have looked 6000 years ago. The visitor centre has full details and staff are happy to explain much more, plus detail the latest discoveries.

Sligo's ultimate rock pile sits atop a magical mountain hike. **Knocknarea Cairn (Cnoc na Riabh)** is popularly believed to be the grave of legendary Queen Maeve (Queen Mab in Welsh and English folk tales). The 40,000 tonnes of stone have never been excavated, despite speculation that a tomb on the scale of the one at Newgrange lies buried below. The site is 2km northwest of Carrowmore. The parking area is off the R292.

The cairn is perched high atop a limestone plateau (328m); a 40-minute (1.2km; the fit and fast can do it in 20 minutes) trek up the mountain reveals spectacular views. From the top you can gaze out over Benbulben, Rosses Point and the Atlantic Ocean beyond. The cairn seems to be looking over your shoulder everywhere you dare tread in its ancestral backyard. Many think the rocks purposely form a giant nipple, which takes on meaning when the overall horizon is viewed from Carrowmore. Believers in underlying powers at the sites say that you can easily make out the shape of a reclining woman, or a mother god. They say that Queen Maeve is buried upright in the cairn, holding a spear and facing her adversaries in Ulster.

WB Yeats was enthralled by the myth and lore of Knocknarea and its magic wormed its way into his verse. In 'Red Hanrahan's Song about Ireland', he writes: 'The wind has bundled up the clouds high over Knocknarea, And thrown the thunder on the stones for all that Maeve can say.'

Having got to the mountain top, signs urge you not to climb the cairn itself. An estimated 100,000 walkers visit the wider site each year, and an increase in the numbers of people clambering up over the stacked stones is causing erosion to this historic structure.

Strandhill Lodge & Suites   GUESTHOUSE €€
(☑ 071-912 2122; www.strandhilllodgeandsuites. com; Top Rd; s €99, d €120-130, ste €130-150; ℗ 🛜) This excellent hillside guesthouse offers 22 bright, spacious rooms with king-sized beds, hotel-quality design and trendy neutral styling. Room sizes vary, but most have terraces or balconies and fabulous ocean views.

🍴 Eating & Drinking

Shells   CAFE €
(☑ 071-912 2938; www.shellscafe.com; Shore Rd; mains €8-12; ⊙ 9am-6pm; 🖌) You'll find flowers on tables and own-grown herbs in the dishes at this sprightly little cafe right across from the beach. Pastries and coffee are excellent, while breakfasts span chorizo and beans to Burren smoked salmon on toast. Lunch brings quality burgers, chilli and calamari salads.

It's deservedly hugely popular; be prepared to take your time.

★ Stoked   IRISH €€
(☑ 071-912 2734; Shore Rd; mains €15-26; ⊙ 6-10pm Wed-Sun; 🖌) With its surf-chic vibe, stripped wooden tables and primary colour scheme, the eatery above Strandhill's shoreside Strand Bar is winning over legions of local fans.

Expect everything from whole spatchcock chicken and juicy steaks, to seared scallops and chargrilled sea bream. Book ahead.

It posts regular menu and events updates to its Facebook page.

Strand Bar PUB
(☏071-916 8140; www.thestrandbar.ie; Shore Rd; ⊙11am-late) Surfers, locals and tourists crowd into the snugs and cosy corners at this convivial pub to be warmed by turf fires. Come summer they'll be listening to the ocean from the seafront terrace outside. Wednesdays bring trad-music sessions and there are live bands at weekends.

Hearty bar food (served from noon; mains from €8) includes its famous Guinness beef stew.

ⓘ Getting There & Away

Strandhill is 8km due west of Sligo town off the R292. Bus Éireann (www.buseireann.ie) bus S2 links it with Sligo (€3, hourly, 20 minutes).

South of Sligo Town

Heading south of Sligo town takes you on a gorgeous scenic shore-line drive to Enniscrone and Killala Bay. From there you can head on into County Mayo or divert to Knocknarea Cairn, a marvellous and breathtaking climb.

If you head inland you'll encounter the ruined Ballymote Castle, the extraordinary Caves of Keash and one of the region's most impressive sights: Carrowkeel Megalithic Cemetery.

Ballymote & Around
POP 1549

This pretty little town merits a visit for opportunities to ponder Irish music, culture and history; for its formidable and sublime castle ruin; and for the chance to make an expedition to the Caves of Keash and take in their magnificent views.

★**Caves of Keash** CAVE
(Keshcorran Caves; off the R295) Set around 6km southeast of Ballymote, these splendid limestone caves high in Keshcorran Hill make for a fun expedition. You can park at the fields at the foot of the slope and climb on up. It doesn't take long to reach the 16 caves, some of which are pretty deep, and afford excellent views over the countryside. Mind your step as it is steep and can be slippery after rain.

Ballymote Castle CASTLE
(Tubbercurry Rd/R296) Just down from the train station, the immense shell of Ballymote Castle is a classic, imposing ruin. It was from this early-14th-century redoubt, fronted by formidable drum towers, that O'Donnell marched to disaster at the Battle of Kinsale in 1601.

CARROWKEEL MEGALITHIC CEMETERY

With a bird's-eye view of the county from high in the Bricklieve Mountains, it's little wonder the hilltop site, **Carrowkeel Megalithic Cemetery**, was sacred in prehistoric times. But for a few sheep, it's undeveloped and spectacular. Dotted with 14 passage cairns, the site dates from the late Stone Age (3000 to 2400 BC).

Carrowkeel is closer to Boyle than Sligo town. It's about 5km from either the R295 in the west or the N4 in the east. Follow the signs.

This windswept and lonely location is simultaneously eerie and uplifting. Just the sweeping views down to south Sligo from the car park make the journey worthwhile; the views further on over Lough Arrow are just as stunning. It's a 2km walk from the car park (look out for the sign that says 'Pedestrians Only') to the first ancient site, **Cairn G**. Above its entrance is a roof-box aligned with the midsummer sunset, which illuminates the inner chamber. The only other such roof-box known in Ireland is that at Newgrange in County Meath. Continue along to another three such cairns (the last one is in a state of collapse) and you'll reach a fence with a piece of plastic tubing over the wire. Cross this and after a short distance you will find a huge **limestone sinkhole** full of small trees, shrubs and vegetation.

Everywhere you look across the surrounding hills in this region there's evidence of early life, including about 140 stone circles – all that remain of the foundations of a large village thought to have been inhabited by the builders of the tombs.

Eagles Flying NATURE CENTRE
(☑071-918 9310; www.eaglesflying.com; off N17; adult/child €14/8; ☉10.30am-12.30pm & 2.30-4.30pm, demonstrations 11am & 3pm Apr-early Nov) Eagles soar straight over your head at this volunteer-run research centre as you learn about these birds of prey during demonstrations. There's also a mini-zoo with ducks, donkeys and other cute critters. It's signposted 3.5km northwest of Ballymote.

Easkey

Easkey is one of Europe's best year-round surfing destinations. But in pubs with names like Lobster Pot and Fisherman's Weir, conversations still revolve around hurling and seafood prices. The road to the beach is just east of town and facilities are few.

When driving in from the east, look out for the Split Rock, a boulder split in two, whose origins have generated much folklore and legend. It is said that if you squeeze through the split three times, it will close on you.

★**Pudding Row** CAFE €
(☑096-49794; www.puddingrow.ie; Main St; mains from €5; ☉9.30am-5pm; ☑) Local, often organic ingredients and own-baked breads and pastries combine with an eye for design and a flair for food at this bright, inviting, spacious cafe. All-day breakfasts feature homemade baked beans; pear and bacon appear in the cheese sandwiches; and there's sea salt in the chocolate caramel squares.

Enniscrone

This very low-key holiday town facing Killala Bay is all about the ocean and the glorious views and sunsets. The stunning **Enniscrone Beach** (www.enniscronebeach.com) stretches for 5km.

Seventh Wave Surf School SURFING
(☑087 971 6389; www.surfsligo.com; Enniscrone Beach; lessons adult/child from €30/25; ☉Apr-Oct) Offers surf lessons and board rental (€20 per wetsuit and board).

Kilcullen's Seaweed Baths SPA
(☑096-36238; www.kilcullenseaweedbaths.net; Cliff Rd; bath from €25; ☉10am-9pm Jun-Aug, noon-8pm Mon-Fri, 10am-8pm Sat & Sun Sep-May, closed Tue & Wed Nov-Mar) Enniscrone is famous for its traditional seaweed baths, which are some of the most atmospheric in the country. The Edwardian bathhouse has buckets of character, with original fittings including vast porcelain baths, solid brass taps and wood cabinets.

The full treatment involves being enclosed in an individual cabinet with your head sticking out, then taking a warm Seaweed Bath followed by a cold sea-water shower.

Pilot Bar IRISH €€
(☑096-36131; www.facebook.com/thepilotbar; Main St; mains €7-24; ☉1-8pm Sun-Thu, 1-9pm Fri & Sat; ☑) Terrace tables let you bask in the sun framed by flowers; inside, fancy yourself a sailor beside porthole motifs. The acclaimed food combines local produce with global

LISSADELL HOUSE

The imposing ancestral home of the Gore-Booth family, **Lissadell House** (☎071-916 3150; www.lissadellhouse.com; Ballinful; adult/child house & grounds €14/6, grounds €10/5; ⊗10.30am-6pm Easter-Oct) is one of Sligo's top sights. Revolutionary nationalist and socialist Constance Goore-Booth (Countess Markievicz) grew up here and WB Yeats used to frequently drop by. The extensive grounds include a gorgeous walled alpine garden that boasts sea views. A 45-minute guided tour leads through the house's grand guest rooms and the servants' quarters. Take the N15 from Sligo to Drumcliff, head along the L3305 through Carney and follow the signs.

In 1918 Countess Markievicz was the first woman elected to the British House of Commons. The tour winds through the rooms she grew up in: the anteroom, drawing room, dining room, billiard room and basement (where the kitchens were), but as it is a home in use, the upstairs rooms are inaccessible. For a cheaper ticket, you can explore the exhibition in the coach house and the grounds, but it's the house, restored at great cost by the current owners, that's worth seeing.

flavours, so perhaps start with a creamy seafood chowder, before tucking into spicy duck with noodles or a hearty beef goulash.

Lough Gill & Around

Beautiful, mirror-like Lough Gill (Lake of Brightness) was a place of great inspiration for Yeats. The lake, which is dotted with some 20 small islands, is a mere 8km southeast of Sligo town and simple to reach. It's shaded by two magical swaths of woodland – Hazelwood and Slish Wood – which have waymarked trails; there are good views of Innisfree Island from the latter.

You can take a cruise on the lake from atmospheric Parke's Castle (p497), in nearby County Leitrim. Watch for the shadows of huge salmon and the ripples of otters.

The lake is immediately southeast of Sligo town. Take the R286 along the north shore for the most interesting views, whether you are driving or riding. The southern route on the R287 is less interesting until you reach Dooney Rock.

Dooney Rock   HILL

Immortalised by Yeats in 'The Fiddler of Dooney' (1899), this fissured limestone knoll bulges awkwardly upward by the lough's southern shore. There's a great lake view from the top and you can park right at the bottom. Photographs over the lake can be stunning as the sun sinks at the end of the day. It's 7km southeast of Sligo town on the R287.

Innisfree Island   ISLAND

This pint-sized island lies tantalisingly close to the lough's southeastern shore, but, alas,

can't be accessed. Still, it's visible from the shore. Its air of tranquillity so moved Yeats that he famously wrote 'The Lake Isle of Innisfree' (1890):

'I will arise and go now, and go to Innisfree,
And a small cabin build there, of clay and wattles made;
Nine bean rows will I have there, a hive for the honey bee,
And live alone in the bee-loud glade.'

Access the best vantage point of the island from a small road that starts at the junction of the R287 and the R290. Follow the winding lane for 4.2km to a small parking area by the water.

North of Sligo Town

Evocative coastal drives and lonely mountain paths highlight the heart of Yeats country – the scenery is nothing short of sublime.

Benbulben

A stolid greenish-grey eminence visible all along Sligo's northern coast, Benbulben (525m), often written Ben Bulben, resembles a table covered by a pleated cloth: its limestone plateau is uncommonly flat, and its near-vertical sides are scored by earthen ribs. Walking here is not for the uninitiated; **High Hopes Mountain Treks** (☎086 345 4045; www.highhopesmountaintreks.com; from €25) leads hikes to the top.

Gortarowey Forest Recreation Area FOREST

(www.coillte.ie/site/gortarowey) FREE The best way to walk around within the shadow of Benbulben is by visiting this area within

Benbulben Forest. There are three trails: the looped longer walks take you along the northern slopes of the mountain, affording spectacular views. The longest is the **Benbulben Loop** (www.coillte.ie/site/gortarowey; off N15), which is clearly signposted, 5.5km long and takes around two hours to complete. Each trail starts and ends in the car park. Download a map from the website.

Drumcliff & Around

Benbulben's beauty was not lost on WB Yeats. Before the poet died in Menton, France, in 1939, he had requested: 'If I die here, bury me up there on the mountain, and then after a year or so, dig me up and bring me privately to Sligo.' His wishes were apparently followed in 1948, when what was thought to be his body was interred in the churchyard at Drumcliff, where his great-grandfather had been rector. Doubts later emerged as to exactly whose bones had been reburied.

Drumcliff itself is a small place, and the main places of interest – Yeats' grave, the round tower remains and high cross – lie very close together, with the Cafe & Crafts Shop in between.

★**Yeats' Grave**   MONUMENT
(☑071-914 4956; off N15; ⊙dawn-dusk) Yeats was long believed to be buried next to the doorway of Drumcliff Parish Church, but recent evidence suggests that the bones shipped here from France in 1948 were not his at all, owing to his actual bones being scattered about an ossuary during the chaos of WWII. Yeats' youthful bride, Georgie Hyde-Lee, however, is buried alongside. Almost three decades her senior, Yeats was 52 when they married.

The poet's epitaph is from his poem 'Under Ben Bulben':
'Cast a cold eye
On life, on death.
Horseman, pass by!'
There's a small **cafe & crafts shop** (☑071-914 4956; www.drumcliffeteahouse.ie; mains from €4; ⊙9am-5.30pm; 🖥) beside the church. It is popular with locals at lunch and has a good selection of books.

In the 6th century, St Colmcille chose this location for a monastery. You can still see the stumpy remains of a **round tower**, which was struck by lightning in 1396, on the main road nearby. Also beside the churchyard is an extraordinary 9th-century **high cross**, etched with intricate biblical scenes that include

INISHMURRAY

It takes a little effort to arrange a visit to Inishmurray (www.inishmurray.com), an island that was abandoned in 1948, leaving behind early Christian remains and fascinating pagan relics. There are three well-preserved churches, beehive cells and open-air altars. The old monastery, surrounded by a thickset oval wall, was founded in the early 6th century by St Molaise.

Although it's only 7km between Inishmurray and the mainland, there's no regular boat service, and the lack of a harbour makes landing subject to the weather. To visit, check with **Inishmurray Island Trips** (☑087 254 0190; www. inishmurrayislandtrips.com; Mullaghmore; trips per person from €40; ⊙Apr-Sep).

Adam and Eve, as well as Daniel in the Lion's Den. There is a car park alongside the church.

Yeats Lodge   B&B €
(☑071-917 3787; www.yeatslodge.com; Drumcliff; s/d €50/80; 🅿🖥) Obliging owners, five large, modern rooms and a tranquil atmosphere make this B&B well worth seeking out. It offers tasteful country-style decor and unbeatable views of Benbulben. It's 300m off the N15, some 8km from Sligo town.

Prices fall by €10 per double room outside July and August.

★**Rathcormac**
Food & Craft Market   MARKET
(N15, Rathcormac; ⊙10am-3pm Sat) Held in the Benbulben Craft Village, this market is worth scheduling your trip around. Although small, the best producers in the region sell ready-to-eat food, produce, cheeses, baked goods and much more. It's a delight to wander about snacking while shopping for your picnic.

Lough Glencar Waterfall

WB Yeats is among those who've fallen for Lough Glencar Waterfall, a 15m tumbling torrent, set in the most beautiful area of Lough Glencar – it features in his poem 'The Stolen Child'. There are astonishing views over the water, especially towards sunset; it's particularly impressive after heavy rain. There's a car park right at the foot of the hill.

Streedagh Strand

Curving, dune-backed, 3km-long Streedagh Strand occasionally sees parts of the Spanish Armada washing up on its shores from three wrecks offshore: *La Juliana*, *La Lavia* and *La Santa Maria de Visón*; over 1000 soldiers and sailors drowned or were killed when the ships were caught in a storm. It's a site of immense archaeological significance, but there are also many examples of fossilised coral, fascinating geological formations, a wedge tomb and views to the island of Inishmurray.

Some people say the wrecks are visible at low tide, but these are actually the ribs of a 'butter boat'.

The best way to appreciate the local wonders is to tag along with Auriel Robinson on one of her Sea Trails (p446) walks. She will fill you in on all the local geology; marine and land-based archaeology; and folklore, legends and stories associated with Streedagh Strand.

Mullaghmore

The sweeping arc of dark-golden sand and the safe shallow waters make the pretty fishing village of Mullaghmore a popular family destination.

Take time to walk, cycle or drive the scenic road loop around Mullaghmore Head, where wide shafts of rock slice into the Atlantic surf. En route you'll pass Classiebawn Castle (closed to the public), which is quite an astonishing sight against the skyline.

◉ Sights & Activities

Classiebawn Castle   CASTLE
Although you can't visit this photogenic neo-Gothic turreted pile, views of it against a dramatic backdrop of mountains and sea make for a terrific sight. It was built for Lord Palmerston in 1856 and was later home to the ill-fated Lord Mountbatten, who was killed near here in 1979 when the IRA rigged his boat with explosives.

Mullaghmore Head   BEACH
Big-wave tow-in surfing competitions are regularly held off Mullaghmore Head. The area is becoming known as one of Ireland's premier big-wave surf spots with swells of up to 30m allowing for Hawaiian-style adventures.

Mullaghmore Adventures   ADVENTURE SPORTS
(☑083 831 0333; www.mullaghmoreadventures. com; Mullaghmore Harbour; ☺Easter-Oct) Mullaghmore's hills and craggy coast set the scene for epic coasteering (from €45), and guided SUP (€35), mountain-bike (€30) and hillwalking tours (25).

Gleniff Horseshoe   TREKKING
(www.sligowalks.ie) Set amid the stark, barren drama of the Dartry Mountains, the Gleniff Horseshoe begs for exploration. A trail follows a tiny lane on a 10km loop through the valley, passing wild babbling streams and the remains of an old mill. To get to the trailhead from Cliffony near Mullaghmore, follow the small road southeast into the broad Gleniff Horseshoe Valley.

The loop is good on foot (allow around 2½ hours), by bike or by car. Hikes also branch off into the hills – Sligo Walks (www. sligowalks.ie) has online maps.

🛏 Sleeping & Eating

Benwiskin Centre   HOSTEL €
(☑071-917 6721; www.benwiskincentre.com; Ballintrillick; dm/d/tr/q from €17/44/55/66; 🅿🛜) At the base of the Gleniff Horseshoe Valley, the Benwiskin Centre is a good hostel with dorms and private rooms.

★Pier Head Hotel   HOTEL €€
(☑071-916 6171; www.pierheadhotel.ie; Mullaghmore Harbour; s/d from €90/140; ☺closed late Dec; 🛜🏊) The panoramic views from this gorgeous quayside hotel are magnificent. The 40 smart rooms feature clean lines, artful lighting and bright colour schemes; the best have extensive ocean or harbour views. Other draws include a sweeping rooftop terrace with hot tub, spa and indoor pool, and very decent food (mains €11 to €22).

★Eithna's by the Sea   SEAFOOD €€
(☑071-916 6407; www.eithnasrestaurant.com; Mullaghmore Harbour; mains €15-35; ☺11am-3.30pm, dinner from 5pm; 🛜🍴) 🍃 With views over the bay at Mullaghmore, bright-blue Eithna's is a joy, with tables outside for sunny dining on lobster, shellfish, crab and squid. Food comes to the kitchen straight from the waters, so it's all fresher than fresh. Eithna delights in innovative uses of seaweed; look out for it in punchy pestos and sweet dishes. Book ahead.

ℹ Getting There & Away

Local Link (www.locallink.ie) bus 982 between Sligo and Rossnowlagh calls in at Mullaghmore (€4, one hour) two to four times daily.

County Donegal

POP 159,000 / AREA 3001 SQ KM

Best Places to Eat

➡ Lemon Tree (p481)

➡ Wild Strands Caife (p490)

➡ Cove (p479)

➡ Danny Minnie's Restaurant (p474)

➡ Nancy's Bar (p471)

➡ Seafood Shack (p466)

Best Places to Stay

➡ Castle Murray (p465)

➡ Sandrock Holiday Hostel (p490)

➡ Rathmullan House (p486)

➡ Glen House (p489)

➡ Carnaween House (p472)

➡ Lough Eske Castle (p463)

Why Go?

County Donegal is the wild child of Ireland and home to some of its most ravishingly sublime scenery and beautiful beaches. This is a county of extremes: at times desolate and battered by brutal weather, yet also a land of unspoilt splendour where stark peaks and sweeping beaches bask in glorious sunshine, and port-side restaurants serve majestic food.

Donegal's rugged interior, with its remote mountain passes and shimmering lakes, is only marginally outdone by the long and labyrinthine coastline with windswept peninsulas and isolated pubs. In recent years the local food scene has been flourishing, and delicious fresh seafood is never far away. Proudly independent, one-third of Donegal is official Gaeltacht territory, with Irish the lingua franca.

After its northern start in Derry, the Wild Atlantic Way really begins to strut its stuff here as the county's untamed craggy coastline truly puts the wild into the way.

When to Go

➡ Donegal's wild and rough-hewn but sublime character is forged by its impetuous weather. In winter the howling winds and sheeting rain can feel Arctic, and brutal storms may arrive unannounced. A lot of accommodation options shut up shop for the cold months.

➡ In spring and summer, the clouds and short-lived bursts of rain regularly break into brilliant sunshine that transforms brooding pewter skies into brilliant blue and dapples Donegal in light of a beautiful quality.

➡ Because everything is open in summer, you'll also get the pick of traditional-music, storytelling and dance festivals that spring up across the county and even in pubs. Summer nights can also see some of the most ravishing sunsets.

County Donegal Highlights

1 Sliabh Liag
(p467) Climbing to the top of the soaring sea cliffs, then sampling seaweed-infused gin at the nearby distillery.

2 Glenveagh Castle (p482)
Touring the flamboyant castle in beautiful Glenveagh National Park.

3 Dunfanaghy
(p477) Dining in style and then catching a trad session.

4 Glengesh Pass
(p470) Pausing at the viewpoint before plunging down the switchbacks towards Ardara.

5 Poisoned Glen
(p476) Taking in the views of this spectacular glen.

6 Rossnowlagh
(p463) Learning to surf on the white-sand beach.

7 Malin Head
(p489) Gazing out to sea as you hike the wildflower-strewn clifftops.

8 Glencolumbcille
(p468) Hillwalking amid the dramatic landscapes and coastal vistas.

9 Maghera Strand
(p470) Running your toes through the sands and admiring a nearby waterfall.

10 Tory Island
(p479) Taking a ferry out to this wild and culturally rich island and spotting seals, basking sharks and puffins.

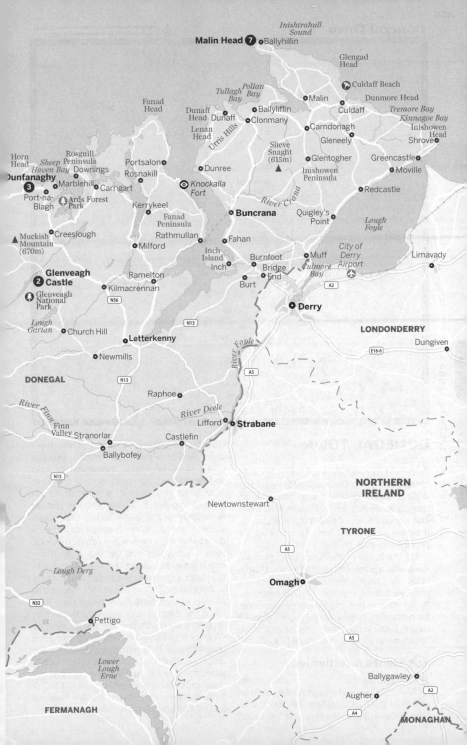

Donegal Town

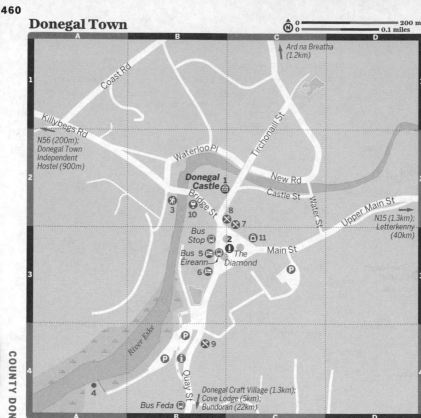

DONEGAL TOWN

POP 2600

Pretty and compact, Donegal town occupies a photogenic spot at the mouth of Donegal Bay. With a backdrop of the Blue Stack Mountains, a handsome and well-preserved castle and a good choice of places to eat and sleep, it makes an excellent base for exploring the popular coastline nearby.

On the banks of the River Eske, Donegal town was a stamping ground of the O'Donnells, the great chieftains who ruled the northwest from the 15th to 17th centuries. Today, despite being the county's namesake, it's neither its largest town (that's the much larger Letterkenny) nor the county town (that's the even smaller town of Lifford).

⊙ Sights & Activities

★ **Donegal Castle**   HISTORIC BUILDING
(☏ 074-972 2405; www.heritageireland.ie; Castle St; adult/child €5/3; ⊘10am-6pm daily Easter–mid-Sep, 9.30am-4.30pm Thu-Mon mid-Sep–Easter)

Guarding a picturesque bend of the River Eske, well-preserved 15th-century Donegal Castle is an imperious monument to Irish and English might. The castle was rebuilt in 1623 by Sir Basil Brooke, along with the adjacent three-storey Jacobean house. Further restoration in the 1990s kicked things into shape; don't miss the magnificent upstairs **Great Hall** with its vast and ornate fireplace, French tapestries and Persian rugs. Afterwards corkscrew down the spiral staircase to the storeroom. There are guided tours hourly.

Built by the O'Donnells in 1474, it served as the seat of their formidable power until 1607, when the English decided to rid themselves of pesky Irish chieftains once and for all. Rory O'Donnell was no pushover, though, torching his own castle before fleeing to France in the infamous Flight of the Earls. Their defeat paved the way for the Plantation of Ulster by thousands of newly arrived Scots and English Protestants, sowing the seeds of the divisions that still afflict Ireland to this day.

Donegal Town

Diamond Obelisk   MONUMENT

(The Diamond) In the early 17th century, four Franciscan friars, fearing that the arrival of the English meant the end of Celtic culture, chronicled the whole of known Celtic history and mythology. Starting 40 years before the biblical flood through AD 1618, *The Annals of the Four Masters* is one of the most important sources of early Irish history. The obelisk (1937), in the Diamond, commemorates the work; copies are displayed in the National Library in Dublin.

Donegal Food Tours   FOOD & DRINK

(☑ 083 841 5848; www.donegalfoodtours.com; per person €75) Offers tours starting in Letterkenny (Taste the North tours) or Donegal town (Taste the South West tours), with stops at up to six local food and drink producers, for tastings and background insights into production processes.

Bank Walk   WALKING

(👣) Follow this lovely flat trail along the west bank of the River Eske and Donegal Bay. The myriad trees offer shade and have labels as to their type; frequent benches allow you to pause and soak up the views. Look out for the little fairy doors in the trees; there's even a postbox for children to write letters to fairies.

It's 1.5km each way and begins on the west side of the Killybeg Rd/N56 bridge.

Donegal Bay Waterbus   BOATING

(☑ 074-972 3666; www.donegalbaywaterbus.com; Donegal Pier; adult/child €20/7; ☺ Easter–Oct) The most enjoyable way to explore the highlights of Donegal Bay is on a 1¼-hour boat tour taking in everything from historic sites to seal-inhabited coves, admiring an island manor and a ruined castle along the way. The tour runs up to three times daily; departure times change daily to match the tides.

🛏 Sleeping

Good B&Bs and stolid hotels are plentiful around Donegal town; for high-end luxury head to nearby Lough Eske.

**Donegal Town
Independent Hostel**   HOSTEL €

(☑ 074-972 2805; www.donegaltownhostel.com; off Killybegs Rd-N56, Doonan; dm/s/d €20/30/46; @🛜) Run by an energetic couple, this IHH hostel, 1.2km northwest of town, is a sociable place with a good kitchen and mix of spacious dorm rooms and bright, modern private rooms with attached bathrooms. Several rooms have quirky murals and some have water views.

Cove Lodge   B&B €€

(☑ 074-972 2302; www.thecovelodgebandb.com; R267, Drumgowan; r €90; ☺ Apr–Oct; 🛜) You'll find subtle floral patterns and rustic charm in the four ground-floor rooms of this tranquil and pretty stone and stucco B&B 2.5km south of town in a rural setting, offering a taste of Irish country living.

Ard na Breatha   B&B €€

(☑ 074-972 2288; www.ardnabreatha.com; Drumrooske Middle; r €85-160; ☺ Feb–Oct; 🛜🍽) 🅿 In an elevated setting 1.5km north of town, this boutique guesthouse on a working farm has tasteful rooms with pine furniture and wrought-iron beds. The six rooms are in a building separate from the main house. Breakfasts are wholesome and filling and a good start to the Donegal day.

Central Hotel   HOTEL €€

(☑ 074-972 1027; www.centralhoteldonegal.com; The Diamond; s/d from €75/110; 🛜🍽) In the town centre, the Central is an adventure – no matter where your room is located in this rambling collection of buildings, you'll take a lift and wander up and down stairs to find it. Ask for a room with a view of the River Eske – the huge windows offer stunning panoramas. The leisure centre has a pool and gym.

Abbey Hotel
HOTEL €€

(☑074-972 1014; www.abbeyhoteldonegal.com; The Diamond; s/d from €80/130; ☜) This serviceable option is on the Diamond, right at the heart of town, with 90 standard rooms. There's a lift for the three floors, and the bar and restaurant are solid. Guests can use the leisure centre at the Central Hotel (p461).

✕ Eating & Drinking

There are several lively pubs in and around the Diamond. Look for the beers from local craft-brewer Donegal Brewing Co.

Aroma
CAFE €

(☑074-972 3222; www.donegalcraftvillage.com; off R267, Donegal Craft Village; mains €5-13.50; ☺9-5pm Mon-Sat) In the far corner of Donegal's craft village, this small cafe has a big, big reputation for fine food. Along with the excellent coffee and luscious cakes, the blackboard specials feature seasonal local produce whipped up into fine soups, salads and wholesome hot dishes as well as international fare. There's seating outside.

Blueberry Tearoom
CAFE €

(☑074-972 2933; Castle St; mains €5-13; ☺9am-7pm Mon-Sat; ☜☝) A perennial and cosy local favourite, this cafe serves simple, honest food in hearty portions as well as fine coffee. Expect soup, toasties, quiche, panini, sticky cakes of all descriptions and killer cheesecake.

★ Quay West
MODERN IRISH €€

(☑074-972 1590; www.quaywestdonegal.ie; Quay St; mains €16-22, early-bird menu 2/3 courses €20/24; ☺5-9pm Mon-Thu, to 10pm Fri & Sat, 3-8.30pm Sun) A light-filled, contemporary dining room is an inviting setting to sample local seafood (Donegal bay mussels, Burtonport crab, Killybegs smoked haddock) and other well-executed dishes like Guinness-braised shank of Donegal lamb or wild-mushroom risotto. Try to get a table upstairs with views out over the bay. An early-bird menu is available from 5pm to 6.30pm Monday to Friday.

★ Olde Castle Bar
IRISH €€

(☑074-972 1262; www.oldecastlebar.com; Castle St; mains €11-32; ☺kitchen noon-9pm; ☝) This ever-busy pub off the Diamond serves some of the area's best food. Look for classics such as Donegal Bay oysters or mussels, Irish stew and seafood platters (€32), plus steaks and burgers. The pub is always rollicking with locals and serves its own excellent pale ale: Red Hugh Brew.

★ Reel Inn
PUB

(Bridge St; ☺11am-midnight) The best craic in town is invariably found at this old-school pub where the owner plays the button-box accordion and pals join in traditional-music sessions every night from 8.30pm (9.30pm on Saturday).

🛍 Shopping

★ Donegal Craft Village
ARTS & CRAFTS

(☑074-972 5928; www.donegalcraftvillage.com; off R267; ☺10am-5pm Mon-Sat Apr-Sep, Tue-Sat Oct) You won't find any canned leprechauns or Guinness T-shirts here. Instead this huddle of craft studios showcases pottery, ironwork, fabrics, glasswork, jewellery and more. It's signposted 1.5km south of town and is an easy walk. There's a cracking cafe too, Aroma.

Magee's
CLOTHING

(☑074-972 2660; www.magee1866.com; The Diamond; ☺10am-6pm Mon-Sat, from 1pm Sun) One room of this small, upmarket and historic department store is devoted to Donegal tweed, which has been produced here since 1866.

ⓘ Information

The **tourist office** (☑074-972 1148; Quay St; ☺9am-5.30pm Mon-Sat, 10am-3pm Sun Jun-Aug, 9am-5pm Mon-Sat Sep-May) is handily located in the Discover Ireland building by the waterfront.

ⓘ Getting There & Away

Bus Éireann (☑074-913 1008; www.buseireann. ie) services connect Donegal with Sligo (€15, 1¼ hours, six daily), Galway (€21, four hours, four daily) and Dublin (€20, four hours, five daily).

Bus Feda (☑074-954 8114; www.busfeda.ie) serves Gweedore, Dunfanaghy and Letterkenny (all €10) two to three times daily.

The bus stop is on The Diamond.

AROUND DONEGAL TOWN

Lough Eske

An easy scenic diversion from Donegal town, picturesque Lough Eske attracts hikers, cyclists, anglers and those in search of placid lake views.

The lake is only 9km from Donegal – a good bike ride away. Otherwise, if you've a car, it's a straightforward and very fast journey.

Arches Country House
B&B €

(☎074-972 2029; www.archescountryhse.com; s/d €60/80; 🖥) For a bucolic getaway in a tranquil spot overlooking Lough Eske, this modern B&B has rooms that blend country-house charm and contemporary style, all with great views. Noreen the owner is a fount of local knowledge.

★ Lough Eske Castle
HOTEL €€€

(☎074-972 5100; www.lougheskecastlehotel.com; r €245-380, mains €26-38; @🖥🏊🐾) Occupying vast woodland and garden grounds at the lake's south end, this imposing and restored 19th-century castle was razed by fire in 1939 and is now the epitome of elegant country living. The 96-room complex, including a spa, swimming pool and smart restaurant, exudes classic sophistication.

The tower suite occupies three levels of the original castle tower, while garden suites are in a modern, purpose-built extension.

Harvey's Point
HOTEL €€€

(www.harveyspoint.com; hotel ste €160-290, lodge r €90-120; ⏰ kitchen 12.30-9pm; 🖥🐾) This well-run lakeside hotel makes a good base for exploring Donegal. As well as spacious and luxurious hotel suites, more economical accommodation is available in cabin-like singles and twin rooms at the Lodge; room rates include the extravagant hotel breakfast. The bar here is a reliable place to stop for a meal, with food served from 12.30pm to 9pm.

Rossnowlagh

POP 50

Rossnowlagh's spectacular 3km-long Blue Flag beach is a broad, sandy stretch of heaven that attracts families, surfers, kitesurfers and walkers throughout the year. The gentle rollers are great for learning to surf or honing your skills. You can easily lose a few hours picnicking and lounging in the dunes.

Despite the small winter population, in summer the holiday homes fill up and numbers swell.

Rossnowlagh is 17km southwest of Donegal town. The best way to get here is by car.

👁 Sights & Activities

Rossnowlagh Beach
BEACH

This stunner of a Blue Flag beach is the main draw in town, with the Atlantic surf rolling onto its broad expanse of sand. You can drive your car straight onto the beach as it is a public right of way (which does unfortunately mean that sometimes the beach resembles a vast car park).

Franciscan Friary
MONASTERY

(☎071-985 1342; www.franciscans.ie; off R231) **FREE** Hidden in a forest at the southern end of the beach, this modern friary was built in the early 1950s and is set in beautiful, tranquil gardens that are open to the public. The Way of the Cross – a religious walk with spectacular views – meanders up a hillside smothered in rhododendrons. The sense of quietude and calmness is enticing. There's a car park here too.

Fin McCool Surf School
SURFING

(☎071-985 9020; www.finmccoolsurfschool.com; Beach Rd; board & wetsuit rental per day €39, 2hr lesson incl gear adult/child €35/25; ⏰10am-5pm daily Jun-Aug, Sat & Sun Sep-May) Tuition, gear rental and accommodation are available at this surf lodge run by Pro Tour surf judge Neil Britton, with the help of his extended family, most of whom have competed on the international circuit.

Rossnowlagh SUP & Kayak
KAYAKING

(☎083 198 4288; www.rossnowlaghsupandpaddle.com; SUP lessons/tours from €35/20, kayak rental/tours from €20/35; ⏰10am-6pm Mon-Fri, 9am-8pm Sat, 11am-6pm Sun) Learn stand-up paddleboarding (SUP) or rent one with this busy outfit near the beach, or rent a kayak. A wide variety of tours take in the many waterways in the estuaries as well as the waters off the beach; watch for full-moon tours.

🛏 Sleeping & Eating

Smugglers Creek
B&B €€

(☎071-985 2367; www.smugglerscreekinn.com; Cliff Rd; s €50-65, d €80-110, mains €13-25; ⏰pub daily Apr-Sep, Thu-Sun Oct-Mar; 🖥) This combined pub-restaurant-guesthouse perches on the hillside above the bay. It's justifiably popular for its excellent food and sweeping views (room 4 has the best vantage point and a balcony). There's live music on summer weekends. Smugglers Creek also has a self-contained one-bedroom cottage behind the inn.

Gaslight Inn
IRISH €€

(☎071-985 1141; www.gaslightinnrossnowlagh.com; Highfield, Coolmore; mains lunch €9-15, dinner €13-36, s/d €85/110; ⏰11am-late daily Jun-Sep, from 5pm Fri, from 11am Sat & Sun Oct-May) Set on the clifftop, the Gaslight Inn offers an extensive menu of well-cooked comfort food and spectacular views over the bay. Upstairs, the B&B has five pleasant rooms; front rooms have killer sea views.

Ballyshannon

POP 2500

Long a strategic spot for its position overlooking the River Erne that flows in from Lower Lough Erne in County Fermanagh, Ballyshannon today has a role guarding the northern approaches to Bundoran. The town is perhaps most famous for being the birthplace of guitarist and singer Rory Gallagher, a musician celebrated both by a statue in the centre of town and by the Rory Gallagher International Tribute Festival.

Regular buses run between Bundoran (€3, 10 minutes) and Ballyshannon; the same buses continue north to Donegal (€5, 20 minutes).

Rory Gallagher International Tribute Festival   MUSIC
(www.rorygallagherfestival.com; ☉ late May) This music festival celebrates Ballyshannon native, rock and blues guitarist Rory Gallagher (1948–95), with around 30 Irish and international artists and bands. Gallagher's connection to his home town is evident throughout the year and you'll often hear his music playing in pubs.

★ Dicey Reillys Bar   PUB
(☎ 071-985 1371; www.diceys.com; Market St; ☉ noon-late) This old city-centre pub – 'Dicey's' to locals – stays vibrant through constant reinvention. In the old pub downstairs there's live rock and blues most nights, and a Rory Gallagher tune always seems to be the next song. It's also a microbrewery, producing a full range of Donegal Brewing Co beer, plus there's a wine shop and off license here, too.

Bundoran

POP 2200

Blinking amusement arcades, hurdy-gurdy fairground rides and fast-food diners give Bundoran the feel of a cheery beach town. But Donegal's best-known seaside resort has solid waves, and attracts a mixed crowd of young families, pensioners and growing legions of surfers. Outside summer, the carnival atmosphere abates and the town can be a bit bleak.

◉ Sights & Activities

Surfing is big in Bundoran. The town has several surf schools, each of which rents out gear and has its own basic hostel-style accommodation. All offer deals on surf and accommodation packages.

Tullan Strand   BEACH
The long strand of surfing beach has a bountiful supply of that gorgeous trademark fine white sand that much of Ireland is famed for. There are rip tides, so swimming can be risky, but the views are stunning and the surfing is grade A. It's north of the town centre; the Roguey Cliff Walk leads here.

Roguey Cliff Walk   WALKING
This scenic, 2.5km clifftop path connects Bundoran town centre with Tullan Strand. It passes a series of sea stacks known as the Fairy Bridges, once believed by locals to be haunted. The path begins at Promenade Rd, just east of the river.

Peak   SURFING
The Peak, an imposing reef break directly in front of the town, is one of Bundoran's two main surf spots. It should only be attempted by experienced surfers. There is a less formidable beach break at Tullan Strand.

Bundoran Surf Co   SURFING
(☎ 071-984 1968; www.bundoransurfco.com; Main St; adult/child surf lessons from €35/25, full surf-gear rental per day from €20; ☉ 9.30am-5.30pm) Bundoran Surf Co conducts surf, kitesurfing and stand-up paddleboarding lessons. Gear rental includes board and wetsuit, plus boots, gloves and hood in winter.

Bike Stop   CYCLING
(☎ 085 248 8317; www.thebikestop.ie; East End; per half-day/day/week €12/18/85; ☉ 9am-6pm Mon-Sat, 11am-4pm Sun) Rents out a range of bikes including good-quality hybrids.

Donegal Adventure Centre   ADVENTURE SPORTS
(☎ 071-984 2418; www.donegaladventurecentre. net; Bayview Ave; adult/child surf lesson from €35/30) Offers adventure-sports activities on land and sea, including kayaking and surfing, plus climbing. Book online or by phone.

★☆ Festivals & Events

Sea Sessions   MUSIC
(www.seasessions.com; ☉ mid-Jun) The Sea Sessions festival – three days of surfing, skating, music and partying – kicks off the summer season, as thousands of attendees camp in fields around town.

Irish National Surfing Championships   SURFING
(www.irishsurfing.ie; ☉ late Apr or Sep) Bundoran hosts the annual Irish National Surfing Championships, usually in April although they have also been held in September.

Check the Irish Surfing Association website for up-to-date information.

🛏 Sleeping & Eating

Bundoran has a decent choice of hostels – nonsurfers are welcome at all the surf-school lodges, which usually charge about €20 for a dorm bed and €50 for a double. Scores of humble B&Bs line the roads in from the N15, so you'll always find somewhere to stay.

Killavil House   B&B €

(☑ 071-984 1556; www.killavilhouse.com; Finner Rd; s/d/tr €50/70/105; P �) A big modern villa at the Ballyshannon end of town, Killavil has smartly appointed bedrooms with polished wooden furniture. Most have multiple beds and are suitable for families. There's a garden with a seating area for enjoying summer evenings, and lovely Tullan Strand is just a five-minute walk away.

Foam   CAFE €

(www.facebook.com/foam.bundoran; Main St; mains €4-10.50; ⊙ 8am-5.30pm Mon-Fri, from 9am Sat & Sun; ☑) With a minimalist, Scandinavian-inspired interior, this speciality coffee shop stands out among the bucket-and-spade shops of Bundoran's main street. The menu includes wholesome dishes like braised lamb with couscous and salad, overnight oats and flaky sausage rolls, as well as vegan options, such as lentil dahl or vegetable curry.

Maddens Bridge Bar   PUB FOOD €€

(☑ 071-984 2050; www.maddensbridgebar.com; Main St; mains €16-29, r €90; ⊙ kitchen 9am-8pm Mon-Thu, to 9pm Fri & Sat, to 7pm Sun, pub to late) This surfers' hang-out manages a bit of minimalist style and packs a decent menu of classic pub grub with mighty fine burgers and fish and chips. There's a trad session on Fridays year-round and most nights during summer, with terrific craic guaranteed. It's located right at its namesake bridge and some of the simple rooms open to great views.

❶ Information

Bundoran centres on one long main street just back from the beach. The **tourist office** (☑ 071-984 1350; info@discoverbundoran.com; Main St, The Bridge; ⊙ 9am-1pm & 2-5pm Mon-Fri, 12.30-5pm Sat & Sun) is a glass-paned kiosk opposite the Holyrood Hotel.

❶ Getting There & Away

Bus Éireann (☑ in Letterkenny 074-912 1309; www.buseireann.ie) buses stop on Main St on

their runs between Donegal (€9, 30 minutes) and Sligo (€11, 45 minutes), passing through Ballyshannon on their way north.

SOUTHWESTERN DONEGAL

Mountcharles

POP 500

The hillside village of Mountcharles is the first settlement along the coastal road (N56) west of Donegal town; in fact you'll barely have the speedometer turning when, bam, you're in Mountcharles.

About 2km south of the village is a safe, sandy **beach**. The shiny, green **pump** at the top of this hillside village is the point where five roads intersect and it was once the backdrop for stories of fairies, ghosts, historic battles and mythological encounters. It was here that native poet and *seanachaí* (traditional storyteller) Séamus MacManus practised the ancient art in the 1940s and '50s.

Visit Mountcharles community website (www.mountcharlescommunity.ie) for local information.

Salthill Gardens   GARDENS

(☑ 074-973 5387; www.donegalgardens.com; Pier Rd; adult/child €5/2; ⊙ 2-6pm Mon-Sat May-Sep) Behind century-old stone walls, the lovely contemporary garden design of Salthill Gardens bursts with perennials, roses, lilies and clematis. It's 2km southwest of the village, towards the coast.

Dunkineely

POP 370

Views out to sea tantalise from the series of small villages along the N56. A scenic and very worthwhile journey heads down the lengthy finger of land from the N56 and Dunkineely to St John's Point.

Slightly further on along the N56, you'll pass the small town of Bruckless, with its attractive – although not ancient – round tower.

★ Castle Murray   BOUTIQUE HOTEL €€

(☑ 074-973 7022; www.castlemurray.com; St John's Point; r from €120; ☜) Overlooking the ruins of the 15th-century McSwyne's Castle, Castle Murray is not a castle, but a boutique hotel in a modern beach house. Most of the 10 guest rooms have fine sea views. Breakfast is a feast of homemade bread and locally sourced produce. It's 1.5km south of Dunkineely on a minor road leading to St John's Point.

The expansive lounge area and bar with views straight out to the water could tempt you to skip the sights and spend the day curled up on the sofa. Thursday to Saturday, from July to September, a dinner is available for residents.

Cyndi Graham Handweaving Studio   TEXTILES

(www.facebook.com/cyndigrahamhandweaving; ⊙10am-5.30pm Mon-Sat) A small thatched cottage on the road to St John's Point houses the studio and shop of weaver Cyndi Graham. Pop inside to see her at work and browse her beautiful scarves, hats, waistcoats, bags and shawls.

Killybegs

POP 1300

The smell of fish and the caw of seagulls waft from the ranks of giant trawlers and vessels moored in Ireland's largest fishing port. Inland the village bustles with the atmosphere of a charming working town.

⊙ Sights & Activities

Fintragh Bay   BEACH

(off R263) The best beach in the Killybegs area is at secluded Fintragh Bay, about 3km west of town, a gorgeous stunner of a Blue Flag beach and a must-see. Go down the steps from the car park and head round to the right to find a lovely cave, full of pebbles, large stones and great photo ops.

Largy Viewpoint   VIEWPOINT

Pull your car in here for serene and sublime views over the sea. It's west of Killybegs along the R263. On a clear day you can see four counties – Donegal, Mayo, Sligo and Leitrim. Sunsets are best from October to February. You can also frequently spy dolphins playing in the bay below Largy, while from November to February flocks of wild geese fly in from Iceland to winter in the field below.

Below the viewpoint there's a short walk down; when the tide is out you can reach a cave by the sea – there's a waterfall beyond the cave.

Killybegs International Carpet Making & Fishing Centre   MUSEUM

(� 074-974 1944; www.visitkillybegs.com; Fintra Rd; adult/child €5/3; ⊙ 9.45am-5pm Mon-Fri, weekends by appointment) The former factory of Donegal Carpets provides a good overview of the town's history. The fun wheelhouse simulator lets you 'steer' a fishing trawler into the harbour. Don't expect to see any carpets being made as the cost to do so is now 'astronomical', they say. The last tour is at 3.45pm.

Killybegs Angling Charters   FISHING

(⊠087 220 0982; www.killybegsangling.com; Blackrock Pier; half-day charter from €300) If you're interested in taking to the water to catch pollack, ling, brill, mackerel or turbot, Brian McGilloway has more than 30 years of experience in charter angling.

🛏 Sleeping & Eating

★ Ritz   GUESTHOUSE €

(⊠074-973 1309; www.theritz-killybegs.com; Chapel Brae; s/d €40/65; 🛜) The name might be ironic and this isn't Piccadilly, but this superbly run guesthouse in the town centre has ritzy facilities, including an enormous kitchen, colourful rooms with private bathroom and TV, and a laundry. The tastefully decorated rooms all have private bathroom.

Drumbeagh House   B&B €

(⊠074-973 1307; www.killybegsbnb.biz.ly; Conlin Rd; s/d from €50/70; 🛜) Accommodating hosts with plenty of local knowledge make this small B&B a great find. The cosy rooms are tastefully decorated in neutral colours and the breakfast of locally smoked salmon is worth the trip alone. Great harbour views; it's a five-minute walk from the centre.

Tara Hotel   HOTEL €€

(⊠074-974 1700; www.tarahotel.ie; Main St; s/d from €80/130; 🅿🛜) This modern hotel across from and overlooking the harbour has 32 comfortable, simple rooms, a decent bar and a small gym with spa bath, sauna and steam room. Not all rooms come with sea views, so check.

★ Seafood Shack   FISH & CHIPS €

(⊠089 239 3094; www.facebook.com/killybegseafoodshack; Killybegs Harbour; fish & chips €9-12; ⊙4-8.30pm Wed, 12.30-8pm Thu-Sun) Superfresh seafood cooked to order is available at this roadside fish and chips stand. Find it next to the harbour on Shore Rd, opposite the very fishing boats that caught the haddock, cod, scampi and calamari in its fryers.

Ahoy Cafe   CAFE €

(⊠074-973 1952; www.facebook.com/ahoycafekillybegs; Shore Rd; mains €4.50-10.50; ⊙9am-5pm Mon-Sat) This inviting cafe slightly out

SLIABH LIAG SEA CLIFFS

The Cliffs of Moher get more publicity, but the cliffs of **Sliabh Liag** (Slieve League; www.
sliabhliag.com) FREE are higher (and free). In fact, these spectacular sea cliffs are among
the highest in Europe, plunging some 600m to the ceaselessly churning sea.

From Teelin, a road through the stark landscape leads to the lower car park (with hiking signs) beside a gate in the road; drive another 1.5km to the upper car park (often full
in summer) right beside the viewpoint (close the gate though).

From the upper car park, a rough footpath leads up and along the top of the near-vertical cliffs to the aptly named **One Man's Pass**, a narrow ridge that reaches the summit
of Sliabh Liag (595m; 10km round-trip). Be aware that mist and rain can roll in unexpectedly and rapidly, making conditions slippery and treacherous. Be especially careful near
the edge of the cliffs. Walking just the first 500m will give you spectacular views.

It's also possible to hike to the summit of Sliabh Liag from Carrick via the **Pilgrim
Path** (signposted along the minor road on the right before the Sliabh Liag cliffs road),
returning via One Man's Pass and the viewpoint road (12km, allow four to six hours).

The cliffs are particularly scenic at sunset when the waves crash dramatically far
below and the ocean reflects the last rays of the day. Looking down, you'll see two rocks
nicknamed the 'giant's desk and chair' for reasons that are immediately obvious.

---

of the centre of things along Shore Rd does,
among other things, a fine seafood chowder,
sandwiches, salads, blueberry scones, excellent coffee and local craft beers, as well as
tasty pancakes and breakfasts.

Mrs B's Coffee House   CAFE €
(☑074-973 2656; www.facebook.com/mrsbscoffee
house; Upper Main St; mains €4-8; ⊙9am-5pm Mon-
Sat; 🛜🖟) Mrs B's is a bright and welcoming
cafe with comfy sofas, local art on the walls,
and a menu of homemade and locally sourced
food, extending from hearty breakfasts and
sandwiches to drool-worthy baked goods.
Watch for the great seafood-chowder special.

ⓘ Information

Killybegs Information Centre (☑074-973
2346; www.killybegs.ie; Shore Rd; ⊙9.30am-
5.30pm Mon-Fri year-round, plus noon-4pm
Sat & Sun Jul & Aug) is in a trailer just west of
the harbour.

ⓘ Getting There & Away

Bus Éireann (p465) buses from Donegal town
(€9, 30 minutes) run several times daily.

Kilcar, Teelin & Carrick

POP 270

Kilcar (Cill Chártha) and its more attractive
neighbour Teelin (Teileann) make good bases for exploring the breathtaking coastline
of southwestern Donegal, especially the
stunning sea cliffs at Sliabh Liag. Inland,
Carrick (An Charraig) is also appealing.

This is fantastic walking country, particularly if you find the prospect of a few hills
bracing. Just outside Kilcar is a small, sandy
beach.

◉ Sights & Activities

Sliabh Liag Distillers   DISTILLERY
(Line Rd, Carrick; adult/child €10/free; ⊙tours
noon, 2pm & 4pm Mon-Sat) This artisan gin distillery produces An Dúlamán using a 500L
hand-hammered copper still and five Donegal
seaweeds that can only be harvested during
a full moon, when the tides are right. Learn
about the gin-making process on distillery
tours, which end with a tasting. At research
time plans were underway to move to a new
whiskey and gin distillery in Ardara, complete
with a *poitín* (illicit Irish whiskey) museum;
check the website for the latest information.

Studio Donegal   MUSEUM
(☑074-973 8194; www.studiodonegal.ie; Glebe Mill,
Kilcar; ⊙9am-5.30pm Mon-Fri) FREE Though
mechanised in the 1960s, there has been a
hand-weaving tweed mill here for more than
a century. Visitors are often invited upstairs
to see spinners and weavers in action, before
browsing jackets, hats, throws and other
tweed items in the shop.

★ **Sliabh Liag Boat Trips**   BOATING
(☑087 628 4688; www.sliabhleagueboattrips.com;
Teelin Pier; tours per person €20-25; ⊙Apr-Oct)
Sightseeing boat trips along the Sliabh Liag
cliffs can be spectacular. Tours aboard the
Nuala Star often spot dolphins and seals,

and sometimes whales and basking sharks. You can also go for a dip in the sea. There are up to six sailings per day; advance booking is recommended. Private trips and angling journeys are also available.

Sleeping & Eating

Derrylahan Independent Hostel HOSTEL €
(☑ 074-973 8079; http://homepage.eircom.net/~derrylahan; Derrylahan, Kilcar; campsites per person €10, dm €18-20, s/d €25/40; @ 🕏) This rustic, well-run IHH hostel is set on a hilly, windy and dramatic site on a working farm. It has 32 beds in 10 comfortable rooms with private bathrooms, plus plenty of scenic spots to pitch a tent. Book ahead for bike rental (€20). Located 3km west of Kilcar on the coast road. Pickups can be arranged from Kilcar.

Inishduff House B&B €€
(☑ 074-973 8542; www.inishduffhouse.com; off R263, Largy, Kilcar; s/d €50/85; 🕏) About 5km east of Kilcar, this modern B&B run by Ethna has large, comfortable rooms, a varied breakfast menu and supreme sea views. The mood matches the sunny hues of the exterior.

Ti Linn Cafe IRISH €
(☑ 074-973 9077; Teelin; mains €5-10.50; ☺ 10.30am-5.30pm daily Easter-Sep, Fri-Tue Feb-Easter & Oct-Nov; 🕏) This artisan cafe and crafts gallery has excellent coffee, baked goods, sandwiches and hot lunches. There's also a craft shop here.

Rusty PUB
(☑ 074-973 9101; Teelin; mains €14-25; ☺ 10.30am-11.30pm daily May-Sep, shorter hours Oct-Apr) A great pub – also called the Rusty Mackerel – with trad music many nights in summer, plus a menu of good bar food. Inside the space is cosy, with peat fires and wooden booths, and there's an outdoor terrace for sunny weather. It's near the junction of the road to Sliabh Liag.

ℹ Information

Áislann Chill Chartha (☑ 074-973 8376; www.aislann.ie; Main St, Kilcar; ☺ 9am-10pm Mon-Fri, 10am-6pm Sat) A community centre with information for tourists.

Sliabh Liag Visitor Centre (☑ 074-973 9620; www.sliabhliag.com/visitor-centre; Teelin; ☺ 9am-5pm) Local information and advice is available at the gleaming new visitor centre in Teelin (Tí Linn), which opened in May 2019. It has an interpretative centre with displays on local legends and the history of the cliffs. It's on the road to Sliabh Liag.

ℹ Getting There & Away

Local Link (☑ 074-974 1644; www.locallink.ie; single/return €4/6) service 293 (two to three buses daily) stops in Carrick and Kilcar on its way from Glencolumbcille (25 minutes) to Donegal town (50 minutes), via Killibegs (15 minutes).

Bus Éireann (p462) service 490 (one bus daily) from Donegal to Glencolumbcille stops in Carrick and Kilcar.

The best way to tackle the region is by car.

Glencolumbcille

POP 270

Once you've sampled Glencolumbcille's tiny village, scalloped beaches, stunning walks and fine little folk museum, the chances are you'll disagree with locals who claim there's little to do here.

Approaching Glencolumbcille (Gleann Cholm Cille) via the Glengesh Pass does, however, reinforce just how isolated this starkly beautiful coastal haven is. You drive past miles and miles of hills and bogs before the ocean appears, followed by a narrow, green valley and the small Gaeltacht village within it.

The Glencolumbcille website (www.glencolmcille.ie) has reams of information on the village, local history and activities.

History

This spot has been inhabited since 3000 BC and lots of Stone Age remains are scattered among the cluster of tiny settlements.

It's believed that the 6th-century St Colmcille (Columba) founded a monastery here (hence the name, meaning 'Glen of Columba's Church'), and incorporated Stone Age standing stones into Christian use by inscribing them with a cross. At midnight on Columba's Feast Day (9 June), penitents perform An Turas Cholm Chille (the Gaelic '*turas*' meaning a pilgrimage or journey), a walking circuit of the stones and the remains of Cholm Cille's chapel, before attending Mass at 3am.

◉ Sights

★**Malinbeg Beach** BEACH
(Silver Strand) At Malinbeg you'll find this stunning, sheltered bay bitten out of low cliffs, with 60 steps descending to a gorgeous little sandy beach. It's 6km past the folk village. You may find it deserted.

★**Doonalt Beach** BEACH
This lovely sandy beach with brisk waves is in Doonalt, immediately west of the village;

access is from the car park opposite the folk museum.

Glencolmcille Folk Village   MUSEUM
(Father McDyer's Folk Village; www.glenfolkvillage.com; Doonalt; adult/child €6/5; ☺10am-6pm Mon-Sat, from noon Sun Easter-Sep, 11am-4.30pm Oct) A museum with a mission, this folk centre was established by the forward-thinking Father James McDyer in 1967 to freeze-frame traditional folklife for posterity. It's housed in a huddle of thatched white cottages recreated in 18th- and 19th-century style, with genuine period fittings. There's a small school and a *shebeen* (illicit drinking place).

It's 3km west of the village, by the beach.

Look out for the small stone sweat house, where the ill were cured by sweating illnesses out. Grab an information leaflet from the craft shop at the entrance.

🏃 Activities

The 19th-century St Columba's Church is the starting point for several excellent walks; see www.glencolmcille.ie for details. The 5.5km pilgrimage route of **An Turas Cholm Cille** (www.glencolmcille.ie/turas.htm) visits a series of prehistoric stone slabs, many carved with early Christian symbols, and an ancient ruined chapel attributed to the saint. Local landowners grant permission for walkers to visit all the stones on Sundays from June to August (some are accessible year-round).

A couple of waymarked loop walks will lead you into the blustery wilds beyond the town. The **Tower Loop** (10km, two to three hours) heads north to a signal tower atop stunning coastal cliffs, while the more arduous **Drum Loop** (13km, three to four hours) heads into the hills northeast of the town.

Oideas Gael   CULTURE
(☎074-973 0248; www.oideas-gael.com; 3-/7-day courses from €110/230; ☺mid-Mar–Oct) The Foras Cultúir Uladh (Ulster Cultural Foundation), 1km west of the village centre, offers a range of cultural-activity holidays – adult courses in Irish language and traditional culture, including dancing, painting and musical instruments. The centre also leads hillwalking programs. Accommodation can be arranged – either homestay or self-catering – at around €30 per person per night.

🛏 Sleeping & Eating

Áras Ghlean Cholm Cille   B&B €
(☎074-973 0077; www.arasgcc.com; Malinmore; s/d from €32/60; ☺) This large place in peaceful

Malinmore is a good choice, with a large variety of rooms from small but serviceable singles to larger doubles, twins and triples. There's a large kitchen and lounge and breakfast is an extra €5. A shuttle service to local pubs is offered and bikes can be rented (per day €15).

Dooey Hostel   HOSTEL €
(☎074-973 0130; www.independenthostelsireland.com; campsites per person €10, dm/s/d €17/18/36; ☺Mar-Nov) Perched high on a hill, Dooey Hostel is entered via a corridor carved out of a plant-strewn rock face. Facilities are rustic, but clean and comfortable, and the campsite's a beauty. If driving, turn left just after Glenhead Tavern and continue for 1.5km; walkers can hike up a path behind the folk village. Cash only.

There are astonishing views of the ocean below from the living room and bedrooms.

Malinbeg Hostel   HOSTEL €
(☎074-973 0006; www.malinbeghostel.com; Malinbeg; dm/s/d €17/30/45; ☺Apr-Oct) Flung out on a remote stretch of coast near Silver Strand beach, the Malinbeg Hostel is the place for simplicity and total seclusion (and no wi-fi or mobile network coverage). There is a cosy living room with a fire and some rooms have fabulous sea views.

An Chistin   CAFE €€
(☎074-973 0213; R263; mains €12-16; ☺10am-8pm) This welcoming cafe is pretty much the cooking hub of the village. The menu spans seafood chowder (€8) and scampi to pizzas, which can also be ordered to take away.

🛍 Shopping

Glencolmcille Woollen Mill   CLOTHING
(☎074-973 0069; www.rossanknitwear.ie; Malinmore; ☺9.30am-7.30pm Jun-Sep, to 6pm Oct-May) This is a great place to shop for Donegal tweed jackets, caps, ties, and lambswool scarves and shawls. You can sometimes see knitters in action. It's about 5km southwest of Glencolumbcille, in Malinmore.

ℹ Getting There & Away

Bus Éireann (p465) runs to/from Killybegs (€9, 45 minutes) one to two times a day; the route ends at Glencolumbcille.

Local Link service 293 (two to three buses daily) connects Glencolumbcille with Donegal town (one hour 10 minutes), via Carrick, Kilcar and Killybegs.

Maghera Strand & Glengesh Pass

POP 630

On the northern coast of the Glencolumbcille peninsula, 9km west of Ardara, tiny Maghera has a stunning and wide, wide beach – one of the most beautiful in Ireland. If you follow the strand westward, you'll reach a rocky promontory full of caves (inaccessible at high tide). Time a visit for sunset to immerse yourself in the full magic of the beach. Note that dangerous currents make the ocean here unsuitable for swimming.

You'll need a car or a bicycle to reach Maghera. The beach can also be reached on the signed 24km St Conall's Walk hike.

Heading south from Ardara, take the second turning (the first turning after the John Malloy factory outlet), marked by a hand-painted sign to 'Maghera'. If you take the first turning by mistake, you won't pass the waterfall and you'll find yourself on the wrong side and unable to get down to the beach.

★ **Maghera Strand**   BEACH

This astonishing beach is a dream come true, especially if you are rewarded with a gorgeous sunset. Get here during lowish tide to explore the **caves** in the south end, where some spectacular geology awaits. If you get clear skies, the sun dipping into the Atlantic is one of Ireland's most treasured and priceless experiences. During Cromwell's 17th-century destruction, 100 villagers sought refuge here but all except one were discovered and massacred.

There's a car park outside a farm just before the dunes that lead to the beach (signed Maghera Caves; €3 per car). You'll need to walk through a metal gate – remember to shut it after you.

Assarancagh Waterfall   WATERFALL

(Maghera Waterfall) These impressive falls are a worthwhile stop on the way to Maghera Strand. There's a small makeshift shrine to the left of the waterfall.

★ **Glengesh Pass**   VIEWPOINT

On a narrow road from Glencolumbcille to Ardara, past remote mountain bogland, magnificent Glengesh Pass (Glean Géis; meaning 'Glen of the Swans'), scoured out aeons ago by implacably vast glacial forces, is approached down several switchbacks that lead towards thatched cottages and a swath of pastoral beauty. There are spots and visitor viewpoints where you can pull over and take in the whole epic scenario before you.

Ardara

POP 740

Gateway to the switchbacks of the Glengesh Pass, the heritage town of Ardara (pronounced arda-rah; Ard an Rátha in Irish, meaning 'Height of the Fort') is the heart of Donegal's tweed and knitwear industry. You can visit the weavers at work and see the region's most traditional crafts in action.

The standout sight, however, is the lovely drive down to gorgeous Maghera Strand, past the stunning Assarancagh Waterfall.

A fantastically remote, 25km single-track road leads from Glencolumbcille to Ardara via the stark and awesome Glengesh Pass, one of Donegal's most scenic driving routes.

◎ Sights & Activities

Ardara Heritage Centre   MUSEUM

(☑ 087 286 8657; Main St; ⊙ usually 10am-5pm Mon-Fri, 11am-4pm Sat Easter-Sep) **FREE** Set in the old courthouse, this volunteer-run centre traces the story of Donegal tweed, from sheep shearing to dye production and weaving.

Don Byrne   CYCLING

(☑ 074-954 1658; www.donbyrnebikes.com; West End; bike rental per day from €17, hybrid per week €80; ⊙ 10am-6pm Tue-Sat) This bike shop has a wide selection and offers good advice on routes.

Cup of Tae Festival   MUSIC

(☑ 087 242 4590; www.cupoftaefestival.com; ⊙ early May) Dancing, storytelling and a school of music are part of the trad-music Cup of Tae Festival. The small-scale but very worthwhile festival takes its name from a local musician, John Gallagher. Free live music fills the pubs.

▧ Sleeping & Eating

Bayview Country House   B&B €

(☑ 074-954 1145; www.bayviewcountryhouse.com; R261; s/d €50/78; ⊙ Apr–mid-Oct; ☜) Just 800m north of town and overlooking the bay, this purpose-built B&B has spacious rooms with pretty floral bedspreads, spotless bathrooms and great views. There's a wood fire, homemade bread and scones, and a genuinely warm welcome for visitors.

Gort na Móna   B&B €

(☑ 074-953 7777; www.gortnamonabandb.com; Donegal Rd, Cronkeerin; s/d €45/75; ☜) The fine mountain views and large but cosy and colourful rooms make this a home away from home, and the breakfast includes preserves made from homegrown strawberries. It's 2km southeast of town on the old Donegal road.

⭐ Woodhill House   HOTEL €€
(📞 074-954 1112; www.woodhillhouse.com; Woodhill; r €120-170; ⊘ dinner 5-9pm; 🛜) Ireland's last commercial whaling family once lived in this grand manor house, parts of which date from the 17th century. It has a well-stocked bar and the atmosphere of a family home, as well as beautiful gardens with views of the hills. It's just 300m east of the town centre and is popular for its three-course Irish dinners (€42.50).

⭐ Nancy's Bar   IRISH €
(📞 074-954 1187; Front St; mains €10-16; ⊘ kitchen noon-8.30pm Mon-Sat, 12.30-8pm Sun, Sat & Sun only Nov-Feb; 🛜) This old-fashioned pub-restaurant, in the same family for seven generations, is one of the best local spots for trad-music sessions. It serves superb seafood and chowder, including fresh oysters, and is also the best place in town for a sociable pint or two.

West End Cafe   IRISH €
(📞 074-954 1656; Main St; mains €5-15; ⊘ 9am-8.30pm Mon-Sat, from 2pm Sun) Long known as 'Whyte's' and stuffed with locals, this curtained cafe run by ever-diligent Philomena is beloved for its superfresh fish and chips, but it also does sandwiches, all-day breakfasts and hot specials. The coffee comes in a pot that goes on forever.

🍺 Drinking & Nightlife

Many of the town's pubs, such as Nancy's Bar, host regular traditional-music sessions; just stroll down the main drag until you hear the good cheer pouring out the door.

Corner House   PUB
(📞 074-954 1736; The Diamond; ⊘ 10.30am-11pm Sun-Thu, from noon Sat & Sun) This is a good spot to listen to an Irish-music session (Friday and Saturday year-round, nightly from June to September). It's the type of place where someone will spontaneously break into song and, if the mood is right, the rest of the pub joins in.

🛍 Shopping

Ardara has a bevy of knitwear vendors and producers, with traditional sweaters to keep out the Atlantic winds starting from around €60.

⭐ Eddie Doherty   CLOTHING
(📞 087 699 6360; www.handwoventweed.com; Main St; ⊘ 10am-6pm Mon-Sat, sometimes Sun) You can usually catch Eddie Doherty hand-weaving here on a traditional loom. He'll cheerfully explain every step of the process.

Donegal Designer Makers   ARTS & CRAFTS
(www.donegaldesignermakers.com; Front St; ⊘ 10.30am-6pm Mon-Sat) This shop sells the work of 14 talented local designers. Pieces include ceramics, prints, knitwear and jewellery.

John Molloy   CLOTHING
(📞 074-954 1133; www.johnmolloy.com; Killybegs Rd; ⊘ 9am-6pm) Handmade and machine-knitted woollies are available here at the flagship establishment.

ℹ️ Information

The volunteer-run **tourist office** (📞 074-954 1704; www.ardara.ie; Main St, Ardara Heritage Centre; ⊘ 10am-6pm Mon-Fri, 11am-4pm Sat Mar-Oct) has lots of good info including a walking-tour map, even if no one is around. The website has reams of local information.

ℹ️ Getting There & Away

Bus Éireann (p465) services from Donegal (€10, 25 minutes) stop outside the Heritage Centre in Ardara two to three times per day en route to Glenties.

Loughrea Peninsula

The twin settlements of Narin and Portnoo nestle at the western end of a gorgeous wishbone-shaped Blue Flag Portnoo beach. In the southwest corner of the peninsula, hemmed in by grassy dunes, is the beautiful Tramore Beach.

⭐ Iniskeel Island   ISLAND
(Narin) You can walk out to this tiny island at low tide from the sandy tip of the Blue Flag beach at Narin. St Connell, a cousin of St Colmcille (Columba), founded a monastery here in the 6th century and the island is studded with early-medieval Christian remains, including two ruined churches and some decorated grave slabs.

Tramore Beach   BEACH
(Kiltoorish; 🅿️) Backed by sand dunes, this remote and beautiful beach is worth a detour. It's south of Kiltoorish; look for a right turn off the R261 just north of Kilcooney. There is space to park where the road ends at the

DONEGAL'S ONLY RAILWAY

Today, Donegal's only operational railway is the **Fintown Railway** (☑ 074-954 6280; www.antraen.com; off R250, Fintown; adult/child €8/5; ⊘ 11am-4pm Mon-Sat, 1-5pm Sun Jul & Aug, Thu-Sun only Jun & Sep). Lovingly restored to its original condition, the red-and-white 1940s diesel railcar runs on a rebuilt 5km section of the former County Donegal Railway track along picturesque Lough Finn. The return trip, which includes commentary, takes around 40 minutes. Call ahead to reserve a place and confirm tour times.

When the first spluttering steam engine arrived in Donegal in 1895, the locals dubbed the belching creature the Black Pig. The railways gave Donegal's isolated communities a new lease of life and a much-needed connection to the rest of the country. Over 300km of narrow-gauge tracks crossed the county in the railway's heyday, but after WWII business declined and the railway closed to passengers in June 1947, and to freight in 1952.

Payment is by cash only; there is no ATM in Fintown. It's 20km northeast of Glenties.

start of the dunes, next to the entrance to Tramore beach caravan park.

In 1588 part of the Spanish Armada ran aground by lovely Tramore Beach. The survivors temporarily occupied O'Boyle's Island in Kiltoorish Lake, but then marched to Killybegs, where they set sail again in the *Girona*. The *Girona* met a similar fate that same year in Northern Ireland, with the loss of more than 1000 crew members.

Dolmen Ecocentre   ARCHAEOLOGICAL SITE
(☑ 074-954 5010; www.facebook.com/dolmen centreportnoo; R261, Kilclooney; ⊘ 9am-5pm Mon-Fri) Learn about several local prehistoric sites, including the grand **Kilclooney More Court Tomb**, as well as a tortoise-like passage tomb a short walk up a track, to the left of the church.

★ Carnaween House   B&B **€€**
(☑ 074-954 5122; www.carnaweenhouse.com; Narin; s/d from €50/90, cottage from €155, restaurant mains €16.50-26.50; ⊘ kitchen 6-9pm Thu-Sun, 1-4pm Sun Jun-Sep, shorter hours Oct-May; 🛜) Carnaween House glows with brilliant white bedrooms in a luxury beach-house style – indeed, the sands on the adjoining beach are *almost* as white. The restaurant serves modern Irish fare, with an emphasis on seafood. Book a window table and thrill to sunset views.

There's also a beach-hut cafe, open 10am to 5pm in good weather, serving sandwiches, seafood chowder, fish and chips, and pizza (mains €5 to €10).

Glenties

POP 800

At the foot of two valleys with a southern backdrop laid on by the Blue Stack Mountains, the proud Tidy Town of Glenties (Na

Gleannta) is a good spot for fishing and has some cracking walks in the surrounding countryside. Glenties is linked with playwright Brian Friel, whose play about five unmarried sisters in 1930s Ireland, *Dancing at Lughnasa*, is set in the town (it was later made into a 1998 film with Meryl Streep).

St Connell's Museum & Heritage Centre   MUSEUM
(☑ 087 292 1016; Mill Rd; adult/child €5/3; ⊘ 11am-3pm Mon-Fri May-Sep) Next to the courthouse, this informative little museum has a wealth of exhibits on local history over several floors and doubles as an info centre and cafe.

Highlands Hotel   HOTEL **€€**
(☑ 074-955 1111; www.highlandshotel.ie; Main St/N56; s/d €70/120, mains €15-26) The Highlands Hotel offers 27 bright, modern rooms with wooden floors and local art on the walls. The restaurant is a reliable option for comfort food like burgers, scampi and fish and chips, and bar food is served throughout the day.

Brennan's B&B   B&B **€€**
(☑ 074-955 1235; www.brennansbnb.com; Main St; s/d from €45/75; 🛜🐾) The welcome is genuinely warm at this B&B, in a beautiful 1860s townhouse run by Kathleen and Francis. Its three comfy guest rooms are lovingly tended to, and it's handily situated at the southern end of the main drag among a crop of pubs and shops.

NORTHWESTERN DONEGAL

Few places in Ireland are more savagely beautiful than Northwestern Donegal. The rocky Gaeltacht area between Dungloe and Crolly is known as the Rosses (Na Rossa), and is scattered with shimmering lakes, grey-pink granite outcrops and golden-sand beaches pounded by Atlantic surf. Further north, between Bunbeg and Gortahork, the scenery is spoiled a little by the uncontrolled sprawl of holiday homes. Offshore, the islands of Arranmore and Tory are fascinating to those eager for a glimpse of a more traditional way of life.

Dungloe

POP 1160

The hub of the Rosses, Dungloe (An Clochán Liath) is a busy if unprepossessing little town with ample services for anyone passing along the spectacular coastal route.

Dungloe River Walk   WALKING

This gentle 3.7km walking trail snakes alongside Dungloe River then tracks around to take in gorgeous views of Cope Mountain. The trailhead is on Carnmore Rd, 800m east of the town centre.

Charlie Bonner's Tackle Shop   FISHING

(☑074-952 1163; www.facebook.com/bonner dungloe; The Bridge; ☺10am-6pm Mon-Sat) Fishing for trout in the River Dungloe and Lough Dungloe is popular; get tackle and permits or hire a guide from helpful Bonner's.

Mary From Dungloe Festival   MUSIC

(☑087 449 1144; www.maryfromdungloe.com; ☺late Jul-early Aug) Each year in summer, Dungloe hosts the 10-day Mary from Dungloe Festival, during which a 'new Mary' is crowned, keeping the flame alive after all these years. A number-one pop song from the late 1960s, 'Mary from Dungloe', by Emmet Spiceland, helped put this little pit stop on the map.

Radharc na Oileain   B&B €

(☑074-952 1093; www.dungloebedandbreakfast. com; Quay Rd; s/d €45/75; ☺Apr-Nov; ☞) This tidy and charming little family-run B&B with a position by the bay has rooms with plenty of brocade and other satiny details. It's down a small lane off Quay Rd; follow the sign.

Waterfront Hotel   HOTEL €€

(☑074-952 2444; www.waterfronthoteldungloe.ie; Mill Rd; d €130-150, mains €13-22; ☞) Opened in 2016, the four-star Waterfront Hotel has well-appointed rooms and excellent service. There are calming water views from the bar and restaurant and plans to add a swimming pool and leisure centre.

ⓘ Getting There & Away

Bus Éireann (p465) service 492 from Donegal runs to Dungloe (€10, 1½ hours) via Killybegs, Ardara and Glenties two to three times daily.
Doherty's Travel (☑074-952 1105; www. dohertyscoaches.com) runs once-daily coach services (except Sunday) between Letterkenny and the Rosses, stopping at Dungloe (€10, 1¼ hours), Burtonport, Kincasslagh and Annagry.

Burtonport & Around

POP 590

Pocket-sized Burtonport (Ailt an Chorráin) is the embarkation point for Arranmore Island, which looks close enough to wade to from here.

North of Burtonport is the charming seaside village of Kincasslagh, with a population of around 40 people. The village is also on the map as the birthplace of famous singer Daniel O'Donnell.

◉ Sights & Activities

Carrickfinn Beach   BEACH

(off R259, Kincasslagh) Head north of Burtonport on the coast road to reach the picturesque village of **Kincasslagh** (Cionn Caslach), with ancient cottages perched on top of rocky outcrops and the stunning Blue Flag beach at Carrick Finn. This sweeping stretch of sand with a backdrop of distant mountains remains wonderfully undeveloped, despite being right alongside and parallel to Donegal Airport.

Rapid Kayaking   KAYAKING

(☑086 151 0979; www.rapidkayaking.com; Carrick Finn, Annagry; 2hr kayak trips adult/child from €30/20; ☺Jun-Sep) Runs a variety of kayak trips on the sea and through inlets. Trips explore caves and often encounter dolphins.

🛏 Sleeping & Eating

Caisleain Oir Hotel   HOTEL €

(☑074-954 8113; www.donegalhotel.ie; Annagry; s/d from €60/100; ☞) Overlooking the tidal inlet, this well-run 20-room hotel has neat rooms with enticing views. The bar has an inviting peat fire and serves a daily menu of pub food like burgers and steak (€14 to €38) plus decadent weekend seafood specials such as local oysters, scallops and lobster (€10 to €38). There's a trad-Irish music session every Saturday night year-round.

DONEGAL'S BEST BEACHES

Donegal's wild and rugged coastline is splashed with broad sweeps of powdery white sand and secluded coves. Here are some of our favourites.

Tramore (p478) Pristine sands on a secluded stretch of coast.

Maghera Strand (p470) A stunning beach with caves to explore and sunsets to die for.

Carrickfinn (p473) A gorgeous stretch of undeveloped sand near Donegal Airport.

Fintragh Bay (p466) Beautiful and serence.

Portnoo (p471) A wishbone-shaped sheltered cove backed by undulating hills.

Ballymastocker Beach (p486) An idyllic stretch of sand lapped by turquoise water.

Culdaff (p491) A long expanse of golden sand, popular with families.

Rossnowlagh (p463) A white-sand beach ideal for learning to surf.

Lobster Pot SEAFOOD €€
(Kelly's; ☑ 074-954 2012; www.lobsterpot.ie; Main St, Burtonport; mains €10-30, whole/half lobster €42/24; ☺ kitchen noon-9pm, pub to late) You can't miss the giant fibreglass lobster clinging to the wall of the Lobster Pot, which looks onto the working fishing port. Serving up a great selection of seafood, this pub-restaurant is packed when big matches are on TV. Seafood fans can go for the Titanic seafood platter (€54), loaded with lobster, crab, mussels, salmon, prawns and more.

★**Danny Minnie's Restaurant** MODERN IRISH €€€
(☑ 074-954 8201; www.dannyminnies.ie; R259, Annagry; mains €16-29; ☺ noon-3.30pm & 6.30-9.30pm Mon-Sat, 1-4pm Sun Jun-Sep, 6.30-9.30pm Thu-Sat Oct-May) A beacon of family-run fine dining since 1962, this very popular village restaurant is known for food that's inventive and seasonal. The chef is Brian O'Donnell, whose menus feature local produce and meats such as venison. Antique-filled bedrooms are sometimes available. During colder months, it's best to phone ahead as it sometimes shuts early in the week.

❶ Getting There & Away

A car is your best way of reaching Burtonport and environs.

Local Link (p468) bus 271 runs twice daily from Monday to Saturday between Burtonpoint and Letterkenny (1½ hours). The afternoon bus also stops in Annagry and Kincasslagh.

Arranmore Island

POP 470
Ringed by dramatic cliffs, cavernous sea caves and clean sandy beaches, Arranmore (Árainn Mhór) lies just 5km from the mainland. Measuring just 9km by 5km, the tiny island has been inhabited since the early Iron Age (800 BC), and a prehistoric promontory fort can be seen near the southeastern corner. The west and north are wild and rugged, with few houses to disturb the sense of isolation.

Up at the northwestern tip of the island is the old coastguard station and Arranmore Lighthouse.

Irish is the main language spoken on Arranmore Island, although most inhabitants are bilingual.

★**Arranmore Way** WALKING
Among many options, the best and most stirring is the Arranmore Way (Slí Árainn Mhór) walking path that circles the island (14km, allow three to four hours). Bring waterproofs, water and snacks.

Island Bike Rental CYCLING
(☑ 074-952 0024, 087 092 3749; adult per 3/4/8hr €3/10/15) Cycling is a fun way to explore the island. This bike-hire company is located close to the pier; book ahead.

Dive Arranmore Charters DIVING
(☑ 086 330 0516; www.divearranmore.com; boat charter half-/full-day €350/600, tours €20-30) For diving, sea angling, seal watching and a 'sea safari' and marine-heritage tour, Jim Muldowney knows the crystal-clear (and cold) waters around the island like the back of his hand. There are dozens of renowned dive sites and Dive Arranmore Charters also has a B&B on the island.

❶ Getting There & Away

Regular ferries run between Burtonport and the island.

Arranmore Fast Ferry (☑ 087 317 1810; www. arranmorefastferry.com; Burtonport; return per person/car €15/30) Usually makes the crossing in under 15 minutes.

Arranmore Island Ferry (☑ 074-954 2233, 074-952 0532; www.arranmoreferry.com; Burtonport; return adult/child €15/7, car & driver €30; ⊘ 4-8 daily sailings year-round) This large car ferry takes 20 minutes to cross.

Gweedore & Around

POP 4300

The Gaeltacht district of Gweedore (Gaoth Dobhair) is a loose agglomeration of small townships scattered between the N56 road and the coast. The most densely populated rural area in Europe and the largest Gaelic-speaking parish in Ireland, it's a heartland of traditional Irish music and culture, and birthplace of Celtic musicians such as Altan, Enya and Clannad.

The scenery is wild and windswept, but much of the coast has been overrun with holiday homes: the 'villages' of Derrybeg (Doirí Beaga) and Bunbeg (Bun Beag) virtually blend into each other, and the sprawl continues north to Bloody Foreland (named for the crimson colour of the rocks at sunset).

It's a wonderful area to explore by bike, following dead-end roads to secluded coves and beaches. Away from the coast, small fishing lakes break up the bleak, beautiful landscape. If you're driving, the N56 heading east out of Gweedore is particularly scenic.

🛏 Sleeping & Eating

Bunbeg Lodge   B&B €€
(☑ 074-956 0428; www.bunbeglodge.ie; R257, Bunbeg; r from €80; 🛜) Excellent B&B accommodation is available at this modern guesthouse. Some of the spacious rooms offer good views over the beach to the sea, so it's worth asking. Breakfasts are hearty and the hosts are very knowledgeable about the local area.

Bunbeg House   B&B €€
(Teach na Céidhe; ☑ 074-953 1305; www.bunbeghouse.com; The Harbour, Bunbeg; s/d from €60/85; ⊘ B&B Easter-Oct, cafe Jun-Sep) This converted corn mill enjoys a lovely location overlooking Bunbeg harbour, within earshot of wooden boats knocking against each other. Nonguests can enjoy home-cooked chowder, fishermen's pie or open crab sandwiches at its summertime cafe-bar, or soak up the sun on the bar terrace raising a pint.

🍷 Drinking & Nightlife

★ **Leo's Tavern**   PUB
(☑ 074-954 8143; www.leostavern.com; Meenaleck, off R259, Crolly; mains €10.50-14.50; ⊘ kitchen 5-8.45pm Mon-Fri, from 1pm Sat & Sun, bar 4pm-midnight Mon-Fri, from noon Sat & Sun; 🛜) You never know who'll drop by for one of the legendary singalongs at famous, long-standing Leo's Tavern. There's live music nightly in summer and regular sessions throughout the winter, with fine Irish pub grub too. From Crolly, take the R259 1km towards the airport, and look for the signs for Leo's.

The pub is owned by Baba Brennan, mother of Enya and her siblings Moya, Ciaran and Pól (the core of the traditional-but-modern group Clannad), and now run by younger son Bartley. The pub glitters with gold, silver and platinum discs. It's open year-round, but it's worth phoning ahead or checking the website in cold months as opening times can change.

Teac Hiudái Beag   PUB
(☑ 074-953 1016; www.tradcentre.com/hiudaibeag; Bunbeg; ⊘ 2pm-1am daily, Thu-Mon only Oct-May) In the tiny town centre and with picnic tables out the front, Teac Hiudái Beag is noted for its Monday- and Friday-night music sessions where up to a dozen musicians play flutes, whistles, fiddles, bodhráns (handheld goatskin drums) and sometimes war pipes (a larger and, consequently, louder precursor of the Highland bagpipes).

TOP FIVE SCENIC DRIVES

Practically any stretch of road qualifies as a scenic drive in this rugged county, but the following are especially captivating. Be ready for frequent stops to enjoy the views.

➡ The coastal highway from Dunfanaghy (p477) to Gweedore

➡ A hundred-mile loop of the isolated Inishowen Peninsula (p487)

➡ The curvaceous road to sweeping views at Horn Head (p477)

➡ Arcing through stunning Glenveagh National Park (p482)

➡ Snaking switchbacks traversing Glengesh Pass (p470)

ERRIGAL MOUNTAIN

The pinkish-grey quartzite peak of Errigal Mountain (752m) dominates the landscape of northwestern Donegal, appearing conical from some angles, but from others like a ragged shark's fin ripping through the heather bogs. Its name comes from the Gaelic *earagail*, meaning 'oratory', as its shape brings to mind a preacher's pulpit. Its looming presence seems to dare walkers to attempt the strenuous but satisfying climb to its pyramid-shaped summit.

If you're keen to take on the challenge, pay close attention to the weather: it can be a dangerous climb on windy or wet days, when the mountain is shrouded in cloud and visibility is minimal.The easiest route to the summit, a steep and badly eroded path, begins at a parking area on the R251, about 2km east of Dunlewey (4.5km round-trip, allow three hours).

❶ Getting There & Away

Bus Feda (☑ 074-954 8114; www.busfeda. ie) runs a service twice daily (three Friday and Sunday) from Gweedore to Letterkenny (€5, 1½ hours), Donegal (€10, 2¼ hours), Sligo (€12, 3¼ hours) and Galway (€20, 5½ hours).

Dunlewey & Around

POP 600

Blink and the chances are you'll miss the tiny hamlet of Dunlewey (Dún Lúiche). You won't miss the spectacular scenery, however, or quartzite cone of Errigal Mountain, whose craggy peak towers over the surrounding area. Plan enough time to get out of your car and do some walking here, as it's a magical spot. It's close to the N56 and the coastal villages.

⊙ Sights

Poisoned Glen   AREA
With a name like this – misnomer that it is – how can you resist its allure? Follow a rough walking path into the rocky fastness of the glen (4km round-trip) and watch out for the green lady – the resident ghost. Some 2km east of the Dunlewey Centre turn-off on the R251, look for a minor road down through the hamlet of Dunlewey, past the magnificently ruined Dunlewey Church, to roadside parking at a hairpin bend where you'll find the walking path.

Legend has it that the huge ice-carved hollow of the Poisoned Glen got its sinister name when the ancient one-eyed giant king of Tory, Balor, was killed here by his exiled grandson, Lughaidh, whereupon the poison from his eye split the rock and poisoned the glen. The less interesting truth, however, lies in a cartographic gaffe. Locals were inspired to name it An Gleann Neamhe (The Heavenly Glen), but when an English cartographer mapped the area, he carelessly marked it An Gleann Neimhe – The Poisoned Glen.

Dunlewey Church   CHURCH
This roofless white-marble, blue-quartzite and brick church, overlooking Dunlewey Lough, was consecrated in 1853 and makes for sublime photos with the mountain behind and the lake beyond. Eventually the Dunlewey Estate declined and the congregation dried up; the roof was taken down in 1955. Some of the lead remains in the arched windows, although the glass is all gone, but it's a picture and the setting is gorgeous.

Dunlewey Centre   CULTURAL CENTRE
(Ionad Cois Locha; ☑ 074-953 1699; www.dun leweycentre.com; Dunlewey; cottage or boat trip adult/child €7.25/5.25, cottage & boat €13.50/9.50; ⊙ 10.30am-5.30pm Easter-Sep, to 4.45pm Oct; 🖐) This great hotchpotch of craft shop, museum, restaurant (mains €7.50 to €10), activity centre and concert venue has something for everyone. Kids will love the farm, but the real highlight for everyone is a boat trip on the lake with a storyteller who vividly brings to life local history and ghoulish folklore. Adults will appreciate the 30-minute tour of the thatched cottage that once belonged to local weaver Manus Ferry, who earned renown for his tweeds (he died in 1975).

🛏 Sleeping

★ **Errigal Hostel**   HOSTEL €
(☑ 074-953 1180; www.anoige.ie; off R251; dm/s/d €20/32/53; ⊙ Mar-Oct; 🖐) 🖐 At the foot of magnificent Errigal Mountain, this gleaming, excellent and purpose-built 60-bed An Óige hostel has superb facilities including a self-catering kitchen, a large laundry room for your muddy climbing gear, light-filled common areas, and pristine dorms and private

rooms. Friendly staff round out the picture and a petrol station sells groceries next door.

Glen Heights B&B
B&B €€

(☑074-956 0844; www.glenheightsbb.com; s €50, d €70-80; 🛜) The three rooms are bright and inviting, and the Donegal charm is in full swing at this fine choice run by Kathleen. Your breakfast may well go cold on the plate in front of you as you stare at the breathtaking views of Dunlewey Lake and the Poisoned Glen from the conservatory.

It's down a minor road off R251, 2km east of the Dunlewey Centre.

Falcarragh & Gortahork
POP 890

Falcarragh (An Fál Carrach) is a workaday real town without the pretensions of nearby Dunfanaghy, while neighbouring Gortahork (Gort an Choirce) is barely a wide spot in the road. Both give an intriguing glimpse into everyday Gaeltacht life.

👁 Sights & Activities

Get on your bike or don your hiking boots and explore the maze of country lanes and old townlands (farming communities) south of Falcarragh, including the old church and burial ground on the ancient mound of **Ballintemple**.

Muckish Mountain
MOUNTAIN

The grey bulk of Muckish Mountain (670m) dominates the view between Gortahork and Dunfanaghy. The easiest route to the top begins southeast of Falcarragh at the highest point of the R256 road through Muckish Gap. Sweeping views to Malin Head and Tory Island unfurl from the summit.

Magheroarty Beach
BEACH

(Meenlaragh; off R257) A beautiful beach that curves for more than 3km, with good walks along the shore and through the dunes. Even better are the views out to the islands, including Tory.

🛏 Sleeping & Eating

Óstán Loch Altan
HOTEL €€

(☑074-913 5267; www.ostanlochaltan.com; N56, Gortahork; s/d from €60/120, mains €16-26; ☺kitchen noon-9pm Mon-Sat, from 3pm Sun; 🛜) Gortahork's main landmark is this big, tidy cream-coloured hotel on the main street. Its 39 rooms are a mix of styles; some have sea views. It's one of few places to stay along this

stretch of coast that's open all year; good bar food is served year-round, while the restaurant opens for lunch and dinner from June to September.

Lóistín Na Seamróige
PUB

(Shamrock Lodge; Main St/N56, Falcarragh; ☺10.30am-12.30am; 🛜) Owner Margaret grew up on these premises and her pub (established in 1959) is the town's living room, especially on Friday mornings when a market sets up outside the front door. During July and August traditional music is in the air.

ℹ Information

Falcarragh Visitor Centre (☑074-918 0655; www.falcarraghvisitorcentre.com; ☺10am-5pm Mon-Fri, from 11am Sat), which has tourist information and a cafe, is housed in a 19th-century police barracks.

ℹ Getting There & Away

Bus Feda (☑074-954 8114; www.feda.ie; 🛜) buses from Crolly stop in Gortahork and Falcarragh on their way to Letterkenny (€5, one hour).

Local Link (p468) service 966 runs two services daily Monday to Saturday between Falcarragh and Dunglow, stopping in Gortahork.

Dunfanaghy & Around
POP 300

Pretty Dunfanaghy is clustered along the southern shore of a sandy inlet and lies ideally at the centre of one of the most varied and attractive parts of Donegal. Moors and meadows, sea cliffs and sandy beaches, forest and lake lie scattered below the humpbacked hill of Muckish, all waiting to be explored on foot or by bike.

👁 Sights

★ Horn Head
VIEWPOINT

The towering headland of Horn Head has some of the Wild Atlantic Way's most spectacular scenery, with dramatic quartzite cliffs, topped with bog and heather, rearing over 180m high. The narrow road from Dunfanaghy (4km) ends at a small parking area where you can walk 150m to a **WWII lookout point** or 1.5km to Horn Head proper.

On a fine day you'll encounter tremendous views of Tory, Inishbofin, Inishdooey and tiny Inishbeg Islands to the west; Sheep Haven Bay and the Rosguill Peninsula to the east; Malin Head to the northeast; and the coast of Scotland beyond.

Ards Forest Park WILDLIFE RESERVE

(off N56; parking €5, €1 & €2 coins only; ⊘ 8am-9pm Apr-Sep, 10am-4.30pm Oct-Mar) Anyone looking to stretch their legs will love this forested park, criss-crossed by marked nature trails varying in length from 2km to 13km. Covering 480 hectares along the northern shore of the Ards Peninsula and 5km southeast of Dunfanaghy, the park is home to some lovely walks, the best of which lead to its clean beaches with views across Clonmass Bay.

The woodlands are home to several native species, including ash, birch and sessile oak, and you may encounter foxes, hedgehogs and otters. In 1930 the southern part of the peninsula was taken over by Capuchin monks; the grounds of their friary are open to the public.

Tramore Beach BEACH

Reaching Dunfanaghy's loveliest beach, Tramore, requires hiking through the grassy dunes to the west of the village for about 2km. It's not safe to swim here due to dangerous currents.

Dunfanaghy Workhouse HISTORIC BUILDING

(☑ 074-913 6540; www.dunfanaghyworkhouse.ie; Main St, Dunfanaghy; adult/child €5/4; ⊘ 10am-5pm daily Easter-Oct, Sat & Sun only Nov-Easter) This prominent stone building on the western edge of town was once the local workhouse, built to keep and employ the destitute. Conditions were horrible. Men, women, children and the sick were segregated, their lives dominated by gruelling work. The building today is a heritage centre, which tells the powerful true tale of 'Wee Hannah' Herrity (1836–1926) and her passage through the institution. It has a cafe, a crafts shop (and craft courses), tourist information and occasional temporary exhibitions.

As the Famine took grip the workhouse was inundated with starving people. Two years after it opened in 1845, it accommodated some 600 people – double the number originally planned.

🏃 Activities

Narosa Life WATER SPORTS

(☑ 086 883 1090, 074-910 0565; www.narosalife.com; Main St, Dunfanaghy; surf lesson adult/child €40/30; ⊘ 10am-5pm Sun-Fri, from 9am Sat) Offers two-hour group surf and SUP (stand-up paddle boarding) lessons and private one-on-one surf lessons (€120, July and August only), as well as seasonal yoga and fitness classes.

Dunfanaghy Golf Club GOLF

(☑ 074-913 6335; www.dunfanaghygolfclub.com; off N56, Dunfanaghy; green fees weekdays/weekends €30/40) This stunning waterside 18-hole links course is just east of the village.

Dunfanaghy Stables HORSE RIDING

(☑ 074-910 0980; www.dunfanaghystables.com; Arnolds Hotel, Main St; adult/child per hr €35/30; ⊘ Easter-Oct) Explore the expansive beaches and surrounding countryside on horseback. Short rides and lessons also available. Book ahead.

Jaws Watersports WATER SPORTS

(☑ 087 237 1152, 086 173 5109; www.jawswatersports.ie; Main St, Dunfanaghy; gear rental per half-day from €20) Offers surfing, rents out surfing gear, bodyboards and kayaks, and offers guided kayaking trips (€35) and stand-up paddleboarding.

🛏 Sleeping

★ Corcreggan Mill GUESTHOUSE €

(☑ 074-913 6409; www.corcreggan.com; Castlebane, off N56; campsites €17.50, r €95, glamping from €80; @ 🛜) 🅿 As well as spotless double and family rooms (only some with private bathrooms) in the lovingly restored former mill-house, Corcreggan has sites for camping and a number of quirky glamping cabins, including luxury bell tents, compartments in a restored railway carriage and a former fishing trawler, with its own barbecue on deck. The mill is 2.5km southwest of town.

There are cosy lounges and kitchens for campers, glampers and B&B guests.

Willows B&B B&B €

(☑ 074-913 6446; www.thewillowsdunfanaghy.com; Main St, Dunfanaghy; s/d from €48/76; 🛜) At the west end of town, this spiffy B&B has comfy rooms and a great terrace and barbecue area with table and chairs so you can enjoy the long nights of summer with billions of stars.

Whins B&B €€

(☑ 074-913 6481; www.thewhinsdunfanaghy.com; off N56; s/d €50/80; 🛜) About 750m east of the town centre opposite the golf course, the colourful, individually decorated rooms at the Whins have patchwork quilts and a real sense of character. A wide choice of breakfasts is served upstairs in a room with a view towards Horn Head. Cash only.

Arnold's Hotel HOTEL €€

(☑ 074-913 6208; www.arnoldshotel.com; Main St, Dunfanaghy; s/d from €80/115; 🅿 🛜) Open since

1922, this family-run hotel at the east end of the village has 30 comfortable and stylish rooms. The hotel's restaurant serves up traditional seafood, roasts and grills (mains €15 to €26). Next door, **Arnou** serves breakfasts (€6 to €8) and lunches (€7 to €12.50) daily, plus gourmet burgers on Saturday and Sunday nights (€13 to €14).

Eating

★**Rusty Oven**   PIZZA €
(www.facebook.com/therustyoven; Main St; pizzas €10-12; ⊙5-9.30pm Fri-Sun; ⚑) Arrive early to avoid a long wait at this popular place serving artisan sourdough pizzas, cooked in a wood-fired oven, with toppings like goat's cheese and pepper, and pear and walnut. Eat in the garden or at one of the indoor tables in the stove-heated, shabby-chic shed. It's located behind Patsy Dan's. Sourdough loaves are available to take away.

Muck 'n' Muffins   CAFE €
(☑074-913 6780; www.mucknmuffins.ie; The Square; mains €4-10; ⊙9.30am-5pm Mon-Sat, from 10.30am Sun; ⚑) A 19th-century stone grain store houses this 1st-floor cafe, pottery studio and crafts shop. Even on rainy winter days, it's packed with locals sipping coffee, quaffing wine, and tucking into sandwiches, breakfast, hot specials (lasagne, quiche etc), tempting cakes and, of course, muffins.

★**Cove**   MODERN IRISH €€
(☑074-913 6300; www.facebook.com/cove restaurantdonegal; off N56, Rockhill, Port-na Blagh; dinner mains €20-30; ⊙6.30-9.30pm Tue-Sun) Owners Siobhan Sweeney and Peter Byrne are perfectionists who tend to every detail in Cove's art-filled dining room, and on your plate. The cuisine is fresh and inventive. Seafood specials are deceptively simple with subtle Asian influences, and after dinner you can enjoy the elegant lounge upstairs. There's an excellent wine list too. Book ahead.

Mill Restaurant & Guesthouse   MODERN IRISH €€€
(☑074-913 6985; www.themillrestaurant.com; N56; set dinner €47.50; ⊙6.30-8.30pm Wed-Sun May-Oct, Fri & Sat only Mar & Apr; ℗) An exquisite country setting and locally sourced, seasonally changing meals make dining here a treat. Set in an old flax mill that was for many years the home of renowned watercolour artist Frank Eggington, it also has six elegant guest rooms (singles/doubles from €75/120). The mill is 1km south of town. Book in advance.

Drinking & Nightlife

★**Patsy Dan's**   PUB
(Main St; ⊙11am-midnight) This traditional pub with peat fires is the best place in town for trad sessions, held throughout the year on Mondays and Fridays, and more often in summer. Everyone is welcome to bring their instruments along and join in and even if you're too shy to sing you'll find it hard to keep your feet from tapping.

Sourdough pizzas are available from the Rusty Oven, behind the pub.

Shopping

Gallery   ART
(☑074-913 6224; www.thegallerydunfanaghy.com; Main St; ⊙11am-5pm Mon-Sat) This lovely shop was once the 'hospital' for the workhouse next door. Today it is a much more cheery place: it displays works and crafts by local artists plus oodles of gift items.

Getting There & Away

Bus Feda (☑074-954 8114; www.feda.ie) Buses between Crolly (€5, 40 minutes), Donegal (€10, 1½ hours) and Galway (€20, five hours) stop in Dunfanaghy square twice daily Monday to Saturday and three times on Friday and Sunday.
John McGinley (☑074-913 5201; www.john-mcginley.com) Buses stop in Dunfanaghy two to four times daily en route to Letterkenny (from €5, one hour) and Dublin (from €22, five hours).

Tory Island
POP 144

Ireland's most remote inhabited island, blasted by sea winds and stung by salt spray, the distant crag of Tory Island (Oileán Thóraí) has taken its fair share of batterings. Although it's only 11km north of the mainland, the rough sea has long consolidated the island's staunch independence and strengthened its sense of remoteness.

The island has its own dialect of Irish and even has an elected 'king', who acts as community spokesperson and welcomes visitors to the island. Over the decades its inhabitants earned a reputation for distilling and smuggling contraband *poitín*. However, the island is perhaps best known for its 'naive' (or outsider) artists, many of whom have attracted the attention of international collectors.

The island has just one pebbly beach and two recognisable villages: West Town (An Baile Thiar), home to most of the island's facilities, and East Town (An Baile Thoir).

TORY ISLAND NAIVE ART

Tory Island's distinctive school of painters came about in the 1950s when the English artist Derrick Hill began to spend much of his time on the island. The islanders often watched him as he worked. As the story goes, one of the islanders approached Hill and said, 'I can do that.' He was James Dixon, a self-taught painter who used boat paint and made his own brushes with donkey hairs. Hill was impressed with the 'painterly' quality of Dixon's work and the two formed a lasting friendship.

Other islanders were soon inspired to follow suit, forging unique folksy, expressive styles portraying rugged island scenes. Among them were Patsy Dan Rodgers, the much-loved elected Rí Thoraí (King of Tory), who passed away in 2018. Ruairí Rodgers has a small gallery of his work at his home; look for it next to the round tower.

The islanders' work has been exhibited worldwide and fetches impressive prices at auctions. Glebe House & Gallery (p483) on the mainland often has exhibitions.

Sights & Activities

Cottages mingle with ancient ecclesiastical treasures in West Town. St Colmcille (Columba) is said to have founded a monastery here in the 6th century, and reminders of the early Church are scattered throughout the town, including the Tau Cross and a round tower.

Tory Island is a wonderful place for birdwatching – more than 100 species of seabirds inhabit the island, including nesting corncrakes and colonies of puffins (thought to number around 1300).

Tory Island Harbour View Hotel rents bikes (€10 per day).

Tau Cross RELIGIOUS SITE
The 12th-century Tau Cross, an odd, T-shaped cruciform that suggests the possibility of seafaring exchanges with early Coptic Christians from Egypt, greets passengers disembarking from the ferry.

An Cloígtheach Bell Tower TOWER
Not far from the Tau Cross, this 6th- or 7th-century round tower has a circumference of nearly 16m and a round-headed doorway high above the ground.

R. L. Rodgers Gallery GALLERY
(☑086 167 1568; www.facebook.com/R-L-Rodgers-Art-400360957033720) Artist Ruairí Rodgers has a small gallery of his work at his home. Look for his house next to the An Cloígtheach Bell Tower. It's painted white, green and gold and there is a sign saying gallery.

★ Tory Way WALKING
(An Slí Thoraí) Tory Way is a waymarked loop walk (the map board is 50m from the ferry landing). It leads you to the lighthouse at the west end, then back to the eastern end of the island, which is dominated by jagged quartzite cliffs and sea stacks, including the spectacular Tor Mór, a 400m-long blade of rock capped with pinnacles.

The 8km trail takes around two to three hours.

Sleeping & Eating

Tory Island Harbour View Hotel HOTEL €€
(Óstan Radharc Na Céibhe; ☑074-913 5920, 087 938 5284; www.hoteltory.com; West Town; s/d from €50/90; ☺Easter-Oct) The island's sole hotel is a friendly place with 12 comfortable bedrooms inside a sunny yellow building. Bar food is served from 12.30pm to 4.30pm, and the hotel's restaurant opens in the evening from 6pm to 8pm (mains €14 to €18.50). The pub is a hotbed of late-night music, dancing and craic. Bikes can be hired here (€10 per day).

Ionad Bhalor CAFE €
(West Town; snacks €5; ☺11am-6pm) Immediately west of the ferry pier, Ionad Bhalor makes an appealing stop for a cup of tea or coffee and a slice of homemade pie or cake. There is also a small gift shop here, where you can buy children's cardigans knitted by the owner's mother. It's a good place to pick up maps of the islands.

☆ Entertainment

Club Sóisialta Thórai COMMUNITY CENTRE
(Tory Social Club; West Town; ☺hours vary) The island's social life revolves around this merry spot, which besides the hotel has the island's only other pub. It usually gets going from around 8pm but don't expect the real craic to start until much, much later.

❶ Information

Information is available from the **Tory Island Co-op** (Comharchumann Thoraí Teo; ☑074-913

5502; www.oileanthorai.com; ⊙9am-5pm Mon-Fri) near the pier, next to the playground. You can also get information at Ionad Bhalor at the top of the pier.

ⓘ Getting There & Away

Passenger ferries (☑ 087 199 3710; www.toryferry.com; adult/child return €25/10; ⊙1-3 daily Apr-Oct, less often Nov-Mar) run to Tory Island from Magheroarty (Machaire Uí Robhartaigh; 45 minutes). Sailing times vary according to weather and tides, and it's not uncommon for travellers to be stranded on the island in bad weather. At times there are extra runs in July and August. Bring waterproof clothes as it can be a wild ride. Magheroarty is 4km northwest of Gortahork on the R257; the road is signposted Coastal Route/Bloody Foreland.

CENTRAL DONEGAL

Letterkenny

POP 19,600

Donegal's largest town has a buzz about it. It's an important market town with atmospheric pubs, some excellent restaurants and impressive cultural centres that host top local and international artists. On the flip side, rash development has resulted in numerous soulless retail parks, and traffic congestion can be a problem.

⊙ Sights

Newmills Corn & Flax Mills HISTORIC BUILDING (☑ 074-912 5115; www.heritageireland.ie; R250; ⊙10am-6pm late May-Sep) FREE Parts of this complex date back four centuries to a time when water was the main source of power for multiple tasks, such as grinding grain. One of Ireland's largest waterwheels spins thanks to the River Swilly. Exhibits explain the function of the many cogs and gears. It's 5km southwest of Letterkenny.

Donegal County Museum MUSEUM (☑ 074-912 4613; High Rd; ⊙10am-12.30pm & 1-4.30pm Mon-Fri, 1-4.30pm Sat) FREE Letterkenny's 19th-century workhouse, built to provide Famine relief, now houses the local museum. The permanent collection offers 8000-plus artefacts from prehistoric times onwards. Look for temporary exhibits.

Main Street STREET Letterkenny's long, sloping main street is graced by a cute little **market square** halfway

down. This is the most attractive part of the town, with a terrace of red-brick Georgian houses at the top, one of which was a holiday retreat of Maud Gonne, actress, revolutionary and lover of poet WB Yeats.

★★ Festivals & Events

Earagail Arts Festival PERFORMING ARTS (☑ 074-912 0777; www.eaf.ie; ⊙mid-Jul) Theatre performances, concerts and art exhibits headline this diverse two-week festival, with events staged across the region.

🛏 Sleeping

Apple Hostel HOSTEL € (☑ 074-911 3291; www.letterkennyhostel.com; Covehill, Port Rd; dm/s/d from €18/28/40; ⊛) This hostel is close to the centre of town, along the road near the bus station. It's a modern bungalow with accommodation to match, from a dorm with eight bunks to doubles and family rooms with private bathrooms. A continental breakfast is included and there's also a guest kitchen. Call ahead to book.

Pearse Road B&B B&B € (☑ 074-912 3002; Pearse Rd; r €80-85; P⊛) This tidy guesthouse has rooms spread over two buildings close to Main St. Rooms are well equipped and there's a speedy laundry right next door.

Station House HOTEL €€ (☑ 074-912 3100; www.stationhouseletterkenny.com; Lower Main St; s/d €90/100; @⊛) Conveniently located in the centre of town but right on a busy corner, this large, modern hotel has 81 red-hued, wood-floored rooms with low lighting and glass-panelled bathrooms.

✕ Eating & Drinking

★Lemon Tree MODERN IRISH €€ (☑ 074-912 5788; www.thelemontreerestaurant.com; 32-34 The Courtyard Shopping Centre; mains €18-24; ⊙5-9pm Mon-Thu, to 9.30pm Fri & Sat, 1-2.30pm & 5-8pm Sun; ⊛✍) This family-run restaurant is widely considered one of the best places in the county to sample contemporary Donegal cooking. The innovative menu offers an excellent choice of fresh seafood, poultry and meat dishes sourced locally and prepared with French flair. There's a good wine list, too.

Brewery PUB FOOD €€ (☑ 074-912 7330; www.thebrewerybar.com; Market Sq; carvery €10, mains €14-29; ⊙kitchen 11am-9pm) Just off Main St, this multilevel pub is a good choice for a casual meal. A carvery buffet lunch is served from 11am to 2.30pm, then a menu of burgers, steaks, pies and seafood is available until 9pm. The wine list is decent and there are good microbrews on tap.

Yellow Pepper
MEDITERRANEAN €€
(☑074-912 4133; www.yellowpepperrestaurant.com; 36 Lower Main St; mains €9.50-21.50; ⊗noon-10pm; ☎☑) Set in a 19th-century former shirt factory with stone walls and polished wooden floors, this atmospheric restaurant is a favourite among locals. The menu, with food procured from the region, is strong on seafood but offers variety including an excellent tapas-style lunch menu. There's a vegan menu too. Book for dinner.

★ Cottage Bar
PUB
(☑074-912 1338; 49 Upper Main St; ⊗10.30am-midnight) Watch your head! All sorts of bric-a-brac hangs precariously from the ceiling of Letterkenny's most atmospheric pub. There's a good beer garden and regular trad sessions.

McGinley's
PUB
(☑074-912 1106; Lower Main St; ⊗11am-1am) The best spot in town to catch some live music, this old-style pub with an open fire has trad sessions on Tuesday and Wednesday nights, and live bands Thursday to Saturday.

☆ Entertainment

An Grianán Theatre
THEATRE
(☑074-912 0777; www.angrianan.com; Port Rd) An Grianán Theatre is a community theatre and major arts venue for the northwest, presenting national and international drama, comedy and music. It also has a good cafe and bar.

Regional Cultural Centre
THEATRE
(RCC; ☑074-912 9186; www.regionalculturalcentre.com; Port Rd) In a striking glass-and-aluminium structure, Letterkenny's cultural centre hosts music and drama, fine arts and film screenings.

ⓘ Information

The **tourist office** (☑074-912 1160; Neil Blaney Rd; ⊗9am-5.30pm Mon-Sat Jun-Aug, 9.15am-5pm Mon-Fri Sep-May) is 1km southeast of Main St at the roundabout junction of the N14 and N56.

ⓘ Getting There & Away

Letterkenny is a major bus hub for northwest Ireland. The bus station is by the roundabout at the junction of Ramelton and Port Rds.
Bus Éireann (☑074-912 1309; www.buseireann.ie) Runs to Dublin (€21, four hours) five

times daily via Omagh and Monaghan. Buses also serve Derry and Galway via Donegal (€12, 45 minutes, eight times daily).
Bus Feda (☑074-954 8114; www.feda.ie) Runs a bus to Crolly (€5, 1½ hours), or to Galway (€20, four hours) twice daily via Donegal, Bundoran and Sligo. Buses stop on the road outside the bus station.
John McGinley (☑074-913 5201; www.johnmcginley.com) Buses run southeast two to five times daily to Dublin Airport (€22, 3¼ hours) and to coastal towns northwest.
Patrick Gallagher Travel (☑074-913 7037; www.patrickgallaghertravel.com)
Most travellers will be coming through by car, to access the Inishowen and Fanad Peninsulas.

Glenveagh National Park

Ireland's second-largest national park, Glenveagh is a sublime panoply of lakes overlooked by brooding mountains, with valleys scooped from the land and scattered with both forest and swaths of bog that offer an enticing, unspoilt landscape coupled with wonderful options for hiking. Its wealth of wildlife includes the golden eagle, which was hunted to extinction here in the 19th century but reintroduced in 2000, and the country's largest herd of red deer.

Such serenity came at a heavy price. The land was once farmed by 244 tenants, who were forcibly evicted by landowner John George Adair in the winter of 1861 following what he called a 'conspiracy', but really because their presence obstructed his vision for the valley. Adair put the final touches on his paradise by building the spectacular lakeside Glenveagh Castle (1870–73), while his wife, Adelia, introduced the park's definitive red deer and rhododendrons.

◉ Sights & Activities

One of the best ways to appreciate this vast and varied park is simply by wandering around it along the R251 and R254. The majestic sweep of its forbidding golden landscape is a powerful experience.

The park features nature trails along lakes and through woods and blanket bog, as well as a viewing point that's a short walk behind the castle. Get advice and study maps at the visitor centre. One good walk follows Lough Beagh.

Glenveagh Castle
CASTLE
(www.glenveaghnationalpark.ie; off R251; adult/child 30min tour €7/5, bus from visitor centre

adult/child €3/2; ⊙9.15am-5.30pm Apr-Oct, 9am-5pm Nov-Mar, last tours 45min before closing) This castle was modelled on Scotland's Balmoral Castle. Henry McIlhenny made it a characterful home with liberal reminders of his passion for deer-stalking. In fact, few rooms lack a representation – or the taxidermied remains – of a stag.

Access is by guided tour only. Cars are not allowed beyond the Glenveagh Visitor Centre; you can walk or cycle the lovely lakeside 3.6km route to the castle, or take the shuttle bus (every 15 minutes).

The most eye-catching of the flamboyantly decorated rooms are in the **round tower**, including the tartan-and-antler-encrusted **music room** and the blue room where guests Greta Garbo and Ella Fitzgerald once stayed.

The exotic **gardens** are similarly spectacular, boasting terraces, an Italian garden, a walled kitchen garden and the Belgian Walk, built by Belgian soldiers who stayed here during WWI. Their cultured charm is in marked contrast to the wildly beautiful landscape that enfolds the area.

The castle was briefly occupied by the Irish Republican Army (IRA) in 1922. Then in 1929 the property was acquired by Kingsley Porter, professor of art at Harvard University, who mysteriously disappeared in 1933 (presumed drowned, but rumoured to have been spotted in Paris afterwards).

Six years later the estate was bought by his former student, Henry McIlhenny, who sold the whole kit and caboodle to the Irish government in 1975.

Grass Routes   CYCLING
(☑087 665 5599; www.grassroutes.ie; L5542, Termon, Letterkenny; bike rental per 3hr €12-18, full day €24-35; ⊙9.30am-5pm) Hires out electric and hybrid bikes in Glenveagh National Park. The website has a wealth of information, including cycling routes.

ⓘ Information

The **Glenveagh Visitor Centre** (☑076-100 2537; www.glenveaghnationalpark.ie; off R251; ⊙9am-5.30pm Apr-Oct, 8.30am-5pm Nov-Mar) has a 20-minute video on the ecology of the park and the infamous Adairs, as well as informative displays on both subjects. Reception sells the necessary midge repellent, as vital as walking boots in summer, and waterproofs in winter. No camping is allowed in the park. It's 24km northwest of Letterkenny.

Lough Gartan

The patriarch of Irish monasticism, St Colmcille (Columba), was born in the 6th century in a lovely setting near glassy Lough Gartan, where some relics associated with the saint can be seen. The lake is 17km northwest of Letterkenny in beautiful and splendid driving country; getting lost is half the fun. There's nary a holiday home in sight in the charming region around Church Hill.

★ **Glebe House & Gallery**   GALLERY
(☑074-913 7071; www.heritageireland.ie; Church Hill; adult/child €5/3; ⊙11am-6.30pm daily Easter, Jul & Aug, Sat-Thu Jun & Sep, last admission 5.30pm) The English painter Derrick Hill bought this 1828 mansion in 1953, providing him with a mainland base close to his beloved Tory Island. Sumptuously decorated with an evident love of all things exotic, the real lure here is Hill's astonishing art collection. Besides paintings by Hill and Tory Island's 'naive' artists are works by Picasso, Landseer, Hokusai, Jack B Yeats and Kokoschka. A guided tour of the house takes about 45 minutes. An additional gallery hosts exhibitions by local artists.

Before Hill arrived, the house served as a rectory and then a hotel. The lavish gardens can also be toured and there is a cute little cafe too.

Colmcille Heritage Centre   MUSEUM
(☑074-912 1160; www.colmcilleheritagecentre.ie; off R251, Church Hill; adult/child €3/2; ⊙10.30am-5pm Mon-Sat, from 1.30pm Sun May-Sep) Colmcille's Hall of Fame is this comprehensive heritage centre on the shore of Lough Gartan in a wooded grove, with a lavish display on the production of illuminated manuscripts. The centre is signposted just southwest of Church Hill.

St Colmcille's mother, on the run from pagans, supposedly haemorrhaged during childbirth and her blood is believed to have changed the colour of the surrounding Gartan clay to pure white. Ever since, the clay has been regarded as a lucky charm.

**St Colmcille's Abbey
& Birthplace**   HISTORIC SITE
(⊙24hr) FREE The 10th-century ruins of Colmcille's abbey lie on a hillside to the north of Lough Gartan and northwest of Lough Nacally, beside a 16th-century chapel and an O'Donnell clan burial ground. It's signposted 1km north of Glebe House along

a country road. There's a car park just up from the main road.

One kilometre south of the ruins, near the southeastern (hikers and cyclists only) entrance to Glenveagh National Park, is the saint's birthplace, marked by a hefty Celtic cross erected in 1911. Beside it is an intriguing prehistoric cup-marked slab strewn with greening copper coins. It's popularly known as the Flagstone of Loneliness on which Colmcille supposedly slept.

NORTHEASTERN DONEGAL

Rosguill Peninsula

The best way to appreciate Rosguill's rugged splendour is by driving, cycling or even walking the 15km Atlantic Drive, a waymarked loop on minor roads signposted to your left as you come into the sprawling village of Carrigart (Carraig Airt) from the south. The sea views are superb, although the remoteness is spoiled somewhat by the growth in holiday homes.

The pretty, secluded beach at Trá na Rossan in the northern part of the peninsula makes a good target, rather than the overcrowded holiday strand at Downings (often written as Downies).

⚡ Activities

Mevagh Dive Centre DIVING
(☑074-915 4708; www.mevaghdiving.com; Milford Rd, Carrigart) This excellent dive centre offers PADI diving courses, equipment rentals and boat charter, and has a heated saltwater swimming pool. The northwest waters are crystal clear and at numerous sites they can take you to see everything from shipwrecks to sharks. It has accommodation (doubles from €76) in its purpose-built, four-bedroom (all with bathroom) B&B. Various packages (dive/stay/lessons) are offered.

Rosapenna Golf Resort GOLF
(☑074-915 5301; www.rosapenna.ie; Downings; green fees €130) The scenery at this renowned golf club – designed by St Andrew's Old Tom Morris in 1891 and remodelled by Harry Vardon in 1906 – is as spectacular as the layout, which can challenge even the lowest handicapper. It has two courses and there's a fully equipped four-star hotel attached.

Carrigart Riding Centre HORSE RIDING
(☑074-915 3583, 087 227 6926; per hr adult/child €20/15; ⊙10am-6pm) Offers beach treks and riding lessons.

🛏 Sleeping & Eating

Trá na Rosann Hostel HOSTEL €
(☑074-915 5374, 087 244 6027; www.anoige. ie; dm €25; ⊙late May-Sep, reception closed 10.30am-5pm; ℗) Knockout views envelop this heritage-listed 24-bed former hunting lodge, designed by Sir Edwin Lutyens. It's an atmospheric spot with a colourful history, just a short walk from lovely Trá na Rosann beach. The trade-off for the tranquil setting is that it's 8km north of Downings and there's no public transport.

Beach HOTEL €€
(Óstán na Trá; ☑074-915 5303; www.beachhotel. ie; R248, Downings; s €80-100, d €110-130; ℗ 🐕 🛜) The bright, modern rooms at this large family-run hotel come in calming neutral tones; many have ocean views. You can refuel in its restaurant (mains €12 to €23). It's in Downings, 4km north of Carrigart.

★ Olde Glen Bar & Restaurant MODERN IRISH €€
(☑083 158 5777; www.oldeglen.ie; Glen, Carrigart; mains €18-28; ⊙kitchen 6-9pm daily Jul & Aug, Sat & Sun only Sep-Jun; ☑) Authentic down to its original 1700s stone floor, this traditional pub serves a fine pint, while its farmhouse-style restaurant serves outstanding blackboard specials. Food is sourced locally so expect top-quality seafood, meat and produce. Be sure to book ahead.

Fanad Peninsula

The second-most northerly point in Donegal, Fanad Head thrusts out into the Atlantic to the east of Rosguill. The peninsula curls around the watery expanses of Mulroy Bay to the west, and Lough Swilly to the east, the latter edged with high cliffs and sandy beaches. Most travellers stick to the peninsula's eastern flank, visiting the beautiful beach at Portsalon and the quiet heritage towns of Ramelton and Rathmullan.

Apart from the ferry that runs in summer between Buncrana and Rathmullan, the only way in, around and out of the Fanad Peninsula is behind a steering wheel: hiring a car is the most sensible, if not the only, option.

HIKING THE URRIS HILLS

The Urris Hills, a rugged ridge of resistant quartzite (a continuation of the Knockalla Mountains on the Fanad Peninsula to the southwest), provide grandstand views of the Inishowen coast and the distant hills of Muckish, Errigal and Glenveagh. A network of waymarked walking trails ranges from 2km to 11km in length. Starting points are at Butler's Bridge and the car park at the north end of the Mamore Gap. Ask for the *Urris Walks* leaflet at Buncrana tourist office (p489).

Starting at Glen House (p489), an easy 800m trail leads to the cascading 10m-high **Glenevin Waterfall**, with benches and picnic tables along the way. From Clonmany, follow the road signed to Tullagh Bay, cross the river and bear right at an intersection. Butler's Bridge and the waterfall car park are about 1km further on.

Ramelton

POP 1250

Historic Ramelton (sometimes called Rathmelton) is a picture-perfect spot with rows of Georgian houses and rough-walled stone warehouses curving along the tidal inlet to the River Lennon.

Walk the colourful, picturesque streets and dawdle by the water. It's worth visiting ruined Tullyaughnish Church but also just wandering around the roads by the river, looking at the historic architecture and out over the rotten ribs of decaying boats in the river.

★ **Frewin House**   B&B **€€**

(☑ 074-915 1246; www.frewinhouse.com; Rectory Rd; s €125, d €160-180; ☺Mar-Oct; 🅿🛜) This fine Victorian rectory in secluded grounds would make every weepy heroine's dreams come true. The house combines antique furniture and open fires with contemporary style. The bedrooms are pretty but uncluttered and overlook lush gardens. There's also a self-catering cottage available.

Ardeen House   B&B **€€**

(☑ 074-915 1243; www.ardeenhouse.com; Aughnish Rd; s/d €45/90; 🅿🛜) The warm welcome and homemade scones on arrival at Ardeen House make you feel like you're coming home. Overlooking the river, it has five pleasingly decorated bedrooms, and the breakfasts are copious and tasty. It's on the east edge of town, on the south side of the river, just beyond the town hall.

★ **Bridge Bar**   SEAFOOD **€€**

(☑ 074-915 1119; R245, Bridgend; mains €12-21.50; ☺kitchen 5-8.30pm Fri-Sun, bar 6-11pm daily) The Bridge Bar is one of those lovely old country pubs you specifically came to Ireland to seek out. Its excellent restaurant (open weekend evenings only) has classic Irish steak and seafood dishes: be sure to try the excellent beers from Kinnegar Craft Brewery while you enjoy a trad-music session.

Ramelton Country Market   MARKET

(Castle St; ☺11am-12.30pm Sat) The limited hours mean there's a real scrum to get the best produce, prepared foods, and baked treats at Ramelton's weekly food and craft market. It's in the town hall.

Rathmullan

POP 530

You wouldn't know it while enjoying the views of Lough Swilly, but the refined little port village of Rathmullan has a tranquillity that belies the momentous events that took place here from the 16th to 18th centuries, notably the end of the power of the Irish chieftains with the Flight of the Earls and the conclusion of the old Gaelic order. The village is home to the historic Rathmullan Priory and offers scenic views over Lough Swilly.

History

In 1587 Hugh O'Donnell, the 15-year-old heir to the powerful O'Donnell clan, was tricked into boarding a ship here and taken to Dublin as a prisoner. He escaped four years later on Christmas Eve and, after unsuccessful attempts at revenge, died in Spain, aged only 30.

In 1607, despairing of fighting the English, Hugh O'Neill, the Earl of Tyrone, and Rory O'Donnell, the Earl of Tyrconnell, boarded a ship in Rathmullan harbour and left Ireland for good. This decisive act, known as the Flight of the Earls, marked the effective end of Gaelic Ireland and the rule of Irish chieftains. Large-scale confiscation of their estates took place, preparing for the Plantation of Ulster with settlers from Britain.

It was also in Rathmullan that Wolfe Tone, leader of the 1798 Rising, was captured.

⊙ Sights & Activities

Rathmullan Priory RUINS
(Main St) Dating from 1508 and facing the water, this ivy-cloaked priory was plundered in 1595 and then used as a barracks; in the early 17th century it was semiconverted to a castle.

Donegal Sea Kayaking KAYAKING
(☑086 313 0523; www.donegalseakayaking.com; Fanad; tours adult/child €30/25; ⊙kayak hire 9am-9pm) This mobile kayaking company runs fantastic offshore tours of the lovely Fanad Peninsula with modern kayaks; it also does training and kayak hire. Locations vary by tides and conditions, so check the website for details.

🛏 Sleeping & Eating

Glenalla Lodge B&B €€
(☑074-915 8750; www.glenallalodge.com; Ray; s/d €40/70) This lodge, 8km southwest of Rathmullan, sits in a remote and bucolic spot, with four rooms (three doubles, one family room) furbished with tasteful wooden furniture and rustic style. There's also the helpful knowledge of a local historian on tap.

★Rathmullan House HERITAGE HOTEL €€€
(☑074-915 8188; www.rathmullanhouse.com; off R247; s/d from €90/160, restaurant mains €18-30; ⊙restaurant 1-2.30pm & 6.30-8.30pm, Tap Room 5-9pm Fri-Sun; P@🕏🌊) This country house is large, luxurious and refreshingly dressed with nonfrumpy furnishings. Sprawled over wooded gardens on the shores of Lough Swilly, the original house dates from the 1780s. The best of the 34 rooms have balconies or terraces. There's a tennis court, two bars and a restaurant.

The glass-paned restaurant, the **Cook & Gardener**, uses organic produce from the property's gardens, while the **Tap Room** serves pizzas (€15) and has six different Kinnegar beers on tap.

★Belle's Kitchen IRISH €€
(www.rathmullanrestaurants.com; Pier Rd; mains €15-20; ⊙10am-9pm Jul-Aug, closed Mon Sep-Jun; 🖶) This nautically themed, family-friendly restaurant serves breakfast until noon, then an extensive menu of sandwiches, salads, burgers, fish and chips, cakes and desserts. The fresh local seafood is particularly good (try the Donegal-crab salad) and there are local craft beers and decent coffee too.

ⓘ Getting There & Away

It's best to have a set of wheels to get to Rathmullan. From early June to late September, a car ferry (p489) operates every 80 minutes or so daily between Rathmullan and Buncrana. The first ferry (40 minutes) from Buncrana is at 10am and the last leaves at 6pm; in the other direction, the first boat leaves Rathmullan at 10.40am and the last departs at 6.40pm.

Portsalon & Fanad Head

A spectacular roller coaster of a road hugs the sea cliffs from Rathmullan to Portsalon (Port an tSalainn), passing the early-19th-century Knockalla Fort, one of six built to defend against a possible French invasion – the history is told at its companion, Fort Dunree, across the lough. You'll see the lovely length of Ballymastocker Beach swing gloriously into view, with Portsalon at its northern end.

From Portsalon, the 8km scenic drive to the lighthouse on the rocky tip of Fanad Head is simply beautiful. The lighthouse and its environs are perfect photographing territory.

★Ballymastocker Beach BEACH
(off R246, Portsalon) Once named the second-most beautiful beach in the world by British newspaper the *Observer,* this tawny-coloured Blue Flag beach is a supremely fine place to while away the hours. It is indeed stunning as you drive round the high headland on the R268 and it rears into view, but put the brakes on – there's a viewpoint you can pull into to take mesmerising shots.

Portsalon Golf Club GOLF
(☑074-915 9459; www.portsalongolfclub.com; off R246; green fees €90) The marvellously scenic Portsalon Golf Club follows the curve of the bay, alongside stunning Ballymastocker Beach.

Lighthouse Tavern PUB FOOD €€
(☑074-915 9212; www.facebook.com/fanadlighthousetavern; Araheera; mains lunch €5-9.50, dinner €10.50-22.50; ⊙kitchen 12.30-7.45pm Sun-Fri, to 8.45pm Sat mid-Mar–mid-Sep, Sat & Sun only mid-Sep–mid-Mar) Just before you reach Fanad Lighthouse, this welcoming and excellently located tavern is at hand for decent pub fare: lunchtime sandwiches and soups, plus seafood chowder with homemade bread, fish and chips, scampi, burgers and steaks. If you have special dietary requirements it's best to call ahead.

Inishowen Peninsula

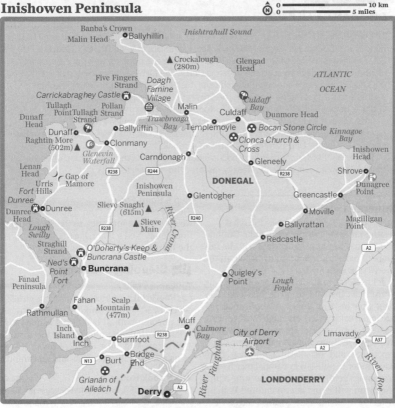

Inishowen Peninsula

The Inishowen Peninsula reaches just far enough into the Atlantic to grab the title of northernmost point on the island of Ireland: Malin Head. It is remote, rugged, desolate and sparsely populated, making it a special and peaceful sort of place. Ancient sites and ruined castles abound, as do traditional thatched cottages that haven't yet been turned into holiday homes.

Surrounded by vast sea loughs and open ocean, Inishowen (meaning 'Island of Eoghain', the chieftain who also gave his name to County Tyrone) attracts a lot of birdlife. The variety is tremendous, with well over 200 resident and migrant species, including well-travelled avian visitors from Iceland, Greenland and North America. Irregular Atlantic winds mean rare and exotic species also blow in from time to time.

Twitchers should visit www.birdsireland.com.

🛈 Getting There & Away

You'll want to be in a car to reach the Inishowen Peninsula; there are a few sporadic bus services and you can get to Magilligan's Point in County Londonderry from Greencastle by ferry, but in the main, you'll need to be driving.

There are two approaches: via Buncrana on the west side of the peninsula to Clonmany, Malin or Culdaff and Malin Head; or immediately east along the lovely southern shore following the R238 to Moville, Greencastle and Inishowen Head before making a route north to Malin Head. You can of course go one way and return by the other.

North West Busways (🖉 074-938 2619; www.northwestbusways.ie) runs three buses daily Monday to Friday and one bus on Saturday between Moville and Letterkenny via Culdaff, Carndonagh, Ballyliffin, Clonmany and Buncrana.

Local Link (p468) bus 955 runs twice daily from Buncrana to Malin Head, via Clonmany, Ballyliffin, Doagh Famine Village, Carndonagh and Malin Town.

GRIANÁN OF AILEÁCH

The amphitheatre-like stone fort of **Grianán of Aileách** (www.heritageireland.ie; off N13, Burt; ⊙9am-8.30pm Jun-Aug, to 7pm May & Sep, 10am-5.30pm Mar & Oct, to 3.30pm Nov-Feb) **FREE** encircles the top of Grianán Hill like a halo with eye-popping views of surrounding loughs. On clear days you can see as far as Derry. The fort may have existed at least 2000 years ago, but it's thought that the site itself goes back to pre-Celtic times as a temple to the god Dagda. Between the 5th and 12th centuries it was the seat of the O'Neills, before being demolished by Murtogh O'Brien, king of Munster.

Most of what you see now is a reconstruction built between 1874 and 1878.

At the foot of the hill is merry-go-round-shaped Burt Church. Built in 1967, it was modelled on the fort by Derry architect Liam McCormack.

The fort is 18km south of Buncrana. Its small arena can resemble a circus whenever a tour bus empties out inside the heavily restored 4m-thick walls.

Buncrana

POP 6800

On the tame side of the peninsula, Buncrana is a busy but appealing town with its fair share of pubs and a long sandy beach on the shores of Lough Swilly.

John Newton, the composer of 'Amazing Grace', was inspired to write his legendary song after his ship the *Greyhound* took refuge in the calm waters of Lough Swilly during a severe storm in 1748. He and his crew were welcomed in Buncrana after their near-death experience and his spiritual journey from slave trader to antislavery campaigner had its beginnings here. He went on to become a prolific hymn writer and later mentored William Wilberforce in his fight against slavery. For more on the story, visit www.amazinggrace.ie.

◉ Sights & Activities

A waymarked Shore Walk heads north for 4.5km along the coast from the park north of the tourist office to **Straghill Strand**, passing to the town's main sights.

O'Doherty's Keep   HISTORIC BUILDING
(Castle Bridge) At the northern end of the seafront, the picture-perfect early-18th-century, six-arched **Castle Bridge** leads to these tower-house ruins originally built by the O'Dohertys, the local chiefs, in 1430. It was burned by the English and then rebuilt for their own use.

Buncrana Castle   HISTORIC BUILDING
(Castle Bridge) At the side of O'Doherty's Keep is the manor-like Buncrana Castle, built in 1718 by John Vaughan, who also constructed the bridge. Wolfe Tone was imprisoned here following the unsuccessful French invasion in 1798. It's closed to the public.

Ned's Point Fort   HISTORIC BUILDING
(Ned's Point) Walk 500m from O'Doherty's Keep (turn left and stick to the shoreline) to find squat Ned's Point Fort (1812), built by the British.

🛏 Sleeping & Eating

Tullyarvan Mill   HOSTEL €
(☑074-936 1613; www.tullyarvanmill.com; off R238; dm/d €17/50; 🖜) Set amid riverside gardens, this purpose-built 51-bed hostel is housed in a modern building attached to the historic Tullyarvan Mill. Just north of town, it also hosts regular cultural events and art exhibits.

Westbrook House   B&B €€
(☑074-936 1067; www.westbrookhouse.ie; Westbrook Rd; s/d from €55/85; 🖜) A handsome Georgian house set in beautiful gardens, Westbrook features chandeliers and antique furniture, giving it a refined sophistication. Cash only. It's right opposite the entrance to **Swan Park**, with a riverside path leading to the waterfront.

Caldra Bed & Breakfast   B&B €€
(☑074-936 3703; www.caldrabandb.com; Pillar Park; s/d from €50/80; 🅿🖜) This large, modern B&B has four spacious rooms ideal for families. The public rooms feature impressive fireplaces and gilt mirrors while guest rooms are more sedate and understated. The garden and patio overlook Lough Swilly and the mountains.

★ Tank & Skinny's   BISTRO €€
(☑074-936 1583; www.facebook.com/tankand skinnysseaside; Swilly Rd; mains lunch €8-10, dinner €12-14.50; ⊙9am-9pm daily Jun-Sep, to 4.30pm Mon-Wed, to 8pm Thu-Sun Oct-May) With picture windows overlooking the lough, this cafe-bistro can easily be your destination for

the day. Breakfast, including fluffy pancakes and freshly baked croissants, is served until midday, followed by a lunch menu of salads and sandwiches and evening burgers and pizzas. There's good coffee and live music on summer weekend evenings.

❶ Information

The **tourist office** (📞074-936 2600; www. visitinishowen.com; Railway Rd; ⊙9.30am-5pm Mon-Fri; 📶) is near the beach and covers the entire peninsula.

❶ Getting There & Away

North West Busways (p487) runs a service between Moville and Letterkenny via Culdaff, Carndonagh, Ballyliffin, Clonmany and Buncrana.

Local Link (p468) bus 955 runs twice daily between Buncrana and Malin Head, via Clonmany, Ballyliffin, Doagh Famine Village, Carndonagh and Malin Town.

McGonagle (📞074-936 1284; www.mcgonaglebushire.com; 29 Main St) runs a bus service to Derry (35 minutes, hourly Monday to Friday, eight on Saturday, two on Sunday).

The **Swilly Ferry** (📞087 211 2331; www.swillyferry.com; adult/car one-way €5/17; ⊙Jun-Sep) to Rathmullan operates seasonally.

Clonmany & Ballyliffin

POP 950

These two quaint villages and their surrounds have plenty to occupy visitors for a day or two. Clonmany has a working atmosphere and lots of characterful pubs, while Ballyliffin feels more upmarket with more hotels and restaurants.

◉ Sights & Activities

Doagh Famine Village MUSEUM
(📞074-938 1901; www.doaghfaminevillage.com; Doagh Island; adult/child €10/6; ⊙10am-5pm mid-Mar–Oct) Set in a reconstructed village of thatched cottages, this open-air museum is packed with interesting tidbits about the tragic Famine of the mid-19th century, and insightful comparisons with famine-stricken countries today. It's worth taking one of the excellent free guided tours, led by knowledgeable local guides who provide fascinating background on aspects of local culture, including Donegal's *poteen*-brewing history and the tradition of funeral wakes. It's about 5km north of Ballyliffin, on Doagh Island (now part of the mainland).

Pollan Strand BEACH
This lovely stretch of beach makes for pleasant walks on the sand; however, the atmospheric crashing breakers make it rather unsafe for swimming.

Tullagh Strand BEACH
Tullagh Strand, 2km northwest of Clonmany, is a little better for swimming than Pollan Strand, although it isn't recommended when the tide's going out.

Ballyliffin Golf Club GOLF
(📞074-937 6119; www.ballyliffingolfclub.com; off R238; green fees €50-200) With two championship courses, the Old Links and the Glashedy Links, Ballyliffin Golf Club is among the best places to play a round of golf in Donegal. The scenery is so beautiful that it can distract even the most focused golfer.

🛏 Sleeping & Eating

⭐**Glen House** GUESTHOUSE €€
(📞074-937 6745; www.glenhouse.ie; Straid, Clonmany; d €90-100; 🅿🖶) Despite the grand surroundings and luxurious rooms, you'll find neither pretension nor high prices at this gem of a guesthouse, where rooms are a lesson in restrained sophistication and the setting is totally tranquil. Rooms at the front have gorgeous views of the lough, and the walking trail to Glenevin Waterfall and the Urris Hills is right next door.

Ballyliffin Lodge & Spa HOTEL €€
(📞074-937 8200; www.ballyliffinlodge.com; off R238, Ballyliffin; s/d from €80/110; 🖶🌊) This rather grand 40-room hotel is set back from the tiny village, with superior rooms looking out onto sublime ocean views. You can treat yourself at the state-of-the-art spa, to a round or two of golf, or to a meal in the relaxed bar.

Rusty Nail GASTROPUB €€
(📞074-937 6116; Clonmany; mains €12-20; ⊙kitchen 4-11.30pm Fri, to 12.30am Sat, 2-11pm Sun) While you might be tempted to sun yourself at the picnic table out the front, you should step inside this atmospheric pub for an excellent meal – it has all the classics and they're great. There's often live music too. It's just west of town.

Malin Head

POP 92

The rolling swells never stop coming across the sea at Malin Head, the island's northern extreme. It's a name familiar to sailors and meteorological buffs, as Malin Head is one of the weather stations mentioned in BBC Radio's daily shipping forecast. You can almost imagine you can see Iceland (you can't) as you peer out through sometimes perfectly crystal blue but ever-blustery skies, which can change from sun to squall at the drop of a sou'wester. The rolling grasslands are dotted with suitably thick-coated donkeys, cows and well-wrapped-up hikers.

On the northernmost tip of Malin Head is Banba's Crown.

The small but very pretty village of Malin, on Trawbreaga Bay, 14km southeast of Malin Head, has a charmingly sedate movie-set quality, arranged around a neat, triangular village green.

◉ Sights & Activities

★ Banba's Crown   VIEWPOINT
(Malin Head) On the northernmost tip of Malin Head, called Banba's Crown, stands a cumbersome 1805 clifftop tower that was built by the British admiralty and later used as a Lloyds signal station. Around it are concrete huts that were used by the Irish army in WWII as lookout posts. To the west from the fort-side car park, a path leads 700m to Hell's Hole, a chasm where the incoming waters crash against the rock forms.

The view to the west takes in, from left to right, the Inishowen Hills, Dunaff Head, low-lying Fanad Head with its lighthouse, the twin 'horns' of Horn Head and the twin bumps of Tory Island; in the far distance, to the left of Fanad lighthouse, are Muckish and Errigal Mountains. To the east lie raised beach terraces, and offshore you can see the lighthouse on the remote island of Inishtrahull. A viewing area has coin-operated telescopes. On a few nights a year you can even see the Northern Lights.

WASHED-UP TREASURES

Beachcombers will find more than empty shells along the Inishowen coast. The area is renowned for its raised beaches, stranded above the high-water mark by postglacial uplift, and littered with semi-precious stones: cornelian, agate, jasper and more. You'll see them on the beaches along the northern coast of Malin Head, near Banba's Crown and Ballyhillin, but don't be tempted to pocket your finds: removing stones from the beach is illegal.

Watch for the truck-based Caffe Banba that is sometimes in the car park selling superb coffees and baked goods. The car park itself can get quickly crowded with cars during the busy season.

Malin Head Tours   TOURS
(☏ 087 458 0033; www.malinheadcommunity.ie/malin-head-tours; off R242, Malin Head Community Centre; ⊘noon Sat) Unlock the secrets of this blustery region on these fascinating driving, walking and boat tours. Book ahead.

🛏 Sleeping & Eating

★ Sandrock Holiday Hostel   HOSTEL €
(☏ 086 325 6323; www.sandrockhostel.com; Port Ronan Pier, Malin Head; dm €15; ☏) The cinematic view from this IHH hostel – at the end of the road, above a rocky bay on the western side of the headland – will take your breath away. Inside are 20 beds in two dorms, plus musical instruments and laundry facilities. There's a good kitchen and a cosy lounge with telescopes on hand for spotting basking sharks and dolphins.

Bike rental (€10 per day) is available. Ask about the very limited community-bus connections to get here.

Whitestrand B&B   B&B €
(☏ 086 822 9163, 074-937 0335; www.whitestrand.net; off R242, Middletown; s €35-37, d €70-74; ☏) Perfectly placed amid the bluffs and hills leading to Malin Head, this comfy B&B has three fine bedrooms. As a welcome you'll receive a hot beverage and tasty home-baked treats.

★ Wild Strands Caife   CAFE €
(☏ 085 105 3893; www.malinheadcommunity.ie/wild-strands-caife; Carnmalin, Malin Head Community Centre; flatbread €9-11; ⊘10am-5pm Fri, Sat & Mon, 11am-4pm Sun; ☏) At the Malin Head Community Centre on the road to Malin Head, Wild Strands Caife is a worthwhile stop for delicious, home-cooked organic food. The menu features flatbreads cooked in the wood-fired oven and topped with seasonal, local ingredients (including vegan options), freshly baked seaweed scones, coffee and brownies. All the food is cooked with locally harvested seaweed.

Caffe Banba   CAFE €
(☏ 074-937 0538; www.caffebanba.com; baked goods €1-2.50; ⊘10am-6pm Easter-Sep) From Easter to September, this little three-wheeler climbs the hill to Banba's Crown, providing coffee, hot chocolate and baked goodies to travellers at Ireland's northernmost tip.

FORT DUNREE

The best preserved and most dramatic of six forts built by the British on Lough Swilly, **Fort Dunree** (☑ 074-936 1817; www.dunree.pro.ie; Dunree Head; adult/child €7/5; ☺ 10.30am-4.30pm Mon-Fri, noon-5pm Sat & Sun) was built following the 1798 Rising of the United Irishmen (which was supported by France), when fears of a French invasion were at fever pitch.

The original fort, built in 1813, houses a military museum, while the surrounding headland is littered with WWI and WWII remains you can explore. There are several good waymarked walks. The Saldanha Suite houses a wildlife discovery room.

The winding fjord of Lough Swilly is one of Ireland's great natural harbours, and has played its part in many historical dramas, from Viking invasions and the Flight of the Earls to the 1798 Rising and WWI.

Huge naval guns were added to the fort in the late 19th century, and during WWI the lough was used as a marshalling area for Atlantic convoys, and as an anchorage for the Royal Navy's Grand Fleet. Unusually, it remained in British hands after the partition of Ireland in 1922, and was only handed over to the Republic of Ireland in 1938.

ⓘ Getting There & Away

You'll need a car to get up here. The best way to approach Malin Head is by the R238/242 from Carndonagh, rather than up the rough road along the eastern side from Culdaff.

Local Link (p468) bus 955 runs twice daily to and from Buncrana to Malin Head, via Clonmany, Ballyliffin, Doagh Famine Village, Carndonagh and Malin Town.

The car park can get full quickly in summer.

Culdaff & Around

POP 270

Sheep vastly outnumber people around the secluded beach village of Culdaff, situated on the remote north coast of Inishowen. If isolation is what you are after, make a beeline here.

★**Culdaff Beach**   BEACH
(off R238) This Blue Flag beach is great for swimming and windsurfing. You can wander its gorgeous length and get lost in the grassy sand dunes, and there's a fun playground for kids too. Lifeguards are on duty from June to September. There's an annual New Year's Day charity swim in the freezing water, which is a hoot.

Clonca Church & Cross   HISTORIC SITE
(Clonca) The gable ends and huge windows of the roofless shell of 17th-century Clonca Church frame views of the Donegal mountains. Inside there is an intricately carved tombstone sporting a sword and hurling-stick motif. Outside, the remains of the cross show the miracle of the loaves and fishes on the eastern face. Heading from Culdaff towards Moville on the R238, turn east after 1.2km at Bocan Church. The Clonca Church

and cross are 1.7km to the north behind some farm buildings.

★**McGrory's of Culdaff**   GUESTHOUSE €€
(☑ 074-937 9104; www.mcgrorys.ie; Malin Rd/R238; s/d from €84/118, mains €14-18; ☺ kitchen 12.30-9pm; ☎) This landmark hotel and bar has 17 bright, modern rooms. Catch live music in the **Backroom**, which books international singer-songwriters and traditional music. McGrory's classic Irish cuisine, served in the **Front Room**, is the best for miles around; the seafood chowder with homemade Guinness bread is especially good. There's an excellent selection of local craft beers and speciality gins too.

Greencastle

POP 820

Seals bob their heads in the hopes of a fish in the busy little fishing port of Greencastle. The sublime 14th-century Northburgh Castle was a supply base for English armies in Scotland, and for this reason was attacked by Robert Bruce in the 1320s. The castle's ivy-shrouded hulk survives – its dark-green stone gives the town its name – surrounded by residential units.

**Inishowen Maritime
Museum & Planetarium**   MUSEUM
(☑ 074-938 1363; www.inishowenmaritime.com; off R241; adult/child museum €5/3, museum & planetarium show €10/6; ☺ 9.30am-5pm Mon-Fri year-round, plus to 5.30pm Sat & from noon Sun Easter-Sep) An eccentric collection of artefacts awaits at this museum in a former coastguard station on a grassy verge right by the waterfront. The most fascinating exhibits are from the

sunken wrecks of Lough Foyle, the displays exploring the demise of the Spanish Armada and the examples of Drontheim fishing boats, once widely used along Ireland's north coast. There's also an astronomy show in the full-dome digital theatre at the Planetarium.

A welcoming **cafe** with tables out the front is right next door. If the sun's out, grab a coffee and savour the harbour views.

★**Kealy's Seafood Bar** SEAFOOD €€
(☑074-938 1010; www.kealysseafoodbar.ie; The Harbour; mains €16-29, early-bird set menu €24-28.50; ⊙12.30-3pm & 5-9.30pm Wed-Sun; 🛜🎔) Family-run for over 25 years, this bistro offers locally caught seafood so fresh you almost have to fight the harbourside seals for it. Its unpretentious nautical-style polished-timber decor belies its numerous culinary awards. It's a splendid spot for anything from a bowl of chowder to monkfish tagine, and every meal has a side serve of delicious views.

The early-bird menu is served from 5pm to 6.30pm every day except Saturday.

Malin Pebbles ARTS & CRAFTS
(☑074-938 1432; www.malinpebbles.com; Church Brae; ⊙hours vary) Local semiprecious stones are transformed into lovely jewellery and unusual gifts by Petra Watzka at her workshop, 100m uphill from the ferry – check the website for exact directions. Call ahead to see if it's open.

Moville & Around

POP 1500

Little more than a tight cluster of streets above an all-business jetty, Moville is a neat little town with old, well-kept buildings. It can be sleepy, but on holiday weekends tourists flood in. Moville was a busy port during the 19th and early 20th centuries, when thousands of emigrants set sail for America from here.

A good reason to stop is to walk the scenic 4km coastal walkway to Greencastle.

Coastal Walkway WALKING
This terrific 4km coastal walkway from Moville to Greencastle takes in the stretch of coast where the emigrant steamers used to moor; there are sublime views along the way.

Inish Adventures WATER SPORTS
(☑087 220 2577; www.inishadventures.com; shore front; 1hr taster €20, half-day tour €40) Offers sea kayaking, stand-up paddle boarding and sailing tours, courses and equipment hire. It is based at the waterfront, but call ahead to check opening times and make a booking.

★**Moville Boutique Hostel** HOSTEL €
(☑074-938 2378; www.movilleboutiquehostel.com; off R238; campsites per person €15, s €40-50, d €70-80, apt €100; 🛜) A small lane leads off the R238, 300m north of town, to a grove of trees and this secluded farmhouse. It's in a nook-and-cranny-filled 18th-century building beside a stream, with some gorgeous spots to pitch a tent. It has a mix of doubles and family rooms, some are split-level, each with a different colour theme and attached bathroom. Includes breakfast.

Breakfast is a self-catering choice of teas, coffees, milk, breakfast cereals and organic sourdough bread, and guests can use the kitchen to prepare meals. The owner is a fount of information on the area's rich history and folklore.

Redcastle Hotel & Spa HOTEL €€
(☑074-938 5555; www.redcastlehoteldonegal. com; R238, Redcastle; s/d from €90/140; 🛜🐕) The peninsula's smartest luxury resort is on the coast 7km southwest of Moville, tucked away off the main road. The 93 rooms are comfortable and spacious; some look straight out to the water. Restaurants include the **Edge**, which has excellent views and modern Irish cuisine.

Facilities include a nine-hole golf course, spa, swimming pool and kids' club during summer.

❶ Getting There & Away

North West Busways (p487) runs three buses daily from Monday and Friday and one bus on Saturday between Moville and Letterkenny, via Culdaff, Carndonagh, Ballyliffin, Clonmany and Buncrana.

The Midlands

POP 358,016 / AREA 10,790 SQ KM

Best Places to Eat

➜ Oarsman (p496)

➜ Spinners on Castle St (p511)

➜ Glasson Village Restaurant (p506)

➜ Hatters Lane Bistro (p505)

➜ Keenans Hotel (p500)

➜ Drumanilra Farm Kitchen (p502)

Best Places to Stay

➜ Lough Key House (p502)

➜ Castle Durrow (p518)

➜ Roundwood House (p519)

➜ Lough Rynn (p495)

➜ Ballyfin House (p519)

➜ Maltings Guesthouse (p510)

Why Go?

If you're in search of a genuine slice of rural Irish life, you'll find it here in the country's heart. Often bypassed by visitors, the Midlands region brims with verdant pastoral landscapes, stately homes, archaeological treasures, sacred monastic sites, lakeside vistas and sleepy towns where the locals are genuinely glad to see you.

Getting lost along the twisting back roads of these six counties is an unhurried pleasure and you're virtually guaranteed to happen upon a local village shop, pub, garage or post office that's scarcely changed in decades. The region is refreshingly free of tour buses and souvenir stalls and well worth at least a pause in your journeys.

The River Shannon dominates the Midlands, meandering through fields and forests, drawing boaters and anglers in shoals. Stylish hotels and gourmet restaurants continue to spring up along its banks, making it a wonderfully scenic and surprisingly cosmopolitan way to travel.

When to Go

➜ Spring is a great time for revelling in Ireland's famous greener-than-green countryside, reflected in the many waterways and lakes, and accented by fields of wildflowers.

➜ During summer, fairs, festivals and special events take place throughout the region as locals spend the long days outside.

➜ July and August are the ideal time for cruising the Shannon with everything open, better weather and a spirited summertime crowd in the riverside pubs and restaurants.

➜ Many museums and other attractions are closed or have greatly reduced hours during the short days from November to March.

The Midlands Highlights

1 Shannon–Erne Waterway (p495) Slowing down a gear while cruising through the Midlands' rolling landscapes.

2 Clonmacnoise (p513) Contemplating the lost land of saints and scholars at Ireland's finest monastic site.

3 Rindoon (p506) Taking a lakeside stroll through this deserted medieval village.

4 Birr (p509) Roaming the Georgian streets and exploring the castle grounds in this elegant town.

5 Strokestown Park (p499) Learning about Ireland's greatest disaster at the harrowing Famine Museum.

6 Corlea (p502) Exploring the amazing Iron Age oak trackway unearthed here.

7 Belvedere House & Gardens (p506) Wandering the magnificent corridors and rambling lakeside gardens of this 18th-century estate.

8 Fore Valley (p508) Visiting this emerald-green valley and discovering impressive Christian ruins and other-worldly views.

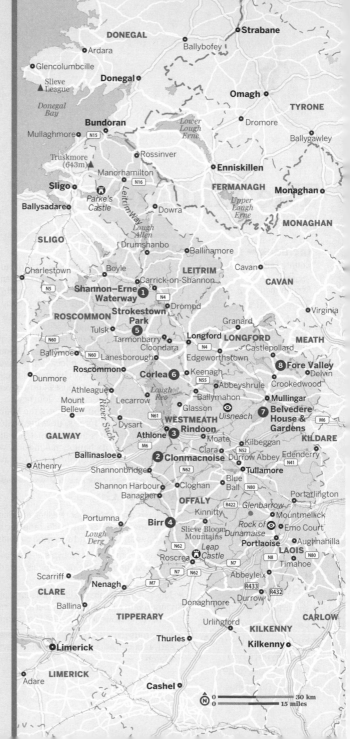

COUNTY LEITRIM

County Leitrim's untamed landscape and authentic rural charm are cherished by those who call it home. Leitrim was ravaged by the Famine in the 19th century and spent subsequent generations struggling with mass emigration and unemployment, but while today it's Ireland's least populated county, it's a hideaway for artists, writers and musicians, and a popular boating centre.

Virtually split in two by Lough Allen, the county is traversed by the mighty River Shannon, which remains its biggest draw. Lively Carrick-on-Shannon, the county town, makes a great base for exploring the region by road or water. Leitrim provides a vital link between Counties Sligo and Donegal, via a 4.7km stretch of the Wild Atlantic Way (N15) where Leitrim meets the ocean.

Carrick-on-Shannon

POP 4062

Since the completion of the Shannon–Erne Waterway, the marina at this charming riverside town has thrived. Carrick-on-Shannon is a hugely popular weekend destination with a good choice of accommodation and restaurants, and a great music and arts scene.

During the 17th and most of the 18th centuries Carrick was a Protestant enclave, and the local residents' wealth can still be seen in the graceful buildings around the town.

◉ Sights

The waterfront is the number-one draw, but Carrick also has some wonderful examples of early-19th-century architecture on St George's Terrace, including **Hatley Manor**, home of the St George family, and the **Old Courthouse**, which now contains the Leitrim Design House (p497) and Dock Arts Centre (p496).

Costello Memorial Chapel   CHAPEL
(www.carrickonshannonparish.com; cnr Bridge & Main Sts; ◔9am-6pm) Measuring just 5m by 3.6m, Ireland's smallest chapel was built in 1877 by Edward Costello, distraught at the early death of his wife, Mary. Both husband and wife now rest within the grey limestone interior lit by a single stained-glass window. Their embalmed bodies were placed in lead coffins, which sit on either side of the door. If the door is locked ask at St George's Heritage Centre for the key.

St George's Heritage Centre   MUSEUM
(☑071-962 1757; www.carrickheritage.com; St Mary's Close; adult/child €5/1.50, with workhouse tour €10/7.50; ◔10am-5pm Mon-Sat) Up the hill in a restored 1827-built church, this heritage centre looks at the history and landscape of Leitrim from old Gaelic traditions through to Plantation times. Bronze plaques lead 800m northeast to the old Famine workhouse, which remains a bleak memorial to desperate times, as well as the Famine Garden of Remembrance; both are visitable by guided tours arranged in advance.

🕭 Activities

Carrick is the Shannon–Erne Waterway's boat-hire capital, with several companies based at the marina. The canal's 16 locks are fully automated, you don't need a licence, and you're given full instructions on handling your boat before you set off.

Moon River   CRUISE
(☑071-962 1777; www.moonriver.ie; The Marina; cruises €15; ◔Mar-Oct) The 110-seat boat *Moon River* runs one-hour cruises on the Shannon. There are one to four sailings, depending on the season; check the information board at the quay or online for times.

Emerald Star   BOATING
(☑071-962 7633; www.emeraldstar.ie; The Marina; boat hire per 24hr from €110; ◔9am-6pm Mon-Fri, 10am-4pm Sat) Emerald Star's huge range of boats range from budget options through to luxury eight-berth cruisers. There's a minimum three-night rental.

🛏 Sleeping

★Lough Rynn   CASTLE €€
(☑071-963 2700; www.loughrynn.ie; Lough Rynn, Mohill; d/ste from €125/255; P❄🛜) Between Lough Rynn and Lough Errew, 21km southeast of Carrick-on-Shannon, this magnificent early-19th-century property sits amid 120 hectares with nature trails and a walled garden. Antique-filled rooms have underfloor heating; 16 are located in the former manager's residence, while 28 are in the castle itself, including two sumptuous suites – one with a Jacuzzi and private crenellated roof terrace.

Local produce stars at its stone-walled restaurant, serving lunch as well as four-course evening menus (€65). At the bottom of a staircase, a secret door leads to the fabulously atmospheric dungeon bar.

Lock View House
B&B €€

(☑ 071-9640790; www.bedandbreakfastleitrim.com; R209, Kilclare; s/d/tr from €45/86/100; P ⓐ) A country retreat 11km northeast of Carrick, this lovely B&B has four large rooms (three with attached private bathroom, one with a separate but private bathroom), while beds range from twins to kings. Tea and cakes are served on arrival. True to its name, you can watch boats navigate the nearby lock on the Shannon–Erne Waterway. Two-night minimum stay.

Bush Hotel
HOTEL €€

(☑ 071-967 1000; www.bushhotel.com; Main St; s/d/tr/f from €69/109/135/150; ⓐ) Dating from the 18th century, this family-run place is one of Ireland's oldest in-town hotels. Black-and-white photos abound in the public spaces, while the 60 rooms, split between the original building and modern rear wing, are more contemporary. Irish history buffs can check into the Michael Collins room (Room 1), where the independence leader stayed in 1917.

Family rooms come with a double and two single beds.

Cryan's Hotel
HOTEL €€

(☑ 071-967 2066; www.cryanshotel.ie; Bridge Lane; s/d/tr from €65/110/160; ⓐ) Right by the riverfront, Cryan's is popular with boaters as well as tourists. The modern facade is nothing special, but the 24 rooms are large and well equipped with timber furnishings, sofas and plenty of storage space, and many have water views. A relative runs the pub of the same name around the corner.

✖ Eating

Lena's Tea Room
CAFE €

(☑ 071-962 2791; www.lenastearoom.ie; Main St; dishes €2.70-7; ☺ 10am-5pm Tue-Thu, to 5.30pm Fri & Sat; ⓐ) Decked out with 1920s-vintage-style decor and comfy sofas, with jazz playing in the background, this cute cafe makes everything in-house daily, including breads, plus soups, savoury tarts and sandwiches. Afternoon tea is a speciality with loose-leaf teas served in china cups accompanied by cakes and scones.

★ Oarsman
GASTROPUB €€

(☑ 071-962 1733; www.theoarsman.com; Bridge St; mains lunch €10-15, dinner €15-27; ☺ kitchen noon-9pm Tue-Thu, to 9.30pm Fri & Sat, bar to midnight; ⓐ) 🖉 Dating from 1781 and run by the seventh generation, this upmarket pub serves seasonal and locally sourced dishes, from gourmet lunchtime sandwiches (eg chicken and pesto on garlic and rosemary bread or maple- and soy-marinated pork on brioche) to evening mains like beetroot- and apple-glazed pork belly with salt-baked celeriac. Irish microbrews include local Carrig Brewing beers.

Cottage
BISTRO €€

(☑ 071-962 5933; www.cottagerestaurant.ie; off N4, Jamestown; mains €18-28; ☺ 6-10pm Thu-Sat, noon-4pm & 6-10pm Sun) Set in a small whitewashed cottage by the River Shannon, 5km southeast of Carrick, this humble-looking place belies its innovative Irish-Asian fusion cuisine. Utilising vegetables from the restaurant garden, meats from local suppliers and west-coast seafood, chef Sham Hanifa's seasonal dishes might include goji berry–glazed duck with miso crème or tandoori lamb shoulder with crispy coconut.

Vittos Restaurant & Wine Bar
ITALIAN €€

(☑ 071-962 7000; www.vittosrestaurant.com; Bridge St; mains €14-24; ☺ 5-9pm Wed-Fri, 1-10pm Sat & Sun; 🖷) In a stone building within the Market Yard Centre, this family-friendly restaurant has an extensive menu of classic Italian dishes, including great pasta and pizza. Burgers and steaks are chargrilled; gluten-free, vegan and kids' menus are available.

🍺 Drinking & Entertainment

Pubs are plentiful. Look for beers by locally based Carrig Brewing; its Poachers Pale Ale and Coalface Black IPA – among others – are superb.

Flynn's Corner House
PUB

(cnr Main & Bridge Sts; ☺ 10.30am-11.30pm Mon-Thu, to 12.30am Fri & Sat, noon-11pm Sun) Renovated in 2018 but retaining its polished timber bar and wood-burning stove, Carrick's landmark corner pub serves a grand pint of Guinness. Live music (all genres) plays during the week year-round as well as on weekends in summer.

Anderson's Thatch Pub
PUB

(☑ 087 228 3288; www.andersonspub.com; Elphin Rd; ☺ 8pm-12.30am) You can hardly miss this traditional thatched pub 4.5km south of town while driving along the R368 towards Elphin. Dating from 1734, it's worth a trip for its live-music sessions (Wednesday, Friday and Saturday), old-world atmosphere and country charm. Hours can vary.

Dock Arts Centre
ARTS CENTRE

(☑ 071-965 0828; www.thedock.ie; St George's Tce; ☺ art exhibitions 10am-6pm Mon-Fri, to 5pm Sat) Set in the grand surroundings of the

19th-century former courthouse, this place hosts performances, concerts, art exhibitions and workshops. Its design shop sells quality arts and crafts.

🛍 Shopping

Market Yard Centre ARTS & CRAFTS
(off Bridge St; ⊙ shop hours vary, farmers market 10am-2pm Thu) In the town centre, these restored 19th-century market buildings now house shops selling everything from nautical gear to crafts. Don't miss the **farmers market**, which draws an impressive array of organic farmers, bakers and food producers.

Leitrim Design House ARTS & CRAFTS
(☑ 071-965 0550; www.leitrimdesignhouse.ie; St George's Tce; ⊙ 10am-6pm Mon-Thu, from 11am Fri, 11am-5pm Sat) Downstairs from the Dock Arts Centre in the 19th-century former courthouse, this retail gallery is a showcase for textiles, ceramics, paintings, toys and gifts from local craftspeople.

❶ Information

The **tourist office** (☑ 071-962 0170; www.leitrimtourism.com; Old Barrel Store, Quay Rd; ⊙ 10am-4pm Mon-Fri, to 5pm Sat & Sun Apr-Sep) has a good walking-tour brochure that takes in Carrick's places of interest.

❶ Getting There & Away

Bus Éireann (www.buseireann.ie) runs from Dublin (€20, 2¾ hours, six daily) via Carrick-on-Shannon to Sligo (€13.50, 50 minutes).

Irish Rail (www.irishrail.ie) runs from Dublin (€15, 2¼ hours, every two hours) via Carrick to Sligo (€9.50, 45 minutes). The station is on Croghan Rd, 1km southwest of the town centre.

North Leitrim

North of Carrick-on-Shannon, the Leitrim landscape comes into its own, with ruffled hills, steel-grey lakes including expansive Lough Gill, and isolated rural cottages. If you fancy taking to the hills on foot, the Leitrim Way walking trail begins in Drumshanbo and ends in Manorhamilton, a distance of 48km.

★ **Parke's Castle** CASTLE
(☑ 071-916 4149; www.heritageireland.ie; off R286, Kilmore; adult/child €5/3; ⊙ 10am-6pm Easter-Sep) The tranquil surrounds of Parke's Castle, with swans drifting by on Lough Gill and neat grass cloaking the old moat, belie the fact that its early Plantation architecture, dating from

the 16th and 17th centuries, was created out of an unwelcome English landlord's insecurity and fear. The restored, three-storey castle forms part of one of the five sides of the *bawn* (area surrounded by walls outside the main castle), which also has three rounded turrets at its corners. It's 11km east of Sligo town.

Rose of Innisfree CRUISE
(☑ 087 259 8869; www.roseofinnisfree.com; Parke's Castle, Kilmore; 1/2hr cruise adult €15/20, child €7.50/10; ⊙ 12.30pm & 3.30pm Easter-Oct) Departing from Parke's Castle, cruises on Lough Gill enjoy the best view of the lough and its island, Innisfree. Trips feature live recitals of Yeats' poetry, and good coffee and fresh scones are available on board. From July to mid-August, additional, longer tours make a stop in Sligo town.

COUNTY ROSCOMMON

Studded with megalithic tombs, ring forts and mounds, Roscommon is shrouded in myth and history. Other historical highlights of this underrated county include restored mansions, monastic ruins and some superb museums. Beyond the romance of times past, Roscommon's rolling countryside is splashed with lakes and cleaved by the Rivers Shannon and Suck, providing fantastic fishing and boating opportunities.

Roscommon Town

POP 5876
The county town of Roscommon is very much a place of local business and commerce, but it has a small, stately centre and some significant and picturesque abbey and castle ruins that make it worth exploration.

◎ Sights & Activities

Roscommon's central square is dominated by its former **courthouse** (now the Bank of Ireland). Opposite, the facade of the **old jail** survives. The principal sights, however, are Roscommon Castle, Roscommon Dominican Priory and the County Museum (p497).

Pick up a brochure and map at tourist offices detailing the **Suck Valley Way**, a 75km walking trail along the River Suck, including some shorter strolls along the river's banks.

★ **Roscommon County Museum** MUSEUM
(☑ 090-662 5613; www.roscommontownheritage.com; The Square; adult/child €2/1; ⊙ 10am-5pm

ARIGNA MINERS WAY & HISTORICAL TRAIL

Covering 128km of north Roscommon, east Sligo and mid-Leitrim, the Miners Way & Historical Trail is a series of well-signposted tracks and hill passes covering the routes taken by miners on their way to work. The route usually takes around five days to complete; a brochure with maps is available from local tourist offices.

Mon-Sat May-Sep) Set in a former Presbyterian church (1863), this volunteer-run museum has an idiosyncratic collection, including an inscribed 9th-century slab from St Coman's monastery and a superb medieval sheila-na-gig (carved female figure with exaggerated genitalia) symbol. The unusual stained-glass Star of David window, representing the Trinity, above the door is another draw. Don't leave without hearing the story of Lady Betty, the 18th-century hanging woman.

The museum also acts as an unofficial tourist office.

Roscommon Castle　　　　CASTLE, RUINS
(www.visitroscommon.com; Castle Lane; ◇dawn-dusk) The impressive ruins of the town's Norman castle stand alone in a field to the north of town, beautifully framed by the landscaped lawns and small lake of the town park. Built in 1269, the castle was almost immediately destroyed by Irish forces, and its turbulent history continued until the final surrender to Cromwell's forces in 1652, who took down the fortifications. A conflagration in 1690 sealed the castle's fate.

Roscommon Dominican Priory　　RUINS
(off Circular Rd; ◇dawn-dusk) At the south end of town, the remains of a 13th-century priory are almost hidden behind a primary school. It merits a quick visit for its unusual 15th-century carving of eight *gallógli* ('gallowglasses' or mercenary soldiers) wielding seven swords and an axe.

🛏 Sleeping & Eating

**Gleeson's Townhouse
& Restaurant**　　　　　　　HOTEL €€
(📞090-662 6954; www.gleesonstownhouse.com; The Square; s/d/tr/ste from €49/89/105/119; 🅿🛜) Set back from the square in its own courtyard, this 19th-century townhouse has 25 individually decorated rooms ranging from simple affairs with pine furniture and buttercup-yellow walls to more extravagant rooms with floral wallpaper, cushions and curtains. The smallest singles are tiny at just 10 sq metres, while suites are a whopping 32 sq metres. Its restaurant is the best in town.

**Gleeson's Restaurant &
Artisan Food & Wine Shop**　　　BISTRO €€
(📞090-662 6954; www.gleesonstownhouse.com; The Square; cafe dishes €4.50-9.50, restaurant mains €13-25; ◇cafe & deli 7.30am-6pm, restaurant noon-9pm; 🛜🖥) Local grass-fed lamb is the speciality of Gleeson's elegant restaurant, particularly the stew with rosemary and thyme. Its more casual cafe serves full Irish breakfasts, porridge and pancakes, followed by lunch dishes like black pudding and organic beetroot salad, seafood chowder, and chargrilled steak sandwiches with caramelised onion and blue cheese.

Kids get an activity-sheet menu featuring dishes (€6.50 to €8.50) like mini beef burgers.

The shop has an array of sweet and savoury pastries, premade salads, cured meats and cheeses, as well as wines, that are ideal to take for a picnic during your explorations of the county's ancient sites.

❶ Information

The county museum is an unofficial tourist office; also check out www.visitroscommon.com.

❶ Getting There & Away

Bus Éireann (www.buseireann.ie) runs four buses daily between Westport (€14, 2¼ hours) and Athlone (€8, 30 minutes).

Roscommon train station is in Abbeytown, on the southwestern side of town. Irish Rail (www.irishrail.ie) runs five trains daily on the line from Dublin (€15, two hours) to Westport (€11.70, 1½ hours).

Strokestown & Around

POP 825

Strokestown's main street is a grand tree-lined avenue that remains a testament to the lofty aspirations of one of the landed gentry who wished it to be Europe's widest. It's a striking feature in what is now a sleepy town most notable for its historic estate and unmissable Famine Museum and Strokestown Park.

Add in the nearby ancient Celtic site of Rathcroghan and you can easily spend a day exploring the area.

◉ Sights

★ Strokestown Park HISTORIC SITE
(☑ 071-963 3013; www.strokestownpark.ie; off N5; adult/child house & Famine Museum €14/6, gardens free; ⊙ 10.30am-5.30pm mid-Mar–Oct, to 4pm Nov–mid-Mar, tours noon, 2.30pm, 4pm mid-Mar–Oct, 2pm Nov–mid-Mar, gardens dawn-dusk) At the end of Strokestown's main avenue, triple Gothic arches lead to Strokestown Park House. The original 120-sq-km estate was granted by King Charles II to Nicholas Mahon for his support in the English Civil War. Nicholas' grandson Thomas commissioned Richard Cassels to build him a Palladian mansion in the early 18th century. The gardens give some idea of the original wealth. Admission to the house is by a 50-minute guided tour, which includes the stable-housed Irish National Famine Museum.

The guided tours also take in a galleried kitchen with original ovens dating from 1740, a schoolroom with an exercise book of neatly written dictation dating from 1934 (and, according to her red pen, deemed disgraceful by the governess), and a toy room complete with 19th-century toys and funhouse mirrors.

Over the centuries, the estate decreased in size along with the family's fortunes. When it was eventually sold in 1979, it had been whittled down to (a still vast) 120 hectares. The estate was bought as a complete lot, so virtually all its remaining contents are intact. The walled garden contains the longest herbaceous border in Ireland, which blooms in a rainbow of colours in summer. Look out too for a folly and a lily pond.

There is a small cafe on-site.

Irish National Famine Museum MUSEUM
(☑ 071-963 3013; www.strokestownpark.ie; Strokestown Park; adult/child incl Strokestown Park €14/6; ⊙ 10.30am-5.30pm mid-Mar–Oct, to 4pm Nov–mid-Mar) In direct and deliberate contrast to the splendour of Strokestown Park is the harrowing Irish National Famine Museum, located in the Stables Yard of the house, which documents the devastating 1840s potato blight. It concisely shows how the industrial age coupled with the Famine devastated the island of eight million (about 1.6 million more than today). Strokestown landlord Major Denis Mahon ruthlessly evicted starving tenants who couldn't pay their rent, chartering boats to transport them away from Ireland.

Around half of these 1000 emigrants died on the overcrowded 'coffin ships', and a further 200 perished while in quarantine in Québec (the cheapest route). Perhaps unsurprisingly, Mahon was assassinated by three of his tenants in 1847 (two of whom were publicly hanged in Roscommon). The gun they used is on display. There's a huge amount of information and you can easily spend an hour or more; exhibits here rise above mere lore thanks to more than 50,000 documents that were preserved from the 19th century and which provide often chilling factual underpinning. You'll emerge with an unblinking insight into the starvation of the poor, and the ignorance, callousness and cruelty of those who were in a position to help.

Guided tours of Strokestown Park's house also take in the Famine Museum.

★ Rathcroghan HISTORIC SITE
(☑ 071-963 9268; www.rathcroghan.ie; N5, Tulsk; adult/child museum €5/3, incl site tour €14/6; ⊙ museum & visitor centre 9am-5pm Mon-Sat year-round, plus noon-4pm Sun May-Aug) Anyone with an interest in Celtic mythology will be enthralled by this area around the village of Tulsk. Containing 60 ancient national monuments, including standing stones, barrows, huge cairns and monumental fortresses, it is Europe's most important Celtic royal site, and the landscape and sacred structures have lain largely undisturbed for the past 3000 years. Site tours lasting 45 minutes take place twice daily from June to August.

Tulsk is 11km west of Strokestown. Bus Éireann's Dublin-to-Westport service stops outside.

It's hard to grasp just how significant Rathcroghan is, as archaeological digs are continuing, but it has already been established that the site is bigger and older than Tara in County Meath and was at one time a major seat of Irish power. The excellent visitor centre is the place to start. It has diagrams, photographs, informative panels and maps that explain the significance of the sites, and it can let you know when access to the monuments is possible (some are privately owned). Most are along a 6km stretch of the N5 to the west. Rathmore and Rathcroghan Mound both have public access and parking.

A 15-minute video includes an introduction to the sites and legends, plus an animated story about the legend of the Táin Bó Cúailnge (Cattle Raid of Cooley), which should appeal to all ages. Also interesting is the timeline with replica artefacts.

According to the legend, Queen Maeve (Medbh) – whose burial cairn is at the summit of Knocknarea in County Sligo – had her palace at Cruachan Aí. The **Oweynagat Cave** (Cave of the Cats), believed to be the entrance to the Celtic otherworld, is also nearby. As it's located on private land, a guide has to accompany anyone who enters the cave. This can be arranged at the visitor centre (€20 per person).

Elphin Windmill   WINDMILL
(☑083 406 2113; www.elphinwindmill.blogspot. com; Windmill Rd, Elphin; adult/child €5/3; ⊙11am-4pm) This charming little whitewashed 18th-century windmill was abandoned in 1837 and repaired in the 1990s, and is now the oldest restored operational windmill in Ireland. Guides at the mill detail its history. It's 12km northwest of Strokestown.

✷ Festivals & Events

International Poetry Festival   LITERATURE
(www.strokestownpoetry.org; ⊙early May) Strokestown's three-day International Poetry Festival takes place over the May Day Bank Holiday weekend.

🛏 Sleeping & Eating

Percy French Hotel   HOTEL €€
(☑071-963 3300; www.thepercyfrenchhotel.com; Bridge St; s/d/f from €60/90/120; P🅿🛜) Centrally located, the Percy French has simple but stylish, contemporary guest rooms and a decent restaurant serving dishes like haddock and chips, pumpkin-and-lentil curry, and roast silverside, overseen by efficient and friendly staff.

Family rooms sleep four; baby cots are available, as are kids' menus at the restaurant.

★Keenans Hotel   GASTROPUB €€
(☑043-332 6098; www.keenanshotel.ie; Harbour Rd, Tarmonbarry; mains €11-27; ⊙kitchen 11am-8.45pm Mon-Sat, to 7.30pm Sun, bar 10am-10.30pm Sun-Thu, to 11.30pm Fri & Sat; 🛜🍴) On the River Shannon's western bank, this mid-19th-century country pub draws on produce from the surrounding area: Roscommon lamb shanks with sweet potato mash, Longford sirloin with sautéed mushrooms, Leitrim goat's cheese tart with wild herbs and beetroot, and Shannon-caught trout with parsnip purée. Upstairs are 12 stylish sage- and olive-toned guest rooms, some with river-view balconies (double/family from €100/150).

Also overlooking the river is a sunny beer garden; if the weather's not cooperating, there's a glassed-in conservatory.

Kids' menus are available, along with baby cots; family rooms sleep four.

ℹ Getting There & Away

Bus Éireann (www.buseireann.ie) runs four times daily from Dublin (€20, two hours) via Longford (€7, 30 minutes) to Strokestown.

Boyle & Around

POP 2568

A quiet town at the foot of the Curlew Mountains, Boyle is a scenic and worthwhile stop, home to beautiful Boyle Abbey, a 4000-year-old dolmen on the far side of a railway line, the hands-on and impressive King House Historic & Cultural Centre, and an activity-packed forest park.

History

The history of Boyle is the history of the King family, former residents of grand King House. In 1603 Staffordshire-born John King was granted land in Roscommon with the aim of 'reducing the Irish to obedience'. Over the next 150 years, through canny marriages and cold-blooded conquests, his descendants made their name and fortune, becoming one of the largest landowning families in Ireland. The town of Boyle subsequently grew around their estate, but suffered badly during the Famine years.

⊙ Sights & Activities

★Arigna Mining Experience   MINE
(☑071-964 6466; www.arignaminingexperience.ie; Derreenavoggy; adult/child €10/6; ⊙10am-6pm, tours hourly) Ireland's first and last coal mine (1600s to 1990) is remembered at the Arigna Mining Experience, set in the hills above Lough Allen, 23km northeast of Boyle. The highlight is the 50-minute underground tour, which takes you 400m down to the coal face and includes a simulated mini-explosion. Tours are led by ex-miners who really bring home the gruelling working conditions and dangers. Wear warm clothing and sturdy shoes as it can be cold and muddy.

There's also an exhibition dedicated to the miners and the equipment they used; plus a short video.

**King House Historic
& Cultural Centre**   HISTORIC BUILDING
(☑071-966 3242; www.kinghouse.ie; Main St; adult/ child €5/3; ⊙11am-5pm Tue-Sat, to 4pm Sun Jun-Aug, 11am-5pm Tue-Sat Apr, May & Sep) Sinister-looking mannequins tell the turbulent history of the Connacht kings, the town of Boyle and the King family, including a grim tale of

tenant eviction during the Famine. Kids can try on replica Irish cloaks, breeches and leather shoes, write with a quill and build a vaulted ceiling from specially designed blocks. One room is devoted to Hollywood star Maureen O'Sullivan (1911–98), who was born nearby on Main St. A worthwhile audio guide costs €1.

After the King family moved to Lough Key, this imposing Georgian mansion became a military barracks for the Connaught Rangers. It then was largely dormant for decades.

The mansion's courtyard is home to a large shop selling local crafts and a cafe (p502), as well as a weekly farmers market (p502).

Boyle Abbey   RUINS
(☑ 071-966 2604; www.heritageireland.ie; Abbeytown Rd; adult/child €5/3; ⊙10am-6pm Easter-late Sep) On the banks of the River Boyle is the finely preserved (and reputedly haunted) Boyle Abbey. Founded in 1161 by monks from Mellifont in County Louth, the abbey captures the transition from Romanesque to Gothic style, best seen in the nave, where a set of arches in each style face each other. A glass wall was added on the northern side in 2011 to prevent the arcade wall and buttresses holding up the roof from collapsing.

Unusually for a Cistercian building, figures and carved animals decorate the capitals to the west along with, more bafflingly, pagan sheila-na-gig fertility symbols. After the Dissolution of the Monasteries, the abbey was occupied by the military and became Boyle Castle; the stone chimney on the southern side of the abbey, which was once the refectory, dates from that period.

Drumanone Dolmen   HISTORIC SITE
(off R294) Constructed before 2000 BC, this striking portal dolmen is one of Ireland's largest, measuring 4.5m by 3.3m. To reach it from Boyle's town centre, follow Patrick St west and then the R294 for 3km, until you pass under a railway arch. Keep going for another 400m and you'll see a small abandoned building on your right; stop the car here and climb up the hill and over the railway line (take care and shut the gates).

★**Lough Key Forest Park**   PARK
(☑ 071-967 3122; www.loughkey.ie; off N4; forest admission free, parking €4; ⊙10am-7pm Jul & Aug, 10am-6pm Apr-Jun, 10am-6pm Wed-Sun Mar, Sep & Oct, 10am-5pm Wed-Sun Nov-Feb) Sprinkled with small islands, the 350-hectare Lough Key Forest Park, 4km east of Boyle, shelters picturesque ruins including a 12th-century abbey on

ABBEYSHRULE AQUEDUCT & ABBEY

Hidden away in the delightfully remote southeast corner of County Longford, Abbeyshrule is a tiny village with a serene setting on the Royal Canal and River Inny. Locals proudly point out that it regularly wins awards for its tidiness.

Just north of town, one of the 19th-century's great engineering feats, the stolid stone **Whitworth Aqueduct** carries the canal over the river. Another highlight is the 12th-century **Cistercian Abbey**. Its ruins are a moody and evocative place for a stroll.

The village is 2km south of the R399 and 7.5km east of the N55.

tiny **Trinity Island** and a 19th-century castle on **Castle Island**. It's a favourite with families for its wishing chair, bog gardens, fairy bridge and viewing tower. Marked walking trails wind through the park.

Bus Éireann services from Sligo to Dublin stop here; in July and August, shuttle buses run from King House.

The park was once part of the Rockingham estate, owned by the King family from the 17th century until 1957. Rockingham House, designed by John Nash, was destroyed by a fire in the same year; all that remains are some stables, outbuildings and eerie tunnels leading to the lake – built to hide the servants from view. There is an informative **visitor centre**, and the **Lough Key Experience** (adult/child €8/5), incorporating a panoramic, 300m-long treetop canopy walk, which rises 9m above the woodland floor with sweeping lake views. Other attractions include the **Boda Borg Challenge** (€19; minimum three people), a series of rooms filled with activities and puzzles, and an outdoor **adventure playground** (day pass €5).

Lough Key Boats (☑086 084 6849; www.loughkeyboats.com; Lough Key Forest Park; boat hire per hr from €25, tours adult/child €12/6; ⊙boat hire 11am-6pm daily Jun-Aug, Sat & Sun Easter-May) runs cruises and hires row boats.

Angling Services Ireland   FISHING
(☑086 601 1878; www.anglingservicesireland.com; Canal View; half-/full-day guided fishing trips for 2 people €130/225; ⊙by reservation) These Boyle-based guides know where to find pike (year-round), and perch and trout (January to September).

✳️ Festivals & Events

Boyle Arts Festival PERFORMING ARTS
(www.boylearts.com; ⊙ Jul) If you're in Boyle in mid- to late July, you can catch the lively 10-day Boyle Arts Festival, which features music, theatre, storytelling and contemporary Irish art exhibitions.

🛏️ Sleeping & Eating

★**Lough Key House** B&B €€
(☑ 071-966 2161; www.loughkeyhouse.com; Carrick-on-Shannon Rd; d/tr from €98/135; P 🛜) This beautifully restored Georgian country house has six guest rooms, all individually decorated with period furniture. The antique-furnished downstairs sitting room is warmed by an open fire; superb breakfasts include eggs from the owner's hens and seasonal fruits from the gardens. It's next to Lough Key Forest Park.

Forest Park House B&B €€
(☑ 071-966 2227; www.unabhan.ie; Carrick-on-Shannon Rd; d/f from €90/140; P 🛜) Just by the entrance to Lough Key Forest Park, 3.5km east of town, this purpose-built guesthouse has six light-filled modern rooms, including two four-person family rooms, with pine woodwork and crisp white linens.

★**Drumanilra Farm Kitchen** CAFE €
(☑ 071-966 2117; www.drumanilra.ie; Elphin St; dishes €5-11; ⊙ 9.30am-5pm Tue-Fri, from 10am Sat; 🛜☑) 🌱 All of the meat and dairy products here come from the family's organic farm on Lough Key. The cafe serves breakfast (eg pancakes with yoghurt and berry compote), lunch (including house-speciality burgers) and afternoon tea, with vegetarian, vegan and gluten-free options. Its attached farm shop is a great place to pick up picnic ingredients.

King House Tearooms CAFE €
(☑ 087 643 0326; www.unabhan.ie; King House, Main St; dishes €2.50-10; ⊙ 8am-5pm Mon-Sat, 10am-4pm Sun) In the King House (p500) courtyard, this little cafe serves coffee, tea and cakes (including a luxurious red velvet cake) and light lunches, like soups, sandwiches and hotel dishes such as chickpea and lentil curry. On Sundays, breakfast is available all day.

Farmers Market MARKET €
(King House, Main St; ⊙ 10am-2pm Sat) On Saturdays, this weekly open-air market at King House (p500) has stalls selling cakes, biscuits, slices, breads, cheeses, jams, preserves, chutneys, fruit and veggies, and rare-breed meats.

ℹ️ Information

In the courtyard of King House, **Úna Bhán Tourism Cooperative** (☑ 071-966 3033; www.unabhan.ie; King House, Main St; ⊙ 9am-5pm Mon-Sat) has tourist information on the Boyle region.

ℹ️ Getting There & Away

Bus Éireann (www.buseireann.ie) runs between Dublin (€20, three hours, six daily) and Sligo (€13, 40 minutes), stopping at King House en route.

Irish Rail (www.irishrail.ie) trains leave eight times daily to Sligo (€7.90, 35 minutes) and Dublin (€17, 2½ hours). The station is on Elphin St on the southern edge of town.

COUNTY LONGFORD

With low hills and pastoral scenes, quiet County Longford attracts anglers from all corners to cast a line around Lough Ree and Lanesborough.

Longford suffered massive emigration during the Famine and never fully recovered. Many Longford emigrants went to Argentina, where one of their descendants, Edelmiro Farrell, became president from 1944 to 1946.

Longford's eponymous county town is a decidedly workaday place, but the county is home to one of Ireland's most important archaeological sites: the Corlea Trackway, and an impressive portal dolmens, Aughnacliffe Dolmen. Both are well worth seeking out.

Longford town has a **tourist office** (☑ 043-334 2577; www.visitlongford.ie; ⊙ 10am-5pm Mon-Fri) on Market Sq.

★**Corlea Trackway** HISTORIC SITE
(☑ 043-332 2386; www.heritageireland.ie; off R392, Keenagh; ⊙ 10am-6pm Easter-Sep) **FREE** Don't miss the extraordinary Corlea Trackway, an Iron Age bog road built in 148 BC. An 18m stretch of the pavement-like oak track has been preserved in a humidified hall at the site's visitor centre, which screens an educational 17-minute film. Highly informative one-hour guided tours detail the bog's unique flora and fauna, and explain how the track was discovered and methods used to preserve it.

The centre is 16km south of Longford town.

The precise purpose of the track has not been fully established, but perhaps it was constructed as a symbol of peace and cooperation between formerly warring regions. Objects found beneath the track also point to similar tracks discovered in other parts of Europe.

Aughnacliffe Dolmen
HISTORIC SITE

(off R198, Aughnacliffe; ⊘ dawn-dusk) Thought to date back 5000 years, this astonishing portal dolmen is one of the three biggest in Ireland, with a height of 2m and two capstones, one almost 3m in length. It's tricky to find: from Aughnacliffe, 22km northeast of Longford town, head 200m north from the petrol station, where you'll see a signposted pedestrian pathway on the road's eastern side. Along this 350m-long track, you'll pass through several wooden gates (close them behind you!) to reach the dolmen.

Longford–Cloondara Trail
CYCLING

Follow the placid waters of the Royal Canal on this walking and cycling path that runs 16km from Longford town. The well-marked trail follows the canal for 8km southwest from Longford before turning northwest for another 8km along the Royal Canal. It's excellent for restful, waterside cycling.

If walking, when you reach the end at the Richmond Harbour in Cloondara you can walk another 2km to Termonbarry to get a bus back to Longford via the N5.

Torc Café & Foodhall
CAFE €

(✆ 043-334 8277; www.torccafe.com; 1 New St, Longford town; dishes €6-15; ⊘ 9.30am-6pm Mon-Thu & Sat, to 9pm Fri; ⑨⊛) Chocolate from a free-flowing fountain awaits as a reward for exploring the county's backroads at this cafe in the centre of Longford town. Fresh, seasonal fare includes bagels, wraps, pies, quiches, salads and more substantial dishes like steak sandwiches and lasagne. Pick up picnic fare or linger for breakfast or lunch. Mini pizzas are a favourite on the kids' menu.

ⓘ Getting There & Away

Bus Éireann (www.buseireann.ie) runs southeast from Longford town to Mullingar (€13, 40 minutes) and northwest to Boyle (€14, 50 minutes) via Carrick-on-Shannon (€12, 35 minutes), but this is a county where you'll need your own wheels to get around to see the sights.

Longford town has a train station and is linked by rail (www.irishrail.ie) with Dublin (€14, 1¾ hours, every two hours) and Sligo town (€12, 1¼ hours).

COUNTY WESTMEATH

Characterised by lakes and pastures grazed by beef cattle, Westmeath has many attractions, ranging from bucolic lakeside vistas and the miraculous Fore Valley to the country's oldest pub in the confident county town, Athlone. The rivers and lakes attract a steady stream of visitors.

Athlone & Around
POP 21,349

The county town of Westmeath, Athlone, is the Midlands' largest town and a great place to base yourself while exploring the region. The River Shannon splits this former garrison town in two, with most businesses and services sitting on its eastern bank. In the shadow of Athlone Castle, the western bank is an enchanting jumble of twisting streets, colourfully painted houses, historic pubs and antique shops.

⊙ Sights & Activities

★ Athlone Castle
CASTLE

(✆ 090-644 2130; www.athlonecastle.ie; Castle St; adult/child €9/4.50; ⊘ 9.30am-6pm Mon-Sat, from 10.30am Sun Jun-Aug, 10am-5.30pm Tue-Sat Mar, 11am-5.30pm Apr, May, Sep & Oct, 10.30am-5pm Mon-Sat, from 11.30am Sun Nov-Feb) Inside this low, hulking 13th-century riverside castle, modern displays bring to life the tumultuous history of the town and detail life here through the ages. The highlight is the cacophonous Siege Experience, which takes place in a circular panoramic gallery.

The ancient river ford at Athlone was an important crossroads on the Shannon and the cause of many squabbles over the centuries. By 1210 the Normans had asserted their power and built a castle here.

In 1690 the Jacobite town survived a siege by Protestant forces, but it fell a year later – under a devastating bombardment of 12,000 cannonballs – to William of Orange's troops. The castle was soon remodelled and further major alterations took place over the following centuries. A lightning strike in 1697, however, ignited the castle's magazine, causing 260 barrels of gunpowder to explode, destroying much of the town in the process.

Church of St Peter & St Paul
CHURCH

(www.sspeterandpaulsparishathlone.com; Barrack St; ⊘ 8am-6pm) Designed by Irish architect Ralph Byrne and completed in 1939, this colossal neoclassical church stands opposite Athlone Castle. Its stained-glass images of St Peter, St Paul, St Patrick, the Last Judgement and Purgatory were created by Richard King in the Harry Clarke Workshop.

ANCIENT UISNEACH

Between Mullingar (16km northeast) and Athlone (31km southeast) on the R390 is **Uisneach** (☑ 087 718 9550; www.uisneach.ie; off R390; suggested donation €10; ☺ tours 1pm Wed-Sun May-Sep, 1pm Sun Apr & Oct), the centre of Ireland during Neolithic times when sea levels were lower (the centre today is 46km to the west). It's a site with great ancient significance. Ancient constructions found so far include earthworks that may have been a royal palace, a possible fort and holy wells. The 2-sq-km site is mostly privately owned; the only way to visit is by an informative two-hour tour.

Tours cover a 3km route; arrive by 12.45pm.

In early May, halfway between the spring equinox and summer solstice, it hosts the Bealtaine Fire Festival.

Dún na Sí Heritage Park   PARK

(☑ 090-648 1183; www.dunnasi.ie; Lake Rd, Moate; adult/child €8/4; ☺ 10am-4pm Easter-Oct) Situated 19km east of Athlone, this engaging folk park has a recreated ring fort, a portal dolmen, a lime kiln, a Mass rock, a farmhouse, a fisherman's cottage and a forge. Also here are a sensory garden, a parkland garden with sculptures made from recycled materials, wetlands with a boardwalk and hides for observing the park's birdlife. Westmeath's genealogy centre is based here. Traditional music, dancing and storytelling sessions take place regularly; schedules are posted online.

Luan Gallery   GALLERY

(☑ 090-644 2154; www.athloneartsandtourism. ie; Grace Park Rd; ☺ 11am-5pm Tue-Sat, from noon Sun) FREE On the river opposite the castle, this contemporary art gallery has rotating exhibitions by top Irish artists.

Shannon Banks Nature Trail   WALKING

(www.athlone.ie) Starting at Athlone Castle, this well-signposted looping 5km walk follows the banks of the River Shannon and the Old Canal Bank. It's an easy stroll; signposts describe flora and fauna along the way.

Viking Ship Cruises   CRUISE

(☑ 086 262 1136; www.vikingtoursireland.ie; The Quay; Lough Ree tour adult/child €14/7, Clonmacnoise tour €20/10; ☺ Easter-Oct) Cruise along the Shannon aboard a Viking-themed canal boat, complete with costumed staff and dress-up clothes. Boats depart next to Athlone Castle and travel north to Lough Ree (75 minutes round trip), or south to Clonmacnoise (90 minutes round trip; alternatively you can spend 90 minutes at Clonmacnoise and return by bus; ticket prices include either option).

Buckley Cycle Hire   CYCLING

(☑ 090-647 8989; www.buckleycycles.ie; Dublin Rd; bike hire per 1/3/7 days from €15/30/50; ☺ 9am-6pm Mon-Fri, to 5.30pm Sat) Helpful staff at Buckley Cycle Hire hire bikes, which come with helmets, locks, repair kits and maps. It has a second location at Tullamore (p515), County Offaly; you can pick up a bike at one location and return it at the other.

🛏 Sleeping

Bastion B&B   GUESTHOUSE €

(☑ 090-649 4954; www.thebastion.net; 2 Bastion St; d €65, without bathroom €55; 🛜) You can't miss Bastion's brightly coloured facade near Athlone Castle. Inside, the white-on-white interiors are a canvas for eclectic artwork, Indian wall hangings and Buddhist ornaments. The seven rooms (five with private bathroom) are crisp and clean, with dark wooden floors. Go for the spacious loft if you can. Despite the name, there's no breakfast; head to its adjacent cafe.

Coosan Cottage
Eco Guesthouse   GUESTHOUSE €€

(☑ 090-647 4184; www.ecoguesthouse.com; Coosan Point Rd; s/d from €50/80; 🅿🛜) 🌿 In tranquil surroundings 3.7km north of town, this ecofriendly 10-bedroom guesthouse blends traditional style with contemporary thinking. Triple-glazed windows, a wood-pellet burner and a heat-recovery system are just some of its green credentials, along with timer-controlled showers and down bedding (hypoallergenic alternatives are available).

Prince of Wales Hotel   HOTEL €€

(☑ 090-647 6666; www.theprinceofwales.ie; Church St; d from €105; 🅿✳🛜) In the commercial heart of town, the landmark Prince of Wales has 46 large, modern, businesslike rooms with blonde timber furniture and cream, brown and red fabrics. Art deco stained glass features in the bar and restaurant; the basement nightclub is a popular venue for hen and stag parties.

✕ Eating & Drinking

Lowe & Co CAFE €
(https://lowe-co.business.site; 8 O'Connell St; dishes €2.50-10.50; ⊙10am-6pm Tue-Sat; ☎🅿) 🌿
Local organic produce forms the basis of the menu at this lovely cafe, which might feature sourdough croissants, cheese, spinach and ham toasties, and spiced lentil and pumpkin soup alongside probiotic juices. Raw, vegan and gluten-free options are plentiful. The upstairs room doubles as a library with comfy vintage sofas.

Bastion Kitchen CAFE €
(www.bastionkitchen.com; 1 Bastion St; dishes €5-11; ⊙8.30am-5pm Mon-Fri, from 9am Sat, from 11am Sun; ☎🅿) 🌿 On Athlone's Left Bank, this boho cafe attracts a laid-back local crowd. All-organic produce is used in breakfast dishes such as avocado toast with poached eggs or black-pepper and chive-sausage baps, and lunch mains like kale and quinoa salad, or Moroccan chickpea tagine with paprika yoghurt.

It's run by the same team as the Bastion B&B located opposite.

★Hatters Lane Bistro BISTRO €€
(☎090-647 3077; www.hatterslane.ie; 9 Custume Pl; mains €16-24, 2-/3-course menu €24/29; ⊙bistro 5.30-10pm Mon-Sat, bar noon-midnight Mon-Sat, to 11.30pm Sun) The intimate bistro at this 11th-century inn has red leather banquettes, chequered tablecloths and timber-panelled walls hung with black-and-white photos of Hollywood stars. Black pudding and smoked-bacon soup; Athlone honey-marinated pork with roast apple compote; and fillet of hake in a Dublin Bay prawn bisque are among its superb dishes. Upstairs is the wood-lined, memorabilia-filled Gertie Browne's Bar.

Pizzeria Il Basilico PIZZA €€
(☎090-647 6784; www.pizzeriailbasilico.ie; North Gate St; pizzas €5.50-18; ⊙5-11.30pm Mon-Thu, from 4pm Fri & Sat, 4-11pm Sun; 🅿) Athlone's best pizza is fired up at 450°C in the wood oven of this pizzeria. Toppings span a simple but stellar Margherita to Rustic (wild mushrooms, salami and olives), Sunny Side Up (bacon, egg and pesto) and Greca (anchovies, oregano and feta) varieties. It's takeaway only; seating is limited to a handful of outdoor tables.

Left Bank Bistro BISTRO €€
(☎090-649 4446; www.leftbankbistro.com; Fry Pl; mains lunch €9.50-16.50, dinner €20-17; ⊙10.30am-9pm Tue-Sat; 🖶) With an airy, whitewashed interior, this sophisticated spot combines superior Irish ingredients with Mediterranean and Asian influences. Lunch features big salads and open sandwiches, while dinner highlights include hazelnut-stuffed duckling with orange and honey glaze, monkfish with chorizo and sweet potato, or grilled squash, goat's cheese mousse and candied walnuts.

Mini burgers are among the kids' dishes (€4 to €8).

★Sean's Bar PUB
(☎090-649 2358; www.seansbar.ie; 13 Main St; ⊙10.30am-11.30pm Mon-Thu, to 12.30am Fri & Sat, 12.30-11pm Sun) You mightn't guess it from the front, but this pub dates from AD 900, making it Ireland's oldest (look for the Guinness World Records certificate). Peat fires warm the low-ceilinged interior, which has uneven floors (to help flood waters run back down to the river), sawdust and curios; live music plays in the riverside beer garden most nights in summer.

ℹ Information

The **tourist office** (☎090-644 2130; www.athlone.ie; Athlone Castle, Market Sq; ⊙10am-6pm Mon-Sat, from noon Sun Jun-Aug, to 5pm Tue-Sun mid-Mar–May, Sep & Oct) is inside the castle's guardhouse.

ℹ Getting There & Away

Bus Éireann (www.buseireann.ie) runs buses to Dublin (€15, 1½ hours, hourly) and Galway (€13.50, 1¾ hours, hourly) and Westport (€14, 3¾ hours, four daily Monday to Saturday, three Sunday).

Irish Rail (www.irishrail.ie) runs trains to Dublin (€14, 1½ hours, hourly), Galway (€10.50, one hour, 10 daily) and Westport (€14, 1¾ hours, four daily).

Lough Ree & Around

Many of the 50-plus islands within Lough Ree were once inhabited by monks and their ecclesiastical treasures, drawing Vikings like bears to honey-laced beehives. These days it draws visitors for sailing, trout and pike fishing, and birdwatching. Migratory birds that nest here include bewick and whooper swans, golden plovers and curlews.

Poet, playwright and novelist Oliver Goldsmith (1728–74), author of *The Vicar of Wakefield*, is closely associated with the area running alongside the eastern shore of Lough Ree. Known as Goldsmith Country, the region is beautifully captured in his writings.

On the County Roscommon side of the lough, the ruined medieval village of **Rindoon** (Lecarrow) is accessible by foot, bicycle or boat.

For boat and bike hire as well as fishing, contact **Lough Ree Boat & Bike Hire** (⏱087 716 8844; www.loughreeboathire.ie; Main St, Lecarrow; fishing boat hire per day from €65, bike hire per day from €12; ☺by reservation), on the County Roscommon side.

Glasson Golf Course　　　GOLF
(⏱090-648 51200; www.glassongolfhotel.ie; off N55, Killinure; green fees €40-50; ☺by reservation) Designed by Christy O'Connor Jr, this par 73 course has water views from all 18 holes (hole 15's green juts right into Killinure Bay). Deep bunkers, mature woodlands, reed beds and plenty of wind make it a challenging prospect. Its elegant hotel (doubles from €140) has 65 contemporary rooms; a panoramic restaurant and bar overlooks the bay.

Wineport Lodge　　　LODGE €€€
(⏱090-643 9010; www.wineport.ie; Portaneena; d/ste from €200/280; P🖥) Wake up to water views: the 29 rooms with floor-to-ceiling windows at this modern-rustic lodge face Killinure Lough and Killinure Island; some rooms open to balconies. On-site amenities include a spa offering treatments and massages, and a fine-dining restaurant serving lunch and dinner daily plus brunch on weekends (mains €20 to €34) utilising local produce from artisan suppliers.

★**Glasson Village Restaurant**　SEAFOOD €€
(⏱090-648 5001; www.glassonvillagerestaurant.ie; Main St, Glasson; mains €20-28; ☺5.30-9pm Tue-Fri, 6-9.30pm Sat, 1-5pm Sun) Inside an ivy-covered, 200-year-old cottage, this romantic restaurant with white-clothed tables and flickering candles specialises in seafood, such as Lissadell oysters with chervil butter, Rossaveal monkfish with red wine Bordelaise sauce, or Kilmore Quay sea bass with samphire and charred lemon. The three-course early-bird menu is a bargain at €29. Bookings are essential in summer.

Kilbeggan

Little Kilbeggan has two big claims to fame: a restored distillery-turned-museum and Ireland's only National Hunt racecourse.

Kilbeggan Distillery Experience　DISTILLERY
(⏱057-933 2134; www.kilbeggandistillery.com; Main St; tour 1hr/90min/3hr €14/26/85; ☺9am-6pm Apr-Oct, 10am-4pm Nov-Mar) Established in 1757, Kilbeggan is Ireland's oldest licensed distillery – after stopping production in 1957, it has been producing whiskey again since 2007. Its basic one-hour Apprentice tour includes three tastings. The 90-minute Distillers tour also visits the old warehouses and distillers, finishing with four tastings. For true whiskey aficionados, the three-hour Connoisseur tour includes lunch with a head distiller, seven tastings and the opportunity to fill your own 200mL bottle from an aged cask using a valinch (whiskey-drawing tube).

Kilbeggan Races　　　HORSE RACING
(⏱057-933 2176; www.kilbegganraces.com; R389; ☺usually fortnightly May-Sep) Punters from all over the country attend the old-time evening meetings at the Kilbeggan Races, 2km north of the town centre. The village is transformed on race nights in summer into a buzzing equine centre, where the thrill of the chase is matched by the craic in the pubs.

Mullingar & Around

POP 20,928

The regional service town of Mullingar hums with the activity of locals going about their daily lives, but nearby visitor attractions include fish-filled lakes and a fantastical mansion, Belvedere House, with an odious, but gripping, history.

James Joyce visited Mullingar in his youth and it appears in both *Ulysses* (1922) and *Finnegans Wake* (1939). Restored sections of the Royal Canal extend in either direction from the town.

◉ Sights & Activities

Trout and salmon fishing is popular in the rivers and lakes around Mullingar. The fishing season runs from 1 March or 1 May (depending on the location) to 12 October; the tourist office (p507) has information.

★**Belvedere House
& Gardens**　　　HISTORIC BUILDING
(⏱044-933 8960; www.belvedere-house.ie; off N52; adult/child €8/4; ☺house 9.30am-5pm Mar-Oct, to 4pm Nov-Feb, gardens 9.30am-8pm May-Aug, to 7pm Apr & Sep, to 6pm Mar & Oct, to 4.30pm Nov-Feb) Belvedere House, 7.5km south of Mullingar, is an unmissable sight. This immense 1740-built hunting and fishing lodge is set in 65 hectares of gardens overlooking Lough Ennell. Designed by Richard Cassels, it contains delicate rococo plasterwork in the upper rooms.

The gardens, with their Victorian glasshouse, walled garden and lakeshore setting, make for wonderful rambling. An airy annex houses a cafe; there's a large children's playground.

More than a few skeletons have come rattling from Belvedere's closets: the first earl, Lord Belfield, accused his wife and younger brother Arthur of adultery. She was placed under house arrest here for 31 years, and Arthur was jailed in London for the rest of his life. Meanwhile, the earl lived a life of decadence and debauchery. On his death, his wife emerged dressed in the fashion of three decades earlier, still protesting her innocence.

Lord Belfield also found time to fall out with his other brother, George, who built a home nearby. Ireland's largest folly, a ready-made 'ruin' called the Jealous Wall, was commissioned by the earl so he wouldn't have to look at George's mansion.

Cathedral of Christ the King CATHEDRAL

(☑ 044-934 8338; www.mullingarparish.com; Bishop's Gate St; ⊗ 7.30am-8pm) Mullingar's most distinctive landmark is this colossal twin-towered cathedral, commenced in 1933 and consecrated on the eve of WWII. Its large mosaics of St Anne and St Patrick were designed by Russian artist Boris Anrep.

Mullingar Equestrian Centre HORSE RIDING

(☑ 044-934 8331; www.mullingarequestrian.com; Athlone Rd, Rathcolman; 1-day lesson & ride adult/child €100/80) Situated 4km west of Mullingar, this equestrian centre offers rides and lessons for adults and children.

🛏 Sleeping & Eating

Novara House B&B €

(☑ 044-933 5209; www.novarahouse.com; Bellview, off Dublin Rd; s/d from €40/80; 🅿🛜) Just a five-minute walk (900m) east from the town centre, this simple B&B is set in a modern bungalow. Rooms are simple but spotless with pine furniture and neutral colour schemes, but it's the amiable hosts, Richie and Margaret, with their warm welcome, homemade scones and cups of tea that guarantee a memorable stay.

Annebrook House Hotel HOTEL €€

(☑ 044-935 3300; www.annebrook.ie; Austin Friars St; d/apt from €99/160; 🅿🛜) Right in the town centre, the hub of this hotel is a lovely early-19th-century stone house. Accommodation is in an annex with 26 contemporary rooms in shades of creams and yellows; apartments come with two bedrooms and open-plan living rooms with cherry-wood kitchens; some have balconies overlooking the River Brosna, which flows through the grounds.

Greville Arms Hotel HOTEL €€

(☑ 044-934 8563; www.grevillearmshotel.ie; Pearse St; s/d/tr from €70/100/120; 🛜) Dating from 1884, this grande-dame hotel with gilt mirrors, statues, dark oil paintings and chandeliers has 40 spacious rooms with plush carpets and patterned wallpaper. James Joyce allegedly frequented the establishment; the James Joyce Restaurant and Ulysses Bar (with a beer garden) are named for him. Its small museum covering Westmeath's and Ireland's ancient history has an early *Ulysses* edition.

Druid's Chair PUB

(www.druidschairmullingar.com; 8 Pearse St; ⊗ 10am-11pm Mon-Thu, to 1am Fri & Sat, noon-11pm Sun; 🛜) Behind its photogenic black-framed stone facade with geranium-filled window boxes, this large pub is a welcoming place for a pint, a sporting fixture on the big screen, or a meal (burgers include a 'Druid's Breakfast Burger' with beef, bacon, eggs, hash browns and tomato relish; mains €13 to €24) until 9pm. Live music plays some Saturday nights.

☆ Entertainment

Mullingar Arts Centre ARTS CENTRE

(☑ 044-934 7777; www.mullingarartscentre.ie; County Hall, Mount St) Mullingar's arts centre runs a regular program of music, comedy, drama and art exhibitions. In summer there are family-friendly traditional music sessions every weekend.

ℹ Information

Tourist Office (☑ 044-934 8650; www.mullingar.ie; Market Sq; ⊗ 9am-5pm Mon-Fri) Right in the centre of town.

ℹ Getting There & Away

Bus Éireann (www.buseireann.ie) runs to Dublin (€16, 1½ hours, half-hourly Monday to Friday, hourly Saturday and Sunday) and Athlone (€13, one hour, one daily Monday to Saturday only).

Irish Rail (www.irishrail.ie) runs 10 direct services to Dublin (€11, 1¼ hours) and Longford (€7.90, 30 minutes, every two hours).

North of Mullingar

The area north of Mullingar is famed for its lakes. The best-known is Lough Derravaragh, an 8km-long lake associated with the legend of the children of Lír, who were turned into swans here by their jealous stepmother. Each winter the legend is recalled by thousands of snow-white migratory swans that flock here from as far away as Russia and Siberia.

Along with the lakes and rolling landscapes you'll find plenty of historical interest around the unassuming town of Castlepollard and bucolic Fore Valley.

⊙ Sights

★ Fore Valley HISTORIC SITE
(off R195; ⊘ dawn-dusk) Near the shores of Lough Lene, the emerald-green Fore Valley, 5km east of Castlepollard, is a superb place to explore by bicycle or on foot. In AD 630 St Fechin founded a monastery just outside the village of Fore. There's nothing left of this early settlement, but three later buildings in the valley are closely associated with 'seven wonders' said to have occurred here. It's a deeply atmospheric place with sweeping views across the valley.

The oldest of the three buildings is **St Fechin's Church**, containing an early-13th-century chancel and baptismal font. Over the Cyclopean entrance is a huge lintel stone carved with a Greek cross and thought to weigh about 2.5 tonnes. It's said to have been put into place by St Fechin's devotions – the wonder of the stone raised by prayer.

A path runs from the church to the attractive little **anchorite cell** – the 'anchorite in a stone' – which dates from the 15th century and was lived in by a succession of hermits. The Fore Abbey Coffee Shop in the village holds the key.

On the other side of the road near the car park is **St Fechin's Well**, filled with water that will not boil. Cynics should beware of testing this claim, as it's said that if you try it, doom will come to your family. Nearby is a branch from the tree that will not burn; the coins pressed into it are a more contemporary superstition.

Further over the plain are the extensive remains of a **13th-century Benedictine priory**, the Monastery of the Quaking Scraw, miraculous because it was built on a bog. In the following century it was turned into a fortification, hence the loophole windows and castle-like square towers. The western tower is in a dangerous state – keep clear.

The last two wonders are the mill without a race and the water that flows uphill. The mill site is marked, and legend has it that St Fechin caused water to flow uphill, towards the mill, by throwing his crosier against a rock near Lough Lene, 1.3km to the southeast.

Tullynally Castle Gardens GARDENS
(☑ 044-966 1856; www.tullynallycastle.ie; Granard Rd, Castlepollard; adult/child €7/3; ⊘ dawn-dusk) The imposing Gothic-revival Tullynally Castle is the seat of the Pakenham family and, although closed to visitors, its 12 hectares of gardens and parkland are an enchanting place to roam. Ornamental lakes, a Chinese and a Tibetan garden, and a stately stretch of 200-year-old yews are some of the highlights. A tearoom in the castle courtyard opens Thursday to Sunday from April to September.

The gardens are 2km northwest of Castlepollard off the R395.

🛏 Sleeping & Eating

Hotel Castlepollard PUB €€
(☑ 044-966 1194; www.facebook.com/hotelcastlepollard; The Square, Castlepollard; d from €95; P 🛜) The closest accommodation to the Fore Valley, this cosy country hotel overlooking Castlepollard's neat, triangular village green has spacious timber-floored rooms and a restaurant serving breakfast, lunch and dinner (mains €8.50 to €13). The bar has live music on Saturdays.

Fore Abbey Coffee Shop CAFE €
(☑ 044-966 1780; R195, Fore; dishes €2.30-6.50; ⊘ 11am-4pm daily Jun-Sep, to 4pm Sun Oct-May) Next to the Fore Valley car park, this small stone cafe serves soups, salads, sandwiches and cakes. It doubles as a tourist information office and screens a short video about the monastery ruins.

COUNTY OFFALY

Beyond the magnificent ecclesiastical remains of Clonmacnoise, the green and watery county of Offaly doesn't feature on many tourist itineraries, which is a shame as it deserves far greater attention. Steeped in history with plentiful castle remains and the atmospheric town of Birr, Offaly also retains vast swaths of bogland (most accessible at the Clara Bog Nature Reserve, recognised for their fertile habitat of plant and animal life, as well as prime fishing and water sports on the River Shannon and the Grand Canal. Other highlights include ancient abbey ruins and the vast river fort at Shannonbridge.

For county-wide information, visit www.offaly.ie and www.visitoffaly.ie.

Birr

POP 5741

Birr is one of the Midlands' unmissable towns. Elegant Georgian buildings with candy-coloured facades are overlooked by a grande dame of a castle. There is excellent accommodation, as well as spirited nightlife. Despite its appeal, Birr remains off the beaten track and can be enjoyed without jostling with the crowds.

◉ Sights

Stroll down tree-lined **Oxmantown Mall** or **John's Mall** to see some of Birr's best Georgian buildings. The corner of Oxmantown Mall was the site of the world's first-ever motor vehicle fatality, a steam-powered car in 1869, an event that is recorded on a sign.

The tourist office has a walking-tour map that details the most important landmarks, including the megalithic **Seffin Stone** (said to be the ancient marker for Umbilicus Hiberniae – the Navel of Ireland – used to mark the centre of the country) and **St Brendan's Old Churchyard**, reputedly the site of the saint's 6th-century settlement.

★**Birr Castle**   CASTLE
(☑057-912 0336; www.birrcastle.com; Rosse Row; adult/child gardens €9/5, gardens, exhibits & castle €18/10; ⊙9am-6pm Mar-Oct, 9.30am-4pm Nov-Feb) It's easy to spend half a day exploring the attractions and gardens of Birr Castle demesne. The castle dates from 1620 and is a private home, but during May to August you can visit the main living quarters on tours (which must be booked in advance). Most of the present building dates from around 1620, with alterations made in the early 19th century.

The 50-hectare castle grounds are famous for their magnificent **gardens** set around a large artificial lake.

The gardens are home to more than 1000 species of plants from all over the world, so there's invariably something in bloom. Look for one of the world's **tallest box hedges** (which has made the *Guinness Book of Records*), planted in the 1780s and now standing 12m high, and the romantic **Hornbeam cloister**. There are waterfalls, wildflower meadows and a pergola festooned with a wisteria planted in 1936.

The Parsons clan, who have owned the castle since 1620, are a remarkable family of pioneering Irish scientists, and their work is documented in the historic **science centre**.

Exhibits include the massive **telescope** built by William Parsons in 1845. The 'leviathan of Parsonstown', as it was known, was the largest telescope in the world for 75 years and attracted a wide variety of scientists and astronomers. It was used to make innumerable discoveries, including the spiral galaxies. After the death of William's son, the telescope slowly fell to bits. It has been completely restored and may be viewed in all its glory.

William Parsons' wife, Mary Ross, was a keen photographer and her dark room was reputed to be one of the first of its kind in the world. You can now view a replica. Other highlights are a children's **adventure playground**, complete with playhouse, hobbit huts and trampolines, and the excellent **Courtyard Cafe** (open daily March to October; weekends only November and December), which showcases local produce. Otherwise you can wander the garden to your heart's content, with over 8km of trails including short walks.

Leap Castle   CASTLE
(☑086 869 0547; www.leapcastle.net; R421; ⊙by arrangement) Leap Castle is reputedly one of the most haunted castles in Europe. Originally an O'Carroll family residence, the 1514-built castle was the scene of many dreadful deeds and is famous for its eerie apparitions – its most renowned inhabitant is the 'smelly ghost', a spirit that apparently leaves a lingering odour after sightings. Another apparition is the self-explanatory 'red lady'.

Renovations are ongoing, but you can arrange a visit. It's 12km southeast of Birr.

🏃 Activities

A leafy **riverside walk** runs 1.1km east along the River Camcor from Oxmantown Bridge to Elmgrove Bridge.

Birr Equestrian Centre   HORSE RIDING
(☑087 244 5545; www.birrequestrian.ie; Kingsborough House, Clareen Rd; 1hr/half-day horse treks €30/80) This equestrian centre, 5.5km east of Birr, runs hour-long treks in the surrounding farmland as well as half-day horse treks in the Slieve Bloom Mountains.

🎊 Festivals & Events

Birr Vintage Week & Arts Festival   ART
(www.birrvintageweek.com; ⊙early Aug) The town celebrates its rich history during this week-long festival, with street parades, theatre, music, exhibitions, workshops, guided walks and a traditional fair.

CRUISING IRELAND'S CANALS

After much debate about linking Dublin to the Shannon by water, work began on the Grand Canal in 1757. The project was beset by problems and encountered huge difficulties and delays. In the meantime, commercial rivals hatched a plan for the competing Royal Canal. The two canals revolutionised transport in Ireland in the early 19th century, but their heyday was short-lived, as they were soon superseded by the railway.

Today the canals are popular for cruising and fishing, while their banks are ideal for walking and cycling, and pass through some truly picturesque villages. With the restoration of the final section of the Royal Canal it is now possible to complete a triangular route by heading from Dublin to the Shannon along either the Royal or the Grand, returning along the other canal. Both waterways link to a much greater network that includes the Shannon–Erne Waterway and the River Suck.

Waterways Ireland (www.waterwaysireland.org) and the Inland Waterways Association of Ireland (www.iwai.ie) have a wealth of information on the canals.

Grand Canal

The Grand Canal threads its way from Dublin through Tullamore to join the River Shannon at Shannonbridge, a total of 132km. The canal passes through relatively unpopulated countryside, with bogs, pretty villages and 44 finely crafted locks lining the journey. Near the village of Sallins in County Kildare, the graceful seven-arched **Leinster Aqueduct** carries the canal across the River Liffey. From nearby Robertstown, a 45km spur turns south to join the River Barrow at the pretty town of Athy.

Royal Canal

The 145km-long Royal Canal follows Kildare's northern border, flowing over a massive **aqueduct** near Leixlip, before it joins the River Shannon at Clondra in County Longford, with 46 locks en route. It's popular with thousands of residents along the north Kildare commuter belt, and both the canal and the towpaths are open all the way to the Shannon.

Barges & Boats

You can hire narrow boats at several locations along the canals, which is an excellent way to journey through the waterways. **Barrowline Cruisers** (⟟057-862 6060; www.barrowline.ie; Vicarstown; boat hire per week from €830; ⊘by reservation Mar-Oct) and **Canalways** (⟟087 243 3879; www.canalways.ie; Spencer Bridge, Rathangan; canal-boat rental per week from €985; ⊘Apr-Oct) are major firms with multiple locations. You can also find rental firms in the boating centres of Banagher (p512) and Carrick-on-Shannon (p495).

🛌 Sleeping

★ **Maltings Guesthouse**　　　　GUESTHOUSE €
(⟟057-912 1345; www.themaltingsbirr.com; Castle St; s/d from €50/80; 🛜) Based in an 1810 malt storehouse once used by Guinness, this guesthouse has a serene location by the River Camcor near the castle. The large, pine-furnished rooms have a lilac-and-green colour scheme; all overlook the water, as does the breakfast room, which is framed by floor-to-ceiling glass and opens to a terrace.

Kids aged under 12 pay half price.

★ **Walcot B&B**　　　　　　　　B&B €€
(⟟057-912 1247; www.facebook.com/Walcotbandb; Rosse Row; s/d from €60/90; 🅿🛜) Set back from the road amid sprawling formal gardens across from Birr Castle, this Georgian townhouse is close to everything. The five large,

antique-furnished bedrooms have period-style bathrooms with large tubs and showers.

Brendan House　　　　　　　　B&B €€
(⟟057-912 1818; www.tinjugstudio.com; Brendan St; s/d without bathroom from €55/80; 🛜) Packed with knick-knacks, books, rugs, art and antiques, this Georgian townhouse is a bohemian delight. The three rooms share a bathroom (allegedly one of Birr's oldest), but the four-poster beds, period charm, superb breakfast and artistic style are the real draws. The owners arrange mountain walks, castle and art tours, holistic treatments and art classes.

Dooly's Hotel　　　　　　　　HOTEL €€
(⟟057-912 0032; www.doolyshotel.com; Emmet Sq; s/d/tr/f from €55/99/119/140; 🛜) Originally a coaching house dating from 1747, Dooly's has an inviting, homey feel and old-world

charm with Georgian-style furnishings, a reliable restaurant and a choice of bars. The 17 spacious rooms have contemporary chocolate-toned furnishings; some look onto Birr's main square.

Family rooms have a double and two single beds; cots are available for babies.

✖ Eating & Drinking

★ **Spinners on Castle St** IRISH €€
(☑ 057-912 3779; www.spinnersbirr.com; Castle St; bar mains €12-18, restaurant mains €14-27; ⊘ restaurant 6-9pm Fri & Sat, 12.30-3.30pm Sun, bar 5-9pm Wed & Thu, 12.30-9pm Fri & Sat, 12.30-7pm Sun; ⑤) By the castle wall, Spinners is part of a complex spanning five restored Georgian houses. The whitewashed wine-cocktail bar is the perfect place for a cheeseboard or burger with black pudding and homemade relish, while the elegant restaurant's seasonal menu might feature Burren Smokehouse mackerel and potato salad followed by baked brill with red lentil broth. Service is excellent.

Tables set up in the tree-shaded enclosed courtyard in fine weather; occasional live music plays in the bar.

Upstairs are stylish rooms (doubles with private bathroom €90 to €140, doubles with shared bathroom from €80).

Thatch IRISH €€
(☑ 057-912 0682; www.thethatchcrinkill.com; Military Rd, Crinkill; lunch mains €12.50-27, 2-/3-course dinner menus €26/32; ⊘ kitchen 4-7.30pm Mon, to 9pm Tue-Thu, 12.30-9pm Fri & Sat, to 7.30pm Sun, bar to 10pm; ⑤ ⏺) ✤ This 200-year-old traditional thatched pub 2.2km southeast of Birr is a great place to sip a pint or enjoy a meal at lunch (à la carte) or dinner (fixed-price menus only) in its brick-and-stone interior warmed by open fires. Alongside traditional roasts, specialities include black pudding–stuffed duck.

Chestnut PUB
(www.thechestnut.ie; Green St; ⊘ 8-11.30pm Mon & Tue, from 5pm Wed & Thu, 5pm-12.30am Fri, 3pm-1am Sat, 3-11pm Sun) Dating from 1823, the Chestnut incorporates dark wood, gilded mirrors, flickering candles, peat fires and a pressed-tin ceiling. Trad sessions take place on Thursdays, with live rock gigs on Fridays; regular special events include evening barbecues and film nights.

Craughwell's PUB
(☑ 057-912 1839; www.craughwellspub.com; Castle St; ⊘ 5-11.30pm Mon-Fri, noon-1am Sat, 11am-11pm Sun) Stop for a pint at Craughwell's, renowned

for its rollicking trad-music sessions and impromptu singalongs. Visitors and locals alike contribute to the bar's baseball cap collection.

☆ Entertainment

Birr Theatre & Arts Centre ARTS CENTRE
(☑ 057-912 2911; www.birrtheatre.com; Oxmantown Mall) On tree-lined Oxmantown Mall, this is a vibrant place with a regular line-up of art exhibitions, films, theatre and concerts.

ⓘ Getting There & Away

Bus Éireann (www.buseireann.ie) runs to Limerick (€19, 1¼ hours) via Birr to Athlone (€12, 45 minutes, three daily), where you can change for Dublin and Galway.

Kearns Transport (www.kearnstransport.com) runs direct buses to Dublin (€10, 2¼ hours, six daily Monday to Friday, two Saturday, three Sunday).

Kinnitty

POP 359

Kinnitty is a quaint village that makes a handy base for exploring the Slieve Bloom Mountains to the east. The scenic R440 runs east from the town across the mountains to Mountrath.

◉ Sights

Stone Pyramid MONUMENT
(St Finian's Church, Ballyshane Rd) Look out for the unexpected 10m-high stone pyramid in the village graveyard behind St Finian's Church. In the 1830s Richard Bernard commissioned this scale replica of the Cheops pyramid in Egypt for the family crypt.

Kinnitty High Cross MONUMENT
(Kinnitty Castle Hotel, R421) The sandstone shaft of the 9th-century Kinnitty High Cross from the Augustinian Abbey now stands in the grounds of the Kinnitty Castle Hotel. Adam and Eve and the Crucifixion are clearly visible on either face.

🛏 Sleeping & Eating

★ **Kinnitty Castle Hotel** CASTLE €€
(☑ 057-913 7318; www.kinnittycastlehotel.com; R421; d/ste from €170/195; ⓟ ⑤) Reached by a long, winding driveway through the forested 265-hectare estate, 1km northeast of town, storybook Kinnitty Castle was built in the 13th century, and extensively renovated in neo-Gothic style in 1811. Its 37 superbly atmospheric rooms have period furnishings such as cast-iron roll-top baths; there's a

dungeon bar-restaurant, gourmet week-end-only restaurant, and a library bar with antiquarian tomes.

Ardmore House
B&B €€

(☑ 057-913 7009; www.kinnitty.com; The Walk; s/d from €60/90; P �) Handily located just off Kinnitty's main street, this rustic Victorian stone farmhouse warmed by peat fires has five cosy rooms with brass beds, antique furniture and views of the nearby Slieve Bloom Mountains, where the owners organise walking tours.

Giltraps Pub
PUB FOOD €

(☑ 057-913 7076; www.giltrapspub.com; R421; dishes €6-18; ⊙ kitchen noon-9pm, bar 11am-11pm; �) A perfect place to stop after exploring the Slieve Bloom Mountains, this lovely country pub scores across the board. Food ranges from simple sandwiches to Irish classics such as steak-and-Guinness pie, plus summer barbecues. Trad music plays on weekends year-round. In fine weather, you can enjoy a pint outside at a picnic table while taking in the mountain vistas.

If you want to stay, Giltraps has rooms in a neighbouring townhouse, as well as log cabins and a yurt; doubles start at €85.

Banagher & Around

POP 1653

Sleepy Banagher bursts into life in the summer months when the busy marina is awash with boaters. Perhaps Banagher's greatest claim to fame is that it was the location for Charlotte Brontë's honeymoon.

◉ Sights

Situated at a crossing point over the River Shannon between the provinces of Leinster and Connacht, Banagher was a place of enormous strategic importance. The modest fortifications by the bridge include the diminutive Cromwell's Castle, a roofless military barracks and Martello tower.

Clonony Castle
CASTLE

(☑ 087 761 4034; www.facebook.com/Clonony Castle; R357, Clonony; admission by donation; ⊙ noon-5pm Fri-Sun Jun-Aug or by appointment) Built in the 1490s, Clonony Castle is enclosed by an overgrown castellated wall. Tales that Henry VIII's second wife, Anne Boleyn, was born here are unlikely to be true, but her cousins Elizabeth and Mary Boleyn are buried beside the ruins. From 1612 to 1620, it

was home to Matthew de Renzi, who compiled the first Irish–English dictionary. Ongoing renovations mean opening hours can vary. It's 7.5km northeast of Banagher.

Cromwell's Castle
FORT

(www.banagher.ie; R356) Defending Banagher Bridge just across the River Shannon in County Galway, this small 'castle' (really, fort) dates to the 1650s. It was modified during the Napoleonic Wars and abandoned just five years later in 1810. The interior is closed to the public.

🏃 Activities

Banagher Marina is a good place to hire cruisers for a trip along the River Shannon or the Royal Canal; try Carrick Craft (☑ 01-278 1666; www.cruise-ireland.com; boat hire per week from €850) or Silverline Cruisers (☑ 057-915 1112; www.silverlinecruisers.com; 3 days from €400). A boat licence isn't required as full training is provided.

Shannon Adventure Canoeing
CANOEING

(☑ 057-915 1411; www.facebook.com/Shannon-AdventureCanoeingHolidayltd; Banagher Marina; 2-person canoe hire per day €50; ⊙ by reservation) You don't need a houseboat to enjoy Ireland's waterways – here you can hire a Canadian touring canoe and leisurely paddle your way along the canals. Canoes come with tents and cooking equipment, though not sleeping bags, so you'll need to bring your own.

🛏 Sleeping

Dún Cromáin
B&B €

(☑ 057-915 3966; www.duncromain.com; Crank Rd; s/d/f from €47.50/75/150; P ᵈ) Surrounded by sweeping lawns, family-run Dún Cromáin has three large rooms simply decorated in pastel colours with light wood and white linens. The breakfast-sitting room has a thoughtful feel-at-home atmosphere and an open fire. Perks include fridges and facilities for drying clothes (handy in these parts). One room is wheelchair accessible.

Babysitting can be arranged.

Charlotte's Way
B&B €€

(☑ 057-915 3864; www.charlottesway.com; Birr Rd; d/tr/f €90/110/130; P ᵈ) This tastefully restored former 18th-century rectory on Banagher Hill has five comfortable rooms with period furniture, old prints and antiques. Charlotte Brontë was a frequent visitor and, after her death, her husband Arthur lived here as the rector. Breakfast features eggs

SHANNON HARBOUR & AROUND

Just 1km east of where the Grand Canal joins the River Shannon, picturesque Shannon Harbour was once a thriving trading centre, constructed to serve the waterways and home to more than 1000 people. Along with cargo boats, passenger barges ran from here, many taking poverty-stricken locals on their first leg of a long journey to North America or Australia.

Today the waterways are again teeming with boats and walking paths stretching in all directions, making the harbour an appealing stop for walkers, fishers, boaters and birders.

fresh from the chickens and produce from the pretty garden.

Drinking & Nightlife

★ **JJ Houghs Singing Pub** PUB
(www.facebook.com/Houghs.Pub; Main St; ⊙noon-11.30pm Sun-Thu, to 1am Fri & Sat) Opening to a lovely beer garden, Hough's is a 250-year-old vine-clad pub renowned for its music sessions. You'll find someone playing here most nights in summer and at weekends in winter. People sing nightly, led by the owner, Michael.

ⓘ Getting There & Away

Kearns Transport (www.kearnstransport.com) links Banagher with Birr (€3, 25 minutes), Tullamore (€6, 55 minutes) and Dublin (€10, three hours) once daily Monday to Saturday, twice on Sunday.

Shannonbridge

POP 650

A small, sleepy village with just one main street, picturesque Shannonbridge gets its name from a narrow 16-span, 18th-century bridge that crosses the river into County Roscommon, with a 19th-century fort on the western bank.

Shannonbridge Fort FORT
(R357) You can't miss the massive 1810-built bridgehead fortifications on the western bank in County Roscommon, where heavy artillery was installed to bombard Napoleon in case he tried to invade by river. Substantial other sections of the fort remain: the adjacent guardhouse is still here and part of the redoubt and defensive wall survive, although some of it was demolished in the 1950s to allow vehicles to pass.

Killeens Village Tavern PUB FOOD €
(☑090-967 4112; www.killeens.ie; Main St; mains €10; ⊙kitchen noon-8.30pm, bar 10am-11.30pm) Old-world pub and shop Killeens

is renowned for its lively traditional music six nights a week from March to September and at weekends during the rest of the year. Traditional pub grub spans steak sandwiches to fish and chips.

ⓘ Information

Visitor Centre & Tourist Information (www.shannonbridge.com; Main St; ⊙10am-6pm Mar-Sep) Information point run by the local council.

Clonmacnoise

Alongside the River Shannon with a nearby ruined castle for company, the setting is sublime at Clonmacnoise (www.heritageireland.ie; R444; adult/child €8/4; ⊙9am-6.30pm Jun-Aug, 10am-6pm mid-Mar–May, Sep & Oct, 10am-5.30pm Nov–mid-Mar) – one of Ireland's holiest and most significant monastic sites. An air of sacred mystery pervades the remains, with its wealth of early church architecture, including some of Ireland's finest high crosses and most ancient round towers arrayed closely together within a walled field. The site is not large, but plan on a visit of a couple of hours.

The surrounding marshy area is known as the Shannon Callows, home to many wild plants and one of Western Europe's last refuges of the endangered corncrake (a pastel-coloured relative of the coot).

If you want to avoid summer crowds, it's a good idea to visit early or late; the tiny country lanes nearby can get clogged with coaches.

History

When St Ciarán founded a monastery here in AD 548, it was the most important crossroads in the country, the intersection of the north–south River Shannon and the east–west Esker Riada (Highway of the Kings).

The giant ecclesiastical city had a humble beginning and Ciarán died just seven months after building his first church. Over the years,

Clonmacnoise

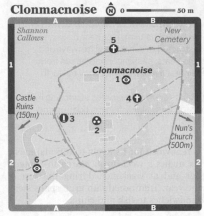

Clonmacnoise ⓝ 0 ▬▬▬ 50 m

of Ireland's finest. It's very distinctive, with unique upward-tilting arms and richly decorated panels depicting the Crucifixion, the Last Judgement, the arrest of Jesus and Christ in the tomb.

Only the shaft of the **North Cross**, which dates from around AD 800, remains. It is adorned by lions, convoluted spirals and a single figure, thought to be the Celtic god Cernunnos. The richly decorated **South Cross** has mostly abstract carvings – swirls, spirals and fretwork – and, on the western face, the Crucifixion plus a few odd cavorting creatures.

The museum also contains the largest collection of early Christian grave slabs in Europe. Many have inscriptions clearly visible, often starting with *oroit do* or *ar* (a prayer for).

Cathedral RUINS
The largest building at Clonmacnoise, the cathedral was originally built in AD 909, but was significantly altered and remodelled over the centuries. Its most interesting feature is the intricate 15th-century Gothic doorway with carvings of Sts Francis, Patrick and Dominic. A whisper carries from one side of the door to the other – a feature believed to have been used by lepers to confess their sins without infecting the priests.

The last High Kings of Tara – Turlough Mór O'Connor (died 1156) and his son Ruairí (Rory; died 1198) – are said to be buried near the altar.

Temple Ciaran CHURCH
The small churches at Clonmacnoise are called temples, a derivation of the Irish word *teampall* (church). Tiny Temple Ciaran is reputed to be the burial place of St Ciarán, the site's founder. Its floor level is lower than outside because local farmers have been taking clay from the church for centuries to protect their crops and cattle. The floor has been covered in slabs, but handfuls of clay are still removed from outside the church in the early spring.

however, Clonmacnoise grew to become an unrivalled bastion of Irish religion, literature and art and attracted a large lay population. Between the 7th and 12th centuries, monks from all over Europe came to study and pray here, helping to earn Ireland the title of the 'land of saints and scholars'.

Most of what you can see today dates from the 10th to 12th centuries. The monks would have lived in small huts surrounding the monastery. The site was burned and pillaged on numerous occasions by both the Vikings and the Irish. After the 12th century it fell into decline, and by the 15th century was home solely to an impoverished bishop. In 1552 the English garrison from Athlone reduced the site to a ruin.

⦿ Sights

Visitor Centre VISITOR CENTRE
(☏090-967 4195; www.heritageireland.ie; R444; adult/child €8/4; ⊙9am-6.30pm Jun-Aug, 10am-6pm mid-Mar–May, Sep & Oct, 10am-5.30pm Nov–mid-Mar, last admission 1hr before closing) Three connected conical huts, echoing the design of early monastic dwellings, house the visitor centre museum. A 20-minute audiovisual show provides an excellent introduction to the historic Clonmacnoise site.

The exhibition area contains the original high crosses (replicas have been put in their former locations outside) and various artefacts uncovered during excavation, including silver pins, beaded glass and an Ogham stone. Textual illustrations and explanations on the walls provide context.

There's a real sense of drama as you descend to the foot of the imposing **Cross of the Scriptures (King Flann's Cross)**, one

O'Rourke's Tower TOWER
Overlooking the River Shannon is the 19.3m-high O'Rourke's Tower. Lightning blasted the top off the tower in 1135, but the remaining structure was used for another 400 years. Some say that the stones that came down after the lightning strike were used to help build Temple Finghin & Tower.

Temple Finghin & Tower CHURCH
Temple Finghin and its round tower are on the northern boundary of the Clonmacnoise monastic site, overlooking the River Shannon. The building dates from around 1160 and has some fine Romanesque carvings. The herringbone-patterned tower roof is the only one in Ireland that has never been altered.

Nun's Church HISTORIC SITE
Beyond the site's boundary wall, about 500m east through the modern graveyard and on the way to the Mongan Bog, is the secluded Nun's Church with wonderful Romanesque arches and minute carvings; one has been interpreted as Ireland's earliest sheila-na-gig, in an acrobatic pose with feet tucked behind the ears.

Castle Ruins RUINS
To the west of the site, on the ridge near the car park, is a motte with the oddly shaped ruins of a 13th-century castle – also known as Clonmacnoise Castle – built by John de Grey, bishop of Norwich, to watch over the Shannon.

⌨ Sleeping & Eating
Clonmacnoise can be easily visited as a day trip from destinations including Athlone, 24km to the north, and Birr, 33km to the south; however, there are nearby B&Bs such as Kajon House if you want to spend the night.

The visitor centre has a small cafe. Near the car park, a **gift shop** (☑ 090-967 4134; ⊙ 10am-6pm mid-Mar–Oct) sells snacks and ice creams.

Kajon House B&B €€
(☑ 090-967 4191; www.kajonhouse.ie; R444, Creevagh; s/d from €60/80; ⊙ Mar-Oct; P 🕏) If you want to stay near the ruins, this is your best option, just 1.7km southwest. It has cosy rooms, comfy beds (warmed by electric blankets), a spacious garden (with a picnic table) and a warm welcome even by Irish standards, with scones and tea or coffee on arrival. Breakfast includes homemade pancakes and compotes.

❶ Getting There & Away
Clonmacnoise is 7km northeast of Shannonbridge on the R444. Bus tours are promoted throughout the region, but the best way to arrive is by car or bicycle.

Tullamore
POP 14,607
Set on the Grand Canal, Offaly's bustling county town, Tullamore, is best known for its namesake Tullamore Dew whiskey, which opened a new distillery in 2014, 60 years after it had shifted all production to County Tipperary. Its state-of-the-art visitor centre is a Midlands highlight.

◉ Sights & Activities

Tullamore Dew Visitor Centre VISITOR CENTRE
(☑ 057-932 5015; www.tullamoredew.com; Bury Quay; guided tour €16; ⊙ 9.30am-6pm Mon-Sat, 11.30am-5pm Sun) Located in an 1829-built canal-side warehouse, this famous whiskey producer's visitor centre has engaging exhibits that spotlight the role of the Grand Canal in the town's development. Tours are led by expert guides and conclude with tastings.

For real aficionados, there is a €29 Whiskey Wise Masterclass that explores the distillery process in depth, and a three-hour Ultimate Distillery Experience (€90; by appointment), which includes a visit to the off-site distillery and lets you create your own whiskey blend.

Charleville Castle CASTLE
(☑ 057-932 3040; www.charlevillecastle.com; off N52; guided tour adult/child €8/4; ⊙ guided tours noon-5.30pm Jun-Aug, by appointment Sep-Apr) Spires, turrets, clinging ivy and creaking trees give this hulking structure a spooky feel (and, yes, it's reputedly haunted). Charleville Castle was the family seat of the Burys, who commissioned the design in 1798 from Francis Johnston, one of Ireland's most famous architects. Admission is by 45-minute tour only. The castle is 3km southwest of Tullamore; look for the grove of huge ancient oaks.

The interior is spectacular, with ornately plastered ceilings, one of the most striking Gothic-revival galleries in Ireland and a kitchen block built to resemble a country church.

Buckley Cycle Hire CYCLING
(☑ 057-935 2240; www.buckleycycles.ie; Bury Quay; bike hire per 1/3/7 days from €15/30/50; ⊙ 9am-6pm Mon-Sat) Buckley's rental bikes come with helmets, repair kits, locks and maps. The company has another branch in Athlone (p504),

COUNTY OFFALY BOGLANDS

Clara Bog is one of the few great expanses of classic bogland in Western Europe to escape being stripped for fuel. Deceptively flat and seemingly lifeless, it offers a fascinating window into the natural world. At the Clara Bog Nature Reserve (www.clarabognaturereserve.ie; Erry Mill Rd; ☉ dawn-dusk), a magical preserved 464-hectare raised bog landscape, you'll hear water coursing, birds chirping and insects buzzing but the most memorable impression is the sense of quiet. A 1km-loop boardwalk leads from a parking area 2km south of Clara village (7.5km southeast of the M6).

Look for tiny wildflowers growing amid the pillowy soft peat and enjoy the sweeping views of distant green hills and the soft Offaly light on boggy pools of water.

A visitor centre is in Clara village.

Much of County Offaly's once-extensive boglands were stripped of peat for electricity generation during the 20th century. Now Lough Boora, 17km north of Kinnitty, is the focus of a scheme for bog restoration. There are more than 50km of walking and cycling trails across the Lough Boora Parklands (☑ 057-934 0010; www.loughboora.com; off R357; ☉ parklands dawn-dusk, visitor centre 9.30am-6pm Mon-Fri Apr-Oct, 11am-4pm Mon-Fri Nov-Mar), with excellent birdwatching, fishing, rare flora and a Mesolithic site. Maps are available at the visitor centre, which has a cafe open April to October, and adjacent bike hire.

Ireland's diversifying renewable energy portfolio, including its growing number of wind farms, will further help in the recovery of the boglands.

County Westmeath, allowing you to collect a bike here and drop it off there or vice versa.

🛏 Sleeping & Eating

Bridge House Hotel   HOTEL €€

(☑ 057-932 5600; www.bridgehousehoteltullamore.ie; Bridge St, enter via Distillery Lane; s/d/f/ste from €79/125/159/180; P❋🕏🐕) Graced by a grand stairway, this four-star hotel is the best in town. Its 70 spacious, antique-styled rooms have crimson colours; suites (only) come with air-conditioning, and some have balconies and Jacuzzis. A swimming pool flanked by arched windows and columns is adjacent to the spa, gym, sauna and steam room; there are several restaurants, bars and a nightclub.

Family rooms sleep up to five; cots and babysitting services are available.

Annaharvey Farm   B&B €€

(☑ 057-934 3544; www.annaharveyfarm.ie; R420, Aharney; d/f from €90/120; ☉ mid-Feb–Nov; P🕏) Ideal for families, this award-winning property in a tranquil rural location 7km southeast of Tullamore has an equestrian centre and a six-room guesthouse in a century-old converted barn, with simple but comfortable pine-furnished rooms with chequered blankets. Combined accommodation and horse-riding packages start at €120; you can also take one-hour riding lessons (adult/child €40/30) even if you're not staying here.

Sirocco's   ITALIAN €€

(☑ 057-935 2839; www.siroccos.net; Patrick St; mains €15-27, pizzas €12-14; ☉ 5-10pm Mon-Thu, noon-3pm & 5-10pm Fri, 1-10.30pm Sat, 1-9.30pm Sun; 🚼) Italian-Irish owned, this popular town-centre bistro has a wide selection of pasta dishes and pizzas named for famous Italian names (eg Versace, with tiger prawns, mussels and crab), as well as more substantial mains (veal escalope with Marsala cream sauce; mushroom- and Gorgonzola-stuffed chicken breast; salt-baked cod with parsley). Reservations are recommended; alternatively, takeaway is available.

Two-/three-course kids' menus cost €8/10.

✦ Getting There & Away

BUS

Bus Éireann (www.buseireann.ie) runs to/from Dublin (€18, 1½ hours, up to two per hour) and Athlone (€11, 40 minutes, two daily Monday to Saturday, one Sunday).

Kearns Transport (www.kearnstransport.com) runs local buses to destinations including Birr (€6, 35 minutes, six daily Monday to Friday, two Saturday, three Sunday).

TRAIN

Irish Rail (www.irishrail.ie) trains run to Dublin (€11.70, 55 minutes, hourly), Galway (€12.50, 1½ hours, hourly) and Westport (€17, 2¼ hours, five daily).

COUNTY LAOIS

Little-visited Laois (pronounced leash) is often overlooked as drivers zoom past to the south and west. Away from the main roads, though, this hidden corner of Ireland has pretty towns such as Abbeyleix making a perfect daytime stop, and the dramatic Slieve Bloom Mountains, which get you right off the beaten track. Laois is also home to magnificent Emo Court, one of Ireland's grandest buildings.

The county's heritage sights are linked via the Laois Heritage Trail, detailed in a free app and booklets available from tourist offices. County-wide information is also available at www.laoistourism.ie.

ℹ️ Getting Around

While Portlaoise has rail services, the county is best explored with your own wheels as bus services are sparse.

Abbeyleix

POP 1770

Abbeyleix (abbey-*leeks*) is a classic heritage town with a Georgian market house, graceful terraced housing and a wide leafy main street. The town grew up around a 12th-century Cistercian monastery, but frequent flooding led to local landowner Viscount de Vesci levelling the village in 1790 and creating a new estate in the present location, which is now Ireland's oldest planned town. During the Famine, de Vesci proved a kinder landlord than many, and the fountain obelisk in the square was erected in gratitude from his tenants.

◉ Sights

Unfortunately for visitors, de Vesci's magnificent mansion is not open to the public, but it's worth taking a look at the elegant Market House.

Heywood Gardens GARDENS
(☑ 087 220 2686; www.heritageireland.ie; Ballinakill; ⊙ 8.30am-9pm May-Aug, to 7pm Apr & Sep, to 5pm Oct-Mar) FREE These lavish gardens with lakes and woodland were designed by Edwin Lutyens and landscaped by Gertrude Jekyll, and completed in 1912. The centrepiece is a sunken garden, where circular terraces lead down to an oval pool with a magnificent fountain surrounded by sculpted stone turtles.

The gardens are 6km southeast of Abbeyleix, off the R432 to Ballinakill, in the grounds of Heywood Community School.

Market House HISTORIC BUILDING
(Market Sq; ⊙ 9.30am-1.30pm & 2.30-5pm Tue, Wed & Fri, 9.30am-1.30pm & 2.30-7.30pm Thu, 10am-2pm Sat) FREE Built in 1836 by Viscount de Vesci as a market house, this landmark building was restored by the council in 2009 and now houses the town library and an exhibition space.

Abbeyleix Heritage House & Museum MUSEUM
(☑ 057-873 1653; www.abbeyleixheritage.com; Ballyroan Rd; adult/child €3/2; ⊙ 9am-5pm Mon-Fri) An old 19th-century school building houses this museum detailing Abbeyleix' rich history. One room looks at the town's carpet-making legacy – the Turkish-influenced carpets once made here were chosen to grace the floors of the *Titanic* – while another showcases memorabilia from the Morrissey family, who ran the town's renowned shop and pub from 1775 to 2004. It also has tourist information and genealogy services.

🛏️ Sleeping & Eating

Farran Farm Hostel HOSTEL €
(☑ 057-873 4032; www.farmhostel.com; Ballacolla; dm from €20; 🅿️) In a beautifully restored limestone grain loft on a working family farm, this independent hostel has 45 beds in dorms with up to five bunks and private bathrooms in the rooms. Continental breakfast is €5; you can arrange in advance for evening meals made from fresh local produce. The hostel is off the R434, 12km west of Abbeyleix. Cash only.

Sandymount House B&B B&B €€
(☑ 057-873 1063; www.sandymounthouse.com; off R433, Old Town; s/d from €60/90; 🛜) Once the de Vesci estate manager's home, this beautifully restored country house dating from 1836 has a grand sweeping staircase, marble fireplaces and mature gardens. The four spacious rooms are well equipped with bathrooms sporting high-pressure showers. It's 2.5km west of Abbeyleix.

Gallic Kitchen CAFE €
(☑ 086 605 8208; www.gallickitchen.com; Main St; dishes €6.50-13; ⊙ 9.30am-5.30pm Wed-Sat, 10am-5pm Sun; 🛜🖶) Set in an old haberdashery shop named Bramley's, framed by floor-to-ceiling windows, this light, bright cafe serves simple dishes, such as quiches, pies, burgers and salads.

Paninis (€2.90 to €3.90) are among the choices for kids.

DONAGHMORE WORKHOUSE

The peaceful farming village of Donaghmore, is home to a quietly horrifying reminder of the Famin.

The unadorned stone **Donaghmore Workhouse** (📞086 829 6685; www. donaghmoremuseum.ie; R435, Donaghmore; adult/child €5/3; ⊙11am-5pm Mon-Fri), 19km west of Durrow, was a last resort for the destitute in the 1850s – one of 130 workhouses in the country at the time. Conditions were intentionally grim so the poor wouldn't stick around. They didn't, as scores died in the harsh conditions before the workhouse closed in 1886. Today the remaining buildings hold a collection of simple displays that detail this cruel story.

A sign near the entrance notes: 'By the time the Donaghmore Workhouse opened in 1853, most of the poor of the area had already perished from starvation or sickness or had emigrated.'

Overcrowding was rife, families were separated (often permanently), meals (no more than a bowl of gruel) were taken in silence, toilets were crude and bedding was limited. The loss of dignity that came with entering the workhouse was a tragic reality for many.

🍺 Drinking & Nightlife

★Morrissey's PUB
(📞057-873 1281; Main St; ⊙10am-11pm) Dating from 1775 (when it opened as a grocery store), this treasure of a pub has withstood the onslaught of modernisation. A hotchpotch of oddities line the shelves above the pew seats and pot-belly stove. It's a wonderful place to soak up the atmosphere with a pint or a coffee. Traditional music sessions take place on Saturday nights.

Durrow

POP 811

Durrow's neat rows of houses, pubs and cafes surround a manicured village green. On the western side stands the imposing gateway to the 18th-century Castle Durrow.

Castle Arms Hotel HOTEL €€
(📞057-873 6117; www.castlearmshotel.ie; The Square; s/d from €65/85; 🛜) Overlooking a corner of Durrow's village centre, this tidy place has 15 snug but comfortable rooms. The bar serves pub standards throughout the day and hosts traditional music and dancing on Sundays.

★Castle Durrow CASTLE €€€
(📞057-873 6555; www.castledurrow.com; The Square; d/ste from €250/330; 🅿🛜) Stately 18th-century Castle Durrow is one of Ireland's top country-house hotels, with 46 rooms including 10 opulent suites with four-poster beds and heavy brocades (though note there's no lift). Activities include tennis, archery, clay pigeon shooting and fishing. Even if you're not staying overnight, it's worth popping into its **restaurant** (mains €15-27, 3-course menu €39.50, afternoon tea €30; ⊙7am-9pm Wed-Sun) or having coffee on the terrace overlooking the vast grounds.

Numerous walks lace the estate.

Bob's Bar PUB
(www.bobsbardurrow.com; The Bridge; ⊙4pm-midnight Mon-Thu, to 1am Fri-Sun; 🛜) On the banks of the River Erkina, with a beer garden overlooking the bridge's stone arches, this cosy pub dating from 1832 has an old fuel bowser out the front, an interior filled with historic photos, and an adjacent museum (free entry) with vintage bikes, old farming implements and other memorabilia. Trad music sessions take place regularly.

Slieve Bloom Mountains

Populated Ireland recedes into your rearview mirror when you drive up into the wild, desolate Slieve Bloom Mountains, which rise dramatically from the Laois plain. The lower slopes are home to generic conifer farms, but higher up the sense of being away from it all permeates as you explore deserted blanket bogs, moorland, pine forests and isolated valleys.

◉ Sights & Activities

For leisurely walking, **Glenbarrow**, southwest of Rosenallis, has an interesting trail by the cascading **Glendine Park**, near the Glendine Gap and the **Cut Mountain Pass**. Look for parking areas with trail maps for more ideas.

For something more challenging you could stride out on the **Slieve Bloom Way**, an 84km-long signposted trail that does a complete circuit of the mountains, taking in most major points of interest. The recommended starting point is the car park at Glenbarrow, 5km from Rosenallis, from where the trail follows tracks, forest firebreaks and old roads around the mountains. The trail's highest point is at **Glendine Gap** (460m).

The website www.slievebloom.ie has comprehensive information and 17 downloadable looped walking routes ranging from 4km to 75km.

★ **Slieve Bloom Mountains**
Nature Reserve   NATURE RESERVE
(www.npws.ie) The mountains' higher elevations are protected by this 2300-hectare nature reserve, which tops out at 527m. Along with good walking suggestions, the website has info about the flora and fauna, including herbs and wildflowers.

Slieve Bloom Walking Club   WALKING
(☑ 086 821 0056; www.slievebloom.ie; €5; ☺ Sun, check website for other days) This club organises three- to four-hour guided walks (departure points vary), as well as an annual three-day walking festival in early May, which has been going strong since 1994.

🛏 Sleeping & Eating

★ **Roundwood House**   GUESTHOUSE €€
(☑ 057-873 2120; www.roundwoodhouse.com; R440, Mountrath; s/d/tr/cottage from €105/160/185/120; ☺ Feb-Dec; ℗ 🛜) Set in secluded woods, Roundwood has six bedrooms in its main building, a stately 18th-century Palladian villa, and another four rooms in the original, 17th-century 'yellow house', plus two self-catering cottages. Convivial communal dinners (three-/five-course menus €45/60) provide the chance to try local specialities like roast lamb with wild blueberry sauce. Kids aged under four stay free; those aged from five to 12 pay €25 per night.

Ballyfin House   LUXURY HOTEL €€€
(☑ 057-875 5866; www.ballyfin.com; off R423, Ballyfin; s/d/ste from €350/580/970; ℗ 🛜 ⛱) At the foot of the Slieve Bloom Mountains, this vast, opulent Regency mansion on a 248-hectare estate is one of Ireland's most luxurious properties. Highlights of its lavish interior include 17th-century Flemish tapestries, a Roman sarcophagus bath, secret doorways and a 'whispering room'. Some of

its 20 chandelier-lit, antique-furnished guest rooms have four-poster beds. Kids aged under nine aren't permitted.

Its 14m-long indoor swimming pool overlooks the courtyard garden; there's also a hydrotherapy pool and a sauna. Other amenities include a personal butler service, a library with 5000 books, clay pigeon shooting and rowing on the lake.

Mountmellick
POP 4777

A quiet Georgian town located on the River Owenass, Mountmellick was renowned for its linen production in the 19th century. It owes much of its history to its Quaker settlers and its place on the Grand Canal.

Starting from the Mountmellick Museum, a 4km looped and signed **heritage trail** leads you on a walking tour of the town.

Mountmellick Museum   MUSEUM
(☑ 057-862 4525; www.mountmellickdevelopment.com; Pearse St; adult/child €5/2; ☺ 9am-1pm & 2-5pm Mon-Fri) For an insight into the town's Quaker and industrial heritage, visit Mountmellick Museum, where you can also see a display of superbly subtle Mountmellick embroidery. Various linens and quilts still being made by locals are on sale, along with lace, threads and patterns. The museum also has a brochure on the heritage trail around town, and genealogical records of the town's Quaker inhabitants dating back to the 17th century.

Portarlington
POP 8368

Straddling County Laois to the south of the River Barrow and County Offaly to the north, Portarlington grew up under the influence of French Huguenot and German settlers and has some fine, if neglected, 18th-century buildings along French and Patrick Sts.

DON'T MISS

ELECTRIC PICNIC

Ireland's answer to Glastonbury, albeit on a smaller scale, the annual Electric Picnic (www.electricpicnic.ie; Stradbally Hall; 3-day pass from €205; ☺ late Aug-early Sep) is a spirited three-day open-air arts and music festival. Known for its eclectic line-up, it hosts big-name and emerging Irish and international performers. Tickets sell out months in advance and most people camp, creating one vast communal party. The festival takes place 11km east of Portlaoise.

Since it began in 2004, performers have included Björk, The Chemical Brothers, Sinéad O'Connor, Massive Attack, Blur, Arctic Monkeys and Wu-Tang Clan.

★ **Emo Court**   HISTORIC BUILDING

(☑ 057-862 6573; www.heritageireland.ie; off R422, Emo; house adult/child €5/3, grounds free; ☺ house 10am-6pm daily Easter-Sep, Sat & Sun Oct, last admission 5pm, grounds dawn-dusk year-round) The neoclassical, copper-domed Emo Court was designed in 1790 by James Gandon, architect of Dublin's Custom House. Originally the country seat of the first Earl of Portarlington, it later became a Jesuit novitiate. Admission is by a compulsory 40-minute guided tour. Studded with Greek statues, the extensive grounds contain over 1000 different trees, including huge sequoias. Enjoy refreshments at the cafe or a leisurely picnic before a scenic stroll through the woodlands to Emo Lake. It's 8km south of Portarlington.

Lea Castle   RUINS

On the banks of the River Barrow, 4.3km east of town, the ivy-covered ruins of 13th-century Lea Castle include a fairly intact towered keep with two outer walls and a twin-towered gatehouse. Access is through a farmyard, 500m to the north off the main Monasterevin road (R420).

St Paul's Church   CHURCH

(French Church St; ☺ 8am-dusk) FREE The 1851 St Paul's Church, on the site of the original 17th-century French church, was built for the Huguenots, some of whose tombstones stand in a corner of the churchyard. Most of the wealthier Huguenots had left Portarlington by 1871; those who stayed were mainly tradespeople and shopkeepers.

Portlaoise & Around

POP 22,050

The busy county town of Portlaoise mainly serves as a commercial centre and you'll probably only find yourself either passing through or stopping off in September for the Electric Picnic music and arts festival.

Timahoe Round Tower   RUINS

(R426, Timahoe) In the tiny, charming village of Timahoe, 12km southeast of Portlaoise, is a tilting 30m-tall, 12th-century round tower with an elaborately carved Romanesque doorway 5m above the ground. Screened by a burbling stream and seemingly straight out of a fairy tale, the tower is part of an ancient site that includes the ruins of a 15th-century church.

The entire place has a certain magical quality, enhanced by a dearth of visitors.

Rock of Dunamase   HISTORIC SITE

(off N80, Aughnahilla; ☺ dawn-dusk) The Rock of Dunamase, 6km east of Portlaoise, is an arresting sight: a craggy limestone outcrop rising 45m out of the flat plains. It offered early settlers a superb natural defensive position looking out across the surrounding countryside. The ruins here are those of a castle built in the 12th century. You'll need some imagination to envisage the site as it was before it was destroyed by Cromwell's henchmen in 1650, but the views from the summit are breathtaking.

The rock was first fortified in the Bronze Age. Over the centuries that followed, successive waves of Viking, Norman, Irish and English invaders fought over its occupation and control. The castle was extensively remodelled in the 15th century, and fell into decline until its 17th-century destruction.

On a clear day, you can see Timahoe round tower to the south, the Slieve Blooms to the west and the Wicklow Mountains to the east.

❶ Getting There & Away

Bus Éireann (www.buseireann.ie) has two services daily Monday to Saturday, one service on Sunday, running north to Mountmellick (€4.30, 10 minutes), Tullamore (€12, 40 minutes) and Athlone (€16, 1¼ hours), and south to Kilkenny (€17, 1½ hours).

The train station is on Station Rd, 300m north of the town centre. Direct trains (www.irishrail.ie) run to Dublin (€15.80, one hour, up to two per hour), Cork (€16, 1¾ hours, up to 10 daily) and Limerick (€16, 1½ hours, three daily).

Counties Meath, Louth, Cavan & Monaghan

POP 460,587 / AREA 6395 SQ KM

Best Places to Eat

➡ MacNean House & Restaurant (p550)

➡ Olde Post Inn (p549)

➡ Browne's Bar (p530)

➡ Strandfield (p544)

➡ Riverbank County Pub (p553)

➡ Ghan House (p547)

Best Places to Stay

➡ Hilton Park (p552)

➡ Castle Leslie (p552)

➡ Scholars Townhouse Hotel (p540)

➡ Rock Farm Glamping (p530)

➡ Station House Hotel (p533)

➡ Carlingford House (p546)

Why Go?

The fertile fields of Counties Meath and Louth attracted Ireland's first settlers, making these two counties the birthplace of Irish civilisation. Today they're part of Dublin's commuter belt, but the earliest inhabitants' legacies endure at the mystical tombs at Brú na Bóinne and Loughcrew – which both predate the Egyptian pyramids – and on the Hill of Tara, the seat of Ireland's high kings and gateway to the otherworld.

Following St Patrick's arrival, the faithful built abbeys, high crosses and round towers to protect their treasured manuscripts. Magnificent ruins recall a time when Ireland was known as the Land of Saints and Scholars.

To the northwest, Counties Cavan and Monaghan's undulating hills and fish-filled lakes are wilder and more remote. Walking trails take in the rugged scenery and expansive views of the Cuilcagh Mountains.

When to Go

➡ If sightseeing is at the top of your list, try to avoid November to March when many of the region's high-profile historic sites have reduced hours or are closed altogether.

➡ April is the driest month of the year in this part of the country. The daffodils are in bloom, along with a riot of wildflowers, making it especially scenic (and less soggy) for walkers.

➡ Summertime is festival time: Drogheda hosts its annual Arts Festival in May, while Carlingford's party atmosphere peaks in August during its famous Oyster Festival. Horses race on Laytown's beach around late August and Monaghan town hosts its Harvest Blues Festival in early September.

Counties Meath, Louth, Cavan & Monaghan Highlights

1 Brú na Bóinne
(p524) Exploring evocative prehistoric remains at Brú na Bóinne's extraordinary ancient burial sites.

2 Hot-Air Balloon Flights (p535) Floating above fascinating ruins and emerald-green fields on a hot-air balloon flight from Trim.

3 Slane Castle (p529) Touring Slane's 18th-century castle and state-of-the-art whiskey distillery in its former stables.

4 Tayto Park (p533) Riding Europe's largest wooden inverted roller coaster and touring Tayto's crisp factory.

5 Tara (p531) Uncovering the secrets of the massive earthworks, passage graves and Stone of Destiny at this sacred hilltop.

6 Cavan Adventure Centre (p549) Canoeing the waterways around Butlersbridge.

7 Listoke Distillery & Gin School (p540) Mixing botanicals to create your own gin, accompanied by G&Ts, on a course at this distillery in Listoke.

8 Cavan Burren Park (p550) Wandering among megalithic stones and tombs near Blacklion.

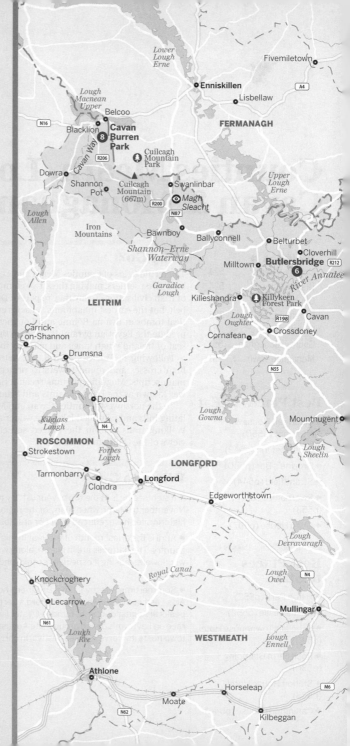

COUNTY MEATH

Meath's rich soil, laid down during the last ice age, drew settlers as early as 8000 BC. They worked their way up the banks of the River Boyne, transforming the landscape from forest to farmland. One of the five provinces of ancient Ireland, Meath was at the centre of Irish politics for centuries.

Today Meath's high-yielding land and plentiful water supply make it a vital agriculture centre. Its proximity to Dublin means larger towns are surrounded by housing estates and roads have heavy traffic at commuter time. For visitors, though, there are numerous must-see attractions here, including many tangible reminders of Meath's absorbing history.

Brú na Bóinne

The vast Neolithic necropolis known as Brú na Bóinne (the Boyne Palace) is one of the most extraordinary sites in Europe. A thousand years older than Stonehenge, it's a powerful testament to the mind-boggling achievements of prehistoric humankind.

The complex was built to house the remains of those in the top social tier and its tombs were the largest artificial structures in Ireland until the construction of the Anglo-Norman castles 4000 years later. The area consists of many different sites; the three principal ones are Newgrange, Knowth and Dowth.

NEWGRANGE WINTER SOLSTICE

At 8.20am on the winter solstice (between 18 and 23 December), the rising sun's rays shine through the roof-box above the entrance, creep slowly down the long passage and illuminate the tomb chamber for 17 minutes. There is little doubt that this is one of the country's most memorable, even mystical, experiences.

There's a simulated winter sunrise for every group taken into the mound. To be in with a chance of witnessing the real thing on one of six mornings around the solstice, enter the free lottery that's drawn in late September; 50 names are drawn and each winner is allowed to take one guest (be aware, however, that over 30,000 people apply each year). Fill out the form at the Brú na Bóinne Visitor Centre or email brunaboinne@opw.ie.

Over the centuries the tombs decayed, were covered by grass and trees, and were plundered by everybody from Vikings to Victorian treasure hunters, whose carved initials can be seen on the great stones of Newgrange. The countryside around the tombs is home to countless other ancient tumuli (burial mounds) and standing stones.

⊙ Sights

★ Brú na Bóinne Visitor Centre   VISITOR CENTRE

(☑ 041-988 0300; www.worldheritageireland.ie; Donore; adult/child visitor centre €4/3, visitor centre & Newgrange €7/4, visitor centre & Knowth €6/4, all 3 sites €13/8; ⊙ 9am-7pm Jun–mid-Sep, 9am-6.30pm May & mid-Sep–early Oct, 9.30am-5.30pm Feb-Apr & early Oct-early Nov, 9am-5pm early Nov-Jan) Built in a spiral design echoing Newgrange, this superb interpretive centre houses interactive exhibits on prehistoric Ireland and its passage tombs. It has regional tourism info, an excellent cafe, plus a book and souvenir shop. Upstairs, a glassed-in observation mezzanine looks out over Newgrange. All visits to Newgrange and/or Knowth depart from here.

★ Newgrange   HISTORIC SITE

(www.worldheritageireland.ie; visitor centre & Newgrange €7/4; ⊙ 9am-7pm Jun–mid-Sep, 9am-6.30pm May & mid-Sep–early Oct, 9.30am-5.30pm Feb-Apr & early Oct-early Nov, 9am-5pm early Nov-Jan) A startling 80m in diameter and 13m high, Newgrange's white round stone walls, topped by a grass dome, look eerily futuristic. Underneath lies the finest Stone Age passage tomb in Ireland – one of the most remarkable prehistoric sites in Europe. Dating from around 3200 BC, it predates Egypt's pyramids by some six centuries.

The tomb's precise alignment with the sun at the time of the winter solstice (p###) suggests it was also designed to act as a calendar. No one is quite sure of its original purpose, however – the most common theories are that it was a burial place for kings or a centre for ritual.

Newgrange's name derives from 'New Granary' (the tomb did in fact serve as a repository for wheat and grain at one stage), although a more popular belief is that it comes from the Irish for 'Cave of Gráinne', a reference to a popular Celtic myth. *The Pursuit of Diarmuid and Gráinne* tells of the illicit love between the woman betrothed to Fionn MacCumhaill (or Finn McCool), leader of the Fianna, and Diarmuid, one of his most trusted lieutenants.

ⓘ BRÚ NA BÓINNE TOP TIPS

Advance planning will help you get the most out of your visit.

→ All visits to Brú na Bóinne start at the Brú na Bóinne Visitor Centre (p524), from where there's a shuttle bus to the tombs. If you turn up at either Newgrange or Knowth first, you'll be sent to the visitor centre, 4km from either site. Walking is discouraged, as the lanes are narrow and dangerous due to passing tour buses.

→ Allow plenty of time: an hour for the visitor centre alone, two hours to include a trip to Newgrange or Knowth, and half a day to see all three.

→ Dowth's tombs are closed to the public but you can freely visit the surrounding site.

→ In summer, particularly at weekends, Brú na Bóinne gets very crowded; on peak days more than 2000 people can show up. As there are only 750 tour slots, you may not be guaranteed a visit to either of the passage tombs. Tickets are sold on a first-come, first-served basis (no advance booking). Arrive early in the morning or visit midweek and be prepared to wait. Alternatively, visiting as part of an organised tour, such as Mary Gibbons Tours (p528), guarantees a spot.

→ Tours are primarily outdoors with no shelter so bring rain gear, just in case.

When Diarmuid was fatally wounded, his body was brought to Newgrange by the god Aengus in a vain attempt to save him, and the despairing Gráinne followed him into the cave, where she remained long after he died. This suspiciously Arthurian tale (substitute Lancelot and Guinevere for Diarmuid and Gráinne) is undoubtedly a myth, but it's still a pretty good story. Newgrange also plays another role in Celtic mythology as the site where the hero Cúchulainn was conceived.

Over time, Newgrange, like Dowth and Knowth, deteriorated and at one stage was even used as a quarry. The site was extensively restored in 1962 and again in 1975.

A superbly carved kerbstone with double and triple spirals guards the tomb's main entrance, but the area has been reconstructed so that visitors don't have to clamber in over it. Above the entrance is a slit, or roof-box, which lets light in. Another beautifully decorated kerbstone stands at the exact opposite side of the mound. Some experts say that a ring of standing stones encircled the mound, forming a great circle about 100m in diameter, but only 12 of these stones remain, with traces of others below ground level.

Holding the whole structure together are the 97 boulders of the kerb ring, designed to stop the mound from collapsing outwards. Eleven of these are decorated with motifs similar to those on the main entrance stone, although only three have extensive carvings.

The white quartzite that encases the tomb was originally obtained from Wicklow, 70km south – in an age before horse and wheel, it was transported by sea and then up the River Boyne. More than 200,000 tonnes of earth and stone also went into the mound.

You can walk down the narrow 19m passage, lined with 43 stone uprights (some of them engraved), which leads into the tomb chamber about one third of the way into the colossal mound. The chamber has three recesses, and in these are large basin stones that held cremated human bones. As well as the remains, the basins would have held funeral offerings of beads and pendants, but these were stolen long before the archaeologists arrived.

Above, the massive stones support a 6m-high corbel-vaulted roof. A complex drainage system means that not a drop of water has penetrated the interior in 40 centuries.

★ **Knowth**   HISTORIC SITE
(www.worldheritageireland.ie; visitor centre & Knowth €6/4; ⏰ 9am-7pm Jun–mid-Sep, 9am-6.30pm May & mid-Sep–early Oct, 9.30am-5.30pm Feb-Apr & early Oct-early Nov, 9am-5pm early Nov-Jan) Northwest of Newgrange, the burial mound of Knowth was built around the same time. It has the greatest collection of passage-grave art ever uncovered in Western Europe. Early excavations cleared a passage leading to the central chamber, which at 34m is much longer than the one at Newgrange. In 1968, a 40m passage was unearthed on the opposite side of the mound.

Also in the mound are the remains of six early Christian souterrains (underground chambers) built into the side. Some 300 carved slabs and 17 satellite graves surround the main mound.

Brú na Bóinne

All visits start at the **①visitor centre**, which has a terrific exhibit that includes a short context-setting film. From here, you board a shuttle bus that takes you to **②Newgrange**, where you'll go past the **③kerbstone** into the **④main passage** and the **⑤burial chamber**. If you're not a lucky lottery winner for the solstice, fear not – there's an artificial illumination ceremony that replicates it. If you're continuing on to tour **⑥Knowth**, you'll need to go back to the visitor centre and get on another bus; otherwise, you can drive directly to **⑦Dowth** and visit, but only from outside (the information panels will tell you what you're looking at).

Newgrange Interior Passage

The passage is lined with 43 orthostats, or standing stones, averaging 1.5m in height: 22 on the left (western) side, 21 on the right (eastern) side.

Knowth

Roughly one third of all megalithic art in Western Europe is contained within the Knowth complex, including more than 200 decorated stones. Alongside typical motifs like spirals, lozenges and concentric circles are rare crescent shapes.

TOP TIP

Best time to visit is early morning mid-week during summer, when there are fewer tourists and no school tours.

Newgrange Entrance Kerbstone

Newgrange is surrounded by 97 kerbstones (24 of which are still buried), numbered sequentially from K1, the beautifully decorated entrance stone.

Newgrange
Newgrange's passage grave is designed to allow for a solar alignment during the winter solstice.

FACT FILE

The winter solstice event is witnessed by a maximum of 50 people selected by lottery and their guests (one each). In 2018, 28,595 people applied.

Dowth
There is no public access to the two passage chambers at Dowth. The crater at the top was due to a clumsy attempt at excavation in 1847.

⑦

Newgrange Burial Chamber
The corbelled roof of the chamber has remained intact since its construction, and is considered one of the finest of its kind in Europe.

①

Brú na Bóinne Visitor Centre
The spiral design of this wonderful interpretative centre is designed to echo the construction and decoration of Newgrange. Inside are exhibits on prehistoric Ireland and passage tombs.

ℹ HERITAGE CARD

If you're planning to visit several archaeological and historic sites, consider investing in a Heritage Card (www.heritageireland.ie; adult/child €40/10), valid for one year and available for purchase at the Battle of the Boyne Site (p529) ticket office, as well as other participating sites throughout the country.

Human activity at Knowth continued for thousands of years after its construction, which accounts for the site's complexity. The Beaker folk, so-called because they buried their dead with drinking vessels, occupied the site in the Early Bronze Age (c 1800 BC), as did the Celts in the Iron Age (c 500 BC). Remnants of bronze and iron workings from these periods have been discovered. Around AD 800 to 900, it was turned into a *ráth* (earthen ring fort), a stronghold of the very powerful O'Neill clan. In 965 it was the seat of Cormac MacMaelmithic, later Ireland's high king for nine years, and in the 12th century the Normans built a motte and a bailey (a raised mound with a walled keep) here. The site was finally abandoned around 1400. Visits start only from the visitor centre (p524).

Dowth   HISTORIC SITE

(L1607; ⊙ 24hr) FREE The circular mound at Dowth is similar in size to Newgrange (p524) – about 63m in diameter – but is slightly taller at 14m high. Due to safety issues, Dowth's tombs are closed to visitors, though you can visit the mound (and its resident grazing sheep) from the L1607 road between Newgrange and Drogheda.

North of the tumulus are the ruins of **Dowth Castle** and **Dowth House**.

Dowth has two entrance passages leading to separate chambers (both sealed), and a 24m early Christian underground passage at either end, which connect with the western passage. This 8m-long passage leads into a small cruciform chamber, in which a recess acts as an entrance to an additional series of small compartments, a feature unique to Dowth. To the southwest is the entrance to a shorter passage and a smaller chamber.

It has suffered badly at the hands of everyone from road builders and treasure hunters to amateur archaeologists, who scooped out the centre of the tumulus in the 19th century. For a time, Dowth even had a tearoom ignobly perched on its summit.

Newgrange Farm   FARM

(☎ 041-982 4119; www.newgrangefarm.com; Newgrange; per person €9, tractor ride €3; ⊙ 10am-6pm mid-Mar–Aug) One for the kids, this hands-on, family-run 135-hectare working farm allows visitors to feed the ducks, lambs and goats, milk a cow, pet a rabbit and take a tractor ride. Children's play areas include a straw maze and toy tractors; there are indoor and outdoor picnic areas and a cafe. Follow the signs on the N51. Sunday at 3pm is a very special time when the 'sheep derby' is run, with teddy bear 'jockeys' tied to the animals' backs. Visiting children are made owners of individual sheep for the race.

☞ Tours

Brú na Bóinne is one of the most popular tourist attractions in Ireland, and there are plenty of organised tours. Most depart from Dublin.

★ Mary Gibbons Tours   TOURS

(☎ 086 355 1355; www.newgrangetours.com; tour incl entrance fees adult/child €40/35) These excellent tours depart from numerous Dublin hotels, beginning at 9.30am Monday to Friday, and 7.30am Saturday and Sunday, and take in the whole of the Boyne Valley including Newgrange and the Hill of Tara. Expert guides offer a fascinating insight into Celtic and pre-Celtic life in Ireland. No credit cards; pay cash on the bus.

🛏 Sleeping

Newgrange Lodge   LODGE €

(☎ 041-988 2478; www.newgrangelodge.com; Staleen Rd, Donore; dm/s/d/f from €22/65/75/119; P🛜) Footsteps east of the Brú na Bóinne Visitor Centre, this converted farmhouse has 23 rooms ranging from dorms with four to 10 beds to hotel-standard doubles with private bathroom. Superb facilities include a self-catering kitchen, two outdoor patios, a lounge with an open fire, board games and books, and free bikes. Rates include continental breakfast with homemade scones.

ℹ Getting There & Away

Bus Éireann (www.buseireann.ie) links the Brú na Bóinne Visitor Centre with Drogheda (€2.85, 25 minutes, two daily), with connections to Dublin.

Battle of the Boyne Site

More than 60,000 soldiers of the armies of King James II and King William III fought in

1690 on this **patch of farmland** (⌨041-980 9950; www.battleoftheboyne.ie; Drybridge; adult/child €5/3; ⊙9am-5pm May-Sep, to 4pm Oct-Apr) on the border of Counties Meath and Louth. William ultimately prevailed and James sailed off to France.

The battle site has an informative visitor centre and parkland walks. It's 6km west of Drogheda's town centre along Rathmullan Rd (follow the river). Buses run to/from Drogheda (€4.80, 20 minutes, two daily).

At the visitor centre you can watch a short film about the battle, see original and replica weaponry of the time, and explore a laser battlefield model. Self-guided walks through the parkland and battle site allow time to ponder the events that saw Protestant interests remain in Ireland. Costumed re-enactments take place in summer.

Boyne Boats
BOATING

(⌨086 361 6420; www.boyneboats.ie; Oldbridge; 90min tour adult/child €20/15; ⊙11am-3pm Wed-Sun Easter-May, 11am-3pm Jun-Oct) One of the most peaceful ways to explore the Boyne Valley is to row a traditional oak-and-spruce, eight-seater *currach* (rowing boat made of a framework of laths covered with tarred canvas). Tours head along the Boyne Navigation canal network past the Battle of the Boyne Site, with commentary relaying its history as well as stories relating to the TV series *Game of Thrones*, in which the boats starred.

The launch point is the lock keeper's cottage 4km west of Drogheda.

Slane
POP 1369

Slane's 18th-century stone houses and cottages slink down a steep hill to the River Boyne, which glides beneath a narrow bridge. The town grew up around the enormous castle (after which it was named), whose stables now house a whiskey distillery. At the main crossroads four identical houses face each other: local lore has it that they were built for four sisters who had taken an intense dislike to one another and kept a beady-eyed watch from their individual residences.

◉ Sights

★Slane Castle
CASTLE

(⌨041-982 0600; www.slanecastle.ie; Main St; guided tour adult/child €12/7.20, combined castle & distillery tour €27/15; ⊙guided tour by reservation early May-Aug) Still the private residence of Henry Conyngham, Earl of Mountcharles, 18th-century Slane Castle is best known for its massive outdoor **concerts** featuring rock-royalty names: past performers include Bon Jovi, U2, the Rolling Stones, Madonna and Metallica.

Guided castle tours lasting 45 minutes include the neo-Gothic Ballroom, completed in 1821, and the Kings Room. Tours and tastings are also available at its stable-housed whiskey distillery. There's a superb restaurant and a bar (p530). It's 1.5km west of the village centre off the N51.

Built in the Gothic-revival style by James Wyatt in 1785, the building was later altered by Francis Johnson for George IV's visits to Lady Conyngham, allegedly his mistress. It's said the road between Dublin and Slane was built especially straight and smooth to speed up the smitten king's journeys. In 1991 the castle was gutted by a fire, whereupon it was discovered that the earl was under-insured. A major fundraising drive, of which the summer concerts were a part, led to a painstaking restoration.

Slane Distillery
DISTILLERY

(⌨041-982 0600; www.slaneirishwhiskey.com; Slane Castle; guided tour adult/child €18/10.80, combined castle & distillery tour €27/15; ⊙11am-5pm except during events) Triple-cask-matured whiskey made on-site at Slane Castle was first released in 2017. The castle's 18th-century horse stables are home to a visitor experience, with one-hour guided tours (hourly from 11am to 4pm) that take you through the heritage and barley rooms, the cooperage, warehouse and production area, where you'll see the copper stills, finishing with a tasting. You can also take a DIY tasting in the distillery's bar.

Hill of Slane
HISTORIC SITE

(off N2) About 1km north of Slane village is the Hill of Slane, a fairly plain-looking mound that stands out only for its association with a thick slice of Celto-Christian mythology. According to legend, St Patrick lit a paschal (Easter) fire here in 433 to proclaim Christianity throughout the land.

On a clear day, climb the evocative ancient stone steps of the tower to enjoy magnificent views of the Hill of Tara and the Boyne Valley, and (it's said) seven Irish counties.

The story goes that Patrick's paschal fire infuriated Laoghaire, the pagan high king of Ireland, who had expressly ordered that no fire be lit within sight of the Hill of Tara. He was restrained by his far-sighted druids, who warned that 'the man who had kindled the flame would surpass kings and princes'. Laoghaire went to meet Patrick, and all but one of the king's attendants, a man called Erc, greeted Patrick with scorn.

Undeterred, Patrick plucked a shamrock from the ground, using its three leaves to explain the paradox of the Holy Trinity: the union of the Father, the Son and the Holy Spirit in one. Laoghaire wasn't convinced, but he agreed to let Patrick continue his missionary work. Patrick's success that day, apart from keeping his own life and giving Ireland one of its enduring national symbols, was good old Erc, who was baptised and later became the first bishop of Slane. To this day, the local parish priest lights a fire here on Holy Saturday.

The Hill of Slane originally had a church associated with St Erc and, later, a round tower and monastery, but only an outline of the foundations remains. You can also see the remains of a ruined church and tower that were once part of an early-16th-century Franciscan friary.

Ledwidge Museum   MUSEUM

(☑ 041-982 4544; www.francisledwidge.com; Janesville; adult/child €3/1; ⊙10am-5pm Apr-Oct, to 3.30pm Nov-Mar) This quaint cottage, 1km east of Slane on the N51, was the birthplace of poet Francis Ledwidge (1887–1917). A keen political activist, Ledwidge was thwarted in his efforts to set up a local Gaelic League branch, but found an outlet in verse. He died on the battlefield at Ypres, having survived Gallipoli and Serbia.

The museum provides an insight into Ledwidge's works, and the cottage itself is a humbling example of how farm labourers lived in the 19th century.

🛌 Sleeping

★ Rock Farm Glamping   CAMPGROUND €

(☑ 041-988 4861; www.rockfarmslane.ie; off N2; d from €60; ⊙yurts Apr-Oct, huts Nov-Apr; P🐕🛜) 🐾 On an organic farm stretching 1.5km along the banks of the River Boyne, shaded by oak, ash and chestnut trees, Rock Farm has stunning yurts and huts with lanterns and wood stoves sleeping up to six. Bathrooms are located in the communal 'Le Shack' alongside a lounge and state-of-the-art kitchen, with a pizza oven outside. There's a two-night minimum stay.

Outdoor hot tubs, electric bike hire (€25), yoga classes (€15) and kayak tours along the river (€50) are all available. Two-day breakfast, barbecue and pizza packs cost €10 to €15.

Slane Farm Hostel   HOSTEL €

(☑ 041-982 4985; www.slanefarmhostel.ie; Harlinstown House, Navan Rd; campsites per person €12, dm/s/d/cottage from €23/40/60/110; P🛜) 🐾 These former stables, built by the Marquis of Conyngham in the 18th century, have been converted into a wonderful hostel that's part of a working dairy farm. Common areas include a games room and a kitchen, with free-range eggs and a vegetable plot for guests to use. Free bikes are available. It's 2.5km west of Slane. Self-catering terraced cottages sleep up to six.

Conyngham Arms   INN €€

(☑ 041-988 4444; www.conynghamarms.ie; Main St; s/d/f from €65/89/109; P🛜) Beautifully restored, this 18th-century stone coaching inn has 15 airy rooms decorated with French country-style furnishings (some with canopied, four-poster beds), a charming, rose-filled garden with a fountain at its centre, a restaurant and excellent breakfasts such as free-range scrambled eggs with Annagassan smoked salmon. Staff are welcoming and professional. Wi-fi is strongest in the front rooms.

🍴 Eating & Drinking

★ Browne's Bar   IRISH €

(www.slanecastle.ie; Slane Castle; mains €8-17; ⊙10am-6pm Mon-Wed, to 8pm Thu-Sat, 10.30am-7.30pm Sun, bar to 7pm Mon-Wed, to 11.30pm Thu-Sat, to 9pm Sun; 🛜) 🐾 Even if you're not touring Slane Castle, don't miss a meal at its bar. Decorated with framed photos of rock stars who've performed at the castle's concerts, it utilises produce from its own organic farm in breakfast specials (eg avocado and Dunany crab eggs Benedict), burgers, cider-steamed mussels, and Boyne Valley charcuterie boards with local cheeses and homemade chutney.

Higher-end dining is available at the castle's grand Gandon Room from Thursday to Saturday evenings (mains €18 to €39.50) and at Sunday lunch (two/three courses €30/36.50).

Inside Out   MEDITERRANEAN €€

(☑ 041-988 4629; www.insideoutslane.ie; Chapel St; mains €13-31.50; ⊙5-10pm Wed-Fri, from 12.30pm Sat, 12.30-9pm Sun; 🛜) Opening to a fairy-lit garden, split-level Inside Out blends premium Irish produce and Mediterranean flavours. Slane Whiskey–marinated spatchcock chicken and Clogherhead prawn, squid and mussel paella are highlights; a wood-fired oven also bakes pizzas like the Gambino (with Slane garlic sausage) or Josip (with black pudding and Boyne Valley blue goat's cheese). Live acoustic sets play in summer.

Conyngham Arms   GASTROPUB €€
(📞 041-988 4444; www.conynghamarms.ie; Main St; mains €12.50-23.50; ⊕kitchen noon-9pm, bar to 11pm; 🖥) At the back of the Conyngham Arms hotel, its restaurant serves upmarket pub fare: smoked cod chowder, herb-crusted Camembert with red-currant jam, spiced pork sausages with stout black pudding, and peat-smoked bacon with mash and cider gravy.

A two-course kids' menu costs €9.

Tankardstown House   IRISH €€€
(📞 041-982 4621; www.tankardstown.ie; Rathkenny; mains lunch €13-17.50, dinner €19.50-29.50; ⊕noon-4.30pm & 6-8.30pm Wed & Thu, noon-4.30pm & 6-9.30pm Fri & Sat, 12.30-3.30pm & 6-8.30pm Sun; 🖥) ✔ Restored by the owners of the Conyngham Arms, this spectacular manor house and orangery on 32 hectares 10km northwest of Slane dates from the 18th century. Its evening restaurant, Brabazon, is its centrepiece, with exquisite dishes such as smoked wood pigeon or wild mushroom ravioli with black truffle and Parmesan foam; casual lunches are served in its 'garden village'.

Eggs come from its own hens, with vegetables sourced from its polytunnels and gardens. The kids' menu will impress junior gourmands. Accommodation is available in the manor and courtyard cottages (double/suite/cottage from €167.50/180/105), but book well ahead as it's a popular wedding venue.

★ Boyles   PUB
(www.boylesofslane.ie; Main St; ⊕noon-11.30pm Mon-Thu, to 12.30am Fri & Sat, to 11pm Sun; 🛜) Behind a fire-engine-red facade, this nook-and-cranny-filled pub has cosy snugs, stained-glass partitions and a toasty wood stove. It's owned by musician Andrew Cassidy, who hosts a knockout line-up of gigs and trad-music sessions. On Wednesdays, when Andrew and his friends jam, the atmosphere is electric. Live music also takes place Fridays, Saturdays and Sundays (plus some Thursdays). Cash only.

❶ Information

Slane's **tourist office** (📞 041-982 4000; www.visitslane.ie; The Hub, 2 Main St; ⊕9.30am-5pm Mon-Sat, noon-4pm Sun) is in the village centre.

❶ Getting There & Away

Bus Éireann (www.buseireann.ie) has a direct service to Drogheda (€5, 30 minutes, hourly), from where you can connect to Dublin.

CHEESE CENTRAL

Renowned **Sheridans Cheesemongers** (www.sheridanscheesemongers.com; Virginia Rd Station, Pottlereagh; ⊕10am-6pm Mon-Sat), with shops in Dublin and Galway, has its warehouses and HQ here in County Meath. A former train station now houses a cavernous barn-style shop crammed with cheeses from across Europe; Irish varieties include Cashel Blue, Durrus, Gubbeen and smoked Knockanore. It also sells chutneys, crackers, freshly baked bread, charcuterie, smoked fish, wines and its own cookbooks.

A small market showcasing local farmers and other producers sets up on Saturdays.

Tara

The Hill of Tara is Ireland's most sacred stretch of turf, occupying a place at the heart of Irish history, legend and folklore. It was the home of the mystical druids, the priest-rulers of ancient Ireland, who practised their particular form of Celtic paganism under the watchful gaze of the all-powerful goddess Maeve (Medbh). Later it was the ceremonial capital of the high kings, all 142 of them, who ruled until the arrival of Christianity in the 5th century. It is also one of the most important ancient sites in Europe, with a Stone Age passage tomb and prehistoric burial mounds that date back some 5000 years.

Although little remains other than humps and mounds on the hill (named from ancient texts), its historic and folkloric significance is immense.

Entrance to Tara is free and the site is always open. There are good explanatory panels by the entrance.

History

Mythology and religion intertwine with historical facts here. The Celts believed that Tara was the sacred dwelling place of the gods and the gateway to the other world. The passage grave was thought to be the final resting place of the Tuatha dé Danann, the mythical fairy folk. They were real enough, but instead of pixies and brownies, they were earlier Stone Age arrivals on the island.

As the Celtic political landscape began to evolve, the druids' power was usurped by warlike chieftains who took kingly titles;

there was no sense of a united Ireland, so at any given time there were countless *rí tuaithe* (regional kings) controlling many small areas. The king who ruled Tara, though, was generally considered the big shot, the high king, even though his direct rule didn't extend too far beyond the provincial border.

The most important event in Tara's calendar was the three-day harvest *feis* (festival) that took place at Samhain, a precursor to modern Halloween. During the festival, the high king pulled out all the stops: grievances were heard, laws passed and disputes settled amid a bacchanalia of eating, drinking and partying. When the early Christians hit town in the 5th century, they targeted Tara straight away. The arrival of Christianity marked the beginning of the end for Celtic pagan civilisation, and the high kings began to desert Tara, though the kings of Leinster continued to be based here until the 11th century.

In August 1843 Tara saw one of the greatest crowds ever to gather in Ireland. Daniel O'Connell, leader of the opposition to union with Great Britain, held one of his galvanising rallies at Tara, and up to 750,000 people came to hear him speak.

⊙ Sights

Rath of the Synods
HISTORIC SITE

Tara's Protestant church grounds and graveyard spill onto the remains of this triple-ringed fort where some of St Patrick's early synods (meetings) supposedly took place. Excavations suggest the enclosure was used between AD 200 and 400 for burials, rituals and dwellings – originally the ring fort would have contained wooden houses surrounded by timber palisades.

Archaeologists have uncovered Roman glass, shards of pottery and seals, showing links with the Roman Empire even though the Romans never extended their power to Ireland.

Royal Enclosure
HISTORIC SITE

South of Tara's church, the Royal Enclosure is a large oval Iron Age hill fort, 315m in diameter and surrounded by a bank and ditch cut through solid rock under the soil. Inside are several smaller earthworks: the **Mound of the Hostages** (closed to the public); **Royal Seat**, a ring fort with a house site; and **Cormac's House**, a barrow (burial mound) in the side of the circular bank, which is topped by the **Stone of Destiny**.

The Mound of the Hostages, a bump in the northern corner of the enclosure, is the most

ancient known part of Tara. A treasure trove of artefacts was unearthed, including some ancient Mediterranean beads of amber and faience (glazed pottery). More than 35 Bronze Age burials were found here, as well as extensive cremated remains from the Stone Age.

There are superb views of the surrounding Boyne and Blackwater Valleys from the Royal Seat and Cormac's House.

Atop Cormac's House is the phallic Stone of Destiny (originally located near the Mound of the Hostages), which represents the joining of the gods of the earth and the heavens. It's said to be the inauguration stone of the high kings, although alternative sources suggest that the actual coronation stone was the Stone of Scone, which was taken to Scotland in the early 6th century and – after several centuries in London's Westminster Abbey – now sits in Edinburgh. The would-be king stood on top of the Stone of Destiny and, if the stone let out three roars, he was crowned. The mass grave of 37 men who died in a skirmish on Tara during the 1798 Rising is next to the stone.

Enclosure of King Laoghaire
HISTORIC SITE

South of Tara's Royal Enclosure is this large but worn ring fort where the king, a contemporary of St Patrick, is said to be buried standing upright and dressed in his armour.

Banquet Hall
HISTORIC SITE

Tara's most unusual feature is a rectangular earthwork measuring 230m by 27m along a north–south axis. Tradition holds that it was built to cater for thousands of guests during feasts.

Its orientation suggests that it was a sunken entrance to Tara, leading directly to the Royal Enclosure. More recent research, however, has uncovered graves within the compound, and it's possible that the banks are in fact the burial sites of some of the kings of Tara.

Gráinne's Fort
HISTORIC SITE

Gráinne was the daughter of King Cormac, the most lauded of all high kings. Betrothed to Fionn MacCumhaill (Finn McCool), she eloped with Diarmuid, one of the king's warriors, on her wedding night. This became the subject of the epic *The Pursuit of Diarmuid and Gráinne*. Gráinne's Fort and the northern and southern Sloping Trenches to the northwest are burial mounds.

Tara Visitor Centre
VISITOR CENTRE

(☑ 046-902 5903; www.heritageireland.ie; adult/child €5/3; ⊙ visitor centre 10am-6pm late Apr–mid-Sep, site open 24hr year-round) A former

Protestant church (with a window by acclaimed stained-glass artist the late Evie Hone) is home to Tara's visitor centre, which screens a 20-minute audiovisual presentation about the site.

Sleeping & Eating

★ Station House Hotel   HERITAGE HOTEL €€
(☑046-902 5239; www.stationhousehotel.ie; Kilmessan; d/ste/f from €149/169/218; P☎) The 19th-century Kilmessan train station ceased operations in 1947 and now houses this atmospheric hotel. Antique-filled rooms are spacious; the signal box houses a separate two-storey bridal suite. In the former waiting room, the bar retains its original stained glass. Other vestiges of its former incarnation include the railway platforms out front and the turntable in the fairy-lit woodland gardens.

Kids get a train-themed activity sheet at its restaurant. Contemporary Irish cuisine (mains €16 to €25) includes seared Clogherhead sea bass with tarragon sauce or Wicklow lamb shanks with sweet potato and mint; cheaper dining is available in the bar.

Bellinter House   HISTORIC HOTEL €€
(☑046-903 0900; www.bellinterhouse.com; Bellinter; d from €120; P☎) Dating from the 18th century, grande dame Bellinter House, 5km northwest of the Hill of Tara (signposted off the R147), is a haven of crackling open fires and rich artworks. There are 34 antique-furnished rooms in the main house, as well as 16 period rooms in the east and west pavilions and five duplexes in the former stables.

Soak in the on-site spa's outdoor hot tubs and dine on top-class fare at its evening-only restaurant Eden (three-course menu €110), which has its own bakery. Lunch is served in its Drawing Room restaurant (mains €15 to €27), where afternoon tea for two costs €50.

Shopping

Old Tara Book Shop   BOOKS
(☺10am-5pm Tue-Sun) At the base of the Hill of Tara, this tiny, jumbled secondhand bookshop is run by Michael Slavin, who has authored an informative little book about the site, *The Tara Walk*, as well as a weightier tome, *The Book of Tara*. Hours can vary.

Getting There & Away

Regular Bus Éireann (www.buseireann.ie) services link Dublin to within 1km of the site (€10, one

TAYTO PARK

An Irish icon, Tayto has been producing much-loved potato crisps since 1954. Alongside the factory, the **Tayto Park** (☑01-835 1999; www.taytopark.ie; Kilbrew, Ashbourne; €15.50, incl day pass €31.50; ☺9.30am-7pm Jul & Aug, shorter hours Apr-Jun & Sep-Dec) amusement park has attractions including Europe's largest wooden inverted roller coaster, a 5D cinema (yes, 5D), a high-speed spinning Rotator and the stomach-churning Air Race ride. There's also a zoo, rock climbing, a zipline and a fantastic playground.

Admission includes a self-guided crisp-factory tour and zoo and playground entry; the wristband day pass is the most economical option for the rides.

It's just off the M2 motorway. Bus Éireann (www.buseireann.ie) buses link it with Dublin (€6, 30 minutes, every 30 minutes).

hour, hourly). Ask the driver to drop you off at Tara Cross, where you take a left turn off the main road.

Dunsany Castle

You can see how the other 1% lives at Dunsany Castle (☑046-902 5169; www.dunsany.com; Dunsany; adult/child €15/free; ☺by appointment 10am-4pm Jul & Aug), 5km south of Tara on the Dunshaughlin–Kilmessan road. The residence of the lords of Dunsany, it's one of the oldest continually inhabited buildings in Ireland. Construction started in the 12th century, with major alterations taking place in the 18th and 19th centuries. Maintenance and restoration are ongoing.

Tours lasting almost two hours offer a fascinating insight into the family's history and impressive private art collection.

The castle houses many treasures related to important figures in Irish history, such as Oliver Plunkett and Patrick Sarsfield, leader of the Irish Jacobite forces at the siege of Limerick in 1691.

You can also buy **Dunsany Home Collection** homewares here: locally made table linen and accessories, as well as various articles designed by the 20th Lord Dunsany (Edward Carlos Plunkett; 1939–2011), who was an acclaimed international designer and artist, famed for his geometrical abstractions and portraits.

Trim

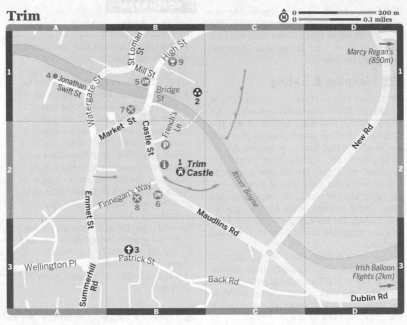

Trim

POP 9194

Dominated by its mighty castle, the quiet town of Trim was an important settlement in medieval times. Five city gates surrounded a busy jumble of streets, and as many as seven monasteries were established in the immediate area.

It's hard to imagine nowadays, but a measure of Trim's importance was that Elizabeth I considered building Trinity College here. One student who did study in Trim was Dublin-born Arthur Wellesley (1769–1852), the first Duke of Wellington, who studied at Talbot Castle and St Mary's Abbey.

Today, Trim's history is everywhere, from atmospheric ruins to streets lined with tiny workers' cottages.

⊙ Sights

★ **Trim Castle** CASTLE
(King John's Castle; www.heritageireland.ie; Castle St; adult/child €5/3; ⊙10am-5pm mid-Mar–Sep, 9.30am-4.30pm mid-Feb–mid-Mar & Oct, 9am-4pm Sat & Sun Nov–mid-Feb) Proof of Trim's medieval importance, this remarkably preserved edifice was Ireland's largest Anglo-Norman fortification. Hugh de Lacy founded Trim Castle in 1173, but it was destroyed by Ruaidrí Ua Conchobair,

Ireland's last high king, within a year. The building you see today was begun around 1200 and has hardly been modified since.

Self-guided tours involve climbing narrow, steep stairs, so aren't suitable for very young children or anyone with restricted mobility.

Throughout Anglo-Norman times the castle occupied a strategic position on the western edge of the Pale, the area where the Anglo-Normans ruled supreme; beyond Trim was the volatile country where Irish chieftains and lords fought with their Norman rivals and vied for position, power and terrain. By the 16th century, the castle had begun to fall into decline and in 1649, when the town was taken by Cromwellian forces, it was severely damaged.

The castle's grassy 2-hectare enclosure is dominated by a massive stone keep, 25m tall and mounted on a Norman motte. Inside are three levels, the lowest divided by a central wall. Just outside the central keep are the remains of an earlier wall.

The principal outer-curtain wall, 450m long and for the most part still standing, dates from around 1250 and includes eight towers and a gatehouse. It also has a number of sally gates from which defenders could exit to confront the enemy. The finest stretch of the outer wall runs from the River Boyne through Dublin Gate to Castle St.

Trim

Fans of the film *Braveheart* might recognise it as Edinburgh Castle, York Castle or the Tower of London (it starred as all three).

Bective Abbey RUINS
(L4010, Bective; ☉24hr) The extraordinarily preserved yet little-visited ruins of Cistercian Bective Abbey are off the R161, 7km northeast of Trim. Founded by Murchadh O'Melaghin, King of Meath, in 1147, the abbey was confiscated by Henry VIII between 1536 and 1541 to fund his military campaign. Like Trim Castle, Bective Abbey also played a starring role in *Braveheart*. The evocative ruins are free to visit and are open round the clock; there's a small car park next to the site.

St Patrick's Cathedral Church CATHEDRAL
(Patrick St; ☉8.30am-5pm) That huge steeple you see belongs to St Patrick's Cathedral Church, parts of which date from the 15th century, although it wasn't granted cathedral status until 1955. Take a look at the beautiful stained-glass windows, including one showing St Patrick preaching on the Hill of Tara. Hours can vary depending on religious services and events.

St Mary's Abbey & Talbot Castle RUINS
(Abbey Lane) Across the River Boyne from Trim Castle are the ruins of the 12th-century Augustinian **St Mary's Abbey**, rebuilt after a fire in 1368 and once home to a wooden statue of Our Lady of Trim, revered by the faithful for its supposedly miraculous powers.

In 1415 part of the abbey was converted into a manor house by Sir John Talbot, then viceroy of Ireland; it came to be known as **Talbot Castle**.

On the northern wall of the castle you can see the Talbot coat of arms. Talbot went to war in France where, in 1429, he was defeated at Orleans by Joan of Arc. He was taken prisoner, released and went on fighting the French until 1453. He became known as 'the scourge of France' and even got a mention in Shakespeare's *Henry VI*: 'Is this the Talbot so much feared abroad/That with his name the mothers still their babes?'

In 1649 Cromwell's soldiers invaded Trim, set fire to the revered statue and destroyed the remaining parts of the abbey. In the early 18th century, Talbot Castle was owned by Esther 'Stella' Johnson, the mistress of Jonathan Swift. He later bought the property from her and lived there for a year. Swift was rector of Laracor, 3km southeast of Trim, from around 1700 until his death in 1745. From 1713 he was also, more significantly, the Dean of St Patrick's Cathedral in Dublin.

Just northwest of the abbey building is the 40m **Yellow Steeple**, once the bell tower of the abbey, dating from 1368 but damaged by Cromwell's soldiers. It takes its name from the colour of the stonework at dusk.

East of the abbey ruins is part of the 14th-century town wall, including the **Sheep Gate**, the lone survivor of the town's original five gates. It used to be closed daily between 9pm and 4am, and a toll was charged for sheep entering to be sold at market.

🏃 Activities

⭐**Irish Balloon Flights** BALLOONING
(☑046-948 3436; www.balloons.ie; 1hr flight per person from €149; ☉Apr-Sep) Float over patchwork fields, ruins, castles and churches aboard a hot-air balloon. The meeting point is the car park of the Knightsbrook Hotel on Dublin Rd, 2.5km southeast of Trim's centre; schedules and launch locations vary according to weather conditions. Flights last an hour, followed by champagne or soft drinks. Kids must be eight or older.

Boyne Valley Activities WATER SPORTS
(☑086 734 2585; www.boynevalleyactivities.ie; Jonathan Swift St; 2hr guided kayaking/rafting tour €45/50, kayak hire per day €50; ☉by reservation) Year-round, this Trim-based company runs guided kayaking trips along the River Boyne;

when the river swells, from January to May, it can also take you white-water rafting. The 35km-long route passes six four-century-old weirs, ruined castles and churches; look out for otters and plentiful birdlife.

🛏 Sleeping

Crannmór House B&B €
(📞 046-943 1635; www.crannmor.com; Dunderry Rd; d €76; 🅿🛜) Rolling farmland and paddocks surround this vine-covered old house with bright rooms and traditional hospitality about 2km along the road to Dunderry. If you're interested in angling, the owner is an experienced *ghillie* (fishing guide).

Bridge House Tourist Hostel HOSTEL €
(📞 046-943 1848; Bridge St; dm/d €20/50; 🅿🛜) Right on the river, this quirky old house has basic four-bed dorm rooms, a couple of doubles and a kitchen for self-caterers. Contact the hostel in advance to confirm your arrival time. Cash only.

Trim Castle Hotel HOTEL €€
(📞 046-948 3000; www.trimcastlehotel.com; Castle St; s/d/f from €85/115/135; 🅿@🛜) Expanses of glossy marble in the foyer set the scene at this contemporary hotel opposite Trim Castle. Some of its stylish rooms come with balconies (try for sprawling corner room 225). Its rooftop sun terrace overlooks Trim Castle, and dining – whether at breakfast, the bar's carvery or upmarket Jules Restaurant (Friday and Saturday evenings and Sunday lunch only) – is top-notch.

🍴 Eating & Drinking

Harvest Home Bakery BAKERY €
(18 Market St; dishes €4-11; ⏰ 9am-5pm Mon-Wed, to 5.30pm Thu-Sat) This little gem sells delicious breads, cakes, pies and biscuits (including sugar- and gluten-free options), as well as homemade soups and full-to-bursting sandwiches. There are outside tables in fine weather.

StockHouse STEAK €€
(📞 046-943 7388; www.stockhouserestaurant.ie; Emmet House, Finnegan's Way; mains €16-30; ⏰ 5-9pm Mon-Thu, 4.30-10pm Fri & Sat, 1-8.30pm Sun) Cooked-to-order dry-aged steaks from local abattoir-butcher Coogan's are the stock-in-trade of this always-packed restaurant, but noncarnivores can choose from vegetarian dishes including sizzling fajitas.

Marcy Regan's PUB
(Lackanash Rd, Newtown; ⏰ usually 5-11.30pm) Filled with welcoming regulars, this small, traditional, sage-green-painted pub beside Norman-era St Peter's Bridge faces Newtown's ruins. It's a no-frills kind of place steeped in old-world atmosphere. Opening days are irregular, but trad-music sessions take place on Friday nights.

James Griffin PUB
(www.jamesgriffinpub.ie; High St; ⏰ 3-11.30pm Mon-Fri, 1pm-12.30am Sat, 1-11pm Sun; 🛜) This award-winning historic pub dates from 1904 and hosts trad-music sessions (Thursday), live bands (Friday and Sunday) and DJs (Saturday). The interior has retained its traditional-Irish-pub atmosphere and visitors are made to feel very welcome.

ℹ Information

In the town hall, Trim's **tourist office** (📞 046-943 7227; www.discoverboynevalley.ie; 6 Castle St; ⏰ 10am-5pm mid-Mar–Sep, shorter hours Oct–mid-Mar) has a handy tourist-trail map, a cafe and a genealogy centre.

ℹ Getting There & Away

Bus Éireann (www.buseireann.ie) links Trim with Dublin (€13, 1¼ hours, hourly) and Drogheda (€13, 1¼ hours, hourly).

Kells

POP 6135

The working market town of Kells is best known for the magnificent illuminated manuscript that bears its name, and which visitors queue to see at Trinity College in Dublin. Although the great book wasn't created here, it was kept in Kells, one of the leading monasteries in the country, from the end of the 9th century until 1541, when it was removed by the Church. You can view a copy at Kells' tourist office.

Remnants of the once-great monastic site include some interesting high crosses and a 1000-year-old round tower.

👁 Sights

St Columba CHURCH
(www.ireland.anglican.org; Cannon St; ⏰ 10am-1pm & 2-5pm Mon-Sat Jun-Aug) The Protestant church of St Columba has a 30m-high 10th-century round tower on the southern side (today without its conical roof). In 1076 the high king of Tara was murdered in its confined apartments.

In the churchyard are four 9th-century high crosses in various states of repair.

The West Cross, at the far end, is the stump of a decorated shaft, which has scenes of the baptism of Jesus, the Fall of Adam and Eve, and the Judgement of Solomon on the eastern face, and Noah's ark on the western .

All that's left of the North Cross is the bowl-shaped base stone.

Near the round tower is the best preserved of the crosses, the Cross of Patrick & Columba, with its semi-legible inscription, 'Patrici et Columbae Crux', on the eastern face of the base.

The other surviving cross is the unfinished East Cross, with a carving of the Crucifixion and a group of four figures on the right arm.

St Colmcille's House   HISTORIC SITE
(Church Lane) This solid structure is a survivor from the old monastic settlement. Its name is a misnomer, as it was built in the 10th century and St Colmcille was alive in the 6th century. Experts have suggested that it was used as a scriptorium, a place where monks illuminated books.

Market Cross   MONUMENT
(Headfort Pl) Until 1996, when it was relocated outside the courthouse on Headfort Pl, the Market Cross had stood for centuries in Cross St, at the heart of the town centre. Besides inviting the pious admiration of the faithful, the cross was used as a gallows in the aftermath of the 1798 Rising; the British garrison hanged rebels from the crosspiece, one on each arm so the cross wouldn't fall over.

🛏 Sleeping & Eating

Headfort Arms Hotel   HOTEL €€
(☎046-924 0063; www.headfortarms.ie; Headfort Pl; s/d from €75/109; 🅿🛜) Right in the town centre, the family-run Headfort Arms has 45 comfortable rooms with classic styling and facilities such as laptop safes. Rooms in the charming old building have the most character. There's a small spa; dining options include the independently run Vanilla Pod bistro.

Vanilla Pod   BISTRO €€
(☎046-924 0063; Headfort Pl; mains €17.50-29.50; ⊗5-10pm Mon-Thu, to 11pm Fri & Sat, 12.30-9.30pm Sun; 🍴🪑) Bright and contemporary, this restaurant inside the Headfort Arms Hotel features an ambitious bistro-style menu. Well-prepared dishes from seasonal, locally sourced ingredients range from venison with blackberry jus and duck fat–fried chips to black pudding–stuffed chicken fillet with roast apples, and sticky toffee pudding with

vanilla bean ice cream. There's a good vegetarian menu, as well as a kids' menu, high chairs and various deals for families.

ℹ Information
In the Kells Civic Offices, the **tourist office** (☎046-924 8856; www.meath.ie; Headfort Pl; ⊗9.30am-1pm & 2-5pm Mon-Fri) has a copy of the famed *Book of Kells* and screens a free 13-minute audiovisual presentation.

ℹ Getting There & Away
Bus Éireann (www.buseireann.ie) has services linking Kells with Dublin (€14, 90 minutes, half-hourly) and Cavan town (€14, 45 minutes).

Loughcrew Cairns
Given the high profile of Brú na Bóinne, the Stone Age passage graves strewn about the Loughcrew Hills, along the R154 near Oldcastle, are often overlooked. They're well off the beaten track and attract relatively few visitors, which means you can enjoy this moody and evocative place in peace.

Like Brú na Bóinne, the graves were all built around 3000 BC, but unlike their better-known and better-excavated peers, the Loughcrew tombs were used at least until 750 BC. Although there are 32 tombs here, most are on private land and inaccessible to the public. It is possible, however, to visit Cairn T at Carnbane East, a steep but scenic 15-minute climb from the car park.

Loughcrew is some 20km west of Kells via the R154 and the L2800. It's not served by public transport, so your own wheels are essential.

★ Cairn T   HISTORIC SITE
(www.heritageireland.ie; off L2800; ⊗10am-6pm late May-Aug, by arrangement Sep-late May) FREE At Carnbane East, Cairn T is 35m in diameter, with numerous carved stones. One of its outlying kerbstones, the Hag's Chair, is covered in gouged holes, circles and other markings.

Light pierces the chamber on the spring and autumn equinoxes, when Heritage Ireland guides are in attendance; guides are also here in summer. Otherwise, pick up the key to enter the passageway from the cafe at Loughcrew Gardens (bring a torch), or book a tour with the Loughcrew Megalithic Centre.

Loughcrew Megalithic Centre   VISITOR CENTRE
(☎086 736 1948; www.loughcrewmegalithiccentre.com; Summerbank, Oldcastle; ⊗11am-5pm)

Centred on a collection of thatched cottages, the Loughcrew Megalithic Centre encompasses a **museum** detailing the megalithic wonders hereabouts, as well as a **cafe** (dishes €3.50 to €7), a **hostel** (dorm/double/glamping yurt €23/45/55), a **campground** (tent per person €10) and a **craft shop** with stunning photography of the area, including cairns that aren't accessible to the public. Special equinox events take place here. It runs tours by arrangement of Cairn T (p537) (€12 including tea, coffee and scones).

Loughcrew Gardens   GARDENS
(☑ 049-854 1356; www.loughcrew.com; L2800, Oldcastle; gardens adult/child €7/3.50, adventure centre per half-/full day €37/57; ☉ 9.30am-5.30pm Mon-Fri, to 6pm Sat & Sun mid-Mar–Oct, by request Mon-Fri, 11am-4pm Sat & Sun Nov–mid-Mar) Loughcrew Gardens incorporates 2.5 hectares of lawns, terraces and herbaceous borders along with a lime avenue, yew walk, canal and 'grotesque grotto' with tortured pillars, frescoes and fantasy sculptures. There's also a medieval moat, a tower house and St Oliver Plunkett's family church, plus a daily opening cafe in a log-built lodge, where you can pick up a key for Cairn T (p537). Advance reservations are essential for its **adventure centre**, which incorporates an assault course, archery, a zipline and a climbing wall.

COUNTY LOUTH

Louth is Ireland's smallest county, hence its moniker, the Wee County. In the 5th and 6th centuries, it was at the centre of ecclesiastical Ireland, with wealthy religious communities at the monastery at Monasterboice and the Cistercian abbey at Mellifont. The 12th-century Norman invaders were responsible for the development of Dundalk and the two towns on opposite banks of the Boyne that united in 1412 to become what is now Drogheda, the county's largest town.

In the north, the picturesque Cooley Peninsula is separated from County Armagh, Northern Ireland, by the waters of Carlingford Lough, home to the lively little town of Carlingford, which retains its medieval architecture.

While Louth can easily be covered as a day trip from Dublin, you'll get more from your visit by spending some time exploring the county.

Drogheda

POP 40,956

Only 48km north of Dublin, Drogheda is a historic fortified town straddling the River Boyne. Stately old buildings, a handsome cathedral and a riveting museum provide plenty of cultural interest, while atmospheric pubs, fine restaurants, numerous sleeping options and good transport links make it a handy base for exploring the region.

⊙ Sights

★ **Millmount Museum & Tower**   MUSEUM
(☑ 041-983 3097; www.millmount.net; off Duleek St, Millmount; adult/child €6/3; ☉ 10am-5.30pm Mon-Sat, 2-5pm Sun) Overlooking Drogheda, Millmount is an artificial hill that may have been a prehistoric burial ground like Newgrange, but has never been excavated. The Normans constructed a motte-and-bailey fort on top of this convenient command post overlooking the bridge. It was followed by a castle, which in turn was replaced by a Martello tower in 1808. A section of the army barracks now houses the **Millmount Museum**, where exhibits include three wonderful late-18th-century guild banners. Several craft workshops are also here.

The tower played a dramatic role in the 1922 Civil War, when it was Drogheda's chief defensive feature and suffered heavy shelling from Free State forces. It has been aesthetically restored and offers great views over the town below.

Other museum highlights include a room devoted to Cromwell's brutal siege of Drogheda and the Battle of the Boyne. The pretty, cobbled basement is full of gadgets and kitchen utensils from bygone times. Across the courtyard, the Governor's House opens for temporary exhibitions.

Just northwest of Millmount, the 13th-century **Butter Gate** (John St) has a distinctive tower and an arched passageway.

★ **St Peter's Roman Catholic Church**   CHURCH
(www.saintpetersdrogheda.ie; West St; ☉ 8.30am-6pm) Displayed in a glittering brass-and-glass case in the north transept, the shrivelled **head of St Oliver Plunkett** (1629–81) is this church's main draw (the rest of the martyr was separated at his hanging in 1681). It's actually two churches in one: the first was designed by Francis Johnston in a classical style

Drogheda

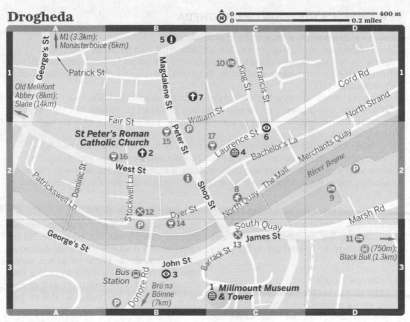

Drogheda

in 1791; the neo-Gothic addition was built in the late 19th century.

Highlanes Gallery   GALLERY
(www.highlanes.ie; 36 Laurence St; suggested donation €2; ◎10.30am-5pm Mon-Sat) Set in a beautifully converted 19th-century monastery, this gallery has a permanent collection of contemporary art, along with regular temporary exhibitions. Attached is a shop featuring Louth craftwork, and a chic cafe (p540).

St Peter's Church of Ireland   CHURCH
(www.drogheda.armagh.anglican.org; William St; ◎8.30am-5pm) St Peter's Church of Ireland (not to be confused with St Peter's Roman Catholic Church) is the church whose spire was burned by Cromwell's men, resulting in the death of 100 people seeking sanctuary inside. Built in 1752, today's church is the second replacement of the original destroyed by Cromwell and, following an arson attack in 1999, was extensively restored. Opening hours can vary.

Magdalene Tower   TOWER
(Magdalene St) The 14th-century Magdalene Tower is the bell tower of a Dominican friary founded in 1224. It was here that England's King Richard II, accompanied by a great

CROMWELL'S INVASION OF DROGHEDA

Lauded as England's first democrat and protector of the people, Oliver Cromwell (1599–1658) was an Irish nightmare. Cromwell hated the Irish for siding with Charles I during the Civil War. So when 'God's own Englishman' landed his 12,000 troops at Dublin in August 1649, he immediately set out for Drogheda, a strategic fort town and bastion of royalist support.

When Cromwell arrived at the walls of Drogheda, he was met by 2300 men led by Sir Arthur Aston, who boasted that 'he who could take Drogheda could take hell'. After Aston refused to surrender, Cromwell let fly with heavy artillery and after two days the walls were breached.

In order to set a terrifying example to any other town that might resist Cromwell's armies, over a period of hours an estimated 3000 people were massacred, mostly royalist soldiers but also priests, women and children. Aston was bludgeoned to death with his own (wooden) leg. Of the survivors, many were captured and sold into slavery in the Caribbean.

army, accepted the submission of the Gaelic chiefs with suitable ceremony in 1395. Peace lasted only a few months, however, and Richard's return to Ireland led to his overthrow in 1399.

St Laurence's Gate GATE
(Laurence St) Astride the eastwards extension of the town's main street is the 13th-century St Laurence's Gate, the finest surviving portion of the city walls (which originally extended for 3km) and a notable landmark.

🎓 Courses

★**Listoke Distillery & Gin School** DISTILLERY
(☑087 240 5283; www.listokedistillery.ie; Ballymakenny Rd, Listoke; gin-making course €95; ⊘by reservation) Brilliant three-hour gin-making courses in the 200-year-old stable of Listoke House and Gardens begin with refreshments and a distillery tour. You then taste three different gins and mix botanicals to create your gin in a miniature copper distiller (accompanied by G&Ts), which you bottle to take home afterwards. It's set in picturesque woodland 3.5km north of central Drogheda.

🎉 Festivals & Events

Drogheda Arts Festival PERFORMING ARTS
(www.droghedaartsfestival.ie; ⊘early May) Theatre, music, film, poetry, visual arts and workshops such as silk painting take place at this week-long festival culminating over the May Day weekend.

🛏 Sleeping

Spoon & the Stars HOSTEL €
(☑041-987 3333; www.spoonandthestars.com; 13 St Mary's Tce, Dublin Rd; dm from €22, d from €77, without bathroom from €60; ⊛) Rory and

Hannah's well-run budget accommodation blends vintage and contemporary furnishings and has a great, laid-back vibe. Rooms range from a double with private bathroom and kitchenette to eight- to 10-bed dorms (one female only). Facilities include a cosy lounge and a breezy courtyard and garden, complete with a barbecue, as well as bike storage.

★**Scholars Townhouse Hotel** HOTEL €€
(☑041-983 5410; www.scholarshotel.com; King St; s/d/f from €79/135/139; P⊛) This former monastery dates from 1867 and was revamped as a family-owned hotel and restaurant. Despite the 16 rooms being on the small side, some have four-poster beds and there's nothing monastic about the facilities, which include an atmospheric bar and a superb restaurant (mains €18 to €32; bookings recommended). The central location is ideal for exploring the town.

D Hotel HOTEL €€
(☑041-987 7700; www.thedhotel.com; Scotch Hall, Marsh Rd; d/tr from €115/175; P⊛) Minimalist rooms at this slick riverside hotel are bathed in light and decked out with designer furniture and cool gadgets. There's a stylish bar and a restaurant, a mini-gym and fantastic views over the skyline. The hotel is popular for hen and stag parties: beware of pounding music (and higher prices) on weekends.

🍴 Eating

Relish CAFE €
(www.relishcafe.ie; Highlanes Gallery, Laurence St; dishes €8-14.50; ⊘9am-7pm Mon-Wed, to 9pm Thu-Sun; ⊛) Located in the Highlanes Gallery (p539), this split-level cafe serves a stylish range of breakfasts, gourmet sandwiches,

savoury tarts and daily specials like lasagne and desserts such as hot apple crumble. Vegetarian and gluten-free options are plentiful; the fun kids' menu includes 'pizzarettes' with smiley faces.

★ **Kitchen** MEDITERRANEAN €€
(✍ 041-983 4630; www.facebook.com/thekitchenrestaurantdrogheda; 2 South Quay; mains lunch €13-17, dinner €19-27; ⊙11am-9pm Wed, to 10pm Thu-Sat, noon-9pm Sun Mar-Oct, noon-7pm Wed & Sun, from 11am Thu, 11am-9pm Fri & Sat Nov-Feb; 🖥) Fronted by a sage-green facade, Drogheda's best restaurant is aptly named for its shiny open kitchen. Organic local produce is used along with worldly ingredients such as Cypriot halloumi and Serrano ham. Breads are made on-site and there's an excellent choice of wine by the glass. Don't miss the salted-caramel baked Alaska for dessert.

Black Bull IRISH €€
(✍ 041-983 7139; www.blackbullinn.ie; Dublin Rd; mains €10.50-28; ⊙kitchen 9.30am-10pm Mon-Sat, to 8pm Sun, bar 9.30am-11.30pm Mon-Thu, to 12.30am Fri & Sat, to 11pm Sun; 🖥) Topped by a gleaming golden (not black) bull, this cosy pub has low ceilings, candlelit corners and a centrepiece glass table filled with illuminated liqueur bottles. The modern extension houses a spacious restaurant serving solidly good pub standards such as chargrilled steaks, burgers, and fish and chips. Afterwards, have a pint in the ingeniously named beer garden, the China Shop.

D'vine BISTRO €€
(✍ 041-980 0440; www.dvine.ie; Dyer St; mains lunch €8-12, dinner €13.50-27.50, tapas €3.50-9; ⊙noon-3pm & 5-11pm Wed & Thu, noon-11pm Fri & Sat, from 1pm Sun) Hidden down a small flight of steps and opening to a sunny courtyard, this convivial cellar bistro has a great selection of Mediterranean tapas dishes, elaborate salads, and steak, seafood and gourmet burgers, plus a long wine list. Service is faultless. Live music performs on Sunday at 7pm.

🍷 Drinking & Nightlife

★ **Grey Goose** BAR
(www.facebook.com/Thegreygoosewestst; 89 West St; ⊙10.30am-11.30pm Mon-Thu, to 12.30am Fri & Sat, 12.30-11pm Sun; 🖥) Grey Goose has a vast downstairs bar with herringbone floors, stained glass and leather sofas, and a grand piano in its upstairs cocktail lounge, the Birdcage, where DJs spin on Fridays and Saturdays, bands play on Sundays and trad

sessions take place on Mondays. Alongside Irish and international craft beers, local spirits include Listoke gin and Slane whiskey.

Gastropub fare (mains €8 to €13), spanning house-speciality wood-fired pizzas to burgers, smoky ribs and salads, is served until 9pm.

Cagney's BAR
(www.facebook.com/CagneysBarDrogheda; 3 Dyer St; ⊙10.30am-11.30pm Mon-Thu, to 12.30am Fri & Sat, 12.30-11pm Sun) With low lighting and a beer garden, Cagney's is a classy spot for wines by the glass, whiskeys and over 300 gins, including locally distilled Listoke 1777.

Clarke & Sons PUB
(www.clarkesofdrogheda.com; 19 Peter St; ⊙1-11.30pm Mon-Thu, noon-12.30am Fri & Sat, 12.30-11pm Sun) This wonderful old 1900 boozer is right out of a time capsule. Clarke's unrestored wooden interior features snugs and leaded-glass doors that read 'Open Bar'.

Peter Matthews PUB
(McPhails; www.facebook.com/McPhailsD; 9 Laurence St; ⊙3pm-1am Mon-Thu, from 1pm Fri, from noon Sat, from 12.30pm Sun) One of Drogheda's top spots for live music, McPhails (as it's always called, no matter what the sign says) features everything from heavy-metal cover bands to trad-music sessions. There's a traditional bar at the front and a beer garden out the back.

ℹ Information

Drogheda's **tourist office** (✍ 041-987 2843; www.drogheda.ie; 1 West St; ⊙9.30am-5.30pm Mon-Sat May-Nov, closed Sat & Sun Dec-Apr; 🖥) is inside the historic Tholsel, an 18th-century limestone town hall.

ℹ Getting There & Away

BUS

The **bus station** (cnr Donore Rd & George's St) is on the south side of the river.

Bus Éireann (www.buseireann.ie) links Drogheda with Dublin (€9, 1½ hours, half-hourly Monday to Saturday, hourly Sunday) and Dundalk (€8, 55 minutes, hourly).

Matthews (www.matthews.ie) also serves Dublin (€10, 45 minutes, half-hourly Monday to Friday, hourly Saturday and Sunday) and Dundalk (€10, 30 minutes, half-hourly Monday to Friday, hourly Saturday and Sunday).

TRAIN

The **train station** (www.irishrail.ie; off Dublin Rd) is just south of the river and east of the town centre. Drogheda is on the main Belfast–Dublin line (Dublin €12.90, one hour; Belfast €14.50, 1½ hours) with hourly or better trains.

❶ Getting Around

Drogheda is compact and walkable. Many of the surrounding sites are within cycling distance; rent bikes from **Quay Cycles** (☑ 041-983 4526; www.quaycycles.com; 11A North Quay; per day from €14; ☺ 9am-6pm Mon-Sat).

Around Drogheda

A number of historic sites lie close to Drogheda, while the coast road between Drogheda and Dundalk makes a scenic alternative to the motorway.

★ Old Mellifont Abbey   RUINS

(☑ 041-982 6459; www.heritageireland.ie; Tullyallen; site admission free, visitor centre adult/student €5/3; ☺ site 24hr year-round, visitor centre 10am-6pm Jun-early Sep) In its Anglo-Norman prime, this abbey, 1.5km off the main Drogheda–Collon road (R168), was the Cistercians' first and most magnificent centre in Ireland. Highly evocative and well worth exploring, the ruins still reflect the site's former splendour.

Mellifont's most recognisable building and one of the country's finest examples of Cistercian architecture is the 13th-century lavabo, the monks' octagonal washing room.

In the mid-12th century Irish monastic orders had grown a little too fond of the good life and were not averse to a bit of corruption. In 1142 an exasperated Malachy, bishop of Down, invited a group of hard-core monks from Clairvaux in France to set up shop in a remote location, where they would act as a sobering influence on the local clergy. Unsurprisingly, the Irish monks didn't get on with their French guests, and the latter soon left for home. Still, the construction of Mellifont continued, and within 10 years, nine more Cistercian monasteries were established. Mellifont was eventually the mother house for 21 lesser monasteries; at one point as many as 400 monks lived here.

In 1556, after the Dissolution of the Monasteries, a fortified Tudor manor house was built on the site.

There's good picnicking next to the rushing stream. The visitor centre describes monastic life in detail.

★ Monasterboice   HISTORIC SITE

(☺ sunrise-sunset) **FREE** Crowing ravens lend an eerie atmosphere to Monasterboice, an intriguing monastic site down a leafy lane in sweeping farmland, which contains a cemetery, two ancient church ruins, one of the finest and tallest round towers in Ireland, and two of the most important high crosses.

Come early or late in the day to avoid the crowds. It's just off the M1 motorway, about 8km north of Drogheda.

The original monastic settlement here is said to have been founded in the 5th or 6th century by St Buithe, a follower of St Patrick, although the site probably had pre-Christian significance. St Buithe's name somehow got converted to Boyne, and the river is named after him. An invading Viking force took over the settlement in 968, only to be comprehensively expelled by Donal, the Irish high king of Tara, who killed at least 300 of the Vikings in the process.

The high crosses of Monasterboice are superb examples of Celtic art. The crosses had an important didactic use, bringing the gospels alive for the uneducated, and they were probably brightly painted originally, although all traces of colour have long disappeared.

The cross near the entrance is known as **Muiredach's Cross**, named after a 10th-century abbot. The western face relates more to the New Testament, and from the bottom depicts the arrest of Christ, Doubting Thomas, Christ giving a key to St Peter, the Crucifixion, and Moses praying with Aaron and Hur.

The **West Cross** is near the round tower and stands 6.5m high, making it one of the tallest high crosses in Ireland. It's much more weathered, especially at the base, and only a dozen or so of its 50 panels are still legible. The more distinguishable ones on the eastern face include David killing a lion and a bear.

A third, simpler cross in the northeastern corner of the compound is believed to have been smashed by Cromwell's forces and has only a few straightforward carvings. This cross makes a great evening silhouette photo, with the round tower in the background.

The **round tower**, minus its cap, is more than 30m tall, and stands in a corner of the complex. Records suggest the tower interior went up in flames in 1097, destroying many valuable manuscripts and other treasures. It's closed to the public.

Laytown Races   SPORTS

(www.laytownstrandraces.ie; ☺ late Aug/early Sep) Bookies, punters and jockeys descend on Laytown, 11.5km southeast of Drogheda, for races that have been held here since 1868.

DROGHEDA TO DUNDALK VIA THE COAST ROAD

Most people zip north along the M1 motorway, but if you want to see a little of rural Ireland, opt for the R166 coast road from Drogheda.

The little village of **Termonfeckin** was, until 1656, the seat and castle of the primate of Armagh. Nothing remains of the castle but a tiny, 15th-century **tower house** (☑086 079 1484; off Strand Rd; key deposit €50; ⊙10am-6pm) FREE, once belonging to a wealthy landowner, is worth a brief stop. Pick up the key from the first house to its right.

A further 3.5km north is the busy seaside and fishing centre of **Clogherhead**, with a good, shallow Blue Flag beach at Lurganboy. Squint to ignore the static-home-filled caravan parks and take in the lovely views of the Cooley and Mourne Mountains instead. At the harbour is **Fisherman's Catch** (☑041-988 9706; www.fishermanscatch.ie; Port Oriel; dishes €5-8; ⊙9am-6pm) run by the Kirwan family, who have been fishing the local waters since 1862, and sell their catch here alongside ready-to-eat fish cakes, chowder and freshly shucked oysters, plus fish and chips in summer. Other local products sold here span Oriel sea salt (try the Teeling Whiskey–infused variety) made across the port. It also sells salmon that's oak-smoked by fisherman Terry Butterly in **Annagassan**, a further 14km north.

At Annagassan's **O'Neills Bakery** (☑042-937 2253; www.oneillsbakery.ie; Main St; ⊙6am-1pm), a cavernous five-generations-old bakery with vast ovens (one more than a century old), you can buy still-warm breads, cakes and buns (cash only). Knock on the door around the side of the building and one of the bakers will let you in. Annagassan is anchored by the 1770-built **Glyde Inn** (☑042-937 2350; www.theglydeinn.ie; Main St; mains €14.50-27; ⊙kitchen noon-9.30pm Mon-Sat, to 4pm Sun, bar 10am-midnight Sun-Thu, to 1am Fri & Sat). The pub has its own specially brewed beer, Linn Duachaill (named for a local Viking settlement currently being excavated), which is also the name of its seafood restaurant where panoramic windows overlook the beer garden, Dundalk Bay's tidal shallows and the Mourne Mountains beyond. If you want to stop for the night, it also has four guest rooms.

The 33km route comes to an end in **Castlebellingham**. The picturesque village grew up around an 18th-century crenellated mansion (www.bellinghamcastle.ie), which is now a luxury wedding venue; ask about midweek B&B options (doubles from €105) between May and October. From Castlebellingham you can continue 12km north to Dundalk along the suburban R132 or join the M1.

For one late-summer's day, Laytown's 3km of golden sands are transformed into a racecourse, attracting a diverse crowd of locals, celebrities and diehard racing fans.

Dundalk

POP 39,004

Midway between Dublin and Belfast, Dundalk, despite its role as an industrial hub, is a surprisingly pleasant town with some interesting sites. In the Middle Ages the city was at the northern limits of the English-controlled Pale, and with partition in 1921 it once again became a border town, this time with South Armagh.

⊙ Sights

County Museum Dundalk   MUSEUM
(www.dundalkmuseum.ie; 8 Jocelyn St; adult/child €2/1; ⊙10am-5pm Tue-Sat) Different floors in this worthwhile museum are dedicated to

the town's early history and archaeology, and to the Norman period. One floor deals with the growth of industry in the area, from the 1750s to the 1960s, including the cult classic Heinkel Bubble Car. Other oddities include Oliver Cromwell's shaving mirror.

St Patrick's Cathedral   CATHEDRAL
(www.stpatricksparishdundalk.com; Roden Pl; ⊙8.30am-5pm) The richly decorated 19th-century St Patrick's Cathedral was modelled on King's College Chapel in Cambridge, England. Hours can vary depending on services and events.

Courthouse   NOTABLE BUILDING
(cnr Crowe & Clanbrassil Sts) Dundalk's courthouse is a photogenic neo-Gothic building with large Doric pillars. The interior is closed to the public. In the front square is the stone *Maid of Erin* statue, commemorating the 1798 Rising.

🛏 Sleeping & Eating

Ballymascanlon House   HISTORIC HOTEL €€
(☑ 042-935 8200; www.ballymascanlon.com; R173;
s/d/tr from €95/155/205; 🚗🖥) Situated 8km
northeast of Dundalk on the edge of the
Cooley Peninsula, this grand old property
(and modern extension) has spacious rooms,
warm, personalised service and atmosphere
in spades. There's an 18-hole golf course (with
a circa 3000 BC, 3m-high standing stone on
the 6th hole), a leisure centre and a restaurant and bar, plus 24-hour room service.

★ Strandfield   CAFE €
(www.strandfield.com; off R173; dishes €5-14; �)8am-
5pm; 🚗🖥) 🍴 On a working farm, this skylit,
retrofitted barn houses a wondrous bakery,
deli, florist and homewares shop as well as an
all-organic vegetarian cafe. For breakfast, expect French toast with walnuts and honey or
smashed avocado on sourdough; lunch sees
wood-fired pizzas, open-faced sandwiches (St
Tola goat's cheese and root vegetables) and
salads (quinoa, tahini and aubergine).

Rum House   PUB
(www.therumhouse.ie; 92 Park St; �) noon-1.30am
Mon-Sat, to midnight Sun; 🚗) Fitted out with
exposed brick walls, copper pipes and
studded Chesterfield sofas, this stylish pub
mixes inventive house cocktails including a
lemon meringue martini and a strawberry

and cucumber caipirinha. High-end pub
food (eg whiskey-marinated barbecue ribs;
mains €13.50 to €24.50) is served from 1pm
to 9pm. DJs spin four nights a week, while
live bands play on weekends.

☆ Entertainment

Spirit Store   LIVE MUSIC
(www.spiritstore.ie; off George's Quay; �) 4-11.30pm
Mon-Thu, to 12.30am Fri & Sat, to 11pm Sun) Downstairs this sunset-pink-painted place is your
typical harbour-front bar, full of character
and characters. Upstairs is a state-of-the-art
live venue, with a terrific sound system that is
beloved of the crowd and the regular streams
of touring musicians that play here. Across
both bars, there's live music Friday to Sunday,
including Sunday-afternoon trad sessions.

On Mondays it hosts a pub quiz with
pints as prizes. Look out for comedy shows
and board-game nights.

ⓘ Information

Dundalk's **tourist office** (☑ 042-935 2111; www.
visitlouth.ie; Jocelyn St; �) 9.30am-5pm Mon-
Fri) is on Market Sq.

ⓘ Getting There & Away

Bus Éireann (www.buseireann.ie) runs an hourly
bus service to Dublin (€10.50, 1½ hours). The **bus
station** (The Long Walk) is near the courthouse.

From the **train station** (www.irishrail.ie;
Carrickmacross Rd), there are hourly or better
services to Dublin (€15.80, 1¼ hours) and Belfast (€10.20, 1¼ hours).

TRACING YOUR ANCESTORS

With advance notice, genealogical centres in the region can help trace your
ancestors.

Meath Contact the **Meath Heritage
Centre** (☑ 046-943 6633; www.meath.
rootsireland.ie; Castle St; �) 9am-1pm &
1.30-5pm Mon-Thu, 9am-2pm Fri) inside
Trim's town hall.

Louth The **Louth County Library**
(☑ 042-932 4323; www.louthcoco.ie; Roden
Pl; �) 10am-8pm Tue & Thu, to 5pm Wed, Fri
& Sat) in Dundalk has information.

Cavan Visit **Cavan Genealogy** (☑ 049-
436 1094; www.cavan.rootsireland.ie;
Farnham St) on the 1st floor of Johnston
Central Library in Cavan town.

Monaghan Monaghan currently has
no genealogy centre, but the website
www.monaghan.rootsireland.ie has
information.

Cooley Peninsula

Forested slopes and multihued hills rise
above the dark waters of Carlingford Lough
cleaving the picturesque Cooley Peninsula.
Country lanes wind their scenic way down
to deserted stony beaches, while sweeping
views stretch north across the water (and
border) to the majestic Mourne Mountains.

The medieval village of Carlingford is
an ideal base. From here, you can continue along the coast road past the village of
Omeath to Newry, at the nexus of Counties
Down and Armagh in Northern Ireland.

Carlingford

POP 2201
Amid the medieval ruins and whitewashed
houses, the vibrant little village of Carlingford buzzes with pubs, restaurants and

boutiques. There's also spirited festivals and gorgeous views of the mountains and across Carlingford Lough to County Down.

◎ Sights

Carlingford Brewing Company   BREWERY
(☑083 328 4040; www.carlingfordbrewing.ie; The Old Mill, Riverstown; tours €18, with lunch €30; ☺tours by reservation 2.30pm Sat) Tours of this craft brewery, 8km southwest of Carlingford on the R173, start with a sample, then take you through the brewing process (one to 1½ hours) and finish with three more tastings. The post-tour lunch of pizzas wood-fired in-house is a great way to wrap up. Its four brews are named for Carlingford landmarks: Tholsel Blonde, Taaffe's Red, Friary Pale Ale and King John's Stout. Live jazz and blues evenings often take place.

King John's Castle   CASTLE
(R173) Carlingford was first settled by the Vikings, and in the Middle Ages became an English stronghold under the protection of the now-ruined castle, which was built on a pinnacle in the 11th to 12th centuries to control the entrance to the lough. King John spent a couple of days here in 1210 en route to battle in Antrim.

At the time of writing, the castle was being restored and was closed to the public, but there are often free tours during Heritage Week (p545).

On the western side, the entrance gateway was built to allow only one horse and rider through at a time.

Taaffe's Castle   HISTORIC BUILDING
(Market St) Today the storeroom of the attached pub of the same name, Taaffe's Castle is an imposing 16th-century tower house that stood on the waterfront until the land in front was reclaimed to build a short-lived train line.

Opposite the castle is a bust commemorating Carlingford-born Thomas D'Arcy McGee (1825–68), one of Canada's founding fathers.

Mint   HISTORIC BUILDING
(Tholsel St) Dating from the 16th century, the Mint, near the village square, has some interesting Celtic-inspired carvings around the windows. Although Edward IV is thought to have granted a charter to a mint in 1467, no coins were produced here.

🏃 Activities

Carlingford is the starting point for the 40km Táin Way, which makes a circuit of the

WORTH A TRIP

FLAGSTAFF VIEWPOINT

Travelling along the Cooley Peninsula from Carlingford to Newry in Northern Ireland, a quick 3km detour to Flagstaff Viewpoint (Flagstaff Rd) rewards you with sweeping views of Carlingford Lough, framed by forested mountains, green fields and the sparkling Irish Sea beyond.

Flagstaff Viewpoint lies just over the border in County Armagh. Heading northwest along the coast road (the R173), follow the signs to your left onto Ferryhill Rd, then turn right up to the viewpoint's car park.

The quickest way to reach Newry from here is to retrace your steps and rejoin the R173.

Cooley Peninsula through the Cooley Mountains along a mix of surfaced roads, forest tracks and green paths.

There's great cycling around the Cooley Peninsula; On Yer Bike (☑087 648 7337; www.onyerbike.ie; Chapel Hill; bike rental per day €20; ☺9am-6.30pm Mon-Fri, to 6pm Sat & Sun) rents out wheels.

Much of the Cooley Peninsula is protected and is home to various species of birds, including godwits, red-breasted mergansers, buzzards, tits and various finches. Ask at the tourist office (p547) for information on the Carlingford Birdwatching Trail.

Carlingford Adventure Centre   ADVENTURE SPORTS
(☑042-937 3100; www.carlingfordadventure.com; Tholsel St) Carlingford Adventure Centre runs a wide range of activities including sailing, kayaking, stand-up paddleboarding, rock climbing and ziplining in its aerial adventure park.

🎊 Festivals & Events

Carlingford Oyster Festival   FOOD & DRINK
(www.carlingfordoysterfestival.com; ☺mid-Aug) This rollicking four-day event toasts Carlingford's famous oysters with an oyster treasure hunt, a fishing competition, music, food markets and a regatta on Carlingford Lough.

Heritage Week   CULTURAL
(www.heritageweek.ie; ☺Aug) Concerts, talks, guided walks, sporting events and family activities are part of this week-long celebration.

FITZPATRICK'S

Overflowing inside and out with bric-a-brac – milk cans, lanterns, antlers, church pews, crockery, street signs, barrels, bellows, bank notes and even tables dangling upside down from the ceiling – Fitzpatrick's (☑042-937 6193; www.fitzpatricks-restaurant.com; Rockmarshall, Jenkinstown; ⊙11.30am-11pm Mon-Thu, to 12.30am Fri & Sat, to 10pm Sun; 🖥️🚫) is a locally patronised treasure with fantastic craic. Excellent pub fare (mains €15.50 to €36) includes steak, seafood, award-winning chowder and 'almost-famous French-onion soup'; book ahead for lunch or dinner.

The flower-filled, umbrella-shaded beer gardens and petting zoo with resident braying donkeys are positively hopping on sunny days. Traditional Irish music strikes up frequently of an evening. There are kids' and babies' menus.

🛏 Sleeping

★Carlingford House   B&B €€
(☑042-937 3118; www.carlingfordhouse.com; Dundalk St; d from €110; 🅿🛜) In the village centre, but set back from the road in manicured grounds, this stately 1844 manor house (once the local doctor's house) is especially stunning in warmer months when it's enveloped by vines. Welcoming hosts Peter and Irene achieve the perfect balance of old-world character and contemporary comfort. Exceptional breakfasts are included in the rate from mid-March to September.

Rates drop the rest of the year, when breakfast isn't served.

Belvedere House   B&B €€
(☑042-938 3848; www.belvederehouse.ie; Newry St; s/d from €74/94; 🛜) An excellent deal, this lovely B&B has seven modern but cosy rooms with antique furniture and subtle lighting, themed around local Celtic history. Breakfast is served in the downstairs Bay Tree restaurant.

Children's cots are available on request.

Ghan House   BOUTIQUE HOTEL €€€
(☑042-937 3682; www.ghanhouse.com; Old Quay Lane; d from €170; 🅿🛜) Set in flower-filled gardens, this 18th-century Georgian house has 12 rooms, each exquisitely decorated with period antiques and original artworks. Book one of the four rooms in the main house for the most character and old-world charm. There's a superb restaurant on-site (with discounts for guests) and a cookery school (courses from €75).

🍴 Eating

Liberty Cafe   CAFE €
(www.facebook.com/LibertyCafeCarlingford; 3 Tholsel St; dishes €6-11; ⊙9am-5pm Mon-Fri, to 5.30pm Sat & Sun; 🚫🖥️) Set over two levels, Liberty has brightly coloured flowers painted on its whitewashed exterior. Freshly made dishes include soups such as spiced lentil and pumpkin or carrot and coconut, hot specials like roast butternut squash, courgette and spinach tart, and open sandwiches, wraps, clubs and toasties (including special toasties for kids). Breakfast is served until noon.

A handful of tables are set up on the pedestrianised street out the front in fine weather.

Ruby Ellen's Tea Rooms   CAFE €
(www.rubyellens.com; Marion House, Newry St; dishes €7-13, afternoon tea €15; ⊙9am-6pm) In a charming cottage with eggshell-blue walls, mismatched chairs and lace tablecloths, Ruby Ellen's serves wraps, bagels, jacket potatoes with gourmet toppings such as smoked salmon, crab meat and lemon zest, or pork sausages and smoked cheese, as well as daily baked cakes. Afternoon tea is a treat. When the sun's shining, the sweetest seats are in the flower-filled courtyard.

Bay Tree   IRISH €€
(☑042-938 3848; www.belvederehouse.ie; Newry St; mains €22-27; ⊙6-9pm Wed-Sat, 1-7.30pm Sun; 🖥️) Simple, stylishly presented dishes made from seasonal locally sourced ingredients (some grown in its own polytunnel) at this little restaurant attached to Belvedere House include squash and mushroom agnolotti with sage and aged Parmesan, confit of duck with pickled rhubarb, and indulgent desserts such as a Valhrona chocolate and berry fondant with raspberry sorbet. Bookings are advised.

Mini gourmet dishes on its kids' menu cost €8.

PJ O'Hares   PUB FOOD €€
(☑042-937 3106; www.pjoharescarlingford.com; Tholsel St; mains €14-24.50, small plates €6.50-13.50; ⊙kitchen 11am-9.30pm Mon-Thu, to 10pm Fri & Sat, noon-8pm Sun, bar 10.30am-midnight daily) Hearty main courses at this popular pub include pies (beef and Guinness or salmon, cod and cockle), but you can easily fill up on tapas-style starters including Carlingford

oysters and garlic crab claws. Weather depending, head for the bustling beer garden or cosy up in front of the roaring fire. Live music plays most nights year-round and afternoons in summer.

There's a second entrance on Newry St.

★ **Ghan House**   IRISH €€€
(☑042-937 3682; www.ghanhouse.com; Old Quay Lane; tasting menus €45-52.50, 3-course Sun lunch €35; ☺6-9.30pm Mon-Sat, 1-3pm Sun) 🍴 The restaurant at boutique hotel Ghan House is renowned for its classic multi-course menus (no à la carte) incorporating its own breads, stocks, ice creams and sauces, and herbs and vegetables from its garden. Dishes might include chestnut dumplings with mushroom fricassée or Mourne mountain lamb with nettle and blackberry jus. Be sure to book.

🛍 Shopping

Mia Mullen   JEWELLERY
(www.facebook.com/miamullen.jewellery; Old Quay Lane; ☺10am-5.30pm Wed-Sat, from 11.30am Sun) The Mourne Mountains and Carlingford Lough inspire the contemporary designs of jeweller Mia Mullen, who works with gold, silver, platinum and precious stones to create rings, earrings, necklaces and bespoke pieces.

ℹ Information

Carlingford's **tourist office** (☑087 957 6989; www.visitcarlingford.com; R173; ☺9.30am-5.30pm) is on the waterfront in the former train station.

ℹ Getting There & Away

BUS

Bus Éireann (www.buseireann.ie) has services to Dundalk (€7.70, one hour, six daily Monday to Saturday) with connections to Newry (€5.50, 25 minutes, four daily Monday to Saturday) and Dublin (€10.50, 1½ hours, hourly).

BOAT

Carlingford Ferry (☑UK 028-4176 2488; www.carlingfordferry.com; Greenore Port; one-way car incl passengers €15, pedestrians & cyclists €3.50; ☺7am-9.30pm Mon-Fri, from 8am Sat, 9am-9.30pm Sun Jul & Aug, shorter hours Sep-Jun) links Carlingford's Greenore Port with Greencastle, County Down, Northern Ireland in just 15 minutes, saving you a 52km journey by road. Payment is accepted in euros and pounds; fares are 10% cheaper if you pre-book online.

LEPRECHAUNS – A PROTECTED SPECIES

The mountains around Carlingford are famed for being the last remaining site of Ireland's leprechauns. Among the believers in the little people was the late publican PJ O'Hare, who found a leprechaun's suit and hat, along with a collection of tiny bones and four gold coins, on Foy mountain in 1989.

Nineteen years later, after a vigorous lobbying campaign by self-acclaimed 'Leprechaun Whisperer' Kevin Woods (who claims he has seen three leprechauns to date), the EU issued a highly unconventional directive establishing a protective leprechaun zone here. According to Woods, this is apparently the last habitat for Ireland's leprechauns and there's even an annual **leprechaun hunt** (www.thelastleprechaunsofireland. com; ☺late Mar/early Apr) and a small **leprechaun garden** (☑087 257 0539; www.thelastleprechaunsofireland.com; Ghan Rd; adult/child €3.50/7; ☺tour 3pm Sat & Sun). Even if you don't spot a little fella, this certainly is a very magical spot.

COUNTY CAVAN

Cavan is a remote paradise for boaters, anglers, walkers and cyclists. Known as the 'Lake Country', there's supposedly a lake for every day of the year (including leap years). Between them is a gentle landscape of meandering streams, bogs and drumlins. Spectacular walking trails wind through the wild Cuilcagh Mountains, which are the source of the 300km River Shannon.

Cavan's lakes create a tangled knot of narrow, twisting roads. Take your time and enjoy the views that appear unexpectedly around each bend.

The area has an intricate history. Magh Sleacht, a plain near the border village of Ballyconnell, was an important Druidic centre in the 5th century when St Patrick was busy converting the pagan Irish to Christianity, and the area is still littered with tombs, standing stones and stone circles dating from this time. The Gaelic O'Reilly clan ruled until the 16th century, when they were defeated by the English. As part of the Ulster Plantation, Cavan was divided among English and Scottish settlers. After the War of Independence in 1922, the Ulster counties of Cavan, Monaghan and Donegal were incorporated into the Republic. Following the UK's 2016 referendum vote to leave the EU, the potential return of a border is one of the key issues to be resolved during Brexit negotiations, and the resulting outcome remains to be seen.

Cavan Town

POP 10,914

Cavan's county town is a solidly workaday place with some handsome Georgian houses. There are few sights, but it's a handy stop for info and supplies.

Bell Tower   HISTORIC SITE

All that remains of the 13th-century Franciscan friary the town grew up around is an ancient bell tower, next to the grave of 17th-century rebel leader Owen Roe O'Neill in Abbey St's cemetery.

Farnham Estate   SPA HOTEL €€€

(☑049-437 7700; www.farnhamestate.ie; d/ste/ self-catering lodge from €139/174/419; P@🖥🐕) Set in misty woodlands, this sprawling 16th-century estate has amenities galore, including a garden-view restaurant, a hydrotherapy pool (off-limits to kids aged under 16), spa treatments and an 18-hole golf course. Luxurious rooms blend contemporary style with period features and character; self-catering lodges sleeping up to eight have a two-night minimum stay. It's 3km west of town on the R198.

Chapter One   CAFE €

(www.chapter1.ie; Convent Bldg, 12 Main St; dishes €2.75-8.25; ⊙8am-6.30pm Mon-Fri, 9am-6pm Sat, from 11am Sun; 🖥☑) Up a short flight of steps,

---

LAKE FISHING

Cavan's exceptional lake fishing reels in anglers, especially to the county's southern and western areas. It's primarily coarse fishing, but there's also some game angling for brown trout and pike. Most lakes are well signposted, and the types of fish available are marked.

For more information, visit www. fishinginireland.info, which lists tackle shops, fishing guides and boat-rental operators. Facilities are few and far between, however, so bringing your own equipment is advised.

Chapter One is crammed at lunchtime when locals descend to dine on the huge range of filled bagels, soups, nachos and hot and cold salads. Vegetarian and/or gluten-free options are plentiful.

ℹ Information

On the 1st floor of the Johnston Central Library, Cavan's **tourist office** (☑049-433 1942; www. thisiscavan.ie; Farnham St; ⊙10am-5pm Mon-Fri) has county-wide info.

ℹ Getting There & Away

Bus Éireann (www.buseireann.ie) has services daily to Dublin (€16.15, two hours, hourly), Enniskillen, County Fermanagh (€13.50, 1¼ hours, hourly) and Donegal town (€14, 1½ hours, every 90 minutes). There are also less frequent services to various small towns throughout the county.

Killykeen Forest Park & Lough Oughter

Sprawling over 240 hectares, **Killykeen Forest Park** (www.coillte.ie; ⊙9am-dusk) FREE, 12km northwest of Cavan, has various nature trails (from 1.5km to 5.8km) that lead you through the woods and along the shore of **Lough Oughter**, which splatters across the map like spilt steely grey ink. It's popular with anglers. Keep an eye out for stoats, badgers, foxes, grey squirrels and hedgehogs, as well as some amazing birdlife.

Many of the low overgrown islands in the lake were *crannógs* (fortified, artificial islands). The most spectacular is home to Clough Oughter Castle, a 13th-century circular tower perched on a tiny speck of land. It was used as a lonely prison, then as a stronghold by rebel leader Owen Roe O'Neill before being destroyed by Cromwell's army in 1653. The castle lies out of reach over the water; canoe trips run by the Cavan Adventure Centre in Butlersbridge head here. The forest trails provide wonderful views.

Butlersbridge

POP 276

The village of Butlersbridge sits on the banks of the River Annalee. There are no sights as such, but it's a pretty spot to break your journey, with a great pub, as well as a gourmet restaurant with a cookery school, and canoeing nearby.

★ **Cavan Adventure Centre** CANOEING
(☑049-489 3630; www.cavanadventure.com; Inishmore; canoe & kayak rentals per half-/full day €30/50, fishing boats incl fuel per day €60; ☺10am-6pm Apr-Oct) Cavan Adventure Centre rents out canoes and kayaks (including all-important wetsuits), and runs tours of the local waterways including to Killykeen Forest Park. You can also hire fishing boats (equipment included). It's 5.5km west of Butlersbridge on the L1511.

Annalee House B&B €
(☑087 235 0289; Main St; s/d €65/95; P❄🐕) In the heart of the village, this sweet little B&B has three rooms in the main house and four in the adjacent cottage (one of which is wheelchair accessible). Guests can fire up the barbecue in the courtyard. Host Anna May is a chef, so breakfast is worth waking up for.

Derragarra Inn PUB FOOD €€
(☑049-433 1033; www.murphsbistro.com; mains €15-29; ☺kitchen noon-9pm Mon-Fri, to 9.30pm Sat, 12.30-3.30pm & 5-9pm Sun, bar noon-11pm Sun-Thu, to midnight Fri & Sat) This delightful ivy-covered pub has a wood-beamed interior and a large, sunny beer garden overlooking the river and St Aidan Church across the way. Its unconventional menu includes seared ostrich steak, kangaroo burgers and Parmesan-crusted chicken with plum sauce. Live music plays at weekends.

★ **Olde Post Inn** GASTRONOMY €€€
(☑047-55555; www.theoldepostinn.com; Cloverhill; 4-/8-course dinner menus €66/88, 3-course Sun lunch €41, cookery courses from €140; ☺6-9pm Wed & Thu, to 9.30pm Fri & Sat, 12.30-2.30pm & 5.30-8.30pm Sun; ☑) The lovely little village of Cloverhill, 4km north of Butlersbridge, is best known for its award-winning gastronomic restaurant housed in an 1884 former post office. Acclaimed chef Gearoid Lynch's contemporary cuisine is based on traditional ingredients such as monkfish, salmon, duck and lamb, with vegetarian and gluten-free options. In the former postmaster's residence are six luxurious guest rooms (single/double from €90/140).

ℹ **Getting There & Away**

Bus Éireann (www.buseireann.ie) has services to Cavan town (€4.90, 10 minutes, every two hours) and Dublin (€26, two hours, every two hours).

Ballyjamesduff & Around
POP 2661

A sleepy market town, Ballyjamesduff was the one-time home of the Earl of Fife, James Duff, an early Plantation landlord. His descendant, Sir James Duff, commanded English troops during the suppression of the 1798 Rising.

Nearby Lough Sheelin is famed for its trout fishing, but you'll need to bring your own equipment. It's a scenic place for walking year-round.

Cavan County Museum MUSEUM
(☑049-854 4070; www.cavanmuseum.ie; Virginia Rd; adult/child €6/4; ☺10am-5pm Tue-Sat, 2-5.30pm Sun Jun-Sep, 10am-5pm Tue-Sat Oct-May) Located inside a former convent, this museum's wide-ranging collection includes a huge array of 18th-, 19th- and 20th-century costumes and relics from the Stone, Bronze, Iron and Middle Ages, including the Celtic Killycluggin stone and the three-faced Corleck Head, as well as a 1000-year-old boat excavated from Lough Errill. There's also a large feature on Irish sports. Outside, the kid-friendly WWI Trench Experience has sound effects along its dug-out, sandbagged trenches.

Ross Castle CASTLE €€
(☑087 125 0911; www.ross-castle.com; Mountnugent; d €120-160; P🐕) Situated 9km south of Ballyjamesduff, this 1590 castle was partially destroyed by Cromwell but rebuilt by the Nugent family. It's not for the fainthearted – the steps get steeper and narrower the higher you climb into its tower (where three of its six rooms are located) and it's reputedly haunted. Its two cheapest rooms, in a ground-level annex, share a bathroom.

Call ahead to confirm your arrival time.

Eastern Cavan

Dún an Rí Forest Park PARK
(☑049-433 1942; www.coillte.ie; cars €5; ☺car park 9am-6pm Apr-Oct, to 4.30pm Nov-Mar) The 225-hectare Dún an Rí Forest Park, 11km southwest of Carrickmacross, has four colour-coded forest walks (all less than 4km long), with picnic places and a wishing well. Look out for mink and otters along the river. The car park accepts coins only.

Cabra Castle CASTLE €€
(☑042-966 7030; www.cabracastle.com; Carrickmacross Rd, Kingscourt; cottage/d from €140/198;

P 🛜) Bordering the Dún an Rí Forest Park, 10km southwest of Carrickmacross, 19th-century Cabra Castle is now a deluxe hotel decked out in plush period furnishings. A dozen rooms are in the castle itself but most are in its courtyard area; there are also simpler self-catering cottages. Wi-fi can be patchy.

Northwestern Cavan

Jampa Ling Buddhist Centre   MEDITATION
(☎ 049-952 3448; www.jampaling.org; Owendoon House, Bawnboy; retreat & workshop per activity free-€60, inclusive weekend retreat €180-275) 🥗 Jampa Ling ('Place of Infinite Loving Kindness') offers courses, retreats and workshops on Buddhist teachings, philosophy, meditation, yoga, and medicinal and culinary herbs. All meals are vegetarian. Accommodation (dorm/single including meals €28/45) may not be available if there is an event on. It's off the N87, 38km northwest of Cavan town.

Slieve Russell Hotel   SPA HOTEL €€
(☎ 049-952 6444; www.slieverussell.ie; N87, Cranaghan; d/ste from €139/199; P @ 🛜 ⛱) A vision of marble columns, fountains, restaurants and bars, the Slieve Russell Hotel has 222 elegantly furnished rooms. There are 18- and nine-hole golf courses (with pro lessons available); spa treatments include flotation tanks, a herbal sauna and a salt grotto. A kids' club makes it a popular choice with families. It's 26km northwest of Cavan town.

BALLYWHO?

All over Ireland you'll see the town prefix 'Bally' (and variations thereof, such as Ballyna and Ballina). The ubiquitous term originates from the Irish phrase 'Baile na'. It's often mistranslated as 'town', but there were very few towns in Ireland when the names came about. A closer approximation is 'place of'; hence Ballyjamesduff, for example, means 'Place of James Duff' (or James Duff's place). Dublin's Irish name is Baile Átha Cliath ('Place of the Hurdle Ford'). If it was anglicised, it too would be a Bally, spelt something like 'Ballycleeagh'.

Other common place-name prefixes include Carrick (or Carrig), meaning 'rock' in Irish, and Dun, from the Irish *dún* (meaning 'fort').

Blacklion & Around
POP 194

This remote corner of the county is traversed by the Cavan Way. The little village of Blacklion lies less than 50m from the River Belcoo, marking the border with County Fermanagh, Northern Ireland.

★ Cavan Burren Park   HISTORIC SITE
(www.cavanburrenpark.ie; Tullygobban Hill; ⊙ 7am-11pm May-Aug, reduced hours Sep-Apr) FREE Just 3km south of Blacklion, within the Cuilcagh Mountain Park and traversed by the Cavan Way walking route, this other-worldly megalithic site was identified in the 1870s but farmed until the 1950s and only established as the Cavan Burren Park in 2014. Highlights include a promontory fort circa 500 BC and the Giant's Grave wedge tomb from 2500 BC. An unstaffed information shed has interpretive panels, but the hilly, wooded area is otherwise pristine and magical to explore.

Cuilcagh Mountain Park   PARK
(www.marblearchcavesgeopark.com) The border between the Republic and Northern Ireland runs along the ridge of Cuilcagh Mountain, the distinctive tabletop summit of Cuilcagh Mountain Park, the world's first cross-border geopark. Its lower slopes are protected peatland habitats, while the upper slopes have dramatic sweeping cliffs. The visitor centre and the park's most high-profile attraction, the Marble Arch Caves (p663), lie over the border from Blacklion in County Fermanagh.

On the Republic side, the megalithic Cavan Burren Park is a highlight.

★ MacNean House & Restaurant   GASTRONOMY €€€
(☎ 071-985 3022; www.nevenmaguire.com; Main St; dinner menu €89, with paired wines €139, Sun lunch €48, cookery class from €200; ⊙ sittings 6pm & 9.30pm Wed-Sat, 12.30pm, 3.30pm & 7pm Sun; 🥗) Award-winning TV chef Neven Maguire grew up in this gorgeous village house and has turned it into one of Ireland's finest restaurants and cookery schools. Book months in advance (or nab a last-minute cancellation online) to feast on inspired creations such as rabbit wrapped in kataifi pastry with chestnut velouté, and to stay in beautiful pastel-hued rooms (double/suite from €134/174).

Vegetarian menus (€85) are available.

HIKING THE CAVAN WAY

The highlight for many walkers in the region is the Cavan Way, a 26km trail between the hamlets of Blacklion and Dowra through the Cuilcagh Mountains. Heading south from Blacklion, it takes you through Cavan Burren Park (p550) and its ancient burial site Magh Sleacht, which is dotted with prehistoric monuments – court cairns, ring forts and tombs – and was one of the last strongholds of Druidism. It continues past the Shannon Pot, the source of Ireland's longest river, then by road to Dowra, passing over the Black Pigs Dyke, an ancient fortification that once divided Ireland in two.

From Blacklion it's mainly hill walking; from Shannon Pot to Dowra it's mainly road. The highest point on the walk is Giant's Grave (260m). You'll need Ordinance Survey map No 26 and the *Cavan Way* map guide. Maps are on display in Blacklion and Dowra. Detailed route information (including downloadable map PDFs) is available online at www.thisiscavan.ie and www.irishtrails.ie. The route can be boggy, so take spare socks!

At Blacklion you can pick up the Ulster Way and at Dowra you can join the Leitrim Way, which runs between Manorhamilton and Drumshanbo.

❶ Getting There & Away

Bus Éireann (www.buseireann.ie) has services to Sligo town, County Sligo (€14, one hour, four daily Monday to Saturday, three Sunday) and Enniskillen, County Fermanagh (€6.60, 30 minutes, four daily Monday to Saturday, three Sunday), from where you can connect to Dublin and Belfast. To explore the area, however, you really need your own wheels.

COUNTY MONAGHAN

Monaghan's quiet, undulating landscape is known for its tiny rounded hills that resemble bubbles in badly pasted wallpaper. Known as drumlins, these bumps are the result of debris left by retreating glaciers during the last ice age. The county's lakes attract plenty of anglers, but few others make it here, making it a tranquil place to explore.

Unlike much of the province, Monaghan was largely left alone during the Ulster Plantation. After the Cromwellian wars, though, local chieftains were forced to sell their land for a fraction of its true value, or else have it seized and redistributed to Cromwell's soldiers.

In the early 19th century, lace-making became an important facet of the local economy, providing work and income for women. Carrickmacross was one of the key centres of the industry and you can still see the fine needlework on display here.

Monaghan Town

POP 8012

It may be the county town, but Monaghan's residents live their lives utterly unaffected by tourism. It's an enjoyable place to wander and admire the elegant 18th- and 19th-century limestone buildings. Many buildings have gently rounded corners, an unusual architectural feature in Ireland.

◉ Sights & Activities

St Macartan's Cathedral   CATHEDRAL
(☑047-81220; www.monaghan-rackwallace.ie; Old Armagh Rd; ⊗8.30am-5pm) In a commanding hilltop position this neo-Gothic Catholic cathedral with stepped buttresses, turrets and an 81m-high spire was built from local grey limestone between 1861 and 1892. Its front doors are flanked by sculptures of St Peter (carrying the keys of authority) and St Paul (holding the sword of martyrdom). Inside its soaring interior are a hand-carved granite altar, a 2000-pipe organ and dazzling rose and lancet stained-glass windows. Opening hours can vary.

Monaghan County Museum   MUSEUM
(www.monaghan.ie; 1-2 Hill St; ⊗11am-5pm Mon-Fri, from noon Sat) FREE More than 70,000 artefacts from the Stone Age to modern times are housed at this excellent regional museum. Its crowning glory is the 14th-century Cross of Clogher, an oak altar cross encased in decorative bronze panels. Other impressive finds include the Lisdrumturk and Altartate Cauldrons, medieval *crannóg* artefacts, and some frightening knuckledusters and cudgels relating to the border with the North.

Rossmore Forest Park   PARK
(www.coillte.ie; off R189; ⊗car park 8am-6pm Apr-Oct, to 4.30pm Nov-Mar) FREE Crumbling remains of the Rossmore family's 19th-century castle, including its entrance

WORTH A TRIP

HILTON PARK

The magnificent country-house retreat **Hilton Park** (☏047-56007; www. hiltonpark.ie; off N54, Scotshouse; d/f from €210/240, gatehouse per week from €780; ☺Apr-Oct; P⚡) has been in the same family since 1734. Its six spacious, light-bathed guest rooms have original furniture, free-standing baths and four-poster or half-tester beds. Top-class cuisine is largely sourced from the estate's farm, lakes and gardens (four-course dinner menu €65; Tuesday to Saturday). It's located on a 240-hectare estate, 27km southwest of Monaghan town.

The gatehouse sleeps up to four and has a wood-burning stove.

Cots and half-price meals are available for kids, who also have their own two-course high tea (€15).

Guests get free access to its 18-hole golf course, fishing lakes and row boats, as well as bikes for exploring the grounds. In spring you can see the farm's newborn lambs.

stairway, buttresses and the family's pet cemetery, can still be seen at Rossmore Forest Park, where rhododendrons and azaleas blaze with colour in early summer. The park contains several giant redwoods, a yew avenue and Iron Age tombs, and is home to badgers, foxes, pygmy shrews, hedgehogs, otters and five of Ireland's seven bat species. There are forest walks and pretty picnic areas. It's 3.5km southwest of central Monaghan.

Birdlife in the park includes warblers, flycatchers and cuckoos.

Venture Sports   FISHING
(☏047-81495; 71 Glaslough St; ☺9am-6pm Mon-Sat) Fine fishing abounds in the area; contact Venture Sports for permits, tackle and local knowledge.

★ Festivals & Events

Harvest Blues Festival   MUSIC
(www.harvestblues.ie; ☺early Sep) Local and international acts feature at this fabulous three-day blues festival.

🛏 Sleeping & Eating

Cafes and restaurants concentrate around the Diamond and Glaslough St. Monaghan's

farmers market (Church Sq; ☺10am-2pm Fri) 🍃 sets up in the centre of town; there are also large supermarkets.

Westenra Arms   HOTEL €€
(☏047-74400; www.westenrahotel.com; The Diamond; s/d/tr/ste from €79/110/150/160; 🛜) A town-centre landmark, this huge red-brick hotel has comfortable rooms (some with four-poster beds) reached by a lift/elevator, and sociable public areas including a glass-roofed restaurant (mains €16 to €30), a bar with live music and a nightclub. But you can still sleep in peace: rooms are well soundproofed. Kids are welcomed with toys and colouring books.

★Castle Leslie   CASTLE €€€
(☏047-88100; www.castleleslie.com; Glaslough; d from €200; P🛜) Castle Leslie, 11km northeast of Monaghan town along the R185, is a magnificent Victorian pile, acquired by the Leslie family (who trace their ancestors back to Attila the Hun) in 1665. Facilities include a Victorian spa and an equestrian centre (per hour from €35); dining options span sophisticated **Snaffles Brasserie** (four-course menu €65) to snug **Conor's Bar**. Public areas have wi-fi.

Each of the 20 guest rooms in the main house has a story: the Red Room, used by WB Yeats, contains the first bath plumbed in Ireland, while in Uncle Norman's Room, guests claim to have been levitated in the Gothic four-poster bed. The Hunting Lodge has a further 51 rooms, with decor ranging from rich traditional drapery to more minimalist contemporary style.

Batch Loaf   BISTRO €€
(☏047-72253; www.thebatchloaf.com; North Rd; mains €14.50-28.50; ☺5-9pm Mon, Wed & Thu, to 10pm Fri & Sat, 3-9pm Sun) A floor-to-ceiling map of County Monaghan occupies one wall of this bright, contemporary two-level bistro, and locally sourced ingredients are used in dishes like roast duck breast with bacon, chestnut and cabbage, maple-cured pork with cider sauce, Monaghan sirloin with roast peppercorn sauce, and grilled hake with wild mushroom crème. Live music plays Friday, Saturday and Sunday.

🍺 Drinking & Entertainment

McKenna's Bar   PUB
(www.facebook.com/Smckennas; 62 Dublin St; ☺7pm-midnight; 🛜) This historic pub is famous throughout the region for its jam ses-

sions, predominantly blues. They take place in its upstairs bar 'the Brewery': the ideal moody venue with its dark wood, barrel tables and exposed brick walls. Its downstairs bar is known as 'the Anchor'.

Market House ARTS CENTRE
(☑ 047-73722; www.monaghan.ie; Market St) This restored 18th-century market hall turned arts venue hosts exhibitions, concerts and drama productions.

ℹ Information

Monaghan's seasonal **tourist office** (☑ 047-81122; www.monaghantourism.com; Market St; ☺10am-5pm Mon-Fri Mar-Sep) is in the Market House.

ℹ Getting There & Away

Daily Bus Éireann (www.buseireann.ie) services include Dublin (€18, two hours, every two hours) via Carrickmacross (€13, 30 minutes).

Carrickmacross & Around

POP 5032

Carrickmacross was first settled by early English and Scottish Planters, and its broad main street is flanked by elegant Georgian houses with gorgeous poster-paint coloured facades. It's most famous as the home of delicate Carrickmacross lace, an industry revived in 1871 by the St Louis nuns.

Carrickmacross has no tourist office, but visitor information is available at www.carrickmacross.ie/visit-carrick.

◉ Sights

Carrickmacross Lace Gallery GALLERY
(☑ 042-966 4176; www.carrickmacrosslace.ie; Market Sq; ☺9.30am-5.30pm Mon-Sat) FREE In the town's former cattle yards, a local cooperative runs this thimble-sized lace gallery, where you can see lace-making demonstrations and check out exquisite designs. Designs are appliquéd on organza using thick thread and close stitches, then embellished with a variety of point stitches, guipure, pops and the lace's distinctive loop edge. Lace makers can take commissions and you can purchase delicate pieces made into fridge magnets, bookmarks and the like.

Carrickmacross lace graced the sleeves of Princess Diana's wedding dress and, more recently, the technique was used on the wedding dress for Kate Middleton's marriage to Prince William in 2011.

St Joseph's Catholic Church CHURCH
(www.carrickmacrossparish.ie; O'Neill St; ☺8am-6pm) Craftsmanship shines at St Joseph's Catholic Church, with 10 windows designed by Harry Clarke, Ireland's most renowned stained-glass artist. Opening hours can vary.

🛌 Sleeping & Eating

Shirley Arms HOTEL €€
(☑ 042-967 3100; www.shirleyarmshotel.ie; Main St; d/f from €128/180; P🖥) Right in the centre of town, the Shirley Arms has a warm stone exterior, behind which lies a superb family-run hotel. White linens, walnut floors and modern bathrooms give the rooms a contemporary flair. The open-plan bar and lounge create an informal setting for excellent Irish classics, which are also served at its elegant restaurant (mains €16 to €38). Family rooms sleep four.

It's a popular wedding venue, so be sure to book ahead, especially on weekends.

Matilda's Artisan Bakehouse BAKERY €
(1 Monaghan St; dishes €3.50-8.50; ☺8.30am-6pm Mon-Sat, 9.30am-4pm Sun) In addition to artisan breads such as sourdough and focaccia, Matilda's bakes cakes, sweet pastries and savoury varieties including fennel sausage rolls. It's ideal for picking up a quick breakfast or picnic ingredients; there's also a small seating area where you can dine on daily specials like quiches, soups and salads.

★ **Riverbank County Pub** GASTROPUB €€
(☑ 041-685 5883; www.theriverbank.ie; Lannette, Killanny; mains €15-28; ☺kitchen 5-9.30pm Wed-Sat, 12.30-9pm Sun, bar noon-11pm Sun-Thu, to midnight Fri & Sat; 🖥🚸) On the banks of the River Glyde (the source of salmon served here), this gem is 7.5km southeast of Carrickmacross off the L4700 on the County Louth border. A roaring fire warms the dining area, with no TV to distract from fantastic dishes like cider-steamed Clogher Head mussels or Monaghan fillet steak with Bellingham blue cheese. Book ahead on weekends.

There's a kids' menu and a playground.

Run by the fourth generation of the same family, the pub was rebuilt using reclaimed timbers and flagstones from the original 18th-century inn. Upstairs are six spacious guest rooms with private bathroom (double/triple from €86/105) with river or garden views.

🍷 Drinking & Nightlife

Fiddlers Elbow
PUB

(www.fiddlers.ie; Main St; ⊙11am-midnight Sun-Thu, to 2am Fri-Sun) On Carrickmacross' wide main street, Fiddlers Elbow contains a buzzing bar, an upmarket restaurant serving dishes like smoked bacon–wrapped chicken (mains €16 to €28) and an upstairs nightclub (open 9pm to 3am Friday and Saturday). Live music in all genres regularly takes place; check the agenda online.

❶ Getting There & Away

Bus Éireann (www.buseireann.ie) services connect with Dublin (€17.50, two hours, hourly) and Dundalk (€7.70, 35 minutes, five daily Monday to Saturday, none Sunday).

Inniskeen

Patrick Kavanagh
Resource Centre
MUSEUM

(☎042-937 8560; www.patrickkavanaghcountry.com; Inniskeen; ⊙11am-4.30pm Tue mid-Mar–mid-Dec or by appointment) FREE Acclaimed poet Patrick Kavanagh (1904–67) was born in the picturesque little village of Inniskeen, 10km northeast of Carrickmacross. The Patrick Kavanagh Resource Centre is housed in the village's old parish church where Kavanagh was baptised; he's buried in the attached graveyard. The centre's staff have a passion for his life and work that is contagious. Download a self-guided literary tour of the village and the picturesque surrounding countryside (5.6km in all) from the website.

The centre hosts events including a Writers' Weekend in late July/early August.

Kavanagh's long work *The Great Hunger* (1942) blasted away the earlier clichés of Anglo-Irish verse and revealed Ireland's poor farming communities as half-starved, broken-backed and sexually repressed. His best-known poem, 'On Raglan Road' (1946), was an ode to his unrequited love. It doubled as the lyrics for the traditional Irish air 'The Dawning of the Day', which has been performed by Van Morrison, Mark Knopfler, Billy Bragg, Sinéad O'Connor and countless others.

On the Road

Belfast

POP 340,220 / AREA 115 SQ KM

Best Places to Eat

➡ Saphyre (p582).

➡ Noble (p583)

➡ Yügo (p580)

➡ Muddlers Club (p582)

➡ Eipic (p581)

Best Places to Stay

➡ Bullitt Hotel (p575)

➡ Titanic Hotel Belfast (p576)

➡ Rayanne House (p580)

➡ Vagabonds (p576)

➡ Merchant Hotel (p575)

➡ Global Village Backpackers (p576)

Why Go?

Belfast is in many ways a brand-new city. Once shunned by travellers unnerved by tales of the Troubles and sectarian violence, in recent years it has pulled off a remarkable transformation from bombs-and-bullets pariah to a hip-hotels-and-hedonism party town.

The old shipyards on the Lagan have given way to the luxury apartments of the Titanic Quarter, whose centrepiece – the stunning, star-shaped edifice housing the Titanic Belfast centre, covering the ill-fated liner's construction here, has become the city's number-one tourist draw. No visitor to Belfast leaves without learning *something* about that ship.

Belfast's rich cultural heritage is reflected in its world-class musicians and thriving arts scene – the Belfast International Arts Festival is one of the largest in the UK and Ireland. It heads a list of attractions that includes beautifully restored Victorian architecture, a glittering waterfront lined with modern art, a fantastic and fast-expanding foodie scene and music-filled pubs.

When to Go

➡ April can be a great time to visit Belfast, with spring flowers blooming throughout the city's parks and gardens, and the Belfast Film Festival showcasing Irish and international filmmakers' works.

➡ August brings good weather for walking and cycling, along with celebrations of Irish music and dance in West Belfast during Féile An Phobail, plus street parties and a carnival parade.

➡ October can start to get chilly, but the Festival at Queen's, the UK's second-largest arts festival (after Edinburgh), warms things up during its three-week run.

Belfast Highlights

1 Titanic Belfast (p564) Learning about the world's most famous ocean liner.

2 St George's Market (p562) Sampling some of Northern Ireland's top produce.

3 Crown Liquor Saloon (p559) Sipping a Guinness in this beautiful Victorian pub.

4 Ulster Museum (p566)

Discovering prehistoric treasures and Armada gold.

5 Cave Hill (p568) Enjoying panoramic city views from the North Belfast viewpoint.

6 Ulster Folk Museum (p570) Wandering recreated farmhouses, forges and mills.

7 Lagan Towpath (p568) Cycling along the riverbank to a former linen town.

8 Botanic Gardens (p567) Visiting the Palm House in the peaceful park.

9 Crumlin Road Gaol (p570) Wandering the cells of the notorious jail.

10 Cathedral Quarter (p584) Drinking and dancing in the lively nightlife district.

History

Belfast takes its name from the River Farset (from the Irish *feirste*, meaning sandbank, or sandy ford), which flows into the River Lagan at Donegall Quay (it is now channelled through a culvert). Its Irish name, Béal Feirste, means 'Mouth of the Farset'.

In 1177 the Norman lord John de Courcy built a castle here, and a small settlement grew up around it. Both were destroyed in battle 20 years later, and the town did not begin to develop in earnest until 1611 when Baron Arthur Chichester built a castle in what is now the city centre (near Castle Pl and Castle St); it was destroyed by fire in 1708.

The early-17th-century Plantation of Ulster brought in the first waves of Scottish and English settlers, followed in the late 17th century by an influx of Huguenots (French Protestants) fleeing persecution in France; they laid the foundations of a thriving linen industry. More Scottish and English settlers arrived, and other industries such as rope-making, tobacco, engineering and shipbuilding developed.

With its textile mills and shipyards, Belfast was the one city in Ireland that truly rode the wave of the Industrial Revolution. Sturdy rows of brick terrace houses were built for the factory and shipyard workers, and a town of around 20,000 people in 1800 grew steadily into a city of 400,000 by the start of WWI, by which time Belfast had nearly overtaken Dublin in size.

The partition of Ireland in 1920 gave Belfast a new role as the capital of Northern Ireland. It also marked the end of the city's industrial growth, although decline didn't really set in until after WWII. With the outbreak of the Troubles in 1969, the city saw more than its fair share of violence and bloodshed, and shocking news images of terrorist bombings, sectarian murders and security forces' brutality made Belfast a household name around the world.

The 1998 Good Friday Agreement, which laid the groundwork for power-sharing among the various political factions in a devolved Northern Ireland Assembly, raised hopes for the future, and a historic milestone was passed on 8 May 2007 when the Reverend Ian Paisley (firebrand Protestant preacher and leader of the Democratic Unionist Party) and Martin McGuinness (Sinn Féin MP and former IRA commander) were respectively sworn in at Stormont as first minister and deputy first minister of a new power-sharing government.

For 10 years the Northern Ireland Assembly remained active, functioning under the terms of the Good Friday Agreement, until in 2017 the power-sharing agreement collapsed and direct rule from Westminster was imposed once again. Meanwhile, since 2000 the economy picked up as investments poured in and a massive, ongoing program of regeneration began. As Belfast's image improved, and with the opening of new attractions like Titanic Belfast, tourists began to visit in large numbers. And while the National Assembly at Stormont has had its share of scandals, Belfast hasn't looked back.

◉ Sights

◉ City Centre

The city centre's most important sights date back to the Victorian era, when Belfast was a prospering centre of trade and industry: the Crown Liquor Saloon, Grand Opera House, St George's Market and City Hall were all built during that time.

★ **City Hall**   HISTORIC BUILDING
(Map p560; ✆028-9027 0456; www.belfastcity. gov.uk; Donegall Sq; ⊙9.30am-5pm Mon-Fri, 10am-5pm Sat & Sun, to 8pm Thu Jun-Sep; ▣Donegall Sq) **FREE** Belfast's classical Renaissance-style City Hall was built in fine, white Portland stone in 1906. Highlights of the free, 45-minute guided tour include the sumptuous, wedding-cake Italian marble of the rotunda; an opportunity to sit on the mayor's throne in the council chamber; and the idiosyncratic portraits of past lord mayors. On the ground floor and accessible outside tour times are a series of commemorative stained-glass windows and a visitor exhibition with displays on Belfast's history spread across 16 rooms.

The Industrial Revolution transformed Belfast in the 19th century. The city's rapid rise to prosperity is reflected in the extravagance of the building. The hall is fronted by a statue of a rather dour 'we are not amused' Queen Victoria. The bronze figures on either side of her symbolise the textile and shipbuilding industries. The child at the back represents education.

At the northeastern corner of the grounds is a statue of Sir Edward Harland, the Yorkshire-born marine engineer who founded Harland & Wolff shipyards and who served as mayor of Belfast from 1885 to 1886. To his south stands a memorial to the victims of the *Titanic*.

Guided tours are at 11am, 2pm and 3pm Monday to Friday and at noon, 2pm and 3pm Saturday and Sunday. From June to September additional tours are offered at 10am and 4pm Monday to Friday and 4pm Saturday and Sunday. Sign up at the reception desk or book by phone.

⭐ **Crown Liquor Saloon**   HISTORIC BUILDING
(Map p560; www.nationaltrust.org.uk/the-crown-bar; 46 Great Victoria St; ⊙ 11.30am-11pm Mon-Sat, 12.30-10pm Sun; ⌨ 8A to 8D, 9A to 9C) There are not many historical monuments that you can enjoy while savouring a pint of Guinness, but the National Trust's Crown Liquor Saloon is one of them. Belfast's most famous bar was refurbished by Patrick Flanagan in the late 19th century and displays Victorian decorative flamboyance at its best (he was looking to pull in a posh clientele from the train station and Grand Opera House opposite). Despite being a tourist attraction, the bar fills up with locals come 6pm.

The exterior (1885) is decorated with ornate and colourful Italian tiles, and boasts a mosaic of a crown on the pavement outside the entrance. Legend has it that Flanagan, a Catholic, argued with his Protestant wife over what the pub's name should be. His wife prevailed and it was named the Crown in honour of the British monarchy. Flanagan took his sneaky revenge by placing the crown mosaic underfoot where customers would tread on it every day.

The interior (1898) sports a mass of stained and cut glass, marble, ceramics, mirrors and mahogany, all atmospherically lit by genuine gas mantles. A long, highly decorated bar dominates one side of the pub, while on the other is a row of ornate wooden snugs. The snugs come equipped with gunmetal plates (from the Crimean War) for striking matches and bell-pushes that once allowed drinkers to order top-ups without leaving their seats (alas, no longer).

⭐ Grand Opera House   HISTORIC BUILDING
(Map p560; ☎ 028-9024 1919; www.goh.co.uk; Great Victoria St; tours £8.50; ⊙ box office 10am-5pm Mon-Sat; ⌨ 8A to 8D, 9A to 9C) One of Belfast's great Victorian landmarks is the Grand Opera House. Opened in 1895 and completely refurbished in the 1970s, it sustained severe IRA-bomb damage in 1991 and 1993. The interior has been restored to its original, over-the-top Victorian pomp, with swirling wood and plasterwork, fancy gilt-work in abundance and carved elephant heads framing the private boxes in the auditorium. Check the website for details of upcoming hour-long backstage tours, during which you'll see the inner-workings of the theatre.

The Opera House is set to close for most of 2020 for renovations, which will include a new visitor exhibition.

Linen Hall Library   LIBRARY
(Map p560; www.linenhall.com; 17 Donegall Sq N; ⊙ 9.30am-5.30pm Mon-Fri; ⌨ G1, G2) 🆓 Established in 1788 to 'improve the mind and excite a spirit of general inquiry', the Linen Hall Library houses some 260,000 books, more than half of which are part of its important Irish and local studies collection. The political collection consists of pretty much everything that has been written about Northern Irish politics since 1966. The library also has a small **coffee shop** (⊙ 10am-4pm Mon-Fri).

The library was moved from its original home in the White Linen Hall (the site is now occupied by City Hall) to the present building a century later. Thomas Russell, the first librarian, was a founding member of the United Irishmen and a close friend of Wolfe Tone – a reminder that this movement for independence from Britain had its origins in Belfast. Russell was hanged in 1803 after Robert Emmet's abortive rebellion.

Entries   STREET
(Map p560; ⌨ 1A to 1G, 2A to 2E) These narrow alleyways running between High St and Ann St were once bustling commercial and residential thoroughfares; **Pottinger's Entry**, for example, had 34 houses in 1822. **Joy's Entry** is named after Francis Joy, who founded the *Belfast News Letter* in 1737, the British Isles' first daily newspaper (it's still in business). **Crown Entry** is where the United Irishmen were founded in 1791 by Wolfe Tone in Peggy Barclay's tavern. On **Wine Cellar Entry**, **White's Tavern** (www.whitesbelfast.com; 1-4 Wine Cellar Entry; ⊙ noon-11pm Mon & Tue, to 1am Wed-Sat, to midnight Sun; ⌨ 1A to 1J, 2A to 2E) is Belfast's oldest tavern.

St Malachy's Church   CHURCH
(Map p560; www.saintmalachysparish.com; 24 Alfred St; ⊙ 8am-5.30pm; ⌨ 13A, 13B) Catholic St Malachy's was built between 1841 and 1844 by Thomas Jackson and extensively renovated in the past decade. Its exterior resembles a Tudor castle complete with arrow slits and turrets, and the jewel-like interior's fan-vaulted ceiling replicates Westminster Abbey's Henry VII Chapel. In 1886 the largest bell in Northern Ireland was installed but swiftly removed

BELFAST

Central Belfast

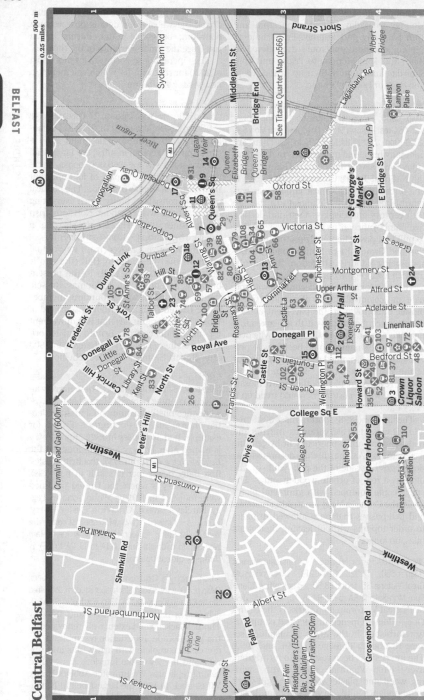

500 m
0.25 miles

See Titanic Quarter Map (p566)

Short Strand

Sydenham Rd

Middlepath St.

Bridge End

River Lagan

Albert Bridge

Lagan Weir

Lanyon Pl

Laganbank Rd

Belfast Lanyon Place

Corporation St

Donegall Quay

Queen's Sq

Queen Elizabeth Bridge

Queen's Bridge

Oxford St

St George's Market

E Bridge St

Grace St

Corporation St

Tomb St

Albert St

Dunbar St

Waring St

Victoria St

Ann St

Chichester St

May St

Montgomery St

Dunbar Link

St Anne's Sq

Hill St

High St

Cornmarket

Upper Arthur St

Alfred St

Adelaide St

Frederick St

York St

Talbot St

Writer's Sq

North St

Bridge St

Rosemary St

Castle La

City Hall

Donegall Sq

Linenhall St

Donegall St

Little Donegall St

Library St

Kent St

North St

Royal Ave

Castle St

Fountain Pl

Donegall Pl

Bedford St

Carrick Hill

Peter's Hill

Francis St

Wellington Pl

Howard St

Crown Liquor Saloon

Crumlin Road Gaol (600m)

Westlink

Townsend St

Divis St

College Sq N

College Sq E

Athol St

Grand Opera House

Great Victoria St Station

Shankill Rd

Shankill Pde

Northumberland St

Albert St

Falls Rd

Grosvenor Rd

Westlink

Peace Line

Conway St

Sinn Féin Headquarters (250m); Bia; Cultúrlann McAdam Ó Fiaich (950m)

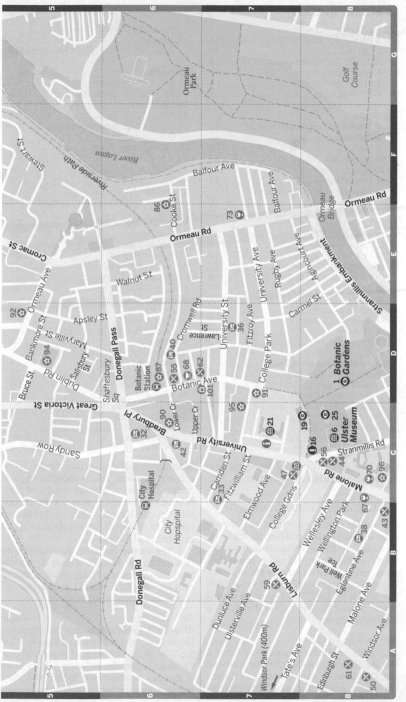

Central Belfast

when local distillers claimed its chimes were interfering with whiskey production.

◎ Laganside Waterfront

Soaring above the waterfront at Donegall Quay is Belfast's tallest building, the 2011-built 27-storey **Obel** (🚇G2), containing apartments. To its south, **Victoria Square** (www.victoria square.com; btwn Ann & Chichester Sts; ⊙9.30am-6pm Mon-Tue, to 9pm Wed-Fri, 9am-6pm Sat, 1-6pm Sun; 🚇11A to 11D, 12A, 12B), set around a soaring atrium topped by a vast glass dome, has a **viewing platform**.

★ **St George's Market**   MARKET
(Map p560; www.belfastcity.gov.uk; cnr Oxford & May Sts; ⊙6am-3pm Fri, 9am-3pm Sat, 10am-4pm Sun; 🚇4) Ireland's oldest continually operating market was built in 1896. This Victorian

beauty hosts a Friday **variety market** (flowers, produce, meat, fish, homewares and secondhand goods), a Saturday **food and craft market** (food stalls to look out for include Suki Tea, Ann's Pantry bakers and Hillstown Farm) and a **Sunday market** (food, local arts and crafts and live music).

A free shuttle bus links the market with Donegall Sq and Adelaide St every 20 minutes from 11am to 3pm on Friday and Saturday. In early December, a two-day Christmas Fair and Market takes place here.

Belfast Barge   MUSEUM
(Map p560; www.facebook.com/TheBelfastBarge; Lanyon Quay; adult/child £4/3; ⊙10am-4pm Tue-Sat; 🚇3A, 5A, 5B) Housed in a barge moored on the River Lagan, this museum tells the story of Belfast's maritime and industrial history, bringing together old photographs, original

drawings and documents, ship models and artefacts, and recordings of interviews with retired engineers, designers and shipyard workers. On the upper floor of the barge is the restaurant Holohan's at the Barge (p580).

Albert Memorial Clock Tower   LANDMARK
(Map p560; Queen's Sq; 🚌3A, 4D, 5A, 6A) At the east end of High St is Belfast's very own leaning tower. Erected in 1865 in honour of Queen Victoria's dear departed husband, it is not as dramatically out of kilter as the more famously tilted tower in Pisa, but does, nevertheless, lean noticeably to the south – as the locals say, 'Old Albert not only has the time, he also has the inclination.' Restoration work has stabilised its foundations and left its Scrabo sandstone masonry sparkling white.

Bigfish   SCULPTURE
(Map p560; Donegall Quay; 🚌3A, 4D, 5A, 6A) The most prominent of several modern artworks on the riverbank between Clarendon Dock and Ormeau Bridge, *Bigfish* (1999), by

Belfast-born artist John Kindness, is a 10m ceramic salmon symbolising the regeneration of the River Lagan. Its blue tiles depict the history of Belfast.

Custom House   HISTORIC BUILDING
(Map p560; Custom House Sq; 🚌3A, 4D, 5A, 6A) Opposite the west end of Lagan Weir is the elegant Custom House, built by Charles Lanyon in Italianate style between 1854 and 1857; the writer Anthony Trollope once worked in the post office here. On the waterfront side, the pediment carries sculpted portrayals of Britannia, Neptune and Mercury. The **Custom House steps** were once a speakers' corner, a tradition memorialised in a bronze statue preaching to an invisible crowd. The building's interior is closed to the public.

◉ Cathedral Quarter

Once run-down and derelict, the area around St Anne's Cathedral has emerged as a cultural and creative hotspot, with a buzzing nightlife,

BELFAST IN...

One Day

If it's Friday, Saturday or Sunday start your day with a look around **St George's Market** (p562) too. Then walk into the city centre and take a free guided tour of **City Hall** (p558). Take a **black taxi tour** (p573) of the West Belfast murals, and ask the taxi driver to drop you off for lunch at **Holohan's at the Barge** (p580). From there, take a stroll across the river and spend the rest of the afternoon exploring **Titanic Belfast** Round off the day with dinner at the **Muddlers Club** (p582) and then drinks at the **Duke of York** (p584) and the bars of buzzing Hill St.

Two Days

On your second day, take a look at **Queen's University** (p567), explore the fascinating exhibits in the **Ulster Museum** (p566) and take a stroll through the **Botanic Gardens** (p567). In the afternoon either take a guided tour around historic **Crumlin Road Gaol** (p570), or go for a hike up **Cave Hill** (p568). Stop for a pint at the **Crown Liquor Saloon** (p559), then have dinner at nearby **Eipic** (p581). End the night with a rooftop cocktail at **Babel Rooftop Bar** (p583).

dynamic arts venues and street art. The cobbled lanes of this former trading quarter are now lined with recording studios, media companies and design offices, as well as hip bars and restaurants. As the bohemian enclave becomes ever more gentrified, the area around North St is set for development; residents have opposed plans to rebrand the area Tribeca and demolish the North Street Arcade.

St Anne's Cathedral CHURCH

(Map p560; www.belfastcathedral.org; Donegall St; adult/child £5/3; ⊘9am-5.15pm Mon-Sat, 1-3pm Sun; 🚌2, 12) Built in imposing Hiberno-Romanesque style, St Anne's Cathedral was started in 1899 but did not reach its final form until 1981. As you enter you'll see that the black-and-white marble floor is laid out in a maze pattern – the black route leads to a dead end, the white to the sanctuary and salvation. Tours run at 10am, noon, 2pm and 4pm Monday to Saturday, or pick up a leaflet for a self-guided tour.

The nave's 10 pillars are topped by carvings symbolising aspects of Belfast life; look out for the Freemasons' pillar (the central one on the south side). In the south aisle is the tomb of Unionist hero Sir Edward Carson (1854–1935). In the baptistry, the stunning mosaic of *The Creation* contains 150,000 pieces of coloured glass; it and the mosaic above the west door are the result of seven years' work by sisters Gertrude and Margaret Martin.

Oh Yeah Music Centre MUSEUM

(Map p560; www.ohyeahbelfast.com; 15-21 Gordon St; ⊘museum 10am-5pm Mon-Fri, 1-5pm Sat; 🚌3A, 4D, 5A, 6A) FREE A charitable organisation that provides rehearsal space for young musicians in a converted whiskey warehouse, the Oh Yeah Music Centre is also home to an exhibition on Northern Ireland's musical history, from folk music to The Undertones to Snow Patrol. Exhibits include electric guitars, historic gig posters, ticket stubs and stage clothing donated by famous bands.

◉ Titanic Quarter

Stretching along the east side of the River Lagan, Belfast's former shipbuilding yards – the birthplace of the RMS *Titanic* – are dominated by the towering yellow Harland & Wolff cranes. Since 2009, the former industrial wasteland has been transformed as part of a £7 billion regeneration project; development of the area is scheduled for completion by 2034. The quarter's centrepiece is the striking star-shaped outline of Titanic Belfast, the city's top tourist attraction. Spaced out in the surrounding docklands are a number of other maritime and *Titanic*-related sites.

★Titanic Belfast MUSEUM

(Map p566; www.titanicbelfast.com; Queen's Rd; adult/child £18.50/8; ⊘9am-7pm Jun & Jul, to 8pm Aug, to 6pm Apr, May & Sep, 10am-5pm Oct-Mar; 🚌G2) The head of the slipway where the *Titanic* was built is now occupied by the gleaming, angular edifice of Titanic Belfast, an unmissable multimedia extravaganza that charts the history of Belfast and the creation of the world's most famous ocean liner. Cleverly designed exhibits enlivened by historical images, animated projections and soundtracks chart Belfast's rise to turn-of-the-20th-century industrial superpower, followed by a high-tech ride through a noisy, smells-and-all recreation of the city's shipyards. Tickets include entry to the SS Nomadic.

You can explore every detail of the *Titanic's* construction, from a computer 'fly-through' from keel to bridge, to replicas of the passenger accommodation. Perhaps most poignant are the few flickering images that constitute the only film footage of the ship in existence.

Saver tickets (adult/child £10/8) are available for speedy visits without the shipyard ride one hour before the museum closes.

Behind the building you can see the massive slipways where the *Titanic* and her sister ship *Olympic* were built and launched.

SS Nomadic HISTORIC SITE

(Map p566; www.nomadicbelfast.com; Hamilton Dock, Queen's Rd; adult/child £7/5; ⊘10am-7pm Sun-Thu, to 8pm Fri & Sat Jul & Aug, 10am-7pm Jun, 10am-6pm Apr, May & Jun, 11am-5pm Oct-Mar; ⛴G2) Built in Belfast in 1911, the SS *Nomadic* is the last remaining vessel of the White Star Line. The little steamship ferried 1st- and 2nd-class passengers between Cherbourg Harbour and the ocean liners that were too big to dock at the French port. On 10 April 1912 it delivered 172 passengers to the ill-fated *Titanic*. Don't miss the luxurious 1st-class toilets. Entry to the SS *Nomadic* (valid for 24 hours) is included in the ticket for Titanic Belfast.

Requisitioned in both world wars, the ship ended up as a floating restaurant in Paris in the 1980s and '90s. In 2006 it was rescued from the breaker's yard and brought to Belfast, where it's berthed in the Hamilton Graving Dock.

Titanic's Dock & Pump House HISTORIC SITE

(Map p566; www.titanicsdock.com; Queen's Rd; adult/child £5/3.50; ⊘10am-5pm Apr-Oct, 10.30am-4pm Nov & Dec, 10.30am-5pm Jan & Feb; ⛴G2) At the far end of Queen's Rd is an impressive monument to the days of the great liners – the vast **Thompson Dry Dock** where the *Titanic* was fitted out. Beside it is the **Pump House.** Self-guided tours include a viewing of original footage from the shipyards, a visit to the inner workings of the pump house and a walk along the floor of the dry dock. Watch your step: parts of the building are in need of repairs.

The dock's huge size gives you some idea of the scale of the ship, which could only just fit into it.

Harland & Wolff Drawing Offices HISTORIC BUILDING

(Map p566; www.titanichotelbelfast.com; Queen's Rd; ⛴G2) The designs for the *Titanic* were first drawn up here at the original Harland & Wolff drawing offices. Now part of the Titanic Hotel (p576), the drawing offices, Thomas Andrews' office, the old Harland & Wolff bathrooms and the room that received the news by telegram that the ship was in trouble have all been preserved. Pop inside to take a look around and have a drink in Drawing Office Two (p585), or see them on the **Titanic Discovery Tour** (☑028-9076 6386; adult/child £9/7.50; ⛴G2).

If the hotel concierge is free he or she may be able to show you around; the best times are before noon or after 5pm. Don't miss John Kempster's photographs of the launch of the *Titanic;* the forgotten album was rediscovered in 2012.

HMS Caroline SHIP

(Map p566; ☑028-9045 4484; www.hmscaroline. co.uk; Alexandra Dock, Queen's Rd; adult/child £13.50/5; ⊘10am-5pm; ⛴G?) The UK's last surviving WWI Royal Navy cruiser has been converted into a floating museum, docked in Titanic Quarter. Audio tours take in the captain's quarters, officers' cabins, marine's mess,

---

CATHEDRAL QUARTER STREET ART

Belfast has a well-established tradition of political and sectarian murals, usually painted on gable ends to stake out territory. But in the Cathedral Quarter, the culture of painting walls has been reset with the emergence of a thriving street art scene.

Much of the neighbourhood's street art was commissioned as part of the annual Hit the North festival (p574), started in 2013 by a local arts organisation as a way to brighten up and improve the shuttered, empty shop houses of North St as the area awaits the imminent arrival of developers.

One piece that is unlikely to be painted over any time soon is the magnificent **Duel of Belfast, Dance by Candlelight** (Map p560; Hill St; ⛴3A, 4D, 5A, 6A) by Irish artist Conor Harrington. Painted as part of the 2012 Cathedral Quarter Arts Festival (p574), it depicts two historical figures fighting over a dead animal, while a third man looks on. The artist has described it as a comment on colonialism.

Find out about the local and international artists behind the works on a weekly Street Art Walking Tour (p571).

BELFAST SIGHTS

Titanic Quarter

sick bay, engine room and galley kitchen, with interactive exhibits and a film dramatisation of HMS *Caroline's* role in the 1916 Battle of Jutland. Tickets are valid for one year; buy them at the office in the pump house.

★ **W5** SCIENCE CENTRE
(Map p566; www.w5online.co.uk; Odyssey Complex, 2 Queen's Quay; adult/child £9.80/7.50; ⊙10am-5pm Mon-Fri, to 6pm Sat, noon-6pm Sun, last entry 1hr before closing; ⚐; ⚐G2) Also known as whowhatwherewhenwhy, W5 is an interactive science centre aimed at children aged three to 11 and filled with more than 250 exhibits. Kids can compose their own tunes by biffing the 'air harp' with a foam rubber bat, try to beat a lie detector, create cloud rings and tornadoes, and design and build robots and racing cars. The newest exhibits are MED-Lab, an interactive medical-themed space, and Amaze, a 360-degree virtual reality experience.

Odyssey Complex LANDMARK
(Map p566; www.theodyssey.co.uk; 2 Queen's Quay; ⚐G2) The cylindrical-shaped Odyssey Complex is a huge sporting and entertainment centre on the eastern side of the river at the edge of the Titanic Quarter. The complex features a hands-on science centre, W5; the 10,800-seat SSE Arena (p587), home to the Belfast Giants (p587) ice-hockey team; and the multiplex Odyssey Cinemas (p587).

◎ Queen's Quarter

South of the city centre are the leafy streets and student bars of the Queen's Quarter, which takes its name from Queen's University. Academic life extends beyond the campus to the neighbouring Ulster Museum – located in a lush park – and is reflected in the Quarter's thriving arts centres. This is Belfast's most ethnically diverse area; in addition to international students, it's where many members of the city's growing Chinese, South Asian and other minority communities live.

★**Ulster Museum** MUSEUM
(Map p560; www.nmni.com; Botanic Gardens, Stranmillis Rd; ⊙10am-5pm Tue-Sun; ⚐; ⚐8A to 8D) **FREE** You could spend hours browsing this state-of-the-art museum, but if you're pressed for time don't miss the **Armada Room**, with artefacts retrieved from the 1588 wreck of the Spanish galleon *Girona;* the **Egyptian Room**, with Takabuti, a 2500-year-old

Egyptian mummy unwrapped in Belfast in 1835; and the Early Peoples Gallery, with the bronze Bann Disc, a superb example of Celtic design from the Iron Age.

On the ground floor, an overview of local history from 1700 leads to a gallery on the Troubles and Beyond, where exhibits include a bomb disposal robot. On the 1st floor, a spectacular collection of prehistoric stone and bronze artefacts helps to provide a context for Ireland's many archaeological sites. Exhibits include the Malone Hoard, a clutch of 16 polished, Neolithic stone axes discovered only a few kilometres from the museum.

The kid-friendly, interactive Nature Zone on the 2nd floor covers geological time, evolution and natural history; highlights include the Snapshot of an Ancient Sea Floor, a fossilised portion of a 200-million-year-old seabed with jumbled ammonite shells and petrified driftwood.

The top floors are given over to Irish and European art, most notably the works of Belfast-born Sir John Lavery (1856–1941).

★ **Botanic Gardens**   GARDENS
(Map p560; ☑028-9031 4762; Stranmillis Rd; ⏱7.30am-sunset; 🚌8A to 8D) **FREE** The showpiece of Belfast's green oasis is Charles Lanyon's beautiful Palm House (⏱10am-5pm Apr-Sep, to 4pm Oct-Mar), built in 1839 and completed in 1852, with its birdcage dome, a masterpiece in cast-iron and curvilinear glass. Nearby is the 1889 Tropical Ravine (⏱10am-5pm Tue-Sun), a huge red-brick greenhouse designed by the garden's curator Charles McKimm. Inside, a raised walkway overlooks a jungle of tropical ferns, orchids, lilies and banana plants growing in a sunken glen. It reopened in 2018 following a £3.8 million renovation.

Just inside the Botanic Gardens' Stranmillis Rd gate is the Lord Kelvin statue of Belfast-born Sir William Thomson (1824–1907), who helped lay the foundation of modern physics and invented the Kelvin scale, which measures temperatures from absolute zero (−273°C or 0°K).

Free hour-long guided tours of the Palm House and Tropical Ravine are offered at 2pm on Tuesday and Thursday and 11am on Wednesday. Book a space by emailing tropicalravine@belfastcity.gov.uk.

Queen's University   HISTORIC BUILDING
(Map p560; www.qub.ac.uk; University Rd; 🚌8A to 8D) Northern Ireland's most prestigious university was founded by Queen Victoria in 1845. In 1908 the Queen's College became the Queen's University of Belfast and today its campus spreads across some 250 buildings.

Just inside the main entrance is the Queen's Welcome Centre (p589), with an information desk and souvenir shop. Pick up a free *Campus Walkbout* booklet that outlines a self-guided tour which highlights the beautiful architectural features of the buildings.

Charles Lanyon built the Queen's College building, a Tudor Revival in red brick and honey-coloured sandstone, in 1849. If it seems to have an Oxbridge air about it, that may be because Lanyon based the design of the central tower on the 15th-century Founder's Tower at Oxford's Magdalen College.

The college was one of three Queen's colleges (the others, still around but no longer called Queen's colleges, are in Cork and Galway), which were created to provide a non-denominational alternative to the Anglican Church's Trinity College in Dublin.

◉ West Belfast

Northwest of Donegall Sq, Divis St leads across the Westlink Motorway to Falls Rd and West Belfast. Though scarred by decades of civil unrest during the Troubles, this former battleground is one of the most compelling places to visit in Northern Ireland. Recent history hangs heavy in the air, but there is a noticeable spirit of optimism and hope for the future. The main attractions are the powerful murals that chart the history of the conflict, as well as the political passions of the moment.

West Belfast grew up around the linen mills that propelled the city into late-19th-century prosperity. It was an area of low-cost, working-class housing, and even in the Victorian era was divided along religious lines. The advent of the Troubles in 1969 solidified the sectarian divide, and since 1970 the ironically named Peace Line (p568) has separated the Loyalist and Protestant Shankill district (from the Irish *sean chill,* meaning 'old church') from the Republican and Catholic Falls district.

Despite its past reputation, the area is safe to visit. The best way to see West Belfast is on an informative and entertaining black taxi tour (p573), but there's nothing to stop you visiting under your own steam, either walking or using the shared black taxis that travel along the Falls and Shankill Rds. Alternatively, the G2 bus goes up the Falls Rd; buses 11A to 11D from Wellington Pl go along Shankill Rd.

LAGAN TOWPATH

Part of Belfast's Laganside redevelopment project was the restoration of the towpath along the west bank of the River Lagan. You can walk or cycle for 20km along the winding riverbank from central Belfast to Lisburn.

A shorter walk along the towpath (10km) starts from **Shaw's Bridge** (🚌77, 78) on the southern edge of the city and heads back towards the city centre. Take bus 8A or 8B from Donegall Sq E to the stop just before the Malone roundabout (where Malone Rd becomes Upper Malone Rd). Bear left at the roundabout (signposted Outer Ring A55) and you'll reach the River Lagan at Shaw's Bridge.

Turn left and follow the towpath downstream on the left bank of the river (waymarked with red '9' signs), passing a restored lock-keeper's cottage and canalside cafe at lock number '3'. The most attractive part of the walk is **Lagan Meadows** (www.laganvalley.co.uk; 🚌8D), a tree-fringed loop in the river to the right of the path and a good place for a picnic on a summer day. Further along, **Cutters Wharf** (📞028-9080 5100; www.cutterswharf. co.uk; 4 Lockview Rd, Stranmillis; bar meals £11-13, restaurant mains £11-24; ⊘kitchen noon-9pm; 🛜; 🚌8A to 8D) is also a great place for a lunch break or refreshing ale. From the pub, the walk continues to Lagan Weir (p569) in Belfast's city centre.

Belfast City Bike Tours (p572) runs 'brew tours' along the towpath to the **Hilden Brewery** (📞028-9266 0800; www.hildenbrewery.com; Hilden House, Grand St; tour £10; ⊘tours by reservation noon Wed-Fri) in Lisburn, returning to Belfast by train. Alternatively, you can rent one of its bikes (from £10/15 per half-/full day) and go by yourself.

Peace Line   WALLS

(Map p560; 🚌G1) The most visible sign of the divisions that have scarred the area for so long are the so-called 'peace walls' that controversially divide Belfast's Protestant and Catholic communities, covering some 34km in all. The longest section divides Falls Rd and the Shankill in West Belfast; its steel gates are generally open during daytime hours.

Begun in 1969 as a 'temporary measure', the 6m-high walls of corrugated steel, concrete and chain link have outlasted the Berlin Wall. In 2013 local government ministers pledged to dismantle 60 of Northern Ireland's 110 peace walls by 2023, but progress has been slow, in part because some local communities feel the walls offer them protection. In 2016 the first peace wall was demolished with the removal of the barrier on Belfast's Crumlin Rd; the peace wall on Springfield Rd was remodelled the following year.

Cultúrlann
McAdam Ó Fiaich   CULTURAL CENTRE

(Map572; www.culturlann.ie; 216 Falls Rd; ⊘9am-6pm Mon-Thu, to 9pm Fri & Sat, 11am-4pm Sun; 🚌G1) **FREE** Housed in a red-brick, former Presbyterian church, this Irish language and cultural centre is the focus for West Belfast's community activity. It's a cosy and welcoming place with a tourist information desk, a shop selling a wide selection of books on Ireland, Irish-language material, crafts and Irish-music CDs, and a good cafe-restaurant, Bia (📞028-9096

4184; mains £6.50-15; ⊘9am-5.30pm Mon-Thu, to 9pm Fri, 10am-5.30pm Sat, to 4pm Sun; 🛜🎫). The centre also has an art gallery and a theatre that stages music, drama and poetry events.

Conway Mill   HISTORIC BUILDING

(Map p560; www.facebook.com/conwaymillflax; 5-7 Conway St; ⊘8am-6pm; 🚌G1, 10A to 10J) **FREE** Conway Mill is a restored 19th-century flax mill that now houses artists' studios and work spaces for local enterprises. It also contains the **Eileen Hickey Irish Republican History Museum** (www.eileenhickeymuseum.com; ⊘10am-2pm Tue-Sat), a collection of artefacts, newspaper articles, photos and archives relating to the Republican struggle.

Sinn Féin Headquarters   NOTABLE BUILDING

(Map p572; www.sinnfein.ie; 51 Falls Rd; 🚌G1) This red-brick building has the famous mural of a smiling **Bobby Sands**, the hunger striker who was elected as MP for West Belfast just a few weeks before he died in 1981. The text reads, in Sands' own words, 'Our revenge will be the laughter of our children'.

⊙ Outside the Centre

★Cave Hill Country Park   PARK

(Map p572; www.belfastcity.gov.uk; Antrim Rd; ⊘7.30am-dusk; 🚌1A to 1J) **FREE** The view from the summit of Cave Hill (368m) takes in the whole sprawl of the city, the docks, Belfast Lough and the Mourne Mountains – on a clear day you can see Scotland. Cave Hill Country

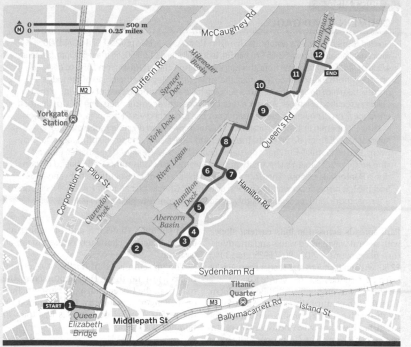

City Walk
Titanic Quarter

START LAGAN WEIR FOOTBRIDGE
END THOMPSON DRY DOCK
LENGTH 3KM; TWO HOURS

Begin at ❶ **Lagan Weir** (Map p560; ☐ G2) and cross the footbridge to Queen's Quay. Turn left and follow the path along the riverbank to the ❷ **Odyssey Complex** (p566). You are now on Queen's Island, formed in 1841 using material that was dredged up to create a shipping channel.

Follow the path to Abercorn Basin, a working marina, and continue to ❸ **Titanic Kit**, a bronze sculpture that depicts the ship in the form of a toy model kit. On the right is the ❹ **Dock Cafe** (p585); pop inside to view an assortment of maritime memorabilia.

Next, cross the footbridge to reach Hamilton Dock and the ❺ **SS Nomadic** (p565). The silhouette statues on your right relate to the *Nomadic*, which ferried the *Titanic's* passengers from Cherbourg harbour to the ship. They represent a Belfast shipyard worker, a French sailor and Charlie Chapman, once a *Nomadic* passenger.

Cross the footbridge on your left to reach the 1867 pump house, which contained the machinery used to drain Hamilton Dock. Now the gleaming, angular structure of ❻ **Titanic Belfast** (p564) comes into full view. Walk around the right-hand side of the Titanic Belfast building. On your right is the former Harland & Wolff headquarters containing the ❼ **drawing offices** (p565) where the *Titanic* was designed; it's now the Titanic Hotel.

Behind Titanic Belfast are the ❽ **slipways** from which *Titanic* and sister ship *Olympic* were launched. Walk to the far end of the slipways, which give a sense of the ships' size, to ❾ **Titanic Studios** (Queen's Rd; ☐ G2); from here there is a good view of the Harland & Wolff gantry cranes, known as Samson and Goliath.

Continue along the path to the ❿ **Great Light** (Map p566; www.greatlighttq.org), a former lighthouse lens, and on to Alexandra Graving Dock, home to naval vessel **HMS Caroline** (p565). Behind it is the pump house used to drain the water from **Thompson Dry Dock** (p565), where the *Titanic* was fitted out. Continue straight to reach Queen's Rd and buses to the city centre.

DON'T MISS

CRUMLIN ROAD GAOL

Guided tours of Belfast's notorious Crumlin Road Gaol (Map p572; ☑ 028-9074 1500; www.crumlinroadgaol.com; 53-55 Crumlin Rd; tour adult/child £12/7.50; ⊘ 10am-5.30pm, last tour 4.30pm; ☐ 12B, 57) take you from the tunnel beneath Crumlin Rd, built in 1850 to convey prisoners from the courthouse across the street (and allegedly the origin of the judge's phrase 'take him down'), through the echoing halls and cramped cells of C-Wing, to the truly chilling execution chamber. Advance tour bookings are recommended. The jail's pedestrian entrance is on Crumlin Rd; the car-park entrance is reached via Cliftonpark Ave to the north.

Since it opened in 1846, Crumlin Road Gaol imprisoned a whole range of historic figures, from Eamon de Valera to the Reverend Ian Paisley, and from suffragette Dorothy Evans to the 'Shankill Butcher' murderer Lenny Murphy. Designed by Charles Lanyon (the architect of Queen's University and many other city landmarks), and based on London's Pentonville prison, 'The Crum' was also the scene of 17 executions between 1854 and 1961. It remained a working prison until 1996. Check the calendar for four-hour 'paranormal tours', and for regular, highly atmospheric concerts held at the jail.

Park spreads across the hill's eastern slopes, with several waymarked walks and an **adventure playground** (☑ 028-9077 6925; child 3-14yr £2.50; ⊘ 10am-8pm Jul & Aug, shorter hours Apr-Jun & Sep, Sat & Sun only Oct-Mar; ☐ 1A to 1G).

The hill was originally called Ben Madigan, after the 9th-century Ulster king, Matudhain. Its distinctive, craggy profile, seen from the south, has been known to locals for two centuries as 'Napoleon's Nose' – it supposedly bears some resemblance to Bonaparte's schnoz, but you might take some convincing. On the summit is an Iron Age earthwork known as McArt's Fort, where members of the United Irishmen, including Wolfe Tone, looked down over the city in 1795 and pledged to fight for Irish independence. The path leading to the summit from Belfast Castle car park passes beneath the five caves that give the hill its name (it's a 7.2km circular trail; allow two hours). To get here, take buses 1A to 1J from Royal Ave to Belfast Castle.

★ Ulster Folk Museum   MUSEUM

(Map p572; www.nmni.com/uftm; 153 Bangor Rd, Cultra; folk museum adult/child £9/5.50, transport & folk museum £11/6; ⊘ 10am-5pm Tue-Sun Mar-Sep, to 4pm Tue-Fri, 11am-4pm Sat & Sun Oct-Feb; ⚙; ☐ Cultra) Farmhouses, forges, churches and a complete village have been reconstructed at this excellent museum, with human and animal extras combining to give a powerful impression of Irish life over the past few hundred years. From industrial times, there are red-brick terraces from 19th-century Belfast and Dromore. Another highlight is the Picture House, a silent cinema that was housed in a County Down hayloft from 1909 to 1931. There's even a corner shop dating from 1889 selling sweets.

In summer, thatching and ploughing are demonstrated by characters dressed in period costume.

The museum is 14km northeast of central Belfast, just north of Holywood, across the road from the Ulster Transport Museum. Buses to Bangor stop nearby. Cultra station on the Belfast–Bangor train line is less than 10 minutes' walk away.

Ulster Transport Museum   MUSEUM

(Map p572; www.nmni.com/uftm; 153 Bangor Rd, Cultra; transport museum adult/child £9/5.50, transport & folk museum £11/6; ⊘ 10am-5pm Tue-Sun Mar-Sep, to 4pm Tue-Fri, 11am-4pm Sat & Sun Oct-Feb; ⚙; ☐ Cultra) Across the road from the Ulster Folk Museum, the Transport Museum has steam locomotives, rolling stock, motorcycles, trams, buses and cars. Most popular is the Titanica exhibit, which includes the original design drawings for the *Titanic* and its sister ship *Olympic*. The highlight of the car collection is the stainless-steel-clad prototype of the ill-fated DeLorean DMC, made in Belfast in 1981. The car achieved everlasting fame in the *Back to the Future* films.

The museum is 14km northeast of central Belfast, just north of Holywood. Buses to Bangor stop nearby. Cultra station on the Belfast–Bangor train line is less than 10 minutes' walk away.

Stormont   NOTABLE BUILDING

(Map p572; www.niassembly.gov.uk; Upper Newtownards Rd; ⊘ 9am-4pm Mon-Fri, guided tours 11am & 2pm; ☐ 4A, 4B) **FREE** Stormont's dazzling white neoclassical facade is one of Belfast's most iconic, occupying a dramatic position at the end of a gently rising 1.5km avenue. Since 1998 it has been the home of the Northern Ireland Assembly.

Free guided tours meet in the elaborate Great Hall, which is made entirely of Italian marble and adorned with five chandeliers; you'll also see the Assembly and Senate Chambers and the Committee Room.

From its completion in 1932 until the introduction of direct rule in 1972, Stormont was the seat of the parliament of Northern Ireland. Following the Good Friday Agreement of 1998 it became home to Northern Ireland's devolved legislative body. However, in 2017 the power-sharing agreement collapsed over the Renewable Heat Incentive scandal, and the assembly lay dormant. At research time, politicians had yet to return to Stormont.

The building is fronted by a defiant statue of the arch-Unionist Sir Edward Carson. Nearby, 19th-century Stormont Castle, like Hillsborough in County Down, is an official residence of the Secretary of State for Northern Ireland.

Take bus 4A or 4B from Donegall Sq W.

Belfast Castle CASTLE
(Map p572; www.belfastcastle.co.uk; Antrim Rd; ⊙9.30am-4pm Mon, to 9pm Tue-Sat, to 4.30pm Sun; ▣1A to 1J) FREE Built in 1870 for the third Marquess of Donegall, in the Scottish Baronial style made fashionable by Queen Victoria's Balmoral, multiturreted Belfast Castle commands the southeastern slopes of Cave Hill. It was presented to the City of Belfast in 1934 and is now used mostly for weddings and other functions. Downstairs there's a small exhibition on the folklore and history of the park and the Cellar Restaurant; most of the castle is closed to the public.

Legend has it that the castle's residents will experience good fortune only as long as a white cat lives there, a tale commemorated in the beautiful formal gardens by nine portrayals of cats in mosaic, painting, sculpture and topiary – a good game for kids is getting them to find all nine.

Belfast Zoo ZOO
(Map p572; www.belfastzoo.co.uk; Antrim Rd; adult/child £13/6.50; ⊙10am-6pm, last entry 5pm Apr-Sep, to 4pm, last entry 2.30pm Oct-Mar; ▣1A to 1J) Home to 120 species, Belfast Zoo has spacious enclosures set on an attractive, sloping site; the sea lion and penguin pool with its underwater viewing is particularly good. Some of the more unusual animals include golden lion tamarins, Malayan sun bears and red pandas, but the biggest attractions are the ultracute

meerkats, the colony of ring-tailed lemurs and the herd of Rothschild's giraffes.

🏃 Activities

Belfast Cookery School COOKING
(Map p560; ☑028-9023 4722; www.belfastcookeryschool.com; 53-54 Castle St; classes £40-60; ▣1A to 1J, 2A to 2E) Classes at the Belfast Cookery School, attached to the Mourne Seafood Bar (p581), feature everything from knife skills to bread making, dinner parties, barbecues and a wide range of international cuisines (Indian, Italian, Thai...), but its seafood courses are especially popular. Book well ahead.

Holywood Golf Club GOLF
(Map p572; ☑028-9042 3135; www.holywoodgolfclub.co.uk; Nuns Walk, Demesne Rd, Holywood; green fees Mon-Thu £40, Sat & Sun £45; ⊙6am-8pm; ▣Holywood) This undulating par-69 parkland course, 11km northeast of Belfast, is Rory McIlroy's home club and has spectacular views over Belfast Lough and the Antrim coast. Discounted rates are often available; check the website's booking page for times and prices.

Vertigo Indoor Skydiving SKYDIVING
(Map p566; www.wearevertigo.com; T13 Bldg, Queen's Rd; from £45; ♿; ▣G2) This indoor skydiving centre replicates the thrill of free-falling from a plane inside a wind tunnel. Flights are measured in distances of 24,000ft to 72,000ft and last for between two and six minutes in winds of up to 200km/h. The full activity takes one hour, including instructions and safety briefings. Suitable for ages four years old and up.

👉 Tours

★Belfast Food Tour FOOD & DRINK
(Map p560; www.tasteandtour.co.uk; 4hr food tour per person £58; ▣4C to 4E) Starting in St George's Market, these fun tours are a great way to tap into Northern Ireland's flourishing food scene, with plenty of samples of the region's most traditional dishes and innovative new produce along the way. The company also runs other food and drink tours, including a gin jaunt (£63), Belfast whiskey walk (£60) and a beer crawl (£45). Book ahead.

Street Art Walking Tour WALKING
(Map p560; www.seedheadarts.com; Commercial Ct; per person £10; ⊙noon-2pm Sun; ▣3A, 4D, 5A, 6A) The Cathedral Quarter is covered with fascinating street art. This tour takes in some impressive works by a range of international artists, most of it commissioned as part of the Hit the North festival (p574). Tours are

Around Central Belfast

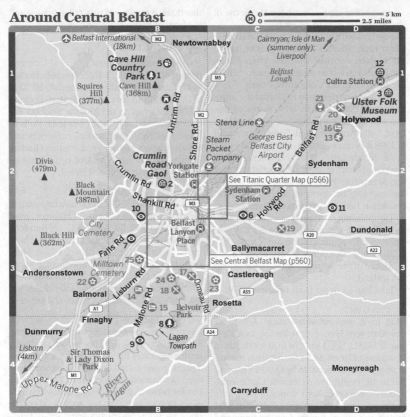

guided by local street artists or the festival founder. The meeting point is outside the Duke of York on Commercial Ct (check availability online first).

Private tours available on request.

Titanic Tours
TOURS

(☑ 028-9065 9971; www.titanictours-belfast.co.uk; 3hr tour per adult/child £30/15) A three-hour luxury tour led by the great-granddaughter of one of the *Titanic's* crew, visiting various *Titanic*-related sites. For groups of two to five people; includes pickup and drop-off at your accommodation. Also offers full-day tours.

Lagan Boat Company
BOATING

(Map p560; ☑ 028-9024 0124; www.laganboat-company.com; Donegall Quay; adult/child £12/10; ⊙ hours vary; ☒ G1, G2) The Lagan Boat Company's excellent Titanic Tour explores the docklands downstream of Lagan Weir, taking in the slipways where the liners *Titanic* and *Olympic* were launched and the huge dry dock where they could just fit, with just 23cm

to spare. There's also a chance to spot seals. Tours depart from Donegall Quay near the Bigfish sculpture (p563). Book ahead.

Belfast Free Walking Tour
WALKING

(Map p560; www.belfastfreewalkingtour.com; Donegall Sq N; tips appreciated; ⊙ 11am & 2.30pm; ☒ G1, G2) FREE These two-hour walking tours of the city centre and Cathedral Quarter are a good introduction for first-time visitors to the city. Tours leave from outside City Hall at 11am and 2.30pm daily.

Belfast City Bike Tours
CYCLING

(Map p560; ☑ 07980 816057; www.belfastcitybike tours.com; 18 Winetavern St, Norm's Bikes; per person 3hr city tour £30, 4hr bike & brew £50; ⊙ 10am Thu-Sun; ☒ 1A to 1J, 2A to 2E) Offers three-hour **city bike tours** through the Cathedral, Titanic and Queen's Quarters and West Belfast, and four-hour bike and **brew tours** along the Lagan Towpath to the Hilden Brewery in Lisburn, returning to Belfast by train. Tours leave at 10am

Around Central Belfast

Thursday to Sunday; book ahead. Also offers bike rentals (from £10/15 per half-/full day).

Belfast Pub Crawl TOURS
(Map p560; ☑07712 603764; www.belfastcrawl.co.uk; per person £10; ⊙8pm Fri & Sat; ⊒G2) A three-hour tour taking in four of the city's historic pubs (including a drink in each, plus live trad music), departing from the Albert Memorial Clock Tower (p563). Booking required.

Wee Tram BUS
(Map p566; www.theweetram.com; adult/child £5/4; ⊙noon-5pm daily May-Aug, Sat & Sun Mar-Apr & Sep-Oct; ⊒G2) These cute replica tram cars make 10 stops around the Titanic Quarter – including the Samson and Goliath cranes – with on-board video commentary en route and pull-down plastic flaps if it rains. Tickets are valid for two days.

Taxi Tours

Black taxi tours of West Belfast's murals – known locally as the 'bombs and bullets' or 'doom and gloom' tours – are offered by a large number of taxi companies and local cabbies. These can vary in quality and content, but in general they're an intimate and entertaining way to see the sights.

Be aware that tours often reflect the personal experiences of the driver, and the recounting of historical events may be coloured by his or her background. The discussion of violence during the Troubles may be distressing for some.

Drivers will pick you up from anywhere in the city centre. Established operators include **Official Black Taxi Tours** (☑07702 449694, 028-9064 2264; www.belfasttours.com; 1-2 passengers £40, plus £17.50 per additional person) and **Paddy Campbell's Famous Black Cab Tours** (☑07990 955227; www.belfastblackcabtours.co.uk; per person tour for 1-2 people £35, for 3-8 people £12).

Game of Thrones Tours

Game of Thrones Tours BUS
(Map p560; ☑028-9568 0023; www.gameofthronestours.com; adult/student £50/45; ⊙Wed-Sun Easter-Sep, reduced tours Oct-Easter; ⊒G1, G2) Offers two full-day itineraries covering 11 iconic *Game of Thrones* filming locations: the Winterfell Locations Trek taking in Castle Ward and Tollymore Forest Park (where the Starks discover a dead direwolf and her pups), and the Iron Islands and Stormlands Adventure, covering sights in north Antrim including Ballintoy Harbour and the Dark Hedges. Tours depart from Victoria Square mall (p562).

McComb's Game of Thrones Tours BUS
(Map p560; ☑028-9031 5333; www.mccombscoaches.com; 22-32 Donegall Rd; £35; ⊙office 8.30am-4.30pm; ⊒8A to 8D, 9A to 9C) The drivers of these *Game of Thrones* tours have also driven the extras and equipment. Filming locations visited include the Dark Hedges (ie King's Road), Cushendun (the sea-cave where the shadow assassin was born), Ballintoy Harbour (Lordsport Harbour) and Larrybane (where the shadow assassin kills Renly). Pickup is from the Belfast Youth Hostel (p576) at 9am.

✿ Festivals & Events

Belfast City Council (www.belfastcity.gov.uk/events) organises a wide range of events throughout the year, covering everything from the St Patrick's Day parade to the Lord Mayor's Show. It has a useful online events calendar, as does the Visit Belfast Welcome Centre (www.visit-belfast.com/whats-on).

CityDance   DANCE
(www.crescentarts.org; ⊙ Nov) Free three-day dance festival, based at the Crescent Arts Centre (p587).

Féile an Earraigh   MUSIC
(Spring Festival; www.feilebelfast.com; ⊙ Mar) This week-long festival of traditional Irish and Celtic music attracts artists from all over Ireland, Europe and America.

St Patrick's Day   CULTURAL
(www.belfastcity.gov.uk/events; ⊙ 17 Mar) A celebration of Ireland's patron saint, marked by various community festivals and culminating in a grand city-centre parade.

Belfast Film Festival   FILM
(www.belfastfilmfestival.org; ⊙ early Apr) Ten-day celebration of Irish and international film; most screenings are at the Queen's Film Theatre (p587).

Festival of Fools   PERFORMING ARTS
(www.foolsfestival.com; ⊙ early May) A four-day festival of street entertainment, with events concentrated in the Cathedral Quarter and city centre.

Belfast City Marathon   SPORTS
(www.belfastcitymarathon.com; ⊙ 1st Sun in May) Avid runners from across the globe come to compete in the marathon, crossing the finish line in Ormeau Park; other events include a walk and a fun run.

Cathedral Quarter
Arts Festival   PERFORMING ARTS
(www.cqaf.com; ⊙ early May) Ten days of drama, music, poetry, street theatre and art exhibitions in and around the Cathedral Quarter.

Hit the North   ART
(www.capartscentre.com; ⊙ May) International street artists paint the walls of Belfast's Cathedral Quarter during this five-day festival, with live street-art jams and artists' talks.

Belfast Book Festival   LITERATURE
(www.belfastbookfestival.com; ⊙ mid-Jun) A week of all things book-related, from films and readings to workshops and meet-the-author events, held at the Crescent Arts Centre (p587) and other nearby venues.

Belfast Titanic Maritime Festival   SAILING
(www.belfastcity.gov.uk/events; ⊙ May, Jun or Jul) A three-day festival centred on Queen's Quay, with sailing ships, street entertainment, a seafood festival and live music. The highlight is the arrival of the tall ships.

Belfast Pride   LGBT
(www.belfastpride.com; ⊙ late Jul-early Aug) A 10-day celebration of gay, lesbian, bisexual and transgender culture, culminating in a huge city-centre parade.

BELFAST FOR CHILDREN

With its excellent museums, green spaces and family-centred attractions, easy-to-navigate Belfast is a fantastic city to visit with kids of all ages. If you're in town in March, look out for cultural and educational events during the **Belfast Children's Festival** (www.youngatart.co.uk; ⊙ early–mid-Mar).

Child-friendly things to do include the following:

Titanic Belfast Interactive exhibits and a shipyard ride will keep kids engaged at this spectacular multimedia museum (p564).

Ulster Museum This museum (p566) has plenty of exhibits and special events designed for children of all ages, including three hands-on discovery rooms with kid-centred activities.

W5 Fantastic hands-on science centre (p566) aimed at children aged three to 11, with themed educational spaces and a virtual-reality room.

Vertigo Indoor Skydiving Children aged four years old and up – and adults – can experience the thrill of skydiving at this indoor centre (p571).

Lagan Boat Company Explore the docklands from the water on a boat tour (p572). You might even spot some seals.

Wee Tram Give little legs a rest and tour the Titanic Quarter on these cute hop-on, hop-off replica trams (p573).

Féile An Phobail CULTURAL

(West Belfast Festival; www.feilebelfast.com; ⏲ early Aug) Said to be the largest community festival in Ireland, the August Féile takes place in West Belfast over 10 days. Events include an opening carnival parade, street parties, theatre performances, concerts and historical tours of the City and Milltown cemeteries.

Belfast International Arts Festival PERFORMING ARTS

(www.belfastinternationalartsfestival.com; ⏲ mid-late-Oct) One of the largest arts festivals in the UK and Ireland stretches over three weeks and features theatre, music, dance and talks.

Sleeping

From backpacker hostels to boutique havens, the range of places to stay in Belfast widens every year. Most budget and midrange accommodation is south of the centre, in the leafy university district around Botanic Ave, University Rd and Malone Rd, around a 20-minute walk from City Hall. Business and luxury boutique hotels proliferate in the city centre.

Book ahead on weekends, in summer and during busy festival periods.

City Centre

★**Bullitt Hotel** HOTEL ££

(Map p560; ☎028-9590 0600; www.bullitthotel.com; 40A Church Lane; d £85-150; @ 📶; 🚌 G1, G2) The Bullitt is a haven for the hip, with super-fast wi-fi, smart TVs, an espresso bar, restaurant and two bars – there's even Bullitt beer on tap. Breakfast is left at your door so party animals can roll out of bed at their leisure. Rest assured: rooms are soundproofed.

★**Ten Square** HOTEL ££

(Map p560; ☎028-9024 1001; www.tensquare.co.uk; 10 Donegall Sq S; s/d/ste from £105/115/195; 📶; 🚌 G1, G2) A former bank houses an opulent 131-room hotel, full of contemporary local art and designer touches. Rooms in the original building have a decadent decor of blue velvet curtains and furnishings, while the new extension has more of a luxe business feel; the Jaffe Suite has a private terrace overlooking City Hall. Service is friendly and attentive.

Flint HOTEL ££

(Map p560; ☎028-9066 6400; www.theflintbelfast.com; 48 Howard St; ste from £105; 📶; 🚌 G1, G2) With smart TVs, super-fast wi-fi and paired-back interior styling, the Flint is a hotel designed to meet the needs of the modern millennial. Each suite has a small kitchen (with a combination microwave oven, hob and fridge) and a table for eating or working, and there's also a free guest laundry room.

There's no bar or restaurant, but the hotel is surrounded by places to eat and drink.

Grand Central HOTEL £££

(Map p560; ☎028-9023 1066; www.grandcentralhotelbelfast.com; 9-15 Bedford St; d from £135; 📶; 🚌 7A, 7D) There are impressive views from the upper floors of this vast, 23-storey hotel – the most expensive hotel to be built in Northern Ireland – which opened in 2018. The 300 rooms are well-equipped and neutrally decorated, with floor-to-ceiling windows.

On the top floor, the **Observatory** bar is open to nonguests, but dress smartly and bring a fat wallet: a pint of the hotel's exclusive Observatory Pale Ale (brewed at Whitewater Brewery) will set you back £8.

Cathedral Quarter

★**Merchant Hotel** HOTEL £££

(Map p560; ☎028-9023 4888; www.themerchanthotel.com; 16 Skipper St; d/ste from £180/350; P @ 📶; 🚌 3A, 4D, 5A, 6A) Belfast's most flamboyant hotel occupies the palatial former Ulster Bank head office. Rooms are individually decorated with a fusion of contemporary styling and old-fashioned elegance; those in the original Victorian building have opulent floor-length silk curtains while newer

WORTH A TRIP

EAST BELFAST

The little explored neighbourhoods of East Belfast were once home to writer CS Lewis, footballer George Best and musician Van Morrison, whose former haunts have been mapped out in self-guided walking trails.

The star stop on the CS Lewis trail is a **square** (Map p572; 280 Newtownards Rd; 👪; 🚌 G1) dedicated to the author, with fabulous sculptures of characters from *The Chronicles of Narnia*.

Fans of 'Van the Man' Morrison can take a neighbourhood walk past sights referenced in his lyrics, including the Hollow (immortalised in 'Brown Eyed Girl'), Cypress Ave and the house where he was born on Hyndford St (at number 125).

You can pick up maps at EastSide Visitor Centre (p589), or download them from www.connswatergreenway.co.uk/trails.

rooms have an art deco–inspired theme. Facilities include a luxurious spa and an eight-person rooftop hot tub.

Its **Great Room** (Map p560; 2-/3-course lunch £27/28, afternoon tea £38-41, dinner mains £15.50-31.50; ⊙12.30-2.15pm & 5.30-9.45pm Mon-Thu, 12.30-2.15pm & 6-10pm Fri & Sat, 12.30-8.30pm Sun) restaurant is magnificent.

Queen's Quarter

Conveniently located within walking distance of the city centre, the Queen's Quarter makes a good base. The city's best hostels and a number of good-value midrange hotels are here.

★ Vagabonds HOSTEL £

(Map p560; ☑028-9023 3017; www.vagabonds belfast.com; 9 University Rd; dm £15-18, d & tw £50-60; @⊚; ☑8A to 8D, 9A to 9C) Comfy bunks, lockable luggage baskets, private shower cubicles, a beer garden, a pool table and a relaxed atmosphere are what you get at one of Belfast's best hostels, run by a couple of experienced travellers. It's conveniently located close to both Queen's and the city centre.

★ Global Village Backpackers HOSTEL £

(Map p560; ☑028-9031 3533; www.globalvillage belfast.com; 87 University St; dm £15.50-17.50, d £50; @⊚; ☑7A to 7D) In a 19th-century brick terrace house, Global Village combines period fireplaces and stained-glass windows with bright wall murals and wall-mounted guitars. There's a sociable kitchen and dining area, a beer garden and a barbecue. Dorms have high ceilings and storage facilities; some dorm beds are in enclosed 'pods', with wooden screens and curtains for added privacy.

Botanical Backpackers HOSTEL £

(Map p560; ☑07572 950502; www.botanicalback packers.co.uk; 63 Fitzwilliam St; dm £14-18; @⊚; ☑9A to 9C) This hostel, set in a quiet terraced house in the university area, has a kitchen and small backyard. Cheery yellow paint and a friendly crowd make it more cosy than cramped. The four- and six-bed dorms are on the small side.

Belfast Youth Hostel HOSTEL £

(Map p560; ☑028-9031 5435; www.hini.org.uk; 22-32 Donegall Rd; dm £13-16.50, tw with/without private bathroom £44/34; @⊚; ☑8A to 8D, 9A to 9C) Handy amenities at this big, bright HI hostel include laundry facilities, secure on-site parking, 24-hour reception (with no lock-out or curfew), and a cafe serving breakfast and lunch. Dorms are spacious and clean, with metal bunks and laminate floors.

Tara Lodge GUESTHOUSE ££

(Map p560; ☑028-9059 0900; www.taralodge. com; 36 Cromwell Rd; s/d from £95/100; P@⊚; ☑7A to 7D) In a great location on a quiet side street just a few paces from the buzz of Botanic Ave, this guesthouse feels more like a boutique hotel with its clean-cut, minimalist decor, friendly and efficient staff, and 34 bright and cheerful rooms. Breakfast options include porridge with Bushmills whiskey.

Malone Lodge Hotel HOTEL ££

(Map p560; ☑028-9038 8000; www.malonelodge hotelbelfast.com; 60 Eglantine Ave; d/f/apt from £95/110/100; P⊚; ☑8A, 8B, 9A to 9C) The centrepiece of a tree-lined Victorian terrace, Malone Lodge has large, comfortable rooms with elegantly understated decor, good breakfasts and pleasant staff. Some bedrooms are in a separate building; it also offers five-star one- and two-bedroom self-catering apartments.

Titanic Quarter

★ Titanic Hotel Belfast BOUTIQUE HOTEL £££

(Map p566; ☑028-9508 2000; www.titanichotelbel fast.com; Queen's Rd; d £110-270; ✱⊚; ☑G2) The Titanic Hotel is a spectacular addition to Belfast. Located in the Harland & Wolff shipping company's old headquarters, it pays tribute in both its location and design to the city's shipbuilding past, with the old drawing office transformed into a light-filled bar and each room decked out with ship-related touches.

Old photographs of the headquarters and posters for Atlantic-crossing liners adorn the walls, the former, renovated business rooms are open to take a peek into, and a large model of the *Titanic* sits by windows that overlook the Titanic Belfast museum and the slipway down which the ill-fated ship was launched. Even if you're not staying, come for a drink, afternoon tea or dinner (book ahead) in the Wolff Grill (p583) to get a feel for this historic building.

Outside the Centre

Old Rectory B&B ££

(Map p572; ☑028-9066 7882; www.anoldrectory. co.uk; 148 Malone Rd; s £58-68, d £88, tw £90; P@⊚; ☑8A, 8B) A lovely Victorian house with lots of original stained glass, this former rectory has spacious bedrooms, a comfortable drawing room, and fancy breakfasts (home-baked bread, porridge with Bushmills whiskey, scrambled eggs with smoked salmon, veggie fry-up and freshly squeezed orange juice).

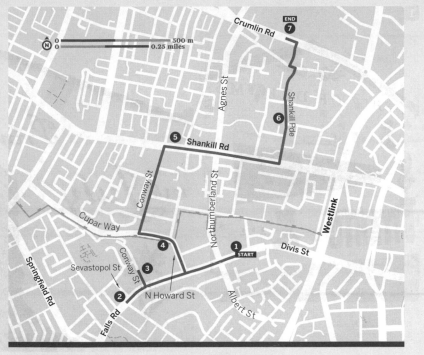

City Walk
West Belfast Murals

START SOLIDARITY WALL
END CRUMLIN ROAD GAOL
LENGTH 3KM; TWO HOURS

Start at the ❶ **Solidarity Wall** (Map p560; 🚌 G1, 10A to 10J) on Divis St (the G2 bus stops here). The collection of murals here express Republican sympathies with, among others, the Palestinians, the Kurds and the Basques; one mural pays tribute to African American abolitionist Frederick Douglass, an advocate of the Irish independence movement in the 19th century.

Walk west for 450m along Divis St, which becomes the Falls Rd. On the right, the redbrick ❷ **Sinn Féin Headquarters** (p568) has a famous mural of a smiling Bobby Sands, the hunger striker who was elected as MP for West Belfast just a few weeks before he died in 1981. The text reads, in Sands' own words, 'Our revenge will be the laughter of our children'.

Backtrack for two blocks and turn left onto Conway St, to reach ❸ **Conway Mill** (p568), a restored 19th-century flax mill. Next to it is the Eileen Hickey Irish Republican History Museum, with items relating to the Republican struggle from 1798 to the Troubles.

Go back to Divis St, walk one block east and turn left onto North Howard St. On your left is the ❹ **Peace Line** (p568), separating the Catholic and Protestant communities. Walk through the opening in the tall steel fencing (the gates are closed at night) and bear left along Cupar Way, walking with the peace wall on your left, then turn right onto Conway St. Continue straight to reach Shankill Rd.

Cross Shankill Rd and walk east, passing the courtyard of the ❺ **Rex Bar**, where photographic and text displays celebrate the signing of the Ulster Covenant against Irish self-governance in 1912. Continue walking east for 450m and turn left onto ❻ **Shankill Parade**. As you walk through the estate you'll see murals on gable ends, including King William III on his prancing white horse on the left; on the right sits *Remember, Respect, Resolution*, three metal columns representing the communities' willingness to embrace the future.

Continue straight along Hopewell Cres and Florence Pl to Crumlin Rd, where the former Courthouse faces ❼ **Crumlin Road Gaol** (p570).

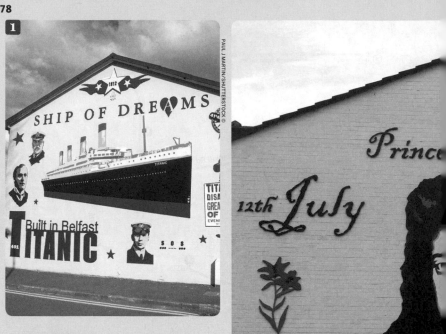

1. RMS *Titanic* **2.** King Billy
3. Bobby Sands **4.** Solidarity Wall

Belfast Murals

Since the start of the Troubles, the gable ends of Belfast's housing estates have been used as informal canvases, painted with colourful murals that serve as territorial markers, political statements and defiant symbols of Loyalist or Nationalist identity. More recently, many nonpolitical murals have appeared.

Hunger Strike

Several Nationalist murals in West Belfast commemorate the Hunger Strike of 1981, when 10 Republican prisoners starved themselves to death. Most prominent is the image of Bobby Sands, who was elected as a local MP shortly before his death. A favourite slogan is '*Tiocfaidh ár lá*', which means 'Our time will come'.

Solidarity Wall

Another popular theme for murals in Republican areas is support for other nationalist and republican movements around the world, including Palestine, the Basque Country and Latin America, notably on the stretch of Falls Rd known as Solidarity Wall.

King Billy

The most iconic of the Protestant murals is the image of King Billy (William of Orange), whose victory over the Catholic King James at the Battle of the Boyne in 1690 is still celebrated annually with parades on 12 July. He is usually shown mounted on a prancing white horse.

Nonpolitical Murals

Since the advent of the peace process there has been a concerted effort to replace aggressively partisan murals with ones that celebrate nonpolitical subjects, such as footballer George Best, novelist CS Lewis, the RMS *Titanic* and the Harland & Wolff shipyards.

The inconspicuous driveway is on the left, just past Deramore Park.

All Seasons B&B
B&B ££

(Map p572; ☑028-9068 2814; 356 Lisburn Rd; s/d £40/60; P ➔; ☐9A to 9C) Away from the centre, but right on the buzzy Lisburn Rd, All Seasons is a red-brick villa with bright, colourful bedrooms, modern bathrooms, a stylish little breakfast room and a comfortable lounge.

★ Rayanne House
GUESTHOUSE £££

(Map p572; ☑028-9042 5859; www.rayannehouse. com; 60 Demesne Rd, Holywood; s £100-120, d £140-160, f £160-165; ➔; ☐Holywood) Just 100m from Holywood Golf Club (p571), this gorgeous 1883 manor house has exquisite rooms – some with balconies and views of Belfast Lough – including a Rory McIlroy–themed room with a shower rail made from an engraved club. Its restaurant (open to nonguests) hosts regular nine-course *Titanic* menus (£69), replicating the last 1st-class meal served aboard.

✕ Eating

From fine dining to market grazing, it's easy to eat well in Belfast. The city is surrounded by lush farming country and located just a few kilometres from bustling fishing ports; this bounty of locally sourced meat, seafood and fresh produce is whipped into a spectacular array of dishes in kitchens of restaurants across the city.

✕ City Centre

Tribal Burger
BURGERS £

(Map p560; www.tribalburger.com; 12 Callender St; burgers £5.50-6.75; ☒11.30am-7pm Mon, to 8pm Tue & Wed, to 9pm Thu-Sat; ☑➔; ☐G1, G2) There's a youthful vibe to this burger joint, with industrial-style decor and spray-painted walls. As well as 6 oz burgers, made fresh daily using local beef, the menu includes vegan options, boozy milkshakes and local craft beers. It gets packed with local office workers at lunchtime.

The original branch is on **Botanic Av** (☑028-9094 5499; 86 Botanic Ave; burgers £5.50-6.75; ☒11.30am-10pm; ➔; ☐7A to 7D)enue.

John Long's
FISH & CHIPS £

(Map p560; ☑028-9032 1848; www.johnlongs.com; 39 Athol St; fish & chips £4.50-7; ☒11.45am-6.30pm Mon-Fri, to 6pm Sat; ☐8A to 8D, 9A to 9C) A wonderfully down-to-earth Belfast institution, this 1914-opened chippie is hidden in an inconspicuous red-brick building adjoining a car park, and is covered in mesh grills (a legacy of having its windows blown out when the nearby Europa Hotel was bombed). Inside, it fries up classic cod and chips in beef dripping, served at 1970s Formica booths. Cash only.

Sawers Deli
DELI £

(Map p560; www.sawersbelfast.com; 5-6 Fountain Centre, College St; sandwiches £6-7; ☒9am-5.30pm Mon-Fri) This excellent deli sells gut-busting sandwiches, bagels and wraps made with produce from the store's charcuterie and cheese counter, available to eat in or take away. In addition to stocking a wide selection of local produce, the deli carries its own range of artisan chutneys, crackers, coffee and tea.

★ Yügo
ASIAN ££

(Map p560; ☑028-9031 9715; www.yugobelfast. com; 3 Wellington St; mains £10-24; ☒noon-3pm & 5-10pm; ☐G1, G2) The contemporary styling at this compact restaurant – exposed brick walls, sleek industrial furniture and bamboo lanterns – sets the scene for fusion cooking that feels fresh and exciting; the dumplings, bao buns and rice dishes are particularly good. Service is excellent. Take a seat at the counter to watch the chefs at work.

★ Holohan's at the Barge
MODERN IRISH ££

(Map p560; ☑028-9023 5973; www.holohansatthe-barge.co.uk; Belfast Barge, Lanyon Quay; mains lunch £9-14, dinner £16-25; ☒1-4pm & 5-11pm Tue-Thu, 1-4pm & 5pm-midnight Fri & Sat, 1-7pm Sun; ☐4, 6) Aboard the Belfast Barge (p562), Holohan's is a sensational find for inspired twists on sea-

---

ORANGE ORDER PARADES

In Northern Ireland the 12 July public holiday marks the anniversary of the Protestant victory at the 1690 Battle of the Boyne. It is celebrated with bonfires, marching bands and parades staged by the Orange Order.

Although the 12 July parades have been associated with sectarian stand-offs and outbursts of violence, there has been an effort in recent years to promote the Belfast parade as a cultural celebration, even rebranding it Orangefest.

However, many people still perceive the parades as divisive and confrontational. Visitors should be alert for signs of trouble and follow local advice.

food and superb cooking of traditional Irish recipes such as *crabachain,* a mushroom, chestnut and tarragon fritter, and boxty, a kind of potato pancake. Desserts are excellent too, and wines are served by the glass.

Home
MODERN IRISH ££

(Map p560; ✆ 028-9023 4946; www.homebelfast. co.uk; 22 Wellington Pl; mains £11-27; ⊙noon-4pm & 5-9.30pm Mon-Thu, noon-4pm & 5-10pm Fri, noon-3.30pm & 5-10pm Sat, 1-4pm & 5-9pm Sun; � 🔊 ✍; 🖳G1, G2) After beginning life as a pop-up restaurant that took the city's food scene by storm, Home moved into permanent premises where it continues to win fans for its creative use of seasonal ingredients. Its menus are tailored for vegetarians, vegans, gluten-free diners, slimmers and theatregoers.

Jumon
ASIAN ££

(Map p560; ✆ 028-9023 1394; www.facebook. com/jumonbelfast; Fountain St; mains £11.50; ⊙5-10pm Mon, noon-4pm & 5-10pm Wed-Sat; ✍) Everything on the menu at Jumon is vegan or vegetarian (vegetarian dishes can be adapted for vegans). The flavour-packed dishes like jackfruit curry and kimchi wantons might challenge some palates, but have proved a hit with the Belfast crowd. The vibe is mellow and welcoming; hip wall murals add to the atmosphere.

Deanes Deli Bistro
BISTRO ££

(Map p560; ✆ 028-9024 8800; www.michaeldeane. co.uk; 44 Bedford St; mains lunch £7-13, dinner £10.50-16; ⊙noon-3pm & 5.30-10pm Mon-Sat; 🖳G1, G2) Enjoy top-notch nosh at this relaxed and informal bistro, with gourmet burgers and posh fish and chips on the menu. The attached Deánes Vin Cafe is a cafe by day and wine bar by night, when it serves snacks and hosts live music on Friday and Saturday.

★Eipic
MODERN IRISH £££

(Map p560; ✆ 028-9033 1134; www.deaneseipic. com; 34-40 Howard St; lunch menu £30-45, dinner menu £45-70; ⊙noon-1.30pm Fri, 6-9.30pm Wed-Sat; ✍; 🖳G1, G2) The finest, seasonal local ingredients are given a creative twist at the flagship restaurant in Michael Deane's portfolio, the Michelin-starred Eipic. Head chef Alex Greene is originally from County Down; his tasting menus are full of theatrical surprises.

Other restaurants in the Deanes portfolio include Love Fish and Meatlocker on Howard St, Deanes at Queen's (p582) and Deanes Deli Bistro.

ⓘ TRACING YOUR ANCESTORS

If you're hoping to track down your Ulster ancestors, **PRONI** (Public Record Office of Northern Ireland; ✆ 028-9053 4800; www. proni.gov.uk; 2 Titanic Blvd; ⊙9am-4.45pm Mon-Wed & Fri, 10am-8.45pm Thu; 🖳G2) has its headquarters in Belfast's Titanic Quarter. Entry is free, but there are charges for copies of documents. Check the website for details of how to register and search the records.

★Mourne Seafood Bar
SEAFOOD £££

(Map p560; ✆ 028-9024 8544; www.mournesea food.com; 34-36 Bank St; mains £12-27.50; ⊙noon-4pm & 5-9.30pm Mon-Thu, noon-3.30pm & 5-9.45pm Fri & Sat, 1-4pm & 5-9pm Sun; 🖳10A, 10B) 🖉 Hugely popular, this informal, pub-like place is all red brick and dark wood with old oil lamps dangling from the ceiling. On the menu are oysters, meltingly sweet scallops, lobster and langoustines sourced from its own shellfish beds, along with luscious fish such as hake, seabream and sea bass. Book for dinner.

The attached Belfast Cookery School (p571) runs a diverse range of culinary classes. Mourne Seafood Bar's sister restaurant (p606) is near County Down's Dundrum Bay.

OX
IRISH £££

(Map p560; ✆ 028-9031 4121; www.oxbelfast.com; 1 Oxford St; 2-/3-course lunch £22/28, 4-/6-course dinner menu £50/60; ⊙6-9.30pm Tue, 12.15-2.30pm & 6-9.30pm Wed-Fri, 1-2.30pm & 6-9.30pm Sat; 🖳G1, G2) 🖉 A high-ceilinged space with cream-painted brick and golden wood creates a theatre-like ambience for the open, Michelin-starred kitchen at the back, which turns out some of Belfast's finest cuisine. The restaurant works with local suppliers and focuses on Irish beef, sustainable seafood, and seasonal vegetables and fruit. The lunch menu is good value. Book several weeks in advance.

James St
MODERN IRISH £££

(Map p560; ✆ 028-9560 0700; www.jamesstandco. com/james-street; 19-21 James St S; mains lunch £9.50-30, dinner £13.50-34; ⊙noon-9pm; 🖳G1, G2) St James' informal but elegant dining room is the perfect stage for a sophisticated but low-key menu of local meat and seafood dishes. The highlights are the Tyrone steaks cooked on the grill, plus seafood dishes and daily specials. Kick things off with a cocktail at the bar. The service is relaxed yet highly professional.

✗ Cathedral Quarter

Curated Kitchen CAFE £

(Map p560; www.curatedkitchen.co.uk; 60 Donegall St; mains £4-8; ⊙8am-4pm Mon-Fri, 9am-4pm Sat, 10am-4pm Sun; ⛱🖉; ▣3A, 4D, 5A, 6A) As well as serving excellent coffee and brunches, this cafe takes a different cookbook as inspiration for its changing weekly lunch menu; check the website to see which books are currently being curated. It's a bright space, with high ceilings, exposed brick walls and cookbooks to browse.

Coppi ITALIAN ££

(Map p560; ☑028-9031 1959; www.coppi.co.uk; Unit 2, St Anne's Sq; mains £11.50-27; ⊙noon-3pm & 5-10pm Mon-Thu, noon-10pm Fri & Sat, to 9pm Sun; ▣G2) In a buzzy dining room with high ceilings and leather booths, Coppi serves modern Italian dishes like Tuscan goat pappardelle and roast wild hake. The sourdough breads and excellent desserts – tiramisu, amaretto panna cotta, and chocolate and salted caramel torta – are freshly prepared daily.

★Muddlers Club MODERN IRISH £££

(Map p560; ☑028-90313199; www.themuddlersclub belfast.com; Warehouse Lane, off Waring St; 6-course tasting menu £55, with wine pairings £90; ⊙noon-2.45pm & 5.30-10pm Tue-Sat; ▣3A, 4D, 5A, 6A) Industrial-style decor, friendly service and rustic dishes that allow fresh local ingredients to shine are a winning combination at one of Belfast's best restaurants. The Muddlers Club is named after a society of Irish revolutionaries who held meetings at the same spot in the 1790s; look for it in an alleyway between Waring St and Commercial Ct.

✗ Queen's Quarter

Maggie May's CAFE £

(Map p560; ☑028-9066 8515; www.maggiemays belfastcafe.co.uk; 50 Botanic Ave; mains £5-11; ⊙8am-9.30pm Mon-Fri, 9am-10.30pm Sat & Sun; ▣7A to 7D) This is a classic little cafe with cosy wooden booths, murals of old Belfast and a host of hungover students wolfing down huge Ulster fry-ups. The all-day breakfast menu includes French toast and pancake stacks, while lunch can be soup and a sandwich or a burger. BYO alcohol (£1.50 corkage per bottle of wine/four beers).There's a newer branch in Stranmillis (2 Malone Rd).

Café Conor CAFE £

(Map p560; ☑028-9066 3266; www.cafeconor.com; 11A Stranmillis Rd; breakfast £4.50-9, mains £6-13; ⊙9am-10pm Mon-Sat, to 9pm Sun; ▣8A to 8C) Set in the glass-roofed former studio of Belfast artist William Conor, this laid-back bistro offers a range of pastas, salads and burgers, along with favourites such as fish and chips with mushy peas and a daily pie special. The breakfast menu, which includes waffles with bacon and maple syrup, is served till 5pm.

★French Village
Patisserie & Brasserie BRASSERIE ££

(Map p560; ☑028-9066 4333; www.frenchvillage bakery.co.uk; 343-353 Lisburn Rd; mains lunch £8.50-11, dinner £14-22; ⊙kitchen 9am-3pm Mon-Wed, to 9pm Thu, to 10pm Fri & Sat, 11am-4pm Sun; ▣9A to 9C) There's an air of sophistication at this excellent brasserie, serving plates like salmon nicoise and pea and shallot ravioli; the home-baked breads are worth the trip alone. Lunch like an elegant Parisian before hitting Lisburn Rd's boutiques. Be sure to stop at the patisserie counter to pick up pastries and cakes to go.

Deanes at Queen's BISTRO ££

(Map p560; ☑028-9038 2111; www.michaeldeane. co.uk; 1 College Gardens; mains lunch £10-13.50, dinner £15-30; ⊙noon-3pm & 5.30-10pm Mon-Sat, 1-6pm Sun; ▣8A to 8D) A chilled-out bar and grill from Belfast's top chef, Michael Deane, in what was once Queen's University's staff club. The menu focuses on what can be described as good-value, gourmet pub grub, taking full advantage of the Mibrasa charcoal grill. A three-course fixed price menu costs £22. The outdoor terrace is perfect on a sunny day.

Shu MODERN IRISH ££

(Map p560; ☑028-9038 1655; www.shu-restaurant. com; 253 Lisburn Rd; mains £12.50-31; ⊙noon-2.30pm & 5.30-9.30pm Mon-Fri, noon-2.30pm & 6-9.30pm Sat; ▣9A to 9D) Lording it over fashionable Lisburn Rd since 2000, Shu is the granddaddy of Belfast chic, and is still winning plaudits for its French-influenced food: slow-cooked blade of beef; Himalayan salt-aged sirloin; and seared scallops with samphire and smoked fennel butter.

★Saphyre MODERN IRISH £££

(Map p560; ☑028-9068 8606; www.saphyrerest aurant.com; 135 Lisburn Rd; mains lunch £10, dinner £24-32; ⊙11am-3pm & 5-10pm Wed-Fri, 10am-3pm & 5-10pm Sat; ▣9A to 9C) Spectacularly set inside the 1924 Ulsterville Presbyterian Church, Saphyre serves some of the most sophisticated cooking in Belfast today. Menus change seasonally and include a five-course tasting menu (£50); each dish is a masterpiece. Brunch is available from 11am to 3pm and there's live music on Saturdays from 1pm to 3pm.

Barking Dog

BISTRO **£££**

(Map p560; ☑028-9066 1885; www.barkingdog belfast.com; 33-35 Malone Rd; mains lunch £8.50-16, dinner £17-32, 5 tapas dishes £16; ⊙noon-2.30pm & 5-10pm Mon-Sat, noon-4pm & 5-9pm Sun; ☑8A, 8B) Chunky hardwood, bare brick, candlelight and modern design create the atmosphere of a stylishly restored farmhouse. The menu completes the feeling of cosiness and comfort with dishes such as the signature burger of tender beef shin with caramelised onion and horseradish cream, and sweet-potato gnocchi.

✖ Titanic Quarter

Paper Cup

CAFE **£**

(Map p566; ☑028-9076 6400; 11 ARC, Queen's Rd; mains £4.50-9; ⊙8am-5pm Mon-Sat, 9am-5pm Sun; ☑G2) With windows looking out on the SS *Nomadic,* this little coffee shop is a good place to stop for lunch (sandwiches, quiche, baked potatoes, soup and stew), cake or ice cream when exploring the Titanic Quarter.

Scullery & Linen Lounge

INTERNATIONAL **£**

(Map p566; ☑028-9026 5170; linenloungebook-ings@belfastmet.ac.uk; Queen's Rd, Belfast Met Titanic Quarter Campus; lunch mains £4, 3-course dinner £10; ⊙term time: noon-1.15pm Mon & Wed-Fri, plus 5.45-7.15pm Thu) During term time, catering students put their skills into practice at the Scullery & Linen Lounge restaurant. Its location on the ground floor of Belfast Met's Titanic Quarter campus building is convenient for nearby sights, service is enthusiastic and the food is excellent value; the menu changes daily and spans the globe. Book ahead for Thursday evening's fine-dining menu.

Wolff Grill

MODERN IRISH **£££**

(Map p566; ☑028-9508 2000; www.titanichotel belfast.com; Titanic Hotel, Queen's Rd; mains £17-29; ⊙6-9.30pm, plus 1-2.30pm Sun; ☑G2) The Titanic Hotel's fine-dining restaurant exudes a sense of history. Expect sophisticated plates featuring unusual combinations, such as duck with pear, ginger, lavender and fennel, and sea bream with kale, cucumber, Earl Grey and lemon. The dessert menu is just as adventurous, with items like parsnip custard and tobacco sabayon making an appearance. Book ahead.

✖ Outside the Centre

★ Bia Rebel

RAMEN **£**

(Map p572; www.biarebel.com; 409 Ormeau Rd; ramen £6-11; ⊙11am-9pm Mon & Wed-Sat, noon-9pm Sun; ☑7A, 7B) It's worth searching out this understated noodle bar that fuses Japanese ramen with locally sourced Irish ingredients. It takes 36 hours to create a bowl of Belfast Shoyu Ramen: fresh, handmade ramen in a deep broth with pork shoulder and an egg poached in tea. There are vegan options, too. The name is a pun: *bia* means food in Irish.

★ Noble

MODERN IRISH **££**

(Map p572; ☑028-9042 5655; www.nobleholy-wood.com; 27A Church Rd, Holywood; mains £15-19; ☒Holywood) You'll need to book ahead to secure a table at this tiny restaurant that serves exceptional food. The menu of modern Irish dishes is nothing revolutionary but everything tastes really good; there's an excellent wine list, too. The service is so warm you'll feel like you're eating with old friends.

★ Il Pirata

ITALIAN **££**

(Map p572; ☑028-9067 3421; www.ilpiratabelfast. com; 279-281 Upper Newtownards Rd, Ballyhackamore; mains £12-21; ⊙noon-3pm & 5-10pm Mon-Thu, noon-3pm & 5-11pm Fri, noon-11pm Sat, noon-9pm Sun; ☑G1) This rustic Italian restaurant is a firm favourite among Belfast's foodies for its flavoursome dishes like duck ragu with gnocchi and Portavogie prawn linguine, served in a contemporary, stripped-back dining room.

🍷 Drinking & Nightlife

Belfast's nightlife is one of its biggest drawcards. In the city centre, traditional pubs are interspersed with sleek bars. The bars and clubs of the Queen's Quarter are especially popular with students. At weekends the party spills out into the street in the Cathedral Quarter, where most bars have live music. Many pubs are also great places to dine.

🍶 City Centre

★ Babel Rooftop Bar

ROOFTOP BAR

(Map p560; www.bullitthotel.com/eat-drink/babel; Ann St; ⊙3pm-1am Mon-Wed, noon-1am Thu-Sat, to midnight Sun; ☑G1, G2) On a summer's night, a cocktail at the Bullitt Hotel's rooftop bar is hard to beat. Come on Sundays for boozy brunches (breakfast and bottomless cocktails) or tipsy tea (sandwiches, cakes, and cocktails served in a teapot).

★ Muriel's Cafe-Bar

BAR

(Map p560; ☑028-9033 2445; 12-14 Church Lane; ⊙11.30am-1am Mon-Fri, 10am-1am Sat, 11.30am-midnight Sun; ☑G1, G2) Hats meet harlotry (ask who Muriel was) in this delightfully snug and welcoming bar with retro-chic decor, old sofas and armchairs, heavy fabrics in shades of olive and dark red, gilt-framed mirrors and a cast-iron fireplace. Gin is Muriel's favourite tipple and there's a range of more than 150 exotic brands to mix with your tonic.

★**Love & Death Inc**   COCKTAIL BAR
(Map p560; www.loveanddeathbelfast.com; 10A Ann St; ⊙4pm-1am; ▣G1, G2) More like a cool inner-city house party than a bar, speakeasy-style Love & Death Inc is secreted up a flight of stairs above a pizza joint. Its living-room-style bar has outrageous decor, feisty cocktails and a wild nightclub in the attic on weekends.

Drop Hopper Coffee Roasters   COFFEE
(Map p560; www.drophoppercoffee.com; Unit 5 St Georges Market, Oxford St; ⊙ shop 7am-3pm Mon-Fri, market stall 6am-2.30pm Fri, 8am-3pm Sat, 9am-4pm Sun; ▣4C to 4E) Drop in for a coffee made with Central and South American beans roasted at their premises near Crossgar in County Down. On weekends, Drop Hopper has a coffee cart inside St George's Market (p562).

Perch   ROOFTOP BAR
(Map p560; www.theperchbelfast.com; 5th fl, The Gate, 42 Franklin St; ⊙1pm-1am Mon-Sat, to midnight Sun Apr-Sep, from 5pm Mon-Fri Oct-Mar; ▣7A to 7D) Piped-in birdsong and flowery murals set the scene as an industrial lift takes you up to the Perch, a rooftop bar in the rafters of a Victorian building. In winter there's boozy hot chocolate, while the summer cocktail menu includes Pimm's punch and Bellinis.

Harlem Cafe   BAR
(Map p560; ✆028-9024 4860; 34-36 Bedford St; ⊙8am-5pm Mon-Thu, to 9pm Fri, 9am-9pm Sat, to 4pm Sun; ☎; ▣7A, 7D) With eclectic art covering the walls, the Harlem is a great place for lounging over coffee, or enjoying a glass of wine after hitting the shops. A full food menu spans breakfast to brunch to pre-theatre dinner.

Bittles Bar   PUB
(Map p560; 103 Victoria St; ⊙11am-11pm Mon-Thu, to 1am Fri & Sat, noon-6pm Sun; ▣G2) A cramped and staunchly traditional bar, Bittles is a 19th-century triangular red-brick building decorated with gilded shamrocks. The wedge-shaped interior is covered in paintings of Ireland's literary heroes by local artist Joe O'Kane. In pride of place on the back wall is a large canvas depicting Yeats, Joyce, Behan, Beckett and Wilde. It has a good range of craft beers.

Kelly's Cellars   PUB
(Map p560; www.facebook.com/kellys.cellars; 30-32 Bank St; ⊙11.30am-1am Mon-Sat, 1pm-midnight Sun; ▣10A, 10B) Kelly's is Belfast's oldest pub (1720) and was a meeting place for Henry Joy McCracken and the United Irishmen when they were planning the 1798 Rising. It pulls in a broad cross-section of Belfast society and is a great place to catch trad sessions on Saturday afternoons and during the week.

Cathedral Quarter

★**Sunflower**   PUB
(Map p560; www.sunflowerbelfast.com; 65 Union St; ⊙noon-midnight Mon-Thu, to 1am Fri & Sat, 5pm-midnight Sun; ▣2A to 2H) In a city full of buzzing bars, the Sunflower is an authentic corner pub, free from gimmicks and commercial glitz. There are local craft beers on tap, a beer garden with a pizza oven, and live music every night. The Sunflower Folk Club meets on Thursday nights.

The security cage on the front door was once a common sight in 1980s Belfast; though it's no longer needed, the Sunflower has preserved it as a relic of Belfast's social history.

★**Established Coffee**   COFFEE
(Map p560; www.established.coffee; 54 Hill St; ⊙7am-6pm Mon-Fri, 8am-6pm Sat, 9am-6pm Sun; ▣3A, 4D, 5A, 6A) Heading up Belfast's burgeoning coffee scene, Established takes its beans seriously, serving a range of specialist drip coffees, as well as light meals like salt beef sandwiches, and roast celeriac with puy lentils. Its corner plot with concrete floors, low-hanging lights and shared wooden counters makes it a popular spot to linger with a laptop.

★**Duke of York**   PUB
(Map p560; ✆028-9024 1062; www.dukeofyork belfast.com; 11 Commercial Ct; ⊙11.30am-11pm Mon, to 1am Tue & Wed, to 2am Thu & Fri, to midnight Sat, 3-9pm Sun; ▣3A, 4D, 5A, 6A) In a cobbled alleyway off buzzing Hill St, the snug, traditional Duke feels like a living museum. There's regular live music; local band Snow Patrol played some of their earliest gigs here. Outside on Commercial Ct, a canopy of umbrellas leads to an outdoor area covered with murals depicting Belfast life; it takes on a street-party atmosphere in warm weather.

The Duke of York is one of several Hill St establishments owned by Willie Jack, whose nearby properties include the **Dark Horse**, a dimly lit, wood-panelled space that contains a *Game of Thrones* door, and the **Harp Bar**, with a Victorian-style interior. Both have live music at weekends.

★**Spaniard**   PUB
(Map p560; www.thespaniardbar.com; 3 Skipper St; ⊙noon-1pm Mon-Sat, to midnight Sun; ▣3A, 4D, 5A,

6A) Specialising in rum, this narrow, crowded bar has more atmosphere in one battered sofa than most 'style bars' have in their shiny entirety. Friendly staff, an eclectic crowd and cool tunes played at a volume that still allows you to talk: bliss. Nearby burger joint **Pablos** (www.pablosbelfast.com; 16 Church Lane; burgers £5.50-7.50; ☺noon-10pm Tue-Thu, to 2am Fri & Sat, 2-10pm Sun; 🖥G1, G2) delivers to the bar.

National
BAR

(Map p560; www.thenationalbelfast.com; 62 High St; ☺8.30am-11pm Mon-Wed, to 1am Thu, to 3am Fri, 9.30am-3am Sat, to 10pm Sun; 🖥3A, 4D, 5A, 6A) Behind the grey ground-floor facade of the 1897 former National Bank building, and through its post-industrial interior, is the National's *pièce de résistance* – the city's biggest beer garden, which hosts regular barbecues and live music. Stop by for breakfast, a sandwich (served until 5pm) or Sunday brunch.

On Friday and Saturday nights DJs spin the tunes at club Sixty6.

John Hewitt
PUB

(Map p560; www.thejohnhewitt.com; 51 Donegall St; ☺11.30am-1am Mon-Fri, noon-1am Sat, 7pm-1am Sun; 🖥3A, 4D, 5A, 6A) Named for the Belfast poet and socialist, the John Hewitt is one of those treasured bars that has no noise but the murmur of conversation. There are trad sessions on Saturday afternoons and regular folk, jazz and bluegrass. It's owned by the Belfast Unemployed Research Centre.

Queen's Quarter

Hatfield House
PUB

(Map p560; www.hatfieldhousebelfast.com; 130 Ormeau Rd; ☺11.30am-1am Mon-Sat, to midnight Sun; 🖥7A to 7D) On the Ormeau Rd, Hatfield House is no fly-by-night – its original timber and brass bar fixtures and ornate ceiling mouldings are the work of the *Titanic's* craftsmen. Live music includes acoustic and folk; it's also a popular spot for watching big-screen sport such as football and GAA (Gaelic Athletics Association) events. On the ground floor is the cocktail bar **Copperplate**.

Eglantine
PUB

(Map p560; www.eglantinebar.com; 32 Malone Rd; ☺11.30am-midnight Sun-Tue, to 1am Wed-Sat; 🖥8A, 8B) The 'Eg' is a local institution, and widely reckoned to be the best of Belfast's student pubs. It serves good-value food, and hosts numerous events: Monday is open-mike night and there are speed pool competitions every Tuesday; other nights see DJs and bands.

Botanic Inn
PUB

(Map p560; www.thebotanicinn.com; 23-27 Malone Rd; ☺11.30am-1am Mon, Tue, Thu & Fri, to 2am Wed & Sat, noon-midnight Sun; 🖥8A, 8B) Wednesday at the 'Bot' is one of Belfast's longest-running student nights, with live music and DJs on the decks in the basement club. The party continues at the weekend; live sport is screened in the beer garden.

Clements
COFFEE

(Map p560; www.clementscoffee.com; 66-68 Botanic Ave; ☺7.30am-11pm Mon-Thu, to 10pm Fri, 9am-10pm Sat & Sun; 🖥7A to 7D) Belfast's answer to Starbucks. Other branches include Donegall Sq West, Rosemary St and Royal Ave.

Titanic Quarter

★Drawing Office Two
BAR

(Map p566; www.titanichotelbelfast.com; Titanic Hotel Belfast, Queen's Rd; mains £12-18.50; ☺kitchen noon-10pm; 🖥G2) At the Titanic Hotel, one of Harland & Wolff's two historic drawing offices has been transformed into a light-filled bar with an impressive barrel-vaulted ceiling. The island bar is decorated with salvaged tiles identical to those used in the pool and Turkish baths on board the *Titanic*. A menu of gastro-pub-style food is served throughout the day.

Dock Cafe
CAFE

(Map p566; www.the-dock.org; ARC Retail, Queen's Rd; by donation; ☺11am-5pm Mon-Sat; 🖥G2) Run by volunteers, Dock Cafe has an honesty box and no price list: pay what you wish for coffee, tea, cakes and soup. Everyone's welcome to lounge on the squishy sofas and mismatched, donated furniture, and even bringing your own food is fine. It's a welcoming space with books and local art to look at.

Outside the Centre

Dirty Duck
PUB

(Map p572; www.thedirtyduckalehouse.co.uk; 3 Kinnegar Rd, Holywood; ☺noon-11pm Sun-Wed, to 1am Thu-Sat; 🖥Holywood) On a sunny afternoon, it's hard to beat the Belfast Lough–facing beer garden at this welcoming local, just footsteps from Holywood train station. It's a great bet at any time for craft ales on tap, frequent live music and its panoramic upstairs restaurant.

☆ Entertainment

Belfast is a great place to hear live music, catch some stand-up comedy or see a play. The city's thriving arts scene nurtures local

LGBTQ+ BELFAST

Belfast's gay and lesbian scene is concentrated in the Cathedral Quarter around Union St. Nightspots include Kremlin, Maverick and Union Street.

Since 2014, civil partnerships (legally binding unions) between same sex couples have been legal in Northern Ireland, but gay marriage is not legal here. Love Equality (www. loveequalityni.org) campaigns for equal marriage rights.

Belfast has a thriving LGBT community and LGBT travellers are unlikely to experience problems based on their sexual orientation. The Rainbow Project (www.rainbow-project. org) provides an advocacy service for victims of hate crimes.

Ireland's largest celebration of gay, lesbian, bisexual and transgender culture, Belfast Pride (p574) in late July to early August, culminates in a huge city-centre parade.

Kremlin (Map p560; www.kremlin-belfast.com; 96 Donegall St; ⊙10pm-2.30am Tue, Thu & Sun, 9pm-3am Fri & Sat; ▣1A to 1E) Gay-owned and -operated, the Soviet-kitsch-themed Kremlin is the heart and soul of Northern Ireland's gay scene. A statue of Lenin guides you into Tsar, the preclub bar, from where the Long Bar leads into the main clubbing zone, Red Square. **Revolution** on Saturdays is the flagship event.

Maverick (Map p560; www.facebook.com/pg/maverickbarbelfast; 1 Union St; ⊙5pm-1am Mon-Sat, to midnight Sun; ▣1A to 1D) Look for the moustached sign to find Maverick, a gay bar that attracts a friendly crowd. Check the Facebook page for the current schedule of cabaret and karaoke nights hosted by drag acts such as the Queens of the Queer Quarter. It's most popular for its **Boombox** nightclub, upstairs from the main bar.

Union Street (Map p560; www.unionstreetbar.com; 8-14 Union St; ⊙noon-1am Mon-Thu, to 1.30am Fri & Sat, 1.30pm-1am Sun; ☏; ▣1A to 1E) A stylish modern bar with retro decor and lots of bare brick and dark wood (check out the Belfast sinks in the loo), Union Street attracts a mixed gay and straight crowd with nightly cabaret and karaoke, and a tempting food menu. Sunday's bingo night pulls in the punters.

talent, while its excellent theatres, concert venues and arts centres also attract world-class international touring productions and musicians. Windsor Park football stadium is the home ground of Northern Ireland's national football team.

For entertainment listings, check out:

➡ Big List (www.thebiglist.co.uk)

➡ Culture Northern Ireland (www.culturenorthernireland.org)

➡ Visit Belfast (www.visitbelfast.com)

Live Music

⭐ **Belfast Empire**　　LIVE MUSIC
(Map p560; www.thebelfastempire.com; 42 Botanic Ave; entry live bands £3-22.50; ⊙11.30am-1am Mon-Sat, 12.30pm-midnight Sun; ▣7A to 7D) A converted late-Victorian church (reputed to be haunted) with three floors of entertainment, the Empire is a legendary live-music venue. Look out for stand-up comedy and quiz nights too.

⭐ **Black Box**　　ARTS CENTRE
(Map p560; www.blackboxbelfast.com; 18-22 Hill St; ▣3A, 4D, 5A, 6A) Black Box is an innovative arts venue, hosting a dynamic program of music, theatre, magic nights, spoken word

events, comedy, film and more on Hill St in the heart of the Cathedral Quarter.

Berts Jazz Bar　　JAZZ
(Map p560; ☏028-9026 2713; www.themerchant hotel.com; High St, Merchant Hotel; ⊙4pm-1am Mon-Fri, 11am-1am Sat, to midnight Sun; ▣1A to 1J, 2A to 2E) This intimate venue has live jazz nightly from 9pm to midnight. Tables next to the stage are reserved for diners (mains £15 to £20, plus £10 per person weekend stage charge; book ahead), but there is no charge to drink or dine in the bar area, from where the music sounds just as good.

Limelight　　LIVE MUSIC
(Map p560; www.limelightbelfast.com; 17-19 Ormeau Ave; ▣13A, 13B) This combined pub and club is one of the city's top venues for live rock and indie music. Past acts have included Oasis, Franz Ferdinand, the Manic Street Preachers and the Kaiser Chiefs.

An Droichead　　LIVE MUSIC
(Map p560; www.androichead.com; 20 Cooke St, Lower Ormeau; ▣7A to 7D) This Irish cultural centre is a great place to hear live Irish folk music performed by big names from around the country, as well as up-and-coming local talent. It also offers Irish-language courses,

stages traditional dance and *céilidh* (traditional music and dancing) workshops.

Sonic Arts Research Centre LIVE MUSIC
(SARC; Map p560; www.sarc.qub.ac.uk; Cloreen Park; ⌨ 8A, 8B) Queen's University's School of Music stages regular free lunchtime recitals and evening concerts in the beautiful, hammerbeam-roofed Harty Room and at the Sonic Arts Research Centre. You can download a program from the website.

SSE Arena CONCERT VENUE
(Map p566; www.ssearenabelfast.com; Odyssey Complex, 2 Queen's Quay; ⌨ G2) Within the Odyssey Complex (p566), this is the venue for big entertainment events such as rock and pop concerts and stage shows. It's also the home stadium of the Belfast Giants ice-hockey team.

Classical Music
Ulster Hall CONCERT VENUE
(Map p560; www.ulsterhall.co.uk; 34 Bedford St; ⌨ 7A to 7D) Dating from 1862, Ulster Hall is a popular venue for a range of events including rock concerts, lunchtime organ recitals and performances by the Ulster Orchestra (www.ulsterorchestra.org.uk).

Waterfront Hall CONCERT VENUE
(Map p560; www.waterfront.co.uk; 2 Lanyon Pl; ⌨ 1, 2, 5, 7) The impressive 2200-seat Waterfront is Belfast's flagship concert venue, hosting local, national and international performers from pop stars to symphony orchestras.

Crescent Arts Centre ARTS CENTRE
(Map p560; www.crescentarts.org; 2-4 University Rd; ⌨ 8A to 8D) The Crescent hosts a range of concerts, plays, workshops, readings and dance classes. It's also the headquarters of the Belfast Book Festival (p574) and the dance festival CityDance (p574).

Harty Room CLASSICAL MUSIC
(Map p560; School of Music, University Sq; ⌨ 7A to 7D) The beautiful, hammerbeam-roofed Harty Room is sometimes used for free recitals by Queen's University's School of Music.

Theatre
MAC ARTS CENTRE
(Metropolitan Arts Centre; Map p560; www.themaclive.com; 10 Exchange St West; ⌨ 3A, 4D, 5A, 6A) The MAC is a beautifully designed venue overlooking the St Anne's Sq development, with its two theatres hosting regular performances of drama, stand-up comedy and talks, including shows for children. The centre's three galleries stage a rolling program of exhibitions, which are generally free. There's also a cafe.

Lyric Theatre THEATRE
(Map p572; www.lyrictheatre.co.uk; 55 Ridgeway St; ⌨ 8A) This stunning modern space overlooking the River Lagan is Northern Ireland's only full-time producing theatre (it produces its own plays rather than staging works produced by other companies).

Cinema
Queen's Film Theatre CINEMA
(Map p560; www.queensfilmtheatre.com; 20 University Sq; ⌨ 7A to 7D, 8A to 8D) A major venue for the Belfast Film Festival (p574), this two-screen art-house cinema is close to the University.

Movie House CINEMA
(Map p560; www.moviehouse.co.uk; 14 Dublin Rd; ⌨ 7A to 7D, 8A to 8D, 9A to 9C) Convenient city-centre 10-screen multiplex.

Odyssey Cinemas CINEMA
(Map p566; www.odysseycinemas.co.uk; Odyssey Complex, 2 Queen's Quay; ⌨ G2) Belfast's biggest multiplex has 12 screens and stadium seats throughout.

Spectator Sports
Casement Park GAELIC FOOTBALL
(Map p572; www.antrimgaa.net; Andersonstown Rd; ⌨ G1) Located in West Belfast; you can see Gaelic football and hurling here.

Windsor Park FOOTBALL
(Map p572; www.irishfa.com; Donegall Ave; ⌨ 9A to 9C) Northern Ireland plays its home games at the National Football Stadium at Windsor Park, 2km south of Belfast city centre; see the website for details of upcoming matches.

Belfast Giants ICE HOCKEY
(Map p566; ✆ 028-9046 0044; www.belfastgiants.com; 2 Queen's Quay; ⌨ G2) The Belfast Giants ice-hockey team draws big crowds to the SSE Arena; the season is September to April. The arena also hosts indoor sporting events including tennis and athletics.

Kingspan Stadium RUGBY
(Map p572; www.ulsterrugby.com; 134 Mount Merrion Ave; ⌨ 6A) This 18,000-capacity stadium is the home of Ulster Rugby.

🔒 Shopping

Belfast's compact city centre is full of high-street stores as well as a number of independent shops selling top-quality local arts and crafts and specialist food and drink. In the south of the city, the Lisburn Rd has high-end boutiques and homewares stores. St George's Market is a great place to browse for art, souvenirs and vintage goods.

ℹ PUBLIC TRANSPORT TICKETS & PASSES

You can pick up a free bus map (and buy tickets) from the **Metro kiosk** (Map p560; Donegall Sq) at the northwest corner of the square. Buy your ticket from the driver (change given); cash fares within the city zone are £2.

You can also buy DayLink cards (£3.50; available from the Metro kiosk, the Visit Belfast Welcome Centre and the Europa Bus Centre), giving you unlimited bus travel within the City Zone all day Monday to Saturday.

If you plan on using city buses a lot, it's worth buying a Metro Smartlink Multi-Journey Card (available from the same places). The card costs an initial fee of £1, plus £12 per 10 journeys – you can get it topped up as you want. When you board the bus, you simply place the card on top of the ticket machine and it automatically issues a ticket.

Belfast Visitor Pass

The Belfast Visitor Pass (per one/two/three days £6.50/11/14.50) allows unlimited travel on bus and train services in Belfast and around, and discounts on admission to Titanic Belfast and other attractions. You can buy it online at www.translink.co.uk and at airports, train and bus stations, the Metro kiosk on Donegall Sq and the Visit Belfast Welcome Centre.

★**Unique Artshop**   ARTS & CRAFTS
(Map p560; www.ulster.ac.uk/artshop; 25-51 York St, Ulster University; ⊙9am-5pm Mon-Fri, 11am-4pm Sat; 🚌2A to 2H) At Ulster University, this dynamic artshop sells pieces by students, alumni and other local designer makers, including graphics and prints, sculptures, pottery and ceramics, textiles, fine art, jewellery and furniture. It's also possible to commission work.

★**Space Craft**   ARTS & CRAFTS
(Map p560; www.craftni.org; Fountain Centre, College St; ⊙10.30am-5.30pm; 🚌G1, G2) This shop and exhibition space displays the work of more than 40 local designers and artists. High-quality pieces include ceramics, artwork, greeting cards and jewellery. Information about each artist is displayed next to their work.

Studio Souk   ARTS & CRAFTS
(Map p560; www.studiosouk.com; 60-62 Ann St; ⊙9.30am-5.30pm Mon-Wed & Fri-Sat, to 8pm Thu, 1-5.30pm Sun; 🚌1, 2) With three floors filled with pieces by local artists and designers, Souk is the perfect place to pick up Belfast-themed items including pottery, printed canvas bags, tea towels and original artwork.

No Alibis Bookstore   BOOKS
(Map p560; www.noalibis.com; 83 Botanic Ave; ⊙9am-5.30pm Mon-Sat, 1-5pm Sun; 🚌7A to 7D) Specialising in crime fiction (and even appearing in print in Colin Bateman's *Mystery Man* series), this small, independent bookshop run by friendly and knowledgable staff hosts regular poetry readings and book signings.

Young Savage   VINTAGE
(Map p560; www.facebook.com/theyoungsavage-belfast; 22 Church Lane; ⊙10am-6pm Mon-Sat, 1.30-5.30pm Sun) This compact shop spread over two floors is packed full with vintage clothing, shoes, records and books.

Keats & Chapman   BOOKS
(Map p560; www.facebook.com/KeatsChapman; 21 North St; ⊙10am-5.30pm Mon-Sat; 🚌2A to 2H) You could lose hours browsing the crammed shelves of this secondhand bookshop, that's been in business since 1928.

Co Couture   CHOCOLATE
(Map p560; www.cocouture.co.uk; 7 Chichester St; ⊙10am-6pm Mon-Sat; 🚌G1, G2) This small subterranean shop has won prizes for its hand-crafted chocolates made using raise trade (a step up from fair trade) chocolate from Madagascar. The range includes dairy-free chocolates, hot chocolate and vegetarian marshmallows. Also runs classes.

Steensons   JEWELLERY
(Map p560; www.thesteensons.com; Bedford House, Bedford St; ⊙10am-5.30pm Mon-Sat; 🚌7A to 7D) This city-centre showroom sells a range of stylish, contemporary, handmade jewellery in silver, gold and platinum, from the Steensons workshop (p647) in County Antrim. Steensons is the creator of *Game of Thrones* jewellery; look out for its similarly inspired designs.

Wicker Man   ARTS & CRAFTS
(Map p560; www.thewickerman.co.uk; 18 High St; ⊙9.30am-6pm Mon-Wed, Fri & Sat, to 9pm Thu, 1.30-6pm Sun; 🚌1A to 1G, 2A to 2G) In addition to offering knitting and crochet classes, arty Wicker Man sells a wide range of contemporary Irish crafts and gifts, including silver jewellery, glassware and knitwear.

ℹ Information

DANGERS & ANNOYANCES

Dissident Republican groups continue a campaign of violent attacks aimed at police and military targets, but have very little public support. Security alerts usually have no effect on visiting tourists (other than roads being closed), but be aware of the potential danger. You can follow the Police Service of Northern Ireland (PSNI) on Twitter (@policeserviceni) and receive immediate notification of any alerts.

➔ Even at the height of the Troubles, Belfast wasn't a particularly dangerous city for tourists. It's still best, however, to avoid the so-called 'interface areas' – near the peace lines in West Belfast, Crumlin Rd and the Short Strand (just east of Queen's Bridge) – after dark.

➔ If in doubt about any area, ask at your hotel or hostel.

➔ You will notice a more obvious security presence than elsewhere in the UK and Ireland, such as armoured police Land Rovers and fortified police stations. There are door attendants at many city-centre pubs.

EMERGENCY PHONE NUMBERS

International access code	☑ 00
Country code	☑ 44
Police, Fire & Ambulance	☑ 999

Victim Support NI (☑ 028-9024 3133; www. victimsupportni.co.uk; 1st fl, Albany House, 73-75 Great Victoria St; ☒ 8A to 8D, 9A to 9C) is an independent charity that supports people affected by crime.

INTERNET ACCESS

Belfast has a network of 104 free wi-fi hotspots at visitor attractions, community and leisure centres and other public buildings. Search for BelfastWiFi. All hostels and hotels and most cafes, restaurants and bars have wi-fi.

LEFT LUGGAGE

A legacy of the Troubles is that, due to security concerns, there are no left-luggage facilities at Belfast's airports, train stations and bus stations. However, most hotels and hostels allow guests to leave their bags for the day, and the Visit Belfast Welcome Centre also offers a daytime left-luggage service.

MEDICAL SERVICES

Everyone receives free emergency treatment at accident and emergency (A&E) departments of state-run NHS hospitals, regardless of nationality. The following hospitals have A&Es:

Belfast City Hospital (☑ 028-9032 9241; www.belfasttrust.hscni.net/hospitals; 51 Lisburn Rd; ☒ 24hr; ☒ 9A to 9C)

Mater Hospital (☑ 028-9074 1211; www. belfasttrust.hscni.net/hospitals/MaterHospital. htm; 45-51 Crumlin Rd; ☒ Mater Hospital)

Royal Victoria Hospital (☑ 028-9024 0503; www.belfasttrust.hscni.net/hospitals/ RVHIntro.htm; 274 Grosvenor Rd; ☒ Falls Rd)

Ulster Hospital (☑ 028-9048 4511; www.se trust.hscni.net/2024.htm; Upper Newtownards Rd, Dundonald; ☒ Ulster Hospital)

POST

There are several branches of the generally reliable UK postal service, the Post Office (www. postoffice.co.uk), in Belfast. International postage costs £1.35 to £2.30 for a standard letter and £4.50 to £5.65 for a 100g parcel. Detailed rates are listed on the website.

Main Post Office (Map p560; www.postoffice. co.uk; 12-16 Bridge St; ☒ 9am-5.30pm Mon-Sat; ☒ 1A to 1G, 2A to 2E)

Donegall Sq (Map p560; 16 Howard St; ☒ 8am-5.30pm Mon-Fri; ☒ G1, G2)

Queen's University (Map p560; 95 University Rd; ☒ 8am-9pm Mon-Fri, 9am-2pm Sat; ☒ 8A to 8D)

TOURIST INFORMATION

Visit Belfast Welcome Centre (Map p560; ☑ 028-9024 6609; www.visitbelfast.com; 9 Donegall Sq N; ☒ 9am-7pm Mon-Sat, 11am-4pm Sun Jun-Sep, 9am-5.30pm Mon-Sat, 11am-4pm Sun Oct-May; ☎; ☒ G1, G2) Stacks of information about Northern Ireland. Services include left luggage (not overnight), tour and accommodation bookings, bus-ticket sales and wi-fi.

EastSide Visitor Centre (☑ 028-9045 1900; www.eastsidepartnership.com; 278-280 Newtownards Rd; ☒ 8am-6pm Mon-Fri, 10am-5pm Sat & Sun; ☒ G1)

Queen's Welcome Centre (Map p560; ☑ 028-9097 5252; www.qub.ac.uk/welcomecentre; University Rd; ☒ 8.30am-5.30pm Mon-Fri, 11am-4pm Sat & Sun; ☒ 8A to 8D)

There are also tourist information desks at George Best Belfast City Airport and **Belfast International Airport** (www.nitga.co.uk; half-day tours from £95).

ℹ Getting There & Away

AIR

Located 30km northwest of Belfast, **Belfast International Airport** (Aldergrove; ☑ 028-9448 4848; www.belfastairport.com; Airport Rd) is a busy local airport; lines at security can be slow so be sure to arrive at least an hour before your flight. There is a **tourist information desk** (☑ 028-9448 4677; ☒ 7.30am-7pm Mon-Fri, to 5.30pm Sat, 8am-11 Sun).

Located 6km northeast of the city centre, **George Best Belfast City Airport** (BHD;

028-9093 9093; www.belfastcityairport.com; Airport Rd) is the smaller of Belfast's two airports, with flights to UK cities and seasonal flights elsewhere in Europe. There is a **tourist information desk** (☑ 028-9093 5372; George Best Belfast City Airport; ⊙ 7.30am-7pm Mon-Fri, to 4.30pm Sat, 11am-6pm Sun) here.

BOAT

Stena Line (☑ 08447 707070; www.stenaline. co.uk; Victoria Terminal, 4 West Bank Rd; trips from £89; ☑ 96) Car ferries to Belfast from Liverpool (England; eight hours) and Cairnryan (Scotland; 2¼ hours) dock at Victoria Terminal, 5km north of the city centre; take the M2 motorway north and turn right at junction No 1. Bus 96 runs from Upper Queen St (£2.10, 20 minutes, nine daily Monday to Friday, three Saturday and Sunday). A taxi costs about £10.

Steam Packet Company (☑ 08722 992 992; www.steam-packet.com; Albert Quay; return fares from £92) Runs car ferries between Belfast and Douglas on the Isle of Man (2¾ hours, two or three per week, April to September only), docking at Albert Quay, 2km north of the city centre. There's no public transport to the ferry terminal; a taxi costs about £5.

Additional car ferries to and from Scotland and England dock at Larne, 37km north of Belfast. Trains to the terminal at Larne Harbour depart from Great Victoria St station.

BUS

There is an **information point** (⊙ 8am-6pm Mon-Fri, 8.30am-5pm Sat) at Belfast's **Europa Bus Centre** (☑ 028-9066 6630; www.translink.co.uk; Great Victoria St, Great Northern Mall; ⊙ 5am-11pm Mon-Fri, 5.45am-11pm Sat, to 10.15pm Sun), where you can pick up regional bus timetables. Contact **Translink** (☑ 028-9066 6630; www. translink.co.uk; Great Victoria St, Europa Bus Centre) for timetable and fares information.

Laganside Buscentre (Oxford St) Near the River Lagan; mainly for buses to eastern County Down, including Bangor and Newtownards.

Aircoach (☑ 028-9033 0655; www.aircoach.ie; single/return adult £14/21, child £8/12) Offers an hourly bus service between Belfast and Dublin City Centre (2¼ hours) via Dublin Airport (1¾ hours). Discounted fares available when you book online. The bus stop is on Glengall St.

National Express (☑ 0871 781 8181; www. nationalexpress.com) Runs a daily coach service between Belfast and London (from £41 one-way, 15½ hours) via the Cairnryan ferry, Dumfries, Manchester and Birmingham. Buses depart from Glengall St.

Scottish Citylink (☑ 0871 266 3333; www. citylink.co.uk; Great Victoria St, Great Northern Mall) Operates three buses a day from Glasgow to Belfast (£28 to £32, six hours), via the Cairnryan ferry.

TRAIN

For information on train fares and timetables, contact Translink.

Belfast Lanyon Place (East Bridge St) East of the city centre. Trains run to Dublin and all destinations in Northern Ireland.

Great Victoria Street Station (Great Victoria St, Great Northern Mall) Next to the Europa Bus Centre. Trains run to Portadown, Lisburn, Bangor, Larne Harbour and Derry.

Northern Ireland Railways (NIR; ☑ 028-9066 6630; www.translink.co.uk/Services/NI-Railways) Runs four routes from Belfast. One links with the system in the Republic via Newry to Dublin; the other three go east to Bangor, northeast to Larne and northwest to Derry via Coleraine.

ⓘ Getting Around

TO/FROM THE AIRPORTS
Belfast International Airport

Airport Express 300 bus runs to the Europa Bus Centre (one-way/return £8/11, 30 to 55 minutes). From Monday to Friday, the first bus from Belfast/the airport is at 4am/4.40am, then buses run at least once an hour until 11.30pm (from Belfast) and 12.15am (from the airport). There are fewer buses on Saturday and Sundays.

A taxi from the airport to the city centre costs about £30.

BUS SERVICES FROM BELFAST

DESTINATION	PRICE (€)	DURATION (HR)	FREQUENCY
Armagh	10	1¼	hourly Mon-Fri, 8 Sat, 5 Sun
Bangor	4	¾	half-hourly Mon-Fri, hourly Sat, 4 Sun
Derry	13	1¾	half-hourly
Downpatrick	6.20	1	at least hourly Mon-Sat, hourly Sun
Dublin	16	2½	hourly
Enniskillen	13	2¼	hourly Mon-Fri, 9 Sat, 5 Sun
Newcastle	8.60	1¼	at least hourly
Omagh	13	1¾	hourly Mon-Fri, 11 Sat, 6 Sun

TRAIN SERVICES FROM BELFAST

DESTINATION	PRICE (€)	DURATION (HR)	FREQUENCY
Bangor	6	½	every 20min Mon-Sat, hourly Sun
Dublin	30	2¼	8 Mon-Sat, 5 Sun
Larne Harbour	7.70	1	hourly
Newry	11.50	¾	7 Mon-Sat, 5 Sun
Portrush	13	1¾	hourly

George Best Belfast City Airport

Airport Express 600 bus runs to the Europa Bus Centre (one-way/return £2.60/4, 15 minutes) every 20 minutes between 5.15am and 9.30pm Monday to Saturday, and every 40 minutes from 7am to 9.30pm on Sunday. A return ticket is valid for one month.

A pedestrian bridge links the airport with Sydenham train station on the Belfast to Bangor train line. Trains to the city centre run several times an hour from 6.30am to 11.45pm (£2, 10 minutes).

A taxi fare to the city centre is about £10.

BICYCLE

National Cycle Network route 9 runs through central Belfast, mostly following the western bank of the River Lagan and the north shore of Belfast Lough.

Belfast Bikes (☑ 034-3357 1551; www.belfast-bikes.co.uk; registration per 3 days £6, bikes per 30min/1hr/2hr/3hr free/£0.50/1.50/2.50; ⊙ 6am-midnight) Belfast's bike-share scheme, introduced in 2015, provides bikes at 40 docking stations throughout the city. Register online or via the app. If the bike is lost, stolen or damaged, your credit card will be charged £120.
Belfast City Bike Tours (p572) Guided tours; also rents out bikes.

BUS

Metro (☑ 028-9066 6630; www.translink. co.uk) services depart from various stops on and around Donegall Sq, at City Hall and along Queen St. Since 2018, articulated, 18m-long **Glider** (☑ 028-9066 6630; www.translink. co.uk) buses have operated along two routes. You must buy a ticket before boarding; there are ticket machines at each stop.

The **G1** runs from Stewartstown Rd in the west to Dundonald park and ride in the east of the city, via the Falls Rd, city centre and Newtownards Rd (about every 10 minutes, 5.30am to midnight Monday to Saturday 7.30am to 10.30pm Sunday).

The **G2** runs from Donegall Sq N along Queen's Rd in Titanic Quarter (every 10 to 15 minutes, 7.15am to 11.30pm Monday to Saturday, every 30 minutes 9.30am to 9.30pm Sunday).

An increasing number of buses are low-floor, 'kneeling' buses with space for one wheelchair. Glider buses are wheelchair accessible.

CAR HIRE

Driving is a convenient way to reach the city's peripheral sights, but traffic can be terrible (especially on the main commuter routes in and out of the city) and parking expensive.

Avis (www.avis.co.uk) **City** (☑ 028-9032 9258; 69-71 Great Victoria St; ⊙ 8am-5pm Mon-Fri); **Belfast International Airport** (☑ 0844 544 6012; ⊙ 7.30am-11pm Mon-Fri, 8am-midnight Sat, noon-7pm Sun, 24hr drop-off); **George Best Belfast City Airport** (☑ 028-9073 1929; ⊙ 7am-10pm, 24hr drop-off)

Budget (www.budgetbelfast.co.uk) **City** (☑ 028-9023 0700; 69-71 Great Victoria St; ⊙ 8am-5pm Mon-Fri); **Belfast International Airport** (☑ 028-9442 3332; ⊙ 5.30am-midnight); **George Best Belfast City Airport** (☑ 028-9045 1111; ⊙ 7am-10pm)

Dooley Car Rentals (☑ 0800 282 189; www. dooleycarrentals.com; Belfast International Airport; ⊙ 6.30am-11pm) This reliable Ireland-wide agency offers good rates – around £250 a week for a compact car, with the option of one-way cross-border rentals.

Europcar (www.europcar.co.uk) **City** (☑ 0371 384 3425; 27 Balmoral Rd; ⊙ 8am-6pm Mon-Fri, to 1pm Sat); **Belfast International Airport** (☑ 0371 384 3426; ⊙ 7am-11pm Mon-Fri & Sun, to 10pm Sat); **George Best Belfast City Airport** (☑ 0371 384 3425; ⊙ 7am-9.30pm Mon-Sat, 8am-9.30pm Sun)

Hertz (www.hertz.co.uk) **George Best Belfast City Airport** (☑ 028-9073 2451; ⊙ 7.30am-9.30pm Mon-Sat, 9am-9.30pm Sun)

TAXI

Fona Cab (☑ 028-9033 3333; www.fonacab. com)
Value Cabs (☑ 028-9080 9080; www.valuecabs. co.uk)

Counties Down & Armagh

POP 706,460 / AREA 3702 SQ KM

Best Places to Eat

➡ Hara (p610)

➡ Balloo House (p600)

➡ Guillemot Kitchen Cafe (p594)

➡ Poacher's Pocket (p600)

➡ Tuk Tuk Too (p597)

Best Places to Stay

➡ Old Inn (p595)

➡ Enniskeen Country House (p604)

➡ Shoreline (p597)

➡ Portaferry Hotel (p596)

➡ Hutt Hostel (p604)

Why Go?

County Down's treasures fan out beyond Belfast. Strangford Lough's sparkling, island-fringed waters stretch south, with the bird-haunted mudflats of Castle Espie and Nendrum's ancient monastery on one shore, and the picturesque Ards Peninsula on the other. The Mourne Mountains' velvet curves sweep down to the sea near Downpatrick and Lecale, the old stamping grounds of Ireland's patron saint. To the south of the Mournes, the coastal road passes the picturesque coastal towns of Rostrevor and Warrenpoint, the respective hosts of summer folk and blues festivals.

Down's neighbour County Armagh is largely rural, from the low, rugged hills of the south to the apple orchards and strawberry fields of the north, with Ireland's ecclesiastical capital, the appealing little city of Armagh, in the middle. South Armagh is a peaceful backwater with enchanting scenery ideal for walkers and cyclists.

When to Go

➡ May brings white clouds of apple blossom to County Armagh's orchards.

➡ Summertime generally has the best weather for hiking and cycling, and late June sees the International Walking Festival in the Mourne Mountains.

➡ Spring and autumn are both good for birdwatching, but keen birders have a big X on their calendars in October, when tens of thousands of overwintering brent geese begin to arrive at Castle Espie on Strangford Lough.

➡ Late July is the time to catch the Fiddler's Green International Festival in Rostrevor; Warrenpoint's Blues on the Bay festival is held in late May.

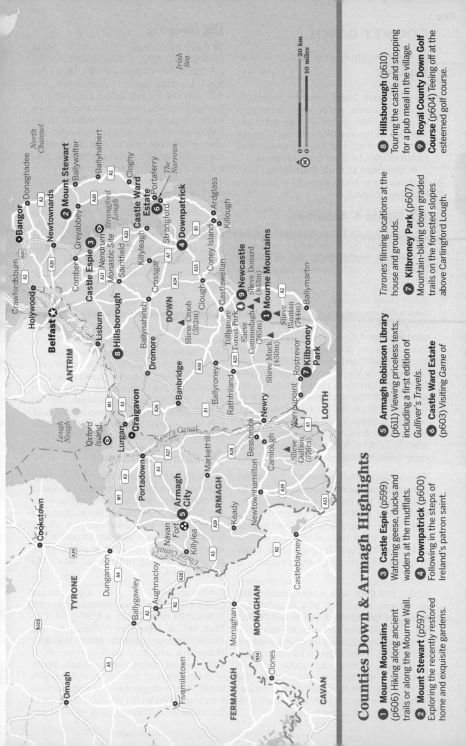

Counties Down & Armagh Highlights

1 Mourne Mountains (p606) Hiking along ancient trails or along the Mourne Wall.

2 Mount Stewart (p597) Exploring the recently restored home and exquisite gardens.

3 Castle Espie (p599) Watching geese, ducks and waders at the mudflats.

4 Downpatrick (p600) Following in the steps of Ireland's patron saint.

5 Armagh Robinson Library (p611) Viewing priceless texts, including a first edition of *Gulliver's Travels*.

6 Castle Ward Estate (p603) Visiting *Game of Thrones* filming locations at the house and grounds.

7 Kilbroney Park (p607) Mountain-biking down graded trails on the forested slopes above Carlingford Lough.

8 Hillsborough (p610) Touring the castle and stopping for a pub meal in the village.

9 Royal County Down Golf Course (p604) Teeing off at the esteemed golf course.

COUNTY DOWN

Bangor

POP 61,000

On the County Down's northern shore, this Victorian seaside resort town first flourished when the Belfast–Bangor train line was built in the late 19th century. In recent years, Bangor has enjoyed a renaissance as an out-of-town base for city commuters.

In the centre of town, Main St and High St (Bangor has both) converge at the huge boat-filled marina.

◉ Sights & Activities

The scenic **North Down Coastal Path** follows the shore from Holywood train station on Belfast's northeastern edge to Bangor Marina (15km), and continues east to Orlock Point.

North Down Museum   MUSEUM
(www.northdownmuseum.com; Castle Park Ave; ☉10am-4.30pm Tue-Sat, noon-4.30pm Sun year-round, plus 10am-4.30pm Mon Jul & Aug) FREE Historical treasures displayed in the converted laundry, stables and stores of Bangor Castle include the *Raven Maps* (the only complete folio of Plantation-era maps in Ireland); the Bronze Age Ballycroghan Swords, dating from around 500 BC; the 9th-century bronze handbell, the Bangor Bell; and a 17th-century sundial by Scottish craftsman John Bonar. Don't miss the model of Bangor Castle made out of sugar cubes, by local artist Brendan Jamison.

Bangor Castle Walled Garden   GARDENS
(www.visitardsandnorthdown.com; Valentine Rd; ☉10am-8pm Mon-Thu, to 6pm Fri-Sun Apr-Aug, shorter hours Sep-Nov) FREE Designed in the 1840s by the Ward family who lived in Bangor Castle, these tranquil gardens make a good picnicking spot. It's particularly pretty in spring, when the tulips are in bloom.

Pickie Funpark   AMUSEMENT PARK
(☎028-9145 0746; www.pickiefunpark.com; Marine Gardens; attractions £1.50-4.50; ☉9am-9pm Jun-Aug, to 7pm Apr-May & Sep, to 4pm Oct-Mar; ▣) This old-fashioned seaside entertainment complex is famous for its swan-shaped pedal boats. There's also a kids' adventure playground, electric-track karts, minigolf, zorbs and a miniature steam train, the *Pickie Puffer*. Family passes include various attractions or you can pay for each ride individually (the park is free to enter).

🛏 Sleeping

⭐ **Cairn Bay Lodge**   B&B ££
(☎028-9146 7636; www.cairnbaylodge.com; 278 Seacliff Rd; s/d from £65/100; ▣ 🖥) Set amid beautiful gardens, this lovely seaside villa exudes Edwardian elegance with its oak-panelled lounge and dining room serving superb gourmet breakfasts. Its six bedrooms (all with private bathroom and organic toiletries, and some with sparkling sea views) blend antique charm with contemporary style. Beauty treatments are available. It's 1km east of the town centre, overlooking Ballyholme Bay.

Ennislare House   B&B ££
(☎028-9127 0858; www.ennislarehouse.com; 7-9 Princetown Rd; s/d from £55/90; ▣ 🖥) Just 300m north of Bangor train station, this lovely Victorian townhouse has big, bright rooms, stylish decor and a friendly owner who can't do enough to make you feel welcome.

Clandeboye Lodge Hotel   HOTEL ££
(☎028-9185 2500; www.clandeboyelodge.com; 10 Estate Rd, Clandeboye; d from £115; ▣ @ 🖥) Resembling a modern red-brick church, the Clandeboye offers informal luxury – big bedrooms, polished granite bathrooms, fluffy bathrobes, champagne and chocolates – with a log fire in winter and a drinks terrace in summer. Its bar-restaurant, the Coq & Bull, serves farm-reared poultry and beef, and local seafood. It sits amid landscaped gardens on the southwest edge of Bangor.

🍴 Eating & Drinking

⭐ **Guillemot Kitchen Cafe**   CAFE £
(www.facebook.com/theguillemotcafe; 2 Seacliff Rd; mains £4-8; ☉kitchen 9am-3pm Mon-Fri, to 4pm Sat & Sun; ✎) Opposite the marina, this snug, sky-blue cafe does excellent all-day breakfasts, gourmet sandwiches, soups and salads, as well as homemade cakes. There are plenty of vegan options, too, as well as an attached deli.

Boat House   MODERN IRISH £££
(☎028-9146 9253; www.boathousebangor.com; 1A Seacliff Rd; mains £18-26; ☉12.30-3pm & 5.30-10pm Wed-Sat, 1-8pm Sun) Tucked into the former harbour master's office, the Boat House is a cosy little nook of stone, brick and designer decor serving fancy plates of deftly prepared local seafood, lamb and game. Five- and seven-course surprise tasting menus (£50/65 per person) are served to the whole table. There's a good wine list too.

THE OLD INN, CRAWFORDSBURN

In the quaint little village of Crawfordsburn, 3km west of Bangor on the B20, the 1614-established **Old Inn** (☏ 028-9185 3255; www.theoldinn.com; 15 Main St; d from £90; P🐕) claims to be Ireland's oldest hotel. Its original thatched cottage (now the bar, with log fires and low ceilings) is flanked by 18th-century additions. Character-filled rooms have Arts and Crafts–style wallpaper and mahogany.

The inn was once a resting place on the coach route between Belfast and Donaghadee (formerly the main ferry port for mainland Britain). As a result, it has been patronised by many famous names, including a young Peter the Great (tsar of Russia), Dick Turpin (highwayman), former US president George HW Bush, and a roll call of literary figures, including Swift, Tennyson, Thackeray, Dickens, Trollope and CS Lewis.

Hop House BAR
(www.facebook.com/Hophousebangor; 44 High St; ⊗11.30am-1am Mon-Sat, noon-midnight Sun, kitchen noon-8pm) Local craft beers and nightly live music or DJs keep this central spot hopping. The awesome beer garden has a pizza oven.

Jenny Watts PUB
(☏028-9127 0401; www.jennywattsbar.com; 41 High St; mains £6-16; ⊗11.30am-11pm Mon & Tue, 11.30am-1am Wed-Sat, 12.30pm-midnight Sun) Bangor's oldest pub (1780) pulls in a mixed-age crowd for live music on Tuesday night (folk), Friday and Saturday night (varying musicians and bands) and Sunday lunchtime (jazz). There's a beer garden out the back. Good pub food is served from noon to 9pm daily (to 8pm Sunday).

Rabbit Rooms BAR
(www.therabbitrooms.com; 30-32 Quay St; ⊗11.30am-1am Mon-Sat, 12.30pm-midnight Sun) In a charcoal-coloured building stencilled with a gigantic white rabbit, this bare-boards space is a wonderland of mismatched vintage furniture like old, cracked-leather cinema seats, with cocktails served in teapots. Live music plays Monday to Thursday and Saturday.

🛍 Shopping

Project 24 ARTS & CRAFTS
(www.project24ni.com; Queen's Parade; ⊗hours vary) A series of brightly-coloured shipping containers house artists' studios and shops; stop by for pet portraits, jewellery, ceramics, paintings or a tattoo.

ℹ Information

Bangor Visitor Information Centre (☏028-9127 0069; www.visitardsandnorthdown.com; 34 Quay St; ⊗approximately 9.15am-5pm Mon, Tue, Thu & Fri, 10am-5pm Wed & Sat year-round, plus 1-5pm Sun May-Aug) Housed in a tower built in 1637 as a fortified customs post.

ℹ Getting There & Away

The bus and train stations are together on Abbey St, at the uphill end of Main St.

Buses 1 and 2 run from Belfast's Laganside Buscentre to Bangor (£4, one hour, hourly). From Bangor, bus 3 goes to Donaghadee (£3.10, 25 minutes, hourly Monday to Saturday, three on Sunday).

Regular train services run from Belfast's Great Victoria St and Central stations to Bangor (£6, 40 minutes, every 30 minutes Monday to Saturday, hourly Sunday).

Ards Peninsula

The low-lying Ards Peninsula (An Aird) is the finger of land that encloses Strangford Lough, pinching against the thumb of the Lecale Peninsula at the Portaferry Narrows. The northern half of the peninsula has some of Ireland's most fertile farmland, with large expanses of wheat and barley, while the south is a landscape of neat fields, white cottages and narrow, winding roads. The eastern coast has some good sandy beaches.

Donaghadee
POP 6900
The small harbour town of Donaghadee (Domhnach Daoi) was the main ferry port for Scotland until 1874, when it was superseded by Larne. These days it's a jolly seaside spot that come summer fills up with local holidaymakers, many of whom have holiday homes in nearby caravan parks.

Pier 36 B&B ££
(☏028-9188 4466; www.pier36.co.uk; 36 The Parade; s £60, d £80-145) An excellent pub with comfortable B&B rooms upstairs and a red-brick and terracotta-tiled restaurant at the back, dominated by a yellow Rayburn stove that turns out home-baked bread and the

daily roast (restaurant mains £11 to £27; open noon to 9pm).

It's a great place to sample local seafood such as Portavogie scampi, sole, monkfish, haddock and cod.

Slice of Heaven
CAFE £

(www.sliceofheavendessertcafe.com; 11 New St; mains £3.50-6, desserts £4; ⊙10am-5pm Tue-Sat, noon-5pm Sun; 🛜) In Donaghadee's lavishly restored former courthouse, you can get fantastic sandwiches like Coronation Chicken (Christmas-style with turkey, ham, stuffing and cranberry sauce), as well as soups and salads. But the showstoppers are the desserts: key lime pie, summer-berry pavlova, sticky toffee pudding and homemade ice cream such as champagne sorbet.

Harbour & Company
BARBECUE ££

(📞028-9188 4466; www.harbourandcompany. com; 31 The Parade; mains £8-20; ⊙kitchen noon-2.30pm & 5-9.30pm Tue-Sat, noon-9.30pm Sun) In a beachy bar and restaurant with good views of the pier, Harbour & Company specialises in meat, fish and seafood dishes cooked over a wood-fired grill, as well as stone-baked pizzas and artisan flat breads.

❶ Getting There & Away

Bus 3 runs to/from Bangor (£3.10, 25 minutes, hourly Monday to Saturday, three on Sunday).

Portaferry

POP 2500

Beneath Windmill Hill, topped by an old windmill tower, Portaferry (Port an Pheire) is a neat huddle of streets around a medieval tower house, which looks across a turbulent stretch of water, the Narrows, to a matching tower house in Strangford.

◉ Sights & Activities

There are pleasant walks on the minor roads along the coast, north for 2.5km to **Ballyhenry Island**, and south for 6km to the National Trust nature reserve at **Ballyquintin Point**. Both are good for birdwatching, seal spotting or just admiring the views of the Mourne Mountains.

Pick up a free *Portaferry Heritage Trail* map at the visitor information office.

★ Exploris
AQUARIUM

(📞028-4272 8062; www.explorisni.com; Rope Walk, Castle St; adult/child £10.50/9; ⊙10am-6pm Apr-Oct, to 5pm Nov-Mar; 👶) This excellent aquarium has displays of marine life from Strangford Lough and the Irish Sea as well as tropical fish, otters and a reptile centre with an African Nile crocodile, geckos and snakes. There's also a sunken gallery with sharks and a seal sanctuary where orphaned, sick and injured seals are nursed back to health before being released into the wild. Last admission is 4.30pm in summer and 4pm in winter.

Portico
NOTABLE BUILDING

(📞028-4272 8808; www.porticoards.com; Steel Dickson Ave; tour per person £10; ⊙tours 11am Tue, 2pm Thu & Sun) This magnificent Greek Revival building, built as a Presbyterian church in 1841, is thought to have been modelled on the ancient temple of Nemesis on the island of Rhamnous. After falling into disrepair, it underwent a £1.5-million restoration, completed in 2015. It continues to operate as a church, and also hosts classical concerts. Hour-long tours explain the fascinating history and architecture of the building.

Portaferry Castle
CASTLE

(Castle St; ⊙10am-5pm Mon-Sat, 1-5pm Sun Easter-Sep) FREE Portaferry's castle is a small 16th-century tower house that, together with the tower house in Strangford, once controlled sea traffic through the Narrows. It's next to the visitor information office.

🛏 Sleeping

Barholm
HOSTEL £

(📞028-4272 9967; www.barholmportaferry.co.uk; 11 The Strand; dm/s/d from £20/30/50; 🅿🛜) Barholm offers basic, hostel-style accommodation in a Victorian villa with a superb seafront location opposite the ferry slipway. It has a kitchen, laundry facilities and a big, sunny conservatory that doubles as a tearoom. Rooms are available with or without breakfast; some share bathrooms. It's popular with groups, so you'll need to book ahead.

★ Portaferry Hotel
HOTEL ££

(📞028-4272 8231; www.portaferryhotel.com; 10 The Strand; d £80-150; ⊙kitchen noon-3pm & 5-9pm Mon-Fri, noon-9pm Sat, noon-3pm Sun; 🅿📶) Converted from a row of 18th-century terrace houses, this charming seafront hotel has an elegant, Georgian look to its rooms. Each is individually decorated with pretty wallpaper and French-style furniture; some have lough views. The hotel is famous for its scampi; it's also a good place to try Strangford Lough mussels and Portavogie prawns (mains £12.50 to £17).

Drinking & Nightlife

Fiddler's Green PUB

(028-42728393; www.fiddlersgreenportaferry.com; 10 Church St; 10am-11pm) The Fiddler's is a fabulous place for trad music, with live bands every weekend and impromptu sessions that get the whole bar joining in. The Guinness is pretty good, and you'll find one of the 10 *Game of Thrones* carved doors from the Dark Hedges (p641) here. In the upstairs B&B, comfortable guest rooms start from £80.

Information

Portaferry Visitor Information Office (028-4272 9882; www.visitstrangfordlough.co.uk; The Stables, Castle St; 10am-5pm Mon-Sat, 1-5pm Sun Easter-Sep) In a restored stable near the tower house at Portaferry Castle.

Getting There & Away

Buses 9 and 10 travel from Belfast's Laganside Buscentre to Portaferry (£7.20, 1½ hours, seven daily Monday to Saturday, three on Sunday) via Newtownards, Mount Stewart and Greyabbey. More frequent services begin from Newtownards (£6.20, one hour); some buses go via Carrowdore and don't stop at Mount Stewart or Greyabbey – check first.

A **car ferry** (028-4488 1637; one-way car & driver £5.80, car passengers & pedestrians £1) from Portaferry to Strangford sails every half-hour at a quarter past and a quarter to the hour, between 7.45am and 10.45pm Monday to Friday, 8.15am to 11.15pm on Saturday and 9.45am to 10.45pm on Sunday. The journey time is about 10 minutes.

Greyabbey

POP 1000

The little village of Greyabbey, 18km north of Portaferry, is synonymous with the splendid ruins of the Cistercian Grey Abbey. It's also popular for its antiques shops.

Off Main St in the village centre, Hoops Courtyard has a cluster of 18 little shops selling antiques and collectables. Opening times vary, but all are open on Wednesday, Friday and Saturday afternoons.

Grey Abbey MONASTERY

(www.friendsoftheabbey.co.uk; Church Rd; ruins 24hr, visitor centre 1-4pm Sat, 2-4pm Sun Feb-Nov) **FREE** This Cistercian abbey was founded in 1193 by Affreca, wife of Norman knight John de Courcy, the builder of Carrickfergus Castle (p649), in thanks for surviving a stormy sea crossing from the Isle of Man. The small visitor centre explains Cistercian life with paintings and panels; there's also a herb garden full of medicinal plants once cultivated by the monks. The abbey's **church**, in use until the 18th century, was the first in Ireland to be built in the Gothic style.

In the visitor centre (moved inside for protection) is a sandstone effigy, possibly depicting Affreca. Even if the visitor centre is closed, the ruins are well labelled with informative signs. The grounds, overlooked by 18th-century Rosemount House, are awash with trees and flowers on spreading lawns, making this an ideal picnic spot.

★ **Shoreline** B&B ££

(028-4278 8800; www.shorelinemountstewart.com; 88A Newtownards Rd; s £70, d £95-120, tr £145; P) Birdwatchers will be in heaven at this B&B situated on the shore of Strangford Lough. Beside a wood-burning stove, huge windows offer views of the water and visiting brent geese, oystercatchers and heron. Rooms are spacious and modern and there's afternoon tea on arrival. It's located 1km south of the entrance to Mount Stewart, on the road to Greyabbey.

★ **Tuk Tuk Too** ASIAN ££

(028-4278 8774; www.tuktukbistro.com; 23-25 Main St; mains £10-16; 5-9pm Wed-Sat, 1-8pm Sun) This Southeast Asian bistro is a surprising find in sleepy Greyabbey, but one well worth visiting. Chef Kelvin was born and raised in Malaysia; his menu is an attempt to recreate the flavours of the home cooking he grew up with. A range of dishes from Thailand, Vietnam and Malaysia are prepared with fresh local ingredients, with lip-smackingly good results. The original Tuk Tuk Bistro (p599) is in Newtownards.

Getting There & Away

Buses 9 and 10 link Greyabbey with Newtownards (£3.10, 15 minutes, every two hours or more Monday to Saturday, six on Sunday). The same service continues to Portaferry (£4, 30 minutes).

Mount Stewart

The magnificent 18th-century **Mount Stewart** (028-4278 8387; www.nationaltrust.org.uk; Portaferry Rd; adult/child £10.50/5.75; house 11am-5pm daily Mar-Oct, 11am-3pm Sat & Sun Nov-Feb, grounds 10am-5pm daily Mar-Oct, to 4pm Nov-Feb) is one of Northern Ireland's grandest stately homes. Entertaining tours tell the story of the house and its contents; treasures include a painting of racehorse Hambletonian in *Hambletonian, Rubbing Down* (1799–1800) by George Stubbs, one of the most important paintings in Ireland. The house overlooks formal gardens filled with colourful subtropical plants and eccentric topiary.

This National Trust property's contents reflect the period when Lord Londonderry and his wife Edith would entertain guests such as WB Yeats, Winston Churchill and Neville Chamberlain; the dining table has place settings for an imagined 1930s dinner party. As part of a three-year restoration project completed in 2017, the central hall's original 1840s Scrabo stone floor was uncovered and the delicate plaster work repaired.

Much of the landscaping of the beautiful gardens was supervised by Lady Edith for the benefit of her children – the Dodo Terrace at the front of the house is populated with unusual creatures from history (dinosaurs and dodos) and myth (griffins and mermaids), accompanied by giant frogs and duck-billed platypuses. There are several walking trails around the gardens and grounds.

Don't miss the 18th-century Temple of the Winds, a folly in the classical Greek style built on a high point above the lough. Tours of the Temple of the Winds interior are only offered on the last Sunday of the month (advance booking required), but it's worth the walk up to see the building from the outside and take in the views.

Mount Stewart is on the A20, 3km northwest of Greyabbey. Buses from Belfast to Portaferry stop at the gate.

Newtownards & Around

POP 28,000

Founded in the 17th century on the site of the 6th-century Movilla monastery, today Newtownards (Baile Nua na hArda) is a busy commercial centre, with some interesting sights nearby. The town is known locally as Ards.

⊙ Sights

Scrabo Tower & Country Park   PARK
(www.visitardsandnorthdown.com; 403 Scrabo Rd; tower adult/child £3/2; ⊙tower 10am-4pm Thu-Sun Jun-Sep) Newtownards is overlooked by Scrabo Hill, 2km southwest of town. It was once the site of extensive prehistoric earthworks, which were largely removed during construction of the 41m 1857 Scrabo Tower, built in honour of the third Marquess of Londonderry, and visible for miles around. Its interior contains a 122-step spiral staircase

leading to a viewing gallery; it's usually open Thursday to Sunday in the summer months, but check ahead. The surrounding country park is a great spot for a scenic picnic.

The sandstone quarries nearby, now disused, provided material for many famous buildings, including Belfast's Albert Memorial Clock Tower.

Avalon Guitar Factory   FACTORY
(☑028-9182 0542; www.avalonguitars.com; 8 Glenford Way; ⊙9am-5pm Mon-Fri, tours 10am-3pm Tue-Thu) FREE See how Avalon's handcrafted acoustic guitars are made on a factory tour. Every stage of the guitar-making process is explained, including how the wood used affects the sound. Custom guitars take eight weeks to make and can be shipped internationally; prices start at around £2000 for a standard guitar. Call ahead to book a tour (there's no pressure to buy).

Ark Open Farm   FARM
(☑028-9182 0445; www.thearkopenfarm.co.uk; 296 Bangor Rd; adult/child £7/6.50; ⊙10am-6pm Mon-Sat, 2-6pm Sun Apr-Oct, to 5pm Nov-Mar; ⊕) The Ark is a family favourite for its rare breeds of sheep, cattle, poultry, llamas and donkeys. Kids get to pet and hand-feed the lambs, piglets and ducklings. There are also pony rides and walks along a dinosaur trail and through a fairy-tale forest.

Somme Heritage Centre   MUSEUM
(www.sommeassociation.com; 233 Bangor Rd; ⊙10am-4pm Mon-Thu & Sat Apr-Nov, 10am-4pm Mon-Thu plus 1st Sat of month Dec-Mar) FREE This grimly fascinating centre illustrates the horrors of the WWI Somme campaign of 1916 from the perspective of men of the 10th (Irish), 16th (Irish) and 36th (Ulster) divisions, and is a memorial to the men and women who died. It has short films and reconstructions of the trenches, plus a photographic display commemorating the suffragette movement and women's roles in WWI.

It's 3km north of Newtownards on the A21 towards Bangor. Bus 6 from Bangor to Newtownards passes the entrance.

✗ Eating

★**McKee's Country
Store & Restaurant**   IRISH £
(☑028-9182 1304; www.mckeesproduce.com; Strangford View, 28 Holywood Rd; mains £6-15; ⊙restaurant 9am-4.30pm Mon-Sat, shop 8.30am-5.30pm Mon-Sat; ☑⊕) 🌿 On a working 162-hectare farm 5km northwest of Newtownards, this

foodie emporium incorporates a bakery, butcher and deli, plus fruit, vegetable and dairy sections. Everything is produced on site or sourced from the surrounding area. If it's not picnic weather, try the restaurant dishes, such as slow-baked lasagne, in a panoramic dining room overlooking farmland, Scrabo and the lough.

Tuk Tuk Bistro ASIAN ££
(☑ 028-9181 2101; www.tuktukbistro.com; 6 William St; mains £10-14; ⊙ noon-2pm & 5-9pm Mon & Wed-Sat, 1-8pm Sun) Fresh local ingredients are used to create a range of Vietnamese, Thai and Malaysian dishes at this popular bistro. There's a second branch in Greyabbey (p597).

ℹ Information

Ards Visitor Information Centre (☑ 028-9182 6846; www.visitardsandnorthdown.com; 31 Regent St; ⊙ 9.15am-5pm Mon-Fri, 9.30am-5pm Sat) Next to the bus station.

ℹ Getting There & Away

Buses 9 and 10 serve Belfast (£3, 20 minutes, every two hours or more Monday to Saturday, six on Sunday) and Portaferry (£6.20, one hour).

West Side of Strangford Lough

Almost landlocked, Strangford Lough (Loch Cuan) is connected to the open sea by a 700m-wide strait, the Narrows, between the towns of Portaferry and Strangford. The lough's western shore is fringed by hump-backed islands – half-drowned mounds of boulder clay (called drumlins) left behind by ice sheets at the end of the last ice age. On the eastern shore, the drumlins have been broken down by the waves into heaps of boulders that form shallow tidal reefs (known locally as 'pladdies').

Large colonies of grey seals frequent the lough, especially at the southern tip of the Ards Peninsula. Birds abound on the shores and tidal mudflats.

◉ Sights

Castle Espie Wildfowl & Wetlands Centre WILDLIFE RESERVE
(☑ 028-9187 4146; www.wwt.org.uk; 78 Ballydrain Rd, Comber; adult/child £9.20/5.10; ⊙ 10am-5pm daily year-round, to 5.30pm Sat & Sun May-Aug) ✎ Situated 2km southeast of Comber, off the Downpatrick road (A22), Castle Espie is a haven for huge flocks of geese, ducks and

COUNTY DOWN'S RURAL RESTAURANTS

Look around at the rich farmland, fields of cows, grazing mountain sheep and busy coastal fisheries – it's little wonder that County Down's restaurants turn out such fine plates of food. Local menus name-check ingredients like Comber potatoes, Kilkeel crab and Mourne lamb in dishes that have been wooing critics and winning awards.

Some of the county's best eateries include Balloo House (p600), Poacher's Pocket (p600) and Hara (p610).

swans. The landscaped grounds are dotted with birdwatching hides, and are great for fledgling naturalists, with family bird-feeding and pond-dipping sessions.

The best months to visit are May and June, when it's overrun with goslings, ducklings and cygnets, and October, when vast flocks of 30,000 light-bellied brent geese (75% of the world's population) arrive from Canada.

There's a rustic children's play area in the woods, with a zip wire, rope swings and tree houses, as well as a good cafe with windows looking out on the ducks.

Nendrum Monastic Site HISTORIC SITE
(Mahee Island; ⊙ site 24hr year-round, visitor centre 10am-5pm Wed, Fri, Sat & Sun May-Sep) FREE In a wonderful island setting, the 5th-century Celtic monastic community of Nendrum was built under the guidance of St Mochaoi (St Mahee). Its scant remains provide a clear outline of its early plan, with the foundations of a number of churches, a round tower, beehive cells, three concentric stone ramparts and a monks' cemetery. The stone sundial was reconstructed using original pieces. There's a small visitor centre.

Nendrum is 5km south of Comber, reached by a causeway and bridge. By the bridge, look for the ruined tower of 15th-century Mahee Castle.

🛏 Sleeping

★ **Dufferin Coaching Inn** B&B ££
(☑ 028-4482 1134; www.dufferincoachinginn.com; 35 High St, Killyleagh; s £65-70, d £90-100; P 🕸) The comfortable lounge in this lovely Georgian house was once Killyleagh's village bank – the manager's office in the corner now houses a little library. Excellent breakfasts include freshly squeezed orange juice, good coffee and

scrambled eggs with smoked salmon. The seven plush rooms have crisp linen and fluffy towels, and some have four-poster beds.

Anna's House B&B
B&B **££**

(☑028-9754 1566; anna@annashouse.com; 35 Lisbarnett Rd, Tullynagee, Lisbane; s £60, d £90-110; ⓟ⑦) Just west of Lisbane, Anna's is a spacious, ecofriendly country house with views over a lake from a glass-walled extension complete with grand piano. The hospitality is second to none, the scones, pancakes and pastries are home baked, and the breakfast menu ranges from an Ulster fry-up or smoked-salmon omelette to fresh fruit salad.

Old Schoolhouse Inn
B&B **££**

(☑028-9754 1182; www.theoldschoolhouseinn. com; 100 Ballydrain Rd, Comber; s/d from £60/80; ⓟ⑦) Just south of Castle Espie, the 1929 Old Schoolhouse Inn has eight comfortable rooms, each named for a former US president, and a sociable guest lounge. Breakfasts are particularly good, with home-baked Guinness bread, local smoked salmon, and fruit salads with rhubarb fresh from the kitchen garden.

✗ Eating & Drinking

★ Old Post Office Tearoom
CAFE **£**

(www.opocafe.co.uk; 191 Killinchy Rd, Lisbane; mains £5-8; ⊘9am-5pm Mon-Sat; ⑦☑) Once the village post office, this thatched cottage has been lovingly converted into a tearoom and art gallery, with cream plaster and bare stone walls and a wood-burning stove. It serves great coffee, cakes and home-baked scones, plus cooked breakfasts and lunch specials such as quiches and lovely fresh salads.

★ Balloo House
MODERN IRISH **££**

(☑028-9754 1210; www.ballooinns.com; 1 Comber Rd, Killinchy; mains £14-22, Sun lunch 2-/3-course £22/26; ⊘noon-9pm Sun-Thu, to 9.30pm Fri & Sat) Balloo House has long been one of County Down's best restaurants. Casual, modern Irish fare is available in the nook-and-cranny-filled, stone-floored downstairs pub, which centres on a warming cast-iron range stove. Upstairs, a fine-dining restaurant (undergoing refurbishment at research time) serves more refined dishes on Saturday nights (book ahead).

There's bluegrass in the bar Wednesday, Thursday and Friday from 9pm.

Poacher's Pocket
MODERN IRISH **££**

(☑028-9754 1589; www.poacherspocketlisbane.com; 181 Killinchy Rd, Lisbane; mains £10-28; ⊘kitchen noon-9pm Sun-Thu, to 9.30pm Fri & Sat, deli 9am-9pm) ⯑ A fresh, contemporary makeover has transformed this roadside pub into a foodie magnet, with a menu that showcases local ingredients like Portavogie prawns, Strangford crab and glazed ham hock. There's a fantastic range of local craft ciders and beers, which it also sells at its attached Poacher's Pantry deli and farm shop.

Dufferin Arms
PUB FOOD **££**

(www.dufferinarms.com; 35 High St, Killyleagh; mains £11-25; ⊘kitchen noon-3pm & 5-8.30pm Mon-Thu, noon-9pm Fri & Sat, noon-8pm Sun) Easy to spot (it's bright pink), this comfortably old-fashioned pub serves decent pub grub, while the cosy, candlelit restaurant offers a more intimate atmosphere. There's live music on Wednesdays from 9pm and Saturday afternoons from 4pm. The pub featured in the 2013 Oscar-nominated film *Philomena*, starring Dame Judi Dench.

Daft Eddy's
PUB

(☑028-9754 1615; www.dafteddysni.co.uk; Sketrick Island, Whiterock; ⊘11.30am-11.30pm Mon-Thu, 11.30am-1am Fri & Sat, noon-10.30pm Sun) Idyllic on a sunny day, this local favourite is hidden away on an island, with panoramic views over Strangford Lough from its bar, timber-decked terrace and gardens below. There's also a cafe, Little Eddy's. It's 4.5km northeast of Killinchy: follow Whiterock Rd east, then veer around to the left to reach the causeway.

Downpatrick

POP 10,900

St Patrick's mission to spread Christianity to Ireland began and ended in Downpatrick. Ireland's patron saint is believed to have made his first convert at nearby Saul, and was buried at Down Cathedral; St Patrick's Day (17 March) sees the town filled with pilgrims and revellers.

Downpatrick – now County Down's administrative centre – was settled long before the saint's arrival. His first church here was constructed inside the earthwork *dún* (fort) of Rath Celtchair, still visible to the southwest of the cathedral. The place later became known as Dún Pádraig (Patrick's Fort), anglicised to Downpatrick in the 17th century.

◉ Sights

★ St Patrick Centre
MUSEUM

(☑028-4461 9000; www.saintpatrickcentre.com; Patrick's Sq, Market St; adult/child £5.75/3.50; ⊘9am-5pm Mon-Sat year-round, plus 1-5pm Sun Jul & Aug) This magnificent glass-and-timber heritage centre houses a multimedia exhibition called 'Ego Patricius', charting the life and legacy of Ireland's patron saint. Audio and video presentations tell St Patrick's story, often in his own words (taken from his *Confession*, written in Latin around the year 450, which begins with the words *'Ego Patricius'*, meaning 'I am Patrick'). At the end is a spectacular widescreen film that takes you on a swooping helicopter ride over the landscapes of Ireland.

Down Cathedral
CATHEDRAL

(☎ 028-4461 4922; www.downcathedral.org; English St; ☺9.30am-4pm Mon-Sat) **FREE** According to legend, St Patrick died in Saul, where angels told his followers to place his body on a cart drawn by two untamed oxen, and to bury the saint wherever they halted. The oxen supposedly stopped at the church on the hill of Down, now the site of the Church of Ireland's Down Cathedral. In the churchyard, a slab of Mourne granite with the inscription 'Patric' (placed in 1900) marks the traditional site of St Patrick's grave.

The cathedral is testimony to 1600 years of building and rebuilding. Viking attacks wiped away all trace of the earliest churches, and the subsequent Norman cathedral and monasteries were destroyed by Scottish raiders in 1316. The rubble was used in a 15th-century church finished in 1512, but after the Dissolution of the Monasteries it was razed to the ground in 1541. Today's building dates largely from the 18th and 19th centuries, with a completely new interior installed in the 1980s.

To get here, from the St Patrick Centre, take the path to its left, uphill through the landscaped grounds.

Down County Museum
MUSEUM

(☎ 028-4461 5218; www.downcountymuseum.com; The Mall; ☺10am-4.30pm Mon-Sat, 1.30-5pm Sun) **FREE** Downpatrick's 18th-century jail now houses the county museum. In a former cell block at the back are models of some of the prisoners once incarcerated there, and details of their sad stories. Displays in the Governor's residence include early flint tools and items from the Norman conquest of Down. The Raising of the Cross exhibition houses the 10th-century Downpatrick High Cross; in 2015 the cross was moved here from its location outside Down Cathedral to protect it from the elements.

Outside the museum, a short signposted trail leads to the Mound of Down, a Norman motte-and-bailey.

ST PATRICK'S WAY

Downpatrick is the terminus of St Patrick's Way, a 132km signposted pilgrim walk from Armagh City, linking sites related to St Patrick. Starting at Navan Fort (p614), the walk passes along the Newry canal towpath to Newry, through Rostrevor and across the Mourne Mountains to Newcastle on the way to Downpatrick. You can pick up a free Pilgrim Walk Passport at the Navan Centre (p614) and tourist offices and collect stamps along the way.

If walking doesn't appeal, pick up a map for the St Patrick's Trail, which highlights St Patrick–related and other Christian sights on a driving route from Armagh to Bangor. You'll find copies of the map in tourist information centres.

Inch Abbey
ABBEY

(Inch Abbey Rd) **FREE** Built by Norman knight John de Courcy for the Cistercians in 1180 on an earlier Irish monastic site, Inch Abbey is visible across the river from Down Cathedral – and yes, it's another *Game of Thrones* filming location. Most of the ruins are just foundations and low walls; the atmospheric setting beside the marshes of the River Quoile is its most attractive feature.

John de Courcy commissioned one of the monks at Inch Abbey to rewrite the legends of St Patrick; it's possible that the story of St Patrick banishing the snakes from Ireland was written here.

Inch Abbey is off the A7 Belfast Rd just across the river, north of Downpatrick.

Downpatrick & County Down Railway
MUSEUM

(☎ 028-4461 5779; www.downrail.co.uk; Market St; adult/child £7.50/5.50; ☺1-4.30pm Sat & Sun mid-Jun–mid-Sep & Dec, plus some bank holidays) From mid-June to mid-September, plus December, St Patrick's Day, Easter, May Day and Halloween, this working railway museum runs steam-hauled trains over a restored section of the former Belfast–Newcastle line, from Downpatrick to Inch Abbey. The ticket price includes a return journey and entrance to the carriage gallery and station museum.

🛏 Sleeping & Eating

Denvir's Hotel & Pub
B&B ££

(☎ 028-4461 2012; www.denvirs.com; 14-16 English St; s/d £40/70; 🛜) Dating from 1642, Denvir's is allegedly Ireland's oldest surviving coaching inn. It offers B&B accommodation in six idiosyncratic rooms with polished floorboards, Georgian windows and period fireplaces. Good food is served in the cosy bar and rustic restaurant, which has an enormous, 17th-century stone fireplace.

Oakley Fayre CAFE £

(☑ 028-4461 2500; www.oakleyfayre.com; 52 Market St; breakfast £3.25-5.25, lunch mains £4.50-7; ☺ 8am-5pm Mon-Sat; 🖽) In business since 1979, Oakley's is the place to go for wholesome fare like east coast haddock chowder, baked potatoes, quiches and freshly baked scones. There is also a deli counter for takeaway; many of the items for sale are locally produced.

ⓘ Information

Downpatrick Visitor Information Centre
(☑ 028-4461 2233; www.visitstrangfordlough.co.uk; Market St; ☺ 9am-5pm Mon-Fri, 9.30am-5pm Sat year-round, plus 1-5pm Sun Jul & Aug) In the St Patrick Centre.

ⓘ Getting There & Away

Downpatrick's bus station is just south of the St Patrick Centre.

Services:

Belfast (Europa Bus Centre) £6.20, one hour, half-hourly Monday to Friday, hourly Saturday, six Sunday

Castlewellan £4, 30 minutes, seven daily Monday to Friday, six Saturday, four Sunday

Dundrum £3.60, 15 minutes, seven daily Monday to Friday, six Saturday, four Sunday

Newcastle £4, 20 minutes, seven daily Monday to Friday, six Saturday, four Sunday

Newry £10, 1¼ hours, seven daily Monday to Friday, six Saturday, four Sunday

Saul

On landing near this spot in 432, St Patrick made his first convert: Díchú, the local chieftain, gave the holy man a sheep barn (*sabhal* in Irish, pronounced sawl) in which to preach. A replica 10th-century church and round tower marks the site to the west of the village.

East of the village is the small hill of Slieve Patrick (120m), with stations of the cross along the path to the top and a massive 10m-high statue of St Patrick on the summit. The hill is a popular pilgrimage site on St Patrick's Day.

Saul Church CHURCH

(www.downcathedral.org/saul-church; Saul Rd; ☺ 9am-5pm) **FREE** At the supposed site of the first church in Ireland, founded by St Patrick in 432, you'll find a replica 10th-century church and round tower, built in 1932 to mark the 1500th anniversary of St Patrick's arrival. The church is west of Saul village.

Struell Wells CHRISTIAN SITE

FREE These supposedly curative spring waters are traditionally associated with St Patrick – it is said he scourged himself here, spending much of the night immersed in what is now the Drinking Well.

The wells are in a scenic, secluded glen 3km east of Downpatrick and 3km south of Saul village. From Downpatrick, take the B1 road towards Ardglass, and turn left after passing the hospital. Patrick must have been a hardy soul – the well-preserved but chilly 17th-century bathhouses here look more likely to induce ill health than cure it! The site has been venerated for centuries, although the buildings are all post-1600.

Between the bathhouses and the ruined chapel stands the Eye Well, whose waters are said to cure eye ailments.

Lecale Peninsula

East of Downpatrick, the low-lying Lecale Peninsula is isolated by the sea and Strangford Lough to the north, south and east, and the marshes of the Rivers Quoile and Blackstaff to the west. Its Irish name Leath Chathail (lay-ca-*hal*) means 'the territory of Cathal' (an 8th-century prince). This region of fertile farmland is fringed by fishing harbours, rocky bluffs and sandy beaches.

Between Ardglass and Killough in the south of the peninsula is Coney Island, vividly described in Van Morrison's spoken-word song of the same name. This little seaside hamlet isn't in fact an island, but has a small peninsula that may once have been cut off by the sea. The Oscar-winning short film *The Shore* (2011) was shot at director Terry George's family cottage here.

Strangford

POP 475

The picturesque fishing village of Strangford (Baile Loch Cuan) lies 16km northeast of Downpatrick. It's dominated by Strangford Castle, a 16th-century tower house (closed to the public) that faces its counterpart in Portaferry across the Narrows.

At the end of Castle St, a footpath called the Squeeze Gut leads over the hill behind the village, with a fine view of the lough, before looping back to Strangford via tree-lined Dufferin Ave (1.5km), or continuing 4.5km around the shoreline to Castle Ward Estate.

Strangford Sea Safari   BOATING
([✆] 028-4372 3933; www.clearsky-adventure.com; Strangford Harbour; adult/child £26/23) Runs one-hour speedboat tours (on most Sundays March to September) into the swirling tidal streams of the Narrows, including visits to the Angus Rock Lighthouse and local seal colonies. Call ahead for the boat-trip schedule and to make a booking.

Cuan   B&B ££
([✆] 028-4488 1222; www.thecuan.com; The Square; s/d £67/85; [P][🖥]) You can't miss the Cuan and its sage-green facade, just around the corner from the ferry slip, or the warm welcome from husband-and-wife managers Peter and Caroline. There are eight neat, comfortable and well-equipped rooms, and an atmospheric, wood-panelled restaurant.

❶ Getting There & Away

Bus 16 serves Downpatrick (£3.60, 25 minutes, nine daily Monday to Friday, five on Saturday, four on Sunday).

A **car ferry** ([✆] 028-4488 1637; one-way car & driver £5.80, car passengers & pedestrians £1; ⊘7.30am-10.30pm Mon-Fri, 8am-11pm Sat, 9.30am-10.30pm Sun) from Strangford to Portaferry sails on the hour and half-hour between 7.30am and 10.30pm Monday to Friday, 8am and 11pm on Saturday, and 9.30am and 10.30pm on Sunday. The journey time is about 10 minutes.

Castle Ward Estate

Famed for its role as Winterfell in *Game of Thrones*, 1760s-built Castle Ward ([✆]028-4488 1204; www.nationaltrust.org.uk; Park Rd; adult/child £9.50/4.75; ⊘buildings noon-5pm Easter-Oct, grounds 10am-5pm Mar-Oct, to 4pm Nov-Feb; [♿]) house has a superb setting overlooking the bay west of Strangford. The estate's history is relayed in entertaining 45-minute tours of the house and servants' quarters. On the extensive grounds are a Victorian laundry museum, a farmyard, 16th-century Plantation tower Old Castle Ward and 15th-century tower house Castle Audley, along with walking and cycling trails.

Castle Ward House was built for Lord and Lady Bangor – Bernard Ward and his wife, Anne – whose widely differing architectural tastes resulted in an eccentric country residence – and a subsequent divorce. Bernard favoured the neoclassical style seen in the front facade and the main staircase, while Anne leaned towards the Strawberry Hill Gothic of the rear facade, which reaches a peak in the incredible fan vaulting of her Gothic boudoir.

There's a caravan park on the estate with pitches for tents.

Clearsky Adventure Centre   CYCLING
([✆] 028-4372 3933; www.clearsky-adventure.com; Castle Ward Estate, Park Rd; ⊘10am-5pm Easter-Sep, to 4pm Oct-Mar) Based at Castle Ward Estate, Clearsky Adventure Centre offers various *Game of Thrones*–themed activities, including archery sessions and bicycle tours to filming locations around the estate, complete with capes and wooden swords. It also rents out bikes and kayaks (£20 for 2½ hours). Book ahead.

Clearsky also runs boat trips with Strangford Sea Safar across the Narrows.

Castle Ward Caravan Park   CARAVAN PARK £
(www.nationaltrust.org.uk; Downpatrick Rd; campsites per tent £22, caravans £23-40, glamping huts £47-67) The caravan park at Castle Ward Estate has pitches for tents and caravans as well as basic glamping huts (bring your own camping equipment and bedding, and book ahead). It's open year-round. National Trust members get discounted rates.

Newcastle
POP 7400

Gloriously set at the foot of the Mourne Mountains on a 5km strand of golden sand, the faded Victorian seaside resort of Newcastle (An Caisleán Nua) has a contemporary sculpture-studded, kilometre-long seafront promenade and an elegant footbridge over the River Shimna.

◉ Sights & Activities

Newcastle's main attraction is the beach, which stretches northeast to the nature reserve.

The little harbour at the south end of town once served the 'stone boats' that exported Mourne granite from the quarries of Slieve Donard.

Royal County Down Golf Course GOLF
(☑ 028-4372 3314; www.royalcountydown.org; 36 Golf Links Rd; green fees £230-250 May-Oct, lower rates Nov-Apr) Set amid flowering heather and gorse, this hallowed par-71 links course was designed by Old Tom Morris and incorporates two awe-inspiring nine-hole loops. It's open to visitors Monday, Tuesday and Friday morning and afternoon, Thursday morning and Sunday afternoon. No handicap is required, but you'll need to book several months ahead.

Rock Pool SWIMMING
(☑ 028-4372 5034; South Promenade; adult/child £2.50/2; ☺ 10am-5pm Mon-Fri, noon-5pm Sat, 2-5.30pm Sun Jul & Aug, weather & tides permitting) This outdoor seawater pool, dating from 1933, is at the south end of Newcastle's seafront.

Granite Trail WALKING
(www.walkni.com/walks/333/granite-trail) Beginning across the road from the water, the 5km Granite Trail is a waymarked footpath up a disused funicular railway line that once carried Mourne Mountains granite blocks to the harbour. The view from the top is worth the steep, 200m climb. Pick up a leaflet at the Newcastle Visitor Information Centre.

Soak SPA
(☑ 028-4372 6002; www.soakseaweedbaths.co.uk; 5-7 South Promenade; 1hr session from £25; ☺ 11.30am-8pm Wed-Mon Jul & Aug, 11.30am-8pm Thu-Mon Sep-Jun) If it's too cold for outdoor bathing, you can simmer away in a hot seaweed bath at Soak.

🛏 Sleeping

★**Hutt Hostel** HOSTEL £
(☑ 028-4372 2133; www.hutthostel.com; 30 Downs Rd; dm/apt £22/100; 🛜) A frisbee's throw from the beach in a renovated Victorian townhouse, the 40-bed Hutt has super amenities including a sociable common room with open fireplace, games room with pool table, self-catering kitchen and laundry. Its self-contained apartment 'the Padd' sleeps up to six people.

★**Enniskeen Country House** BOUTIQUE HOTEL ££
(☑ 028-4372 2392; www.enniskeenhotel.co.uk; 98 Bryansford Rd; s/d from £77/105; ☺ restaurant 12.30-8.30pm; 🛜) In a stately 19th-century stone manor house 2km northwest of Newcastle, delightfully old-fashioned Enniskeen has a dozen period-furnished rooms, most with mountain, sea or forest views (try for room 15, tucked in the turret). Its refined Oak Restaurant opens to a terrace and serves traditional Northern Irish cuisine, including afternoon tea using hand-churned butter and honey from a local apiary.

Briers Country House B&B ££
(☑ 028-4372 4347; www.thebriers.co.uk; 39 Middle Tollymore Rd; d £85-125, cottage £150-200; 🅿 🛜) A peaceful farmhouse B&B with views of the Mournes, Briers is just 1.5km northwest of Newcastle's town centre (signposted off the road between Newcastle and Bryansford). Huge breakfasts – vegetarian if you like – are served with a view over the garden. There's also a self-contained three-bedroom cottage (minimum three-night stay).

Slieve Donard Resort & Spa HOTEL £££
(☑ 028-4372 1066; www.hastingshotels.com; Downs Rd; s/d from £160/180; 🅿 🛜 🏊) Established in 1897, the Slieve Donard is a magnificent Victorian red-brick pile on 2.5 hectares of beachfront land, with several restaurants and a fancy spa. Adjoining Royal County Down Golf Course, it's where golf legends Tom Watson, Tiger Woods and Rory McIlroy stay when they're in town.

🍴 Eating

Olive Bizarre CAFE £
(☑ 028-4372 5576; www.olivebizarre.com; 67 South Promenade; mains £5-8; ☺ 9am-5pm; 🛜 ☑ 🍴) 🌱 Vegetarian and vegan options abound at this chilled little cafe: think soups, quiches, pies, jacket potatoes, sandwiches and daily specials such as organic falafel balls with Ballymaloe spiced tomato relish and hummus.

Niki's Kitchen Café CAFE £
(☑ 028-4372 6777; www.facebook.com/NikisKitchenCafe; 107 Central Promenade; mains £5-10; ☺ 8am-5pm; 🛜 🍴) The crowds testify to the success of this large, airy eatery, where the menu focuses on quality versions of classic cafe cuisine. There are high chairs, a kids' menu and sofas for loafing over coffee.

Strand Cafe & Bakery ICE CREAM £
(53-55 Central Promenade; ice cream from £1.50; ☺ 9am-6pm Mon-Fri, to 7.30pm Sat & Sun) Yes, there's a cafe and bakery here, but the real reason to stop by is to order a cone of award-winning ice cream, made here since 1930. Classic flavours include raspberry ripple, honeycomb, and chocolate and orange.

★**Brunel's** MODERN IRISH ££
(☑ 028-4372 3951; www.brunelsrestaurant.co.uk; 9 Bryansford Rd; mains lunch £8-10, dinner £16-28; ☺ 10am-2.30pm & 5-8pm Mon & Tue, 10am-

CLIMBING SLIEVE DONARD

You can hike to the summit of **Slieve Donard** (853m; the highest hill in Northern Ireland) from various starting points in and around Newcastle, but it's a stiff climb and you shouldn't attempt it without proper walking boots, waterproofs and a map and compass.

On a good day, the view from the top extends to the hills of Donegal, the Wicklow Mountains, the coast of Scotland, the Isle of Man and even the hills of Snowdonia in Wales. Two cairns near the summit were long believed to have been cells of St Donard, who retreated here to pray in early Christian times.

The shortest route to the top is via the River Glen from Newcastle. Begin at Donard Park car park, at the edge of town, 1km south of the bus station. At the far end of the car park, turn right through the gate and head into the woods, with the river on your left. A gravel path leads up the River Glen valley to the saddle between Slieve Donard and Slieve Commedagh. From here, turn left and follow the Mourne Wall to the summit. Return by the same route (round-trip 9km; allow at least three hours).

2.30pm & 5-9.30pm Wed-Sat, 10am-8pm Sun) 🍴
At Brunel's, chef Paul Cunningham uses locally sourced and foraged ingredients in his beautifully presented dishes, such as rhubarb-cured Kilkeel salmon with foraged wood sorrel and black olive powder, and rabbit cooked five ways. The restaurant also opens for brunch, serving dishes like buttermilk pancakes and Jameson-cured sea trout with treacle soda, scrambled eggs and rocket.

Vanilla   TAPAS **££**
(📞028-4372 2268; www.vanillarestaurant.co.uk; 67 Main St; mains £8-13; ⊘5-9pm Thu, noon-3pm & 5-10pm Fri & Sat, noon-3pm & 5-8pm Sun; 🍴) Tapas are the stars of the show at this sleek town-centre wine bar: Iberian ham and cheeses, crispy polenta chips with truffle mayo and spiced sausage roll with apricot, chilli and apple puree. There is also an eclectic selection of Spanish- and Asian-influenced main course dishes, including plenty of veggie options. Over-18s only.

ℹ Information

There's free public wi-fi along the promenade.
Newcastle Visitor Information Centre (📞028-4372 2222; www.visitmournemountains.co.uk; 10-14 Central Promenade; ⊘9.30am-7pm Mon-Sat, 1-7pm Sun Jul & Aug, 9.30am-5pm Mon-Fri, 10am-5pm Sat, 2-5pm Sun Sep-Jun; 📶) Sells local interest books and maps, and traditional and contemporary crafts.

ℹ Getting There & Away

Buses 18 and 20 run to Newcastle from Belfast's Europa Bus Centre (£8.60, 1¼ hours, at least hourly Monday to Saturday, every two hours on Sunday) via Dundrum (£2.50, 15 minutes).

Bus 240 takes the inland route from Newry to Newcastle (£8.60, 55 minutes, six daily Monday to Saturday, four on Sunday) and continues to Downpatrick (£4, 15 minutes).

Dundrum & Around

POP 1500

Sheltered Dundrum Bay is famous for its oysters and mussels, making Dundrum village a good place to stop for seafood. There are spectacular views of the Mourne Mountains and the coastline from Dundrum Castle, and a nearby nature reserve is a great spot for a walk across the dunes.

Murlough National
Nature Reserve   WILDLIFE RESERVE

(www.nationaltrust.org.uk; Dundrum Rd; car park Mar-Oct £5, Nov-Feb £3; ⊘dawn-dusk) At the Murlough National Nature Reserve, footpaths and boardwalks meander among the grassy dunes leading to a wide sandy beach with great views back towards the Mournes. It's a haul-out site for common and grey seals.

Seaforde Gardens &
Tropical Butterfly House   GARDENS

(www.seafordegardens.com; Seaforde House, Seaforde; gardens & butterfly house adult/child £10.80/6.15; ⊘10am-5pm Mon-Sat, 1-5pm Sun Apr-Sep; ♿) Adults and kids alike will enjoy this oasis in the Seaforde demesne, which is home to an 18th-century walled garden with ornamental flower beds, a hedge maze, spiral-staircase tower with viewing platform and strutting iridescent-blue peacocks. Its rainforest-like butterfly house is filled with hundreds of fluttering butterflies as well as parrots. A simple but cosy timber cafe is located by the entrance. The gardens are 7km north of Dundrum (13km north of Newcastle) on the A2.

Dundrum Castle   CASTLE

(Castle Hill) **FREE** Founded in 1177 by John de Courcy of Carrickfergus, this Norman fortress overlooks Dundrum Bay. Enter the castle for views across to the Mourne Mountains and rural County Down from de Lacey's keep.

Mourne Seafood Bar SEAFOOD ££
(📞 028-4375 1377; www.mourneseafood.com; 10 Main St; mains £8-26; ⊙ 12.30-3pm & 5-9.30pm Wed-Fri, 12.30-9.30pm Sat & Sun) Set in a Victorian house hung with local art, this friendly and informal spot serves oysters three ways, plus seafood chowder, crab, langoustines and daily fish specials, all sourced locally (including from its own shellfish beds). Its Belfast outpost (p581) has a cookery school.

❶ Getting There & Away

Bus 240 from Newcastle (£2.50, 10 minutes, seven daily Monday to Friday, six on Saturday, four on Sunday) to Downpatrick (£3.60, 15 minutes) stops in Dundrum.

Mourne Mountains

The Mourne Mountains dominate the horizon as you head south from Belfast towards Newcastle. This is one of the most beautiful corners of Northern Ireland, with a distinctive landscape of grey granite, yellow gorse and whitewashed cottages, the lower slopes of the hills latticed with a neat patchwork of drystone walls cobbled together from huge, rounded granite boulders.

The hills were made famous in a popular song penned by Irish songwriter William Percy French in 1896 – the chorus, 'Where the Mountains of Mourne sweep down to the sea', captures perfectly their scenic blend of ocean, sky and hillside.

History

The crescent of low-lying land on the southern side of the mountains is known as the Kingdom of Mourne. Cut off for centuries by its difficult approaches (the main overland route passed north of the hills), it developed a distinctive landscape and culture. Until the coast road was built in the early 19th century, the only access was on foot or by sea.

Smuggling provided a source of income in the 18th century. Boats carrying French spirits would land at night and packhorses would carry the casks through the hills to the inland road, avoiding the excise men at Newcastle. The Brandy Pad, a former smugglers' path from Bloody Bridge to Tollymore, is a popular walking route today.

⊙ Sights & Activities

The Mournes offer some of the best hillwalking and rock climbing in the North. You can buy maps at the Newcastle Visitor Information Centre (p605).

Tollymore Forest Park FOREST
(Bryansford Rd; car park £5; ⊙ 10am-dusk) FREE This scenic forest park, 3km west of Newcastle, offers lovely walks and bike rides along the River Shimna and across the Mournes' northern slopes. Victorian follies include the Clanbrassil Barn, as well as grottoes, caves, bridges and stepping stones (and yes, the park is a *Game of Thrones* filming location). You can pitch a tent at the campground here.

Castlewellan Forest Park FOREST
(Main St, Castlewellan; car park £5; ⊙ 10am-dusk) FREE Castlewellan Forest Park offers gentle walks around the castle grounds, one of the world's largest hedge mazes, the Peace Maze (entry free), and, from March to October, trout fishing in its lovely lake (three-day licence and permit £9.50). There's also a network of mountain-bike trails – see www.mountainbikeni.com for details. Bike hire is available from Life Adventure Centre.

Silent Valley Reservoir LAKE
(www.niwater.com; car/motorcycle £4.50/2, plus per adult/child £1.60/60p; ⊙ 10am-6.30pm May-Sep, to 4pm Oct-Apr) At the heart of the Mournes is the beautiful Silent Valley Reservoir, where the River Kilkeel, which supplies Belfast and County Down with water, was dammed in 1933. There are scenic, waymarked walks around the grounds and an interesting exhibition on the dam's construction.

Life Adventure Centre OUTDOORS
(📞 028-4377 0714; www.onegreatadventure.com; Grange Courtyard, Castlewellan Forest Park) If you fancy trying hillwalking, rock climbing, canoeing or a range of other outdoor activities, this centre in Castlewellan Forest Park offers one-day, have-a-go sessions for individuals, couples and families, as well as Sunday afternoon taster sessions. It also rents out canoes (£35 per two hours), kayaks (£20) and mountain bikes (from £20).

Mountpleasant Trekking Centre HORSE RIDING
(📞 028-4377 8651; www.mountpleasantcentre.com; Bannonstown Rd, Castlewellan; per hr £20; ⊙ by reservation) Catering for both experienced riders and beginners, this horse-riding and pony-trekking centre offers various guided

treks into Castlewellan Forest Park. Short and long rides, beach rides and pony trekking can also be arranged.

Hotrock Climbing Wall CLIMBING
(☑ 028-4372 2188; www.tollymore.com; 32 Hilltown Rd, Tollymore National Outdoor Centre; adult/child £5/2.50; ⊙ 10am-10pm Tue-Thu, to 5pm Fri-Mon) If the weather is wet, you can go climbing at this indoor wall; it rents out rock boots and harnesses for £3.50. The entrance is on the B180, on the western side of Tollymore Forest Park, off Bryansford Rd.

🎊 Festivals & Events

Mourne International
Walking Festival SPORTS
(www.walkni.com; 1/2/3 days £12/24/30; ⊙ late Jun) This three-day festival is a great opportunity for glorious mountain walks, with guided hikes ranging from 9km to 20km.

🛏 Sleeping & Eating

★ Mourne Lodge HOSTEL £
(☑ 07991 819700, 028-4176 5859; www.themourne lodge.com; Bog Rd, Atticall; dm/s/d from £20/45/50; P@🛜) This purpose-built 31-bed hostel offers bright and appealing budget accommodation. As well as a self-catering kitchen and barbecue patio, there's a restaurant that serves breakfast, lunch and dinner (bookings essential). It's in the village of Atticall, 6km north of Kilkeel, off the B27 Hilltown road, and 3km west of the entrance to Silent Valley.

Tollymore Forest Park CAMPGROUND £
(☑ 028-4372 2428; 176 Tullybranigan Rd; campsites £18) Many of Newcastle's camping sites are for caravans only; the nearest place you can pitch a tent is here amid the attractive scenery of Tollymore Forest Park, in the foothills of the Mourne Mountains, 3km northwest of the town centre. You can hike here (along Bryansford Ave and Bryansford Rd) in 45 minutes.

Meelmore Lodge HOSTEL £
(☑ 028-4372 6657; www.meelmorelodge.co.uk; 52 Trassey Rd, Bryansford; campsites per adult/child £10/5, dm/s/d/f £20/40/65/80; P) On the northern slopes of the Mournes, 5km west of Bryansford village, wonderfully remote Meelmore has a cosy lounge and kitchen, two four-bunk dorms, a couple of private rooms with private bathrooms, a tent-only campsite and a good cafe. You can hike into the hills from the hostel's front door.

THE MOURNE WALL
The spectacular drystone Mourne Wall marches across the summits of 15 surrounding peaks, including the highest, Slieve Donard (853m). You can walk the 2m-high, 1m-thick, 35km-long wall's entire length, or just a short section.

ℹ Getting There & Away
The summertime **Mourne Rambler bus** (Bus 405; www.translink.co.uk; unlimited day travel adult/child £9.50/4.75; ⊙ Jun-Aug) runs a circular route from Newcastle around the Mournes, making 18 stops that include Tollymore Forest Park, Castlewellan and Silent Valley.

Mourne Coast Road
The A2 coast road between Newcastle and Newry is one of the region's most scenic drives.

There are plenty of places to stop for a meal along the Mourne Coast Road, including some excellent restaurants in Newcastle and Rostrevor. The road passes through Kilkeel, the main fishing port on the Down coast; look out for Kilkeel crab, langoustines and lobster on local menus.

ℹ Getting There & Around
Bus 39 links Newry with Kilkeel (£6.20, 50 minutes, hourly Monday to Saturday, four on Sunday) via Warrenpoint and Rostrevor. From Kilkeel, bus 37 continues along the coastal road to Newcastle (£4.60, 35 minutes, hourly Monday to Saturday, eight on Sunday).

Rostrevor & Around
POP 2400

The pretty seaside resort of Rostrevor (Caislean Ruairi) is best known for its pubs and the hills of nearby Kilbroney Park, with fabulous mountain-biking trails. CS Lewis once said that the part of Rostrevor that overlooks Carlingford Lough was his idea of Narnia.

Each year in late July, folk musicians converge on the village for the week-long Fiddler's Green International Festival.

⊙ Sights & Activities

★ Kilbroney Park FOREST
(www.visitmournemountains.co.uk; Shore Rd; ⊙ car park 9am-10pm Jun-Aug, to 9pm May & Sep, to 7pm Apr & Oct, to 5pm Nov-Mar) FREE This 16-sq-km forest park has walking paths offering awesome views, as well as Northern Ireland's best

downhill mountain-biking trails. The main park entrance is 1km east of Rostrevor. From the lower car park, you can continue to the top of the forest drive, from where a 10-minute hike leads up to a superb view over the lough to Carlingford Mountain, as well as to the **Cloughmore Stone**, a 30-tonne granite boulder inscribed with Victorian-era graffiti.

If walking from town, follow Bridge St east to reach Kilbroney River; from here the **Fairy Glen** path leads along the riverbank, connecting with other trails; continue east to reach the **Narnia Trail**, a children's woodland path dotted with characters from *The Lion, the Witch and the Wardrobe* (Kilbroney was the inspiration behind CS Lewis' fantastical tale).

Bike hire and uplift are available from East Coast Adventure at the trailhead. There's also a **caravan park**, with a grass area suitable for tents (campsites with/without electricity hook-up £23/18.50).

East Coast Adventure   MOUNTAIN BIKING
(office weekdays 028-4173 8516, trail office weekends 07876 681197; www.eastcoastadventure.com; bike hire per half-/full day £30/45, uplift per half-day £17.50; bike hire by prior reservation, uplift service Sat & Sun only, plus Fri & Mon Jul-Aug) Kilbroney Park is home to Northern Ireland's best downhill mountain-biking trails; bike hire and uplift are available at the trailhead. Book ahead. See www.mountainbikeni.com/rostrevor for more info about mountain biking.

✿ Festivals & Events

Fiddler's Green
International Festival   MUSIC
(www.fiddlersgreenfestival.eu; late Jul) Folk musicians converge on the village of Rostrevor for the week-long Fiddler's Green International Festival in late July.

🛏 Sleeping & Eating

Rostrevor Inn   INN **££**
(www.therostrevorinn.com; 33 Bridge St; s £50-60, d £70-90, tr £90-110; restaurant 12.30-3pm & 5.30-9pm Mon-Sat, noon-8pm Sun) The Rostrevor Inn's seven modern rooms are a comfortable place to rest your head after a night of traditional or folk music in the inn's Crawford's Bar; the other village pubs are all within stumbling distance. The inn's restaurant (mains £11 to £20) is also excellent. It's in an 18th-century building by the Kilbroney River.

Church   CAFE **££**
(www.thechurchrostrevor.com; Cloughmore Rd; mains lunch £5-10, dinner £12-22; 10am-5pm

Mon-Thu, 10am-8pm Fri, 9am-9pm Sat, 9am-8pm Sun) This bright cafe in a converted church makes a lovely breakfast or lunch spot between walks or cycles in Kilbroney Park. From Friday to Sunday, an evening bistro menu of local seafood, burgers and steaks is served. Indoor seating includes pew benches; outdoor tables have views of the forest.

🍷 Drinking & Nightlife

⭐**Crawford's Bar**   PUB
(33 Bridge St; 11am-11pm) Crawford's is the best bar in town for local craft beers and ciders and hosts Wednesday folk nights (with music and storytelling by the fire), as well as Friday night folk sessions, live bands on Saturdays and trad music on Sundays from 4pm. It's at the Rostrevor Inn.

Corner House   PUB
(1 Bridge St; noon-midnight Mon-Sat, to 8pm Sun) A favourite with locals, this traditional pub hosts Tuesday night live music from 10pm.

ⓘ Getting There & Away

Bus 39 serves Newry (£3.60, 25 minutes, at least hourly Monday to Saturday, six on Sunday).

Warrenpoint

POP 8700

Warrenpoint (An Pointe) is a Victorian resort at the head of Carlingford Lough, with a shingle beach and beautiful mountain views. Its seaside appeal is somewhat diminished by the large industrial harbour at the west end of town, but its broad streets, main square and renovated prom warrant a stop.

Narrow Water Castle   CASTLE
About 2km northwest of Warrenpoint's town centre, you'll see Narrow Water Castle, a fine Elizabethan tower house built in 1568 to command the entrance to the River Newry. It's closed to the public, unless, that is, you stay at its apartment.

Blues on the Bay   MUSIC
(www.bluesonthebay.co.uk; late May) The spring bank holiday weekend sees some of the world's leading blues musicians descend on Warrenpoint for the Blues on the Bay festival.

Narrow Water
Castle Apartment   APARTMENT **££**
(07784 730826; www.narrowwatercastle.co.uk; Apartment 2, Narrow Water Castle; apt from £120) Within historic Narrow Water Castle, but with its own entrance, this apartment has

two bedrooms (one with a private bathroom, and both with Hungarian down pillows and beautiful linens), an antique-furnished lounge with an open fireplace, a main bathroom with a free-standing, double-slipper bath, a fully equipped kitchen and access to the castle gardens. There is a minimum three-night stay.

Whistledown Hotel BOUTIQUE HOTEL **££**
(📞 028-4175 4174; www.thewhistledownhotel.com; 6 Seaview; s £80-110, d £80-120; 🛜) In a superb waterfront setting, the Whistledown has 21 stylish bedrooms with cherry and pistachio crushed-velvet trimmings, flat-screen TVs and bathrooms with colourful designer tiling.

ⓘ Getting There & Away

Bus 39 serves Newry (£3.10, 20 minutes, at least hourly Monday to Saturday, six on Sunday).

Newry

POP 26,970

Newry has long been a frontier town, guarding the land route from Dublin to Ulster through the 'Gap of the North', the pass between Slieve Gullion and the Carlingford hills, which is still followed by the main Dublin–Belfast road and railway. Its name derives from a yew tree (An tÍúr) supposedly planted here by St Patrick.

The opening of the Newry Canal in 1742, linking the town with the River Bann at Portadown, made Newry a busy trading port, exporting coal, linen and butter. Today it's a shopping centre.

⊙ Sights

Bagenal's Castle MUSEUM
(www.bagenalscastle.com; Castle St; ⊙ 10am-4.30pm Mon-Sat, 1.30-5pm Sun) FREE Bagenal's Castle, the town's oldest surviving building, houses the **Newry & Mourne Museum** with exhibits on the Newry Canal and local archaeology, culture and folklore. The 16th-century castle was rediscovered in 2000, having been incorporated into more recent buildings; it was built for Nicholas Bagenal, grand marshal of the English army in Ireland.

Derrymore House HISTORIC BUILDING
(www.nationaltrust.org.uk; Camlough Rd; ⊙ gardens dawn-dusk) FREE Just south of Bessbrook, and 4km west of Newry, is Derrymore House. The elegant thatched cottage was built in 1776 for Isaac Corry, the Irish MP for Newry for 30 years; the Act of Union was drafted in the drawing room here in 1800. The house is

only open on a handful of days each year – call or check the National Trust website. The surrounding parkland offers scenic trails with views to the Ring of Gullion.

The grounds were laid out by John Sutherland (1745–1826), one of the most celebrated disciples of English landscape gardener Capability Brown.

🛌 Sleeping & Eating

Canal Court Hotel HOTEL **££**
(📞 028-3025 1234; www.canalcourthotel.com; 34 Merchants Quay; s £100-120, d £130-185; P @ 🛜 ☒) Overlooking Newry Canal, this 110-room hotel is relatively new but has a charmingly old-fashioned atmosphere, with leather sofas dotted around the vast wood-panelled lobby, a low-lit bar with trad music and good pub food, and a grand staircase up to the spacious rooms. Its leisure centre has a 20m pool. Staff are a pleasure to deal with.

Brass Monkey PUB FOOD **££**
(📞 028-3026 3176; 1-4 Sandy St; mains £11-24; ⊙ 10am-midnight Mon-Thu, 10am-2am Fri & Sat, noon-midnight Sun) Newry's most popular pub has a Victorian brass, brick and timber decor with contemporary lighting and velvet sofas. It serves good bar meals ranging from lasagne and burgers to seafood and steaks. There's live music on Saturday and Sunday.

★ **Finegan & Son** COFFEE
(www.facebook.com/fineganandson; 9 Kildare St; ⊙ 8.30am-5pm; 🛜) Named for the owner and his young son, this light-filled corner cafe serves some seriously good coffee. There are three single-origin drip coffees available that change weekly, as well as cold brews and flat whites from the machine. It also does good brunches and gourmet sandwiches. Book ahead for blind, five-course tasting menu events on Saturday nights (£40).

ⓘ Information

Newry Visitor Information Centre (📞 028-3031 3170; www.visitmournemountains.co.uk; Castle St; ⊙ 9am-5pm Mon-Fri, 10am-4pm Sat, plus 1-5pm Sun Jun-Sep) In Bagenal's Castle.

ⓘ Getting There & Away

BUS
Newry's bus station is on the Mall, opposite the Canal Court Hotel.

Services include the following:

Armagh £6.20, 50 minutes, hourly Monday to Saturday, three Sunday

Belfast (Europa Bus Centre) £10, 1¼ hours, at least hourly Monday to Saturday, eight Sunday

Hillsborough £7.20, 50 minutes, at least hourly Monday to Saturday, eight Sunday

Rostrevor £3.60, 25 minutes, at least hourly Monday to Saturday, six Sunday

Warrenpoint £3.10, 20 minutes, at least hourly Monday to Saturday, six Sunday

TRAIN

The train station is 2.5km northwest of the centre, on the A25; bus 341 (free for train passengers) links train arrivals and departures to the bus station.

Newry is on the line linking Dublin (£20, 1¼ hours, eight daily) and Belfast (£11.50, one hour 10 minutes, 10 Monday to Saturday, five Sunday).

Hillsborough & Around

POP 3400

The elegant little town of Hillsborough, 19km south of Belfast, was founded in the 1640s by Colonel Arthur Hill, who built a fort here to quell Irish insurgents. Fine Georgian architecture rings the square and lines Main St.

Most famously, Hillsborough Castle is the official residence of the Secretary of State for Northern Ireland, and is used to entertain visiting heads of state (US presidents George W Bush and Bill Clinton have both been guests). It is the Queen's official residence when she's in Northern Ireland.

⊙ Sights

Hillsborough Castle HISTORIC BUILDING
(⌨028-9268 1300; www.hrp.org.uk; Main St; adult/child £11.40/5.70; ⊙9.30am-6pm Apr-Oct, to 4pm Nov-Mar) The British monarch's official Northern Ireland residence is this rambling, late-Georgian mansion, which was built in 1797 for Wills Hill, the first Marquess of Downshire, and extensively remodelled in the 1830s and '40s. Hour-long guided tours take in the throne room, state drawing room and dining rooms, and the Lady Grey Room where, in 2003, Tony Blair and George W Bush held talks on Iraq. Highlights of the lovely gardens include the lime-tree walk and the restored, 18th-century walled garden.

The car park is accessed from the A1, just south of the turn-off for the village (follow signs). Last admission is one hour before closing.

Hillsborough Courthouse HISTORIC BUILDING
(The Square; ⊙9am-5.30pm Mon-Sat, 11am-4pm Sun Apr-Sep, 9.30am-3.30pm Mon-Fri Oct-Mar)

FREE Dating from 1765, this fine old Georgian market house was used as a courthouse from 1810 until 1986. It now contains a few displays describing the working of the courts.

St Malachy's Parish Church CHURCH
(www.hillsboroughparish.org.uk; Main St; ⊙8.30am-7pm) FREE Overlooking Hillsborough village is St Malachy's, a splendid 18th-century church, with twin towers at the ends of the transepts and a tall spire at the western end. A tree-lined avenue leads to the church from a statue of Arthur Hill, fourth Marquess of Downshire, at the bottom of Main St.

Hillsborough Fort HISTORIC BUILDING
(Main St; ⊙grounds 10am-4pm Mon-Sat, 11am-4pm Sun) FREE Built as an artillery fort by Colonel Hill in 1650 (William of Orange stayed here on his way to the Boyne in 1690), Hillsborough Fort was remodelled as a Gothic-style tower house in 1758. A tree-lined path opposite the Courthouse leads to the fort, which sits on the edge of Hillsborough Forest Park. Only the grounds are open to the public.

In 1771 Benjamin Franklin spent five days at the fort as the guest of Wills Hill, then Secretary of State for the Colonies. Reportedly the meeting went so badly that it helped convince Franklin that revolution was America's only option.

🛌 Sleeping & Eating

Fortwilliam Country House B&B ££
(⌨028-9268 2255; www.fortwilliamcountryhouse.com; 210 Ballynahinch Rd; s/d £60/85; Ⓟ🛜) The Fortwilliam's four luxurious rooms include the Victorian room, with rose wallpaper, a huge antique mahogany wardrobe and a view over the garden. Breakfast includes fresh eggs from the chickens in the yard, and the smell of home-baked wheaten bread wafts from the Aga stove. From Hillsborough, take the B177 towards Anahilt; it's 5.6km along on the right.

★ **Hara** MODERN IRISH ££
(⌨028-7116 1467; www.harahillsborough.co.uk; 16 Lisburn St; mains £15-28; ⊙5-9.30pm Thu, noon-2.30pm & 5-9.30pm Fri & Sat, 12.30-6.30pm Sun) Hara gets even the little details right: the wheaten bread is served warm from the oven and the side orders are divine. The menu changes regularly, but usually features unusual and creative dishes alongside more classic Irish cooking, all of it highlighting local ingredients. Service is chatty and the dining room is bright and modern. Book ahead.

Parson's Nose · MODERN IRISH ££
(www.ballooinns.com; 48 Lisburn St; mains £13-28; ⊙ kitchen noon-9pm Sun-Thu, to 10pm Fri & Sat) Housed in a beautiful Georgian building, this popular gastropub has a cosy ground-floor bar and a bright restaurant at the back, with views of the grounds of Hillsborough Castle. Upstairs, chefs whip local ingredients into appealing dishes, in a theatrical open kitchen complete with a wood-fired pizza oven.

Plough Inn · BISTRO ££
(☑ 028-9268 2985; www.ploughgroup.com; 3 The Square; mains lunch £10-13, dinner £14-16; ⊙ kitchen 11.30am-9pm Mon-Fri, 11.30am-9.30pm Sat, noon-8pm Sun) This fine old pub, with its maze of dark, wood-panelled nooks and crannies, has been offering 'beer and banter' since 1758. It serves gourmet bar lunches and evening bistro meals in the bar and upstairs dining room, where stone walls, low ceilings and a roaring fireplace make a cosy setting. There's live music on Friday and Saturday nights.

Vintage Rooms · BISTRO ££
(www.ploughgroup.com; 3 The Square; mains lunch £9-13, dinner £16.50-28; ⊙ kitchen 9am-2.30pm Mon-Thu, 9am-2.30pm & 5-9.30pm Fri & Sat, 9am-noon Sun) The Vintage Rooms is a cafe by day (serving breakfast, lunchtime sandwiches, cake, pies and scones), a cocktail bar by night, and a seafood bistro on Friday and Saturday evenings.

ⓘ Information

Hillsborough Visitor Information Centre
(☑ 028-9244 7640; www.visitlisburncastlereagh.com; The Square; ⊙ 9am-5.30pm Mon-Sat year-round, plus 11am-4pm Sun Apr-Sep) In the Georgian Hillsborough Courthouse in the centre of the village.

ⓘ Getting There & Away

Bus 238 from Belfast's Europa Bus Centre (£4, 20 minutes, at least hourly) continues to Newry (£7.20, 50 minutes).

COUNTY ARMAGH

Armagh City

POP 14,800

The attractive little cathedral city of Armagh (Ard Macha) has been an important religious centre since the 5th century, and remains the ecclesiastical capital of Ireland, the seat of both the Anglican and Roman Catholic archbishops of Armagh, and Primates of All Ireland. Their two cathedrals, both named for St Patrick, look across at each other from their respective hilltops.

History

When St Patrick began his mission to spread Christianity throughout Ireland, he chose a site close to Emain Macha (Navan Fort), the nerve centre of pagan Ulster, for his power base. In 445 he built Ireland's first stone church on a hill nearby (now home to the Church of Ireland cathedral), and later decreed that Armagh should have pre-eminence over all the churches in Ireland.

By the 8th century, Armagh was one of Europe's best-known centres of religion, learning and craftwork. The city was divided into three districts (called *trians*), centred around English, Scottish and Irish streets. Armagh's fame was its undoing, however, as the Vikings plundered the city 10 times between 831 and 1013.

The city gained a new prosperity from the linen trade in the 18th century, a period whose legacy includes a Royal School, an astronomical observatory, a renowned public library and a fine crop of Georgian architecture.

⊙ Sights

★ Armagh Robinson Library · LIBRARY
(☑ 028-3752 3142; http://armaghrobinsonlibrary.co.uk; 43 Abbey St; ⊙ 10am-1pm & 2-4pm Mon-Fri) **FREE** A first edition of *Gulliver's Travels*, published in 1726 and annotated by Swift himself, is the most prized possession of the wonderful Armagh Robinson Library, founded in 1771 by Archbishop Robinson. Other treasures include Sir Walter Raleigh's 1614 *History of the World*, the *Claims of the Innocents* (pleas to Oliver Cromwell) and engravings by Hogarth and others. The oldest manuscripts here are theological works dating from the 1480s.

Nearby, you can see ancient coins, early Christian artefacts and other curiosities at **No 5 Vicar's Hill** (☑ 028-3751 1420; www.armaghrobinsonlibrary.co.uk/wp/no-5-vicars-hill; 5 Vicar's Hill; adult/child £2/free; ⊙ 10am-1pm & 2-4pm Tue-Sat Apr-Sep, Thu-Sat Oct-Mar), a depository for Church of Ireland records.

★ St Patrick's Church of Ireland Cathedral · CATHEDRAL
(☑ 028-3752 3142; www.stpatricks-cathedral.org; Cathedral Close; adult/child £3/free; ⊙ 9am-5pm Apr-Oct, to 4pm Nov-Mar) The city's Anglican cathedral occupies the site of St Patrick's

Armagh City

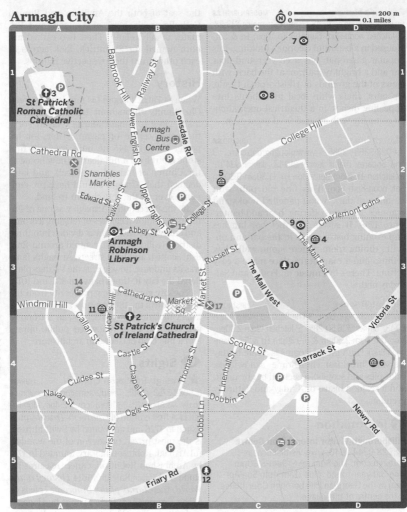

original stone church. The present cathedral's ground plan is 13th century, but the building itself is a Gothic restoration dating from 1834 to 1840. A stone slab on the exterior wall of the north transept marks the **burial place of Brian Ború**, the high king of Ireland, who died near Dublin during the last great battle against the Vikings in 1014.

Within the church are the remains of an 11th-century **Celtic Cross** that once stood nearby, and the **Tandragee Idol**, a curious granite figure dating from the Iron Age. In the south aisle is a **memorial to Archbishop Richard Robinson** (1709–94), who founded Armagh's observatory and public library.

★ **St Patrick's Roman Catholic Cathedral**   CATHEDRAL
(www.armagharchdiocese.org; Cathedral Rd; admission by donation; ⊙8.30am-7.30pm) Huge twin towers dominate the approach to Armagh's Roman Catholic Cathedral, built between 1838 and 1873 in Gothic Revival style. Inside it seems almost Byzantine, with every piece of wall and ceiling covered in coloured mosaics. The sanctuary was modernised in 1981 and has a very distinctive tabernacle holder and crucifix that seem out of place among the mosaics and statues of the rest of the church.

Armagh City

⊙ Top Sights
1 Armagh Robinson Library B3
2 St Patrick's Church of Ireland
   Cathedral.. B4
3 St Patrick's Roman Catholic
   Cathedral... A1

⊙ Sights
4 Armagh County Museum D3
5 Armagh Courthouse C2
6 Armagh Gaol...................................... D4
7 Armagh Observatory C1
8 Armagh Planetarium C1

9 Charlemont Place C3
10 Mall C3
11 No 5 Vicar's Hill A3
12 Palace Demesne Public Park B5

⊟ Sleeping
13 Armagh City Hotel C5
14 Armagh Hostel A3
15 Seven Houses..................................... B3

⊗ Eating
16 Mulberry Bistro A2
17 Uluru Bar & Grill C3

Armagh County Museum   MUSEUM
(☑ 028-3752 3070; www.nmni.com/acm; The Mall
E; ⊙10am-5pm Mon-Fri, 10am-1pm & 2-5pm Sat)
FREE Prehistoric axe heads, artefacts found in
bogs, corn dollies and straw-boy outfits, and
military costumes and equipment are among
the items on display at the county museum,
housed in a former art school on the Mall.
Don't miss the gruesome cast-iron skull that
once graced the top of the Armagh gallows.

Mall   PARK
This long grassy expanse east of Armagh's
centre was a horse-racing, cock-fighting and
bull-baiting venue until the 18th century,
when Archbishop Robinson decided that it
was all a tad vulgar for a city of learning,
and transformed it into an elegant Georgian park. It's flanked by notable buildings,
including the working and therefore closed
to the public **Armagh Courthouse** (The Mall
N), **Armagh Gaol** (The Mall S), and Georgian
terraces, including **Charlemont Place**.

Armagh Planetarium   PLANETARIUM
(☑ 028-3752 3689; www.armaghplanet.com; College Hill; exhibition area free, shows adult/child
£6/5; ⊙10am-2pm Mon, to 5pm Tue-Sat year-round,
plus 10am-5pm Sun Jul & Aug) Aimed mainly at
educating young people, the Armagh Planetarium has an interactive exhibition on space
exploration, and a digital theatre that screens
a range of spectacular half-hour shows on its
domed ceiling (prebooking is essential; check
the website for show times).

A path connects the planetarium with the
Armagh Observatory.

Armagh Observatory   OBSERVATORY
(www.armagh.ac.uk; College Hill; ⊙grounds 9.30am-
4.30pm Mon-Fri) The Armagh Observatory was
founded by Archbishop Robinson in 1789 and
is still Ireland's leading astronomical-research
institute. The observatory building is closed to

the public but the grounds (open during daylight hours) contain sundials, a scale model of
the solar system and a human orrery showing
the positions and orbits of the earth.

Palace Demesne Public Park   PARK
(www.armagh.co.uk; 1 Greenpark; ⊙park dawn-dusk,
palace 9am-5pm Mon-Fri) **FREE** This palace and
surrounding 121-hectare estate were home to
the archbishops of the Church of Ireland from
the 1770s to the 1970s. The palace now houses
Armagh's city council, but it's possible to go
inside the elegant Armstrong Room (formerly the palace dining room and now the Lord
Mayor's parlour). The palace grounds contain
walking trails and a children's playground.

🛏 Sleeping & Eating

Armagh Hostel   HOSTEL £
(☑ 028-3751 1800; www.hini.org.uk; 39 Abbey
St; dm/s/tw/f £19/31/42/48; ⊙8.30-11am &
4-9.30pm Apr-Oct, groups only Nov-Mar; ℗ 🖥)
This modern, purpose-built hostel near the
St Patrick's Church of Ireland Cathedral has
six small but comfortable twin rooms, two
family rooms and 10 small dorms (all with
private bathroom), plus TV and tea-and-
coffee facilities, a well-equipped kitchen, a
laundry, lounge and reading room.

Seven Houses   B&B ££
(☑ 028-3751 1213; www.sevenhouses.co.uk; 3 Upper
English St; d £80-120; 🖥) This lovely B&B in a
central location has two bright rooms with
period features and a one-bedroom apartment with a small kitchen and dining area.
On the ground floor there's an elegant bar
and lounge. Breakfast is in the Bagel Bean
cafe across the road.

Armagh City Hotel   HOTEL ££
(☑ 028-3751 8888; www.armaghcityhotel.com; 2
Friary Rd; s/d/tr from £99/119/180; @ 🖥 🌊) What
this immense 120-room contemporary hotel

lacks in character, it makes up for in amenities: a state-of-the-art leisure centre with a gym, steam room and swimming pool plus a beauty salon, restaurant, bar and nightclub. Executive rooms have balconies overlooking a golf course. Ask for one of the deluxe rooms with floor-to-ceiling windows and views of both of Armagh's cathedrals.

Mulberry Bistro   BISTRO £
(☑ 028-3751 0128; www.facebook.com/Mulberry-Bistro; Cathedral Rd; mains £7.50-11; ☺ 8am-8pm Mon-Sat, 9am-3pm Sun) This welcoming cafe with mulberry-coloured walls serves good breakfasts, coffee and cakes, and a lunchtime and evening menu of sandwiches, burgers, lasagne and daily specials.

★ Uluru Bar & Grill   BISTRO ££
(☑ 028-3751 8051; www.ulurubarandgrill.com; 3-5 Market St; mains lunch £7-13, dinner £13-20; ☺ 10am-9pm Mon-Fri, 9am-10pm Sat, noon-9pm Sun) Aussie-run Uluru brings a bit of antipodean flair to Armagh, with Indigenous art on the walls and a menu that includes Bondi burgers (melted Brie and bacon), chargrilled kangaroo and rustic stone-baked pizzas. It's a good place to try local craft beers and ciders, and the wine list spans the globe.

ⓘ Information

Armagh Visitor Information Centre (☑ 028-3752 1800; www.armagh.co.uk; 40 Upper English St; ☺ 9am-5.30pm Mon-Sat, 1-5.30pm Sun Apr-Sep, 9am-5pm Mon-Sat Oct-Mar)

ⓘ Getting There & Away

Bus 251 serves Belfast's Europa Bus Centre (£10, 1½ hours, hourly Monday to Friday, six Saturday, five Sunday). Bus 40 serves Newry (£6.20, 50 minutes, hourly Monday to Friday, six Saturday). Buses depart from the **Armagh Bus Centre** near the town centre.

Navan Fort

Perched atop a drumlin, Ulster's most important archaeological site, **Navan Fort** (Emain Macha; Navan Fort Rd) `FREE`, is linked in legend with the tales of Cúchulainn and named as capital of Ulster and the seat of the legendary Knights of the Red Branch.

Known as Emain Macha in Irish, Navan Fort was an important centre from around 1150 BC until the coming of Christianity; the discovery of the skull of a Barbary ape on the site indicates trading links with North Africa.

The main circular **earthwork enclosure** is a whopping 240m in diameter, and encloses a smaller circular structure and an Iron Age **burial mound**. The circular structure has intrigued archaeologists – it appears to be some sort of temple, whose roof was supported by concentric rows of wooden posts, and whose interior was filled with a vast pile of stones. Stranger still, the whole thing was set on fire soon after its construction around 95 BC, possibly for ritual purposes.

From April to September, actors in period costume are on hand to demonstrate life in an Iron Age settlement as part of the Navan Centre's excellent living history tours (included in the centre's entrance fee).

Navan Fort is 3km west of Armagh City; take bus 73 (seven daily Monday to Friday).

Navan Centre   MUSEUM
(☑ 028-3752 9644; www.armagh.co.uk; 81 Killylea Rd; adult/child £5.60/3.40; ☺ 10am-6.30pm Apr-Sep, to 4pm Oct-Mar, last entry 90min before closing, 1hr before closing in winter) The Navan Centre has exhibitions that put the Navan Fort in its historical context, and a recreation of an Iron Age settlement. From April to September, actors in period costume are on hand to demonstrate life in the Iron Age settlement as part of excellent living history tours.

Lough Neagh

Lough Neagh (pronounced 'nay') is the largest freshwater lake in Britain and Ireland, big enough to swallow the city of Birmingham (UK or Alabama, USA – either one would fit). Though vast (around 32km long and 16km wide), the lough is relatively shallow – never more than 9m deep – and is an important habitat for waterfowl. Its waters are home to the pollan, a freshwater herring found only in Ireland, and the dollaghan, a subspecies of trout unique to Lough Neagh.

Connected to the sea by the River Bann, the lough has been a vital waterway and food source since prehistoric times, and is still home to Europe's largest eel fishery. The lough's main points of access include Oxford Island in the south, Antrim town on the eastern shore, and Ardboe in the west.

Towns with hotels and B&Bs near Lough Neagh include Cookstown and Dungannon in East Tyrone and Antrim Town. Cyclists on the Loughshore Trail can download a leaflet with accommodation listings from www.cycleni.com.

OXFORD ISLAND

Despite its name, the Oxford Island (www.oxfordisland.com; 📶) FREE nature reserve is not an island but a peninsula of land on Lough Neagh's southern edge. The reserve protects a range of habitats – woodland, wildflower meadows, reedy shoreline and shallow lake margins – and is criss-crossed by walking and cycling trails, with information boards and birdwatching hides. There's also a playground and cafe at the Lough Neagh Discovery Centre.

Oxford Island is north of Lurgan, signposted from Junction 10 on the M1; you'll need your own transport. Birds to look out for include great crested grebes, little grebes, black-headed and black-backed gulls, coots and moorhens.

Half-hour boat trips on Lough Neagh (📞 028-3832 7573; Kinnego Marina, Annaloist Rd, Oxford Island; ⊙ every 30min 1.30-5pm Sat & Sun Mar-Oct) depart from Kinnego Marina, aboard the 12-seat cabin cruiser *Master McGra* (adult/child £5/3). Three-hour trips to Coney Island run on Thursday and Friday from May to August, departing at 10am and 2pm (adult/child £12.50/10.50, minimum six people). Book ahead.

In the middle of a reed-fringed pond inhabited by waterfowl, the Lough Neagh Discovery Centre (📞 028-3832 2205; www.oxfordisland.com; Oxford Island; ⊙ 9am-6pm Mon-Fri, 10am-6pm Sat & Sun Apr-Sep, to 5pm Oct-Mar; 📶) has a tourist information desk, gift shop, gallery and a great little cafe with lake-shore views.

Loughshore Trail
CYCLING
(www.cycleni.com/75/loughshore-trail) Encircling Lough Neagh is the 180km Loughshore Trail cycle route. For most of its length it follows quiet country roads set back from the shore. A downloadable leaflet on www.cycleni.com lists accommodation, places to eat and cycle-hire shops along the route.

Ring of Gullion

The Ring of Gullion (www.ringofgullion.org) is a magical region steeped in Celtic legend, centred on Slieve Gullion (Sliabh gCuillinn), where the Celtic warrior Cúchulainn is said to have taken his name after killing the dog *(cú)* belonging to the smith Culainn. The 'ring' is a necklace of rugged hills strung between Newry and Forkhill, 15km to the southwest, encircling the central whaleback ridge of Slieve Gullion. This unusual concentric formation is a geological structure known as a ring dyke.

★ Slieve Gullion Forest Park
FOREST
(www.ringofgullion.org; 89 Drumintee Rd, Meigh; ⊙ 8am-dusk; 📶) FREE A 10km scenic drive through this forest park provides picturesque views over the surrounding hills. From the parking and picnic area at the top of the drive, you can hike to the summit of Slieve Gullion (576m), the highest point in County Armagh, topped by two early Bronze Age cairns and a tiny lake (1.5km round-trip). Slieve Gullion is 10km southwest of Newry on the B113 road to Forkhill.

At the main entrance to the forest park there's a fantastic adventure playpark and a magical Giant's Lair children's storybook trail through the forest, with hidden fairy houses, teacups and soup bowls abandoned by giants and other fantastical sights along the way; the trail is inspired by local legends. There's a good cafe in the courtyard by the main car park, and a tourist information point.

Killeavy Old Churches
HISTORIC SITE
(Killeavy; Church Rd; ⊙ 24hr) FREE Surrounded by beech trees, these ruined, conjoined churches, 6km south of Camlough, were constructed on the site of a 5th-century nunnery founded by St Moninna. The eastern church dates from the 15th century and shares a gable wall with the 12th-century western one. The west door, with a massive lintel and granite jambs, may be 200 years older still. At the side of the churchyard, a footpath leads uphill to a white cross that marks St Moninna's holy well.

Synge & Byrne
CAFE £
(www.syngeandbyrne.com; 89 Drumintee Rd, Meigh; mains £5-8; ⊙ 8.30am-5pm Mon-Fri, 9am-5pm Sat & Sun; 📶📷) In the courtyard at the main entrance to Slieve Gullion Forest Park, this cafe – part of a local chain – serves soups, sandwiches, quiches and cakes.

❶ Getting There & Around

Bus 43 links Newry with Forkhill via Meigh (for Slieve Gullion Forest Park) and Killeavy (£3.10, 20 minutes, seven daily Monday to Friday, five on Sunday).

National cycle route 9 links Newry with Slieve Gullion Forest Park via the Killevy Old Churches.

Counties Londonderry & Antrim

POP 865,240 / AREA 4918 SQ KM

Best Places to Eat

➡ Ursa Minor (p641)

➡ Pyke 'n' Pommes (p625)

➡ Ocho Tapas (p633)

➡ Morton's Fish & Chips (p641)

➡ Angler's Rest (p630)

➡ Primrose Restaurant (p625)

Best Places to Stay

➡ Saltwater House (p631)

➡ Ballyeamon Barn (p647)

➡ Shola Coach House (p633)

➡ Manor House (p643)

➡ Galgorm Resort & Spa (p651)

➡ Bishop's Gate Hotel (p625)

Why Go?

Northern Ireland's spectacular north coast is a giant geology classroom. The patient work of the ocean has laid bare the black basalt and white chalk that underlies much of County Antrim, and has dissected the rocks into a scenic extravaganza of sea stacks, pinnacles, cliffs and caves. This mystical landscape's extraordinary rock formations, ruined castles and wooded glens made the region an atmospheric backdrop for the TV series *Game of Thrones,* with numerous filming locations here.

To the west, County Londonderry's chief attraction is the spirited city of Derry. Ireland's only walled city sits alongside a broad sweep of the River Foyle and echoes with centuries of often-turbulent history. Since 2010, Derry has undergone a renaissance, with a profusion of creative enterprises, public artworks and vibrant drinking and dining scenes. It also makes an ideal jumping-off point for the Wild Atlantic Way.

When to Go

➡ May is the best month for walking along the Causeway Coast, as you'll avoid the summer crowds at the Giant's Causeway and enjoy a colourful sprinkling of spring flowers.

➡ The months of June and July bring the best beach weather, and are the peak of the seabird nesting season – an ideal time to visit the Rathlin West Light Seabird Centre on gloriously remote Rathlin Island.

➡ The traditional festivities of Ballycastle's Ould Lammas Fair, dating from the 17th century, take place on the last Monday and Tuesday of August, marking the end of summer and the beginning of the harvest.

COUNTY LONDONDERRY

Derry (Londonderry)

POP 107,900

Northern Ireland's second-largest city continues to flourish as an artistic and cultural hub. The city centre was given a striking makeover for its year as the UK City of Culture 2013, with the construction of the Peace Bridge, Ebrington Sq, and the redevelopment of the waterfront and Guildhall area making the most of the city's splendid riverside setting.

There's lots of history to absorb here, from the Siege of Derry to the Battle of the Bogside and Bloody Sunday. A stroll around the 17th-century city walls that encircle the city is a must, as is a tour of the Bogside murals, along with taking in the burgeoning live-music scene in the city's lively pubs.

History

A defining moment of Derry's history was the Siege of Derry in 1688–89, an event that reverberates to this day. King James I granted the city a royal charter in 1613, and gave the London livery companies (trade guilds) the task of fortifying Derry and planting the county of Coleraine (soon to be renamed County Londonderry) with Protestant settlers.

In Britain, the Glorious Revolution of 1688 saw the Catholic King James II ousted in favour of the Protestant Dutch prince, William of Orange. Derry was the only garrison in Ireland that was not held by forces loyal to King James, and so, in December 1688, Catholic forces led by the earl of Antrim arrived on the east bank of the River Foyle, ready to seize the city. They sent emissaries to discuss terms of surrender, but in the meantime troops were being ferried across the river in preparation for an assault. On seeing this, 13 apprentice boys barred the city gates with a cry of 'There'll be no surrender!'.

And so, on 7 December 1688, the Siege of Derry began. For 105 days the Protestant citizens of Derry withstood bombardment, disease and starvation (the condition of the besieging forces was not much better). By the time a relief ship burst through and broke the siege, an estimated half of the city's inhabitants had died. In the 20th century, the Siege of Derry became a symbol of Ulster Protestants' resistance to rule by a Catholic Irish Republic, and 'No surrender!' remains a Loyalist battle cry to this day. The Siege Museum (p620) commemorates the events of the siege.

In the 19th century, Derry was one of the main ports of emigration to the US, a fact commemorated by *Emigrants,* the Eamonn O'Doherty–designed sculptures depicting an emigrant family standing on Derry Quay.

Derry was a flashpoint during the Troubles, particularly during the Battle of the Bogside and Bloody Sunday. More recently, its role as the UK City of Culture 2013 has helped revitalise the city.

In 2019, rumblings of unrest returned. In January a car bomb was detonated outside a courthouse on Bishop St, and in April journalist Lyra McKee was killed in gunfire during a night of rioting in the Creggan estate; dissident republican group the New IRA later acknowledged responsibility and apologised to her family for her death.

⊙ Sights

⊙ Walled City

Derry's walled city is Ireland's earliest example of town planning. It's thought to have been modelled on the French Renaissance town of Vitry-le-François, designed in 1545 by Italian engineer Hieronimo Marino – both are based on the grid plan of a Roman military camp, with two main streets at right angles to each other, and four city gates, one at either end of each street.

★ **Derry's City Walls** WALLS
(⊙dawn-dusk) FREE The best way to get a feel for Derry's layout and history is to walk the 1.5km circumference of the city's walls. Completed in 1619, Derry's city walls are 8m high and 9m thick, and are the only city walls in Ireland to survive almost intact. The four original gates (Shipquay, Ferryquay, Bishop's and Butcher's) were rebuilt in the 18th and 19th centuries, when three new gates (New, Magazine and Castle) were added.

The walls were built under the supervision of the Honourable The Irish Society, an organisation created in 1613 by King James and the London livery companies to fund and oversee the fortification of Derry and the plantation of the surrounding county with Protestant settlers. The society still exists today (though now its activities are mainly charitable) and it still owns Derry's city walls.

Derry's nickname, the Maiden City, derives from the fact that the walls have never been breached by an invader.

Counties Londonderry & Antrim Highlights

1 **Giant's Causeway** (p636) Hiking the Causeway Coast to the other-worldly collection of hexagonal rocks.

2 **Rathlin Island** (p642) Spotting seabirds and seals on the remote, rugged island.

3 **Derry** (p617) Discovering ancient walls, modern murals, fabulous dining and foot-stomping music in this history-steeped city.

4 **Carrick-a-Rede Rope Bridge** (p637) Wobbling across the narrow, swaying bridge.

5 **Ballycastle seafood and craft beer** (p641) Sampling Atlantic seafood and washing it down with local craft beers.

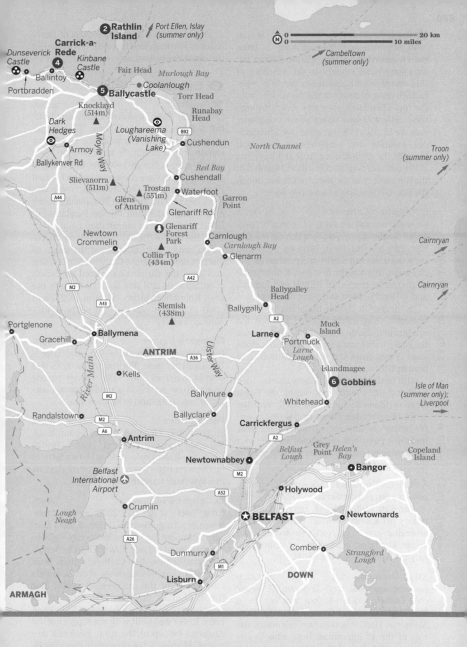

2 Rathlin Island   Port Ellen, Islay (summer only)

Carrick-a-Rede 4   Kinbane Castle

Dunseverick Castle

Ballintoy

Portbradden

Fair Head   *Murlough Bay*

● Coolanlough

5 Ballycastle   Torr Head

Knocklayd (514m) ▲

Dark Hedges

Armoy

Ballykenver Rd

Slievanorra (511m) ▲

Loughareema (Vanishing Lake)   Cushendun

Runabay Head

North Channel

Troon (summer only)

Cambeltown (summer only)

0   20 km
0   10 miles

B92

Red Bay

Cushendall

Trostan (551m) ▲   Waterfoot

Garron Point

Glens of Antrim   Glenariff Rd

Newtown Crommelin

Glenariff Forest Park

Collin Top (434m) ▲

Carnlough

Carnlough Bay

Glenarm

A42

A44

M2

A43

Slemish (438m) ▲

Ballygalley Head

Ballygalley

A2

Portglenone

Gracehill ●

Ballymena ●

Kells ●

River Main

ANTRIM

A36

Ulster Way

Larne

Muck Island

Portmuck

Larne Lough

Islandmagee

6 Gobbins

Isle of Man (summer only); Liverpool

Cairnryan

Cairnryan

M2

Ballynure ●

Whitehead ●

Randalstown ●

M2

A6

Ballyclare ●

Carrickfergus

A2

Antrim ●

Newtownabbey ●

Belfast International Airport

Crumlin ●

Lough Neagh

M2

A52

Belfast Lough

Grey Point

Helen's Bay

Bangor

Copeland Island

Holywood ●

☆ **BELFAST**

Newtownards ●

A26

Dunmurry ●

Comber ●

Strangford Lough

M1

DOWN

Lisburn ●

ARMAGH

---

6 Gobbins (p648) Crossing tubular bridges on a dramatic cliff walk.

7 Portrush (p632) Surfing the Atlantic breakers and golfing at the prestigious Royal Portrush Golf Club, host of the 2019 Open Championship.

8 Old Bushmills Distillery (p634) Learning the secrets of Irish whiskey making on a behind-the-scenes tour.

9 Downhill Demesne (p630) Soaking up spectacular coastal views from Mussenden Temple, one of the region's many iconic *Game of Thrones* filming locations.

★ Tower Museum   MUSEUM

(www.derrystrabane.com/towermuseum; Union Hall Pl; adult/child £3/1.50; ⊙10am-5.30pm, last entry 4pm) Head straight to the 5th floor of this award-winning museum inside a replica 16th-century tower house for a view from the top. Then work your way down through the excellent **Armada Shipwreck** exhibition, and the **Story of Derry**, where well-thought-out exhibits and audiovisuals lead you through the city's history, from the founding of the monastery of St Colmcille (Columba) in the 6th century to the Battle of the Bogside in the late 1960s. Allow at least two hours.

St Columb's Cathedral   CATHEDRAL

(www.stcolumbscathedral.org; 17 London St; suggested donation £2; ⊙9am-5pm Mon-Sat Mar-Oct, 10am-2pm Nov-Feb) Built between 1628 and 1633 from the same grey-green schist as the city walls, this was the first post-Reformation church to be erected in Britain and Ireland, and is Derry's oldest surviving building.

In the **porch** (under the spire, by the St Columb's Court entrance) you can see the original foundation stone of 1633 that records the cathedral's completion. The smaller stone inset comes from the original church built here in 1164.

Also in the porch is a hollow mortar shell fired into the churchyard during the Great Siege of 1688–89; inside the shell were the terms of surrender. The neighbouring **chapter house** contains more historical artefacts, including paintings, old photos and the four huge padlocks used to secure the city gates in the 17th century.

Centre for Contemporary Art   GALLERY

(www.cca-derry-londonderry.org; 10-12 Artillery St; ⊙noon-6pm Tue-Sat) FREE Derry's contemporary art gallery provides a showcase for emerging artists in Northern Ireland and stages changing exhibitions of contemporary art from around the world.

Siege Museum   MUSEUM

(www.thesiegemuseum.org; 13 Society St; adult/child £4/free; ⊙10am-4.30pm Mon-Sat) In a building adjoining the Apprentice Boys Memorial Hall, this museum celebrates the role of the 13 apprentice boys who in December 1688 locked the city gates against the approaching Jacobite army. Derry was surrounded and during the 105-day siege no supplies could reach the city, its starving citizens resorting to eating dogs and rats until English ships brought relief.

The Protestant Apprentice Boys of Derry Association marches in commemoration of the event every August.

⊙ Outside the Walls

★ Guildhall   NOTABLE BUILDING

(☑028-7137 6510; www.derrystrabane.com/Guildhall; Guildhall St; ⊙10am-5.30pm) FREE Standing just outside the city walls, the neo-Gothic Guildhall was originally built in 1890, then rebuilt after a fire in 1908. Its fine stained-glass windows were presented by the London livery companies, and its clock tower was modelled on London's Big Ben. Inside, there's a historical exhibition on the Plantation of Ulster, and a tourist information point.

As the seat of the old Londonderry Corporation, which institutionalised the policy of discriminating against Catholics for housing and jobs, the Guildhall incurred the wrath of nationalists and was bombed twice by the Irish Republican Army (IRA) in 1972. From 2000 to 2005 it was the seat of the Bloody Sunday Inquiry.

Ebrington Square   SQUARE

Originally a 19th-century fort, and later a British Army base, Ebrington Barracks was demilitarised in 2003. The former parade ground now serves as a public square, performance venue and exhibition space.

Peace Bridge   BRIDGE

Sinuous and elegant, this 2011-completed, S-shaped pedestrian and cyclist bridge spans the River Foyle, linking the walled city on the west bank to Ebrington Sq on the east in a symbolic handshake.

St Columba's Church   CHURCH

(Long Tower; ☑028-7126 2301; www.longtower-church.org; Long Tower St; ⊙9am-8.30pm Mon-Sat, 7.30am-7pm Sun) Outside the city walls to the southwest is Long Tower Church, Derry's first post-Reformation Catholic church. Built in 1784 in neo-Renaissance style, it stands on the site of the medieval Teampall Mór (Great Church), built in 1164, whose stones were used to help build the city walls in 1609. Long Tower was built with the support of the Anglican bishop at the time, Frederick Augustus Harvey, who presented the capitals for the four Corinthian columns framing the ornate high altar.

Hands Across the Divide   MONUMENT

As you enter the city across Craigavon Bridge, the first thing you see is the *Hands*

Across the Divide monument. This striking bronze sculpture of two men reaching out to each other symbolises the spirit of reconciliation and hope for the future; it was unveiled in 1992, 20 years after Bloody Sunday.

◉ Bogside

The Bogside district, to the west of the walled city, developed in the 19th and early 20th centuries as a working-class, predominantly Catholic, residential area. By the 1960s, its serried ranks of small, terrace houses had become overcrowded and beset by poverty and unemployment, a focus for the emerging Civil Rights Movement and a hotbed of nationalist discontent.

In August 1969, the three-day Battle of the Bogside – a running street battle between local youths and the Royal Ulster Constabulary (RUC) – prompted the UK government to send British troops into Northern Ireland. The residents of the Bogside and neighbouring Brandywell districts – 33,000 of them – declared themselves independent of the civil authorities and barricaded the streets to keep the security forces out. 'Free Derry', as it was known, was a no-go area for the police and army, its streets patrolled by IRA volunteers. In January 1972, the area around Rossville St witnessed the horrific events of Bloody Sunday (p628). 'Free Derry' ended with Operation Motorman on 31 July 1972, when thousands of British troops and armoured cars moved in to occupy the Bogside.

The area's population is currently around 8000, following extensive redevelopment that has seen the old houses and flats demolished and replaced with modern housing.

★ **People's Gallery Murals**   PUBLIC ART
(Rossville St) The 12 murals that decorate the gable ends of houses along Rossville St, near Free Derry Corner, are popularly referred to as the People's Gallery. They are the work of 'the Bogside Artists' (Kevin Hasson, Tom Kelly, and William Kelly, who passed away in 2017). The three men lived through the worst of the Troubles in Bogside. The murals can be clearly seen from the northern part of the City Walls.

Mostly painted between 1997 and 2001, the murals commemorate key events in the Troubles, including the Battle of the Bogside, Bloody Sunday, Operation Motorman and the 1981 hunger strike. The most powerful images are those painted largely in monochrome, consciously evoking journalistic imagery: *Operation Motorman,* showing a British soldier

breaking down a door with a sledgehammer; *Bloody Sunday,* with a group of men led by local priest Father Daly carrying the body of Jackie Duddy (the first fatality on that day); and *The Petrol Bomber,* a young boy wearing a gas mask and holding a petrol bomb.

The most moving image is *The Death of Innocence,* which shows the radiant figure of 14-year-old schoolgirl Annette McGavigan, killed in crossfire between the IRA and the British Army on 6 September 1971, the 100th victim of the Troubles. Representing all the children who died in the conflict, she stands against the brooding chaos of a bombed-out building, the roof beams forming a crucifix in the top right-hand corner. At the left, a downward-pointing rifle, broken in the middle, stands for the failure of violence, while the butterfly symbolises resurrection and the hope embodied in the peace process.

The final mural in the sequence, completed in 2004, is the *Peace Mural,* a swirling image of a dove (symbol of peace and of Derry's patron saint, Columba) rising out of the blood and sadness of the past towards the sunny yellow hope of a peaceful future.

Museum of Free Derry   MUSEUM
(www.museumoffreederry.org; 55 Glenfada Park; adult/child £6/5; ⊙9.30am-4.30pm Mon-Fri, 1-4pm Sat year-round, plus 1-4pm Sun Jul-Sep) Just off Rossville St, this excellent museum chronicles the history of the Bogside, the Civil Rights Movement and the events of Bloody Sunday through photographs, newspaper reports, film clips, interactive displays and the accounts of firsthand witnesses, including some of the original photographs that inspired the murals of the nearby People's Gallery.

Free Derry Corner   MONUMENT
(cnr Fahan & Rossville Sts) The Free Derry Corner, where the gable end of a house painted with the famous slogan 'You are Now Entering Free Derry' still stands, is all that remains of a row of terraced houses in the old Bogside district.

Bloody Sunday Memorial   MONUMENT
(Joseph Pl) A simple granite obelisk that commemorates the 14 civilians who were shot dead by the British Army on Bloody Sunday, 30 January 1972.

Hunger Strikers' Memorial   MONUMENT
(Rossville St) The H-shaped Hunger Strikers' Memorial is near the Free Derry Corner.

Derry

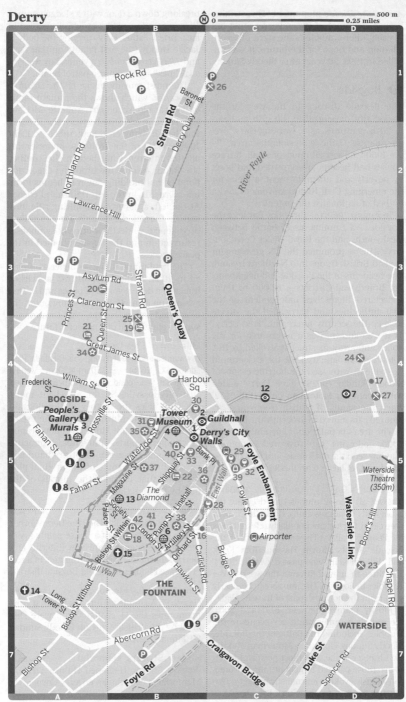

River Foyle

Rock Rd

Strand Rd

Baronet St

Derry Quay

26

Northland Rd

Lawrence Hill

Queen's Quay

Asylum Rd

Strand Rd

Princes St

Clarendon St

Queen St

20

25
19

21

Great James St

34

William St

Frederick St

Harbour Sq

12

24

17

7

27

BOGSIDE

People's Gallery Murals

3

Rossville St

30

Tower Museum

2

Guildhall

11

35

31

4

Derry's City Walls

1

5

Fahan St

10

Waterloo St

40

33

Bank Pl

29

32

Foyle Embankment

8

Fahan St

Magazine St

37

Shipquay St

22

36

39

East Wall

The Diamond

13

Society St

Palace St

42

41

Pump St

Linehall St

38

28

18

London St

6

Artillery St

Foyle St

Bishop St Within

15

Orchard St

Airporter

Waterside Theatre (350m)

Waterside Link

Bond's Hill

Mall Wall

Carlisle Rd

Hawkin St

Bridge St

23

Chapel Rd

14

Long Tower St

Bishop St Without

THE FOUNTAIN

9

WATERSIDE

Bishop St

Abercorn Rd

Foyle Rd

Craigavon Bridge

Duke St

Spencer Rd

Derry

👉 Tours

Free Derry Tours   CULTURAL
(📞07793 285972; www.freederry.tours) The Museum of Free Derry offers walking tours of the Bogside, taking in the People's Gallery murals, Free Derry Corner, the Hunger Strikers' Memorial and the Bloody Sunday Memorial.

Made in Derry Food Tour   FOOD & DRINK
(www.madeinderryfoodtour.com; per person £50; ⊘noon Sat) Four-hour tours of Derry's emerging artisan food and drink scene, meeting chefs and producers and sampling 20 local specialities – such as cheeses and craft beer – along the way. The tour starts outside the Eighty81 building on Ebrington Sq. Book ahead.

City Walking Tours   WALKING
(📞028-7127 1996; www.derrycitytours.com; Carlisle Rd; adult/under 12yr £4/free; ⊘Historic Derry tours 10am, noon, 2pm and 4pm year-round) One-hour Historic Derry walking tours start from outside the Carlisle Rd entrance to the Foyleside Shopping Centre. There are also tours of the Bogside and of Derry's murals. Recommended.

🎊 Festivals & Events

City of Derry Jazz Festival   MUSIC
(www.cityofderryjazzfestival.com; ⊘late Apr/early May) Five days of jazz at various venues around the city.

Walled City Marathon   SPORTS
(www.thewalledcitymarathon.com; ⊘Jun) Runners take on the challenge of the 42km course that takes them through Derry city and rural villages along the banks of the River Foyle.

Gasyard Féile   CULTURAL
(www.facebook.com/gasyardwallfeile; ⊘Aug) Live music, street performers, carnival, theatre and Irish-language events all feature at this major cultural festival.

City of Derry Guitar Festival   MUSIC
(www.facebook.com/cityofderryguitarfestival; Culturlann Ui Chanain; ⊘late Aug) Over two days, Culturlann Ui Chanain hosts performances and master classes by guitarists from around the world, from all genres including classical, acoustic, electric, flamenco and bass.

Halloween Carnival   CARNIVAL
(www.derryhalloween.com; ⊘25 Oct-1 Nov) The city dresses up for Ireland's biggest street

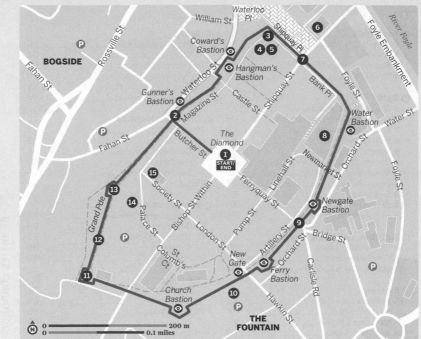

Walking Tour
Derry's Walled City

START THE DIAMOND
END THE DIAMOND
LENGTH 2KM; ONE HOUR

Start your walk at the Diamond, Derry's central square, dominated by the ❶ **war memorial**. Head along Butcher St, where the town's butchers once had their shops, to ❷ **Butcher's Gate**, and climb the steps to the left of the gate to the top of the city walls.

Stroll downhill to ❸ **Magazine Gate**, named for the powder magazine that used to be close by. Inside the walls is the modern ❹ **O'Doherty's Tower**, housing the excellent ❺ **Tower Museum** (p620); outside the walls stands the red-brick, neo-Gothic ❻ **Guild-hall** (p620).

The River Foyle used to come up to the northeastern wall here. In the middle is the ❼ **Shipquay Gate**. The walls turn southwest and climb beside the ❽ **Millennium Forum** (p627) to the ❾ **Ferryquay Gate**, where the apprentice boys barred the gate at the start of the Great Siege of 1688–89.

The stretch of wall beyond overlooks the ❿ **Fountain housing estate**, the last significant Protestant community on the western bank of the Foyle. The round, empty gravel area on the ground outside New Gate is where a 10m-high bonfire is lit on the night before the annual Apprentice Boys' march

Continue around the southern stretch of wall to the ⓫ **Double Bastion** at the south-western corner, home to the most famous of the cannons used during the Siege of Derry. The next section of wall is known as the ⓬ **Grand Parade**, and offers an excellent view of the murals painted by the Bogside Artists.

An empty plinth on ⓭ **Royal Bastion** marks the former site of a monument to the Reverend George Walker, joint governor of the city during the Great Siege; it was blown up by the IRA in 1973. Behind the Royal Bastion is the 1872 Church of Ireland ⓮ **Chapel of St Augustine**, built on the site of St Colmcille's 6th-century monastery. A little further along is the ⓯ **Apprentice Boys' Memorial Hall**, with a high mesh fence to protect it from paint bombs hurled from below.

party, which features fireworks, live music, a haunted house, ghost tours and more.

Foyle Film Festival FILM
(www.foylefilmfestival.org; Nerve Centre, 7-8 Magazine St; ⊙ mid-Nov) This week-long event is the North's biggest film festival.

🛏 Sleeping

Hostel Connect HOSTEL £
(☑ 028-7137 2101; www.hostelconnect.co.uk; 51 Strand Rd; dm £15-18, d £34-45; @ �) This bright, centrally located hostel offers small but neat doubles and twins as well as six-, nine- and 15-bed dorms with wooden bunks. There's a big living room, a kitchen for preparing meals, and a breakfast of bagels, fruit and toast is included. All rooms share bathrooms.

★ Merchant's House B&B ££
(☑ 028-7126 9691; www.thesaddlershouse.com; 16 Queen St; d from £75; @ �) This historic, Georgian-style townhouse is a gem of a B&B. It has an elegant lounge and dining room with marble fireplaces and antique furniture, TV, coffee-making facilities, homemade marmalade at breakfast and bathrobes in the bedrooms (some rooms have shared bathroom). Call at Saddler's House first to pick up a key.

Beech Hill Country House HISTORIC HOTEL ££
(☑ 028-7134 9279; www.beech-hill.com; 32 Ardmore Rd; s/d from £65/85; �) Secluded in a picturesque patch of woodland 4.3km southeast of Derry, this wonderfully atmospheric 18th-century manor house is surrounded by magnificent gardens and steeped in history – it was a WWII base for US marines, and former US president Bill Clinton stayed here several times. All 30 rooms incorporate Georgian-era colours and furnishings. The lake-view restaurant is excellent.

Saddler's House B&B ££
(☑ 028-7126 9691; www.thesaddlershouse.com; 36 Great James St; d from £75; �) Centrally located within a five-minute walk of the walled city, this friendly B&B is set in a lovely Victorian townhouse. All seven rooms have private bathrooms, and you get to enjoy a huge breakfast in the family kitchen.

Shipquay Hotel HOTEL ££
(☑ 028-7126 7266; www.shipquayhotel.com; 15-17 Shipquay St; s/d from £105/130; �) Housed in a historic building – a former bank dating from 1895 – this contemporary boutique hotel is located right in the middle of town, close to the city's sights and nightlife. Rooms are well

appointed, service is top-notch, breakfast is a banquet and the restaurant is excellent.

Arkle House B&B ££
(☑ 028-7127 1156; www.derryhotel.co.uk; 2 Coshquin Rd; s/d £55/65; P �) 2km northwest of the city centre, this grand Victorian house is set in private gardens and offers five large, lush bedrooms and a private kitchen.

★ Bishop's Gate Hotel HOTEL £££
(☑ 028-7114 0300; www.bishopsgatehotelderry.com; 24 Bishop St; s/d/ste from £120/130/210) The former Northern Counties gentleman's club has been transformed into a stylish 30-room hotel located within Derry's city walls. Rooms combine period features with plush carpets and contemporary furnishings in greys and yellows. Leather armchairs, wood panelling and open fires create a cosy atmosphere in the bar, and there's good food available at the restaurant. Staff are friendly and helpful.

🍴 Eating

Derry is gaining a reputation as a foodie city, with several excellent restaurants specialising in fresh local produce opening in recent years.

★ Pyke 'n' Pommes STREET FOOD £
(No. 57; www.pykenpommes.ie; 57 Strand Rd; 1/2/3 tacos £5/8/10, burgers £8.50-13; ⊙ noon-9pm Sun-Thu, to 10pm Fri & Sat; 🖉) For years Pyke 'n' Pommes POD has been serving up the best food in Derry; in 2019 chef Kevin Pyke opened this licensed restaurant, serving a mouth-watering menu of tacos (fillings include fried cauliflower and tequila-battered haddock), and burgers like the Legenderry (made with wagyu beef) and the Veganderry (chickpeas, lemon and coriander).

The dining room has a street vibe, with industrial touches and roughly finished concrete walls.

Pyke 'n' Pommes POD STREET FOOD £
(www.pykenpommes.ie; behind Foyle Marina, off Baronet St; mains £4-16; ⊙ noon-8.30pm Fri & Sat, to 6pm Sun-Thu; 🖉) Stop by this quayside shipping container to sample Kevin Pyke's delectable street food: his signature Notorious PIG (pulled pork, crispy slaw, beetroot and crème fraiche), the Veganderry burger, the Legenderry Burger, and tacos.

★ Primrose Restaurant IRISH ££
(☑ 028-7137 3744; www.primrose-ni.com; 53-55 Strand Rd; mains lunch £6.50-11.50, dinner £12-18; ⊙ 8am-5pm Mon & Tue, 8am-9.30pm Wed-Sat, 10am-5pm Sun) In its chic new Strand Rd premises,

DERRY/LONDONDERRY

Derry-Londonderry is a city with two names. Nationalists always use Derry, and the 'London' part of the name is often crossed through on road signs. Some staunch Unionists insist on Londonderry, which is still the city's (and county's) official name. All the same, most people, regardless of political persuasion, call it Derry in everyday speech.

The settlement was originally named Doíre Calgaigh (Oak Grove of Calgach), after a pagan warrior-hero; in the 10th century it was renamed Doíre Colmcille (Oak Grove of Columba), in honour of the 6th-century saint who established the first monastic settlement here. In the following centuries, the name was shortened and anglicised to Derrie or Derry. In 1613, in recognition of the Corporation of London's role in the 'plantation' of northwest Ulster with Protestant settlers, Derry was granted a royal charter and was renamed Londonderry.

A new County Londonderry was created from what was originally County Coleraine, along with parts of Tyrone and Antrim; unlike the city, there has never been an officially sanctioned county called Derry. Nevertheless, those with nationalist leanings, including the county's Gaelic football team, prefer to use County Derry.

Traditionally, road signs in Northern Ireland point to Londonderry and those in the Republic point to Derry (or Doíre in Irish). Attempts by the council to change the city's official name to Derry were foiled by a 2007 High Court ruling that the city's legal name could only be changed by legislation or royal prerogative. In 2015, Derry and Strabane District Council again voted in favour of a name change, but for the time being the clunky 'Derry-Londonderry' moniker remains the destination announced on trains and buses and used by most of the city's businesses.

Primrose has expanded beyond home baking and brunches. Owners Ciaran (a butcher) and Melanie (a baker) Breslin have designed a sophisticated lunch and dinner bistro menu using local ingredients; look out for cider-battered Donegal haddock and house butchery beef burger, plus brunch items, scones, cakes and desserts, all made fresh daily.

★ **Walled City Brewery** GASTROPUB ££
(☑ 028-7134 3336; www.walledcitybrewery.com; 70 Ebrington Sq; mains £14-25; ⊙kitchen 5-11pm Tue-Thu, 12.30-3pm & 5-11pm Fri & Sat, 2-8pm Sun; ♠) Housed in the former army barracks on Ebrington Sq, Walled City Brewery is a craft brewery and restaurant run by master brewer and Derry local James Huey. As well as having 10 craft beers on tap, Walled City serves top-notch grub, such as house-smoked pork neck. It also runs home-brewing courses.

Ollies IRISH ££
(☑ 028-7132 9751; www.facebook.com/loveollies; 59 Ebrington Sq; mains £10.50-17; ⊙9am-9pm; ♠♪) All the food at this bright cafe/bistro is homemade using local ingredients, from the fluffy pancakes and waffles at breakfast to the creamy Greencastle seafood chowder and the breads, cakes and pastries. There's a good range of vegetarian and gluten-free options.

Brown's Restaurant IRISH £££
(☑ 028-7134 5180; www.brownsrestaurant.com; 1 Bond's Hill, Waterside; 3 courses £35; ⊙noon-3pm Tue-Sat, 5.30-9pm Tue-Thu, 5-10pm Fri & Sat, noon-3pm Sun; ♠) ♪ From the outside, Brown's may not have the most promising appearance, but step inside and you're in an elegant little enclave of brandy-coloured banquettes and ornate metal light fittings, with vintage monochrome prints adorning the walls. The ever-changing menu is a gastronome's delight, making creative use of fresh local produce.

🍷 Drinking & Nightlife

Derry's pubs are friendly and atmospheric and there is live music happening somewhere every night of the week. Most bars and pubs are within crawling distance of each other in and around the walled city, but across the Peace Bridge, a number of new places have opened on Ebrington Sq.

★ **Peadar O'Donnell's** PUB
(www.facebook.com/Peadarsderry; 59-63 Waterloo St; ⊙11.30am-1.30am Mon-Sat, 12.30pm-12.30am Sun) Done up as a typical Irish pub and grocery (with shelves of household items, shopkeeper's scales on the counter and a museum's-worth of old bric-a-brac), Peadar's has rowdy traditional-music sessions every night and often on weekend afternoons as well. The adjacent Gweedore Bar hosts live rock bands every night, and a Saturday-night disco upstairs.

Sandino's Cafe-Bar
BAR
(www.sandinoscafebar.com; 1 Water St; ⊙11.30am-1am Mon-Sat, noon-midnight Sun) From the posters of Che to the Free Palestine flag to the fairtrade coffee and gluten-free beer, this relaxed cafe-bar exudes a liberal, left-wing vibe. DJs spin from Thursday to Saturday in Club Havana; there's regular live music, too.

Guildhall Taphouse
BAR
(www.facebook.com/Guildhalltaphouse; 4 Custom House St; ⊙noon-1am Mon-Sat, to midnight Sun) Housed in a wooden-beamed, 19th-century building brightened with fairy lights, the Taphouse is a cosy place to sample an excellent selection of craft beers or a sophisticated cocktail. There's regular live music including trad sessions every Wednesday.

Sugar
CLUB
(www.facebook.com/sugarniteclub; 33 Shipquay St; ⊙11pm-2am Wed, Fri & Sat) Above Quays Bar, Derry's hottest club spreads over two floors, and has the city's largest rooftop terrace. Guest and resident DJs play; see the Facebook page for details of upcoming nights.

Blackbird
PUB
(☑028-7136 2111; www.blackbirdderry.com; 24 Foyle St; ⊙11.30am-1am Mon-Sat, to midnight Sun) With wooden booths, leather sofas and roaring fires, the Blackbird hasn't sacrificed comfort and cosiness in its bid to create a modern space. The kitchen serves snacks, wraps and burgers (mains £8 to £8.50). There's a good cocktail list, too. Live music most weekends.

Badgers Bar
PUB
(16-18 Orchard St; ⊙11.30am-1am Mon-Sat, noon-1am Sun) A fine polished-brass and stained-glass Victorian pub with wood-panelled nooks and crannies, and an outdoor terrace, Badgers overflows at lunchtime with shoppers enjoying quality pub grub, and offers a quiet haven in the evenings.

☆ Entertainment

Cultúrlann Uí Chanáin
ARTS CENTRE
(www.culturlann.org; 37 Great James St; ⊙8am-5pm Mon-Fri, 9am-4pm Sat) This cultural centre devoted to the Irish language stages performances of traditional Irish music, poetry and dance.

Gweedore Bar
LIVE MUSIC
(www.facebook.com/GweedoreRocks; 59-63 Waterloo St; ⊙11.30am-1.30am Mon-Sat, 12.30pm-12.30am Sun) Adjoining Peadar O'Donnell's, the Gweedore Bar hosts live rock bands every night, while the DJ bar upstairs is home to a regular Saturday-night disco.

Playhouse
THEATRE
(www.derryplayhouse.co.uk; 5-7 Artillery St; ⊙box office 10am-5.30pm Mon-Fri, to 4pm Sat) Housed in beautifully restored former school buildings with an award-winning modern extension at the rear, this community arts centre stages music, dance and theatre by local and international performers.

Nerve Centre
ARTS CENTRE
(www.nerve-centre.org.uk; 7-8 Magazine St) Set up in 1990 to encourage young, local talent in the fields of music and film, the Nerve Centre has a performance area, with live music at weekends, a theatre and an art-house cinema.

Millennium Forum
THEATRE
(www.millenniumforum.co.uk; 98 Newmarket St) With a capacity of 1000 and Ireland's largest theatre stage, this auditorium is a major venue for dance, drama, opera and musicals.

Waterside Theatre
THEATRE
(www.watersidetheatre.com; Glendermott Rd) Housed in a former factory 500m east of the River Foyle, Waterside stages drama, dance, comedy, children's theatre and live music.

🛍 Shopping

★ Smart Swag
DESIGN
(www.smartswag.co.uk; 12 London St; ⊙10am-6pm Tue-Sat) Run by local artists and designers, Smart Swag sells original and unusual pieces such as jewellery made from vinyl records, upcycled furniture, screen-printed T-shirts and dresses, and traditional Irish tapestries that have been given a contemporary twist. The illustrations of Derry city make great souvenirs.

Cool Discs Music
MUSIC
(www.cooldiscsmusic.com; 6 Lesley House, Foyle St; ⊙9am-6pm Mon-Thu & Sat, 9am-8pm Fri, 2-8pm Sun) One of Northern Ireland's best independent record shops, Cool Discs has a wide selection of music by Irish artists old and new and sells concert tickets.

Craft Village
ARTS & CRAFTS
(www.derrycraftvillage.com; off Shipquay St; ⊙hours vary) A handful of craft shops sell Derry crystal, handwoven cloth, ceramics, jewellery and other local craft items in this renovated courtyard. One of the best is **Derry Designer Makers**, a collective of 15 artists and craftspeople who take turns staffing the shop. Enter from Shipquay St, Magazine St or Tower Museum.

SUNDAY, BLOODY SUNDAY

Tragically echoing Dublin's Bloody Sunday of November 1920, when British security forces shot dead 14 spectators at a Gaelic football match in Croke Park, Derry's Bloody Sunday was a turning point in the history of the Troubles.

On Sunday 30 January 1972, the Northern Ireland Civil Rights Association organised a peaceful march through Derry in protest against internment without trial, which had been introduced by the British government the previous year. Some 15,000 people marched from Creggan through the Bogside towards the Guildhall, but they were stopped by British Army barricades at the junction of William and Rossville Sts. The main march was diverted along Rossville St to Free Derry Corner, but a small number of youths began hurling stones and insults at the British soldiers.

The exact sequence of events was disputed, but it has since been established that soldiers of the 1st Battalion, Parachute Regiment opened fire on unarmed civilians. Fourteen people were shot dead (13 outright; one who died four-and-a-half months later from his injuries), some of them shot in the back; six were aged just 17. A similar number were injured, most by gunshots and two from being knocked down by armoured personnel carriers. The Catholic population of Derry, who had originally welcomed the British troops as a neutral force protecting them from Protestant violence and persecution, now saw the army as the enemy and occupier. The ranks of the Provisional Irish Republican Army (IRA) swelled with a fresh surge of volunteers.

The **Widgery Commission**, set up in 1972 to investigate the affair, failed to find anyone responsible. None of the soldiers who fired at civilians, nor the officers in charge, were brought to trial or even disciplined; records disappeared and weapons were destroyed.

Long-standing public dissatisfaction with the Widgery investigation led to the massive **Bloody Sunday Inquiry**, headed by Lord Saville, which sat from March 2000 till December 2004. The inquiry heard from 900 witnesses, received 2500 witness statements and allegedly cost British taxpayers £400 million; its report (available on www.official-documents.gov.uk) was finally published in June 2010.

Lord Saville found that 'The firing by soldiers of 1 PARA on Bloody Sunday caused the deaths of 13 people and injury to a similar number, none of whom was posing a threat of causing death or serious injury. What happened on Bloody Sunday strengthened the Provisional IRA, increased nationalist resentment and hostility towards the Army and exacerbated the violent conflict of the years that followed. Bloody Sunday was a tragedy for the bereaved and the wounded, and a catastrophe for the people of Northern Ireland.'

Following publication of the report, Prime Minister David Cameron publicly apologised on behalf of the UK government, describing the killings as 'unjustified and unjustifiable'. In 2010, the Police Service of Northern Ireland (PSNI) launched a murder inquiry into the deaths, which remains ongoing. In 2019, Northern Ireland's Public Prosecution Service announced its decision to bring murder and attempted charges against a member of the Parachute Regiment, known as Soldier F.

The events of Bloody Sunday inspired rock band U2's most overtly political song, 'Sunday Bloody Sunday' (1983), and are commemorated in the Museum of Free Derry (p621), the People's Gallery Murals (p621) and the Bloody Sunday Memorial (p621), all in the Bogside.

Whatnot ANTIQUES
(www.thewhatnot.co.uk; 22 Bishop St; ⊙10am-5pm Tue-Sat) Jewellery, militaria, bric-a-brac and collectables cram this interesting little antique shop.

ⓘ Information

Visit Derry Information Centre (☑028-7126 7284; www.visitderry.com; 44 Foyle St; ⊙9am-7pm Mon-Fri, 9am-6pm Sat, 10am-5pm Sun Jun-Aug, shorter hours Sep-May; ⓢ) A large tourist information centre with helpful staff and stacks of brochures for attractions in Derry and beyond. Also sells books and maps and can book accommodation.

ⓘ Getting There & Away

AIR

City of Derry Airport (☑028-7181 0784; www.cityofderryairport.com; Airport Rd, Eglinton) is about 13km east of Derry along the A2 towards Limavady. There are direct flights to London

Stansted (daily), Manchester (daily), Liverpool (three days a week), Glasgow International (five days a week) and Edinburgh (five days a week).

BUS

The **bus station** (⌨ 028-7126 2261; Foyle St) is just northeast of the walled city.

Services to Northern Ireland destinations are operated by Translink (www.translink.co.uk); destinations in the Republic are served by Bus Éireann (www.buseireann.ie).

Belfast Europa Bus Centre £13, 1¾ hours, half-hourly Monday to Friday, hourly Saturday and Sunday

Coleraine £8.60, one hour, eight daily Monday to Friday, two Sunday; no Saturday service

Donegal town £12.60, 1½ hours, 10 daily

Galway £16.50, 5½ hours, four daily

Letterkenny £5.50, 40 minutes, 12 daily

Limavady £5.40, 30 minutes, at least hourly Monday to Saturday, six Sunday

Omagh £8.60, one hour, hourly Monday to Saturday, six Sunday

Sligo £16.80, 2½ hours, seven daily

Airporter (⌨ 028-7126 9996; www.airporter. co.uk; Foyleside Shopping Centre Coach Park, Foyle St; single/return £20/30; 🖥) buses run directly from Derry to Belfast International Airport (£20, 1½ hours) and George Best Belfast City Airport (£20, two hours) at least once an hour Monday to Friday and slightly less frequently Saturday and Sunday. Buses depart from Foyleside Shopping Centre Coach Park, near the Visit Derry Information Centre.

TRAIN

Derry's train station is on the eastern side of the River Foyle. At research time, major works were underway to create a new transport hub at the site of the former Waterside Railway Station, 100m north of the current train station. The new North-West Transport Hub, scheduled for completion in 2020, will house the new train terminus, bus stands, park-and-ride facilities and a green way link to the city via the Peace Bridge.

Belfast £13, two hours, hourly Monday to Saturday, six on Sunday

Coleraine £10, 40 minutes, hourly Monday to Saturday, six on Sunday

🛈 Getting Around

Bus 234 stops at City of Derry Airport (£3.60, 20 minutes, at least hourly Monday to Saturday, six Sunday). A taxi costs about £15.

The Foyle Valley cycle route runs through Derry, along the west bank of the river.

Claudy Cycles (⌨ 028-7133 8128; www.claudy cycles.com; Visit Derry Information Centre, 44 Foyle St; bike hire per half-/full day £8/12) rents out bikes.

Local buses leave from Foyle St, outside the bus station, leading to the suburbs and surrounding villages.

Taxi services in Derry include **Derry Taxis** (⌨ 028-7126 0247) and **Foyle Taxis** (⌨ 028-7127 9999; www.foyletaxis.com).

Limavady

POP 12,000

Enchanted by a folk tune played by a blind fiddler outside her window in 1851, Limavady (Léim an Mhadaidh) resident Jane Ross (1810–79) jotted down the melody – then known as 'O'Cahan's Lament', and later as the 'Londonderry Air'. The tune came to be known around the world as 'Danny Boy' – probably the most famous Irish song of all time. A blue plaque on the wall at 51 Main St, opposite the Alexander Arms, commemorates the home of Jane Ross. Other sights in the neat little town are few, but it makes for a pleasant stop.

Roe Valley Country Park PARK (Dogleap Rd; ⊙ 9am-dusk) FREE This country park, 3km south of Limavady, has walks stretching for 5km either side of the River Roe. The river is famed for its salmon and trout fishing; the season runs from early June until late October. To fish you'll need a ticket (£20 for one day); see www.roeangling.com.

The area is associated with the O'Cahans, who ruled the valley until the Plantation. The 17th-century settlers saw the flax-growing potential of the damp river valley and it became an important linen-manufacturing centre.

Danny Boy Jazz and Blues Festival MUSIC (www.dannyboyjazzandblues.com; ⊙ mid-Jun) Limavady's Danny Boy Jazz and Blues Festival runs over four days at venues across town.

Lime Tree IRISH £££ (⌨ 028-7776 4300; www.limetreerest.com; 60 Catherine St; mains lunch £12-13.50, dinner £17-23; ⊙ 5.30-8.30pm Tue & Wed, noon-1.30pm & 5.30-8.30pm Thu, noon-1.30pm & 5.30-9pm Fri, 5.30-9pm Sat; 🖥) Streamlined decor in shades of burgundy and beige softened by flickering tea lights creates a relaxing atmosphere in Limavady's best restaurant. The menu promotes local produce, from Caldeirada Galician fish stew to catch-of-the-day seafood thermidor and sirloin steak from McAtamney's butchers.

🛈 Information

Visitor Information Centre (⌨ 028-7776 0650; 24 Main St; ⊙ 9.30am-5pm Mon-Sat) In the Roe Valley Arts Centre.

ⓘ Getting There & Around

Bus 143 serves Derry (£5.40, 30 minutes, at least hourly Monday to Saturday, five Sunday). **Roe Valley Cycles** (☏ 028-7776 6406; www. roevalleycycles.co.uk; 35 Catherine St; bikes per day £15; ⏱ 9am-6pm Mon-Sat) Rents out bikes for a spin through the Roe Valley.

Magilligan Point

The huge triangular spit of land that almost closes off the mouth of Lough Foyle is mostly taken up by a military firing range, and is home to a once-notorious prison. Still, it's worth a visit for its vast sandy beaches: Magilligan Strand to the west, and the 9km sweep of Benone Strand to the northeast. The latter provides a superb venue for kite buggies and mini land yachts.

The family-friendly campsite **Benone Tourist Complex** (☏ 028-7775 0555; www. benoneni.com; 53 Benone Ave; tent sites £23-25.50, camping huts £55-60; ⏱ 9am-9pm Jul & Aug, to dusk Apr-Jun & Sep, to 4pm Oct-Mar; ▧) is connected to Benone Strand by a boardwalk across the dunes.

Magilligan Martello Tower   HISTORIC BUILDING
(Point Rd) On Magilligan Point itself, watching over the entrance to Lough Foyle, stands a well-preserved Martello tower, built during the Napoleonic Wars in 1812 to guard against French invasion. The tower's interior is closed to the public but the surrounding dunes make for a pleasant walk.

Long Line Surf School   SURFING
(☏ 07738 128507; http://longlinesurfschool.co.uk; Benone Tourist Complex; ⏱ 9.30am-5pm Easter-Sep, by appointment rest of year) Long Line has a cabin at Benone Tourist Complex and rents gear from Sea Shed Coffee & Surf at Benone Strand. You can also take 2½-hour group lessons in surfing (£25) and stand-up paddleboarding (SUP; £30).

★ **Angler's Rest**   GASTROPUB ££
(☏ 028-7775 0600; www.facebook.com/anglersrestbenone; 660 Seacoast Rd; mains lunch £9.50-20, dinner £12-23.50; ⏱ 11.30am-11pm Wed-Sat, to 10pm Sun) The best meal for miles can be had in this cosy pub with bench seats, wooden beams and roaring log fires. Local ingredients are treated with great care to create dishes like seafood chowder with homemade Guinness bread and Abernethy butter, north coast seafood pie, triple cheese macaroni and slow-cooked ham hock that glides off the bone.

Sea Shed Coffee & Surf   COFFEE
(☏ 07738 128507; Benone Strand; ⏱ 10am-4pm) This chic beachside hut sells single-origin coffee, cold brews, hot chocolate, teas and pastries and rents out surf equipment (per half-day/day bodyboard with wetsuit £10/15, surfboard with wetsuit £15/25). It's at the entrance to Benone Strand.

ⓘ Getting There & Away

Bus 134 between Coleraine and Limavady goes along Sea Coast Rd roughly once an hour Monday to Friday, less frequently on Saturdays and Sundays, and stops close to Benone Strand. The nearest stop to Magilligan Point is at the corner of Point Rd, from where it's a 4km walk.

The **Lough Foyle Ferry** (www.loughfoyleferry. com; single/return car £13/17, foot passenger £2.50/4; ⏱ 9am-8.30pm mid-Jul–Sep, hours vary Apr-Jun) connects Magilligan Point and Greencastle in County Donegal.

Downhill

The twin draws of this stretch of coast are the sprawling Downhill Demesne and sweeping surf beach below.

From Downhill, the scenic Bishop's Rd climbs steeply up through a ravine and heads over the hills to Limavady. There are spectacular views over Lough Foyle, Donegal and the Sperrin Mountains from the Gortmore picnic area, and from the clifftop at Binevenagh Lake.

★ **Downhill Demesne**   HISTORIC SITE
(www.nationaltrust.org.uk; Mussenden Rd; adult/child £6.20/3.10; ⏱ dawn-dusk) In 1774, the bishop of Derry (fourth earl of Bristol, Frederick Augustus Hervey), built a palatial home amid a 160-hectare demesne. The house burnt down in 1851, was rebuilt in 1876, and abandoned after WWII. The ruins now stand forlornly on a clifftop, with beautiful landscaped gardens below. The colonnaded, dome-capped **Mussenden Temple**, built by the bishop for his library (some say his mistress), is a *Game of Thrones* icon. Enter via the Lion's Gate or Bishop's Gate.

Nearby is whitewashed, 17th-century **Hezlett House** (open 11am to 5pm from June to September, weekends only April to June), one of Ireland's oldest thatched cottages, which belonged to the same family of dairy farmers for over 300 years. The rooms are set up as they would have looked in Victorian times. It's 2km southeast of Downhill Demesne on the Mussenden Rd.

Downhill Beach House
HOSTEL **££**

(📞 028-7084 9077; www.downhillbeachhouse.com; 12 Mussenden Rd; d £65, s/d/q without bathroom £35/50/80; ⊗ Easter-Halloween; 🅿 @ 🛜) Tucked beneath the sea cliffs overlooking the beach, this beautifully restored late-19th-century house offers comfortable accommodation in seven-bed dorms (for group bookings), doubles and family rooms. There's a big lounge with an open fire and a view of the sea, and a self-catering kitchen (there are no shops nearby so bring supplies with you).

ⓘ Getting There & Away

Bus 134 between Limavady (£4.60, 35 minutes, seven daily Monday to Friday, six Saturday and Sunday) and Coleraine (£3.10, 15 minutes) stops at Downhill.

Portstewart

POP 8030

Ever since Victorian times, when English novelist William Thackeray described it as having an 'air of comfort and neatness', the seaside and golfing resort of Portstewart has cultivated a sedate, upmarket atmosphere that distinguishes it from populist Portrush, 6km further east. However, there's also a sizeable student community from the University of Ulster in Coleraine.

⊙ Sights & Activities

Portstewart's central **Promenade** is dominated by the castellated facade of a Dominican college, looming over the seaside.

The **Port Path** is a 10.5km coastal footpath (part of the Causeway Coast Way) that stretches from Portstewart Strand to Whiterocks, 3km east of Portrush.

Portstewart Strand
BEACH

(www.nationaltrust.org.uk/portstewart-strand) The broad, 2.5km beach of Portstewart Strand is a 20-minute walk south of the centre along a coastal path, or a short bus ride along Strand Rd. Parking is allowed on the firm sand, which can accommodate over 1000 cars (open year-round, £6.50 per car from Easter to October).

Aquaholics
DIVING

(📞 028-7083 2584; www.aquaholics.co.uk; 14 Portmore Rd; ⊗ dive shop 9am-5pm Mon-Sat) The waters around Portstewart abound with marine life and shipwrecks, offering fantastic diving. Aquaholics runs PADI-accredited introductory courses (£89) and Open Water courses

(£499), as well as dives (from £89) and multi-dive packages to locations including Skerries Cavern and HMS *Drake* near Rathlin Island.

Portstewart Golf Club
GOLF

(📞 028-7083 2015; www.portstewartgc.co.uk; 117 Strand Rd; green fees Strand course £60-170, Riverside course £25-29, Old Course £10-15) Dating from 1894, renowned Portstewart Golf Club has three courses: the Strand par-72 championship links course, the par-68 Riverside course and the par-64 Old Course. It's on the western side of Portstewart, on the road to Portstewart Strand.

✵ Festivals & Events

North West 200 Motorcycle Race
SPORTS

(www.northwest200.org; ⊗ mid-May) Ireland's biggest outdoor sporting event is run on a road circuit taking in Portrush, Portstewart and Coleraine; you can see the starting grid painted on the main road at Portstewart's eastern edge. It attracts up to 100,000 spectators; if you're not one of them, it's best to avoid the area on the race weekend.

🛏 Sleeping

Rick's Causeway Coast Hostel
HOSTEL **£**

(📞 028-7083 3789; causewaycoasthostel@gmail. com; 4 Victoria Tce; dm/d/tr from £15/40/54; 🛜) This neat terrace house just northeast of the harbour has spacious four-, six- and eight-bed dorms plus a double room, and good power showers. It has its own kitchen, laundry and, in winter, a welcoming open fire.

Cul-Erg House
B&B **££**

(📞 028-7083 6610; www.culerg.co.uk; 9 Hillside, Atlantic Circle; s £50-60, d £95-120; 🅿 🛜) Warm and welcoming, this family-run B&B inside a modern terrace house is just a couple of minutes' walk from the Promenade in a quiet cul-de-sac. There is a cosy guest lounge and a small kitchen for preparing meals.

★ Saltwater House
B&B **£££**

(📞 028-7083 3872; www.saltwaterhouse.co.uk; 63 Strand Rd; d £130-150) More like a boutique hotel than a B&B, Saltwater House has four beautiful wooden-shuttered rooms with pale grey and blue hues, bike rental and an ocean-facing terrace. It also serves scrumptious organic and/or free-range breakfasts (green superfood breakfast smoothies, and cinnamon French toast with maple poached banana, blueberries and almonds). Minimum two-night stay.

Strand House
B&B **£££**

(☑ 028-7083 1000; www.strandguesthouse.com; 105 Strand Rd; s/d from £95/125; **P** **��**) This smart, eight-bed property, located a short walk west of town near Portstewart Strand, has welcoming hosts, bright modern rooms and top-notch facilities (dressing gowns and slippers; Nespresso coffee machines and homemade cookies in the rooms). Breakfast includes carefully sourced meats and eggs from local organic farms and home-baked breads.

🍴 Eating & Drinking

Warke's Deli
CAFE **£**

(☑ 028-7083 3388; www.warkesdeli.com; 1 The Promenade; mains £4-6.50; ⊙9am-5.30pm; ��) Warke's makes everything on the premises – Bircher muesli, pancakes, soups, salads and bruschetta included. If you'd rather take a picnic to the beach, you can get hampers made up. Its corner building (where Portmore Rd meets the Promenade) looks out over the prom, harbour and ocean beyond.

Morelli's
CAFE **£**

(www.morellisofportstewart.co.uk; 53 The Promenade; ice creams from £2.20, mains £5-11; ⊙9am-10pm, hot food to 8pm, shorter hours in winter; ��) Morelli's is a local institution, founded by Italian immigrants and serving up its own ice cream (since 1911), along with cafe classics. Its ice-cream sundaes are legendary.

★ Harry's Shack
BISTRO **££**

(☑ 028-7083 1783; www.facebook.com/Harrys Shack; Portstewart Strand; mains £12-19; ⊙11am-8.30pm Mon-Thu, 11am-9pm Fri, 10am-9pm Sat, 10am-7pm Sun) Bang on Portstewart Strand beach, this wooden shack has one of the north coast's best restaurants (book ahead for lunch and dinner). Harry's uses fruit, vegetables and herbs from its own organic farm plus local meat and seafood in simple but sensational dishes like megrim sole with cockles and seaweed butter, and Mulroy Bay mussels in Irish cider.

The drinks list includes craft beers from seven local breweries including Lacada Brewery in Portrush and Northbound from Derry. Breakfast is served from Saturday to Sunday.

Anchor Bar
PUB

(www.theanchorbar.co.uk; 87-89 The Promenade; ⊙11.30am-1am Mon-Thu, to 1.30am Fri & Sat, to 12.30am Sun) Hugely popular with students from the University of Ulster, the Anchor offers a well-stocked bar and decent pub grub, and has live bands Friday and Saturday. The complex includes the Anchorage Bistro, Aura nightclub and a 20-room hotel (doubles from £90).

ⓘ Getting There & Away

Buses 140A and 140B make the trip from Coleraine and Portstewart (£2.80, 20 minutes, every 20 minutes Monday to Saturday, five Sunday) and continue to Portrush (£2.50, 10 minutes).

COUNTY ANTRIM

Portrush
POP 7355

The seaside resort of Portrush (Port Rois) bursts at the seams with holidaymakers in high season and, not surprisingly, many of its attractions are focused unashamedly on good old-fashioned family fun. However, it's also one of Ireland's top surfing centres and home to the North's most prestigious golf club, host of the 2019 Open Championship. In preparation for the tournament, money has been spent on beautifying the town centre with new granite paving, benches and lighting, and renovating the train station.

◉ Sights & Activities

East Strand
BEACH

(Curran Strand) Portrush's main attraction is the beautiful sandy East Strand beach that stretches for 3km to the east of town, ending at the scenic chalk cliffs of Whiterocks.

★ Royal Portrush Golf Club
GOLF

(☑ 028-7082 2311; www.royalportrushgolfclub.com; Dunluce Rd; green fees Dunluce £90-220, Valley £25-50) Spectacularly situated alongside the Atlantic at the town's eastern edge, 1888-founded Royal Portrush first hosted the Open Championship in 1951. It's home to two courses: the Dunluce, with its water's-edge White Rock (5th) and ravine-set Calamity (14th) holes, and the Valley. Substantial improvements were made to the Dunluce Course ahead of hosting the Open Championship again in 2019, including the building of five new greens and two new holes. See the website for visitor times.

Troggs Surf Shop
SURFING

(☑ 028-7082 5476; www.troggs.com; 88 Main St; ⊙10am-6pm Mon-Sat, closed Tue Oct-Mar) Friendly Troggs Surf Shop offers year-round bodyboard/surfboard hire (per day £6/12) and wetsuit hire (per day £8). It also provides surf reports and general advice, as well as surfing lessons and surf camps.

🛏 Sleeping

★Portrush Holiday Hostel — HOSTEL £
(☑028-7082 1288; www.portrushholidayhostel.com; 24 Princess St; dm/d from £17/46; ⑨) Just a few minutes' walk from both beach and harbour, this popular hostel is set in a Victorian terrace house, and feels cosy rather than cramped. Rooms and dorms are brightly decorated and there's a large kitchen and comfortable lounge. Staff are friendly and helpful, and facilities include a washing machine and barbecue area. Check-in is from 3pm to 9pm.

Portrush Townhouse — HOSTEL £
(☑028-7082 5699; www.portrushtownhouseaccommodation.com; 6 Bath St; tw/q/6-bed without bathroom £45/60/90, q/7-bed with bathroom £110/150; ⑨) Billing itself as a boutique hostel, this centrally located townhouse has a few luxury touches – quality mattresses and bed linen, polished wood floors, artwork on the walls – that are a step up from your average backpackers. Facilities include a modern kitchen and a barbecue area. Good for families and groups.

★Shola Coach House — B&B £££
(☑028-7082 5925; www.sholabandb.com; 110A Gateside Rd; r £110-140) Housed in a converted stable block dating from 1840, this luxurious B&B has four gorgeous guest rooms and a stylish lounge with wooden beams and a welcoming fire. There are home-baked cakes on arrival and the breakfast menu includes porridge with Bushmills whiskey and locally sourced smoked salmon and pork sausages. It's 3km south of Portrush. Two-night minimum stay.

Royal Court Hotel — HOTEL £££
(☑028-7082 2236; www.royalcourthotel.co.uk; 233 Ballybogey Rd; d/ste from £140/220; ⑨) Overlooking Whiterocks beach and Royal Portrush Golf Club 3.5km east of Portrush town centre is this well-run, traditional hotel in a spectacular location. The best rooms have large balconies with ocean views, while suites have huge picture windows and four-poster beds.

🍴 Eating

Arcadia — CAFE £
(www.arcadiaportrush.co.uk; East Strand; mains £3-6; ⊙9am-5pm Apr-Sep) A Portrush landmark, this 1920s art deco pavilion houses a breezy

beach cafe on the ground floor, serving big breakfasts, bagels, salads and ice cream for a post-surf refuel, and a free art gallery on the upper floor, which also hosts workshops and classes (yoga, painting et al).

★Ocho Tapas — SPANISH ££
(☑028-7082 4110; www.ochotapas.com; 92-94 Main St; tapas £4-12; ⊙5-9pm Mon-Thu, 5-9.30pm Fri, 12.30-2.30pm & 5-9.30pm Sat, 12.30-2.30pm & 5-9pm Sun) After living in Spain for 20 years, chef Trudy Brolly opened this authentic tapas restaurant in her hometown of Portrush. Locally sourced and Spanish ingredients are combined in dishes such as Fivemiletown goats' cheese croquettas with beetroot panna cotta and cherry sour cream. Order three to four tapas per person, or six of the smaller, exquisite *pintxos*, with sherry pairings.

Also runs paella cookery classes (£35).

Ramore Wine Bar — IRISH ££
(☑028-7082 4313; www.ramorerestaurant.com; The Harbour; mains £8-19; ⊙12.15-2.15pm & 5-9pm Mon-Thu, 12.15-2.15pm & 5-9.30pm Fri, 12.15-2.30pm & 4.45-10pm Sat, 12.15-3pm & 5-9pm Sun; 🔊) Part of a complex of six restaurants at Portrush harbour, the perennially popular, family-friendly Ramore Wine Bar serves an extensive menu of pub grub like chilli chicken pitta, monkfish and tiger prawns, pizzas, and burgers with tobacco onions. The oversized, homemade cakes and pies on display at the dessert counter make regular appearances on Instagram.

Other restaurants at the Ramore complex include **Neptune & Prawn** (mains £9 to £18), serving Asian dishes, and Mermaid (sharing plates £17 to £18), specialising in seafood.

Drinking & Nightlife

Koko COFFEE
(www.facebook.com/kokoportrush; 2 Castle Erin Rd; ⊙9am-5pm) Great coffee and fantastic sea views are the main draws of this beach cafe. Snuggle up by the wood-burning stove and look out through the picture windows in winter, or if the sun's shining, sip your flat white outside on the deck. Also serves sandwiches and cakes.

Kiwis Brew Bar BAR
(www.kiwisbrewbar.com; 47 Main St; ⊙5pm-1am Mon-Fri, 1pm-1am Sat & Sun) Craft beers at this good-time, Kiwi-owned bar include New Zealand's Tui, as well as hard-to-find Irish brews like Pokertree from County Tyrone, and Long Meadow Cider from County Armagh. Its TVs screen rugby, of course, and surfing. There's live music most weekends, including blues on Sundays.

Kelly's Complex CLUB
(Lush!; www.kellysportrush.co.uk; Bushmills Rd; ⊙9pm-late Wed & Sat) Plain and small-looking from the outside, the Tardis effect takes over as you enter a wonderland of five bars and three dance floors at the North's hottest club, just east of Portrush. It's been around since 1996, and Lush! remains one of Ireland's best club nights.

Getting There & Away

The bus terminal is near the Dunluce Centre. Buses 140A to 140D link Portrush with Portstewart (£2.50, 10 minutes, every 20 minutes) and Coleraine (£2.80, 20 minutes). It's also served by the seasonal **Causeway Rambler** (Bus 402; ☏028-9066 6630; www.translink.co.uk; day ticket adult/child £9.50/4.75; ⊙Mar-Sep) bus service.

The train station is just south of the harbour. Portrush is served by trains from Coleraine (£2.40, 12 minutes, hourly), where there are connections to Belfast and Derry.

Dunluce Castle

The ruins of Dunluce Castle (87 Dunluce Rd; adult/child £5.50/3.50; ⊙10am-5pm Feb-Nov, to 4pm Dec & Jan, last entry 30min before closing) perch atop a dramatic basalt crag 5km east of Portrush, a one-hour walk away along the coastal path. A narrow bridge leads from the former guest lodgings and stables on the mainland across a dizzying gap to the main part of the fortress. Below, a path leads down from the gatehouse to the Mermaid's Cave beneath the castle crag (the path was closed for repairs at research time).

In the 16th and 17th centuries, the castle was the seat of the MacDonnell family (the earls of Antrim from 1620), who built a Renaissance-style manor house within the walls.

Bushmills

POP 1290

The nearest town to the Giant's Causeway (5km), Bushmills has long been a place of pilgrimage for connoisseurs of Irish whiskey, and is an attractive stop for hikers exploring the Causeway Coast.

Sights & Activities

Old Bushmills Distillery DISTILLERY
(☏028-2073 3218; www.bushmills.com; 2 Distillery Rd; tour adult/child £9/5; ⊙9.15am-4.45pm Mon-Sat, noon-4.45pm Sun) Bushmills is the world's oldest licensed distillery, having been given permission to produce whiskey by King James I in 1608. The whiskey is made with Irish barley and water from St Columb's Rill, a tributary of the River Bush, and matured in oak barrels. During ageing, the alcohol content drops from around 60% to 40%; the spirit lost through evaporation is known as 'the angels' share'. After the tour, you can try a free sample of your choice from Bushmills' range.

Giant's Causeway & Bushmills Railway TRAIN
(☏028-2073 2844; infogcbr@btconnect.com; return adult/child £5/3) Trains run at noon, 2pm and 4pm from the Causeway, returning at 12.30pm, 2.30pm and 4.30pm from Bushmills, daily in July and August, and on weekends only from Easter to June and September and October.

Brought from a private line on the shores of Lough Neagh, the narrow-gauge line and locomotives (two steam and one diesel) follow the route of a 19th-century tourist tramway for 3km from Bushmills to below the Giant's Causeway Visitor Experience.

A path alongside the full length of the Giants Causeway & Bushmills Railway track makes for a pleasant 5km walk or cycle.

Sleeping

Bushmills Hostel HOSTEL £
(☏028-2073 1222; www.hini.org.uk; 49 Main St; dm £16-20, s £30-35, tw £50-60, tr £60-75; ⊙closed

11.30am-2.30pm Jul & Aug, to 3.30pm Mar-Jun, Sep & Oct; @🛜) Just off the Diamond in the centre of town, this modern, purpose-built hostel has mostly four- to six-bed dorms, all with attached bathrooms. There's also a kitchen, laundry and bike shed. The hostel is open daily April to October, but only accepts groups from November to March. Call ahead to check it's staffed before turning up.

Bushmills Inn Hotel   HOTEL **£££**
(📞028-2073 3000; www.bushmillsinn.com; 9 Dunluce Rd; d/ste from £220/360; 🅿@🛜) The Bushmills Inn is an old coaching inn dating to around 1608, complete with peat fires, gas lamps, a secret library and a round tower. The old part of the hotel has been given over to the restaurant; the luxurious accommodation is in the neighbouring, modern Mill House complex. Low-season discounts cut room rates in half.

★ **Bushmills Inn**   IRISH **££**
(📞028-2073 3000; www.bushmillsinn.com; 9 Dunluce Rd; mains lunch £7-13, dinner £14-28; ⊙noon-9.30pm Mon-Sat, 12.30-3pm & 5-9.30pm Sun; 🛜) Set in the old 17th-century stables of the Bushmills Inn, this haven has intimate wooden booths and blazing fires, and uses fresh local produce in dishes like Greencastle cod, Laney Valley lamb and traditional Dalriada Cullen skink (wood-smoked haddock poached in cream, with poached eggs and new potatoes). Book ahead. There's trad music in the bar on Saturday nights.

Tartine   IRISH **££**
(📞028-2073 1044; www.distillersarms.com; 140 Main St; mains £12-24; ⊙5-8pm Wed & Thu, to 9pm Fri, to 9.30pm Sat, 12.30-2.15pm & 5-7.30pm Sun) Inside a former pub, with bare boards, exposed stone and glowing fire, Tartine's three interconnecting dining rooms are adorned with Irish art. Local produce is given a French twist: Guinness and molasses cured salmon on a baked seafood thermidor and Irish oysters in a Pernod-infused cream.

A two-course menu for £19, including a drink, is available until 6.30pm.

French Rooms   FRENCH **££**
(📞028-2073 0033; www.thefrenchrooms.com; 45 Main St; mains breakfast £5-8, lunch £8-18, dinner £14-22; ⊙10-11.30am & noon-3pm Wed & Thu, 10-11.30am, noon-3pm & 6-9pm Fri & Sat) Incorporating a homewares shop and gourmet deli counter, this French-themed emporium with zinc-topped tables is an especially good option for breakfast (*croques monsieur* and *madame*,

crêpes, eggs royale, brioche bacon butty). Lunch and dinner choices span supreme of guinea fowl to cajun-seasoned sea bass.

At research time luxury B&B rooms were being constructed.

🛍 Shopping

★ **Designerie**   ARTS & CRAFTS
(www.thedesignerie.co.uk; 88 Main St; ⊙10am-5pm Mon-Sat) This nonprofit social enterprise sells handcrafted ceramics, soaps, art and textiles by some 60 Irish designer makers. There are some fine pieces to be found here, including soft leather bags, glass sculptures and handwoven blankets. Upstairs the **Makers House** contains the shared work space of eight local designers, who are happy to discuss their work.

Gallery 1608   ART
(www.gallery1608.co.uk; 83-85 Main St; ⊙9am-5.30pm Mon-Sat, 11am-5pm Sun) Some of Ireland's top artists are represented at this small gallery that's packed full with paintings, photography, ceramics and sculptures. The collection includes paintings by acclaimed Belfast-based artist Colin Watson.

ℹ Information

Bushmills Visitor Information Centre
(📞028-2073 0390; www.visitcausewaycoastandglens.com; Main St; ⊙10am-6pm daily Jul & Aug, 10am-5pm daily May, Jun & Sep, 10am-5pm Sat & Sun Mar, Apr & Oct)

ℹ Getting There & Away

Bus 172 serves Coleraine (£3.60, 20 minutes, eight daily Monday to Friday, three Saturday and Sunday), the Giant's Causeway (£2.10, five minutes) and Ballycastle (£4.60, 45 minutes).

Seasonal services include the Causeway Rambler hop-on, hop-off bus and the Giant's Causeway & Bushmills Railway.

A free park-and-ride shuttle bus runs from the Bushmills Visitor Information Centre to the Giant's Causeway every 20 minutes, from 9am to 4pm (to 5pm June to September). The bus is free but you must buy a ticket to the Giant's Causeway Visitor Experience (p636), sold on board.

Giant's Causeway

When you first see it you'll understand why the ancients believed the Causeway was not a natural feature. This spectacular rock formation is one of Ireland's most impressive and atmospheric landscape features, but it can get very crowded. If you can, try to visit midweek or out of season to experience it at its most evocative. Sunset in spring or autumn is the best time for photographs.

◉ Sights & Activities

A pleasant way to reach the Giant's Causeway (and avoid paying the combined parking and visitor centre entrance fee) is to walk from Bushmills along the path running parallel to the Giant's Causeway & Bushmills Railway. The walk takes about 45 minutes and there are pretty views across the sand dunes to the coast.

★ **Giant's Causeway**   LANDMARK
(www.nationaltrust.org.uk; ⊘dawn-dusk) `FREE`
This extraordinary rock formation – Northern Ireland's only Unesco World Heritage site – is a vast expanse of regular, closely packed, hexagonal stone columns looking for all the world like the handiwork of giants. The phenomenon is explained in the Giant's Causeway Visitor Experience, housed in a state-of-the-art ecofriendly building half-hidden in the hillside above the sea.

Visiting the Giant's Causeway itself is free of charge but you pay to use the car park on a combined ticket with the visitor centre; parking-only tickets aren't available.

From the centre it's a 10- to 15-minute walk downhill to the Causeway itself, but a more interesting approach is to follow the clifftop path then descend the **Shepherd's Steps**. For the less mobile, a minibus shuttles from the visitor centre to the Causeway (£2 return).

The lower coastal path leads east as far as the **Amphitheatre viewpoint** at Port Reostan, passing impressive rock formations such as the **Organ** (a stack of vertical basalt columns resembling organ pipes).

You can also follow the clifftop path east past the **Chimney Stacks headland** as far as Dunseverick or beyond.

Giant's Causeway
Visitor Experience   MUSEUM
(☑ 028-2073 1855; www.nationaltrust.org.uk; 60 Causeway Rd; adult/child £12.50/6.25; ⊘9am-7pm Jun-Sep, to 6pm Mar-May & Oct, to 5pm Nov-Feb) 🖋 Built into the hillside and walled with tall black basalt slabs that mimic the basalt columns of the Causeway, the Giant's Causeway Visitor Experience houses an exhibition explaining the geology of the region, and has a tourist information desk, restaurant and shop. Admission includes an audio guide to listen to as you explore the rocks. Guided tours leave every hour.

The Visitor Experience admission fee is reduced by £1.50 if you arrive by bus, bike or on foot.

🛏 Sleeping & Eating

Staying at the Giant's Causeway itself makes it easy to explore the coastline early morning and late evening, without the crowds. A better range of accommodation is available in Bushmills, 5km south of the Causeway.

If you've worked up an appetite clambering among the stones, there's a cafe at the Giant's Causeway Visitor Experience, a restaurant in the Causeway Hotel and pub grub at the **Nook** (☑ 028-2073 2993; 48 Causeway Rd; mains £10.50-14; ⊘kitchen 11am-9pm Mar-Oct, to 6pm Nov-Feb).

Causeway Hotel   HOTEL £££
(☑ 028-9073 1210; www.thecausewayhotel.com; 40 Causeway Rd; d £150-200; 🅿 🎅) On the cliffs

---

THE MAKING OF THE CAUSEWAY

The story goes that the Irish giant Finn McCool built the Causeway so he could cross the sea to fight the Scottish giant Benandonner. Benandonner pursued Finn back across the Causeway, but in turn took fright and fled back to Scotland, ripping up the Causeway as he went. All that remains are its ends – the Giant's Causeway in Ireland, and the island of Staffa in Scotland (which has similar rock formations).

The scientific explanation is that the Causeway rocks were formed 60 million years ago, when a thick layer of molten basaltic lava flowed along a valley in the existing chalk beds. As the lava flow cooled and hardened – from the top and bottom surfaces inward – it contracted, creating a pattern of hexagonal cracks at right angles to the cooling surfaces (think of mud contracting and cracking in a hexagonal pattern as a lake bed dries out). As solidification progressed towards the centre of the flow, the cracks spread down from the top and up from the bottom, until the lava was completely solid. Erosion has cut into the lava flow, and the basalt has split along the contraction cracks, creating the hexagonal columns.

above the Giant's Causeway, this 28-room National Trust–owned hotel is an ideal base for exploring the coast early or late in the day without the crowds. Ask for one of the rooms at the western end, with outdoor terraces that enjoy sunset views over the Atlantic. Low-season discounts cut rates in half.

Parking is free for guests and diners at its restaurant.

❶ Getting There & Away

As well as the seasonal Causeway Rambler (p634) and the Giant's Causeway & Bushmills Railway (p634), bus 172 from Ballycastle (£4.60, 30 minutes, eight daily Monday to Friday, three Saturday and Sunday) to Coleraine (£3.60, 25 minutes) and Bushmills (£2.10, five minutes) stops here year-round. From Coleraine, trains run to Belfast or Derry.

❶ Getting Around

It's an easy 1km walk from the Giant's Causeway Visitor Experience car park down to the Causeway, although you can take one of the minibuses that plies the route (one-way/return £1/2, every 15 minutes). The buses are wheelchair accessible.

Ballintoy & Around

POP 170

The pretty village of Ballintoy (Baile an Tuaighe) tumbles down the hillside to a picture-postcard harbour, better known to *Game of Thrones* fans as the Iron Islands' Lordsports Harbour (among other scenes filmed here). The restored limekiln on the quayside once made quicklime using stone from the chalk cliffs and coal from Ballymoney.

Ballintoy lies roughly halfway between Ballycastle and the Giant's Causeway on the most scenic stretch of the Causeway Coast, with sea cliffs of contrasting black basalt and white chalk, rocky islands and broad sweeps of sandy beach.

◎ Sights & Activities

The main attractions can be reached by car or bus, but the 16.5km stretch between the Carrick-a-Rede car park and the Giant's Causeway is best enjoyed on a walk following the waymarked Causeway Coast Way (www.walkni.com).

About 9.5km east of the Giant's Causeway is the tiny seaside hamlet of Portbradden, with half a dozen harbourside houses. Visible from Portbradden and accessible via the next junction off the A2 is the spectacular White

Park Bay, with its wide, sweeping sandy beach. Some 3km further east is Ballintoy.

★Carrick-a-Rede Rope Bridge BRIDGE
(☎ 028-2073 3335; www.nationaltrust.org.uk/carrick-a-rede; 119 Whitepark Rd, Ballintoy; adult/child £9/4.50; ◎ 9.30am-6pm Apr-Oct, to 3.30pm Nov-Mar) This 20m-long, 1m-wide bridge of wire rope spans the chasm between the sea cliffs and the little island of Carrick-a-Rede, swaying 30m above the rock-strewn water. Crossing the bridge is perfectly safe, but frightening if you don't have a head for heights, especially if it's breezy (in high winds the bridge is closed). From the island, views take in Rathlin Island and Fair Head to the east.

There's a small National Trust information centre and cafe (mains £3.50-6; ◎ 9.30am-5.15pm) at the car park.

The impetus for the crossing first came from fishermen, who would stretch their nets out from the tip of the island to intercept the passage of salmon migrating along the coast to their home rivers.

Now firmly on the tour-bus route, Carrick-a-Rede has become so popular that the National Trust has introduced ticketed one-hour time slots to visit the bridge. Book your ticket online in advance, especially during high season. Mornings tend to be quieter; the coaches arrive in the afternoon.

Kinbane Castle CASTLE
(Whitepark Rd) FREE On a limestone headland jutting out from the basalt cliffs, with stupendous views of Rathlin Island and Scotland, this castle, now ruined, was built in 1547 by Colla MacDonnell (son of Alexander MacDonnell, lord of Islay and Kintyre, and Catherine, daughter of the lord of Ardnamurchan), then rebuilt in 1555 following an English siege. It was inhabited until the 17th century, when it was abandoned. From the car park, 140 steep steps lead down to the castle.

🛏 Sleeping & Eating

Whitepark Bay Hostel HOSTEL £
(☎ 028-2073 1745; www.hini.org.uk; 157 Whitepark Rd; dm £16-18.50, tw £44; ◎ mid-Mar–Oct; P 🐾) Near the west end of White Park Bay, this modern, purpose-built hostel has mostly four-bed dorms, plus twin rooms with TV, all with private bathroom. The common room is warmed by a fireplace and positioned to soak up the view, and the beach is just a few minutes' walk through the dunes. It's often booked by groups, so call ahead.

1. Ballintoy Harbour (p637) **2.** Giant's Causeway (p635)
3. Carrick-a-Rede Rope Bridge (p637) **4.** White Park Bay (p637)

DACOWLEY/GETTY IMAGES ©

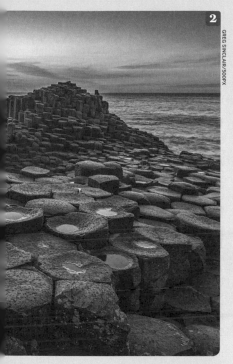

GREG SINCLAIR/500PX

Causeway Coast

Known as the Causeway Coast, the north shore of County Antrim from Ballycastle to Portrush is one of the most scenic stretches of coastline in all of Ireland. Whether you drive, cycle or walk its length, it's not to be missed.

Giant's Causeway

The grand geological centrepiece of the Antrim coast is the Giant's Causeway, a spectacular rock formation composed of countless hexagonal basalt columns. A Unesco World Heritage site, it is the north coast's most popular tourist attraction.

Causeway Coast

The Causeway Coast isn't just about the scenery. There are picturesque villages at Ballintoy (famous as the Iron Islands' Lordsports Harbour in *Game of Thrones*) and Portbradden, historic ruined fortresses at Dunluce and Dunseverick Castles, and the chance to savour a dram of Irish whiskey at Old Bushmills Distillery.

Carrick-a-Rede Rope Bridge

Originally rigged and used by local salmon fishermen, the famous Carrick-a-Rede Rope Bridge is now a popular test of nerve for Causeway Coast visitors, swaying gently 30m above the rocks and the sea.

Antrim Coast

Although famous for its dramatic sea-cliff scenery, the Antrim coast also has some excellent sandy beaches. As well as the family-friendly strand at Ballycastle, there's the harder-to-reach but twice-as-beautiful White Park Bay.

Sheep Island View Hostel HOSTEL £

(☑ 028-2076 9391; www.sheepislandview.com; 42A Main St; dm/s/tw from £18/25/45; P @ ⚋) This family-run independent hostel offers dorm and basic rooms with private bathrooms. There's a kitchen and laundry, and a village store nearby. It's on the main coast road near the turn-off to Ballintoy Harbour, with a bus stop at the door, and makes a handy overnight stop if you're hiking between Bushmills and Ballycastle.

Whitepark House B&B £££

(☑ 028-2073 1482; www.whiteparkhouse.com; 150 Whitepark Rd; s/d £90/130; P ⚋) A beautifully restored 18th-century house overlooking White Park Bay, this B&B has traditional features such as antique furniture and a peat fire complemented by Asian artefacts gathered during the welcoming owners' travels. There are three rooms – ask for one with a sea view.

Red Door Cottage IRISH £

(☑ 028-2076 9048; www.facebook.com/thereddoortearoom; 14A Harbour Rd; mains £7-11; ⚋11am-4pm Tue-Sun May-Oct, 10am-4pm Sat & Sun Mar & Apr) Fronted by a fire engine–red door, this little cottage sits 200m off the main coast road along the side road to Ballintoy Harbour. Everything is homemade: soups, chowders, Irish stew, burgers and cakes. The garden's picnic tables are idyllic in the sunshine; when it's chilly there's a turf fire indoors. It's worth booking ahead in peak holiday season.

GAME OF THRONES

If you're driving around Northern Ireland, you'll discover *Game of Thrones* filming locations aplenty, or alternatively there are day-long bus tours departing from Belfast. Visit www.discovernorthernireland.com/gameofthrones for details.

Northern Ireland locations associated with *Game of Thrones* include the following:

➡ Dark Hedges (p641)

➡ Ballintoy Harbour (p637)

➡ Downhill Demesne (p630)

➡ Cushendun Caves (p644)

➡ Castle Ward Estate (p603)

➡ Inch Abbey (p601)

➡ Tollymore Forest Park (p606)

➡ Fiddler's Green (p597)

➡ Blakes of the Hollow (p658)

Roark's Kitchen CAFE £

(Harbour Rd, Ballintoy Harbour; mains £4.25-9; ⚋11am-5.30pm Apr-Sep, noon-4pm Oct-Mar; P) On the quayside at Ballintoy Harbour, this cute little chalk-built tearoom serves teas, coffees, ice cream, home-baked apple, cherry and rhubarb tart, and lunch dishes such as Irish stew or chicken and ham pie. Cash only.

ℹ Getting There & Away

Bus 172 (eight daily Monday to Friday, three daily Saturday and Sunday) connects Ballintoy with Coleraine (£6.20, 40 minutes), Ballycastle (£3.10, 20 minutes), Giant's Causeway (£3.10, 20 minutes) and Bushmills (£3.60, 25 minutes). Causeway Rambler (p634) buses cover the route in season.

Ballycastle & Around

POP 5000

The harbour town and holiday resort of Ballycastle (Baile an Chaisil) marks the eastern end of the Causeway Coast. It's a pretty town with a family-friendly promenade, a good bucket-and-spade beach and a thriving food scene. Ferries to Rathlin Island depart from here. Castle St and the Diamond are where most of the action is.

◉ Sights & Activities

Marconi Memorial MONUMENT

In the harbour car park, a plaque at the foot of a rock pinnacle commemorates the day in 1898 when Guglielmo Marconi's assistants contacted Rathlin Island by radio from Ballycastle to prove to Lloyds of London that wireless communication was a viable proposition. The idea was to send notice to London or Liverpool of ships arriving safely after a transatlantic crossing – most vessels on this route would have to pass through the channel north of Rathlin.

Sea Haven Therapy SPA

(www.seahaventherapy.com; 18 Bayview Rd; ⚋10am-6pm Mon-Sat) Immerse yourself in a relaxing seaweed bath (good for muscular aches, joint pain and circulation; £25) while enjoying views of Rathlin Island and beyond. Or try the salt therapy room (45 minutes; £20) or a massage (30 minutes from £30). Next to the Rathlin Island ferry terminal at Ballycastle Harbour.

Ballycastle Food Tour FOOD & DRINK

(☑ 07718 276612; www.irishfeast.com; per person £40) This three-hour walking tour makes stops at five of the town's eateries to sample items such as local black pudding, seafood chowder and craft ale. Book ahead via the website or at the Ballycastle Visitor Information Centre. Also offers tours of Bushmills and Rathlin Island.

✳️ Festivals & Events

Ould Lammas Fair CULTURAL
(☺ last Mon & Tue Aug) Ballycastle's Ould Lammas Fair dates back to 1606. Thousands of people descend on the town for the market stalls and fairground rides, and to sample 'yellowman' (a hard, chewy, toffee-like honeycomb) and dulse (dried edible seaweed).

🛏️ Sleeping

Watertop Open Farm CAMPGROUND £
(☎ 028-2076 2576; www.watertopfarm.co.uk; 188 Cushendall Rd; camp sites for 2 people £15, per additional person £5, caravan sites from £25; ☺ Easter-Oct) About 10km east of Ballycastle on the road to Cushendun, family favourite Watertop is based at a working farm and activity centre (open 11am to 5.30pm daily July and August, weekend only May; admission £3.50), offering pony trekking, sheep-shearing and farm tours.

Castle Hostel HOSTEL £
(☎ 028-2076 2845; Quay Rd; dm £15; ⊛) This centrally located hostel in a Victorian terrace has a good kitchen and dining area and a friendly, helpful owner. Rooms have bay windows and wooden floors; most share bathrooms.

An Caislean Guesthouse GUESTHOUSE ££
(☎ 028-2076 2845; www.ancaislean.co.uk; 42 Quay Rd; s £35, d £70-80; P ⊛) Originally two guesthouses, now linked by a covered walkway, An Caislean has a large guest lounge and a warm and welcoming family atmosphere. Rooms are spacious and comfortable, if a bit creaky, but the trump card is the location, just a few minutes' walk from the beach. Some rooms share bathrooms.

Ballycastle Backpackers HOSTEL ££
(☎ 077-7323 7890; www.ballycastlebackpackers.net; 4 North St; dm £17.50, d with/without bathroom £60/40; P @ ⊛) Overlooking the harbour, this small, homey terrace house has one six-bed dorm, a family room and a couple of twin and double rooms. There's a well-equipped kitchen and a cosy living room. Four further, more luxuriously appointed family rooms with attached bathrooms are available in **Quayside** in the adjoining terrace (£75 to £100).

WORTH A TRIP

KINGSROAD

Planted by the Stuart family in the 18th century as the formal entrance to their property, the shadowy, gnarled, entwined beech trees at **Dark Hedges** (Bregagh Rd, Ballymoney) are now among Northern Ireland's most photographed sights after doubling as the Kingsroad in *Game of Thrones*. Coach tours stop here and getting a photo without crowds isn't easy. The Dark Hedges are 14km southwest of Ballycastle via the A44 and Ballykenver Rd. Bregagh Rd is closed to traffic; parking is available at the Hedges Hotel (signed).

In 2016 when Storm Gertrude uprooted several of the 200-year-old trees, the wood was salvaged and used to create 10 intricately carved *Game of Thrones* doors. These are scattered across Northern Ireland; pick up the free 'Journey of the Doors' passport at tourist information points.

🍴 Eating & Drinking

With artisan bakeries, craft breweries and fine local seafood, Ballycastle is emerging as something of a foodie destination. Local produce items to look out for include smoked fish from North Coast Smokehouse (www.northcoastsmokehouse.com) and beer from Glens of Antrim Craft Ale & Beers (www.glensofantrimcraftaleandbeers.com).

★ Morton's Fish & Chips FISH & CHIPS £
(☎ 028-2076 1100; The Harbour, Bayview Rd; dishes £2.30-7; ☺ noon-8pm Sun-Thu, to 9pm Fri & Sat) Fish and chips don't come fresher: local boats unload their daily catch right alongside this little harbourside hut. The cod, haddock, scallops, scampi and crab cakes, along with chips made from locally farmed potatoes, draw long queues in summer (expect to wait).

★ Ursa Minor BAKERY £
(www.ursaminorbakehouse.com; 45 Ann St; dishes £2.50-5, loaves £3; ☺ 10am-4pm Tue-Sat; ⊛) Artisan bakers Dara and Ciara Ó Hartghaile use only three ingredients in their sourdough loaves: flour, water and salt. You can see the bread being made in the downstairs bakehouse; panels explain the process. Upstairs, a bright cafe serves vegetarian breakfasts and lunches, as well as pastries and excellent coffee. Look out for regular sourdough-making classes (£90 per person).

Thyme & Co
CAFE **£**

(☑ 028-2076 9851; www.thymeandco.co.uk; 5 Quay Rd; mains £6-9; ☺ 9am-4pm Mon-Tue, Thu & Fri, 9am-3.30pm & 5-9pm Sat, 10am-3pm Sun; 🛜🥗) 🥗 Lush salads, shepherd's pie, salmon and egg crumble and plenty of vegetarian and vegan options are among the homemade dishes prepared using local produce at this welcoming cafe. Many of its cakes and bakes are gluten free; there's excellent coffee too. Saturday nights offer various specials, such as BYO pizza nights.

Cellar Restaurant
IRISH **££**

(☑ 028-2076 3037; www.cellarballycastle.com; 11B The Diamond; mains £14-25; ☺ 5-10pm Sun-Fri, noon-10pm Sat) Down a flight of steps from the street, this cosy little basement restaurant with intimate wooden booths and a big slate fireplace is a good place to sample Ulster produce like locally caught crab claws, north coast salmon and Atlantic prawns, along with Irish beef and lamb.

O'Connor's
PUB

(www.oconnorsbar.ie; 5-7 Ann St; ☺ 11.30am-1am) Just off the Diamond, O'Connor's is Ballycastle's best pub for music, with trad Thursday nights year-round. From Easter to September, there are also bands in the bar and DJs in the beer garden on Saturday, and jam sessions on Sunday. Hearty food is served nonstop until 9pm.

ℹ Information

Ballycastle Visitor Information Centre (☑ 028-2076 2024; www.visitcausewaycoastandglens.com; 14 Bayview Rd; ☺ 9.30am-5pm Mon-Fri, 10am-4pm Sat Sep-Jun, plus noon-4pm Sun Jul & Sep, longer hours Jul & Aug) Helpful tourist information office near the Rathlin Island ferry terminal at the harbour.

ℹ Getting There & Away

The bus station is on Station Rd, just east of the Diamond. Bus 217 links Ballycastle with Ballymena (£7.20, 50 minutes, hourly Monday to Friday, five Saturday), where you can connect to Belfast.

Bus 172 goes along the coast to Coleraine (£7.20, one hour, eight daily Monday to Friday, three Saturday and Sunday) via Ballintoy, the Giant's Causeway and Bushmills. The seasonal Causeway Rambler (p634) covers the same route.

High-speed passenger ferries with **Kintyre Express** (☑ 01586 555895; www.kintyreexpress.com; ☺ Easter-Sep) link Ballycastle with Campbeltown, Scotland (one-way/return £50/90, 1½ hours, daily May to September). A separate service runs to Port Ellen on Islay, Scotland (one-way/return £60/95, one hour, daily May to September).

Rathlin Island
POP 160

Rugged Rathlin Island sits 6km offshore from Ballycastle. An L-shaped island just 6.5km long and 4km wide, Rathlin is home to hundreds of seals and thousands of nesting seabirds in late spring and summer.

Scottish hero Robert the Bruce spent time here in 1306 while hiding out after being defeated by the English king. Watching a spider's resoluteness in repeatedly trying to spin a web gave him the courage to have another go at the English, whom he subsequently defeated at Bannockburn. The cave where he is said to have stayed is beneath the East Lighthouse, at the northeastern tip of the island.

⊙ Sights & Activities

Rathlin is famous for its spectacular coastal scenery and the seabirds, especially puffins, who nest on the sea cliffs at the island's western tip.

From the harbour in Church Bay, there are three main walking routes: 7km to the Rathlin West Light Seabird Centre (p642), to the **East Lighthouse** (3km) and to the **Rue Point Lighthouse** in the south (4.5km). The roads are all suitable for cycling; bikes (p644) can be hired.

There are also some fabulous off-road walking trails including the **Ballyconagan Trail** to the Old Coastguard Station on the north coast, with great views along the sea cliffs and across to the Scottish islands of Islay and Jura; and the clifftop **Roonivoolin Trail** in the south, where you can spot choughs (the rarest of the crow family), hear the singing of skylarks and spot Irish hares.

The island is surrounded by some 40 shipwrecks, including the HMS *Drake,* which can be dived with Aquaholics (p631).

★ Rathlin West Light Seabird Centre
LIGHTHOUSE

(☑ 028-2076 3948; www.rspb.org.uk/rathlinisland; adult/child £5/2.50; ☺ 10am-5pm May-Aug, 11am-4pm Apr & Sep) This Royal Society for the Protection of Birds (RSPB) centre offers spectacular views of a thriving seabird colony, where every summer thousands of puffins can be seen. It's located at Rathlin's upside-down west lighthouse (the lamp is at the building's base). Built into the cliff face, the lighthouse was a feat of engineering when it was completed in 1919. The lighthouse tower now contains exhibits on Rathlin's marine life and history.

Above the lighthouse, viewing platforms look out to the neighbouring sea stacks, where every year thousands of seabirds return to breed, including guillemots, razorbills, kittiwakes and fulmars. The best times to see puffins are mid-May (when the birds gather on the cliffs), mid-June (when the chicks begin hatching) and late July (when the puffins prepare to return to sea). Binoculars and telescopes are provided for close-up views of the birds and their chicks.

Boathouse Visitor Centre   MUSEUM
(www.rathlincommunity.org; ⊙10am-12.30pm & 1-4.30pm Apr-Jun, to 5pm Jul & Aug, to 4pm Sep) South of the harbour, this combined visitor centre/museum details the fascinating history, culture and ecology of Rathlin Island, and can give advice on walks and wildlife.

Paul Quinn   WALKING
(☑07745 566924; www.rathlinwalkingtours.com) Insightful guide Paul Quinn offers entertaining walking tours of Rathlin Island.

Rathlin Sound Maritime Festival   CULTURAL
(www.rathlinsoundmaritimefestival.com; ⊙late May) This 10-day festival centres around the stretch of water between Rathlin Island and Ballycastle. Events and activities on land (in both Rathlin and Ballycastle) and sea include a sailing regatta, live music, talks and tours and a chowder championship.

🛌 Sleeping

Kinramer Cottage   HOSTEL £
(☑028-2076 3948; www.kinramercottage.com; Kinramer; dm £12) Kinramer is a basic bunkhouse located on an organic farm, 5km west from the harbour (a one-hour walk) in a beautifully remote location; however it is usually booked out by Seabird Centre volunteers, so check availability well ahead. You'll need to bring your own food.

★Manor House   GUESTHOUSE ££
(☑028-2076 0046; www.manorhouserathlin.com; Church Bay; s £70-80, d £130-145) Rathlin's 18th-century manor house has been fully renovated and transformed into a stylish 11-room guesthouse with stunning views across Church Bay. Rooms combine modern furnishings with period features and the bright reception area has a welcoming fire. There's also a good restaurant serving fresh local seafood.

Rathlin Glamping   CABIN ££
(☑07702 706882, 07715 897773; www.rathlinglamping.co.uk; d £75) Located a 10-minute walk south of the harbour, these four, neat glamping pods looking directly out to the ocean come equipped with attached bathrooms and small kitchenettes; bring your own bedding. There is a barbecue area and outdoor tables for dining. Pods sleep up to four people; third and fourth occupants are charged £12.50 per adult and £5 per child.

Rathlin Island Hostel   HOSTEL ££
(☑07563 814378; www.rathlinhostel.com; dm/d/f £20/50/70; 🕿) Just a five-minute walk south of the harbour, Rathlin Island Hostel has five simple but bright rooms with four to 12 beds, with the option to book each as a private room (good for families). All share bathrooms. There's a self-catering kitchen and fantastic ocean views from nearly every room.

🍴 Eating & Drinking

Rathlin has a pub, a shop and a handful of eating options (many of them seasonal), all located in and around Church Bay. Bring supplies if you're heading out walking or cycling elsewhere on the island. There are vending machines selling chocolate bars and coffee at the Rathlin West Light Seabird Centre.

Manor House   IRISH ££
(☑028-2076 0046; Church Bay; mains lunch £5-7, dinner £12-22; ⊙noon-3pm & 6.30-9pm; 🕿) The restaurant at the Manor House is a good option for a freshly baked scone and coffee (served all day), a light lunch or an evening meal. The menu features daily seafood specials including freshly caught crab and lobster when it's in season. Book ahead for dinner.

McCuaig's Bar   PUB
(☑028-2076 0011; The Harbour; ⊙11am-11pm, kitchen noon-8pm; 🕿📶) Rathlin Island's pub and beer garden overlook the harbour, with wooden picnic tables providing an idyllic spot for a pint and a plate of hearty pub food like Irish stew or fish and chips (mains £6 to £12). There's an ATM here.

ℹ️ Getting There & Away

Rathlin Island Ferry (☑028-2076 9299; www.rathlinballycastleferry.com; return trip adult/child/bicycle £12/6/3.30) operates daily from Ballycastle; advance bookings are essential. From April to mid-September there are up to 10 crossings a day, half of which are express services (25 minutes), the rest via a slower car ferry (40 minutes). In winter, the service is reduced.

ⓘ Getting Around

Only residents can take their car to Rathlin (except for disabled drivers), but nowhere on the island is more than 6km (about 1½ hours' walk) from the ferry pier.

McGinn's **Puffin Bus** (☑ 07752 861788, 07759 935192; adult/child £5/3) shuttles visitors between the ferry and Rathlin West Light Seabird Centre from April to September; contact the company for other transport requests.

Bicycle hire (☑ 028-2076 3954; john_jennifer@btinternet.com; per day £10; ☺ 10am-5pm May-Sep) is available at Soerneog View Hostel, south of the harbour (book in advance; cash only).

Glens of Antrim

The northeastern corner of Antrim is a high plateau of black basalt lava overlying beds of white chalk. Along the coast, between Cushendun and Glenarm, the plateau has been dissected by a series of scenic, glacier-gouged valleys known as the Glens of Antrim.

Two waymarked footpaths traverse the region: the Ulster Way sticks close to the sea, passing through all the coastal villages, while the 32km Moyle Way runs inland across the high plateau from Glenariff Forest Park to Ballycastle.

Torr Head Scenic Road

A few kilometres east of Ballycastle, a minor road signposted 'Scenic Route' branches north off the A2. This alternative route to Cushendun is not for the faint-hearted driver (nor for caravans), as it clings, precarious and narrow, to steep slopes high above the sea. Side roads lead off to the main points of interest. On a clear day, there are superb views across the sea to Scotland, from the Mull of Kintyre to the peaks of Arran.

The first turn-off ends at the National Trust car park at Coolanlough, the starting point for a waymarked 5km return hike to Fair Head. The second turn-off leads steeply down to Murlough Bay. From the parking area at the end of this road, you can walk north along the shoreline to some ruined miners' cottages (10 minutes); coal and chalk were once mined in the cliffs above, and burned in a limekiln (south of the car park) to make quicklime.

The third turn-off leads you past some ruined coastguard houses to the rocky headland of Torr Head, crowned with a 19th-century coastguard station (abandoned in the 1920s).

This is Ireland's closest point to Scotland – the Mull of Kintyre is a mere 19km away across the North Channel. In late spring and summer, a fixed-net salmon fishery operates here. The ancient ice house beside the approach road was once used to store the catch.

Cushendun

POP 150

The pretty seaside village of Cushendun is famous for its distinctive Cornish-style cottages, now owned by the National Trust. Built between 1912 and 1925 at the behest of the local landowner, Lord Cushendun, they were designed by Clough Williams-Ellis, the architect of Portmeirion in north Wales.

Cushendun has a wide sandy beach, various short coastal walks and some impressive caves – a *Game of Thrones* filming location – cut into the overhanging conglomerate sea cliffs south of the village (follow the trail around the far end of the holiday apartments south of the river mouth).

Some 6km north of the village on the A2 road to Ballycastle is Loughareema, also known as the Vanishing Lake. Three streams flow in but none flow out. The lough fills up to a respectable size (400m long and 6m deep) after heavy rain, but the water gradually drains away through fissures in the underlying limestone, leaving a dry lake bed.

🛏 Sleeping & Eating

★ **Villa Farmhouse**   B&B ££
(☑ 028-2176 1252; www.thevillafarmhouse.com; 185 Torr Rd; s/d £35/70; ⓟ �ⓢ) This lovely old whitewashed farmhouse is set on a hillside 1km north of Cushendun, with great views over the bay and the warm atmosphere of a family home, decorated with photos of children and grandchildren. The owner is an expert chef, and breakfast will be a highlight of your stay.

Cloneymore House   B&B ££
(☑ 028-2176 1443; ann.cloneymore@btinternet.com; 103 Knocknacarry Rd; s £60, d £75-85; ⓟ ⓢ) A traditional family B&B on the B92 road 500m southwest of Cushendun, Cloneymore has three spacious and spotless rooms named after Irish and Scottish islands – Aran is the biggest. There are wheelchair ramps and a stairlift, and rooms are equipped for visitors with limited mobility.

Mary McBride's   PUB FOOD ££
(☑ 028-2176 1511; www.facebook.com/Mcbrides cushendun; 2 Main St; bar mains £10-15, restaurant

mains £14-35; ⊙food noon-6pm Wed, 11am-9pm Thu-Sat, 11am-6pm Sun) The original bar here (on the left as you go in) is the smallest in Ireland (2.7m by 1.5m), but there's plenty of elbow-bending room in the rest of the pub. Good pub grub is served downstairs and there's live music on weekends. Upstairs is the **Little Black Door** (6pm to 9pm Thursday to Saturday), specialising in seafood and steak.

Drinking & Nightlife

Randal's PUB
(☑028-2176 1266; 10 Strand View Park; ⊙11.30am-11.30pm) By the bridge in Cushendun, this eccentric place occupies a pair of vintage rooms in what was the Cushendun Hotel. There are just two choices on tap – Guinness and Harp – but also a great selection of whiskeys. On sunny days, the best seats are on the front pavement overlooking the River Dun. Opening hours are irregular.

Corner House CAFE
(☑028-2176 1560; 1 Main St; ⊙10am-5pm Fri-Sun) The National Trust–owned Corner House serves coffee, cakes, scones, cooked breakfasts, and lunchtime soups and salads.

Getting There & Away

Bus 150 links Cushendun with Cushendall (£2.80, 15 minutes, six daily Monday to Friday, three Saturday), Glenariff Forest Park (£4, 30 minutes) and Ballymena (£7.20, one hour).

Cushendall

POP 1240
Cushendall is a holiday centre with a small and shingly beach. The village, which can be a traffic bottleneck, sits at the foot of Glenballyeamon, overlooked by the prominent flat-topped hill of Lurigethan.

Sights

Layd Old Church CHURCH
(Layde Rd) FREE From the car park beside the beach (follow the golf-club signs), a coastal path leads 1km north to the picturesque ruins of Layd Old Church, with views across to Ailsa Craig (a prominent conical island also known as 'Paddy's Milestone') and the Scottish coast. Founded by the Franciscans, it was used as a parish church from the early 14th century until 1790. The graveyard contains several grand MacDonnell memorials.

Near the gate stands an ancient, weathered ring-cross (with the arms missing), much older than the 19th-century inscription on its shaft.

Curfew Tower HISTORIC BUILDING
The unusual red sandstone Curfew Tower at the central crossroads was built in 1817 and based on a building the landowner had seen in China. It was originally a prison. The tower is closed to the public.

Sleeping & Eating

Cullentra House B&B ££
(☑028-2177 1762; www.cullentrahouse.com; 16 Cloughs Rd; s/d from £40/54; P�) This modern bungalow sits high above the village, offering good views of the craggy Antrim coast. The three rooms are spacious and comfy, and the breakfasts (accompanied by home-baked wheaten bread) are as hearty as the owners' hospitality.

Village B&B B&B ££
(☑028-2177 2366; www.thevillagebandb.com; 18 Mill St; s/d/f from £50/75/110; P索) Right in the middle of town, the Village offers spotless rooms with private bathrooms and fireplaces, and huge hearty breakfasts (including a vegetarian option).

★**Harry's Restaurant** BISTRO ££
(☑028-2177 2022; 10 Mill St; mains lunch £11-14, dinner £12-22; ⊙noon-9pm; 索) With its cosy lounge-bar atmosphere and friendly welcome, Harry's is a local institution, serving pub grub staples from noon to 5pm, plus an à la carte evening menu that ranges from steak to seafood.

★**McCollam's** PUB
(Johnny Joe's; ☑028-2177 2849; www.johnnyjoes.co.uk; 23 Mill St; ⊙noon-11.30pm daily, kitchen noon-9pm Wed-Sun) Locally known as Johnny Joe's, this rhubarb-coloured pub is the town's liveliest. The original ground-floor bar was built in the 1800s; behind it is a tiny lounge dominated by an old range cooker. There are regular trad-music sessions and great craic. The excellent restaurant **Upstairs at Joes** (mains £13 to £22) serves modern Irish dishes and daily seafood specials.

Information

Tourist office (☑028-2177 1180; 24 Mill St; ⊙10am-1pm Mon-Sat Apr-Sep) Run by the Glens of Antrim Historical Society.

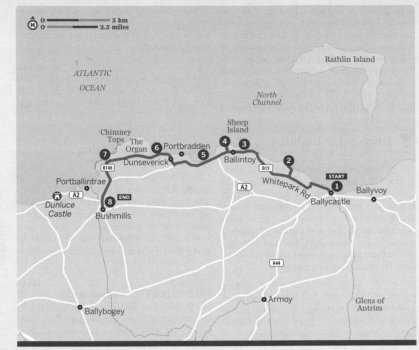

Driving Tour
Ballycastle to Bushmills

START BALLYCASTLE MARINA
END OLD BUSHMILLS DISTILLERY
LENGTH 30KM; FOUR HOURS

From **1** **Ballycastle Marina** car park, turn right onto North St, which becomes Clare Rd, and begin the steep climb onto the clifftops and out of town. Turn right onto Whitepark Rd (A2), and after 2km follow signs to turn right down a single track lane to **2** **Kinbane Castle** (p637), dramatically positioned on a limestone headland with stunning views of Rathlin Island. Steep steps lead down to the castle.

Return to Whitepark Rd, turn right, and continue west along the coast for 5km to reach **3** **Carrick-a-Rede Rope Bridge** (p637), where you can cross the bridge – if you dare.

Turn right on Whitepark Rd, driving west through Ballintoy village, then turn right onto Harbour Rd, following signs to **4** **Ballintoy Harbour**. The road snakes around some tight turns as you descend to a picturesque, sheltered bay, which *Game of Thrones* fans might recognise as the Iron Islands' Harbour.

Go back up to Whitepark Rd and continue west past **5** **Whitepark Bay**, a 2km-long expanse of glistening white sand; there is a car park (signed) at the western end of the beach.

Two kilometres beyond Whitepark Bay, look for a right turn onto the B147 Causeway Rd (signed 'Giant's Causeway'). Soon you'll see signs for **6** **Dunseverick Castle**; park in the lay-by on the right-hand side for views of the modest ruins; over the years most of the castle has been lost to the sea.

Continue along Causeway Rd for 4.5km to reach the **7** **Giant's Causeway** (p636). To park here you will need to pay for a ticket to the Giant's Causeway Visitor Experience. Alternatively, continue on the Causeway Rd then turn right onto Whitepark Rd to reach Bushmills, where you can park in the free park-and-ride car park and walk back to the Causeway along the path running parallel to the Giant's Causeway & Bushmills Railway.

Drive south along Main St through Bushmills town to reach **8** **Old Bushmills Distillery** (p634), where you can take a tour and learn about its famous whiskeys.

ⓘ Getting There & Away

Bus 150 links Cushendall with Cushendun (£2.80, 15 minutes, six daily Monday to Friday, three Saturday), Glenariff Forest Park (£3.10, 15 minutes) and Ballymena (£6.20, one hour).

Glenariff

About 2km south of Cushendall is the village of Waterfoot, with a 2km-long sandy beach, the best on Antrim's east coast. From here the A43 Ballymena road runs inland along Glenariff, the loveliest of Antrim's glens. Views of the valley led the writer Thackeray to exclaim that it was 'Switzerland in miniature' (a claim that makes you wonder if he'd ever been to Switzerland).

Glenariff Forest Park FOREST
(www.nidirect.gov.uk; 98 Glenariff Rd; car/motorcycle £5/2.50; ☺9am-dusk, teahouse 11am-5pm Easter-Sep) At the head of the Glenariff Valley is Glenariff Forest Park, where the main attraction is **Ess-na-Larach Waterfall**, an 800m walk from the visitor centre. You can also walk to the waterfall from Laragh Lodge, 600m downstream. Wonderful hikes in the park include the 9km circular scenic trail. There's also a teahouse selling scones and hot drinks and lunches.

★Ballyeamon Barn HOSTEL £
(☑028-2175 8451; www.ballyeamonbarn.com; 127 Ballyeamon Rd; dm/d £15/40; ℗ 🖥) Run by professional storyteller Liz Weir, this whitewashed barn has hostel accommodation for hikers and hosts regular sessions of traditional Irish music, poetry, dance and storytelling. It's 8km southwest of Cushendall on the B14 (1km north of its junction with the A43), close to the Moyle Way and about a 1.5km walk from the main entrance to Glenariff Forest Park.

Upstairs, the spacious loft bedroom with attached bathroom is good for couples or families. There's secure parking for bikes and a well-equipped kitchen.

Laragh Lodge IRISH ££
(☑028-2175 8221; www.laraghlodge.co.uk; 120 Glen Rd; mains £12-16; ☺11am-9pm Mar-Oct; 🖥) A renovated Victorian tourist lodge, the Laragh dates from 1890 and serves hearty meals like steak sandwiches, burgers and fish and chips, as well as a traditional roast lunch on Sunday – perfect after a long walk. It's on a side road off the A43, 3km northeast of the main Glenariff Forest Park entrance.

ⓘ Getting There & Away

You can reach Glenariff Forest Park on bus 150 from Cushendall (£3.10, 15 minutes, six daily Monday to Friday, three Saturday) and Ballymena (£4.60, 30 minutes).

Glenarm

POP 1800
Delightful little Glenarm (Gleann Arma) is the oldest village in the Glens of Antrim. It's well worth a visit for the fabulous gardens at Glenarm Castle, rows of pretty Georgian houses and forest park. Take a stroll into the old village (off the main road, south of the river). Where the street opens into the broad expanse of Altmore St, look right to see the **Barbican Gate** (1682), the entrance to the grounds of Glenarm Castle.

Up steep Vennel St, turn left after the last house along the Layde Path to the viewpoint, which has a grand view of the village and the coast.

◉ Sights & Activities

Glenarm Castle & Walled Garden CASTLE
(www.glenarmcastle.com; 2 Castle Lane; walled garden adult/child £6/3; ☺garden 10am-4pm Mar & Oct, to 5pm Apr-Sep) Since 1750, Glenarm has been the family seat of the McDonnell family, earls of Antrim; it's currently the home of Lord and Lady Dunluce. The castle itself is closed to the public – except during the Tulip Festival on the May bank-holiday weekend, and during the Dalriada Festival in July – but you can visit the lovely walled garden and take a walk around the estate along the castle trail. Admission is free for children under 12.

The estate's organic farm is renowned for its Glenarm shorthorn beef; the smokehouse produces organic smoked salmon. Both are sold at the Glenarm Castle Tea Room & Shop.

Steensons JEWELLERY
(www.thesteensons.com; New Rd; ☺10am-5.30pm Mon-Sat) Watch craftspeople at work at Steensons, the designer jewellery workshop that produced the jewellery worn in *Game of Thrones*. Pieces are also available to buy.

Dalriada Festival MUSIC
(www.dalriadafestival.co.uk; day pass adult/child £33/22; ☺Jul) This family-friendly three-day music and food festival at Glenarm Castle features performances from some big-name bands and top local acts, as well as a street food market and cooking demonstrations.

Camping and caravan pitches are available in the castle grounds.

🛏 Sleeping & Eating

★ **Water's Edge Glenarm**   B&B **££**
(☎028-2884 1117; www.watersedgeglenarm.com; 11-13 The Cloney; r £100-120) In a beautifully renovated former police station, Water's Edge has three spacious rooms with hand-woven bed quilts and fabulous sea views. There's a bright guest lounge area and secure storage for bikes. Breakfast options include Glenarm organic smoked salmon and scrambled eggs on wheaten bread.

Granny Shaw's Fudge Factory   SWEETS **£**
(www.grannyshawsfudgefactory.co.uk; 12 Castle Demesne; 4 bars of fudge £9, ice cream £2-3.50; ☺11am-4pm Mon-Sat, noon-4pm Sun Mar-Oct) The artisan fudge sold here is handmade in the adjoining factory, visible through a window from inside the shop. Flavours include lemon meringue, raspberry ripple and salted caramel. There's coffee and ice cream, too.

Glenarm Castle Tea Room & Shop   CAFE **£**
(☎028-2884 1984; www.glenarmcastle.com; 2 Castle Lane; mains £5-11.50; ☺10am-5pm Mar–mid-Oct) Sample Glenarm's famous shorthorn beef at this excellent tearoom. Produce from the estate farm and kitchen garden are used in its shorthorn beefburger with walled-garden relish, haddock and chips, sandwiches and salads. The homemade cakes – including fluffy Victoria sponge – are irresistible. There's also a shop selling Glenarm estate beef, salmon, infused rapeseed oils and relishes.

ℹ Information

Glenarm Visitor Information Centre (☎028-2884 1087; www.glenarmtourism.org; 17 New Rd; ☺9.30am-1.30pm Tue-Fri)

ℹ Getting There & Away

Bus 162 connects Glenarm with Larne (£4.60, 25 minutes, seven daily Monday to Friday, five Saturday) and Carnlough (£4, 10 minutes). In July and August buses run hourly from Monday to Friday, and seven times on Saturday.

Larne

POP 32,000

As a major port for ferries from Scotland, Larne (Lutharna) is one of Northern Ireland's main gateways. However, with its concrete overpasses and the huge chimneys of Ballylumford power station opposite the harbour, poor old Larne is a little lacking in the charm department. After a visit to the excellent Larne Visitor Information Centre, there's no real reason to linger.

Most visitors to Larne don't stop for long on their way to or from the ferry port – it's close enough to Belfast to make an overnight stay unnecessary – but there are some cosy rooms available at Billy Andy's.

Billy Andy's   IRISH **££**
(☎028-2827 0648; www.billyandys.com; 66 Browndod Rd; mains lunch £10-11.50, dinner £12-22.50; ☺kitchen 5-8.30pm Mon-Thu, noon-4pm & 5-9pm Fri & Sat, noon-7pm Sun) In a bucolic setting 7km southwest of Larne, this 19th-century

---

THE GOBBINS

Tubular bridges, rocky surfaces, tunnels, caves and narrow crevices form a dramatic cliff path at Islandmagee, the slender peninsula that runs parallel to the coastline between Whitehead and Larne. The **Gobbins coastal path** (Coastal Walk; ☎028-9337 2318; www.thegobbinscliffpath.com; 68 Middle Rd, Islandmagee; adult/child £15/12; ☺9.30am-6.30pm Mar-Nov) is accessible on 2½-hour-long guided tours. A good level of fitness, a minimum height of 1.2m and suitable footwear are essential. Book in advance.

The Gobbins first opened as a tourist attraction in 1902, when the new railway made the area accessible to visitors. The path was closed in the 1930s and fell into disrepair; a £7.5-million investment saw the attraction reopen in 2015.

Tours leave from the visitor centre, from where it's a five-minute bus ride to the path. The most strenuous part of the walk is the return climb up the steep access path; otherwise the path is not physically demanding. Guides explain the history of the Gobbins and highlight geological and natural features of the coastline. As well as spectacular views out to the Irish Sea, you might spot dolphins and puffins on the walk.

There's a playground, cafe and souvenir shop at the visitor centre.

To reach Islandmagee, take the A2 Belfast–Larne road, turn right onto the B90 Island Lower Rd and follow the signs. The nearest train station is Ballycarry (3km), on the Belfast–Larne line.

SEAMUS HEANEY HOME PLACE

Nobel Prize–winning poet Seamus Heaney's home town of Bellaghy, 54km northwest of Belfast, is the location of a wonderful museum and arts centre, **Seamus Heaney Home Place** (⏹ 028-7938 7444; www.seamusheaneyhome.com; 45 Main St; adult/child £7/4.50; ⊙ 10am-5pm Mon-Sat, 1-5pm Sun). References in Heaney's poetry to the local landscape, everyday village life and the people who influenced him are highlighted in a creatively laid-out exhibition, which places his work in the context of his home and surroundings. Audio guides allow you to listen to poems read by Heaney himself as you walk around, bringing his words to life.

The centre also hosts regular poetry-reading events and writing workshops; see the website for details. It's easiest to drive here, but the 127 bus from Ballymena stops in Bellaghy (six daily, 50 minutes) and continues to Magherafelt (15 minutes).

The museum can be visited on a day trip from Derry or Belfast, but Heaney fans should consider spending the night at **Laurel Villa** (⏹ 028-7930 1459; www.laurel-villa.com; 60 Church St; s/d from £70/90; 🖥) in nearby Magherafelt. Owner Eugene Kielt offers recommended **Seamus Heaney Tours** (⏹ 028-7930 1459; www.laurel-villa.com; half-day private tour £90) of the surrounding area, and the characterful B&B contains his extensive collection of Heaney poetry and memorabilia.

country pub with open log and peat fires, low ceilings, and live trad sessions on Saturday afternoons rewards a detour, not least for its fine gastropub fare, with dishes like braised Mounthill lamb shank, platter of rare-breed pork, and spiced pear and star anise crumble.

Upstairs, cosy single/double rooms cost from £50/65.

ⓘ Information

Larne Visitor Information Centre (⏹ 028-2826 2450; www.midandeastantrim.gov.uk; Narrow Gauge Rd; ⊙ 9am-5pm Mon-Fri, 10am-4pm Sat year-round, plus 11am-3pm Sun Jun-Sep) Extensive information on all of Northern Ireland, and an exhibition on local history and wildlife.

ⓘ Getting There & Away

Bus 153 runs between the town centre and Belfast (£5.20, one hour 15 minutes, five Monday to Friday, four Saturday); the trains are quicker and more frequent.

P&O Ferries (www.poferries.com) links Larne with Cairnyan in Scotland.

Larne has two train stations, Larne Town and Larne Harbour. Trains run from Larne Town to Belfast Central (£7.70, 50 minutes, hourly Monday to Friday, every two hours Saturday and Sunday); those from the harbour are timed to connect with ferries.

Carrickfergus

POP 28,000

Northern Ireland's most impressive medieval fortress commands the entrance to Belfast

Lough from the rocky promontory of Carrickfergus (Carraig Fhearghais), just 18km northeast of Belfast. The old town centre opposite Carrickfergus Castle has some attractive 18th-century houses and you can still trace a good part of the 17th-century city walls.

⊙ Sights

Carrickfergus Castle   CASTLE
(⏹ 028-9335 1273; Marine Hwy; adult/child £5.50/3.50; ⊙ 9.30am-5pm, last admission 4.30pm) The central keep of Ireland's first and finest Norman fortress was built by John de Courcy soon after his 1177 invasion of Ulster. The massive walls of the outer ward were completed in 1242, while the red-brick gun ports were added in the 16th century. Inside, the keep is set up to recreate the days of de Courcy, and the site is dotted with life-size figures illustrating the castle's history. Guided tours run roughly every hour.

The castle overlooks the harbour where William of Orange landed on 14 June 1690, on his way to the Battle of the Boyne. A blue plaque on the old harbour wall marks the site where he stepped ashore, and a bronze statue of 'King Billy' himself stands on the shore nearby.

Carrickfergus Museum   MUSEUM
(⏹ 028-9335 8241; www.midandeastantrim.gov. uk; 11 Antrim St; ⊙ 10am-5pm Mon-Fri, to 4pm Sat) 🆓 The glass-fronted Museum and Civic Centre on Antrim St houses the local museum, which has an interesting collection of artefacts relating to the town's history.

Items of note include silver coins made in Carrickfergus for John de Courcy, Elizabethan and Jacobean town charters, a medieval tower house window, a collection of bone and clay pipes, and a steam fire engine dating from 1908. There is also a tribute to local poet Louis MacNeice.

Andrew Jackson Centre
HISTORIC SITE

(2 Boneybefore; ⊗by appointment 11am-3pm Thu-Sat, 1-4pm Sun May-Oct, 11am-3pm Fri & Sat Nov-Apr) FREE The seventh US president's parents left Carrickfergus in the 18th century. His ancestral home was demolished in 1860, but a replica thatched cottage now houses this memorial 2km north of Carrickfergus Castle. Displays cover the Jackson family in Ulster, and Ulster's US connections.

Next door, the US Rangers Centre commemorates the first US Rangers, who trained during WWII in Carrickfergus before heading for Europe.

Contact Carrickfergus' visitor information centre in advance to arrange your visit.

🛏 Sleeping & Eating

Dobbins Inn Hotel
HOTEL ££

(☑ 028-9335 1905; www.dobbinsinn.co.uk; 6-8 High St; s £58-62, d £78-85; 🖝) In the centre of the old town, Dobbin's is a friendly and informal place with 15 small and creaky-floored but comfortable rooms (one of them supposedly haunted). The building has been around for over three centuries, and has a priest's hole and an original 16th-century fireplace.

Restoration work has left the hotel's facade resembling a 12th-century tower house once again, and returned the windows to their original arched shape.

Nix
CAFE £

(☑ 028-9332 6060; www.facebook.com/nixbistroltd; 2 North St; mains £5-10; ⊗8am-5pm Mon-Thu, to 9pm Fri & Sat; 🖝🖝) Local favourite Nix is an unpretentious spot with friendly service and a menu of homemade savoury scones, sandwiches and salads through to lasagne, steaks and ribs. It's tiny, so book ahead for dinner.

Ownies
PUB

(☑ 028-9335 1850; www.owniesbarbistro.com; 16-18 Joymount; ⊗9am-midnight Sun-Wed, to 1am Thu-Sat) Carrickfergus' most traditional bar – formerly the Joymount Arms, dating from 1846 – has a cosy interior complete with snugs, fireplaces, a beer garden and a bistro serving breakfast, lunch (mains £6 to £14) and dinner (mains £10 to £17).

Windrose
BAR

(☑ 028-9335 1164; www.thewindrose.co.uk; Rodgers Quay; ⊗10am-midnight Mon-Thu, 10am-1am Fri, 9am-1am Sat, 9am-midnight Sun) This modern bar-bistro has dining on two levels, but the real reason to drop by is for a drink on the sun-drenched terrace overlooking the forest of yacht masts in the marina.

ⓘ Information

Carrickfergus Visitor Information Centre
(☑ 028-9335 8222; www.midandeastantrim.gov.uk; Marine Hwy; ⊗10am-5pm Apr-Sep, to 4pm Oct-Mar; 🖝) At Carrickfergus Castle.

ⓘ Getting There & Away

Trains link Carrickfergus with Belfast Lanyon Place (£4.70, 25 minutes, every 30 minutes Monday to Saturday, hourly Sunday).

Antrim Town

POP 23,400

The county town of Antrim (Aontroim) straddles the Six Mile Water river, close to the shores of Lough Neagh. The landscaped gardens at the site of the long-demolished Antrim Castle are a pleasant spot to stretch your legs, and there are waymarked walking and cycling paths along the riverbank and lough shore.

During the 1798 Rising, the United Irishmen fought a pitched battle along the length of Antrim town's High St.

Pick up a map at the tourist office, housed in the beautifully restored Old Courthouse (1762), a gem of Georgian architecture.

A walking and cycling trail leads west along the river from the Antrim Castle Gardens to Antrim Lough Shore Park, where the vast size of Lough Neagh is apparent. There are picnic tables, a children's playground and lakeside walking trails. At research time, a new Lough Neagh Gateway Centre, to house a cafe, interpretation centre and conference rooms, was under construction.

Antrim Castle Gardens & Clotworthy House
GARDENS

(Randalstown Rd; ⊗9.30am-7pm, or dusk if earlier) FREE Pass through the Barbican Gate (1818), a portion of the old castle walls, and the underpass beyond to reach Antrim Castle Gardens. The castle burned down many years ago, but the grounds remain as one of the few surviving examples of a 17th-century ornamental garden. Clotworthy House, the castle's former coach house and stable block, now houses an exhibition on the history of the castle and gardens as well as a cafe and gift shop.

Round Tower
HISTORIC BUILDING

(Steeple Rd) Antrim's 10th-century Round Tower, on the northeast edge of town, is 28m tall, and is one of the finest examples of these monastic towers in Ireland. The tower itself is closed to the public, but you're free to explore the surrounding site.

ℹ Information

Tourist office (☑ 028-9442 8331; www.antrimandnewtownabbey.gov.uk; Market Sq; ⊙10am-4.30pm Mon-Fri) Inside the Old Courthouse.

ℹ Getting There & Away

Bus 120 connects Belfast and Antrim (£4.60, 55 minutes, seven daily Monday to Friday, five on Saturday).

Trains link Belfast Central with Antrim (£6, 30 minutes, hourly), continuing to Derry (£12, 1¾ hours).

Ballymena & Around

POP 29,470

Ballymena (An Baile Meánach) is a bustling market town with good shops, making it a handy place for stocking up if you're heading for remoter pastures. Sights are sparse but there are a few good places to sleep, eat and drink near the town.

★ Galgorm Resort & Spa
HOTEL £££

(☑ 028-2588 1001; www.galgorm.com; 136 Fenaghy Rd, Cullybackey; cottages/d/ste from £175/185/275; P@🅐🅢) About 6km west of Ballymena in a pretty spot overlooking the River Main is the Galgorm. Accommodation is in pleasant, classically decorated rooms, suites and cottages, but the Galgorm's biggest draw is the state-of-the-art Thermal Village spa, with hydrotherapy pools, snow cabin, steam rooms, open-air hot tubs and a daily Celtic sauna meditation ritual led by the sauna master.

There are several excellent restaurants and bars, including one in the former stables.

Blackstone
MODERN IRISH ££

(☑ 028-2564 8566; www.facebook.com/blackstonebarandrestaurant; 15-17 Hill St; mains lunch £7.50-11, dinner £13-18; ⊙noon-2.30pm & 5-9pm Mon-Thu, noon-9pm Fri & Sat, noon-7.30pm Sun) Just off Ballymena's main street, this gastropub is worth seeking out for its seriously good cooking. The menu changes regularly, but often features Asian dishes (Malaysian butternut squash

SLEMISH MOUNTAIN

The skyline to the east of Ballymena is dominated by the distinctive craggy peak of **Slemish Mountain** (438m; Carnstroan Rd, Broughshane). The hill is one of many sites in the North associated with Ireland's patron saint – the young St Patrick is said to have tended goats on its slopes. On St Patrick's Day, thousands of people make a pilgrimage to its summit; the rest of the year it's a pleasant climb, though steep and slippery in wet weather, rewarded with a fine view.

There is a toilet block and picnic tables at the car park but no shop or cafe; bring your own snacks and water. Allow one hour return from the parking area.

curry or Chinese black bean beef) as well as more traditional Irish fare, such as Portavogie scampi with pea-and-mint purée.

★ Crosskeys Inn
PUB

(https://crosskeys-inn.com; 40 Grange Rd, near Toomebridge; ⊙11.30am-1am Mon-Sat, noon-11pm Sun) Dating from 1654, Ireland's oldest thatched pub is an absolute treasure, with tiny, antique-filled rooms, a crackling turf fire, the best Guinness for miles around and fabulous craic. Live traditional music plays every Saturday, with impromptu sessions on Wednesday, Friday and Sunday. It's 13km southwest of Ballymena.

Slemish Market Garden
FOOD & DRINKS

(www.facebook.com/slemishmarketgarden; Kernohans Lane, Ecos Nature Park; ⊙9.30am-5pm Mon-Sat) At the Ecos Nature Park, this food shop sells organic and biodynamic produce from the on-site gardens and local farms. Pick up seasonal fruit and fresh-from-the-ground vegetables, locally produced honey, oils and vinegar, and recently laid eggs from the hens that roam the gardens.

ℹ Getting There & Away

Buses 217 and 131 link Ballymena with Ballycastle (£7.20, 50 minutes, eight daily Monday to Friday, five Saturday). Bus 120 serves Belfast's Laganside Bus Centre (£7.20, 70 minutes, two services daily Monday to Saturday); there is one daily express bus to Belfast Europa Bus Centre (50 minutes, Monday to Friday only).

Trains link Ballymena with Belfast Central (£8.40, 50 minutes, hourly); some continue from Ballymena to Derry (£12, 1½ hours, every two hours).

Counties Fermanagh & Tyrone

POP 240,170 / AREA 4954 SQ KM

Best Places to Eat

➡ 28 Darling St (p658)

➡ Thatch Coffee Shop
(p662)

➡ Jolly Sandwich Bar (p657)

➡ Watermill Restaurant
(p659)

➡ Brewer's House (p668)

➡ Cafe Merlot (p657)

Best Places to Stay

➡ Finn Lough (p662)

➡ Watermill Lodge (p659)

➡ Tullylagan Country House
(p667)

➡ Killyhevlin Hotel (p657)

➡ Enniskillen Hotel (p657)

➡ Mullaghmore House
(p665)

Why Go?

The ancient landscape of Fermanagh was shaped by ice and water, with rugged hills rising above quilted plains of half-drowned drumlins (rounded hills formed by retreating glaciers) and shimmering, reed-fringed lakes. A glance at the map shows the county is around one-third water – as the locals will tell you, the lakes are in Fermanagh for six months of the year; for the other six, Fermanagh is in the lakes. This watery maze is a natural playground for boaters, kayakers and anglers. The surrounding landscape is laced with good walks.

County Tyrone – from Tír Eoghain (Land of Owen, a legendary chieftain) – is dominated by the tweed-tinted moorlands of the Sperrin Mountains, whose southern flanks are dotted with prehistoric sites. Apart from hiking these heather-clad hills, visitors can enjoy several excellent sights that celebrate its heritage, including the historic ties to the USA.

When to Go

➡ May marks the start of the mayfly season, the most exciting time for trout fishing on Lough Erne, while June is ideal for cruising the lakes.

➡ If hiking is more to your taste, July is great for hillwalking in the Sperrins. You can join a mass pilgrimage to the summit of Mullaghcarn, above Gortin, on Cairn Sunday, the last Sunday in the month.

➡ The tail end of summer is enlivened by the Ulster American Folk Park's annual Appalachian and Bluegrass Music Festival, which takes place in late August/early September.

COUNTY FERMANAGH

The least populated of Northern Ireland's six counties, Fermanagh is dominated by lakes and waterways. About 80km long, Lough Erne is made up of two sections: the Upper Lough to the south of Enniskillen, and the Lower Lough to the north. The two are connected by the River Erne, which begins its journey in County Cavan and meets the sea at Donegal Bay west of Ballyshannon. This is a great region for exploring with your own wheels, picnicking at will and enjoying no end of water sports and other aquatic activities.

Enniskillen & Around

POP 13,800

Perched amid the web of waterways that link Upper and Lower Lough Erne, Enniskillen (Inis Ceithleann, meaning 'Ceithleann's Island', after a legendary female warrior) is an appealing island town. Its attractive waterside setting, bustling with boats in summer, plus its range of lively pubs and restaurants, make Enniskillen a good base for exploring Upper and Lower Lough Erne, Florence Court and the Marble Arch Caves.

Though neither was born here, both Oscar Wilde and Samuel Beckett were pupils at Enniskillen's Portora Royal School (Wilde from 1864 to 1871, Beckett from 1919 to 1923); it was here that Beckett first studied French, a language he would later write in. The town's name is also prominent in the history of the Troubles – on Remembrance Sunday in 1987 an IRA bomb killed 11 people during a service at Enniskillen's war memorial.

◉ Sights

Castle Coole HISTORIC BUILDING
(☑ 028-6632 2690; www.nationaltrust.org.uk; off A4; adult/child house tour & grounds £11/5.50, grounds only £4.50/2.25; ⊗ house 11am-5pm daily Jul & Aug, Fri-Wed Jun, Sat, Sun & public holidays mid-Mar–May & Sep, grounds 10am-7pm Mar-Oct, to 4pm Nov-Feb) This National Trust–owned neoclassical palace sits in 600 hectares of beautiful parkland containing a lake that's home to the UK's only nonmigratory colony of greylag geese. The house's double cantilever staircase, Italian marble fireplaces, Regency furniture and basement servants quarters can be seen on one-hour guided tours.

Designed by James Wyatt, the Palladian mansion was built between 1789 and 1795 for Armar Lowry-Corry, the first earl of Belmore, and is probably the purest expression of late-18th-century neoclassical architecture in Ireland. When King George IV visited Ireland in 1821, the second earl of Belmore had a state bedroom specially prepared at Castle Coole in anticipation of the monarch's visit. The king, however, was more interested in dallying with his mistress at Slane Castle and never turned up. The bedroom, draped in red silk and decorated with paintings depicting *A Rake's Progress,* is one of the highlights of the house tour.

Castle Coole is 2.5km southeast of Enniskillen; it's a pleasant 5km walk or cycle along the Castle to Castle path from Enniskillen Castle.

Enniskillen Castle Museums MUSEUM
(☑ 028-6632 5000; www.enniskillencastle.co.uk; off Wellington Rd; adult/child £5/3.50; ⊗ 10am-5pm Mon-Fri, from 11am Sat year-round, plus 11am-5pm Sun Jun-Sep) Enniskillen Castle, a former stronghold of the 16th-century Maguire chieftains, guards the western end of the town's central island, its twin-turreted Watergate looming over passing fleets of cabin cruisers. Within the walls is the refurbished **Fermanagh County Museum**, which has excellent displays and interactive exhibits on the county's history, archaeology, landscape and wildlife. It includes a fascinating gallery dedicated to the history of Fermanagh's waterways as a route for pilgrims travelling via Devenish Island to Lough Derg in Donegal.

In the ground-floor Lakelands Gallery, look for the 1000-year-old 35lb block of bog butter, uncarthed by a Fermanagh farmer in 1980; it was probably buried in the bog to preserve it for consumption during winter.

The 15th-century castle keep contains the **Inniskilling Museum**, full of guns, uniforms and medals, including eight Victoria Crosses awarded in WWI; it's dedicated to the regiment that was raised at the castle in 1689 to support the army of William I.

Headhunters Barber Shop & Railway Museum MUSEUM
(☑ 028-6632 7488; www.facebook.com/headhuntersmuseum; 5 Darling St; ⊗ 9am-5.30pm Tue-Sat) **FREE** This museum and barber shop (open for haircuts) displays the Johnston family's impressive collection of local railway memorabilia, from old station signs to timetables, uniforms, tickets and passes. There's a display case containing items frequently smuggled on Fermanagh's trains (which stopped running in 1957), and even a violin made by former station-master Thomas

Counties Fermanagh & Tyrone Highlights

1 Mysterious stone figures (p661) Pondering the meaning of the ancient carvings on White Island and Boa Island, including those at Caldragh Graveyard.

2 Ulster American Folk Park (p665) Revelling in the historical links between Ireland and the USA.

3 Marble Arch Caves (p663) Discovering an amazing network of underground caverns.

4 Canoeing (p659) Exploring the reed-fringed backwaters of Lough Erne.

5 Devenish Island (p660) Exploring the Celtic monastic settlement and ancient round tower.

6 Florence Court (p663) Taking a house tour and exploring the forest walks and cycle trails.

7 Cuilcagh Mountain Park (p663) Striding along boardwalks to the summit of Fermanagh's highest peak.

8 Castle Coole (p653) Seeing how the Irish aristocracy enjoyed the high life in this elegant country house.

9 Enniskillen Castle (p653) Viewing the illuminating exhibits at the Fermanagh County Museum.

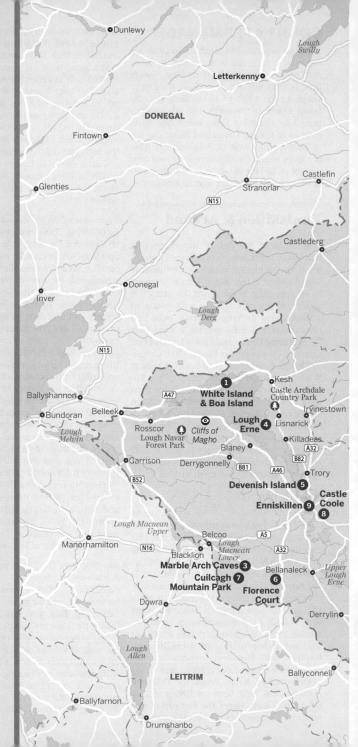

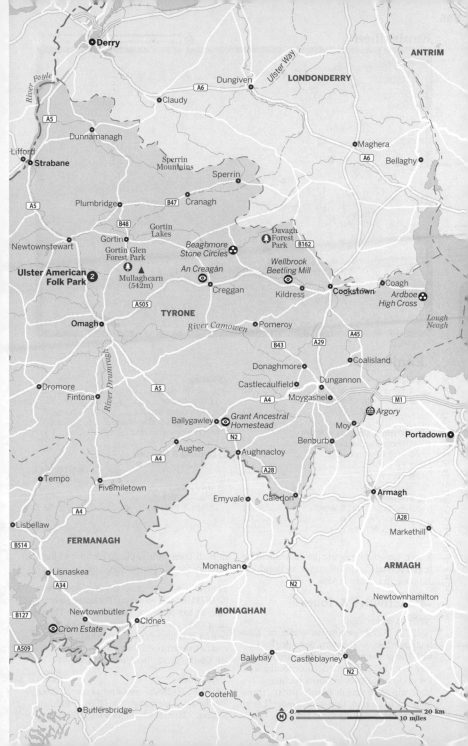

Enniskillen

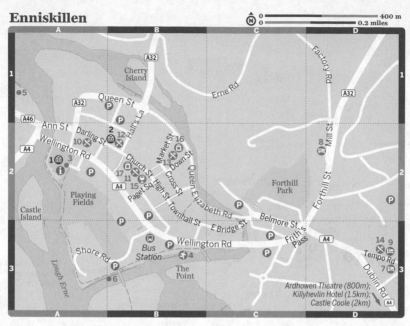

Enniskillen

⊙ Sights
1 Enniskillen Castle Museums A2
2 Headhunters Barber Shop &
　Railway Museum B2

⊕ Activities, Courses & Tours
3 Enniskillen Taste Experience A2
4 Erne Boat Hire B3
5 Erne Tours A1
6 Erne Water Taxi B3

⊟ Sleeping
7 Belmore Court & Motel D3
8 Enniskillen Hotel D2
9 Westville Hotel D3

⊗ Eating
10 28 Darling St A2
11 Cafe Merlot B2
12 Jolly Sandwich Bar B2
13 Rebecca's Coffee Shop B2
14 Terrace Restaurant D3

⊙ Drinking & Nightlife
15 Blakes of the Hollow B2

⊟ Shopping
16 Buttermarket... B2
17 Home, Field & Stream B2

Moore, known for playing the instrument between arrivals and departures at Bundoran Junction in County Tyrone.

🏃 Activities & Tours

★ Erne Water Taxi　　　　BOATING
(☑ 07719 770588; www.ernewatertaxi.com; Lakeland Forum Leisure Centre jetty, Wellington Rd; tours for 1-8 people per hr £70) Offers a range of private tours led by knowledgeable local guides for up to eight people. Tours include a 1½-hour trip to Devenish Island (p660), three-hour trips around Upper or Lower Lough Erne and full-day (seven-hour) trips taking

in both lakes. Add a picnic hamper of local produce for £15 per person.

Enniskillen Taste Experience　　FOOD & DRINK
(☑ 07734 055452; www.enniskillentasteexperience. com; 3hr tour per person £45; ⊙ 11am Sat) Three-hour food and drink tours that take in the best of Fermanagh's local produce, from ice cream to craft beer. Tours begin at Enniskillen Castle (p653); book in advance.

Erne Tours　　　　BOATING
(☑ 028-6632 2882; www.ernetours.com; Brook Park, Round 'O' Jetty; adult/child £10/6; ⊙ 10.30am, 12.15pm, 2.15pm & 4.15pm Jul & Aug, 2.15pm daily

Jun, Tue, Sat & Sun May & Sep; 🚤) Operates 1¾-hour cruises on Lower Lough Erne aboard the 56-seat waterbus MV *Kestrel,* calling at Devenish Island (p660) (May to September) along the way. It departs from the Round 'O' Quay, just west of the town centre on the A46 to Belleek.

Erne Boat Hire BOATING
(☑ 07523 423232; www.erneboathireltd.com; Regal Pass Jetty, Wellington Rd; boat for 2/4/8hr £35/55/85) Rents boats year-round for self-guided trips out on the lake. Devenish Island (p660) can be reached in 30 minutes. Tutorials can be given to inexperienced boaters. Boats hold up to six people; fuel and buoyancy aids included. Book ahead on weekends.

Erne Angling FISHING
(☑ 07884 472121; www.erneangling.com; 2 anglers half-/full-day trip £80/130) Hook the pike of your dreams on Lough Erne with these experienced guides.

Kingfisher Trail CYCLING
(www.kingfishercycletrail.com) The Kingfisher Trail is a waymarked, long-distance cycling trail that starts in Enniskillen and wends its way through the back roads of Counties Fermanagh, Leitrim, Cavan and Monaghan. You can get a trail map from the Enniskillen tourist office (p658) or online.

The full route is around 370km long, but a shorter loop, starting and finishing in Enniskillen, and travelling via Kesh, Belleek, Garrison, Belcoo and Florencecourt, is 115km – easily done in two days with an overnight stay at Belleek.

🛌 Sleeping

Enniskillen Hotel HOTEL ££
(☑ 028-6632 1177; www.enniskillenhotel.com; 72 Forthill St; hotel/motel d from £75/60; 🅿) Enniskillen's newest hotel has contemporary decor and a central location. Rooms are on the snug side but are nonetheless comfortable and stylish, with a contemporary grey-and-black colour scheme and flash bathrooms with rain showers. A separate block houses budget motel rooms, which come with continental breakfast bags, rather than full breakfasts.

Westville Hotel HOTEL ££
(☑ 028-6632 0333; www.westvillehotel.co.uk; 14-20 Tempo Rd; s/d from £80/100; 🅿🖧🛜) Starting with its grand lobby, the Westville adds a dash of four-star comfort to Enniskillen's hotel scene with designer fabrics, sophisticated colour combinations and good food at the

Terrace Restaurant (mains £12-24; ⊙6-10pm Mon-Sat, noon-4pm Sun). Rooms come with cookies made by the hotel's pastry chef and triple-glazed windows to block out road noise.

Belmore Court & Motel HOTEL ££
(☑ 028-6632 6633; www.motel.co.uk; Tempo Rd; d/f from £70/100; 🛜) Set in a centrally located row of terrace houses linked to a large modern extension, the Belmore offers spacious, well-equipped rooms in the new building and family rooms with small kitchens in the old section. Some motel-style rooms sleep up to four.

Killyhevlin Hotel HOTEL £££
(☑ 028-6632 3481; www.killyhevlin.com; off A4, Killyhevlin; s/d from £115/170; 🅿🛜🏊) The luxurious Killyhevlin occupies an idyllic setting overlooking Upper Lough Erne, 1.5km south of Enniskillen on the road to Maguiresbridge. Many of its 71 elegant rooms have lovely views over landscaped gardens to the lough; self-catering accommodation is offered in two-bedroom, timber-clad lakeside lodges. There's also a fancy spa and health club.

🍴 Eating & Drinking

⭐ Jolly Sandwich Bar CAFE £
(☑ 028-6632 2277; 3 Darling St; mains £4-7; ⊙7.30am-4.15pm Mon-Sat) This cheery place sells divine baked goods and a wide range of sandwiches to eat in or takeaway. Ingredients include seasonal and local produce. The freshly baked rhubarb and ginger scones are a favourite among cafe regulars.

Rebecca's Coffee Shop CAFE £
(☑ 028-6632 9376; Buttermarket; mains £4-6.20; ⊙9am-5.30pm Mon-Sat) At the Buttermarket (p658), Rebecca's serves good sandwiches, salads, scones and pastries as well as a few hot dishes; locals rave about the cottage pie. There are outdoor courtyard tables in summer.

Cafe Merlot MODERN IRISH ££
(☑ 028-6632 0918; www.cafemerlot.co.uk; 6 Church St; mains lunch £8-11, dinner £16-30; ⊙noon-3pm &

ℹ GETTING AFLOAT
It's easy to hire out day boats at Enniskillen (try Erne Boat Hire) and Castle Archdale Country Park (contact Castle Archdale Boat Hire, p661). Rates range from about £15 per hour for an open rowing boat with outboard motor to £65/90 per half/full day for a six-seater with cabin and engine.

FISHING ON LOUGH ERNE

The lakes of Fermanagh are renowned for both coarse and game fishing. The Lough Erne trout-fishing season runs from the beginning of March to the end of September. Salmon fishing begins in June and also continues to the end of September. The mayfly season usually lasts a month from the second week in May.

You'll need a combined licence and permit, which costs £9.50 for three days. See www.nidirect.gov.uk/angling for full details. Licences and permits can be purchased from the Fermanagh Visitor Information Centre and Home, Field & Stream in Enniskillen, plus from the marina at Castle Archdale Country Park (p661), which also hires out fishing rods.

Hire an experienced guide through Erne Angling (p657).

5.30-9pm Mon-Thu & Sun, to 9.30pm Fri & Sat) Located below street level in a beautiful space with vaulted brick ceilings, Cafe Merlot serves seasonal specials in addition to its regular menu of contemporary meat, fish and vegetarian dishes. Try the dry-aged rib-eye steak (Fermanagh beef is highly regarded). The wine list is the best in town. It's below the pub Blakes of the Hollow; book ahead.

★ **28 Darling St**　　　　　　　IRISH £££
(028-6632 8224; www.28darlingstreet.com; 28 Darling St; mains £18.50-26, tasting menu £55; 5.30-9.30pm Thu-Fri, 6-9pm Sat, noon-5.30pm Sun) After working in European and American Michelin-starred restaurants, chef Glen Wheeler has returned to his native Fermanagh to open 28 Darling St. The stripped-back menu features deceptively simple dishes that allow local ingredients to shine. A lavishly decorated dining room adds to the experience (gilded mirrors, velvet upholstery and a chandelier so big it took eight men to fit it).

★ **Blakes of the Hollow**　　　　　　PUB
(William Blake; 028-6632 2143; 6 Church St; noon-late) This traditional pub has barely changed since 1887, with a marble-topped bar, huge sherry casks, antique silver lamp holders, and ancient wood panelling kippered by a century of cigarette smoke. A newer addition is the *Game of Thrones* door, one of 10 doors made from wood felled by a 2016 storm and intricately carved with themes from the HBO series.

☆ Entertainment

Ardhowen Theatre　　　　　　THEATRE
(028-6632 5440; www.ardhowentheatre.com; 97 Dublin Rd; box office 9.30am-4.30pm Mon-Fri, to 8pm before performances, 11am-1pm, 2-5pm & 6-8pm Sat) The program here includes concerts, local amateur and professional drama and musical productions, pantomimes and films. The theatre is about 1km southeast of the town centre

on the A4, in an impressive glass-fronted lakeside building. It has a good cafe.

🛍 Shopping

Buttermarket　　　　　　ARTS & CRAFTS
(Down St; 9am-5pm Mon-Sat) The restored buildings in the old marketplace house an appealing variety of craft shops and studios selling paintings, ceramics and jewellery, and Rebecca's Coffee Shop.

Home, Field & Stream　　　SPORTS & OUTDOORS
(028-6632 2114; www.hfs-online.com; 18-20 Church St; 9am-5.30pm Mon-Sat) Has a wide range of fishing tackle and also sells fishing licences and permits.

ℹ Information

Fermanagh Visitor Information Centre (028-6632 3110; www.fermanaghlakelands.com; 9.30am-5pm Mon-Fri, from 11am Sat year-round, plus 11am-5pm Sun Jun-Sep;) Helpful and well-stocked tourist information office at Enniskillen Castle. Staff can book accommodation and help with fishing licences and permits. There's a good cafe here.

ℹ Getting There & Away

From the **bus station** (Wellington Rd; facilities 8.45am-5.25pm Mon-Fri, 8am-2.30pm Sat), Ulsterbus and Bus Éireann services run to/from Belfast (£13, 2¼ hours, hourly Monday to Saturday, two on Sunday), Omagh (£8.60, one hour, one daily Monday to Saturday) and Dublin (€20, 2½ hours, eight daily).

The Bus Éireann service Route 30 stops in Enniskillen on its way between Dublin (2½ hours, about once an hour) and Donegal (one hour). The 458 links Enniskillen with Sligo (1½ hours, eight daily).

Upper Lough Erne

Upper Lough Erne is not so much a lake as a watery maze of more than 150 islands, inlets, reedy bays and meandering backwaters.

Birdlife is abundant: flocks of whooper swan and goldeneye overwinter here; great crested grebes nest in the spring; and you'll find Ireland's biggest heronry in a 400-year-old oak grove on the island of Inishfendra, just south of Crom Estate.

◉ Sights & Activities

Crom Estate
PARK

(☑ 028-6773 8118; www.nationaltrust.org.uk/crom; Crom Rd, Newtownbutler; adult/child £6.50/3.25; ☺ grounds 10am-7pm May-Aug, to 6pm mid-Mar–Apr, Sep & Oct, visitor centre 11am-5pm daily Easter-Sep, Sat & Sun only Oct) Home to the largest area of natural woodland in Northern Ireland, the National Trust's beautiful Crom Estate is a haven for pine martens, bats and many species of bird. You can walk from the visitor centre to the old castle ruins, an ancient walled garden, gnarled yew trees and views over the reed-fringed lough. Castle Crom itself is privately owned and closed to the public.

The estate is on the eastern shore of Upper Lough Erne, 5km west of Newtownbutler.

For views of Crom from the lake, rent a rowing boat (per hour £7.50) or outboard-engine boat (per day £45); ask at the visitor centre and book ahead in summer. See the website for details of upcoming events. Camping is available.

Share Canoeing & Kayaking
CANOEING

(☑ 028-6772 2122; www.sharevillage.org; off Newbridge Rd, Share Discovery Village; 2hr kayak £12, 1hr canoe £8) Share Discovery Centre offers canoeing and kayaking sessions on Upper Lough Erne; book online. The centre is 5km southwest of Lisnaskea.

Inishcruiser
BOATING

(☑ 028-6772 2122; www.sharevillage.org/inish cruiser; off Newbridge Rd, Share Discovery Village; adult/child £10/6; ☺ 2.30pm Sun Easter-end Aug) The *Inishcruiser* offers 1½- to two-hour cruises of the Upper Lough Erne, leaving from Share Discovery Village.

🛏 Sleeping & Eating

Crom Campsite
CAMPGROUND £

(☑ 028-6773 8118; Crom Estate, Crom Rd, Newtownbutler; campsites per tent/adult/child £12/8/3, glamping pods £55-65; ☺ Mar-Oct) Camping is available in the peaceful grounds of the National Trust's Crom Estate. Book well in advance for glamping huts, which sleep two adults and up to three children.

★ Watermill Lodge
B&B ££

(☑ 028-6772 4369; www.watermillrestaurant fermanagh.com; Kilmore Quay, Lisnaskea; s/d £70/100) A secluded lakeside setting makes for a peaceful night's rest in one of the seven lake-view guest rooms here. It's next to the excellent thatch-roofed Watermill Restaurant.

Kissin' Crust
CAFE £

(☑ 028-6772 2678; www.facebook.com/the kissincrust; 152 Main St, Lisnaskea; mains £3-7; ☺ 8.30am-5pm Mon-Sat) Popular with locals, this coffee shop is stacked with home-baked pies, quiches and scones, and serves up a lunch menu of homemade soup, sandwiches and hot dishes. It's good for picnic shopping.

★ Watermill Restaurant
FRENCH £££

(☑ 028-6772 4369; www.watermillrestaurant fermanagh.com; Kilmore Quay, Lisnaskea; 3-course lunch/dinner £24/29; ☺ 5-9.30pm Mon-Sat, noon-8pm Sun) Seasonal Irish fare is given a French twist at this award-winning restaurant in a peaceful lakeside setting. Chef Pascal Brissaud uses produce from the restaurant's own vegetable and herb garden in dishes like chicken cassoulet, duck cooked two ways and lamb casserole. The cellar contains a vast array of French wines.

➊ Getting There & Away

From Enniskillen, Ulsterbus service 95 runs along the east side of the lough to Maguiresbridge (£4, 25 minutes, six daily Monday to Friday, four on Saturday). Bus 58 goes down the west side to Derrylin (£4.60, 40 minutes, five

---

LOUGH ERNE CANOE TRAIL

The Lough Erne Canoe Trail (www.canoeni.com) highlights the attractions along the 50km of lough and river between Belleek and Belturbet. The wide open expanses of the Lower Lough can build up big waves in a strong breeze and are best left to experts, but the sheltered backwaters of the Upper Lough are ideal for beginners and families. You can download maps and info from the website. The Fermanagh Visitor Information Centre in Enniskillen can help you find where to rent canoes and boats, plus it has full details on angling.

Castle Archdale Boat Hire (p661) offers canoe and kayak rentals. You can try kayaking and canoeing in supervised sessions at Share Discovery Village.

HIKING THE ULSTER WAY

The Ulster Way **long-distance walking trail** makes a circuit around the six counties of Northern Ireland. In total the route covers 1000km, so walking all of it might take four to five weeks. Sections of the way are on minor roads rather than footpaths; to get around this, the route has been divided into two categories: 'Quality Sections' – good, scenic, mostly off-road walking – separated by 'Link Sections', which can be covered by public transport. Check the website of WalkNI (www.walkni.com) for details.

Short sections of the Ulster Way that make good day walks include Cuilcagh Mountain Park (p663) and the Causeway Coast Way (p637).

Short sections of the Ulster Way that make good day walks include Cuilcagh Mountain Park (p663) and the Causeway Coast Way (p637).

daily Monday to Friday, two on Saturday), and continues to Belturbet in County Cavan.

Lower Lough Erne

Lower Lough Erne is more of an open expanse of water than the Upper Lough, with its 90-odd islands clustered mainly in the southern reaches. In early Christian times, when overland travel was difficult, Lough Erne was an important highway between the Donegal coast and inland Leitrim, and there are many ancient religious sites and other antiquities dotted around its shores. In medieval times the lough was part of an important pilgrimage route.

🛈 Getting There & Around

On the eastern side of the lough, Ulsterbus runs from Enniskillen to Pettigo via Irvinestown (three to five Monday to Saturday) and stops near Castle Archdale Country Park (35 minutes) and Kesh (one hour).

Trory Jetty to Devenish Island (☑ 028-6882 1892; www.castlearchdaleboathire.com; off A32 Irvinestown Rd; adult/child £5/4; ⊙10am-5pm daily Jul & Aug, Thu-Mon Sep, Sat & Sun Oct) To get to Trory Jetty, take the A32 towards Irvinestown and look for a left turn (signed Trory jetty) onto a minor road, just south of Trory village. The licence to run this ferry service is renewed annually; call ahead to confirm sailing times.

Devenish Island

From Daimh Inis, meaning 'Ox Island', Devenish Island, is the biggest of several 'holy islands' in Lough Erne. The remains of an Augustinian monastery, founded here in the 6th century by St Molaise, include a superb 12th-century round tower in near-perfect condition, the ruins of St Molaise's Church and St Mary's Abbey and a 15th-century high cross.

The island is accessible by boat from Trory Jetty, 6km north of Enniskillen, or from Enniskillen with Erne Tours (p656) or Erne Water Taxi (p656).

A small **visitors centre** outlines the fascinating history of the monastic site, where up to 1000 monks once lived and worked. When the monastery was founded, most of Ireland was covered in thick forest; the island site would have been chosen for its accessibility on one of the country's major waterways. The island was raided by Vikings in 837 and again in 923, but by the 12th century Devenish was a large and important community. The stonemasons and builders responsible for the round tower were some of the most skilled craftsmen of their day, and Devenish continued to thrive as a centre of learning and arts until the 16th-century Dissolution of the Monasteries under Henry VIII.

The licence to run the Trory Jetty to Devenish boat service is renewed annually; call ahead to confirm it's operational. To get to Trory Jetty, take the A32 towards Irvinestown and look for a left turn (signed 'Trory jetty') onto a minor road, just south of Trory village.

Castle Archdale

Castle Archdale has a popular forest park with walking and cycling trails as well as an adjoining country park with a caravan site and a marina. From here boats make the crossing to the monastic ruins on White Island.

◉ Sights & Activities

White Island   ISLAND
(☑028-6862 1156; www.castlearchdaleboathire.com; Castle Archdale Bay; ferry per person £5; ⊙ferry 10.30am-4.30pm daily Jul & Aug, plus Easter & May bank-holiday weekends, call to confirm) White Island is the most haunting of Lough Erne's monastic sites. At the eastern tip of the island are the ruins of a small 12th-century church with a beautiful Romanesque door on its southern side. Inside are eight extraordinary stone figures, thought to date from the 9th century, lined up along the wall like miniature Easter Island statues.

The line-up is a modern arrangement; most of the figures were discovered buried in the walls of the church in the 19th century, where the medieval masons had used them as ordinary building stones. The six main figures, all created by the same hand, are flanked on the left by a sheila-na-gig (carved female figure with exaggerated genitalia), which is probably contemporary with the church, and flanked on the right by a scowling stone face. The age and interpretation of these figures have been the subject of much debate; it has been suggested that the two central pairs, of equal height, were pillars that once supported a pulpit, and that they represent either saints or aspects of the life of Christ.

A ferry makes the 15-minute crossing to the island from the marina at Castle Archdale.

Castle Archdale Country Park
PARK

(☎028-6634 4803; off B82, Rossmore; ☺visitor centre 10am-5pm daily Jun-Aug, from 1pm Sat & Sun May & Sep) **FREE** This park has pleasant woodland and lakeshore walks and cycle tracks, in the former estate of 18th-century Archdale Manor and the adjacent **forest park**, which also contains the ruins of 17th-century Archdale Castle. The island-filled bay was used in WWII as a base for Catalina flying boats, a history explained in the small **museum** in the country park visitor centre.

Castle Archdale Boat Hire
BOATING

(☎028-6862 1156; www.castlearchdaleboathire.com; Castle Archdale Marina; 6-person boat hire per half/full day £65/90, per hr kayak/canoe £15/25; ☺10.30am-4.30pm daily Jul & Aug, plus Easter & May bank-holiday weekends) Rents six- and eight-person boats (no previous experience or special licence required), as well as bicycles (per hour/half-day £5/10) and fishing rods. Also runs the ferry to White Island.

🛏 Sleeping & Eating

Castle Archdale
Caravan Park
CAMPGROUND £

(☎028-6862 1333; www.castlearchdale.com; off B82, Rossmore; campsites per tent £10-40, caravan £25-30; ☺Easter-Oct; 🛜) This attractive, tree-sheltered site in Castle Archdale Country Park is dominated by on-site caravans, but has pitches for tents and good facilities, including a shop, launderette, playground and pub.

Dollakis in the Park
FOOD TRUCK £

(☎028-6634 2616; www.dollakis.com; Castle Archdale Caravan Park; mains £4-8; ☺noon-5pm daily Jul & Aug) This fabulous food truck serves authentic Greek street food such as spit-roast gyros, beef and lamb burgers, grilled chicken souvlaki,

falafel, halloumi, flatbreads and calamari. Eat at picnic tables in a giant tepee tent.

ⓘ Getting There & Away

The park is 16km northwest of Enniskillen, near Lisnarick. Bus 194 goes from Lisnarick to Enniskillen (£4.60, 25 minutes, eight daily Monday to Friday, four Saturday).

Boa Island

Boa Island, at the northern end of Lower Lough Erne, is connected to the mainland at both ends – the main A47 road runs along its length. It's worth a stop here to see the mysterious stone figures at the small and unkempt Caldragh Graveyard.

Caldragh Graveyard
CEMETERY

Spooky, moss-grown Caldragh Graveyard contains the intriguing **Dreenan Figure**. It's often called a Janus figure, but it's actually two separate figures placed back to back. It's thought to date from the early Christian period and perhaps represent the war goddess Badhbh, a frightening figure in local folklore. Nearby is a smaller figure called **Lusty Man**, brought here from Lusty More island.

There's a sign indicating the graveyard about 1.5km from the bridge at the western tip of Boa Island.

The exact origins and meanings of the figures remain unclear. The Dreenan Figure, which has been in the graveyard since at least 1841, was believed for many years to date from the pagan Iron Age and be as much as 2000 years old; it's now thought to date from the early Christian period, from 500 to 1000 AD.

CRUISING HOLIDAYS ON LOUGH ERNE

If you fancy exploring Lough Erne as captain of your own motor cruiser, you can – and without any previous experience or qualifications. Several companies in Fermanagh hire out self-drive, liveaboard cabin cruisers by the week, offering a crash course (not literally, hopefully) in boat-handling and navigation at the start of your holiday. Weekly rates in high season (July and August) range from about £800 for a two-berth to £1250 for a four-berth and £1525 for a six-berth boat.

Check out www.fermanaghlakelands.com for details on holidays and boat-hire companies.

There's no information about the enigmatic figures at the graveyard itself.

Lusty Beg Island
RESORT ££

(☑ 028-6863 3300; www.lustybegisland.com; s/d/cabin from £100/140/165, minimum 3 nights; P @ ⊛) This private island retreat, reached by ferry (use a telephone at the dock) from a jetty halfway along Boa Island, has self-catering cabins and chalets that sleep two to six people, as well as B&B rooms in its rustic 40-room courtyard block. There's a spa and swimming pool, tennis court, nature trail and canoeing on the lough for guests.

Lusty Beg's informal **restaurant** (mains £10.50-20, Sun carvery adult/child £23/8; ☺ noon-9.30pm) is open to all.

★ Finn Lough
RESORT £££

(☑ 028-6838 0360; www.finnlough.com; 41 Letter Rd, off B136; d from £160, bubble domes from £245, cottages 2 nights from £520; @ ☎) On the mainland shore overlooking Boa Island is this wonderful complex with a range of luxurious accommodation and a friendly, relaxed atmosphere. The most special rooms here are the forest bubble domes: transparent globes with uninterrupted views of the night sky, attached bathrooms and four-poster beds, hidden among the trees; the largest have free-standing baths. Book well ahead.

There are also three rooms in the main house, and self-catering cottages sleeping six people, some with great water views. The resort's superb restaurant serves fresh, locally sourced fare including produce grown in the kitchen garden or foraged from the forest. Activities at the lush complex include water sports, kayaking, tennis and cycling, and a range of treatments at the spa.

Belleek

Belleek's (Beal Leice) village street of colourful, flower-bedecked houses slopes up from a bridge across the River Erne where it flows out of the Lower Lough towards Ballyshannon and the sea. The village is right on the border – the road south across the bridge passes through a finger of the Republic's territory for about 200m before leaving again – and shops accept both euros and pounds sterling.

★ Belleek Pottery Visitor Centre
ARTS CENTRE

(☑ 028-6865 9300; www.belleekpottery.ie; 3 Main St; tours adult/child £5/free; ☺ 9am-6pm Mon-Fri, from 10am Sat, noon-5.30pm Sun Jul-Sep, shorter hours Oct-Jun, closed Sat & Sun Jan & Feb) The imposing Georgian-style building beside Belleek's main bridge houses the world-famous Belleek Pottery, founded in 1857. It has been producing fine Parian china ever since, and is especially noted for its delicate basketware; pieces are available to buy in the shop. You can see the pottery being made on guided tours of the factory floor, which run every half-hour from 9.30am to 12.15pm and 1.45pm to 4pm weekdays year-round (to 3pm on Fridays), plus summer weekends.

There's also a small museum, showroom and cafe.

Fiddlestone Bar & B&B
B&B ££

(☑ 028-6865 8008; www.facebook.com/fiddlestone.bar; 15-17 Main St; s/d from £40/70; ☺ pub noon-11pm; ☎) This classic village-centre pub has six basic rooms that are just right after a long day touring followed by hours spent enjoying the trad-music sessions downstairs.

★ Thatch Coffee Shop
CAFE £

(☑ 028-6865 8181; 20 Main St; mains £4-8; ☺ 9am-5pm Mon-Sat) This cosy little thatched cottage is Belleek's oldest building (late 18th century); the original rafters are visible above an old church bench on the back wall. The sandwiches and soups are freshly prepared using organic ingredients, and the homemade cakes (such as caramelised apple tart) and scones are superb. The traditional breakfasts (available until noon) are excellent too.

Black Cat Cove
PUB

(☑ 028-6865 8942; www.facebook.com/theblackcatcove; 28 Main St; mains £9; ☺ kitchen noon-9pm) This family-run pub with antique furniture and an open fire serves good bar meals. It also has live music most nights in summer, and on weekends in winter.

ⓘ Getting There & Away

The 194 bus links Belleek with Enniskillen (£7.20, about 1¼ hours, three daily Monday to Saturday).

Lough Navar Forest Park

The **Lough Navar Forest Park** (www.marblearchcavesgeopark.com/attraction/lough-navar; ☺ 10am-dusk) FREE lies at the western end of Lower Lough Erne, where the **Cliffs of Magho** – a 250m-high and 9km-long limestone escarpment – rise above a fringe of bog, heath and native woodland on the southern shore. A 10km scenic drive leads to the Magho Viewpoint; there are plenty of good walking trails in the forest too.

The entrance is on the Glennasheevar road between Garrison and Derrygonnelly, 20km southeast of Belleek; follow signs for the 'Forest Scenic Drive'.

The panorama from the Magho clifftop is one of the finest in Ireland: it looks out over the shimmering expanse of lough and river to the Blue Stack Mountains, the sparkling waters of Donegal Bay and the sea cliffs of Sliabh Liag.

West of Lough Erne

The remote hills west of Lough Erne are home to some worthwhile sights and spectacular scenery. The area falls within the Unesco-protected Marble Arch Caves Global Geopark.

The bus service in this area of rural Fermanagh is limited and you'll need your own vehicle to get around. National cycle route 91 links Enniskillen with Florence Court and Marble Arch Caves.

★**Marble Arch Caves**   CAVE
(⌂028-6634 8855; www.marblearchcaves-geopark.com; 43 Marlbank Rd, Legnabrocky; adult/child £11/7.50; ⊙10am-6pm Jul & Aug, to 4pm mid-Mar–Jun & Sep, 10.30am-3pm Oct) To the south of Lower Lough Erne lies a limestone plateau, where Fermanagh's abundant rainwater has carved out a network of subterranean caverns. The largest of these are the star attraction of the Marble Arch Caves Global Geopark. Popular 1¼-hour tours feature spectacular chambers and underwater rivers.

The caves are 16km southwest of Enniskillen, and 4km west of Florence Court, reached via the A4 and the A32. Book tours in advance in summer.

Tours begin with a short boat trip along the peaty, foam-flecked waters of the underground River Cladagh to Junction Jetty, where three subterranean streams meet up. You then continue on foot past the Pool Chamber, regaled all the time with jokes from your guide. An artificial tunnel leads into the New Chamber, from which the route follows the underground River Owenbrean through the Moses Walk (a walled pathway sunk waist-deep into the river) to the Calcite Cradle, where the most picturesque formations are found.

Unexpected serious flooding of the caves in the 1990s was found to have been caused by mechanised peat-cutting in the blanket bog on the slopes of Cuilcagh Mountain, whose rivers feed the caves. Cuilcagh Mountain Park was established to restore and preserve the bog environment, and in 2001 the entire area was designated a Unesco geopark. The park's geology and ecology are explained in the caves' visitor centre.

The caves take their name from a natural limestone arch that spans the River Cladagh where it emerges from the caves; you can reach it via a short walk along a signposted footpath from the visitor centre. They were first explored by the French caving pioneer Édouard Martel in 1895.

★**Florence Court**   HISTORIC BUILDING
(⌂028-6634 8249; www.nationaltrust.org.uk; Swanlinbar Rd; adult/child grounds only £7/3.50, grounds & house tour £11.50/5.75; ⊙house 11am-5pm daily Apr-Sep, weekends only Mar & Apr, grounds 10am-7pm Mar-Oct, to 4pm Nov-Feb) Set in lovely wooded grounds in the shadow of Cuilcagh Mountain, Florence Court, 12km southwest of Enniskillen, is famous for its rococo plasterwork and antique Irish furniture, viewable on a guided tour, which also takes in the servants' quarters downstairs. In the grounds you can explore the walled garden and, on the edge of Cottage Wood, admire an ancient Irish yew tree said to be the mother plant of all Irish yews.

Florence Court was the home of three generations of the Cole family starting with Sir John Cole, who named the house after his wife Florence. In the 1770s his son William Willoughby Cole, the first Earl of Enniskillen, oversaw the addition of grand Palladian wings to this beautiful, baroque country house. It was badly damaged by fire in 1955 and much of what you see on the tour is the result of meticulous restoration, but the magnificent plasterwork on the dining-room ceiling is original.

Check the website for upcoming costume tours, where you'll see characters such as the cook at work in the kitchen, and special children's tours.

Within the estate's 35-sq-km grounds are 15km of trails for walking and cycling; bikes can be hired from the visitor centre (£7.50/15 for three hours/full day).

Cuilcagh Mountain Park   MOUNTAIN
(www.marblearchcavesgeopark.com; Marlbank Rd) Part of the Marble Arch Caves Global Geopark, Cuilcagh Mountain Park was established to restore and preserve the blanket bog

CUILCAGH MOUNTAIN

Rising above Marble Arch and Florence Court, Cuilcagh (*cull*-kay) Mountain (666m) is the highest point in Counties Fermanagh and Cavan, its summit right on the border between Northern Ireland and the Republic.

The mountain is a geological layer cake, with a cave-riddled limestone base, shale and sandstone flanks draped with a shaggy tweed skirt of blanket bog, and a high grit-stone plateau ringed by steep, craggy slopes, all part of the **Marble Arch Caves Global Geopark**.

Hidden among the sphagnum moss, bog cotton and heather of the blanket bog is the sticky-fingered sundew, an insect-eating plant, while the crags echo to the 'krok-krok-krok' of ravens and the mewing of peregrine falcons. The other-worldly summit plateau is a breeding ground for golden plover and is rich in rare plants such as alpine clubmoss.

The **hike** to the summit is a 12km round-trip (allow four or five hours). Start at the car park of the Cuilcagh Mountain Park (p663), 300m west of the turn-off to the visitor centre of the Marble Arch Caves (p663), where there is an information desk and maps. Right next to the car park is the **Monastir sinkhole**, a deep depression ringed by limestone cliffs where the River Aghinrawn disappears underground for its journey through the Marble Arch Caves system.

The **Legnabrocky Trail** begins as a well-groomed gravel track that winds through rich green limestone meadows for 4km. From here you begin your ascent of Cuilcagh Mountain along a 2km section of **boardwalk** (built to protect the sensitive bog blanket below), climbing steeply to the summit ridge, with great views west to the crags above little Lough Atona. The boardwalk comes to an end here, but a rough path continues 1km east across the rock-strewn plateau to the prominent cairn on the summit (turn back when you reach the end of the boardwalk unless you have good boots, a compass and map).

The **summit cairn** is actually a Bronze Age burial mound; about 100m south of the summit are two rings of boulders, the foundations of prehistoric huts. On a clear day the view extends from the Blue Stack Mountains of Donegal to Croagh Patrick, and from the Atlantic Ocean to the Irish Sea.

For downloadable maps of other walks in the area, visit www.marblearchcaves geopark.com.

– one of Ireland's biggest – on the slopes of Cuilcagh Mountain (666m). The Marble Arch Caves (p663) visitor centre has an information desk and maps; the mountain is accessed from a car park 300m west of the caves. A 2.5km stretch of boardwalk, constructed in 2015 to protect the bog, has proved popular with walkers climbing the mountain along the Legnabrocky Trail.

Lough Melvin   LAKE

Lough Melvin is famous for its salmon and trout fishing, and is home to two unusual trout species that are unique to the lough – the sonaghan, with its distinctive black spots, and the crimson-spotted gillaroo (if caught, gillaroo must be returned to the lake unharmed). You'll need a licence and a permit from Garrison Anglers (www.garrisonandloughmelvinanglersassoc.co.uk; permits £10 to £20 per day).

Lough Melvin is situated along the border with the Republic, on the B52 road from Belcoo to Belleek.

Sheelin Antique Irish Lace Shop   MUSEUM

(☑ 028-6634 8052; www.sheelinlace.com; 178 Derrylin Rd, Bellanaleck; ⊙ 10am-6pm Mon-Sat) This lace shop also houses a small collection of Irish lace dating from 1850 to 1900. Lace-making was an important cottage industry in the region both before and after the Famine – prior to WWI there were at least 10 lace schools in County Fermanagh. The shop is 6km south of Enniskillen in Bellanaleck.

COUNTY TYRONE

Tyrone's three largest towns – Omagh, Dungannon and Cookstown – form a triangle across its centre, but the county's biggest draw lies in the untouched wildness of the Sperrin Mountains, their southern foothills scattered with prehistoric sites. There's also an excellent outdoor museum near Omagh that explores the history and legacy of emigration from Ulster to the US.

Omagh

POP 18,100

Situated at the confluence of the Rivers Camowen and Drumragh, which join to form the River Strule, Omagh (An Óghmagh) is a busy market town with a handful of historic Georgian buildings.

Memorial Obelisk
MEMORIAL

(Market St) For a long time to come, Omagh will be remembered for the devastating 1998 car bomb that killed 29 people and injured 200. Planted by the breakaway Real IRA group, the bomb was the worst single atrocity in the 30-year history of the Troubles.

An impressive 4.5m-high glass obelisk marks the spot of the explosion. It's part of a project that includes a **memorial garden** 300m north across the river on Drumragh Ave.

Mullaghmore House
B&B ££

(☑ 07710 539449, 028-8224 2314; 94 Old Mountfield Rd; s £40, d £78-88; 🖙) Offering affordable country-house charm, this beautifully restored Georgian house has a period mahogany-panelled library, an orangery and a full-sized snooker table. The bedrooms have cast-iron fireplaces and antique furniture (some share bathrooms). The owner runs courses on antique restoration and the house feels like a living museum. Guests can use the kitchen. It's 1.5km northeast of Omagh's town centre.

Rooms at Rue
HOTEL ££

(☑ 028-8225 7575; ww.roomsatrue.com; 12 Main St; r from £75; 🅿🖙) Centrally located right on Omagh's Main St, Rooms at Rue has 13 modern rooms decorated with a plush cream and purple colour scheme, and exceptionally friendly staff. It's located above Rue restaurant and close to Omagh's nightlife (it can be noisy at weekends). The car park is accessed from Kevlin Ave.

Grant's Restaurant
IRISH ££

(☑ 028-8225 0900; 29 George's St; mains £10-26; ⊘4-10pm Mon-Thu, to 10.30pm Fri, from 3pm Sat, noon-10pm Sun) Named for Ulysses S Grant, this family-run restaurant is a good bet for a meal in Omagh. The traditional, wood-panelled interior and cosy timber booths will make you want to linger over your steak and chips or Sunday roast. There's a good cocktail and wine list, and excellent desserts too.

🛈 Getting There & Away

The bus station is on Mountjoy Rd, just north of the town centre along Bridge St.

Bus 273 goes from Belfast to Omagh (£13, 1¾ hours, hourly Monday to Saturday, six on Sunday) via Dungannon (£7.20, 45 minutes) and on to Derry (£8.60, 1¼ hours). Bus 94 goes to Enniskillen (£8.60, one hour, six or seven Monday to Friday, three on Saturday, one on Sunday).

Ulster American Folk Park

In the 18th and 19th centuries more than two million Ulster people left their homes to forge a new life across the Atlantic. Their story is told here at the **Ulster American Folk Park** (☑ 028-8224 3292; www.nmni.com/uafp; 2 Mellon Rd; adult/child £9/5.50; ⊘10am-5pm Tue-Sun Mar-Sep, to 4pm Tue-Fri, from 11am Sat & Sun Oct-Feb), one of Ireland's best museums, which features a sprawling **outdoor history park**. Exhibits are split into Old World cottages and New World log cabins, with actors in period costume on hand to bring the stories to life.

The park is 8km northwest of Omagh. Last admission is 1½ hours before closing.

Original buildings from various parts of Ulster have been dismantled and re-erected here, including a blacksmith's forge, a weaver's thatched cottage, a Presbyterian meeting house and a schoolhouse. The two parts of the park are cleverly linked by passing through a mock-up of an emigrant ship. In the American section of the park you can visit a genuine 18th-century settler's stone cottage and a log house, both shipped across the Atlantic from Pennsylvania, and a Tennessee plantation house, plus many more original buildings.

The **Exhibition Hall** explains the close connections between Ulster and the USA – the American Declaration of Independence was signed by several Ulstermen – and includes an original Calistoga wagon.

Costumed guides and artisans explain the arts of spinning, weaving, candle-making and so on. Various **special events** are held throughout the year, including American Independence Day celebrations in July and the Appalachian and Bluegrass Music Festival in late August/September. At least half a day is needed to do the place justice.

Translink Goldline bus 273 from Belfast to Derry stops in Omagh, and will stop on request at the park gates.

DAVAGH FOREST PARK MTB TRAILS

Remote Davagh Forest Park provides some of the best mountain biking in Ireland, ranging from family-friendly green and blue trails along a wooded stream to 16km of red trails leading to the top of Beleevenamore Mountain, with several challenging rock slabs and drop-offs on the descents.

Walking gives you time to enjoy this landscape of rolling hills and sweeping forests. A 3km loop trail takes in the forests and red-hued stream.

The trailhead is on a minor road, 10km northwest of Cookstown, signposted from the A505 Cookstown–Omagh road at Dunnamore. For details see www.mountainbikeni.com and www.walkni.com.

Sperrin Mountains

On a sunny spring day, when the russet bogs and yellow gorse stand out against a clear blue sky, the Sperrin Mountains can offer some grand walking. The moorland hills are also dotted with standing stones and prehistoric tombs.

Ulsterbus service 403 runs twice daily from Monday to Saturday between Omagh (to Gortin £3.60, 25 minutes) and Magherafelt (to Gortin £9.30, 1½ hours).

Gortin

The village of Gortin (pronounced Gorchin) lies 15km north of Omagh at the foot of Mullaghcarn (542m), the southernmost of the Sperrin summits, and makes a good base for exploring the hills. There are several good walks around the village, a forest park with walking and mountain-biking trails and a scenic drive to Gortin Lakes, with views north to the main Sperrin ridge.

Hundreds of hikers converge for a mass ascent of Mullaghcarn on Cairn Sunday (the last Sunday in July), a revival of an ancient pilgrimage.

Gortin Glen Forest Park   FOREST
(Glenpark Rd; car park £4; ⊙10am-dusk) FREE Originally planted for timber production, this coniferous forest is now a 15-sq-km park. The main car park is the starting point for a series of walking trails and an 8km scenic forest drive. In the northern section of the park are three graded trails for mountain biking. The trails are accessed 1km from the park exit on Lisnaharney Rd.

Gortin Glen is 5km south of Gortin on the B48 road to Omagh.

Gortin Hostel   HOSTEL £
(☑028-8164 8346; www.gortincommunity.com; 62 Main St; dm/f/cottages £20/45/65; ☎) Part of a community enterprise, this hostel, with simple dorms and family rooms with attached bathrooms, is a great option for walkers and cyclists. Staff are helpful and there's a well-equipped kitchen, cosy lounge with a working fireplace, and a washing machine. There are also four spacious self-catering cottages. The reception is in the outdoor activity centre; call ahead.

Hidden Pearl   IRISH ££
(☑028-8164 8157; 16 Main St; mains £12-25; ⊙4-9pm Tue-Thu, noon-10pm Fri & Sat, to 9pm Sun) This relaxed village restaurant and wine bar serves sophisticated plates such as maple duck breast with rhubarb, sweet potato and pistachio, and slow-cooked lamb shoulder with charred onion and pea puree. There's a good selection of vegetarian options and a range of tempting desserts.

ⓘ Getting There & Away

Ulsterbus service 403 runs twice daily from Monday to Saturday between Omagh (£3.60, 25 minutes) and Magherafelt (£9.30,1½ hours), stopping at Gortin. Bus 92 links Gortin with Omagh (£3.60, 25 minutes, seven daily from Monday to Friday) and Plumbridge (£2.50, 10 minutes, three daily from Monday to Friday).

An Creagán

Beaghmore Stone Circles   ARCHAEOLOGICAL SITE
(Blackrock Rd; ⊙24hr) FREE What these Neolithic stone circles lack in stature – the stones are all less than 1m tall – they make up for in complexity; the impressive complex has seven stone circles and rows, one filled with smaller stones, nicknamed 'dragon's teeth'.

The site is signposted about 8km east of An Creagán, and 4km north of the A505. The scenic drive to the stones offers wonderful views of the Sperrins.

An Creagán   VISITOR CENTRE
(☑028-8076 1112; www.an-creagan.com; A505, Creggan; bike rental per day £10; ⊙9am-5pm

Mon-Fri; 🖢) FREE Meaning 'stony site' in Irish, An Creagán (20km east of Omagh) is a great starting point for exploring the ecology of the surrounding bogs and the archaeology of the region. Pick up a free map with information on the Neolithic and Bronze Age sites in the area, including the Beaghmore Stone Circles, from the information desk. There are also 5km of nature trails through bogs and forest, a woodland children's play area, self-catering cottages and a good restaurant.

The grounds contain stones and prehistoric artefacts collected from the surrounding countryside, as well as a mock Bronze Age round house.

An Creagán Cottages   COTTAGE **£**
(📞 028-8076 1116; www.an-creagan.com; Creggan Rd, Creggan; 1-/2-/3-bed cottages 2 nights from £120/160/180) An Creagán's eight modern, self-catering cottages have an idyllic setting near nature trails in the foothills of the Sperrins. Each one comes fully equipped with a working fireplace, flat-screen TV, good kitchen and contemporary furnishings.

An Creagán Restaurant   IRISH **££**
(www.an-creagan.com; Creggan Rd, Creggan; mains £8.50-18; ⊘ 10am-3pm Mon-Thu, to 8pm Fri & Sun, to 9pm Sat) The restaurant at An Creagán serves a range of pasta, steak, chicken and seafood dishes prepared using herbs, vegetables and salad leaves from the kitchen garden. There's traditional Irish music in the bar on Saturday nights.

East Tyrone

The market towns of Cookstown and Dungannon are the main settlements in the eastern part of County Tyrone, but the key sights here are in the surrounding countryside.

🅾 Sights

Wellbrook Beetling Mill   HISTORIC BUILDING
(📞 028-8674 8210; www.nationaltrust.org.uk; 20 Wellbrook Rd, Corkhill; adult/child £5.50/free; ⊘ 2-5pm Sat, Sun & public holidays mid-Mar–late Sep) Beetling, the final stage of linen-making, involves pounding the cloth with wooden hammers, or beetles, to give it a smooth sheen. This 18th-century mill still has its original machinery and stages loud demonstrations of the linen-making process during hour-long guided tours. The whitewashed building is on a pretty stretch of the Ballinderry River, 8km west of Cookstown, just off the A505.

Ardboe High Cross   RELIGIOUS SITE
(Ardboe Rd, off B73) FREE This 6th-century monastic site overlooking Lough Neagh is home to one of Ireland's best-preserved and most elaborately decorated Celtic stone crosses. The 10th-century Ardboe High Cross stands 5.5m tall, with 22 carved panels depicting biblical scenes. It's an evocative yet remote place, 16km east of Cookstown, with distant views and a nearby cemetery. Take the B73 through Coagh and watch for the signs for Ardboe High Cross, which will lead you along a narrow country road.

The western side of the cross (facing the road) has New Testament scenes including the Adoration of the Magi and Christ's entry into Jerusalem; the more weathered eastern face (towards the lough) shows Old Testament scenes.

Grant Ancestral Homestead   HISTORIC SITE
(📞 028-8555 7133; 45 Dergenagh Rd, Ballygawley; ⊘ 9am-5pm) FREE Ulysses Simpson Grant (1822–85) led Union forces to victory in the American Civil War and later served as the 18th US president. His maternal grandfather, John Simpson, emigrated from County Tyrone to Pennsylvania in 1760, but the farm he left behind at Dergina has been restored in the style of a typical Ulster smallholding, as it would have been during the time of Grant's presidency.

The farm outbuildings contain exhibitions on local history, famine and emigration and the American Civil War.

The site is 20km west of Dungannon, signposted south of the A4.

Donaghmore High Cross   RELIGIOUS SITE
The village of Donaghmore, 5km northwest of Dungannon on the road to Pomeroy, is famed for its 10th-century Celtic high cross. It was cobbled together from two different crosses in the 18th century (note the obvious join halfway up the shaft) and now stands outside the church graveyard. The carved biblical scenes are similar to those on the Ardboe High Cross.

🛏 Sleeping & Eating

★**Tullylagan Country House**   HOTEL **££**
(📞 028-8676 5100; www.tullylaganhotel.com; 40b Tullylagan Rd, Cookstown; s/d from £75/110; 🛜) Set amid beautiful riverside gardens, the ivy-clad Tullylagan has a Victorian country-manor feel, with gilt-framed mirrors, polished wooden floors and marble-effect bathrooms; some have been updated with plush velvet

and a contemporary grey scheme. It's 4km south of Cookstown (off the A29).

Grange Lodge
B&B **££**

(📱 028-8778 4212; www.grangelodgecountryhouse. com; 7 Grange Rd, Dungannon; s/d from £90/110; 📶) The five-room Grange is a period gem set on its own 8-hectare grounds. Parts of the antique-packed house date from 1698, though most are Georgian with Victorian additions. The proprietor is an accomplished cook; expect homemade oatmeal cookies and excellent breakfasts. It's 5km southeast of Dungannon, signposted off the A29.

Brewer's House
MODERN IRISH **££**

(📱 028-8776 1932; www.thebrewershouse.com; 73 Castlecaulfield Rd, Donaghmore; mains £15-19; ⊘ kitchen 4.30-8.30pm Mon & Wed-Thu, noon-9pm Fri, to 10pm Sat, to 8pm Sun; 🍴) This much-loved old village pub combines welcoming open fires and cosy nooks and crannies with a menu of creative, modern dishes including locally sourced meat and seafood, burgers, and fish and chips. The beer, wine and cocktail lists are excellent and there are tables outside for sunny afternoons. It's 5km north-west of Dungannon.

Kitchen Restaurant
IRISH **££**

(📱 028-8676 5100; www.tullylaganhotel.com; 40B Tullylagan Rd, Cookstown; mains £12.50-26; ⊘ noon-3pm daily, plus 5-9pm Mon, Tue, Fri & Sat) The restaurant at Tullylagan Country House (p667)

sources its ingredients locally for dishes such as its Tullylagan Estate wild-mushroom risotto and slow-braised duck ragu.

🛍 Shopping

Linen Green Designer Village
SHOPPING CENTRE

(📱 028-8775 3761; www.thelinengreen.co.uk; off A29, Moygashel; ⊘ 10am-5.30pm Mon-Sat) Housed in the former Moygashel Linen Mills, this complex includes a range of designer shops and factory outlets. It's a good place to shop for men's and women's fashion, shoes and accessories. It's southeast of Dungannon.

ⓘ Information

Ranfurly House Arts & Visitor Centre
(📱 028-8772 8600; www.dungannon.info; 26 Market Sq, Dungannon; ⊘ 9am-9pm Mon-Fri, to 5pm Sat, from 1pm Sun Apr-Sep, 9am-5pm Mon-Fri Oct-Mar; 📶) Tourist information for County Tyrone, with an exhibition on the Flight of the Earls. There's a good coffee shop too.

ⓘ Getting There & Away

Bus 273 links Dungannon to Belfast (£10, 50 minutes, hourly Monday to Saturday, six on Sunday) and Omagh (£7.20, 45 minutes). Bus 80 connects Dungannon and Cookstown (£4, 45 minutes, hourly Monday to Friday, seven on Saturday). Bus 209 links Cookstown to Belfast (£10, about 1¼ hours, five daily Monday to Friday, three on Saturday, two on Sunday).

Understand
Ireland

History

From pre-Celts to Celtic cubs, Ireland's history has been a search for identity, which would have been a little more straightforward if this small island hadn't been of such interest to a host of foreign parties: Celtic tribes, Viking marauders, Norman invaders and, most particularly, the English, whose close-knit, fractious and complicated relationship with Ireland provides the prism through which a huge part of the Irish identity is reflected.

The Native Irish

It took the various Celtic tribes roughly 500 years to settle in Ireland, beginning in the 8th century BC. The last of the tribes, commonly known as the Gaels (which in the local language came to mean 'foreigner'), came ashore in the 3rd century BC and proceeded to divide the island into five provinces – Leinster, Meath, Connaught, Ulster and Munster (Meath later merged with Leinster) – that were subdivided into territories controlled by as many as 100 minor kings and chieftains, all of whom nominally paid allegiance to a high king who sat at Tara, in County Meath.

The Celts set about creating the basics of what we now term 'Irish' culture – they devised a sophisticated code of law called the Brehon Law, which remained in use until the early 17th century, and their swirling, maze-like design style, evident on artefacts nearly 2000 years old, is considered the epitome of Irish design. Some excellent ancient Celtic designs survive in the Broighter Hoard in the National Museum in Dublin. The Turoe Stone in County Galway is another fine representation of Celtic artwork.

For a concise, 10-minute read on who the Celts were, see www. ibiblio.org/gaelic/ celts.html.

The Arrival of Christianity

Although St Patrick gets all the credit, Ireland was Christianised by a host of missionaries between the 3rd and 5th centuries. They converted pagan tribes by fusing their local druidic rituals with the new Christian teaching, thereby creating a hybrid known as Celtic or Insular Christianity.

Irish Christian scholars excelled in the study of Latin and Greek philosophy and Christian theology in the monasteries that flourished at, among other places, Clonmacnoise in County Offaly, Glendalough in County Wicklow and Lismore in County Waterford. It was the golden age, and

TIMELINE	10,000–8000 BC	4500 BC	700–300 BC
	After the last ice age ends, humans arrive in Ireland during the Mesolithic era, originally crossing a land bridge between Scotland and Ireland. Few archaeological traces remain of this group.	The first Neolithic farmers arrive in Ireland by boat from as far afield as the Iberian peninsula, bringing cattle, sheep and crops, marking the beginnings of a settled agricultural economy.	Iron technology gradually replaces bronze. The Celtic culture and language arrive, ushering in 1000 years of cultural and political dominance and leaving a legacy still visible today.

the arts of manuscript illumination, metalworking and sculpture flourished, producing such treasures as the *Book of Kells*, ornate jewellery and the many carved stone crosses that dot the 'island of saints and scholars'.

The Vikings Are Coming!

The next group to try their luck were the Vikings, who first showed up in AD 795 and began plundering the prosperous monasteries. In self-defence the monks built round towers, which served as lookout posts and places of refuge during attacks. You can see surviving examples throughout the country, including some fine ones at Glendalough, Kells and Steeple, near Antrim.

Despite the monks' best efforts, the Vikings had their way, mostly due to superior weaponry but also thanks to elements of the local population, who sided with the marauders for profit or protection. By the 10th century the Norsemen were well established in Ireland, having founded towns such as Wicklow, Waterford and Wexford and their capital Dyfflin, which later became Dublin. The Vikings were defeated at the Battle of Clontarf in 1014 by Brian Ború, king of Munster, but Ború was killed and the Vikings, much like the Celts before them, eventually settled, giving up the rape-rob-and-run policy in favour of integration and assimilation. By intermarrying with the Celtic tribes, they introduced red hair and freckles to the Irish gene pool.

The English Invade

The '800 years' of English rule in Ireland nominally began with the Norman invasion of 1169, which was really more of an invitation as the barons, led by Richard Fitz Gilbert de Clare, earl of Pembroke (1130–76; aka Strongbow), had been asked to assist the king of Leinster in a territorial squabble. Two years later King Henry II of England came ashore with a substantial army and a request from Pope Adrian IV to bring the rebel Christian missionaries to heel.

Despite the king's overall authority, the Anglo-Norman barons carved Ireland up between them and over the next 300 years set about consolidating their feudal power. Once again the effects of assimilation were in play, as the Anglo-Normans and their hirelings became, in the oft-quoted phrase, *Hiberniores Hibernis ipsis* (more Irish than the Irish themselves). They dotted the country with castles, but their real legacy is in the cities they built, such as magnificent Kilkenny, which today retains much of its medieval character. The Anglo-Normans may have pledged allegiance to the English king, but in truth they were loyal only to themselves, and by the turn of the 16th century, the Crown's direct rule didn't extend any further than a cordon surrounding Dublin known as the Pale. But you can only ignore an English king for so long…

Top Monastic Sites

....

Cashel (County Tipperary)

....

Clonmacnoise (County Offaly)

....

Glendalough (County Wicklow)

HISTORY THE VIKINGS ARE COMING!

AD 431–2	550–800	795–841	1014
Pope Celestine I sends Bishop Palladius to Ireland to minister to those 'already believing in Christ'; St Patrick arrives the following year to continue the mission.	The flowering of early monasticism in Ireland. The great monastic teachers begin exporting their knowledge across Europe, ushering in Ireland's 'golden age'.	Vikings plunder Irish monasteries; their raping and pillaging urges sated, they establish settlements throughout the country, including Dublin, which they soon turn into a centre of economic power.	The Battle of Clontarf takes place on Good Friday between the forces of the high king, Brian Ború, and forces led by the king of Leinster, Máelmorda mac Murchada.

ST PATRICK

Ireland's patron saint is remembered all around the world on 17 March, when people of all ethnicities drink Guinness and wear green clothing. But behind the hoopla was a real man with a serious mission. For it was Patrick (AD 389–461) who introduced Christianity to Ireland.

The plain truth of it is that he wasn't Irish. This symbol of Irish pride hailed from what is now Wales, which at the time of his birth was under Roman rule.

Patrick's arrival in Ireland was made possible by Irish raiders who kidnapped him when he was 16, and took him across the channel to work as a slave. He found religion, escaped from captivity and returned to Britain. But he vowed that his life's work would be to make Christians out of the Irish. He was ordained, then appointed Bishop of Ireland. Back he went across the channel.

He based himself in Armagh, where St Patrick's Church of Ireland Cathedral stands on the site of his old church. Patrick quickly converted peasants and nobles in great numbers. Within 30 years much of Ireland had been baptised and the country was divided into Catholic dioceses and parishes. He also established monasteries throughout Ireland, which would be the foundations of Irish scholarship for many centuries.

So next St Paddy's Day, as you're swilling Guinness and champing down corned beef and cabbage, think of who the man really was.

Ireland & the Tudors

When Henry VIII declared himself head of the Church in England in 1534, following his split with the papacy over his divorce from Catherine of Aragon, the Anglo-Normans cried foul and some took up arms against the Crown. Worried that an Irish rising would be of help to Spain or France, Henry responded firmly, quashing the rebellion, confiscating the rebels' lands and (as in England) dissolving all Irish monasteries. He then had himself declared King of Ireland.

The Course of Irish History by TW Moody and FX Martin is a hefty volume by two Trinity College professors tracing much of Ireland's history back to its land and its proximity to England.

Elizabeth I (1533–1603) came to the throne in 1558 with the same uncompromising attitude as her father to Ireland. Ulster was the most hostile to her, with the Irish fighting doggedly under the command of Hugh O'Neill, earl of Tyrone, but they too were finally defeated in 1603. O'Neill, though, achieved something of a pyrrhic victory when he refused to surrender until after he heard of Elizabeth's death. He and his fellow earls then fled the country in what became known as the Flight of the Earls. It left Ulster open to English rule and to the policy of Plantation, which involved confiscating the lands of the flown earls and redistributing them to subjects loyal to the Crown. Though the confiscations happened all over the country, they were most thorough in Ulster.

1169	1171	1350–1530	1366
Henry II's Welsh and Norman barons land in Wexford and capture Waterford and Wexford with MacMurrough's help. It's the beginning of an 800-year occupation by Britain.	King Henry II invades Ireland, forcing the Cambro-Norman warlords and some of the Gaelic Irish kings to accept him as their overlord.	The Anglo-Norman barons establish power bases independent of the English Crown. Over the following two centuries, English control gradually recedes to an area around Dublin known as 'the Pale'.	The English Crown enacts the Statutes of Kilkenny, outlawing intermarriage, the Irish language and other Irish customs to stop the Anglo-Normans from assimilating too much with the Irish. It doesn't work.

Oliver Cromwell Invades Ireland

At the outset of the English Civil War in 1642, the Irish threw their support behind Charles I against the very Protestant parliamentarians in the hope that victory for the king would lead to the restoration of Catholic power in Ireland. When Oliver Cromwell and his Roundheads defeated the Royalists and took Charles' head off in 1649, Cromwell turned his attention to the disloyal Irish. His nine-month campaign was effective and brutal (Drogheda was particularly mistreated). Yet more lands were confiscated – Cromwell's famous utterance that the Irish could 'go to hell or to Connaught' seems odd given the province's beauty, but there wasn't much arable land out there – and Catholic rights restricted even more.

The Boyne & Penal Laws

Catholic Ireland's next major setback came in 1690. Yet again the Irish had backed the wrong horse, this time supporting James II after his deposition in the Glorious Revolution by the Dutch Protestant King William of Orange (who was married to James' daughter Mary). After James had unsuccessfully laid siege to Derry for 105 days (the Loyalist cry of 'No surrender!', in use to this day, dates from the siege), he fought William's armies by the banks of the Boyne in County Louth in July and was roundly defeated.

The final ignominy for Catholics came in 1695 with the passing of the Penal Laws, which prohibited them from owning land or entering any higher profession. Irish culture, music and education were banned in the hope that Catholicism would be eradicated. Most Catholics continued to worship at secret locations, but some prosperous Irish converted to Protestantism to preserve their careers and wealth. Land was steadily transferred to Protestant owners, and a significant majority of the Catholic population became tenants living in wretched conditions. By the late 18th century Catholics owned barely 5% of the land.

Revolt Against British Rule

Beginning towards the end of the 18th century, the main thrust of opposition to Irish inequalities resulting from the Penal Laws came from an unlikely source. A handful of liberal Protestants, versed in the ideologies of the Enlightenment and inspired by the revolutions in France and the newly established United States of America, began organising direct opposition to British rule.

The best known was Theobald Wolfe Tone (1763–98), a young Dublin lawyer who led a group called the United Irishmen in their attempts to reform and reduce British power in Ireland (Loyalist Protestants prepared for the possibility of conflict by forming the Protestant Orange Society, later known as the Orange Order). Wolfe Tone attempted to enlist French help in his uprising, but the French failure to land an army of

The expression 'beyond the Pale' came into use when the Pale was the Anglo-Norman-controlled part of Ireland. To them the rest of Ireland was an uncivilised territory populated by barbarians.

A History of Ulster by Jonathan Bardon is a serious and far-reaching attempt to come to grips with Northern Ireland's saga.

1536–41	1585	1594	1601
Henry VIII orders the Dissolution of the Monasteries and confiscation of church property. In 1541 he arranges for the Irish Parliament to declare him King of Ireland.	Potatoes from South America are introduced to Ireland, where they eventually become a staple on nearly every table in the country.	Hugh O'Neill, earl of Tyrone, orders lead from England to reroof his castle, but instead uses it for bullets, instigating the start of the Nine Years' War.	The Battle of Kinsale is fought between Queen Elizabeth I's armies and the combined rebel forces led by Hugh O'Neill. O'Neill surrenders and the back of the Irish rebellion against the Crown is broken.

succour in 1796 left the organisation exposed to retribution and the men met their bloody end in the Battle of Vinegar Hill in 1798. Three years later the British sought to put an end to Irish agitation with the Act of Union, but the nationalist genie was already out of the bottle.

The Famine, O'Connell & Parnell

The 19th century was marked by repeated efforts to wrest some kind of control from Britain. There were the radical Republicans, who advocated use of force to found a secular, egalitarian republic that tried – and failed – in 1848 and 1867. And there were the moderates, who advocated non-violent and legal action to force the government into concession.

The Great Liberator

Dominating the moderate landscape for nearly three decades was Kerry-born Daniel O'Connell (1775–1847), who tirelessly devoted himself to the cause of Catholic emancipation. In 1828 he was elected to the British Parliament but, being a Catholic, he couldn't actually take his seat. To avoid the possibility of an uprising, the government was forced to pass the 1829 Catholic Emancipation Act, allowing some well-off Catholics voting rights and the right to be elected as MPs.

O'Connell continued to fight for Irish self-determination and became known as a powerful speaker, not only on behalf of Ireland but against all kinds of injustice, including slavery – the abolitionist leader Frederick Douglass was one of his greatest admirers (their relationship was specifically referred to by President Barack Obama during his 2011 visit). O'Connell, known as 'the Liberator', was adored by the Irish, who turned out in their tens of thousands to hear him speak, but his unwillingness to step outside the law was to prove his undoing: when the government banned one of his rallies from going ahead, O'Connell stood down – ostensibly to avoid the prospect of violence and bloodshed. But Ireland was in the midst of the Potato Famine, and his failure to defy the British was seen as capitulation. He was imprisoned for a time and died a broken man in 1847.

The Uncrowned King of Ireland

Charles Stewart Parnell (1846–91) was the other great 19th-century statesman. Like O'Connell, he was a powerful orator, but the primary focus of his artful attentions was land reform, particularly the reduction of rents and the improvement of working conditions (conveniently referred to as the 'Three Fs': fair rent, free sale and fixity of tenure). Parnell championed the activities of the Land League, which instigated the strategy of 'boycotting' (named after one particularly unpleasant agent called Charles Boycott) tenants, agents and landlords who didn't adhere

Cromwell: An Honourable Enemy by Tom Reilly advances the wildly unpopular view that perhaps the destruction of Cromwell's campaign is grossly exaggerated. You're no doubt familiar with the common view; here's the contrary position. (Yes, Reilly is Irish.)

For the Cause of Liberty: A Thousand Years of Ireland's Heroes by Terry Golway vividly describes the struggles of Irish nationalism.

1607	1649–53	1688–90	1695
O'Neill and 90 other Ulster chiefs sail to Europe, leaving Ireland forever. Known as the Flight of the Earls, it leaves Ulster open to English rule and the policy of Plantation.	Cromwell lays waste to Ireland in 1649 after the Irish support Charles I in the English Civil War; this includes the mass slaughter of Catholic Irish and the confiscation of 2 million hectares of land over the next four years.	Following the deposition of King James II, James' Catholic army fights the Protestant forces of his successor, King William, resulting in William's victory at the Battle of the Boyne, 12 July 1690.	The Penal Laws (aka the 'popery code') prohibit Catholics from owning a horse, marrying outside their religion, building churches out of anything but wood, and buying or inheriting property.

THE GREAT FAMINE

As a result of the Great Famine of 1845–51, it's estimated that up to one million people died and some two million were forced to emigrate from Ireland. This great tragedy is all the more inconceivable given that the scale of suffering was attributable to selfishness as much as to natural causes. Potatoes were the staple food of a rapidly growing, desperately poor population and, when a blight hit the crops, prices soared. The repressive Penal Laws ensured that farmers, already crippled with high rents, could ill afford the few subsistence potatoes provided. Inevitably most tenants fell into arrears, with little or no concession given by the mostly indifferent landlords, and were evicted or sent to the dire conditions of the workhouses.

During this time there were abundant harvests of wheat and dairy produce – the country was producing more than enough grain to feed the entire population and it's said that more cattle were sold abroad than there were people on the island. But while millions of its citizens were starving, Ireland was forced to export its food to Britain and overseas.

The Poor Law, in place at the height of the Famine, deemed landlords responsible for the maintenance of their poor and encouraged many to 'remove' tenants from their estates by paying their way to America. Many Irish were sent unwittingly to their deaths on board the notoriously scourged 'coffin ships'. British prime minister Sir Robert Peel made well-intentioned but inadequate gestures at famine relief, and some – but far too few – landlords did their best for their tenants.

Mass emigration continued to reduce the population during the next 100 years and huge numbers of Irish emigrants who found their way abroad, particularly to the USA, carried with them a lasting bitterness.

---

to the Land League's aims: these people were treated like lepers by the local population. In 1881 they won an important victory with the passing of the Land Act, which granted most of the League's demands.

Parnell's other great struggle was for a limited form of autonomy for Ireland. Despite the nominal support of the Liberal leader William Gladstone, Home Rule bills introduced in 1886 and 1892 were uniformly rejected by Parliament. Like O'Connell before him, Parnell's star plummeted dramatically, and in 1890 he was embroiled in a divorce proceeding that scandalised puritanical Ireland. The 'uncrowned king of Ireland' was forced to resign and died less than a year later.

The Border: The Legacy of a Century of Anglo-Irish Politics by Diarmaid Ferriter (2019) is a fresh look at the tumultuous history of cross-border relations between north and south.

Fomenting Revolution

Ireland's struggle for some kind of autonomy picked up pace in the second decade of the 20th century. The radicalism that had always been at the fringes of Irish nationalist aspirations was once again beginning to assert itself, partly in response to a hardening of attitudes in Ulster. Mass opposition to any kind of Irish independence had resulted in the

1795	1798	1801	1828–29
Concerned at the attempts of the Society of United Irishmen to secure equal rights for nonestablishment Protestants and Catholics, a group of Protestants create the Orange Order.	The flogging and killing of potential rebels sparks a rising led by the United Irishmen and their leader, Wolfe Tone. Wolfe Tone is captured and taken to Dublin, where he commits suicide.	The Act of Union comes into effect, uniting Ireland politically with Britain. The Irish Parliament votes itself out of existence following a campaign of bribery. Around 100 MPs move to the House of Commons in London.	Daniel O'Connell exploits a loophole in the law to win a seat in Parliament but is unable to take it because he is Catholic. The prime minister passes the Catholic Emancipation Act, giving limited rights to Catholics.

formation of the Ulster Volunteer Force (UVF), a Loyalist vigilante group whose 100,000-plus members swore to resist any attempt to impose Home Rule on Ireland. Nationalists responded by creating the Irish Volunteer Force (IVF) and a showdown seemed inevitable.

Home Rule was finally passed in 1914, but the outbreak of WWI meant that its enactment was shelved for the duration. For most Irish the suspension was disappointing but hardly unreasonable, and the majority of the volunteers enlisted to help fight the Germans.

The Great Hunger by Cecil Woodham-Smith is the classic study of the Great Famine of 1845–51.

The Easter Rising

A few, however, did not heed the call. Two small groups – a section of the Irish Volunteers under Pádraig Pearse and the Irish Citizens' Army led by James Connolly – conspired in a rebellion that took the country by surprise. A depleted Volunteer group marched into Dublin on Easter Monday 1916 and took over a number of key positions in the city, claiming the General Post Office on O'Connell St as its headquarters. From its steps, Pearse read out to passers-by a declaration that Ireland was now a republic and that his band was the provisional government. Less than a week of fighting ensued before the rebels surrendered to the superior British forces. The rebels weren't popular and had to be protected from angry Dubliners as they were marched to jail.

The Easter Rising would probably have had little impact on the Irish situation had the British not made martyrs of the rebel leaders. Of the 77 given death sentences, 15 were executed, including the injured Connolly, who was shot while strapped to a chair. This brought about a sea change in public attitudes, and support for the Republicans rose dramatically.

The Irish in America by Michael Coffey takes up the history of the Famine where many histories leave off: the turbulent experiences of Irish immigrants in the USA.

War with Britain

By the end of WWI, Home Rule was far too little, far too late. In the 1918 general election, the Republicans stood under the banner of Sinn Féin and won a large majority of the Irish seats. Ignoring London's Parliament, where technically they were supposed to sit, the newly elected Sinn Féin deputies, many of them veterans of the 1916 Easter Rising, declared Ireland independent and formed the first Dáil Éireann (Irish assembly or lower house), which sat in Dublin's Mansion House under the leadership of Eamon de Valera (1882–1975). The Irish Volunteers became the Irish Republican Army (IRA) and the Dáil authorised it to wage war on British troops in Ireland.

As wars go, the War of Independence was pretty small fry. It lasted 2½ years and cost around 1200 casualties. But it was a nasty affair, as the IRA fought a guerrilla-style, hit-and-run campaign against the British, whose numbers were swelled by returning veterans of WWI known as Black and Tans (on account of their uniforms, which were a mix of army

1845–51	1879–82	1890s	1916
A mould ravages the potato harvest. The British government adopts a laissez-faire attitude, resulting in the deaths of between 500,000 and one million people, and the emigration of up to two million others.	The Land War, led by the Land League, sees tenant farmers defying their landlords en masse to force the passing of the Land Act in 1881, which allows for fair rent, fixity of tenure and free sale.	The Gaelic Revival, championed by poet WB Yeats, sees a focused interest in the Irish language and Irish culture, including folklore, sport, music and the arts.	The Easter Rising: a group of Republicans take Dublin's General Post Office and announce the formation of an Irish republic. After less than a week of fighting, the rebels surrender to the superior or British forces.

khaki and police black), many of whom were so traumatised by their wartime experiences that they were prone to all kinds of brutality.

A Kind of Freedom

A truce in July 1921 led to intense negotiations between the two sides. The resulting Anglo-Irish Treaty, signed on 6 December 1921, created the Irish Free State, made up of 26 of 32 Irish counties. The remaining six – all in Ulster – remained part of the UK. The Treaty was an imperfect document: not only did it cement the geographic divisions on the island that 50 years later would explode into the Troubles, it also caused a split among nationalists – between those who believed the Treaty to be a necessary stepping stone towards full independence, and those who saw it as capitulation to the British and a betrayal of Republican ideals. This division was to determine the course of Irish political affairs for virtually the remainder of the century.

For articles exploring the whole gamut of Irish history, check out the National Library's historical blog at www. nli.ie/blog.

Civil War

The Treaty was ratified after a bitter debate and the June 1922 elections resulted in a victory for the pro-Treaty side. But the anti-Treaty forces rallied behind de Valera, who, though president of the Dáil, had not been a member of the Treaty negotiating team (affording him, in the eyes of his critics and opponents, maximum deniability should the negotiations go pear-shaped) and objected to some of the Treaty's provisions, most notably the oath of allegiance to the British monarch.

Within two weeks of the elections, civil war broke out between comrades who, a year previously, had fought alongside each other. The most prominent casualty of this particularly bitter conflict was Michael Collins (1890–1922), mastermind of the IRA's campaign during the War of Independence and a chief negotiator of the Anglo-Irish Treaty. He was shot in an ambush in his native Cork. Collins himself had presaged the bitterness that would result from the Treaty: upon signing it, he is said to have declared 'I tell you, I have signed my own death warrant'.

Brendan O'Brien's popular *Pocket History of the IRA* summarises a lot of complex history in a mere 150 pages; it's a good introduction.

The Making of a Republic

The Civil War ground to an exhausted halt in 1923 with the victory of the pro-Treaty side, which governed the new state until 1932. Defeated but unbowed, de Valera founded a new party in 1926 called Fianna Fáil (Soldiers of Ireland) and won a majority in the 1932 elections; they would remain in charge until 1948. In the meantime de Valera created a new constitution in 1937 that did away with the hated oath of allegiance, reaffirmed the special position of the Catholic Church and once again laid claim to the six counties of Northern Ireland. In 1948 Ireland officially left the Commonwealth and became a republic but, as historical irony

1919–21	1921	1921–22	1922–23
Irish War of Independence, aka the Black and Tan War on account of British irregulars wearing mixed police (black) and army (khaki) uniforms, begins in January 1919.	Two years and 1200 casualties later, the war ends in a truce on 11 July 1921 that leads to peace talks. After negotiations in London, the Irish delegation signs the Anglo-Irish Treaty on 6 December.	The Treaty gives 26 counties of Ireland independence and allows six largely Protestant Ulster counties the choice of opting out. The Irish Free State is founded in 1922.	Unwilling to accept the terms of the Treaty, forces led by Eamon de Valera take up arms against their former comrades, led by Michael Collins. The brief but bloody Civil War ensues, resulting in the death of Collins.

would have it, it was Fine Gael, as the old pro-Treaty party was now known, that declared it – Fianna Fáil had surprisingly lost the election that year. After 800 years, Ireland – or at least a substantial chunk of it – was independent.

Growing Pains & Roaring Tigers

Neil Jordan's movie *Michael Collins*, starring Liam Neeson as the revolutionary, depicts the Easter Rising, the founding of the Free State and Collins' violent demise.

Unquestionably the most significant figure since independence, Eamon de Valera made an immense contribution to an independent Ireland but, as the 1950s stretched into the 1960s, his vision for the country was mired in a conservative and traditional orthodoxy that was at odds with the reality of a country in desperate economic straits. Chronic unemployment and emigration were but the more visible effects of inadequate policy. De Valera's successor as Taoiseach (Republic of Ireland prime minister) was Sean Lemass, whose tenure began in 1959 with the dictum 'a rising tide lifts all boats'. By the mid-1960s his economic policies had halved emigration and ushered in a new prosperity that was to be mirrored 30 years later by the Celtic Tiger.

Partners in Europe

In 1972 the Republic (along with Northern Ireland) became a member of the European Economic Community (EEC). This brought an increased measure of prosperity thanks to the benefits of the Common Agricultural Policy, which set fixed prices and guaranteed quotas for Irish farming produce. Nevertheless, the broader global depression, provoked by the oil crisis of 1973, forced the country into yet another slump and emigration figures rose again, reaching a peak in the mid-1980s.

The Celtic Tiger

The events leading up to the Anglo-Irish War and their effect on ordinary people are movingly and powerfully related in JG Farrell's novel *Troubles*, first published in 1970.

In the early 1990s European funds helped kick-start economic growth. Huge sums of money were invested in education and physical infrastructure, while the policy of low corporate tax rates coupled with attractive incentives made Ireland very appealing to high-tech businesses looking for a door into EU markets. In less than a decade Ireland went from being one of the poorest countries in Europe to one of the wealthiest: unemployment fell from 18% to 3.5%, the average industrial wage somersaulted to the top of the European league, and the dramatic rise in GDP meant that the country laid claim to an economic model of success that was the envy of the entire world. Ireland became synonymous with the term 'Celtic Tiger'.

Recession Looms

From 2002 the Irish economy was kept buoyant by a gigantic construction boom that was completely out of step with any measure of respon-

1932	1948	1969	1972
After 10 years in the political wilderness, de Valera leads his Fianna Fáil party into government and goes about weakening the ties between the Free State and Britain.	Fianna Fáil loses the general election to Fine Gael in coalition with the new Republican Clann an Poblachta. The new government declares the Free State to be a republic at last.	Marches by the Northern Ireland Civil Rights Association are disrupted by Loyalist attacks and police action, resulting in rioting and culminating in the Battle of the Bogside. The Troubles begin.	The Republic and Northern Ireland become members of the EEC. On Bloody Sunday, 13 civilians are killed by British troops; Westminster suspends the Stormont government and introduces direct rule.

sible growth forecasting. The out-of-control international derivatives market flooded Irish banks with cheap money, and they lent it freely.

Then in 2008 American global financial services firm Lehman Bros collapsed and the credit crunch happened. The Irish banks nearly went to the wall, but were bailed out at the last minute, and before Ireland could draw breath, the International Monetary Fund (IMF) and the EU held the chits of the country's midterm economic future. The resulting program of austerity led to deep cuts and tough times for most Irish, but the country turned a corner in 2015 and the economy once again began to grow – with property prices exceeding the boom years by 2018.

It's (Not So) Grim Up North

Since 8 May 2007 Northern Ireland has been governed in relative harmony by a constituent assembly led by a First Minister and a Deputy First Minister, drawn from the largest parties on either side of the sectarian divide. Until 2017 it was the Democratic Unionist Party (DUP) and Sinn Féin respectively, but their generally pacific alliance was scuttled by, firstly, a scandal that saw Sinn Féin pull out of government (triggering new elections) and, secondly, the emergence of the DUP as the Conservative Party's parliamentary lifeline following the British general election in June 2017, wherein the party's 10 MPs agreed to a 'supply and confidence' arrangement with the government. Meanwhile the Northern Ireland Assembly remains suspended, but the tragic killing in April 2019 of young journalist Lyra McKee in Derry by republican dissidents – shot during rioting in the Creggan area of the city – has forced both sides to make positive noises about resolving the political impasse.

In 1870, after the Great Famine and ongoing emigration, more than a third of all native-born Irish lived outside Ireland.

Ireland Divided

Following the Anglo-Irish Treaty, a new Northern Ireland Parliament was constituted on 22 June 1922, with James Craig as the first prime minister. His Ulster Unionist Party (UUP) was to rule the new state until 1972, with the minority Catholic population (roughly 40%) stripped of any real power or representative strength by a Parliament that favoured the Unionists through economic subsidy, bias in housing allocations and gerrymandering – Derry's electoral boundaries were redrawn so as to guarantee a Protestant council, even though the city was two-thirds Catholic. The overwhelmingly Protestant Royal Ulster Constabulary (RUC) and its paramilitary force, the B-Specials, made little effort to mask its sectarian bias.

We Shall Overcome

The first challenge to the unionist hegemony came with the long-dormant IRA's border campaign in the 1950s, but it was quickly quashed and its leaders imprisoned. A decade later, however, the authorities met

1973–74	1981	1993	Mid-1990s
The Sunningdale Agreement results in a new Northern Ireland Assembly. Unionists oppose the agreement and the Ulster Workers' Council calls a strike that paralyses the province and brings an end to the Assembly.	Ten Republican prisoners die from a hunger strike. The first to die, Bobby Sands, had three weeks earlier been elected to Parliament on an Anti-H-Block ticket. More than 100,000 people attend Sands' funeral.	Downing Street Declaration is signed by British Prime Minister John Major and Irish Prime Minister Albert Reynolds. It states that Britain has no 'selfish, strategic or economic interest in Northern Ireland'.	Low corporate tax, restraint in government spending, transfer payments from the EU and a low-cost labour market result in the 'Celtic Tiger' boom, transforming Ireland into one of Europe's wealthiest countries.

with a far more defiant foe in the shape of the Civil Rights Association, founded in 1967 and heavily influenced by its US counterpart as it sought to redress the blatant sectarianism in Derry. In October 1968 a mainly Catholic march in Derry was violently broken up by the RUC amid rumours that the IRA had provided 'security' for the marchers. Nobody knew it at the time, but the Troubles had begun.

In January 1969 another civil rights movement, called People's Democracy, organised a march from Belfast to Derry. As the marchers neared their destination, they were attacked by a group of Protestants. The police first stood to one side and then swept through the predominantly Catholic Bogside district. Further marches, protests and violence followed, with many Republicans arguing that the police only added to the problem. In August British troops went to Derry and then Belfast to maintain law and order. The British army was initially welcomed in some Catholic quarters, but soon it too came to be seen as a tool of the Protestant majority. Overreaction by the army actually fuelled recruitment into the long-dormant IRA, whose numbers especially increased after Bloody Sunday (30 January 1972), when British troops killed 13 civilians in Derry.

Books on the Troubles

Lost Lives, David McKittrick

Ten Men Dead, David Beresford

The Faithful Tribe: An Intimate Portrait of the Loyal Institutions, Ruth Dudley Edwards

The Troubles

Following Bloody Sunday the IRA more or less declared war on Britain. While continuing to target people in Northern Ireland, it moved its campaign of bombing to the British mainland, targeting innocents and earning the condemnation of citizens and parties from both sides of the sectarian divide. Meanwhile Loyalist paramilitaries began a sectarian campaign against Catholics. Passions reached fever pitch in 1981 when Republican prisoners in the North went on a hunger strike, demanding the right to be recognised as political prisoners. Ten of them fasted to death, the best known being an elected MP, Bobby Sands.

The waters were further muddied by an incredible variety of parties splintering into subgroups with different agendas. The IRA had split into 'official' and 'provisional' wings, from which sprang more extreme Republican organisations such as the Irish National Liberation Army (INLA). Myriad Protestant, Loyalist paramilitary organisations sprang up in opposition to the IRA, and violence was typically met with violence.

Overtures of Peace

By the early 1990s it was clear to Republicans that armed struggle was a bankrupted policy. Northern Ireland was a transformed society – most of the injustices that had sparked the conflict in the late 1960s had long since been rectified and most ordinary citizens were desperate for an end to hostilities. A series of negotiated statements between the unionists, nationalists and the British and Irish governments – brokered in part by

1994	1998	1998	2005
Sinn Féin leader Gerry Adams announces a 'cessation of violence' on behalf of the Irish Republican Army (IRA) on 31 August. In October the Combined Loyalist Military Command also announces a ceasefire.	On 10 April negotiations culminate in the Good Friday Agreement, under which the new Northern Ireland Assembly is given full legislative and executive authority.	The 'Real IRA' detonates a bomb in Omagh, killing 29 people and injuring 200. It's the worst single atrocity in the history of the Troubles; public outrage and swift action by politicians prevent a Loyalist backlash.	The IRA orders its units not to engage in 'any other activities' apart from assisting 'the development of purely political and democratic programmes through exclusively peaceful means'.

George Mitchell, Bill Clinton's special envoy to Northern Ireland – eventually resulted in the historic Good Friday Agreement of 1998.

The agreement called for the devolution of legislative power from Westminster (where it had been since 1972) to a new Northern Ireland Assembly, but posturing, disagreement, sectarianism and downright obstinance on both sides made slow work of progress, and the Assembly was suspended four times – the last from October 2002 until May 2007.

During this period, the politics of Northern Ireland polarised dramatically, resulting in the falling away of the more moderate UUP and the emergence of the hardline DUP, led by Ian Paisley; and on the nationalist side, the emergence of the IRA's political wing, Sinn Féin, as the main torchbearer of nationalist aspirations, under the leadership of Gerry Adams and Martin McGuinness.

Many films depict events related to the Troubles, including *Bloody Sunday* (2002), *The Boxer* (1997; starring Daniel Day-Lewis) and *In the Name of the Father* (1994; also starring Day-Lewis).

HISTORY IT'S (NOT SO) GRIM UP NORTH

A New Northern Ireland

Eager to avoid being seen to surrender any ground, the DUP and Sinn Féin dug their heels in on key issues, with the main sticking points being decommissioning of IRA weapons and the identity and composition of the new police force ushered in to replace the RUC. Paisley and the Unionists made increasing demands of the decommissioning bodies (photographic evidence, Unionist witnesses etc) as they refused to accept anything less than an open and complete surrender of the IRA. Sinn Féin refused to join the police board that monitored the affairs of the Police

AMERICAN CONNECTIONS

Today more than 40 million Americans have Irish ancestry, a legacy of successive waves of emigration, spurred by events from the Potato Famine of the 1840s to the Depression of the 1930s. Many of the legendary figures of American history, from Davy Crockett to John Steinbeck, and 18 of the 45 US presidents to date, are of Irish descent – including Barack Obama, whose mother's family includes an emigrant called Falmouth Kearney, from Moneygall, County Offaly.

Following is a list of places that have links to past US presidents, or deal with the experience of Irish emigrants to the USA:

➡ Andrew Jackson Centre (p650), County Antrim

➡ Cobh, The Queenstown Story (p240), County Cork

➡ Dunbrody Famine Ship (p191), County Wexford

➡ Grant Ancestral Homestead (p667), County Tyrone

➡ Kennedy Homestead (p190), County Wexford

➡ Ulster American Folk Park (p665), County Tyrone

2007	2008	2010	2011
The Northern Ireland Assembly resumes after a five-year break when talks between unionists and Republicans remain in stalemate. They resolve their primary issues.	The Irish banking system is declared virtually bankrupt following the collapse of American global financial services firm Lehman Bros; Ireland is on the brink of economic disaster as the extent of the crisis is revealed.	Ireland receives an €85-billion bailout package from the International Monetary Fund (IMF) and the EU, which alleviates the banking crisis but leaves the country in strict financial shackles.	Queen Elizabeth II is the first British monarch to visit the Republic of Ireland; the visit is heralded as a resounding affirmation of the close ties between the two nations.

Service of Northern Ireland (PSNI), effectively making no change to their policy of total noncooperation with the security forces.

But the IRA did finally decommission all of its weapons, and Sinn Féin eventually agreed to join the police board. The DUP abandoned its intransigence towards its former Republican enemies and the two sides got down to the business of governing a province whose pressing needs had long been shunted aside by sectarianism. Proof that Northern Ireland had finally achieved some kind of normality came with the 2011 Assembly elections, which returned the DUP and Sinn Féin as the two largest parties, mandating them to keep going.

But old enmities die hard. The murder of a young PSNI officer called Ronan Kerr in April 2011 was a bitter reminder of the province's violent history, but even in tragedy there was a sense that something fundamental had shifted. Kerr was a Catholic member of a police force that had gone to great lengths to disavow its traditionally pro-Protestant bias and his murder was condemned with equal strength by both sides of the divide. Perhaps most tellingly, the then–First Minister Peter Robinson's presence at the funeral was the first time Robinson had ever been to a Catholic requiem mass.

A History of Ireland by Mike Cronin summarises all of Ireland's history in less than 300 pages. It's an easy read, but doesn't offer much in the way of analysis.

2013	2015	2017	2018
Ireland becomes the first stricken eurozone country to successfully exit the terms of the bailout.	Ireland becomes the first country in the world to introduce marriage equality for same-sex couples by plebiscite.	Leo Varadkar, the gay son of an Indian immigrant, becomes Taoiseach (Republic of Ireland prime minister); he is the fourth openly gay leader in European history.	Ireland votes to remove the constitutional ban on abortion by 66.4%; Donegal is the only constituency to vote against its removal, by a narrow majority of 51.87%.

The Irish Way of Life

The Irish reputation for being affable is largely well deserved, but it only hints at a more profound character, one more complex and contradictory than the image of the silver-tongued master of blarney might suggest. This dichotomy is best summarised by a quote usually ascribed to the poet William Butler Yeats: 'Being Irish, he had an abiding sense of tragedy, which sustained him through temporary periods of joy.'

The Irish Pulse

The Irish are famous for being warm and friendly, which is just another way of saying the Irish love a chat, whether with friends or strangers. They will entertain you with their humour, alarm you with their willingness to get stuck into a good debate, and cut you down with their razor-sharp wit. Slagging – the Irish version of teasing – is an art form, which may seem caustic to unfamiliar ears, but is quickly revealed as an intrinsic element of how the Irish relate to one another. It is commonly assumed that the mettle of friendship is proven by how well you can take a joke rather than by the payment of a cheap compliment.

Yet beneath all of the garrulous sociability and self-deprecating twaddle lurks a dark secret, which is that at heart the Irish have traditionally been low on self-esteem. This is partly why they're so suspicious of easy compliments, but the last three decades have seen a paradigm shift in the Irish character.

Prosperity and its related growth in expectations have gone a long way towards transforming the Irish from a people who wallowed in false modesty like a sport, to a nation eager to celebrate its achievements and successes. Inevitably this personality shift has been largely driven by the appetites and demands of Generation Y, but there's no doubt that many older Irish, for too long muted by a fear of appearing unseemly or boastful, have wholeheartedly embraced the change.

This cultural shift survived the trauma of the financial crash and the austerity that followed, even if many blamed a tawdry and materialistic culture of exaggerated excess for Ireland's woes, an attitude memorably summarised by a government minister who sheepishly declared on TV that 'we all partied!' But with the economy (largely) back on track, Ireland is once again hammering down on the pedal of its ambitions and watching the worst ravages of austerity quickly disappear in its rear-view mirror.

> According to the 2016 census, the average number of children per family has fallen to 1.38, the lowest in Irish history.

Nurse & Curse of the People

Despite a 25% drop-off in alcohol consumption over the last decade (according to a 2017 report by the World Health Organization), Ireland has a fractious relationship with alcohol. The country regularly tops the list of the world's biggest binge drinkers, and while there is an increasing awareness of, and alarm at, the devastation caused by alcohol to Irish society (especially to young people), drinking remains the country's most popular social pastime, with no sign of letting up. Spend a weekend night walking around any town in the country and you'll get a firsthand feel of the influence and effect of the booze.

Some experts put Ireland's binge-drinking antics down to the dramatic rise in the country's economic fortunes, but statistics have long suggested that Ireland has had an unhealthy fondness for 'taking the cure', though the acceptability of public drunkenness is a far more recent phenomenon – the older generations are never done reminding the youngsters that they would *never* have been seen staggering in public.

Lifestyle

The Irish may like to grumble – about work, the weather, the government and those *feckin' eejits* on reality TV shows – but if pressed will tell you that they live in the best country on earth. There's loads *wrong* with the place, but isn't it the same way everywhere else?

> In 2016 37.3% of the population lived in rural areas.

Traditional Ireland – of the large family, closely linked to church and community – has largely disappeared as the increased urbanisation of the country continues to break up the social fabric of community interdependence that was a necessary element of relative poverty. Contemporary Ireland is therefore not altogether different from any other European country, and you have to travel further to the margins of the country – the islands and the isolated rural communities – to find an older version of society.

In the North daily concerns largely echo those south of the border and across the UK, but the province's particular history has inevitably had a huge impact on the society at large. Despite younger generations' concerted efforts to bridge the religious divide, Protestant and Catholic communities are still mostly segregated from each other: tricolours and Union Jacks are a clear sign of partisanship in some neighbourhoods, but in many others the divide is invisible to all but those in the community itself. Most Northern Irish are hyperaware of the sectarian breakdown of virtually every hamlet in the province and adjust their lives accordingly.

Gay-Friendly Ireland

A gay Taoiseach (Republic of Ireland prime minister). The first country in the world to introduce marriage equality for same-sex couples by popular vote. It's been an extraordinary road for a country that only decriminalised same-sex activity in 1993.

The rise to power of Taoiseach Leo Varadkar, who only came out five months before the country voted for marriage equality in May 2015, is a powerful example of the paradigm shift that has occurred in attitudes toward the LGBT community in Ireland. The vote in favour of same-sex marriage was 62.4% – all but one constituency voted in favour.

> In 2016 there were 978 males per 1000 females in the Republic, the lowest it's been since 1981.

Varadkar is very much a product of a new Ireland, where sexual orientation is considered not quite irrelevant, but not worthy of any kind of discrimination. In this new Ireland, pride celebrations – in Dublin, Cork, Galway and elsewhere – are now firmly fixed on the festival calendar, with rural Ireland lagging not too far behind their urban brethren.

Which isn't to say that the inhabitants of a small rural community would necessarily be comfortable with a pride march through their village or the opening of a gay bar on the main street. For many the new attitudes have simply evolved from an older notion that people are entitled to do as they please so long as they keep it in the private sphere, and that includes same-sex marriage.

At an official level, Northern Ireland remains troublingly regressive as it's the only part of the United Kingdom where same-sex marriage remains illegal. Whatever LGBT-friendly legislation there is (civil partnership, removal of the ban on blood donations by gay men) has been the result of either direct rule by Westminster or court action rather than legislative reform, this is mostly due to the intransigence of the anti-LGBT Democratic Unionist Party. DUP attitudes, however, are severely at odds with the views of most people under 30, regardless of their political affiliations, who are as progressive in their attitudes toward LGBT issues as their counterparts on the rest of the island and the UK.

Multiculturalism

Ireland has long been a pretty homogenous country, but the arrival of thousands of immigrants from all over the world – 17% of the population is foreign-born – has challenged the mores of racial tolerance and integration. To a large extent the integration has been successful – though, if you scratch beneath the surface, racial tensions can be exposed.

The tanking of the economy exacerbated these tensions and the 'Irish jobs for Irish people' opinion has been expressed with greater vehemence and authority: the rise of right-wing movements across Europe and the US has emboldened Irish ultranationalists to take a more vocal and visible stance. Their numbers remain relatively insignificant for now, even though in 2019 one of these groups was involved in a series of protests against plans to house groups of immigrants in several Irish towns.

Antiracism groups have reported a rise in racist incidents, particularly Islamophobia, but the bulk of these are generally verbal and nonphysical, which perhaps also explains the statistic that 75% of these incidents go unreported. In spite of this, most Muslims and people of colour living in Ireland feel that the country is safe and welcoming and that racism is not the norm for the vast majority of the white Irish population.

Religion

According to the census of 2016, about 3.7 million residents in the Republic (or 78% of the population) call themselves Roman Catholic, followed by 2.6% Church of Ireland (Protestant), 1.3% Muslim, 1.3% Orthodox, and other religions 3.9%; 9.8% declared themselves to have no religion – a 74% rise from 2011.

In the North the breakdown is about 48% Protestant and 45% Catholic (with 7% other or no religion). Most Irish Protestants are members of the Church of Ireland, an offshoot of the Church of England, and the Presbyterian and Methodist churches.

Catholicism remains a powerful cultural identifier, but more in a secular rather than religious way, as many Irish now reject the Church's stance on a host of social issues, from contraception to divorce and homosexuality. In part this is the natural reaction of an increasingly cosmopolitan country with an ever-broadening international outlook, but the Church's failure to satisfactorily take responsibility and atone for its role in the clerical abuse scandals of decades past has breached the bond of trust between many parishioners and their parish.

TV & Radio

Of the country's four terrestrial TV channels, three are operated by the national broadcaster, Raidió Teilifís Éireann (RTE), while the other is a privately owned commercial station. The Irish-language station TG4 shows movies and dramas, mostly *as gaeilge* (in Irish). The main British TV stations – BBC, ITV and Channel 4 – are also available in most Irish homes, through satellite or cable; in Northern Ireland they're the main players.

The Irish are avid radio listeners – up to 85% of the population tunes in on any given day. RTE Radio 1 (88.2FM–90FM; mostly news and discussion) is the main player, followed by two privately owned national stations, Newstalk 106FM–108FM and Today FM, found at 100FM–102FM.

The rest of the radio landscape is filled out by the 25-or-so local radio stations that represent local issues and tastes and are often a great insight into the local mindset: the northwest's Highland Radio is Europe's most successful local radio station, with an 84% market share. In Northern Ireland the BBC rules supreme

THE IRISH WAY OF LIFE MULTICULTURALISM

Polish people have overtaken UK nationals as the largest non-Irish group living in Ireland, making up 2.57% of the population.

The number of respondents on the 2016 census who declared to have no religion rose by 73.6% from 2011 – from 269,800 to 468,400.

Music

Ireland's literary tradition may have the critics nodding sagely, but it's the country's ability to render music to the ear that will remain with you long after your Irish day is done. There's music for every occasion and every mood, from celebration to sorrow. The Irish do popular music as well as anyone, but it is its traditional forms that make Ireland a special place to hear live music, especially in the intimate environment of a pub session.

Traditional & Folk

Irish music (known in Ireland as traditional music, or just trad) has retained a vibrancy not found in other traditional European forms, which have lost out to the overbearing influence of pop music. Although Irish music has kept many of its traditional aspects, it has itself influenced many forms of music, most notably US country and western – a fusion of Mississippi Delta blues and Irish traditional tunes that, combined with other influences such as gospel, is at the root of rock and roll.

The music was never written down; it was passed on from one player to another and so endured and evolved – regional 'styles' only developed because local musicians sought to play just like the one who seemed to play better than everybody else. The blind itinerant harpist Turlough O'Carolan (1670–1738) 'wrote' more than 200 tunes – it's difficult to know how many versions their repeated learning has spawned. This characteristic of fluidity is key to an appreciation of traditional music, and explains why it is such a resilient form today.

Nevertheless in the 1960s composer Seán Ó Riada (1931–71) tried to impose a kind of structure on the music. His ensemble group, Ceoltóirí Chualann, was the first to reach a wider audience, and from it were born The Chieftains, arguably the most important traditional group of all. They started recording in 1963 – any one of their nearly 40 albums are worth a listen, but you won't go wrong with their 10-album eponymous series.

The other big success of the 1960s were The Dubliners. More folksy than traditional, they made a career out of bawdy drinking songs that got everybody singing along. Other popular bands include The Fureys, comprising four brothers originally from the travelling community (no, not like the Wilburies) along with guitarist Davey Arthur. And if it's rousing renditions of Irish rebel songs you're after, you can't go past The Wolfe Tones.

Since the 1970s various bands have tried to blend traditional with more progressive genres, with mixed success. The Bothy Band were formed in 1975 and were a kind of trad supergroup: bouzouki player Dónal Lunny, uillean piper Paddy Keenan, flute and whistle player Matt Molloy (later a member of The Chieftains), fiddler Paddy Glackin and accordion player Tony MacMahon were all superb instrumentalists and their recordings are still as electrifying today as they were four decades ago.

Musicians tend to come together in collaborative projects. A contemporary group worth checking out are The Gloaming, who've taken traditional reels and given them a contemporary sound – their eponymous debut album (2011) is sensational. A key member of the group, fiddler

Top Trad-Music Venues

....

Hughes' Bar (Dublin)

....

Crane Bar (Galway)

....

De Barra's Folk Club (Clonakilty, County Cork)

....

McDermott's (Doolin, County Clare)

....

Leo's Tavern (Crolly, County Donegal)

Caoimhín Ó Raghallaigh, is also worth checking out in his own right. His latest album, *The Gloaming 3,* displays both his beautiful fiddle playing and his superb understanding of loops and electronic texturing.

If you want to check out a group that melds rock, folk and traditional music, you won't go far wrong with The Spook of the Thirteenth Lock, who've released a couple of albums since 2008; in 2017 they released an EP called *The Bullet in the Brick.*

No discussion of traditional music would be complete without a mention of *Riverdance,* which made Irish dancing sexy and became a worldwide phenomenon, despite the fact that most aficionados of traditional music are seriously underwhelmed by its musical worth. Good stage show, crap music.

Popular Music

From the 1960s onward, Ireland produced its fair share of great rock musicians, including Van Morrison, Thin Lizzy, Celtic rockers Horslips, punk poppers The Undertones and Belfast's own Stiff Little Fingers (SLF), Ireland's answer to The Clash. And then there was Bob Geldof's Boomtown Rats, who didn't like Mondays or much else either.

But they all paled in comparison to the supernova that is U2, formed in 1976 in North Dublin and becoming one of the world's most successful rock bands since the late 1980s. What else can we say about them that hasn't already been said? After 13 studio albums, 22 Grammy awards and upwards of 170 million album sales they have nothing to prove to anyone – and not even their minor faux pas in 2014, when Apple 'gave' copies of their latest release, *Songs of Innocence,* to iTunes subscribers whether they wanted it or not, has managed to dampen their popularity. Their iNNOCENCE + eXPERIENCE tour (note the typographic ode to Apple), which ran until the end of 2018, was a massive success.

Of all the Irish acts that followed in U2's wake during the 1980s and early 1990s, only a few managed to comfortably avoid being tarred with 'the next U2' burden. The Pogues' mix of punk and Irish folk kept everyone going for a while, but the real story there was the empathetic songwriting of Shane MacGowan, whose genius has been overshadowed by his chronic drinking – but he still managed to pen Ireland's favourite song, 'A Fairytale of New York', sung with emotional fervour by everyone around Christmas. Sinéad O'Connor thrived by acting like a U2 antidote – whatever they were into she wasn't – and by having a damn fine voice; the raw emotion on *The Lion and the Cobra* (1987) makes it a great offering. And then there were My Bloody Valentine, the pioneers of late-1980s guitar-distorted shoegazer rock: *Loveless* (1991) is one of the best Irish albums of all time.

The 1990s were largely dominated by DJs, dance music and a whole new spin on an old notion – the boy band. Behind Ireland's most successful groups (Boyzone and Westlife) is the Svengali of Saccharine, impresario Louis Walsh, whose musical sensibilities seem mired in '60s

Trad Playlist

The Quiet Glen (Tommy Peoples)

Paddy Keenan (Paddy Keenan)

The Chieftains 6: Bonaparte's Retreat (The Chieftains)

Old Hag You Have Killed Me (The Bothy Band)

THE NUTS & BOLTS OF TRAD MUSIC

Despite popular perception, the harp isn't widely used in traditional music. The bodhrán (*bow*-rawn) goat-skin drum is much more prevalent, though it makes for a lousy symbol. The uillean pipes, played by squeezing bellows under the elbow, provide another distinctive sound, though you're not likely to see them in a pub. The fiddle isn't unique to Ireland but it is one of the main instruments in the country's indigenous music, along with the flute, tin whistle, accordion and bouzouki (a version of the mandolin). Music fits into five main categories (jigs, reels, hornpipes, polkas and slow airs), while the old style of singing unaccompanied versions of traditional ballads and airs is called *sean-nós*.

showband schmaltz. Since 2004 he has been a judge on the popular *X Factor* talent show in Britain, but still found time to unleash a series of new groups on the music scene, including identical twins Jedward – who can't sing a note, but are liked for their wacky antics – and Hometown, a six-piece boy band from all over Ireland.

The Contemporary Scene

Alternative music has never been in ruder health in Ireland – and Dublin, as the largest city in the country, is where everyone comes to make noise. Local artists to look out for include Saint Sister, whose 'atmosfolk' sound is a blend of harp, synth and harmony; their 2018 debut album *Shape of Silence* was one of the year's best releases.

Wyvern Lingo's eponymous debut album was also very well received, with their harmonious R & B sound a harbinger of even better things to come, while Kojaque, aka Kevin Smith, is one of the most interesting new voices of recent years. His unique brand of hip-hop is flawlessly expressed on his debut, *Deli Daydreams*.

More established artists still making waves include Kodaline, whose fusion of American rock and British pop has made them one of Ireland's most popular bands; their third album, *Politics of Living*, was released in 2018. Bray-born, blues-influenced Hozier (full name Andrew Hozier-Byrne), whose 2013 smash hit *Take Me to Church* made him a global name, released his second album, *Wasteland, Baby!*, in 2019. It debuted at the top of the US Billboard 200 chart. Although he spends a lot of his time in New York these days, Glen Hansard (of *Once* fame) is still a major presence in Ireland; in 2019 he released his fourth solo album, *The Wild Willing*.

Hugely successful Dublin trio The Script have parlayed their melodic brand of pop-rock onto all kinds of TV shows, from *90210* to *Made in Chelsea*. In 2017 they released their fifth album, the chart-topping *Freedom Child*. They mightn't sell as many records, but Villagers (which is really just Conor O'Brien and a selection of collaborators) has earned universal acclaim for his brand of indie-folk rock – and in 2018 his fourth album, *The Art of Pretending to Swim*, moved him away from the more folksy sound of the earlier stuff into a more electronic feel, without forgoing the brilliant songwriting that cemented his position as one of the country's best overall talents.

But it's not just about musicians with grave intent. If Boyzone and Westlife were big, their success pales in comparison to that of One Direction, another product of 'the X Factory'. One of their members, Niall Horan, is from Mullingar, County Westmeath – about an hour west of Dublin – which inevitably meant that when One Direction played Croke Park in 2015 it was a kind of homecoming. The band has since split, but Niall has launched a successful solo career – 2017 saw the release of his first solo album, *Flicker*. Inevitably it debuted at the top of the US album charts.

Perhaps the most esoteric musician of all is also one of the most successful, as nobody can quite hold a candle to the phenomenon that is Enya, the best-selling solo artist in Irish history and one of the best-selling female artists in the world. The Donegal-born composer and instrumentalist was raised in Irish traditional music, but in the early 1980s she and her siblings in the group Clannad created Celtic New Age music, based around synthesizers and heavy, looping effects. Enya broke out on her own and, 80 million record sales and four Grammy awards later, she stands alone atop the New Age music pyramid. She hasn't released anything since 2015's *Dark Sky Island*, generally considered one of her best.

Best Irish Rock Albums

....

The Joshua Tree (U2)

....

Becoming a Jackal (Villagers)

....

Loveless (My Bloody Valentine)

....

Live & Dangerous (Thin Lizzy)

....

I Do Not Want What I Haven't Got (Sinéad O'Connor)

Literary Ireland

Of all their cultural expressions, it's perhaps the way the Irish speak and write that best distinguishes them. Their love of language has contributed to Ireland's legacy of world-renowned writers and storytellers. And all this in a language imposed on them by a foreign invader. The Irish responded to this act of cultural piracy by mastering a magnificent hybrid – English in every respect but flavoured and enriched by the rhythms, pronunciation patterns and grammatical peculiarities of Irish.

The Mythic Cycle

Before there was anything like modern literature there was the Ulaid (Ulster) Cycle – Ireland's version of the Homeric epic – written down from oral tradition between the 8th and 12th centuries. The chief story is the Táin Bó Cúailnge (Cattle Raid of Cooley), about a battle between Queen Maeve of Connaught and Cúchulainn, the principal hero of Irish mythology. Cúchulainn appears in the work of Irish writers right up to the present day, from Samuel Beckett to Frank McCourt.

Modern Literature

From the mythic cycle, zip forward 1000 years, past the genius of Jonathan Swift (1667–1745) and his *Gulliver's Travels,* stopping to acknowledge acclaimed dramatist Oscar Wilde (1854–1900), *Dracula* creator Bram Stoker (1847–1912) – some have claimed that the name of the count may have come from the Irish *droch fhola* (bad blood) – to the literary giant that was James Joyce (1882–1941), whose name and books elicit enormous pride in Ireland.

The majority of Joyce's literary output came when he had left Ireland for the artistic hotbed that was Paris, which was also true for another great experimenter of language and style, Samuel Beckett (1906–89). Beckett's work centres on fundamental existential questions about the human condition and the nature of self. He is probably best known for his play *Waiting for Godot,* but his unassailable reputation is based on a series of stark novels and plays.

Of the dozens of 20th-century Irish authors to have achieved published renown, some names to look out for include playwright and novelist Brendan Behan (1923–64), who wove tragedy, wit and a turbulent life into

Listowel Writers' Week takes place over the last weekend in May in Listowel, County Kerry, and is one of the most popular of all literary festivals – mostly because it gives readers a chance to meet their favourite writers in person.

THE GAELIC REVIVAL

While Home Rule was being debated and shunted, something of a revolution was taking place in Irish arts, literature and identity. The poet William Butler Yeats (1865–1939; p452) and his coterie of literary friends (including Lady Gregory, Douglas Hyde, John Millington Synge and George Russell) championed the Anglo-Irish literary revival, unearthing old Celtic tales and writing with fresh enthusiasm about a romantic Ireland of epic battles and warrior queens. For a country that had suffered centuries of invasion and deprivation, these images presented a much more attractive version of history.

TOP IRISH READS

Angela's Ashes (Frank McCourt; 1996) The Pulitzer Prize–winning novel tells the relentlessly bleak autobiographical story of the author's poverty-stricken Limerick childhood in the Depression of the 1930s.

Amongst Women (John McGahern; 1990) McGahern's simple, economical piece centres on a west-of-Ireland family in the social aftermath of the War of Independence.

Milkman (Anna Burns; 2018) Northern Ireland's first Booker Prize winner explores the Troubles through the eyes of an anonymous 18-year-old narrator being stalked by a much older paramilitary figure.

The Sea (John Banville; 2005) The Booker Prize–winning novel is an engrossing meditation on mortality, grief, death, childhood and memory; it was made into a film in 2013.

Conversations With Friends (Sally Rooney; 2017) Rooney's debut novel is a keenly observed exploration of the complex dynamics between four privileged friends in post-crash Dublin.

The Butcher Boy (Patrick McCabe; 1992) A brilliant, gruesome tragicomedy about an orphaned Monaghan boy's descent into madness. It was later made into a successful film by Neil Jordan.

his best works, including *Borstal Boy, The Quare Fellow* and *The Hostage,* before dying young of alcoholism.

Belfast-born CS Lewis (1898–1963) died a year earlier, but he left us *The Chronicles of Narnia,* a series of allegorical children's stories, three of which have been made into films. Other Northern writers have, not surprisingly, featured the Troubles in their work: Bernard MacLaverty's *Cal* (also made into a film) and his more recent *The Anatomy School* are both wonderful.

The Contemporary Scene

The literary scene is flourishing, thanks in part to the proliferation of smaller presses and printing houses giving authors a chance to publish, which in turn has helped engender a generation of new writers more confident in seeing the fruits of their labours reach an audience.

The #MeToo movement has also played its indirect part, with publishers keen to promote female voices that in previous eras may not have been given the opportunity to be heard. Sally Rooney is perhaps the biggest star in the new firmament. Her first novel, *Conversations with Friends* (2017), established her as a writer of huge talent, while her follow-up, *Normal People* (2018), about the difficult relationship between two friends during the economic downturn, won best novel at the Costa Book Awards, book of the year at the British Book Awards, and was a New York Times bestseller.

Belfast-born Anna Burns is the first Northern Irish author to win the Booker Prize, picking up the award in 2018 for her third novel, *Milkman,* about an 18-year-old girl being stalked by a much older paramilitary figure. Emilie Pine burst onto the scene in 2018 with a superb collection of non-fiction essays, *Notes to Self,* an unflinching look at addiction, sexual assault and mental health.

Melatu Oche Okorie was born in Nigeria, but moved to Ireland in 2006, where she spent 8½ years in direct provision (the processing system for asylum seekers), experiences she recounts in the three stories of *This Hostel Life* (2018), which cast an important light on the migrant experience in Ireland.

Sinéad Gleeson is another important voice on the literary scene. Her 2019 memoir, *Constellations: Reflections from a Life,* is a stunning col-

One of the most successful Irish authors is Eoin Colfer, creator of the *Artemis Fowl* series, eight fantasy novels following the adventures of Artemis Fowl II as he grows from criminal antihero to saviour of the fairies.

lection of linked essays exploring the fraught relationship between the physical body and identity. Dubliner Karl Geary left home for New York in the late '80s, but tells the story of a love affair between a teenager and an older woman in his debut novel, *Montpelier Parade* (2017).

Irish Poets

Ireland's greatest modern bard was Derry-born Nobel laureate Seamus Heaney (1939–2013), whose enormous personal warmth and wry humour flows through each of his evocative works. He was, unquestionably, the successor to Yeats and one of the most important contemporary poets of the English language. After winning the Nobel Prize in 1995 he compared the ensuing attention to someone mentioning sex in front of their mammy. *Opened Ground – Poems 1966–1996* (1998) is excellent.

Dubliner Paul Durcan (1944–) is one of the most reliable chroniclers of changing Dublin. He won the prestigious Whitbread Prize for Poetry in 1990 for *Daddy, Daddy* and is a funny, engaging, tender and savage writer. Eavan Boland (1944–) is a prolific and much-admired writer, best known for her poetry, who combines Irish politics with outspoken feminism. *In a Time of Violence* (1994) and *The Lost Land* (1998) are two of her most celebrated collections. More recently Derek Mahon's (1941–) *Against the Clock* (2018) is as much a melancholic meditation on the passage of time as it is a light-hearted acceptance of the fact. Galway-born Elaine Feeney (1979–) is one of the country's best-known contemporary poets: 2017's *Rise* is her fourth collection of poems.

To find out more about poetry in Ireland in general, visit the website of the excellent Poetry Ireland (www.poetryireland.ie), which showcases the work of new and established poets. For a taste of modern Irish poetry in print, try *Contemporary Irish Poetry,* edited by Fallon and Mahon. *A Rage for Order,* edited by Frank Ormsby, is a vibrant collection of the poetry of the North.

When James Joyce – unathletic and losing his eyesight – got into drunken fights while living in Paris in the 1920s, he would often hide behind his drinking companion, the much more physically imposing Ernest Hemingway.

Irish Landscapes

Irish literature, song and painting make it pretty clear that the landscape – spread across 486km north to south and only 275km from east to west – exerts a powerful sway on the people who have lived in it. This is especially true for those who have left, for whom the aul' sod is still a land worth pining for. For many visitors the vibrant greenness of gentle hills and the fearsome violence of jagged coasts are an integral part of experiencing Ireland.

Cliffs & Stones

Massive rocky outcrops, such as The Burren in County Clare, are for the most part inhospitable to grass, and though even there the green stuff does sprout up in enough patches for sheep and goats to graze on, these vast, other-worldly landscapes are mostly grey and bleak. Nearby, the dramatic Cliffs of Moher are a sheer drop into the thundering surf. Similarly there is no preparing for the extraordinary hexagonal stone columns of the Giant's Causeway in County Antrim or the rugged drop of County Donegal's Sliabh Liag, Europe's highest sea cliffs. Sand dunes buffer many of the more gentle stretches of coast. Smaller islands dot the shores of Ireland, many of them barren rock piles supporting unique ecosystems – Skellig Michael is a breathtakingly jagged example just off the Kerry coast (and featured in the recent *Star Wars* films).

The rural farms of the west coast have a rugged, hard-earned look to them, due mostly to the rock that lies so close to the surface. Much of this rock has been dug up to create tillable soil and converted into stone walls that divide tiny paddocks. The Aran Islands stand out for their spectacular networks of stone walls.

In 1821 the body of an Iron Age man was found in a bog in Galway with his cape, shoes and beard still intact.

Mountains & Forests

The west of Ireland is a bulwark of cliffs, hills and mountains and is the country's most mountainous area. The highest mountains are in the southwest – the tallest mountain in Ireland is Carrantuohil (1040m) in County Kerry's Macgillycuddy's Reeks.

The Irish frequently lament the loss of their woodlands, much of which were cleared by the British (during the reign of Elizabeth I) to build ships for the Royal Navy – and for the indoor panels and seating of Westminster. Little of the island's once-plentiful oak forests survive today, and much of what you'll see is the result of relatively recent planting. Instead the countryside largely comprises green fields divided by hedgerows and stone walls. Use of this land is divided between cultivated fields and pasture for cattle and sheep.

Look for *Reading the Irish Landscape* by Frank Mitchell and Michael Ryan for info on Ireland's geology, archaeology, urban growth, agriculture and afforestation.

Plants

Although Ireland is sparsely wooded, the range of surviving plant species is larger here than in many other European countries, thanks in part to the comparatively late arrival of agriculture.

There are remnants of the original oak forests in Killarney National Park and in southern Wicklow near Shillelagh. Far more common are pine plantations, which are growing steadily. Hedgerows, planted to divide fields and delineate land boundaries throughout Ireland, actually host many of the native plant species that once thrived in the oak forests – it's an intriguing example of nature adapting and reasserting itself. The Burren in County Clare is home to a remarkable mixture of Mediterranean, alpine and Arctic species.

The bogs of Ireland are home to a unique flora adapted to wet, acidic, nutrient-poor conditions, the survival of which is threatened by the depletion of bogs for energy use. Sphagnum moss is the key bog plant and is joined by other species such as bog rosemary, bog cotton, black-beaked sedge (whose spindly stem grows up to 30cm in height) and various types of heather and lichen. Carnivorous plants also thrive, such as the sundew, which has sticky tentacles to trap insects, and bladderwort, with its tiny explosive bladders that trap aquatic animals in bog pools.

Mammals

Apart from the fox and badger, which tend to shy away from humans and are rarely seen, the wild mammals of Ireland are mostly of the ankle-high 'critter' category, such as rabbits, hedgehogs and shrews. Hikers often spot the Irish hare, or at least glimpse the blazing-fast blur of one running away. Red deer roam the hillsides in many of the wilder parts of the country, particularly the Wicklow Mountains and in Killarney National Park, which holds the country's largest herd.

For most visitors, the most commonly sighted mammals are those inhabiting the sea and waterways. The otter, rarely seen elsewhere in Europe, is thriving in Ireland. Seals are a common sight in rivers and along the shore, as are dolphins, which follow the warm waters of the Gulf Stream towards Ireland. Some colonise the coast of Ireland year-round, frequently swimming into the bays and inlets along the western coast.

Bird Life

Many travellers visit Ireland specifically for the birding. Ireland is a stopover for migrating birds, many of them from the Arctic, Africa and North America. Additionally, irregular winds frequently deliver exotic blow-overs rarely seen in Western Europe.

In autumn the southern counties become a temporary home to the American waders (mainly sandpipers and plovers) and warblers. Migrants from Africa, such as shearwaters, petrels and auks, begin to arrive in spring in the southwestern counties.

The reasonably rare corncrake, which migrates from Africa, can be found in the western counties, in Donegal, around the Shannon Callows and on islands such as Inishbofin in Galway. In late spring and early summer the rugged coastlines, particularly cliff areas and islands, become a haven for breeding seabirds, mainly gannets, kittiwakes, Manx shearwaters, fulmars, cormorants and herons. Puffins, resembling penguins with their tuxedo colour scheme, nest in large colonies on coastal cliffs.

For information on parks, gardens, monuments and inland waterways, see www.heritage ireland.ie.

The illustrated pocket guide *Animals of Ireland* by Gordon D'Arcy is a handy, inexpensive introduction to Ireland's varied fauna.

THE BOG

The boglands, which once covered one-fifth of the island, are more of a whiskey hue than green – that's the brown of heather and sphagnum moss, which cover uncut bogs. Visitors will likely encounter a bog in County Kildare's Bog of Allen or while driving through the western counties – much of the Mayo coast is covered by bog, and huge swathes also cover Donegal.

The lakes and low-lying wetlands attract large numbers of Arctic and northern European waterfowl and waders such as whooper swans, lapwings, barnacle geese, white-fronted geese and golden plovers. The important Wexford Wildfowl Reserve holds half the world's population of Greenland white-fronted geese, and little terns breed on the beach there, protected by the dunes. Also found during the winter are teals, redshanks and curlews. The main migration periods are April to May and September to October.

The magnificent peregrine falcon has been making something of a recovery and can be found nesting on cliffs in Wicklow and elsewhere. In 2001 46 golden-eagle chicks from Scotland were released into Glenveagh National Park in Donegal in an effort to reintroduce the species. The project has been afflicted by adverse weather and, sadly, by unknowns poisoning and shooting the birds, but a small number of pairs continue to thrive. More recent reintroductions include the white-tailed sea eagle, with a pair called Saoirse and Caimin successfully breeding a chick in 2014 – the first native-born sea eagle in 110 years. Twenty-three other chicks followed and, thankfully, most have survived. For more information (and live cam action), check out www.goldeneagle.ie.

Irish Birds by David Cabot is a pocket guide describing birds and their habitats, outlining the best places for serious birdwatching.

Environmental Issues

Ireland does not rate among the world's biggest offenders when it comes to polluting the environment, but economic growth has led to an increase in industry and consumerism, which in turn generate more pollution and waste. While the population density is among Europe's lowest, the population is rising. The last 30 years have seen a massive expansion of suburban developments around all of Ireland's major towns and cities; the biggest by far is inevitably around Dublin, especially in the broadening commuter belt of Counties Meath and Kildare. The collapse of the construction bubble in 2008 put an end to much of this development, but the rows of semidetached houses still remain. As more people drive cars and fly in planes, Ireland grows more dependent on nonrenewable sources of energy. The amount of waste has risen substantially since the early 1990s.

Needless to say, concern for the environment is growing and the government has taken some measures to offset the damage that a thriving economy can cause. Since 2007 the Sustainable Energy Authority of Ireland (www.seai.ie) has been charged with promoting and assisting the development of renewable energy resources, including solar, wind, hydropower, geothermal and biomass resources. As it stands the country is only tapping a fraction of these: in 2019 10.6% of the country's energy requirements (heat, electricity and transport) were being met by renewables.

The European Renewables Directive set Ireland a target of sourcing 16% of all energy requirements from renewables by 2020, as well as the management of grid access for electricity for renewable sources, and adherence to

NATIONAL NATURE RESERVES

There are 66 state-owned and 10 privately owned national nature reserves (NNRs) in the Republic, represented by the National Parks & Wildlife Service (www.npws.ie). These reserves are defined as areas of importance for their special flora, fauna or geology. Northern Ireland has more than 45 NNRs, which are leased or owned by the Department of the Environment. These include the Giant's Causeway and Glenariff in Antrim, and North Strangford Lough in County Down. More information is available from the Northern Ireland Environment Agency (www.ni-environment.gov.uk).

FRACKING

Fracking, or hydraulic fracturing, is banned in both the Republic and Northern Ireland. There's been great interest in the shale-rich areas of the Northwest Ireland Carboniferous Basin, roughly covering parts of counties Leitrim, Roscommon, Sligo, Cavan, Donegal and Fermanagh, with pro-fracking groups lobbying hard for the exploitation of the area's reserves of shale gas. A 2016 report by the Environmental Protection Agency (EPA), however, found that while many of the environmental problems related to the process could be overcome, not enough was known to ensure the protection of human health. Similarly the North's environment minister, Mark Durkan, banned fracking until such time as there is 'sufficient and robust evidence on all environmental impacts of fracking'.

sustainability criteria for biofuels and bioliquids. It has long been clear that Ireland won't meet those requirements, which has earned it ongoing fines.

On a more practical level a number of recycling programmes have been very successful, especially the 'plastax' – a €0.24 levy on all plastic bags used within the retail sector, which has seen their use reduced by a whopping 90%.

While this is a positive sign it doesn't really put Ireland at the vanguard of the environmental movement. Polls seem to indicate the Irish are slightly less concerned about the environment than the citizens of most other European countries, and the country is a long way from meeting its Kyoto Protocol requirement for reduced emissions. The government isn't pushing the environmental agenda much beyond ratifying EU agreements, though it must be said that these have established fairly ambitious goals for reduced air pollution and tighter management of water quality.

Sustainable Tourism

The annual number of tourists in Ireland far exceeds the number of residents (by a ratio of about 1½ to one), so visitors can have a huge impact on the local environment. Tourism is frequently cited as potentially beneficial to the environment – that is, responsible visitor spending can help stimulate ecofriendly sectors of the economy. Ecotourism is not really burgeoning in a formalised way, although EcoTourism Ireland (www.ecotourismireland.ie) is charged with maintaining standards for ecotourism on the island and promotes tour companies that comply with these standards. The rising popularity of outdoor activities such as diving, surfing and fishing creates economic incentives for maintaining the cleanliness of Ireland's coasts and inland waters, but increased activity in these environments can be harmful if not managed carefully.

Ireland's comprehensive and efficient bus network makes it easy to avoid the use of a car, and the country is well suited to cycling and walking holidays. Many hotels, guesthouses and hostels tout green credentials, and organic ingredients are frequently promoted on restaurant menus. It's not difficult for visitors to minimise their environmental footprint while in Ireland.

Ireland's National Parks

The Burren (p408)

Connemara (p408)

Glenveagh (p482)

Killarney (p282)

Wicklow Mountains (p153)

Ballycroy (p440)

Sporting Ireland

For many Irish sport is akin to religion. For some it's all about faith through good works such as jogging, cycling and organised team sports. For everybody else observance is enough, especially from the living-room couch or the pub stool, where the mixed fortunes of their favourite teams are followed with elevated hope and vocalised despair.

Gaelic Football & Hurling

Gaelic games are at the core of Irishness. They are enmeshed in the fabric of Irish life and hold a unique place in the heart of its culture. Their resurgence towards the end of the 19th century was entwined with the whole Gaelic revival and the march towards Irish independence. The beating heart of Gaelic sports is the Gaelic Athletic Association (www.gaa.ie), set up in 1884 'for the preservation and cultivation of National pastimes'. The GAA is still responsible for fostering these amateur games. It warms our hearts to see that after all this time – and amid the onslaught of globalisation and the general commercialisation of sport – they are still far and away the most popular sports in Ireland.

Gaelic games are fast, furious and not for the faint-hearted. Challenges are fierce, and contact between players is extremely aggressive. Both sports are county-based games. The dream of every club player is to represent their county, with the hope of perhaps playing in an All-Ireland final in September at Croke Park in Dublin, the climax of a knockout championship that is played first at a provincial and then interprovincial level.

Football

There is huge support in Ireland for the 'world game', though there is generally greater enthusiasm for British teams such as Manchester United, Liverpool and the two Glasgow teams (Rangers and particularly Celtic) than for the struggling pros and part-timers who make up the League of Ireland (www.fai.ie) in the Republic and the Irish League (www.irishfa.com) in Northern Ireland.

Nevertheless the over-hyped, billion-dollar global glitz of the Premier League has led some fans to 'rediscover' the charms of local football, which in turn has seen attendances at some League of Ireland matches rise, especially those between stalwart rivals such as Bohemians, Shamrock Rovers, Cork City, Dundalk and Drogheda.

YOU SAY SOCCER, I SAY FOOTBALL

To distinguish it from Gaelic football, you'll often hear football referred to as 'soccer' (especially in Gaelic strongholds, where doing so implies scorn on so-called 'garrison sports'). This will allay American confusion but only irritate the Brits. Regardless, Irish fans of Association Football (the official name of the sport) will always call it football and the other, Gaelic football or, in Dublin, 'gah' – which is just the pronunciation of the letters GAA (Gaelic Athletic Association).

WOMEN & THE GAA

In 2018 50,141 fans watched Dublin beat Cork in the All-Ireland Final, the first women's game to break the 50,000 barrier and the most attended women's sport final in the world that year.

Women's football – or Ladies Gaelic Football, to give it its proper name – is one of the fastest growing participation sports in Europe. There are over 1000 clubs nationwide, a remarkable achievement given the sport was only properly established in 1974 (curiously, women's football is governed by the Ladies Gaelic Football Association, not the GAA, even though they play by the same rules in the same grounds). The game's growth has accelerated apace in recent years, thanks in part to a cash injection and big promotional push by primary sponsor Lidl, the German supermarket group.

The women's version of hurling is camogie, which bar a few rule differences (and shorter games) is virtually identical to hurling. It was first established in 1903 by cultural nationalists and Irish language enthusiasts Máire Ní Chinnéide (anglicised as Mary O'Kennedy) and Cáit Ní Dhonnchadha (Kathleen Donnehy), and its name derives from *camóg*, the diminutive of *camán*, the Irish for hurley stick. Although there are more than 500 camogie clubs throughout Ireland, it's most popular in the same counties in which hurling is popular, with Cork, Dublin, Kilkenny and Tipperary at the top of the list.

The women's All-Ireland finals in both sports are held at Croke Park, with the football final on the last Sunday in September (occasionally the first Sunday in October) and the camogie final on the Sunday in between the men's hurling and football finals.

At an international level the Republic and Northern Ireland field separate teams, but both struggle to qualify for major tournaments. It's all a far cry from their respective moments of glory – the 1980s for Northern Ireland and 1988 to 2002 for the Republic.

In order to avoid competing (and losing) with the more popular English Premier League, the season for which runs from mid-August to mid-May, the League of Ireland runs its season from April to November and is the only European league to do so. Northern Ireland's Irish League still follows the British winter timetable.

Rugby

Although traditionally the preserve of Ireland's middle classes, rugby captures the mood of the whole island in February and March during the annual Six Nations Championships, because the Irish team is drawn from both sides of the border and is supported by both nationalists and unionists. It also helps that Ireland is going through a major purple patch – in 2018 it was ranked the second-best team in the world after New Zealand.

At a provincial level Leinster and Munster are major players on the European stage, having won the European Champions Cup four times and twice respectively; Ulster is a step behind with one win.

Golf

Scotland may be the home of golf, but Ireland is where golf goes on holiday.

With over 400 courses to choose from, there's no shortage of choice when it comes to teeing it up. These include a host of parkland (or inland) courses; worth checking out are the wonderful, American-style resort courses built over the last couple of decades, with immaculate, lawn-like fairways, white-sand bunkers and strategically placed water features ready to swallow any chunkily hit shot.

But the essence of Irish golf is to be found on seaside links, dotted in a spectacular string of scenery along virtually the entire coastline. Here nature provides the perfect raw material, and the very best of them are

---

Best Places to Watch a GAA Match

Croke Park (Dublin)

Semple Stadium (Thurles, County Tipperary)

Fitzgerald Stadium (Killarney, County Kerry)

Inisheer (County Galway)

Nowlan Park (Kilkenny)

less built into the landscape than found within it, much like Michelangelo 'found' his figures hiding in the blocks of marble.

Finally, a word about the Irish golfer. Clubhouse snobs and high-handicap etiquette junkies aside, the real Irish golfer is the person who puts their shoes on in the car park and can't wait to tee it up on the first; they know all the safe spots to land the ball and see it as their duty to share local knowledge. If you land up in the club on your own and they're doing a little putting practice before heading out, they're the ones who will offer a twosome because it's just not right to play on your own. The Irish golfer is friendly, easy-going and always recognises that you will never win at golf, and that today's bad round is just for today and tomorrow will turn up something different. And they know that golf is played over 19 holes – what's the point of playing unless you can laugh about it all over a drink when the round is done?

Horse Racing & Greyhound Racing

A passion for horse racing is deeply entrenched in Irish life and comes without the snobbery of its English counterpart. If you fancy a flutter on the gee-gees you can watch racing from around Ireland and England on the TV in bookmakers shops every day. No money ever seems to change hands in the betting, however, and every Irish punter will tell you they 'broke even'.

Ireland has a reputation for producing world-class horses for racing and other equestrian events such as showjumping, which is also very popular, albeit in a much less egalitarian kind of way. Major annual races include the Irish Grand National (Fairyhouse, April), Irish Derby (the Curragh, June) and Irish Leger (the Curragh, September). For more information on events contact Horse Racing Ireland (www.hri.ie).

Traditionally the poor-man's punt, greyhound racing ('the dogs') has been smartened up in recent years and partly turned into a corporate outing. It offers a cheaper, more accessible and more local alternative to horse racing. There are 20-odd tracks across the country, administered by the Irish Greyhound Board (www.igb.ie).

Road Bowling

The object of this sport is to throw a cast-iron ball weighing approximately 800g along a public road (normally one with little traffic) for a designated distance, usually 1km or 2km, with speed, control and accuracy. The person who does it in the least number of throws is the winner. Participants traditionally bet during the game.

The ball is known as a bowl or bullet. A shot is a throw and a kitter-paw is a left-handed thrower. If you hear someone talking about their butt, they are referring to the throwing mark on the road. Breaking butt means someone has stepped over the mark before releasing the ball. *Faugh an Bheallach* is a traditional Irish battle cry and means you should get out of the way. A sop is a tuft of grass placed where the bowl should first strike the road and a score is a match.

The main centre for road bowling is Cork, which has 200 clubs, and, to a lesser extent, Armagh. Competitions take place throughout the year, attracting considerable crowds. The sport has been taken up in various countries around the world, including the US, the UK, Germany and the Netherlands, and a world championship competition has been set up (see www.irishroadbowling.ie). In Ireland the sport is governed by the Irish Road Bowling Association.

Survival Guide

Directory A-Z

Accessible Travel

All new buildings have wheelchair access, and many hotels (especially urban ones that are part of chains) have installed lifts, ramps and other facilities such as hearing loops. Others, particularly B&Bs, have not invested in making their properties accessible.

Public Transport

In big cities most buses have low-floor access and priority spaces on board, but only 63% of the Bus Éireann coach fleet that operates on Commuter and Expressway services is wheelchair-accessible. Note, too, that many of its rural stops are not accessible.

Trains are accessible with help. Call 1850 366 222 (outside Republic of Ireland +353 1 836 6222) or email access@irishrail.ie 24 hours in advance to arrange assistance with boarding, alighting and transferring at intermediate stations. Note that there is a limited number of wheelchair-accessible spaces on each train. Newer trains have audio and visual information systems for visually impaired and hearing-impaired passengers. Assistance dogs may travel without restriction. A full list of station facilities as at 2019 can be downloaded from www.irishrail.ie/travel-information/disabled-access.

Resources

➜ For an informative article with links to accessibility information for transport and tourist attractions, visit www.ireland.com/en-us/accommodation/articles/accessibility.

➜ Two review sites covering accommodation, eating and drinking, and places of interest that are worth checking out are https://mobilitymojo.com, which has a searchable database that's expanding outside its base of Dublin and Galway, and www.accessibleireland.com, which also hosts short introductions to public transport.

➜ Download Lonely Planet's free Accessible Travel guides from http://lptravel.to/AccessibleTravel.

➜ The **Citizens' Information Board** (☑0761 079 000; www.citizensinformationboard.ie) in the Republic and **Disability Action** (☑028-9029 7880; www.disabilityaction.org; 189 Airport Rd W, Portside Business Pk; ☑28) in Northern Ireland can give some advice to travellers with disabilities.

Accommodation

From basic hostels to five-star hotels, you'll find every kind of accommodation in Ireland. Advance bookings are generally recommended and are an absolute necessity during the July–August holiday period.

Hotels From chain hotels with comfortable digs to Norman castles with rainfall showers and wi-fi – with prices to match.

B&Bs From a bedroom in a private home to a luxurious Georgian townhouse, the ubiquitous B&B is the bedrock of Irish accommodation.

Hostels Every major town and city has a selection of hostels, with clean dorms and wi-fi – some have laundry and kitchen facilities.

Booking Services

Daft.ie (www.daft.ie) Online property portal includes holiday homes and short-term rentals.

Elegant Ireland (www.elegant.ie) Specialises in self-catering castles, period houses and unique properties.

Imagine Ireland (www.imagineireland.com) Holiday cottage rentals throughout the whole island, including Northern Ireland.

Irish Landmark Trust (www.irishlandmark.com) Not-for-profit conservation group that rents self-catering properties of historical and cultural significance, such as castles, tower houses, gate lodges, schoolhouses and lighthouses.

Lonely Planet (www.lonelyplanet.com/Ireland/hotels) Recommendations and bookings.

Dream Ireland (www.dreamireland.com) Lists self-catering

SLEEPING PRICE RANGES

Accommodation prices can vary according to demand, or there may be different rates for online, phone or walk-in bookings. B&B rates are more consistent, but virtually every other accommodation will charge wildly different rates depending on the time of year, day, festival schedule and even your ability to do a little negotiating. The following price ranges are based on a double room with private bathroom in high season.

BUDGET	REPUBLIC	DUBLIN	NORTHERN IRELAND
€/£	less than €80	less than €150	less than £50
€€/££	€80–€180	€150–€250	£50–£120
€€€/£££	more than €180	more than €250	more than £120

holiday cottages and apartments.

B&Bs & Guesthouses

Bed and breakfasts are small, family-run houses, farmhouses and period country houses, generally with fewer than five bedrooms. Standards vary enormously, but most have some bedrooms with private bathroom at a cost of roughly €40 to €60 (£35 to £50) per person per night (at least €100 in Dublin). In luxurious B&Bs, expect to pay €70 (£60) or more per person. Off-season rates – usually October through to March – are usually lower, as are midweek prices.

Guesthouses are like upmarket B&Bs, but a bit bigger. Facilities are usually better and sometimes include a restaurant.

Other tips:

➡ Facilities in B&Bs range from basic (bed, bathroom, kettle, TV) to beatific (whirlpool baths, rainforest showers) as you go up in price. Wi-fi is standard and most have parking (but check).

➡ Most B&Bs take credit cards, but the occasional rural one might not; check when you book.

➡ Advance reservations are strongly recommended, especially in peak season (June to September).

➡ Some B&Bs and guesthouses in more remote regions may only be open

from Easter to September or other months.

➡ If full, B&B owners may recommend another house in the area (possibly a private house taking occasional guests, not in tourist listings).

➡ To make prices more competitive at some B&Bs, breakfast may be optional.

Camping, Caravanning & Canal Boats

Camping and caravan parks aren't as common in Ireland as they are elsewhere in Europe. Some hostels have camping space for tents and also offer house facilities, which makes them better value than the main camping grounds. At commercial parks the cost is typically somewhere between €15 and €25 (£12 to £20) for a tent and two people. Prices given for campsites are for two people unless stated otherwise. Caravan sites cost around €20 to €30 (£17 to £25). Most parks are open only from Easter to the end of September or October.

Alternative forms of mobile accommodation include the following:

Horse-drawn caravan In high season you can hire a traditional horse-drawn caravan for around €690 for three nights. Search the **Fáilte Ireland** (☑Republic 1850 230 330, UK 0800 039 7000; www.discoverireland.ie) website for 'horse drawn caravan', or see www.irishhorse drawncaravans.com.

Canal barge Another unhurried and pleasurable way to see the countryside (with slightly less maintenance) is by barge on one of the country's canal systems. Contact Fáilte Ireland for a list of rental companies.

Cabin cruiser Yet another option is to hire a motorboat, which you can live aboard while cruising Ireland's inland waterways. One of several companies offering boats for hire on the Shannon-Erne Waterway is **Emerald Star** (☑071-962 7633; www.emeraldstar.ie; per week from €1100).

Hostels

Prices quoted for hostel accommodation apply to those aged over 18. A high-season dorm bed generally costs €12 to €25, or €18 to €30 in Dublin (£15 to £20 in Northern Ireland). Many hostels now have family and double rooms.

Relevant hostel associations:

An Óige (www.anoige.ie) HI-associated national organisation with 26 hostels scattered around the Republic.

HINI (www.hini.org.uk) HI-associated organisation with five hostels in Northern Ireland.

Independent Holiday Hostels of Ireland (www.hostels-ireland.com) Fifty-five tourist-board-approved hostels throughout all of Ireland.

Independent Hostel Owners of Ireland (www.independent hostelsireland.com) Independent hostelling association.

BOOK YOUR STAY ONLINE

For more accommodation reviews by Lonely Planet authors, check out http://lonelyplanet.com/hotels/. You'll find independent reviews, as well as recommendations on the best places to stay. Best of all, you can book online.

Hotels

Hotels range from the local pub to a medieval castle. Booking online or negotiating directly will almost always net you a better rate than the published one, especially out of season or midweek (except for business hotels, which offer cheaper weekend rates).

The bulk of the country's hotels are of the midrange variety, with clean rooms and a range of facilities, from restaurants to gyms. The trend towards offering free wi-fi is stubbornly resisted by many – usually more expensive – hotels that still charge for the privilege.

House Swapping

House swapping can be a popular and affordable way to enjoy a real home away from home. There are several agencies in Ireland that, for an annual fee, facilitate international swaps. The fee pays for access to a website and a book giving house descriptions, photographs and the owners' details. After that it's up to you to make arrangements. Use of the family car is sometimes included.

Homelink International House Exchange (www.homelink.ie) Home-exchange service running for more than 60 years.

Intervac International Holiday Service (www.intervac-home exchange.com) Long-established, with agents all over the world.

Rental Accommodation

Self-catering accommodation is often rented on a weekly basis and usually means an apartment, house or cottage where you look after yourself. The rates vary from one region and season to another. **Fáilte Ireland** (☑ Republic 1850 230 330, UK 0800 039 7000; www.discover ireland.ie) publishes a guide for registered self-catering accommodation; you can check listings on its website.

Children

Ireland loves kids. Everywhere you go you'll find locals to be enthusiastic and inquisitive about your beloved progeny. This admiration, however, hasn't always translated into child services such as widespread and accessible baby-changing facilities, or high chairs in restaurants, especially in smaller towns and rural areas.

Children between 15 and 17 are allowed into pubs unaccompanied; under 15s must be accompanied and can only be in a licensed premises between 10.30am (12.30pm on Sunday) and 9pm (10pm between May and September), after which they must leave. In rural areas, however, some publicans will allow children to remain in the bar so long as they're under proper parental supervision.

The bulk of the country's visitor attractions cater to kids almost as much as they do the adults that accompany them. Many visitor experiences feature activities tailor-made for young 'uns, which are often ramped up during the school holidays. Most activity centres offer kids' programs for all ages, while many museums have kid-friendly exhibits and some even cater guided tours to suit younger ages.

Resources

BabyGoes2 (www.babygoes2. com) Travel site with family-friendly accommodation worldwide.

eumom (www.eumom.ie) For pregnant women and parents with young children.

Failte Ireland (www.discover ireland.ie) Some good ideas for family-friendly things to see and do.

Lonely Planet (www.lonely planet.com/family-travel) Inspirational articles about travelling as a family.

Northern Ireland Tourist Board (https://discovernorthernireland. com) Has a dedicated section to family travel.

Customs Regulations

Both the Republic of Ireland and Northern Ireland have a two-tier customs system: one for goods bought duty-free outside the EU, the other for goods bought in another EU country where tax and duty is paid. There is technically no limit to the amount of goods transportable within the EU, but customs will use certain guidelines to distinguish personal use from commercial purpose. Allowances are as follows:

Duty-free For duty-free goods from outside the EU, limits include 200 cigarettes, 1L of spirits or 2L of wine, 60mL of perfume and 250mL of eau de toilette.

Tax and duty paid Amounts that officially constitute personal use include 3200 cigarettes (or 400 cigarillos, 200 cigars or 3kg of tobacco) and either 10L of spirits, 20L of fortified wine, 60L of sparkling wine, 90L of still wine or 110L of beer.

Electricity

**Type G
230V/50Hz**

Embassies & Consulates

Following is a selection of embassies in Dublin and consular offices in Belfast. For a complete list, see the website of the Department of Foreign Affairs (www.dfa.ie), which also lists Ireland's diplomatic missions overseas.

Australian Embassy (☑01-664 5300; www.ireland.embassy. gov.au; 3rd fl, 47-49 St Stephen's Green E; ⊙8.30am-4.30pm Mon-Fri; ➁37 from city centre)

Canadian Embassy (☑01-234 4000; www.canada.ie; 7-8 Wilton Tce, Dublin 2; ⊙9am-

1pm & 2-4.30pm; ➁37 from city centre)

Dutch Embassy (☑01-269 3444; www.netherlandsandyou. nl/your-country-and-the-netherlands/ireland; 160 Merrion Rd, Ballsbridge, Dublin 4; ⊙By appointment only; ➁4, 7, 8 from city centre)

Dutch Consulate (☑Carson McMullan 07484-717280) in Belfast

French Embassy (☑01-277 5000; www.ambafrance-ie.org; 66 Fitzwilliam Lane; ⊙9-10am & noon-4pm Mon-Fri; ➁46A from city centre)

German Embassy (☑01-269 3011; www.dublin.diplo.de; 31 Trimleston Ave, Booterstown, Blackrock; ⊙8am-5pm Mon-Thu, to 2pm Fri, consular service 9am-noon Mon, Tue & Fri, 8.30-11.30am & 2-4pm Wed; ➂Booterstown)

Italian Embassy (☑01-660 1744; www.ambdublino.esteri.it/ Ambasciata_Dublino; 63 Northumberland Rd, Ballsbridge, Dublin 4; ⊙by appointment only; ➁4, 7, 63, 84 from city centre)

UK Embassy (☑01-205 3700; www.gov.uk; 29 Merrion Rd, Ballsbridge, Dublin 4; ⊙9am-5pm Mon-Fri; ➁4, 7, 8 from city centre)

US Embassy (☑01-630 6200; http://ie.usembassy.gov/ embassy; 42 Elgin Rd, Ballsbridge, Dublin; ⊙by appointment only; ➁4, 7, 8 from city centre)

US Consulate (☑028-9038 6100; https://uk.usembassy. gov/embassy-consulates/ belfast; Danesfort House, 223 Stranmillis Rd; ⊙8.30am-5pm

Mon-Fri; ➂Broomhill Pk) in Belfast

Food

Booking ahead is recommended in cities and larger towns; same-day reservations are usually fine except for top-end restaurants – book those two weeks in advance.

Health

No jabs are required to travel to Ireland.

Excellent health care is readily available. For minor, self-limiting illnesses, pharmacists can give valuable advice and sell over-the-counter medication. They can also advise when more specialised help is required and point you in the right direction.

EU citizens equipped with a European Health Insurance Card (EHIC), available from health centres or, in the UK, post offices, will be covered for most medical care – but not nonemergencies or emergency repatriation. While other countries, such as Australia, also have reciprocal agreements with Ireland and Britain, many do not.

In Northern Ireland everyone receives free emergency treatment at accident and emergency (A&E) departments of state-run NHS hospitals, irrespective of nationality.

EATING PRICE RANGES

The following price ranges refer to the cost of a main course at dinner.

BUDGET	REPUBLIC	DUBLIN	NORTHERN IRELAND
€/£	less than €12	less than €15	less than £12
€€/££	€12–€25	more than €28	£12–£20
€€€/£££	more than €25	more than €28	more than £20

Insurance

Comprehensive travel insurance to cover theft, loss and medical problems is highly recommended. Worldwide travel insurance is available at www.lonelyplanet.com/travel-insurance. You can buy, extend and claim online anytime – even if you're already on the road.

Internet Access

Wi-fi and 3G/4G networks are making internet cafes largely redundant (except to gamers). The few that are left will charge around €6 per hour. Most accommodation places have wi-fi, either free or for a daily charge (up to €10 per day).

Legal Matters

Illegal drugs are widely available, especially in clubs. The possession of small quantities of marijuana attracts a fine or warning, but harder drugs are treated more seriously. Public drunkenness is illegal but commonplace – the police will usually ignore it unless you're causing trouble. Should you find yourself under arrest, you have the right to remain silent and to contact either an attorney or your embassy.

Once you are charged and cautioned you will either be released on bail (known as 'station bail') or, in the event of a more serious offence, transferred from the police station to the District Court as early as possible (usually within 12 hours), where you will either be bailed or remanded in custody by the judge.

Contact the following for assistance:

Legal Aid Board (☎066-947 1000, in Republic 1890 615 200; www.legalaidboard.ie; ☺9am-5pm Mon-Fri) Has a network of local law centres.

Legal Services Agency Northern Ireland (☎028-9076 3000; www.justice-ni.gov.uk/topics/legal-aid) Administers the statutory legal-aid scheme for Northern Ireland, but cannot offer legal advice.

LGBT+ Travellers

Ireland is a generally tolerant place for the LGBTQ community. Bigger cities such as Dublin, Galway and Cork have well-established gay scenes, as do Belfast and Derry in Northern Ireland. Same-sex marriage has been legal in the Republic since 2015; Northern Ireland is the only region of the United Kingdom where it is not.

While the cities and main towns tend to be progressive and tolerant, you'll still find pockets of homophobia throughout the island, particularly in smaller towns and rural areas.

Resources include the following:

Gaire (www.gaire.com) Message board and info for a host of gay-related issues.

Gay & Lesbian Youth Northern Ireland (www.cara-friend.org.uk) Voluntary counselling, information, health and social-space organisation for the gay community.

Gay Men's Health Project (☎01-660 2189; www.hse.ie/go/GMHS) Practical advice on men's health issues.

National LGBT Federation (NLGF; ☎01-671 9076; http://nxf.ie) Publishes the monthly Gay Community News (www.gcn.ie).

Northern Ireland Gay Rights Association (☎028-9066 4111; www.nigra.org.uk; Belfast LGBT Centre, 23-31 Waring St) Represents the rights and interests of the LGBTQ community in Northern Ireland. It offers phone and online support, but is not a call-in centre.

Outhouse (☎01-873 4932; www.outhouse.ie; 105 Capel St; ☺10am-6pm Mon-Fri, noon-5pm Sat; ☐all city centre) Top gay, lesbian and bisexual resource centre. Great stop-off point to see what's on, check noticeboards and meet people. It publishes the free Pink Pages, a directory of gay-centric services, which is also accessible on the website.

Money

The Republic of Ireland uses the euro (€). Northern Ireland uses the pound sterling (£), though the euro is also accepted in many places.

The best exchange rates are at banks, though bureaux de change and other exchange facilities usually open for more hours.

PRACTICALITIES

Newspapers Irish Independent (www.independent.ie), Irish Times (www.irishtimes.com), Irish Examiner (www.examiner.ie), Belfast Telegraph (www.belfasttelegraph.co.uk).

Radio RTE Radio 1 (88MHz–90MHz), Today FM (100MHz–103MHz), Newstalk 106-108 (106MHz–108MHz), BBC Ulster (92MHz–95MHz; Northern Ireland only).

Smoking It is illegal to smoke indoors everywhere except private residences and prisons.

Weights & Measures The metric system is used; the exception is for liquid measures of alcohol, where pints are used.

ATMs

All banks have ATMs that are linked to international money systems such as Cirrus, Maestro or Plus. Each transaction incurs a currency-conversion fee, and credit cards can incur immediate and exorbitant cash-advance interest-rate charges. Watch out for ATMs that have been tampered with, as card-reader scams ('skimming') have become a real problem.

Credit & Debit Cards

Visa and MasterCard credit and debit cards are widely accepted. American Express is only accepted by the major chains, and virtually no one will accept Diners or JCB. Chip-and-PIN is the norm for card transactions – only a few places will accept a signature.

Smaller businesses, such as pubs and some B&Bs, prefer debit cards (and will charge a fee for credit cards), and a small number of rural B&Bs only take cash.

Taxes & Refunds

Most goods come with value-added tax (VAT) of 21% (20% in Northern Ireland), which non-EU residents can claim back so long as the store in which the goods are purchased operates either the Cash-back or Taxback refund programme (the Tax-Free Shopping refund scheme in Northern Ireland), usually indicated by a display sticker on the window.

To claim the VAT you must fill in the voucher that comes with your purchase, which must be stamped at the *last point of exit* from the EU. If you're travelling on to Britain or mainland Europe from Ireland, hold on to your voucher until you pass through your final customs stop in the EU. It can then be stamped and you can post it back for a refund of duty paid.

Goods such as books, children's clothing and educational items are excluded from VAT.

Tipping

Hotels A tip of €1/£1 per bag is standard; tip cleaning staff at your discretion.

Pubs Not expected unless table service is provided, then €1/£1 for a round of drinks.

Restaurants For decent service 10%; up to 15% in more expensive places.

Taxis Tip 10% or round up fare to nearest euro/pound.

Toilet attendants Loose change; no more than 50c/50p.

Opening Hours

Banks 10am–4pm Monday to Friday (to 5pm Thursday)

Pubs 10.30am–11.30pm Monday to Thursday, 10.30am–12.30am Friday and Saturday, noon–11pm Sunday (30 minutes 'drinking up' time allowed); closed Christmas Day and Good Friday

Restaurants noon–10.30pm; many close one day of the week

Shops 9.30am–6pm Monday to Saturday (to 8pm Thursday in cities), noon–6pm Sunday

Photography

➜ Natural light can be very dull, so use higher ISO speeds than usual, such as 400 for daylight shots.

➜ In Northern Ireland get permission before taking photos of fortified police stations, army posts or other military or quasi-military paraphernalia.

➜ Don't take photos of people in Protestant or Catholic strongholds of West Belfast without permission; always ask and be prepared to accept a refusal.

➜ Lonely Planet's *Guide to Travel Photography* is full of helpful tips for photography while on the road.

Public Holidays

Public holidays can cause road chaos as everyone tries to get somewhere else for the break. It's wise to book accommodation in advance for these times.

The following are public holidays in both the Republic and Northern Ireland:

New Year's Day 1 January

St Patrick's Day 17 March

Easter (Good Friday to Easter Monday inclusive) March/April

May Holiday 1st Monday in May

Christmas Day 25 December

St Stephen's Day (Boxing Day) 26 December

St Patrick's Day and St Stephen's Day holidays are taken on the following Monday when they fall on a weekend. Nearly everywhere in the Republic closes on Good Friday even though it isn't an official public holiday. In the North most shops open on Good Friday, but close the following Tuesday.

Northern Ireland

Spring Bank Holiday Last Monday in May

The Twelfth 12 July

August Holiday Last Monday in August

Republic of Ireland

June Holiday 1st Monday in June

August Holiday 1st Monday in August

October Holiday Last Monday in October

Safe Travel

Ireland is safer than most countries in Europe, but normal precautions should be observed.

➜ Don't leave anything visible in your car when you park.

➜ Skimming at ATMs is an ongoing problem; be sure to cover the keypad with your hand when you input your PIN.

➜ In Northern Ireland exercise extra care in 'interface' areas where sectarian neighbourhoods adjoin.

➜ Best avoid Northern Ireland during the climax of the Orange marching season on 12 July. Sectarian passions are usually inflamed and even many Northerners leave the province at this time.

Telephone

When calling Ireland from abroad, dial your international access code, followed by 353 and the area code (dropping the 0). Area codes in the Republic have three digits, eg 021 for Cork, 091 for Galway and 061 for Limerick. The only exception is Dublin, which has a two-digit code (01).

To make international calls from Ireland, first dial 00 then the country code, followed by the local area code and number. Always use the area code if calling from a mobile phone, but you don't need it if calling from a fixed-line number within the area code.

In Northern Ireland the area code for all fixed-line numbers is 028, but you only need to use it if calling from a mobile phone or from outside Northern Ireland. To call Northern Ireland from the Republic, use 048 instead of 028, without the international dialling code.

Mobile Phones

All European and Australasian phones work in Ireland, as do North American phones not locked to a local network. Check with your provider. Prepaid SIM cards cost from €10/£10.

➜ Both the Republic and Northern Ireland use the GSM 900/1800 cellular phone system, which is compatible with European and Australian, but not North American or Japanese, phones.

➜ Pay-as-you-go mobile-phone packages with any of the main providers start at around €40 and usually include a basic handset and credit of around €10.

➜ SIM-only packages are also available, but make sure your phone is compatible with the local provider.

Time

In winter Ireland is on Greenwich Mean Time (GMT), also known as Universal Time Coordinated (UTC), the same as Britain. In summer the clock shifts to GMT plus one hour, so when it's noon in Dublin and London, it's 4am in Los Angeles and Vancouver, 7am in New York and Toronto, 1pm in Paris, 7pm in Singapore and 9pm in Sydney.

Toilets

There are no on-street facilities in Ireland. All shopping centres have public toilets (either free or 20c/20p). If you're stranded, go into any bar or hotel.

Tourist Information

In both the Republic and the North there's a tourist office or information point in almost every big town. Most can offer a variety of services, including accommodation and attraction reservations, currency-changing services, map and guidebook sales and free publications.

In the Republic the tourism purview falls to **Fáilte Ireland** (☑Republic 1850 230 330, UK 0800 039 7000; www. discoverireland.ie); in Northern Ireland, it's **Discover Northern Ireland** (☑head office 028-9023 1221; www. discovernorthernireland.com). Outside Ireland both organisations unite under the banner Tourism Ireland (www. tourismireland.com).

Visas

If you're a European Economic Area (EEA) national, you don't need a visa to visit (or work in) either the Republic or Northern Ireland. Citizens of Australia, Canada, New Zealand, South Africa and the US can visit the Republic for up to three months, and Northern Ireland for up to six months. They are not allowed to work, unless sponsored by an employer.

Full visa requirements for visiting the Republic are available online at www.dfa. ie; for Northern Ireland's visa requirements see www. gov.uk/government/ organisations/uk-visas-and-immigration.

To stay longer in the Republic, contact the local *garda* (police) station or the **Garda National Immigration Bureau** (☑01-666 9100; www.garda.ie; 13-14 Burgh Quay, Dublin; ⊙8am-9pm Mon-Fri; 🖥all city centre). To stay

USEFUL CALLING CODES

	REPUBLIC	NORTHERN IRELAND
Country Code	☑353	☑44
International Access Code	☑00	☑00
Directory Enquiries	☑11811/11850	☑118 118/118 192
International Directory Enquiries	☑11818	

longer in Northern Ireland, contact the Home Office (www.gov.uk/government/organisations/uk-visas-and-immigration).

Volunteering

Volunteering opportunities are limited, but there are projects where you can lend a helping hand.

Women Travellers

Ireland should pose no problems for women travellers. Finding contraception is not the problem it once was, though anyone on the pill should bring adequate supplies.

Rape Crisis Network Ireland (☑091-563 676; www.rcni.ie) In the Republic. App available.

Work

EEA citizens are entitled to work legally in the Republic of Ireland and Northern Ireland. Non-EEA citizens with an Irish parent or grandparent are eligible for dual citizenship (and the right to work), though this procedure can be quite lengthy – inquire at an Irish embassy or consulate in your own country.

Full-time US students aged 18 and over can get a four-month work permit for Ireland, plus insurance and support information, through **Work & Travel Ireland**

(☑01-602 1788; www.workandtravelireland.org).

Most Commonwealth citizens with a UK-born parent are entitled to work in the North (and the rest of the UK) through the 'Right of Abode'. Most Commonwealth citizens under 31 are eligible for a Working Holidaymaker Visa. Valid for two years, it allows you to work for a total of 12 months and must be obtained in advance of your arrival. Check with the UK Border Agency (www.gov.uk/government/organisations/uk-visas-and-immigration) for more info.

Transport

GETTING THERE & AWAY

Entering the Country

Dublin is the primary point of entry for most visitors to Ireland, but you can also fly into Shannon or Belfast.

➔ The overwhelming majority of airlines fly into Dublin.

➔ For travel to the US, Dublin and Shannon airports operate preclearance facilities, which means you pass through US immigration *before* boarding your aircraft.

➔ Dublin is home to two seaports that serve as the main points of sea transport with Britain; ferries from France arrive in the southern ports of Rosslare and Cork.

➔ Dublin is the nation's rail hub.

Air

Airports

Ireland's main airports:

Cork Airport (☎021-431 3131; www.corkairport.com) Airlines

DEPARTURE TAX

Departure tax is included in the price of a ticket.

---

servicing the airport include Aer Lingus and Ryanair.

Dublin Airport (☎01-814 1111; www.dublinairport.com) Ireland's major international gateway airport, with direct flights from the UK, Europe, North America and the Middle East.

Shannon Airport (SNN; ☎061-712 000; www.shannonairport.ie; ☎) Has a few direct flights from the UK, Europe and North America.

Northern Ireland:

Belfast International Airport (Aldergrove; ☎028-9448 4848; www.belfastairport.com; Airport Rd) Has direct flights from the UK, Europe and North America.

The Irish flag-carrier airline is Aer Lingus (www.aerlingus.com), which was founded by the Irish government but since 2015 is a fully owned subsidiary of the IAG group which also owns British Airways and Iberia. Ireland's biggest carrier, however, is Ryanair (www.ryanair.com), the low-cost behemoth that carries more passengers than any other European airline. Neither airline has had any crash fatalities.

Land

Eurolines (www.eurolines.com) has a daily coach and ferry service from London's Victoria Station to Dublin Busáras.

Sea

The main ferry routes between Ireland and the UK and mainland Europe:

➔ Belfast to Liverpool (England; eight hours)

➔ Belfast to Cairnryan (Scotland; 2½ hours)

➔ Cork to Roscoff (France; 14 hours; April to October only)

➔ Dublin to Liverpool (England; fast ferry four hours, slow ferry 8½ hours)

➔ Dublin to Holyhead (Wales; fast ferry two hours, slow ferry 3½ hours)

➔ Dublin to Roscoff (France; 18 hours)

➔ Larne to Cairnryan (Scotland; two hours)

➔ Rosslare to Cherbourg (France; 18 hours)

➔ Rosslare to Fishguard and Pembroke (Wales; 3½ hours) Competition from budget airlines has forced ferry operators to discount heavily and offer flexible fares.

A useful website is www.aferry.co.uk, which covers all sea-ferry routes and operators to Ireland.

Main operators include the following:

Brittany Ferries (Map p228; ☎021-427 7801; www.brittanyferries.ie; 42 Grand Pde) Cork to Roscoff; April to October.

Irish Ferries (☎0818 300 400; www.irishferries.com; Ferryport,

Terminal Rd South) Dublin to Holyhead (up to five per day year-round) and Dublin to France (four times per week).

P&O Ferries (☎01-686 9467; www.poferries.com; Terminal 3, Dublin Port) Daily sailings year-round from Dublin to Liverpool, and Larne to Cairnryan.

Stena Line Daily sailings from Holyhead to Dublin, Belfast to Liverpool and Cairnryan, and Rosslare to Fishguard and Cherbourg.

GETTING AROUND

The big decision in getting around Ireland is whether to go by car or use public transport. Your own car will make the best use of your time and help you reach even the most remote of places. It's usually easy to get very cheap rentals – €30 per day, or even less, is common – and if two or more are travelling together, the fee for rental and petrol can be cheaper than bus fares.

The bus network, made up of a mix of public and private operators, is extensive and generally quite competitive, though journey times can be slow and lots of the points of interest outside towns are not served. The rail network is quicker but more limited, serving only some major towns and cities. Both buses and trains get busy during peak times; you'll need to book in advance to be guaranteed a seat.

BUS, TRAIN & FERRY COMBOS

It's possible to combine bus, ferry and train tickets from major UK centres to most Irish towns. This might not be as quick as flying on a budget airline but leaves less of a carbon footprint. The journey between London and Dublin takes about 12 hours by bus, eight hours by train; the London-to-Belfast trip takes 13 to 16 hours by bus. Both can be had for as little as £29 one way. Eurolines (www.eurolines.com) has bus-ferry combos while Virgin Trains (www.virgintrains.co.uk) has combos that include London to Dublin. For more options, look for SailRail fares.

Air

Ireland's size makes domestic flying unnecessary, but there are flights between Dublin and Belfast, Cork, Derry, Donegal, Galway, Kerry, Shannon and Sligo aimed at passengers connecting from international flights. Flights linking the mainland to the Aran Islands are popular.

Bicycle

Ireland's compact size and scenic landscapes make it a good cycling destination. However, unreliable weather, very narrow roads and some very fast drivers are major concerns. Special tracks such as the 42km Great Western Greenway (p434) in County Mayo are a delight. A good tip for cyclists in the west is that the prevailing winds make it easier to cycle from south to north.

Buses will carry bikes, but only if there's room. For trains, bear the following in mind:

➡ Intercity trains charge up to €10.50 per bike.

➡ Book in advance (www.irishrail.ie), as there's only room for two bikes per service.

Companies that arrange cycle tours in Ireland include the following:

Go Visit Ireland (☎066-976 2094; www.govisitireland.com) Guided and independent tours.

Irish Cycling Safaris (☎01-260 0749; www.cyclingsafaris.com; tours from €860) Organises numerous tours across Ireland.

Boat

Ireland's offshore islands are all served by boat.

Ferries also operate across rivers, inlets and loughs, providing useful shortcuts, particularly for cyclists.

Cruises are popular on a 258km section of the Shannon–Erne Waterway (p495)

CLIMATE CHANGE & TRAVEL

Every form of transport that relies on carbon-based fuel generates CO_2, the main cause of human-induced climate change. Modern travel is dependent on aeroplanes, which might use less fuel per kilometre per person than most cars but travel much greater distances. The altitude at which aircraft emit gases (including CO_2) and particles also contributes to their climate change impact. Many websites offer 'carbon calculators' that allow people to estimate the carbon emissions generated by their journey and, for those who wish to do so, to offset the impact of the greenhouse gases emitted with contributions to portfolios of climate-friendly initiatives throughout the world. Lonely Planet offsets the carbon footprint of all staff and author travel.

Ferry & Fast Boat Routes

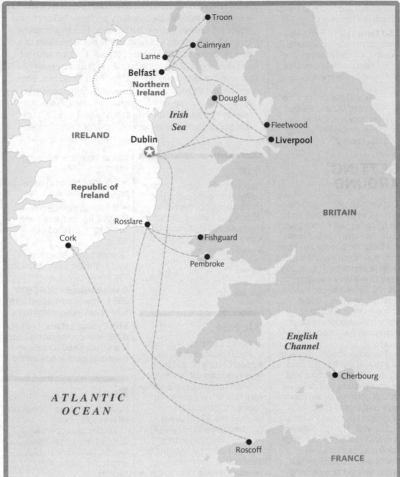

and on a variety of other lakes and loughs.

Bus

Private buses compete – often very favourably – with Bus Éireann in the Republic and also run where the national buses are irregular or absent.

Distances are not especially long: few bus journeys will last longer than five hours. Bus Éireann bookings

can be made online, but you can't reserve a seat for a particular service. Dynamic pricing is in effect on many routes, so book early to get the lowest fares.

Note the following:

➡ Bus routes and frequencies are slowly contracting in the Republic.

➡ The National Journey Planner app by Transport for Ireland is very useful for planning bus and train trips.

The main bus services in Ireland:

Bus Éireann (☑1850 836 6111; www.buseireann.ie) The Republic's primary bus line.

Translink (☑028-9066 6630; www.translink.co.uk) Northern Ireland's main bus service; includes Ulsterbus and Goldline.

Car & Motorcycle

Travelling by car or motorbike means greater flexibility and independence. The road system is extensive and the network of motorways has cut driving times considerably. Also note, however, that many secondary roads are very narrow and at times rather perilous.

All cars on public roads must be insured. If you are bringing your own vehicle, check that your insurance will cover you in Ireland.

Car Hire

Advance hire rates start at around €20 a day for a small car (unlimited mileage). Shop around and use price-comparison sites as well as company sites (which often have deals not available on booking sites).

Other tips:

➤ Most cars are manual; automatic cars are available, but they're more expensive to hire.

➤ If you're travelling from the Republic into Northern Ireland, it's important to be sure that your insurance covers journeys to the North.

➤ The majority of hire companies won't rent you a car if you're under 23 and haven't had a valid driving licence for at least a year.

Motoring Organisations

The two main motoring organisations:

Automobile Association (AA; ✆Northern Ireland breakdown 00 800 8877 6655, Republic breakdown 1800 66 77 88; www.theaa.ie)

Royal Automobile Club (RAC; ✆Northern Ireland breakdown 0333 200 0999, Republic breakdown 0800 015 6000; www.rac.ie)

Parking

All big towns and cities have covered and open short-stay car parks that are conveniently signposted.

➤ On-street parking is usually by 'pay and display' tickets available from on-

street machines or disc parking (discs, which rotate to display the time you park your car, are usually provided by rental agencies). Costs range from €1.50 to €6 per hour; all-day parking in a car park will cost around €25.

➤ Yellow lines (single or double) along the edge of the road indicate restrictions. Double yellow lines mean no parking at any time. Always look for the nearby sign that spells out when you can and cannot park.

Road Rules

Ireland may be one of the few countries where the posted speed limits are often much faster than you'll find possible.

➤ Motorways (marked by M+number on a blue background): modern, divided highways.

➤ Primary roads (N+number on a green background in the Republic, A+number in Northern Ireland): usually

well-engineered two-lane roads.

➤ Secondary and tertiary roads (marked as R+number in the Republic, B+number in Northern Ireland): can be very winding and exceedingly narrow.

➤ Tolls are charged on many motorways, usually by machine at a plaza. On the M50, pay the automated tolls between junctions 6 and 7 at www.eflow.ie.

➤ Directional signs are often not in evidence.

➤ GPS navigation via your smartphone or device is very helpful.

➤ EU licences are treated like Irish licences.

➤ Non-EU licences are valid in Ireland for up to 12 months.

➤ If you plan to bring a car from Europe, it's illegal to drive without at least third-party insurance.

The basic rules of the road:

ROAD DISTANCES (KM)

	Athlone	Belfast	Cork	Derry	Donegal	Dublin	Galway	Kilkenny	Killarney	Limerick	Rosslare Harbour	Shannon Airport	Sligo	Waterford
Belfast	242													
Cork	219	424												
Derry	209	117	428											
Donegal	183	180	402	69										
Dublin	127	167	256	237	233									
Galway	93	306	209	272	204	212								
Kilkenny	116	284	148	335	309	129	172							
Killarney	232	436	87	441	407	304	193	198						
Limerick	363	323	105	328	287	202	98	113	111					
Rosslare Harbour	201	330	208	397	391	153	274	98	275	211				
Shannon Airport	133	346	128	351	282	218	93	135	135	25	234			
Sligo	117	206	336	135	66	214	138	245	343	227	325	218		
Waterford	164	333	126	383	357	163	220	48	193	129	82	152	293	
Wexford	184	309	187	378	372	135	253	80	254	190	19	213	307	61

➡ Drive on the left; overtake to the right.

➡ Safety belts must be worn by the driver and all passengers.

➡ Children aged under 12 aren't allowed to sit in the front passenger seat.

➡ When entering a roundabout, give way to the right.

➡ In the Republic, speed-limit and distance signs are in kilometres; in the North, speed-limit and distance signs are often in miles.

Speed limits:

Republic 120km/h on motorways, 100km/h on national roads, 80km/h on regional and local roads, and 50km/h or as signposted in towns.

Northern Ireland 70mph (112km/h) on motorways, 60mph (96km/h) on main roads, 30mph (48km/h) in built-up areas.

Drinking and driving is taken very seriously. You're allowed a maximum blood-alcohol level of 50mg/100mL (0.05%) in the Republic, and 35mg/100mL (0.035%) in Northern Ireland.

Hitching

Hitching is not especially popular in Ireland anymore, except in rural communities – and then over short distances. Hitching is never entirely safe, and we don't recommend it. Travellers who hitch should understand that they are taking a potentially serious risk. It's illegal to hitch on motorways.

Local Transport

Dublin and Belfast have comprehensive local bus networks, as do some other large towns.

➡ The Dublin Area Rapid Transport (DART) rail line runs roughly the length of Dublin's coastline, while the Luas tram system has two popular lines.

➡ Taxis tend to be expensive: flagfall is daytime/night-time €3.60/4 plus €1.10/1.40 per kilometre after the first 500m.

➡ Uber is in Dublin but is not as popular as the taxi app MyTaxi (www.mytaxi.com).

Train

Given Ireland's relatively small size, train travel can be quick and advance-purchase fares are competitive with buses. Worth noting:

➡ Many of the Republic's most beautiful areas, such as whole swathes of the Wild Atlantic Way, are not served by rail.

➡ Most lines radiate out from Dublin, with limited ways of interconnecting between lines, which can complicate touring.

➡ There are four routes from Belfast in Northern Ireland. One links with the system in the Republic via Newry to Dublin.

Train Routes

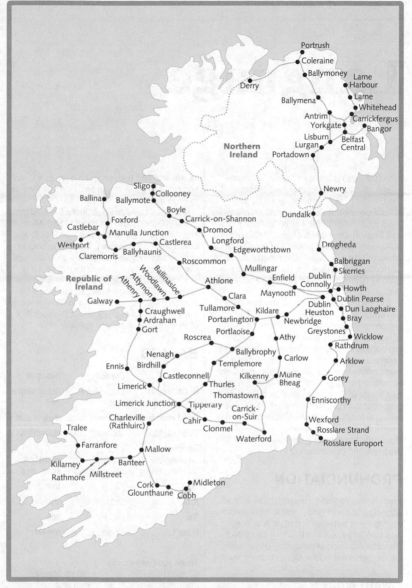

→ True 1st class only exists on the Dublin–Cork and Dublin–Belfast lines. On all other trains seats are the same size as in standard class, despite any marketing come-ons such as 'Premier' class.

Irish Rail (Iarnród Éireann; ☏01-836 6222; www.irishrail. ie) operates trains in the Republic.

Translink NI Railways (☏028-9066 6630; www.translink. co.uk) operates trains in Northern Ireland.

Language

Irish (Gaeilge) is the country's official language. In 2003 the government introduced the Official Languages Act, whereby all official documents, street signs and official titles must be either in Irish or in both Irish and English. Despite its official status, Irish is really only spoken in pockets of rural Ireland known as the Gaeltacht, the main ones being Cork (Corcaigh), Donegal (Dún na nGall), Galway (Gaillimh), Kerry (Ciarraí) and Mayo (Maigh Eo).

Ask people outside the Gaeltacht if they can speak Irish and nine out of 10 of them will probably reply, *'ah, cupla focal'* (a couple of words), and they generally mean it. Irish is a compulsory subject in both primary and secondary schools, but Irish classes have traditionally been rather academic and unimaginative, leading many students to resent it as a waste of time. As a result, many adults regret not having a greater grasp of it. In recent times, at long last, a new Irish curriculum has been introduced cutting the hours devoted to the subject but making the lessons more fun, practical and celebratory.

PRONUNCIATION

Irish divides vowels into long (those with an accent) and short (those without) and also disinguishes between broad (**a**, **á**, **o**, **ó**, **u**) and slender (**e**, **é**, **i** and **í**), which can affect the pronunciation of preceding consonants. Other than a few odd-looking clusters, such

as **mh** and **bhf** (pronounced both as w), consonants are generally pronounced as they are in English.

Irish has three main dialects: Connaught Irish (in Galway and northern Mayo), Munster Irish (in Cork, Kerry and Waterford) and Ulster Irish (in Donegal). The blue pronunciation guidelines given here are an anglicised version of modern standard Irish, which is essentially an amalgam of the three – if you read them as if they were English, you'll be able to get your point across in Gaeilge without even having to think about the specifics of Irish pronunciation or spelling.

BASICS

Hello.	*Dia duit.*	deea gwit
Hello. (reply)	*Dia is Muire duit.*	deeas moyra gwit
Good morning.	*Maidin mhaith.*	mawjin wah
Good night.	*Oíche mhaith.*	eekheh wah
Goodbye.		
(when leaving)	*Slán leat.*	slawn lyat
(when staying)	*Slán agat.*	slawn agut
Yes.	*Tá.*	taw
It is.	*Sea.*	sheh
No.	*Níl.*	neel
It isn't.	*Ní hea.*	nee heh

Thank you (very much).
Go raibh (míle) maith agat. — goh rev (meela) mah agut

Excuse me.
Gabh mo leithscéal. — gamoh lesh scale

I'm sorry.
Tá brón orm. — taw brohn oruhm

I don't understand.
Ní thuigim. — nee higgim

WANT MORE?

For in-depth language information and handy phrases, check out Lonely Planet's *Irish Language & Culture*. You'll find it at **shop.lonelyplanet.com**, or you can buy Lonely Planet's iPhone phrasebooks at the Apple App Store.

Do you speak Irish?
An bhfuil Gaeilge agat? — on wil gaylge oguht

What is this?
Cad é seo? — kod ay shoh

What is that?
Cad é sin? — kod ay shin

I'd like to go to...
Ba mhaith liom — baw wah lohm
dul go dtí... — dull go dee...

I'd like to buy...
Ba mhaith liom... — bah wah lohm...
a cheannach. — a kyanukh

| another/ one more | *ceann eile* | kyawn ella |
| nice | *go deas* | goh dyass |

MAKING CONVERSATION

Welcome.
Ceád míle fáilte. — kade meela fawlcha
(lit: 100,000 welcomes)

How are you?
Conas a tá tú? — kunas aw taw too

..., (if you) please.
...más é do thoil é. — ...maws ay do hall ay

What's your name?
Cad is ainm duit? — kod is anim dwit

My name is (Sean Frayne).
(Sean Frayne) is — (shawn frain) is
ainm dom. — anim dohm

DAYS OF THE WEEK

Monday	*Dé Luaín*	day loon
Tuesday	*Dé Máirt*	day maart
Wednesday	*Dé Ceádaoin*	day kaydeen
Thursday	*Déardaoin*	daredeen
Friday	*Dé hAoine*	day heeneh
Saturday	*Dé Sathairn*	day sahern
Sunday	*Dé Domhnaigh*	day downick

SIGNS

Fir	fear	Men
Gardaí	gardee	Police
Leithreas	lehrass	Toilet
Mna	mnaw	Women
Oifig An Phoist	iffig ohn fwisht	Post office

CUPLA FOCAL

Here are a few phrases *os Gaeilge* (in Irish) to help you impress the locals:

Tóg é gobogé.
Take it easy.
tohg ay gobogay

Ní féidir é!
Impossible!
nee faydir ay

Ráiméis!
Nonsense!
rawmaysh

Go huafásach!
That's terrible!
guh hoofawsokh

Ní ólfaidh mé go brách arís!
I'm never ever drinking again!
knee ohlhee mey gu brawkh ureeshch

Slainte!
Your health!/Cheers!
slawncha

Táim go maith.
I'm fine.
thawm go mah

Nollaig shona!
Happy Christmas!
nuhlig hona

Cáisc shona!
Happy Easter!
kawshk hona

Go n-éirí an bóthar leat!
Bon voyage!
go nairee on bohhar lat

NUMBERS

1	*haon*	hayin
2	*dó*	doe
3	*trí*	tree
4	*ceathaír*	kahirr
5	*cúig*	kooig
6	*sé*	shay
7	*seacht*	shocked
8	*hocht*	hukt
9	*naoi*	nay
10	*deich*	jeh
11	*haon déag*	hayin jague
12	*dó dhéag*	doe yague
20	*fiche*	feekhe

GLOSSARY

12 July – the day the *Orange Order* marches to celebrate Protestant King William III's victory over the Catholic King James II at the Battle of the Boyne in 1690

An Óige – literally 'the Youth'; Republic of Ireland Youth Hostel Association

Anglo-Norman – Norman, English and Welsh peoples who invaded Ireland in the 12th century

Apprentice Boys – *Loyalist* organisation founded in 1814 to commemorate the Great Siege of Derry in August every year

ard – literally 'high'; Irish place name

Ascendancy – refers to the Protestant aristocracy descended from the Anglo-Normans and those who were installed here during the *Plantation*

bailey – outer wall of a castle

bawn – area surrounded by walls outside the main castle, acting as a defence and as a place to keep cattle in times of trouble

beehive hut – see *clochán*

Black & Tans – British recruits to the Royal Irish Constabulary shortly after WWI, noted for their brutality

Blarney Stone – sacred stone perched on top of Blarney Castle; bending over backwards to kiss the stone is said to bestow the gift of gab

bodhrán – hand-held goatskin drum

Bronze Age – earliest metalusing period, around 2500 BC to 300 BC in Ireland; after the Stone Age and before the *Iron Age*

B-Specials – Northern Irish auxiliary police force, disbanded in 1971

bullaun – stone with a depression, probably used as a mortar for grinding medicine or food, often found at monastic sites

caher – circular area enclosed by stone walls

cairn – mound of stones over a prehistoric grave

cashel – stone-walled *ring fort*; see also *ráth*

céilidh – session of traditional music and dancing; also called 'ceili'

Celtic Tiger – nickname of the Irish economy during the growth years from 1990 to about 2002

Celts – *Iron Age* warrior tribes that arrived in Ireland around 300 BC and controlled the country for 1000 years

chancel – eastern end of a church, where the altar is situated, reserved for the clergy and choir

chipper – slang term for fish-and-chips fast-food restaurant

cill – literally 'church'; Irish place name; also 'kill'

Claddagh ring – ring worn in much of *Connaught* since the mid-18th century, with a crowned heart nestling between two hands; if the heart points towards the hand then the wearer is partnered or married, if towards the fingertip he or she is looking for a mate

clochán – circular stone building, shaped like an oldfashioned beehive, from the early Christian period

Connaught – one of the four ancient provinces of Ireland, made up of Counties Galway, Leitrim, Mayo, Roscommon and Sligo; sometimes spelled 'Connacht'; see also *Leinster, Munster* and *Ulster*

craic – conversation, gossip, fun, good times; also known as 'crack'

crannóg – artificial island made in a lake to provide habitation in a good defensive position

currach – rowing boat made of a framework of laths covered with tarred canvas; also known as 'cúrach'

Dáil – lower house of the parliament of the Republic of Ireland; see also *Oireachtas* and *Seanad*

DART – Dublin Area Rapid Transport train line

demesne – landed property close to a house or castle

diamond – town square

dolmen – tomb chamber or portal tomb made of vertical stones topped by a huge capstone; from around 2000 BC

drumlin – rounded hill formed by retreating glaciers

Dúchas – government department in charge of parks, monuments and gardens in the Republic; formerly known as the Office of Public Works

dún – fort, usually constructed of stone

DUP – Democratic Unionist Party; founded principally by Ian Paisley in 1971 in hardline opposition to *Unionist* policies held by the *UUP*

Éire – Irish name for the Republic of Ireland

esker – raised ridge formed by glaciers

Fáilte Ireland – 'Welcome Board'; Irish Tourist Board

Fianna – mythical band of warriors who feature in many tales of ancient Ireland

Fianna Fáil – literally 'Warriors of Ireland'; a major political party in the Republic, originating from the *Sinn Féin* faction opposed to the 1921 treaty with Britain

Fine Gael – literally 'Tribe of the Gael'; a major political party in the Republic, originating from the *Sinn Féin* faction that favoured the 1921 treaty with Britain; formed the first government of independent Ireland

fir – men (singular 'fear'); sign on men's toilets; see also *leithreas* and *mná*

fleadh – festival

GAA – Gaelic Athletic Association; promotes Gaelic football and hurling, among other Irish games

Gaeltacht – Irish-speaking

gallóglí – mercenary soldiers of the 14th to 15th century; anglicised to 'gallowglasses'

garda – Irish Republic police; plural 'gardai'

ghillie – fishing or hunting guide; also known as 'ghilly'

gort – literally 'field'; Irish place name

hill fort – a hilltop fortified with ramparts and ditches, usually dating from the *Iron Age*

HINI – Hostelling International of Northern Ireland

Hunger, the – colloquial name for the Great Famine of 1845–51

hurling – Irish sport similar to hockey

Iarnród Éireann – Republic of Ireland Railways

INLA – Irish National Liberation Association; formed in 1975 as an *IRA* splinter group; it has maintained a ceasefire since 1998

IRA – Irish Republican Army; the largest Republican paramilitary organisation, founded 80 years ago with the aim to fight for a united Ireland; in 1969 the IRA split into the Official IRA and the Provisional IRA; the Official IRA is no longer active and the PIRA has become the IRA

Iron Age – metal-using period that lasted from the end of the *Bronze Age*, around 300 BC (the arrival of the Celts), to the arrival of Christianity, around the 5th century AD

jarvey – driver of a *jaunting car*

jaunting car – Killarney's traditional horse-drawn transport; see also *jarvey*

Leinster – one of the four ancient provinces of Ireland, made up of Counties Carlow, Dublin, Kildare, Kilkenny, Laois, Longford, Louth, Meath, Offaly, West Meath, Wexford and Wicklow; see also *Connaught, Munster* and *Ulster*

leithreas – toilets; see also *mná* and *fir*

leprechaun – mischievous elf or sprite from Irish folklore

lough – lake, or long narrow bay or arm of the sea

Loyalist – person, usually a Northern Irish Protestant, insisting on the continuation of Northern Ireland's links with Britain

Luas – light-rail transit system in Dublin; Irish for 'speed'

marching season – *Orange Order* parades, which take place from Easter and throughout summer to celebrate the victory by Protestant King William III of Orange over Catholic James II in the Battle of the Boyne on 12 July 1690, and the union with Britain

Mesolithic – also known as the Middle Stone Age; time of the first human settlers in Ireland, about 8000 BC to 4000 BC; see also *Neolithic*

mná – women; sign on women's toilets; see also *fir* and *leithreas*

motte – early Norman fortification consisting of a raised, flattened mound with a keep on top; when attached to a *bailey* it is known as a motte-and-bailey fort, many of which were built in Ireland until the early 13th century

Munster – one of the four ancient provinces of Ireland, made up of Counties Clare, Cork, Kerry, Limerick, Tipperary and Waterford; see also *Connaught, Leinster* and *Ulster*

nationalism – belief in a re-united Ireland

Nationalist – proponent of a united Ireland

Neolithic – also known as the New Stone Age; a period characterised by settled agriculture lasting from around 4000 BC to 2500 BC in Ireland; followed by the *Bronze Age*; see also *Mesolithic*

NIR – Northern Ireland Railways

NITB – Northern Ireland Tourist Board

NNR – National Nature Reserves

North, the – political entity of Northern Ireland, not the northernmost geographic part of Ireland

NUI – National University of Ireland; made up of branches in Dublin, Cork, Galway and Limerick

Ogham stone – a stone etched with Ogham characters, the earliest form of writing in Ireland, with a variety of notched strokes

Oireachtas – Parliament of the Republic of Ireland, consisting of the *Dáil*, the lower house, and the *Seanad*, the upper house

Orange Order – the largest Protestant organisation in Northern Ireland, founded in 1795, with a membership of up to 100,000; name commemorates the victory of King William of Orange in the Battle of the Boyne

óstán – hotel

Palladian – style of architecture developed by Andrea Palladio (1508–80), based on ancient Roman architecture

paramilitaries – armed illegal organisations, either *Loyalist* or *Republican*, usually associated with the use of violence and crime for political and economic gain

partition – division of Ireland in 1921

passage grave – Celtic tomb with a chamber reached by a narrow passage, typically buried in a mound

penal laws – laws passed in the 18th century forbidding Catholics from buying land and holding public office

Plantation – settlement of Protestant immigrants (known as Planters) in Ireland in the 17th century

poitín – illegally brewed whiskey, also spelled 'poteen'

provisionals – Provisional IRA, formed after a break with the official *IRA* (who are now largely inconsequential); named after the provisional government declared in 1916, they have been the main force combating the

British army in *the North;* also known as 'provos'

PSNI – Police Service of Northern Ireland

ráth – *ring fort* with earthen banks around a timber wall; see also *cashel*

Real IRA – splinter movement of the *IRA;* opposed to *Sinn Féin's* support of the Good Friday Agreement; responsible for the Omagh bombing in 1998 in which 29 people died; subsequently called a ceasefire but has been responsible for bombs in Britain and other acts of violence

Republic of Ireland – the 26 counties of *the South*

Republican – supporter of a united Ireland

republicanism – belief in a united Ireland, sometimes referred to as militant nationalism

ring fort – circular habitation area surrounded by banks and ditches, used from the *Bronze Age* right through to the Middle Ages, particularly in the early Christian period

RTE – Radio Telifís Éireann; the national broadcasting service of the Republic of Ireland, with two TV and four radio stations

RUC – Royal Ulster Constabulary, the former name for the armed Police Service of Northern Ireland *(PSNI)*

Seanad – upper house of the parliament of the Republic of Ireland; see also *Oireachtas* and *Dáil*

shamrock – three-leafed plant said to have been used by St Patrick to illustrate the Holy Trinity

shebeen – from the Irish 'síbín'; illicit drinking place or speakeasy

sheila-na-gig – literally 'Sheila of the teats'; female figure with exaggerated genitalia, carved in stone on the exteriors of some churches and castles; explanations include male clerics warning against the perils of sex to the idea that they represent Celtic war goddesses

Sinn Féin – literally 'We Ourselves'; a *Republican* party with the aim of a united Ireland; seen as the political wing of the *IRA* but it maintains that both organisations are completely separate

slí – hiking trail or way

snug – partitioned-off drinking area in a pub

souterrain – underground chamber usually associated with *ring* and *hill forts;* probably provided a hiding place or escape route in times of trouble and/or storage space for goods

South, the – Republic of Ireland

standing stone – upright stone set in the ground, common across Ireland and dating from a variety of periods; some are burial markers

Taoiseach – Republic of Ireland prime minister

teampall – church

trá – beach or strand

Treaty – Anglo-Irish Treaty of 1921, which divided Ireland and gave relative independence to the South; cause of the 1922–23 Civil War

tricolour – green, white and orange Irish flag symbolising the hoped-for union of the 'green' Catholic Southern Irish with the

'orange' Protestant Northern Irish

turlough – a small lake that often disappears in dry summers; from the Irish 'turlach'

UDA – Ulster Defence Association; the largest *Loyalist* paramilitary group; it has observed a ceasefire since 1994

uillean pipes – Irish bagpipes with a bellow strapped to the arm; 'uillean' is Irish for 'elbow'

Ulster – one of the four ancient provinces of Ireland; sometimes used to describe the six counties of *the North,* despite the fact that Ulster also includes Counties Cavan, Monaghan and Donegal (all in the Republic); see also *Connaught, Leinster* and *Munster*

Unionist – person who wants to retain Northern Ireland's links with Britain

United Irishmen – organisation founded in 1791 aiming to reduce British power in Ireland; it led a series of unsuccessful risings and invasions

UUP – Ulster Unionist Party; the largest *Unionist* party in Northern Ireland and the majority party in the Assembly; founded in 1905 and led by *Unionist* hero Edward Carson from 1910 to 1921; from 1921 to 1972 the sole *Unionist* organisation but is now under threat from the *DUP*

UVF – Ulster Volunteer Force; an illegal *Loyalist* Northern Irish paramilitary organisation

Volunteers – offshoot of the IRB that came to be known as the *IRA*

Behind the Scenes

SEND US YOUR FEEDBACK

We love to hear from travellers – your comments keep us on our toes and help make our books better. Our well-travelled team reads every word on what you loved or loathed about this book. Although we cannot reply individually to your submissions, we always guarantee that your feedback goes straight to the appropriate authors, in time for the next edition. Each person who sends us information is thanked in the next edition – the most useful submissions are rewarded with a selection of digital PDF chapters.

Visit **lonelyplanet.com/contact** to submit your updates and suggestions or to ask for help. Our award-winning website also features inspirational travel stories, news and discussions.

Note: We may edit, reproduce and incorporate your comments in Lonely Planet products such as guidebooks, websites and digital products, so let us know if you don't want your comments reproduced or your name acknowledged. For a copy of our privacy policy visit lonelyplanet.com/privacy.

OUR READERS

Many thanks to the travellers who used the last edition and wrote to us with helpful hints, useful advice and interesting anecdotes: Molly Bentley, Simon Britt, Valerie Carter, Eamon Oxley, Karin Schwenk, Seth Vannaman.

WRITER THANKS

Neil Wilson

Thanks to the friendly and helpful tourist office staff in Cork, Kerry, Limerick and Tipperary; to Mortimer at Mannix Point; to Warren at Curraghchase; to Hilary at Fleming's; to George at Glen of Aherlow; and, as ever, to Carol Downie. Thanks also to my co-authors, and to Cliff and the editorial team at Lonely Planet.

Isabel Albiston

I'm grateful for the help of many people whose friendly advice and warm encouragement made researching and writing this guide such a pleasure. Huge thanks to Caroline Wilson for the foodie tips, to Hazel at Dunluce Castle for the tour and to Philip Bingham for helping with endless bus prices. Most of all, thanks to my family for all their help and support, for lending me the car and for accompanying me to restaurants and windswept castles.

Fionn Davenport

Dublin's forever changing, and to update it properly I need more than two eyes and one brain, so a huge thanks to everyone who helped me along. To the staff in the Dublin office, thanks for your tips, suggestions and recommendations; to Nicola Brady, for her invaluable assistance in knowing all of the right places to eat; and to Cliff Wilkinson, the ever-present, ever-helpful editor who answered all of my questions.

Belinda Dixon

To everyone encountered along the way: *go raibh maith agat* for the warmth and wit that makes your wild, creative country so irresistible. To Cliff for these fantastic opportunities, my sincere thanks; it's been a blast. All LP's in-house teams: thank you so much for helping turn my rain-sodden notes into beautiful books, maps and tech. To fellow LP writers: shall we meet for a pint next time? And to Laura for keeping me grounded and making me laugh.

Catherine Le Nevez

Sláinte first and foremost to Julian, and to all of the locals and fellow travellers throughout Ireland who provided insights, information and great times. Huge thanks too to Cliff Wilkinson and the Ireland team, and to everyone at LP. As ever, merci encore to my parents, brother, belle-sœur, neveu and nièce.

ACKNOWLEDGEMENTS

Climate map data adapted from Peel MC, Finlayson BL & McMahon TA (2007) 'Updated World Map of the Köppen-Geiger Climate Classification', *Hydrology and Earth System Sciences*, 11, 1633–44.

Cover photograph: Carrick-a-Rede Rope Bridge, Lauz83/Getty Images©

Illustrations p74–5, p158–9 by Javier Zarracina.

Illustrations p338–9, p526–7 by Michael Weldon.

THIS BOOK

This 14th edition of Lonely Planet's *Ireland* guidebook was researched and written by Neil Wilson, Isabel Albiston, Fionn Davenport, Belinda Dixon and Catherine Le Nevez. The previous edition was researched and written by Neil Wilson, Isabel Albiston, Fionn Davenport, Damian Harper and Catherine Le Nevez. This guidebook was produced by the following:

Destination Editor
Clifton Wilkinson

Senior Product Editor
Jessica Ryan

Regional Senior Cartographer
Mark Griffiths

Product Editor
Amy Lynch

Book Designer
Fergal Condon

Assisting Editors
Andrew Bain, Imogen Bannister, Nigel Chin, Carly Hall, Kellie Langdon, Anne Mulvaney, Rosie Nicholson, Kristin Odijk, Maja Vatrić, Simon Williamson

Assisting Cartographers
Julie Dodkins, Mick Garrett

Cover Researcher
Naomi Parker

Thanks to Katie Connolly, Barbara Delissen, Sandie Kestell, Claire Rourke

Index

Map Legend

Sights

- Beach
- Bird Sanctuary
- Buddhist
- Castle/Palace
- Christian
- Confucian
- Hindu
- Islamic
- Jain
- Jewish
- Monument
- Museum/Gallery/Historic Building
- Ruin
- Shinto
- Sikh
- Taoist
- Winery/Vineyard
- Zoo/Wildlife Sanctuary
- Other Sight

Activities, Courses & Tours

- Bodysurfing
- Diving
- Canoeing/Kayaking
- Course/Tour
- Sento Hot Baths/Onsen
- Skiing
- Snorkelling
- Surfing
- Swimming/Pool
- Walking
- Windsurfing
- Other Activity

Sleeping

- Sleeping
- Camping
- Hut/Shelter

Eating

- Eating

Drinking & Nightlife

- Drinking & Nightlife
- Cafe

Entertainment

- Entertainment

Shopping

- Shopping

Information

- Bank
- Embassy/Consulate
- Hospital/Medical
- Internet
- Police
- Post Office
- Telephone
- Toilet
- Tourist Information
- Other Information

Geographic

- Beach
- Gate
- Hut/Shelter
- Lighthouse
- Lookout
- Mountain/Volcano
- Oasis
- Park
- Pass
- Picnic Area
- Waterfall

Population

- Capital (National)
- Capital (State/Province)
- City/Large Town
- Town/Village

Transport

- Airport
- Border crossing
- Bus
- Cable car/Funicular
- Cycling
- Ferry
- Metro station
- Monorail
- Parking
- Petrol station
- S-Bahn/Subway station
- Taxi
- T-bane/Tunnelbana station
- Train station/Railway
- Tram
- U-Bahn/Underground station
- Other Transport

Routes

- Tollway
- Freeway
- Primary
- Secondary
- Tertiary
- Lane
- Unsealed road
- Road under construction
- Plaza/Mall
- Steps
- Tunnel
- Pedestrian overpass
- Walking Tour
- Walking Tour detour
- Path/Walking Trail

Boundaries

- International
- State/Province
- Disputed
- Regional/Suburb
- Marine Park
- Cliff
- Wall

Hydrography

- River, Creek
- Intermittent River
- Canal
- Water
- Dry/Salt/Intermittent Lake
- Reef

Areas

- Airport/Runway
- Beach/Desert
- Cemetery (Christian)
- Cemetery (Other)
- Glacier
- Mudflat
- Park/Forest
- Sight (Building)
- Sportsground
- Swamp/Mangrove

Note: Not all symbols displayed above appear on the maps in this book

Belinda Dixon

Counties Mayo & Sligo; County Clare; County Galway Only happy when her feet are suitably sandy, Belinda has been (gleefully) travelling, researching and writing for Lonely Planet since 2006. It's seen her navigating mountain passes and soaking in hot-pots in Iceland's Westfjords, marvelling at Stonehenge at sunrise; scrambling up Italian mountain paths; horse riding across Donegal's golden sands; gazing at Verona's frescoes; and fossil hunting on Dorset's Jurassic Coast. Then there's the food and drink: truffled mushroom pasta in Salo; whisky in Aberdeen, Balti in Birmingham, grilled fish in Dartmouth; wine in Bardolino. And all in the name of research. Belinda is also a podcaster and adventure writer and helps lead wilderness expeditions. See her blog posts at https://belindadixon.com.

Catherine Le Nevez

Counties Meath, Louth, Cavan and Monaghan; the Midlands; Counties Wicklow and Kildare; Counties Wexford, Waterford, Carlow and Kilkenny Catherine's wanderlust kicked in when she roadtripped across Europe from her Parisian base aged four, and she's been hitting the road at every opportunity since, travelling to some 60 countries and completing her Doctorate of Creative Arts in Writing, Masters in Professional Writing, and postgrad qualifications in Editing and Publishing along the way. Over the past decade-and-a-half she's written scores of Lonely Planet guides and articles covering Paris, France, Europe and far beyond. Her work has also appeared in numerous online and print publications. Topping Catherine's list of travel tips is to travel without any expectations.

OUR STORY

A beat-up old car, a few dollars in the pocket and a sense of adventure. In 1972 that's all Tony and Maureen Wheeler needed for the trip of a lifetime – across Europe and Asia overland to Australia. It took several months, and at the end – broke but inspired – they sat at their kitchen table writing and stapling together their first travel guide, *Across Asia on the Cheap*. Within a week they'd sold 1500 copies. Lonely Planet was born.

Today, Lonely Planet has offices in Franklin, London, Melbourne, Oakland, Dublin, Beijing and Delhi, with more than 600 staff and writers. We share Tony's belief that 'a great guidebook should do three things: inform, educate and amuse'.

OUR WRITERS

Neil Wilson

Counties Limerick & Tipperary; County Cork; County Kerry Neil was born in Scotland and has lived there most of his life. Based in Perthshire, he has been a full-time writer since 1988, working on more than 80 guidebooks for various publishers, including the Lonely Planet guides to Scotland, England, Ireland and Prague. He has climbed and tramped in four continents, including ascents of Jebel Toubkal in Morocco, Mount Kinabalu in Borneo, the Old Man of Hoy in Scotland's Orkney Islands and the Northwest Face of Half Dome in California's Yosemite Valley. Like most Lonely Planet writers, Neil fell into the guidebook-writing business by accident. He began by producing articles for a Scottish magazine, but was soon off to photograph Corfu for a guidebook. Neil also contributed to the Plan, Understand and Survival Guide chapters.

Isabel Albiston

Belfast; Counties Down & Armagh, Counties Derry & Antrim; Counties Fermanagh & Tyrone; County Donegal After six years working for the *Daily Telegraph* in London, Isabel left to spend more time on the road. A job as writer for a magazine in Sydney, Australia was followed by a four-month overland trip across Asia and five years living and working in Buenos Aires, Argentina. Isabel started writing for Lonely Planet in 2014 and has contributed to 12 guidebooks. She's currently based in Ireland. Isabel also contributed to the Plan, Understand and Survival Guide chapters.

Fionn Davenport

Dublin Irish by birth and conviction, Fionn has spent the last two decades focusing on the country of his birth and its nearest neighbour, England, which he has written about extensively for Lonely Planet and others. In between writing gigs he's lived in Paris and New York, where he was an editor, actor, bartender and whatever else paid the rent. He moved to Manchester a few years ago where he lives with his wife, Laura, but he commutes back and forth to Dublin, only 40 minutes away. He posts his travel shots on instagram – @fionndavenport. Fionn also contributed to the Plan, Understand and Survival Guide chapters.

OVER MORE
PAGE WRITERS

Published by Lonely Planet Global Limited
CRN 554153
14th edition – Mar 2020
ISBN 978 1 78701 580 7
© Lonely Planet 2020   Photographs © as indicated 2020
10 9 8 7 6 5 4 3 2 1
Printed in China